Florida

HOLT McDOUGAL

Earth SCIENCE

Mead A. Allison

Arthur T. DeGaetano

Jay M. Pasachoff

HOLT McDOUGAL

 HOUGHTON MIFFLIN HARCOURT

About the Authors

Mead A. Allison, Ph.D.
The University of Texas, Austin, Texas
Mead Allison received his Ph.D. in oceanography from State University of New York. Formerly a professor of Earth and environmental science at Tulane University in Louisiana, Dr. Allison is now a Senior Research Scientist at the Institute for Geophysics, Jackson School of Geosciences at The University of Texas at Austin.

Arthur T. DeGaetano, Ph.D.
Cornell University, Ithaca, New York
Arthur DeGaetano received his Ph.D. in meteorology from Rutgers University. He is a professor of Earth and atmospheric sciences at Cornell University in New York, where he teaches introductory climatology and upper-level courses in atmospheric thermodynamics and physical meteorology. Dr. DeGaetano is also the director of the Northeast Regional Climate Center.

Jay M. Pasachoff, Ph.D.
Williams College, Williamstown, Massachusetts
Jay Pasachoff received his Ph.D. in astronomy from Harvard University. He is the Field Memorial Professor of Astronomy and the director of the Hopkins Observatory at Williams College in Massachusetts, where he teaches introductory and upper-level courses in astronomy. In addition, Dr. Pasachoff has written several popular college-level astronomy textbooks and an astronomy field guide.

Acknowledgments

Authors

Mead A. Allison, Ph.D.
Senior Research Scientist
Institute for Geophysics
Jackson School of Geosciences
The University of Texas
Austin, Texas

Arthur T. DeGaetano, Ph.D.
Director, Northeast Regional
  Climate Center
Professor
Department of Earth and
  Atmospheric Science
Cornell University
Ithaca, New York

Jay M. Pasachoff, Ph.D.
Director, Hopkins Observatory
Field Memorial Professor of Astronomy
Williams College
Williamstown, Massachusetts

Academic Reviewers

Paul Asimow, Ph.D.
Associate Professor of Geology
  and Geochemistry
Geological and Planetary Sciences
California Institute of Technology
Pasadena, California

Nolan Aughenbaugh
Professor
Department of Geology and
  Geological Engineering
The University of Mississippi
University, Mississippi

Loren E. Babcock, Ph.D.
Professor
School of Earth Sciences
The Ohio State University
Columbus, Ohio

John A. Brockhaus, Ph.D.
Professor & Program Director of
  Geospatial Information Science
Geospatial Information Science
  Program
United States Military Academy
West Point, New York

Jim Burt, Ph.D.
Professor of Geography
Department of Geography
University of Wisconsin-Madison
Madison, Wisconsin

Scott A. Darveau, Ph.D.
Professor of Chemistry
Chemistry Department
University of Nebraska at Kearney
Kearney, Nebraska
Faculty Associate
Nebraska Center for Materials and
  Nanoscience
University of Nebraska-Lincoln
Lincoln, Nebraska

Deborah Hanley, Ph.D.
Meteorologist
Florida Division of Forestry
Department of Agriculture and
  Consumer Services
Tallahassee, Florida

Brennan Jordan, Ph.D.
Assistant Professor
Department of Earth Sciences
University of South Dakota
Vermillion, South Dakota

Daniel Leavell, Ph.D.
Assistant Professor
Department of Geology
The Ohio State University
  at Newark
Newark, Ohio

Sten Odenwald, Ph.D.
Senior Astronomer/Author
Astronomy and Space Physics
NASA-Goddard Space
  Flight Center
Greenbelt, Maryland

Jim Price, Ph.D.
Senior Scientist
Physical Oceanography
  Department
Woods Hole Oceanographic
  Institution
Woods Hole, Massachusetts

Kenneth H. Rubin, Ph.D.
Professor
Department of Geology
  and Geophysics
School of Ocean and Earth Science
University of Hawaii
Honolulu, Hawaii

Dork Sahagian, Ph.D.
Director of Environmental Initiative
Professor of Earth and
  Environmental Sciences
Department of Earth and
  Environmental Sciences
Lehigh University
Bethlehem, Pennsylvania

Vatche P. Tchakerian, Ph.D.
Professor of Geology and Geophysics
Associate Dean for Academic Affairs
College of Geosciences
Texas A&M University
College Station, Texas

Teacher Reviewers

Lowell S. Bailey
Earth Science Educator
Bedford-North Lawrence High School
Bedford, Indiana

Daniel Brownstein, MAT/MA
Science Department Chair
Hastings High School
Hastings, New York

Jeanne Endrikat
Science Chair (Retired)
Lake Braddock Secondary School
Burke, Virginia

Anthony P. LaSalvia
Curriculum Coordinator and Science Teacher
New Lebanon Central Schools
New Lebanon, New York

Keith McKain
Earth Science Teacher
Colonel Richardson High School
Federalsburg, Maryland

Mike McKee
Program Director of The Greater Orlando Graduate Fellows in K-12 Education Program Director of Florida Science Olympiad
University of Central Florida
Orlando, Florida

Christine V. McLelland
Distinguished Earth Science Educator in Residence
Education and Outreach
Geological Society of America
Boulder, Colorado

Tammie Niffenegger
Science Chair and Teacher
Port Washington High School
Port Washington, Wisconsin

Scott Robertson
Earth Science and Physics Teacher
North Warren Central School District
Chestertown, New York

Sharon M. Stroud
Earth Science Teacher and Consultant
Colorado Springs, Colorado

Teresa Tucker
Earth Science Teacher and High School Science Curriculum Chair
Northwest Community Schools
Jackson, Michigan

Lab Reviewers

Randa Flinn, M.S.
Teacher and Science Curriculum Facilitator
Northeast High School
Broward County, Florida

Tammie Niffenegger
Science Chair and Teacher
Port Washington High School
Port Washington, Wisconsin

Scott Robertson
Earth Science and Physics Teacher
North Warren Central School District
Chestertown, New York

Florida Teacher Reviewers

J. Paul DeWise
Jim C. Bailey Middle School
Pensacola, FL

Mary C. Exum
NBCT Science
Pensacola, FL

Pam Hicks
Science Chair
Booker T. Washington High
Pensacola, FL

Loretta Lucas
Belleview High School
Belleview, FL

Miriam Sawyer
Cantonment, FL

Overview of Florida Student Edition

Look for the Florida Standards symbol throughout the book. It tells you which standards are covered in each section.

© Robin Hill/Digital Vision/Getty Images

CONTENTS IN BRIEF

Florida Table of Contents

CONTENTS

Unit 1 Studying the Earth

Environmental
Connection

Unit 2 | Composition of the Earth

Unit 3 — History of the Earth

SC.912.N.1.1
SC.912.N.3.2
SC.912.N.2.5

✹ Environmental
Connection

© Layne Kennedy/CORBIS

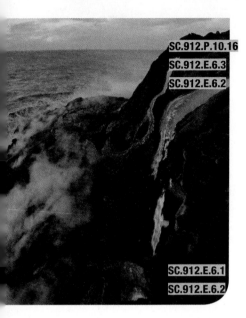

Contents   **FL11**

Unit 5		**Reshaping the Crust**	

Environmental
Connection

© Jim Wark/Airphoto

© Ralph A. Clevenger/CORBIS

Environmental Connection

© Chris Noble/Getty Images

🍂 Environmental Connection

© Jean-Charles Cuillandre/Canada-France-Hawaii Telescope/SPL/Photo Researchers, Inc.

Reference

© NOAO/AURA/NSF

Labs

Short Labs

These short *Inquiry Labs* and *QuickLabs* are designed to be done quickly during any class period (or at home!) with simple materials.

Inquiry Labs

Quick Labs

Chapter Labs

Each chapter includes an in-depth, hands-on lab that lets you experience science first-hand.

Inquiry Labs

Skills Practice Labs

Making Models Labs

MAPS in Action

Maps are important tools of the Earth scientist. This collection of map-skills activities will help you read and understand a variety of maps.

READING TOOLBOX

Reading a textbook is different from reading a novel. The *Reading ToolBoxes* suggest ways to help you organize the concepts in each chapter to get the most out of your reading.

Why It Matters

Have you ever wondered why you need to learn science? Check out these short, interesting articles to learn how science relates to the world around you.

Contents   **FL21**

Florida Student Guide

This page shows you how to read the standards that you will find throughout your textbook. Starting on page FL23, you will find a listing of all the Florida Performance Standards covered in this book. You will also see where the standards are addressed and examples of how they are tested.

SECTION 2 Science as a Process

Key Ideas	Key Terms	Why It Matters
› Explain how science is different from other forms of human endeavor. › Identify the steps that make up scientific methods. › Analyze how scientific thought changes as new information is collected. › Explain how science affects society.	observation hypothesis independent variable dependent variable peer review theory	Science helps us understand Earth, nature, and the universe. Science also helps us apply our knowledge to develop technologies which, in turn, help us solve problems and improve the condition of human society.

Art, architecture, philosophy, and science are all forms of human endeavor. Although artists, architects, and philosophers may use science in their work, science does not have the same goals as other human endeavors do.

The goal of science is to explain natural phenomena. Scientists ask questions about natural events and then work to answer those questions through experiments and examination. Scientific understanding moves forward through the work of many scientists, who build on the research of the generations of scientists before them.

Behavior of Natural Systems

Scientists start with the assumption that nature is understandable, and they expect that similar forces in a similar situation will cause similar results. But the forces involved in natural events are complex. For example, changes in temperature and humidity can cause rain in one city, but the same changes in temperature and humidity may cause fog in another city. These different results might be due to differences in the two cities or due to complex issues, such as differences in climate.

Scientists also expect that nature is predictable, which means that the future behavior of natural forces can be anticipated. So, if scientists understand the forces and materials involved in a process, they can predict how that process will evolve. The scientists in **Figure 1**, for example, are studying ice cores in Antarctica. Ice cores can provide clues to Earth's past climate changes. Because natural systems are complex, however, a high level of understanding and predictability can be difficult to achieve. To increase their understanding, scientists follow the same basic processes of studying and describing natural events.

FLORIDA STANDARDS

SC.912.N.2. Formulate hypotheses referencing prior research and knowledge; SC.912.N.2.2 Conduct controlled experiments or simulations to test hypotheses; SC.912.N.2.3 Collect, organize and analyze data accurately and precisely; SC.912.N.2.4 Apply statistical methods to the data to reach and support conclusions; SC.912.N.2. Formulate hypotheses referencing prior research and kit; SC.912.N.2.2 Apply statistical methods to the data to reach and support conclusions. Apply statistical methods to the data to

Figure 1 Scientists use ice cores to study past compositions of Earth's atmosphere. This information can help scientists learn about past climate changes.

9

Standards Alignment

Throughout your textbook you will see standards listed. This shows what standards are covered in that section.

Figure 8 The Alaskan pipeline has carried more than 15 billion barrels of oil since it was built in 1977. The pipeline has also sparked controversy about the potential dangers to nearby Alaskan wildlife.

SCLINKS.
www.scilinks.org
Topic: Careers in Earth Science
Code: HQX0222

Publication of Results and Conclusions

Scientists commonly present the results of their work in scientific journals or at professional meetings, such as the one shown in **Figure 6**. Results published in journals are usually written in a standard scientific format. Many journals are now being published online to allow scientists quicker access to the results of other scientists and to reduce the costs of printing journals.

Peer Review

Scientists in any one research group tend to view scientific ideas similarly. Therefore, they may be biased in their experimental design or data analysis. To reduce bias, scientists submit their ideas to other scientists for peer review. **Peer review** is the process in which several experts on a given topic review another expert's work on that topic before the work gets published. These experts determine if the results and conclusions of the study merit publication. Peer reviewers commonly suggest improvements to the study, or they may determine that the results or conclusions are flawed and recommend that the study not be published. Scientists follow an ethical code that states that only valid experimental results should be published. The peer review process serves as a filter that allows only well-supported ideas to be published.

Section 2 Review **SC.912.** SC.912.N.2.3; SC.912.N.2.1; SC.912.N.2.1

Key Ideas

1. **Describe** one reason that a scientist conduct research.
2. **Identify** the steps that make up scientific methods.
3. **Compare** a hypothesis with a theory.
4. **Describe** how scientists test hypotheses.
5. **Describe** the difference between a dependent variable and an independent variable.
6. **Describe** the conditions under which scientific laws and theories can be changed.
7. **Summarize** how scientific methods contribute to the development of modern science.
8. **Explain** how technology can affect scientific research.

Critical Thinking

9. **Analyzing Ideas** An observation can be precise but inaccurate. Do you think it is possible for an observation to be accurate but not precise? Explain.
10. **Making Comparisons** When an artist paints a picture of a natural scene, what aspects of his or her work are similar to the methods of a scientist? What aspects are different?
11. **Demonstrating Reasoned Judgment** A new technology is known to be harmful to a small group of people. How does this knowledge affect whether you would use this new technology? Explain.

Concept Mapping

12. Use the following terms to create a concept map: *independent variable, observation, experiment, dependent variable, hypothesis, scientific methods,* and *conclusion.*

5 Chapter 1 **Introduction to Earth Science**

Florida Standards Review

Small codes next to items in the Section Assessment and Chapter Assessment indicate questions that address a standard.
Every item in the Benchmark Review at the end of each chapter addresses a standard.

Sunshine State Standards: Science

FLORIDA STANDARD 1

The Practice of Science

A: Scientific inquiry is a multifaceted activity; The processes of science include the formulation of scientifically investigable questions, construction of investigations into those questions, the collection of appropriate data, the evaluation of the meaning of those data, and the communication of this evaluation.

B: The processes of science frequently do not correspond to the traditional portrayal of "the scientific method."

C: Scientific argumentation is a necessary part of scientific inquiry and plays an important role in the generation and validation of scientific knowledge.

D: Scientific knowledge is based on observation and inference; it is important to recognize that these are very different things. Not only does science require creativity in its methods and processes, but also in its questions and explanations.

WHAT IT MEANS TO YOU

When scientists observe the natural world, they often think of a question or problem. But scientists don't just guess at answers. Instead, they follow series of steps called the scientific method. Scientific methods are a series of steps that scientists use to answer questions and solve problems. Although scientific methods have several steps, there is not a set procedure. Scientists may use all of the steps or just some of the steps. They may even repeat some of the steps or do them in a different order. The goal of scientific methods is to come up with reliable answers and solutions. Scientists use scientific methods to gain ins ight into the problems they investigate.

SC.912.N.1.1 Define a problem based on a specific body of knowledge, for example: biology, chemistry, physics, and earth/space science, and do the following: 1. pose questions about the natural world, 2. conduct systematic observations, 3. examine books and other sources of information to see what is already known, 4. review what is known in light of empirical evidence, 5. plan investigations, 6. use tools to gather, analyze, and interpret data (this includes the use of measurement in metric and other systems, and also the generation and interpretation of graphical representations of data, including data tables and graphs), 7. pose answers, explanations, or descriptions of events, 8. generate explanations that explicate or describe natural phenomena (inferences), 9. use appropriate evidence and reasoning to justify these explanations to others, 10. communicate results of scientific investigations, and 11. evaluate the merits of the explanations produced by others.

SC.912.N.1.2 Describe and explain what characterizes science and its methods.

SC.912.N.1.3 Recognize that the strength or usefulness of a scientific claim is evaluated through scientific argumentation, which depends on critical and logical thinking, and the active consideration of alternative scientific explanations to explain the data presented.

Florida Student Guide

SC.912.N.1.4 Identify sources of information and assess their reliability according to the strict standards of scientific investigation.

SC.912.N.1.5 Describe and provide examples of how similar investigations conducted in many parts of the world result in the same outcome.

SC.912.N.1.6 Describe how scientific inferences are drawn from scientific observations and provide examples from the content being studied.

SC.912.N.1.7 Recognize the role of creativity in constructing scientific questions, methods and explanations.

SAMPLE QUESTIONS

1 Experimental results that do not support a hypothesis can often be very valuable. Why?

   A. They can be labeled as a theory instead of a law.

   B. They can be changed to match the hypothesis for the published article.

   C. They can cause scientists to develop new experiments that produce additional data.

   D. They can cause incompetent scientists to lose their jobs and make room for better scientists.

2 Which of the following attributes would contribute to a good scientific mind?

   F. empathetic nature

   G. willingness to travel

   H. desire to conduct experiments

   I. continual questioning of observations

Answers: 1C, 2I

Illustration by Dan Stuckenschneider (Uhl Studios)

FLORIDA STANDARD 2

The Characteristics of Scientific Knowledge

A: Scientific knowledge is based on empirical evidence, and is appropriate for understanding the natural world, but it provides only a limited understanding of the supernatural, aesthetic, or other ways of knowing, such as art, philosophy, or religion.

B: Scientific knowledge is durable and robust, but open to change.

C: Because science is based on empirical evidence it strives for objectivity, but as it is a human endeavor the processes, methods, and knowledge of science include subjectivity, as well as creativity and discovery.

WHAT IT MEANS TO YOU
From time to time, there are big changes in the way that scientists think the world works. Usually, only very small changes take place. Big changes in the way that scientists think usually take place after one or more scientists discover something new or find a new way of thinking about an old discovery.

SC.912.N.2.1 Identify what is science, what clearly is not science, and what superficially resembles science (but fails to meet the criteria for science).

SC.912.N.2.2 Identify which questions can be answered through science and which questions are outside the boundaries of scientific investigation, such as questions addressed by other ways of knowing, such as art, philosophy, and relgion.

SC.912.N.2.3 Identify examples of pseudoscience (such as astrology, phrenology) in society.

SC.912.N.2.4 Explain that scientific knowledge is both durable and robust and open to change. Scientific knowledge can change because it is often examined and re-examined by new investigations and scientific argumentation. Because of these frequent examinations, scientific knowledge becomes stronger, leading to its durability

SC.912.N.2.5 Describe instances in which scientists' varied backgrounds, talents, interests, and goals influence the inferences and thus the explanations that they make about observations of natural phenomena and describe that competing interpretations (explanations) of scientists are a strength of science as they are a source of new, testable ideas that have the potential to add new evidence to support one or another of the explanations.

Florida Student Guide

Photograph by Sharon Hoogstraten

SAMPLE QUESTIONS

3 What happens when an observation is submitted for peer review?
   A. The article is proofread before it is published.
   B. A professor gives a lecture based on a published article.
   C. The results are looked at closely by other scientific experts.
   D. Information on the experimental design is included in published works.

Answers: 3C

The Role of Theories, Laws, Hypotheses, and Models

The terms that describe examples of scientific knowledge, for example: "theory," "law," "hypothesis" and "model" have very specific meanings and functions within science

SC.912.N.3.1 Explain that a scientific theory is the culmination of many scientific investigations drawing together all the current evidence concerning a substantial range of phenomena; thus, a scientific theory represents the most powerful explanation scientists have to offer.

SC.912.N.3.2 Describe the role consensus plays in the historical development of a theory in any one of the disciplines of science.

SC.912.N.3.3 Explain that scientific laws are descriptions of specific relationships under given conditions in nature, but do not offer explanations for those relationships.

SC.912.N.3.4 Recognize that theories do not become laws, nor do laws become theories; theories are well supported explanations and laws are well supported descriptions.

SC.912.N.3.5 Describe the function of models in science, and identify the wide range of models used in science.

> ## WHAT IT MEANS TO YOU
>
> A hypothesis is a possible explanation for a problem, and a theory is an explanation that is consistent with all existing tests. Scientific theories also make predictions that can be tested. A model is a description, representation, or imitation of an object, system, process, or concept. Scientists use models to simulate conditions in the natural world.

SAMPLE QUESTIONS

4 A possible explanation for a scientific problem is called a(n)

- **F.** experiment.
- **G.** theory.
- **H.** observation.
- **I.** hypothesis.

5 The model that is most useful in studies of global warming is a

- **A.** physical model of the ocean.
- **B.** mathematical model of the ocean.
- **C.** physical model of the atmosphere.
- **D.** mathematical model of the atmosphere.

Answers: 4I, 5D

Florida

FLORIDA STANDARD 4

Science and Society

As tomorrows citizens, students should be able to identify issues about which society could provide input, formulate scientifically investigable questions about those issues, construct investigations of their questions, collect and evaluate data from their investigations, and develop scientific recommendations based upon their findings.

SC.912.N.4.1 Explain how scientific knowledge and reasoning provide an empirically-based perspective to inform society's decision making.

SC.912.N.4.2 Weigh the merits of alternative strategies for solving a specific societal problem by comparing a number of different costs and benefits, such as human, economic, and environmental.

SAMPLE QUESTIONS

6 When scientists pose questions about how nature operates and attempt to answer those questions through testing and observation, they are conducting

   F. research.

   G. predictions.

   H. examinations.

   I. peer reviews.

7 How do scientists determine that there was no bias in an experiment?

   A. The researcher repeats the experiment many times before reporting it.

   B. Independent researchers repeat the experiment.

   C. They know which researchers are biased and which are unbiased.

   D. They trust one another to be careful not to have bias.

Answers: 6F, 7B

Florida Student Guide

Earth in Space and Time

The origin and eventual fate of the Universe still remains one of the greatest questions in science. Gravity and energy influence the development and life cycles of galaxies, including our own Milky Way Galaxy, stars, the planetary systems, Earth, and residual material left from the formation of the Solar System. Humankind's need to explore continues to lead to the development of knowledge and understanding of the nature of the Universe.

SC.912.E.5.1 Cite evidence used to develop and verify the scientific theory of the Big Bang (also known as the Big Bang Theory) of the origin of the universe.

SC.912.E.5.2 Identify patterns in the organization and distribution of matter in the universe and the forces that determine them.

SC.912.E.5.3 Describe and predict how the initial mass of a star determines its evolution.

SC.912.E.5.4 Explain the physical properties of the Sun and its dynamic nature and connect them to conditions and events on Earth.

SC.912.E.5.5 Explain the formation of planetary systems based on our knowledge of our Solar System and apply this knowledge to newly discovered planetary systems.

SC.912.E.5.6 Develop logical connections through physical principles, including Kepler's and Newton's Laws about the relationships and the effects of Earth, Moon, and Sun on each other.

SC.912.E.5.7 Relate the history of and explain the justification for future space exploration and continuing technology development.

SC.912.E.5.8 Connect the concepts of radiation and the electromagnetic spectrum to the use of historical and newly-developed observational tools.

SC.912.E.5.9 Analyze the broad effects of space exploration on the economy and culture of Florida.

SC.912.E.5.10 Describe and apply the coordinate system used to locate objects in the sky.

SC.912.E.5.11 Distinguish the various methods of measuring astronomical distances and apply each in appropriate situations.

WHAT IT MEANS TO YOU

The big bang theory is the accepted explanation for the formation of the universe. According to the theory, about 14 billion years ago, all the matter and energy of the universe was compressed into an extremely small volume. An explosion of this matter and energy in all directions formed our expanding universe. The nebular hypothesis, developed in the late 18th century, states that the solar system formed from a huge rotating cloud of interstellar gas and dust that contracted under the force of its own gravity. Other theories have contributed to our understanding of the formation of our solar system. Using robot explorers in the outer solar system could provide important information about the early history of the solar system.

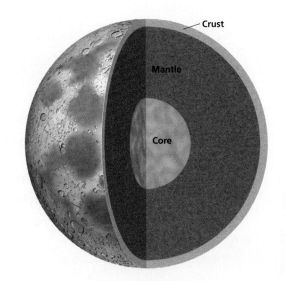

SAMPLE QUESTIONS

8 The hypothesis that states that the sun and the planets develop out of the same cloud of gas and dust is called the

F. Copernicus hypothesis

G. solar hypothesis

H. nebular hypothesis

I. Galileo hypothesis

9 A spectrum reveals the elements in a star. Over a long period, what change would be expected in the sun's spectrum?

A. The amount of hydrogen would increase.

B. The amount of hydrogen would decrease.

C. The amount of helium would decrease.

D. The amount of heavy elements would decrease.

Answers: 8H, 9B

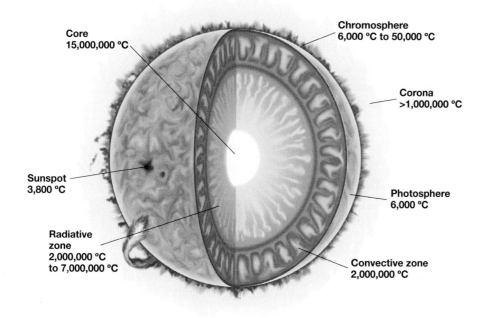

Core
15,000,000 °C

Chromosphere
6,000 °C to 50,000 °C

Corona
>1,000,000 °C

Sunspot
3,800 °C

Photosphere
6,000 °C

Radiative
zone
2,000,000 °C
to 7,000,000 °C

Convective zone
2,000,000 °C

Florida Student Guide

Earth Structures

The scientific theory of plate tectonics provides the framework for much of modern geology. Over geologic time, internal and external sources of energy have continuously altered the features of Earth by means of both constructive and destructive forces. All life, including human civilization, is dependent on Earth's internal and external energy and material resources.

SC.912.E.6.1 Describe and differentiate the layers of Earth and the interactions among them.

SC.912.E.6.2 Connect surface features to surface processes that are responsible for their formation.

SC.912.E.6.3 Analyze the scientific theory of plate tectonics and identify related major processes and features as a result of moving plates.

SC.912.E.6.4 Analyze how specific geologic processes and features are expressed in Florida and elsewhere.

SC.912.E.6.5 Describe the geologic development of the present day oceans and identify commonly found features.

SC.912.E.6.6 Analyze past, present, and potential future consequences to the environment resulting from various energy production technologies.

WHAT IT MEANS TO YOU

Tectonic plates move around on the asthenosphere. This motion occurs because density changes caused by the outward flow of thermal energy from deep within Earth. When magma is heated, it expands, becomes less dense, and tends to rise towards the surface of Earth. As the magma gets near the surface it cools, becomes denser, and tends to sink. Where tectonic plates collide, land features that start as folds and faults can eventually become large mountain ranges. Mountains exist because tectonic plates are continually moving around and colliding with one another. For example, the Andes Mountains formed above the subduction zone where two tectonic plates converge.

SAMPLE QUESTIONS

10 Mountains and other major landforms on Earth result from forces generated by

    F. the separation, collision, and movement of tectonic plates.

    G. high winds during sandstorms.

    H. waves crashing against the coast.

    I. meteors striking Earth's surface.

11 What is a mantle plume?

    A. a rising column of magma

    B. a formation under a mid-ocean ridge

    C. part of a geyser

    D. the center of a volcano

Answers: 10F, 11A

FLORIDA STANDARD 7

Earth Systems and Patterns

The scientific theory of the evolution of Earth states that changes in our planet are driven by the flow of energy and the cycling of matter through dynamic interactions among the atmosphere, hydrosphere, cryosphere, geosphere, and biosphere, and the resources used to sustain human civilization on Earth.

WHAT IT MEANS TO YOU
The evolution of the Earth system is a result of the interaction between the two most basic components of the universe; matter and energy. The Earth system is composed of "spheres" that are the storehouses of all of the planet's matter. The energy that flows through the Earth system takes the form of heat, light, vibrations and electromagnetic waves.

SC.912.E.7.1 Analyze the movement of matter and energy through the different biogeochemical cycles, including water and carbon.

SC.912.E.7.2 Analyze the causes of the various kinds of surface and deep water motion within the oceans and their impacts on the transfer of energy between the poles and the equator.

SC.912.E.7.3 Differentiate and describe the various interactions among Earth systems, including: atmosphere, hydrosphere, cryosphere, geosphere, and biosphere.

SC.912.E.7.4 Summarize the conditions that contribute to the climate of a geographic area, including the relationships to lakes and oceans.

SC.912.E.7.5 Predict future weather conditions based on present observations and conceptual models and recognize limitations and uncertainties of such predictions.

SC.912.E.7.6 Relate the formation of severe weather to the various physical factors.

SC.912.E.7.7 Identify, analyze, and relate the internal (Earth system) and external (astronomical) conditions that contribute to global climate change.

SC.912.E.7.8 Explain how various atmospheric, oceanic, and hydrologic conditions in Florida have influenced and can influence human behavior, both individually and collectively.

SC.912.E.7.9 Cite evidence that the ocean has had a significant influence on climate change by absorbing, storing, and moving heat, carbon, and water.

SAMPLE QUESTIONS

12 Why is the energy generated at a hydroelectric dam dependent on the sun?

    F. The sun's gravity causes water to flow.

    G. Energy from the sun powers the water cycle.

    H. Sunlight gets rid of the pollution created by hydroelectric dams.

    I. Sunlight is the source of energy in the fuels burned by hydroelectric dams.

Answers: 12G

Florida Student Guide

LAB SAFETY

In the laboratory or in the field, you can engage in hands-on explorations, test your scientific hypotheses, and build practical lab skills. However, while you are working, it is your responsibility to protect yourself and your classmates by conducting yourself in a safe manner. You will avoid accidents by following directions, handling materials carefully, and taking your work seriously. Read the following safety guidelines before working in the lab or field. Make sure that you understand all safety guidelines before entering the lab or field.

Before You Begin

- **Read the entire activity before entering the lab.** Be familiar with the instructions before beginning an activity. Do not start an activity until you have asked your teacher to explain any parts of the activity that you do not understand.
- **Wear the right clothing for lab work.** Before beginning work, tie back long hair, roll up loose sleeves, and put on any required personal protective equipment as directed by your teacher. Remove your wristwatch and any necklaces or jewelry that could get caught in moving parts or contact electrical connections. Avoid or confine loose clothing that could knock things over, catch on fire, get caught in moving parts, contact electrical connections, or absorb chemical solutions. Wear pants rather than shorts or skirts. Nylon and polyester fabrics burn and melt more readily than cotton does. Protect your feet from chemical spills and falling objects. Do not wear open-toed shoes, sandals, or canvas shoes in the lab.
- **Know the location of all safety and emergency equipment used in the lab.** Know proper fire-drill procedures and the location of all fire exits. Ask your teacher where the nearest eyewash stations, safety blankets, safety shower, fire extinguisher, first-aid kit, and chemical spill kit are located. Be sure that you know how to operate the equipment safely.

While You Are Working

- **Always wear a lab apron and safety goggles.** Wear these items while in the lab, even if you are not working on an activity. Labs contain chemicals that can damage your clothing, skin, and eyes. Aprons and goggles also protect against many physical hazards. If your safety goggles cloud up or are uncomfortable, ask your teacher for help. Lengthening the strap slightly, washing the goggles with soap and warm water, or using an anti-fog spray may help the problem.
- **NEVER work alone in the lab.** Work in the lab only when supervised by your teacher.
- **NEVER leave equipment unattended while it is in operation.**
- **Perform only activities specifically assigned by your teacher.** Do not attempt any procedure without your teacher's direction. Use only materials and equipment listed in the activity or authorized by your teacher. Steps in a procedure should be performed only as described in the activity or as approved by your teacher.
- **Keep your work area neat and uncluttered.** Have only books and other materials that are needed to conduct the activity in the lab. Keep backpacks, purses, and other items in your desk, locker, or other designated storage areas.
- **Always heed safety symbols and cautions listed in activities, listed on handouts, posted in the room, provided on equipment or chemical labels (whether provided by the manufacturer or added later), and given verbally by your teacher.** Be aware of the potential hazards of the required materials and procedures, and follow all precautions indicated.
- **Be alert, and walk with care in the lab.** Be aware of others near you and your equipment and be aware of what they are doing.
- **Do not take food, drinks, chewing gum, or tobacco products into the lab.** Do not store or eat food in the lab. Either finish these items or discard them before coming into the lab or beginning work in the field.
- **NEVER taste chemicals or allow them to contact your skin.** Keep your hands away from your face and mouth, even if you are wearing gloves. Only smell vapors as instructed by your teacher and only in the manner indicated.

- **Exercise caution when working with electrical equipment.** Do not use electrical equipment with frayed or twisted wires. Check that insulation on wiring is intact. Be sure that your hands are dry before using electrical equipment. Do not let electrical cords dangle from work stations. Dangling cords can catch on apparatus on tables, can cause you to trip and can cause an electrical shock. The area under and around electrical equipment should be dry; cords should not lie in puddles of spilled liquid, under sink spigots, or in sinks themselves.

- **Use extreme caution when working with hot plates and other heating devices.** Keep your head, hands, hair, and clothing away from the flame or heating area. Remember that metal surfaces connected to the heated area will become hot by conduction. Gas burners should be lit only with a spark lighter, not with matches. Make sure that all heating devices and gas valves are turned off before you leave the lab. Never leave a heating device unattended when it is in use. Metal, ceramic, and glass items do not necessarily look hot when they are hot. Allow all items to cool before storing them.

- **Do not fool around in the lab.** Take your lab work seriously, and behave appropriately in the lab. Lab equipment and apparatus are not toys; never use lab time or equipment for anything other than the intended purpose. Be considerate and be aware of the safety of your classmates as well as your safety at all times.

© Sam Dudgeon/Harcourt

Emergency Procedures

- **Follow standard fire-safety procedures.** If your clothing catches on fire, do not run; WALK to the safety shower, stand under it, and turn it on. While doing so, call to your teacher. In case of fire, alert your teacher and leave the lab.

- **Report any accident, incident, or hazard—no matter how trivial—to your teacher immediately.** Any incident involving bleeding, burns, fainting, nausea, dizziness, chemical exposure, or ingestion should also be reported immediately to the school nurse or to a physician. If you have a close call, tell your teacher so that you and your teacher can find a way to prevent it from happening again.

- **Report all spills to your teacher immediately.** Call your teacher rather than trying to clean a spill yourself. Your teacher will tell you whether it is safe for you to clean up the spill; if it is not safe, your teacher will know how to clean up the spill.

- **If you spill a chemical on your skin, wash the chemical off in the sink and call your teacher.** If you spill a solid chemical onto your clothing, using an appropriate container, brush it off carefully without scattering it onto somebody else and call your teacher. If you spill corrosive substances on your skin or clothing, use the safety shower or a faucet to rinse. Remove affected clothing while you are under the shower, and call to your teacher. (It may be temporarily embarrassing to remove clothing in front of your classmates, but failure to thoroughly rinse a chemical off your skin could result in permanent damage.)

- **If you get a chemical in your eyes, walk immediately to the eyewash station, turn it on, and lower your head so your eyes are in the running water.** Hold your eyelids open with your thumbs and fingers, and roll your eyeballs around. You have to flush your eyes continuously for at least 15 minutes. Call your teacher while you are doing this.

When You Are Finished

- **Clean your work area at the conclusion of each lab period as directed by your teacher.** Broken glass, chemicals, and other waste products should be disposed of in separate, special containers. Dispose of waste materials as directed by your teacher. Put away all material and equipment according to your teacher's instructions. Report any damaged or missing equipment or materials to your teacher.

- **Even if you wore gloves, wash your hands with soap and hot water after each lab period.** To avoid contamination, wash your hands at the conclusion of each lab period, and before you leave the lab.

SAFETY SYMBOLS

Before you begin working on an activity, familiarize yourself with the following safety symbols, which are used throughout your textbook, and the guidelines that you should follow when you see these symbols.

Eye Protection

- **Wear approved safety goggles as directed.** Safety goggles should be worn in the lab at all times, especially when you are working with a chemical or solution, a heat source, or a mechanical device.

- **If chemicals get into your eyes, flush your eyes immediately.** Go to an eyewash station immediately, and flush your eyes (including under the eyelids) with running water for at least 15 minutes. Use your thumb and fingers to hold your eyelids open and roll your eyeballs around. While doing so, call your teacher or ask another student to notify your teacher.

- **Do not look directly at the sun or any intense light source or laser.** Do not look at these through any optical device or lens system. Do not reflect direct sunlight to illuminate a microscope. Such actions concentrate light rays to an intensity that can severely burn your retinas, causing blindness.

Clothing Protection

- **Wear an apron or lab coat at all times in the lab to prevent chemicals or chemical solutions from contacting skin or clothes.**

- **Tie back long hair, secure loose clothing, and remove loose jewelry so that they do not knock over equipment, get caught in moving parts, or come into contact with hazardous materials or electrical connections.**

- **Do not wear open-toed shoes, sandals, or canvas shoes in the lab.** Splashed chemicals directly contact skin or quickly soak through canvas. Hard shoes will not allow chemicals to soak through as quickly and they provide more protection against dropped or falling objects.

Hand Safety

- **Do not cut an object while holding the object in your hand.** Cut objects on a suitable work surface. Always cut in a direction away from your body.

- **Wear appropriate protective gloves when working with an open flame, chemicals, solutions, or wild or unknown plants.** Your teacher will provide the type of gloves necessary for a given activity.

- **Use a heat-resistant mitt to handle resistors, light sources, and other equipment that may be hot.** Allow all equipment to cool before storing it.

Hygienic Care

- **Keep your hands away from your face, hair, and mouth while you are working on any activity.**

- **Wash your hands thoroughly before you leave the lab or when you finish any activity.**

- **Remove contaminated clothing immediately.** If you spill corrosive substances on your skin or clothing, use the safety shower or a faucet to rinse. Remove affected clothing while you are under the shower, and call to your teacher. (It may be temporarily embarrassing to remove clothing in front of your classmates, but failure to thoroughly rinse a chemical off your skin could result in permanent damage.)

Sharp-Object Safety

- **Use extreme care when handling all sharp and pointed instruments, such as scalpels, sharp probes, and knives.**

- **Do not cut an object while holding the object in your hand.** Cut objects on a suitable work surface. Always cut in a direction away from your body.

- **Do not use double-edged razor blades in the lab.**

- **Be aware of sharp objects or protrusions on equipment or apparatus.**

Glassware Safety

- **Inspect glassware before use; do not use chipped or cracked glassware.** Use heat-resistant glassware for heating materials or storing hot liquids, and use appropriate tongs or a heat-resistant mitt to handle this equipment.
- **Notify your teacher immediately if a piece of glassware or a light bulb breaks.** Do not attempt to clean up broken glass or remove broken bulbs unless your teacher directs you to do so.

 Proper Waste Disposal

- **Clean and sanitize all work surfaces and personal protective equipment after each lab period as directed by your teacher.**
- **Dispose of contaminated materials (biological or chemical) in special containers only as directed by your teacher.** Never put these materials into a regular waste container or down the drain.
- **Dispose of sharp objects (such as broken glass) in the appropriate sharps or broken-glass container as directed by your teacher.**

 Electrical Safety

- **Do not use equipment with frayed electrical cords or loose plugs.** Do not attempt to remove a plug tine if it breaks off in the socket. Notify your teacher and stay away from the outlet.
- **Fasten electrical cords to work surfaces by using tape.** Doing so will prevent tripping and will ensure that equipment will not be pulled or fall off the table.
- **Do not use electrical equipment near water or when your clothing or hands are wet.**
- **Hold the plug housing when you plug in or unplug equipment.** Do not touch the metal prongs of the plug, and do not unplug equipment by pulling on the cord.
- **Wire coils in circuits may heat up rapidly.** If heating occurs, open the switch immediately and use a hot mitt to handle the equipment.

 Heating Safety

- **Be aware of any source of flames, sparks, or heat (such as open flames, electric heating coils, or hot plates) before working with flammable liquids or gases.**
- **Avoid using open flames.** If possible, work only with hot plates that have an on/off switch and an indicator light. Do not leave hot plates unattended. Do not use alcohol lamps. Turn off hot plates and open flames when they are not in use.
- **Never leave a hot plate unattended while it is turned on or while it is cooling off.**
- **Know the location of lab fire extinguishers and fire-safety blankets.**
- **Use tongs or appropriate insulated holders when handling heated objects.** Heated objects often do not appear to be hot. Do not pick up an object with your hand if it could be warm.
- **Keep flammable substances away from heat, flames, and other ignition sources.**
- **Allow all equipment to cool before storing it.**

 Fire Safety

- **Know the location of lab fire extinguishers and fire-safety blankets.**
- **Know your school's fire-evacuation routes.** Always evacuate the building when the fire alarm is activated.
- **If your clothing catches on fire, walk (do not run) to the emergency lab shower to put out the fire.** If the shower is not working, STOP, DROP, and ROLL! Smother the fire by stopping immediately, dropping to the floor, and rolling until the fire is out.

 Safety with Gases

- **Do not inhale any gas or vapor unless directed to do so by your teacher.** Never inhale pure gases.
- **Handle materials that emit vapors or gases in a well-ventilated area.** This work should be done in an approved chemical fume hood. Always work at least four to six inches inside the front edge of the hood.

 Caustic Substances

- **If a chemical gets on your skin, on your clothing, or in your eyes, rinse it immediately (shower, faucet or eyewash fountain) and alert your teacher.**
- **If you spill a chemical on the floor or lab bench, alert your teacher, but do not clean it up yourself unless your teacher directs you to do so.**

How to Use Your Textbook

This textbook might seem confusing to you when you first look through it. But by reading the next few pages, you will learn how the different parts of this textbook will help you to become a successful science student. You may be tempted to skip this section, but you should read it. This textbook is an important tool in your exploration of science. Like any tool, the more you know about how to use this textbook, the better your results will be.

Step into Science
The beginning of each chapter is designed to get you involved with science. You will immediately see that science matters!

Chapter Outline You can get a quick overview of the chapter by looking at the chapter's outline. In the outline, the section titles and the topics within that section are listed.

Why It Matters The photo that starts each chapter was selected not only to be interesting but also to relate to the content you will learn about in the chapter. The photo caption lets you know how this content applies to the real world.

Inquiry Lab This lab gives you a chance to get some hands-on experience right away. It is designed to help focus your attention on the concepts that you will learn in the chapter.

Read for Meaning

At the beginning of each chapter you will find tools that will help you grasp the meaning of what you read. Each section also introduces what is important in that section and why.

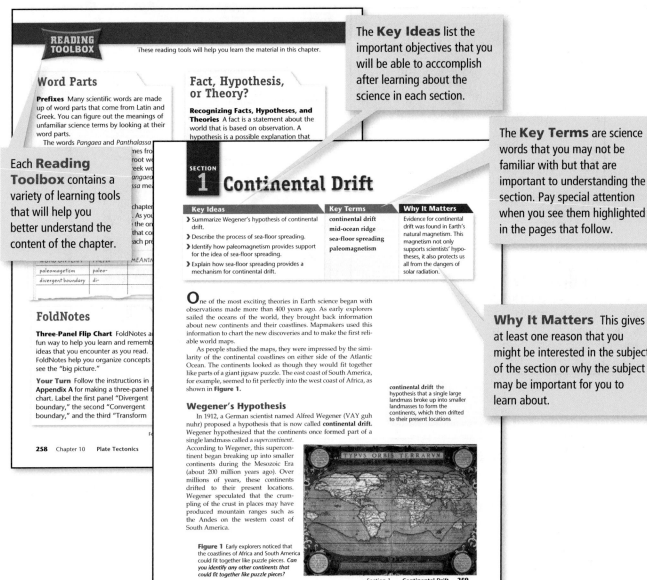

The **Key Ideas** list the important objectives that you will be able to acccomplish after learning about the science in each section.

The **Key Terms** are science words that you may not be familiar with but that are important to understanding the section. Pay special attention when you see them highlighted in the pages that follow.

Each **Reading Toolbox** contains a variety of learning tools that will help you better understand the content of the chapter.

Why It Matters This gives at least one reason that you might be interested in the subject of the section or why the subject may be important for you to learn about.

Keep an Eye on Headings

Notice that the headings in this textbook are different sizes and different colors. The headings help you organize your reading and form a simple outline, as shown below.

Blue: Section titles

Red: Main heading

Green: Sub-heading

Science Is Doing

You will get many opportunities throughout this textbook to actually do science. After all, doing is what science is about.

Build your reasoning and problem-solving skills by following the example problems in **Math Skills**.

Check your reading comprehension with the **Reading Check** questions. Answers are found in Appendix G.

SciLinks lets you use the Internet to link to interesting topics and activities related to the section.

Almost every section in the textbook has at least one **Quick Lab** or slightly more-involved **Inquiry Lab** to help you get real experience doing science.

The **Chapter Lab** at the end of the chapter helps you build your understanding of scientific methods. These labs reinforce the chapter with hands-on activity.

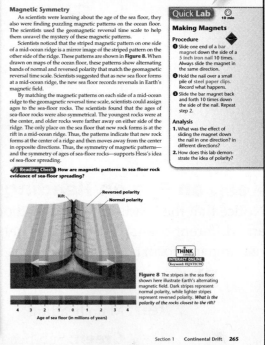

Review What You Have Learned

You can't review too much when you are learning science. To help you review, a **Section Review** appears at the end of every section and a **Chapter Summary** and **Chapter Review** appear at the end of every chapter. These reviews not only help you study for tests but also help further your understanding of the content.

Just a few clicks away, each **Super Summary** gives you even more ways to review and study for tests using a computer and the Internet.

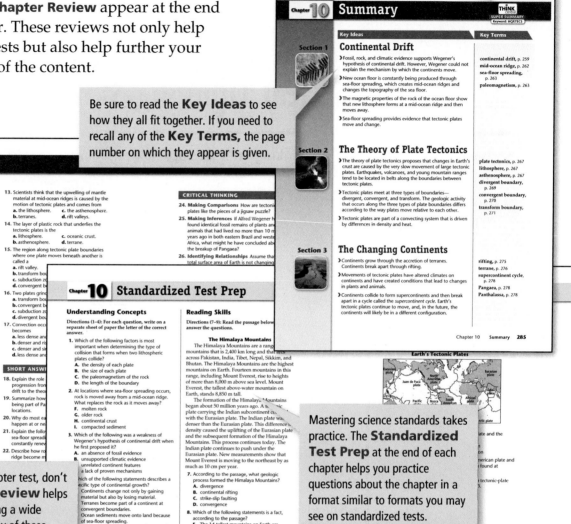

Be sure to read the **Key Ideas** to see how they all fit together. If you need to recall any of the **Key Terms**, the page number on which they appear is given.

When it is time for a chapter test, don't panic. The **Chapter Review** helps you get ready by providing a wide variety of questions. Many of these questions help you develop a better understanding of the content. Once you understand the content, you will be ready for any test!

Mastering science standards takes practice. The **Standardized Test Prep** at the end of each chapter helps you practice questions about the chapter in a format similar to formats you may see on standardized tests.

↗ Be Resourceful—Use the Web!

Your Online Textbook

If your teacher gives you a special password to log onto the thinkcentral.com site, you will find your complete textbook on the Web in an online format. In addition, you will find some great learning tools and interactive materials. You can now access your textbook anywhere and anytime via the Internet.

Take a Test Drive

How well can you use this book now? Take Chapter 1 out for a spin and see how you do. Log onto thinkcentral.com and enter the keyword **HQX TEST DRIVE** for a short list of questions that will test your ability to navigate this book.

Science Testing and Critical Thinking Skills

What Are Critical Thinking Skills?

Critical thinking skills are not a new phenomenon on the education scene. In 1956, Benjamin Bloom published a book that listed critical thinking skills in the form of a taxonomy, as shown in the illustration below.

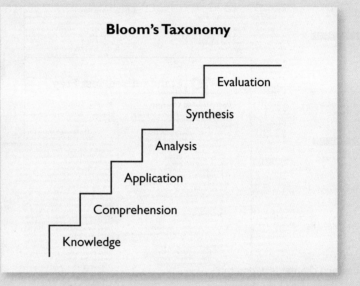

Bloom's Taxonomy

Evaluation
Synthesis
Analysis
Application
Comprehension
Knowledge

- **Knowledge** is the simplest level of education objectives and is not considered a higher-order thinking skill. It requires the learner to remember information without having to fully understand it. Tasks that students perform to demonstrate knowledge are recalling, identifying, recognizing, citing, labeling, listing, reciting, and stating.

EXAMPLES

1. What is physical science?
2. Define *osmosis*.
3. Label the following laboratory equipment.

- **Comprehension** is not considered a higher-order thinking skill either. Learners demonstrate comprehension when they paraphrase, describe, summarize, illustrate, restate, or translate. Information isn't useful unless it's understood. Students can show they've understood by restating the information in their own words or by giving an example of the concept.

EXAMPLES

1. Explain and give an example of a pure substance.
2. Use the terms *element* and *pure substance* in the same sentence.
3. In your own words, write a definition for the term *motion*.

Many teachers tend to focus the most on knowledge and comprehension—and the tasks performed at these levels are important because they provide a solid foundation for the more complex tasks at the higher levels of Bloom's pyramid.

However, offering students the opportunity to perform at still higher cognitive levels provides them with more meaningful contexts in which to use the information and skills they have acquired, thus allowing them to more easily retain what they have learned.

When teachers incorporate **application, analysis, synthesis,** and **evaluation** as objectives, they allow students to utilize **higher-order thinking skills.**

- **Application** involves solving, transforming, determining, demonstrating, and preparing. Information becomes useful when students apply it to new situations—predicting outcomes, estimating answers—this is application.

EXAMPLES

1. Explain what happens to the temperature of an ice cube when it melts.
2. An athlete swims a distance from one end of a 50-meter pool to the other end in a time of 25 seconds. What is the athlete's average speed?
3. List 3 forces that you exert when riding a bicycle.

- **Analysis** includes classifying, comparing, making associations, verifying, seeing cause-and-effect relationships, and determining sequences, patterns, and consequences. You can think of analysis as taking something apart in order to better understand it. Students must be able to think in categories in order to analyze.

  EXAMPLES

  1. When finding net force, why must you know the directions of the forces acting on an object?
  2. How is Newton's third law of motion related to the law of conservation of momentum?
  3. How do fluids exert pressure on a container?

- **Synthesis** requires generalizing, predicting, imagining, creating, making inferences, hypothesizing, making decisions, and drawing conclusions. Students create something which is new to them when they use synthesis. It's important to remember, though, that students can't create until they have the skills and information they have received in the comprehension through analysis levels.

  EXAMPLES

  1. Why do airplanes need to be pressurized for passenger safety when flying high in the atmosphere?
  2. Create a demonstration that shows the effects of buoyant force.
  3. Research the lives and works of Anders Celsius and Gabriel Fahrenheit and present your findings in a skit.

- **Evaluation** involves assessing, persuading, determining value, judging, validating, and solving problems. Evaluation is based on all the other levels. When students evaluate, they make judgments, but not judgments based on personal taste. These judgments must be based on criteria. It is important for students to evaluate because they learn to consider different points of view and to know how to validate their judgments.

  EXAMPLES

  1. Defend the following statement:
     Integrated circuits for computer and game chips have changed the world.
  2. Create a set of criteria for evaluating the success of an experiment.
  3. Validate the correctness of this statement:
     Rock + Waves = Sand

Why is it Important for Students to Work with Higher-Order Thinking Skills?

For one thing, if students can determine the levels of questions that will appear on their tests, they will be able to study using appropriate strategies. Bloom's leveling of questions provides a useful structure in which to categorize test questions, since tests will characteristically ask questions within particular levels.

Also, thinking is a skill that can be taught. When you have students practice answering questions at all the levels of Bloom's taxonomy, you are helping to scaffold their learning. Information just becomes trivia unless that information is understood well enough to build more complicated concepts or generalizations. When students can comprehend—not just recall—the information, it becomes useful for future problem solving or creative thought. Think of information as a building material—like a board. It could be used to build something, but it is just useless litter unless you understand how to make use of it.

Below are some question stems you—or your students—could use to create questions for each of the levels of higher-order thinking:

Application

1. Make a timeline to show _____.
2. Use the key vocabulary words in this chapter to write a paragraph about _____.
3. Write a letter to (the main character, inventor, historical figure).
4. Explain how the (principle, theorem, concept) is evident in _____.
5. In what way is _____ a _____?

Analysis

1. Analyze the organizational structure of _____.
2. Evaluate the relevancy of the data in _____.
3. What other (stories, books, chapters, etc.) have similar messages/themes? Explain.
4. Compare and contrast the (main characters, theorems, classes, etc.).
5. On the basis of your observation of _____, which variables could you eliminate as _____factors?

Synthesis

1. Change the setting and rewrite the (story, novel, chapter, etc.) based on the new setting and the changes it would cause.

2. Show how the fictional work _____ actually reflects the ideas in the nonfiction work _____.

3. Create a new way to classify _____.

4. Design your own _____ to show _____.

5. Create a new way to _____.

Evaluation

1. Which (poet, general, experiment, etc.) did you like more? Why?

2. What is _____'s most important contribution? Support your answer.

3. Is this _____ relevant for today's _____? Explain.

4. Justify your opinion of _____.

5. Were _____'s actions in this (battle, crisis, etc.) correct? Defend your answer.

Unit 1 Studying the Earth

1

Chapter 1

Introduction to Earth Science

Why It Matters

Scientists who study Earth explore the relationships among human society and the air, water, and soil of Earth. They also solve mysteries, such as how this heavy boulder moves on its own across a flat plain in Death Valley, California.

Inquiry Lab

⏱ 15 min

How Observant Are You?

Working in groups, make and record as many observations about your classroom as you can in 10 min. Use a **magnifying glass**, a **thermometer**, and a **meterstick** to help you. Compare your observations with the observations made by other students.

Questions to Get You Started

1. Which of your observations were qualitative? Which were quantitative?

2. Think of a question about your classroom that could be answered by making more observations. What observations would you make to answer your question?

SC.912.N.1.1.6

3

READING TOOLBOX

These reading tools will help you learn the material in this chapter.

Word Parts

Suffixes When you add the suffix *-logy* to a root word or a prefix, you form a word that means "the science of." For example, when you combine *-logy* with the prefix *bio-* (which means "life"), you form the word *biology*. Biology is the study of life.

Your Turn Two key terms in Section 1 use the suffix *-logy*. (Key terms in sections are indicated by bold text with yellow highlights.) Copy the table below and add the second key term.

Key term	Root and its meaning	Suffix	Definition
geology	geo-, means "Earth"	-logy	the study of the origin, history, processes, and structure of the solid Earth

Graphic Organizers

Spider Maps Spider maps show how details are organized into categories that, in turn, are related to a main idea. To make a spider map, follow these steps.

1 For your title, write the main topic. Draw an oval around it.

2 From the oval, draw legs. Each leg represents a category of the main topic.

3 From each leg, draw horizontal lines. Write details about each category on these lines.

Your Turn As you read Section 2, complete a spider map like the one started here to organize the ideas you learn about scientific measurement.

Finding Examples

Words That Signal Examples As you are reading, certain words or phrases can serve as signals that an example is about to be introduced. Two of these signal phrases are "for example" and "such as."

Your Turn In Chapter 1, there are ten sentences with examples that are signaled by

"for example" and ten sentences with examples that are signaled by "such as." Search the chapter to find and record three sentences that use "for example" and four sentences that use "such as."

For more information on how to use these and other tools, see **Appendix A**.

What Is Earth Science?

Key Ideas	Key Terms	Why It Matters
❯ Describe two cultures that contributed to modern scientific study. ❯ Name the four main branches of Earth science. ❯ Discuss how Earth scientists help us understand the world around us.	**Earth science** **geology** **oceanography** **meteorology** **astronomy**	Earth scientists help us understand our place in Earth's history and in the universe. They can also help us gain access to Earth's resources and use these resources wisely.

For thousands of years, people have looked at the world around them and wondered what forces shaped it. Throughout history, many cultures have been terrified and fascinated by seeing volcanoes erupt, feeling the ground shake during an earthquake, or watching the sky darken during an eclipse.

Some cultures developed myths or stories to explain these events. Modern science searches for natural causes and uses careful observations to explain these same events and to understand Earth and its changing landscape.

The Scientific Study of Earth

Scientific study of Earth began with careful observations. Scientists in China began keeping records of earthquakes as early as 780 BCE. The ancient Greeks compiled a catalog of rocks and minerals around 200 BCE. Other ancient peoples, including the Maya, tracked the movements of the sun, the moon, and the planets at observatories like the one shown in **Figure 1.** The Maya used these observations to create accurate calendars.

For many centuries, scientific discoveries were limited to observations of phenomena that could be seen with the unaided eye. Then, in the 16th and 17th centuries, the inventions of the microscope and the telescope made seeing previously hidden worlds possible. Eventually, the body of knowledge about Earth became known as Earth science. **Earth science** is the study of Earth and of the universe around it. Earth science, like other sciences, assumes that natural events, or phenomena, can be explained through careful observation and experimentation.

FLORIDA STANDARDS

LA.910.2.2.3 The student will organize information to show understanding or relationships among facts, ideas, and events (e.g., representing key points within text through charting, mapping, paraphrasing, summarizing, comparing, contrasting, or outlining); **MA.912.S.3.2** Collect, organize, and analyze data sets, determine the best format for the data and present visual summaries from the following: bar graphs, line graphs, stem and leaf plots, circle graphs, histograms, box and whisker plots, scatter plots, cumulative frequency graphs.

Earth science the scientific study of Earth and the universe around it

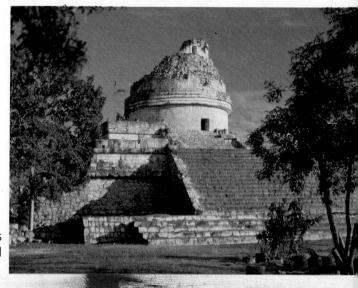

Figure 1 El Caracol, an observatory built by the ancient Maya of Central America, is one of the oldest known observatories in the Americas. Mayan calendars include the celestial movements that the Maya tracked by using observatories.

Branches of Earth Science

The ability to make observations improves when <u>technology</u>, such as new processes or equipment, is developed. Technology has allowed scientists to explore the ocean depths, Earth's unseen interior, and the vastness of space. Earth scientists have used technology and hard work to build an immense body of knowledge about Earth.

Most Earth scientists specialize in one of four major areas of study: the solid Earth, the oceans, the atmosphere, and the universe beyond Earth. Examples of Earth scientists working in these areas are shown in **Figure 2.**

Geology

The study of the origin, history, processes, and structure of the solid Earth is called **geology.** Geology includes many specialized areas of study. Some geologists explore Earth's crust for deposits of coal, oil, gas, and other resources. Other geologists study the forces within Earth to predict earthquakes and volcanic eruptions. Some geologists study fossils to learn more about Earth's past. Often, new knowledge forms new areas of study.

Oceanography

Oceans cover nearly three-fourths of Earth's surface. The study of Earth's oceans is called **oceanography.** Some oceanographers work on research ships that are equipped with special instruments for studying the sea. Other oceanographers study waves, tides, and ocean currents. Some oceanographers explore the ocean floor to obtain clues to Earth's history or to locate mineral deposits.

READING TOOLBOX

Spider Map
Create a spider map that summarizes the branches of Earth science. Use the green heads in this section as the legs of your spider map, and add one or two branches to each leg.

geology the scientific study of the origin, history, and structure of Earth and the processes that shape Earth

oceanography the scientific study of the ocean, including the properties and movements of ocean water, the characteristics of the ocean floor, and the organisms that live in the ocean

Academic Vocabulary

technology (tek NAHL uh jee) tools, including electronic devices

Figure 2 Fields of Study in Earth Science

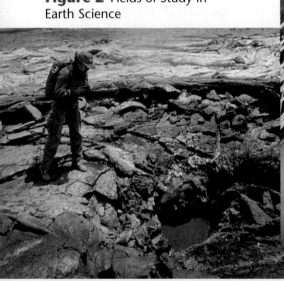

Geologists who study volcanoes are called volcanologists. This volcanologist is measuring the properties of moving lava.

This astronomer is linking a telescope with a specialized instrument called a spectrograph. Information gathered will help her catalog the composition of more than 100 galaxies.

This meteorologist is studying ice samples to learn about past climate. Studying past climate patterns gives scientists information about possible future changes in climate.

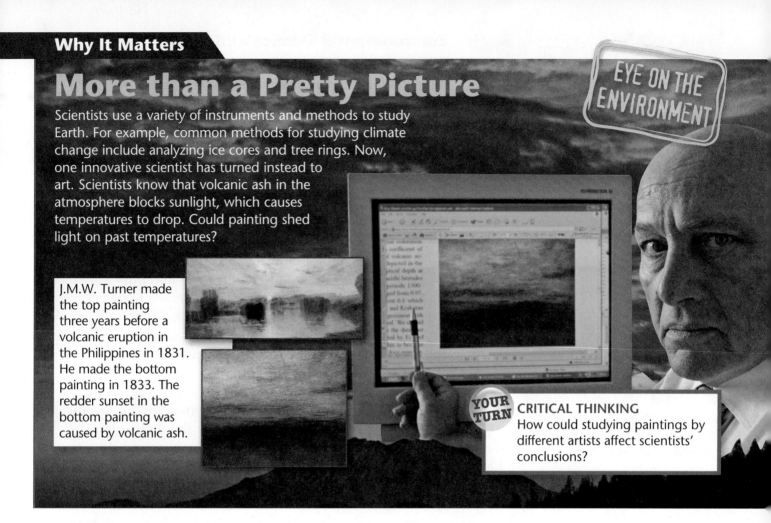

More than a Pretty Picture

EYE ON THE ENVIRONMENT

Scientists use a variety of instruments and methods to study Earth. For example, common methods for studying climate change include analyzing ice cores and tree rings. Now, one innovative scientist has turned instead to art. Scientists know that volcanic ash in the atmosphere blocks sunlight, which causes temperatures to drop. Could painting shed light on past temperatures?

J.M.W. Turner made the top painting three years before a volcanic eruption in the Philippines in 1831. He made the bottom painting in 1833. The redder sunset in the bottom painting was caused by volcanic ash.

YOUR TURN

CRITICAL THINKING
How could studying paintings by different artists affect scientists' conclusions?

Meteorology

The study of Earth's atmosphere is called **meteorology**. Using satellites, radar, and other technologies, meteorologists study the atmospheric conditions that produce weather. Many meteorologists work as weather observers and measure factors such as wind speed, temperature, and rainfall. This weather information is then used to prepare detailed weather maps. Other meteorologists use weather maps, satellite images, and computer models to make weather forecasts. Some meteorologists study *climate*, the patterns of weather that occur over long periods of time.

Astronomy

The study of the universe beyond Earth is called **astronomy.** Astronomy is one of the oldest branches of Earth science. In fact, the ancient Babylonians charted the positions of planets and stars nearly 4,000 years ago. Modern astronomers use Earth-based and space-based telescopes as well as other instruments to study the sun, the moon, the planets, and the universe. Technologies such as rovers and space probes have also provided astronomers with new information about the universe.

meteorology the scientific study of Earth's atmosphere, especially in relation to weather and climate

astronomy the scientific study of the universe

SC*L*INKS.

www.scilinks.org
Topic: Branches of Earth Science
Code: HQX0191

Reading Check **What information is used for weather maps?**
(See Appendix G for answers to Reading Checks.)

Environmental Science and Earth Science

Some Earth scientists study the ways in which humans interact with their environment in a relatively new field of science called *environmental science*. Many fields of study, such as Earth science, biology, and the social sciences, contribute to environmental science. The goal of environmental science is to understand and solve problems that result from how we use natural resources and how our actions affect the environment.

The Importance of Earth Science

Natural forces not only shape Earth but also affect life on Earth. For example, a volcanic eruption may bury a town under ash. And an earthquake may produce huge ocean waves that destroy shorelines. By understanding how natural forces shape our environment, Earth scientists, such as those in **Figure 3,** can better predict potential disasters and help save lives and property.

The work of Earth scientists also helps us understand our place in the universe. Astronomers studying distant galaxies have come up with new ideas about the origins of our universe. Geologists studying rock layers have found clues to Earth's past environments and to the evolution of life on this planet.

Earth provides the resources that make life as we know it possible. Earth also provides the materials to enrich the quality of people's lives. The fuel that powers a jet, the metal used in surgical instruments, and the paper and ink in this book all come from Earth's resources. The study of Earth science can help people gain access to Earth's resources, but Earth scientists also strive to help people use those resources wisely.

Figure 3 These meteorologists are risking their lives to gather information about tornadoes. If scientists can better predict when tornadoes will occur, many lives may be saved each year.

Section 1 Review

LA.910.2.2.3; SC.912.N.1.2; SC.912.N.4.1

Key Ideas

1. **Discuss** how one culture contributed to modern science.

2. **Name** the four major branches of Earth science.

3. **Describe** two specialized fields of geology.

4. **Describe** the work of oceanographers and meteorologists.

5. **Explain** how the work of astronomers has been affected by technology.

Critical Thinking

6. **Analyzing Ideas** How have Earth scientists improved our understanding of the environment?

7. **Analyzing Concepts** Give two examples of how exploring space and exploring the ocean depths are similar.

Concept Mapping

8. Use the following terms to create a concept map: *Earth science, geology, meteorology, climate, environmental science, astronomy,* and *oceanography.*

Key Ideas	Key Terms	Why It Matters
❯ Explain how science is different from other forms of human endeavor. ❯ Identify the steps that make up scientific methods. ❯ Analyze how scientific thought changes as new information is collected. ❯ Explain how science affects society.	observation hypothesis independent variable dependent variable peer review theory	Science helps us understand Earth, nature, and the universe. Science also helps us apply our knowledge to develop technologies which, in turn, help us solve problems and improve the condition of human society.

Art, architecture, philosophy, and science are all forms of human endeavor. Although artists, architects, and philosophers may use science in their work, science does not have the same goals as other human endeavors do.

The goal of science is to explain natural phenomena. Scientists ask questions about natural events and then work to answer those questions through experiments and examination. Scientific understanding moves forward through the work of many scientists, who build on the research of the generations of scientists before them.

FLORIDA STANDARDS

SC.912.N.1.2 Describe and explain what characterizes science and its methods; **SC.912.N.1.4** Identify sources of information and assess their reliability according to the strict standards of scientific investigation; **SC.912.N.1.5** Describe and provide examples of how similar investigations conducted in many parts of the world result in the same outcome; **SC.912.N.1.7** Recognize the role of creativity in constructing scientific questions, methods and explanations.

Behavior of Natural Systems

Scientists start with the assumption that nature is understandable, and they expect that similar forces in a similar situation will cause similar results. But the forces involved in natural events are complex. For example, changes in temperature and humidity can cause rain in one city, but the same changes in temperature and humidity may cause fog in another city. These different results might be due to differences in the two cities or due to complex issues, such as differences in climate.

Scientists also expect that nature is predictable, which means that the future behavior of natural forces can be anticipated. So, if scientists understand the forces and materials involved in a process, they can predict how that process will evolve. The scientists in **Figure 1,** for example, are studying ice cores in Antarctica. Ice cores can provide clues to Earth's past climate changes. Because natural systems are complex, however, a high level of understanding and predictability can be difficult to achieve. To increase their understanding, scientists follow the same basic processes of studying and describing natural events.

Figure 1 Scientists use ice cores to study past compositions of Earth's atmosphere. This information can help scientists learn about past climate changes.

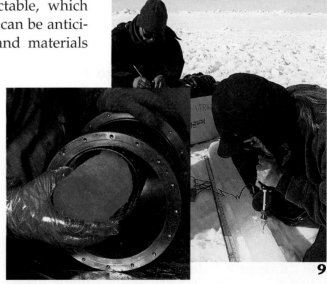

9

Scientific Methods

Over time, the scientific community has developed organized and logical approaches to scientific research. These approaches are known as *scientific methods*. Scientific methods are not a set of sequential steps that scientists always follow. Rather, these methods are guidelines to scientific problem solving. **Figure 2** shows a basic flowchart of scientific methods.

Ask a Question

Scientific methods often begin with observations. **Observation** is the process of using the senses of sight, touch, taste, hearing, and smell to gather information about the world. When you see thunderclouds form in the summer sky, you are making an observation. And when you feel cool, smooth, polished marble or hear the roar of river rapids, you are making observations.

Observations can often lead to questions. What causes tornadoes to form? Why is oil discovered only in certain locations? What causes a river to change its course? What causes some plants to grow faster than others? Simple questions such as these have fueled years of scientific research and have been investigated through scientific methods.

Form a Hypothesis

Once a question has been asked and basic information has been gathered, a scientist may propose a tentative answer, which is also known as a hypothesis (hie PAHTH uh sis). A **hypothesis** (plural, *hypotheses*) is a possible explanation or solution to a problem. Hypotheses can be developed through close and careful observation. Most hypotheses are based on known facts about similar events. One example of a hypothesis is that plants that are given a large amount of sunlight will grow faster than plants given a smaller amount of sunlight. This hypothesis could be made from observing how and where other plants grow.

Reading Check Name two ways scientific methods depend on careful observations.

---

observation the process of obtaining information by using the senses; the information obtained by using the senses

hypothesis a testable idea or explanation that leads to scientific investigation

www.scilinks.org
Topic: Scientific Methods
Code: HQX1359

Figure 2 Scientific Method Flowchart

Making observations → Asking questions → Forming a hypothesis → Testing a hypothesis → Drawing conclusions → Communicating results

Figure 3 Astronaut Shannon Lucid observes wheat plants as a part of a controlled experiment in orbit around Earth.

independent variable in an experiment, the factor that is deliberately manipulated

dependent variable in an experiment, the factor that changes as a result of manipulation of one or more other factors (the independent variables)

Test the Hypothesis

After a hypothesis is proposed, it is often tested by performing experiments. An *experiment* is a procedure that is carried out according to certain guidelines. Factors that can be changed in an experiment are variables. **Independent variables** are factors that are changed by the person performing the experiment. **Dependent variables** are variables that change as a result of a change in independent variables.

In most experiments, only one independent variable is tested. For example, to test how sunlight affects plants, a scientist would grow identical plants. The plants would receive the same amount of water and fertilizer but different amounts of sunlight. Thus, sunlight would be the independent variable. How the plants respond to the different amounts of sunlight would be the dependent variable. Most experiments include a control group. A *control group* is a group that serves as a standard of comparison with another group to which the control group is identical except for one factor. In this experiment, the plants that receive a natural amount of sunlight would be the control group. An experiment that contains a control is called a *controlled experiment*. Most scientific experiments are controlled experiments. The "zero gravity" experiment shown in **Figure 3** is a controlled experiment.

Draw Conclusions

After many experiments and observations, a scientist may reach conclusions about his or her hypothesis. If the hypothesis fits the known facts, it may be accepted as true. If the experimental results differ from what was expected, the hypothesis may be changed or discarded. Expected and unexpected results lead to new questions and further study. The results of scientific inquiry may also lead to new knowledge and new methods of inquiry that further scientific aims.

 SC.912.N.1.1.2

Quick **Lab**   5 min

Making Observations

Procedure

❶ Get an ordinary **candle** of any shape and color.

❷ Record all the observations you can make about the candle.

❸ Light the candle with a **match**, and watch it burn for 1 min.

❹ Record as many observations about the burning candle as you can. When you are finished, extinguish the flame. Record any observations.

Analysis

1. Share your results with your class. How many things that your classmates observed did you not observe? Explain this phenomenon.

Good accuracy and good precision

Poor accuracy but good precision

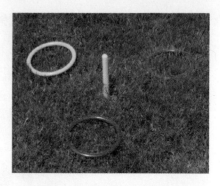

Good overall accuracy but poor precision

Figure 4 Accuracy and Precision

THINK
central
INTERACT ONLINE
Keyword: HQXIESF4

Scientific Measurements and Analysis

During an experiment, scientists must gather information. An important method of gathering information is measurement. Measurement is the comparison of some aspect of an object or event with a standard unit. Scientists around the world can compare and analyze each other's measurements because scientists use a common system of measurement called the *International System of Units,* or SI. This system includes standard measurements for length, mass, temperature, and volume. All SI units are based on intervals of 10. The Reference Tables section of the Appendix contains a chart of SI units.

Accuracy and Precision

Accuracy and precision are important in scientific measurements. *Accuracy* refers to how close a measurement is to the true value of the thing being measured. *Precision* is the exactness of the measurement. For example, a distance that is measured in millimeters is more precise than a distance that is measured in centimeters. Measurements can be precise and yet inaccurate. The relationship between accuracy and precision is shown in **Figure 4.**

SC.912.N.1.1.6

Quick Lab   Sample Size and Accuracy

15 min

Procedure

❶ Shuffle a **deck of 52 playing cards** eight times.

❷ Lay out 10 cards. Record the number of red cards.

❸ Reshuffle, and repeat step 2 four more times.

❹ Which trials showed the highest number and lowest number of red cards? Calculate the total range of red cards by finding the difference between the highest number and lowest number.

❺ Determine the mean number of red cards per trial by adding the number of red cards in the five trials and then dividing by 5.

Analysis

1. A deck of cards has 50% red cards. How close is your average to the percentage of red cards in the deck?

2. Pool the results of your classmates. How close is the new average to the percentage of red cards in the deck?

3. How does changing the sample size affect accuracy?

Error

Error is an expression of the amount of imprecision or variation in a set of measurements. Error is commonly expressed as percentage error or as a confidence interval. Percentage error is the percentage of deviation of an experimental value from an accepted value. A *confidence interval* describes the range of values for a set percentage of measurements. For example, imagine that the average length of all of the ears of corn in a field is 23 cm, and 90% of the ears are within 3 cm of the average length. A scientist may report that the average length of all of the ears of corn in a field is 23 ± 3 cm with 90% confidence.

Observations and Models

In Earth science, using controlled experiments to test a hypothesis is often impossible. When experiments are impossible, scientists make additional observations to gather evidence. The hypothesis is then tested by examining how well the hypothesis fits or explains all of the known evidence.

Scientists also use models to simulate conditions in the natural world. A *model* is a description, representation, or imitation of an object, system, process, or concept. Scientists use several types of models, two of which are shown in **Figure 5.** Physical models are three-dimensional models that can be touched. Maps and charts are examples of graphical models.

Conceptual models are verbal or graphical models that represent how a system works or is organized. Mathematical models are mathematical equations that represent the way a system or process works. Computer models are a kind of mathematical model that use the high speed and efficiency of a computer to make calculations and display results. After a good computer model has been created, scientists can perform experiments by manipulating variables much as they would when performing a physical experiment.

Reading Check **Name three types of models.**

Figure 5 Two models of Mount Everest are shown below. The computer model on the right is used to track erosion along the Tibetan Plateau. The model on the left is a physical model.

Mt. Everest

Figure 6 Meteorologists at a conference in California are watching the "Science On a Sphere™" exhibit. They are wearing 3-D glasses to better see the complex and changing three-dimensional display of global temperatures.

Acceptance of Scientific Ideas

When scientists reach a conclusion, they introduce their findings to the scientific community. New scientific ideas undergo review and testing by other scientists before the ideas are accepted.

Publication of Results and Conclusions

Scientists commonly present the results of their work in scientific journals or at professional meetings, such as the one shown in **Figure 6.** Results published in journals are usually written in a standard scientific format. Many journals are now being published online to allow scientists quicker access to the results of other scientists and to reduce the costs of printing journals.

Peer Review

Scientists in any one research group tend to view scientific ideas similarly. Therefore, they may be biased in their experimental design or data analysis. To reduce bias, scientists submit their ideas to other scientists for peer review. **Peer review** is the process in which several experts on a given topic review another expert's work on that topic before the work gets published. These experts determine if the results and conclusions of the study merit publication. Peer reviewers commonly suggest improvements to the study, or they may determine that the results or conclusions are flawed and recommend that the study not be published. Scientists follow an ethical code that states that only valid experimental results should be published. The peer review process serves as a filter that allows only well-supported ideas to be published.

Reading Check **Name two places scientists present the results of their work.**

Formulating a Theory

After results are published, they usually lead to more experiments, which are designed to test and expand the original idea. This process may continue for years until the original idea is disproved, is modified, or becomes generally accepted. Sometimes, elements of different ideas are combined to form <u>concepts</u> that are more complete.

When an idea has undergone much testing and reaches general acceptance, that idea may help form a theory. A **theory** is an explanation that is consistent with all existing tests and observations. Theories are often based on scientific laws. A *scientific law* is a general statement that describes how the natural world behaves under certain conditions and for which no exceptions have been found. Like theories, laws are discovered through scientific research. Theories and scientific laws can be changed if conflicting information is discovered in the future.

Academic Vocabulary

concept (KAHN sept) an idea or a thought

theory a system of ideas that explains many related observations and is supported by a large body of evidence acquired through scientific investigation

The Importance of Interdisciplinary Science

Scientists from many disciplines commonly contribute the information necessary to support an idea. The free exchange of ideas between fields of science allows scientists to identify explanations that fit a wide range of scientific evidence. When an explanation is supported by evidence from a variety of fields, the explanation is more likely to be accurate. New disciplines of science sometimes emerge as a result of new connections that are found between more than one branch of science. An example of the development of a widely accepted hypothesis that is based on interdisciplinary evidence is shown in **Figure 7.**

Figure 7 The hypothesis that the dinosaurs were killed by an asteroid impact was developed over many years and through the work of many scientists from different disciplines.

Impact Hypothesis of Extinction of the Dinosaurs

Paleontology

No dinosaur fossils exist in rock layers younger than 65 million years old.

Geology

A large impact crater about 65 million years old exists in the ocean near the Yucatan Peninsula.

Astronomy

A layer of iridium occurs in rocks about 65 million years old all around Earth. Iridium is rare on Earth, but is common in asteroids.

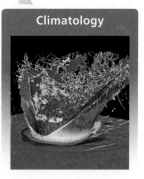

Climatology

Climate models predict that a large impact would change Earth's climate and affect life on Earth.

Figure 8 The Alaskan pipeline has carried more than 15 billion barrels of oil since it was built in 1977. The pipeline has also sparked controversy about the potential dangers to nearby Alaskan wildlife.

Science and Society

Scientific knowledge helps us understand our world. The work of people, including scientists, is influenced by their cultural and personal beliefs. Science is a part of society, and advances in science can have important and long-lasting effects on both science and society. Examples of these far-reaching advances include the theory of plate tectonics, quantum mechanics, and the theory of evolution.

Science is also used to develop new technology, including new tools, machines, materials, and processes. Sometimes, technologies are designed to address a specific human need. In other cases, technology is an indirect result of science that was directed at another goal. For example, technology that was designed for space exploration has been used to improve computers, cars, medical equipment, and airplanes.

However, new technology may also create new problems. Scientists involved in research that leads to new technologies may or may not consider the possible negative effects of their work. Before making decisions about the technology they adopt, people should consider alternatives, risks, and costs and benefits to humans, to other life, and to Earth. Even after decisions are made, society often continues to debate them. For example, the Alaskan pipeline, part of which is shown in **Figure 8,** transports oil. But the transport of oil in the United States is part of an ongoing debate about how we use oil resources and how these uses affect our natural world.

www.scilinks.org
Topic: Careers in Earth
Science
Code: HQX0222

SC.912.N.1.1; SC.912.N.1.2 ; SC.912.N.1.4; SC.912.N.1.5; SC.912.N.1.7;
SC.912.N.2.1; SC.912.N.2.2; SC.912.N.2.4; SC.912.N.3.1; SC.912.N.3.2;
SC.912.N.3.3; SC.912.N.3.4; SC.912.N.3.5; SC.912.N.4.1

Section 2 Review

Key Ideas

1. **Describe** one reason that a scientist might conduct research.

2. **Identify** the steps that make up scientific methods.

3. **Compare** a hypothesis with a theory.

4. **Describe** how scientists test hypotheses.

5. **Describe** the difference between a dependent variable and an independent variable.

6. **Describe** the conditions under which scientific laws and theories can be changed.

7. **Summarize** how scientific methods contribute to the development of modern science.

8. **Explain** how technology can affect scientific research.

Critical Thinking

9. **Analyzing Ideas** An observation can be precise but inaccurate. Do you think it is possible for an observation to be accurate but not precise? Explain.

10. **Making Comparisons** When an artist paints a picture of a natural scene, what aspects of his or her work are similar to the methods of a scientist? What aspects are different?

11. **Demonstrating Reasoned Judgment** A new technology is known to be harmful to a small group of people. How does this knowledge affect whether you would use this new technology? Explain.

Concept Mapping

12. Use the following terms to create a concept map: *independent variable, observation, experiment, dependent variable, hypothesis, scientific methods,* and *conclusion.*

The Boundaries of Science

What makes a question scientific?

You have read that scientific investigations generally begin with a question, but what kinds of questions can be answered by science? Science deals with questions about the natural world that can be answered through observation, experimentation, and the collection and analysis of data.

Many other kinds of questions lie outside of science. For example, science cannot answer questions about beliefs or values. Instead, these questions are addressed by religion and philosophy. Similarly, science does not answer questions about art or aesthetics, such as what makes something beautiful or useful.

How is pseudoscience similar to and different from science?

Sometimes people claim to have scientific evidence to support an explanation when in fact they do not. Pseudoscience is a set of beliefs or practices falsely claimed as findings acquired through scientific methods. Pseudoscience is like science in that it often involves topics related to the natural world. People who practice pseudoscience have explanations that sound logical and plausible. Like science, pseudoscience uses technical language or at least scientific-sounding terms. Both science and pseudoscience claim to be supported by empirical evidence.

The biggest difference between science and pseudoscience is that pseudoscience does not use accepted scientific methods. When asked for evidence, people who rely on pseudoscience generally provide only vague information that lacks any measurements. Often their explanations can't be tested using scientific methods because they are not specific. Unlike science, pseudoscience often claims that results not proven false must be true. Pseudoscience often provides only anecdotes and personal experiences as supporting evidence. The table below summarizes the key differences between science and pseudoscience.

Science	Pseudoscience
Based on logic	Not necessarily based on logic
Has testable explanations	Explanations generally not testable
Relies on empirical evidence	Empirical evidence is not available
Results can be reproduced by others	Only anecdotes and personal experiences are used as evidence
Explanations that are not proven false continue to be tested	Explanations that are not proven false are assumed to be true
	Results can't be reproduced by others
Explanations are modified by new evidence	Explanations do not change with new evidence

YOUR TURN **ONLINE RESEARCH**
Do some Internet research about a pseudoscience, such as astrology or phrenology. Write down three forms of "evidence" that proponents cite to support their claims.

⏱ **90 min**

Scientific Methods

What You'll Do

> **Observe** natural phenomena.
> **Propose** hypotheses to explain natural phenomena.
> **Evaluate** hypotheses.

What You'll Need

hand lens
meterstick

Not all scientists think alike, and scientists don't always agree about various concepts. However, all scientists use scientific methods, part of which are the skills of observing, inferring, and predicting. In this lab, you will apply scientific methods as you examine a place where puddles often form after rainstorms. You can study the puddle area even when the ground is dry, but it would be best to observe the area again when it is wet. Because water is one of the most effective agents of change in our environment, you should be able to make many observations.

Make Observations

1 Examine the area of the puddle and the surrounding area carefully. Make a numbered list of what can be seen, heard, smelled, or felt. Sample observations are as follows: "The ground where the puddle forms is lower than the surrounding area, and there are cracks in the soil." Remember to avoid making any suggestions of causes.

Form a Hypothesis

2 Review your observations, and write possible hypotheses for those observations. A sample hypothesis might be "Cracks in the soil (Observation 2) may have been caused by a lack of rain (Observation 5)."

3 Review your observations and possible hypotheses, and place them into similar groups, if possible. Can one hypothesis or set of hypotheses explain several observations? Is each hypothesis reasonable when compared with the others? Does any hypothesis contradict any of the other observations?

Step 1

Test the Hypothesis

4 Based only on your hypotheses, make some predictions about what will happen at the puddle as conditions change. Describe the changes you expect and your reasoning. A sample prediction is the following: "If the puddle dries out, the crack will grow wider because of the loss of water."

5 Revisit the puddle several times to see if the changes that you observe match your predictions.

Step 2

Analyze the Results

1. **Evaluating Results** Which of your predictions were correct, and which predictions were incorrect?

2. **Analyzing Methods** Which of your senses did you use most to make your observations? How could you improve your observations by using this sense? by using other senses?

3. **Evaluating Methods** What could you have used to measure, or quantify, many of your observations? Is quantitative observation better than qualitative observation? Explain your answer.

Draw Conclusions

4. **Drawing Conclusions** Examine your incorrect predictions. What new knowledge have you gained from them?

5. **Analyzing Results** Reexamine your hypotheses. What can you say now about the ones that were correct?

6. **Drawing Conclusions** When knowledge is derived from observation and prediction, this process uses *scientific methods*. After reporting the results of a prediction, how might a scientist continue his or her research?

Extension

Designing Experiments Choose another small area to examine, but look for changes caused by a different factor, such as wind. Follow the steps outlined in this lab to predict changes that will occur in the area. Use scientific methods to design an experiment. Briefly describe your experiment, including how you would perform it.

MAPS in Action

Geologic Features and Political Boundaries in Europe

Map ▶ Skills Activity

This map shows the political boundaries of a part of Europe. The map also shows some surface features. Use the map to answer the questions below.

1. **Using a Key** What do the blue lines represent?

2. **Analyzing Data** How many countries are represented on the map?

3. **Examining Data** What country has two smaller countries within its borders?

4. **Applying Ideas** What type of surface features define the political boundary between Romania and Moldova and the political boundary between Switzerland and Germany?

5. **Applying Ideas** What type of surface feature defines the political boundary between Poland and Slovakia?

6. **Making Inferences** Why do you think that political boundaries commonly correspond with surface features?

Summary

Key Ideas

Key Terms

Section 1

What Is Earth Science?

❯ Many cultures, including the ancient Greeks and Maya, contributed to the development of modern scientific study.

❯ The four main branches of Earth science are geology, oceanography, meteorology, and astronomy.

❯ Earth scientists help us understand how Earth formed and the natural forces that affect human society.

Earth science, p. 5
geology, p. 6
oceanography, p. 6
meteorology, p. 7
astronomy, p. 7

Section 2

Science as a Process

❯ Science differs from other human endeavors by following a procedure of testing to help understand natural phenomena.

❯ The steps that make up scientific methods include asking questions, forming hypotheses, testing hypotheses, and drawing conclusions.

❯ New scientific thought undergoes review and testing by other scientists before new ideas are accepted.

❯ Science affects society by helping us understand our world. Science is also used to develop new technology that can help solve existing problems as well as create new problems that require solutions.

observation, p. 10
hypothesis, p. 10
independent variable, p. 11
dependent variable, p. 11
peer review, p. 14
theory, p. 15

1. **Word Parts** Write the word *astronomy* and its definition. Then use a dictionary to look up the meanings of *astro-* and *-nomy*. Do this for two more words that have the suffix *-nomy*.

USING KEY TERMS

Use each of the following terms in a separate sentence.

2. *observation* SC.912.N.1.1

3. *peer review* SC.912.N.1.1

4. *theory* SC.912.N.1.1

For each pair of terms, explain how the meanings of the terms differ.

5. *hypothesis* and *theory* SC.912.N.1.1

6. *geology* and *astronomy*

7. *oceanography* and *meteorology*

8. *dependent variable* and *independent variable* SC.912.N.1.1

9. *Earth science* and *geology*

UNDERSTANDING KEY IDEAS

10. The study of solid Earth is called
    a. geology.
    c. oceanography.
    b. meteorology.
    d. astronomy.

11. The Earth scientist most likely to study storms is a(n)
    a. geologist.
    b. meteorologist.
    c. oceanographer.
    d. astronomer.

12. The study of the origin of the solar system and the universe in general is
    a. geology.
    b. ecology.
    c. meteorology.
    d. astronomy.

13. How long ago were the first scientific observations about Earth made?
    a. a few years ago
    b. a few decades ago
    c. hundreds of years ago
    d. several thousand years ago

14. The Earth scientist most likely to study volcanoes is a(n)
    a. geologist.
    b. meteorologist.
    c. oceanographer.
    d. astronomer.

15. One possible first step in scientific problem solving is to SC.912.N.1.1
    a. form a hypothesis.
    b. ask a question.
    c. test a hypothesis.
    d. state a conclusion.

16. A possible explanation for a scientific problem is called a(n) SC.912.N.1.1
    a. experiment.
    c. observation.
    b. theory.
    d. hypothesis.

17. A statement that consistently and correctly explains a natural phenomenon is SC.912.N.1.1
    a. a hypothesis.
    c. an observation.
    b. a theory.
    d. a control.

18. When scientists pose questions about how nature operates and attempt to answer those questions through testing and observation, they are conducting SC.912.N.1.2
    a. research.
    c. examinations.
    b. predictions.
    d. peer reviews.

SHORT ANSWER

19. How does accuracy differ from precision in a scientific measurement? SC.912.N.1.1

20. Why do scientists use control groups in experiments?

21. A meteorite lands in your backyard. What two branches of Earth science would help you explain that natural event?

22. Write a short paragraph about the relationship between science and technology.

23. Give two reasons why interdisciplinary science is important to society.

24. Explain how peer review affects scientific knowledge. SC.912.N.1.5

25. How did some ancient cultures explain natural phenomena? SC.912.N.2.1

CRITICAL THINKING

26. **Making Connections** How could knowing how our solar system formed affect our understanding of the universe?

27. **Evaluating Hypotheses** Some scientists have hypothesized that meteorites have periodically bombarded Earth and caused mass extinctions every 26 million years. How might this hypothesis be tested? SC.912.N.1.1

28. **Determining Cause and Effect** Name some possible negative effects of a new technology that uses nuclear fuel to power cars.

29. **Analyzing Ideas** A scientist observes that each eruption of a volcano is preceded by a series of small earthquakes. The scientist then makes the following statement: "Earthquakes cause volcanic eruptions." Is the scientist's statement a hypothesis or a theory? Why? SC.912.N.3.1

30. **Forming a Hypothesis** You find a yellow rock and wonder if it is gold. How could you apply scientific methods to this problem? SC.912.N.1.1

CONCEPT MAPPING

31. Use the following terms to create a concept map: *control group, accuracy, precision, variable, technology, Earth science, experiment,* and *error.*

MATH SKILLS

32. **Making Calculations** One kilogram is equal to 2.205 lb at sea level. At the same location, how many kilograms are in 100 lb?

33. **Making Calculations** One meter is equal to 3.281 ft. How many meters are in 5 ft?

34. **Making Calculations** The accepted value of the average distance between Earth and the moon is 384,467 km. If a scientist measures that the moon is 384,476 km from Earth, what is the measurement's percentage error?

WRITING SKILLS

35. **Expressing Original Ideas** Imagine that you must live in a place that has all the benefits of only one of the Earth sciences. Which branch would you choose? Defend your choice in an essay.

36. **Outlining Topics** Explain the sequence of events that happens as a scientific hypothesis becomes a theory. SC.912.N.3.1

INTERPRETING GRAPHICS

The graph below shows error in measuring tectonic plate movements. The blue bars represent confidence intervals. Use this graph to answer the questions that follow.

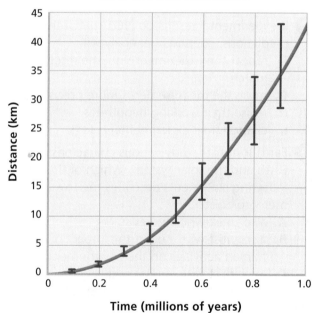

37. How much error is there in the smallest measurement of plate movement? SC.912.N.1.1

38. How much error is there in the largest measurement of plate movement? SC.912.N.1.1

39. How would you explain the difference between the error in the smallest measurement and the error in the largest measurement? SC.912.N.1.1

Understanding Concepts

Directions (1–9): For each question, write on a separate sheet of paper the letter of the correct answer.

1 What is the difference between a theory and a hypothesis?
  A. A hypothesis is a possible explanation for a problem, and a theory is an explanation that is consistent with all existing tests.
  B. A hypothesis is an explanation that is consistent with all existing tests, and a theory is a general statement about the natural world for which no exceptions have been found.
  C. A hypothesis changes during an experiment, which results in a change in a theory.
  D. A hypothesis never changes during an experiment, while a theory is often changed as observations produce new data.

2 If experimental results do NOT match their predictions, scientists generally will
  F. repeat the experiment until the results match.
  G. make the measurements more precise.
  H. revise their working hypothesis.
  I. change their experimental results.

3 Earth scientists study various characteristics of Earth and the solar system. Which of the following statements describes the role of a meteorologist?
  A. a scientist who studies stars
  B. a scientist who studies the impact of human activities on the environment
  C. a scientist who studies rock layers
  D. a scientist who studies weather patterns

4 Which of the following is an example of a new technology?
  F. a tool that is designed to help a doctor better diagnose patients
  G. a previously unknown element that is discovered in nature
  H. a law that is passed to fund scientists conducting new experiments
  I. scientists that record observations on the movement of a star

5 Which of the following statements describes an example of a physical model?
  A. a model that consists of a graph
  B. a model made up of molded clay, soil, and chemicals
  C. a model that includes equations
  D. a model created using a program

6 During an experiment, scientists control conditions to avoid error. In a controlled experiment, which of the following factors is changed by the scientist?
  F. control group
  G. dependent variable
  H. independent variable
  I. observation

7 Which of the following describes a relationship between accuracy and precision that most likely would NOT result in experimental error?
  A. Measurements are precise, but inaccurate.
  B. Measurements are both accurate and precise.
  C. Measurements are imprecise and inaccurate.
  D. Measurements are accurate, but imprecise.

8 A scientist has developed a new technology that may benefit humans. Before the scientist introduces the new technology in society, the scientist should
  F. consider the possible negative effects of the technology.
  G. develop a new scientific theory.
  H. run an experiment that involves humans.
  I. address a specific human need.

9 If scientists make an observation that does NOT agree with an accepted scientific theory, the scientists should
  A. assume that their observations are incorrect.
  B. conclude that the theory is wrong.
  C. perform more experiments to determine if the observation is the result of error or if the theory is wrong.
  D. publish their results so other scientists can test the theory.

Interpreting Graphics

Directions (10–11): For each question below, record the correct answer on a separate sheet of paper.

Branches of Earth Science

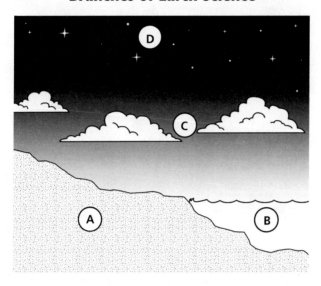

10 The diagram above shows the four major areas studied by Earth scientists. A scientist studying the events that take place in area C would be primarily concerned with which of the following?

F. Earth's age

G. Earth's weather

H. movement of waves and tides

I. movement of the stars across the sky

Using a Scientific Method

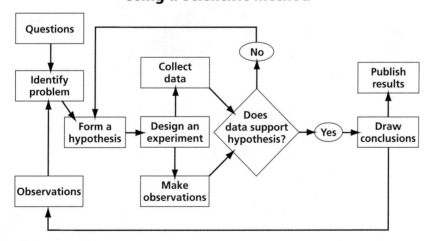

11 In the illustration above, during which step do scientists develop a possible explanation for a problem?

A. collect data

B. form a hypothesis

C. make observations

D. draw conclusions

Test Tip

If you are unsure of an answer, eliminate the answers that you know are wrong before choosing your response.

Chapter 2

Earth as a System

Chapter Outline

Why It Matters

Earth's supply of matter is finite and cycles continuously among Earth's four major reservoir systems. Energy, on the other hand, must be supplied constantly to maintain this cycling and support life processes.

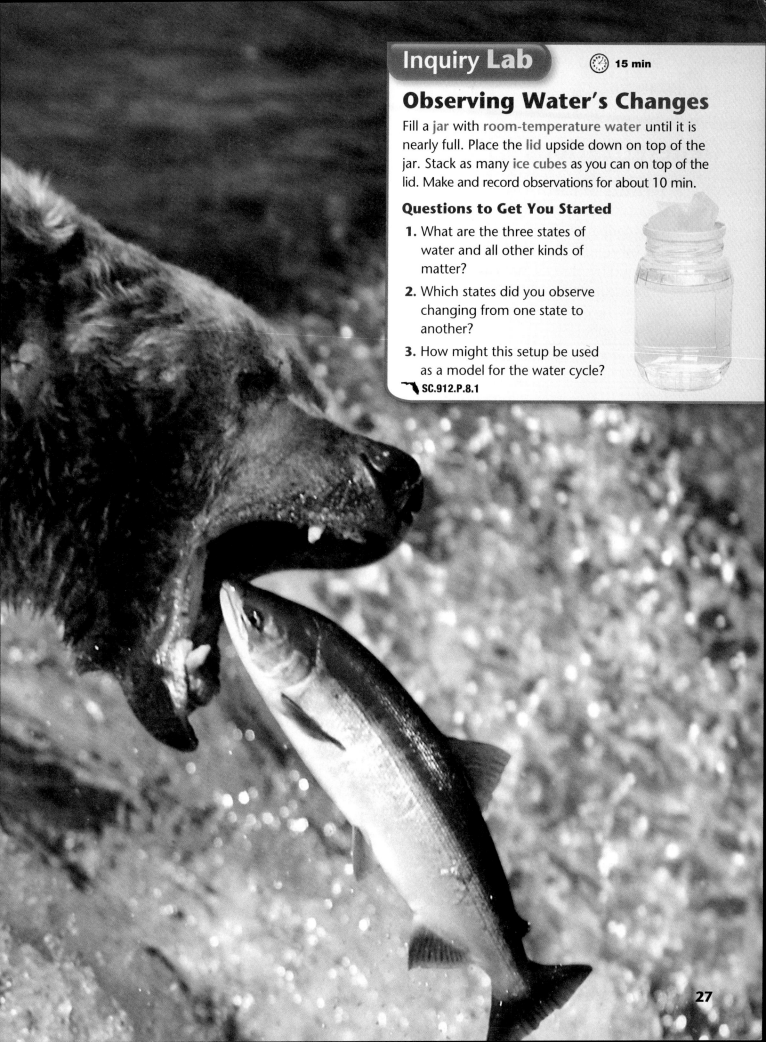

Observing Water's Changes

Fill a jar with room-temperature water until it is nearly full. Place the lid upside down on top of the jar. Stack as many ice cubes as you can on top of the lid. Make and record observations for about 10 min.

Questions to Get You Started

1. What are the three states of water and all other kinds of matter?

2. Which states did you observe changing from one state to another?

3. How might this setup be used as a model for the water cycle?

SC.912.P.8.1

27

These reading tools will help you learn the material in this chapter.

Generalizations

Characteristics of Earth Generalizations are statements that apply to a large group of things (or people). Generalizations may be signaled by words, such as *most, mostly,* or *generally,* and by phrases, such as *in general* or *for the most part.* Many generalizations, however, are not signaled by any words or phrases.

> **Example of a generalization:**
> Earth is made mostly of rock.

This statement is a generalization because
- it applies to most—but not all—of Earth's matter
- water (which covers Earth's surface) and air (which surrounds Earth's surface) are exceptions.

Your Turn Record two statements in Section 2 or 3 that are generalizations. Give one or two reasons why each is a generalization.

Fact, Hypothesis, or Theory?

Scientific Laws A scientific law describes or summarizes a pattern in nature. Scientific theories are sometimes confused with scientific laws, but they are not the same thing. Theories explain. Laws describe. The following statements apply to scientific laws:
- They describe patterns in nature.
- They are different from theories.
- They have been confirmed by experiments, or they have been observed so often that they are assumed to be true.

Your Turn As you read Section 2, record the name of each law that is discussed. Also record the pattern that the law describes or summarizes. Include an example of a situation to which the law applies to help you remember it.

Note Taking

Outlining Outlining the content of a section or chapter is a simple and effective way to take notes. To make an outline, follow the steps below.
1. List each main idea or topic, such as a section title, after a Roman numeral.
2. Add major points that give you important information about the idea or topic. List these points after capitalized letters.
3. Add subpoints that describe or explain the major points. List these subpoints after numerals.

4. Add supporting details for each subpoint. List these details after lowercase letters.

Your Turn Use outlining to take notes for Section 1. The example below, for part of Section 1, can help you get started.

> I. Earth's Gravity
>   A. Gravity: force of attraction between all matter
>   1. Law of Gravitation: The force of attraction depends on masses of objects and distance between objects.

For more information on how to use these and other tools, see **Appendix A.**

Earth: A Unique Planet

Key Ideas	Key Terms	Why It Matters
❯ Describe the size and shape of Earth. ❯ Describe the compositional and structural layers of Earth's interior. ❯ Identify the possible source of Earth's magnetic field. ❯ Summarize Newton's law of gravitation.	crust mantle core lithosphere asthenosphere mesosphere	Understanding Earth's structure and composition helps us not only study other bodies in the universe, but also appreciate the features that make our own planet unique.

Earth is unique for several reasons. It is the only known planet in the solar system that has liquid water on its surface and an atmosphere that contains a large proportion of oxygen. Earth is also the only planet—in our solar system or in any other solar system—that is known to support life. Scientists study the characteristics of Earth that make life possible in order to know what life-supporting conditions to look for on other planets.

Earth Basics

Earth is the third planet from the sun in our solar system. Earth formed about 4.6 billion years ago and is made mostly of rock. Approximately 71% of Earth's surface is covered by a relatively thin layer of salt water called the *global ocean.*

As viewed from space, Earth is a blue sphere covered with white clouds. Earth appears to be a perfect sphere but is actually an *oblate spheroid*, or slightly flattened sphere, as **Figure 1** shows. The spinning of Earth on its axis makes the polar regions flatten and the equatorial zone bulge. Earth's circumference from pole to pole is 40,007 km. Its equatorial circumference is 40,074 km.

Earth's surface is relatively smooth. That is, distances between surface high points and low points are small when compared with Earth's size. The difference between the height of the tallest mountain and the depth of the deepest ocean trench is about 20 km. This distance is small compared with Earth's average diameter of 12,756 km.

FLORIDA STANDARDS

SC.912.E.5.6 Develop logical connections through physical principles, including Kepler's and Newton's Laws about the relationships and the effects of Earth, Moon, and Sun on each other; **SC.912.E.6.1** Describe and differentiate the layers of Earth and the interactions among them; **SC.912.P.10.10** Compare the magnitude and range of the four fundamental forces (gravitational, electromagnetic, weak nuclear, strong nuclear).

Perfect sphere   Oblate spheroid

Equator

Axis of rotation

Figure 1 Although from afar Earth looks like a sphere (left), it is an oblate spheroid. In this illustration, Earth's shape has been exaggerated to show that Earth bulges at the equator.

Figure 2 Changes in the speed and direction of seismic waves were used to determine the locations and properties of Earth's interior zones.

crust the thin and solid outermost layer of the Earth above the mantle

mantle in Earth science, the layer of rock between Earth's crust and core

core the central part of the Earth below the mantle

Earth's Interior

Direct observation of Earth's interior has been limited to the upper few kilometers that can be reached by drilling. So, scientists rely on indirect methods to study Earth at greater depths. For example, scientists have made important discoveries about Earth's interior through studies of seismic waves. *Seismic waves* are vibrations that travel through Earth. Earthquakes and explosions near Earth's surface produce seismic waves. By studying these waves as they travel through Earth, scientists have determined that Earth is made up of three major compositional zones and five major structural zones, as shown in **Figure 2.**

Compositional Zones of Earth's Interior

The thin, solid, outermost zone of Earth is called the **crust.** The crust makes up only 1% of Earth's mass. The crust beneath the oceans is called *oceanic crust*. Oceanic crust is only 5 to 10 km thick. The part of the crust that makes up the continents is called *continental crust*. The continental crust varies in thickness and is generally between 15 and 80 km thick. Continental crust is thickest beneath high mountain ranges.

The lower boundary of the crust, which was named for its discoverer, is called the *Mohorovičić* (MOH hoh ROH vuh CHICH) *discontinuity*, or *Moho*. The **mantle,** the layer that underlies the crust, is denser than the crust. The mantle is nearly 2,900 km thick and makes up almost two-thirds of Earth's mass.

The center of Earth is a sphere whose radius is about 3,500 km. Scientists think that this center sphere, called the **core,** is composed mainly of iron and nickel.

✓ Reading Check **Explain why scientists have to rely on indirect observations to study Earth's interior.** (See Appendix G for answers to Reading Checks.)

Structural Zones of Earth's Interior

The three compositional zones of Earth's interior are divided into five structural zones. The uppermost part of the mantle is cool and brittle. This part of the mantle and the crust above it make up the **lithosphere,** a rigid layer 15 to 300 km thick. Below the lithosphere is a less rigid layer, known as the **asthenosphere.** The asthenosphere is about 200 to 250 km thick. Because of enormous heat and pressure, the solid rock of the asthenosphere has the ability to flow. This ability to flow is called *plasticity.* Below the asthenosphere is a layer of solid mantle rock called the **mesosphere.**

At a depth of about 2,900 km lies the boundary between the mantle and the *outer core.* Scientists think that the outer core is a dense liquid. The inner core begins at a depth of 5,150 km. The inner core is a dense, rigid solid. The inner and outer core together make up nearly one-third of Earth's mass.

Earth as a Magnet

Earth has two magnetic poles. The lines of force of Earth's magnetic field extend between the North geomagnetic pole and the South geomagnetic pole. Earth's magnetic field, shown in **Figure 3,** extends beyond the atmosphere and affects a region of space called the *magnetosphere.*

The source of Earth's magnetic field may be the liquid iron in Earth's outer core. Scientists hypothesize that motions within the core produce electric currents that in turn create Earth's magnetic field. However, recent research indicates that the magnetic field may have another source. Scientists have learned that the sun and moon also have magnetic fields. Because the sun contains little iron and the moon does not have a liquid outer core, discovering the sources of the magnetic fields of the sun and moon may help identify the source of Earth's magnetic field.

lithosphere the solid, outer layer of Earth that consists of the crust and the rigid upper part of the mantle

asthenosphere the solid, plastic layer of the mantle beneath the lithosphere; made of mantle rock that flows very slowly, which allows tectonic plates to move on top of it

mesosphere literally, the "middle sphere"; the strong, lower part of the mantle between the asthenosphere and the outer core

READING TOOLBOX

Generalizations
Find at least two generalizations in Section 1. Record them in a list, and underline any words or phrases that signal the generalizations. As you read the rest of the chapter, find other generalizations and add them to your list.

www.scilinks.org
Topic: Zones of Earth
Code: HQX1684

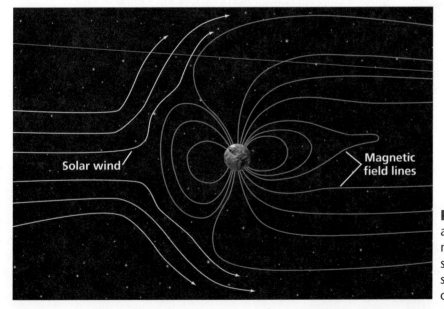

Solar wind

Magnetic field lines

Figure 3 The magnetic field lines around Earth show the shape of Earth's magnetosphere. Earth's magnetosphere is compressed and shaped by solar wind, which is the flow of charged particles from the sun.

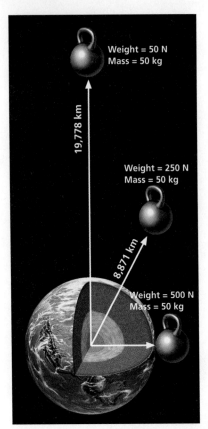

Figure 4 As the distance between an object and Earth's center changes, weight changes but mass remains constant.

THINK central
INTERACT ONLINE
Keyword: HQXEASF4

Earth's Gravity

Earth, like all objects in the universe, is affected by gravity. *Gravity* is the force of attraction that exists between all matter in the universe. The 17th-century scientist Isaac Newton was the first to explain the phenomenon of gravity. Newton described the effects of gravity in his *law of gravitation*. According to the law of gravitation, the force of attraction between any two objects depends on the masses of the objects and the distance between the objects. The larger the masses of two objects and the closer together that the two objects are, the greater the force of gravity between the objects will be.

Weight and Mass

Earth exerts a gravitational force that pulls objects toward the center of Earth. Weight is a measure of the strength of the pull of gravity on an object. The newton (N) is the SI unit used to measure weight. On Earth's surface, a kilogram of mass weighs about 10 N. The mass of an object does not change with location, but the weight of the object does. An object's weight depends on its mass and its distance from Earth's center. According to the law of gravitation, the force of gravity decreases as the distance from Earth's center increases, as shown in **Figure 4**.

Weight and Location

Weight varies according to location on Earth's surface. As you may recall, Earth spins on its axis, and this motion causes Earth to bulge near the equator. Therefore, the distance between Earth's surface and its center is greater at the equator than at the poles. This difference in distance means that your weight at the equator would be about 0.3% less than your weight at the North Pole.

Section 1 Review

LA.910.2.2.3; SC.912.E.5.6; SC.912.E.6.1; SC.912.N.2.5; SC.912.N.3.3; SC.912.N.3.4; SC.912.P.10.10; SC.912.P.10.16; SC.912.P.10.19; SC.912.P.12.4

Key Ideas

1. **Describe** the size and shape of Earth.

2. **Describe** two characteristics that make Earth unique in our solar system.

3. **Summarize** how scientists learn about Earth's interior.

4. **Compare** Earth's compositional layers with its structural layers.

5. **Identify** the possible source of Earth's magnetic field.

6. **Summarize** Newton's law of gravitation.

Critical Thinking

7. **Making Inferences** What does the difference between your weight at the equator and your weight at the poles suggest about Earth's shape?

8. **Making Comparisons** How does the asthenosphere differ from the mesosphere?

9. **Analyzing Ideas** Why would you weigh less on a high mountain peak than you would at sea level?

Concept Mapping

10. Use the following terms to create a concept map: *crust, mantle, core, lithosphere, asthenosphere, mesosphere, inner core,* and *outer core.*

Energy in the Earth System

Key Ideas	Key Terms	Why It Matters
❯ Compare an open system with a closed system. ❯ List the characteristics of Earth's four major spheres. ❯ Identify the two main sources of energy in the Earth system. ❯ Identify four processes in which matter and energy cycle on Earth.	system atmosphere hydrosphere geosphere biosphere	Viewing Earth as a system helps scientists study ways that matter and energy interact to create and support Earth's life forms and living conditions.

Traditionally, different fields of Earth science have been studied separately. Geologists studied Earth's rocks and interior, oceanographers studied the oceans, and meteorologists studied the atmosphere. But now, some scientists are combining knowledge of several fields of Earth science in order to study Earth as a system.

Earth-System Science

An organized group of related objects or components that interact to create a whole is a **system.** Systems vary in size from subatomic to the size of the universe. All systems have boundaries, and many systems have matter and energy that flow through them. Even though each system can be described separately, all systems are linked. A large and complex system, such as the Earth system, operates as a result of the combination of smaller, interrelated systems, as shown in **Figure 1.**

The operation of the Earth system is a result of interaction between the two most basic components of the universe: matter and energy. *Matter* is anything that has mass and takes up space. Matter can be atoms or molecules, such as oxygen atoms or water molecules, and matter can be larger objects, such as rocks, living organisms, or planets. *Energy* is defined as the ability to do work. Energy can be transferred in a variety of forms, including heat, light, vibrations, or electromagnetic waves. A system can be described by the way that matter and energy are transferred within the system or to and from other systems. Transfers of matter and energy are commonly accompanied by changes in the physical or chemical properties of the matter.

FLORIDA STANDARDS

SC.912.E.5.2 Identify patterns in the organization and distribution of matter in the universe and the forces that determine them; **SC.912.E.7.1** Analyze the movement of matter and energy through the different biogeochemical cycles, including water and carbon; **SC.912.E.7.3** Differentiate and describe the various interactions among Earth systems, including: atmosphere, hydrosphere, cryosphere, geosphere, and biosphere.

system a set of particles or interacting components considered to be a distinct physical entity for the purpose of study

Figure 1 This threadfin butterflyfish is part of a system that includes other living organisms, such as coral. Together, the organisms are part of a larger system, a coral reef system in Micronesia.

Figure 2 Energy is exchanged in both the open system (left) and the closed system (right). In the open system, matter is also exchanged.

Open Systems

An *open system* is a system in which both energy and matter are exchanged with the surroundings. The open jar in **Figure 2** is an open system. A lake is also an open system. Water molecules enter a lake through rainfall and streams. Water exits a lake through streams, evaporation, and absorption by the ground. Sunlight and air exchange heat with the lake. Wind's energy is transferred to the lake as waves.

Closed Systems

A *closed system* is a system in which energy, but not matter, is exchanged with the surroundings. The sealed jar in **Figure 2** is a closed system. Energy in the form of light and heat can be exchanged through the jar's sides. But because the jar is sealed, matter cannot exit or enter the system. Most aquariums are open systems because oxygen and food must be added to them, but some are closed systems. Closed-system aquariums contain a variety of organisms: plants, which produce oxygen, and aquatic animals, some of which are food for others. Some of the animals feed on the plants. Animal wastes and organic matter nourish the plants. Only sunlight enters from the surroundings.

The Earth System

Technically, all systems that make up the Earth system are open. But the Earth system is almost a closed system because matter exchange is limited. Energy enters the system in the form of sunlight and is released into space as heat. Only a small amount of dust and rock from space enters the system, and only a fraction of the hydrogen atoms in the atmosphere escape into space.

Reading Check What types of matter and energy are exchanged between Earth and space?

Earth's Four Spheres

Matter on Earth is in solid, liquid, and gaseous states. The Earth system is composed of four "spheres" that are storehouses of all of the planet's matter. These four spheres are shown in **Figure 3.**

The Atmosphere

The blanket of gases that surrounds Earth's surface is called the **atmosphere.** The atmosphere provides the air that you breathe and shields Earth from the sun's harmful radiation. Earth's atmosphere is made up of 78% nitrogen and 21% oxygen. The remaining 1% includes other gases, such as argon, carbon dioxide, and helium.

atmosphere a mixture of gases that surrounds a planet, moon, or other celestial body

hydrosphere the portion of the Earth that is water

geosphere the mostly solid, rocky part of the Earth; extends from the center of the core to the surface of the crust

biosphere the part of Earth where life exists; includes all of the living organisms on Earth

The Hydrosphere

Water covers much of Earth's surface, and 97% of this water is contained in the salty oceans. The remaining 3% is fresh water. Fresh water can be found in lakes, rivers, and streams, frozen in glaciers and the polar ice sheets, and underground in soil and bedrock. All of Earth's water makes up the **hydrosphere.**

The Geosphere

The mostly solid part of Earth is known as the **geosphere.** This sphere includes all of the rock and soil on the surface of the continents and on the ocean floor. The geosphere also includes the solid and molten interior of Earth, which makes up the largest volume of matter on Earth. Natural processes, such as volcanism, bring matter from deep inside Earth's interior to the surface. Other processes move surface matter back into Earth's interior.

Figure 3 The Earth system is composed of the atmosphere, hydrosphere, geosphere, and biosphere. *Can you identify elements of the four spheres in this photo?*

The Biosphere

Another one of the four subdivisions of the Earth system is the biosphere. The **biosphere** is composed of all of the forms of life in the geosphere, in the hydrosphere, and in the atmosphere. The biosphere also contains any organic matter that has not decomposed. Once organic matter has completely decomposed, it becomes a part of the other three spheres. The biosphere extends from the deepest parts of the ocean to the atmosphere a few kilometers above Earth's surface.

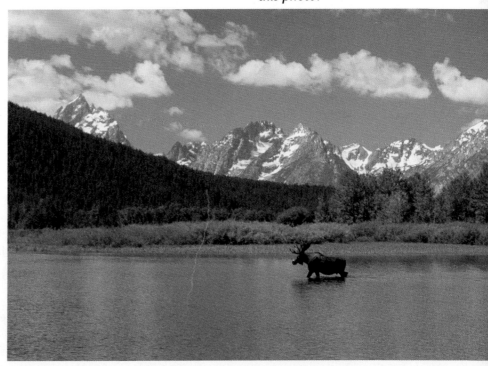

Figure 4 Incoming solar energy is balanced by solar energy reflected or reradiated by several of Earth's systems.

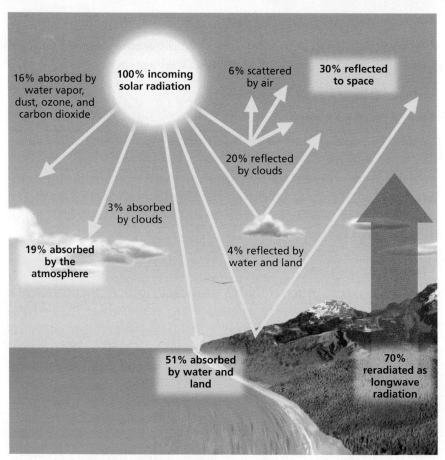

16% absorbed by water vapor, dust, ozone, and carbon dioxide

100% incoming solar radiation

6% scattered by air

30% reflected to space

20% reflected by clouds

3% absorbed by clouds

19% absorbed by the atmosphere

4% reflected by water and land

51% absorbed by water and land

70% reradiated as longwave radiation

Earth's Energy Budget

Exchanges and flow of energy on Earth happen in predictable ways. According to the *first law of thermodynamics*, energy is transferred between systems, but it cannot be created or destroyed. The transfers of energy between Earth's spheres can be thought of as parts of an *energy budget*, in which additions in energy are balanced by subtractions. This concept is shown in **Figure 4**, which shows how solar energy is transferred through Earth's systems. Solar energy is absorbed and reflected in such a way that the solar energy input is balanced by the solar energy output. Like energy, matter can be transferred but cannot be created or destroyed.

The *second law of thermodynamics* states that when energy transfer takes place, matter becomes less organized with time. The overall effect of this natural law is that the universe's energy is spread out more and more uniformly over time.

Earth's four main spheres are open systems that can be thought of as huge storehouses of matter and energy. Matter and energy are constantly being exchanged between the spheres. This constant exchange happens through chemical reactions, radioactive decay, the radiation of energy (including light and heat), and the growth and decay of organisms.

Reading Check Define *energy budget.*

Internal Sources of Energy

When Earth formed about 4.6 billion years ago, its interior was heated by radioactive decay and gravitational contraction. Since that time, the amount of energy as heat generated by radioactive decay has declined. But the decay of radioactive atoms still generates enough energy to keep Earth's interior hot. Earth's interior also retains much of the energy from the planet's formation.

Because Earth's interior is warmer than its surface layers, hot materials move toward the surface in a process called *convection*. As material is heated, the material's density decreases, and the hot material rises and releases energy as heat. Cooler, denser material sinks and displaces the hot material. As a result, the energy in Earth's interior is transferred through the layers of Earth and is released at Earth's surface as heat. On a large scale, this process drives the motions in the surface layers of the geosphere that create mountain ranges and ocean basins.

External Energy Sources

In order for the life-supporting processes on Earth to continue operating for billions of years, energy must be added to the Earth system. Earth's most important external energy source is the sun. Solar radiation warms Earth's atmosphere and surface. This heating causes the movement of air masses, which generates winds and ocean currents. Plants, such as the wheat shown in **Figure 5**, use solar energy to fuel their growth. Because many animals feed on plants, plants provide the energy that acts as a base for the energy flow through the biosphere. Even the chemical reactions that break down rock into soil require solar energy. Another important external source of energy is gravitational energy from the moon and sun. The pull of the sun and the moon on the oceans, combined with Earth's rotation, generates tides that cause currents and drive the mixing of ocean water.

Quick Lab
10 min

SC.912.E.7.7

Effects of Solar Energy

Procedure

1. Wrap one small glass jar with black construction paper so that no light can enter it. Get a second glass jar. Make sure that the second jar has a clean, transparent surface.

2. Use a hammer and large nail to punch a hole in each jar lid.

3. Place a thermometer through the hole in each jar lid. Place the lids tightly onto the jars.

4. Place the jars on the windowsill. Wait 5 min. Then, read the temperature from each jar's thermometer.

Analysis

1. Which jar had the higher temperature?

2. Which jar represents a system in which energy enters from outside the system?

Figure 5 Solar energy is changed into stored energy in the wheat kernels by chemical processes in the wheat plant. When the wheat is eaten, the stored energy is released from the wheat and used or stored by the consumer.

Cycles in the Earth System

A *reservoir* is a place where matter or energy is stored. A *cycle* is a group of processes in which matter repeatedly moves through a series of reservoirs. Many elements on Earth cycle between reservoirs. These cycles rely on energy sources to drive them. The length of time that energy or matter spends in a reservoir can vary from a few hours to several million years.

The Nitrogen Cycle

Organisms on Earth use the element nitrogen to build proteins, which are then used to build cells. Nitrogen gas makes up 78% of the atmosphere, but most organisms cannot use the atmospheric form of nitrogen. The nitrogen must be altered, or *fixed*, before organisms can use it. Nitrogen fixing is an important step in the *nitrogen cycle*, which is shown in **Figure 6.**

In the nitrogen cycle, nitrogen moves from air to soil, from soil to plants and animals, and back to air again. Nitrogen is removed from air mainly by the action of nitrogen-fixing bacteria. These bacteria live in soil and on the roots of certain plants. The bacteria chemically change nitrogen from air into nitrogen compounds, which are vital to the growth of all plants. When animals eat plants, nitrogen compounds in the plants become part of the animals' bodies. These compounds are returned to the soil by the decay of dead animals and in animals' excretions. After nitrogen compounds enter the soil, chemical processes release nitrogen back into the atmosphere. Water-dwelling plants and animals take part in a similar nitrogen cycle.

Reading Check **Identify two nitrogen reservoirs on Earth.**

Figure 6 The balance of nitrogen in the atmosphere and biosphere is maintained through the nitrogen cycle. *What role do animals play in the nitrogen cycle?*

Atmospheric nitrogen, N_2

Lightning converts some atmospheric nitrogen into nitrates that organisms can use.

Runoff

Nitrogen-fixing bacteria in soil and root nodules produce ammonia, NH_3.

Aquatic bacteria also process nitrogen.

Bacteria in soil and water add nitrogen to the atmosphere.

Atmospheric carbon dioxide, CO$_2$

RESPIRATION

PHOTOSYNTHESIS

RESPIRATION

COMBUSTION (human and natural)

RESPIRATION

EROSION

DECOMPOSITION

Natural gas

CO$_2$ dissolved in water

Limestone

Marine plankton remains

Plant and animal remains

Coal

Natural gas

Oil

Figure 7 Carbon moves through Earth's four spheres in a combination of short-term and long-term cycles.

The Carbon Cycle

Carbon is an essential substance in the fuels used for life processes. Carbon moves through all four spheres in a process called the *carbon cycle*, as **Figure 7** shows. Part of the carbon cycle is a short-term cycle. In this short-term cycle, plants convert carbon dioxide, CO$_2$, from the atmosphere into carbohydrates, such as glucose, C$_6$H$_{12}$O$_6$. Then, organisms eat the plants and obtain the carbon from the carbohydrates. Next, organisms' bodies break down the carbohydrates and release some of the carbon back into the air as CO$_2$. Organisms also release carbon into the air through their organic wastes and by the decay of their remains, which release carbon into the air as CO$_2$ or as methane, CH$_4$.

Part of the carbon cycle is a long-term cycle in which carbon moves through Earth's four spheres over a very long time. Carbon is stored in the geosphere in buried plant or animal remains and in a type of rock called a *carbonate*, such as limestone. Carbonate forms from shells and bones of once-living organisms.

The Phosphorus Cycle

The element phosphorus is part of some molecules that organisms need to build cells. During the *phosphorus cycle*, phosphorus moves through every sphere except the atmosphere, because phosphorus is rarely a gas. Phosphorus enters soil and water when rock breaks down and when phosphorus dissolves in water. Some organisms excrete their excess phosphorus in their waste, and this phosphorus may enter soil and water. Plants absorb this phosphorus through their roots. The plants then incorporate it into their tissues. Animals absorb the phosphorus when they eat the plants. When the animals die, the phosphorus returns to the environment through decomposition.

SCI LINKS.

www.scilinks.org
Topic: Carbon Cycle
Code: HQX0216
Topic: Nitrogen Cycle
Code: HQX1036

CONDENSATION

EVAPORATION
TRANSPIRATION

PRECIPITATION

Figure 8 The water cycle is the continuous movement of water from the atmosphere to Earth's surface and back to the atmosphere.

The Water Cycle

The movement of water from the atmosphere to Earth's surface and back to the atmosphere is always taking place. This continuous movement of water is called the *water cycle*, which is shown in **Figure 8.** In the water cycle, water changes from liquid water to water vapor through the energy transfers involved in evaporation and transpiration. Evaporation occurs when energy is absorbed by liquid water and the energy changes the water into water vapor. Transpiration is the release of moisture from plant leaves. During these processes, water absorbs energy and changes state. When the water loses energy, it condenses to form water droplets, such as those that form clouds. Eventually, water falls back to Earth's surface as precipitation, such as rain, snow, or hail.

Humans and the Earth System

All natural cycles can be altered by human activities. The carbon cycle is affected when humans use fossil fuels. Fossil fuels form over millions of years. Carbon dioxide is returned to the atmospheric reservoir rapidly when humans burn these fuels. Also, both the nitrogen and phosphorus cycles are affected by agriculture. Some farming techniques can strip the soil of nitrogen and phosphorus. Many farmers replace these nutrients by using fertilizers, which can upset the balance of these elements in nature. 🦗

Section 2 Review

LA.910.2.2.3; MA.912.S.1.2; SC.912.E.5.2; SC.912.E.7.1; SC.912.E.7.3; SC.912.N.1.1; SC.912.P.8.1; SC.912.P.10.4

Key Ideas

1. **Explain** how Earth can be considered a system.

2. **Compare** an open system with a closed system.

3. **List** two characteristics of each of Earth's four major spheres.

4. **Identify** the two main sources of energy in Earth's system.

5. **Identify** four processes in which matter cycles on Earth.

6. **Explain** how carbon cycles in Earth's system.

7. **Explain** how nitrogen cycles in Earth's system.

Critical Thinking

8. **Identifying Relationships** For each of Earth's four spheres, describe one way that the water cycle affects the sphere.

9. **Determining Cause and Effect** What effect, if any, would you expect a massive forest fire to have on the amount of carbon dioxide in the atmosphere? Explain your answer.

10. **Analyzing Ideas** Early Earth was constantly being bombarded by meteorites, comets, and asteroids. Was early Earth an open system or a closed system? Explain your answer.

11. **Analyzing Relationships** Explain the role of energy in the carbon cycle.

Concept Mapping

12. Use the following terms to create a concept map: *closed system, system, open system, matter, atmosphere, biosphere, energy, geosphere,* and *hydrosphere.*

SECTION 3 Ecology

Key Ideas	Key Terms	Why It Matters
❯ Define *ecosystem*. ❯ Identify three factors that control the balance of an ecosystem. ❯ Summarize how energy is transferred through an ecosystem. ❯ Describe one way that ecosystems respond to environmental change.	ecosystem carrying capacity food web	The study of ecology demonstrates, and helps us appreciate, the inter-connectedness of all the Earth systems that support and sustain humans and all other living things.

One area of science in which life science and Earth science are closely linked is called *ecology*. Ecology is the study of the complex relationships between living things and their nonliving, or *abiotic*, environment. Some ecologists also investigate how communities of organisms change over time.

Ecosystems

Organisms on Earth inhabit many different environments. A community of organisms and the abiotic environment that the organisms inhabit is called an **ecosystem.** The terms *ecology* and *ecosystem* come from the Greek word *oikos*, which means "house." Each ecosystem on Earth is a distinct, self-supporting system. An ecosystem may be as large as an ocean or as small as a drop of water. The largest ecosystem is the entire biosphere.

Most of Earth's ecosystems contain a variety of plants and animals. Plants are important to an ecosystem because they use energy from the sun to produce their own food. Organisms that make their own food are called *producers*. Producers are a source of food for other organisms. *Consumers* are organisms that get their energy by eating other organisms. Consumers may get energy by eating producers or by eating other consumers, as the consumers shown in **Figure 1** are doing. Some consumers get energy by breaking down dead organisms. These consumers are called *decomposers*. To remain healthy, an ecosystem needs to have a balance of producers, consumers, and decomposers.

FLORIDA STANDARDS

SC.912.E.7.1 Analyze the movement of matter and energy through the different biogeochemical cycles, including water and carbon; **SC.912.E.7.3** Differentiate and describe the various interactions among Earth systems, including: atmosphere, hydrosphere, cryosphere, geosphere, and biosphere.

ecosystem a community of organisms and their abiotic environment

Figure 1 Vultures and a spotted hyena are feeding on an elephant carcass in Chobe National Park in Botswana. *Name two consumers that are shown in this photo.*

41

Figure 2 The fur of this elk calf was singed in a forest fire in Yellowstone National Park.

carrying capacity the largest population that an environment can support at any given time

Balancing Forces in Ecosystems

Organisms in an ecosystem use matter and energy. Because amounts of matter and energy in an ecosystem are limited, population growth within the ecosystem is limited, too. The largest population that an environment can support at any given time is called the **carrying capacity.** Carrying capacity depends on available resources. The carrying capacity of an ecosystem is also affected by how easily matter and energy are transferred between life-forms and the environment in that ecosystem. So, a given ecosystem can support only the number of organisms that allows matter and energy to be transferred efficiently through the ecosystem.

Ecological Responses to Change

Changes in any one part of an ecosystem may affect the entire system in unpredictable ways. However, in general, ecosystems react to changes in ways that maintain or restore balance in the ecosystem.

Environmental change in the form of a sudden disturbance, such as a forest fire, can greatly damage and disrupt ecosystems, as shown in **Figure 2.** But over time, organisms will migrate back into damaged areas in predictable patterns. First, grasses and fast-growing plants will start to grow. Then, shrubs and small animal species will return. Eventually, larger tree species and larger animals will return to the area. Ecosystems are resilient and tend to restore a community of organisms to a state like its original state unless the physical environment is permanently altered.

✓ Reading Check Explain the relationship between carrying capacity and the amount of matter and energy in an ecosystem.

Why It Matters

How Does Life Form on Bare Rock?

REAL WORLD

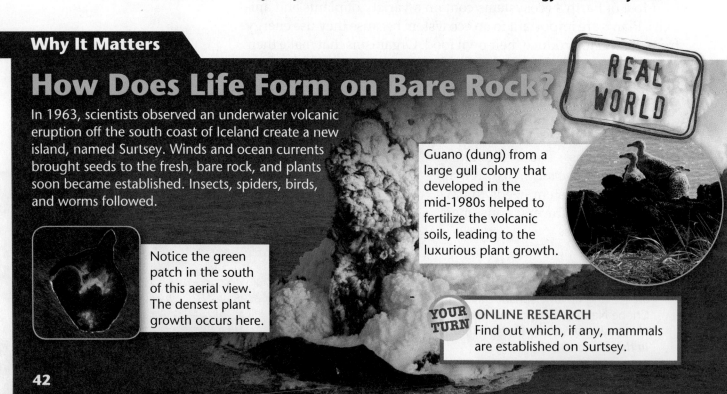

In 1963, scientists observed an underwater volcanic eruption off the south coast of Iceland create a new island, named Surtsey. Winds and ocean currents brought seeds to the fresh, bare rock, and plants soon became established. Insects, spiders, birds, and worms followed.

Notice the green patch in the south of this aerial view. The densest plant growth occurs here.

Guano (dung) from a large gull colony that developed in the mid-1980s helped to fertilize the volcanic soils, leading to the luxurious plant growth.

YOUR TURN ONLINE RESEARCH Find out which, if any, mammals are established on Surtsey.

Energy Transfer

The ultimate source of energy for almost every ecosystem is the sun. Plants capture solar energy by a chemical process called *photosynthesis*. This captured energy then flows through ecosystems from the plants, to the animals that feed on the plants, and finally to the decomposers of animal and plant remains. Matter also cycles through an ecosystem by this process.

As matter cycles and energy flows through an ecosystem, chemical elements are combined and recombined. Each chemical change results in either the temporary storage of energy or the loss of energy. One way to see how energy is lost as it moves through the ecosystem is to draw an energy pyramid. Producers form the base of the pyramid. Consumers that eat producers are the next level of the pyramid. Animals that eat those consumers form the upper levels of the pyramid. As you move up the pyramid, more energy is lost at each level. Therefore, the least amount of total energy is available to organisms at the top of the pyramid.

Food Chains and Food Webs

The sequence in which organisms consume other organisms can be represented by a *food chain*. However, ecosystems are complex and generally contain more organisms than are on a single food chain. In addition, many organisms eat more than just one other species. Therefore, a **food web**, such as the one shown in **Figure 3**, is used to represent the relationships between multiple food chains. Each arrow points to the organism that eats the organism at the base of the arrow.

Quick Lab **20 min**

SC.912.E.7.1

Studying Ecosystems

Procedure

❶ Find a small natural area near your school.

❷ Choose a 5 m by 5 m section of the natural area to study. This area may include the ground or vegetation such as trees or bushes.

❸ Spend 10 min documenting the number and types of organisms that live in the area.

Analysis

1. How many kinds of organisms live in the area that you studied?

2. Draw a food web that describes how energy may flow through the ecosystem that you studied.

food web a diagram that shows the feeding relationships among organisms in an ecosystem

THINK central
INTERACT ONLINE
(Keyword: HQXEASF3)

Figure 3 This food web shows how, in an ocean ecosystem, the largest organisms, such as killer whales, depend on the smallest organisms, such as algae. *Which organisms would be near the top of a food pyramid?*

Human Stewardship of the Environment

All of Earth's systems are interconnected, and changes in one system may affect the operation of other systems. Earth's ecosystems provide a wide variety of resources on which people depend. People need water and air to survive. Changes in ecosystems can affect the ability of an area to sustain a human population. For example, the quality of the atmosphere, the productivity of soils, and the availability of natural resources can affect the availability of food.

Ecological balances can be disrupted by human activity. Populations of plants and animals can be destroyed through overconsumption of resources. When humans convert large natural areas to agricultural or urban areas, natural ecosystems are often destroyed. Another serious threat to ecosystems is pollution. *Pollution* is the contamination of the environment with harmful waste products or impurities.

When people, such as those in **Figure 4,** strive to prevent ecological damage to an area, they are trying to be responsible stewards of Earth. To help ensure the ongoing health and productivity of the Earth system, many people work to use Earth's resources wisely. By using fossil fuels, land and water resources, and other natural resources wisely, many people are helping keep Earth's ecosystems in balance.

Figure 4 These hikers are acting responsibly by choosing to remain on marked trails in the rain forest. In this way, they are helping prevent ecological damage to the area.

Section 3 Review

LA.910.2.2.3; SC.912.E.7.3; SC.912.N.1.1; SC.912.N.1.6; SC.912.N.1.7; SC.912.N.4.1; SC.912.P.10.19

Key Ideas

1. **Define** *ecosystem.*

2. **Explain** why the entire biosphere is an ecosystem.

3. **Identify** three factors that control the balance of an ecosystem.

4. **Summarize** how energy is transferred between the sun and consumers in an ecosystem.

5. **Describe** one way that ecosystems respond to environmental change.

6. **Compare** a food chain with a food web.

7. **Summarize** the importance of good stewardship of Earth's resources.

Critical Thinking

8. **Making Inferences** Discuss two ways that the expansion of urban areas might be harmful to nearby ecosystems.

9. **Analyzing Ideas** Why would adapting to a gradual change in environment be easier for an ecosystem than adapting to a sudden disturbance would be?

10. **Making Inferences** Why does energy flow in only one direction in a given food chain of an ecosystem?

Concept Mapping

11. Use the following terms to create a concept map: *ecology, ecosystem, producer, decomposer, carrying capacity, consumer,* and *food web.*

Fish that Feed the Forest

Food webs and cycles can involve some unlikely participants. Did you know that salmon nourish the forests of North America's Pacific coast? Up to 77% of the nitrogen in coastal rain-forest trees comes from the ocean. Trees that grow close to inland salmon-spawning streams, such as Sitka spruce, grow faster than trees that do not. By understanding the links between different Earth systems, scientists have pieced together an unexpected relationship between nitrogen from the ocean, bears, salmon, and inland rain-forest trees.

Salmon spend most of their lives in the ocean. Before they die, they migrate from the ocean, up freshwater rivers and into inland streams to spawn. In the shallow waters of their spawning grounds, salmon are easy prey to predators, such as bears.

Bears often drag the salmon they catch into the forest. They often eat only their favorite parts of the fish and leave the rest to decay on the forest floor. The decaying nitrogen-rich carcasses become the fertilizer that ensures the health of the rain forest.

YOUR TURN

UNDERSTANDING CONCEPTS
How does nitrogen from the ocean end up in inland coastal trees?

CRITICAL THINKING
What could happen to the coastal rain forests if salmon populations decreased dramatically?

Testing the Conservation of Mass

What You'll Do

> **Measure** the masses of reactants and products in a chemical reaction.

> **Describe** how measuring masses of reactants and products can illustrate the law of conservation of mass.

What You'll Need

bag, plastic sandwich, zipper-type closure
baking soda (sodium bicarbonate)
balance (or scale), metric
beaker, 400 mL
cup, clear plastic, 150 mL (2)
graduated cylinder, 100 mL
paper, weighing (2 pieces)
twist tie
vinegar (acetic acid solution)
water

Safety

As matter cycles through the Earth system, the matter can undergo chemical changes that cause it to change its identity. However, although the matter may change, it is not destroyed. This principle is known as the *law of conservation of mass.* In this lab, you will cause two chemicals to react to form products that differ from the two reacting chemicals. Then, you will determine whether the amount of mass in the system (the experiment) has changed.

Procedure

1. On a blank sheet of paper, prepare a table like the one shown on the next page.

2. Place a piece of weighing paper on a balance. Place 4 to 5 g of baking soda on the paper. Carefully transfer the baking soda to a plastic cup.

3. Using a graduated cylinder, measure 50 mL of vinegar. Pour the vinegar into a second plastic cup.

4. Place both cups on the balance, and determine the combined mass of the cups, baking soda, and vinegar to the nearest 0.01 g. Record the combined mass in the first row of your table under "Initial mass."

5. Take the cups off the balance. Carefully and slowly pour the vinegar into the cup that contains the baking soda. To avoid splattering, add only a small amount of vinegar at a time. Gently swirl the cup to make sure that the reactants are well mixed.

Step 2

The content includes a table, numbered steps, and analysis questions.

	Initial mass (g)	Final mass (g)	Change in mass (g)
Trial 1			
Trial 2			

DO NOT WRITE IN THIS BOOK

6. When the reaction has finished, place both cups back on the balance. Determine the combined mass to the nearest 0.01 g. Record the combined mass in the first row of your table under "Final mass."

7. Subtract final mass from initial mass, and record the difference in the first row of your table under "Change in mass."

8. Repeat step 2, but carefully transfer the baking soda to one corner of a plastic bag rather than the cup.

9. To seal the baking soda in the corner of the bag, twist the corner of the bag above the baking soda and wrap the twist tie tightly around the twisted part of the bag.

10. Add 50 mL of vinegar to the bag. Zipper-close the bag so that the vinegar cannot leak out and the bag is airtight.

11. Place the bag in the beaker, and measure the mass of the beaker, the bag, and the reactants. Record the combined mass in the second row of your table under "Initial mass."

12. Remove the twist tie from the bag, and mix the reactants.

13. When the reaction has finished, repeat steps 6 and 7 by using the beaker, bag, twist tie, and products. Record the final mass and change in mass in the table's second row.

Step 11

Analysis

1. **Analyzing Data** Compare the change in mass that you calculated for the first trial with the change in mass that you calculated for the second trial. What evidence of the conservation of mass does the second trial show?

2. **Analyzing Results** Was the law of conservation of mass violated in the first trial? Explain your answer.

3. **Drawing Conclusions** Was the first trial an example of a closed system or an open system? Which type of system was the second trial? Explain your answer.

Extension

Designing an Experiment Brainstorm other ways to demonstrate the law of conservation of mass in a laboratory. Describe the materials that you would need, and describe any difficulties that you foresee.

MAPS in Action

Concentration of Plant Life on Earth

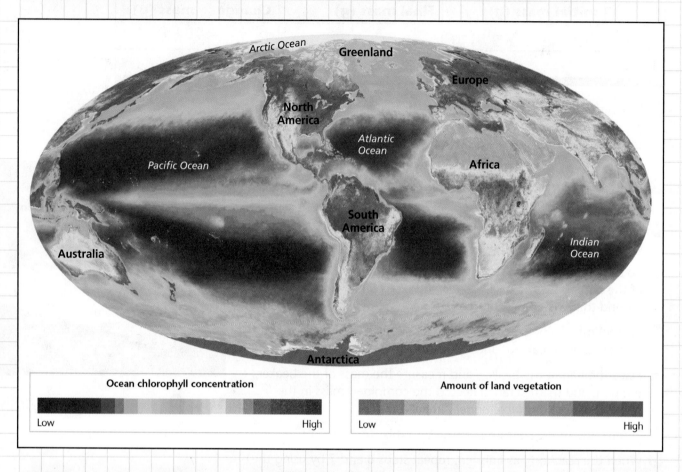

Map Skills Activity

This map shows the concentration of plant life on land and in the oceans. Each color in the key represents a concentration of plant life as indicated by the concentration of chlorophyll. The higher the concentration of chlorophyll is, the higher the concentration of plant life is. Use the map to answer the questions below.

1. **Using a Key** How can you distinguish between high chlorophyll concentration in the ocean and high chlorophyll concentration on land?

2. **Comparing Areas** List three areas that have very low chlorophyll concentration on land. What characteristics of these areas cause such low chlorophyll concentrations?

3. **Comparing Areas** Why do you think Antarctica, Greenland, and the Arctic Ocean lack chlorophyll?

4. **Identifying Trends** Where are the highest chlorophyll concentrations in the ocean located? Why do you think that these locations have high chlorophyll concentrations?

5. **Identifying Trends** Plants use sunlight and chlorophyll to produce energy. What can you infer about the amount of sunlight around the equator that could help explain why areas along the equator tend to have higher concentrations of chlorophyll than surrounding areas do?

48 Chapter 2 **Earth as a System**

THINK central
SUPER SUMMARY
Keyword: HQXEASS

Key Ideas	Key Terms

Section 1

Earth: A Unique Planet

❯ Earth is an oblate spheroid that has an average diameter of 12,756 km.

❯ The compositional layers of Earth's interior are the thin, solid outermost crust, the rocky mantle beneath the crust, and the central core. These layers are divided into five structural zones: lithosphere, asthenosphere, mesosphere, outer core, and inner core.

❯ Liquid iron in the outer core may be a source of Earth's magnetic field.

❯ Newton's law of gravitation states that the force of attraction between any two objects depends on their masses and the distance between them.

crust, p. 30
mantle, p. 30
core, p. 30
lithosphere, p. 31
asthenosphere, p. 31
mesosphere, p. 31

Section 2

Energy in the Earth System

❯ In an open system, both energy and matter enter and exit the system. In a closed system, energy enters and exits, but matter neither enters nor exits.

❯ The atmosphere is gaseous. The hydrosphere is mostly liquid water but may also appear in solid or vapor form. The geosphere is the solid part of Earth. The biosphere contains all the life in the other three spheres.

❯ The sun (external) and radioactive decay (internal) are the two main sources of energy in the Earth system.

❯ Matter moves through Earth systems in cycles such as the nitrogen, carbon, phosphorus, and water cycles.

system, p. 33
atmosphere, p. 35
hydrosphere, p. 35
geosphere, p. 35
biosphere, p. 35

Section 3

Ecology

❯ An ecosystem is a community of organisms and the environment that they inhabit.

❯ Carrying capacity, disturbance, and energy transfer are three factors that control the balance of an ecosystem.

❯ Energy is transferred through an ecosystem via feeding relationships.

❯ In general, an ecosystem responds to changes in ways that maintain or restore balance in the ecosystem.

ecosystem, p. 41
carrying capacity, p. 42
food web, p. 43

1. **Outlining** Choose one of the scientific laws in this chapter. Explain why it is an example of a scientific law rather than a scientific theory. Include an example of a scientific theory for comparison.

   SC.912.N.3.4

USING KEY TERMS

Use each of the following terms in a separate sentence.

2. *system*

3. *carrying capacity*

4. *lithosphere* SC.912.N.6.1

For each pair of terms, explain how the meanings of the terms differ.

5. *system* and *ecosystem* SC.912.N.7.3

6. *biosphere* and *geosphere* SC.912.N.7.3

7. *hydrosphere* and *atmosphere* SC.912.N.7.3

8. *mantle* and *asthenosphere* SC.912.N.6.1

9. *energy pyramid* and *food web*

UNDERSTANDING KEY IDEAS

10. The diameter of Earth is greatest at the
    a. poles.
    b. equator.
    c. oceans.
    d. continents.

11. The element that makes up the largest percentage of the atmosphere is
    a. oxygen.
    b. nitrogen.
    c. carbon dioxide.
    d. ozone.

12. The gravitational attraction between two objects is determined by the mass of the two objects and the SC.912.E.5.6
    a. distance between the objects.
    b. weight of the objects.
    c. diameter of the objects.
    d. density of the objects.

13. Energy can enter the Earth system from internal sources through convection and from external sources through SC.912.E.7.7
    a. radioactive decay.   c. wind energy.
    b. wave energy.   d. solar energy.

14. Closed systems exchange energy but do *not* exchange
    a. gravity.   c. sunlight.
    b. matter.   d. heat.

15. Which of the following is *not* an ecosystem?
    a. a lake   c. a tree
    b. an ocean   d. a population

16. Which of the following processes is *not* involved in the water cycle?
    a. evaporation
    b. transpiration
    c. combustion
    d. precipitation

17. A jar with its lid on tightly is one example of a(n)
    a. open system.
    b. biosphere.
    c. closed system.
    d. ecosystem.

18. Phosphorus cycles through all spheres except the
    a. geosphere.
    b. atmosphere.
    c. biosphere.
    d. hydrosphere.

SHORT ANSWER

19. What characteristic of Earth's interior is likely to be responsible for Earth's magnetic field? SC.912.E.6.1

20. What is the role of decomposers in the cycling of matter in the biosphere?

21. Corrolate the three compositional zones of Earth to the five structural zones of Earth. SC.912.E.6.1

22. Restate the first and second laws of thermodynamics, and explain how they relate to ecosystems on Earth.

23. Describe two ways that your daily activities affect the water cycle.

24. Explain three reasons that stewardship of Earth's resources is important.

25. Describe three ways in which the atmosphere interacts with the geosphere. `SC.912.N.7.3`

26. Identify two distinguishing factors of a nearby ecosystem, and name five kinds of organisms that live in that ecosystem.

CRITICAL THINKING

27. **Analyzing Ideas** What happens to the matter and energy in fossil fuels when the fuels are burned?

28. **Making Inferences** Draw an energy pyramid that includes the organisms shown in the food web diagram in this chapter.

29. **Making Predictions** How would the removal of decomposers from Earth's biosphere affect the carbon, nitrogen, and phosphorus cycles? `SC.912.N.7.3`

30. **Analyzing Relationships** Do you think that Earth has a carrying capacity for humans? Explain your reasoning.

CONCEPT MAPPING

31. Use the following terms to create a concept map: *biosphere, magnetosphere, mantle, atmosphere, geosphere, hydrosphere, ecosystem, crust,* and *core.* `SC.912.E.6.1`

MATH SKILLS

32. **Making Calculations** In one year, the plants in each square meter of an ecosystem obtained 1,460 kilowatt·hours (kWh) of the sun's energy by photosynthesis. In that year, each square meter of plants stored 237 kWh. What percentage of the sun's energy did the plants use for life processes in that year?

33. **Making Calculations** The average radius of Earth is 6,371 km. If the average thickness of oceanic crust is 7.5 km and the average thickness of continental crust is 35 km, what fraction of Earth's radius is each type of crust?

WRITING SKILLS

34. **Creative Writing** If you noticed that pollution was harming a nearby lake, how would you convince your community of the need to take action to solve the problem? Describe three research tools you would use to find materials that support your opinion.

35. **Communicating Main Ideas** Explain why closed systems typically do not exist on Earth. Suggest two examples of a closed system created by humans.

INTERPRETING GRAPHICS

The graphs below show the difference in energy consumption and population size in developed and developing countries. Use the graphs to answer the questions that follow.

Commercial Energy Consumption

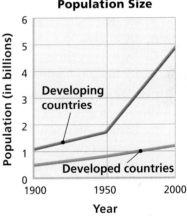

Population Size

36. Describe the differences in energy consumption and population growth between developed and the developing countries. `SC.912.N.1.1`

37. Do you think that the percentage of commercial energy consumed by developing countries will increase or decrease? Explain your answer. `SC.912.N.1.1`

38. Why is information on energy consumption represented in a pie graph, while population size is shown in a line graph? `SC.912.N.1.1`

Understanding Concepts

Directions (1–9): For each question, write on a separate sheet of paper the letter of the correct answer.

1 Carbon cycles through the Earth system. During photosynthesis, carbon is
 A. released from wood as carbon dioxide when wood is burned.
 B. broken down and released from the remains of living organisms.
 C. converted by organisms from a gas to carbohydrates.
 D. released by organisms as carbon dioxide.

2 Because phosphorus rarely occurs as a gas, the phosphorus cycle mainly occurs between the
 F. biosphere, geosphere, and hydrosphere.
 G. biosphere, geosphere, and atmosphere.
 H. geosphere, hydrosphere, and atmosphere.
 I. biosphere, hydrosphere, and atmosphere.

3 How are scientists able to study the composition and size of the interior layers of Earth?
 A. by direct observation
 B. by analyzing surface rock samples
 C. by using seismic waves
 D. by deep-drilling into the interior layers

4 Convection is the internal energy transfer that drives volcanic activity. During convection,
 F. Earth's interior is heated by radioactive decay.
 G. hot materials in Earth's interior move toward Earth's surface.
 H. the materials inside Earth are heated by gravitational contraction.
 I. the sun warms Earth's surface, making its interior warm.

5 Earth has internal energy, but it also receives a lot of external energy. Which of the following statements describes an external source of energy on Earth?
 A. Earth's core is hot because of the force of Earth's gravity.
 B. Radioactive atoms keep Earth's interior hot.
 C. Earth gets all of its energy from its formation.
 D. The sun warms Earth's atmosphere and surface.

6 Plants act as the base for the flow of energy through the biosphere. What is the function of plants in the flow of energy?
 F. They capture solar energy and use it to make food.
 G. They consume other organisms, absorbing energy.
 H. They break down other organisms, releasing energy into the environment.
 I. They absorb solar energy and make it directly available to other organisms.

7 Acid rain is precipitation that has a pH lower than the pH of normal precipitation. Acid rain results from the combustion of carbon. Which of the following activities would contribute most to acid rain?
 A. the use of fossil fuels at power plants
 B. the breakdown of carbohydrates by animals
 C. the breakdown of dead organisms by decomposers
 D. the use of light energy by plants to convert carbon dioxide to carbohydrates

8 The flow of energy in an ecosystem can be illustrated by a pyramid. Why is less energy available at the top of the pyramid than at the bottom of the pyramid?
 F. Organisms at the top of the pyramid use less energy than organisms at the bottom of the pyramid do.
 G. Organisms at the bottom of the pyramid need more energy to survive than organisms at the top of the pyramid do.
 H. At the bottom of the pyramid, organisms must consume other organisms to get energy.
 I. As energy moves up the pyramid, some energy is lost.

9 Energy flows through an ecosystem, starting as solar energy. Which of the following sequences shows the proper flow of energy through an ecosystem?
 A. solar energy → consumers → decomposers
 B. solar energy → decomposers → scavengers
 C. solar energy → producers → consumers
 D. solar energy → scavengers → producers

Interpreting Graphics

Directions (10–11): For each question below, record the correct answer on a separate sheet of paper.

Structure of the Earth

10 The diagram above shows the interior layers of Earth. One type of seismic wave, S waves, cannot travel through liquids. Which layer of the Earth's interior does not transmit S waves?

F. layer B

G. layer C

H. layer D

I. layer E

Worldwide Energy Consumption By Source

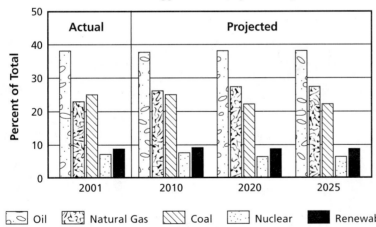

11 The graph above shows predicted worldwide energy consumption by fuel type between the years 2001 and 2025. Which of the following sources of energy is predicted to see the greatest increase in usage between 2001 and 2025?

A. oil

B. natural gas

C. coal

D. renewable

Test Tip

If time permits, take short mental breaks during the test to improve your concentration.

Chapter 3

Models of the Earth

Why It Matters

Using past and present technologies, scientists can create extremely accurate models of Earth's surface. These models, commonly called maps, help people navigate and find locations. Scientists use maps to study changes in Earth's four "spheres."

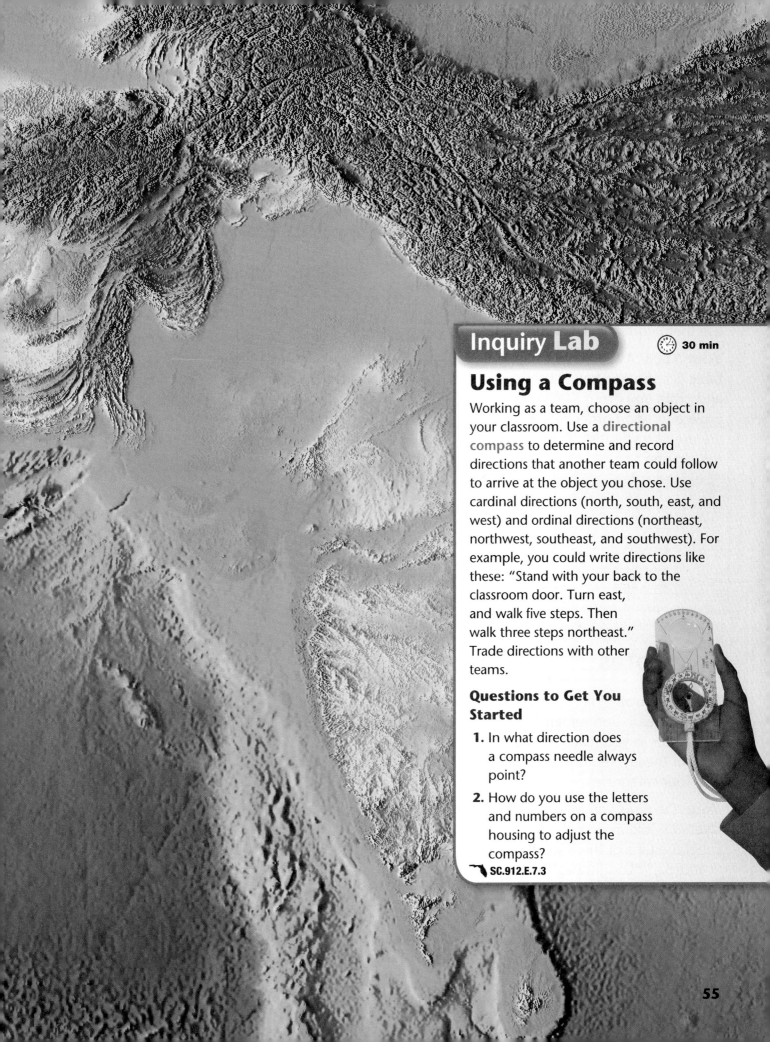

Inquiry **Lab**

⏱ **30 min**

Using a Compass

Working as a team, choose an object in your classroom. Use a directional compass to determine and record directions that another team could follow to arrive at the object you chose. Use cardinal directions (north, south, east, and west) and ordinal directions (northeast, northwest, southeast, and southwest). For example, you could write directions like these: "Stand with your back to the classroom door. Turn east, and walk five steps. Then walk three steps northeast." Trade directions with other teams.

Questions to Get You Started

1. In what direction does a compass needle always point?

2. How do you use the letters and numbers on a compass housing to adjust the compass?

SC.912.E.7.3

These reading tools will help you learn the material in this chapter.

Science Terms

Everyday Words Used in Science All the key terms in this textbook are words that scientists use. Many words that are used in science are also used in everyday speech. You should pay attention to the definitions of these words so that you can use them correctly in scientific contexts.

Your Turn As you read Chapter 3, make a table like the one below for the terms *relief* and *projection* (from the key term *map projection*). Add other everyday words that are used by scientists as you find them in the chapter.

Term	Scientific context	Everyday meaning
relief	the difference between the highest and lowest elevations in a given area	a lessening or easing of a burden or anxiety, pain, or stress

Frequency

Always, Sometimes, or Never? Many statements include a word that tells you how often they are true. Examples include words such as *always, often, sometimes,* and *never.* Words such as *all, some, many,* and *most* tell you about frequency in number.

Your Turn As you read this chapter, make a list of statements that contain frequency words. For each statement in your list, underline the word or phrase that tells how frequently the statement is true. Here is an example: Air and sea routes <u>often</u> travel along great circles.

FoldNotes

Layered Book FoldNotes are a fun way to help you learn and remember ideas that you encounter as you read. You can use the four flaps of the layered book to divide the ideas into four categories.

Your Turn As you read Section 1, make a layered book, as described in **Appendix A**. Label the tabs of the layered book with "Latitude," "Longitude," "Great Circles," and "Finding Direction." Write notes on the appropriate layer as you read the section.

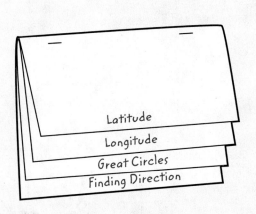

For more information on how to use these and other tools, see **Appendix A**.

Finding Locations on Earth

Key Ideas	Key Terms	Why It Matters
❯ Distinguish between latitude and longitude. ❯ Explain how latitude and longitude can be used to locate places on Earth's surface. ❯ Explain how a magnetic compass can be used to find directions on Earth's surface.	parallel latitude meridian longitude	Latitude and longitude form a frame of reference that is based on Earth's axis of rotation, making it possible to identify and locate any point on Earth.

The points at which Earth's axis of rotation intersects Earth's surface are used as reference points for defining direction. These reference points are the geographic North and South Poles. Halfway between the poles, a circle called the *equator* divides Earth into the Northern and Southern Hemispheres. A reference grid of additional circles is used to locate places on Earth's surface.

Latitude

One set of circles describes positions north and south of the equator. These circles are called **parallels** because they run east and west around the world, parallel to the equator. The angular distance north or south of the equator is called **latitude.**

Degrees of Latitude

Latitude is measured in degrees, and the equator is designated as 0° latitude. Because the distance from the equator to either of the poles is one-fourth of a circle, and a circle has 360°, the latitude of both the North Pole and the South Pole is one-quarter of 360°, or 90°, as shown in **Figure 1.** In actual distance, 1° of latitude equals 1/360 of Earth's circumference, or about 111 km. Parallels north of the equator are labeled N; those south of the equator are labeled S.

Minutes and Seconds

Each degree of latitude consists of 60 equal parts, called *minutes*. One minute (symbol: ') of latitude equals 1.85 km. In turn, each minute is divided into 60 equal parts, called *seconds* (symbol: "). So, the latitude of the center of Washington, D.C., could be expressed as 38°53'23"N.

FLORIDA STANDARDS

SC.912.P.10.16 Explain the relationship between moving charges and magnetic fields, as well as changing magnetic fields and electric fields, and their application to modern technologies; **SC.912.P.10.19** Explain that all objects emit and absorb electromagnetic radiation and distinguish between objects that are blackbody radiators and those that are not.

parallel any circle that runs east and west around Earth and that is parallel to the equator; a line of latitude

latitude the angular distance north or south from the equator; expressed in degrees

Figure 1 Parallels are circles that describe positions north and south of the equator. Each parallel forms a complete circle around the globe.

Figure 2 Meridians are semicircles reaching around Earth from pole to pole.

meridian any semicircle that runs north and south around Earth from the geographic North Pole to the geographic South Pole; a line of longitude

longitude the angular distance east or west from the prime meridian; expressed in degrees

Academic Vocabulary

location (loh KAY shuhn) place or position

Figure 3 A great-circle route from Chicago to Rome is much shorter than a route following a parallel is.

Longitude

The latitude of a particular place indicates only its position north or south of the equator. To determine the specific location of a place, you also need to know how far east or west that place is along its circle of latitude. East-west locations are established by using meridians. As **Figure 2** shows, a **meridian** is a semicircle (half of a circle) that runs from pole to pole.

By international agreement, one meridian was selected to be 0°. This meridian, called the *prime meridian*, passes through Greenwich, England. **Longitude** is the angular distance, measured in degrees, east or west of the prime meridian.

Degrees of Longitude

Because a circle is 360°, the meridian opposite the prime meridian, halfway around the world, is labeled 180°. All locations east of the prime meridian have longitudes between 0° and 180°E. All locations west of the prime meridian have longitudes between 0° and 180°W. Washington, D.C., which lies west of the prime meridian, has a longitude of 77°W. Like latitude, longitude can be expressed in degrees, minutes, and seconds. So, a more precise location for Washington, D.C., is 38°53'23"N, 77°00'33"W.

Distance Between Meridians

The distance covered by a degree of longitude depends on where the degree is measured. At the equator, or 0° latitude, a degree of longitude equals approximately 111 km. However, all meridians meet at the poles. Because meridians meet, the distance measured by a degree of longitude decreases as you move from the equator toward the poles. At a latitude of 60°N, for example, 1° of longitude equals about 55 km. At 80°N, 1° of longitude equals only about 20 km.

Great Circles

A great circle is often used in navigation, especially by long-distance aircraft. A *great circle* is any circle that divides the globe into halves, or marks the circumference of the globe. Any circle formed by two meridians of longitude that are directly across the globe from each other is a great circle. The equator is the only line of latitude that is a great circle. Great circles can run in any direction around the globe. Just as a straight line is the shortest distance between two points on a flat surface or plane, the route along a great circle is the shortest distance between two points on a sphere, as shown in **Figure 3**. As a result, air and sea routes often travel along great circles.

Reading Check **Why is the equator the only parallel that is a great circle?** (See Appendix G for answers to Reading Checks.)

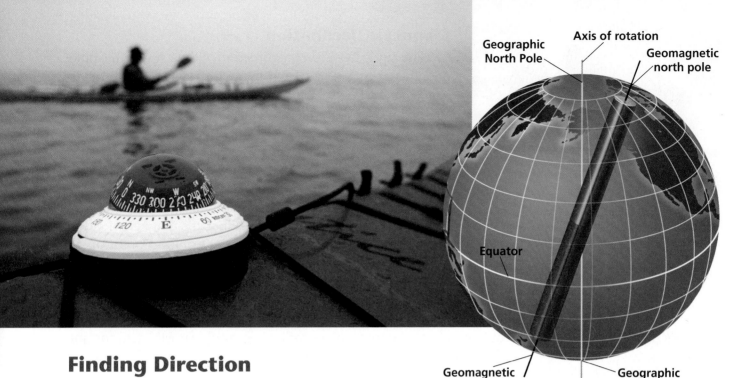

Figure 4 Earth's magnetic poles are at an angle to Earth's axis of rotation.

Finding Direction

One way to find direction on Earth is to use a magnetic compass. A magnetic compass can indicate direction because Earth has magnetic properties as if a powerful bar-shaped magnet were buried at Earth's center at an angle to Earth's axis of rotation, as shown in **Figure 4.**

The areas on Earth's surface where the poles of the imaginary magnet would be are called the *geomagnetic poles*. The geomagnetic poles and the geographic poles are different and are located in different places. The north end of a compass needle points in the direction of the geomagnetic north pole.

Geocaching

SCIENCE & SOCIETY

Finding direction is not only for when you're lost. In geocaching, people hide a cache of "treasure" and post the coordinates (latitude and longitude) online. Other people then use GPS (Global Positioning System) receivers to find the cache.

People hide a cache of items, including a logbook, in a safe place.

The cache's coordinates are posted on a geocaching Web site.

People can trade items that they find and write an entry in the logbook.

YOUR TURN

ONLINE RESEARCH
Research how a GPS receiver uses satellite signals to pinpoint its location.

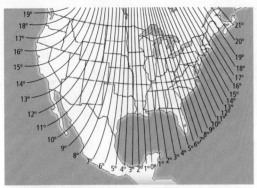

Figure 5 This map shows the pattern of magnetic declinations over North America. The lines connect points that have the same magnetic declination.

www.scilinks.org
Topic: Global Positioning
        System
Code: HQX0680

Magnetic Declination

The angle between the direction of the geographic pole and the direction in which the compass needle points is called *magnetic declination*. In the Northern Hemisphere, magnetic declination is measured in degrees east or west of the geographic North Pole. A compass needle will align with both the geographic North Pole and the geomagnetic north pole for all locations along the line of 0° magnetic declination, which is shown as the red line in **Figure 5**.

Magnetic declination has been determined for points all over Earth. However, because Earth's magnetic field is constantly changing, the magnetic declinations of locations around the globe also change constantly. **Figure 5** shows recent magnetic declinations for most of the United States. By using magnetic declination, a person can use a compass to determine geographic north for any place on Earth. Current declination at any location can be obtained from the Internet. Locating geographic north is important in navigation and in mapmaking.

The Global Positioning System

Another way people can find their location on Earth is by using the *global positioning system*, or *GPS*. GPS is a satellite navigation system that is based on a global network of satellites that transmit radio signals to Earth's surface. The first GPS satellite, known as NAVSTAR, was launched in 1978.

A GPS receiver held by a person on the ground receives signals from at least three satellites, which it uses to calculate the latitude, longitude, and altitude of the receiver on Earth. Personal GPS receivers are accurate to within 10 to 15 m of their position, but high-tech receivers designed for military or commercial use can be accurate to within several centimeters of their location.

Section 1 Review

LA.910.2.2.3; SC.912.P.10.16; SC.912.P.10.19

Key Ideas

1. **Describe** the difference between lines of latitude and lines of longitude.

2. **Explain** how latitude and longitude are used to find specific locations on Earth.

3. **Summarize** why great-circle routes are commonly used in navigation.

4. **Explain** how a magnetic compass can be used to find directions on Earth.

Critical Thinking

5. **Applying Concepts** How might GPS technology be beneficial when used in airplanes or on ships?

6. **Making Comparisons** How do parallels differ from latitude?

7. **Identifying Patterns** Explain why the distance between parallels is constant but the distance between meridians decreases as the meridians approach the poles.

Concept Mapping

8. Use the following terms to create a concept map: *equator, second, parallel, degree, Earth, minute, longitude, meridian, prime meridian,* and *latitude*.

Mapping Earth's Surface

Key Ideas	Key Terms	Why It Matters
❯ Explain two ways that scientists get data to make maps. ❯ Describe the characteristics and uses of three types of map projections. ❯ Summarize how to use keys, legends, and scales to read maps.	remote sensing map projection legend scale isogram	Maps are models of Earth's surface that can be made or chosen to display characteristics for a specific purpose, such as plotting the best route for your next road trip.

A globe is a familiar model of Earth. Because a globe is spherical like Earth, a globe can accurately represent the locations, relative areas, and relative shapes of Earth's surface features. A globe is especially useful for studying large surface features, such as continents and oceans. But most globes are too small to show details of Earth's surface, such as streams and highways. For that reason, a great variety of maps have been developed for studying and displaying detailed information about Earth.

How Scientists Make Maps

The science of making maps, called *cartography*, is a subfield of Earth science and geography. Scientists who make maps are called *cartographers*.

Cartographers use data from a variety of sources to create maps. They may collect data by conducting a field survey, shown in **Figure 1.** During a field survey, cartographers walk or drive through an area to be mapped and make measurements of that area. The information they collect is then plotted on a map. Because surveyors cannot take measurements at every site in an area, they often use their measurements to make estimated measurements for sites between surveyed points.

By using remote sensing, cartographers can collect information about a site without being at that site. In **remote sensing,** equipment on satellites or airplanes obtains images of Earth's surface. Maps are often made by combining information from images gathered remotely with information from field surveys.

FLORIDA STANDARDS

LA.910.2.2.3 The student will organize information to show understanding or relationships among facts, ideas, and events (e.g., representing key points within text through charting, mapping, paraphrasing, summarizing, comparing, contrasting, or outlining).

remote sensing the process of gathering and analyzing information about an object without physically being in touch with the object

Figure 1 Cartographers in the field use technology to enhance the precision of their measurements. Electronic devices can be used to measure the distance between an observer and a distant point with a high degree of accuracy.

Making Projections

Procedure

❶ Use a **fine-tip marker** to draw a variety of shapes on a **small glass ivy bowl** or **clear plastic hemisphere.**

❷ Shine a **flashlight** through the bottom of the bowl.

❸ Shape a **piece of white paper** into a cylinder around the bowl.

❹ Trace the shapes projected from the bowl onto the paper.

❺ Using a cone of paper, repeat steps 3 and 4.

Analysis

1. What type of projection did you create in steps 3 and 4? in step 5?

2. Compare the sizes of the shapes on the bowl with those on your papers. What areas did each projection distort?

map projection a flat map that represents a spherical surface

Map Projections

A map is a flat representation of Earth's curved surface. However, transferring a curved surface to a flat map results in a distorted image of the curved surface. An area shown on a map may be distorted in size, shape, distance, or direction. The larger the area being shown is, the greater the distortion tends to be. A map of the entire Earth would show the greatest distortion. A map of a small area, such as a city, would show only slight distortion.

Over the years, cartographers have developed several ways to transfer the curved surface of Earth onto flat maps. A flat map that represents the three-dimensional curved surface of a globe is called a **map projection.** No projection is an entirely accurate representation of Earth's surface. However, each kind of projection has certain advantages and disadvantages that must be considered when choosing a map.

Cylindrical Projections

Imagine Earth as a transparent sphere that has a light inside. If you wrapped a cylinder of paper around this lighted globe and traced the outlines of continents, oceans, parallels, and meridians, a *cylindrical projection,* shown in **Figure 2,** would result. Meridians on a cylindrical projection appear as straight, parallel lines that have an equal amount of space between them. On a globe, however, the meridians come together at the poles. A cylindrical projection is accurate near the equator but distorts distances and sizes near the poles.

Though distorted, cylindrical projections have some advantages. One advantage is that parallels and meridians form a grid, which makes locating positions easier. Also, the shapes of small areas are usually well preserved. When a cylindrical projection is used to map small areas, distortion is minimal.

▶ **Reading Check** Why do meridians and parallels appear as a grid when shown on a cylindrical projection?

Figure 2 A light at the center of a transparent globe would project lines on a cylinder of paper (left) that would produce a cylindrical projection (right).

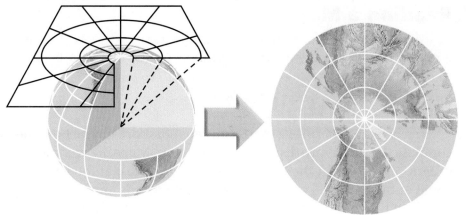

Figure 3 When a sheet of paper is placed so that it touches a lighted globe at only one point (left), the lines projected on the paper form an azimuthal projection (right).

Azimuthal Projections

A projection made by placing a sheet of paper against a transparent, lighted globe such that the paper touches the globe at only one point is called an *azimuthal* (AZ uh MYOOTH uhl) *projection,* as shown in **Figure 3.** On an azimuthal projection, little distortion occurs at the point of <u>contact</u>, which is commonly one of the poles. However, an azimuthal projection shows unequal spacing between parallels that causes a distortion in both direction and distance. This distortion increases as distance from the point of contact increases.

Despite distortion, an azimuthal projection is a great help to navigators in plotting routes used in air travel. As you know, a great circle is the shortest distance between any two points on the globe. When projected onto an azimuthal projection, a great circle appears as a straight line. Therefore, by drawing a straight line between any two points on an azimuthal projection, navigators can readily find a great-circle route.

Conic Projections

A projection made by placing a paper cone over a lighted globe so that the axis of the cone aligns with the axis of the globe is known as a *conic projection.* The cone touches the globe along one parallel of latitude. As shown in **Figure 4,** areas near the parallel where the cone and globe are in contact are distorted the least.

A series of conic projections may be used to increase accuracy by mapping a number of neighboring areas. Each cone touches the globe at a slightly different latitude. Fitting the adjoining areas together then produces a continuous map. Maps made in this way are called *polyconic projections.* The relative size and shape of small areas on the map are nearly the same as those on the globe.

READING TOOLBOX

Layered Book
Make a layered book FoldNote. Label the tabs with the three types of map projections. Write notes on the appropriate tab to list the advantages and disadvantages of each type of map projection.

Academic Vocabulary

contact (KON takt) state of touching; coming together of objects or surfaces

Figure 4 A light at the center of a transparent globe would project lines on a paper cone (left) that would produce a conic projection (right).

Reading a Map

Maps provide information through the use of symbols. To read a map, you must understand the symbols on the map and be able to find directions and calculate distances.

Direction on a Map

To correctly interpret a map, you must first determine how the compass directions are displayed on the map. Maps are commonly drawn with north at the top, east at the right, west at the left, and south at the bottom. Parallels run from side to side, and meridians run from top to bottom. Direction should always be determined in relation to the parallels and meridians.

On maps published by the United States Geological Survey (USGS), such as the one shown in **Figure 5,** north is located at the top of the map and is marked by a parallel. The southern boundary, at the bottom of a map, is also marked by a parallel. At least two additional parallels are usually drawn in or indicated by cross hairs at 2.5' intervals. Meridians of longitude indicate the eastern and western boundaries of USGS maps. Additional meridians may also be shown. All parallels and meridians shown on these maps are labeled in degrees, minutes, and seconds.

Many maps also include a compass rose, as shown in **Figure 5.** A *compass rose* is a symbol that indicates the cardinal directions. The *cardinal directions* are north, east, south, and west. Some maps replace the compass rose with a single arrow that points to geographic north. This arrow is generally labeled and may not always point to the top of the map.

Figure 5 Maps may show locations by marking parallels and meridians. Direction is commonly shown with a compass rose (inset).

Figure 6 The map legend explains the symbols used on the map.

Symbols

Maps often have symbols for features such as cities and rivers. The symbols are explained in the map **legend,** a list of the symbols and their meanings, such as the one shown in **Figure 6.** Some symbols resemble the features that they represent. Others, such as those for towns and urban areas, are more abstract.

legend a list of map symbols and their meanings

scale the relationship between the distance shown on a map and the actual distance

Map Scales

To be accurate, a map must be drawn to **scale.** The scale of a map indicates the relationship between distance shown on the map and actual distance. A map scale can be expressed as a graphic scale, a fractional scale, or a verbal scale.

A *graphic scale* is a printed line that has markings on it that are similar to those on a ruler. The line represents a unit of measure, such as the kilometer or the mile. Each part of the scale represents a specific distance on Earth. To find the actual distance between two points on Earth, you first measure the distance between the points as shown on the map. Then, you compare that measurement with the map scale.

A second way of expressing scale is by using a ratio, or a *fractional scale.* For example, a fractional scale such as 1:25,000 indicates that 1 unit of distance on the map represents 25,000 of the same unit on Earth. A fractional scale remains the same with any system of measurement. In other words, the scale 1:100 could be read as 1 in. equals 100 in. or as 1 cm equals 100 cm.

A *verbal scale* expresses scale in sentence form. An example of a verbal scale is "One centimeter is equal to one kilometer." In this scale, 1 cm on the map represents 1 km on Earth.

Math Skills

Determining Distance You notice that the scale on a map of the United States says, "One centimeter equals 120 kilometers." By measuring the straight-line distance between Brooklyn, New York, and Miami, Florida, you determine that the cities are about 14.5 cm apart on the map. What is the approximate distance in kilometers between the two cities?

Reading Check Name three ways to express scale on a map.

Figure 7 Areas connected by the isobars on the map share equal atmospheric pressure.

isogram a line on a map that represents a constant or equal value of a given quantity

Isograms

A line on a map that represents a constant or equal value of a given quantity is an **isogram.** The prefix *iso-* is Greek for "equal." The second part of the word, *-gram*, means "drawing." This part of the word can be changed to describe the measurement being graphed. For example, when a line connects points of equal temperature, the line is called an *isotherm* because *iso-* means "equal" and *therm* means "heat." All locations along an isogram share the value that is being measured.

Isograms can be used to plot many types of data. Meteorologists use these lines to show changes in atmospheric pressure on weather maps. Isograms used for this purpose on a weather map are called *isobars,* as shown in **Figure 7.** All points along an isobar share the same pressure value. Because one location cannot have two air pressures, isobars never cross one another.

Scientists can use isograms on a map to plot data that represent almost any type of measurement. Isograms are commonly used to show areas that have similar measurements of precipitation, temperature, gravity, magnetism, density, elevation, or chemical composition.

Section 2 Review

LA.910.2.2.3; SC.912.N.1.1

Key Ideas

1. **Identify** two methods that scientists use to get the data needed to make maps.

2. **Describe** three types of map projections in terms of their different characteristics and uses.

3. **Explain** why all maps are in some way inaccurate representations.

4. **Summarize** how to use legends and scales to read maps.

5. **Describe** what isograms show.

6. **Explain** why maps are more useful than globes are for studying small areas on the surface of Earth.

7. **Summarize** how to find directions on a map.

Critical Thinking

8. **Applying Concepts** If a cartographer is making a map for three countries that do not use a common unit of measurement, what type of scale should the cartographer use on the map? Explain your answer.

9. **Making Inferences** Why would a conic projection produce a better map for exploring polar regions than a cylindrical projection would?

Concept Mapping

10. Use the following terms to create a concept map: *cartography, map projection, cylindrical projection, azimuthal projection, conic projection, map, legend, scale,* and *symbol.*

Key Ideas	Key Terms	Why It Matters
❯ Explain how elevation and topography are shown on a map. ❯ Describe three types of information shown in geologic maps. ❯ Identify two uses of soil maps.	topography elevation contour line relief	Different types of maps enable scientists to display detailed three-dimensional information about the surface and below-surface features of Earth.

Earth scientists use a wide variety of maps that show many distinct characteristics of an area. Some of these characteristics include types of rocks, differences in air pressure, and varying depths of groundwater in a region. Scientists also use maps that show locations, elevations, and surface features of Earth.

Topographic Maps

One of the most widely used maps is called a *topographic map*. Topographic maps show the surface features, or **topography,** of Earth. Most topographic maps show both natural features, such as rivers and hills, and constructed features, such as buildings and roads. Topographic maps are made by using both aerial photographs and survey points collected in the field. A topographic map shows the **elevation,** or height above sea level, of the land. Elevation is measured from *mean sea level,* the point midway between the highest and lowest tide levels of the ocean. The elevation at mean sea level is 0.

Advantages of Topographic Maps

An aerial view of an island is shown in **Figure 1.** Although the drawing shows the shape of the island, it does not indicate the island's size or elevation. A typical map projection would show the island's size and shape but would not show the island's topography. A topographic map provides more detailed information about the surface of the island than either the drawing or a projection map does. The advantage of a topographic map is that it shows the island's size, shape, and elevation.

FLORIDA STANDARDS

SC.912.N.1.4 Identify sources of information and assess their reliability according to the strict standards of scientific investigation; **SC.912.N.1.6** Describe how scientific inferences are drawn from scientific observations and provide examples from the content being studied; **SC.912.N.3.5** Describe the function of models in science, and identify the wide range of models used in science.

topography the size and shape of the land surface features of a region, including its relief

elevation the height of an object above sea level

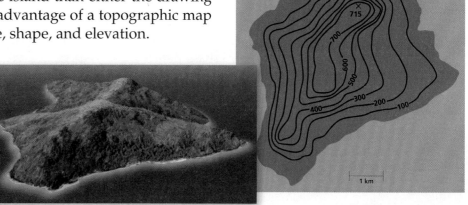

Figure 1 A drawing gives little information about the elevation of the island (left). In the topographic map (right), contour lines have been drawn to show elevation. An ✕ marks the highest point on this map.

Figure 2 On a topographic map, the contour interval for this mountain would be very large because of the mountain's steep slope.

contour line a line that connects points of equal elevation on a map

relief the difference between the highest and lowest elevations in a given area

Elevation on Topographic Maps

On topographic maps, **contour lines** are used to show elevation. Each contour line is an isogram that connects points that have the same elevation. Because points at a given elevation are connected, the shape of the contour lines reflects the shape of the land.

The difference in elevation between one contour line and the next is called the *contour interval*. A cartographer chooses a contour interval suited to the scale of the map and the relief of the land. **Relief** is the difference in elevation between the highest and lowest points of the area being mapped. On maps of areas where the relief is high, such as the area shown in **Figure 2,** the contour interval may be as large as 50 or 100 m. Where the relief is low, the interval may be only 1 or 2 m.

To make reading the map easier, a cartographer makes every fifth contour line bolder than the four lines on each side of it. These bold lines, called *index contours*, are labeled by elevation. A point between two contour lines has an elevation between the elevations of the two lines. For example, if a point is halfway between the 50 and 100 m contour lines, its elevation is about 75 m. Exact elevations are marked by an × and are labeled.

SC.912.N.3.5

Quick Lab Topographic Maps

20 min

Procedure

❶ Make a model mountain that is 6 to 8 cm high out of modeling clay. Work on a flat surface, and smooth out the mountain's shape. Make one side of the mountain slightly steeper than the other side.

❷ Run a paper clip down one side of the model to form a valley that is several millimeters wide.

❸ Place the model in the center of a large waterproof container that is at least 8 cm deep.

❹ Use tape to hold a ruler upright in the container. One end of the ruler should rest on the bottom of the container. Make sure that the container is level.

❺ Using the ruler as a guide, add water to the container to a depth of 1 cm. Use a sharp pencil to inscribe the clay by tracing around the model along the waterline.

❻ Raise the water level 1 cm at a time until you reach the top of the model. Each time you add water to the container, inscribe another contour line in the clay along the waterline.

❼ When you have finished, carefully drain the water and remove the model from the container.

Analysis

1. What is the contour interval of your model?

2. Observe your model from directly above. Try to duplicate the size and spacing of the contour lines on a sheet of paper to create a topographic map.

3. Compare the contour lines on a steep slope with those on a gentle slope. How do they differ?

4. How is a valley represented on your topographic map?

Landforms on Topographic Maps

As shown in **Figure 3**, the spacing and the direction of contour lines indicate the shapes of the landforms represented on a topographic map. Contour lines spaced widely apart indicate that the change in elevation is gradual and that the land is relatively level. Closely spaced contour lines indicate that the change in elevation is rapid and that the slope is steep.

A contour line that bends to form a V shape indicates a valley. The bend in the V points toward the higher end of the valley. If a stream or river flows through the valley, the V in the contour line will point upstream, the direction from which the water flows. A river always flows from higher to lower elevation. The width of the V formed by the contour line shows the width of the valley.

Contour lines that form closed loops indicate a hilltop or a depression. Generally, a depression is indicated by *depression contours*, which are closed-loop contour lines that have short, straight lines perpendicular to the inside of the loop. These short lines point toward the center of the depression.

Reading Check Why do V-shaped contour lines along a river point upstream?

Topographic Map Symbols

Symbols are used to show certain features on topographic maps. Symbol color indicates the type of feature. For example, constructed features, such as buildings, boundaries, roads, and railroads, are generally shown in black. Major highways are shown in red. Bodies of water are shown in blue, and forested areas are shown in green. Contour lines are brown or black. Often, areas whose map information has been updated based on aerial photography but not verified by field exploration are shown in purple. A key to common topographic map symbols is provided for your reference in Appendix E.

Figure 3 The features of the area's coastal valley are represented by contour lines on the topographic map of the area.

THINK central
INTERACT ONLINE
Keyword: HQXMODF3

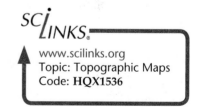
SCi LINKS.
www.scilinks.org
Topic: Topographic Maps
Code: HQX1536

Figure 4 Each color on this geologic map represents a distinct type of rock and shows where in this region that type of rock occurs.

Geologic Maps

Geologic maps, such as the one shown in **Figure 4,** are designed to show the distribution of geologic features. In particular, geologic maps show the types of rocks found in a given area and the locations of faults, folds, and other structures.

Geologic maps are created on top of another map, called a *base map*. The base map provides surface features, such as topography or roads, to help identify the location of the geologic units. The base map is commonly printed in light colors or as gray lines so that the geologic information on the map is easy to read and understand.

Rock Units on Geologic Maps

A volume of rock of a given age range and rock type is a *geologic unit*. On geologic maps, geologic units are distinguished by color. Units of similar ages are generally assigned colors in the same color family, such as different shades of blue. In addition to assigning a color, geologists assign a set of letters to each rock unit. This set of letters is commonly one capital letter followed by one or more lowercase letters. The capital letter symbolizes the age of the rock, usually by geologic period. The lowercase letters represent the name of the unit or the type of rock.

Other Structures on Geologic Maps

Other markings on geologic maps are contact lines. A *contact line* indicates places at which two geologic units meet, called *contacts*. The two main types of contacts are faults and depositional contacts. Depositional contacts show where one rock layer formed above another. Faults are cracks where rocks have moved past each other. Also on geologic maps are strike and dip symbols for rock beds. *Strike* indicates the direction in which the beds run, and *dip* indicates the angle at which the beds tilt.

Soil Maps

Another type of map that is commonly used by Earth scientists is called a *soil map*. Scientists construct soil maps to classify, map, and describe soils. Soil maps are based on soil surveys that record information about the properties of soils in a given area. Soil surveys can be performed for a variety of areas, but they are most commonly performed for a county.

The government agency that is in charge of overseeing and compiling soil data is the Natural Resources Conservation Service (NRCS). The NRCS is part of the United States Department of Agriculture (USDA). The NRCS has been mapping the distribution of soils in the United States for more than a century.

Academic Vocabulary

distribution (DIS tri BYOO shuhn) relative arrangement of objects or organisms in time or space

Reading Check   **Why do scientists create soil maps?**

Soil Surveys

A soil survey consists of three main parts: text, maps, and tables. The text of soil surveys includes general information about the geology, topography, and climate of the area being mapped. The tables describe the types and volumes of soils in the area. Soil surveys generally include two types of soil maps. The first type is a very general map that shows the approximate location of different types of soil within the area, such as the one shown in **Figure 5.** The second type shows detailed information about soils in the area.

Uses of Soil Maps

Soil maps are valuable tools for agriculture and land management. Knowing the properties of the soil in an area helps farmers, agricultural engineers, and government agencies identify ways to conserve and use soil and to plan sites for future development.

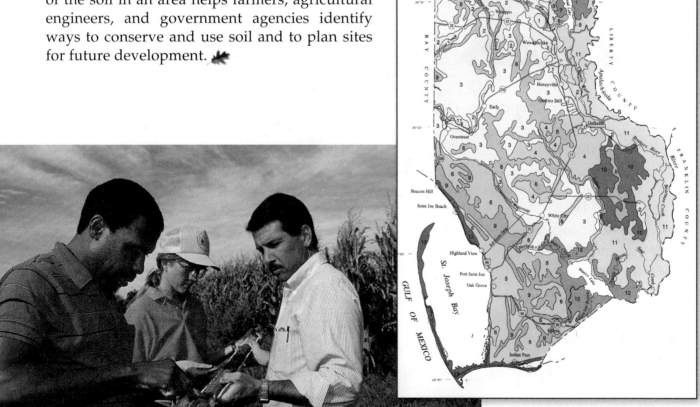

Figure 5 Scientists gather data to make a soil map by taking soil samples. Soil maps help scientists determine the potential abilities and limitations of the land to support development and agriculture.

Figure 6 This map was created by using satellite data. The map shows the global distribution of lightning based on the average number of strikes per square kilometer. The highest frequency of strikes is shown in black, and the lowest frequency is shown in white.

Other Types of Maps

Earth scientists also use maps to show the location and flow of both water and air. These maps are commonly constructed by plotting data from various points around a region and then using isograms to connect the points whose data are identical.

Maps are useful to every branch of Earth science. For example, meteorologists use maps such as the one shown in **Figure 6** to record and predict weather events. Maps may be used to plot the amount of precipitation that falls in a given area. Maps are also used to show the locations of areas of high and low air pressure and the weather fronts that move across Earth's surface. These maps are updated constantly and are used by meteorologists to communicate to the public important information on daily weather conditions and emergency situations.

The location and direction of the flow of groundwater can be recorded on maps. Data from these maps can be used to determine where and when water shortages may occur. Scientists use map information to identify potential locations for power plants, waste disposal sites, and new communities.

Other types of Earth scientists use maps to study changes in Earth's surface over time. Such changes include changes in topography, changes in amounts of available resources, and changes in factors that affect climate. Maps generated by satellites are particularly useful for studying changes in Earth's surface.

Section 3 Review

MA.912.S.1.2; SC.912.N.1.1; SC.912.N.1.3; SC.912.N.1.4; SC.912.N.1.6; SC.912.N.3.5

Key Ideas

1. **Explain** how elevation is shown on a topographic map.

2. **Define** *contour interval.*

3. **Summarize** how you can use information on a topographic map to compare the steepness of slopes on the map.

4. **Describe** how geologic units of similar ages are shown on a geologic map.

5. **Identify** the three main parts of a soil survey.

6. **Identify** two primary uses for soil maps.

7. **Identify** three types of maps other than topographic maps, geologic maps, and soil maps.

Critical Thinking

8. **Applying Ideas** How can you use lines on a topographic map to identify the direction of river flow?

9. **Making Inferences** In what ways might topographic maps be more useful than simple map projections to someone who wants to hike in an area that he or she has never hiked in before?

10. **Identifying Patterns** What type of map would be the most useful to a scientist studying earthquake patterns: a geologic map or a topographic map?

Concept Mapping

11. Use the following terms to create a concept map: *topographic map, elevation, mean sea level, contour interval, contour line,* and *index contour.*

Is There Anywhere That Isn't Mapped?

Lost in the city? Consult a map. Lost in the woods? Check your handy GPS receiver. With our ever-improving models of Earth, it is getting harder to "get lost"—harder, but not impossible. While much of Earth's surface is mapped, a detailed view of many features on and below its surface remains incomplete. Parts of rain forests around the world remain uncharted, and there are many kilometers of caves and sinkholes (cenotes) that no human has ever entered.

Inventor and explorer Bill Stone used a robotic submarine, DEPTHX, to survey Mexico's unexplored El Zacatón cenote in 2007. The same technology may one day be used to map the moons of the outer planets.

The Darien Gap borders Panama and Columbia. It is a dense, 26,000 km², area containing forest and swamp—and the only part of the Pan-American Highway that is not fully mapped.

Mammoth Cave in Kentucky has more than 600 km of surveyed passages and perhaps twice as many that are still unmapped.

YOUR TURN

CRITICAL THINKING
What are three locations on or under Earth that you think have yet to be mapped?

ONLINE RESEARCH
Research these three locations to find out whether or not they have been mapped.

Contour Maps: Island Construction

A map is a drawing that shows a simplified version of some detail of Earth's surface. There are many types of maps. Each type has its own special features and purpose. One of the most useful types of maps is the topographic map, or contour map. This type of map shows elevation and other important features of the landscape. Scientists make a contour map by using data obtained from a careful survey and photographic study of the area that the map represents.

What You'll Do

> **Build** a scale model based on a map.

> **Identify** contour intervals and landscape features based on a map.

What You'll Need

basin, flat (or large pan), 8 cm deep
clay, modeling (4 lb)
dowel, thick wooden (or rolling pin)
knife, plastic
paper, white
pencil
ruler, metric
scissors
topographic map from Reference Tables section of the Appendix
water

Safety

Procedure

1. Study the topographic map in the Reference Tables section of the Appendix. Record the contour interval used on the island contour map. Then, count the number of contour lines that appear on the map.

2. Use the dowel to press out as many flat pieces of clay as there were contour lines counted in step 1. Each piece of clay should be 1 cm thick and large enough to cover the island shown on the map.

3. On a blank sheet of paper, trace the island contour map. Cut out the island from your copy of the contour map along the outermost contour line.

4. Place this cutout on top of one of the pieces of clay. Trace the edge of the cutout in the clay. Cut the piece of clay to match the shape of the island.

Step **2**

5 Cut the paper tracing along the next contour line, making sure not to damage the outer ring of paper as you cut.

6 Using the new paper shape and a new layer of clay, repeat step 4.

7 Place the paper ring from the first cut on the first clay shape that you cut out so that the outer edges of the paper ring line up with the edges of the clay. Stack the second layer of clay on the first layer so that the second layer fits inside the paper contour ring. This gives you the same contour spacing as shown on the map. Remove the paper ring.

Step 5

8 Continue steps 4–7 for each of the contour layers.

9 Use leftover clay to smooth the terraced edges into a more natural profile.

10 Make a mark inside a pan approximately 1 cm down from the rim. Put the clay model of the island into the pan, and add water to a depth of 1 cm.

11 Compare the shoreline of the model with the lines on the contour map. Continue to add water at 1 cm intervals until the water reaches the mark on the pan.

Step 6

Analysis

1. **Making Inferences** What is the contour interval of your map?

2. **Understanding Relationships** How could you tell the steepest slope from the gentlest slope by observing the spacing of the contour lines?

3. **Analyzing Data** What is the elevation above sea level for the highest point of your model?

4. **Applying Ideas** How do you know if your model contains any areas that are below sea level? If there are any such areas, where are they and what are their elevations?

5. **Evaluating Models** What landscape feature is located at point C on your model, as indicated on the original map? What is the elevation of point B on your model?

Extension

Making Predictions From observations of your model, what conclusions can you make about where people might live on this island? Explain your answer.

MAPS *in Action*

Topographic Map of the Desolation Watershed

Scale: 1:24,000

0   1,000 ft   2,000 ft

Contour interval = 40 ft
Contour line
Index contour
River
Improved road
Unimproved road
Trail
Benchmark   ×

Map ▶ Skills Activity

This map, produced by the United States Geological Survey (USGS), shows the topography of the area around the Desolation watershed located in eastern Oregon. Note that the USGS uses English and metric units when measuring distance. Use the map to answer the questions below.

1. **Using a Key** What is the distance between the location on the northwest corner of the map labeled "4681T" and the location on the eastern side of the map labeled "5212T"?

2. **Analyzing Data** In what direction does Park Creek flow? How are you able to determine this information by looking at the map?

3. **Making Comparisons** Which area has the steeper slopes: the area around Park Creek or the

area around Bruin Creek? How are you able to determine this information by looking at the map?

4. **Inferring Relationships** What is the elevation of the contour line that circles the point 4550T, located on the northwest of the map?

5. **Identifying Trends** Desolation Creek, Park Creek, and Bruin Creek enter the map from different geographic directions. Use the information on the map to determine what these creeks have in common in terms of their direction of flow.

6. **Analyzing Relationships** What is the total change in elevation between two index contours?

THINK central
SUPER SUMMARY
Keyword: HQXMODS

Key Ideas	Key Terms

Section 1

Finding Locations on Earth

❯ Lines of latitude are parallels that run east and west around Earth. Lines of longitude are meridians that run north and south from pole to pole.

❯ Lines of latitude and longitude form a system of intersecting lines (a grid system). The points at which lines intersect may be used to identify places on Earth's surface.

❯ The needle of a compass points to the geomagnetic north pole. Once north is located, south, east, and west may be determined.

parallel, p. 57
latitude, p. 57
meridian, p. 58
longitude, p. 58

Section 2

Mapping Earth's Surface

❯ Two ways that scientists get data to make maps are by using field surveys and by using images of Earth's surface obtained by remote sensing.

❯ For cylindrical projections, distances and sizes are accurate near the equator but distorted at the poles. Azimuthal projections are commonly used to map the poles, where distortion is minimal; distortion increases, however, farther from the poles. Conic projections are useful for mapping mid-latitude regions.

❯ The keys and legends of maps list map symbols and their meanings. Map scales show the relationship between distance shown on a map and actual distance.

remote sensing, p. 61
map projection, p. 62
legend, p. 65
scale, p. 65
isogram, p. 66

Section 3

Types of Maps

❯ Contour lines are used to show elevation and topography on a map.

❯ Geologic maps show the types and locations of rocks, faults, folds, and other geologic features.

❯ Soil maps are used to classify, map, and describe soils.

topography, p. 67
elevation, p. 67
contour line, p. 68
relief, p. 68

Chapter 3 Review

USING KEY TERMS

1. **Layered Book** You have made a layered book for concepts within a section. Now make a layered book with the names of the three sections themselves and summarize the key ideas in the chapter.

READING TOOLBOX

Use each of the following terms in a separate sentence.

2. *cartography*
3. *map projection*
4. *contour lines*

For each pair of terms, explain how the meanings of the terms differ.

5. *parallel* and *latitude*
6. *meridian* and *longitude*
7. *legend* and *scale*
8. *topography* and *relief*
9. *index contour* and *contour interval*

UNDERSTANDING KEY IDEAS

10. The distance in degrees east or west of the prime meridian is
    a. latitude.
    b. longitude.
    c. declination.
    d. projection.

11. The distance covered by a degree of longitude
    a. is 1/180 of Earth's circumference.
    b. is always equal to 11 km.
    c. increases as you approach the poles.
    d. decreases as you approach the poles.

12. The needle of a magnetic compass points toward the
    a. geomagnetic pole.
    b. geographic pole.
    c. parallels.
    d. meridians.

13. The shortest distance between any two points on the globe is along
    a. the equator.
    b. a line of latitude.
    c. the prime meridian.
    d. a great circle.

14. If 1 cm on a map equals 1 km on Earth, the fractional scale would be written as
    a. 1:1.   **c.** 1:100,000.
    b. 1:100.   **d.** 1:1,000,000.

15. On a topographic map, elevation is shown by means of
    a. great circles.
    b. contour lines.
    c. verbal scale.
    d. fractional scale.

16. What type of map is commonly used to locate faults and folds in beds of rock?
    a. geologic map
    b. topographic map
    c. soil map
    d. isogram map

17. The contour interval is a measurement of
    a. the change in elevation between two adjacent contour lines.
    b. the distance between mean sea level and any given contour line.
    c. the length of a contour line.
    d. the time needed to travel between any two contour lines.

SHORT ANSWER

18. How much distance on Earth's surface does one second of latitude equal?

19. What is the difference between latitude and longitude?

20. What are the three main types of map projections? How do they differ?

21. Compare the advantages and disadvantages of the three main types of map projections.

22. How do legends and scales help people interpret maps?

23. How do contour lines on a map illustrate topography?

CRITICAL THINKING

24. Applying Ideas What is wrong with the following location: 135°N, 185°E?

25. Identifying Trends As you move from point A to point B in the Northern Hemisphere, the length of a degree of longitude progressively decreases. In which direction are you moving?

26. Understanding Relationships Imagine that you are at a location where the magnetic declination is 0°. Describe your position relative to magnetic north and true north.

27. Making Inferences You examine a topographic map on which the contour interval is 100 m. In general, what type of terrain is probably shown on the map?

28. Applying Ideas A topographic map shows two hiking trails. Along trail A, the contour lines are widely spaced. Along trail B, the contour lines are almost touching. Which path would probably be easier and safer to follow? Why?

CONCEPT MAPPING

29. Use the following terms to create a concept map: *latitude, longitude, relief, map projection, cylindrical projection, elevation, map, azimuthal projection, contour line, conic projection, topography, legend,* and *scale.*

MATH SKILLS   `Math Skills`

30. Making Calculations A topographic map has a contour interval of 30 m. By how many meters would your elevation change if you crossed seven contour lines?

31. Applying Quantities A map has a fractional scale of 1:24,000. How many kilometers would 3 cm on the map represent?

32. Making Calculations A city to which you are traveling is located along the same meridian as your current position but is 11° of latitude to the north of your current position. About how far away is the city?

WRITING SKILLS

33. Writing from Research Research the navigation instrument known as the *sextant*. Make a diagram explaining how the sextant can be used to determine latitude.

34. Writing from Research Use the Internet and library resources to research global positioning systems. Write a short essay describing the different ways that GPS devices are currently being used in everyday situations. Then, make a prediction about how the technology might be used in the future.

INTERPRETING GRAPHICS

The map below shows contour lines of groundwater. The lines show elevation of the water table in meters above sea level. Use the map to answer the questions that follow.

35. What is the contour interval for this map? `SC.912.N.1.1`

36. What is the highest measured level of the water table? `SC.912.N.1.1`

37. Groundwater flows from highest to lowest elevation. In which direction is the groundwater flowing? `SC.912.N.1.1`

Understanding Concepts

Directions (1–10): For each question, write on a separate sheet of paper the letter of the correct answer.

1 How can you determine whether the contours on a topographic map show a gradual slope?
   A. Look for V-shaped contour lines.
   B. Look for widely spaced contour lines.
   C. Look for short, straight lines inside the loop.
   D. Look for tightly spaced, circular contour lines.

2 What is the maximum difference in elevation between two successive index contours on a map that has a contour interval of 5 meters?
   F. 5 meters
   G. 10 meters
   H. 20 meters
   I. 25 meters

3 What part of a road map would you use in order to measure the distance from your current location to your destination?
   A. latitude lines
   B. map scale
   C. longitude lines
   D. map legend

4 Meteorologists use isobars on a weather map in order to
   F. show changes in atmospheric air pressure.
   G. connect points of equal temperature.
   H. plot local precipitation data.
   I. show elevation above or below sea level.

5 No map projection is entirely accurate. However, each type of projection has certain advantages and disadvantages. Which of the following is a disadvantage of a conic projection?
   A. It distorts distances near the poles.
   B. It causes distortion in both direction and distance.
   C. It has unequal spacing between parallels.
   D. It causes distortion in areas away from the parallel that contacts the globe.

6 If you wanted to easily locate a position on a map, which type of projection would you use?
   F. a conic projection, which has straight lines of longitude and curved lines of latitude
   G. a cylindrical projection, which has lines of latitude and lines of longitude that form a grid
   H. an azimuthal projection, which has straight lines of longitude and circular lines of latitude
   I. a polyconic projection, which is made up of multiple conic projections

7 A soil map classifies, maps, and describes soils based on the properties of the soils in a certain area. Which of the following individuals would find a soil map most useful?
   A. meteorologist
   B. hiker
   C. seismologist
   D. farmer

8 What characteristic is particularly advantageous of topographic maps?
   F. They are the most accurate maps.
   G. They show elevation.
   H. They have no distortion.
   I. They can be used to identify a location easily.

9 Which of the following statements about cylindrical projections is true?
   A. Because latitude and longitude form a grid, plotting great circles can be done by using a straight-edged ruler.
   B. When showing small areas, cylindrical projections have little distortion.
   C. Cylindrical projections often show the greatest distortion where the projection contacts the globe.
   D. Cylindrical projections often show polar regions as being much smaller than they actually are.

10 On a topographic map, which lines illustrate a depression?
   F. lines that bend in a V
   G. lines that form a closed loop
   H. closed loops that have short perpendicular lines
   I. bold lines

Interpreting Graphics

Directions (11–13): For each question below, record the correct answer on a separate sheet of paper.

Topographic Map of the Orr River

11 What location on the map has the steepest gradient?
- **A.** location A
- **B.** location B
- **C.** location C
- **D.** location D

12 In which direction is the river in the topographic map flowing?
- **F.** south to north
- **G.** east to west
- **H.** northwest to southeast
- **I.** northeast to southwest

Latitude and Longitude

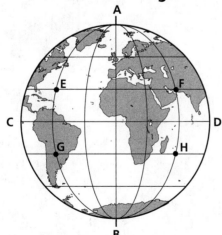

13 The lines in the map are drawn in 30° increments. Which point is located at 30°N 60°E?
- **A.** point E
- **B.** point F
- **C.** point G
- **D.** point H

Test Tip

Choose an answer to a question based on both what you already know as well as any information presented in the question.

Unit 2 Composition of the Earth

Chapter 4

Earth Chemistry

Chapter Outline

Why It Matters

New Zealand's geothermal Champagne Pool is steaming hot, at 74 °C. Its water contains dissolved elements, such as gold, silver, mercury, and arsenic. In fact, the entire Earth is made of chemical elements. Understanding the chemical structure of elements and molecules will help you understand the properties of the substances that make up Earth.

Inquiry Lab

🕐 **20 min**

Classifying Matter

Examine each of the **six solids** provided by your teacher, and record your observations. Consider properties such as mass, shininess, color, texture, size, and hardness. Determine whether the solids are made up of only one component, or two or more different components. Add each solid to a **beaker** with **water**, and observe how it behaves. Based on your observations, classify the solids into two or three groups.

Questions to Get You Started

1. Some properties help you distinguish one solid from another, and some do not. Explain which properties are the most and least helpful for developing a classification system.

2. How did you decide on your classification system? Explain your reasoning.

3. Compare your classification system with another group's classification system. Explain the similarities and differences.

SC.912.P.8.2

READING TOOLBOX

These reading tools will help you learn the material in this chapter.

FoldNotes

Double-Door Fold This type of FoldNote can help you identify the similarities and differences between topics.

Your Turn Use a double-door fold to compare the terms *element* and *atom* in Section 1. For Section 2, compare the terms *compound* and *mixture*.

Note Taking

Comparison Table You can use a comparison table to organize your notes as you compare related terms or topics. A table that compares chemical and physical properties has been started for you below.

Your Turn As you read Section 1, complete a table like the one started here.

Type of Property	Physical	Chemical
How the property is observed	can be observed without changing the composition of the substance	
Examples		

Science Terms

Everyday Words Used in Science Many words that are used in science are also used in everyday speech. These words often have different or more precise meanings in science contexts than in everyday speech. Pay attention to the definitions of these words so that you can use them correctly in scientific contexts.

Your Turn As you read Chapter 4, complete a table like the one shown. For each term, write its everyday meaning and its scientific meaning.

Term	Everyday meaning	Scientific meaning
matter	a subject or problem	anything that takes up space and has mass
element	a piece or component of something	
compound		
mixture		
solution		

For more information on how to use these and other tools, see **Appendix A**.

Earth Chemistry

Key Ideas	Key Terms	Why It Matters
❭ Compare chemical properties and physical properties of matter. ❭ Describe the basic structure of an atom. ❭ Compare atomic number, mass number, and atomic mass. ❭ Define *isotope*. ❭ Describe the arrangement of elements in the periodic table.	matter element atom proton electron neutron isotope	To understand the world around you, it helps to understand what Earth is made of—matter. From Earth's rocks to the oceans and air (and even your own body), matter really matters.

Every object in the universe is made of particles of some kind of substance. Scientists use the word *matter* to describe the substances of which objects are made. **Matter** is anything that takes up space and has mass. The amount of matter in any object is its *mass*.

Properties of Matter

All matter has two types of distinguishing characteristics—physical properties and chemical properties. *Physical properties* can be observed without changing the composition of the substance. Physical properties include density, color, hardness, freezing point, boiling point, and the ability to conduct an electric current.

Chemical properties describe how a substance reacts with other substances. For example, a chemical property of iron is that iron reacts with oxygen to form rust. Understanding the chemical properties of a substance requires knowing some basic information about the particles that make up all substances.

Elements

An **element** is a substance that cannot be broken down into simpler, stable substances by chemical means. Each element has physical and chemical properties that can be used to identify it. **Figure 1** shows common elements in Earth's crust. Approximately 90 elements occur naturally on Earth. Eight of these make up more than 98% of Earth's crust.

FLORIDA STANDARDS

SC.912.E.5.2 Identify patterns in the organization and distribution of matter in the universe and the forces that determine them; **SC.912.P.10.10** Compare the magnitude and range of the four fundamental forces (gravitational, electromagnetic, weak nuclear, strong nuclear).

matter anything that has mass and takes up space

element a substance that cannot be separated or broken down into simpler substances by chemical means

Figure 1 This graph shows the percentage of total mass that each common element makes up in Earth's continental crust.

Aluminum 8.1%
Iron 5.0%
Calcium 3.6%
Sodium 2.8%
Potassium 2.6%
Magnesium 2.1%
All others 1.5%
Silicon 27.7%
Oxygen 46.6%

Atoms

Elements consist of atoms. An **atom** is the smallest unit of an element that has the chemical properties of that element. Atoms cannot be broken down into smaller particles that will have the same chemical and physical properties as the atom. A single atom is so small that its size is difficult to imagine. To get an idea of how small it is, look at the thickness of this page. About a million atoms lined up side by side would be equal to that thickness.

Atomic Structure

Even though atoms are very tiny, they are made up of even smaller parts called *subatomic particles*. The three major kinds of subatomic particles are protons, electrons, and neutrons. **Protons** are subatomic particles that have a positive charge. **Electrons** are subatomic particles that have a negative charge. **Neutrons** are subatomic particles that are neutral, which means that they have no charge.

The Nucleus

As shown in **Figure 2**, the protons and neutrons of an atom are packed close to one another. Together they form the *nucleus*, which is a small region in the center of an atom. The nucleus has a positive charge because protons have a positive charge and neutrons have no charge.

The nucleus makes up most of an atom's mass but very little of an atom's volume. If an atom's nucleus were the size of a gumdrop, the atom itself would be as big as a football stadium.

The Electron Cloud

The electrons of an atom move in a certain region of space called an *electron cloud* that surrounds the nucleus. Because opposite charges attract each other, the negatively charged electrons are attracted to the positively charged nucleus. This attraction is what holds electrons in the atom.

atom the smallest unit of an element that maintains the chemical properties of that element

proton a subatomic particle that has a positive charge and that is located in the nucleus of an atom; the number of protons of the nucleus is the atomic number, which determines the identity of an element

electron a subatomic particle that has a negative charge

neutron a subatomic particle that has no charge and that is located in the nucleus of an atom

Academic Vocabulary
region (REE juhn) a specific surface or space; an area

Figure 2 The nucleus of the atom is made up of protons and neutrons. The protons give the nucleus a positive charge. The negatively charged electrons are in the electron cloud that surrounds the nucleus.

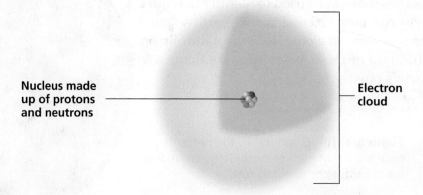

Nucleus made up of protons and neutrons

Electron cloud

Hydrogen
1 proton
1 electron
0 neutrons
Atomic number 1
Mass number 1

Helium
2 protons
2 electrons
2 neutrons
Atomic number 2
Mass number 4

Lithium
3 protons
3 electrons
4 neutrons
Atomic number 3
Mass number 7

Figure 3 Hydrogen, helium, and lithium are unique, as indicated by their atomic numbers.

 SC.912.P.8.4

Atomic Number

The number of protons in the nucleus of an atom is called the *atomic number*. All atoms of any given element have the same atomic number. An element's atomic number sets the atoms of that element apart from the atoms of all other kinds of elements, as shown in **Figure 3**. Because an uncharged atom has an equal number of protons and electrons, the atomic number is also equal to the number of electrons in an atom of any given element.

Elements on the periodic table are ordered according to their atomic numbers. The *periodic table,* shown on the following pages, is a system for classifying elements. Elements in the same column on the periodic table have similar arrangements of electrons in their atoms. Elements that have similar arrangements of electrons have similar chemical properties.

Atomic Mass

The sum of the number of protons and neutrons in an atom is the *mass number*. The mass of a subatomic particle is too small to be expressed easily in grams. So, a special unit called the *unified atomic mass unit* (u) is used. Protons and neutrons each have an atomic mass that is close to 1 u. In contrast, electrons have much less mass than protons and neutrons do. The mass of 1 proton is equal to the combined mass of about 1,840 electrons. Because electrons add little to an atom's total mass, their mass can be ignored when calculating an atom's approximate mass.

> **Reading Check** What is the difference between atomic number, mass number, and unified atomic mass unit? (See Appendix G for answers to Reading Checks.)

Isotopes

Although all atoms of a given element contain the same number of protons, the number of neutrons may differ. For example, while most helium atoms have two neutrons, some helium atoms have only one neutron. An atom that has the same number of protons (or the same atomic number) as other atoms of the same element do but has a different number of neutrons (and thus a different atomic mass) is called an **isotope** (IE suh TOHP).

A helium atom that has two neutrons is more massive than a helium atom that has only one neutron. Because of their different numbers of neutrons and their different masses, different isotopes of the same element have slightly different properties.

Quick Lab

⏱ 10 min

Using the Periodic Table

Procedure

❶ Use the periodic table to find the atomic numbers of the following elements: carbon, iron, molybdenum, and iodine.

❷ Determine the number of protons and electrons that are in each neutral atom of the elements listed in step 1.

❸ Find the average atomic masses of the elements listed in step 1.

Analysis

1. Use the atomic number and average atomic mass of each element to estimate the average number of neutrons in each atom of the elements listed in step 1 of this activity.

2. Which element has the largest difference between its average number of neutrons and the number of protons? Describe any trends that you observe.

isotope one of two or more atoms that have the same number of protons (atomic number) but different numbers of neutrons (atomic mass)

The Periodic Table of Elements

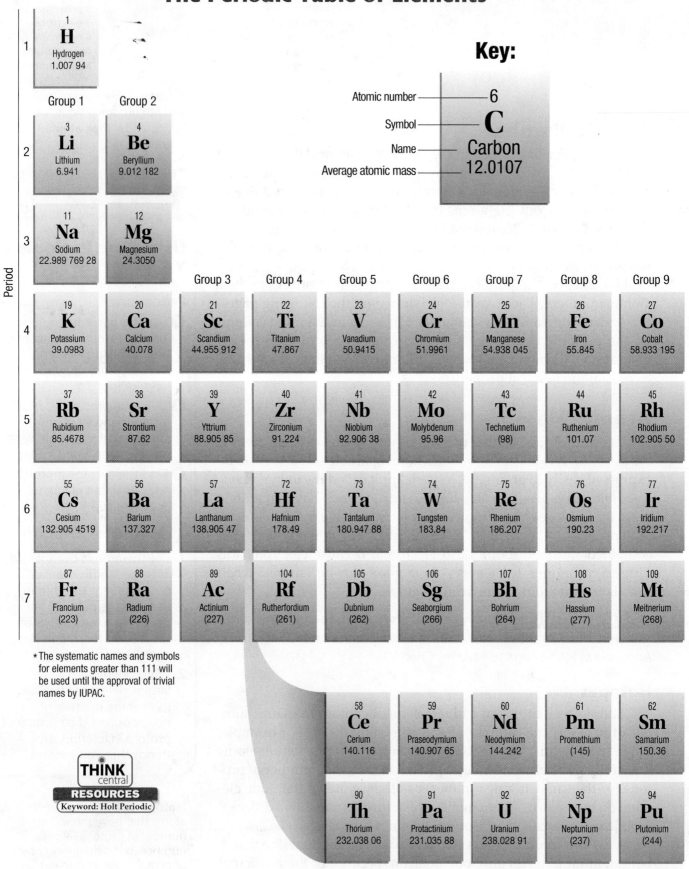

Key:

Atomic number — 6
Symbol — **C**
Name — Carbon
Average atomic mass — 12.0107

Period	Group 1	Group 2		Group 3	Group 4	Group 5	Group 6	Group 7	Group 8	Group 9
1	1 **H** Hydrogen 1.007 94									
2	3 **Li** Lithium 6.941	4 **Be** Beryllium 9.012 182								
3	11 **Na** Sodium 22.989 769 28	12 **Mg** Magnesium 24.3050								
4	19 **K** Potassium 39.0983	20 **Ca** Calcium 40.078		21 **Sc** Scandium 44.955 912	22 **Ti** Titanium 47.867	23 **V** Vanadium 50.9415	24 **Cr** Chromium 51.9961	25 **Mn** Manganese 54.938 045	26 **Fe** Iron 55.845	27 **Co** Cobalt 58.933 195
5	37 **Rb** Rubidium 85.4678	38 **Sr** Strontium 87.62		39 **Y** Yttrium 88.905 85	40 **Zr** Zirconium 91.224	41 **Nb** Niobium 92.906 38	42 **Mo** Molybdenum 95.96	43 **Tc** Technetium (98)	44 **Ru** Ruthenium 101.07	45 **Rh** Rhodium 102.905 50
6	55 **Cs** Cesium 132.905 4519	56 **Ba** Barium 137.327		57 **La** Lanthanum 138.905 47	72 **Hf** Hafnium 178.49	73 **Ta** Tantalum 180.947 88	74 **W** Tungsten 183.84	75 **Re** Rhenium 186.207	76 **Os** Osmium 190.23	77 **Ir** Iridium 192.217
7	87 **Fr** Francium (223)	88 **Ra** Radium (226)		89 **Ac** Actinium (227)	104 **Rf** Rutherfordium (261)	105 **Db** Dubnium (262)	106 **Sg** Seaborgium (266)	107 **Bh** Bohrium (264)	108 **Hs** Hassium (277)	109 **Mt** Meitnerium (268)

* The systematic names and symbols
for elements greater than 111 will
be used until the approval of trivial
names by IUPAC.

THINK central
RESOURCES
Keyword: Holt Periodic

58 **Ce** Cerium 140.116	59 **Pr** Praseodymium 140.907 65	60 **Nd** Neodymium 144.242	61 **Pm** Promethium (145)	62 **Sm** Samarium 150.36
90 **Th** Thorium 232.038 06	91 **Pa** Protactinium 231.035 88	92 **U** Uranium 238.028 91	93 **Np** Neptunium (237)	94 **Pu** Plutonium (244)

Group 18

| 2 |
| **He** |
| Helium |
| 4.002 602 |

Group 13	Group 14	Group 15	Group 16	Group 17	
5 **B** Boron 10.811	6 **C** Carbon 12.0107	7 **N** Nitrogen 14.0067	8 **O** Oxygen 15.9994	9 **F** Fluorine 18.998 4032	10 **Ne** Neon 20.1797
13 **Al** Aluminum 26.981 5386	14 **Si** Silicon 28.0855	15 **P** Phosphorus 30.973 762	16 **S** Sulfur 32.065	17 **Cl** Chlorine 35.453	18 **Ar** Argon 39.948

Group 10	Group 11	Group 12						
28 **Ni** Nickel 58.6934	29 **Cu** Copper 63.546	30 **Zn** Zinc 65.38	31 **Ga** Gallium 69.723	32 **Ge** Germanium 72.64	33 **As** Arsenic 74.921 60	34 **Se** Selenium 78.96	35 **Br** Bromine 79.904	36 **Kr** Krypton 83.798
46 **Pd** Palladium 106.42	47 **Ag** Silver 107.8682	48 **Cd** Cadmium 112.411	49 **In** Indium 114.818	50 **Sn** Tin 118.710	51 **Sb** Antimony 121.760	52 **Te** Tellurium 127.60	53 **I** Iodine 126.904 47	54 **Xe** Xenon 131.293
78 **Pt** Platinum 195.084	79 **Au** Gold 196.966 569	80 **Hg** Mercury 200.59	81 **Tl** Thallium 204.3833	82 **Pb** Lead 207.2	83 **Bi** Bismuth 208.980 40	84 **Po** Polonium (209)	85 **At** Astatine (210)	86 **Rn** Radon (222)
110 **Ds** Darmstadtium (271)	111 **Rg** Roentgenium (272)	112 **Uub*** Ununbium (285)	113 **Uut*** Ununtrium (284)	114 **Uuq*** Ununquadium (289)	115 **Uup*** Ununpentium (288)	116 **Uuh*** Ununhexium (292)		118 **Uuo*** Ununoctium (294)

The discoveries of elements with atomic numbers 112 through 116 and 118 have been reported but not fully confirmed.

63 **Eu** Europium 151.964	64 **Gd** Gadolinium 157.25	65 **Tb** Terbium 158.925 35	66 **Dy** Dysprosium 162.500	67 **Ho** Holmium 164.930 32	68 **Er** Erbium 167.259	69 **Tm** Thulium 168.934 21	70 **Yb** Ytterbium 173.054	71 **Lu** Lutetium 174.9668
95 **Am** Americium (243)	96 **Cm** Curium (247)	97 **Bk** Berkelium (247)	98 **Cf** Californium (251)	99 **Es** Einsteinium (252)	100 **Fm** Fermium (257)	101 **Md** Mendelevium (258)	102 **No** Nobelium (259)	103 **Lr** Lawrencium (262)

The atomic masses listed in this table reflect the precision of current measurements. (Each value listed in parentheses is the mass number of that radioactive element's most stable or most common isotope.)

Hydrogen–1, ^1_1H
1 proton
1 electron
0 neutrons
Atomic number 1
Mass number 1

Hydrogen–2, ^2_1H
1 proton
1 electron
1 neutron
Atomic number 1
Mass number 2

Hydrogen–3, ^3_1H
1 proton
1 electron
2 neutrons
Atomic number 1
Mass number 3

Figure 4 There are three naturally occurring isotopes of hydrogen. The main difference between these isotopes is their mass numbers.

www.scilinks.org
Topic: Valence Electrons
Code: HQX1591

Average Atomic Mass

Because the isotopes of an element have different masses, the periodic table uses an average atomic mass for each element. The *average atomic mass* is the weighted average of the atomic masses of the naturally occurring isotopes of an element.

As shown in **Figure 4**, hydrogen has three isotopes. Each isotope has a different mass because each has a different number of neutrons. By calculating the weighted average of the atomic masses of the three naturally occurring hydrogen isotopes, you can determine the average atomic mass. As noted on the periodic table, the average atomic mass of hydrogen is 1.007 94 u.

Valence Electrons and Periodic Properties

Based on similarities in their chemical properties, elements on the periodic table are arranged in columns, which are called *groups*. An atom's chemical properties are largely determined by the number of the outermost electrons in an atom's electron cloud. These electrons are called *valence* (VAY luhns) *electrons*.

Within each group, the atoms of each element generally have the same number of valence electrons. For Groups 1 and 2, the number of valence electrons in each atom is the same as that atom's group number. Atoms of elements in Groups 3–12 have 2 or more valence electrons. For Groups 13–18, the number of valence electrons in each atom is the same as that atom's group number minus 10, except for helium, He. It has only two valence electrons. Atoms in Group 18 have 8 valence electrons. When an atom has 8 valence electrons, it is considered stable, or chemically unreactive. Unreactive atoms do not easily lose or gain electrons.

Elements whose atoms have only one, two, or three valence electrons tend to lose electrons easily. These elements have metallic properties and are generally classified as *metals*. Elements whose atoms have from four to seven valence electrons are more likely to gain electrons. Many of these elements, which are in Groups 13–17, are classified as *nonmetals*.

Section 1 Review

LA.910.2.2.3; SC.912.E.5.2; SC.912.N.1.1; SC.912.P.8.4

Key Ideas

1. **Compare** the physical properties of matter with the chemical properties of matter.

2. **Describe** the basic structure of an atom.

3. **Name** the three basic subatomic particles.

4. **Compare** atomic number, mass number, and atomic mass.

5. **Explain** how isotopes of an element differ from each other.

Critical Thinking

6. **Evaluating Data** Oxygen combines with hydrogen and becomes water. Is this combination a result of the physical or chemical properties of hydrogen?

7. **Making Comparisons** What sets an atom of one element apart from atoms of all other elements?

Concept Mapping

8. Use the following terms to create a concept map: *matter, element, atom, electron, proton, neutron, atomic number,* and *periodic table.*

Combinations of Atoms

Key Ideas

> Define *compound* and *molecule*.
> Interpret chemical formulas.
> Describe two ways that electrons form chemical bonds between atoms.
> Explain the differences between compounds and mixtures.

Key Terms

compound
molecule
ion
ionic bond
covalent bond
mixture
solution

Why It Matters

Most of the matter in the universe consists of a collection of electrons and ions. This state of matter, called plasma, is used in televisions, light bulbs, and other technologies.

Elements rarely occur in pure form in Earth's crust. They generally occur in combination with other elements. A substance that is made of two or more elements that are joined by chemical bonds between the atoms of those elements is called a **compound.** The properties of a compound differ from those of the elements that make up the compound, as shown in **Figure 1.**

The smallest unit of a compound that can exist by itself and retain all of the compound's chemical properties is a molecule. A **molecule** is made of atoms that are chemically bonded together.

Some elements occur naturally as *diatomic molecules*, which are molecules that are made up of only two atoms. For example, the oxygen in the air you breathe is the diatomic molecule O_2. The O in this notation is the symbol for oxygen. The subscript 2 indicates the number of oxygen atoms that are bonded together.

Chemical Formulas

In any given compound, the elements that make up the compound occur in the same relative proportions. Therefore, a compound can be represented by a chemical formula. A *chemical formula* is a combination of letters and numbers that shows which elements make up a compound. It also shows the number of atoms of each element that are required to make a molecule of a compound.

The chemical formula for water is H_2O, which indicates that each water molecule consists of two atoms of hydrogen and one atom of oxygen. In a chemical formula, the subscript that appears after the symbol for an element shows the number of atoms of that element that are in a molecule.

FLORIDA STANDARDS

SC.912.P.8.1 Differentiate among the four states of matter; **SC.912.P.8.4** Explore the scientific theory of atoms (also known as atomic theory) by describing the structure of atoms in terms of protons, neutrons and electrons, and differentiate among these particles in terms of their mass, electrical charges and locations within the atom.

compound a substance made up of atoms of two or more different elements joined by chemical bonds

molecule a group of atoms that are held together by chemical forces

Figure 1 Sodium, a silvery metal, and chlorine, a poisonous, greenish-yellow gas, are both components of table salt, which you can eat.

Figure 2 Methane, CH_4, and oxygen gas, O_2, react during combustion to form the products carbon dioxide, CO_2, and water, H_2O. *How many hydrogen atoms are on each side of this reaction?*

Methane
CH_4

Oxygen
$2O_2$

Carbon dioxide
CO_2

Water
$2H_2O$

THINK
central
INTERACT ONLINE
Keyword: HQXCHMF2

Chemical Equations

Elements and compounds often combine through chemical reactions to form new compounds. The reaction of these elements and compounds can be described in a *chemical equation*.

Equation Structure

In a chemical equation, such as the one shown below, the *reactants*, which are on the left-hand side of the arrow, form the *products*, which are on the right-hand side of the arrow. In a chemical equation, the arrow means "gives" or "yields."

$$CH_4 + 2O_2 \rightarrow CO_2 + 2H_2O$$

In this equation, one molecule of methane, CH_4, reacts with two molecules of oxygen, O_2, to yield one molecule of carbon dioxide, CO_2, and two molecules of water, H_2O, as shown in **Figure 2.**

Balanced Equations

Chemical equations are useful for showing the types and amounts of the products that could form from a particular set of reactants. However, the equation must be balanced to show this information. A chemical equation is balanced when the number of atoms of each element on the right side of the equation is equal to the number of atoms of the same element on the left side.

To balance an equation, you cannot change the chemical formulas. Changing the formulas would mean that different substances were in the reaction. To balance an equation, you must put numbers called *coefficients* in front of chemical formulas.

On the left side of the equation above, the methane molecule has four hydrogen atoms, which are indicated by the subscript 4. On the right side, each water molecule has two hydrogen atoms, which are indicated by the subscript 2. A coefficient of 2 is placed in front of the formula for water to balance the number of hydrogen atoms. A coefficient multiplies the subscript in a formula. For example, four hydrogen atoms are in the formula $2H_2O$.

A coefficient of 2 is also placed in front of the oxygen molecule on the left side of the equation so that both sides of the equation have four oxygen atoms. When the number of atoms of each element is the same on both sides of the equation, the equation is balanced.

Math Skills

Balancing Equations
Magnesium, Mg, reacts with oxygen gas, O_2, to form magnesium oxide, MgO. Write a balanced chemical equation for this reaction by placing the coefficients that are needed to obtain an equal number of magnesium and oxygen atoms on either side of the equation.

Chemical Bonds

The forces that hold together the atoms in molecules are called *chemical bonds*. Chemical bonds form because of the attraction between positive and negative charges. Atoms form chemical bonds by either sharing or transferring valence electrons from one atom to another. Transferring or sharing valence electrons from one atom to another changes the properties of the substance. Variations in the forces that hold molecules together are responsible for a wide range of physical and chemical properties.

As shown in **Figure 3**, scientists can study interactions of atoms to predict which kinds of atoms will form chemical bonds together. Scientists do this by comparing the number of valence electrons that are present in a particular atom with the maximum number of valence electrons that are possible. For example, a hydrogen atom has only one valence electron. But because hydrogen can have two valence electrons, it will give up or accept another electron to reach a more chemically unreactive state.

Reading Check In what two ways do atoms form chemical bonds?

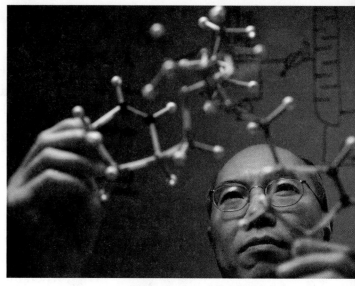

Figure 3 Scientists sometimes make physical models of molecules to better understand how chemical bonds affect the properties of compounds.

Academic Vocabulary

transfer (TRANS fuhr) to carry or cause to pass from one thing to another

Why It Matters

How Can Diamond and Graphite Both Be Carbon?

Diamonds are valued for their sparkle, and diamond-coated blades can cut through granite. The soft black graphite in your pencil is also used in powdered form as an industrial lubricant. But diamonds and graphite are both made of pure carbon. The extreme differences in their properties are because of differences in how their carbon atoms are bonded together.

Graphite is made of carbon atoms arranged in layers, with weak bonds between the layers.

Diamond is made of carbon atoms joined in a tetrahedral arrangement, forming a rigid three-dimensional crystal.

YOUR TURN

ONLINE RESEARCH
Research artificial diamonds. Make a poster to display how they are made and used.

ion an atom or molecule that has gained or lost one or more electrons and has a negative or positive charge

ionic bond the attractive force between oppositely charged ions, which form when electrons are transferred from one atom or molecule to another

www.scilinks.org
Topic: Covalent and Ionic Bonds
Code: HQX0362

Double-Door Fold

Create a double-door fold. Label one door "Ionic bond" and the other door "Covalent bond." Write notes about these terms behind each door.

Ions

When an electron is transferred from one atom to another, both atoms become charged. A particle, such as an atom or molecule, that carries a charge is called an **ion.**

Neutral sodium atoms have 11 electrons. And because a sodium atom has 1 valence electron, sodium is a Group 1 element on the periodic table. If a sodium atom loses its outermost electron, the next 8 electrons in the atom's electron cloud become the outermost electrons. Because the sodium atom now has 8 valence electrons, it is unlikely to share or transfer electrons and, therefore, is stable.

However, the sodium atom is missing the 1 electron that was needed to balance the number of protons in the nucleus. When an atom no longer has equal numbers of positive and negative charges, it becomes an ion. The sodium atom became a positive sodium ion, Na^+, when the atom released its valence electron.

Suppose a chlorine atom accepts the electron that the above sodium atom lost. A chlorine atom has a total of 17 electrons, 7 of which are valence electrons. This chlorine atom now has a complete set of 8 valence electrons and is chemically stable. The extra electron, however, changes the neutral chlorine atom into a negatively charged chloride ion, Cl^-.

Ionic Bonds

The attractive force between oppositely charged ions that result from the transfer of electrons from one atom to another is called an **ionic bond.** A compound that forms through the transfer of electrons is called an *ionic compound*. Most ionic compounds form when electrons are transferred between the atoms of metallic and nonmetallic elements.

Sodium chloride, or common table salt, is an ionic compound. The positively charged sodium ions and negatively charged chloride ions attract one another because of their opposite charges. This attraction between the positive sodium ions and the negative chloride ions is an ionic bond. The attraction creates cube-shaped crystals, such as in the table salt shown in **Figure 4.**

Figure 4

Ionic Bonds		
+ −	A sodium atom, Na, transfers an electron to a chlorine atom, Cl, to form table salt, NaCl. The chlorine atom with the added electron becomes a negatively charged ion, Cl^-, and the sodium atom, which lost the electron, becomes a positively charged ion, Na^+. The oppositely charged ions attract each other and form an ionic bond.	Table salt, NaCl

Figure 5

Covalent Bonds		
	Covalent bonds form when atoms share one or more pairs of electrons. In a covalent compound, pairs of electrons are shared between most of the atoms that make up the compound. Some elements also contain covalent bonds. In molecules of chlorine, two chlorine atoms are bonded together by sharing electrons.	Chlorine gas, Cl_2

Covalent Bonds

A bond that is formed by the attraction between atoms that share electrons is a **covalent bond.** When atoms share electrons, the positive nucleus of each atom is attracted to the shared negative electrons, as shown in **Figure 5.** The pull between the positive and negative charges is the force that keeps these atoms joined.

Water is an example of a *covalent compound*—that is, a compound formed by the sharing of electrons. Two hydrogen atoms can share their single valence electrons with an oxygen atom that has six valence electrons. The sharing of electrons creates a bond and gives oxygen a stable number of eight outermost electrons. At the same time, the oxygen atom shares two of its electrons—one for each hydrogen atom—which gives each hydrogen atom a more stable number of two electrons. Thus, a water molecule consists of two atoms of hydrogen bonded with one atom of oxygen.

Polar Covalent Bonds

In many cases, atoms that are covalently bonded do not equally share electrons. The reason for this is that the ability of atoms of some elements to attract electrons from atoms of other elements differs. A covalent bond in which the bonded atoms have an unequal attraction for the shared electrons is called a *polar covalent bond*. Water is an example of a molecule that forms as a result of polar covalent bonds. Two hydrogen atoms bond covalently with an oxygen atom and form a water molecule. Because the oxygen atom has more ability to attract electrons than the hydrogen atoms do, the electrons are not shared equally between the oxygen and hydrogen atoms. Instead, the electrons remain closer to the oxygen nucleus, which has the greater pull. As a result, the water molecule as a whole has a slightly negative charge at its oxygen end and slightly positive charges at its hydrogen ends. The slightly positive ends of a water molecule attract the slightly negative ends of other water molecules.

Reading Check **Why do water molecules form from polar covalent bonds?**

covalent bond a bond formed when atoms share one or more pairs of electrons

SC.912.P.8.2

Quick Lab
10 min

Compounds

Procedure

❶ Place **4 g of compound A** in a **clear plastic cup.**

❷ Place **4 g of compound B** in a **second clear plastic cup.**

❸ Observe the color and texture of each compound. Record your observations.

❹ Add **5 mL of vinegar** to each cup. Record your observations.

Analysis

1. What physical and chemical differences between the two compounds did you record? How do physical properties and chemical properties differ?

2. Vinegar reacts with baking soda but not with powdered sugar. Which of these compounds is compound A, and which is compound B?

Mixtures

On Earth, elements and compounds are generally mixed together. A **mixture** is a combination of two or more substances that are not chemically combined. The substances that make up a mixture keep their individual properties. Therefore, unlike a compound, a mixture can be separated into its parts by physical means. For example, you can use a magnet to separate a mixture of powdered sulfur, S, and iron, Fe, filings. The magnet will attract the iron, which is magnetic, and leave behind the sulfur, which is not magnetic.

Heterogeneous Mixtures

Mixtures in which two or more substances are not uniformly distributed are called *heterogeneous mixtures*. For example, the igneous rock granite is a heterogeneous mixture of crystals of the minerals quartz, feldspar, hornblende, and biotite.

Homogeneous Mixtures

In chemistry, the word *homogeneous* means "having the same composition and properties throughout." A homogeneous mixture of two or more substances that are uniformly dispersed throughout the mixture is a **solution.**

Any part of a given sample of the solution known as sea water, for example, will have the same composition. Sodium chloride, NaCl, (along with many other ionic compounds) is dissolved in sea water. The positive ends of water molecules attract negative chloride ions. And the negative ends of water molecules attract positive sodium ions. Eventually, all of the sodium and chloride ions become uniformly distributed among the water molecules.

Gases and solids can also be solutions. An *alloy* is a solution composed of two or more metals. The steel shown in **Figure 6** is an example of such a solution, both in liquid and solid states.

Figure 6 The steel that is being smelted in this steel mill in Iowa is a solution of iron, carbon, and various other metals such as nickel, chromium, and manganese.

mixture a combination of two or more substances that are not chemically combined

solution a homogeneous mixture throughout which two or more substances are uniformly dispersed

Section 2 Review

SC.912.N.1.6; SC.912.P.8.4

Key Ideas

1. **Define** the term *compound.*

2. **Determine** the number of each type of atom in the following chemical formula: $C_6H_{12}O_6$.

3. **Explain** why atoms join to form molecules.

4. **Describe** the difference between ionic and covalent bonds.

5. **Explain** why a water molecule has polar covalent bonds.

6. **Compare** compounds and mixtures.

7. **Identify** two common solutions.

Critical Thinking

8. **Applying Ideas** What happens to the chemical properties of a substance when it becomes part of a mixture?

9. **Evaluating Data** If you were given two mixtures and told that one is a solution, how might you determine which one is the solution?

Concept Mapping

10. Use the following terms to create a concept map: *compound, molecule, ionic compound, ionic bond, ion, covalent compound,* and *covalent bond.*

Not Such a Strange State

In elementary school, you learned about the three states of matter. But over 99.9% of the matter in the universe is not in the gas, liquid, or solid state. Instead, it is in a state called *plasma*. Very large amounts of energy can split gaseous atoms apart. The resulting matter is plasma—a collection of negatively charged electrons and positively charged ions. All stars, including our sun, are giant plasmas. On Earth, natural plasmas are formed in very hot fires and during lightning. Artificial plasmas are used in fluorescent lamps and flat-screen televisions.

The huge current in a lightning bolt supplies the energy to heat the air to 30,000 °C, creating a plasma.

A high voltage in a noble gas, such as neon or xenon, produces the plasma in displays like this.

Electrical energy converts mercury vapor into plasma inside the tube of a compact fluorescent lamp.

YOUR TURN

UNDERSTANDING CONCEPTS
How is a gas different from a plasma?

ONLINE RESEARCH
Find out about other applications of plasma technology, besides televisions and lights. Describe at least two of these applications.

Inquiry Lab

What You'll Do

> **Design** an experiment to test the physical properties of different metals.

> **Identify** unknown metals by comparing the data you collect and reference information.

What You'll Need

balance
beakers (several)
graduated cylinder
hot plate
magnet
metal samples, unknown, similarly shaped (several)
ruler, metric
stopwatch
water
wax

Safety

Physical Properties of Elements

In this lab, you will identify samples of various metals by collecting data and comparing the data with the reference information listed in the table below. Use at least two of the physical properties listed in the table to identify each metal.

Ask a Question

1 How can you use an element's physical properties to identify the element?

Form a Hypothesis

2 Use the table below to identify which physical properties you will test. Write a few sentences that describe your hypothesis and the procedure you will use to test those physical properties.

Test the Hypothesis

3 With your lab partner(s), decide how you will use the available materials to identify each metal that you are given. Because there are many ways to measure some of the physical properties that are listed in the table below, you may need to use only some of the materials that are provided.

4 Before you start to test your hypothesis, list each step that you will need to perform.

5 After your teacher approves your plan, perform your experiment. Keep in mind that the more exact your measurements are, the easier it will be for you to identify the metals that you have been provided.

6 Record all the data that you collect and any observations that you make.

Physical Properties of Some Metals

Metal	Density (g/cm³)	Relative hardness	Relative heat conductivity	Magnetic attraction
Aluminum, Al	2.7	28	100	No
Iron, Fe	7.9	50	34	Yes
Nickel, Ni	8.9	67	38	Slight
Tin, Sn	7.3	19	28	No
Tungsten, W	19.3	100	73	No
Zinc, Zn	7.1	28	49	No

How to Measure Physical Properties of Metals

Physical property	Description	How to measure the property
Density	mass per unit volume	If the metal is box-shaped, measure its length, height, and width, and then use these measurements to calculate the metal's volume. If the shape of the metal is irregular, add the metal to a known volume of water and determine what volume of water is displaced.
Relative hardness	how easy it is to scratch the substance	An object that has a high hardness value can scratch an object that has a lower value, but not vice versa.
Relative heat conductivity	how quickly a metal heats or cools	A metal that has a value of 100 will heat or cool twice as quickly as a metal that has a value of 50.
Magnetism	whether an object is magnetic	If a magnet placed near a metal attracts the metal, the metal is magnetic.

Analyze the Results

1. **Summarizing Data** Make a table that lists which physical properties you compared and what data you collected for each of the metals that you tested.

2. **Making Comparisons** Which physical properties were the easiest for you to measure and compare? Which were the most difficult to measure and compare? Explain why.

3. **Applying Ideas** What would happen if you tried to use zinc to scratch aluminum?

Draw Conclusions

4. **Summarizing Results** Which metals were given to you? Explain how you identified each metal.

5. **Analyzing Methods** Explain why you would have difficulty distinguishing between iron and nickel unless you were to measure each metal's density.

Extension

Evaluating Data Suppose you find a metal fastener that has a density of 7 g/cm³. What are two ways to determine whether the unknown metal is tin or zinc?

MAPS in Action

Element Resources in the United States

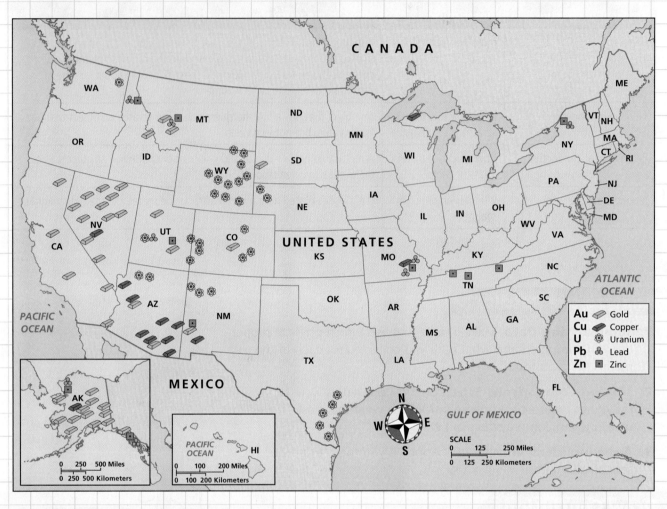

Key:
- Au — Gold
- Cu — Copper
- U — Uranium
- Pb — Lead
- Zn — Zinc

Map Skills Activity

This map shows the distribution of five elements that are used as resources in the United States. Use the map to answer the questions below.

1. **Using a Key** Use the map to locate the state in which you live. Are any of the elements from the key found in your state?

2. **Analyzing Relationships** Can you identify any relationship between the locations of lead deposits and the locations of zinc deposits? Explain your reasoning.

3. **Inferring Relationships** Is it possible to use this map to find out which states have the highest production of the mineral resources that are listed on the map? Why or why not?

4. **Inferring Relationships** Silver is mainly recovered as a byproduct of the bulk mining of other metals such as copper, lead, zinc, and gold. Where in the United States do you think silver recovery would happen?

5. **Using a Key** Use the map to identify the states where uranium can be found.

Summary

THINK central SUPER SUMMARY Keyword: HQXCHMS

Key Ideas

Key Terms

Section 1

Matter

❯ A physical property of matter can be observed without changing the composition of the substance. In contrast, a chemical property describes how a substance reacts with other substances to produce different substances.

❯ An atom consists of electrons surrounding a nucleus that is made up of protons and neutrons.

❯ The atomic number of an atom is equal to the number of protons in the atom. The mass number is equal to the sum of the protons and neutrons in the atom. Atomic mass is the mass of an atom, expressed in atomic mass units (amu). Protons and neutrons each have an atomic mass that is close to 1 amu.

❯ An isotope is an atom that has the same number of protons as other atoms of the same element, but different numbers of neutrons.

❯ Elements on the periodic table are arranged in groups that are based on similarities in the chemical properties of the elements.

matter, p. 87
element, p. 87
atom, p. 88
proton, p. 88
electron, p. 88
neutron, p. 88
isotope, p. 89

Section 2

Combinations of Atoms

❯ A compound is a substance made up of atoms of two or more different elements joined by chemical bonds. A molecule is a group of atoms bonded together.

❯ A chemical formula describes which elements and how many atoms of each of those elements make up a molecule of a compound.

❯ Ionic bonds occur when electrons are transferred from one atom to another. Covalent bonds occur when electrons are shared between atoms.

❯ A compound is a made up of atoms of two or more different elements joined by chemical bonds. A mixture consists of two or more substances that are not chemically bonded.

compound, p. 93
molecule, p. 93
ion, p. 96
ionic bond, p. 96
covalent bond, p. 97
mixture, p. 98
solution, p. 98

1. **Everyday Words Used in Science** The words *compound* and *mixture* have different meanings in science contexts than in everyday speech. Write one sentence using each term in its science context. Write another sentence using each term in an everyday context. SC.912.P.8.2

READING TOOLBOX

USING KEY TERMS

Use each of the following terms in a separate sentence.

2. *matter* SC.912.P.8.4

3. *neutron* SC.912.P.8.4

4. *ion* SC.912.P.8.4

For each pair of terms, explain how the meanings of the terms differ.

5. *atom* and *molecule* SC.912.P.8.4

6. *element* and *compound* SC.912.P.8.4

7. *proton* and *electron* SC.912.P.8.4

8. *compound* and *mixture* SC.912.P.8.2

9. *covalent bond* and *ionic bond* SC.912.P.8.6

UNDERSTANDING KEY IDEAS

10. Color and hardness are examples of a substance's SC.912.P.8.2
    a. physical properties.
    b. chemical properties.
    c. atomic structure.
    d. molecular properties.

11. Subatomic particles in atoms that do not carry an electric charge are called SC.912.P.8.4
    a. neutrons.
    b. protons.
    c. nuclei.
    d. ions.

12. Atoms of the same element that differ in mass are SC.912.P.8.4
    a. ions.
    b. neutrons.
    c. isotopes.
    d. molecules.

13. A combination of letters and numbers that indicates which elements make up a compound is a SC.912.P.8.7
    a. coefficient.
    b. reactant.
    c. chemical bond.
    d. chemical formula.

14. The type of chemical bond that forms between oppositely charged ions is a(n) SC.912.P.8.6
    a. covalent bond.
    b. mixture.
    c. ionic bond.
    d. solution.

15. Two or more elements whose atoms are chemically bonded form a(n) SC.912.P.8.7
    a. mixture.
    b. ion.
    c. nucleus.
    d. compound.

16. The outermost electrons in an atom's electron cloud are called SC.912.P.8.4
    a. ions.
    b. isotopes.
    c. valence electrons.
    d. neutrons.

17. A molecule of water, or H_2O, has one atom of SC.912.P.8.7
    a. hydrogen.
    b. oxygen.
    c. helium.
    d. osmium.

SHORT ANSWER

18. How do chemical properties differ from physical properties? SC.912.P.8.2

19. Define the term *element*.

20. Name three basic subatomic particles. SC.912.P.8.2

21. In terms of valence electrons, what is the difference between metallic elements and nonmetallic elements?

22. Which type of bonding includes the sharing of electrons? SC.912.P.8.6

23. Using the periodic table to help you to understand the following chemical formulas, list the name and number of atoms of each element in each compound: $NaCl$, H_2O_2, Fe_3O_4, and SiO_2. SC.912.P.8.5

CRITICAL THINKING

24. What sets an atom of one element apart from the atoms of all other elements? **SC.912.P.8.4**

25. Applying Ideas Is a diatomic molecule more likely to be held together by a covalent bond or by an ionic bond? Explain your answer. **SC.912.P.8.6**

26. Making Inferences Calcium chloride is an ionic compound. Carbon dioxide is a covalent compound. Which of these compounds forms as a result of the transfer of electrons from one atom to another? Explain your answer. **SC.912.P.8.6**

27. Analyzing Relationships What happens to the chemical properties of a substance when it becomes part of a mixture? Explain your answer. **SC.912.P.8.2**

28. Classifying Information Oxygen combines with hydrogen to form water. Is this process due to the physical or chemical properties of oxygen and hydrogen? **SC.912.P.8.2**

CONCEPT MAPPING

29. Use the following terms to create a concept map: *chemical property, element, atom, electron, proton, neutron, atomic number, mass number, isotope, compound,* and *chemical bond.* **SC.912.P.8.4**

MATH SKILLS

30. Making Calculations How many neutrons does a potassium atom have if its atomic number is 19 and its mass number is 39? **SC.912.P.8.4**

31. Using Formulas The covalent compound formaldehyde forms when one carbon atom, two hydrogen atoms, and one oxygen atom bond. Write a chemical formula for formaldehyde. **SC.912.P.8.7**

32. Balancing Equations Zinc metal, Zn, will react with hydrochloric acid, HCl, to produce hydrogen gas, H_2, and zinc chloride, $ZnCl_2$. Write and balance the chemical equation for this reaction. **SC.912.P.8.7**

WRITING SKILLS

33. Organizing Data Choose one of the eight most common elements in Earth's crust, and write a brief report on the element's atomic structure, its chemical properties, and its economic importance. **SC.912.P.8.4**

34. Communicating Main Ideas Write a brief essay that describes how an element's chemical properties determine what other elements are likely to bond with that element.

35. Making Comparisons Write a brief essay that describes the differences between atoms, elements, ions, and isotopes. **SC.912.P.8.4**

INTERPRETING GRAPHICS

The table below shows the average atomic masses and the atomic numbers of five elements. Use this table to answer the questions that follow.

Element	Symbol	Average atomic mass	Atomic number
Magnesium	Mg	24.3050	12
Tungsten	W	183.84	74
Copper	Cu	63.546	29
Silicon	Si	28.0855	14
Bromine	Br	79.904	35

36. If an atom of magnesium has 12 neutrons, what is its mass number? **SC.912.P.8.4**

37. Estimate the average number of neutrons in an atom of tungsten and in an atom of silicon.

38. Which element has the largest difference between the number of protons and the number of neutrons in the nucleus of one of its atoms? Explain your answer. **SC.912.P.8.4**

Understanding Concepts

Directions (1–9): For each question, write on a separate sheet of paper the number of the correct answer.

1 Why is soil described as a mixture?
A. Soil is made up of different substances that are uniformly dispersed.
B. Soil is made up of two or more elements that are joined by chemical bonds between them.
C. Soil is a combination of different substances that are not chemically combined.
D. Soil is made up of the smallest units of matter, which cannot be broken down without changing their properties.

2 Isotopes are atoms of the same element that has different mass numbers. This difference is caused by
F. a different number of electrons in the atoms.
G. a different number of protons in the atoms.
H. a different number of neutrons in the atoms.
I. a different number of nuclei in the atoms.

3 One of the most economically important elements is gold, which has the chemical symbol Au. The atomic number of gold is 79 and its atomic mass is 197. Which of the following describes the electron, proton, and neutron makeup of gold?
A. 79 electrons, 79 protons, 118 neutrons
B. 197 electrons, 79 protons, 118 neutrons
C. 118 electrons, 118 protons, 79 neutrons
D. 118 electrons, 79 protons, 197 neutrons

4 An element is located on the periodic table according to
F. when the element was discovered.
G. the letters of the element's chemical symbol.
H. the element's chemical name.
I. the element's physical and chemical properties.

5 A scientist is studying a compound in which the chemical bonds are characterized by unequally shared electrons. Which type of substance is the scientist studying?
A. ionic compound
B. covalent compound
C. polar covalent compound
D. homogeneous mixture

6 A typical balanced chemical equation has coefficients, products, reactants, and subscripts, all of which show the elements and molecules that are broken down, joined, and formed during a chemical reaction. To show the conversion from one substance to another, the equation is separated by an arrow. Which parts of a chemical equation always follow the arrow?
F. coefficients
G. products
H. reactants
I. subscripts

7 What does a subscript in a chemical formula represent?
A. Subscripts represent the number of atoms of the chemical symbol that they directly follow that are present in the molecule.
B. Subscripts represent the number of atoms of the chemical symbol that they directly precede that are present in the molecule.
C. Subscripts represent the number of protons that are present in each atom's nucleus.
D. Subscripts represent the total number of atoms that are present in a molecule.

8 A material has different substances and different crystals. Which of the following statements best describes this material?
F. a homogenous mixture, which contains substances that are uniformly distributed
G. a compound, which has two or more elements that are chemically bonded
H. a heterogenous mixture, which contains substances that are unevenly distributed
I. a molecule, which cannot retain all of its characteristics if it is broken down

9 Silver is produced as a byproduct of gold production. Gold and silver are part of Group 11 on the periodic table. What does this indicate about silver?
A. Silver has fewer valence electrons than gold does.
B. Silver is a metal, but gold is not.
C. Silver and gold have the same number of valence electrons.
D. Silver has eight valence electrons.

Interpreting Graphics

Directions (10–12): For each question below, record the correct answer on a separate sheet of paper.

Segment of the Periodic Table

18					
					2 **He** 4.00

13	14	15	16	17	
5 **B** 10.81	6 **C** 12.01	7 **N** 14.01	8 **O** 16.00	9 **F** 19.00	10 **Ne** 20.18
13 **Al** 26.98	14 **Si** 28.09	15 **P** 30.97	16 **S** 32.07	17 **Cl** 35.45	18 **Ar** 39.95

10 The graphic above shows the upper right segment of the periodic table. Which pair of elements would most likely have a similar arrangement of outer electrons and have similar chemical behaviors?
  F. boron and aluminum
  G. helium and fluoride
  H. carbon and nitrogen
  I. chlorine and oxygen

11 What is the atomic mass of helium?
  A. 2.00
  B. 4.00
  C. 6.00
  D. 18.00

States of Matter

A   B   C

12 The graphic above shows matter in three different states. In what physical state is the matter in jar A?
  F. solid
  G. liquid
  H. gas
  I. plasma

Test Tip

Double check (with a calculator, if permitted) all mathematical computations involved in answering a question.

Chapter 5

Minerals of Earth's Crust

Why It Matters

Understanding the properties of minerals is important for being able to identify and use them. Minerals are used to make millions of products, from airplanes to zippers.

Magnetic Minerals

Use a **bar magnet** to decide which of the **mineral samples** given to you have magnetic properties. Then, test the magnetic minerals using a **directional compass**. Use your observations of their effect on the compass needle to arrange the minerals in order of increasing magnetic strength.

Questions to Get You Started

1. How can a bar magnet help you to distinguish certain types of minerals from others?

2. How can a directional compass be used to compare magnetic strength?

3. Which element or elements do you think are present in a magnetic mineral?

🏴 SC.912.P.8.2

READING TOOLBOX

These reading tools will help you learn the material in this chapter.

Classification

Kinds of Minerals Classification is a tool for organizing objects and ideas by grouping them into categories. Groups are classified by defining characteristics. One of the ways that minerals can be classified is on the basis of their composition. For example, some minerals contain the element silicon and others do not. Based on this fact, minerals can be classified into two major groups.

Your Turn In Section 1, you will learn about two major groups of minerals. As you learn about these groups, make a table with three columns. In the first column, list each of the kinds of minerals. In the second column, describe the basis for classifying minerals as one of these kinds. In the third column, list examples and descriptions of each kind of mineral.

Note Taking

Two-Column Notes Two-column notes can help you learn the key ideas from each section.
• Write the key ideas in the left column.
• In your own words, record notes and examples in the right column.

Your Turn Complete the two-column notes for Section 1, adding another row for each key idea.

KEY IDEA #1	A mineral is a solid that meets all four of these criteria:
Define mineral.	• It is inorganic. • It occurs naturally. • It is crystalline. • It has a consistent chemical composition.

FoldNotes

Key-Term Fold The key-term fold can help you learn key terms from this chapter, such as the physical properties that help distinguish one mineral from another.

Your Turn Create a key-term fold, as described in **Appendix A.**

❶ Write one of the physical properties of minerals on the front of each tab.

❷ Write a definition or description for each term under its tab.

❸ Use this FoldNote to help you study the key terms in this chapter.

For more information on how to use these and other tools, see **Appendix A.**

Key Ideas	Key Terms	Why It Matters
❯ Define *mineral*. ❯ Compare the two main groups of minerals. ❯ Identify the six types of silicate crystalline structures. ❯ Describe three common nonsilicate crystalline structures.	mineral silicate mineral nonsilicate mineral crystal silicon-oxygen tetrahedron	Almost everything you do each day—from brushing your teeth in the morning to setting your alarm clock at night—involves minerals in some way.

A ruby, a gold nugget, and a grain of salt look very different from one another, but they have one thing in common. They are minerals, the basic materials of Earth's crust. A **mineral** is a natural, usually inorganic solid that has a characteristic chemical composition, an orderly internal structure, and a characteristic set of physical properties.

Characteristics of Minerals

To determine whether a substance is a mineral or a nonmineral, scientists ask four basic questions, as shown in **Table 1.** If the answer to all four questions is yes, the substance is a mineral.

First, is the substance inorganic? An inorganic substance is one that is not made up of living things or the remains of living things. Coal, for example, is organic—it is composed of the remains of ancient plants. Thus, coal is not a mineral.

Second, does the substance occur naturally? Minerals form and exist in nature. Thus, a manufactured substance, such as steel or brass, is not a mineral.

Third, is the substance a solid in crystalline form? The volcanic glass obsidian is a naturally occurring substance. However, the atoms in obsidian are not arranged in a regularly repeating crystalline structure. Thus, obsidian is not a mineral.

Finally, does the substance have a consistent chemical composition? The mineral fluorite has a consistent chemical composition of one calcium ion for every two fluoride ions. Granite, however, can have a variety of substances. The ratio of these substances commonly varies in each sample of granite.

FLORIDA STANDARDS

LA.910.2.2.3 The student will organize information to show understanding or relationships among facts, ideas, and events (e.g., representing key points within text through charting, mapping, paraphrasing, summarizing, comparing, contrasting, or outlining); **SC.912.N.3.5** Describe the function of models in science, and identify the wide range of models used in science.

mineral a natural, usually inorganic solid that has a characteristic chemical composition, an orderly internal structure, and a characteristic set of physical properties

SC_ILINKS.
www.scilinks.org
Topic: Minerals
Code: HQX0966

Table 1 Four Criteria for Minerals

Questions to Identify a Mineral	Coal	Brass	Obsidian	Basalt	Fluorite
Is it inorganic?	No	Yes	Yes	Yes	Yes
Does it occur naturally?		No	Yes	Yes	Yes
Is it a crystalline solid?			No	Yes	Yes
Does it have a consistent chemical composition?				No	Yes

Kinds of Minerals

Earth scientists have identified more than 4,000 minerals, but fewer than 20 of the minerals are common. The common minerals are called *rock-forming minerals* because they form the rocks that make up Earth's crust. Three of these minerals are shown in **Figure 1.** Of the 20 rock-forming minerals, about half are so common that they make up 90% of the mass of Earth's crust. These include quartz, orthoclase, plagioclase, muscovite, biotite, calcite, dolomite, halite, gypsum, and ferromagnesian minerals. All minerals, however, can be classified into two main groups—silicate minerals and nonsilicate minerals—based on the chemical compositions of the minerals.

Silicate Minerals

A mineral that contains a combination of silicon, Si, and oxygen, O, is a **silicate mineral.** The mineral quartz has only silicon and oxygen atoms. However, other silicate minerals have one or more additional elements. Feldspars are the most common silicate minerals. The type of feldspar that forms depends on which metal combines with the silicon and oxygen atoms. Orthoclase forms when the metal is potassium, K. Plagioclase forms when the metal is sodium, Na, calcium, Ca, or both.

In addition to quartz and the feldspars, ferromagnesian minerals—which are rich in iron, Fe, and magnesium, Mg—are silicates. These minerals include olivines, pyroxenes, amphiboles, and biotite. Silicate minerals make up 96% of Earth's crust. Feldspars and quartz alone make up more than 50% of the crust.

Figure 1 Plagioclase feldspar (left), muscovite mica (center), and orthoclase feldspar (right) are 3 of the 20 common rock-forming minerals.

silicate mineral a mineral that contains a combination of silicon and oxygen and that may also contain one or more metals

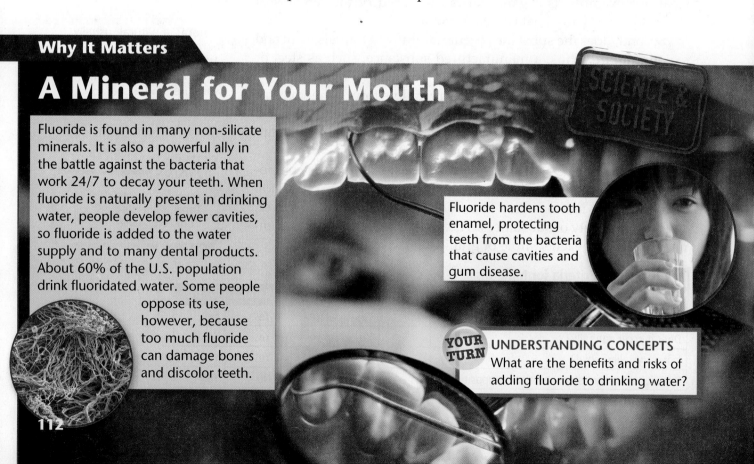

Why It Matters

A Mineral for Your Mouth

SCIENCE & SOCIETY

Fluoride is found in many non-silicate minerals. It is also a powerful ally in the battle against the bacteria that work 24/7 to decay your teeth. When fluoride is naturally present in drinking water, people develop fewer cavities, so fluoride is added to the water supply and to many dental products. About 60% of the U.S. population drink fluoridated water. Some people oppose its use, however, because too much fluoride can damage bones and discolor teeth.

Fluoride hardens tooth enamel, protecting teeth from the bacteria that cause cavities and gum disease.

YOUR TURN UNDERSTANDING CONCEPTS
What are the benefits and risks of adding fluoride to drinking water?

Table 2 Major Classes of Nonsilicate Minerals

Carbonates		
compounds that contain a carbonate group (CO_3)	Dolomite, $CaMg(CO_3)_2$	Calcite, $CaCO_3$
Halides		
compounds that consist of chlorine or fluorine combined with sodium, potassium, or calcium	Halite, NaCl	Fluorite, CaF_2
Native elements		
elements uncombined with other elements	Silver, Ag	Copper, Cu
Oxides		
compounds that contain oxygen and an element other than silicon	Corundum, Al_2O_3	Hematite, Fe_2O_3
Sulfates		
compounds that contain a sulfate group (SO_4)	Gypsum, $CaSO_4 \bullet 2H_2O$	Anhydrite, $CaSO_4$
Sulfides		
compounds that consist of one or more elements combined with sulfur	Galena, PbS	Pyrite, FeS_2

Nonsilicate Minerals

Approximately 4% of Earth's crust is made up of minerals that do not contain compounds of silicon and oxygen, or **nonsilicate minerals. Table 2** organizes the six major groups of nonsilicate minerals by their chemical compositions: carbonates, halides, native elements, oxides, sulfates, and sulfides.

nonsilicate mineral a mineral that does not contain compounds of silicon and oxygen

Reading Check **What compounds will you never find in a nonsilicate mineral?** (See Appendix G for answers to Reading Checks.)

crystal a solid whose atoms, ions, or molecules are arranged in a regular, repeating pattern

silicon-oxygen tetrahedron the basic unit of the structure of silicate minerals; a silicon ion chemically bonded to and surrounded by four oxygen ions

Crystalline Structure

All minerals in Earth's crust have a crystalline structure. Each type of mineral crystal is characterized by a specific geometric arrangement of atoms. A **crystal** is a solid whose atoms, ions, or molecules are arranged in a regular, repeating pattern. A large mineral crystal displays the characteristic geometry of that crystal's internal structure. The conditions under which minerals form, however, often hinder the growth of single, large crystals. As a result, minerals are commonly made up of masses of crystals that are so small you can see them only with a microscope. But, if a crystal forms where the surrounding material is not restrictive, the mineral will develop as a single, large crystal that has one of six basic crystal shapes. Knowing the crystal shapes is helpful in identifying minerals.

One way that scientists study the structure of crystals is by using X rays. X rays that pass through a crystal and strike a photographic plate produce an image that shows the geometric arrangement of the atoms that make up the crystal.

Crystalline Structure of Silicate Minerals

Even though there are many kinds of silicate minerals, their crystalline structure is made up of the same basic building blocks. Each building block has four oxygen atoms arranged in a pyramid with one silicon atom in the center. **Figure 2** shows this four-sided structure, which is known as a **silicon-oxygen tetrahedron.**

Silicon-oxygen tetrahedra combine in different arrangements to form different silicate minerals. The various arrangements are the result of the kinds of bonds that form between the oxygen atoms of the tetrahedra and other atoms. The oxygen atoms of tetrahedra may be shared with those of neighboring tetrahedra. Bonds may also form between the oxygen atoms in the tetrahedra and other elements' atoms outside of the tetrahedra.

Reading Check What is the building block of the silicate crystalline structure?

Figure 2 The structure of a silicon-oxygen tetrahedron can be shown by two different models. The model on the left represents the relative size and proximity of the atoms to one another in the molecule. The model on the right shows the tetrahedral shape of the molecule.

THINK central
INTERACT ONLINE
(Keyword: HQXMINF2)

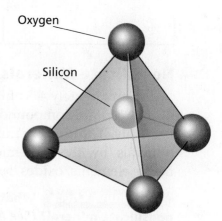

Oxygen

Silicon

Isolated Tetrahedral Silicates and Ring Silicates

Six kinds of arrangements that tetrahedra form are shown in **Figure 3.** In minerals that have *isolated tetrahedra,* only atoms other than silicon and oxygen atoms link silicon-oxygen tetrahedra. For example, olivine is a mineral that forms when the oxygen atoms of tetrahedra bond to magnesium, Mg, and iron, Fe, atoms.

Ring silicates form when shared oxygen atoms join the tetrahedra to form three-, four-, or six-sided rings. The rings can align to create channels that can contain a variety of ions, molecules, and neutral atoms. Beryl and tourmaline are minerals that have ring-silicate structures.

Single-Chain Silicates and Double-Chain Silicates

In *single-chain silicates,* each tetrahedron shares corner oxygen atoms with two others. In *double-chain silicates,* two single chains of tetrahedra link to each other by sharing oxygen atoms. Most single-chain silicate minerals are called *pyroxenes,* and those made up of double chains are called *amphiboles.*

Sheet Silicates and Framework Silicates

In the *sheet silicates,* each tetrahedron shares three oxygen atoms with other tetrahedra. The unshared oxygen atoms bond with aluminum, Al, or magnesium atoms that hold other sheets of silicon-oxygen tetrahedra together. The mica minerals, such as muscovite and biotite, are examples of sheet silicates.

In the *framework silicates,* each tetrahedron shares all of its oxygen atoms with four neighboring tetrahedra to form a three-dimensional network. Frameworks that contain only silicon-oxygen tetrahedra form the mineral quartz. The chemical formula for quartz is SiO_2. Other framework silicates, such as the feldspars, contain some tetrahedra in which atoms of aluminum substitute for some of the silicon atoms.

Figure 3 Six Kinds of Silicate-Mineral Arrangements

1 Isolated tetrahedra do not link with other silicon or oxygen atoms.

2 Ring silicates form rings by sharing oxygen atoms.

3 Single-chain silicates form a chain by sharing oxygen atoms.

4 Double-chain silicates form when two single chains of tetrahedra link to each other by sharing oxygen atoms.

5 Sheet silicates form when each tetrahedron shares three of its oxygen atoms with other tetrahedra.

6 Framework silicates form when each tetrahedron is bonded to four other tetrahedra.

Figure 4 Gold (left) commonly has a dendritic shape. Halite (center) commonly has cubic crystals. Diamond (right) commonly has an octahedral crystal shape. All three of these minerals are nonsilicates.

Academic Vocabulary

similar (SIM uh luhr) alike; almost the same

Key-Term Fold
Create a key-term fold for the key terms in Section 1. Add other terms that you want to remember, such as the six kinds of silicate crystal structures.

Crystalline Structure of Nonsilicate Minerals

Because nonsilicate minerals have diverse chemical compositions, nonsilicate minerals display a vast variety of crystalline structures. Common crystal structures for nonsilicate minerals include cubes, hexagonal prisms, and irregular masses. Some of these structures are shown in **Figure 4**.

Nonsilicates may form tetrahedra that are <u>similar</u> to those in silicates. However, the ions at the center of these tetrahedra are not silicon. Minerals that have the same ion at the center of the tetrahedron commonly share similar crystal structures. Thus, the classes of nonsilicate minerals can be divided into smaller groups based on the structural similarities of the minerals' crystals.

The structure of a nonsilicate crystal determines the nonsilicate's characteristics. For example, the native elements have very high densities because their crystal structures are based on the packing of atoms as close together as possible. This crystal structure is called *closest packing*. In this crystal structure, each metal atom is surrounded by 12 other metal atoms that are as close to each other as the charges of the atomic nuclei will allow.

Section 1 Review

LA.910.2.2.3; SC.912.N.1.1; SC.912.P.8.7

Key Ideas

1. **Define** *mineral*.

2. **Summarize** the characteristics that are necessary to classify a substance as a mineral.

3. **Compare** the two main groups of minerals.

4. **Identify** the two elements that are in all silicate minerals.

5. **Name** six types of nonsilicate minerals.

6. **Describe** the six main crystalline structures of silicate minerals.

7. **Explain** why nonsilicate minerals have a wider variety of crystalline structures than silicate minerals do.

Critical Thinking

8. **Predicting Consequences** If silicon bonded with three oxygen atoms, how might the crystalline structures of silicate minerals be different?

9. **Applying Ideas** Gold is an inorganic substance that forms naturally in Earth's crust. Gold is also a solid and has a definite chemical composition. Is gold a mineral? Explain your answer.

Concept Mapping

10. Use the following terms to create a concept map: *mineral, crystal, silicate mineral, nonsilicate mineral, ring silicate, framework silicate, single-chain silicate,* and *silicon-oxygen tetrahedron*.

SECTION 2 Identifying Minerals

Key Ideas

> Describe seven physical properties that help to distinguish one mineral from another.

> List five special properties that may help to identify certain minerals.

Key Terms

mineralogist
streak
luster
cleavage

fracture
Mohs hardness scale
density

Why It Matters

Some minerals glow in the dark; others are magnetic. The properties of minerals help people to identify and use them.

Earth scientists called **mineralogists** examine, analyze, and classify minerals. To identify minerals, mineralogists study the properties of the minerals. Some properties are simple to study, while special equipment may be needed to study other properties.

Physical Properties of Minerals

Each mineral has specific properties that are a result of its chemical composition and crystalline structure. These properties provide useful clues for identifying minerals. Many of these properties can be identified by simply looking at a sample of the mineral. Other properties can be identified through simple tests.

Color

One property of a mineral that is easy to observe is the mineral's color. Some minerals have very distinct colors. For example, sulfur is bright yellow, and azurite is deep blue. Color alone, however, is generally not a reliable clue for identifying a mineral sample. Many minerals are similar in color, and very small amounts of certain elements may greatly affect the color of a mineral. For example, corundum is a colorless mineral composed of aluminum and oxygen atoms. However, corundum that has traces of chromium, Cr, forms the red gem called *ruby*. Sapphire, which is a type of corundum, gets its blue color from traces of iron, Fe, and titanium, Ti. **Figure 1** compares colorless, pure quartz with purple amethyst. Amethyst is quartz that has manganese, Mn, and iron, Fe, which cause the purple color.

Color is also an unreliable identification clue because weathered surfaces may hide the color of minerals. For example, the golden color of iron pyrite ranges from dark yellow to black when iron pyrite is weathered. When examining a mineral for color, you should inspect only the mineral's freshly exposed surfaces.

FLORIDA STANDARDS

LA.910.2.2.3 The student will organize information to show understanding or relationships among facts, ideas, and events (e.g., representing key points within text through charting, mapping, paraphrasing, summarizing, comparing, contrasting, or outlining); **LA.910.4.2.2** The student will record information and ideas from primary and/or secondary sources accurately and coherently, noting the validity; **MA.912.S.1.2** Determine appropriate and consistent standards of measurement for the data to be collected in a survey or experiment.

mineralogist a person who examines, analyzes, and classifies minerals

Figure 1 Pure quartz (above) is colorless. Amethyst (right) is a variety of quartz that is purple because of the presence of small amounts of manganese and iron.

Figure 2 All minerals have either a metallic luster, as platinum does (top), or a nonmetallic luster, as talc does (bottom).

streak the color of a mineral in powdered form

luster the way in which a mineral reflects light

cleavage the tendency of a mineral to split along specific planes of weakness to form smooth, flat surfaces

fracture the manner in which a mineral breaks along either curved or irregular surfaces

Academic Vocabulary

specific (spuh SIF ik) unique; peculiar to or characteristic of; exact

Streak

A more reliable clue to the identity of a mineral is the color of the mineral in powdered form, which is called the mineral's **streak.** The easiest way to observe the streak of a mineral is to rub some of the mineral against a piece of unglazed ceramic tile called a *streak plate.* The streak's color may differ from the color of the solid form of the mineral. Metallic minerals generally have a dark streak. For example, the streak of gold-colored pyrite is black. For most non-metallic minerals, however, the streak is either colorless or a very light shade of the mineral's standard color. Minerals that are harder than the ceramic plate will leave no streak.

Luster

Light that is reflected from a mineral's surface is called **luster.** A mineral is said to have a *metallic luster* if the mineral reflects light as polished metal does, as shown in **Figure 2.** All other minerals have a *nonmetallic luster.* Mineralogists distinguish several types of nonmetallic luster. Transparent quartz and other minerals that look like glass have a glassy luster. Minerals that have the appearance of candle wax have a waxy luster. Some minerals, such as the mica minerals, have a pearly luster. Diamond is an example of a mineral that has a brilliant luster. A mineral that lacks any shiny appearance has a dull or earthy luster.

Cleavage and Fracture

The tendency of a mineral to split along specific planes of weakness to form smooth, flat surfaces is called **cleavage.** When a mineral has cleavage, as shown in **Figure 3,** it breaks along flat surfaces that generally run parallel to planes of weakness in the crystal structure. For example, the mica minerals, which are sheet silicates, tend to split into parallel sheets.

Many minerals, however, do not break along cleavage planes. Instead, they **fracture,** or break unevenly, into pieces that have curved or irregular surfaces. Mineralogists describe a fracture according to the appearance of the broken surface. For example, a rough surface has an *uneven* or *irregular fracture.* A broken surface that looks like a piece of broken wood has a *splintery* or *fibrous fracture.* Curved surfaces are *conchoidal fractures* (kahng KOYD uhl FRAK chuhr), as shown in **Figure 3.**

Figure 3 Calcite is a mineral that cleaves in three directions. Quartz (right) tends to have a conchoidal fracture.

Table 1 Mohs Hardness Scale

Mineral	Hardness	Common test	Mineral	Hardness	Common test
Talc	1	easily scratched by fingernail	Feldspar	6	scratches glass, but does not scratch steel
Gypsum	2	can be scratched by fingernail	Quartz	7	easily scratches both glass and steel
Calcite	3	barely can be scratched by copper penny	Topaz	8	scratches quartz
Fluorite	4	easily scratched with steel file or glass	Corundum	9	scratches topaz
Apatite	5	can be scratched by steel file or glass	Diamond	10	scratches everything

Hardness

The measure of the ability of a mineral to resist scratching is called *hardness*. Hardness does not mean "resistance to cleavage or fracture." A diamond, for example, is extremely hard but can be split along cleavage planes more easily than calcite, a softer mineral, can be split.

To determine the hardness of an unknown mineral, you can scratch the mineral against those on the **Mohs hardness scale,** which is shown in **Table 1.** This scale lists 10 minerals in order of increasing hardness. The softest mineral, talc, has a hardness of 1. The hardest mineral, diamond, has a hardness of 10. The difference in hardness between two consecutive minerals is about the same throughout the scale except for the difference between the two hardest minerals. Diamond (10) is much harder than corundum (9), which is listed on the scale before diamond.

To test an unknown mineral for hardness, you must determine the hardest mineral on the scale that the unknown mineral can scratch. For example, galena can scratch gypsum but not calcite. Thus, galena has a hardness that ranges between 2 and 3 on the Mohs hardness scale. If neither of two minerals scratches the other, the minerals have the same hardness.

The strength of the bonds between the atoms that make up a mineral's internal structure determines the hardness of that mineral. Both diamond and graphite consist only of carbon atoms. However, diamond has a hardness of 10, while the hardness of graphite is between 1 and 2. A diamond's hardness results from a strong crystalline structure in which each carbon atom is firmly bonded to four other carbon atoms. In contrast, the carbon atoms in graphite are arranged in layers that are held together by much weaker chemical bonds.

Reading Check **What determines the hardness of a mineral?**

www.scilinks.org
Topic: Mineral Identification
Code: **HQX0965**

Mohs hardness scale the standard scale against which the hardness of minerals is rated

READING TOOLBOX

Two-Column Notes
Create two-column notes to outline all the physical properties of minerals, including special properties, that mineralogists can use to help them identify minerals. Put the physical properties in the first column, and add notes and examples in the second column.

Table 2 The Six Basic Crystal Systems

Isometric or Cubic System Three axes of equal length intersect at 90° angles.		**Orthorhombic System** Three axes of unequal length intersect at 90° angles.	
Tetragonal System Three axes intersect at 90° angles. The two horizontal axes are of equal length. The vertical axis is longer or shorter than the horizontal axes.		**Hexagonal System** Three horizontal axes of the same length intersect at 120° angles. The vertical axis is longer or shorter than the horizontal axes.	
Monoclinic System Two of the three axes of unequal length intersect at 90° angles. The third axis is oblique to the others.		**Triclinic System** Three axes of unequal length are oblique to one another.	

Crystal Shape

A mineral crystal forms in one of six basic shapes, as shown in **Table 2.** A certain mineral always has the same basic crystal system because the atoms that form its crystals always combine in the same geometric pattern. But the six basic shapes can become more complex as a result of environmental conditions during crystal growth, such as temperature and pressure.

Density

When handling equal-sized specimens of various minerals, you may notice that some feel heavier than others do. For example, a piece of galena feels heavier than a piece of quartz of the same size does. However, a more precise comparison can be made by measuring the density of a sample. **Density** is the ratio of the mass of a substance to the volume of the substance.

The density of a mineral depends on the kinds of atoms that the mineral has and on how closely the atoms are packed. Most of the common minerals in Earth's crust have densities between 2 and 3 g/cm³. However, the densities of minerals that contain heavy metals, such as lead, uranium, gold, and silver, range from 7 to 20 g/cm³. Thus, density helps identify heavier minerals more readily than it helps identify lighter ones.

density the ratio of the mass of a substance to the volume of the substance; commonly expressed as grams per cubic centimeter for solids and liquids and as grams per liter for gases

Special Properties of Minerals

All minerals exhibit the properties that were described earlier in this section. However, a few minerals have some additional, special properties that can help identify those minerals.

Fluorescence and Phosphorescence

The mineral calcite is usually white in ordinary light, but in ultraviolet light, calcite often appears red. This ability to glow under ultraviolet light is called *fluorescence*. Fluorescent minerals absorb ultraviolet light and then produce visible light of various colors, as shown in **Figure 4**.

When subjected to ultraviolet light, some minerals will continue to glow after the ultraviolet light is turned off. This property is called *phosphorescence*. It is useful in the mining of phosphorescent minerals such as eucryptite, which is an ore of lithium.

Chatoyancy and Asterism

In reflected light, some minerals display a silky appearance that is called *chatoyancy* (shuh TOY uhn see). This effect is also called the *cat's-eye effect*. The word *chatoyancy* comes from the French word *chat*, which means "cat," and from *oeil*, which means "eye." Chatoyancy is the result of closely packed parallel fibers within the mineral. A similar effect called *asterism* is the phenomenon in which a six-sided star shape appears when a mineral reflects light.

 Reading Check What is the difference between chatoyancy and asterism?

Figure 4 The fluorescent minerals calcite and willemite within this rock change colors as they are exposed to ordinary light (top) and ultraviolet light (bottom).

SC.912.P.8.2

Quick Lab
⏱ 15 min

Determining Density

Procedure

❶ Use a **triple-beam balance** to determine the mass of three similarly sized **mineral samples** that have different masses. Record the mass of each mineral sample.

❷ Fill a **graduated cylinder** with **70 mL of water.**

❸ Add one mineral sample to the water in the graduated cylinder. Record the new volume after the mineral sample is added to the water.

❹ Calculate the volume of the mineral sample by subtracting 70 mL from the new volume.

❺ Repeat steps 3 and 4 for the other two mineral samples.

❻ Convert the volume of the mineral samples that you calculated in step 4 from milliliters to cubic centimeters by using the conversion: $1 \text{ mL} = 1 \text{ cm}^3$.

Analysis

1. Calculate the density of each mineral sample by using the following equation:

$$density = mass/volume$$

2. Compare the density of each mineral sample with the density of common minerals in Earth's crust. Compare the density of each mineral sample with minerals that contain a high percentage of heavy metals.

3. Do any of the mineral samples contain a high percentage of heavy metals? Explain your answer.

Figure 5 Some forms of the mineral calcite exhibit double refraction when light rays enter the crystal and split.

Double Refraction

Light rays bend as they pass through transparent minerals. This bending of light rays as they pass from one substance, such as air, to another, such as a mineral, is called *refraction*. Crystals of calcite and some other transparent minerals bend light in such a way that they produce a double image of any object viewed through them, as shown in **Figure 5**. This property is called *double refraction*. Double refraction takes place because light rays are split into two parts as they enter the crystal.

Magnetism

Magnets may attract small particles of some minerals that contain iron. Those minerals are also sometimes magnetic. In general, nonsilicate minerals that contain iron, such as magnetite, are more likely to be magnetic than other nonsilicate minerals are. Lodestone is a form of magnetite. Like a bar magnet, some pieces of lodestone have a north pole at one end and a south pole at the other. The needles of the first magnetic compasses were made of tiny slivers of lodestone.

Radioactivity

Some minerals have a property known as *radioactivity*. The arrangement of protons and neutrons in the nuclei of some atoms is unstable. Radioactivity results as unstable nuclei decay over time into stable nuclei by releasing particles and energy. A *Geiger counter* can be used to detect the released particles and, thus, to identify minerals that are radioactive. Uranium, U, and radium, Ra, are examples of radioactive elements. Pitchblende is the most common mineral that contains uranium. Other uranium-bearing minerals are carnotite and autunite.

Section 2 Review

LA.910.2.2.3; SC.912.P.8.2

Key Ideas

1. **Describe** seven physical properties that help distinguish one mineral from another.

2. **Identify** the two main types of luster.

3. **Summarize** how you would determine the hardness of an unidentified mineral sample.

4. **Explain** why color is an unreliable clue to the identity of a mineral.

5. **List** five special properties that may help to identify certain minerals.

6. **Explain** how magnetism can be useful for identifying minerals.

Critical Thinking

7. **Evaluating Data** An unknown mineral has a black streak and a density of 18 g/cm³. Is the mineral more likely to be metallic or nonmetallic?

8. **Analyzing Methods** Explain how phosphorescence is helpful in mining eucryptite. Describe other ways in which phosphorescent minerals might be used.

Concept Mapping

9. Use the following terms to create a concept map: *luster, streak, fracture, hardness, Mohs hardness scale, streak plate, nonmetallic luster, metallic luster,* and *conchoidal fracture.*

Know by the Glow

FORENSIC SCIENCE

Fluorescence is one of the special properties of some minerals. This same property is used for identification and authentication purposes. Invisible fluorescent inks are used on checks and important documents. These inks cannot be copied by scanners or reproduced by color printers, but they are seen when exposed to ultraviolet light (also called black light). Many plant and animal tissues fluoresce under black light. Crime investigators can use fluorescent chemicals to reveal traces of blood that otherwise would be invisible.

Fluorescent inks are used in hand stamps at amusement parks to allow re-entry privileges. The stamp does not leave a visible mark, but it easily identifies paying customers.

Fingerprints glow when illuminated by black light. Fluorescent dyes of different colors may be used to give better contrast.

Highlighter pens are available in a variety of colors. When used on paper or fabric with similar color, you can write or create designs only visible in black light.

Real amber, especially if it contains an insect, is expensive. Fake amber is easily made using colored plastic. A black light can detect a fake, because only real amber fluoresces.

U.S. currency is the most counterfeited money in the world. Security features on a $20 bill include a plastic strip to the left of President Jackson's portrait. The strip fluoresces green in ultraviolet light.

YOUR TURN

CRITICAL THINKING
Explain how a service technician could use fluorescent dye to find a leak in an air conditioner.

ONLINE RESEARCH
The fluorescent strip in paper money is one of many security features used in bills. Find out about special inks, watermarks, and fine printing details that help foil counterfeiters.

Mineral Identification

A mineral identification key can be used to compare the properties of minerals so that unknown mineral samples can be identified. Mineral properties that are often used in mineral identification keys are color, hardness, streak, luster, cleavage, and fracture. Hardness is determined by a scratch test. The Mohs hardness scale classifies minerals from 1 (soft) to 10 (hard). Streak is the color of a mineral in a finely powdered form. The streak shows less variation than the color of a sample does and thus is more useful in identification. The luster of a mineral is either metallic (having an appearance of metals) or nonmetallic. Cleavage is the tendency of a mineral to split along a plane. Planes may be in several directions. Other minerals break into irregular fragments in a process called *fracture*. In this lab, you will use these properties to classify several mineral samples.

What You'll Do

› **Identify** several unknown mineral samples.

› **Evaluate** which properties of minerals are most useful in identifying mineral samples.

What You'll Need

file, steel
Guide to Common Minerals (in the Reference Tables section of the Appendix)
hand lens
mineral samples (5)
penny, copper
square, glass
streak plate

Safety

Procedure

1 Make a table with columns for sample number, color/luster, hardness, streak, cleavage/fracture, and mineral name.

2 Observe and record in your table the color of each mineral sample. Note whether the luster of each mineral is metallic or nonmetallic.

3 Rub each mineral against the streak plate, and determine the color of the mineral's streak. Record your observations.

Step 4

Sample number	Color/ luster	Hardness	Streak	Cleavage/ fracture	Mineral name
1					
2					
3					
4					
5					

DO NOT WRITE IN THIS BOOK

4 Using a fingernail, copper penny, glass square, and steel file, test each mineral to determine its hardness based on the Mohs hardness scale. Arrange the minerals in order of hardness. Record your observations in your table.

5 Determine whether the surface of each mineral displays cleavage and/or fracture. Record your observations.

6 Use the Guide to Common Minerals in the Reference Tables section of the Appendix to help you identify the mineral samples. Remember that samples of the same mineral will vary somewhat.

Analysis

1. **Analyzing Results** For each mineral, compare the streak with the color of the mineral. Which minerals have the same color as their streak? Which do not?

2. **Classifying Information** Of the mineral samples you identified, how many were silicate minerals? How many were nonsilicate minerals?

3. **Analyzing Methods** Did you find any properties that were especially useful or especially not useful in identifying each sample? Identify these properties, and explain why they were or were not useful.

4. **Evaluating Methods** If you had to write a manual to explain, step by step, how to identify minerals, in what order would you test different properties? Explain your reasoning.

Extension

Understanding Relationships Corundum, rubies, and sapphires have different colors but are considered to be the same mineral. Diamonds and graphite are made of the element carbon but are not considered to be the same mineral. Research these minerals, and explain why they are classified in this way.

Rock and Mineral Production in the United States

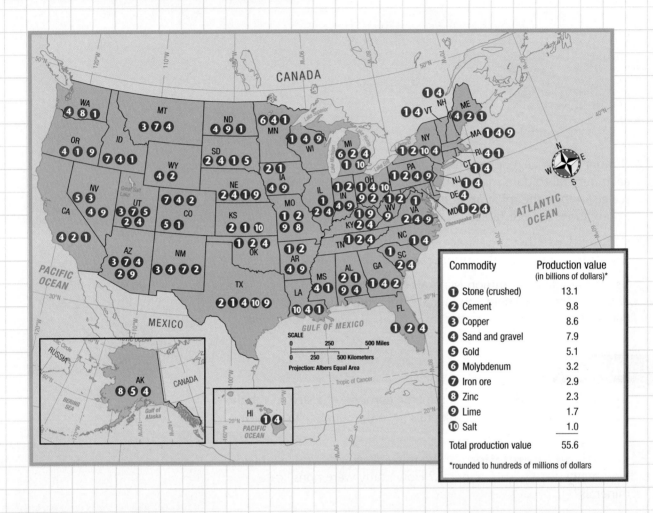

Commodity	Production value (in billions of dollars)*
❶ Stone (crushed)	13.1
❷ Cement	9.8
❸ Copper	8.6
❹ Sand and gravel	7.9
❺ Gold	5.1
❻ Molybdenum	3.2
❼ Iron ore	2.9
❽ Zinc	2.3
❾ Lime	1.7
❿ Salt	1.0
Total production value	55.6

*rounded to hundreds of millions of dollars

Map Skills Activity

This map shows the distribution of the top 10 rock and mineral commodities produced in the United States. The key provides production values for these commodities. Use the map to answer the questions below.

1. **Using a Key** According to the map, which commodity has the highest production value?

2. **Evaluating Data** Gold, copper, iron ore, and zinc are metals in the top 10 mineral commodities produced. What percentage of the total production value do these metals represent? Which of the states produce these metals?

3. **Using a Key** Find your state on the map. Which of the top 10 mineral commodities are produced in your state?

4. **Evaluating Data** Stone, sand, and gravel are collectively known as *aggregates*. What percentage of the total production value of the 10 commodities listed do aggregates represent?

5. **Analyzing Relationships** According to the map, the states that produce enough iron ore to make the top-10 list are located in the western part of the United States. What geologic feature do most of these states share?

Key Ideas

Key Terms

Section 1

What Is a Mineral?

> A mineral is a natural, usually inorganic solid that has a characteristic chemical composition, an orderly internal structure, and a characteristic set of physical properties.

> The two main types of minerals, silicates and nonsilicates, are classified based on differences in their composition. Silicates contain compounds of silicon and oxygen; nonsilicates do not.

> Six types of silicate crystalline structures are isolated tetrahedral, ring, single-chain, double-chain, sheet, and framework.

> The three common nonsilicate crystalline structures commonly include cubes, hexagonal prisms, and irregular masses, but may also include tetrahedrons.

mineral, p. 111
silicate mineral, p. 112
nonsilicate mineral, p. 113
crystal, p. 114
silicon-oxygen tetrahedron, p. 114

Section 2

Identifying Minerals

> Seven physical properties that help distinguish one mineral from another are color, streak, luster, cleavage and fracture, hardness, crystal shape, and density.

> Special properties that can aid in identifying certain minerals include fluorescence and phosphorescence, chatoyancy and asterism, double refraction, magnetism, and radioactivity.

mineralogist, p. 117
streak, p. 118
luster, p. 118
cleavage, p. 118
fracture, p. 118
Mohs hardness scale, p. 119
density, p. 120

USING KEY TERMS

1. **Two-Column Notes** You already have two-column notes for the Key Ideas of Section 1. Complete your notes for the whole chapter by creating two-column notes for the Key Ideas of Section 2.

Use each of the following terms in a separate sentence.

2. *silicon-oxygen tetrahedron*

3. *mineral*

4. *Mohs hardness scale*

5. *cleavage*

For each pair of terms, explain how the meanings of the terms differ.

6. *mineral* and *crystal*

7. *silicate mineral* and *nonsilicate mineral*

8. *luster* and *streak*

9. *fluorescence* and *phosphorescence*

UNDERSTANDING KEY IDEAS

10. The most common silicate minerals are the
   a. feldspars.
   b. halides.
   c. carbonates.
   d. sulfates.

11. Ninety-six percent of Earth's crust is made up of
   a. sulfur and lead.
   b. silicate minerals.
   c. copper and aluminum.
   d. nonsilicate minerals.

12. An example of a mineral that has a basic structure consisting of isolated tetrahedra linked by atoms of other elements is
   a. mica.
   b. olivine.
   c. quartz.
   d. feldspar.

13. When two single chains of tetrahedra bond to each other, the result is called a **SC.912.P.8.6**
   a. single-chain silicate.
   b. sheet silicate.
   c. framework silicate.
   d. double-chain silicate.

14. The words *waxy, pearly,* and *dull* describe a mineral's
   a. luster.
   b. hardness.
   c. streak.
   d. fluorescence.

15. The words *uneven* and *splintery* describe a mineral's
   a. cleavage.
   b. fracture.
   c. hardness.
   d. luster.

16. The ratio of a mineral's mass to its volume is the mineral's
   a. atomic weight.
   b. density.
   c. mass.
   d. weight.

17. Double refraction is a property of some crystals of
   a. mica.
   b. feldspar.
   c. calcite.
   d. galena.

SHORT ANSWER

18. List six major classes of nonsilicate minerals.

19. List eight of the most common rock-forming minerals.

20. Why do minerals that have the nonsilicate crystalline structure called *closest packing* have high density?

21. Which of the two main groups of minerals is more abundant in Earth's crust?

22. Which of the following mineral groups, if any, contain silicon: carbonates, halides, or sulfides?

23. Describe the tetrahedral arrangement of olivine.

24. Summarize the characteristics that a substance must have to be classified as a mineral.

25. How many oxygen ions and silicon ions are in a silicon-oxygen tetrahedron?

CRITICAL THINKING

26. **Classifying Information** Natural gas is a substance that occurs naturally in Earth's crust. Is it a mineral? Explain your answer.

27. **Making Comparisons** Which of the following are you more likely to find in Earth's crust: the silicates feldspar and quartz or the nonsilicates copper and iron? Explain your answer.

28. Applying Ideas Iron pyrite, FeS_2, is called *fool's gold* because it looks a lot like gold. What simple test could you use to determine whether a mineral sample is gold or pyrite? Explain what the test would show.

29. Drawing Conclusions Can you determine conclusively that an unknown substance contains magnetite by using only a magnet? Explain your answer.

CONCEPT MAPPING

30. Use the following terms to create a concept map: *mineral, silicate mineral, nonsilicate mineral, silicon-oxygen tetrahedron, color, density, crystal shape, magnetism, native element, sulfate,* and *phosphorescence.*

MATH SKILLS

31. Applying Quantities Hematite, Fe_2O_3, has three atoms of oxygen and two atoms of iron in each molecule. What percentage of the atoms in a hematite molecule are oxygen atoms? `SC.912.P.8.7`

32. Making Calculations A sample of olivine contains 3.4 billion silicon-oxygen tetrahedra. How many oxygen atoms are in the sample?

33. Applying Quantities A mineral sample has a mass of 51 g and a volume of 15 cm³. What is the density of the mineral sample?

WRITING SKILLS

34. Writing from Research Use the Internet or your school library to find a mineral map of the United States. Write a brief report that outlines how the minerals in your state are discovered and mined.

35. Communicating Main Ideas Write and illustrate an essay that explains how six different crystal structures form from silicon-oxygen tetrahedra.

INTERPRETING GRAPHICS

This table provides information about the eight most abundant elements in Earth's crust. Use the table to answer the questions that follow.

The Eight Most Abundant Chemicals in Earth's Crust

Element	Chemical symbol	Weight (% of Earth's crust)	Volume (% of Earth's crust)*
Oxygen	O	46.60	93.8
Silicon	Si	27.72	0.9
Aluminum	Al	8.13	0.5
Iron	Fe	5.00	0.4
Calcium	Ca	3.63	1.0
Sodium	Na	2.83	1.3
Potassium	K	2.59	1.8
Magnesium	Mg	2.09	0.3
	Total	98.59	100.0

*The volume of Earth's crust comprised by all other elements is so small that it is essentially 0% when the numbers are rounded to the nearest tenth of a percent.

36. What percentage of the weight of Earth's crust is made of silicon? `SC.912.N.1.1`

37. Oxygen makes up 93.8% of Earth's crust by volume, but oxygen is only 46.60% of Earth's crust by weight. How is this possible? `SC.912.N.1.1`

38. By comparing the volume and weight percentages of aluminum and calcium, determine which element has the higher density. `SC.912.N.1.1`

Understanding Concepts

Directions (1–10): For each question, write on a separate sheet of paper the number of the correct answer.

1 Coal provides much of the energy that people use each day. Coal is
  A. organic and a mineral.
  B. inorganic and a mineral.
  C. organic and not a mineral.
  D. inorganic and not a mineral.

2 What determines the hardness of a mineral?
  F. the strength of the bonds among atoms in the mineral
  G. the number of bonds among atoms in the mineral
  H. the tendency of the mineral to split along specific planes
  I. the tendency of the mineral to leave a streak

3 In many cases, minerals can be identified by all of the following properties *except*
  A. specimen color.
  B. specimen shape.
  C. specimen hardness.
  D. specimen luster.

4 A scientist thinks that a new mineral has been discovered. Which of the following characteristics would NOT characterize the substance as a mineral?
  F. It is organic.
  G. It occurs naturally.
  H. It is a crystalline solid.
  I. It has a consistent chemical composition.

5 Fluorescence and phosphorescence are two properties of minerals that relate to light. How do they differ?
  A. Fluorescent minerals continue to glow after exposure light.
  B. Phosphorescent minerals continue to glow after exposure to light.
  C. Fluorescent minerals have a silky appearance in reflected light.
  D. Phosphorescent minerals appear silky in reflected light.

6 A scientist models a crystal which forms a perfect cube. Which type of crystal system did the scientist model?
  F. a hexagonal system, which has three axes of equal length that intersect at 120° angles
  G. a monoclinic system, which has two axes of unequal length that intersect at 90° angles
  H. a tetragonal system, which has two axes of equal length and axes that intersect at 90° angles
  I. an isometric system, which has three axes of equal length that intersect at 90° angles

7 Geiger counters detect the particles released by unstable atoms. What characteristic of minerals results in the release of these particles?
  A. refraction
  B. magnetism
  C. hardness
  D. radioactivity

8 Tourmaline has a ring-silicate structure. Which of the following describes tourmaline?
  F. Shared oxygen atoms join the tetrahedra to form rings.
  G. Each tetrahedron is joined to two other tetrahedra by shared oxygen atoms.
  H. Two chains of tetrahedra join together.
  I. Each tetrahedron is joined to four other tetrahedra.

9 A mineral consists of an element that is combined with sulfur. To which class of minerals does the mineral belong?
  A. carbonates
  B. oxides
  C. sulfates
  D. sulfides

10 Density is one of the characteristics of minerals that is used to help identify them. Which of the following is NOT true of density?
  F. It is the same for all minerals that have the same size.
  G. It is a ratio of mass to volume.
  H. It depends on how closely atoms are packed in the mineral.
  I. It depends on the type of atoms in the mineral.

Interpreting Graphics

Directions (11–13): For each question below, record the correct answer on a separate sheet of paper.

Elements in Earth's Crust

11 The figure above shows the abundance of various elements in Earth's crust. What portion of the crust is made up of silicon?
 A. 46.6%
 B. 27.7%
 C. 8.1%
 D. 5.0%

12 Halides are compounds that consist of chlorine or fluorine, combined with sodium, potassium, or calcium. Based on the figure above, what percentage of the crust could be a part of a halide?
 F. 3.6%
 G. 6.2%
 H. 9.0%
 I. 27.7%

Common Silicates

Mineral	Idealized formula	Cleavage
Olivine	$(Mg,Fe)_2SiO_4$	none
Pyroxene group	$(Mg,Fe)SiO_3$	two planes at right angles
Amphibole group	$Ca_2(Mg,Fe)_5Si_8O_{22}(OH)_2$	two planes at 60° and 120°
Micas, biotite	$K(Mg,Fe)_3AlSi_3O_{10}(OH)_2$	one plane
Micas, muscovite	$KAl_2(AlSi_3O_{10})(OH)_2$	one plane
Feldspars, orthoclase	$KAlSi_3O_8$	two planes at 90°
Feldspars, plagioclase	$(Ca,Na)AlSi_3O_8$	two planes at 90°
Quartz	SiO_2	none

13 How is the cleavage of amphibole minerals similar to that of feldspar minerals?
 A. Both have two planes.
 B. Both have one plane.
 C. Both cleave at 60°.
 D. Both cleave at 90°.

> **Test Tip**
>
> If a question or an answer choice contains an unfamiliar term, try to break the word into parts to determine its meaning.

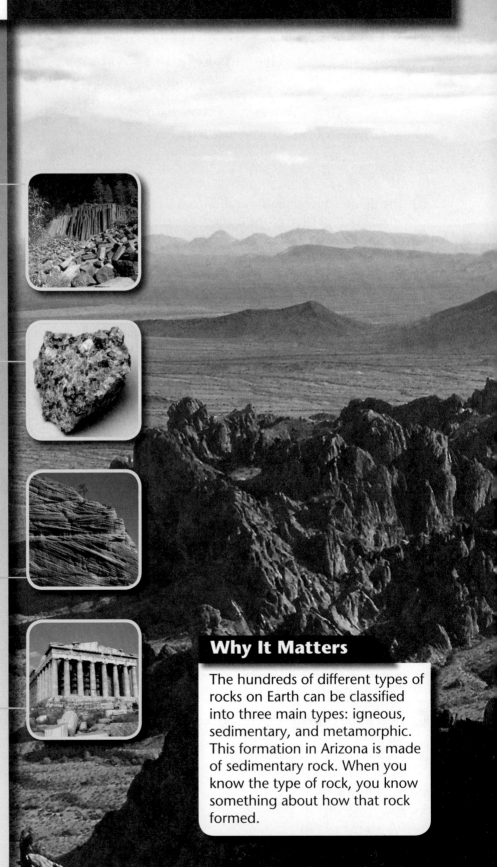

Chapter 6 Rocks

Why It Matters

The hundreds of different types of rocks on Earth can be classified into three main types: igneous, sedimentary, and metamorphic. This formation in Arizona is made of sedimentary rock. When you know the type of rock, you know something about how that rock formed.

Inquiry Lab · Sedimentary Sandwich

15 min

Use slices of different types of bread to model layers of different types of sediment deposits. Next, put your model in a plastic bag. Place a weight on top of the bag to simulate the process of compacting sediment into rock. Then, use an empty film canister to obtain a core sample of the sedimentary sandwich. Trade samples with another group and observe the other group's sample. Identify the different layers of rock and determine if rock layers are the same thickness or if some are thicker than others.

Questions to Get You Started

1. Make a labeled diagram showing the rock layers in the sample you observed.

2. Which factors might affect the thickness of a rock layer in a real rock formation?

3. Your model has layers of different types of rocks. In a real formation, what might changes in rock type indicate about the formation's geological history?

SC.912.E.6.2

133

READING TOOLBOX

These reading tools will help you learn the material in this chapter.

FoldNotes

Pyramid Pyramid FoldNotes help you compare words or ideas in sets of three.

Your Turn Before you read this chapter, make a Pyramid FoldNote as described in **Appendix A.** Label the sides of the pyramid with "Igneous rock," "Sedimentary rock," and "Metamorphic rock." As you read the chapter, define each type of rock, and write characteristics of each type of rock on the appropriate side of the pyramid.

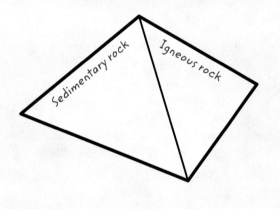

Graphic Organizer

Chain-of-Events Chart A chain-of-events chart is similar to a flow chart. A chain-of-events chart shows the order in which the steps of a process occur.

Your Turn In Section 3, you will read about the formation of sedimentary rocks. Make a chain-of-events chart like the one started below to describe *compaction,* one of the processes that form sedimentary rock. Use as many boxes as you need to record all steps of the process.

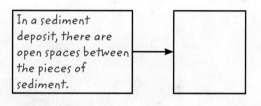

Note Taking

Summarizing Ideas Summarizing the content of each paragraph or set of paragraphs under a heading is a simple way to take notes. A few tips on summarizing are listed below.

❶ Summary statements should be short, but fully express the idea.

❷ Use the green subheadings for guidance in forming summary statements.

❸ Many paragraphs start or end with a sentence that summarizes the main idea of the paragraph.

Your Turn As you read each section, take notes by summarizing the main ideas. You may add structure to your notes by also writing the section title and red headings in the appropriate places.

For more information on how to use these and other tools, see **Appendix A.**

Rocks and the Rock Cycle

Key Ideas	Key Terms	Why It Matters
❯ Identify the three major types of rock, and explain how each type forms. ❯ Summarize the steps in the rock cycle. ❯ Explain Bowen's reaction series. ❯ Summarize the factors that affect the stability of rocks.	rock cycle Bowen's reaction series	Some rocks crumble and others make for solid buildings. The physical and chemical properties of rock are determined by the conditions under which the rock forms.

The material that makes up the solid parts of Earth is known as *rock*. Rock can be a collection of one or more minerals, or rock can be made of solid organic matter. In some cases, rock is made of solid matter that is not crystalline, such as glass. Geologists study the forces and processes that form and change the rocks of Earth's crust. Based on these studies, geologists have classified rocks into three major types by the way the rocks form.

Three Major Types of Rock

Volcanic activity produces *igneous rock*. The word *igneous* is derived from a Latin term that means "from fire." Igneous rock forms when *magma,* or molten rock, cools and hardens. Magma is called *lava* when it is exposed at Earth's surface.

Over time, natural processes break down all types of rock into small fragments. Rocks, mineral crystals, and organic matter that have been broken into fragments are known as *sediment*. Sediment is carried away and deposited by water, ice, and wind. When these sediment deposits are compressed, cemented together, and harden, *sedimentary rock* forms.

Certain forces and processes, including tremendous pressure, extreme heat, and chemical processes, also can change the form of existing rock. The rock that forms when existing rock is altered is *metamorphic rock*. The word *metamorphic* means "changed form." **Figure 1** shows an example of each major type of rock.

FLORIDA STANDARDS

LA.910.2.2.3 The student will organize information to show understanding or relationships among facts, ideas, and events (e.g., representing key points within text through charting, mapping, paraphrasing, summarizing, comparing, contrasting, or outlining); SC.912.E.6.4 Analyze how specific geologic processes and features are expressed in Florida and elsewhere; SC.912.E.7.3 Differentiate and describe the various interactions among Earth systems, including: atmosphere, hydrosphere, cryosphere, geosphere, and biosphere.

Figure 1 These rocks are examples of the three major rock types.

Sandstone (sedimentary)

Gneiss (metamorphic)

Granite (igneous)

Figure 2 The rock cycle illustrates the changes that igneous, sedimentary, and metamorphic rocks undergo.

Sedimentary rock

Erosion, deposition, and cementation

Melting and cooling

Changing temperature and pressure

Erosion, deposition, and cementation

Melting and cooling

Metamorphic rock

Changing temperature and pressure

Igneous rock

rock cycle the series of processes in which rock forms, changes from one type to another, is destroyed, and forms again by geological processes

The Rock Cycle

Any of the three major types of rock can be changed into another of the three types. Geologic forces and processes cause rock to change from one type to another. This series of changes is called the **rock cycle,** which is shown in **Figure 2.**

One starting point for examining the steps of the rock cycle is igneous rock. When a body of igneous rock is exposed at Earth's surface, a number of processes break down the igneous rock into sediment. When sediment from igneous rocks is compacted and cemented, the sediment becomes sedimentary rock. Then, if sedimentary rocks are subjected to changes in temperature and pressure, the rocks may become metamorphic rocks. Under certain temperature and pressure conditions, the metamorphic rock will melt and form magma. Then, if the magma cools, new igneous rock will form.

Much of the rock in Earth's continental crust has probably passed through the rock cycle many times during Earth's history. However, as **Figure 2** shows, a particular body of rock does not always pass through each stage of the rock cycle. For example, igneous rock may never be exposed at Earth's surface where the rock could change into sediment. Instead, the igneous rock may change directly into metamorphic rock while still beneath Earth's surface. Sedimentary rock may be broken down at Earth's surface, and the sediment may become another sedimentary rock. Metamorphic rock can be altered by heat and pressure to form a different type of metamorphic rock.

Properties of Rocks

All rock has physical and chemical properties that are determined by how and where the rock formed. The physical characteristics of rock reflect the chemical composition of the rock as a whole and of the individual minerals that make up the rock. The rate at which rock weathers and the way that rock breaks apart are determined by the chemical stability of the minerals in the rock.

Bowen's Reaction Series

In the early 1900s, a Canadian geologist named N. L. Bowen began studying how minerals crystallize from magma. He learned that as magma cools, certain minerals tend to crystallize first. As these minerals form, they <u>remove</u> specific elements from the magma, which changes the magma's composition. The changing composition of the magma allows different minerals that contain different elements to form. Thus, different minerals form at different times during the solidification (cooling) of magma, and they generally form in the same order.

In 1928, Bowen proposed a simplified pattern that explains the order in which minerals form as magma solidifies. This simplified flow chart is known as **Bowen's reaction series** and is shown in **Figure 3.** According to Bowen's hypothesis, minerals form in one of two ways. The first way is characterized by a gradual, continuous formation of minerals that have similar chemical compositions. The second way is characterized by sudden, or discontinuous, changes in mineral types. As magma cools, the discontinuous and continuous reaction series occur simultaneously, or at the same time.

Reading Check **Summarize Bowen's reaction series.** (See Appendix G for answers to Reading Checks.)

Figure 3 Different minerals crystallize at different times during the solidification of magma. Thus, as minerals crystallize from magma, the composition of the magma changes.

Figure 4 Devils Postpile National Monument in California is one of the world's finest examples of the igneous rock structures known as columnar joints.

Chemical Stability of Minerals

The rate at which a mineral chemically breaks down is dependent on the chemical stability of the mineral. *Chemical stability* is a measure of the tendency of a chemical compound to maintain its original chemical composition rather than break down to form a different chemical. In general, the minerals that are most stable are minerals that formed at the lowest temperatures, under conditions similar to those on Earth's surface. Minerals that formed at the highest temperatures, under conditions very different than those on Earth's surface, are least stable.

Physical Stability of Rocks

Rocks have natural zones of weakness that are determined by how and where the rocks form. For example, sedimentary rocks may form as a series of layers of sediment. These rocks tend to break between layers. Some metamorphic rocks also tend to break in layers that form as the minerals in the rocks align during metamorphism.

Massive igneous rock structures commonly have evenly spaced zones of weakness, called *joints*, that form as the rock cools and contracts. Devils Postpile, shown in **Figure 4**, is igneous rock that has joints that cause the rock to break into columns.

Zones of weakness may also form when the rock is under intense pressure inside Earth. When rock that formed under intense pressure is uplifted to Earth's surface, decreased pressure allows the joints and fractures to open. Once these weaknesses are exposed to air and water, chemical and physical processes begin to break down the rock.

Section 1 Review

LA.910.2.2.3; SC.912.E.7.3

Key Ideas

1. **Identify** the three major types of rock.

2. **Explain** how each major type of rock forms.

3. **Describe** the steps in the rock cycle.

4. **Summarize** Bowen's reaction series.

5. **Explain** how the chemical stability of a mineral is related to the temperature at which the mineral forms.

6. **Describe** how the conditions under which rocks form affect the physical stability of rocks.

Critical Thinking

7. **Applying Ideas** Does every rock go through the complete rock cycle by changing from igneous rock to sedimentary rock, to metamorphic rock, and then back to igneous rock? Explain your answer.

8. **Identifying Relationships** How could a sedimentary rock provide evidence that the rock cycle exists?

Concept Mapping

9. Use the following terms to create a concept map: *rock, igneous rock, sedimentary rock, metamorphic rock,* and *rock cycle.*

Igneous Rock

Key Ideas

❯ Summarize three factors that affect whether rock melts.

❯ Describe how the cooling rate of magma and lava affects the texture of igneous rocks.

❯ Classify igneous rocks according to their composition and texture.

❯ Describe intrusive and extrusive igneous rock.

Key Terms

igneous rock

intrusive igneous rock

extrusive igneous rock

felsic

mafic

Why It Matters

The many different compositions and textures of igneous rocks make sense once you understand the processes by which they form. Useful applications of these properties include nuclear-waste disposal.

When magma cools and hardens, it forms **igneous rock.** Because minerals usually crystallize as igneous rock forms from magma, most igneous rock can be identified as *crystalline,* or made of crystals.

The Formation of Magma

Magma forms when rock melts. Rock melts when the temperature of the rock increases to above the melting point of minerals in the rock. The chemical composition of minerals determines their melting temperatures. In general, rock melts at lower temperatures under lower pressures. If excess pressure is removed from rock that is close to melting, the rock may melt. Hot rock may also melt when fluids such as water are added. The addition of fluids generally decreases the melting point of certain minerals in the rock, which can cause those minerals to melt.

Partial Melting

Different minerals have different melting points, and minerals that have lower melting points are the first minerals to melt. When the first minerals melt, the magma that forms has a specific composition. As the temperature increases and as other minerals melt, the magma's composition changes. The process by which different minerals in rock melt at different temperatures is called *partial melting.* Partial melting is shown in **Figure 1.**

FLORIDA STANDARDS

LA.910.2.2.3 The student will organize information to show understanding or relationships among facts, ideas, and events (e.g., representing key points within text through charting, mapping, paraphrasing, summarizing, comparing, contrasting, or outlining); **SC.912.E.6.4** Analyze how specific geologic processes and features are expressed in Florida and elsewhere.

igneous rock rock that forms when magma cools and solidifies

Figure 1 How Magma Forms by Partial Melting

This solid rock contains the minerals quartz (yellow), feldspar (gray), biotite (brown), and hornblende (green).

The first minerals that melt are quartz and some types of feldspars. The orange background represents magma.

Minerals such as biotite and hornblende generally melt last, which changes the composition of the magma.

Figure 2 As the temperature decreases, the first minerals to crystallize from magma are minerals that have the highest freezing points. As the magma changes composition and cools, minerals that have lower freezing points form.

Fractional Crystallization

When magma cools, the cooling process is the reverse of the process of partial melting. Chemicals in magma combine to form minerals, and each mineral has a different freezing point. Minerals that have the highest freezing points crystallize first. As minerals crystallize, they remove specific chemicals from the magma. As the composition of the magma changes, new minerals begin to form. The crystallization and removal of different minerals from the cooling magma, as occurs in Bowen's reaction series, is called *fractional crystallization* and is shown in **Figure 2.**

Minerals that form during fractional crystallization tend to settle to the bottom of the magma chamber or to stick to the ceiling and walls of the magma chamber. Crystals that form early in the process are commonly the largest because they have the longest time to grow. In some crystals, the chemical composition of the inner part of the crystal differs from the composition of the outer parts of the crystal. This difference occurs because the magma's composition changed while the crystal was growing.

Quick Lab   Crystal Formation

      20 min

Procedure

❶ Add the following until **three glasses** are 2/3 full: glass 1—water and **ice cubes**; glass 2—water at room temperature; and glass 3—hot tap water.

❷ In a small **sauce pan**, mix 120 mL of **Epsom salts** in **120 mL of water.** Heat the mixture on a **hot plate** over low heat. Do not let the mixture boil. Stir the mixture with a **spoon or stirring rod** until no more crystals dissolve.

❸ Using a **funnel,** carefully pour equal amounts of the Epsom salts mixture into **three test tubes.** Use **tongs** to steady the test tubes as you pour. Drop a few crystals of Epsom salt into each test tube, and gently shake each one. Place one test tube into each glass.

❹ Observe the solutions as they cool for 15 minutes. Let the glasses sit overnight, and examine the solutions again after 24 hours.

Analysis

1. In which test tube are the crystals the largest?

2. In which test tube are the crystals the smallest?

3. How does the rate of cooling affect the size of the crystals that form? Explain your answer.

4. How are the differing rates of crystal formation you observed related to igneous rock formation?

5. How would you change the procedure to obtain larger crystals of Epsom salts? Explain your answer.

Textures of Igneous Rocks

Igneous rocks may form beneath Earth's surface or on Earth's surface. Magma that cools deep inside the crust forms **intrusive igneous rock.** The magma that forms these rocks intrudes, or enters, into other rock masses beneath Earth's surface. The magma then slowly cools and hardens. Lava that cools at Earth's surface forms **extrusive igneous rock.**

Intrusive and extrusive igneous rocks differ from each other not only in where they form but also in the size of their crystals or grains. The texture of igneous rock is determined by the size of the crystals in the rock. The size of the crystals is determined mainly by the cooling rate of the magma. Examples of different textures of igneous rocks are shown in **Figure 3.**

Coarse-Grained Igneous Rock

Intrusive igneous rocks commonly have large mineral crystals. The slow loss of heat allows the minerals in the cooling magma to form large, well-developed crystals. Igneous rocks that are composed of large mineral grains are described as having a *coarse-grained texture.* An example of a coarse-grained igneous rock is granite. The upper part of the continental crust is made mostly of granite.

Fine-Grained Igneous Rock

Many extrusive igneous rocks are composed of small mineral grains that cannot be seen by the unaided eye. Because these rocks form when magma cools rapidly, large crystals are unable to form. Igneous rocks that are composed of small crystals are described as having a *fine-grained texture.* Examples of common fine-grained igneous rocks are basalt and rhyolite (RIE uh LIET).

Other Igneous Rock Textures

Some igneous rock forms when magma cools slowly at first but then cools more rapidly as it nears Earth's surface. This type of cooling produces large crystals embedded within a mass of smaller ones. Igneous rock that has a mixture of large and small crystals has a *porphyritic texture* (POHR fuh RIT ik TEKS chuhr).

When a highly viscous, or thick, magma cools quickly, few crystals are able to grow. Quickly cooling magma may form a rock that has a *glassy* texture, such as obsidian. When magma contains a large amount of dissolved gases and cools rapidly, the gases become trapped as bubbles in the rock that forms. The rapid cooling process produces a rock full of holes called *vesicles,* such as those in pumice. This type of rock is said to have a *vesicular texture.*

> **Reading Check** What is the difference between fine-grained and coarse-grained igneous rock?

intrusive igneous rock rock formed from the cooling and solidification of magma beneath Earth's surface

extrusive igneous rock rock that forms from the cooling and solidification of lava at Earth's surface

Figure 3 Igneous Rock Textures

Coarse-grained (granite)

Fine-grained (rhyolite)

Porphyritic (granite)

Glassy (obsidian)

Vesicular (pumice)

Figure 4 Felsic rocks, such as the outcropping and hand sample shown above (left), have light coloring. Mafic rocks (right) are usually darker in color.

felsic describes magma or igneous rock that is rich in feldspars and silica and that is generally light in color

mafic describes magma or igneous rock that is rich in magnesium and iron and that is generally dark in color

READING TOOLBOX

Pyramid
Create a pyramid FoldNote to record your notes on the three families of igneous rock—felsic, mafic, and intermediate. For each term, write the definition and include an example of a rock from that family.

Composition of Igneous Rocks

The mineral composition of an igneous rock is determined by the chemical composition of the magma from which the rock formed. Each type of igneous rock has a specific mineral composition. Geologists divide igneous rock into three families—felsic, mafic (MAF ik), and intermediate. Each of the three families has a different mineral composition. Examples of rock from the felsic and mafic families are shown in **Figure 4.**

Felsic Rock

Rock in the **felsic** family forms from magma that contains a large proportion of silica. Felsic rock generally has the light coloring of its main mineral components, potassium feldspar and quartz. Felsic rock commonly also contains plagioclase feldspar, biotite mica, and muscovite mica. The felsic family includes many common rocks, such as granite, rhyolite, obsidian, and pumice.

Mafic Rock

Rock in the **mafic** family forms from magma that contains lower proportions of silica than felsic rock does and that is rich in iron and magnesium. The main mineral components of rock in this family are plagioclase feldspar and pyroxene minerals. Mafic rock may also include dark-colored *ferromagnesian minerals,* such as hornblende. These ferromagnesian components, as well as the mineral olivine, give mafic rock a dark color. The mafic family includes the common rocks basalt and gabbro.

Intermediate Rocks

Rocks of the intermediate family are made up of the minerals plagioclase feldspar, hornblende, pyroxene, and biotite mica. Rocks in the intermediate family contain lower proportions of silica than rocks in the felsic family do but contain higher proportions of silica than rocks in the mafic family contain. Rocks in the intermediate family include diorite and andesite.

Intrusive Igneous Rock

Igneous rock masses that form underground are called *intrusions*. Intrusions form when magma intrudes, or enters, into other rock masses and then cools deep inside Earth's crust. A variety of intrusions are shown in **Figure 5.**

Batholiths and Stocks

The largest of all intrusions are called *batholiths*. Batholiths are intrusive formations that spread over at least 100 km^2 when they are exposed on Earth's surface. The word *batholith* means "deep rock." Batholiths were once thought to extend to great depths beneath Earth's surface. However, studies have determined that many batholiths extend only several thousand meters below the surface. Batholiths form the cores of many mountain ranges, such as the Sierra Nevadas in California. The largest batholith in North America forms the core of the Coast Range in British Columbia. Another type of intrusion is called a *stock*. Stocks are similar to batholiths but cover less than 100 km^2 at the surface.

Laccoliths

When magma flows between rock layers and spreads upward, it sometimes pushes the overlying rock layers into a dome. The base of the intrusion is parallel to the rock layer beneath it. This type of intrusion is called a *laccolith*. The word *laccolith* means "lake of rock." Laccoliths commonly occur in groups and can sometimes be identified by the small dome-shaped mountains they form on Earth's surface. Many laccoliths are located beneath the Black Hills of South Dakota.

✔ **Reading Check** What is the difference between stocks and batholiths?

Sills and Dikes

When magma flows between the layers of rock and hardens, a *sill* forms. A sill lies parallel to the layers of rock that surround it, even if the layers are tilted. Sills vary in thickness from a few centimeters to hundreds of meters.

Magma sometimes forces itself through rock layers by following existing vertical fractures or by creating new ones. When the magma solidifies, a *dike* forms. Dikes cut across rock layers rather than lying parallel to the rock layers. Dikes are common in areas of volcanic activity.

SCI
LINKS.
www.scilinks.org
Topic: Igneous Rock
Code: HQX0783

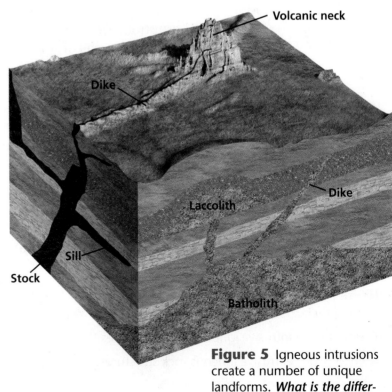

Figure 5 Igneous intrusions create a number of unique landforms. *What is the difference between a dike and a sill?*

Figure 6 Shiprock, in New Mexico, is an example of a volcanic neck that was exposed by erosion.

Extrusive Igneous Rock

A *volcano* is a vent through which magma, gases, or volcanic ash is expelled. When a volcanic eruption stops, the magma in the vent may cool to form rock. Eventually, the soft parts of the volcano are eroded by wind and water, and only the hardest rock in the vent remains. The solidified central vent is called a *volcanic neck*. Narrow dikes that sometimes radiate from the neck may also be exposed. A dramatic example of a volcanic neck called Shiprock is shown in **Figure 6.**

Igneous rock masses that form on Earth's surface are called *extrusions.* Many extrusions are simply flat masses of rock called *lava flows.* A series of lava flows that cover a vast area with thick rock is known as a *lava plateau.* Volcanic rock called *tuff* forms when a volcano releases ash and other solid particles during an eruption. Tuff deposits can be several hundred meters thick and can cover areas of several hundred kilometers.

Section 2 Review

LA.910.2.2.3; SC.912.E.6.4

Key Ideas

1. **Summarize** three factors that affect the melting of rock.

2. **Contrast** partial melting and fractional crystallization.

3. **Describe** how the cooling rate of magma affects the texture of igneous rock.

4. **Name** the three families of igneous rocks, and identify their specific mineral compositions.

5. **Describe** five intrusive igneous rock structures.

6. **Identify** four extrusive igneous rock structures.

Critical Thinking

7. **Applying Ideas** If you wanted to create a rock that has large crystals in a laboratory, what conditions would you have to control? Explain your answer.

8. **Applying Ideas** An unidentified, light-colored igneous rock is made up of potassium feldspar and quartz. To what family of igneous rocks does the rock belong? Explain your answer.

Concept Mapping

9. Use the following terms to create a concept map: *igneous rock, magma, coarse grained, fine grained, felsic, mafic,* and *intermediate.*

Sedimentary Rock

Key Ideas	Key Terms	Why It Matters
❯ Explain the processes of compaction and cementation. ❯ Describe how chemical and organic sedimentary rocks form. ❯ Describe how clastic sedimentary rock forms. ❯ Identify seven sedimentary rock features.	compaction cementation chemical sedimentary rock organic sedimentary rock clastic sedimentary rock	Sedimentary rock is a common building material. Understanding its properties is crucial to public safety. The ways in which it is formed affects the rock's properties.

Loose fragments of rock, minerals, and organic material that result from natural processes, including the physical breakdown of rocks, are called *sediment*. Most sedimentary rock is made up of combinations of different types of sediment. The characteristics of sedimentary rock are determined by the source of the sediment, the way the sediment was moved, and the conditions under which the sediment was deposited.

Formation of Sedimentary Rocks

After sediments form, they are generally transported by wind, water, or ice to a new location. The source of the sediment determines the sediment's composition. As the sediment moves, its characteristics change as it is physically broken down or chemically altered. Eventually, the loose sediment is deposited.

Two main processes convert loose sediment to sedimentary rock—compaction and cementation. **Compaction,** as shown in **Figure 1,** is the process in which sediment is squeezed and in which the size of the pore space between sediment grains is reduced by the weight and pressure of overlying layers. **Cementation** is the process in which sediments are glued together by minerals that are deposited by water.

Geologists classify sedimentary rocks by the processes by which the rocks form and by the composition of the rocks. There are three main classes of sedimentary rocks—chemical, organic, and clastic.

FLORIDA STANDARDS

LA.910.2.2.3 The student will organize information to show understanding or relationships among facts, ideas, and events (e.g., representing key points within text through charting, mapping, paraphrasing, summarizing, comparing, contrasting, or outlining); SC.912.E.6.4 Analyze how specific geologic processes and features are expressed in Florida and elsewhere.

compaction the process in which the volume and porosity of a sediment is decreased by the weight of overlying sediments as a result of burial beneath other sediments

cementation the process in which minerals precipitate into pore spaces between sediment grains and bind sediments together to form rock

Figure 1 Processes That Form Sedimentary Rock

When mud is deposited, there may be a lot of space between grains. During compaction, the grains are squeezed together, and the rock that forms takes up less space.

Overlying layers squeeze sediment.

50-60% water

10-20% water

When sand is deposited, there are many spaces between the grains. During cementation, water deposits minerals such as calcite or quartz in the spaces around the sand grains, which glues the grains together.

Pore spaces between sediment grains are empty.

Water moves through pore spaces.

Minerals deposited by water cement the grains together.

145

Chemical Sedimentary Rock

Minerals made up of ions such as calcium, potassium, and chloride can dissolve in water. **Chemical sedimentary rock** forms when the ions from dissolved minerals precipitate out of water because of changing concentrations of chemicals.

One reason minerals precipitate is due to evaporation. When water evaporates, the minerals that were dissolved in the water are left behind. Eventually, the concentration of minerals in the remaining water becomes high enough to cause minerals to precipitate out of the water. The minerals left behind form rocks called *evaporites*. Gypsum and halite, or rock salt, are two examples of evaporites. The Bonneville Salt Flats near the Great Salt Lake in Utah are a good example of evaporite deposits.

Organic Sedimentary Rock

The second class of sedimentary rock is **organic sedimentary rock.** Organic sedimentary rock is rock that forms from the remains of living things. Coal and some limestones are examples of organic sedimentary rocks. Coal forms from plant remains that are buried before they decay and are then compacted into matter that is composed mostly of carbon.

While chemical limestones precipitate from chemicals dissolved in water, organic limestones form when marine organisms, such as coral, clams, oysters, and plankton, remove the chemical components of the minerals calcite and aragonite from sea water. These organisms make their shells from these minerals. When they die, their shells eventually become limestone. This process of limestone formation is shown in **Figure 2.** Chalk is one example of limestone made up of the shells of tiny, one-celled marine organisms that settle to the ocean floor.

chemical sedimentary rock sedimentary rock that forms when minerals precipitate from a solution or settle from a suspension

organic sedimentary rock sedimentary rock that forms from the remains of plants or animals

READING TOOLBOX

Chain-of-Events Chart

Make a chain-of-events chart to show the steps in the formation of organic sedimentary rocks. Write the first step of the process in a box. Add boxes with additional steps, and connect the boxes with arrows.

Figure 2 Organic Limestone Formation

Organisms that live in lakes or oceans take chemicals from the water and produce the mineral calcium carbonate, $CaCO_3$. They use the $CaCO_3$ to build their shells or skeletons.

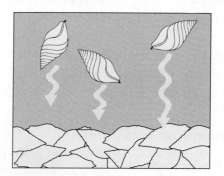

When the organisms die, the hard remains that are made of $CaCO_3$ settle to the lake or ocean floor.

The shells of the dead organisms pile up. Eventually, the layers are compacted and cemented to form limestone.

Figure 3 Types of Clastic Sedimentary Rock

Sandstone is made of small mineral grains that are cemented together.

Conglomerate is composed of rounded, pebble-sized fragments that are held together by a cement.

Breccia is similar to conglomerate, but breccia contains angular fragments.

Shale is made of flaky clay particles that compress into flat layers.

Clastic Sedimentary Rock

The third class of sedimentary rock is made of rock fragments that are carried away from their source by water, wind, or ice and left as deposits. Over time, the individual fragments may become compacted and cemented into solid rock. The rock formed from these deposits is called **clastic sedimentary rock.**

Clastic sedimentary rocks are classified by the size of the sediments they contain, as shown in **Figure 3.** One group consists of large fragments that are cemented together. Rock that is composed of rounded fragments that range in size from 2 mm to boulders is called a *conglomerate.* If the fragments are angular and have sharp corners, the rock is called a *breccia* (BRECH ee uh). In conglomerates and breccias, the individual pieces of sediment can be easily seen.

Another group of clastic sedimentary rocks is made up of sand-sized grains that have been cemented together. These rocks are called *sandstone.* Quartz is the major component of most sandstones. Many sandstones have pores between the sand grains through which fluids, such as groundwater, natural gas, and crude oil, can move.

A third group of clastic sedimentary rocks, called *shale,* consists of clay-sized particles that are cemented and compacted. The flaky clay particles are usually pressed into flat layers that will easily split apart.

Reading Check Name three groups of clastic sedimentary rock.

clastic sedimentary rock sedimentary rock that forms when fragments of preexisting rocks are compacted or cemented together

Math Skills

Sedimentation Rates The rate at which sediment accumulates is called the *sedimentation rate.* The sedimentation rate of an area is 1.5 mm per year. At this rate, how many years must pass for 10 cm of sediment to be deposited?

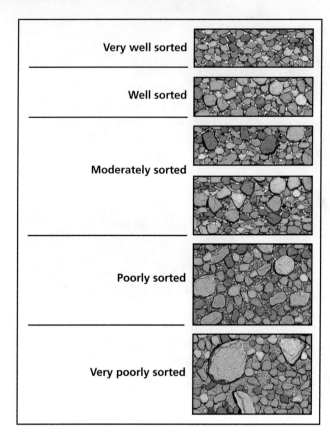

Very well sorted

Well sorted

Moderately sorted

Poorly sorted

Very poorly sorted

Figure 4 Sorting of Sediments

Academic Vocabulary

transport (trans POHRT) to carry from one place to another

www.scilinks.org
Topic: Sedimentary Rock
Code: HQX1365

Characteristics of Clastic Sediments

The physical characteristics of sediments are determined mainly by the way sediments were transported to the place where they are deposited. Sediments are transported by four main agents: water, ice, wind, and the effects of gravity. The size of sediment particles that can be carried and the distance that the particles will move depends on the speed with which the sediment is moved. In general, both the distance the sediment is moved and the agent that moves the sediment determine the characteristics of that sediment.

Sorting

The tendency for currents of air or water to separate sediments according to size is called *sorting*. Sediments can be very well sorted, very poorly sorted, or somewhere in between, as shown in **Figure 4.** In well-sorted sediments, all of the grains are roughly the same size and shape. Poorly sorted sediment consists of grains that are many different sizes. The sorting of a sediment is the result of changes in the speed of the agent that is moving the sediment. For example, when a fast-moving stream enters a lake, the speed of the water decreases sharply. Because large grains are too heavy for the current to carry, these grains are deposited first. Fine grains can stay suspended in the water for much longer than large grains can. So, fine particles are commonly deposited farther from shore or on top of coarser sediments.

Angularity

As sediment is transported from its source to where it is deposited, the particles collide with each other and with other objects in their path. These collisions can cause the particles to change size and shape. When particles first break from the source rock, they tend to be angular and uneven. Particles that have moved long distances from the source tend to be more rounded and smooth. In general, the farther sediment travels from its source, the finer and smoother the particles of sediment become.

Sedimentary Rock Features

The place or setting in which sediment is deposited is called a *depositional environment*. Common depositional environments include rivers, deltas, beaches, and oceans. Each depositional environment has different characteristics that create specific structures in sedimentary rock. These features allow scientists to identify the depositional environment in which the rock formed.

Stratification

Layering of sedimentary rock, as shown in **Figure 5**, is called *stratification*. Stratification occurs when the conditions of sediment deposition change. The conditions may vary when there is a change in sediment type or of depositional environment. For example, a rise in sea level may cause an area that was once a beach to become a shallow ocean, which changes the type of sediment that is deposited in the area.

Stratified layers, or *beds*, vary in thickness depending on the length of time during which sediment is deposited and how much sediment is deposited. *Massive beds*, or beds that have no internal structures, form when similar sediment is deposited under similar conditions for long periods of time or when a large amount of sediment is deposited at one time.

Cross-beds and Graded Bedding

Some sedimentary rocks are characterized by slanting layers called *cross-beds* that form within beds. Cross-beds, which generally form in sand dunes or river beds, are shown in **Figure 5.**

When various sizes and kinds of materials are deposited within one layer, a type of stratification called *graded bedding* may occur. Graded bedding occurs when different sizes and shapes of sediment settle to different levels. Graded beds commonly transition from largest grains on the bottom to smallest grains on the top. However, certain depositional events, such as some mudflows, may cause *reverse grading,* in which the smallest grains are on the bottom and the largest grains are on top.

Reading Check What is graded bedding?

Quick Lab

10 min

SC.912.E.6.4

Graded Bedding

Procedure

❶ Place **20 mL of water** into a **small glass jar.**

❷ Pour **10 mL of poorly sorted sediment** into the jar. Place a **lid** securely on the jar.

❸ Shake the jar vigorously for **1 min,** and then let it sit still for **5 min.**

❹ Observe the settled sediment.

Analysis

1. Describe any sedimentary structures you observed.

2. Name two factors responsible for the sedimentary structures you observed.

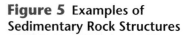

Figure 5 Examples of Sedimentary Rock Structures

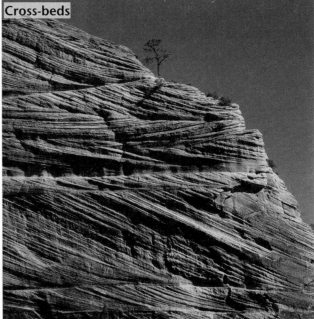

Ripple Marks

Some sedimentary rocks clearly display *ripple marks*. Ripple marks are caused by the action of wind or water on sand. When the sand becomes sandstone, the ripple marks may be preserved. When scientists find ripple marks in sedimentary rock, the scientists know that the sediment was once part of a beach or a river bed.

Mud Cracks

The ground in **Figure 6** shows mud cracks, which are another feature of sedimentary rock. Mud cracks form when muddy deposits dry and shrink. The shrinking causes the drying mud to crack. A river's flood plain or a dry lake bed is a common place to find mud cracks. Once the area is flooded again, new deposits may fill in the cracks and preserve their features when the mud hardens to solid rock.

Figure 6 This dry and mud-cracked river bed is in Nagasaki, Japan.

Fossils and Concretions

The remains or traces of ancient plants and animals, called *fossils*, may be preserved in sedimentary rock. As sediments pile up, plant and animal remains are buried. Hard parts of these remains may be preserved in the rock. More often, even the hard parts dissolve and leave only impressions in the rock. Sedimentary rocks sometimes contain lumps of rock that have a composition that is different from that of the main rock body. These lumps are known as *concretions*. Concretions form when minerals precipitate from fluids and build up around a nucleus. Groundwater sometimes deposits dissolved minerals inside cavities in sedimentary rock. The minerals may crystallize inside the cavities to form a special type of rock called a *geode*.

Section 3 Review

LA.910.2.2.3; SC.912.E.6.2; SC.912.E.6.4

Key Ideas

1. **Explain** how the processes of compaction and cementation form sedimentary rock.

2. **Describe** how chemical and organic sedimentary rocks form, and give two examples of each.

3. **Describe** how clastic sedimentary rock differs from chemical and organic sedimentary rock.

4. **Explain** how the physical characteristics of sediments change during transport.

5. **Identify** seven features that you can use to identify the depositional environment in which sedimentary rocks formed.

Critical Thinking

6. **Making Comparisons** Compare the histories of rounded, smooth rocks and angular, uneven rocks.

7. **Identifying Relationships** Which of the following would most effectively sort sediments: a fast-moving river or a small, slow-moving stream? Explain your answer.

Concept Mapping

8. Use the following terms to create a concept map: *cementation, clastic sedimentary rock, sedimentary rock, chemical sedimentary rock, compaction,* and *organic sedimentary rock.*

Metamorphic Rock

Key Ideas

❭ Describe the process of metamorphism.

❭ Explain the difference between regional and contact metamorphism.

❭ Distinguish between foliated and nonfoliated metamorphic rocks, and give an example of each.

Key Terms

metamorphism

contact metamorphism

regional metamorphism

foliation

nonfoliated

Why It Matters

Metamorphism can produce marble and gemstones, such as rubies. Materials such as these are important to civilization, both ancient and modern.

The process by which heat, pressure, or chemical processes change one type of rock to another is called **metamorphism.** Most metamorphic rock, or rock that has undergone metamorphism, forms deep within Earth's crust. All metamorphic rock forms from existing igneous, sedimentary, or metamorphic rock.

Formation of Metamorphic Rocks

During metamorphism, heat, pressure, and hot fluids cause some minerals to change into other minerals. Minerals may also change in size or shape, or they may separate into parallel bands that give the rock a layered appearance. Hot fluids from magma may circulate through the rock and change the mineral composition of the rock by dissolving some materials and by adding others. All of these changes are part of metamorphism.

The type of rock that forms because of metamorphism can indicate the conditions that were in place when the original rock changed, as shown in **Figure 1.** The composition of the rock being metamorphosed, the amount and direction of heat and pressure, and the presence or absence of certain fluids cause different combinations of minerals to form.

Two types of metamorphism occur in Earth's crust. One type occurs when small volumes of rock come into contact with magma. The second type occurs when large areas of Earth's crust are affected by the heat and pressure that is caused by the movement and collisions of Earth's giant tectonic plates.

FLORIDA STANDARDS

SC.912.E.6.4 Analyze how specific geologic processes and features are expressed in Florida and elsewhere; **SC.912.N.4.1** Explain how scientific knowledge and reasoning provide an empirically-based perspective to inform society's decision making; **SC.912.P.10.11** Explain and compare nuclear reactions (radioactive decay, fission and fusion), the energy changes associated with them and their associated safety issues.

metamorphism the process in which one type of rock changes into metamorphic rock because of chemical processes or changes in temperature and pressure

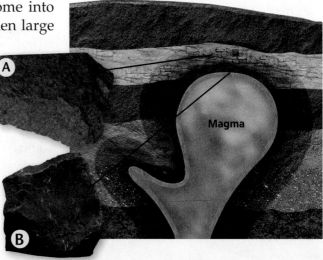

Figure 1 Indicators of Metamorphic Conditions

Magma

Slate (A) is a metamorphic rock that commonly forms in the outer zone of metamorphism around a body of magma where clay-rich rock is exposed to relatively small amounts of heat.

Hornfels (B) is a metamorphic rock that forms in the innermost zone of metamorphism, where clay-rich rock is exposed to large amounts of heat from the magma.

Contact Metamorphism

When magma comes into contact with existing rock, heat from the magma can change the structure and mineral composition of the surrounding rock by a process called **contact metamorphism.** This process forms the hornfels shown on the previous page. During contact metamorphism only a small area of rock that surrounds the hot magma is changed by the magma's heat. Hot chemical fluids moving through fractures may also cause changes in the surrounding rock during contact metamorphism.

Regional Metamorphism

Metamorphism sometimes occurs over an area of thousands of square kilometers during periods of high tectonic activity, such as when mountain ranges form. The type of metamorphism that occurs over a large area is called **regional metamorphism.**

Tectonic activity <u>generates</u> tremendous heat and pressure, which cause chemical changes in the minerals of rock. Most metamorphic rock forms as a result of regional metamorphism. However, volcanism and the movement of magma often accompany tectonic activity. Thus, rocks that are formed by contact metamorphism are also commonly discovered in locations where regional metamorphism has occurred.

✓ Reading Check How are minerals affected by regional metamorphism?

contact metamorphism a change in the texture, structure, or chemical composition of a rock due to contact with magma

regional metamorphism a change in the texture, structure, or chemical composition of a rock due to changes in temperature and pressure over a large area, generally as a result of tectonic forces

Academic Vocabulary

generate (JEN uhr AYT) to bring about; to produce

Why It Matters

Why Are Rubies so Rare?

REAL WORLD

The pressure and heat that form metamorphic rock may also result in the formation of certain gemstones, such as rubies. Natural rubies are rare because they made of the rare mineral corundum, Al_2O_3, and form only in very specific conditions. These natural conditions can be replicated in a laboratory to form synthetic, or human-made, rubies.

Synthetic rubies can be produced by mixing the right chemicals at extremely high temperatures. Only an expert can distinguish a synthetic ruby from a natural ruby.

Gneiss, schist, and marble are metamorphic rocks that may contain rubies. A gem in its natural form is called a rough gem. It may then be cut in special patterns to make it sparkle.

YOUR TURN COMPARING PROCESSES
In what ways are the natural and synthetic processes that form rubies similar? In what ways are they different?

Classification of Metamorphic Rocks

Minerals in the original rock help determine the mineral composition of the metamorphosed rock. As the original rock is exposed to changes in heat and pressure, the minerals in the original rock often combine chemically to form new minerals. While metamorphic rocks are classified by chemical composition, they are first classified according to their texture. Metamorphic rocks have either a foliated texture or a nonfoliated texture.

Foliated Rocks

The metamorphic rock texture in which minerals are arranged in planes or bands is called **foliation.** Foliated rock can form in one of two ways. Extreme pressure may cause the mineral crystals in the rock to realign or regrow to form parallel bands. Foliation also occurs as minerals that have different compositions separate to produce a series of alternating dark and light bands.

Foliated metamorphic rocks include the common rocks slate, schist, and gneiss (NIES). Slate forms when pressure is exerted on the sedimentary rock shale, which contains clay minerals that are flat and thin. The fine-grained minerals in slate are compressed into thin layers, which split easily into flat sheets. Flat sheets of slate are used in building materials, such as roof tiles or walkway stones.

When large amounts of heat and pressure are exerted on slate, a coarse-grained metamorphic rock known as *schist* may form. Deep underground, intense heat and pressure may cause the minerals in schist to separate into bands as the minerals recrystallize. The metamorphosed rock that has bands of light and dark minerals is called *gneiss*. Gneiss is shown in **Figure 2.**

Summarizing Ideas
As you read this page and the next, summarize the main ideas about the classification of metamorphic rocks. Include a summary of the differences between foliated and nonfoliated rocks.

foliation the metamorphic rock texture in which mineral grains are arranged in planes or bands

SC*LINKS*.
www.scilinks.org
Topic: Metamorphic Rock
Code: HQX0949

Figure 2 Large amounts of heat and pressure may change rock into the metamorphic rock gneiss, which shows pronounced foliation.

Figure 3 Marble is a nonfoliated metamorphic rock that is used as building and sculpting material.

nonfoliated the metamorphic rock texture in which mineral grains are not arranged in planes or bands

Nonfoliated Rocks

Rocks that do not have bands or aligned minerals are **nonfoliated.** Most nonfoliated metamorphic rocks share at least one of two main characteristics. First, the original rock that is metamorphosed may contain grains of only one mineral or contains very small amounts of other minerals. Thus, the rock does not form bands of different mineral compositions when it is metamorphosed. Second, the original rock may contain grains that are round or square. Because the grains do not have some long and some short sides, these grains do not change position when exposed to pressure in one direction.

Quartzite is one common nonfoliated rock. Quartzite forms when quartz sandstone is metamorphosed. Quartzite is very hard and does not wear away easily. For this reason, quartzite remains after weaker rocks around it have worn away and may form hills or mountains.

Marble, the beautiful stone that is used for building monuments and statues, is a metamorphic rock that forms from the compression of limestone. The Parthenon, which is shown in **Figure 3,** has been standing in Greece for more than 1,400 years. However, the calcium carbonate in marble reacts with acid rain, which is caused by air pollution. Many ancient marble structures and sculptures are being damaged by acid rain.

Section 4 Review

LA.910.2.2.3; SC.912.E.6.2; SC.912.E.6.4

Key Ideas

1. **Describe** the process of metamorphism.

2. **Explain** the difference between regional and contact metamorphism.

3. **Distinguish** between foliated and nonfoliated metamorphic rocks.

4. **Identify** two foliated metamorphic rocks and two nonfoliated metamorphic rocks.

Critical Thinking

5. **Analyzing Relationships** What do a butterfly and metamorphic rock have in common?

6. **Making Comparisons** If you have samples of the two metamorphic rocks slate and hornfels, what can you say about the history of each rock?

7. **Identifying Relationships** The Himalaya Mountains are located on a boundary between two colliding tectonic plates. Would most of the metamorphic rock in that area occur in small patches or in wide regions? Explain your answer.

Concept Mapping

8. Use the following terms to create a concept map: *contact metamorphism, foliated, regional metamorphism, metamorphic rock,* and *nonfoliated.*

A Nuclear Waste Basket

EYE ON THE ENVIRONMENT

Each day, about 6 tons of highly reactive used fuel rods from nuclear reactors are added to the 30,000 tons held at various sites across the country. These rods and other radioactive waste must be stored for thousands of years, away from people and water. But where? One solution is to place the waste 300 m below ground, in the very stable rock under Yucca Mountain in Nevada.

Used fuel rods are only part of the nuclear waste problem. A large volume of low- and medium-level radioactive waste is piling up in drums like these.

Nuclear waste will be placed in containers for transportation to Yucca Mountain. Tens of thousands of truck and train shipments will be required.

A ramp into the mountain will lead to a network of storage tunnels for the containers.

YOUR TURN

CRITICAL THINKING
Nuclear waste at Yucca Mountain may remain hazardous for 10,000 years. What changes might occur in that time period that could affect the safety of the site?

APPLYING INFORMATION
Use what you know about different types of rock to predict the likely type of rock under Yucca Mountain. Explain your reasoning.

Classification of Rocks

What You'll Do

› **Observe** the characteristics of common rocks.

› **Compare and contrast** the features of igneous, sedimentary, and metamorphic rocks.

› **Identify** igneous, sedimentary, and metamorphic rocks.

What You'll Need

hand lens
hydrochloric acid, 10% dilute
medicine dropper
rock samples

Safety

There are many different types of igneous, sedimentary, and metamorphic rocks. Therefore, it is important to know distinguishing features of the rocks to identify the rocks. The classification of rocks is generally based on the way in which they formed, their mineral composition, and the size and arrangement (or texture) of their minerals.

Igneous rocks differ in the minerals they contain and the sizes of their crystals. Metamorphic rocks often look similar to igneous rocks, but they may have bands of minerals. Most sedimentary rocks are made of fragments of other rocks that are compressed and cemented together. Some common features of sedimentary rocks are parallel layers, ripple marks, cross-bedding, and the presence of fossils. In this lab, you will use these features to identify various rock samples.

Procedure

1 In your notebook, make a table that has columns for sample number, description of properties, rock class, and rock name. List the numbers of the rock samples you received from your teacher.

2 Examine the rocks carefully. You can use a hand lens to study the fine details of the rock samples. Look for characteristics such as the shape, size, and arrangement of the mineral grains. For each sample, list in your table the distinguishing features that you observe.

Step **2**

3 Refer to the Guide to Common Rocks in the Reference Tables section of the Appendix. Compare the properties for each rock sample that you listed with the properties listed in the identification table. If you are unable to identify certain rocks, examine these rock samples again.

Sample	Descriptions of Properties	Rock Class	Rock Name

DO NOT WRITE IN THIS BOOK

4 Certain rocks react with acid, which indicates that they are composed of calcite. If a rock contains calcite, the rock will bubble and release carbon dioxide. Using a medicine dropper and 10% dilute hydrochloric acid, test various samples for their reactions. **CAUTION** Wear goggles, gloves, and an apron when you work with hydrochloric acid. Rinse each sample and wash your hands thoroughly afterward.

5 Complete your table by identifying the class of rock—igneous, sedimentary, or metamorphic—that each sample belongs to, and then name the rock.

Analysis

1. **Analyzing Methods** Which properties were most useful and least useful in identifying each rock sample? Explain.

2. **Evaluating Results** Were there any samples that you found difficult to identify? Explain.

3. **Making Comparisons** Describe any characteristics common to all of the rock samples.

4. **Evaluating Ideas** How can you distinguish between a sedimentary rock and a foliated metamorphic rock if both have observable layering?

Extension

Applying Conclusions Collect a variety of rocks from your area. Use the Guide to Common Rocks to see how many you can classify. How many igneous rocks did you collect? How many sedimentary rocks did you collect? How many metamorphic rocks did you collect? After you identify the class of each rock, try to name the rock.

MAPS in Action

Geologic Map of Virginia

Virginia

SCALE

Miles

Kilometers

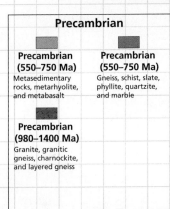

Precambrian

Precambrian (550–750 Ma)
Metasedimentary rocks, metarhyolite, and metabasalt

Precambrian (550–750 Ma)
Gneiss, schist, slate, phyllite, quartzite, and marble

Precambrian (980–1400 Ma)
Granite, granitic gneiss, charnockite, and layered gneiss

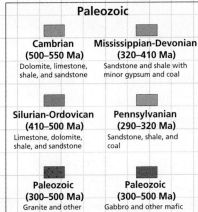

Paleozoic

Cambrian (500–550 Ma)
Dolomite, limestone, shale, and sandstone

Mississippian-Devonian (320–410 Ma)
Sandstone and shale with minor gypsum and coal

Silurian-Ordovician (410–500 Ma)
Limestone, dolomite, shale, and sandstone

Pennsylvanian (290–320 Ma)
Sandstone, shale, and coal

Paleozoic (300–500 Ma)
Granite and other felsic igneous rocks

Paleozoic (300–500 Ma)
Gabbro and other mafic igneous rocks

Mesozoic

Cretaceous (65–140 Ma)
Partly lithified sand, clay, and sandstone

Triassic-Jurassic (200–225 Ma)
Red and gray shale, sandstone, and conglomerate intruded by diabase and basalt

Cenozoic

Quaternary (20 ka–2 Ma)
Sand, mud, and gravel

Holocene (present–20 ka)
Sand, mud, and peat deposited in beaches, marshes, swamps, and estuaries

Tertiary (2–65 Ma)
Sand, mud, limy sand, and marl

Map ▶ Skills Activity

The colors on this map of Virginia represent rocks that formed at different times in Earth's past. These time spans are divisions of the geologic time scale, which divides Earth's history into eons, eras, periods, and epochs. Use the map to answer the questions below.

1. **Using a Key** From what geologic era and period are rocks found in Roanoke, Virginia?

2. **Analyzing Data** Near which cities in Virginia are the oldest rocks in the state found?

3. **Analyzing Data** Near which city in Virginia are the youngest rocks in the state found?

4. **Inferring Relationships** Some of the youngest sediments in Virginia are found along rivers. What do you think might explain this pattern?

5. **Identifying Trends** What are the differences between the three types of Precambrian rocks found in Virginia? Why do you think they are all located near each other?

6. **Analyzing Relationships** What are the age ranges of the oldest of each of the three rock types—igneous, metamorphic, and sedimentary—found in Virginia?

158 Chapter 6 **Rocks**

Key Ideas

Key Terms

Section 1

Rocks and the Rock Cycle

❯ The three major types of rock are igneous rock, sedimentary rock, and metamorphic rock.

❯ The rock cycle describes the natural processes through which each type of rock can change into any other type of rock.

❯ Bowen's reaction series describes the order in which different minerals form as magma cools.

❯ Chemical factors, such as mineral make up, and physical factors, such as joints and fractures, affect the stability of rocks.

rock cycle, p. 136

Bowen's reaction series, p. 137

Section 2

Igneous Rock

❯ Three factors that affect whether rock melts are temperature, pressure, and the presence of fluids in the rock.

❯ The rate at which magma cools determines the texture of the igneous rock that forms.

❯ Igneous rocks may be classified according to their composition and their texture.

❯ Intrusive igneous rock structures form underground and extrusive igneous rock structures form above ground.

igneous rock, p. 139

intrusive igneous rock, p. 141

extrusive igneous rock, p. 141

felsic, p. 142

mafic, p. 142

Section 3

Sedimentary Rock

❯ Compaction and cementation are two main processes that form sedimentary rock.

❯ Chemical sedimentary rock forms from minerals that were once dissolved in water, and organic sedimentary rocks form from the remains of living things.

❯ Clastic sedimentary rock forms from fragments of preexisting rocks that get compacted and cemented together.

❯ Seven sedimentary rock features are stratification, cross-beds, graded bedding, ripple marks, mud cracks, fossils, and concretions.

compaction, p. 145

cementation, p. 145

chemical sedimentary rock, p. 146

organic sedimentary rock, p. 146

clastic sedimentary rock, p. 147

Section 4

Metamorphic Rock

❯ Metamorphism changes one type of rock into another.

❯ Regional metamorphism occurs over a large geographic area. Contact metamorphism occurs in a small area near magma.

❯ Foliated metamorphic rocks have minerals arranged in bands, while nonfoliated metamorphic rocks do not.

metamorphism, p. 151

contact metamorphism, p. 152

regional metamorphism, p. 152

foliation, p. 153

nonfoliated, p. 154

1. **Summarizing Ideas** Look back at your summaries of each section. Now, summarize your summaries. For each section, write one or two sentences that summarize the main ideas of the whole section.

USING KEY TERMS

Use each of the following terms in a separate sentence.

2. *rock cycle* SC.912.E.6.2
3. *Bowen's reaction series* SC.912.E.6.2
4. *sediment* SC.912.E.6.2

For each pair of terms, explain how the meanings of the terms differ.

5. *igneous rock* and *metamorphic rock* SC.912.E.6.4
6. *intrusive igneous rock* and *extrusive igneous rock*
7. *chemical sedimentary rock* and *organic sedimentary rock*
8. *contact metamorphism* and *regional metamorphism*
9. *foliated* and *nonfoliated*

UNDERSTANDING KEY IDEAS

10. Intrusive igneous rocks are characterized by a coarse-grained texture because they contain SC.912.E.6.4
    a. heavy elements.
    b. small crystals.
    c. large crystals.
    d. fragments of different sizes and shapes.

11. Light-colored igneous rocks are generally part of the
    a. basalt family.
    b. intermediate family.
    c. felsic family.
    d. mafic family.

12. Magma that solidifies underground forms rock masses that are known as SC.912.E.6.4
    a. extrusions.
    b. volcanic cones.
    c. lava plateaus.
    d. intrusions.

13. One example of an extrusion is a
    a. stock.
    b. dike.
    c. batholith.
    d. lava plateau.

14. Sedimentary rock formed from rock fragments is called SC.912.E.6.4
    a. organic.
    b. chemical.
    c. clastic.
    d. granite.

15. One example of chemical sedimentary rock is
    a. an evaporite.
    b. coal.
    c. sandstone.
    d. breccia.

16. The splitting of slate into flat layers illustrates its
    a. contact metamorphism.   SC.912.E.6.4
    b. formation.
    c. sedimentation.
    d. foliation.

SHORT ANSWER

17. Describe partial melting and fractional crystallization. SC.912.E.6.4
18. Name and define the three main types of rock.
19. How do clastic sedimentary rocks differ from chemical and organic sedimentary rocks?
20. What is Bowen's reaction series? SC.912.E.6.4
21. What factors affect the chemical and physical stability of rock? SC.912.E.6.4
22. Describe three factors that affect whether rock melts. SC.912.E.6.4
23. Why are some metamorphic rocks foliated while others are not?
24. How does transport affect the size and shape of sediment particles?

CRITICAL THINKING

25. **Making Inferences** A certain rock is made up mostly of plagioclase feldspar and pyroxene minerals. It also includes olivine and hornblende. Will the rock have a light or dark coloring? Explain your answer. SC.912.E.6.4

26. **Classifying Information** Explain how metamorphic rock can change into either of the other two types of rock through the rock cycle. SC.912.E.6.4

27. **Applying Ideas** Imagine that you have found a piece of limestone, which is a sedimentary rock, that has strange-shaped lumps on it. Will the lumps have the same composition as the limestone? Explain your answer. SC.912.E.6.4

28. **Analyzing Ideas** Which would be easier to break, the foliated rock slate or the nonfoliated rock quartzite? Explain your answer. SC.912.E.6.4

CONCEPT MAPPING

29. Use the following terms to create a concept map: *rock cycle, foliated, igneous rock, intrusive, sedimentary rock, clastic sedimentary rock, metamorphic rock, chemical sedimentary rock, extrusive, organic sedimentary rock,* and *nonfoliated.*

MATH SKILLS   Math Skills

30. **Making Calculations** The gram formula weight (weight of one mole) of the mineral quartz is 60.1 g, and the gram formula weight of magnetite is 231.5 g. If you had 4 moles of magnetite, how many moles of quartz would be equal to the weight of the magnetite? SC.912.P.8.9

31. **Making Calculations** The gram formula weight (weight of one mole) of the mineral hematite, Fe_2O_3, is 159.7 g, and the gram formula weight of magnetite, Fe_3O_4, is 231.5 g. Which of the following would weigh more: half a mole of hematite or one-third of a mole of magnetite? SC.912.P.8.9

WRITING SKILLS

32. **Outlining Topics** Outline the essential steps in the rock cycle.

33. **Writing from Research** Find out what types of rock are most abundant in your state. Research the geologic processes that form those types of rock, and write a brief report that describes how the rocks in your state most likely formed. SC.912.E.6.4

INTERPRETING GRAPHICS

The graph below is a ternary diagram that shows the classification of some igneous rocks. Refer to Graphing Skills in Appendix B for instructions on how to read a ternary diagram. Use the diagram to answer the questions that follow.

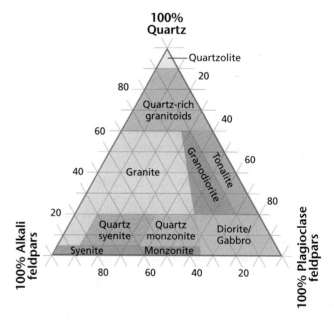

34. What is the maximum amount of quartz in a quartz syenite? SC.912.N.1.1

35. What would a rock that contains 30% quartz, 20% alkali feldspar, and 50% plagioclase feldspar be called? SC.912.N.1.1

Understanding Concepts

Directions (1–10): For each question, write on a sheet of paper the number of the correct answer.

1 Which of the following statements best describes the formation of fossils?
   A. An organism is caught in a lava flow.
   B. An organism is covered by layers of sediment.
   C. An organism is enveloped in magma that contains a high level of silica.
   D. An organism is covered by rock during a landslide.

2 The large, well-developed crystals found in some samples of granite are a sign that
   F. the lava from which it formed cooled rapidly.
   G. the magma contained a lot of dissolved gases.
   H. the lava from which it formed cooled slowly.
   I. water deposited minerals in the rock cavities.

3 How does coal differ from breccia?
   A. Coal is an example of sedimentary rock, and breccia is an example of metamorphic rock.
   B. Coal is an example of metamorphic rock, and breccia is an example of igneous rock.
   C. Coal is an example of organic rock, and breccia is an example of clastic rock.
   D. Coal is an example of clastic rock, and breccia is an example of a conglomerate.

4 How does the order in which igneous rocks form relate to their ability to resist weathering agents?
   F. Rocks that form last weather faster.
   G. Rocks that form first are the most resistant.
   H. Rocks that form last are the most resistant.
   I. There is no relationship between the order of igneous rock formation and weathering.

5 To make a statue, an artist uses a stone that formed from another type of stone by compression and that lacks bands. Which type of rock is the artist using?
   A. sedimentary
   B. igneous
   C. foliated metamorphic
   D. nonfoliated metamorphic

6 Igneous rock forms many intrusive structures. Which of the following statements describes a large igneous structure that forms on Earth's surface?
   F. a batholith, which spreads over at least 100 km^2
   G. a stock, which covers less than 100 km^2
   H. a laccolith, which forms when lava flows up between layers and forms a dome
   I. a sill, which lies parallel to the layers of rock around it

7 Dikes and sills are two types of igneous intrusions. What is the difference between dikes and sills?
   A. A dike is larger than a sill is.
   B. A sill is larger than 100 km^2 while a dike is smaller than 100 km^2.
   C. A dike cuts across rock layers while a sill lies between rock layers.
   D. A sill forms on Earth's surface while a dike forms beneath Earth's surface.

8 What occurs when heat from nearby magma causes changes in the surrounding rocks?
   F. contact metamorphism
   G. fluid metamorphism
   H. intrusive metamorphism
   I. regional metamorphism

9 A mountain in the desert is found to be made from the remains of ancient ocean organisms. Which type of rock makes up the mountain?
   A. chemical sedimentary rock
   B. clastic sedimentary rock
   C. organic sedimentary rock
   D. fossilized sedimentary rock

10 Which of the following statements about the texture of sedimentary rock is most likely true?
   F. Sedimentary rocks are always lumpy and made up of large pieces of older rocks.
   G. Sedimentary rocks all contain alternating bands of lumpy and smooth textures.
   H. Sedimentary rocks are always smooth and made up of small pieces of older rocks.
   I. Sedimentary rocks have a variety of textures that depend on the size and type of pieces that make up the rock.

Interpreting Graphics

Directions (11–12): For each question below, record the correct answer on a separate sheet of paper.

The Rock Cycle

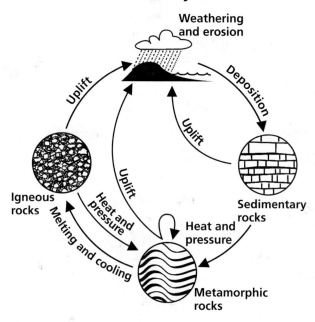

11 The diagram above shows several igneous rock formations. Which of the following processes brings rocks to Earth's surface, where they can be eroded?
- **A.** deposition
- **B.** weathering
- **C.** melting
- **D.** uplift

Rock Types

Rock sample	Characteristics
Rock A	multiple compacted, round, gravel-sized fragments
Rock B	coarse, well-developed, crystalline mineral grains
Rock C	small, sand-sized grains, tan coloration
Rock D	gritty texture; many small, embedded seashells

12 Of the rocks described in the table above, which most likely formed from organic sediments?
- **F.** rock A
- **G.** rock B
- **H.** rock C
- **I.** rock D

Test Tip

When several questions refer to the same graph, table, or diagram, or text passage, answer the questions you are sure of first.

Chapter 7

Resources and Energy

Chapter Outline

Modeling Mining

From your teacher, obtain a **pie plate** containing **birdseed** and **colored beads** that represents an area to "mine" using a **plastic spoon**. As you find sunflower seeds and different colors of beads, place them in separate piles. Determine the total value of your resources using these values: yellow beads, $25; green beads, $15; and sunflower seeds, $5. Your teacher will tell you the value that each white bead represents.

Questions to Get You Started

1. Determine your group's profit.

2. Why do you think the beads and seeds had different values?

SC.912.E.6.6

Why It Matters

People convert many types of energy to energy that is more useful. The energy of water moving through Hoover Dam is used to generate electricity. Supplies of some resources are diminishing. By understanding how these resources are used, scientists can search for sustainable, alternative resources.

Science Terms

Everyday Words Used in Science Many words used in science are familiar words from everyday speech. However, when these words are used in science, their meanings are often different from the everyday meanings.

Your Turn As you read Section 1, make a table like the one below for the terms *placer deposit, native element,* and *hydrothermal solution.* Write the scientific context of each term in the second column. Then, write the everyday meaning of each word listed in the third column.

Term	Scientific Context	Everyday Meaning
placer deposit		deposit—
native element		native—
hydrothermal solution		solution—

Predictions

The Language of Prediction Scientific theories can be used to explain things that happened in the past. They can also be used to make predictions about what will happen in the future. To recognize a statement of prediction, look for words such as these:

- the word *will* before a verb
- words such as *might* or *may*
- the word *if* followed first by a condition and then by a result

Your Turn As you read Sections 2 and 3, make a list of statements of prediction. In each statement, underline the key words that tell you the statement is a prediction. Some examples are given below.

Prediction Statements
- If a fission reaction is allowed to continue uncontrolled, the reaction will escalate quickly and may result in an explosion.
- If a nucleus is struck by a free neutron, however, the nucleus of the atom may split.

Graphic Organizers

Chain-of-Events Chart Use a chain-of-events chart when you need to remember the steps in a process.

Your Turn As you read Section 2, complete the chain-of-events chart that outlines the formation of coal.

For more information on how to use these and other tools, see **Appendix A.**

SECTION 1 Mineral Resources

Key Ideas	Key Terms	Why It Matters
❯ Explain what ores are and where they form. ❯ Identify why mineral resources are important. ❯ Describe four methods by which humans obtain mineral resources.	ore lode placer deposit gemstone	Minerals are sources of many types of useful materials. People use various mining techniques to obtain minerals.

Earth's crust contains useful mineral resources. The processes that formed many of these resources took millions of years. Many of these mineral resources are mined for human use. Mineral resources can be either *metals*, such as gold, Au, silver, Ag, and aluminum, Al, or *nonmetals*, such as sulfur, S, and quartz, SiO_2.

Ores

Metallic minerals, such as gold, silver, and copper, Cu, are called *native elements* and can exist in Earth's crust as nuggets of pure metal. But most other minerals in Earth's crust are *compounds* of two or more elements. Mineral deposits from which metals and nonmetals can be removed profitably are called **ores**. For example, the metal iron, Fe, can be removed from naturally occurring deposits of the minerals magnetite and hematite. Mercury, Hg, can be separated from cinnabar. Aluminum can be separated from bauxite.

Ores Formed by Cooling Magma

Ores form in a variety of ways, as shown in **Figure 1.** Some ores, such as ores of chromium, Cr, nickel, Ni, and lead, Pb, form within cooling magma. As the magma cools, dense metallic minerals sink. As the minerals sink, layers of these minerals accumulate at the bottom of the magma chamber to form ore deposits.

FLORIDA STANDARDS

LA.910.2.2.3 The student will organize information to show understanding or relationships among facts, ideas, and events (e.g., representing key points within text through charting, mapping, paraphrasing, summarizing, comparing, contrasting, or outlining);

ore a natural material whose concentration of economically valuable minerals is high enough for the material to be mined profitably

Figure 1 The Formation of Ores

Groundwater moving downward through rock is heated by magma. Dissolved metals crystallize out of the hot fluid to form new minerals.

When a body of water evaporates, minerals such as halite (rock salt) and gypsum crystallize.

Dissolved minerals that are carried into bodies of water crystallize on the bottom.

Magma

As magma moves upward through the crust, minerals form from the slow-cooling liquid.

lode a mineral deposit within a rock formation

placer deposit a deposit that contains a valuable mineral that has been concentrated by mechanical action

Academic Vocabulary

release (ri LEES) to set free; to let go

Ores Formed by Contact Metamorphism

Some ores of lead, copper, and zinc, Zn, form through the process of contact metamorphism. *Contact metamorphism* is a process that occurs when magma comes into contact with existing rock. Heat and chemical reactions with hot fluids from the magma can change the composition of the existing rock. These changes sometimes form ores.

Contact metamorphism can also form ore deposits when hot fluids called *hydrothermal solutions* move through small cracks in a large mass of rock. In this process, minerals from the surrounding rock dissolve into the hydrothermal solution. Over time, new minerals precipitate from the solution and form narrow zones of rock called *veins*. Veins commonly consist of ores of valuable heavy minerals, such as gold, tin, Sn, lead, and copper. When many thick mineral veins form in a relatively small region, the ore deposit is called a **lode.** Stories of a "mother lode" kept people coming to California during the California gold rush in the late 1840s and 1850s.

Ores Formed by Moving Water

The movement of water helps to form ore deposits. First, tiny fragments of native elements, such as gold, are released from rock as it breaks down by weathering. Then, streams carry the fragments until the currents become too weak to carry these dense metals. Finally, because of the mechanical action of the stream, the fragments become concentrated at the bottom of stream beds in **placer deposits.** A placer deposit is shown in **Figure 2.**

Reading Check Name two ways water creates ore deposits.
(See Appendix G for answers to Reading Checks.)

Figure 2 Placer deposits may occur at a river bend (left) or in holes downstream from a waterfall (right). Gold is a mineral that is commonly found in placer deposits. A stream carries heavy gold grains and nuggets, and then drops them where the current is weak.

Placer deposits

Placer deposits

Table 1 Minerals and Their Uses

Metallic minerals	Uses
Hematite and magnetite (iron)	for making steel
Galena (lead)	in car batteries; in solder
Gold, silver, and platinum	in electronics and dental work; as objects such as coins, jewelry, eating utensils, and bowls
Chalcopyrite (copper)	as wiring; in coins and jewelry; as building ornaments
Sphalerite (zinc)	for making brass and galvanized steel
Nonmetallic minerals	**Uses**
Diamond (carbon)	in drill bits and saws (industrial grade); in jewelry (gemstone quality)
Graphite (carbon)	in pencils, paint, lubricants, and batteries
Calcite	in cement; as building stone
Halite (salt)	for food preparation and preservation
Kaolinite (clay)	in ceramics, paper, cement, and bricks
Quartz (sand)	in glass and computer chips
Sulfur	in gunpowder, medicines, and rubber
Gypsum	in plaster and wallboard

Uses of Mineral Resources

Some metals, such as gold, platinum, Pt, and silver, are prized for their beauty and rarity. Metallic ores are sources of these valuable minerals and elements. Certain rare nonmetallic minerals called **gemstones** display extraordinary brilliance and color when they are specially cut for jewelry. Other nonmetallic minerals, such as calcite and gypsum, are used as building materials. **Table 1** shows some metallic and nonmetallic minerals and their common uses.

gemstone a mineral, rock, or organic material that can be used as jewelry or an ornament when it is cut and polished

Mineral Exploration and Mining

Companies that mine and recover minerals are often looking for new areas to mine. These companies identify areas that may contain enough minerals for economic recovery through mineral exploration. In general, an area is considered for mining if it has at least 100 to 1,000 times the concentration of minerals that are found elsewhere.

During mineral exploration, people search for mineral deposits by studying local geology. Airplanes that carry special equipment are used to measure and identify patterns in magnetism, gravity, radioactivity, and rock color. Exploration teams collect and test rock samples to determine whether the rock contains enough metal to make a mine profitable.

SCLINKS.

www.scilinks.org
Topic: Using Mineral
Resources
Code: HQX1587
Topic: Mining Minerals
Code: HQX0968

Subsurface Mining

Many mineral deposits are located below Earth's surface. These minerals are mined by miners who work underground to recover the deposits. This type of mining is called *subsurface mining*.

Surface Mining

When mineral deposits are located close to Earth's surface, they may be mined by using *surface mining* methods. In these methods, the overlying rock material is stripped away to reveal the mineral deposits. A large openpit copper mine is shown in **Figure 3.**

Placer Mining

Minerals in placer deposits are mined by dredging. In placer mining, large buckets are attached to a floating barge. The buckets scoop up the sediments in front of the barge. Dense minerals from placer deposits are separated from the surrounding sediments. Then, the remaining sediments are released into the water.

Undersea Mining

The ocean floor also contains mineral resources. *Nodules* are lumps of minerals on the deep-ocean floor that contain iron, manganese, Mn, and nickel, and that could become economically important if they could be recovered efficiently. However, because of their location, these deposits are very difficult to mine. Mineral deposits on land can be mined less expensively than deposits on the deep-ocean floor can.

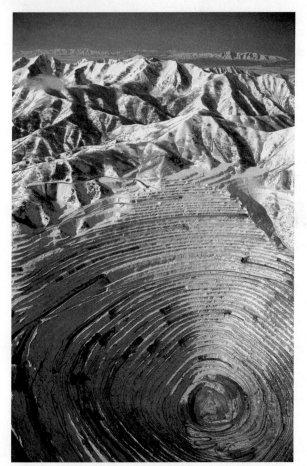

Figure 3 With a rim diameter of 4 km and a depth of almost 1 km, the Bingham Canyon Mine in Utah is the largest copper mine in the world.

Section 1 Review

LA.910.2.2.3; SC.912.E.6.2; SC.912.E.6.4

Key Ideas

1. **Define** *ore*.

2. **Describe** three ways that ore deposits form.

3. **Identify** two uses for each of the following minerals: sulfur, copper, and diamond.

4. **Summarize** the four main types of mining.

Critical Thinking

5. **Applying Ideas** Which properties of gold and copper make these metals suitable for use in electronics?

6. **Understanding Relationships** Why are dense minerals more likely to form placer deposits than less dense minerals are?

7. **Making Inferences** Why do you think that mining on land is less costly than mining in the deep ocean is?

Concept Mapping

8. Use the following terms to create a concept map: *mineral, ore, magma, contact metamorphism, vein, lode, placer deposit,* and *mine*.

SECTION 2 Nonrenewable Energy

Key Ideas	Key Terms	Why It Matters
❯ Explain why coal is a fossil fuel. ❯ Describe the formation of petroleum and natural gas. ❯ Describe how fossil fuels are used today. ❯ Explain how nuclear fission generates electricity.	nonrenewable resource fossil fuel nuclear fission nuclear fusion	Nonrenewable resources, such as fossil fuels, are limited in supply. People use fossil fuels as an energy resource. People use nuclear energy to generate electricity.

Many of Earth's resources are used to generate energy. Energy is used for transportation, manufacturing, and countless other activities that are important to society as we know it. Energy resources that exist in limited amounts and cannot be replaced quickly once they are used are examples of **nonrenewable resources.**

Fossil Fuels

Some of the most important nonrenewable resources are buried within Earth's crust. These natural resources—coal, petroleum, and natural gas—formed from the remains of living things. Because of their organic origin, coal, petroleum, and natural gas are called **fossil fuels.** Fossil fuels consist primarily of compounds of carbon and hydrogen called *hydrocarbons*. These compounds contain stored energy originally obtained from sunlight by plants and animals that lived millions of years ago. When hydrocarbons are burned, the formation of chemical bonds with oxygen (oxidation) releases energy as heat and light. Much of the energy humans use every day comes from the burning of fossil fuels.

Formation of Coal

The most commonly burned fossil fuel is coal. The coal deposits of today are the remains of plants that have undergone a complex process called *carbonization*. Carbonization occurs when partially decomposed plant material is buried in swamp mud and becomes peat. Bacteria consume some of the peat and release the gases methane, CH_4, and carbon dioxide, CO_2. As gases escape, the chemical content of the peat gradually changes until mainly carbon remains. The complex chemical and physical changes that produce coal happen only if there is no oxygen in the swamp. If the conditions are not right for carbonization or if the time required for coal formation has not elapsed, peat remains. Peat can also be used as an energy source, as shown in **Figure 1.**

FLORIDA STANDARDS

SC.912.N.4.1 Explain how scientific knowledge and reasoning provide an empirically-based perspective to inform society's decision making; **SC.912.P.10.10** Compare the magnitude and range of the four fundamental forces (gravitational, electromagnetic, weak nuclear, strong nuclear); **SC.912.P.10.11** Explain and compare nuclear reactions (radioactive decay, fission and fusion), the energy changes associated with them and their associated safety issues.

nonrenewable resource a resource that forms at a rate that is much slower than the rate at which the resource is consumed

fossil fuel a nonrenewable energy resource formed from the remains of organisms that lived long ago

Figure 1 Some people in Ireland and Scotland heat their houses with peat.

Figure 2 Types of Coal

Stage 1: Peat

The partial decomposition of plant remains forms a brownish-black material called *peat*.

Peat

Stage 2: Lignite

Peat is buried by other sediment. As heat and pressure increase, peat becomes lignite. Lignite is also called *brown coal*.

Lignite

Stage 3: Bituminous Coal

Increased temperature and pressure turn lignite into bituminous coal, which is 80% carbon. Bituminous coal is also called *soft coal*.

Bituminous coal

Stage 4: Anthracite

Under high temperature and pressure conditions, bituminous coal eventually becomes anthracite, which is the hardest form of coal.

Anthracite

Types of Coal Deposits

As peat is covered by layers of sediments, the weight of these sediments squeezes out water and gases. A denser material called *lignite* forms, as shown in the second stage of **Figure 2.** The increased temperature and pressure of more sediments compacts the lignite and forms *bituminous coal*. Bituminous coal is the most abundant type of coal. Where the folding of Earth's crust produces high temperatures and pressure, bituminous coal changes into *anthracite*, the hardest form of coal. Bituminous coal is made of 80% carbon, and anthracite is made of 90% carbon. Both release large amounts of energy as heat when they burn.

Formation of Petroleum and Natural Gas

When microorganisms and plants died in shallow prehistoric oceans and lakes, their remains accumulated on the ocean floor and lake bottoms and were buried by sediment. As more sediments accumulated, heat and pressure increased. Over millions of years, the heat and pressure caused chemical changes to convert the remains into petroleum and natural gas.

Petroleum and natural gas are mixtures of hydrocarbons. Petroleum, which is also called *oil*, is made of liquid hydrocarbons. Natural gas is made of hydrocarbons in the form of gas.

Math Skills

Coal Reserves There is thought to be more than 1,000 billion tons of coal on Earth that can be mined. If 4.5 billion tons are used worldwide every year, for how many years will Earth's coal reserves last? If coal use increases to 10 billion tons per year, for how many years will Earth's coal reserves last?

Petroleum and Natural Gas Deposits

Petroleum and natural gas are very important sources of energy for transportation, farming, and many other industries. Because of their importance, petroleum and natural gas deposits are valuable and are highly sought after. Petroleum and natural gas are most often mined from permeable sedimentary rock. *Permeable rocks* have interconnected spaces through which liquids can easily flow.

As sediments accumulate and sedimentary rock forms, pressure increases. This pressure forces fluids, including oil and gas, out of the pores and up through the layers of permeable rock. The fluids move upward until they reach a layer of *impermeable rock*, or rock through which liquids cannot flow, called *cap rock*. Petroleum that accumulates beneath the cap rock fills all the spaces to form an oil reservoir. Because petroleum is less dense than water, petroleum rises above any trapped water. Similarly, natural gas rises above petroleum, because natural gas is less dense than both oil and water.

Oil Traps

Geologists explore Earth's crust to discover the kinds of rock structures that may trap oil or gas. They look for oil trapped in places such as the ones shown in **Figure 3.** When a well is drilled into an oil reservoir, the petroleum and natural gas often flow to the surface. When the pressure of the overlying rock is removed, fluids rise up and out through the well.

Figure 3 Oil Traps

Many oil traps are anticlines, or upward folds in rock layers.

Another common type of oil trap is a fault, or crack, in Earth's crust that seals the oil- or gas-bearing formation.

Fossil-Fuel Supplies

Fossil fuels, like minerals, are nonrenewable resources. Globally, fossil fuels are one of the main sources of energy. *Crude oil*, or unrefined petroleum, is also used in the production of plastics, synthetic fabrics, medicines, waxes, synthetic rubber, insecticides, chemical fertilizers, detergents, shampoos, and many other products.

Coal is the most abundant fossil fuel in the world. Every continent has coal, but almost two-thirds of known deposits occur in three countries—the United States, Russia, and China. Scientists estimate that most of the petroleum reserves in the world have been discovered. However, scientists think that there are undiscovered natural gas reserves. There is also a relatively abundant material called *oil shale* that contains petroleum. But the cost of mining oil from shale is far greater than the present cost of recovering oil from other sedimentary rocks.

Reading Check What is cap rock?

SCI**LINKS**®

www.scilinks.org
Topic: Nonrenewable
    Resources
Code: **HQX1044**
Topic: Fossil Fuels
Code: **HQX0614**

Nuclear Energy

When scientists discovered that atoms had smaller <u>fundamental</u> parts, scientists wondered if atoms could be split. In 1919, Ernest Rutherford first studied and explained the results of bombarding atomic nuclei with high-energy particles. In the 30 years that followed his research, scientists developed nuclear (NOO klee uhr) technologies that allowed atomic weapons to be made and allowed nuclear reactions to be used to generate electricity. Energy that is produced by using these technologies is called *nuclear energy*.

Nuclear Fission

One form of nuclear energy is produced by splitting the nuclei of heavy atoms. This splitting of the nucleus of a large atom into two or more smaller nuclei is called **nuclear fission.** The process of nuclear fission is shown in **Figure 4.**

The forces that hold the nucleus of an atom together are more than 1 million times stronger than the strongest chemical bonds between atoms. If a nucleus is struck by a free neutron, however, the nucleus of the atom may split. When a large nucleus splits, it releases additional neutrons as well as energy. The newly released neutrons strike other nearby nuclei, which causes those nuclei to split and to release more neutrons and more energy. A chain reaction occurs as more neutrons strike neighboring nuclei. If a fission reaction is allowed to continue uncontrolled, the reaction will escalate quickly and may result in an explosion. However, controlled fission produces heat that can be used to generate electricity.

✓ Reading Check **What causes a chain reaction during nuclear fission?**

Academic Vocabulary

fundamental (FUHN duh MENT'l)
basic

nuclear fission the process by which the nucleus of a heavy atom splits into two or more fragments; the process releases neutrons and energy

www.scilinks.org
Topic: Nuclear Energy
Code: HQX1047

THINK central
INTERACT ONLINE
Keyword: HQXRENF4

Figure 4 An Example of a Nuclear Fission Reaction

Fission product

Proton

Neutron

ENERGY

ENERGY

ENERGY

❶ An intact nucleus is about to be struck by a neutron.

❷ When struck by a neutron, the nucleus splits, forms new elements, and releases neutrons plus energy.

❸ The released neutrons strike other nuclei.

❹ The nuclei split and release more neutrons and energy.

Figure 5 How a Nuclear Power Plant Generates Electricity

2 The superheated water is pumped into a heat exchanger, which transfers the heat of the first circuit to the second circuit. Water in the second circuit flashes into high-pressure steam.

3 Steam is directed against a turbine, setting it in motion. The turbine sets the generator in motion, generating electricity.

Cooling tower

Control rod

Steam

Electric current from generator

Second circuit

Water

Pump

Fuel rod

First circuit

Third circuit

1 Energy released by the nuclear reaction heats water in the pressurized first circuit to a high temperature.

4 A third circuit cools the steam from the turbine and the waste heat is released from the cooling tower in the form of steam.

How Fission Generates Electricity

When a nuclear power plant is working correctly, the chain reaction that occurs during nuclear fission is controlled. The flow of neutrons into the fission reaction is regulated so that the reaction can be slowed down, speeded up, or stopped as needed. The specialized equipment in which controlled nuclear fission is carried out is called a *nuclear reactor*.

During fission, a tremendous amount of heat energy is released. This heat energy can, in turn, be used to generate electricity. **Figure 5** shows how nuclear fission inside a nuclear reactor can be used to generate electricity. Currently, only one kind of naturally occurring element is used for nuclear fission. It is a rare isotope of the element uranium called *uranium-235*, or ^{235}U. Because ^{235}U is rare, the ore that is mined is processed into fuel pellets that have a high ^{235}U content. After this process is complete, the fuel pellets are said to be uranium-enriched pellets.

These enriched fuel pellets are placed into rods to make *fuel rods*. Bundles of these fuel rods are then bombarded by neutrons. When struck by a neutron, the ^{235}U nuclei in the fuel rods split and release neutrons and energy. The resulting chain reaction causes the fuel rods to become very hot.

Water is pumped around the fuel rods to absorb and remove the heat energy. The water is then pumped into a second circuit, where the water becomes steam. The steam turns the turbines that provide power for electric generators. A third water circuit carries away excess heat and releases it into the environment.

READING TOOLBOX

Chain-of-Events Chart
Create a chain-of-events chart to describe the process by which fission is used to generate electricity.

Figure 6 These water pools store radioactive wastes. The blue glow indicates that the waste products are highly radioactive.

nuclear fusion the process by which nuclei of small atoms combine to form a new, more massive nucleus; the process releases energy

Advantages and Disadvantages of Nuclear Fission

Nuclear power plants burn no fossil fuels and produce no air pollution. But because nuclear fission uses and produces radioactive materials that have very long half-lives, wastes must be safely stored for thousands of years. These waste products give off high doses of radiation that can destroy plant and animal cells and can cause harmful changes in the genetic material of living cells.

Currently, nuclear power plants store their nuclear wastes in dry casks or in onsite water pools, as shown in **Figure 6.** Other wastes are either stored onsite or transported to one of three disposal facilities in the United States. The U.S. Department of Energy has plans for a permanent disposal site for highly radioactive nuclear wastes.

Nuclear Fusion

All of the energy that reaches Earth from the sun is produced by a kind of nuclear reaction, called nuclear fusion. During **nuclear fusion,** the nuclei of hydrogen atoms combine to form larger nuclei of helium. This process releases energy. Fusion reactions occur only at temperatures of more than 15,000,000 °C.

For more than 50 years, scientists have been trying to harness the energy released by nuclear fusion to produce electricity. More research is needed before a commercial fusion reactor can be built. If such a reactor could be built in the future, hydrogen atoms from ocean water might be used as the fuel. With ocean water as fuel, the amount of energy available from nuclear fusion would be almost limitless. Scientists also think that wastes from fusion would be much less dangerous than wastes from fission. The only byproducts of fusion are helium nuclei, which are harmless to living cells.

Section 2 Review

LA.910.2.2.3; SC.912.E.6.2; SC.912.E.6.4; SC.912.P.10.11

Key Ideas

1. **Explain** why coal, petroleum, and natural gas are called *fossil fuels.*

2. **Compare** how coal, petroleum, and natural gas form.

3. **Describe** the kinds of rock structures in which petroleum reservoirs form.

4. **Identify** the naturally occurring element that is used for nuclear fission.

5. **Explain** how nuclear fission generates electricity.

6. **Summarize** the process of nuclear fusion.

Critical Thinking

7. **Analyzing Relationships** Why have we been able to build nuclear power plants for only the last 50 years?

8. **Recognizing Relationships** Can the waste products of nuclear fission be safely disposed of in rivers or lakes? Explain your answer.

9. **Making Comparisons** How do the processes of nuclear fusion and nuclear fission differ?

Concept Mapping

10. Use the following terms to create a concept map: *nonrenewable resource, fossil fuel, coal, carbonization, peat, lignite, bituminous coal, anthracite coal, petroleum,* and *natural gas.*

Renewable Energy

Key Ideas

❯ Explain how geothermal energy may be used as a substitute for fossil fuels.

❯ Describe two methods for harnessing energy from the sun.

❯ Describe four sources of renewable alternative energy.

Key Terms

renewable resource

geothermal energy

solar energy

hydroelectric energy

biomass

Why It Matters

Sources of renewable energy can be replaced quickly. Using renewable energy sources reduces pollution caused by the burning of fossil fuels.

If current trends continue and worldwide energy needs increase, the world's supply of fossil fuels may be used up in the next 200 years. Nuclear energy does not use fossil fuels, but numerous safety concerns are associated with it. Therefore, many nations are researching alternative energy sources to ensure that safe energy resources will be available far into the future. Resources that can be replaced within a human life span or as they are used are called **renewable resources.**

Geothermal Energy

In many locations, water flows far beneath Earth's surface. This water may flow through rock that is heated by nearby magma or by hot gases that are released by magma. This water becomes heated as it flows through the rock. The hot water, or the resulting steam, is the source of a large amount of heat energy. This heat energy is called **geothermal energy,** which means "energy from the heat of Earth's interior."

Engineers and scientists have harnessed geothermal energy by drilling wells to reach the hot water. Sometimes, water is first pumped down into the hot rocks if water does not already flow through them. The resulting steam and hot water can be used as a source of heat. The steam and hot water also serve as sources of power to drive turbines, which generate electricity.

The city of San Francisco, for example, obtains some of its electricity from a geothermal power plant located in the nearby mountains. In Iceland, 85% of the homes are heated by geothermal energy. Italy and Japan have also developed power plants that use geothermal energy. A geothermal power plant is shown in **Figure 1.**

FLORIDA STANDARDS

LA.910.2.2.3 The student will organize information to show understanding or relationships among facts, ideas, and events (e.g., representing key points within text through charting, mapping, paraphrasing, summarizing, comparing, contrasting, or outlining); **MA.912.S.1.2** Determine appropriate and consistent standards of measurement for the data to be collected in a survey or experiment.

renewable resource a natural resource that can be replaced at the same rate at which the resource is consumed

geothermal energy the energy produced by heat within Earth

Figure 1 These swimmers are enjoying the hot water near a geothermal power plant in Svartsbening, Iceland.

Solar Energy

Another source of renewable energy is the sun. Every 15 minutes, Earth receives enough energy from the sun to meet the energy needs of the world for one year. Energy from the sun is called **solar energy.** The challenge engineers face is how to capture even a small part of the energy that travels to Earth from the sun.

Converting sunshine into heat energy can be done in two ways. A house that has windows facing the sun collects solar energy through a *passive system.* The system is passive because it does not use moving parts. Sunlight enters the house and warms the building material, which stores some heat for the evening. An *active system* includes the use of solar collectors. One type of *solar collector* is a box that has a glass top. The box is commonly placed on the roof of a building. Water circulates through tubes within the box. The sun heats the water as it moves through the tubes, which provides heat and hot water. On cloudy days, however, there may not be enough sunlight to heat the water. So, the system must use heat that was stored from previous days.

Photovoltaic cells are another active system that converts solar energy directly into electricity. Photovoltaic cells work well for small objects, such as calculators. Producing enough electricity from these cells to power cities is under investigation.

solar energy the energy received by Earth from the sun in the form of radiation

SC.912.E.6.6

Quick Lab   Solar Collector

30 min

Procedure

1. Line the inside of a **small, shallow pan** with **black plastic.** Use **tape** to attach a **thermometer** to the inside of the pan. Fill the pan with enough **room-temperature water** to cover the end of the thermometer. Fasten **plastic wrap** over the pan with a **rubber band.** Be sure you can read the thermometer.

2. Place the pan in a sunny area. Use a **stopwatch** to record the temperature every 5 min until the temperature stops rising. Discard the water.

3. Repeat steps 1 and 2, but do not cover the pan with plastic wrap.

4. Repeat steps 1 and 2, but do not line the pan with black plastic.

5. Repeat steps 1 and 2. But do not line the pan with black plastic, and do not cover the pan with plastic wrap.

6. Calculate the rate of temperature change for each trial by subtracting the beginning temperature from the ending temperature. Divide your result by the number of minutes the temperature increased to find the rate of temperature change.

Analysis

1. What are the variables in this investigation? Which trial had the greatest rate of temperature change? the smallest rate of temperature change?

2. Which variable that you tested has the most significant effect on temperature change?

3. What materials would you use to design and build an efficient solar collector? Explain your answer.

Power lines

Dam

Water is discharged into a river or stream.

Penstock

Turbine

River or stream **Discharge pipe**

Reservoir

Generator

Water supply flows down the penstock from the reservoir.

Flowing water turns the turbine, which then turns the generator that generates electricity.

Figure 2 Hydroelectric power plants use moving water to turn turbines. The movement of each turbine powers a generator that generates electricity.

Energy from Moving Water

One of the oldest sources of energy comes from moving water. Energy can be harnessed from the running water of rivers and streams or from ocean tides. In some areas of the world, energy needs can be met by **hydroelectric energy,** or the energy produced by running water. Today, 6% of the electricity in the United States comes from hydroelectric power plants. At a hydroelectric plant, massive dams hold back running water and channel the water through the plant. Inside the plant, the water spins turbines, which turn generators that produce electricity. An example of a hydro-electric plant is shown in **Figure 2.**

Another renewable source of energy that comes from moving water is the tides. Tides are the rising and falling of sea level at certain times of the day. To make use of this tidal flow, people have built dams to trap the water at high tide and then release it at low tide. As the water is released, it turns the turbines within the dams.

Energy from Biomass

Other renewable resources are being <u>exploited</u> to help supply our energy needs. Renewable energy sources that come from plant material, manure, and other organic matter, such as sawdust or paper waste, are called **biomass.** Biomass is a major source of energy in many developing countries. More than half of all trees that are cut down are used as fuel for heating or cooking. Bacteria that decompose the organic matter produce gases, such as methane, that can also be burned. Liquid fuels, such as ethanol, also form from the action of bacteria on biomass. All of these resources can be burned to generate electricity.

Reading Check Name three sources of renewable energy.

hydroelectric energy electrical energy produced by the flow of water

biomass plant material, manure, or any other organic matter that is used as an energy source

Academic Vocabulary

exploit (EKS PLOYT) to use to the greatest possible advantage

www.scilinks.org
Topic: Renewable Resources
Code: HQX1291

Figure 3 The spinning blades of a wind turbine are connected to a generator. When winds cause the blades to spin faster, the generator produces more energy.

Energy from Wind

Wind is the movement of air over Earth's surface. Wind results from air-pressure differences caused by the sun's uneven heating of Earth's surface. Wind turbines use the movement of air to convert wind energy into mechanical energy, which is used to generate electricity.

Wind energy is now being used to produce electricity in locations that have constant winds. Small, wind-driven generators are used to meet the energy needs of individual homes. *Wind farms,* such as the one shown in **Figure 3,** may have hundreds of giant wind turbines that can produce enough energy to meet the electricity needs of entire communities. However, wind generators are not practical everywhere. Even in the most favorable locations, such as in windy mountain passes, the wind does not always blow. Because the wind does not always blow, wind energy cannot be depended on as the only energy source for most locations.

Section 3 Review

LA.910.2.2.3; SC.912.E.6.6

Key Ideas

1. **Explain** why many nations are researching alternative energy resources.

2. **Explain** how geothermal energy may be used as a substitute for fossil fuels.

3. **Describe** both passive and active methods of harnessing energy from the sun.

4. **Summarize** how electrical energy is generated from running water.

5. **Describe** how biomass can be used as fuel to generate electricity.

6. **Explain** how water and wind can be harnessed to generate electricity.

Critical Thinking

7. **Making Comparisons** Both fossil fuels and biomass fuels come from plant and animal matter. Why are fossil fuels considered to be nonrenewable, while biomass fuels are considered to be renewable?

8. **Demonstrating Reasoned Judgment** If you were asked to construct a power plant that uses only renewable energy sources in your area, what type of energy would you use? Explain.

Concept Mapping

9. Use the following terms to create a concept map: *renewable resource, solar collector, geothermal energy, solar energy, passive system, active system, hydroelectric energy, biomass,* and *wind energy.*

SECTION 4 Resources and Conservation

Key Ideas	Key Terms	Why It Matters
❯ Describe the importance of using fossil fuels wisely. ❯ Explain how the environmental impacts of mining can be reduced. ❯ Identify how conservation protects natural resources.	conservation recycling	The supply of fossil fuels is limited. Wise use of natural resources decreases waste and helps to protect the environment.

Scientists estimate that worldwide coal reserves will last about 200 years at the present rate of use. Many scientists also think that humans have already used half of Earth's oil supply. This limited supply of fossil fuels and other traditional energy resources has inspired research into possible new energy sources.

Scientists are also studying how the use of traditional energy sources affects Earth's ecosystems. We have learned that mining can damage or destroy fragile ecosystems. Fossil fuels and nuclear power generation may add pollution to Earth's air, water, and soil. However, people can reduce the environmental impact of their resource use. Many governments and public groups have worked to create and enforce policies that govern the use of these natural resources.

FLORIDA STANDARDS

SC.912.N.3.5 Describe the function of models in science, and identify the wide range of models used in science; **SC.912.N.4.1** Explain how scientific knowledge and reasoning provide an empirically-based perspective to inform society's decision making; **SC.912.P.10.11** Explain and compare nuclear reactions (radioactive decay, fission and fusion), the energy changes associated with them and their associated safety issues.

Environmental Impacts of Mining

Mining for minerals can cause a variety of environmental problems. Mining may cause both air and noise pollution. Nearby water resources may also be affected by water that carries toxic substances from mining processes. Surface mining is particularly destructive to wildlife habitats. For example, surface mining often uses controlled explosions to remove layers of rock and soil, as shown in **Figure 1.** Some mining practices cause increased erosion and soil degradation. Regions above subsurface mines may sink, or subside, because of the removal of the materials below. This sinking results in the formation of sinkholes. Fires in coal mines are also very difficult to extinguish and are commonly left to burn out, which may take several decades or centuries.

Figure 1 The surface of this gold mine in Nevada is being blasted to remove layers of rock.

Quick Lab

30 min

SC.912.E.6.6

Reclamation

Procedure

❶ Use a **plastic spoon** to remove the first layer of gelatin from a **multi-layered gelatin dessert cup** into a **small bowl**.

❷ Remove the next layer of gelatin, and discard it.

❸ Restore the dessert cup by replacing the first layer of gelatin.

Analysis

1. What does the first layer of gelatin on the restored dessert cup represent?

2. Does the "reclaimed" dessert cup resemble the original, untouched dessert cup?

3. What factors would you address to make reclamation more successful?

Academic Vocabulary

procure (proh KYUR) to get as a result of effort; obtain or acquire

Figure 2 Emissions testing and maintenance of pollution-reducing devices in today's vehicles can help reduce air pollution.

Mining Regulations

In the United States, federal and state laws regulate the operation of mines. These laws are designed to prevent mining operations from contaminating local air, water, and soil resources. Some of these federal laws include the Clean Water Act; the Safe Drinking Water Act; and the Comprehensive Environmental Response, Compensation, and Liability Act. All mining operations must also comply with the federal Endangered Species Act, which protects threatened or endangered species and their habitats from being destroyed by mining practices.

Mine Reclamation

To reduce the amount of damage done to ecosystems, mining companies are required to return mined land to its original condition after the mining has been completed. This process, called *reclamation*, helps reduce the long-lasting environmental impact of mining. In addition to reclamation, some mining operations work hard to reduce environmental damage through frequent inspections and by using processes that reduce environmental impacts.

Fossil Fuels and the Environment

Fossil-fuel procurement affects the environment. Strip mining of coal can leave deep holes where coal was removed. Without plants and topsoil to protect it, exposed land often erodes quickly. When rocks that are exposed during mining get wet, they can weather to form acids. If runoff carries the acids into nearby rivers and streams, aquatic life may be harmed.

Fossil-fuel use also contributes to air pollution. The burning of coal that has a high sulfur content releases large amounts of sulfur dioxide, SO_2, into the atmosphere. When SO_2 combines with water in the air, acid precipitation forms. When petroleum and natural gas are burned, they also release pollutants that can damage the environment. The burning of gasoline in cars is a major contributor to air pollution. But emissions testing, which is shown in **Figure 2**, and careful maintenance help reduce the amount of pollutants released into the air. Emissions testing and maintenance include the testing of a car's catalytic converter, a device that removes numerous pollutants from the exhaust before the exhaust leaves the car.

Reading Check Name two ways the use of fossil fuel affects the environment.

182

Conservation

Many people and businesses around the world have adopted practices that help reduce the negative effects of the burning of fossil fuels and the use of other natural resources. This preservation and wise use of natural resources is called **conservation.** By conserving natural resources, people can ensure that limited natural resources last longer. Conservation can also help reduce the environmental damage and amount of pollution that can result from the mining and use of natural resources.

Mineral Conservation

Earth's mineral resources are being used at a faster rate each year. Every new person added to the world's population represents a need for additional mineral resources. In developing countries, people are using more mineral resources as their countries become more industrialized. This increased demand for minerals has led many scientists to look for ways to conserve Earth's minerals.

One way to conserve minerals is to use other abundant or renewable materials instead of scarce or nonrenewable minerals. Another way to conserve minerals is by recycling them. **Recycling** is the process of using materials more than once. Some metals, such as iron, copper, and aluminum, are often recycled, as shown in **Figure 3.** Glass and many building materials can also be efficiently recycled. Recycling does require energy, but recycling uses less energy than the mining and manufacturing of new resources does.

Figure 3 These cubes are made up of metals that have been compacted and are being sent to a recycling plant. *Can you identify the source of these metals?*

conservation the preservation and wise use of natural resources

recycling the process of recovering valuable or useful materials from waste or scrap; the process of reusing some items

Why It Matters

Disposing of Electronic Waste

Consumers purchase millions of cell phones, MP3 players, and computers every year, often to replace broken or slightly outdated equipment. But electronic devices contain toxic materials such as heavy metals. Recycling electronics instead of throwing them in the trash prevents toxins from entering the environment.

HEAVY METALS PLAY FOREVER.
Don't dump lead and mercury—recycle your electronics.
www.RecycleWorks.org

Some recycled electronics can be reused or repaired. Others can be taken apart to recover components and materials.

YOUR TURN
ONLINE RESEARCH
Where in your area can you recycle electronic waste?

Figure 4 Fiberglass insulation is used in homes to reduce the energy required for heating and cooling.

Fossil-Fuel Conservation

Fossil fuels can be conserved by reducing the amount of energy used every day. If less energy is used, fewer fossil fuels must be burned every day to supply the smaller demand for energy. Energy can be conserved in many ways. **Figure 4** shows insulation being installed into a new house to reduce the amount of energy that will be needed for cooling and heating. Using energy-efficient appliances also reduces the amount of electricity used every day. In addition, simple actions, such as turning off lights when you leave a room and washing only full loads of laundry and dishes will reduce energy use.

Reducing the amount of driving you do also conserves fossil fuels. There is evidence that an average car produces more than 8 kg of carbon dioxide for every 3.8 L (1 gal) of gasoline burned. Even fuel-efficient and hybrid cars release some pollutants into the air. When making short trips, consider walking or riding a bicycle. If you need to use a car, combine errands so that you can make fewer trips.

Conservation of Other Natural Resources

Conservation is important for other natural resources, such as water. Some scientists estimate that by the year 2025, the world will have a critical shortage of freshwater resources because of the increased need by a larger human population. Water can be conserved by using water-saving shower heads, faucets, and toilets. By turning off the faucet as you brush your teeth, you can conserve up to 1 gallon of water every day. If you have a garden, you can help to conserve water by watering plants in the morning or at night and by planting native plants.

READING TOOLBOX

The Language of Prediction

As you read this page, make a list of statements of prediction. Underline the key words that tell you each statement is a prediction.

Section 4 Review

LA.910.2.2.3; SC.912.N.1.7; SC.912.N.4.1; SC.912.E.6.6; SC.912.P.10.11

Key Ideas

1. **Name** two environmental problems associated with the mining and use of coal.

2. **Explain** two ways the environmental impacts of mining can be reduced.

3. **Describe** two reasons why scientists are looking for alternatives to fossil fuels.

4. **Define** the term *reclamation* in your own words.

5. **Identify** three ways that you can conserve natural resources every day.

6. **State** one way that recycling can help conserve energy.

Critical Thinking

7. **Analyzing Concepts** How do you think fossil-fuel use affects soil resources?

8. **Applying Ideas** Why does recycling require less energy than developing a new resource does?

9. **Drawing Conclusions** List 10 ways a small community can conserve energy and resources.

Concept Mapping

10. Use the following terms to create a concept map: *recycling, conservation, alternative energy source, renewable energy source, environmental impact, acid precipitation,* and *reclamation.*

What Does Your Dream Car Run On?

Why pay lots of money for fuel that pollutes the environment? Scientists are developing cleaner alternatives to fossil fuels. One day you may be able to drive a zero-emission solar vehicle. People now build and race solar-powered cars, but the cars are not practical for day-to-day use. Adding features to the cars for safety and comfort would add too much weight and make the cars unacceptably slow. Right now, however, some mass-produced vehicles use hybrid technologies that reduce their need for fossil fuels.

Alternative-fuel vehicles

Because golf carts are lightweight, low-speed vehicles, **solar cells** can provide enough energy to run them.

Biofuels, such as the biodiesel this bus runs on, are made from plant and animal wastes.

Hybrid cars use two or more power sources. They produce fewer emissions than cars that run only on gasoline.

Cars that run mainly on **compressed air** are being developed. They produce little to no pollution.

BIODIESEL
B99

Biodiesel Fuel (B99.9)

14 13

YOUR TURN
UNDERSTANDING CONCEPTS
What are advantages of using alternatives to fossil fuels?

Blowing in the Wind

What You'll Do

> **Prepare** a detailed sketch of your solution to the design problem.

> **Design and build** a functional windmill that lifts a specific weight as quickly as possible.

What You'll Need

blow-dryer, 1,500 W
dowel or smooth rod
foam board
glue, white
paper clips, large (30)
paper cup, small
spools of thread, empty (2)
string, 50 cm
optional materials for windmill blades:
    foam board, paper plates, paper cups, or any other lightweight materials

Safety

MEMO

To: Division of Research and Development

Quixote Alternative Energy Systems is accepting design proposals to develop a windmill that can be used to lift window washers to the tops of buildings. As part of the design engineering division, your team has been asked to develop a working model of such a windmill. Your task is to design and build a model that can lift 30 large paper clips a vertical distance of 50 cm. The job will be given to the team whose model can lift the paper clips the fastest.

Ask a Question

1 What is the best windmill design?

Form a Hypothesis

2 Brainstorm with a partner or small group of classmates to design a windmill using only the objects listed in the materials list. Sketch your design, and write a few sentences about how you think your windmill will perform.

Test the Hypothesis

3 Have your teacher approve your design before you begin construction. Build the base for your windmill by using glue to attach the two spools to the foam board. Pass a dowel rod through the center of the spools. Make sure the spools are parallel and the dowel can rotate freely before you glue the spools. Attach one end of the string securely to the dowel between the two spools.

Step **3**

4 Poke a hole through the middle of the foam board to allow the string to pass through. Place your windmill base between two lab tables or in any area that will allow the string to hang freely.

5 After you have decided on your final design, attach the windmill blades to the base.

6 If you have time, you may want to try using different materials to construct your windmill blades. Test the various blades to determine whether they improve the original design. You may also want to vary the number and size of the blades on your windmill.

7 Attach the cup to the end of the string. Fill the cup with 30 paper clips. Turn on the blow-dryer, and measure the time it takes for your windmill to lift the cup.

Step 2
Sample windmill blade designs

Analysis and Conclusion

1. **Evaluating Methods** As a class, test all the designs to determine which design takes the shortest amount of time to lift the cup with the paper clips. What elements of the design do you think made the winning design the fastest?

2. **Evaluating Models** Describe how you would change your design to make your windmill work better or faster.

Extension

Research Windmills have been used for more than 2,000 years. Research the three basic types of vertical axis machines and the applications in which they are used. Prepare a report of your findings.

Making Models Adapt your design to make a water wheel. You will find that a water wheel can lift much more weight than a windmill can. Find designs on the Internet for micro-hydropower water wheels, such as the Pelton wheel, and use the designs as inspiration for your model. You can even design your own dam and reservoir.

Wind Power in the United States

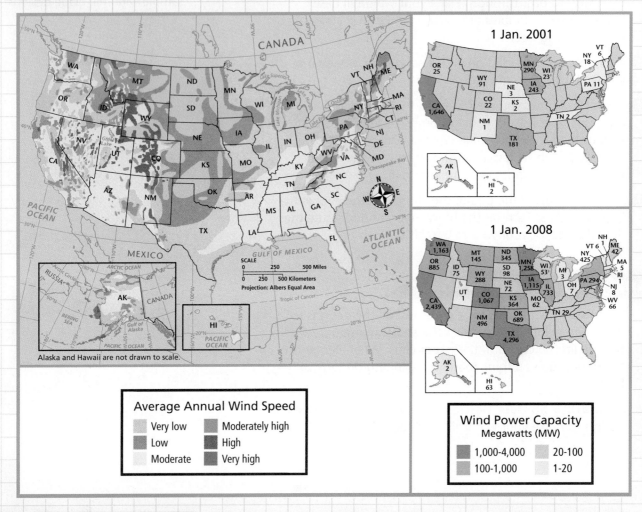

1 Jan. 2001

1 Jan. 2008

Wind Power Capacity
Megawatts (MW)

1,000-4,000	20-100
100-1,000	1-20

Average Annual Wind Speed

Very low	Moderately high
Low	High
Moderate	Very high

Map Skills Activity

This map shows average wind speeds and the locations of wind power projects throughout the United States. Use the map to answer the questions below.

1. **Using a Key** Name two states that have areas of very high wind speed.

2. **Using a Key** Which two states had the most wind power capacity in 2001?

3. **Making Comparisons** Did the two states with the most wind power capacity in 2001 still hold that rank in 2008? Explain.

4. **Analyzing Data** According to the map, which state has an area with the highest average annual wind speed?

5. **Inferring Relationships** Examine Idaho, Wyoming, Montana, and Colorado. What landscape feature might account for the strong winds in those states?

6. **Identifying Trends** Which states increased their wind power capacity by at least 10 times between 2001 and 2008?

7. **Making Comparisons** Because of their potential for wind power projects, the Great Plains states (MT, WY, CO, ND, SD, NE, KS, OK, TX, MN, and IA) have been called the "Saudi Arabia of wind energy." Why do you think this comparison has been made?

THINK
central
SUPER SUMMARY
Keyword: HQXRENS

| Key Ideas | Key Terms |

Section 1

Mineral Resources

❯ Ores are mineral deposits in Earth's crust from which metallic and nonmetallic minerals can be profitably removed.

❯ Minerals are important sources of many useful and valuable materials.

❯ Humans obtain mineral resources through subsurface, surface, placer, and undersea mining.

ore, p. 167
lode, p. 168
placer deposit, p. 168
gemstone, p. 169

Section 2

Nonrenewable Energy

❯ Chemical and physical processes changed the remains of ancient plants into coal.

❯ Petroleum and natural gas formed from the remains of ancient microorganisms.

❯ Today, fossil fuels provide much of the world's energy.

❯ The energy released by nuclear fission—the splitting of the nuclei of heavy atoms—can be used to generate electricity.

**nonrenewable
  resource,** p. 171
fossil fuel, p. 171
nuclear fission, p. 174
nuclear fusion, p. 176

Section 3

Renewable Energy

❯ Geothermal energy is energy from the heat of Earth's interior. Unlike fossil fuels, it can be replaced as it is used.

❯ Solar energy from the sun can be harnessed by both passive and active methods.

❯ Alternative sources of renewable energy include hydroelectric, tidal, solar, and wind energy.

renewable resource,
  p. 177
geothermal energy,
  p. 177
solar energy, p. 178
hydroelectric energy,
  p. 179
biomass, p. 179

Section 4

Resources and Conservation

❯ Fossil fuels are nonrenewable resources. Once a nonrenewable resource is depleted, the resource may take millions of years to be replenished.

❯ Responsible mining operations work hard to return mined land to good condition through reclamation.

❯ Conservation is the preservation and wise use of natural resources to ensure that they last longer.

conservation, p. 183
recycling, p. 183

Chapter 7 Review

1. **The Language of Prediction** In your own words, rephrase in the form of statements of prediction the explanation in Section 4 of how obtaining and using fossil fuels affect the environment.

READING TOOLBOX

USING KEY TERMS

Use each of the following terms in a separate sentence.

2. *placer deposit* SC.912.E.6.2

3. *solar energy*

4. *conservation*

For each pair of terms, explain how the meanings of the terms differ.

5. *renewable resource* and *nonrenewable resource* SC.912.E.6.6

6. *ore* and *lode*

7. *nuclear fission* and *nuclear fusion* SC.912.E.6.6

8. *fossil fuel* and *biomass* SC.912.E.6.6

9. *geothermal energy* and *hydroelectric energy* SC.912.E.6.6

UNDERSTANDING KEY IDEAS

10. Metals are known to
    a. have a dull surface.
    b. provide fuel.
    c. conduct heat and electricity well.
    d. occur only in placer deposits.

11. Energy resources that formed from the remains of once-living things are called
    a. minerals.   c. metals.
    b. gemstones.   d. fossil fuels.

12. Impermeable rock that occurs at the top of an oil reservoir is called
    a. coal.
    b. peat.
    c. cap rock.
    d. water.

13. Plastics, synthetic fabrics, and synthetic rubber are composed of chemicals that are derived from
    a. anthracite.   c. peat.   .
    b. petroleum.   d. minerals.

14. The splitting of the nucleus of an atom to produce energy is called
    a. geothermal energy.
    b. nuclear fission.
    c. nuclear fusion.
    d. hydroelectric power.

15. Energy experts have harnessed geothermal energy by
    a. building dams.
    b. building wind generators.
    c. drilling wells.
    d. burning coal.

16. In a hydroelectric power plant, running water produces energy by spinning a
    a. turbine.
    b. windmill.
    c. fan.
    d. reactor.

SHORT ANSWER

17. Compare the three ways that ores commonly form. SC.912.E.6.2

18. Name two regulations that mining operations must follow to reduce the impact they have on the environment. SC.912.E.6.6

19. Identify and describe the uses for three mineral resources.

20. Describe one advantage and one disadvantage of obtaining energy from nuclear fission. SC.912.E.6.6

21. Describe one advantage and one disadvantage of the use of solar energy. SC.912.E.6.6

22. Identify two ways recycling can reduce energy use. SC.912.E.6.6

23. Explain two ways that moving water can be used to generate electricity.

24. Compare two types of mining, and describe the possible environmental impact of each type. SC.912.E.6.6

25. **Applying Ideas** You learn that the price of iron is higher than it has been in 20 years. Do you think it might be profitable for a company to mine hematite? Explain your answer.

26. **Understanding Relationships** A certain area has extensive deposits of shale. Why might a petroleum geologist be interested in examining the area?

27. **Identifying Trends** Hybrid cars have efficient gasoline and electric motor combinations. They have other design elements that make them extremely fuel efficient. Do you expect that there will be more or fewer hybrid cars on the road in the future? Explain.

28. **Making Inferences** A certain company in your area produces ^{235}U pellets and fuel rods. With which energy source is the company involved? Explain.

CONCEPT MAPPING

29. Use the following terms to create a concept map: *resource, renewable, nonrenewable, fossil fuel, nuclear energy, geothermal energy, solar energy, hydroelectric energy,* and *conservation.* SC.912.E.6.6

MATH SKILLS

Math Skills

30. **Making Calculations** In one year, the United States produced 95,000 megawatts of power from renewable energy sources. If 3% of this power came from wind energy, how much energy did wind power produce that year? SC.912.E.6.6

31. **Making Calculations** A water-efficient washing machine uses 16 gallons of water per load of laundry. Older washing machines use more than 40 gallons of water per load of laundry. If you wash an average of 10 loads of laundry a month, how many gallons of water would you save in a year if you switched to the water-efficient washer?

WRITING SKILLS

32. **Researching Information** A debate surrounds municipal recycling programs. Do some research, and write a paragraph explaining each side of the debate. Write another paragraph explaining your view on whether recycling programs should be continued.

33. **Writing Persuasively** Research the pros and cons of building dams to harness energy. Write a letter to the editor of a local newspaper to express your opinion about whether dams should be used for generating electricity. SC.912.E.6.6

INTERPRETING GRAPHICS

The graph below shows the different contributions of various fuels to the U.S. energy supply since 1850. Use this graph to answer the questions that follow.

Energy Use in the United States

34. What were the two main energy sources used in 1875? SC.912.N.1.1

35. When did oil first become a more widely used energy source than coal? SC.912.N.1.1

36. The use of oil and natural gas rise and fall together. How do you explain this pattern? SC.912.N.1.1

Understanding Concepts

Directions (1–11): For each question, write on a separate sheet of paper the letter of the correct answer.

1 Nonmetallic minerals include gemstones and materials that are used in some building materials. Which of the following is an example of a nonmetallic mineral resource?
A. gold, which is used in jewelry
B. quartz, which is used in glass
C. aluminum, which is used in foil
D. galena, which is used in car batteries

2 Nonmetals are identified by their
F. ability to conduct heat.
G. ability to be mined.
H. ability to conduct electricity.
I. dull surfaces.

3 A mineral deposit called a *lode* is formed by
A. metal fragments deposited in stream beds.
B. layers accumulating in cooling magma.
C. hot mineral solutions in cracks in rock.
D. precipitation of minerals from seawater.

4 Which of the following is an example of a nonrenewable resource?
F. natural gas
G. sunlight
H. falling water
I. wind

5 Which of the following statements best describes coal?
A. It is a nonrenewable resource that formed from ancient plants.
B. It is a renewable resource that formed from the sun's energy.
C. It is a nonrenewable resource that forms in the presence of oxygen.
D. It is a renewable resource that contains hydrocarbons.

6 Fossil fuels are made up of organic remains and are a major source of energy for many people. From where does the energy in fossil fuels originate?
F. burning
G. heat
H. sunlight
I. carbonization

7 What process in the sun produces the energy that reaches Earth?
A. fusion of hydrogen atoms to form helium
B. fission of uranium isotopes
C. the splitting of atoms into smaller atoms
D. the burning of helium nuclei

8 Solar energy is one renewable resource that people often use. How do people collect solar energy?
F. They harness the energy by building dams.
G. They use boxes that have glass tops and allow the heating of water.
H. They drill wells to reach hot water.
I. They burn organic material to release energy.

9 Wind energy can be used to produce electricity. From where does wind energy originate?
A. giant wind turbines
B. uneven heating of the Earth's surface by the sun
C. within Earth
D. the movement of water in the ocean

10 How are biomass and fossil fuels similar?
F. They are both renewable forms of energy.
G. They both contain carbon.
H. They both result from nuclear reactions.
I. They have little impact on the environment when used for energy.

11 A material from which mineral resources can be mined profitably is a(n)
A. gemstone.
B. ore.
C. nodule.
D. renewable resource.

FLORIDA STANDARDS   LA.910.2.2.3; MA.912.S.3.2; SC.912.E.5.4; SC.912.E.6.2

Interpreting Graphics

Directions (12–13): For each question below, record the correct answer on a separate sheet of paper.

U.S. Energy Use from 1850 to 2100

12 The graph above illustrates the sources of energy used in the United States since 1850. Future statistics are predicted based on current trends and technology development. Which of the following is the main reason that coal became a more widely used energy source than wood in the mid-1800s?

F. Coal burns more easily than wood does.

G. Coal is a renewable resource, unlike wood.

H. Coal is a more efficient energy-producer than wood.

I. Coal produces fewer byproducts and waste than wood does.

Minerals and Their Uses

Minerals	Uses
Gold	electronics, coins, dental work, and jewelry
Galena	solder and batteries
Quartz	glass
Sulfur	medicines, gunpowder, and rubber
Graphite	pencils, paint, and lubricants
Hematite	making steel
Chalcopyrite	coins, jewelry, and cables

13 Electronic devices, such as radios and cell phones, contain components and substances that can harm the environment when the materials used to construct these devices are mined and when these devices are thrown away. Based on the table above, which of the following minerals are most likely found in these devices?

A. gold and galena

B. quartz and sulfur

C. graphite and hematite

D. chalcopyrite and graphite

> **Test Tip**
>
> When a question refers to a graph, study the data plotted on the graph to determine any trends or anomalies before you try to answer the question.

Geology Connections

Science, technology, and society are closely linked. This flowchart shows just a few of the connections in the history of geology.

359–299 Ma Forests, swamps, and oceans cover large areas of Earth's surface during the warm, humid Carboniferous Period.

1751 Benjamin Franklin publishes his theory of electricity.

8,000 B.C.E. Stone-age people in what is now China begin to mine coal for fuel use.

1882 The first electrical power generating plants open in Britain and the United States.

1200 B.C.E. The Iron Age begins in India, Greece, and the Near East. Early steel is produced in Africa.

1849 Frenchman Joseph Monier invents steel-reinforced concrete.

1824 Joseph Aspdin invents Portland cement.

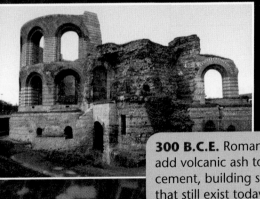

300 B.C.E. Roman builders add volcanic ash to cement, building structures that still exist today.

HISTORY IN SCIENCE

1859 Edwin Drake drills the first oil well in Western Pennsylvania, which leads to the growth of the modern oil industry in the Americas.

2006 The Venturi *Astrolab* becomes the world's first commercially available solar-electric hybrid car.

1886 Karl Benz receives a patent for inventing the first gasoline-fueled car.

1855 The Bessemer process makes steel abundant and inexpensive.

GAS SHORTAGE! Sales Limited to 10 GALS. OF GAS. PER CUSTOMER

1970s Oil shortages promote interest in conservation and alternative energy resources.

1935 Hoover Dam is the world's first major dam to be constructed from concrete.

1982 Solar One, the first large-scale solar power plant, begins operation near Barstow, California.

2007 Alamosa Skatepark Environment opens in Albuquerque, New Mexico.

YOUR TURN

UNDERSTANDING CONCEPTS
When did people first start using iron?

CRITICAL THINKING
How are the forests and swamps of the Carboniferous Period related to the coal we use today?

195

Chapter **8**

The Rock Record

Chapter Outline

Why It Matters

Rocks contain clues that show how and when they formed. Scientists study these clues to learn about Earth's history. Scientists also study fossils, such as the crinoids shown here. These animals have been living in aquatic environments on Earth for almost 490 million years.

Modeling Rock Layers

Use several types of small items to make layers in a beaker or jar. Each layer should be made up of only one type of item. Sketch the beaker or jar and the layers it contains.

Questions to Get You Started

1. Compare your sketch with other groups' sketches. Identify the oldest layer and the youngest layer. How can you tell?

2. Can you tell at what time each layer was made? Explain.

SC.912.E.6.4

These reading tools will help you learn the material in this chapter.

FoldNotes

Key-Term Fold A key-term fold can help you learn the key terms in this chapter.

Your Turn Create a key-term fold, as described in **Appendix A**.

1 Write one key term from the Summary page on the front of each tab.

2 As you read the chapter, write the definition of each term under its tab.

3 Use this FoldNote to study the key terms.

uniformitarianism
relative age
law of superposition
unconformity
law of crosscutting relationships
absolute age

Cause and Effect

Signal Words Certain words or phrases can signal cause-and-effect relationships. Words and phrases that signal causes include *cause, affect,* and *because.* Words and phrases that signal effects include *therefore, results in,* and *thus.* Sentences can also express cause-and-effect relationships without using explicit markers.

Your Turn In this chapter, you will read about cause-and-effect relationships that allow scientists to draw conclusions about the ages of rock layers and structures. Complete a table of cause-and-effect pairs like the table below.

CAUSE	EFFECT	MARKER(S)
movements of Earth's crust	Buried rock layers can be lifted up and exposed to erosion.	(none)

Note Taking

Outlining Taking notes in outline form can help you see how information is organized in a chapter. You can use your outline notes to review the chapter before a test.

Your Turn As you read through this chapter, make notes about the chapter in outline form. An example from Section 1 is shown on the right to help you get started.

1. DETERMINING RELATIVE AGE
   A. Uniformitarianism
      1. The principle of uniformitarianism states that current geologic processes are the same ones that operated in the past.
         a. Uniformitarianism was developed by James Hutton in the 18th century.
         b. Uniformitarianism is one of the basic foundations of geology.
      2. Geologists after Hutton noted that, although geologic processes are the same through time, their rates may vary.

For more information on how to use these and other tools, see **Appendix A**.

Determining Relative Age

Key Ideas

❯ State the principle of uniformitarianism.

❯ Explain how the law of superposition can be used to determine the relative ages of rocks.

❯ Compare three types of unconformities.

❯ Apply the law of crosscutting relationships to determine the relative ages of rocks.

Key Terms

uniformitarianism

relative age

law of superposition

unconformity

law of crosscutting relationships

Why It Matters

By determining the relative ages of rock layers and structures, we can better understand the processes that shape the world around us.

Geologists estimate that Earth is about 4.6 billion years old. The idea that Earth is billions of years old originated with the work of James Hutton, an 18th-century Scottish physician and farmer. Hutton, who is shown in **Figure 1**, wrote about agriculture, weather, climate, physics, and even philosophy. Hutton was also a keen observer of the geologic changes taking place on his farm. Using scientific methods, Hutton drew conclusions based on his observations. Today, he is most famous for his ideas and writings about geology.

Uniformitarianism

Hutton concluded that the same forces that changed the landscape of his farm had changed Earth's surface in the past. He thought that by studying the present, people could learn about Earth's past. Hutton's principle of **uniformitarianism** is that current geologic processes, such as volcanism and erosion, are the same processes that were at work in the past. This principle is one of the basic foundations of the science of geology. Geologists later refined Hutton's ideas by pointing out that although the processes of the past and present are the same, the rates of the processes may vary over time.

FLORIDA STANDARDS

SC.912.N.2.5 Describe instances in which scientists' varied backgrounds, talents, interests, and goals influence the inferences and thus the explanations that they make about observations of natural phenomena and describe that competing interpretations (explanations) of scientists are a strength of science as they are a source of new, testable ideas that have the potential to add new evidence to support one or another of the explanations.

uniformitarianism a principle that geologic processes that occurred in the past can be explained by current geologic processes

Figure 1 James Hutton (left) thought that studying the present is the key to understanding the past. This modern-day geologist (right) is looking for clues to Earth's past.

What's Your Relative Age?

Procedure

❶ Form a group with 5 to 10 of your classmates.

❷ Work together to arrange group members in order from oldest to youngest.

Analysis

1. How did you determine your classmates' relative ages?

2. How did the relative ages compare to the absolute ages of your classmates?

3. How is this process of determining relative and absolute age different from the way scientists date rocks?

Academic Vocabulary

sequence (SEE kwuhns) the order in which things come or events happen

relative age the age of an object in relation to the ages of other objects

Earth's Age

Before Hutton's research was undertaken, many people thought that Earth was only about 6,000 years old. They also thought that all geologic features had formed at the same time. Hutton's principle of uniformitarianism raised some serious questions about Earth's age. Hutton observed that the forces that changed the land on his farm operated very slowly. He reasoned that millions of years must be needed for those same forces to create the complicated rock structures observed in Earth's crust. He concluded that Earth must be much older than previously thought. Hutton's observations and conclusions about the age of Earth encouraged other scientists to learn more about Earth's history. One way to learn about Earth's past is to determine the order in which rock layers and other rock structures formed.

Reading Check **What evidence did Hutton propose to show that Earth is very old?** (See Appendix G for answers to Reading Checks.)

Relative Age

In the same way that a history book shows an order of events, layers of rock, called *strata*, show the sequence of events that took place in the past. Using a few basic principles, scientists can determine the order in which rock layers formed. Once they know the order, a relative age can be determined for each rock layer. **Relative age** indicates that one layer is older or younger than another layer but does not indicate the rock's age in years.

Various types of rock form layers. Igneous rocks form layers when successive lava flows stack on top of each other. Metamorphic rocks that formed from layered rocks can have layers. To determine the relative ages of rocks, however, scientists commonly study the layers in sedimentary rocks, such as those shown in **Figure 2.**

Figure 2 The layers of sedimentary rock that make up this butte near Caineville, Utah were deposited over millions of years.

Skeletons and shells of dead marine organisms settle to the ocean bottom and pile up.

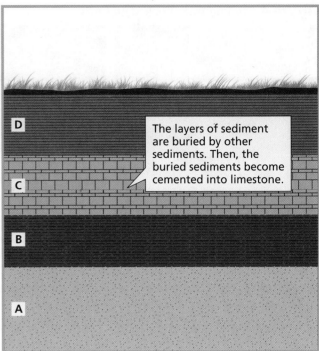

The layers of sediment are buried by other sediments. Then, the buried sediments become cemented into limestone.

Law of Superposition

Sedimentary rocks form when new sediments are deposited on top of old layers of sediment. As the sediments accumulate, they are compressed and become naturally cemented into sedimentary rock layers that are called *beds*. The boundary between two beds is called a *bedding plane*.

Scientists use a basic principle called the law of superposition to determine the relative age of a layer of sedimentary rock. The **law of superposition** states that an undeformed sedimentary rock layer is older than the layers above it and younger than the layers below it. According to the law of superposition, layer A, shown in **Figure 3**, was the first layer deposited, and thus it is the oldest layer. The last layer deposited was layer D, and thus it is the youngest layer.

Principle of Original Horizontality

Scientists also know that sedimentary rock generally forms in horizontal layers. The *principle of original horizontality* states that sedimentary rocks left undisturbed will remain in horizontal layers. Therefore, scientists can assume that sedimentary rock layers that are not horizontal have been tilted or deformed by crustal movements that happened after the layers formed.

In some cases, tectonic forces push older layers on top of younger layers or overturn a group of rock layers. In such cases, the law of superposition cannot be easily applied. So, scientists must look for clues to the original position of layers and then apply the law of superposition.

Figure 3 By applying the law of superposition, geologists are able to determine that layer D is the youngest bed in this rock section. *According to the law of superposition, is layer B older or younger than layer C?*

law of superposition the principle that a sedimentary rock layer is older than the layers above it and younger than the layers below it if the layers are not disturbed

www.scilinks.org
Topic: Law of Superposition
Code: HQX0858

Figure 4 Sedimentary Rock Structures

Graded Bedding Heavy particles settle to the bottom of a lake or river faster than smaller particles do and create graded beds like these.

Cross-Beds As sand slides down the slope of a large sand dune, the sand forms slanting layers like the ones shown here.

Ripple Marks When waves move back and forth on a beach, ripple marks like these commonly form.

Graded Bedding

One possible clue to the original position of rock layers is the size of the particles in the layers. In some depositional environments, the largest particles of sediment are deposited in the bottom layers, as shown in **Figure 4.** The arrangement of layers in which coarse and heavy particles are located in the bottom layers is called *graded bedding*. If larger particles are located in the top layers, the layers may have been overturned by tectonic forces.

Cross-Beds

Another clue to the original position of rock layers is in the shape of the bedding planes. When sand is deposited, sandy sediment forms beds at an angle to the bedding plane. These beds are called *cross-beds* and are shown in **Figure 4.** The tops of these layers commonly erode before new layers are deposited. So, the sediment appears to be curved at the bottom of the layer and to be cut off at the top. By studying the shape of the cross-beds, scientists can determine the original position of these layers.

Ripple Marks

Ripple marks are small waves that form on the surface of sand because of the action of water or wind. When the sand becomes sandstone, the ripple marks may be preserved, as shown in **Figure 4.** In undisturbed sedimentary rock layers, the crests of the ripple marks point upward. By examining the orientation of ripple marks, scientists can establish the original arrangement of the rock layers. The relative ages of the rocks can then be determined by using the law of superposition.

Reading Check How can ripple marks indicate the original position of rock layers?

Unconformities

Movements of Earth's crust can lift up rock layers that were buried and expose them to erosion. Then, if sediments are deposited, new rock layers form in place of the eroded layers. The missing rock layers create a break in the geologic record in the same way that pages missing from a book create a break in a story. A break in the geologic record is called an **unconformity.** An unconformity shows that deposition either stopped for a period of time, or rock may have been removed by erosion before deposition resumed.

As shown in **Table 1,** there are three types of unconformities. An unconformity in which stratified rock rests upon unstratified rock is called a *nonconformity.* The boundary between a set of tilted layers and a set of horizontal layers is called an *angular unconformity.* The boundary between horizontal layers of old sedimentary rock and younger, overlying layers that are deposited on an eroded surface is called a *disconformity.* According to the law of superposition, all rocks beneath an unconformity are older than the rocks above the unconformity.

unconformity a break in the geologic record created when rock layers are eroded or when sediment is not deposited for a long period of time

Table 1 Types of Unconformities

Type	Example	Description
Nonconformity		Unstratified igneous or metamorphic rock may be uplifted to Earth's surface by crustal movements. Once the rock is exposed, it erodes. Sediments may then be deposited on the eroded surface. The boundary between the new sedimentary rock and the igneous or metamorphic rock is a *nonconformity.* The boundary represents an unknown period of time during which the older rock was eroded.
Angular unconformity		An angular unconformity forms when rock deposited in horizontal layers is folded or tilted and then eroded. When erosion stops, a new horizontal layer is deposited on top of a tilted layer. When the bedding planes of the older rock layers are not parallel to those of the younger rock layers deposited above them, an angular unconformity results.
Disconformity		Sometimes, layers of sediments are uplifted without folding or tilting and are eroded. Eventually, the area subsides and deposition resumes. The layers on either side of the boundary are deposited horizontally. Although the rock layers look as if they were deposited continuously, a large time gap exists where the upper and lower layers meet. This gap is known as a *disconformity.*

Figure 5 The law of crosscutting relationships can be used to determine the relative ages of rock layers and the faults and intrusions within them.

Igneous intrusion   Fault

Crosscutting Relationships

When rock layers have been disturbed by faults or intrusions, determining relative age may be difficult. A *fault* is a break or crack in Earth's crust along which rocks shift their position. An *intrusion* is a mass of igneous rock that forms when magma is injected into rock and then cools and solidifies. In such cases, scientists may apply the law of crosscutting relationships. The **law of crosscutting relationships** is that a fault or igneous intrusion is always younger than the rock layers it cuts through. If a fault or intrusion cuts through an unconformity, the fault or intrusion is younger than all the rocks it cuts through above and below the unconformity.

Figure 5 shows a series of rock layers that contains both a fault and an igneous intrusion. As you can see, an intrusion cuts across layers A, B, and C. According to the law of crosscutting relationships, the intrusion is younger than layers A, B, and C. The fault is younger than the intrusion and all four layers.

law of crosscutting relationships the principle that a fault or body of rock is younger than any other body of rock that it cuts through

---

Section 1 Review

LA.910.2.2.3; SC.912.E.6.2; SC.912.E.6.4

Key Ideas

1. **Explain** why it is important for scientists to be able to determine the relative ages of rocks.

2. **State** the principle of uniformitarianism in your own words.

3. **Explain** how the law of superposition can be used to determine the relative age of sedimentary rock.

4. **Explain** the difference between an unconformity and a nonconformity.

5. **Compare** an angular unconformity with a disconformity.

6. **Describe** how the law of crosscutting relationships helps scientists determine the relative ages of rocks.

Critical Thinking

7. **Making Comparisons** Which would be more difficult to recognize: a nonconformity or a disconformity? Explain your answer.

8. **Analyzing Relationships** Suppose that you find a series of rock layers in which a fault ends at an unconformity. Explain how you could apply the law of crosscutting relationships to determine the relative age of the fault and of the rock layers that were deposited above the unconformity.

Concept Mapping

9. Use the following terms to create a concept map: *principle of original horizontality, relative age, graded bedding, law of superposition, cross-bed,* and *ripple mark.*

Determining Absolute Age

Key Ideas	Key Terms	Why It Matters
> Summarize the limitations of using the rates of erosion and deposition to determine the absolute age of rock formations. > Describe the formation of varves. > Explain how the process of radioactive decay can be used to determine the absolute ages of rocks.	absolute age varve radiometric dating half-life	The absolute age of a rock can be determined using radioactive elements. This information helps us understand how our planet formed and continues to change.

Relative age indicates only that one rock formation is younger or older than another rock formation. To learn more about Earth's history, scientists often need to determine the numeric age, or **absolute age,** of a rock formation.

Absolute Dating Methods

Scientists use a variety of methods to measure absolute age. Some methods involve geologic processes that can be observed and measured over time. Other methods involve the chemical composition of certain materials in rock.

Rates of Erosion

One way to <u>estimate</u> absolute age is to study rates of erosion. For example, if scientists measure the rate at which a stream erodes its bed, they can estimate the age of the stream. But determining absolute age by using the rate of erosion is practical only for geologic features that formed within the past 10,000 to 20,000 years. One example of such a feature is Niagara Falls, which is shown in **Figure 1.** For older surface features, such as the Grand Canyon, which formed over millions of years, the method is less dependable because rates of erosion may vary greatly over millions of years.

FLORIDA STANDARDS

SC.912.N.3.5 Describe the function of models in science, and identify the wide range of models used in science; SC.912.P.10.11 Explain and compare nuclear reactions (radioactive decay, fission and fusion), the energy changes associated with them and their associated safety issues.

absolute age the numeric age of an object or event, often stated in years before the present, as established by an absolute-dating process, such as radiometric dating

Academic Vocabulary

estimate (ES tuh MAYT) to calculate approximately

Figure 1 The rocky ledge that forms Niagara Falls has been eroding at a rate of about 1.3 m per year for nearly 9,900 years. *How many kilometers has the ledge been eroded in the last 9,900 years?*

Math Skills

Deposition If 30 cm of sediments are deposited every 1,000 years, how long would 10 m of sediments take to accumulate?

READING TOOLBOX

Key-Term Fold Make a FoldNote for methods that can be used to determine absolute age. List each method and give three facts about how it is used.

varve a pair of sedimentary layers (one coarse, one fine) that is deposited in an annual cycle, commonly in glacial lakes, and that can be used to determine absolute age

Rates of Deposition

Another way to estimate absolute age is to calculate the rate of sediment deposition. By using data collected over a long period of time, geologists can estimate the average rates of deposition for common sedimentary rocks such as limestone, shale, and sandstone. In general, about 30 cm of sedimentary rock are deposited over a period of 1,000 years. However, any given sedimentary layer that is being studied may not have been deposited at an average rate. For example, a flood can deposit many meters of sediment in just one day. In addition, the rate of deposition may change over time. Therefore, this method of determining absolute age is not always accurate; it merely provides an estimate.

Varve Count

You may know that a tree's age can be estimated by counting the growth rings in its trunk. Scientists have devised a similar method for estimating the age of certain sedimentary deposits. Some sedimentary deposits show definite annual layers, called **varves,** that consist of a light-colored band of coarse particles and a dark band of fine particles.

Varves generally form in glacial lakes. During the summer, when snow and ice melt rapidly, a rush of water can carry large amounts of sediment into a lake. Most of the coarse particles settle quickly to form a layer on the bottom of the lake. With the coming of winter, the surface of the lake begins to freeze. Fine clay particles still suspended in the water settle slowly to form a thin layer on top of the coarse sediments. A coarse summer layer and the overlying, fine winter layer make up one varve. Thus, each varve represents one year of deposition. Some varves are shown in **Figure 2.** By counting the varves, scientists can estimate the age of the sediments.

Reading Check How are varves like tree rings?

Figure 2 Varves (below), which form in glacial lakes (right), can be counted to determine the absolute age of sediments.

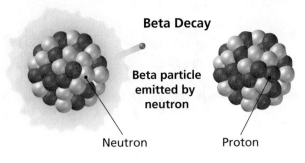
Beta Decay

Beta particle emitted by neutron

Neutron   Proton

Alpha Decay

Alpha particle (two protons and two neutrons) emitted by nucleus

Radiometric Dating

Rocks generally contain small amounts of radioactive material that can act as natural clocks. Atoms of the same element that have different numbers of neutrons are called *isotopes. Radioactive isotopes* have nuclei that emit particles and energy at a constant rate regardless of surrounding conditions. **Figure 3** shows two of the ways that radioactive isotopes decay. During the emission of the particles, large amounts of energy are released. Scientists use this natural breakdown of isotopes to accurately measure the absolute age of rocks. The method of using radioactive decay to measure absolute age is called **radiometric dating.**

As an atom emits particles and energy, the atom changes into a different isotope of the same element or an isotope of a different element. Scientists measure the concentrations of the original radioactive isotope, or *parent isotope,* and of the newly formed isotopes, or *daughter isotopes*. Using the known decay rate, the scientists compare the proportions of the parent and daughter isotopes to determine the absolute age of the rock.

Figure 3 Beta decay and alpha decay are two forms of radioactive decay. In all forms of radioactive decay, an atom emits particles and energy.

radiometric dating a method of determining the absolute age of an object by comparing the relative percentages of a radioactive (parent) isotope and a stable (daughter) isotope

Exposing a Fake Mummy

FORENSIC SCIENCE

"Genuine 2,600-year-old artifact for sale!" How could a potential buyer know whether this claim is true or false? Radiometric dating, based on carbon isotopes, can help. As well as being used to determine the age of rocks, radiometric dating is used in forensics to unmask art forgers and unethical antiquities dealers.

Preparation Steps

🔥 Burn a tiny sample of the coffin's wood and collect the gas.

☢ Analyze the proportions of carbon isotopes in the gas.

👤 Determine the age of the wood. At only 250 years old, it is too young to be genuine.

YOUR TURN UNDERSTANDING CONCEPTS
How is radiometric dating used to expose archaeological frauds?

Figure 4 After each half-life, one-half of the parent isotope (shown in red) is converted into a daughter isotope (shown in blue). After four half-lives, only 1/16 of the parent isotope remains.

half-life the time required for half of a sample of a radioactive isotope to break down by radioactive decay to form a daughter isotope

Half-Life

Radioactive decay happens at a relatively constant rate that is not changed by temperature, pressure, or other environmental conditions. Scientists have determined that the time required for half of any amount of a particular radioactive isotope to decay is always the same and can be determined for any isotope. Therefore, a **half-life** is the time it takes half the mass of a given amount of a radioactive parent isotope to decay into its daughter isotopes. If you began with 10 g of a parent isotope, you would have 5 g of that isotope after one half-life of that isotope. At the end of a second half-life, one-fourth, or 2.5 g, of the original isotope would remain. Three-fourths of the sample would now be the daughter isotope. This process is shown in **Figure 4.**

By comparing the amounts of parent and daughter isotopes in a rock sample, scientists can determine the age of the sample. The greater the percentage of daughter isotopes present in the sample, the older the rock is. But comparing parent and daughter isotopes works only when the sample has not gained or lost either parent or daughter isotopes through leaking or contamination.

SC.912.E.6.4

Quick Lab   Radioactive Decay

Procedure
1 Use a **clock or watch that has a second hand** to record the time.
2 Wait 20 s, and then use **scissors** to carefully cut a **sheet of paper** in half. Select one piece, and set the other piece aside.
3 Repeat step 2 until nine 20 s intervals have elapsed.

Analysis
1. What does the whole piece of paper used in this investigation represent?
2. What do the pieces of paper that you set aside in each step represent?
3. What is the half-life of your paper isotope?
4. How much of your paper isotope was left after the first three intervals? after six intervals? after nine intervals? Express your answers as percentages.
5. What two factors in your model must remain constant so that your model is accurate? Explain your answer.

Table 1 Radiometric Dating Methods

Radiometric dating methods	Parent isotope	Daughter isotope	Half-life	Effective dating range
Radiocarbon dating	carbon-14, ^{14}C	nitrogen-14, ^{14}N	5,730 years	less than 70,000 years
Argon-argon dating, ^{39}Ar/^{40}Ar	potassium-40, ^{40}K irradiated to form argon-39, ^{39}Ar	argon-40, ^{40}Ar	1.25 billion years	10,000 to 4.6 billion years
Potassium-argon dating, ^{40}K/^{40}Ar	potassium-40, ^{40}K	argon-40, ^{40}Ar	1.25 billion years	50,000 to 4.6 billion years
Rubidium-strontium dating, ^{87}Rb/^{87}Sr	rubidium-87, ^{87}Rb	strontium-87, ^{87}Sr	48.1 billion years	10 million to 4.6 billion years
Uranium-lead dating, ^{235}U/^{207}Pb	uranium-235, ^{235}U	lead-207, ^{207}Pb	704 million years	10 million to 4.6 billion years
Uranium-lead dating, ^{238}U/^{206}Pb	uranium-238, ^{238}U	lead-206, ^{206}Pb	4.5 billion years	10 million to 4.6 billion years
Thorium-lead dating ^{232}Th/^{208}Pb	thorium-232, ^{232}Th	lead-208, ^{208}Pb	14.0 billion years	greater than 200 million years

Radioactive Isotopes

The amount of time that has passed since a rock formed determines which radioactive element will give a more accurate age measurement. If too little time has passed since radioactive decay began, there may not be enough of the daughter isotope for accurate dating. If too much time has passed, there may not be enough of the parent isotope left for accurate dating.

Uranium-238, ^{238}U (which is read as "U two thirty-eight"), has an extremely long half-life of 4.5 billion years. ^{238}U is most useful for dating geologic samples that are more than 10 million years old, as long as they contain uranium. In addition to ^{238}U, several other radioactive isotopes are used to date rock samples. One such isotope is potassium-40, ^{40}K, which has a half-life of 1.25 billion years. ^{40}K occurs in mica, clay, and feldspar and is used to date rocks that are between 50,000 and 4.6 billion years old. Rubidium-87, ^{87}Rb, has a half-life of about 48 billion years. ^{87}Rb, which commonly occurs in minerals that contain ^{40}K, can be used to verify the age of rocks previously dated by using ^{40}K. **Table 1** provides a list of other radiometric dating methods.

www.scilinks.org
Topic: Radiometric Dating
Code: HQX1261

Reading Check How does the half-life of an isotope affect the accuracy of the radiometric dating method?

Carbon Dating

Figure 5 This scientist is preparing a mammoth's tooth for carbon-14 dating, which will determine the tooth's absolute age.

Younger rock layers may be dated indirectly by dating organic material found within the rock. The ages of wood, bones, shells, and other organic remains that are included in the layers and that are less than 70,000 years old can be determined by using a method known as *carbon-14 dating,* or *radiocarbon dating,* as shown in **Figure 5.** The isotope carbon-14, ^{14}C, combines with oxygen to form radioactive carbon dioxide, CO_2. Most CO_2 in the atmosphere contains nonradioactive carbon-12, ^{12}C. Only a small amount of CO_2 in the atmosphere contains ^{14}C.

Plants absorb CO_2, which contains either ^{12}C or ^{14}C, during photosynthesis. Then, when animals eat the plants or the plant-eating animals, the ^{12}C and ^{14}C become part of the animals' body tissues. Thus, all living organisms contain both ^{12}C and ^{14}C.

To find the age of a small amount of organic material, scientists first determine the ratio of ^{14}C to ^{12}C in the sample. Then, they compare that ratio with the ratio of ^{14}C to ^{12}C known to exist in a living organism. While organisms are alive, the ratio of ^{12}C to ^{14}C remains relatively constant. When a plant or an animal dies, however, the ratio begins to change. The half-life of ^{14}C is only about 5,730 years. Because the organism is dead, it no longer absorbs ^{12}C and ^{14}C, and the amount of ^{14}C in the organism's tissues decreases steadily as the radioactive ^{14}C decays to nonradioactive nitrogen-14, ^{14}N.

Section 2 Review

LA.910.2.2.3; SC.912.E.6.2; SC.912.E.6.4; SC.912.P.10.11

Key Ideas

1. **Differentiate** between relative and absolute age.

2. **Summarize** why calculations of absolute age based on rates of erosion and deposition can be inaccurate.

3. **Describe** varves, and describe how and where they form.

4. **Explain** how radiometric dating is used to estimate absolute age.

5. **Define** half-life, and explain how it helps determine an object's absolute age.

6. **List** three methods of radiometric dating, and explain the age range for which they are most effective.

Critical Thinking

7. **Demonstrating Reasoned Judgment** Suppose you have a shark's tooth that you suspect is about 15,000 years old. Would you use ^{238}U or ^{14}C to date the tooth? Explain your answer.

8. **Making Inferences** You see an advertisement for an atomic clock. You also know that radioactive decay emits harmful radiation. Do you think the atomic clock contains decaying isotopes? Explain.

Concept Mapping

9. Use the following terms to create a concept map: *absolute age, varve, radiometric dating, parent isotope, daughter isotope,* and *carbon dating.*

The Fossil Record

Key Ideas	Key Terms	Why It Matters
❯ Describe four ways in which entire organisms can be preserved as fossils. ❯ List five examples of fossilized traces of organisms. ❯ Describe how index fossils can be used to determine the age of rocks.	fossil paleontology trace fossil index fossil	Fossils give information about the ages of rocks. They also give information about changes in life forms and the environment throughout time.

The remains or traces of animals or plants that lived in a previous geologic time are called **fossils.** Fossils, such as the one shown in **Figure 1,** are an important source of information for finding the relative and absolute ages of rocks. Fossils also provide clues to past geologic events, climates, and the evolution of living things over time. The study of fossils is called **paleontology.**

Almost all fossils are discovered in sedimentary rock. The sediments that cover the fossils slow or stop the process of decay and protect the body of the dead organism from damage. Fossils are rare in igneous rock or highly metamorphosed rock because intense heat, pressure, and chemical reactions that occur during the formation of these rock types destroy all organic structures.

FLORIDA STANDARDS

SC.912.N.3.5 Describe the function of models in science, and identify the wide range of models used in science; **SC.912.P.10.11** Explain and compare nuclear reactions (radioactive decay, fission and fusion), the energy changes associated with them and their associated safety issues.

Interpreting the Fossil Record

The fossil record provides information about the geologic history of Earth. By revealing how organisms have changed throughout the geologic past, fossils provide important clues to the environmental changes that occurred in Earth's past. For example, fossils of marine animals and plants have been discovered in areas far from any ocean. These fossils tell us that such areas were covered by an ocean in the past. Scientists can use this information to learn about how environmental changes have affected living organisms.

fossil the trace or remains of an organism that lived long ago, most commonly preserved in sedimentary rock

paleontology the scientific study of fossils

Figure 1 Paleontologists are unearthing the remains of rhinoceroses that are 10 million years old at this site in Orchard, Nebraska.

Fossilization

Normally, dead plants and animals are eaten by other animals or decomposed by bacteria. If left unprotected, even hard parts such as bones decay and leave no record of the organism. Only dead organisms that are buried quickly or protected from decay can become fossils. Generally, only the hard parts of organisms, such as wood, bones, shells, and teeth, become fossils. In rare cases, an entire organism may be preserved. In some types of fossils, only a replica of the original organism remains. Other fossils merely provide <u>evidence</u> that life once existed. **Table 1** describes different ways that fossils can form.

Academic Vocabulary

evidence (EV uh duhns) information showing whether an idea is true or valid

READING TOOLBOX

Outlining
Create an outline using the main ideas from this section. Include all key ideas, key terms, and red topic headings. Use your outline to review the material.

Table 1 How Fossils Form

Mummification Mummified remains are often found in very dry places, because most bacteria, which cause decay, cannot survive in these places. Some ancient civilizations mummified their dead by carefully extracting the body's internal organs and then wrapping the body in carefully prepared strips of cloth.

Amber Hardened tree sap is called *amber*. Insects become trapped in the sticky sap and are preserved when the sap hardens. In many cases, delicate features such as legs and antennae have been preserved. In rare cases, DNA has been recovered from amber.

Tar Seeps When thick petroleum oozes to Earth's surface, the petroleum forms a tar seep. Tar seeps are commonly covered by water. Animals that come to drink the water can become trapped in the sticky tar. Other animals prey on the trapped animals and can also become trapped. The remains of the trapped animals are covered by the tar and preserved.

Freezing The low temperatures of frozen soil and ice can protect and preserve organisms. Because most bacteria cannot survive freezing temperatures, organisms that are buried in frozen soil or ice do not decay.

Petrification Minerals that precipitate from groundwater solutions replace original organic materials that have been buried under layers of sediment. Some common petrifying minerals are silica, calcite, and pyrite. The substitution of minerals for organic material often results in the formation of a nearly perfect mineral replica of the original organism.

Table 2 Types of Fossils

Carbon films Carbonized residue of leaves, stems, flowers, and fish have been found preserved in sedimentary rock made of soft mud or clay. When original organic material partially decays, it leaves behind a carbon-rich film that displays the surface features of the organism.

Molds and Casts Shells often leave empty spaces called *molds* within hardened sediment. When a shell is buried, its remains eventually dissolve and leave an empty space. When sand or mud fills a mold and turns into rock, a natural cast forms. A cast is a replica of the original organism.

Coprolites Fossilized dung or waste materials from ancient animals are called *coprolites*. They can be cut into thin sections and observed through a microscope. The materials identified in these sections reveal the feeding habits of ancient animals, such as dinosaurs.

Gastroliths Some dinosaurs had stones in their digestive systems to help grind their food. In many cases, these stones, which are called *gastroliths*, survive as fossils. Gastroliths can often be recognized by their smooth, polished surfaces and by their close proximity to dinosaur remains.

Types of Fossils

Fossils can show a remarkable amount of detail about ancient organisms. **Table 2** describes some of these fossils. In some cases, no part of the original organism survives in fossil form. But **trace fossils,** or fossilized evidence of past animal movement such as tracks, footprints, borings, and burrows, can still provide information about prehistoric life.

A trace fossil, such as the footprint of an animal, is an important clue to the animal's appearance and activities. Suppose that a giant dinosaur left deep footprints in soft mud. Sand or silt may have blown or washed into the footprint so gently that the footprints remained intact. Then, more sediment may have been deposited over the prints. As time passed, the mud containing the footprints turned into sedimentary rock and preserved the footprints. Scientists have discovered ancient footprints of reptiles, amphibians, birds, and mammals.

trace fossil a fossilized mark that formed in sedimentary rock by the movement of an animal on or within soft sediment

Reading Check What is a trace fossil?

SCI*LINKS*

www.scilinks.org
Topic: Fossil Record
Code: HQX0615

Index Fossils

Paleontologists can use fossils to determine the relative ages of the rock layers in which the fossils are located. Fossils that occur only in rock layers of a particular geologic age are called **index fossils.** To be an index fossil, a fossil must meet certain requirements. First, it must be present in rocks scattered over a large region. Second, it must have features that clearly distingish it from other fossils. Third, the organisms from which the fossil formed must have lived during a short span of geologic time. Fourth, the fossil must occur in fairly large numbers within the rock layers.

Figure 2 If you discovered fossils such as these ammonites, you would know that the surrounding rock formed between 180 million and 206 million years ago.

index fossil a fossil that is used to establish the age of rock layers because it is distinct, abundant, and widespread and existed for only a short span of geologic time

Index Fossils and Absolute Age

Scientists can use index fossils to estimate absolute ages of specific rock layers. Because organisms that formed index fossils lived during short spans of geologic time, the rock layer in which an index fossil was discovered can be dated accurately. The ammonite fossils in **Figure 2** show that the rock in which the fossils were observed formed between 180 million and 206 million years ago.

Scientists can also use index fossils to date rock layers in separate areas. So, an index fossil discovered in rock layers in different areas of the world indicates that the rock layers in these areas formed during the same time period.

Geologists also use index fossils to help locate rock layers that are likely to contain oil and natural gas deposits. These deposits form from plant and animal remains that change by chemical processes over millions of years.

Section 3 Review

LA.910.2.2.3; SC.912.E.6.2; SC.912.E.6.4

Key Ideas

1. **Describe** four ways in which an entire organism can be preserved as a fossil.

2. **List** four types of fossils that can be used to provide indirect evidence of organisms.

3. **Explain** how geologists use fossils to date sedimentary rock layers.

4. **Compare** the process of mummification with the process of petrification.

5. **Describe** how index fossils can be used to determine the ages of rocks.

Critical Thinking

6. **Applying Ideas** What characteristic do all good sources of animal fossils have in common?

7. **Identifying Relationships** If a rock layer in Mexico and a rock layer in Australia contain the same index fossil, what do you know about the absolute ages of the layers in both places? Explain your answer.

Concept Mapping

8. Use the following terms to create a concept map: *fossils, mummification, amber, tar seep, freezing,* and *petrification.*

A Record of Yellowstone's Explosive Past

Would you feel safe camping on top of an active volcano with a destructive past? At Yellowstone National Park, people do, every day! Yellowstone's geysers are perched on one of Earth's largest active volcanoes. The rock record shows that three giant eruptions took place at Yellowstone, throwing massive amounts of volcanic ash into the air between 2.1 million and 640,000 years ago.

As a geyser's water heats up, pressure mounts underground, eventually forcing water high into the air.

Yellowstone's largest eruption created the Huckleberry Ridge ash bed, which formed this hillside.

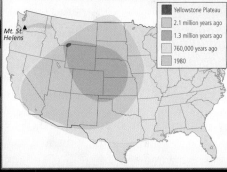

Ash deposits from a Yellowstone eruption have been identified more than 2,000 km away from the eruption site!

Yellowstone Plateau
2.1 million years ago
1.3 million years ago
760,000 years ago
1980

Mt. St. Helens

Yellowstone is shaped like a basin. Its giant eruptions expelled so much material that the ground collapsed into the magma chamber below.

YOUR TURN

CRITICAL THINKING

How do you think scientists made the map that shows the extent of the volcanic deposits from Yellowstone's giant eruptions?

Making Models **Lab**

What You'll Do

> **Model** how different types of fossils form.

> **Demonstrate** how certain types of fossils form.

What You'll Need

clay, modeling
container, plastic
hard objects such as a shell, key, paper clip, or coin
leaf
newspaper
paper, carbon, soft
paper, white (1 sheet)
pencil (or wood dowel)
plaster of Paris
spoon, plastic
tweezers
water
wax paper

Safety

Types of Fossils

Paleontologists study fossils to find evidence of the kinds of life and conditions that existed on Earth in the past. Fossils are the remains of ancient plants and animals or evidence of their presence. In this lab, you will use various methods to make models of fossils.

Procedure

1 Place a ball of modeling clay on a flat surface that is covered with wax paper.

2 Press the clay down to form a flat disk about 8 cm in diameter. Turn the clay over so that the smooth, flat surface is facing up.

3 Choose a small, hard object. Press the object onto the clay carefully so that you do not disturb the indentation. Is the indentation left by the object a mold or a cast? What features of the object are best shown in the indentation? Sketch the indentation.

4 On a second piece of smooth, flat clay, make a shallow imprint to represent the burrow or footprint of an animal. Sketch your fossil imprint.

5 Fill the plastic container with water to a depth of 1 to 2 cm. Stir in enough plaster of Paris to make a paste that has the consistency of whipped cream.

6 Using the plastic spoon, fill both indentations with plaster. Allow excess plaster to run over the edges of the imprints. Let the plaster set for about 15 min, until it hardens.

Step **3**

7 After the plaster has hardened, remove both pieces of plaster from the clay. Do the pieces of hardened plaster represent molds or casts?

8 Place the carbon paper on a flat surface with the carbon facing up. Gently place the leaf on the carbon paper, and cover it with several sheets of newspaper. Roll the pencil or wooden dowel back and forth across the surface of the newspaper several times, and press firmly to bring the leaf into full contact with the carbon paper.

9 Remove the newspaper. Lift the leaf by using the tweezers, and place it on a clean sheet of paper with the carbon-coated side facing down. Cover the leaf with clean wax paper, and roll your pencil across the surface of the wax paper.

10 Remove the wax paper and leaf. Observe and describe the carbon film left by the leaf.

Step 6

Step 9

Analysis

1. **Analyzing Results** Look at the molds and casts made by others in your class. Identify as many of the objects used to make the molds and casts as you can.

2. **Making Comparisons** How does the carbon film you made differ from an actual carbonized film fossil?

3. **Applying Ideas** Trace fossils are evidence of the movement of an animal on or within soft sediment. Why are carbon films, molds, and casts not considered trace fossils?

Extension

Making Predictions Which organism—a rabbit, a housefly, an earthworm, or a snail—would be most likely to form fossils? Which of these organisms would leave trace fossils? Explain.

MAPS *in Action*

Geologic Map of Bedrock in Ohio

KEY

- Permian
- Pennsylvanian
- Mississippian
- Devonian
- Silurian
- Ordovician

Glacial boundary

0   20   40 miles
0 10 30   50 kilometers

Springfield — Columbus — Zanesville — Permian — WEST VIRGINIA
INDIANA
- - - Cambrian and Ordovician
Precambrian

Map Skills Activity

This map shows the ages of the bedrock in Ohio. Bedrock is the solid rock that lies underneath all surface soil and other loose material. Use the map to answer the questions below.

1. **Using a Key** What geologic periods are represented by the bedrock in Ohio?

2. **Analyzing Data** Where is the youngest bedrock in Ohio? Where is the oldest bedrock in Ohio?

3. **Identifying Trends** If you traveled from east to west across Ohio, how would the ages of the rock beneath you change?

4. **Analyzing Relationships** Based on the geologic cross section, how does the shape of the rock beds cause rocks of different ages to be exposed at different places in Ohio?

5. **Identifying Relationships** Why is Mississippian rock likely to be located next to Devonian rock?

6. **Using a Key** The first reptiles appeared in the fossil record during the Pennsylvanian Period. If you wanted to look for fossils of these reptiles in Ohio, in what part of the state would you look? Explain your answer.

Key Ideas

Key Terms

Determining Relative Age

❯ According to the principle of uniformitarianism, the forces that are changing Earth's surface today are the same forces that changed Earth's surface in the past.

❯ In undeformed rock layers, the youngest layer is on the top and the oldest layer is on the bottom, according to the law of superposition.

❯ Nonconformities, angular unconformities, and disconformities are interruptions in the sequence of rock layers and are collectively known as unconformities.

❯ According to the law of crosscutting relationships, a geologic feature is always younger than the rock it cuts through.

uniformitarianism,
  p. 201
relative age, p. 202
law of superposition,
  p. 203
unconformity, p. 205
law of crosscutting
  relationships, p. 206

Determining Absolute Age

❯ Because rates of erosion and deposition can change over time, they are imprecise methods for determining absolute ages of rocks.

❯ Varves are layers of sediment that form in glacial lakes as a result of the annual cycle of freezing and thawing of the glacier.

❯ Radioactive elements decay at constant and measurable rates and can be used to determine absolute age.

absolute age, p. 207
varve, p. 208
radiometric dating,
  p. 209
half-life, p. 210

The Fossil Record

❯ Entire organisms may be preserved in amber, in tar seeps, or through freezing or mummification.

❯ Fossilized evidence of organisms includes trace fossils, carbon films, molds, casts, coprolites, and gastroliths.

❯ Index fossils occur only in rock layers of a particular geologic age, and they can help geologists estimate the age of rock formations.

fossil, p. 213
paleontology, p. 213
trace fossil, p. 215
index fossil, p. 216

1. **Key-Term Fold** Use the FoldNote that you made at the beginning of the chapter to study the key terms for this chapter. See if you know all of the definitions. When you have reviewed the terms, use each term in a sentence.

USING KEY TERMS

Use each of the following terms in a separate sentence.

2. *uniformitarianism*

3. *varve*

4. *radiometric dating*

5. *half-life*

For each pair of terms, explain how the meanings of the terms differ.

6. *relative age* and *absolute age*

7. *law of superposition* and *law of crosscutting relationships*

8. *trace fossil* and *index fossil*

UNDERSTANDING KEY IDEAS

9. Varves are layers of SC.912.E.6.4
   a. limestone mixed with coarse sediments.
   b. alternating coarse and fine sediments.
   c. fossils.
   d. sediments that have gaps that represent missing time in the rock sequence.

10. An unconformity that results when new sediments are deposited on eroded horizontal layers is a(n) SC.912.E.6.4
    a. angular unconformity.
    b. disconformity.
    c. crosscut unconformity.
    d. nonconformity.

11. A fault or intrusion is younger than the rock it cuts through, according to the SC.912.E.6.4
    a. type of unconformity.
    b. law of superposition.
    c. law of crosscutting relationships.
    d. principle of uniformitarianism.

12. The age of a rock in years is the rock's numerical age, or
    a. index age.
    b. relative age.
    c. half-life age.
    d. absolute age.

13. A gap in the sequence of rock layers is a(n) SC.912.E.6.4
    a. bedding plane.
    b. varve.
    c. unconformity.
    d. uniformity.

14. The process by which the remains of an organism are preserved by drying is called SC.912.E.6.4
    a. petrification.
    b. mummification.
    c. erosion.
    d. superposition.

15. Molds that fill with sediment sometimes produce
    a. casts.
    b. gastroliths.
    c. coprolites.
    d. carbon films.

SHORT ANSWER

16. What prompted James Hutton to formulate the principle of uniformitarianism?

17. Describe how the law of superposition helps scientists determine relative age.

18. Compare and contrast the three types of unconformities.

19. How do scientists use radioactive decay to determine absolute age? SC.912.E.6.4

20. Besides radiometric dating, what are three other methods of estimating absolute age?

21. List and describe five ways that organisms can be preserved. SC.912.E.6.4

22. List the four characteristics that define an index fossil.

CRITICAL THINKING

23. **Making Inferences** James Hutton developed the principle of uniformitarianism by observing geologic changes on his farm. What changes might he have observed? SC.912.E.6.4

24. **Applying Ideas** How might a scientist determine the original positions of the sedimentary layers beneath an angular unconformity? SC.912.E.6.4

25. Analyzing Relationships One intrusion cuts through all the rock layers. Another intrusion is eroded and lies beneath several layers of sedimentary rock. Which intrusion is younger? Explain your answer. SC.912.E.6.4

26. Analyzing Concepts A fossil that has unusual features is found in many areas on Earth. It represents a brief period of geologic time but occurs in small numbers. Would this fossil make a good index fossil? Explain.

27. Making Comparisons Compare the processes of mummification and freezing. SC.912.E.6.4

CONCEPT MAPPING

28. Use the following terms to create a concept map: *relative age, law of superposition, unconformity, law of crosscutting relationships, absolute age, radiometric dating, carbon dating,* and *index fossil.*

MATH SKILLS
Math Skills

29. Making Calculations Scientists know that 1 million grams of ^{238}U will undergo radioactive decay to produce 1/7,600 g of ^{206}Pb per year. How many grams of ^{238}U would be left after 1 million years? SC.912.E.6.4

30. Applying Quantities A sample contains 1,000 g of an isotope that has a half-life of 500 years. How many half-lives will have to pass before the sample contains less than 10 g of the parent isotope?

31. Making Calculations The half-life of ^{238}U is 4.5 billion years. How many years would 16 g of ^{238}U take to decay into 0.5 g of ^{238}U and 15.5 g of daughter products?

WRITING SKILLS

32. Writing Persuasively Imagine that you are James Hutton. Write a letter to a fellow scientist to convince him or her of the validity of the principle of uniformitarianism.

33. Outlining Topics Describe what happens to the amount of an isotope as it undergoes radioactive decay through three half-lives. SC.912.E.6.4

INTERPRETING GRAPHICS

The illustration below shows crosscutting relationships in an outcrop of rock. Use this illustration to answer the questions that follow.

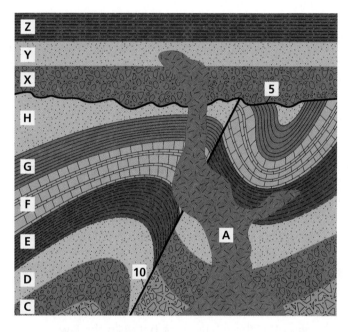

34. Is intrusion A older or younger than fault 10? Explain your answer. SC.912.E.6.4

35. What type of unconformity does feature 5 represent? Explain your answer. SC.912.E.6.4

36. Which rock formation is older: layer X or layer Y? Explain your answer. SC.912.E.6.4

Understanding Concepts

Directions (1–9): For each question, write on a separate sheet of paper the letter of the correct answer.

1 A scientist used radiometric dating during an investigation. The scientist used this method because she wanted to determine the
A. relative ages of rocks.
B. absolute ages of rocks.
C. climate of a past era.
D. fossil types in a rock.

2 Fossils that provide direct evidence of the feeding habits of ancient animals are known as
F. coprolites.
G. molds and casts.
H. carbon films.
I. trace fossils.

3 One way to estimate the absolute age of rock is
A. nonconformity.
B. varve count.
C. the law of superposition.
D. the law of crosscutting relationships.

4 To be an index fossil, a fossil must
F. be present in rocks that are scattered over a small geographic area.
G. contain remains of organisms that lived for a long period of geologic time.
H. occur in small numbers within the rock layers.
I. have features that clearly distinguish it from other fossils.

5 Which of the following statements best describes the relationship between the law of superposition and the principle of original horizontality?
A. Both describe the deposition of sediments in horizontal layers.
B. Both conclude that Earth is more than 100,000 years old.
C. Both indicate the absolute ages of layers of rock.
D. Both recognize that the geologic processes in the past are the same as those at work now.

6 James Hutton developed his theory of uniformitarianism after making what observation?
F. An undeformed sedimentary rock layer is older than the layers above it and younger than the layers below it.
G. Sedimentary rocks will remain in horizontal layers if they remain undeformed.
H. Forces that change a farm work very slowly.
I. The largest particles of sediment are deposited on the bottom of a layer.

7 Which of the following is NOT a way to determine absolute age?
A. examining unconformities
B. studying rates of erosion
C. calculating rates of deposition
D. counting varves

8 When dating the remains of an organism that lived within the last five thousand years, which radiometric dating method should be used?
F. argon-argon dating
G. rubidium-strontium dating
H. radiocarbon dating
I. uranium-lead dating

9 A scientist found an unconformity in a certain area. The unconformity consisted of tilted layers of rock that were covered by horizontal layers of rock. Which type of unconformity did the scientist find?
A. angular unconformity
B. cross-bed
C. disconformity
D. nonconformity

Interpreting Graphics

Directions (10–11): For each question below, record the correct answer on a separate sheet of paper.

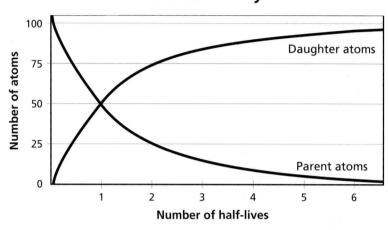

Radioactive Decay

🔟 The graph above shows the rate of radioactive decay. How many half-lives have passed when the number of daughter atoms is approximately three times the number of parent atoms?

F. one
G. two
H. three
I. four

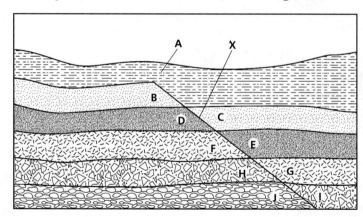

Layers of Rock with a Crosscutting Fault

⓫ The diagram above shows crosscutting taking place in layers of rock. Which of the letter combinations below belonged to the same layer of rock before the fault disrupted the layer?

A. C and D
B. C and F
C. G and I
D. G and F

Test Tip

If time permits, take short mental breaks to improve your concentration during a test.

A View of Earth's Past

Chapter Outline

Why It Matters

The rock and fossil records show that Earth's surface is constantly changing. Fossils provide valuable information about extinct organisms. This illustration shows an artist's idea of how a mother *Hypacrosaurus* might have looked as she fed her hatchlings. Because fossils do not record such characteristics as skin color, they are left to our imagination.

Inquiry Lab

🕐 **20 min**

Exploring Geologic Evidence

Obtain a box from your teacher. Use a spoon to dig carefully through the layers in the box to find "fossils." Transfer material removed from the box to a sheet of newspaper. Record the layer in which each fossil was found. Sketch the layers, including the number and type of each fossil found, to produce a geologic history.

Questions to Get You Started

1. Which fossils are the oldest? How do you know?

2. Which fossils are found only in older layers? What are possible reasons for this distribution?

SC.912.E.6.4

These reading tools will help you learn the material in this chapter.

Word Parts

Prefixes Many scientific words contain prefixes or suffixes that come from Latin and Greek. You can use the meanings of prefixes and suffixes to help you figure out the meanings of science terms.

The term *Paleozoic Era* contains the prefix *paleo-*, from the Greek word *palaio,* meaning "ancient," and the suffix *-zoic,* from the Greek word *zoe,* meaning "life." The Paleozoic Era is the time in which many early forms of life became abundant.

Your Turn As you read this chapter, make a table of terms containing a prefix and the suffix *-zoic.* Using a dictionary, enter the meanings of the prefixes in the table.

TERM	PREFIX	MEANING OF PREFIX
Paleozoic Era	paleo-	ancient
Mesozoic Era	meso-	
Cenozoic Era		

Describing Time

Temporal Language Temporal language is language that is used to describe time. Paying careful attention to temporal language can help you understand events and processes in the environment.

Your Turn Make a two-column table. As you read this chapter, look for words and phrases that refer to time. Write these words and phrases in the first column of your table. In the second column, write whether each word or phrase describes a specific time, duration, frequency, or sequence of events.

TEMPORAL WORD	DESCRIBES...
19th century	specific time
timeline	sequence
rate	frequency

Graphic Organizers

Spider Maps Spider maps show how details are organized into categories that relate to a main idea.

To make a spider map, follow these steps.

❶ Write a main topic title, and draw an oval around it.

❷ From the oval, draw legs. Each leg represents a category of the main topic.

❸ From each leg, draw horizontal lines. Write details about each category on these lines.

Your Turn As you read Section 1, complete a spider map like the one started here to organize the ideas you learn about the geologic column.

Order of rock layers

Geologic column

For more information on how to use these and other tools, see **Appendix A**.

Geologic Time

Key Ideas	Key Terms	Why It Matters
❯ Summarize how scientists worked together to develop the geologic column. ❯ List the major divisions of geologic time.	geologic column era period epoch	The geologic time scale provides a framework for understanding the geologic processes that shape our planet.

Earth's surface is constantly changing. Mountains form and erode; oceans rise and recede. As conditions on Earth's surface change, some organisms flourish and then later become extinct. Evidence of these changes is recorded in the rock layers of Earth's crust. To describe the sequence and length of these changes, scientists have developed a *geologic time scale*. This scale outlines the development of Earth and life on Earth.

FLORIDA STANDARDS

LA.910.2.2.3 The student will organize information to show understanding or relationships among facts, ideas, and events (e.g., representing key points within text through charting, mapping, paraphrasing, summarizing, comparing, contrasting, or outlining).

The Geologic Column

By studying fossils and applying the principle that old layers of rock are below young layers, 19th-century scientists determined the relative ages of sedimentary rock in different areas around the world. No single area on Earth contained a record of all geologic time. So, scientists combined their observations to create a standard arrangement of rock layers. As shown in the example in **Figure 1,** this ordered arrangement of rock layers is called a **geologic column.** A geologic column represents a timeline of Earth's history. The oldest rocks are at the bottom of the column.

Rock layers in a geologic column are distinguished by the types of rock the layers are made of and by the kinds of fossils the layers contain. Fossils in the upper, more-recent layers resemble modern plants and animals. Most of the fossils in the lower, older layers are of plants and animals that are different from those living today. In fact, many of the fossils discovered in old layers are from species that have been extinct for millions of years.

geologic column an ordered arrangement of rock layers that is based on the relative ages of the rocks and in which the oldest rocks are at the bottom

Reading Check Where would you find fossils of extinct animals on a geologic column?
(See Appendix G for answers to Reading Checks.)

Figure 1 By combining observations of rock layers in areas A, B, and C, scientists can construct a geologic column. *Why is relative position important for determining the ages of rock layers?*

A   B   C   Geologic column

Figure 2 This scientist is collecting rock samples that contain fossilized fungal spores that date the rock to the Triassic Period.

Academic Vocabulary

investigate (in VES ti geyt) to examine or study an object in detail in an attempt to learn the facts about it

Using a Geologic Column

When the first geologic columns were being developed, scientists estimated the ages of rock layers by using factors such as the average rates of sediment deposition. The development of radiometric dating methods, however, allowed scientists to determine the absolute ages of rock layers with more accuracy.

Scientists can now use geologic columns to estimate the ages of rock layers that cannot be dated radiometrically. To determine the age of a given rock layer, scientists compare the rock layer with a similar layer in a geologic column that contains the same fossils or that has the same relative position. If the two layers match, they likely formed at about the same time. The scientist in **Figure 2** is investigating the ages of sedimentary rocks.

Divisions of Geologic Time

The geologic history of Earth is marked by major changes in Earth's surface, climate, and types of organisms. Geologists use these indicators to divide the geologic time scale into smaller units. Rocks grouped within each unit contain similar fossils. In fact, a unit of geologic time is generally characterized by fossils of a dominant lifeform. A simplified geologic time scale is shown in **Table 1.**

Because Earth's history is so long, geologists commonly use abbreviations when they discuss geologic time. For example, Ma stands for *mega-annum*, which means "million years."

SC.912.N.3.5

Quick Lab

30 min

Geologic Time Scale

Procedure

❶ Copy the table shown at right onto a piece of paper.

❷ Complete the table by using the scale 1 cm is equal to 10 million years.

❸ Lay a **5-m strip of adding-machine paper** flat on a hard surface. Use a **meterstick**, a **metric ruler**, and a **pencil** to mark off the beginning and end of Precambrian time according to the time scale you calculated. Do the same for the three eras. Label each time division, and color each a different color with **colored pencils.**

❹ Pick two periods from the geologic time scale. Using the same scale that was used in step 2, calculate the scale length for each period listed. Mark the boundaries of each period on the paper strip, and label the periods on your scale.

Era	Length of time (years)	Scale length
Precambrian	4,058,000,000	
Paleozoic	291,000,000	
Mesozoic	185,500,000	
Cenozoic	65,500,000 (to present)	

DO NOT WRITE IN THIS BOOK

❺ Decorate your strip by adding names or drawings of the organisms that lived in each division of time.

Analysis

1. When did humans appear? What is the scale length from that time to the present?

2. Add the lengths of the Paleozoic, Mesozoic, and Cenozoic Eras. What percentage of the geologic time scale do these combined eras represent? What percentage of the geologic time scale does Precambrian time represent?

Table 1 Geologic Time Scale

Era	Period	Epoch	Beginning of interval in Ma	Characteristics from geologic and fossil evidence
Cenozoic	Quaternary	Holocene	0.0115	The last glacial period ends; complex human societies develop.
		Pleistocene	1.8	Woolly mammoths, rhinos, and humans appear.
	Tertiary	Pliocene	5.3	Large carnivores (bears, lions) appear.
		Miocene	23.0	Grazing herds are abundant; raccoons and wolves appear.
		Oligocene	33.9	Deer, pigs, camels, cats, and dogs appear.
		Eocene	55.8	Horses, flying squirrels, bats, and whales appear.
		Paleocene	65.5	Age of mammals begins; first primates appear.
Mesozoic	Cretaceous		146	Flowering plants and modern birds appear; mass extinctions mark the end of the Mesozoic Era.
	Jurassic		200	Dinosaurs are the dominant life-form; primitive birds and flying reptiles appear.
	Triassic		251	Dinosaurs appear; ammonites are common; cycads and conifers are abundant; mammals appear.
Paleozoic	Permian		299	Pangaea comes together; mass extinctions mark the end of the Paleozoic Era.
	Carboniferous	Pennsylvanian Period	318	Giant cockroaches and dragonflies are common; coal deposits form; reptiles appear.
		Mississippian Period	359	Amphibians flourish; brachiopods are common in oceans; forests and swamps cover most land.
	Devonian		416	Age of fishes begins; amphibians appear; giant horsetails, ferns, and seed-bearing plants develop.
	Silurian		444	Eurypterids, land plants and animals appear.
	Ordovician		488	Echinoderms appear; brachiopods increase; trilobites decline; graptolites flourish.
	Cambrian		542	Shelled marine invertebrates appear; trilobites and brachiopods are common; first vertebrates appear; atmosphere reaches modern O_2-rich state.
Precambrian time			4,600	Earth forms; continental shields appear; fossils are rare; cyanobacteria are the most common organism.

Sarcosuchus imperator lived from 110 million to 90 million years ago.

The family of modern crocodiles that includes *Crocodylus intermedius* has lived on Earth for 65 million years.

Figure 3 Crocodilians have lived on Earth for more than two geologic eras without major anatomical changes.

Eons and Eras

The largest unit of geologic time is an *eon*. Geologic time is divided into four eons: the Hadean Eon, the Archean Eon, the Proterozoic Eon, and the Phanerozoic Eon. The first three eons of Earth's history are part of a time interval commonly known as *Precambrian time*. This 4-billion-year interval contains most of Earth's history. Very few fossils exist in early Precambrian rocks, so dividing Precambrian time into smaller time units is difficult.

After Precambrian time, the Phanerozoic Eon began. This eon, as well as most eons, is divided into smaller units of geologic time called **eras.** The first era of the Phanerozoic Eon was the *Paleozoic Era*, which lasted about 291 million years. Paleozoic rocks contain fossils of a wide variety of marine and terrestrial life-forms. After the Paleozoic Era, the *Mesozoic Era* began and lasted about 186 million years. Mesozoic fossils include early forms of birds and reptiles, such as the giant crocodilian shown in **Figure 3.** The present geologic era is the *Cenozoic Era*, which began about 65 million years ago. Fossils of mammals are common in Cenozoic rocks.

Periods and Epochs

Eras are divided into shorter time units called **periods.** Each period is characterized by specific fossils and is usually named for the location in which the fossils were first discovered. Where the rock record is most complete and least deformed, a detailed fossil record may allow scientists to divide a period into shorter time units called **epochs.** An epoch may be divided into smaller units of time called *ages*. Ages are defined by the occurrence of distinct fossils in the fossil record.

era a unit of geologic time that includes two or more periods

period a unit of geologic time that is longer than an epoch but shorter than an era

epoch a subdivision of geologic time that is longer than an age but shorter than a period

Section 1 Review

LA.910.2.2.3; SC.912.N.1.1

Key Ideas

1. **Summarize** the reasons why many scientists had to work together to develop the geologic column.

2. **Describe** the major events in any one period of geologic time.

3. **Explain** why constructing geologic columns is useful to Earth scientists.

4. **List** the following units of time in order of length from shortest to longest: *year, period, era, eon, age,* and *epoch.*

5. **Name** the three eras of the Phanerozoic Eon, and identify how long each one lasted.

6. **Compare** geologic time with the geologic column.

Critical Thinking

7. **Analyzing Relationships** When a scientist discovers a new type of fossil, what characteristic of the rock around the fossil would he or she want to learn first?

8. **Predicting Consequences** How would our understanding of Earth's past change if a scientist discovered a mammal fossil from the Paleozoic Era?

Concept Mapping

9. Use the following terms to create a concept map: *geologic time, Precambrian time, Paleozoic Era, Mesozoic Era, Cenozoic Era, period,* and *epoch.*

SECTION 2
Precambrian Time and the Paleozoic Era

Key Ideas	Key Terms	Why It Matters
❯ Summarize how evolution is related to geologic change. ❯ Identify two characteristics of Precambrian rock. ❯ Identify one major geologic and two major biological developments during the Paleozoic Era.	evolution Precambrian time Paleozoic Era	The rock and fossil records show that Earth changes over time. One of these changes allowed the oxygen we breathe to begin accumulating in the atmosphere.

History is a record of past events. Just as the history of civilizations is written in books, the geologic history of Earth is recorded in rock layers. The types of rock and the fossils that occur in each layer reveal information about the environment when the layer formed. For example, the presence of a limestone layer in an area indicates that the area was once covered by water.

Evolution

Fossils indicate the kinds of organisms that lived when rock formed. By examining rock layers and fossils, scientists have discovered evidence that species of living things have changed over time. Scientists call this process evolution. **Evolution** is the gradual development of new organisms from preexisting organisms. Scientists think that evolution occurs by means of natural selection. Evidence for evolution includes the similarity in skeletal structures of animals, as shown in **Figure 1.** The theory of evolution by natural selection was proposed in 1859 by Charles Darwin, an English naturalist.

Evolution and Geologic Change

Major geologic and climatic changes can affect the ability of some organisms to survive. For example, dramatic changes in sea level greatly affect organisms that live in coastal areas. By using geologic evidence, scientists try to determine how environmental changes affected organisms in the past. The fossil record shows that some organisms survived environmental changes, while other organisms disappeared. Scientists use fossils to learn why some organisms survived long periods of time without changing, while other organisms changed or became extinct.

FLORIDA STANDARDS

SC.912.L.15.1 Explain how the scientific theory of evolution is supported by the fossil record, comparative anatomy, comparative embryology, biogeography, molecular biology, and observed evolutionary change; **SC.912.N.3.2** Describe the role consensus plays in the historical development of a theory in any one of the disciplines of science.

evolution the process of change by which new species develop from preexisting species over time

Figure 1 Bones in the front limbs of these animals are similar, even though the limbs are used in different ways. Similar structures indicate a common ancestor.

Human arm

Dolphin flipper

Cat leg

Bat wing

Precambrian time (4,600 Ma to 542 Ma)

Cenozoic Era
Mesozoic Era
Paleozoic Era

4,600 Ma

542 Ma
251 Ma
65.5 Ma
present

First crustal rocks form.

Earth's surface is cool enough for liquid water.

First known unicellular life appears.

Earth's atmosphere starts to become oxygen rich.

First known multicellular life appears.

First fungi appear.

First shelled organisms, such as arthropods and mollusks, appear.

Figure 2 Precambrian Timeline *How many million years ago did the first unicellular life appear?*

Precambrian time the interval of time in the geologic time scale from Earth's formation to the beginning of the Paleozoic era, from 4.6 billion to 542 million years ago

Precambrian Time

Most scientists agree that Earth formed about 4.6 billion years ago as a large cloud, or *nebula*, spun around the newly formed sun. As material spun around the sun, particles of matter began to clump together and eventually formed Earth and the other planets of the solar system. The time interval that began with the formation of Earth and ended about 542 million years ago is known as **Precambrian time.** This division of geologic time makes up about 88% of Earth's history, as shown in **Figure 2.**

Even though Precambrian time makes up such a large part of Earth's history, we know relatively little about what happened during that time. We lack information partly because the Precambrian rock record is difficult to interpret. Most Precambrian rocks have been so severely deformed and altered by tectonic activity that the original order of rock layers is rarely identifiable.

Reading Check How old is Earth?

Long-Term Survivors

EYE ON THE ENVIRONMENT

Some species alive today have survived for billions of years. Cyanobacteria—sometimes called blue-green bacteria—are one important example. Earth's early atmosphere contained no free oxygen, so it would be toxic to most organisms living today. Along with other photosynthetic organisms, cyanobacteria produced oxygen that built up in the atmosphere. This alteration of the atmosphere allowed oxygen-breathing animals to evolve.

Modern cyanobacteria such as these belong to species that have survived essentially unchanged through the vast span of geologic time.

These cyanobacteria fossils come from rock that is one billion years old. Other cyanobacteria fossils are more than 3.5 billion years old.

YOUR TURN UNDERSTANDING CONCEPTS How did early photosynthetic organisms such as cyanobacteria affect Earth's atmosphere?

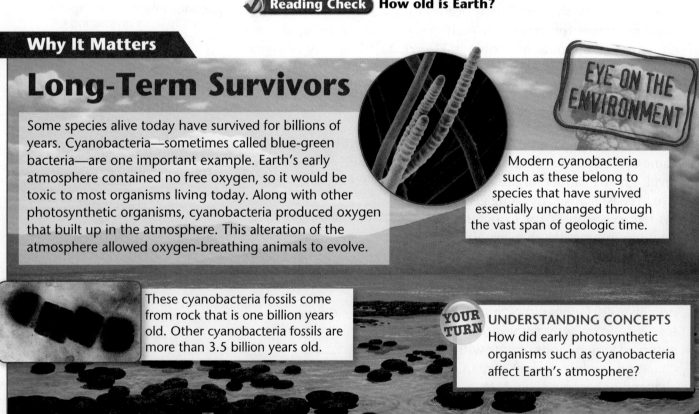

Precambrian Rocks

Large areas of <u>exposed</u> Precambrian rocks, called *shields*, exist on every continent except Antarctica. Precambrian shields are the result of several hundred million years of volcanic activity, mountain building, sedimentation, and metamorphism. After they were metamorphosed and deformed, the rocks of North America's Precambrian shield were uplifted and exposed at Earth's surface. Nearly half of the valuable mineral deposits in the world occur in the rocks of Precambrian shields. These valuable minerals include nickel, iron, gold, and copper.

Precambrian Life

Fossils are rare in Precambrian rocks, probably because Precambrian life-forms lacked bones, shells, or other hard parts that commonly form fossils. Also, Precambrian rocks are extremely old. Some date back nearly 3.9 billion years. Over this long period of time, volcanic activity, erosion, and extensive crustal movements, such as folding and faulting, probably destroyed most of the fossils that may have formed during Precambrian time.

Of the few Precambrian fossils that have been discovered, the most common are cyanobacteria in *stromatolites*, or layered, reef-like deposits. Stromatolites form today in warm, shallow waters, as shown in **Figure 3.** The presence of stromatolites in Precambrian rocks indicates that shallow seas covered much of Earth during intervals of Precambrian time. Fossils of marine worms, jellyfish, and single-celled organisms have also been discovered in rocks from late Precambrian time.

Figure 3 Stromatolites contain layers of sediments that are cemented together by mats of cyanobacteria. Cyanobacteria are the most common Precambrian fossils.

Academic Vocabulary

expose (eks POHZ) to present to view; to reveal; to uncover

SC.912.L.15.13

Quick Lab Chocolate Candy Survival

10 min

Procedure

1. Lay a piece of colorful cloth on a table.
2. Randomly sprinkle a handful of candy-coated chocolate bits on the cloth.
3. Look away for 1 min; then look back.
4. For 10 s, pick up chocolate bits one at a time. Record the colors of candy you picked up.
5. Repeat steps 1–4 with a piece of colorful cloth that has a different pattern.

Analysis

1. What colors were you more likely to pick up in the first trial? What about those candies made you pick them up?
2. When you changed the color of the cloth, did the color of the candies you picked up change?
3. How could camouflage help an organism survive?

Precambrian time | Paleozoic Era (542 Ma to 251 Ma) | Mesozoic Era

542 Ma | Cambrian Period | 488 Ma | Ordovician Period | 444 Ma | Silurian Period | 416 Ma | Devonian Period | 359 Ma | Carboniferous Period (Mississippian Period, Pennsylvanian Period) | 318 Ma | 299 Ma | Permian Period | 251 Ma

First possible vertebrates appear.

Modern, oxygen-rich atmosphere has formed.

First land plants appear.

First arthropods appear on land.

First amphibians appear.

First reptiles appear.

Formation of Pangaea is complete.

Permian mass extinction results from major environmental changes.

Figure 4 Paleozoic Timeline

Paleozoic Era the geologic era that followed Precambrian time and that lasted from 542 million to 251 million years ago

The Paleozoic Era

As shown in **Figure 4,** the geologic era that began about 542 million years ago and ended about 251 million years ago is called the **Paleozoic Era.** At the beginning of the Paleozoic Era, Earth's landmasses were scattered around the world. By the end of the Paleozoic Era, these landmasses had collided to form the supercontinent Pangaea. This tectonic activity created new mountain ranges and lifted large areas of land above sea level.

Unlike Precambrian rocks, Paleozoic rocks hold an abundance of fossils. The number of plant and animal species on Earth increased dramatically at the beginning of the Paleozoic Era. Because of this rich fossil record, North American geologists have divided the Paleozoic Era into six periods.

The Cambrian Period

The Cambrian Period is the first period of the Paleozoic Era. A variety of marine life-forms appeared during this period. These Cambrian life-forms were more advanced than previous life-forms and quickly displaced the primitive organisms as the dominant life-forms. The explosion of Cambrian life may have been partly due to the warm, shallow seas that covered much of the continents during the time period. Marine *invertebrates,* or animals that do not have backbones, thrived in the warm waters. The most common of the Cambrian invertebrates were *trilobites,* such as the one shown in **Figure 5.** Scientists use many trilobites as *index fossils* to date rocks to the Cambrian Period.

Another group of common animals in the Cambrian Period were the *brachiopods,* which are shelled animals. Fossils indicate that at least 15 different families of brachiopods existed during this period. A few kinds of brachiopods exist today, but modern brachiopods are rare. Other Cambrian invertebrates included worms, jellyfish, snails, and sponges. However, little evidence of land-dwelling plants or animals has been discovered in Cambrian rocks.

Reading Check **Name three common invertebrates from the Cambrian Period.**

Figure 5 During the early Paleozoic Era, various types of trilobites, such as this fossilized trilobite of the genus *Modocia*, flourished in the warm, shallow seas.

Figure 6 During the Silurian Period, eurypterids lived in shallow lagoons. Eurypterids had one pair of legs for swimming and had four or five pairs for walking.

The Ordovician Period

During the Ordovician (AWR duh VISH uhn) Period, the number of trilobite species began to shrink. Brachiopods, bryozoans, and cephalopod mollusks became the dominant invertebrate life-forms. Large numbers of corals appeared. Colonies of tiny invertebrates called *graptolites* also flourished in the oceans, and primitive fish appeared. By this period, *vertebrates*, or animals that have backbones, had appeared. The most primitive vertebrates were fish. Unlike modern fish, Ordovician fish did not have jaws or teeth, and their bodies were covered with thick, bony plates. During the Ordovician Period, as during the Cambrian Period, there was little plant life on land.

The Silurian Period

Vertebrate and invertebrate marine life continued to thrive during the Silurian Period. Echinoderms, relatives of modern sea stars, and corals became more common. Scorpion-like sea creatures called *eurypterids* (yoo RIP tuhr IDZ), such as the one shown in **Figure 6,** also existed during the Silurian Period. Fossils of giant eurypterids about 2 m long have been discovered in western New York. Near the end of this period, the earliest vascular land plants as well as animals, such as scorpions, evolved on land.

The Devonian Period

The Devonian Period is called the *Age of Fishes* because fossils of many bony fishes were discovered in rocks of this period. One type of fish, called a *lungfish*, had the ability to breathe air. Other air-breathing fish, called *rhipidistians* (RIE puh DIS tee uhnz), had strong fins that may have allowed them to crawl onto the land for short periods of time. Early amphibians probably evolved from rhipidistians. *Ichthyostega* (IK thee oh STEG uh), early amphibians that resembled huge salamanders, are thought to be the ancestors of modern amphibians such as frogs and toads. During the Devonian Period, land plants, such as giant horsetails, ferns, and seed-bearing plants, also began to develop. In the sea, brachiopods and mollusks continued to thrive.

READING TOOLBOX

Spider Map
Make a spider map that has six legs and several lines on each leg. Use the map to describe the six periods in the Paleozoic Era.

The Carboniferous Period

During the Carboniferous Period, the climate was generally warm, and the humidity was at times very high over most of the world. Forests and swamps covered much of the land. Coal deposits in Pennsylvania, Ohio, and West Virginia are the fossilized remains of these forests and swamps. During this period, the rock in which some major oil deposits occur also formed. *Carboniferous* means "carbon bearing." In North America, the Carboniferous Period is divided into the Mississippian and Pennsylvanian Periods.

Amphibians and fish continued to flourish during the Carboniferous Period. *Crinoids*, like the one shown in **Figure 7**, were common in the oceans. Insects, such as giant cockroaches and dragonflies, were common on land. Toward the end of the Carboniferous Period, vertebrates that were adapted to life on land appeared. These early reptiles resembled large lizards.

Figure 7 During the Carboniferous Period, crinoids, such as the one shown here, were common in the oceans. Crinoids are thought to be ancestors of modern animals called sea lillies.

The Permian Period

The Permian Period marks the end of the Paleozoic Era. A *mass extinction* of a large number of Paleozoic life-forms occurred at the end of the Permian Period. The continents had joined to form the supercontinent Pangaea. The collision of tectonic plates created the Appalachian Mountains. On the northwest side of the mountains, areas of desert and dry savanna climates developed. The shallow inland seas that had covered much of Earth disappeared. As the seas retreated, many species of marine invertebrates, including trilobites and eurypterids, became extinct. However, fossils indicate that reptiles and amphibians survived the environmental changes and dominated Earth in the millions of years that followed the Paleozoic Era.

Section 2 Review

LA.910.2.2.3; SC.912.L.15.1; SC.912.N.3.1; SC.912.N.3.2; SC.912.N.3.4

Key Ideas

1. **Summarize** how evolution is related to geologic change.

2. **Identify** two characteristics of most Precambrian rocks.

3. **Explain** why fossils are rare in Precambrian rocks.

4. **Identify** one life-form from each of the six periods of the Paleozoic Era.

5. **Explain** why the Devonian Period is commonly called the *Age of Fishes*.

6. **Describe** the kinds of life-forms that became extinct during the mass extinction at the end of the Permian Period.

Critical Thinking

7. **Drawing Conclusions** Identify one way in which the formation of Pangaea affected Paleozoic life.

8. **Identifying Relationships** Why is Precambrian time—about 88% of geologic time—not divided into smaller units based on the fossil record?

9. **Analyzing Processes** Explain two ways in which the geologic record of the Paleozoic Era supports the theory of evolution.

Concept Mapping

10. Use the following terms to create a concept map: *Paleozoic Era, invertebrate, Cambrian Period, Ordovician Period, vertebrate,* and *Silurian Period.*

The Mesozoic and Cenozoic Eras

Key Ideas
❯ List the periods of the Mesozoic and Cenozoic Eras.
❯ Identify two major geologic and biological developments during the Mesozoic Era.
❯ Identify two major geologic and biological developments during the Cenozoic Era.

Key Terms
mass extinction
Mesozoic Era
Cenozoic Era

Why It Matters
The movement of tectonic plates and the evolution and extinction of organisms have shaped the world we live in today. Our world continues to change as these processes continue.

At the end of the Permian Period, 90% of marine organisms and more than 70% of land organisms died. This episode during which an enormous number of species died, or **mass extinction,** left many resources available for the surviving life-forms. Because resources and space were readily available, an abundance of new life-forms appeared. These new life-forms evolved, and some flourished while others eventually became extinct.

The Mesozoic Era

As shown in **Figure 1,** the geologic era that began about 251 million years ago and ended about 65 million years ago is called the **Mesozoic Era.** Earth's surface changed dramatically during the Mesozoic Era. As Pangaea broke into smaller continents, the tectonic plates drifted and collided. These collisions uplifted mountain ranges such as the Sierra Nevada in California and the Andes in South America. Shallow seas and marshes covered much of the land. In general, the climate was warm and humid.

Conditions during the Mesozoic Era favored the survival of reptiles. Lizards, turtles, crocodiles, snakes, and a variety of dinosaurs flourished during the Mesozoic Era. Thus, this era is also known as the *Age of Reptiles*. The Mesozoic Era has a rich fossil record and is divided into three periods.

FLORIDA STANDARDS

SC.912.N.2.5 Describe instances in which scientists' varied backgrounds, talents, interests, and goals influence the inferences and thus the explanations that they make about observations of natural phenomena and describe that competing interpretations (explanations) of scientists are a strength of science as they are a source of new, testable ideas that have the potential to add new evidence to support one or another of the explanations.

mass extinction an episode during which large numbers of species become extinct

Mesozoic Era the geologic era that lasted from 251 million to 65.5 million years ago; also called the *Age of Reptiles*

Figure 1 Mesozoic Timeline

Paleozoic Era | Mesozoic Era (251 Ma to 65.5 Ma) | Cenozoic Era

251 Ma — Triassic Period — 200 Ma — Jurassic Period — 146 Ma — Cretaceous Period — 65.5 Ma

Pangaea begins to break apart.

First mammals appear.

First primitive birds appear.

First flowering plants (angiosperms) appear.

First modern birds appear.

The last dinosaurs become extinct. Catastrophic asteroid impact occurs.

Figure 2 A group of dinosaurs of the genus *Coelophysis* race through a Triassic conifer forest in what is now New Mexico.

The Triassic Period

Dinosaurs flourished during the Triassic Period of the Mesozoic Era. Some dinosaurs were the size of squirrels. Others weighed as much as 15 tons and were nearly 30 m long. However, most of the dinosaurs of the Triassic Period were about 2 m to 5 m long and moved very quickly. As shown in **Figure 2,** these dinosaurs roamed through lush forests of cone-bearing trees and *cycads*, which are thick-stemmed plants with crowns of fern-like leaves.

Reptiles called *ichthyosaurs* lived in the Triassic oceans. New forms of marine invertebrates also evolved. The most distinctive was the ammonite, a type of shellfish that is similar to the modern nautilus. Ammonites serve as Mesozoic index fossils. The first mammals, small rodent-like forest dwellers, also appeared.

The Jurassic Period

Dinosaurs became the dominant life-form during the Jurassic Period. Fossil records indicate that two major groups of dinosaurs evolved. These groups are distinguished by their hip-bone structures. One group, called *saurischians*, or "lizard-hipped" dinosaurs, included herbivores, which are plant eaters, and carnivores, which are meat eaters. Among the largest saurischians were herbivores of the genus *Apatosaurus*, once known as *Brontosaurus*, which weighed up to 50 tons and grew up to 25 m long.

The other major group of Jurassic dinosaurs, called *ornithischians*, or "bird-hipped" dinosaurs, were herbivores. Among the best known of the ornithischians were herbivores of the genus *Stegosaurus*, which were about 9 m long and about 3 m tall at the hips. In addition, flying reptiles called *pterosaurs* were common during the Jurassic Period. Like modern bats, pterosaurs flew on skin-covered wings. Fossils of the earliest birds, such as the one shown in **Figure 3,** also occur in Jurassic rocks.

Reading Check **Name two fossils that were discovered in the fossil record of the Jurassic Period.**

Figure 3 The *Archaeopteryx* (AWR kee AUP tuhr IKS) was one of the first birds that appeared during the Jurassic Period.

Figure 4 This 12.5-m-long *Tyrannosaurus rex* was discovered near Faith, South Dakota. This specimen, named Sue, was displayed in the Field Museum in Chicago in 2000.

The Cretaceous Period

Dinosaurs continued to dominate Earth during the Cretaceous Period. Among the most spectacular dinosaurs was the carnivore *Tyrannosaurus rex*, such as the one shown in **Figure 4.** The *Tyrannosaurus rex* stood nearly 6 m tall and had huge jaws with sharp teeth that were up to 15 cm long. Also, among the common Cretaceous dinosaurs were the armored *ankylosaurs*, horned dinosaurs called *ceratopsians*, and duck-billed dinosaurs called *hadrosaurs*.

Plant life had become very sophisticated by the Cretaceous Period. The earliest flowering plants, or *angiosperms*, appeared during this period. The most common of these plants were trees such as magnolias and willows. Later, trees such as maples, oaks, and walnuts became abundant. Angiosperms became so successful that they are the dominant type of land plant today.

The Cretaceous-Tertiary Mass Extinction

The Cretaceous Period ended in another mass extinction. No dinosaur fossils have been found in rocks that formed after the Cretaceous Period. Some scientists think that this extinction was caused by environmental changes resulting from the movement of continents and increased volcanic activity.

However, many scientists accept the *impact hypothesis* as the explanation for the extinction of the last dinosaurs. This hypothesis is that about 65 million years ago, an asteroid crashed into Earth. The impact of the collision raised enough dust to block the sun's rays for many years. As Earth's climate became cooler, plant life began to die, and many animal species became extinct. As the dust settled over Earth, the dust formed a layer of iridium-laden sediment. Iridium is a chemical element that is uncommon in rocks on Earth but that is common in meteorites.

www.scilinks.org
Topic: Mass Extinctions
Code: HQX0916
Topic: Geologic Time Scale
Code: HQX0669

Figure 5 Cenozoic Timeline

Mesozoic Era

Cenozoic Era (65.5 Ma to present)

Holocene Epoch
Pleistocene Epoch
Pliocene Epoch

Tertiary Period

Quaternary Period

| 65.5 Ma | Paleocene Epoch | 55.8 Ma | Eocene Epoch | 33.9 Ma | Oligocene Epoch | 23.0 Ma | Miocene Epoch | 5.3 Ma | 1.8 Ma | 0.0115 Ma | present |

Most modern mammal families, including whales, carnivores, hoofed animals, and primates, have appeared.

First grasses appear.

India collides with Asia, and Antarctica drifts over South Pole.

First hominids (early human ancestors) appear.

Modern Ice Age begins.

Modern humans appear.

The Cenozoic Era

As shown in **Figure 5**, the **Cenozoic Era** is the division of geologic time that began about 65 million years ago and that includes the present period. During this era, the continents moved to their present-day positions. As tectonic plates collided, huge mountain ranges, such as the Alps and the Himalayas in Eurasia, formed.

During the Cenozoic Era, dramatic changes in climate have occurred. At times, continental ice sheets covered nearly one-third of Earth's land. As temperatures decreased during the ice ages, new species that were adapted to life in cooler climates appeared. Mammals became the dominant life-form and underwent many changes. The Cenozoic Era is thus commonly called the *Age of Mammals*.

The Tertiary and Quaternary Periods

The Cenozoic Era is divided into two periods. The Tertiary Period includes the time before the last ice age. The Quaternary Period began with the last ice age and includes the present. These periods have been divided into seven epochs. The Paleocene, Eocene, Oligocene, Miocene, and Pliocene Epochs make up the *Tertiary Period*. The Pleistocene and Holocene Epochs make up the *Quaternary Period*.

The Paleocene and Eocene Epochs

The fossil record indicates that during the Paleocene Epoch, many new mammals, such as small rodents, evolved. The first primates also evolved during the Paleocene Epoch. A modern survivor of an early primate group is shown in **Figure 6**.

Other mammals, including the earliest known ancestor of the horse, evolved during the Eocene Epoch. Fossil records indicate that the first whales, flying squirrels, and bats appeared during this epoch. Small reptiles continued to flourish. Worldwide, temperatures dropped by about 4 °C at the end of the Eocene Epoch.

Cenozoic Era the current geologic era, which began 65.5 million years ago; also called the *Age of Mammals*

Prefixes
Make a table that lists the names of the epochs of the Cenozoic Era. Give the meaning of each prefix attached to the suffix *-cene*.

Figure 6 The *tarsier* is the sole modern survivor of a group of primates common during the earlier Cenozoic Era. *Why are mammals better suited to cool climates than reptiles are?*

The Oligocene and Miocene Epochs

During the Oligocene Epoch, the Indian subcontinent began to collide with the Eurasian continent, which caused the uplifting of the Himalayas. The worldwide climate became significantly cooler and drier. This change in climate favored grasses as well as cone-bearing and hardwood trees. Many early mammals became extinct. However, large species of deer, pigs, horses, camels, cats, and dogs flourished. Marine invertebrates, especially clams and snails, also continued to flourish.

During the Miocene Epoch, circumpolar currents formed around Antarctica, and the modern Antarctic icecap began to form. By the late Miocene Epoch, tectonic forces and dropping sea levels caused the Mediterranean Sea to dry up and refill several times. The largest known land mammals existed during this epoch. Miocene rocks contain fossils of horses, camels, deer, rhinoceroses, pigs, raccoons, wolves, foxes, and the earliest saber-toothed cats, which are now extinct. The earliest human ancestors may date to this epoch.

SCI
LINKS.
www.scilinks.org
Topic: Geologic Periods and Epochs
Code: HQX0667

The Pliocene Epoch

During the Pliocene Epoch, predators—including members of the bear, dog, and cat families—evolved into modern forms. Herbivores, such as the giant ground sloth shown in **Figure 7,** flourished. The first modern horses also appeared in this epoch.

Toward the end of the Pliocene, dramatic climatic changes occurred, and the continental ice sheets began to spread. With more and more water locked in ice, sea level fell. The Bering land bridge appeared between Eurasia and North America. Changes in Earth's crust between North America and South America formed the Central American land bridge. Various species migrated between the continents across these two land bridges.

Reading Check **Why did sea level fall in the Pliocene Epoch?**

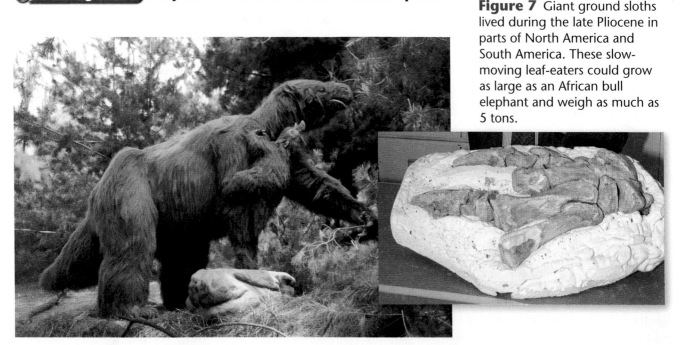

Figure 7 Giant ground sloths lived during the late Pliocene in parts of North America and South America. These slow-moving leaf-eaters could grow as large as an African bull elephant and weigh as much as 5 tons.

Figure 8 This painting from the Stone Age was made by early humans between 15,000 and 13,000 years ago in a cave in Lascaux, France.

The Pleistocene Epoch

The Pleistocene Epoch began 1.8 million years ago. In Eurasia and North America, ice sheets advanced and retreated several times. Some animals had characteristics that allowed them to endure the cold climate, such as the thick fur that covered woolly mammoths and woolly rhinoceroses. Many other species survived by moving to warmer regions. Some species, such as giant ground sloths and dire wolves, became extinct.

Fossils of the earliest modern humans (*Homo sapiens*) were discovered in Pleistocene sediments. Evidence of modern humans, such as the cave painting shown in **Figure 8**, indicates that early humans may have been hunters.

The Holocene Epoch

The Holocene Epoch, which includes the present, began about 11,500 years ago, as the last glacial period ended. As the ice sheets melted, sea level rose about 140 m, and the coastlines took on their present shapes. The North American Great Lakes also formed as the last ice sheets retreated. During the early Holocene Epoch, modern humans developed agriculture and began to make and use tools made of bronze and iron.

Human history is extremely brief. If you think of the entire history of Earth as one year, the first multicellular organisms would have appeared in September. The dinosaurs would have disappeared at 8 P.M. on December 26. Modern humans would not have appeared until 11:48 P.M. on December 31.

Section 3 Review

LA.910.2.2.3; SC.912.N.1.1; SC.912.L.15.1

Key Ideas

1. **List** the periods of the Mesozoic Era, and describe one major life-form in each period.

2. **Identify** two major geologic and two major biological developments of the Mesozoic Era.

3. **List** the periods and epochs of the Cenozoic Era, and describe one major life-form in each division.

4. **Identify** two major geologic and two major biological developments of the Cenozoic Era.

5. **Explain** how the ice ages affected animal life during the Cenozoic Era.

6. **Identify** the era, period, and epoch we are in today.

7. **Describe** the worldwide environmental changes that set the stage for the Age of Mammals.

Critical Thinking

8. **Drawing Conclusions** Explain the criteria that scientists may have used to divide the Cenozoic Era into the Tertiary and Quaternary Periods.

9. **Identifying Relationships** Suppose that you are a geologist who is looking for the boundary between the Cretaceous and Tertiary Periods in an outcrop. What characteristics would you look for to determine the location of the boundary? Explain your answer.

Concept Mapping

10. Use the following terms to create a concept map: *Mesozoic Era, Age of Reptiles, Jurassic Period, Triassic Period, Cretaceous Period, Cenozoic Era, Age of Mammals, Tertiary Period,* and *Quaternary Period.*

Reconstructing the Past

From films and books, most people can visualize the walk and long, swaying neck of an *Apatosaurus,* such as the one shown reaching for tree leaves. Dinosaurs became extinct millions of years ago. How do we know so much about them? Scientists use fossil evidence to reconstruct the bodies and lives of dinosaurs.

Scanning technology lets scientists analyze fossil evidence in a new way. By digitizing bones using CT and X-ray scanners, researchers can build detailed computer models of dinosaur skeletons.

These models show how dinosaur bones functioned in living animals, helping us understand how dinosaurs looked and behaved, without resorting to cutting or slicing up the specimens.

Scientists have digitized a *Triceratops* skeleton for study and to replace missing bones.

Each color of the digital *Triceratops* skull indicates data collected by a different pass of a 3D surface scanner. The passes were combined to "build" a complete skull.

Fossilized dinosaur tracks show that *Apatosaurus* behaved like modern herd animals, with the youngest animals in the center for protection.

Scientists use a digitized *Triceratops* skeleton to study the mechanics of this huge creature. This sequence shows how *Triceratops* moved as it walked.

YOUR TURN

UNDERSTANDING CONCEPTS
How has technology aided in the study of dinosaurs?

ONLINE RESEARCH
Research techniques used to digitize a *Triceratops* at the National Museum of Natural History. Describe the importance of this work.

History in the Rocks

What You'll Do

> **Apply** the law of superposition to sample rock columns.

> **Demonstrate** the use of index fossils for determining relative and absolute ages.

> **Evaluate** the usefulness of different methods for determining relative and absolute ages.

What You'll Need

paper
pencil

Geologists have discovered much about the geologic history of Earth by studying the arrangement of fossils in rock layers, as well as by studying the arrangement of the rock layers themselves. Fossils provide clues about the environment in which the organisms that formed the fossils existed. Scientists can determine the age of the rocks in which fossils occur because the ages of many fossils have been determined by radiometric dating of associated igneous rocks. Radiometric dating, fossil age, and rock arrangement are all used to determine changes that have occurred in the arrangement of the rock layers through geologic time. In this lab, you will discover how the geologic history of an area can be determined by examining the arrangement of fossils and rock layers.

Procedure

1. Study the index fossils shown in **Figure A.** Note their placement in related groups and the geologic periods in which they lived.

2. Select one of the four rock columns shown in **Figure B.** This figure shows how some of these fossils may occur in a series of rock layers. Record the number of the arrangement that you are using.

3. Using **Figure A,** identify all the fossils in your column and the geologic time in which the organisms that formed the fossils lived.

4. List the fossil names in order from bottom to top.

5. Do the fossils in your column appear in the order of geologic time?

6. Do the fossils in your column show a complete sequence of geologic periods? If not, which periods are missing?

7. Repeat steps 2–6 with each of the other three rock columns.

Figure A

Name of Animal Group

Geologic period / Brachiopoda / Echinodermata / Mollusca / Arthorpoda / Chordata

Cretaceous — Gastropod, Shark, Echinoid, Cephalopod
Jurassic — Pelecypod
Triassic — Cephalopod
Permian — Gastropod
Pennsylvanian — Brachiopod
Mississippian — Blastoid, Brachiopod, Cephalopod
Devonian — Brachiopod, Trilobite
Silurian — Brachiopod
Ordovician — Cephalopod, Trilobite

Figure B

Analysis

1. **Analyzing Processes** What processes or events might explain the order of the fossils in each of the rock columns?

2. **Evaluating Assumptions** Based on your observations in the procedure, why is it necessary that a fossil be found in a wide variety of geographic areas for it to be considered an index fossil?

3. **Explaining Events** Study arrangement 3 in **Figure B**. Note that there is a rock layer that contains no fossils between two rock layers that contain fossils. How might this have occurred?

Extension

Examining Data Collect fossils in your area. Identify the fossils you have collected, and describe what your area was like when the organisms existed.

Research Find out how index fossils are used to help petroleum geologists locate oil reservoirs. Then, use that information to give an oral report to your class.

MAPS *in Action*

Fossil Evidence for Gondwanaland

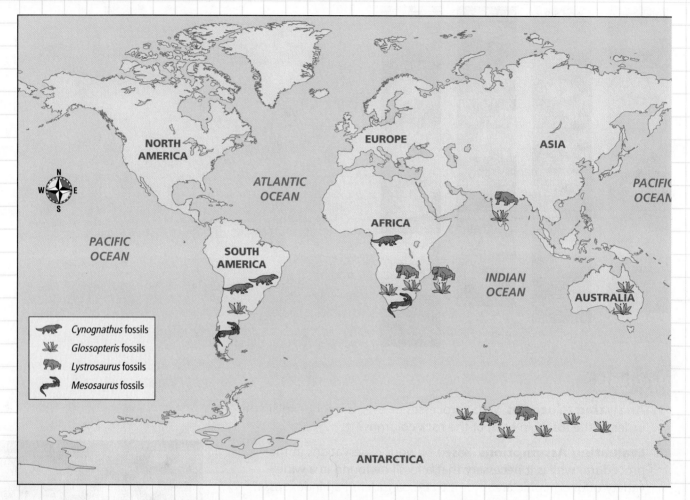

Map Skills Activity

This map shows areas where selected fossils have been found. Use the map to answer the questions below.

1. **Using a Key** On which continents have fossils of plants of the genus *Glossopteris* been found?

2. **Using a Key** On which continents have fossils of organisms of the genus *Lystrosaurus* been found?

3. **Making Comparisons** Which fossil shown on the map was spread over the smallest area?

4. **Inferring Relationships** Based on the map, which continents were connected to Africa when the continents formed a supercontinent?

5. **Inferring Relationships** Based on the map, which continents were connected to Antarctica when the continents formed a supercontinent?

6. **Analyzing Relationships** How would you argue against a claim that plants of the genus *Glossopteris* evolved independently on separate continents or were transported between continents that were not connected? Explain your answer.

7. **Identifying Trends** If the continents were to continue the motion they have had since the time when they formed Gondwanaland, would you expect the east coast of South America and the west coast of Africa to be moving closer together or farther apart? Explain your answer.

Key Ideas

Key Terms

Geologic Time

❯ Scientists developed the geologic column based on observations of the relative ages of rock layers throughout the world.

❯ Scientists used major changes in Earth's climate and extinctions recorded in the fossil record to divide the geologic time scale into smaller units. Geologic time is subdivided into eons, eras, periods, epochs, and ages.

geologic column, p. 229
era, p. 232
period, p. 232
epoch, p. 232

Precambrian Time and the Paleozoic Era

❯ Evolution is the gradual development of organisms from other organisms. Evidence for the theory of evolution occurs throughout the fossil record.

❯ Precambrian rock contains valuable minerals but few fossils.

❯ The rock record reveals the formation of Pangaea and the evolution of marine invertebrates and vertebrates during the Paleozoic Era.

evolution, p. 233
Precambrian time, p. 234
Paleozoic Era, p. 236

The Mesozoic and Cenozoic Eras

❯ The periods of the Mesozoic Era are the Triassic, Jurassic, and Cretaceous Periods; the periods of the Cenozoic Era are the Tertiary and Quaternary Periods.

❯ During the Mesozoic Era, Pangaea began to break apart, mountain ranges such as the Sierra Nevada formed, and the first mammals and flowering plants appeared.

❯ During the Cenozoic Era, India collided with Asia, Antarctica moved over the South Pole, and most modern mammal families, including humans, appeared.

mass extinction, p. 239
Mesozoic Era, p. 239
Cenozoic Era, p. 242

1. **Spider Map** Make a spider map for mass extinctions. Add one leg for the Permian mass extinction and one leg for the Cretaceous-Tertiary mass extinction. To each leg, add details about the mass extinction.

USING KEY TERMS

Use each of the following terms in a separate sentence.

2. *evolution* SC.912.L.15.1

3. *geologic column*

4. *period*

For each pair of terms, explain how the meanings of the terms differ.

5. *era* and *epoch*

6. *period* and *era*

7. *Mesozoic Era* and *Cenozoic Era* SC.912.L.15.1

8. *Precambrian time* and *Paleozoic Era* SC.912.L.15.1

UNDERSTANDING KEY IDEAS

9. The geologic time scale is a SC.912.L.15.1
   a. scale for weighing rocks.
   b. scale that divides Earth's history into time intervals.
   c. rock record of Earth's past.
   d. collection of the same kind of rocks.

10. Scientists are able to determine the absolute ages of most rock layers in a geologic column by using
   a. the law of superposition.
   b. radiometric dating.
   c. rates of deposition.
   d. rates of erosion.

11. To determine the age of a specific rock, scientists might correlate it with a layer in a geologic column that has the same relative position and SC.912.L.15.1
   a. fossil content.
   b. weight.
   c. temperature.
   d. density.

12. Geologic periods can be divided into
   a. eras.
   b. epochs.
   c. days.
   d. months.

13. Precambrian time ended about
   a. 4.6 billion years ago.
   b. 542 million years ago.
   c. 65 million years ago.
   d. 25 thousand years ago.

14. The most common fossils that occur in Precambrian rock are SC.912.L.15.1
   a. graptolites.
   b. trilobites.
   c. eurypterids.
   d. cyanobacteria.

15. The first vertebrates appeared during SC.912.L.15.1
   a. Precambrian time.
   b. the Paleozoic Era.
   c. the Mesozoic Era.
   d. the Cenozoic Era.

16. The *Age of Reptiles* is the name commonly given to SC.912.L.15.1
   a. Precambrian time.
   b. the Paleozoic Era.
   c. the Mesozoic Era.
   d. the Cenozoic Era.

17. The first flowering plants appeared during the SC.912.L.15.1
   a. Cretaceous Period.
   b. Triassic Period.
   c. Carboniferous Period.
   d. Ordovician Period.

18. The *Age of Mammals* is the name commonly given to SC.912.L.15.1
   a. Precambrian time.
   b. the Paleozoic Era.
   c. the Mesozoic Era.
   d. the Cenozoic Era.

SHORT ANSWER

19. Write a short paragraph describing the evolution of plants that is indicated by the fossil record. SC.912.L.15.1

20. Describe the events that may have led to the Cretaceous-Tertiary mass extinction. What evidence have scientists discovered that supports their hypothesis? SC.912.L.15.3

21. Describe the criteria that scientists use to divide a geologic column into different layers.

22. Identify two organisms that are found in the fossil record of a different geologic era but that are still living on Earth today. Identify what characteristic(s) have given them their long-term success. SC.912.L.15.1

CRITICAL THINKING

23. **Analyzing Ideas** Why can Precambrian time not be divided into periods by using fossils?

24. **Applying Ideas** Many coal and oil deposits formed during the Carboniferous Period. What element would you expect to find in both oil and coal? SC.912.P.8.12

25. **Identifying Relationships** What information in the geologic record might lead scientists to infer that shallow seas covered much of Earth during the Paleozoic Era? SC.912.L.15.1

26. **Making Comparisons** Compare the causes of the Permian mass extinction with those of the Cretaceous mass extinction. SC.912.L.15.3

CONCEPT MAPPING

27. Use the following terms to create a concept map: *geologic time, Paleozoic Era, Mesozoic Era, stromatolite, Precambrian time, eurypterid, crinoid, Cenozoic Era, trilobite, saurischian, ornithischian, dinosaur, mammal,* and *human.* SC.912.L.15.1

MATH SKILLS

Math Skills

28. **Scientific Notation** Write the beginning and end dates of each geologic era in scientific notation.

29. **Making Calculations** The Methuselah tree in California is 4.6×10^3 years old. How many times older than this tree is Earth ?

WRITING SKILLS

30. **Creative Writing** Write an essay about a trip back in time. Include descriptions of the organisms that lived during one of the geologic periods described in this chapter.

31. **Writing from Research** Research the discoveries made by British anthropologists Louis S.B. Leakey and Mary Leakey in Olduvai Gorge in Tanzania, Africa. Write a report about your findings.

INTERPRETING GRAPHICS

The graph below shows average global temperatures since Precambrian time. Use this graph to answer the questions that follow.

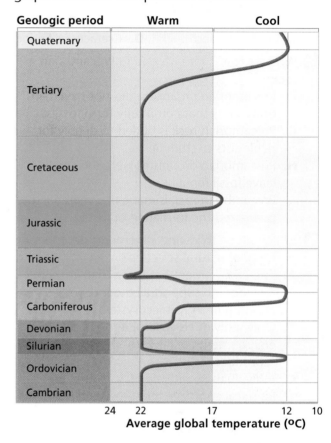

Average global temperature (°C)

32. During which two periods was Earth's average global temperature the highest? SC.912.N.1.1

33. During which periods did Earth's average global temperature decrease? SC.912.N.1.1

34. Based on the graph, could long-term climate change have caused the Permian mass extinction? Is long-term climate change a likely cause of the mass extinction at the Cretaceous-Tertiary boundary? Explain your answer. SC.912.N.1.1

Understanding Concepts

Directions (1–9): For each question, write on a separate sheet of paper the letter of the correct answer.

1 Dinosaurs first became the dominant life-forms during which geologic period?
 A. Quaternary Period   C. Triassic Period
 B. Jurassic Period   D. Cretaceous Period

2 Why are fossils rarely found in Precambrian rock?
 F. Precambrian organisms did not have hard body parts that commonly form fossils.
 G. Precambrian rock is buried to deeply for geologists to study it.
 H. Precambrian organisms were too small to leave fossil remains.
 I. Precambrian rock is made of a material that prevented the formation of fossils.

3 Which of the following statements describes a principle of natural selection?
 A. The environment has more than enough resources to support all the individuals that are born in a given ecosystem.
 B. Only individuals well suited to the environment are likely to survive and reproduce.
 C. Individuals in a healthy population are identical and have the same traits.
 D. Most species produce plentiful offspring that will all live until maturity and reproduce.

4 During various times in Earth's history, mass extinctions have occurred. During a mass extinction, enormous numbers of species die. How do mass extinctions benefit the surviving organisms?
 F. The surviving organisms can consume the dead organisms.
 G. The mass extinction makes resources available for the surviving organisms.
 H. Mass extinctions prevent the spread of disease to surviving organisms.
 I. The surviving organisms can adapt to the environment more easily.

5 Eons are the longest period of geologic time, followed by eras, then periods, and finally epochs. If a scientist wanted to describe when complex human societies evolved, which geologic time period would the scientist most likely use?
 A. eon
 B. era
 C. period
 D. epoch

6 Which of the following statements best describes the relationship between evolution and geologic change?
 F. Geologic change does not affect evolution.
 G. Dramatic geologic changes can drive evolutionary change.
 H. Evolution can cause geologic change.
 I. Geologic change always causes extinctions.

7 Which of the following is NOT true of the geologic column?
 A. It was developed by 19th century scientists and remains in use today.
 B. It represents a timeline of Earth's history.
 C. Most of the fossils in the lower layers are of plants and animals that no longer exist.
 D. Scientists can use the geologic column to determine the absolute age of a rock layer.

8 Which of the following is true of Precambrian time?
 F. It began about 251 million years ago.
 G. It ended with a large mass extinction.
 H. It makes up about 88% of Earth's history.
 I. It is called the Age of Mammals.

9 How is the Carboniferous Period important to modern humans?
 A. It is the period during which humans evolved.
 B. It is the period during which the rocks that hold oil formed.
 C. A mass extinction during this period allowed the evolution of human ancestors.
 D. Fossils from this period are similar to the organisms that live today.

Interpreting Graphics

Directions (10–12): For each question below, record the correct answer on a separate sheet of paper.

The Mesozoic and Cenozoic Eras

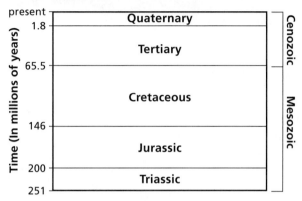

10 Human civilization developed during which of the following periods of time?

F. Triassic Period
G. Jurassic Period
H. Tertiary Period
I. Quaternary Period

11 If Earth formed about 4.6 billion years ago, what percentage of Earth's total history has the Cenozoic Era filled?

A. about 1.5%
B. about 10.5%
C. about 15%
D. about 50%

The Medieval Warm Period and the Little Ice Age

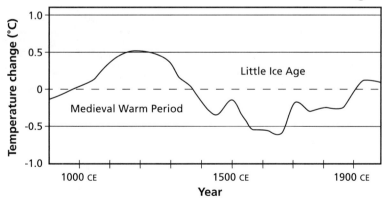

12 Between what years did the Little Ice Age occur?
F. 900 ce to 2000 ce
G. 1000 ce to 1350 ce
H. 1500 ce to 1700 ce
I. 1900 ce to 2000 ce

Test Tip

Simply keeping a positive attitude during any test will help you focus on the test and likely improve your score.

Unit 4 The Dynamic Earth

Chapter 10

Plate Tectonics

Chapter Outline

Why It Matters

Huge, moving slabs of rock called tectonic plates constantly reshape Earth's surface. For example, the island of Iceland is being torn where two tectonic plates are moving apart. Iceland is one of the few places where this process can be seen on land.

Inquiry Lab

⏱ **15 min**

Reconstructing Landmasses

Draw a map of a large landmass on a piece of paper. Use colored pencils or markers to show geological features, such as mountain ranges and types of rock at the surface. Using scissors, cut your map into irregular pieces. Trade map pieces with another group, and then reconstruct the other group's landmass.

Questions to Get You Started

1. What features of the interiors of the pieces did you use to put the pieces back together?

2. What features of the edges of the pieces did you use for your reconstruction?

🔹 SC.912.E.6.2

READING TOOLBOX

These reading tools will help you learn the material in this chapter.

Word Parts

Prefixes Many scientific words are made up of word parts that come from Latin and Greek. You can figure out the meanings of unfamiliar science terms by looking at their word parts.

The words *Pangaea* and *Panthalassa* contain the prefix *pan-*. *Pan-* comes from a Greek word meaning "all." The root words *gaea* and *thalassa* come from Greek words meaning "land" and "ocean." *Pangaea* means "all lands," and *Panthalassa* means "all oceans."

Your Turn Prefixes found in this chapter include *paleo-*, *di-*, *trans-*, and *pan-*. As you read this chapter, make a table like the one started below. List words or terms that contain prefixes and give the meaning of each prefix.

WORD OR TERM	PREFIX	MEANING
paleomagetism	paleo-	
divergent boundary	di-	

Fact, Hypothesis, or Theory?

Recognizing Facts, Hypotheses, and Theories A fact is a statement about the world that is based on observation. A hypothesis is a possible explanation that can be tested. A scientific theory is a model or explanation that ties together many hypotheses and observations.

Your Turn Make a table like the one shown below. List statements of fact, hypotheses, and theories from Sections 1 and 2. Identify the type of statement, and write any language from the text that signals the type of statement.

STATEMENT	FACT, HYPOTHESIS, OR THEORY	KEY WORDS
	hypothesis	"proposed a hypothesis..."
	fact	"scientists found that..."
	theory	"lead to a theory called _____"

FoldNotes

Three-Panel Flip Chart FoldNotes are a fun way to help you learn and remember ideas that you encounter as you read. FoldNotes help you organize concepts and see the "big picture."

Your Turn Follow the instructions in **Appendix A** for making a three-panel flip chart. Label the first panel "Divergent boundary," the second "Convergent boundary," and the third "Transform boundary." Open the appropriate flap to take notes about each type of boundary discussed in Section 2 and make a sketch.

For more information on how to use these and other tools, see **Appendix A**.

Continental Drift

Key Ideas	Key Terms	Why It Matters
❯ Summarize Wegener's hypothesis of continental drift. ❯ Describe the process of sea-floor spreading. ❯ Identify how paleomagnetism provides support for the idea of sea-floor spreading. ❯ Explain how sea-floor spreading provides a mechanism for continental drift.	continental drift mid-ocean ridge sea-floor spreading paleomagnetism	Evidence for continental drift was found in Earth's natural magnetism. This magnetism not only supports scientists' hypotheses, it also protects us all from the dangers of solar radiation.

One of the most exciting theories in Earth science began with observations made more than 400 years ago. As early explorers sailed the oceans of the world, they brought back information about new continents and their coastlines. Mapmakers used this information to chart the new discoveries and to make the first reliable world maps.

As people studied the maps, they were impressed by the similarity of the continental coastlines on either side of the Atlantic Ocean. The continents looked as though they would fit together like parts of a giant jigsaw puzzle. The east coast of South America, for example, seemed to fit perfectly into the west coast of Africa, as shown in **Figure 1.**

Wegener's Hypothesis

In 1912, a German scientist named Alfred Wegener (VAY guh nuhr) proposed a hypothesis that is now called **continental drift.** Wegener hypothesized that the continents once formed part of a single landmass called a *supercontinent.* According to Wegener, this supercontinent began breaking up into smaller continents during the Mesozoic Era (about 200 million years ago). Over millions of years, these continents drifted to their present locations. Wegener speculated that the crumpling of the crust in places may have produced mountain ranges such as the Andes on the western coast of South America.

SC.912.P.10.16 Explain the relationship between moving charges and magnetic fields, as well as changing magnetic fields and electric fields, and their application to modern technologies;
SC.912.P.10.19 Explain that all objects emit and absorb electromagnetic radiation and distinguish between objects that are blackbody radiators and those that are not.

continental drift the hypothesis that a single large landmass broke up into smaller landmasses to form the continents, which then drifted to their present locations

Figure 1 Early explorers noticed that the coastlines of Africa and South America could fit together like puzzle pieces. *Can you identify any other continents that could fit together like puzzle pieces?*

Figure 2 Fossils of *Mesosaurus*, such as the one shown below, were found in both South America and western Africa. Mountain chains of similar ages also exist on different continents, as shown in the map at right.

NORTH AMERICA

ATLANTIC OCEAN

EUROPE

ASIA

AFRICA

SOUTH AMERICA

PACIFIC OCEAN

INDIAN OCEAN

Mountains formed ~ 410 million years ago
Mountains formed ~ 250 million years ago
Distribution of *Mesosaurus* fossils
Distribution of *Glossopteris* fossils

SCiLINKS.
www.scilinks.org
Topic: Continental Drift
Code: HQX0351

Fossil Evidence

In addition to seeing the similarities in the coastlines of the continents, Wegener found other evidence to support his hypothesis. He reasoned that if the continents had once been joined, fossils of the same plants and animals should be found in areas that had once been connected. Wegener knew that identical fossils of *Mesosaurus,* a small, extinct land reptile, had been found in both South America and western Africa. *Mesosaurus,* a fossil of which is shown in **Figure 2**, lived 270 million years ago (during the Paleozoic Era). Wegener knew that it was unlikely these reptiles had swum across the Atlantic Ocean. He also saw no evidence that land bridges had once connected the continents. So, he concluded that South America and Africa had been joined at one time in the past.

Evidence from Rock Formations

Geologic evidence also supported Wegener's hypothesis of continental drift. The ages and types of rocks in the coastal regions of widely separated areas, such as western Africa and eastern South America, matched closely. Mountain chains that ended at the coastline of one continent seemed to continue on other continents across the ocean, as shown in **Figure 2**. The Appalachian Mountains, for example, extend northward along the eastern coast of North America, and mountains of similar age and structure are found in Greenland, Scotland, and northern Europe. If the continents are assembled into a model supercontinent, the mountains of similar age fit together in continuous chains.

Climatic Evidence

Changes in climatic patterns provided more evidence that the continents have not always been located where they are now. Geologists discovered layers of debris from ancient glaciers in southern Africa and South America. Today, those areas have climates that are too warm for glaciers to form. Other fossil evidence—such as the plant fossil shown in **Figure 3**—indicated that tropical or subtropical swamps covered areas that now have much colder climates. Wegener suggested that if the continents were once joined and positioned differently, evidence of climatic differences would be easy to explain.

Missing Mechanisms

Despite the evidence that supported the hypothesis of continental drift, Wegener's ideas were strongly opposed. Other scientists of the time rejected the mechanism proposed by Wegener to explain how the continents moved. Wegener suggested that the continents plowed through the rock of the ocean floor. However, this idea was shown to be physically impossible. Wegener spent the rest of his life searching for a mechanism that would gain scientific consensus. Unfortunately, Wegener died in 1930 before he identified a plausible explanation.

Reading Check **Why did many scientists reject Wegener's hypothesis of continental drift?** (See Appendix G for answers to Reading Checks.)

READING TOOLBOX

Three-Panel Flip Chart
Make a three-panel flip chart. Label the panels "Fossil evidence," "Evidence from rock formations," and "Climatic evidence." Open the appropriate flap to take notes about evidence Wegener used to support his hypothesis.

Academic Vocabulary

mechanism (MEK uh NIZ uhm) any system or means by which something gets done

Figure 3 The climate of Antarctica was not always as harsh and cold as it is today. When the plant that became this fossil lived, the climate of Antarctica was warm and tropical.

Figure 4 Black smokers are vents on the sea floor that form as hot, mineral-rich water rushes from the hot rock at mid-ocean ridges and mixes with the surrounding cold ocean water. This photo was taken from a submersible.

mid-ocean ridge a long, undersea mountain chain that has a steep, narrow valley at its center, that forms as magma rises from the asthenosphere, and that creates new oceanic lithosphere (sea floor) as tectonic plates move apart

Mid-Ocean Ridges

The evidence that Wegener needed to support his hypothesis was discovered nearly two decades after his death. The evidence lay on the ocean floor. In 1947, a group of scientists set out to map the Mid-Atlantic Ridge. The Mid-Atlantic Ridge is part of a system of **mid-ocean ridges,** which are undersea mountain ranges through the center of which run steep, narrow valleys. A special feature of mid-ocean ridges is shown in **Figure 4.** While studying the Mid-Atlantic Ridge, scientists noticed two surprising trends. First, they noticed that the sediment that covers the sea floor is thinner closer to a ridge than it is farther from the ridge. This evidence suggests that sediment has been settling on the sea floor farther from the ridge for a longer time than it has been settling near the ridge. Scientists then examined the remains of tiny ocean organisms found in the sediment to date the sediment. The distribution of these organisms showed that the closer the sediment is to a ridge, the younger the sediment is. This evidence indicates that rocks closer to the ridge are younger than rocks farther from the ridge, as shown in **Figure 5.**

Second, scientists learned that the ocean floor is very young. While rocks on land are as much as 4 billion years old, none of the oceanic rocks are more than 200 million years old. Radiometric dating also showed evidence that sea-floor rocks closer to a mid-ocean ridge are younger than sea-floor rocks farther from a ridge.

Figure 5 Rocks closer to a mid-ocean ridge are younger than rocks farther from the ridge. In addition, rocks closer to the ridge are covered with less sediment, which indicates that sediment has had less time to settle on them.

Mid-ocean ridge

Rift

Sediment

Oceanic crust

Magma

LITHOSPHERE

ASTHENOSPHERE

Sea-Floor Spreading

In the late 1950s, a geologist named Harry Hess suggested a new hypothesis. He proposed that the valley at the center of the ridge was a crack, or *rift,* in Earth's crust. At this rift, molten rock, or *magma,* from deep inside Earth rises to fill the crack. As the ocean floor moves away from the ridge, rising magma cools and solidifies to form new rock that replaces the ocean floor. This process is shown in **Figure 6.** During this process, named **sea-floor spreading** by geologist Robert Dietz, new ocean lithosphere forms as magma rises to Earth's surface and solidifies at a mid-ocean ridge. Hess suggested that if the ocean floor is moving, the continents might be moving, too. Hess thought that sea-floor spreading was the mechanism that Wegener had failed to find.

Still, Hess's ideas were only hypotheses. More evidence for sea-floor spreading would come years later, in the mid-1960s. This evidence would be discovered through **paleomagnetism,** the study of the magnetic properties of rocks.

Reading Check How does new sea floor form?

sea-floor spreading the process by which new oceanic lithosphere (sea floor) forms when magma rises to Earth's surface at mid-ocean ridges and solidifies, as older, existing sea floor moves away from the ridge

paleomagnetism the study of the alignment of magnetic minerals in rock, specifically as it relates to the reversal of Earth's magnetic poles; *also* the magnetic properties that rock acquires during formation

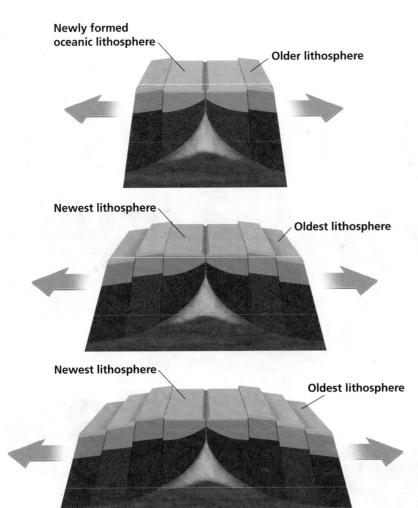

Newly formed oceanic lithosphere

Older lithosphere

Newest lithosphere

Oldest lithosphere

Newest lithosphere

Oldest lithosphere

Figure 6 As the ocean floor spreads apart at a mid-ocean ridge, magma rises to fill the rift and then cools to form new rock. As this process is repeated over millions of years, new sea floor forms.

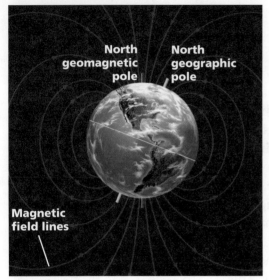

Figure 7 Earth acts as a giant magnet because of currents in Earth's core.

Paleomagnetism

If you have ever used a compass to determine direction, you know that Earth acts as a giant magnet. Earth has north and south geomagnetic poles, as shown in **Figure 7.** The compass needle aligns with the field of magnetic force that extends from one pole to the other.

As magma solidifies to form rock, iron-rich minerals in the magma align with Earth's magnetic field in the same way that a compass needle does. When the rock hardens, the magnetic orientation of the minerals becomes permanent. This residual magnetism of rock is called *paleomagnetism.*

Magnetic Reversals

Geologic evidence shows that Earth's magnetic field has not always pointed north, as it does now. Scientists have discovered rocks whose magnetic orientations point opposite to Earth's current magnetic field. Scientists have dated rocks of different magnetic polarities. All rocks with magnetic fields that point north, or *normal polarity*, are classified in the same time intervals. All rocks with magnetic fields that point south, or *reversed polarity*, also fall into specific time intervals. When scientists placed these periods of normal and reverse polarity in chronological order, they discovered a pattern of alternating normal and reversed polarity in the rocks. Scientists used this pattern to create the *geomagnetic reversal time scale.*

Why It Matters

Our Own Space Shield

Earth's magnetic field is not just an interesting topic for scientists. It makes life on Earth possible. Earth's magnetic field acts like a giant space shield, protecting our planet from the solar wind — electrically charged particles that stream away from the sun in all directions. Even with Earth's magnetic field in place, temporary increases in the strength of the solar wind can disrupt telecommunications systems and disable electric power grids. Without the magnetic field, Earth's atmosphere would be gradually swept away into the depths of space.

The solar wind moves along Earth's magnetic field toward the poles, so auroras are commonly seen at high latitudes.

Auroras, commonly known as the northern and southern lights, are a sign that Earth's protective space shield is working.

YOUR TURN

UNDERSTANDING CONCEPTS
What could happen to our atmosphere if Earth had no magnetic field?

Magnetic Symmetry

As scientists were learning about the age of the sea floor, they also were finding puzzling magnetic patterns on the ocean floor. The scientists used the geomagnetic reversal time scale to help them unravel the mystery of these magnetic patterns.

Scientists noticed that the striped magnetic pattern on one side of a mid-ocean ridge is a mirror image of the striped pattern on the other side of the ridge. These patterns are shown in **Figure 8.** When drawn on maps of the ocean floor, these patterns show alternating bands of normal and reversed polarity that match the geomagnetic reversal time scale. Scientists suggested that as new sea floor forms at a mid-ocean ridge, the new sea floor records reversals in Earth's magnetic field.

By matching the magnetic patterns on each side of a mid-ocean ridge to the geomagnetic reversal time scale, scientists could assign ages to the sea-floor rocks. The scientists found that the ages of sea-floor rocks were also symmetrical. The youngest rocks were at the center, and older rocks were farther away on either side of the ridge. The only place on the sea floor that new rock forms is at the rift in a mid-ocean ridge. Thus, the patterns indicate that new rock forms at the center of a ridge and then moves away from the center in opposite directions. Thus, the symmetry of magnetic patterns—and the symmetry of ages of sea-floor rocks—supports Hess's idea of sea-floor spreading.

Reading Check How are magnetic patterns in sea-floor rock evidence of sea-floor spreading?

Rift

Reversed polarity

Normal polarity

Figure 8 The stripes in the sea floor shown here illustrate Earth's alternating magnetic field. Dark stripes represent normal polarity, while lighter stripes represent reversed polarity. *What is the polarity of the rocks closest to the rift?*

4 3 2 1 0 1 2 3 4

Age of sea floor (in millions of years)

Figure 9 Scientists collected samples of these sedimentary rocks in California and used the magnetic properties of the samples to date the rocks by using the geomagnetic reversal time scale.

Wegener Redeemed

Another group of scientists discovered that the reversal patterns seen in rocks on the sea floor also appeared in rocks on land, such as those shown in **Figure 9.** The reversals in the land rocks matched the geomagnetic reversal time scale. Because the same pattern occurs in rocks of the same ages on both land and the sea floor, scientists became confident that magnetic patterns show changes over time. Thus, the idea of sea-floor spreading gained further favor in the scientific community.

Scientists reasoned that sea-floor spreading provides a way for the continents to move over Earth's surface. Continents are carried by the widening sea floor in much the same way that objects are carried by a conveyor belt. The molten rock from a rift cools, hardens, and then moves away in opposite directions on both sides of the ridge. Here, at last, was the mechanism that verified Wegener's hypothesis of continental drift.

Section 1 Review

SC.912.N.1.3; SC.912.N.2.5; SC.912.P.10.16; SC.912.P.10.19

Key Ideas

1. **Describe** the observation that first led to Wegener's hypothesis of continental drift.

2. **Summarize** the evidence that supports Wegener's hypothesis.

3. **Compare** sea-floor spreading with the formation of mid-ocean ridges.

4. **Explain** how scientists know that Earth's magnetic poles have reversed many times during Earth's history.

5. **Identify** how magnetic symmetry can be used as evidence of sea-floor spreading.

6. **Explain** how scientists date sea-floor rocks.

Critical Thinking

7. **Making Inferences** How does evidence that rocks farther from a ridge are older than rocks closer to the ridge support the idea of spreading?

8. **Analyzing Ideas** Explain how sea-floor spreading provides an explanation for how continents move over Earth's surface.

Concept Mapping

9. Use the following terms to create a concept map: *continental drift, paleomagnetism, fossils, climate, sea-floor spreading, geologic evidence, supercontinent,* and *mid-ocean ridge.*

The Theory of Plate Tectonics

Key Ideas	Key Terms	Why It Matters
❭ Summarize the theory of plate tectonics. ❭ Identify and describe the three types of plate boundaries. ❭ List and describe three causes of plate movement.	plate tectonics lithosphere asthenosphere divergent boundary convergent boundary transform boundary	Plate tectonics is not just a scientific theory. Because of plate tectonics, you are able to enjoy the use of a cell phone, MP3 player, or any number of other electronic devices.

By the 1960s, evidence supporting continental drift and sea-floor spreading led to the development of a theory called *plate tectonics.* **Plate tectonics** is the theory that explains why and how continents move and is the study of the formation of features in Earth's crust.

How Continents Move

Earth's crust and the rigid, upper part of the mantle form a layer of Earth called the **lithosphere.** The lithosphere forms the thin outer shell of Earth. It is broken into several blocks, called *tectonic plates,* that ride on a deformable layer of the mantle called the *asthenosphere* in much the same way that blocks of wood float on water. The **asthenosphere** (as THEN uh sfir) is a layer of "plastic" rock just below the lithosphere. Plastic rock is a solid, not a liquid, but it is so hot that it flows very slowly, like putty does. **Figure 1** shows what tectonic plates may look like.

Earth's crust is classified into two types—*oceanic crust* and *continental crust.* Oceanic crust is dense and is made of rock that is rich in iron and magnesium. Continental crust has a low density and is made of rock that is rich in silica. Tectonic plates can include continental crust, oceanic crust, or both. The crust is carried along on the moving tectonic plates in the same way that passengers are carried by a bus.

FLORIDA STANDARDS

SC.912.E.6.1 Describe and differentiate the layers of Earth and the interactions among them; **SC.912.P.10.4** Describe heat as the energy transferred by convection, conduction, and radiation, and explain the connection of heat to change in temperature or states of matter.

plate tectonics the theory that explains how large pieces of the lithosphere, called *plates,* move and change shape

lithosphere the solid, outer layer of Earth that consists of the crust and the rigid upper part of the mantle

asthenosphere the solid, plastic layer of the mantle beneath the lithosphere

Figure 1 Tectonic plates fit together on Earth's surface like three-dimensional puzzle pieces.

Tectonic Plates

Scientists have identified 15 major tectonic plates and many smaller plates. While plates are often bordered by major surface features, such as mountain ranges or deep trenches in the oceans, the boundaries of the plates are not always easy to identify. As shown in **Figure 2**, the familiar outlines of the continents and oceans often do not match the outlines of plate boundaries. Some plate boundaries are located within continents far from mountain ranges.

Earthquakes

Scientists identify plate boundaries primarily by studying data from earthquakes. When tectonic plates move, sudden shifts can occur along their boundaries. These sudden movements are called *earthquakes*. Frequent earthquakes in a given zone are evidence that two or more plates may meet in that area.

Volcanoes

The locations of volcanoes can also help to identify the locations of plate boundaries. Some volcanoes form when plate motions generate magma that erupts on Earth's surface. For example, the Pacific Ring of Fire is a zone of active volcanoes that encircles the Pacific Ocean. This zone is also one of Earth's major earthquake zones. The characteristics of this zone indicate that the Pacific Ocean is surrounded by plate boundaries.

Reading Check **How do scientists identify locations of plate boundaries?**

Math Skills

The Rate of Plate Movement Tectonic plates move slowly on Earth's surface. The rate of plate movement can be calculated by using the following equation:

$$rate = \frac{distance}{time}$$

In kilometers, how far would a plate that moves 4 cm per year move in 2 million years?

Figure 2 Tectonic plates may contain both oceanic and continental crust. Notice that the boundaries of plates do not always match the outlines of continents.

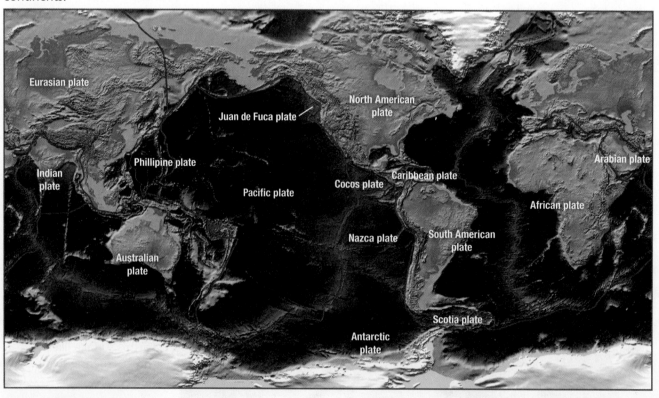

Eurasian plate

North American plate

Juan de Fuca plate

Arabian plate

Phillipine plate

Indian plate

Caribbean plate

Cocos plate

Pacific plate

African plate

Nazca plate

South American plate

Australian plate

Scotia plate

Antarctic plate

Rift

Mid-ocean ridge

Oceanic crust

Continental crust

Figure 3 At divergent boundaries, plates separate. A divergent boundary exists in the Red Sea between the Arabian Peninsula and Africa.

Types of Plate Boundaries

Some of the most dramatic changes in Earth's crust, such as earthquakes and volcanic eruptions, happen along plate boundaries. Plate boundaries may be in the middle of an ocean basin, around the edges of continents, or even within continents. There are three types of plate boundaries. These plate boundaries are: divergent boundaries, convergent boundaries, and transform boundaries. Each type of plate boundary is associated with a characteristic type of geologic activity.

Divergent Boundaries

The way that plates move relative to each other determines how the plate boundary affects Earth's surface. At a **divergent boundary,** two plates move away from each other. A divergent boundary is illustrated in **Figure 3.**

At divergent boundaries, magma from the asthenosphere rises to the surface as the plates move apart. The magma then cools to form new oceanic lithosphere. The newly formed rock at the ridge is warm and light. This warm, light rock sits higher than the surrounding sea floor because it is less dense. This rock forms undersea mountain ranges known as *mid-ocean ridges.* Along the center of a mid-ocean ridge is a *rift valley,* a narrow valley that forms where the plates separate.

Most divergent boundaries are located on the ocean floor. However, rift valleys may also form where continents are separated by plate movement. For example, the Red Sea occupies a huge rift valley formed by the separation of the African plate and the Arabian plate, as shown in **Figure 3.**

divergent boundary the boundary between tectonic plates that are moving away from each other

Convergent Boundaries

As plates pull apart at one boundary, they push into neighboring plates at other boundaries. **Convergent boundaries** are plate boundaries that form where two plates collide.

Three types of collisions can happen at convergent boundaries. One type happens when oceanic lithosphere collides with continental lithosphere, as shown in **Figure 4.** Because oceanic lithosphere is denser, it *subducts,* or sinks, under the less dense continental lithosphere. The region along a plate boundary where one plate moves under another plate is called a *subduction zone.* Deep-ocean trenches form at subduction zones. As the oceanic plate subducts, it heats up and releases fluids into the mantle above it. The addition of these fluids causes material in the overlying mantle to melt to form magma. The magma rises to the surface and forms volcanic mountains.

A second type of collision happens when two plates made of continental lithosphere collide. In this type of collision, neither plate subducts because neither plate is dense enough to subduct under the other plate. Instead, the colliding edges crumple and thicken, which causes uplift that forms large mountain ranges. The Himalaya Mountains formed in this type of collision.

The third type of collision happens between two plates that are made of oceanic lithosphere. One plate subducts under the other plate, and a deep-ocean trench forms. Fluids released from the subducted plate cause mantle rock to melt and form magma. The magma rises to the surface to form an *island arc,* which is a chain of volcanic islands. Japan is an example of an island arc.

Reading Check **Describe the three types of collisions that happen at convergent boundaries.**

convergent boundary the boundary between tectonic plates that are colliding

READING TOOLBOX

Prefixes
The term *convergent boundary* contains the prefix *con-.* Give the definition of the term and the prefix.

Figure 4 Plates collide at convergent boundaries. The islands of Japan are formed by the subduction of the Pacific plate and the Philippine plate under the Eurasian plate.

Ocean trench

Active volcano

Magma

Subduction zone

Pacific plate   **North American plate**

Asthenosphere

Figure 5 Plates slide past each other at transform boundaries. The course of the stream in the photo changed because the plates moved past each other at the San Andreas Fault in California.

Transform Boundaries

The boundary at which two plates slide past each other horizontally, as shown in **Figure 5,** is called a **transform boundary.** However, the plate edges usually do not slide along smoothly. Instead, they scrape against each other in a series of sudden spurts of motion that are felt as earthquakes. Unlike other types of boundaries, transform boundaries do not produce magma. The San Andreas Fault in California is a major transform boundary between the North American plate and the Pacific plate.

Transform motion also occurs along mid-ocean ridges. Short segments of a mid-ocean ridge are connected by transform boundaries called *fracture zones*.

Table 1 summarizes the three types of plate boundaries. The table also describes how each type of plate boundary changes Earth's surface and includes examples of each type of plate boundary.

transform boundary the boundary between tectonic plates that are sliding past each other horizontally

Table 1 Plate Boundary Summary

Type of boundary		Description	Example
Divergent		plates moving away from each other to form rifts and mid-ocean ridges	North American and Eurasian plates at the Mid-Atlantic Ridge
Convergent		plates moving toward each other and colliding to form ocean trenches, mountain ranges, volcanoes, and island arcs	South American and Nazca plates at the Chilean trench along the west coast of South America
Transform		plates sliding past each other while moving in opposite directions	North American and Pacific plates at the San Andreas Fault in California

Causes of Plate Motion

The movement of tectonic plates is part of the mantle convection system. *Convection* is the movement of heated material due to differences in density that are caused by differences in temperatures. This process can be modeled by boiling water in a pot on a stove. As the water at the bottom of the pot is heated, it expands and becomes less dense than the cooler water above it. The cooler, denser water sinks, and the warmer water rises to the surface to create a cycle called a *convection cell*.

Mantle Convection

Scientists think that Earth is also a convecting system. Energy generated by Earth's core and radioactivity within the mantle heat mantle material. This heated material rises through the cooler, denser material around it. As the hot material rises, the cooler, denser material flows away from the hot material and sinks into the mantle to replace the rising material. As the mantle material moves, the overlying tectonic plates move along with it, as shown in **Figure 6.**

Convection currents and the resulting movement of tectonic plates can explain many aspects of plate movement. But scientists have identified two specific mechanisms of convection that help to drive the process of plate motion.

Academic Vocabulary

process (PROH ses) a set of steps, events, or changes

Figure 6 Scientists think that tectonic plates are part of a convection system. *How is the rising of hot material related to the location of divergent boundaries?*

Convergent boundary

Divergent boundary

Convergent boundary

Rising hot material

Convection cell

Sinking cold material

MESOSPHERE

OUTER CORE

272

Ridge Push

Newly formed rock at a mid-ocean ridge is warmer and less dense than older rock nearby. The warmer, less dense rock is elevated above nearby rock, and older, denser rock slopes downward away from the ridge. As the newer, warmer rock cools and becomes denser, it begins to slide down the slope between the lithosphere and the asthenosphere.

As the cooling rock slides down the slope of the ridge, it exerts force on the rest of the plate. This force is called *ridge push*. This force pushes the rest of the plate away from the mid-ocean ridge. Ridge push is illustrated in **Figure 7.**

Scientists think that ridge push may help to drive plate motions. However, most scientists agree that ridge push is not the main driving force of plate motion. So, scientists looked to convergent boundaries for other clues about forces that drive plate motion.

Figure 7 As the cooling lithosphere slides down the slope formed by the elevation of the mid-ocean ridge, it pushes on the rest of the plate. This process contributes to the movement of the entire plate.

Reading Check How may density differences in the rock at a mid-ocean ridge help to drive plate motion?

SC.912.E.6.3

Quick Lab
30 min

Tectonic Plate Boundaries

Procedure

① Using a ruler, draw two 7 cm × 12 cm rectangles on a piece of paper. Cut them out with scissors.

② Use a rolling pin to flatten two different-colored pieces of clay to about 0.5 cm thick.

③ Use a plastic knife to cut each piece of clay into a 7 cm × 12 cm rectangle. Place a paper rectangle on each piece of clay.

④ Place the two clay models side by side on a flat surface, paper side down.

⑤ Place one hand on each piece of clay, and slowly push the blocks together until the edges begin to buckle and rise off the surface of the table.

⑥ Turn the clay models around so that the unbuckled edges are touching each other.

⑦ Place one hand on each clay model. Apply slight pressure toward the plane where the two

blocks meet. Slide one clay model forward 7 cm and the other model backward about 7 cm.

Analysis

1. What type of plate boundary are you modeling in step 5?

2. What type of plate boundary are you modeling in step 7?

3. How do you think the processes you modeled in this activity might affect the appearance of Earth's surface?

Direction of plate motion

Figure 8 The leading edge of the subducting plate pulls the rest of the subducting plate into the asthenosphere in a process called *slab pull*.

Resulting plate motion

Sinking due to density

Slab Pull

Where plates pull away from each other at mid-ocean ridges, magma from the asthenosphere rises to the surface. The magma then cools to form new lithosphere. As the lithosphere moves away from the mid-ocean ridge, the lithosphere cools and becomes denser. Where the lithosphere is dense enough, it begins to subduct into the asthenosphere. As the leading edge of the plate sinks, it pulls the rest of the plate along behind it, as shown in **Figure 8.** The force exerted by the sinking plate is called *slab pull*. In general, plates that are subducting move faster than plates that are not subducting. This evidence indicates that the downward pull of the subducting lithosphere is a strong driving force for tectonic plate motion.

All three mechanisms of Earth's convecting system—movement as part of a convection cell, ridge push, and slab pull—work together to drive plate motions. These mechanisms form a system that makes Earth's tectonic plates move constantly.

SCI*LINKS*®

www.scilinks.org
Topic: Plate Tectonics
Code: HQX1171

Section 2 Review

LA.910.2.2.3; SC.912.E.6.1; SC.912.E.6.3; SC.912.E.7.3;
SC.912.N.3.1; SC.912.N.3.2; SC.912.N.3.4; SC.912.P.10.4

Key Ideas

1. **Summarize** the theory of plate tectonics.

2. **Explain** why most earthquakes and volcanoes happen along plate boundaries.

3. **Identify** and describe the three major types of plate boundaries.

4. **Compare** the changes in Earth's surface that happen at a convergent boundary with those that happen at a divergent boundary.

5. **Describe** the role of convection currents in plate movement.

6. **Describe** how ridge push and slab pull contribute to the movement of tectonic plates.

Critical Thinking

7. **Making Inferences** How do convergent boundaries add material to Earth's surface?

8. **Determining Cause and Effect** Explain how the outward transfer of energy as heat from inside Earth drives the movement of tectonic plates.

Concept Mapping

9. Use the following terms to create a concept map: *tectonic plate, divergent, convergent, convection, transform, ridge push, slab pull, subduction zone,* and *mid-ocean ridge.*

The Changing Continents

Key Ideas	Key Terms	Why It Matters
❯ Identify how movements of tectonic plates change Earth's surface. ❯ Summarize how movements of tectonic plates have influenced climates and life on Earth. ❯ Describe the supercontinent cycle.	rifting terrane supercontinent cycle Pangaea Panthalassa	Global warming is a big concern in today's world. But movements of Earth's tectonic plates have had an effect on climates both past and present.

The continents did not always have the same shapes that they have today. And geologic evidence indicates that they will not remain the same shapes forever. In fact, the continents are always changing. Slow movements of tectonic plates change the sizes and shapes of the continents over millions of years.

Reshaping Earth's Crust

All the continents that exist today contain large areas of stable rock, called *cratons,* that are older than 540 million years. Rocks within the cratons that have been exposed at Earth's surface are called *shields.* Cratons represent ancient cores around which the modern continents formed.

Rifting and Continental Breakup

One way that continents change shape is by breaking apart. **Rifting** is the process by which a continent breaks apart. New, smaller continents may form as a result of this process. The reason that continents rift is not entirely known. Because continental crust is thick and has a high silica content, continental crust acts as an insulator. This insulating property prevents heat in Earth's interior from escaping. Scientists think that as heat from the mantle builds up beneath the continent, continental lithosphere becomes thinner and begins to weaken. Eventually, a rift forms in this zone of weakness, and the continent begins to break apart, as shown in **Figure 1.**

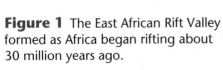

Figure 1 The East African Rift Valley formed as Africa began rifting about 30 million years ago.

FLORIDA STANDARDS

SC.912.E.6.1 Describe and differentiate the layers of Earth and the interactions among them; **SC.912.E.6.2** Connect surface features to surface processes that are responsible for their formation; **SC.912.E.6.3** Analyze the scientific theory of plate tectonics and identify related major processes and features as a result of moving plates; **SC.912.E.7.3** Differentiate and describe the various interactions among Earth systems, including: atmosphere, hydrosphere, cryosphere, geosphere, and biosphere.

rifting the process by which Earth's crust breaks apart; can occur within continental crust or oceanic crust

275

Terranes and Continental Growth

Continents change not only by breaking apart but also by gaining material. Most continents consist of cratons surrounded by a patchwork of terranes. A **terrane** is a piece of lithosphere that has a unique geologic history that differs from the histories of the surrounding lithosphere. A terrane can be identified by three characteristics. First, a terrane contains rock and fossils that differ from the rock and fossils of neighboring terranes. Second, there are major faults at the boundaries of a terrane. Third, the magnetic properties of a terrane generally do not match those of neighboring terranes.

Terranes become part of a continent at convergent boundaries. When a tectonic plate carrying a terrane subducts under a plate made of continental crust, the terrane is scraped off the subducting plate, as shown in **Figure 2.** The terrane then becomes part of the continent. Some terranes may form mountains, while other terranes simply add to the surface area of a continent. The process in which a terrane becomes part of a continent is called *accretion* (uh KREE shuhn).

A variety of materials can form terranes. Terranes may be small volcanic islands or underwater volcanoes called *seamounts.* Small coral islands, or *atolls,* that form on top of seamounts can also become terranes. And large chunks of continental crust can be terranes. When large terranes and continents collide, major mountain chains often form. For example, the Himalaya Mountains formed when India began colliding with Asia about 50 million years ago (during the Cenozoic Era).

terrane a piece of lithosphere that has a unique geologic history and that may be part of a larger piece of lithosphere, such as a continent

Reading Check **Describe the process of accretion.**

Figure 2 As oceanic crust subducts, a terrane is scraped off the ocean floor and becomes part of the continental crust. *What would you expect to happen to sediments on the sea floor when the plate they are on subducts?*

As the oceanic plate subducts, terranes are carried closer to the continent.

When the terrane reaches the subduction zone, the terrane is scraped off the subducting plate and added to the edge of the continent.

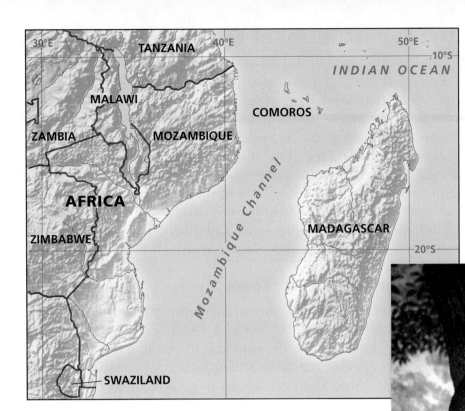

Figure 3 Madagascar separated from Africa about 165 million years ago and separated from India about 88 million years ago. This separation isolated the plants and animals on the island of Madagascar. As a result, unique species of plants and animals evolved on Madagascar. These species, such as the fossa (below), are found nowhere else on Earth.

Effects of Continental Change

Modern climates are a result of past movements of tectonic plates. A continent's location in relation to the equator and the poles affects the continent's overall climate. A continent's climate is also affected by the continent's location in relation to oceans and other continents. Mountain ranges affect air flow and wind patterns around the globe. Mountains also affect the amount of moisture that reaches certain parts of a continent. When continents move, the flow of air and moisture around the globe changes and causes climates to change.

Changes in Climate

Geologic evidence shows that ice once covered most of Earth's continental surfaces. Even the Sahara in Africa, one of the hottest places on Earth today, was once covered by a thick ice sheet. This ice sheet formed about 450 million years ago when all of the continents were close together and were located near the South Pole. As the continents began to drift around the globe, however, global temperatures changed and much of the ice sheet melted.

Changes in Life

As continents rift or as mountains form, populations of organisms are separated. When populations are separated, new species may evolve from existing species. Sometimes, isolation protects organisms from competitors and predators, and may allow the organisms to evolve into unique organisms, as shown in **Figure 3.**

The Supercontinent Cycle

Using evidence from many scientific fields, scientists can construct a general picture of continental change throughout time. Scientists think that, at several times in the past, the continents were arranged into large landmasses called *supercontinents*. These supercontinents broke apart to form smaller continents that moved around the globe. Eventually, the smaller continents joined again to form another supercontinent. When the last supercontinent broke apart, the modern continents formed. A new supercontinent is likely to form in the future. The process by which supercontinents form and break apart over time is called the **supercontinent cycle** and is shown in **Figure 4.**

Why Supercontinents Form

The movement of plates toward convergent boundaries eventually causes continents to collide. Because continental lithosphere does not subduct, the convergent boundary between two continents becomes inactive, and a new convergent boundary forms. Over time, all the continents collide to form a supercontinent. Then, heat from Earth's interior builds up under the supercontinent, and rifts form in the supercontinent. The supercontinent breaks apart, and plates carrying separate continents move around the globe.

Formation of Pangaea

The supercontinent **Pangaea** (pan JEE uh) formed about 300 million years ago (during the Paleozoic Era). As the continents collided to form Pangaea, mountains formed. The Appalachian Mountains of eastern North America and the Ural Mountains of Russia formed during these collisions. A body of water called the Tethys Sea cut into the eastern edge of Pangaea. The single, large ocean that surrounded Pangaea was called **Panthalassa.**

supercontinent cycle the process by which supercontinents form and break apart over millions of years

Pangaea the supercontinent that formed 300 million years ago and that began to break up 200 million years ago

Panthalassa the single, large ocean that covered Earth's surface during the time the supercontinent Pangaea existed

Figure 4 Over millions of years, supercontinents form and break apart in a cycle known as the *supercontinent cycle.*

About 450 million years ago Earth's continents were separated, as they are today.

225 million to 200 million years ago Pangaea had formed and was beginning to break apart.

Breakup of Pangaea

About 200 million years ago (during the Mesozoic Era), Pangaea began to break into two continents—*Laurasia* and *Gondwanaland*. A large rift split the supercontinent from east to west. Then, Laurasia began to drift northward and rotate slowly, and a new rift formed. This rift separated Laurasia into the continents of North America and Eurasia, and eventually formed the North Atlantic Ocean. The rotation of Laurasia also caused the Tethys Sea to shrink, leaving a remnant that eventually became the Mediterranean Sea.

As Laurasia began to break apart, Gondwanaland also broke into two continents. One of these continents broke apart to become the continents of South America and Africa. About 150 million years ago (during the Mesozoic Era), a rift between Africa and South America opened to form the South Atlantic Ocean. The other continent separated to form India, Australia, and Antarctica. As India broke away from Australia and Antarctica, it started moving northward toward Eurasia. About 50 million years ago (during the Cenozoic Era), India collided with Eurasia, and the Himalaya Mountains began to form.

SC*LINKS*

www.scilinks.org
Topic: Pangaea
Code: HQX1105

The Modern Continents

Slowly, the continents moved into their present positions. As the continents drifted, they collided with terranes and other continents. These collisions welded new crust onto the continents and uplifted the land. Mountain ranges, such as the Rocky Mountains, the Andes, and the Alps, formed. Tectonic plate motion also caused new oceans to open up and caused others to close.

Reading Check **What modern continents formed from Gondwanaland?**

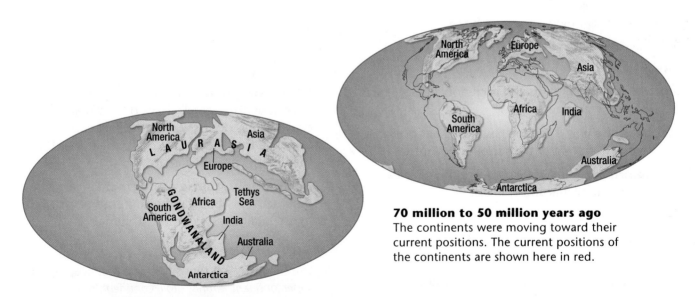

70 million to 50 million years ago
The continents were moving toward their current positions. The current positions of the continents are shown here in red.

160 million to 140 million years ago
Pangaea split into two continents: Laurasia to the north and Gondwanaland to the south.

Geography of the Future

As tectonic plates continue to move, Earth's geography will change dramatically. If plate movements continue at current rates, in about 150 million years, Africa will collide with Eurasia, and the Mediterranean Sea will close. New subduction zones will form off the east coast of North and South America after North America collides with Eurasia. North and South America will then move east across the Atlantic Ocean. The Atlantic Ocean will close as North and South America collide with Africa.

In North America, Mexico's Baja Peninsula and the part of California that is west of the San Andreas Fault will move to where Alaska is today. If this plate movement occurs as predicted, Los Angeles will be located north of San Francisco's current location. Scientists predict that, in 250 million years, the continents will come together again to form a new supercontinent, as shown in **Figure 5.**

Recognizing Facts, Hypotheses, and Theories
Make a three-column table. In the first column, list statements from this page and the preceding page about the past and future positions of continents. In the second column, identify whether each is a fact, hypothesis, or theory. In the third column, write any language from the text that signals which type of statement each is.

Academic Vocabulary
predict (pree DIKT) to tell in advance

Figure 5 Scientists predict that movements of tectonic plates will cause a supercontinent to form in the future.

Section 3 Review

SC.912.E.6.1; SC.912.E.6.2; SC.912.E.6.3; SC.912.E.7.3; SC.912.N.2.5; SC.912.N.3.1; SC.912.N.3.2; SC.912.N.3.4

Key Ideas

1. **Identify** how rifting and accretion change the shapes of continents.

2. **Describe** why a terrane has a different geologic history from that of the surrounding area.

3. **Summarize** how continental rifting may lead to changes in plants and animals.

4. **Describe** the supercontinent cycle.

5. **Explain** how the theory of plate tectonics relates to the formation and breakup of Pangaea.

6. **Compare** Pangaea and Gondwanaland.

7. **List** three changes in geography that are likely to happen in the future.

Critical Thinking

8. **Identifying Relationships** The interior parts of continents generally have drier climates than coastal areas do. How does this fact explain the evidence that the climate on Pangaea was drier than many modern climates?

9. **Determining Cause and Effect** Explain how mountains on land can be composed of rocks that contain fossils of marine animals.

Concept Mapping

10. Use the following terms to create a concept map: *supercontinent, rifting, atoll, continent, terrane, seamount, accretion,* and *Pangaea.*

Copper from Plate Margins

You can find copper almost everywhere around you—in electronics, air conditioners, coins, and cookware. You depend on copper every time you log onto the Internet or use a cell phone. Copper even makes up the outer skin of the Statue of Liberty!

Most of the copper that is mined today formed at ancient tectonic plate margins. Some of this copper formed at hydrothermal vents along divergent plate boundaries. As superheated seawater rises through hydrothermal vents, it deposits metal-rich minerals that had been dissolved in it. More than half of the world's copper, however, comes from areas that were once subduction zones. Hot fluids rising from subduction zones can become enriched with metals. Then, the fluids deposit the metals in fractures in the crust.

When geologists look for copper, they identify ancient plate boundaries to help them target likely search areas.

Deposits of minerals rich in copper and other metals build up around hydrothermal vents at divergent boundaries.

The word's largest copper deposits formed at convergent margins. Open-pit mines such as this one are used when ore is near the surface.

Underground mines are used to extract ore far below Earth's surface.

The mineral chalcopyrite consists of copper and iron combined with sulfur. It is a common copper ore.

Copper nugget

YOUR TURN

UNDERSTANDING CONCEPTS
Why do geologists look for ancient plate margins when they are searching for large bodies of copper ore?

ONLINE RESEARCH
Research a copper mine. What geologic processes formed the ore being mined there?

⏱ **90 min**

What You'll Do

❭ **Model** the formation of sea floor.

❭ **Identify** how magnetic patterns are caused by sea-floor spreading.

What You'll Need

marker
paper, unlined
ruler, metric
scissors or utility knife
shoebox

Safety

Sea-Floor Spreading

The places on Earth's surface where plates pull apart have many names. They are called divergent boundaries, mid-ocean ridges, and spreading centers. The term *spreading center* refers to the fact that sea-floor spreading happens at these locations. In this lab, you will model the formation of new sea floor at a divergent boundary. You will also model the formation of magnetic patterns on the sea floor.

Procedure

1. Cut two identical strips of unlined paper, each 7 cm wide and 30 cm long.

2. Cut a slit 8 cm long in the center of the bottom of a shoebox.

3. Lay the strips of paper together on top of each other and end-to-end so that the ends line up. Push one end of the strips through the slit in the shoe box, so that a few centimeters of both strips stick out of the slit.

4. Place the shoe box flat on a table, open side down, and make sure the ends of the paper strips are sticking up.

Step ❸

Step 6

5. Separate the strips, and hold one strip in each hand. Pull the strips apart. Then, push the strips down against the shoe box.

6. Use a marker to mark across the paper strips where they exit the box. One swipe with the marker should mark both strips.

7. Pull the strips evenly until about 2 cm have been pulled through the slit.

8. Mark the strips with the marker again.

9. Repeat steps 7 and 8, but vary the length of paper that you pull from the slit. Continue this process until both strips are pulled out of the box.

Analysis

1. **Evaluating Models** How does this activity model sea-floor spreading?

2. **Analyzing Models** What do the marker stripes in this model represent?

3. **Analyzing Methods** If each 2 cm on the paper is equal to 3 million years, how could you use your model to determine the age of certain points on the sea floor?

4. **Applying Conclusions** Suppose that you are given paper strips with marks already drawn on them. How would you use the paper strips to reconstruct the way in which the sea floor formed?

Extension

Making Models Design a model that shows what happens at a convergent boundary and what happens at a transform boundary. Present these models to the class.

MAPS *in Action*

Locations of Earthquakes in South America

Earthquake Depth (km)
- 0
- 25
- 75
- 150
- 300
- 600

Map ▶ Skills Activity

This map shows the locations and depths of earthquakes that registered magnitudes greater than 5 and that happened in South America over a recent one-year span. Use the map to answer the questions below.

1. **Using a Key** How many earthquakes happened at a depth greater than 300 km?

2. **Analyzing Data** Deep earthquakes are earthquakes that happen at a depth greater than 300 km. Which earthquakes happen more frequently: deep earthquakes or shallow earthquakes?

3. **Making Comparisons** How does the earthquake activity on the eastern edge of South America differ from the earthquake activity on the western edge?

4. **Inferring Relationships** The locations of earthquakes and plate boundaries are related. Where would you expect to find a major plate boundary?

5. **Identifying Trends** In what part of South America do most deep earthquakes happen? What relationships do you see between the locations of shallow earthquakes and deep earthquakes in South America?

6. **Analyzing Relationships** Most deep earthquakes happen where subducting plates move deep into the mantle. What type of plate boundary is indicated by the earthquake activity in South America? Explain your answer.

Summary

THINK central
SUPER SUMMARY
Keyword: HQXTECS

Key Ideas

Key Terms

Continental Drift

❯ Fossil, rock, and climatic evidence supports Wegener's hypothesis of continental drift. However, Wegener could not explain the mechanism by which the continents move.

❯ New ocean floor is constantly being produced through sea-floor spreading, which creates mid-ocean ridges and changes the topography of the sea floor.

❯ The magnetic properties of the rock of the ocean floor show that new lithosphere forms at a mid-ocean ridge and then moves away.

❯ Sea-floor spreading provides evidence that tectonic plates move and change.

continental drift, p. 259
mid-ocean ridge, p. 262
sea-floor spreading,
  p. 263
paleomagnetism, p. 263

The Theory of Plate Tectonics

❯ The theory of plate tectonics proposes that changes in Earth's crust are caused by the very slow movement of large tectonic plates. Earthquakes, volcanoes, and young mountain ranges tend to be located in belts along the boundaries between tectonic plates.

❯ Tectonic plates meet at three types of boundaries—divergent, convergent, and transform. The geologic activity that occurs along the three types of plate boundaries differs according to the way plates move relative to each other.

❯ Tectonic plates are part of a convecting system that is driven by differences in density and heat.

plate tectonics, p. 267
lithosphere, p. 267
asthenosphere, p. 267
divergent boundary,
  p. 269
convergent boundary,
  p. 270
transform boundary,
  p. 271

The Changing Continents

❯ Continents grow through the accretion of terranes. Continents break apart through rifting.

❯ Movements of tectonic plates have altered climates on continents and have created conditions that lead to changes in plants and animals.

❯ Continents collide to form supercontinents and then break apart in a cycle called the *supercontinent cycle*. Earth's tectonic plates continue to move, and, in the future, the continents will likely be in a different configuration.

rifting, p. 275
terrane, p. 276
supercontinent cycle,
  p. 278
Pangaea, p. 278
Panthalassa, p. 278

1. **Three-Panel Flip Chart** Make a three-panel flip chart. Label the first panel "Crust," the second "Lithosphere," and the third "Asthenosphere." Under the appropriate flap, list the location and characteristics of each of these layers.

READING TOOLBOX

USING KEY TERMS

Use each of the following terms in a separate sentence.

2. *sea-floor spreading* SC.912.E.6.3

3. *convection* SC.912.E.6.3

4. *divergent boundary* SC.912.E.6.3

5. *terrane* SC.912.E.6.3

For each pair of terms, explain how the meanings of the terms differ.

6. *convergent boundary* and *subduction zone* SC.912.E.6.3

7. *continental drift* and *plate tectonics* SC.912.E.6.3

8. *ridge push* and *slab pull* SC.912.E.6.3

9. *Pangaea* and *Panthalassa* SC.912.E.6.3

UNDERSTANDING KEY IDEAS

10. Support for Wegener's hypothesis of continental drift includes evidence of changes in
    a. climatic patterns. SC.912.E.6.3
    b. Panthalassa.
    c. terranes.
    d. subduction.

11. New ocean floor is constantly being produced through the process known as SC.912.E.6.3
    a. subduction.
    b. continental drift.
    c. sea-floor spreading.
    d. terranes.

12. An underwater mountain chain that formed by sea-floor spreading is called a SC.912.E.6.3
    a. divergent boundary.
    b. subduction zone.
    c. mid-ocean ridge.
    d. convergent boundary.

13. Scientists think that the upwelling of mantle material at mid-ocean ridges is caused by the motion of tectonic plates and comes from SC.912.E.6.3
    a. the lithosphere.   c. the asthenosphere.
    b. terranes.   d. rift valleys.

14. The layer of plastic rock that underlies the tectonic plates is the SC.912.E.6.3
    a. lithosphere.   c. oceanic crust.
    b. asthenosphere.   d. terrane.

15. The region along tectonic plate boundaries where one plate moves beneath another is called a SC.912.E.6.3
    a. rift valley.
    b. transform boundary.
    c. subduction zone.
    d. convergent boundary.

16. Two plates grind past each other at a SC.912.E.6.3
    a. transform boundary.
    b. convergent boundary.
    c. subduction zone.
    d. divergent boundary.

17. Convection occurs because heated material becomes SC.912.E.6.3
    a. less dense and rises.
    b. denser and rises.
    c. denser and sinks.
    d. less dense and sinks.

SHORT ANSWER

18. Explain the role of technology in the progression from the hypothesis of continental drift to the theory of plate tectonics. SC.912.E.6.3

19. Summarize how the continents moved from being part of Pangaea to their current locations. SC.912.E.6.3

20. Why do most earthquakes and volcanoes happen at or near plate boundaries? SC.912.E.6.3

21. Explain the following statement: "Because of sea-floor spreading, the ocean floor is constantly renewing itself." SC.912.E.6.3

22. Describe how rocks that form at a mid-ocean ridge become magnetized. SC.912.E.6.3

23. How might continental rifting influence the evolution of plants and animals? SC.912.E.6.3

CRITICAL THINKING

24. Making Comparisons How are tectonic plates like the pieces of a jigsaw puzzle? `SC.912.E.6.3`

25. Making Inferences If Alfred Wegener had found identical fossil remains of plants and animals that had lived no more than 10 million years ago in both eastern Brazil and western Africa, what might he have concluded about the breakup of Pangaea? `SC.912.E.6.3`

26. Identifying Relationships Assume that the total surface area of Earth is not changing. If new material is being added to Earth's crust at one boundary, what would you expect to be happening at another boundary? `SC.912.E.6.3`

27. Making Predictions About 150 million years from now, the continents will have drifted to new locations. How might these changes affect life on Earth? `SC.912.E.6.3`

CONCEPT MAPPING

28. Use the following terms to create a concept map: *asthenosphere, lithosphere, divergent boundary, convergent boundary, transform boundary, subduction zone, mid-ocean ridge, plates, convection, continental drift, theory of plate tectonics,* and *sea-floor spreading.* `SC.912.E.6.3`

MATH SKILLS   Math Skills

29. Making Calculations The coasts of Africa and South America began rifting about 150 million years ago. Today, the coast of South America is about 6,660 km from the coast of Africa. Using the equation *velocity = distance ÷ time,* determine how fast the continents moved apart, in millimeters per year. `SC.912.E.6.3`

30. Using Equations Assume that scientists know the rate at which the North American and Eurasian plates are moving away from each other. If t = time, d = distance, and v = velocity, what equation can they use to determine when North America separated from Eurasia during the breakup of Pangaea? `SC.912.E.6.3`

WRITING SKILLS

31. Writing Persuasively Imagine that you are Alfred Wegener. Write a persuasive essay to explain your idea of continental drift. Use only evidence originally used by Wegener to support his hypothesis. `SC.912.E.6.3`

32. Communicating Main Ideas Explain how the research of Wegener, Hess, and others led to the theory of plate tectonics. `SC.912.E.6.3`

INTERPRETING GRAPHICS

The graph below shows the relationship between the age of sea-floor rocks and the depth of the sea floor beneath the ocean surface. Use the graph to answer the questions that follow.

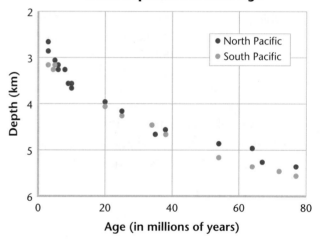

Ocean Depth vs. Sea-Floor Age

33. How old is the sea floor at a depth of 4 km?

34. Approximately how deep is the sea floor when it is 55 million years old? `SC.912.E.6.3`

35. What can you infer about the age of very deep sea floor from the data in the graph? `SC.912.E.6.3`

36. The ridge in the South Pacific Ocean is spreading faster than the ridge in the North Pacific Ocean. If this graph showed the depth of the sea floor in relation to the distance from the ridge, how would graphs for the North Pacific and South Pacific ridges differ? `SC.912.E.6.3`

Understanding Concepts

Directions (1–10): For each question, write on a separate sheet of paper the letter of the correct answer.

1 Which of the following factors is most important when determining the type of boundary that forms when two lithospheric plates collide?
A. the density of each plate
B. the size of each plate
C. the paleomagnetism of the rock
D. the length of the boundary

2 At locations where sea-floor spreading occurs, rock is moved away from a mid-ocean ridge. What replaces the rock as it moves away?
F. molten rock
G. older rock
H. continental crust
I. compacted sediment

3 Which of the following was a weakness of Wegener's proposal of continental drift when he first proposed the hypothesis?
A. an absence of fossil evidence
B. unsupported climatic evidence
C. unrelated continent features
D. a lack of proven mechanisms

4 Which of the following statements describes a specific type of continental growth?
F. Continents change not only by gaining material but also by losing material.
G. Terranes become part of a continent at convergent boundaries.
H. Ocean sediments move onto land because of sea-floor spreading.
I. Rifting adds new rock to a continent and causes the continent to become wider.

5 Modern climates result from
A. the past movements of tectonic plates.
B. changes in populations of organisms.
C. the flow of air in ancient times.
D. isolation.

6 Which of the following statements best describes magma formation at a divergent boundary?
F. One plate subducts under another as two plates collide, forming magma.
G. Magma rises as the plates move apart.
H. Magma forms as two plates slide against each other.
I. A plate subducts as two plates pull apart, forming magma.

7 The San Andreas Fault is a major boundary between the North American plate and Pacific plate. Earthquakes occur along this fault because
A. the plates are spreading.
B. one of the plates subducts under the other.
C. the plates slide against each other.
D. one plate is denser than the other.

8 Rocks on the ocean floor
F. are the same age as rocks on land.
G. are much younger than rocks on land.
H. are older the closer they are to mid-ocean ridges.
I. become magma as they get older.

9 Which of the following best describes the supercontinent cycle that resulted in the continents?
A. Pangaea→Gondwanaland and Laurasia→ separate continents
B. Pangaea→separate continents→ Gondwanaland and Laurasia
C. separate continents→Gondwanaland and Laurasia→Pangaea
D. Gondwanaland and Laurasia→ separate continents→Pangaea

10 Which of the following is NOT true of magnetic reversals?
F. They can be used to assign age to sea floor rocks.
G. They form mirror images on either side of a mid-ocean ridge.
H. They are rarely used to create a time scale.
I. They record changes in Earth's magnetic field.

Interpreting Graphics

Directions (11–13): For each question below, record the correct answer on a separate sheet of paper.

The map below shows the locations of the Earth's major tectonic plate boundaries.

Earth's Tectonic Plates

⑪ What type of boundary is found between the South American plate and the African plate?

A. convergent   **C.** transform

B. divergent   **D.** subduction

⑫ What surface features are most often found at boundaries such as those between the South American and African plates?

F. mountains

G. deep-ocean trenches

H. mid-ocean ridges

I. faults

Plate Boundaries

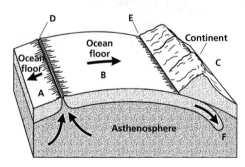

⑬ The illustration above shows a strike-slip fault that formed along a transform boundary. What type of crustal interaction is indicated by the letter E?

A. continental rifting   **C.** divergence

B. sea-floor spreading   **D.** subduction

Test Tip

If you become short on time, quickly scan the unanswered questions to see which questions are easiest to answer.

Deformation of the Crust

Why It Matters

Understanding how rock deforms by bending or breaking helps us understand the processes that shape Earth's surface. When building Highway 14 in California, construction crews cut through this hill. The exposed rock layers were folded by stress that was caused by movement along the nearby San Andreas fault.

Inquiry Lab

🕐 5 min

Types of Deformation

Hold the ends of a wooden craft stick. Apply pressure to bend the stick, and then release the pressure. Apply pressure again, but this time bend the stick until it breaks.

Questions to Get You Started

1. Describe how the shape of the craft stick changed when you bent and released it, and then when you broke it.

2. Which change in shape was temporary? Which change was permanent?

3. How was the pressure that caused the permanent change different from the pressure that caused the temporary change?

SC.912.E.6.2

READING TOOLBOX

These reading tools will help you learn the material in this chapter.

Science Terms

Everyday Words Used in Science Many words that are used in science are also used in everyday speech. When these words are used in science, however, their meanings are often different from their everyday meanings, or more precise. Pay special attention to the definitions of such words so that you use the words correctly in scientific contexts.

Your Turn As you read Section 1, complete a table like the one below.

Word	Everyday meaning	Scientific meaning
stress	an emphasis; a state of anxiety	the amount of force per unit area that acts on a rock
strain	make an intense effort	
fault		

Comparisons

Analyzing Comparisons When you compare two things, you describe how they are similar or different. Words that may signal comparisons include *like*, *unlike*, *more*, and *less*, as well as words formed by using the suffixes *-er* and *-est*.

Your Turn Make a table like the one below. As you read the chapter, list the two things being compared in the first two columns. In the third column, describe how they are similar or different. In the last column, note any words or phrases that signal the comparison. The sample entry below is for the sentence "Like folds, faults vary greatly in size."

First thing	Second thing	Similarity or difference	Signaling word or phrase
folds	faults	Both can be very small or very large.	like

Graphic Organizers

Cause-and-Effect Maps You can use cause-and-effect maps to show how processes are related to each other. To make a cause-and-effect map, follow these steps.

1 Draw a box, and write a cause inside it. Add as many cause boxes as you want.

2 Draw another box to represent an effect. Add as many effect boxes as you want.

3 Connect each cause box to one or more effect boxes with arrows.

4 An effect can be the cause of one or more other effects. You may want to connect an effect box to one or more other effect boxes.

Your Turn As you read Section 1, use a separate sheet of paper to complete the cause-and-effect map started below. Add at least two more effects.

The weight of a portion of Earth's crust changes. → Vertical movement of the lithosphere occurs.

For more information on how to use these and other tools, see **Appendix A.**

How Rock Deforms

Key Ideas	Key Terms	Why It Matters
> Summarize the principle of isostasy. > Identify the three main types of stress. > Compare folds and faults.	deformation isostasy stress strain fold fault	Both folding and faulting can create tall mountains and deep valleys. Understanding how deformed rock behaves can help engineers determine how stable a hillside or a cliff is.

Mountain ranges are visible reminders that the shape of Earth's surface is constantly changing. These changes result from **deformation,** or the bending, tilting, and breaking of Earth's crust.

Isostasy

Deformation sometimes occurs because the weight of some part of Earth's crust changes. When the lithosphere (of which the crust is a part) thickens and becomes heavier, it sinks deeper into the asthenosphere. If the lithosphere thins and becomes lighter, it rises higher in the asthenosphere.

Vertical movement of the lithosphere depends on two opposing forces. One force is the force due to gravity, or weight, of the lithosphere pressing down on the asthenosphere. The other force is the buoyant force of the asthenosphere pressing up on the lithosphere. When these two forces are balanced, the lithosphere and asthenosphere are in a state called **isostasy.** However, when the weight of the lithosphere changes, the lithosphere sinks or rises until a balance of the forces is reached again. One type of this isostatic adjustment is shown in **Figure 1.** As these adjustments occur, areas of the crust are bent up and down. This bending causes rock in these areas to deform.

FLORIDA STANDARDS

SC.912.E.6.1 Describe and differentiate the layers of Earth and the interactions among them; **SC.912.E.6.2** Connect surface features to surface processes that are responsible for their formation; **SC.912.E.7.3** Differentiate and describe the various interactions among Earth systems, including: atmosphere, hydrosphere, cryosphere, geosphere, and biosphere.

deformation the bending, tilting, and breaking of Earth's crust; the change in the shape of rock in response to stress

isostasy a condition of gravitational and buoyant equilibrium between Earth's lithosphere and asthenosphere

Figure 1 (A) When gravitational and buoyant forces are equal, a state of isostasy exists. (B) As erosion wears away the crust, the lithosphere becomes lighter and rises. (C) As erosion continues, the isostatic adjustment also continues.

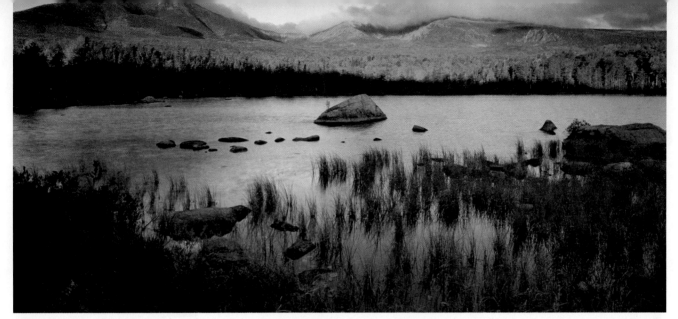

Figure 2 Mt. Katahdin in Baxter State Park, Maine, has been worn down by weathering and erosion. As the mountain shrinks, the crust underneath it is uplifted.

 SC.912.E.6.1

Mountains and Isostasy

In mountainous regions, isostatic adjustments constantly occur. Over millions of years, the rock that forms mountains is worn away by the erosive actions of wind, water, and ice. This erosion can significantly reduce the height and weight of a mountain range, such as the one shown in **Figure 2.** As a mountain becomes smaller and lighter, the area may rise by isostatic adjustment in a process called *uplift*.

Deposition and Isostasy

Another type of isostatic adjustment occurs in areas where rivers carrying large amounts of mud, sand, and gravel flow into larger bodies of water. When a river flows into the ocean, most of the material that the river carries is deposited on the nearby ocean floor. The added weight of the deposited material causes the ocean floor to sink by isostatic adjustment in a process called *subsidence*. This process is occurring in the Gulf of Mexico at the mouth of the Mississippi River, where a thick accumulation of deposited materials has formed.

Glaciers and Isostasy

Isostatic adjustments also occur as a result of the growth and retreat of glaciers and ice sheets. When a large amount of water is held in glaciers and ice sheets on land, the weight of the ice causes the lithosphere beneath the ice to sink. Simultaneously, the ocean floor rises because the weight of the overlying ocean water is less. When glaciers and ice sheets melt, the land that was covered with ice slowly rises as the weight of the crust decreases. As the water returns to the ocean, the ocean floor sinks.

Stress

As Earth's lithosphere moves, the rock in the crust is squeezed, stretched, and twisted. These actions exert force on the rock. The amount of force that is exerted on each unit of area is called **stress.** For example, during isostatic adjustments, the lithosphere sinks and rises atop the asthenosphere. As the lithosphere sinks, the rock in the crust is squeezed and the direction of stress changes. As the lithosphere rises, the rock in the crust is stretched and the direction of stress changes again. Similarly, stress occurs in Earth's crust when tectonic plates collide, separate, or scrape past each other. **Figure 3** shows the three main types of stress.

stress the amount of force per unit area that acts on a rock

Compression

The type of stress that squeezes and shortens a body, such as rock, is called *compression*. Compression can reduce the amount of space that rock occupies. More commonly, however, compression changes the shape of the rock while pushing it higher up or deeper down into the crust. Much of the stress that occurs at or near convergent boundaries, where tectonic plates collide, is compression.

Tension

Another type of stress is tension. *Tension* is stress that stretches and pulls a body apart. When rock is pulled apart by tension, it tends to become thinner. Much of the stress that occurs at or near divergent boundaries, where tectonic plates pull apart, is tension.

Shear Stress

The third type of stress is shear stress. *Shear stress* distorts a body by pushing parts of the body in opposite directions. Sheared rock bends, twists, or breaks apart as it slides past neighboring rock. Shear stress is common at transform boundaries, where tectonic plates slide horizontally past each other. However, each type of stress occurs at or near all types of plate boundaries and in various other regions of the crust, too.

THINK central INTERACT ONLINE Keyword: HQXDEFF3

Figure 3 Types of Stress

Compression

Tension

Shear Stress

Academic Vocabulary

distort (di STOHRT) to change the natural appearance of something

Reading Check Which two kinds of stress pull rock apart?
(See Appendix G for answers to Reading Checks.)

Figure 4 This rock deformation in Kingman, Arizona, is an example of brittle strain.

strain any change in a rock's shape or volume caused by stress

SC.912.E.6.2

Strain

When stress is applied to rock, rock may deform. Any change in the shape or volume of rock that results from stress is called **strain**. When stress is applied slowly, the deformed rock may regain its original shape when the stress is removed. However, the amount of stress that rock can withstand without permanently changing shape is limited. This limit varies with the type of rock and the conditions under which the stress is applied. If a stress exceeds the rock's limit, the rock's shape permanently changes.

Types of Permanent Strain

Materials that respond to stress by breaking or fracturing are *brittle*. Brittle strain appears as cracks or fractures, as **Figure 4** shows. *Ductile* materials respond to stress by bending or deforming without breaking. Ductile strain is a change in the volume or shape of rock in which the rock does not crack or fracture. Brittle strain and ductile strain are types of permanent strain.

Factors That Affect Strain

The composition of rock determines whether rock is ductile or brittle. Temperature and pressure also affect how rock deforms. Near Earth's surface, where temperature and pressure are low, rock is likely to deform in a brittle way. At higher temperature and pressure, rock is more likely to deform in a ductile way.

The type of strain that stress causes is determined by the amount and type of stress and by the rate at which stress is applied to rock. The greater the stress on rock is, the more likely rock is to undergo brittle strain. The more quickly stress is applied to rock, the more likely rock is to respond in a brittle way.

Quick Lab   Modeling Stress and Strain

 15 min

Procedure

❶ Put on a pair of gloves, and pick up a 5 cm × 5 cm square of frozen plastic play putty. Hold one edge of the frozen putty in each hand.

❷ Try to pull the putty apart by pulling the edges away from each other.

❸ Push the edges of the frozen putty toward each other. (You may have to reshape the putty between steps.)

❹ Push one edge of the frozen putty away from you, and pull the other edge toward you.

❺ Repeat steps 2–4, but use a 5 cm × 5 cm square of warm plastic play putty.

Analysis

1. What types of stress did you model in steps 2, 3, and 4?

2. Make a table that lists the characteristics of the two substances that you modeled, the stresses that you modeled, and the resulting strain on each model.

3. How does the frozen putty respond to the stress? How does the warm putty's response to the stress differ from the frozen putty's response?

Folds

When rock responds to stress by deforming in a ductile way, folds commonly form. A **fold** is a bend in rock layers that results from stress. A fold is most easily observed where flat layers of rock were compressed or squeezed inward. As stress was applied, the rock layers bent and folded. Cracks sometimes appear in or near a fold, but most commonly the rock layers remain intact. Although a fold commonly results from compression, it can also form as a result of shear stress.

fold a form of ductile strain in which rock layers bend, usually as a result of compression

Anatomy of a Fold

Folds have features by which they can be identified. Scientists use these features to describe folds. The main features of a fold are shown by the illustration in **Figure 5.** The sloping sides of a fold are called *limbs*. The limbs meet at the bend in the rock layers, which is called the *hinge*. Some folds also contain an additional feature. If a fold's structure is such that a plane could slice the fold into two symmetrical halves, the fold is symmetrical. The plane is called the fold's *axial plane*. However, the two halves of a fold are rarely symmetrical.

Many folds bend vertically, but folds can have many other shapes, as shown by the photograph in **Figure 5.** Folds are usually asymmetrical. Sometimes, one limb of a fold dips more steeply than the other limb does. If a fold is *overturned,* the fold appears to be lying on its side. Folds can have open shapes or be as tight as a hairpin. A fold's hinge can be a smooth bend or may come to a sharp point. Each fold is unique because the combination of stresses and conditions that caused the fold was unique.

Math Skills

Units of Stress Two units are commonly used to describe stress or pressure. One unit is the pascal (Pa). A pascal is a measure of force (in newtons) divided by area (in square meters). The other unit of stress is the pound per square inch (psi). If the pressure in a region of Earth's crust is measured as 25 MPa (megapascals) and as 3,626 psi, how many pounds per square inch does 1 MPa equal? (Note: 1 MPa = 1,000,000 Pa)

Reading Check Name two features of a fold.

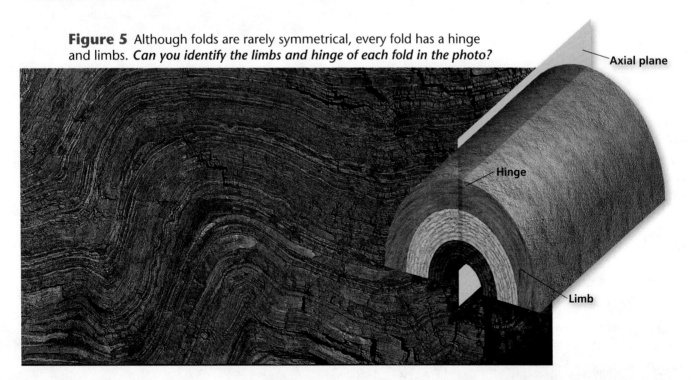

Figure 5 Although folds are rarely symmetrical, every fold has a hinge and limbs. *Can you identify the limbs and hinge of each fold in the photo?*

Axial plane

Hinge

Limb

Oldest rock

Youngest rock

Figure 6 The three major types of folds are anticlines (top), synclines (middle), and monoclines (bottom).

Types of Folds

To categorize a fold, scientists study the relative ages of the rocks in the fold. The rock layers of the fold are identified by age from youngest to oldest. An *anticline* is a fold in which the oldest layer is in the center of the fold. Anticlines are commonly arch shaped. A *syncline* is a fold in which the youngest layer is in the center of the fold. Synclines are commonly bowl shaped. A *monocline* is a fold in which both limbs are horizontal or almost horizontal. Monoclines form when one part of Earth's crust moves up or down relative to another part. The three major types of folds are shown in **Figure 6.**

Sizes of Folds

Folds, which appear as wavelike structures in rock layers, vary greatly in size. Some folds are small enough to be contained in a hand-held rock specimen. Other folds cover thousands of square kilometers and can be seen only from the air.

Sometimes, a large anticline forms a ridge. A *ridge* is a large, narrow strip of elevated land that can occur near mountains. Nearby, a large syncline may form a valley. Over time, however, the varying resistance to erosion of rock in anticlines and synclines can change this simple landscape pattern.

Why It Matters

Which Features Are Fit to Climb?

On a sheer rock face, there's nothing to hold on to. Climbers look for such features as ledges and fractures when planning a route up a cliff. But highly deformed rock can be dangerous—it might crumble unexpectedly.

Movement along a fault zone broke up this rock, making it unstable.

A vertical fracture allows a skilled climber to ascend a cliff.

Climbers may use tools to help them ascend safely. This device spreads to fit tightly in a fracture.

YOUR TURN ONLINE RESEARCH
Find out the name of the device shown above and describe two other devices used by climbers.

Figure 7 Normal and Reverse Faults

Footwall

Hanging wall

Reverse fault

Normal fault

Thrust fault

Faults

Stress does not always cause rock to fold. Near Earth's surface, where temperatures and pressure are low, stresses may simply cause rock to break. Breaks in rock are divided into two categories. A break along which there is no movement of the surrounding rock is called a *fracture*. A break along which the surrounding rock moves is called a **fault.** The surface or plane along which the motion occurs is called the *fault plane*. In a nonvertical fault, the *hanging wall* is the rock above the fault plane. The *footwall* is the rock below the fault plane.

fault a break in a body of rock along which one block slides relative to another; a form of brittle strain

Normal Faults

As shown in **Figure 7,** a *normal fault* is a fault in which the hanging wall moves downward relative to the footwall. Normal faults commonly form at divergent boundaries, where the crust is being pulled apart by tension. Normal faults may occur as a series of parallel fault lines, forming steep, steplike landforms. The Great Rift Valley of East Africa formed by large-scale normal faulting.

Reverse Faults

When compression causes the hanging wall to move upward relative to the footwall, also shown in **Figure 7,** a *reverse fault* forms. A *thrust fault* is a special type of reverse fault in which the fault plane is at a low angle or is nearly horizontal. Because of the low angle of the fault plane, the rock of the hanging wall is pushed up and over the rock of the footwall. Reverse faults and thrust faults are common in mountain ranges, such as the Rockies and the Alps, that formed mainly due to compression.

www.scilinks.org
Topic: Folding and Faulting
Code: HQX0589

Reading Check How does a thrust fault differ from a reverse fault?

Strike-Slip Faults

In a *strike-slip fault,* the rock on either side of the fault plane slides horizontally in response to shear stress. Strike-slip faults got their name because they slide, or *slip,* parallel to the direction of the length, or *strike,* of the fault. Some strike-slip fault planes are vertical, but many are sloped.

Strike-slip faults commonly occur at transform boundaries, where tectonic plates grind past each other as they move in opposite directions. These motions cause shear stress on the rocks at the edges of the plates. Strike-slip faults also occur at fracture zones between offset segments of mid-ocean ridges. Commonly, strike-slip faults occur as groups of smaller faults in areas where large-scale deformation is happening.

Figure 8 The San Andreas fault system stretches more than 1,200 km across California and is the result of two tectonic plates moving in different directions.

Sizes of Faults

Like folds, faults vary greatly in size. Small faults may affect only a few layers of rock in a small region. Other faults are thousands of kilometers long and may extend many kilometers below Earth's surface. Generally, large faults that cover thousands of kilometers are composed of systems of many smaller, related faults, rather than a single fault. The San Andreas fault in California, shown in **Figure 8,** is an example of a large fault system.

Section 1 Review

LA.910.2.2.3; SC.912.E.6.1; SC.912.E.6.2; SC.912.E.7.3

Key Ideas

1. **Summarize** how isostatic adjustments affect isostasy.

2. **Identify and describe** three types of stress.

3. **Compare** stress and strain.

4. **Describe** one type of strain that results when rock responds to stress by permanently deforming without breaking.

5. **Identify** features that all types of folds share and features that only some types of folds have.

6. **Describe** four types of faults.

7. **Compare** folding and faulting as responses to stress.

Critical Thinking

8. **Applying Ideas** Why is faulting most likely to occur near Earth's surface and not deep within Earth?

9. **Making Comparisons** How would the isostatic adjustment that results from the melting of glaciers differ from the isostatic adjustment that may occur when a large river empties into the ocean?

10. **Analyzing Relationships** You are examining a rock outcrop that shows a fold in which both limbs are horizontal but occur at different elevations. What type of fold does this outcrop show, and what can you say about the type of stress that the rock underwent?

11. **Predicting Consequences** You are watching a lab experiment in which a rock sample is being gently heated and slowly bent. Would you expect the rock to fold or to fracture? Explain your reasoning.

Concept Mapping

12. Use the following terms to create a concept map: *stress, compression, strain, tension, shear stress, folds,* and *faults.*

How Mountains Form

Key Ideas	Key Terms	Why It Matters
❯ Identify the types of plate collisions that form mountains. ❯ Identify four types of mountains. ❯ Compare how folded and fault-block mountains form.	mountain range folded mountain fault-block mountain dome mountain	Many mountain ranges and volcanoes are growing taller. Scientists can measure the rate at which Earth's surface is moving and deforming.

Many mountains form due to extreme deformation. Mount Everest, whose elevation is more than 8 km above sea level, is Earth's highest mountain. Forces inside Earth cause Mount Everest to grow taller every year. Some mountains form by volcanic activity. Mount St. Helens is a volcano that captured the world's attention in 1980 when its explosive eruption devastated the surrounding area.

Mountain Ranges and Systems

A group of adjacent mountains that are related to each other in shape and structure is called a **mountain range.** Mount Everest is part of the Great Himalaya Range, and Mount St. Helens is part of the Cascade Range. A group of adjacent mountain ranges is called a *mountain system*. In the eastern United States, for example, the Great Smoky, Blue Ridge, Cumberland, Green, and White mountain ranges make up the Appalachian mountain system.

The largest mountain systems are part of two larger systems called *mountain belts*. Earth's two youngest major mountain belts, the circum-Pacific belt and the Eurasian-Melanesian belt, are shown in **Figure 1.**

FLORIDA STANDARDS

SC.912.E.6.1 Describe and differentiate the layers of Earth and the interactions among them; **SC.912.E.6.2** Connect surface features to surface processes that are responsible for their formation; **SC.912.E.6.3** Analyze the scientific theory of plate tectonics and identify related major processes and features as a result of moving plates.

mountain range a series of mountains that are closely related in orientation, age, and mode of formation

Figure 1 Most tall, young mountain ranges lie along either the Eurasian-Melanesian mountain belt or the circum-Pacific mountain belt.

Plate Tectonics and Mountains

Both the circum-Pacific and the Eurasian-Melanesian mountain belts are located along convergent plate boundaries. The location of these two mountain belts provides evidence that most mountains form as a result of <u>collisions</u> between tectonic plates. Some mountains, such as the Appalachians, do not lie along active convergent plate boundaries. However, evidence indicates that the places at which these ranges formed were previously active plate boundaries.

Collisions Between Continental and Oceanic Crust

Some mountains form when oceanic lithosphere and continental lithosphere collide at convergent plate boundaries. When the moving plates collide, the oceanic lithosphere subducts beneath the continental lithosphere, as shown in **Figure 2.** This type of collision produces such large-scale deformation of rock that high mountains are uplifted. In addition, the subduction of the oceanic lithosphere causes partial melting of the overlying mantle and crust. This melting produces magma that may eventually erupt to form volcanic mountains on Earth's surface. The mountains of the Cascade Range in the northwest region of the United States formed in this way. The Andes mountains on the western coast of South America are another example of mountains that formed by this type of collision.

Some mountains at the boundary between continental lithosphere and oceanic lithosphere may form by a different process. As the oceanic lithosphere subducts, pieces of crust called *terranes* are scraped off. These terranes then become part of the continent and may form mountains.

Academic Vocabulary

collision (kuh LIZH uhn) the event in which two bodies merge or combine; the act of colliding

READING TOOLBOX

Analyzing Comparisons
As you read about different mountain ranges and belts, look for comparisons among them. Make a table of their similarities and differences.

Figure 2 The Andes, shown below, are being uplifted as the Pacific plate subducts beneath the South American plate.

Ocean trench

Active volcano

Magma

SUBDUCTION ZONE

Figure 3 The Mariana Islands in the North Pacific Ocean are volcanic mountains that formed by the collision of two oceanic plates.

Collisions Between Oceanic Crust and Oceanic Crust

Volcanic mountains commonly form where two plates whose edges consist of oceanic lithosphere collide. In this collision, the denser oceanic plate subducts beneath the other oceanic plate, as shown in **Figure 3.** As the denser oceanic plate subducts, fluids from the subducting lithosphere cause partial melting of the overlying mantle and crust. The resulting magma rises and breaks through the oceanic lithosphere. These eruptions of magma form an arc of volcanic mountains on the ocean floor. The Mariana Islands are the peaks of volcanic mountains that rose above sea level.

Figure 4 The Himalayas formed when India collided with Eurasia.

Collisions Between Continents

Mountains can also form when two continents collide, as **Figure 4** shows. The Himalaya Mountains formed from such a collision. About 165 million years ago, India broke apart from Africa and Antarctica and became a separate continent. The Indian plate then began moving north toward Eurasia. The oceanic lithosphere of the Indian plate subducted beneath the Eurasian plate. This subduction continued until the continental lithosphere of India collided with the continental lithosphere of Eurasia. Because the two continents have equally dense lithosphere, subduction stopped but the collision continued. The intense deformation that resulted from the collision uplifted the Himalayas. Because the plates are still colliding, the Himalayas are still growing taller.

Reading Check Why are the Himalayas growing taller today?

www.scilinks.org
Topic: Types of Mountains
Code: HQX1568

Types of Mountains

Mountains are more than just elevated parts of Earth's crust. Mountains are complicated structures whose rock formations provide evidence of the stresses that created the mountains. Scientists classify mountains according to the way in which the crust was deformed and shaped by mountain-building stresses. Examples of several types of mountains are shown in **Figure 5.**

Folded Mountains and Plateaus

Many of the highest mountain ranges in the world consist of folded mountains that form when continents collide. **Folded mountains** form when tectonic movements squeeze rock layers together into accordion-like folds. Parts of the Alps, the Himalayas, the Appalachians, and Russia's Ural Mountains consist of very large and complex folds.

The same stresses that form folded mountains also uplift plateaus. *Plateaus* are large, flat areas of rock high above sea level. Most plateaus form when thick, horizontal layers of rock are slowly uplifted so that the layers remain flat instead of faulting and folding. Most plateaus are located near mountain ranges. For example, the Tibetan Plateau is next to the Himalaya Mountains, and the Colorado Plateau is next to the Rockies. Plateaus can also form when layers of molten rock harden and pile up on Earth's surface or when large areas of rock are eroded.

folded mountain a mountain that forms when rock layers are squeezed together and uplifted

Figure 5 Mountains in the United States

The Colorado Plateau is near the Rockies.

The Sierra Nevada range in California contains many fault-block mountains.

Death Valley is a graben that lies between two mountain chains and has the lowest elevation in the United States.

Fault-Block Mountains and Grabens

Where parts of Earth's crust have been stretched and broken into large blocks, faulting may cause the blocks to tilt and drop relative to other blocks. The relatively higher blocks form **fault-block mountains.** The Sierra Nevada range of California consists of many fault-block mountains.

The same type of faulting that forms fault-block mountains also forms long, narrow valleys called *grabens.* Grabens develop when steep faults break the crust into blocks and one block slips downward relative to the surrounding blocks. Grabens and fault-block mountain ranges commonly occur together. For example, the Basin and Range Province of the western United States consists of grabens separated by fault-block mountain ranges.

Dome Mountains

A less common type of mountain forms when magma rises through the crust and pushes up the rock layers above the magma. The result is a **dome mountain,** a circular structure made of rock layers that slope gently away from a central point. Dome mountains may also form when tectonic forces gently uplift rock layers. The Black Hills of South Dakota and the Adirondack Mountains of New York are examples of dome mountains.

Reading Check Name three types of mountains found in the United States.

fault-block mountain a mountain that forms where faulting breaks Earth's crust into large blocks, which causes some blocks to drop down relative to other blocks

dome mountain a circular or elliptical, almost symmetrical elevation or structure in which the stratified rock slopes downward gently from the central point of folding

This dome mountain is part of the Hudson Highlands in New York.

The Appalachian Mountains stretch from Georgia to Canada and contain many older, more eroded mountains.

The Ouachita Plateau in Arkansas has a lower average elevation than the Colorado Plateau.

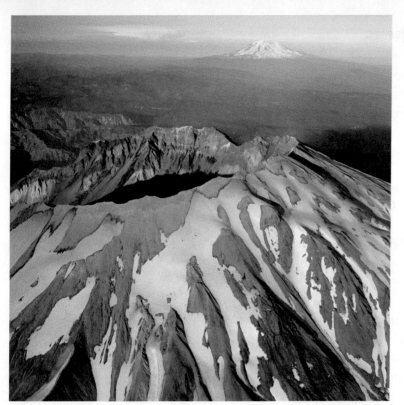

Figure 6 Mount St. Helens (front) and Mount Rainier (back) in the Cascade Range of the western United States are volcanic mountains that formed along a convergent boundary.

Volcanic Mountains

Mountains that form when magma erupts onto Earth's surface are called *volcanic mountains*. Volcanic mountains commonly form along convergent plate boundaries. The Cascade Range of Washington, Oregon, and northern California is composed of this type of volcanic mountain, two of which are shown in **Figure 6.**

Some of the largest volcanic mountains are part of the mid-ocean ridges along divergent plate boundaries. Magma rising to Earth's surface at divergent boundaries makes mid-ocean ridges volcanically active areas. The peaks of these volcanic mountains sometimes rise above sea level to form volcanic islands, such as the Azores in the North Atlantic Ocean.

Other large volcanic mountains form at hot spots. *Hot spots* are volcanically active areas that can lie far from tectonic plate boundaries. These areas seem to correspond to places where hot material rises through Earth's interior and reaches the lithosphere. The Hawaiian Islands are an example of this type of volcanic mountain. The main island of Hawaii is a volcanic mountain that reaches over 10 km above the ocean floor and has a base that is more than 160 km wide.

Section 2 Review

LA.910.2.2.3; SC.912.E.6.1; SC.912.E.6.2; SC.912.E.6.3; SC.912.E.7.3

Key Ideas

1. **Describe** three types of tectonic plate collisions that form mountains.

2. **Summarize** the process by which folded mountains form.

3. **Compare** how plateaus form with how folded mountains form.

4. **Describe** the formation of fault-block mountains.

5. **Explain** how dome mountains form.

6. **Explain** how volcanic mountains form.

Critical Thinking

7. **Making Connections** Explain two ways in which volcanic mountains might get smaller.

8. **Making Connections** Explain why fault-block mountains and grabens are commonly found near each other.

9. **Analyzing Ideas** You are standing on a large, flat area of land and are examining the nearby mountains. You notice that many of the mountains have large folds. Are you standing on a plateau or a graben? Explain your answer.

10. **Making Predictions** Igneous rocks form from cooled magma. Near what types of mountains would you expect to find new igneous rocks?

Concept Mapping

11. Use the following terms to create a concept map: *mountain range, fault-block mountains, mountain belt, folded mountains, mountain system, dome mountains,* and *volcanic mountains.*

Spying on Earth's Movements

SCIENCE & SOCIETY

Earth's surface often changes too slowly or over too large an area for humans to detect, but technology reveals the truth. By comparing satellite images produced at different times, scientists can identify areas where Earth's surface has undergone deformation. This background image shows surface movement caused by an earthquake in California. Areas of deformation are shown in false colors. The color bands are closer together where the ground moved farther. In the future, these types of measurements may help scientists predict such events as volcanic eruptions or earthquakes.

A satellite uses radar energy to produce detailed images of Earth's surface at two different times. A computer digitally compares the images and displays any differences.

Mauna Loa Volcano makes up much of Hawaii's Big Island. It is carefully monitored for signs of an imminent eruption.

Averaged interferogram 2002-2005
RADARSAT-1

Satellite data show deformation of Mauna Loa and Kilauea Volcanoes. Movement of magma inside the crust causes changes to the ground at the surface. The areas of greatest deformation are shown in dark blue and dark red.

YOUR TURN

UNDERSTANDING CONCEPTS
How are satellite data used to measure deformation of Earth's crust?

CRITICAL THINKING
Why are false colors used to show movement of the ground?

90 min

What You'll Do

> **Model** collisions between continents.

> **Explain** how mountains form at convergent boundaries.

What You'll Need

blocks, wooden, 3 cm × 3 cm × 6 cm
bobby pins, long (5)
cardboard, thick, 15 cm × 30 cm
napkins, paper, light- and dark-colored
paper, adding-machine, 6 cm × 35 cm
ruler, metric
scissors
tape, masking

Safety

Continental Collisions

When the subcontinent of India broke away from Africa and Antarctica and began to move northward toward Eurasia, the oceanic crust on the northern side of India began to subduct beneath the Eurasian plate. The deformation of the crust resulted in the formation of the Himalaya Mountains. Earthquakes in the Himalayan region suggest that India is still pushing against Eurasia. In this lab, you will create a model to help explain how the Himalaya Mountains formed as a result of the collision of the Indian and Eurasian tectonic plates.

Procedure

1 To assemble the continental-collision model, cut a 7-cm slit in the cardboard. The slit should be about 6 cm from (and parallel to) one of the short edges of the cardboard. Cut the slit wide enough such that the adding-machine paper will feed through the slit without being loose.

2 Securely tape one wood block along the slit between the slit and the near edge of the cardboard. Tape the other block across the paper strip about 6 cm from one end of the paper. The blocks should be parallel to one another, as shown in the illustration on the next page.

Step 8

Wood block
Cardboard
Bobby pins
Wood block
Paper strip

Taped to paper strip only
Light napkins
Dark napkins
Tape

3. Cut two strips of the light-colored paper napkin that are about 6 cm wide and 16 cm long. Cut two strips of the dark-colored paper napkin that are about 6 cm wide and 32 cm long. Fold all four strips in half along their width.

4. Stack the napkin strips on top of each other such that all of the folds are along the same side. Place the two dark-colored napkins on the bottom.

5. Place the napkin strips lengthwise on the paper strip. The nonfolded ends of the napkin strips should be butted up against the wood block that is taped to the paper strip.

6. Using the bobby pins, attach the napkins to the paper strip, as shown in the illustration above.

7. Push the long end of the paper strip through the slit in the cardboard until the first fold of the napkin rests against the fixed wood block.

8. Hold the cardboard at about eye level, and pull down gently on the paper strip. You may need a partner's help. Observe what happens as the dark-colored napkins contact the fixed wood block and as you continue to pull down on the paper strip. Stop pulling when you feel resistance from the strip.

Analysis

1. **Evaluating Methods** Explain what is represented by the dark napkins, the light napkins, and the wood blocks.

2. **Analyzing Processes** What plate-tectonics process is represented by the motion of the paper strip in the model? Explain your answer.

3. **Applying Ideas** What type of mountain would result from the kind of collision shown by the model?

4. **Evaluating Models** Explain how the process modeled here differs from the process that formed the Himalaya Mountains.

Extension

Analyzing Data Obtain a world map of earthquake epicenters. Study the map. Describe the pattern of epicenters in the Himalayan region. Does the pattern suggest that the Himalaya Mountains are still rising?

Writing from Research Read about the breakup of Gondwanaland and the movement of India toward the Northern Hemisphere. Write about stages in India's movement. List the time frame in which each important event occurred.

MAPS in Action

Shear Strain in New Zealand

Map Skills Activity

The map above shows the plate boundary zone of New Zealand. In this region, the Australian plate is moving north, while the Pacific plate is moving west. These complex plate movements create areas of tension, compression, and shear stress, which result in strain. Strain is measured in parts per million (ppm) per year (yr). The map on the right shows strain in New Zealand. Use the two maps to answer the questions below.

1. **Using a Key** What is the highest amount of shear strain shown in the map on the right?

2. **Identifying Locations** Using latitude and longitude, describe the location of the area that has the highest amount of shear strain.

3. **Using a Key** What is the approximate length of the area of maximum shear strain?

4. **Understanding Relationships** What type of plate boundary is located along the east coast of the North Island? Explain your answer.

5. **Comparing Areas** In what areas might you expect to find compression? Explain your answer.

6. **Making Inferences** What type of fault is the Alpine Fault? Explain your answer.

7. **Drawing Conclusions** A mountain range known as the Southern Alps runs through the center of the South Island. What type of mountains do you think the Southern Alps are? Explain your answer.

Key Ideas	Key Terms

Section 1

How Rock Deforms

❯ Isostasy occurs when there is a balance between the gravitational force of the lithosphere pressing downward and the buoyant force of the asthenosphere pressing upward.

❯ The three main types of stress are compression, which squeezes rock together; tension, which pulls rock apart; and shear stress, which bends and twists rock.

❯ Folds form when rock is bent without breaking. Faults form when a block of rock on one side of a fracture moves relative to the block on the other side.

deformation, p. 293
isostasy, p. 293
stress, p. 295
strain, p. 296
fold, p. 297
fault, p. 299

Section 2

How Mountains Form

❯ Collisions that form mountains can occur between an oceanic plate and a continental plate, between an oceanic plate and another oceanic plate, or between two continental plates.

❯ Four types of mountains are folded mountains, fault-block mountains, dome mountains, and volcanic mountains.

❯ Folded mountains form as tectonic movements squeeze Earth's crust into folds. Faulted mountains form as large blocks of crust tilt and move relative to other blocks of crust.

mountain range, p. 301
folded mountain,
   p. 304
fault-block mountain,
   p. 305
dome mountain, p. 305

1. **Everyday Words Used in Science** The word *range* is used to describe mountains that are related by size and structure. What does the word *range* mean in everyday speech? What does it mean in a scientific context?

USING KEY TERMS

Use each of the following terms in a separate sentence.

2. *isostasy* SC.912.E.6.2

3. *compression* SC.912.E.6.2

4. *shear stress* SC.912.E.6.2

For each pair of terms, explain how the meanings of the terms differ.

5. *stress* and *strain* SC.912.E.6.2

6. *fold* and *fault* SC.912.E.6.2

7. *syncline* and *monocline* SC.912.E.6.2

8. *dome mountains* and *volcanic mountains* SC.912.E.6.3

9. *folded mountains* and *fault-block mountains* SC.912.E.6.3

UNDERSTANDING KEY IDEAS

10. When the weight of an area of Earth's crust increases, the lithosphere SC.912.E.6.3
    a. sinks.
    b. melts.
    c. rises.
    d. collides.

11. The force per unit area that changes the shape and volume of rock is SC.912.E.6.3
    a. footwall.
    b. isostasy.
    c. rising.
    d. stress.

12. Shear stress SC.912.E.6.3
    a. bends, twists, or breaks rock.
    b. causes isostasy.
    c. causes rock to melt.
    d. causes rock to expand.

13. When stress is applied under conditions of high pressure and high temperature, rock is more likely to SC.912.E.6.2
    a. fracture.
    b. sink.
    c. fault.
    d. fold.

14. Folds in which both limbs remain horizontal are called SC.912.E.6.2
    a. monoclines.
    b. fractures.
    c. synclines.
    d. anticlines.

15. When a fault is not vertical, the rock above the fault plane makes up the SC.912.E.6.2
    a. tension.
    b. footwall.
    c. hanging wall.
    d. compression.

16. A fault in which the rock on either side of the fault plane moves horizontally in nearly opposite directions is called a SC.912.E.6.2
    a. normal fault.
    b. reverse fault.
    c. strike-slip fault.
    d. thrust fault.

17. The largest mountain systems are part of still larger systems called SC.912.E.6.2
    a. continental margins.
    b. ranges.
    c. belts.
    d. synclines.

18. Large areas of flat-topped rock high above the surrounding landscape are SC.912.E.6.2
    a. grabens.
    b. footwalls.
    c. hanging walls.
    d. plateaus.

SHORT ANSWER

19. Name two types of deformation in Earth's crust, and explain how each type occurs. SC.912.E.6.2

20. Explain how to identify an anticline. SC.912.E.6.2

21. Identify the two major mountain belts on Earth. SC.912.E.6.2

22. Describe how the various types of mountains are categorized. SC.912.E.6.2

23. Identify the two forces that are kept in balance by isostatic adjustments.

24. Compare the features of dome mountains with those of fault-block mountains. SC.912.E.6.2

CRITICAL THINKING

25. **Evaluating Ideas** If thick ice sheets covered large parts of Earth's continents again, how would you expect the lithosphere to respond to the added weight of the continental ice sheets? Explain your answer. **SC.912.E.6.2**

26. **Analyzing Relationships** When the Indian plate collided with the Eurasian plate and produced the Himalaya Mountains, which type of stress most likely occurred? Which type of stress is most likely occurring along the Mid-Atlantic Ridge? Which type of stress would you expect to find along the San Andreas fault? Explain your answers. **SC.912.E.6.3**

27. **Making Predictions** If the force that causes a rock to deform slightly begins to ease, what may happen to the rock? What might happen if the force causing the deformation becomes greater? **SC.912.E.6.2**

28. **Analyzing Processes** Why do you think that dome mountains do not always become volcanic mountains? **SC.912.E.6.2**

CONCEPT MAPPING

29. Use the following terms to create a concept map: *stress, strain, brittle, ductile, folds, faults, normal fault, reverse fault, thrust fault,* and *strike-slip fault.* **SC.912.E.6.2**

MATH SKILLS

30. **Making Calculations** Scientists calculate that parts of the Himalayas are rising at a rate of 6.1 mm per year. At this rate, in how many years will the Himalayas be 1 m taller than they are today? **SC.912.E.6.3**

31. **Analyzing Data** Rock stress is measured as 48 MPa at point A below Earth's surface. At point B nearby, stress is measured as 12 MPa. What percentage of the stress at point A is the stress at point B equal to? **SC.912.E.6.2**

WRITING SKILLS

32. **Creative Writing** Write a short story from the perspective of a rock that is being deformed. Describe the stresses that are affecting the rock and the final result of the stress.

33. **Writing from Research** Look for photos or illustrations of folding and faulting in a particular area. Then, research the geologic history of the area, and write a report based on your findings. Use any photos or drawings that you find to illustrate your report. **SC.912.E.6.4**

INTERPRETING GRAPHICS

The diagram below shows a fault. Use this diagram to answer the questions that follow.

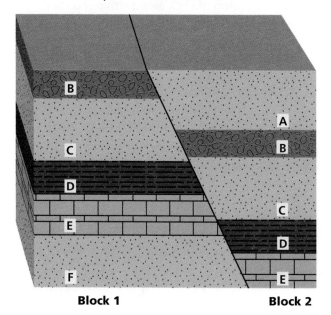

Block 1   Block 2

34. Is Block 2 a footwall or a hanging wall? Explain your answer. **SC.912.E.6.2**

35. What type of fault is illustrated? Explain your answer. **SC.912.E.6.2**

36. What type of stress generally causes this type of fault? **SC.912.E.6.2**

Understanding Concepts

Directions (1–9): For each question, write on a separate sheet of paper the letter of the correct answer.

1 Where are most plateaus located?
- **A.** near mountain ranges
- **B.** bordering ocean basins
- **C.** beneath grabens
- **D.** alongside diverging boundaries

2 Mountains form at various boundaries. Mountains do NOT form at which of the following boundaries?
- **F.** between continental and oceanic lithosphere
- **G.** between two oceanic crusts
- **H.** between continents
- **I.** between fault lines

3 Which of the following statements describes the formation of rock along strike-slip faults?
- **A.** Rock on either side of the fault plane slides vertically.
- **B.** Rock on either side of the fault plane slides horizontally.
- **C.** Rock in the hanging wall is pushed up and over the rock of the footwall.
- **D.** Rock in the hanging wall moves down relative to the footwall.

4 Which does NOT result in mountain formation?
- **F.** collisions between continental and oceanic crust
- **G.** subduction of one oceanic plate beneath another oceanic plate
- **H.** deposition and isostasy
- **I.** deformation caused by collisions between two or more continents

5 When erosion of the lithosphere occurs, what happens between the lithosphere and asthenosphere?
- **A.** The lithosphere and asthenosphere reach isostasy by making adjustments.
- **B.** The lithosphere becomes heavier and pushes down on the asthenosphere.
- **C.** The gravitational force and buoyant force between the lithosphere and asthenosphere are balanced.
- **D.** The area that is eroded undergoes subsidence.

6 Volcanoes such as those found in the Cascades of northern California form
- **F.** at hot spots that lie far from tectonic plate boundaries.
- **G.** along convergent plate boundaries.
- **H.** when magma rises through the crust and pushes up the rock layers above it.
- **I.** along mid-ocean ridges.

7 Which of the following statements best describes fault-block mountains?
- **A.** They form when tectonic movements squeeze rock layers together.
- **B.** Earth's crust is stretched and broken into large pieces that are tilted and drop relative to other pieces.
- **C.** Magma rises through the crust and pushes up the layers above the magma.
- **D.** They form when magma erupts onto Earth's surface.

8 Subduction is NOT a factor in which type of plate collision?
- **F.** collision between continental crust and oceanic crust
- **G.** collision between oceanic crust and oceanic crust
- **H.** collision between continents
- **I.** collision between crusts of varying densities

9 Explorers find a new island in the middle of an oceanic plate. How did the island form?
- **A.** Subduction of an oceanic plate during collision with another oceanic plate resulted in the formation of a volcanic island.
- **B.** Volcanic activity at a divergent boundary results in the formation of a volcanic island.
- **C.** A hot spot in the ocean floor releases magma that eventually forms a volcanic island.
- **D.** Magma rose beneath the crust and pushed up the layers above it to form a dome.

Interpreting Graphics

Directions (10–12): For each question below, record the correct answer on a separate sheet of paper.

Divergent and Convergent Plate Boundaries

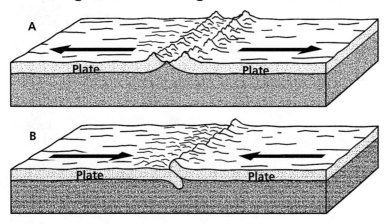

10 The diagrams above show a divergent and a convergent plate boundary. Which of the following is NOT likely to be found at or occur at the boundary found in diagram A?
  F. volcanoes   **H.** earthquakes
  G. lava flows   **I.** subduction

11 How does the subduction of the oceanic crust shown in diagram B produce volcanic mountains?
  A. Magma rises between the plates at a divergent boundary.
  B. Subduction produces hot spots, which in turn produce volcanoes.
  C. Magma pushes up the layers of rock above it, forming a dome.
  D. The mantle and crust of the subducted plate melt, and the resulting magma forms volcanoes.

Rock Deformation

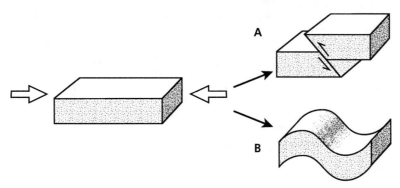

12 The diagram above shows two possible outcomes when pressure, which is represented by the large arrows, is applied to the rock on the left. What type of strain is seen in the rock labeled A?
  F. brittle   **H.** folding
  G. ductile   **I.** monocline

Test Tip

Carefully study all of the details of a diagram before answering the question or questions that refer to it.

Chapter 12 Earthquakes

Chapter Outline

Why It Matters

Understanding how, where, and why earthquakes happen can help scientists and engineers reduce earthquake damage and save lives. This expressway in Kobe, Japan, was toppled by an earthquake that caused the ground to shake for 20 s.

Modeling Earthquake Waves

Have two people stretch a spring toy along the floor. Hold one end of the spring still. Use push-pull motion at the other end to make a wave. Observe how the wave moves along the spring.

Shake one end of the spring from side to side to make a wave. Observe how this wave moves along the spring.

Draw a diagram showing characteristics of each wave.

Questions to Get You Started

1. Which wave moved parallel to the spring?

2. Which wave moved perpendicular to the spring?

SC.912.E.6.4

READING TOOLBOX

These reading tools will help you learn the material in this chapter.

Word Parts

Root Words Many scientific words are made up of word parts derived from ancient or foreign languages. Understanding the meanings of these word parts can help you understand new scientific terms. Consider the term *seismic wave*. It contains the root word *seism-*, which comes from the Greek word *seismos*, meaning "earthquake."

Your Turn On a separate sheet of paper, start a table like the one below. As you read Section 2, find words that contain the root *seismo-* or *seism-* and make entries in the table for them.

Word or Term	Root	Definition
seismic wave	seism-	vibration that travels through Earth; often caused by an earthquake
seismology	seismo-	
seismograph		

Classification

Classifying Seismic Waves Classification is a tool for organizing objects and ideas by grouping them into categories. Groups are classified by defining characteristics. For example, the table below shows how seismic waves can be classified by their speed and type of movement they cause in Earth's crust.

Your Turn As you read Section 1, make a table like the one below for the following classes of seismic waves: P waves, S waves, Love waves, and Rayleigh waves.

CLASS	DEFINING CHARACTERISTICS
P waves	a type of body wave; fastest seismic wave; causes particles to travel in a direction parallel to the direction of travel of the wave
S waves	

FoldNotes

Layered Book FoldNotes are a fun way to help you learn and remember ideas that you encounter as you read.

Your Turn Make a layered book, as described in **Appendix A**. Label the tabs of the layered book with "Causes of Earthquakes," "Locating an Epicenter,"

and "Earthquake Safety." Write notes on the appropriate layer as you read the chapter.

Causes of Earthquakes
Locating an Epicenter
Earthquake Safety

For more information on how to use these and other tools, see **Appendix A**.

How and Where Earthquakes Happen

Key Ideas	Key Terms	Why It Matters
❯ Describe elastic rebound. ❯ Compare body waves and surface waves. ❯ Explain how the structure of Earth's interior affects seismic waves. ❯ Explain why earthquakes generally occur at plate boundaries.	earthquake surface wave elastic rebound P wave focus S wave epicenter shadow zone body wave fault zone	Understanding earthquakes helps people limit the destruction and loss of life that earthquakes can cause. Studying earthquakes also helps scientists understand Earth's interior.

Earthquakes are one of the most destructive natural disasters. A single earthquake can kill many thousands of people and cause billions of dollars in damage. **Earthquakes** are defined as movements of the ground that are caused by a sudden release of energy when rocks along a fault move. Earthquakes usually occur when rocks under stress suddenly shift along a fault. A *fault* is a break in a body of rock along which one block slides relative to another.

Why Earthquakes Happen

The rocks along both sides of a fault are commonly pressed together tightly. Although the rocks may be under stress, friction prevents them from moving past each other. In this immobile state, a fault is said to be *locked*. Parts of a fault remain locked until the stress becomes so great that the rocks suddenly slip past each other. This slippage causes the trembling and vibrations of an earthquake.

Elastic Rebound

Earthquakes are a result of elastic rebound. **Elastic rebound** is the sudden return of elastically deformed rock to its undeformed shape. This process is shown in **Figure 1.**

SC.912.E.6.3 Analyze the scientific theory of plate tectonics and identify related major processes and features as a result of moving plates; **SC.912.P.10.20** Describe the measurable properties of waves and explain the relationships among them and how these properties change when the wave moves from one medium to another.

earthquake a movement or trembling of the ground that is caused by a sudden release of energy when rocks along a fault move

elastic rebound the sudden return of elastically deformed rock to its undeformed shape

Figure 1 Elastic Rebound

Two blocks of crust pressed against each other at a fault are under stress but do not move because friction holds them in place.

As stress builds up at the fault, the crust deforms. When rock is stressed past the point at which it can maintain integrity, it fractures.

When the rock fractures, it separates at the weakest point and snaps back, or *rebounds,* to its original shape, which causes an earthquake.

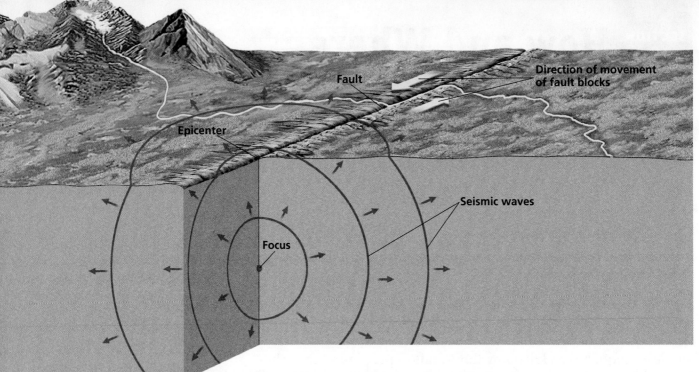

Fault

Direction of movement of fault blocks

Epicenter

Seismic waves

Focus

Figure 2 The epicenter of an earthquake is the point on the surface directly above the focus.

focus the location within Earth along a fault at which the first motion of an earthquake occurs

epicenter the point on Earth's surface directly above an earthquake's starting point, or focus

body wave a seismic wave that travels through the body of a medium

surface wave a seismic wave that travels along the surface of a medium and that has a stronger effect near the surface of the medium than it has in the interior

Anatomy of an Earthquake

The location within Earth along a fault at which the first motion of an earthquake occurs is called the **focus** (plural, *foci*). The point on Earth's surface directly above the focus is called the **epicenter** (EP i SENT uhr), as shown in **Figure 2.**

Although the focus depths of earthquakes vary, about 90% of continental earthquakes have shallow foci. Earthquakes that have shallow foci take place within 70 km of Earth's surface. Earthquakes that have intermediate foci take place at depths between 70 km and 300 km. Earthquakes that have deep foci take place at depths between 300 km and 650 km. Earthquakes that have deep foci usually occur in subduction zones and occur farther from the surface location of the plate boundary than shallower earthquakes do.

By the time the vibrations from an earthquake that has an intermediate or deep focus reach the surface, much of their energy has dissipated. For this reason, the earthquakes that cause the most damage usually have shallow foci.

Seismic Waves

As rocks along a fault slip into new positions, the rocks release energy in the form of vibrations called *seismic waves*. These waves travel outward in all directions from the focus through the surrounding rock. This wave action is similar to what happens when you drop a stone into a pool of still water and circular waves ripple outward from the center.

Earthquakes generally produce two main types of waves. **Body waves** are waves that travel through the body of a medium. **Surface waves** travel along the surface of a body rather than through the middle. Each type of wave travels at a different speed and causes different movements in Earth's crust.

Body Waves

Body waves can be placed into two main categories: P waves and S waves. **P waves,** also called *primary waves* or *compression waves,* are the fastest seismic waves and are always the first waves of an earthquake to be detected. P waves cause particles of rock to move in a back-and-forth direction that is parallel to the direction in which the waves are traveling, as shown in **Figure 3.** P waves can move through solids, liquids, and gases. The more rigid the material is, the faster the P waves travel through it.

S waves, also called *secondary waves* or *shear waves,* are the second-fastest seismic waves and arrive at detection sites after P waves. S waves cause particles of rock to move in a side-to-side direction that is perpendicular to the direction in which the waves are traveling. Unlike P waves, however, S waves can only travel through solid material.

Surface Waves

Surface waves form from motion along a shallow fault or from the conversion of energy when P waves and S waves reach Earth's surface. Although surface waves are the slowest-moving waves, they may cause the greatest damage during an earthquake. The two types of surface waves are Love waves and Rayleigh waves. *Love waves* cause rock to move side to side and perpendicular to the direction in which the waves are traveling. *Rayleigh waves* cause the ground to move with an elliptical, rolling motion.

Reading Check **Describe the two types of surface waves.** (See Appendix G for answers to Reading Checks.)

Figure 3 The different types of seismic waves cause different rock movements, which have different effects on Earth's crust.

P wave a primary wave, or compression wave; a seismic wave that causes particles of rock to move in a back-and-forth direction parallel to the direction in which the wave is traveling

S wave a secondary wave, or shear wave; a seismic wave that causes particles of rock to move in a side-to-side direction perpendicular to the direction in which the wave is traveling

Why It Matters

Do All Seismic Waves Come from Earthquakes?

Have you felt the ground shake as a large truck rumbles past? Seismic waves are produced not only by earthquakes but also by such events as explosions and even the movement of heavy equipment.

Many seismic stations detected this explosion of a gas pipeline in New Mexico.

This meteorite impact in Peru produced measurable seismic waves.

Landslides produce seismic waves as large quantities of soil and rock suddenly collapse downhill.

YOUR TURN CRITICAL THINKING
What are some sources of seismic waves you may have felt?

Seismic Waves and Earth's Interior

Seismic waves are useful to scientists who are exploring Earth's interior. The composition of the material through which P waves and S waves travel affects the speed and direction of the waves. For example, P waves travel fastest through materials that are very rigid and are not easily compressed. By studying the speed and direction of seismic waves, scientists can learn more about the makeup and structure of Earth's interior.

Earth's Internal Layers

In 1909, Andrija Mohorovičić (мон hoh ROH vuh chɪch), a Croatian scientist, discovered that the speed of seismic waves increases abruptly at about a 30-km depth beneath the surface of continents. The location at which the speed of the waves increases marks the boundary between the crust and the mantle. The depth of this boundary varies from about 10 km below the oceans to about 30 km below continents. This increase in speed takes place because the mantle is denser than the crust. By studying the speed of seismic waves, scientists have been able to locate boundaries between other internal layers of Earth. The three main compositional layers of Earth are the *crust,* the *mantle,* and the *core.* Earth is also composed of five mechanical layers—the *lithosphere,* the *asthenosphere,* the *mesosphere,* the *outer core,* and the *inner core.*

Shadow Zones

Recordings of seismic waves around the world reveal shadow zones. **Shadow zones** are locations on Earth's surface where no body waves from a particular earthquake can be detected. Shadow zones exist because the materials that make up Earth's interior are not uniform in rigidity. When seismic waves travel through materials of differing rigidities, the speed of the waves changes. The waves also bend and change direction as they pass through different materials.

As shown in **Figure 4,** a large S-wave shadow zone covers the side of Earth that is opposite an earthquake. S waves do not reach the S-wave shadow zone because they cannot pass through the liquid outer core. Although P waves can travel through all of the layers, the speed and direction of the waves change as the waves pass through each of Earth's layers. The waves bend in such a way that P-wave shadow zones form.

Reading Check What causes the speed of a seismic wave to change?

shadow zone an area on Earth's surface where no direct seismic waves from a particular earthquake can be detected

Figure 4 P waves and S waves behave differently as they pass through different structural layers of Earth.

← P waves
← S waves

Epicenter

Mantle

105°

P wave shadow zone

140°

Solid inner core

Liquid outer core

THINK central
INTERACT ONLINE
Keyword: HQXEQKF4

105°

140°

S wave shadow zone

P wave shadow zone

Earthquakes and Plate Tectonics

Earthquakes are the result of stresses in Earth's lithosphere. Most earthquakes occur in three main tectonic environments, as shown in **Figure 5.** These environments are generally located at or near tectonic plate boundaries, where stress on the rock is greatest.

Convergent Oceanic Environments

At convergent plate boundaries, plates move toward each other and collide. The plate that is denser subducts, or sinks into the asthenosphere below the other plate. As the plates move, the overriding plate scrapes across the top of the subducting plate, and earthquakes occur. Convergent oceanic boundaries can occur between two oceanic plates or between one oceanic plate and one continental plate.

Divergent Oceanic Environments

At the divergent plate boundaries that make up the mid-ocean ridges, plates are moving away from each other. Earthquakes occur along mid-ocean ridges because oceanic lithosphere is pulling away from both sides of each ridge. This spreading motion causes earthquakes along the ocean ridges.

Continental Environments

Earthquakes also occur at locations where two continental plates converge, diverge, or move horizontally in opposite directions. As the continental plates interact, the rock surrounding the boundary experiences stress. The stress may cause mountains to form and also causes frequent earthquakes.

Figure 5 Earthquakes are the result of tectonic stresses in Earth's crust and occur in three main tectonic environments: mid-ocean ridges, subduction zones, and continental collisions.

READING TOOLBOX

Classification
As you read about the three main tectonic environments in which earthquakes occur, make a table classifying the direction of movement of tectonic plates in each environment.

Fault Zones

At some plate boundaries, there are regions of numerous, closely spaced faults called **fault zones.** Fault zones form at plate boundaries because of the intense stress that results when the plates separate, collide, subduct, or slide past each other. One such fault zone is the North Anatolian fault zone, shown in **Figure 6,** which extends almost the entire length of the country of Turkey. Where the edge of the Arabian plate pushes against the Eurasian plate, the small Turkish microplate is squeezed westward. When enough stress builds up, movement occurs along one or more of the individual faults in the fault zone and sometimes causes major earthquakes.

Figure 6 A series of parallel transform faults, seen in the center of this photo, make up part of the North Anatolian fault zone in Turkey.

fault zone a region of numerous, closely spaced faults

Academic Vocabulary

series (SEER eeze) a number of related events or objects coming one after another in succession

Earthquakes Away from Plate Boundaries

Not all earthquakes result from movement along plate boundaries. A widely felt <u>series</u> of earthquakes occurred in the United States far from any active plate boundary. Instead, these earthquakes occurred in the middle of the continent, near New Madrid, Missouri, in 1811 and 1812. The vibrations from the earthquakes that rocked New Madrid were so strong that they caused damage as far away as South Carolina.

It was not until the late 1970s that studies of the Mississippi River region revealed an ancient fault zone deep within Earth's crust. This zone is thought to be part of a major fault zone in the North American plate. Scientists have determined that the fault formed at least 600 million years ago and that it was later buried under many layers of sediment and rock.

Section 1 Review

LA.910.2.2.3; SC.912.E.6.1; SC.912.E.6.3; SC.912.E.7.3; SC.912.P.10.20

Key Ideas

1. **Describe** elastic rebound.

2. **Explain** the difference between the epicenter and the focus of an earthquake.

3. **Compare** body waves and surface waves.

4. **Explain** how seismic waves help scientists learn about Earth's interior.

5. **Explain** how the structure of Earth's interior affects seismic wave speed and direction.

6. **Explain** why earthquakes generally take place at plate boundaries.

7. **Describe** a fault zone, and explain how earthquakes occur along fault zones.

Critical Thinking

8. **Applying Ideas** In earthquakes that cause the most damage, at what depth would movement along a fault most likely occur?

9. **Identifying Patterns** If a seismologic station measures P waves but no S waves from an earthquake, what can you conclude about the earthquake's location?

10. **Making Inferences** If an earthquake occurs in the center of Brazil, what can you infer about the geology of that area?

Concept Mapping

11. Use the following terms to create a concept map: *earthquake, seismic wave, body wave, surface wave, P wave, S wave, Rayleigh wave,* and *Love wave.*

Studying Earthquakes

Key Ideas	Key Terms	Why It Matters
❯ Describe the instrument used to measure and record earthquakes. ❯ Summarize the method scientists use to locate an epicenter. ❯ Describe the scales used to measure the magnitude and intensity of earthquakes.	seismograph seismogram magnitude intensity	Determining an earthquake's location and intensity allows aid to be sent quickly after a significant earthquake occurs.

The study of earthquakes and seismic waves is called *seismology*. Many scientists study earthquakes because earthquakes are the best tool available for investigating Earth's internal structure and dynamics. These scientists have developed special sensing equipment to record, locate, and measure earthquakes.

Recording Earthquakes

Vibrations in the ground can be detected and recorded by using an instrument called a **seismograph** (SIEZ MUH graf), such as the one shown in **Figure 1.** A modern three-component seismograph consists of three sensing devices. One device records the vertical motion of the ground. The other two devices record horizontal motion—one for east-west motion and the other for north-south motion. Seismographs record motion by tracing wave-shaped lines on paper or by translating the motion into electronic signals. The electronic signals can be recorded on magnetic tape or can be loaded directly into a computer that analyzes seismic waves. A tracing of earthquake motion that is recorded by a seismograph is called a **seismogram.**

Because P waves are the fastest-moving seismic waves, they are the first waves to be recorded by a seismograph. S waves travel much slower than P waves. Therefore, S waves are the second waves to be recorded by a seismograph. Surface waves are the slowest-moving waves and are the last waves to be recorded by a seismograph.

FLORIDA STANDARDS

LA.910.2.2.3 The student will organize information to show understanding or relationships among facts, ideas, and events (e.g., representing key points within text through charting, mapping, paraphrasing, summarizing, comparing, contrasting, or outlining); **SC.912.E.6.3** Analyze the scientific theory of plate tectonics and identify related major processes and features as a result of moving plates.

seismograph an instrument that records vibrations in the ground

seismogram a tracing of earthquake motion that is recorded by a seismograph

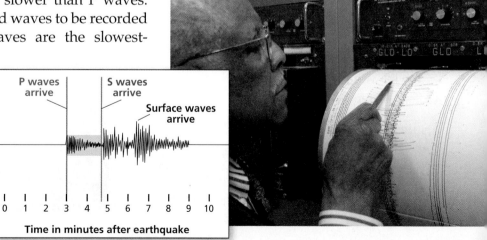

Figure 1 A seismograph station has banks of seismographs to record earthquakes. Each type of seismic wave leaves a unique "signature" on a seismogram (inset).

P waves arrive

S waves arrive

Surface waves arrive

0 1 2 3 4 5 6 7 8 9 10

Time in minutes after earthquake

Locating an Earthquake

Academic Vocabulary

analyze (AN uh LIEZ) study in detail

To determine the distance to an epicenter, scientists analyze the arrival times of the P waves and the S waves. The longer the lag time between the arrival of the P waves and the arrival of the S waves is, the farther away the earthquake occurred. Scientists use computers to calculate how far an earthquake is from a given seismograph station. Before computers were widely available, scientists consulted a lag-time graph. This graph translates the difference in arrival times of the P waves and S waves into distance from the epicenter to each station. The start time of the earthquake can also be determined by using this graph.

To locate the epicenter of an earthquake, scientists use computers to perform complex triangulations based on information from several seismograph stations. An earlier technique was simpler but less precise. On a map, scientists drew circles around at least three seismograph stations that recorded vibrations from the earthquake. The radius of each circle represented the distance from that station to the earthquake's epicenter. The point at which all of the circles intersected indicated the location of the epicenter of the earthquake.

SC**i**LINKS®

www.scilinks.org
Topic: Earthquake
Measurement
Code: HQX0452

SC.912.E.6.4

Quick Lab   Seismographic Record

   20 min

Procedure

1. Line a shoe box with a plastic bag. Fill the box to the rim with sand. Put on the lid.

2. Mark an X near the center of the lid.

3. Fasten a felt-tip pen to the lid of the box with a tight rubber band so that the pen extends slightly beyond the edge of the box.

4. Have a partner hold a pad of paper so that the paper touches the pen.

5. Hold a ball over the X at a height of 30 cm. As your partner slowly moves the paper horizontally past the pen, drop the ball on the X.

6. Label the resulting line with the type of material in the box.

7. Replace about 2/3 of the sand with crumpled newspaper. Put on the lid, and fasten the pen to the lid with the rubber band.

8. Repeat steps 4–6.

Analysis

1. What do the lines on the paper represent?

2. What do the sand and newspaper represent?

3. Compare the lines made in steps 4–6 with those made in step 8. Which material vibrated more when the ball was dropped on it? Explain why one material might vibrate more than the other.

4. How might different types of crustal material affect seismic waves that pass through it?

5. How might the distance of the epicenter of an earthquake from a seismograph affect the reading of a seismograph?

READING TOOLBOX

Layered Book
Make a layered book, and label the tabs with "Richter Scale," "Moment Magnitude Scale," and "Modified Mercalli Intensity Scale." Write notes on the appropriate tab as you read this section.

Earthquake Measurement

Scientists who study earthquakes are interested in the amount of energy released by an earthquake. Scientists also study the amount of damage done by the earthquake. These properties are studied by measuring magnitude and intensity.

Magnitude

The measure of the strength of an earthquake is called **magnitude.** Magnitude is determined by measuring the amount of ground motion caused by an earthquake. Seismologists express magnitude by using a magnitude scale, such as the Richter scale or the moment magnitude scale.

The *Richter scale* measures the ground motion from an earthquake to find the earthquake's strength. While the Richter scale was widely used for most of the 20th century, scientists now prefer the moment magnitude scale. *Moment magnitude* is a measurement of earthquake strength based on the size of the area of the fault that moves, the average distance that the fault blocks move, and the rigidity of the rocks in the fault zone. Although the moment magnitude and the Richter scales provide similar values for small earthquakes, the moment magnitude scale is more accurate for large earthquakes, such as the one shown in **Figure 2.**

The moment magnitude of an earthquake is expressed by a number. The larger the number, the stronger the earthquake. The largest earthquake that has been recorded (in Chile) registered a moment magnitude of 9.5. The earthquake in China in 2008 had a moment magnitude of 7.9 and devastated the country just before it hosted the Olympic Games that year. Earthquakes that have moment magnitudes of less than 2.5 usually are not felt by people.

✓ Reading Check **What is the difference between the Richter scale and the moment magnitude scale?**

magnitude a measure of the strength of an earthquake

Math Skills

Magnitudes On both the moment magnitude scale and the Richter scale, the energy of an earthquake increases by a factor of about 30 for each increment on the scale. Thus, a magnitude 4 earthquake releases 30 times as much energy as a magnitude 3 earthquake does. How much more energy does a magnitude 6 earthquake release than a magnitude 3 earthquake does?

Table 1 Modified Mercalli Intensity Scale

Intensity	Description
I	is not felt except by very few under especially favorable conditions
II	is felt by only few people at rest; delicately suspended items may swing
III	is felt by most people indoors; vibration is similar to the passing of a large truck
IV	is felt by many people; dishes and windows rattle; sensation is similar to a building being struck
V	is felt by nearly everyone; some objects are broken; unstable objects are overturned
VI	is felt by all people; some heavy objects are moved; causes very slight damage to structures
VII	causes slight to moderate damage to ordinary buildings; some chimneys are broken
VIII	causes considerable damage (including partial collapse) to ordinary buildings
IX	causes considerable damage (including partial collapse) to earthquake-resistant buildings
X	destroys some to most structures, including foundations; rails are bent
XI	causes few structures, if any, to remain standing; bridges are destroyed and rails are bent
XII	causes total destruction; distorts lines of sight; objects are thrown into the air

Intensity

intensity in Earth science, the amount of damage caused by an earthquake

Before the development of magnitude scales, the size of an earthquake was determined based on the earthquake's effects. A measure of the effects of an earthquake is the earthquake's **intensity.** The modified *Mercalli scale,* shown in **Table 1,** expresses intensity in Roman numerals from I to XII and provides a description of the effects of each earthquake intensity. The highest-intensity earthquake is designated by Roman numeral XII and is described as total destruction. The intensity of an earthquake depends on the earthquake's magnitude, the distance between the epicenter and the affected area, the local geology, the earthquake's duration, and human infrastructure.

Section 2 Review

LA.910.2.2.3; SC.912.N.1.1

Key Ideas

1. **Describe** the instrument that is used to record seismic waves.

2. **Compare** a seismograph and a seismogram.

3. **Summarize** the method that scientists used to identify the location of an earthquake before computers became widely used.

4. **Describe** the scales that scientists use to measure the magnitude of an earthquake.

5. **Explain** the difference between magnitude and intensity of an earthquake.

Critical Thinking

6. **Analyzing Methods** Explain why it would be difficult for scientists to locate the epicenter of an earthquake if they have seismic wave information from only two locations.

7. **Evaluating Data** Explain why an earthquake with a moderate magnitude might have a high intensity.

Concept Mapping

8. Use the following terms to create a concept map: *seismograph, seismogram, epicenter, P wave, S wave, magnitude,* and *intensity.*

Earthquakes and Society

Key Ideas

❯ Discuss the relationship between tsunamis and earthquakes.

❯ Describe two possible effects of a major earthquake on buildings.

❯ List three safety techniques to prevent injury caused by earthquake activity.

❯ Identify four methods scientists use to forecast earthquake risks.

Key Terms

tsunami

seismic gap

Why It Matters

Knowing where powerful earthquakes are likely to occur and preparing for them in advance can save many lives, perhaps your own. Several safety rules should be followed by those living in areas prone to earthquakes.

Movement of the ground during an earthquake seldom directly causes many deaths or injuries. Instead, most injuries result from the collapse of buildings and other structures or from falling objects and flying glass. Other dangers include landslides, fires, explosions caused by broken electric and gas lines, and floodwaters released from collapsing dams.

Tsunamis

An earthquake whose epicenter is on the ocean floor may cause a giant ocean wave called a **tsunami** (tsoo NAH mee), which may cause serious destruction if it crashes into land. A tsunami may begin to form when a sudden drop or rise in the ocean floor occurs because of faulting associated with undersea earthquakes. The drop or rise of the ocean floor causes a large mass of sea water to also drop or rise suddenly. This movement sets into motion a series of long, low waves that increase in height as they near the shore. These waves are tsunamis.

Destruction to Buildings and Property

Most buildings are not designed to withstand the swaying motion caused by earthquakes. Buildings whose walls are weak may collapse completely. Very tall buildings may sway so violently that they tip over and fall onto lower neighboring structures, as shown in **Figure 1**.

The type of ground beneath a building can affect the way in which the building responds to seismic waves. During an earthquake, the loose soil and rock can vibrate like jelly. Buildings constructed on top of this kind of ground experience exaggerated motion and sway violently.

FLORIDA STANDARDS

SC.912.E.7.3 Differentiate and describe the various interactions among Earth systems, including: atmosphere, hydrosphere, cryosphere, geosphere, and biosphere; **SC.912.P.10.20** Describe the measurable properties of waves and explain the relationships among them and how these properties change when the wave moves from one medium to another; **SC.912.E.6.3** Analyze the scientific theory of plate tectonics and identify related major processes and features as a result of moving plates.

tsunami a giant ocean wave that forms after a volcanic eruption, submarine earthquake, or landslide

Figure 1 Rescue workers surround a building that toppled in Taipei, Taiwan, during the earthquake of 1999.

Figure 2 In Tokyo, Japan—an area that has a high earthquake-hazard level—earthquake safety materials are available at disaster control centers.

 SC.912.E.6.4

Quick **Lab**

🕐 **10 min**

Earthquake-Safe Buildings

Procedure

❶ On a tabletop, build a structure by stacking building blocks on top of each other.

❷ Pound gently on the side of the table. Record what happens to the structure.

❸ Using rubber bands, wrap sets of three blocks together. Build a second structure by using these blocks.

❹ Repeat step 2.

Analysis

1. Which of your structures was more resistant to damage caused by the "earthquake"?

2. How could this model relate to building real structures, such as elevated highways?

Academic Vocabulary

instruction (in STRUHK shun) information given; a direction

Earthquake Safety

A destructive earthquake may take place in any region of the United States. However, destructive earthquakes are more likely to occur in certain geographic areas, such as California or Alaska. People who live near active faults should be ready to follow a few simple earthquake safety rules. These safety rules may help prevent death, injury, and property damage.

Before an Earthquake

Before an earthquake occurs, be prepared. Keep on hand a supply of canned food, bottled water, flashlights, batteries, and a portable radio. Some safety materials are shown in **Figure 2**. Plan what you will do if an earthquake strikes while you are at home, at school, or in a car. Discuss these plans with your family. Learn how to turn off the gas, water, and electricity in your home.

During an Earthquake

When an earthquake occurs, stay calm. During the few seconds between tremors, you can move to a safer position. If you are indoors, protect yourself from falling debris by standing in a doorway or crouching under a desk or table. Stay away from windows, heavy furniture, and other objects that might topple over. If you are in school, follow the instructions given by your teacher or principal. If you are in a car, stop in a place that is away from tall buildings, tunnels, power lines, or bridges. Then, remain in the car until the tremors cease.

After an Earthquake

After an earthquake, be cautious. Check for fire and other hazards. Always wear shoes when walking near broken glass, and avoid downed power lines and objects touched by downed wires.

Earthquake Warnings and Forecasts

Humans have long sought methods by which to predict earthquakes. Accurate earthquake predictions could help prevent injuries and deaths that result from earthquakes.

Today, scientists study past earthquakes to predict where future earthquakes are most likely to occur. Using records of past earthquakes, scientists can make approximate forecasts of future earthquake risks. However, there is currently no reliable way of predicting exactly when or where an earthquake will occur. Even the best forecasts may be off by several years.

To make forecasts that are more accurate, scientists are trying to detect changes in Earth's crust that can signal an earthquake. Faults near many population centers have been located and mapped. Instruments placed along these faults measure small changes in rock movement around the faults and can detect an increase in stress. Currently, however, these methods cannot provide reliable or accurate predictions of earthquakes.

Seismic Gaps

Scientists have identified zones of low earthquake activity, or seismic gaps, along some faults. A **seismic gap** is an area along a fault where relatively few earthquakes have occurred recently but where strong earthquakes occurred in the past. Some scientists think that seismic gaps are likely locations of future earthquakes. Several gaps that exist along the San Andreas Fault zone may be sites of major earthquakes in the future. A couple of seismic gaps in California are illustrated in **Figure 3.**

Reading Check Why do scientists think that seismic gaps are areas where future earthquakes are likely to occur?

READING TOOLBOX

Root Words
Explain how you can use the meaning of the root word *seism-* to understand the term *seismic gap.*

seismic gap an area along a fault where relatively few earthquakes have occurred recently but where strong earthquakes are known to have occurred in the past

Figure 3 Each red dot in the cross sections of the San Andreas Fault represents an earthquake or aftershock before the 1989 Loma Prieta earthquake. Note how seismic gap 2 was filled by the 1989 earthquake and its aftershocks, which are represented by the blue dots.

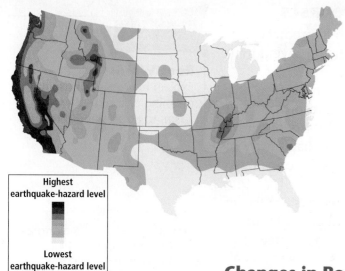

Foreshocks

Some earthquakes are preceded by little earthquakes called *foreshocks*. Foreshocks can precede an earthquake by a few seconds or a few weeks. In 1975, geophysicists in China recorded foreshocks near the city of Haicheng, which had a history of earthquakes. The city was evacuated the day before a major earthquake. The earthquake caused widespread destruction, but few lives were lost thanks to the warning. However, the Haicheng earthquake is the only example of a successful prediction made by using this method.

Figure 4 California, which has experienced severe earthquakes recently, has the highest earthquake-hazard level in the contiguous United States.

www.scilinks.org
Topic: Earthquakes and
        Society
Code: HQX0455

Changes in Rocks

Scientists use a variety of sensors to detect slight tilting of the ground and to identify the strain and cracks in rocks caused by the stress that builds up in fault zones. When cracks in rocks are filled with water, the magnetic and electrical properties of the rocks may change. Scientists also monitor natural gas seepage from rocks that are strained or fractured from seismic activity. Scientists hope that they will one day be able to use these signals to predict earthquakes.

Reliability of Earthquake Forecasts

Unfortunately, not all earthquakes have foreshocks or other precursors. Earthquake prediction is mostly unreliable. However, scientists have been able to determine areas that have a high earthquake-hazard level, as shown in **Figure 4.** Scientists continue to study seismic activity so that they may one day make accurate forecasts and save more lives.

Section 3 Review

LA.910.2.2.3; SC.912.E.7.3; SC.912.P.10.20

Key Ideas

1. **Discuss** the relationship between tsunamis and earthquakes.

2. **Describe** two possible effects of a major earthquake on buildings.

3. **List** three safety rules to follow when an earthquake strikes.

4. **Describe** how identifying seismic gaps may help scientists predict earthquakes.

5. **Identify** changes in rocks that may signal earthquakes.

Critical Thinking

6. **Applying Concepts** What type of building construction and location regulations should be included in the building code of a city that is located near an active fault?

7. **Applying Concepts** You are a scientist assigned to study an area that has a high earthquake-hazard level. Describe a program that you could set up to predict potential earthquakes.

Concept Mapping

8. Use the following terms to create a concept map: *earthquake, earthquake-hazard level, damage, tsunami, safety,* and *prediction.*

Detecting Earthquakes

The first known seismic wave detector was invented in China by Zhang Heng in 132 A.D. During an earthquake, a pendulum inside a large urn would move, causing one of eight dragons to drop a ball into the mouth of a frog below. The first "modern" seismograph was installed by Luigi Palmieri on Mount Vesuvius, Italy, in 1856. Today, the Global Seismographic Network has seismic detection stations around the world. Rapid detection of earthquakes allows tsunami warnings to be issued and aid efforts to be started quickly.

The direction of ground movement determined which dragon released its ball into the frog's mouth.

1. Palmieri's electromagnetic seismograph could measure both horizontal and vertical ground motions as well as duration and magnitude. **2.** This Global Seismographic Network station in Antarctica is part of the worldwide monitoring network. **3.** Early warning systems that alert commuter transit systems to slow down or stop at the first signs of shaking could help to save lives.

YOUR TURN

CRITICAL THINKING
What is the relationship between detecting earthquakes and quickly issuing tsunami warnings?

Skills Practice **Lab**

⏱ 45 min

Finding an Epicenter

What You'll Do

› **Analyze** P waves and S waves to determine the distance from a city to the epicenter of an earthquake.

› **Determine** the location of an earthquake epicenter by using the distance from three different cities to the epicenter.

What You'll Need

calculator
drawing compass
ruler

An earthquake releases energy that travels through Earth in all directions. This energy is in the form of waves. Two kinds of seismic waves are P waves and S waves. P waves travel faster than S waves and are the first to be recorded at a seismograph station. The S waves arrive after the P waves. The time difference between the arrival of the P waves and the arrival of the S waves increases as the waves travel farther from their origin. This difference in arrival time, called *lag time*, can be used to find the distance to the epicenter of the earthquake. Once the distance from three different locations is determined, scientists can find the approximate location of the epicenter.

Procedure

1. The average speed of P waves is 6.1 km/s. The average speed of S waves is 4.1 km/s. Calculate the lag time between the arrival of P waves and S waves over a distance of 100 km.

2. The graph below shows seismic records made in three cities following an earthquake. The records begin at the left. The arrows indicate the arrival of the P waves. The beginning of the next wave on each record indicates the arrival of the S wave. Use the time scale to find the lag time between the P waves and the S waves for each city. Draw a table similar to **Table 1.**

3. Record the lag time for each city in your table.

4. Use the lag times found in step 2 and the lag time per 100 km found in step 1 to calculate the distance from each city to the epicenter of the earthquake by using the equation below.

$$distance = \frac{measured\ lag\ time\ (s) \times 100\ km}{lag\ time\ for\ 100\ km}$$

Table ❶

City	Lag time (seconds)	Distance from city to epicenter
Austin		
Bismarck		
Portland		

DO NOT WRITE IN THIS BOOK

❺ Record the distances in your table.

❻ Copy the map below, which shows the location of the three cities. Using the map scale on your copy of the map, adjust the compass so that the radius of the circle with Austin at the center represents the distance calculation for Austin from step 4. Put the point of the compass on Austin. Draw a circle on your copy of the map.

❼ Repeat step 6 for Bismarck and for Portland. The epicenter of the earthquake is located near the point at which the three circles intersect.

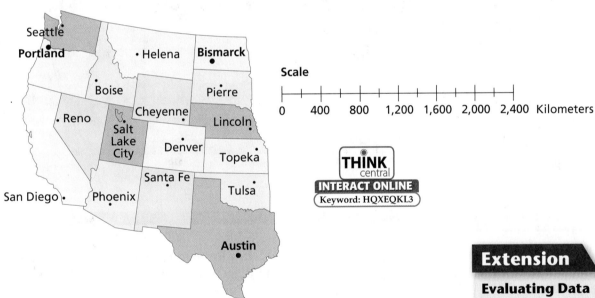

Scale

0   400   800   1,200 1,600 2,000 2,400 Kilometers

THINK central
INTERACT ONLINE
Keyword: HQXEQKL3

Analysis

1. **Evaluating Data** Describe how to locate an earthquake's epicenter. The epicenter that you found is closest to which city?

2. **Analyzing Processes** Why must measurements from three locations be used to find the epicenter of an earthquake?

Extension

Evaluating Data Research earthquakes in the United States. What is the probability of a major earthquake occurring in the area where you live? If an earthquake did occur in your area, what would most likely cause the earthquake?

MAPS in Action

Earthquake Hazard Map

Robinson Projection
Scale: 1:35,000,000 At The Equator

LOW HAZARD | MODERATE HAZARD | HIGH HAZARD | VERY HIGH HAZARD

Map ▸ Skills Activity

This map shows the earthquake-hazard levels for Europe, Asia, Africa, and Australia. Use the map to answer the questions below.

1. **Using a Key** Which areas of the map have a very high earthquake-hazard level?

2. **Using a Key** Which areas of the map have very low earthquake-hazard levels?

3. **Inferring Relationships** Most earthquakes take place near tectonic plate boundaries. Based on the hazard levels, describe the areas of the map where you think tectonic plate boundaries are located.

4. **Analyzing Relationships** In Asia, just below 60° north latitude, there are areas that have high earthquake-hazard levels but no plate boundaries. Explain why these areas might experience earthquakes.

5. **Forming a Hypothesis** There is a tectonic plate boundary between Africa and Saudi Arabia. However, the earthquake-hazard level in that region is low. Explain the low earthquake-hazard level.

6. **Analyzing Relationships** A divergent plate boundary began to tear apart the continent of Africa about 30 million years ago. Where on the continent of Africa would you expect to find landforms created by this boundary? Explain your answer.

Key Ideas

Key Terms

Section 1

How and Where Earthquakes Happen

> In the process of elastic rebound, stress builds in rocks along a fault until they break and spring back to their original shape.

> The two major types of seismic waves are body waves, which travel through a medium, and surface waves, which travel along the surface of a medium.

> Different seismic waves act differently depending on the material of Earth's interior through which they pass.

> Most earthquakes occur near tectonic plate boundaries, because stress on rock is highest in these areas.

earthquake, p. 319
elastic rebound, p. 319
focus, p. 320
epicenter, p. 320
body wave, p. 320
surface wave, p. 320
P wave, p. 321
S wave, p. 321
shadow zone, p. 322
fault zone, p. 324

Section 2

Studying Earthquakes

> Seismographs are instruments that record earthquake vibrations.

> The difference in the times that P waves and S waves take to arrive at a seismograph station helps scientists locate the epicenter of an earthquake.

> Earthquake magnitude scales describe the strength of an earthquake. Intensity is a measure of the effects of an earthquake.

seismograph, p. 325
seismogram, p. 325
magnitude, p. 327
intensity, p. 328

Section 3

Earthquakes and Society

> Tsunamis often are caused by ocean-floor earthquakes.

> During a major earthquake, buildings can sway violently or collapse.

> Earthquake safety techniques include developing a safety plan before an earthquake, moving to a safer location during an earthquake, and avoiding downed power lines after an earthquake.

> Seismic gaps, tilting ground, foreshocks, and variations in rock properties are some of the changes in Earth's crust that scientists use when trying to predict earthquakes.

tsunami, p. 329
seismic gap, p. 331

1. **Layered Book** Make a layered book, and label the tabs with "Seismic Gaps," "Changes in Rocks," and "Earthquake Hazard Levels." Write notes on the appropriate tab to summarize your understanding of earthquake prediction.

READING TOOLBOX

USING KEY TERMS

Use each of the following terms in a separate sentence.

2. *elastic rebound* SC.912.E.6.2
3. *fault zone* SC.912.E.6.2
4. *seismic gap* SC.912.E.6.2

For each pair of terms, explain how the meanings of the terms differ.

5. *focus* and *epicenter* SC.912.E.6.2
6. *body wave* and *surface wave* SC.912.E.6.2
7. *P wave* and *S wave*
8. *seismograph* and *seismogram*
9. *intensity* and *magnitude*

UNDERSTANDING KEY IDEAS

10. Vibrations in Earth that are caused by the sudden movement of rock are called SC.912.E.6.2
    a. epicenters.
    b. earthquakes.
    c. faults.
    d. tsunamis.

11. In the process of elastic rebound, as rock becomes stressed, it first SC.912.E.6.2
    a. deforms.
    b. melts.
    c. breaks.
    d. shrinks.

12. Earthquakes that cause severe damage are likely to have what characteristic? SC.912.E.6.2
    a. a deep focus
    b. an intermediate focus
    c. a shallow focus
    d. a deep epicenter

13. Most earthquakes occur SC.912.E.6.2
    a. in mountains.
    b. along major rivers.
    c. at plate boundaries.
    d. in the middle of tectonic plates.

14. P waves travel SC.912.E.6.1
    a. only through solids.
    b. only through liquids and gases.
    c. through solids, liquids, and gases.
    d. only through liquids.

15. S waves cannot pass through SC.912.E.6.1
    a. solids.
    b. the mantle.
    c. Earth's outer core.
    d. the asthenosphere.

16. Most injuries during earthquakes are caused by
    a. the collapse of buildings. SC.912.E.6.2
    b. cracks in Earth's surface.
    c. the vibration of S waves.
    d. the vibration of P waves.

17. Which of the following is not a method used to forecast earthquake risks? SC.912.E.6.2
    a. identifying seismic gaps
    b. determining moment magnitude
    c. recording foreshocks
    d. detecting changes in rock

SHORT ANSWER

18. How do seismic waves help scientists understand Earth's interior? SC.912.E.6.1

19. Why is the S-wave shadow zone larger than the P-wave shadow zones are? SC.912.E.6.1

20. How do scientists determine the location of an earthquake's epicenter? SC.912.E.6.1

21. Why do scientists prefer the moment magnitude scale to the Richter scale?

22. How might tall buildings respond during a major earthquake? SC.912.E.6.2

23. What should you do if you are in a car when an earthquake happens?

24. List three changes in rock that may one day be used to help forecast earthquakes. SC.912.E.6.2

CRITICAL THINKING

25. Understanding Relationships Why might surface waves cause the greatest damage during an earthquake? `SC.912.E.6.2`

26. Determining Cause and Effect Two cities are struck by the same earthquake. The cities are the same size, are built on the same type of ground, and have the same types of buildings. The city in which the earthquake produces a maximum intensity of VI on the Mercalli scale suffers $1 million in damage. The city in which the earthquake produces a maximum intensity of VIII on the Mercalli scale suffers $50 million in damage. What might account for this great difference in the costs of the damage?

27. Recognizing Relationships Would an earthquake in the Rocky Mountains in Colorado be likely to cause a tsunami? Explain your answer. `SC.912.E.6.2`

CONCEPT MAPPING

28. Use the following terms to create a concept map: *earthquake, elastic rebound, surface wave, body wave, seismic wave, tsunami, seismograph, magnitude, intensity, moment magnitude scale,* and *Richter scale*. `SC.912.E.6.2`

MATH SKILLS

Math Skills

29. Making Calculations If a P wave traveled 6.1 km/s, how long would the P wave take to travel 800 km? `SC.912.E.6.2`

30. Using Equations An earthquake with a magnitude of 3 releases 30 times more energy than does an earthquake with a magnitude of 2. How much more energy does an earthquake with a magnitude of 8 release than an earthquake with a magnitude of 6 does? `SC.912.E.6.2`

31. Making Calculations Of the approximately 420,000 earthquakes recorded each year, about 140 have a magnitude greater than 6. What percentage of all earthquakes have a magnitude greater than 6? `SC.912.E.6.2`

WRITING SKILLS

32. Writing from Research Find out how and why the worldwide network of seismograph stations was formed. Also, find out how all the stations in the network work together. Prepare a report about your findings.

33. Communicating Main Ideas Find out which earthquake registered the highest intensity in history. Write a brief report that describes the effects of this earthquake. `SC.912.E.6.3`

INTERPRETING GRAPHICS

The graph below shows three seismograms from a single earthquake. Use the graph to answer the questions that follow.

Seismic Wave Lapse Time

34. How far from the epicenter is seismograph B?

35. How far from the epicenter is seismograph C?

36. Which seismograph is farthest from the epicenter? `SC.912.E.6.3`

37. Why is there an 8 min interval between P waves and S waves in seismogram B but an 11 min interval between P waves and S waves in seismogram C? `SC.912.E.6.3`

Chapter 12 Florida Benchmark Review

Understanding Concepts

Directions (1–9): For each question, write on a separate sheet of paper the letter of the correct answer.

1 Which of the following statements describes the relationship between the epicenter and focus of an earthquake?
  A. The focus is the point on Earth's surface where the epicenter of an earthquake is located.
  B. The epicenter is the point on Earth's surface that lies directly above the focus.
  C. The epicenter is the point where an earthquake occurs, and the focus is where seismic waves reach Earth's surface.
  D. The focus is deeper within the Earth than the epicenter is.

2 Earthquakes result from
  F. the immobilization of faults.
  G. the sudden return of elastically deformed rock to its undeformed shape.
  H. zones where body waves cannot be detected.
  I. movement between the layers that make up Earth.

3 Most earthquake-related injuries are caused by
  A. tsunamis.
  B. collapsing buildings.
  C. rolling ground movements.
  D. sudden cracks in the ground.

4 Which of the following is least likely to cause deaths during an earthquake?
  F. floodwaters from collapsing dams
  G. falling objects and flying glass
  H. actual ground movement
  I. fires from broken electric and gas lines

5 California has the highest earthquake hazard level in the United States, as indicated by geological hazard maps. Why might scientists use geologic hazard maps?
  A. to determine areas that are at higher risk from a geologic hazard
  B. to predict when an earthquake might occur
  C. to identify stress-related strain in rocks
  D. to monitor gas seepage from strained or fractured rocks

6 The magnitude of an earthquake can be expressed numerically by using
  F. only the Richter scale.
  G. only the Mercalli scale.
  H. both the Mercalli scale and the moment magnitude scale.
  I. both the Richter scale and the moment magnitude scale.

7 Which of the following statements about shadow zones is NOT true?
  A. They are locations on Earth's surface where no body waves from a particular earthquake can be detected.
  B. Waves bend and change directions as they pass through Earth.
  C. They exist because the materials that make up Earth's interior have uniform rigidity.
  D. A large S-wave shadow zone covers the side of Earth opposite an earthquake.

8 How is the intensity of an earthquake measured?
  F. by measuring the amount of ground motion caused by the earthquake
  G. by measuring the strength of the earthquake based on the size of the area of the fault that moves
  H. by measuring the amount of destruction caused by the earthquake
  I. by measuring the number of seismic waves that occur during the earthquake

9 What is the relationship between seismic gaps and earthquakes?
  A. A seismic gap is the area where an earthquake originates.
  B. A seismic gap is an area where numerous, closely-spaced faults produce earthquakes.
  C. A seismic gap occurs because the interior of Earth is not uniformly rigid and seismic waves travel through Earth's core at varying speeds.
  D. A seismic gap is an area along a fault where relatively few earthquakes have occurred recently but where strong earthquakes have occurred in the past.

Interpreting Graphics

Directions (10–12): For each question below, record the correct answer on a separate sheet of paper.

The diagram below shows a recording of data by a seismograph.

Reading a Seismogram

10 What type of seismic waves are indicated by the points on the seismogram marked by the letter A?

   F. Love waves   **H.** P waves

   G. Rayleigh waves   **I.** S waves

11 How are the waves at point C different from the waves at point B?

   A. The waves at point C are slower than the waves at point B are.

   B. The waves at point C are less damaging than the waves at point B are.

   C. The waves at point C are S waves, while the waves at point B are surface waves.

   D. The waves at point B get their energy from the waves at point C.

Earthquake Damage

12 Based on the illustration above, the people that lived in this area would be at most danger from what during an earthquake?

   F. tsunamis   **H.** surface waves

   G. collapsing power lines   **I.** aftershocks

> **Test Tip**
>
> Always read the full question to make sure you understand what is being asked before you look at the answer choices.

Chapter 13 Volcanoes

Why It Matters

Volcanic eruptions can build landforms such as mountains and islands. Volcanic eruptions can also be dangerous to human life and property. Learning about volcanoes helps scientists better predict eruptions and warn people to leave an area where an eruption is likely.

READING TOOLBOX

These reading tools will help you learn the material in this chapter.

Science Terms

Everyday Words Used in Science Many words used in science are familiar words from everyday speech. However, when these words are used in science, their meanings are often different from the everyday meanings. Knowing the definitions of such words lets you use them correctly in scientific contexts.

Your Turn As you read Section 2, make a table like the one below for the terms *volcanic ash, volcanic dust, volcanic bombs,* and *volcanic blocks.* Include the scientific context of the term and the everyday meaning of the word that comes after the word *volcanic.*

Term	Scientific Context	Everyday Meaning
volcanic ash	pyroclastic particles that are less than 2 mm in diameter	ash—the powder that is left after something is burned

Frequency

Some, Many, or Most? Many statements include a word that tells you how often the statement is true. Examples of frequency words are *sometimes, commonly,* and *usually.* Words such as *some, many,* and *most* tell you about frequency in number.

Your Turn As you read Section 2, make a list of statements that contain frequency words. For each statement in your list, underline the word or phrase that tells how frequently the statement is true. An example is given below.

> Frequency Statement:
> <u>Most</u> volcanic dust and ash settles on the land that immediately surrounds the volcano.

Note Taking

Summarizing Ideas Summarizing the text under a heading is a simple way to take notes. Tips on summarizing are listed below.

1. Summary statements should be short but should fully express the idea.
2. Many paragraphs start or end with a sentence that summarizes the main idea of the paragraph.
3. In some cases, you may need more than one sentence to summarize a paragraph.

Your Turn Use summarizing to take notes for Section 1. Include the section titles and red or green headings. The example below can help you get started.

> Section 1—Volcanoes and Plate Tectonics
> • Many volcanic eruptions are caused by the movement of tectonic plates.
> Formation of Magma
> • Rock can melt into magma when the rock's temperature rises, the pressure on the rock is lowered, or fluids are added.

For more information on how to use these and other tools, see **Appendix A.**

SECTION 1
Volcanoes and Plate Tectonics

Key Ideas	Key Terms	Why It Matters
❯ Describe the three conditions under which magma can form. ❯ Explain what volcanism is. ❯ Identify three tectonic settings where volcanoes form. ❯ Describe how magma can form plutons.	magma volcanism lava volcano hot spot	The heat associated with volcanic activity can be used as a source of nonpolluting geothermal energy. Volcanoes are a window into this underground resource.

Volcanic eruptions can cause some of the most dramatic changes to Earth's surface. Some eruptions can be more powerful than the explosion of an atomic bomb. The cause of many of these eruptions is the movement of tectonic plates. The movement of tectonic plates is driven by Earth's internal heat.

By studying temperatures within Earth, scientists can learn more about volcanic eruptions. **Figure 1** shows estimates of Earth's inner temperatures and pressures. The combined temperature and pressure in the lower part of the mantle keeps the rocks below their melting point.

Formation of Magma

Despite the high temperature in the mantle, most of this zone remains solid because of the large amount of pressure from the surrounding rock. Sometimes, however, solid mantle and crust melt to form **magma,** or liquid rock that forms under Earth's surface.

Magma can form under three conditions. First, if the temperature of rock rises above the melting point of the minerals the rock is composed of, the rock will melt. Second, if enough pressure is removed from the rock, the melting point will decrease and the rock will melt. Third, the addition of fluids, such as water, may decrease the melting point of some minerals in the rock and cause the rock to melt.

FLORIDA STANDARDS

SC.912.E.6.3 Analyze the scientific theory of plate tectonics and identify related major processes and features as a result of moving plates; **SC.912.E.7.3** Differentiate and describe the various interactions among Earth systems, including: atmosphere, hydrosphere, cryosphere, geosphere, and biosphere; **SC.912.P.10.4** Describe heat as the energy transferred by convection, conduction, and radiation, and explain the connection of heat to change in temperature or states of matter.

magma liquid rock produced under Earth's surface

Figure 1 Temperature and pressure increase as depth beneath Earth's surface increases. So, rock in the lower mantle stays below its melting point.

Volcanism

Any activity that includes the movement of magma onto Earth's surface is called **volcanism.** Magma rises upward through the crust because the magma is less dense than the surrounding rock. As bodies of magma rise toward the surface, they can become larger in two ways. First, because they are so hot, they can melt some of the surrounding rock. Second, as the magma rises, it is forced into cracks in the surrounding rock. This process causes large blocks of overlying rock to break off and melt. Both of these processes add material to the magma body.

When magma erupts onto Earth's surface, the magma is then called **lava.** As lava flows from an opening, or *vent*, it might build up as a cone of material that eventually forms a mountain. The vent in Earth's surface through which magma and gases are expelled is called a **volcano.**

Major Volcanic Zones

If you were to plot the locations of the volcanoes that have erupted in the past 50 years, you would see that the locations form a pattern across Earth's surface. Like earthquakes, most active volcanoes occur in zones near both convergent and divergent boundaries of tectonic plates, as shown in **Figure 2.**

A major zone of active volcanoes encircles the Pacific Ocean. This zone, called the Pacific Ring of Fire, is formed by the subduction of plates along the Pacific coasts of North America, South America, Asia, and the islands of the western Pacific Ocean. The Pacific Ring of Fire is also one of Earth's major earthquake zones.

volcanism any activity that includes the movement of magma toward or onto Earth's surface

lava magma that flows onto Earth's surface; the rock that forms when lava cools and solidifies

volcano a vent or fissure in Earth's surface through which magma and gases are expelled

Academic Vocabulary

expel (ek SPEL) to eliminate or drive out a contained substance

READING TOOLBOX

Some, Many, or Most?
As you read this section, make a list of frequency statements that describe volcanism.

Figure 2 This map shows the locations of major tectonic plate boundaries and active volcanoes.

— Plate boundary
· Active volcanoes

Subduction Zones

Many volcanoes are located along *subduction zones*, where one tectonic plate moves under another. When a plate that consists of oceanic lithosphere meets a plate that consists of continental lithosphere, the denser oceanic lithosphere moves beneath the continental lithosphere. A deep *trench* forms on the ocean floor along the edge of the continent where the plate is subducted. The plate that consists of continental lithosphere buckles and folds to form a line of mountains along the edge of the continent.

As the oceanic plate sinks into the asthenosphere, fluids such as water from the subducting plate combine with crust and mantle material. These fluids decrease the melting point of the rock and cause the rock to melt and form magma. When the magma rises through the lithosphere and erupts on Earth's surface, lines of volcanic mountains form along the edge of the tectonic plate.

If two plates that have oceanic lithosphere at their boundaries collide, one plate subducts, and a deep trench forms. As when oceanic lithosphere collides with continental lithosphere, magma forms as fluids are introduced into the mantle. Some of the magma breaks through the overriding plate to Earth's surface. Over time, a string of volcanic islands, called an *island arc*, forms on the overriding plate, as shown in **Figure 3**. The early stages of this type of subduction produce an arc of small volcanic islands, such as the Aleutian Islands, which are in the North Pacific Ocean and between Alaska and Siberia. As more magma reaches the surface, the islands become larger and join to form one landmass, such as the volcanic islands that joined to form present-day Japan.

✓ **Reading Check** When a plate that consists of oceanic crust and a plate that consists of continental crust meet, which plate subducts beneath the other plate? (See Appendix G for answers to Reading Checks.)

Quick Lab 5 min

SC.912.E.6.4
Changing Melting Point

Procedure

❶ Place a **piece of ice** on a small **paper plate**.

❷ Wait 1 min, and observe how much ice has melted. Remove the meltwater from the plate.

❸ Pour **1/4 teaspoon of salt** onto a **second piece of ice**.

❹ Wait 1 min, and observe how much ice has melted.

Analysis

1. What happened to the rate of melting when you added salt to the ice?

2. In this model, what is represented by the ice? by the salt?

Figure 3 The Aleutian Islands (below) formed when oceanic lithosphere subducted beneath oceanic lithosphere and caused magma to rise to the surface and erupt to form volcanic islands (left).

Island arc volcanoes

Trench

Oceanic lithosphere

Oceanic lithosphere

Asthenosphere

Subduction zone

Mid-Ocean Ridges

The largest amount of magma comes to the surface where plates are moving apart at mid-ocean ridges. Thus, the interconnected mid-ocean ridges that circle Earth form a major zone of volcanic activity. As plates pull apart, magma flows upward along the rift zone. The upwelling magma adds material to the mid-ocean ridge and creates new lithosphere along the rift. This magma erupts to form underwater volcanoes. **Figure 4** shows pillow lava, an example of volcanic rock that forms underwater at a mid-ocean ridge. Pillow lava is named for its pillow shape, which is caused by the water that rapidly cools the outer surface of the lava.

Most volcanic eruptions that happen along mid-ocean ridges are unnoticed by humans because the eruptions take place deep in the ocean. An exception is found on Iceland. Iceland is one part of the Mid-Atlantic Ridge that is above sea level. One-half of Iceland is on the North American plate and is moving westward. The other half is on the Eurasian plate and is moving eastward. The middle of Iceland is cut by large *fissures*, which are cracks through which lava flows to Earth's surface.

Figure 4 When water rapidly cools hot lava, a hard, pillow-shaped crust forms. As the crust cools, it contracts and cracks. Hot lava flows through the cracks in the crust and then cools quickly to form another pillow-shaped structure.

Why It Matters

Energy Underfoot

EYE ON THE ENVIRONMENT

Volcanic activity and heat go together! People can harness this energy as a clean and renewable power source. Iceland, a volcanic island, is rich in geothermal resources. Swimmers enjoy Iceland's Blue Lagoon, formed by water released from a geothermal power plant. Using geothermal energy decreases the need for oil and other fuels.

The Geysers, near San Francisco, is a group of power plants that use geothermal energy to produce non-polluting steam. The steam turns turbines that generate electricity.

California uses geothermal energy to generate some of the electricity it consumes. This map shows California's major geothermal fields in red.

YOUR TURN

UNDERSTANDING CONCEPTS
What are some advantages of using geothermal energy?

348

Ni'ihau (5 Ma)
Kauai (5 Ma)
Oahu (3 Ma)
Molokai (2 Ma)
Maui (0.75 Ma to 1.3 Ma)
Hawaii (currently active)
Direction of plate movement
Lanai (1.3 Ma)
Kahoolawe (1 Ma)
Hot spot
Mantle plume

Figure 5 As a tectonic plate moves over a stationary mantle plume, volcanic mountains form (above). The Hawaiian Islands (left) formed in this way. The ages of the islands are shown in Ma, or millions of years.

THINK central
INTERACT ONLINE
Keyword: HQXVOLF5

Hot Spots

Not all volcanoes develop along plate boundaries. Areas of volcanism within the interiors of lithospheric plates are called **hot spots.** Most hot spots form where columns of solid, hot material from the deep mantle, called *mantle plumes*, rise and reach the lithosphere. When a mantle plume reaches the lithosphere, the plume spreads out. As magma rises to the surface, it breaks through the overlying crust. Volcanoes can then form in the interior of a tectonic plate, as shown in **Figure 5.**

Mantle plumes appear to remain nearly stationary. However, the lithospheric plate above a mantle plume continues to drift slowly. So, the volcano on the surface is eventually carried away from the mantle plume. The activity of the volcano stops because it has moved away from the hot spot that supplied it with magma. A new volcano forms, however, at the point on the plate's surface that is now over the mantle plume.

Some mantle plumes are long and linear. As magma generated by these plumes rises through cracks in Earth's crust, a line of hot-spot volcanoes forms. Unlike volcanoes that form individually as a plate moves over a mantle plume, hot-spot volcanoes that form in lines over a long plume do not have any particular age relationship to each another.

hot spot a volcanically active area of Earth's surface, commonly far from a tectonic plate boundary

Reading Check **Explain how one mantle plume can form several volcanic islands.**

Figure 6 Devils Tower in Wyoming is an example of a pluton, a formation caused by the cooling of magma beneath Earth's surface. Erosion of surrounding rock has revealed this igneous formation.

www.scilinks.org
Topic: Volcanic Zones
Code: HQX1618

Intrusive Activity

Because magma is less dense than solid rock, magma rises through the crust toward the surface. As the magma moves upward, it pushes into, or *intrudes*, the overlying rock. Because of magma's high temperature, magma affects surrounding rock in a variety of ways. Magma may melt surrounding rock, or it may change the rock. Magma may also fracture surrounding rock and cause fissures to form, or it may cause the surrounding rock to break apart and fall into the magma. Rock that falls into the magma may eventually melt, or the rock may be included as foreign pieces within the new *igneous rock*, which is rock that forms when the magma cools.

When magma does not reach Earth's surface, the magma may cool and solidify inside the crust. This process results in large formations of igneous rock called *plutons*, as shown in **Figure 6**. Plutons can vary greatly in size and shape. Small plutons called *dikes* are tabular in shape and may be only a few centimeters wide. *Batholiths* are large plutons that cover an area of at least 100 km^2 when they are exposed on Earth's surface.

Section 1 Review

LA.910.2.2.3; SC.912.E.6.3 ; SC.912.E.7.3; SC.912.P.10.4

Key Ideas

1. **Describe** three conditions that affect whether magma forms.

2. **Explain** how magma reaches Earth's surface.

3. **Compare** magma with lava.

4. **Describe** how subduction produces magma.

5. **Identify** three tectonic settings where volcanoes commonly occur.

6. **Summarize** the formation of hot spots.

7. **Describe** two igneous structures that form under Earth's surface.

Critical Thinking

8. **Identifying Relationships** Describe how the presence of ocean water in crustal rock might affect the formation of magma.

9. **Applying Ideas** Yellowstone National Park in Wyoming is far from any plate boundary. How would you explain the volcanic activity in the park?

Concept Mapping

10. Use the following terms to create a concept map: *magma, volcanism, vent, volcano, subduction zone, hot spot, dike,* and *pluton.*

Key Ideas	Key Terms	Why It Matters
❭ Explain how the composition of magma affects volcanic eruptions and lava flow. ❭ Describe the five major types of pyroclastic material. ❭ Identify the three main types of volcanic cones. ❭ Describe how a caldera forms. ❭ List three events that may signal a volcanic eruption.	mafic felsic pyroclastic material caldera	Understanding factors that lead to a quiet or explosive volcanic eruption lets scientists determine hazards associated with a particular volcano. By recognizing signs that an eruption may soon occur, scientists can issue warnings and save lives.

Volcanoes can be thought of as windows into Earth's interior. Lava that erupts from them provides an opportunity for scientists to study the nature of Earth's crust and mantle. By analyzing the composition of volcanic rocks, geologists have concluded that there are two general types of magma. **Mafic** (MAF ik) describes magma or rock that is rich in magnesium and iron and is commonly dark in color. **Felsic** (FEL sik) describes magma or rock that is rich in light-colored silicate materials. Mafic rock commonly makes up the oceanic crust, whereas felsic rock is more common than mafic rock in continental crust.

FLORIDA STANDARDS

SC.912.E.6.3 Analyze the scientific theory of plate tectonics and identify related major processes and features as a result of moving plates; **SC.912.E.7.3** Differentiate and describe the various interactions among Earth systems, including: atmosphere, hydrosphere, cryosphere, geosphere, and biosphere.

Types of Eruptions

The *viscosity*, or resistance to flow, of magma affects the force with which a particular volcano will erupt. The viscosity of magma is determined by the magma's composition. Because mafic magmas produce runny lava that has a low viscosity, they typically cause quiet eruptions. Because felsic magmas produce sticky lava that has a high viscosity, they typically cause explosive eruptions. Magma that contains large amounts of trapped, dissolved gases is more likely to produce explosive eruptions than is magma that contains small amounts of dissolved gases.

mafic describes magma or igneous rock that is rich in magnesium and iron and that is generally dark in color

felsic describes magma or igneous rock that is rich in feldspars and silica and that is generally light in color

Quiet Eruptions

Oceanic volcanoes commonly form from mafic magma. Because of mafic magma's low viscosity, gases can easily escape from mafic magma. Eruptions from oceanic volcanoes, such as those in Hawaii, shown in **Figure 1,** are usually quiet.

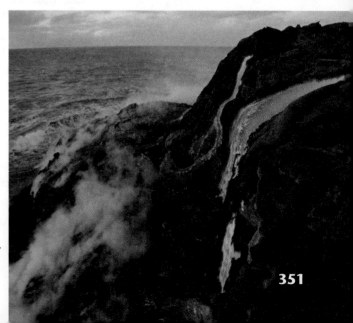

Figure 1 Lava flows from a quiet eruption like a red-hot river would flow. This lava flowed several miles from the Kilauea volcano to the sea.

351

Figure 2 Types of Mafic Lava Flows

Pahoehoe is the least viscous type of mafic lava. It forms wrinkly volcanic rock when it cools.

Aa lava is more viscous than pahoehoe lava and forms sharp volcanic rock when it cools.

Blocky lava is the most viscous type of mafic lava and forms chunky volcanic rock when it cools.

Lava Flows

When mafic lava cools rapidly, a crust forms on the surface of the flow. If the lava continues to flow after the crust forms, the crust wrinkles to form a volcanic rock called *pahoehoe* (pah HOH ee HOH ee), which is shown in **Figure 2**. Pahoehoe forms from hot, fluid lava. As it cools, it forms a smooth, ropy texture. Pahoehoe actually means "ropy" in Hawaiian.

If the crusted-over surface of the lava deforms rapidly or grows too thick to form wrinkles, the surface breaks into jagged chunks to form *aa* (AH AH). Aa forms from lava that has the same composition as pahoehoe lava. Aa lava's texture results from differences in gas content and in the rate and slope of the lava flow.

Blocky lava has a higher silica content than aa lava does, which makes blocky lava more viscous than aa lava. The high viscosity causes the cooled lava at the surface to break into large chunks, while the hot lava underneath continues to flow. This process gives the lava flow a blocky appearance.

Reading Check How do flow rate and gas content affect the appearance of lavas?

Explosive Eruptions

Unlike the fluid lavas produced by oceanic volcanoes, the felsic lavas of continental volcanoes, such as Mount St. Helens, tend to be cooler and stickier. Felsic lavas also contain large amounts of trapped gases, such as water vapor and carbon dioxide. When a volcano erupts, the dissolved gases within the lava escape and send molten and solid particles shooting into the air. So, felsic lava tends to explode and throw pyroclastic material into the air. **Pyroclastic material** consists of fragments of rock that form during a volcanic eruption.

pyroclastic material fragments of rock that form during a volcanic eruption

Types of Pyroclastic Material

Some pyroclastic materials form when magma breaks into fragments during an eruption because of the rapidly expanding gases in the magma. Other pyroclastic materials form when fragments of erupting lava cool and solidify as they fly through the air.

Scientists classify pyroclastic materials according to the sizes of the particles, as shown in **Figure 3.** Pyroclastic particles that are less than 2 mm in diameter are called *volcanic ash*. Volcanic ash that is less than 0.25 mm in diameter is called *volcanic dust*. Usually, most volcanic ash settles on the land surrounding the volcano. However, some of the smallest dust particles may travel around Earth in the upper atmosphere.

Large pyroclastic particles that are less than 64 mm in diameter are called *lapilli* (luh PIL ie), which is from a Latin word that means "little stones." Lapilli generally fall near the vent.

Large clots of lava may be thrown out of an erupting volcano while they are red-hot. As they spin through the air, they cool and develop a round or spindle shape. These pyroclastic particles are called *volcanic bombs*. The largest pyroclastic materials, known as *volcanic blocks*, form from solid rock that is blasted from the vent. Some volcanic blocks are the size of a small house.

READING TOOLBOX

Summarizing Ideas
As you read about types of pyroclastic material, summarize their characteristics.

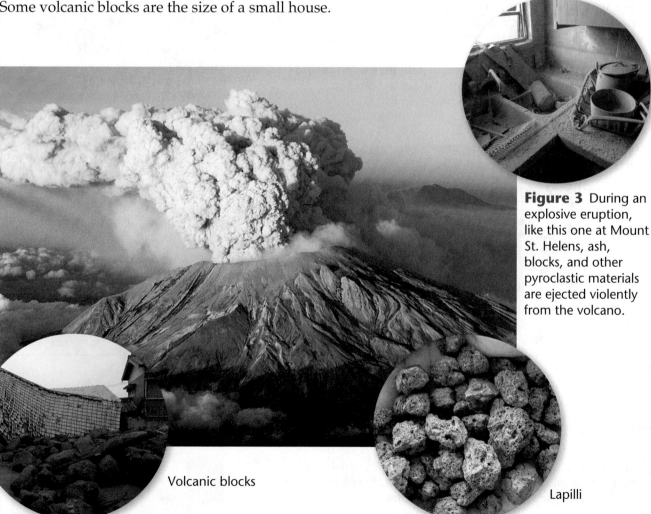

Volcanic ash

Figure 3 During an explosive eruption, like this one at Mount St. Helens, ash, blocks, and other pyroclastic materials are ejected violently from the volcano.

Volcanic blocks

Lapilli

Types of Volcanoes

Volcanic activity produces a <u>variety</u> of characteristic features that form during both quiet and explosive eruptions. The lava and pyroclastic material that are ejected during volcanic eruptions build up around the vent and form volcanic cones. There are three main types of volcanic cones, as described in **Table 1.**

The funnel-shaped pit at the top of a volcanic vent is known as a *crater*. The crater forms when material is blown out of the volcano by explosions. A crater usually becomes wider as weathering and erosion break down the walls of the crater and allow loose materials to collapse into the vent. Sometimes, a small cone forms within a crater. This formation occurs when subsequent eruptions cause material to build up around the vent.

Academic Vocabulary

variety (vuh RIE uh tee) a collection of things that are very different from each other; diversity

Table 1 Volcanic cones are classified into three main categories. *Which type of volcano would form from lava that is highly viscous?*

Types of Volcanoes

Shield Volcanoes Volcanic cones that are broad at the base and have gently sloping sides are called *shield volcanoes*. A shield volcano covers a wide area and generally forms from quiet eruptions. Layers of hot, mafic lava flow out around the vent, harden, and slowly build up to form the cone. The Hawaiian Islands are a chain of shield volcanoes that built up from the ocean floor at a hot spot, forming the largest volcanoes on Earth.

Cinder Cones A type of volcano that has very steep slopes is a cinder cone. The slope angles of cinder cones can be close to 40°, and the cones are rarely more than a few hundred meters high. Cinder cones form from small explosive eruptions and are made of pyroclastic material. Cinder cones are usually quite small in comparison to shield volcanoes or composite volcanoes.

Composite Volcanoes Composite volcanoes are made of alternating layers of hardened lava flows and pyroclastic material. During a quiet eruption, lava flows cover the sides of the cone. Then, when an explosive eruption occurs, large amounts of pyroclastic material are deposited around the vent. The explosive eruption is followed again by quiet lava flows. Composite volcanoes, also known as *stratovolcanoes*, commonly develop to form large volcanic mountains.

Figure 4 Formation of a Caldera

A cone forms from volcanic eruptions.

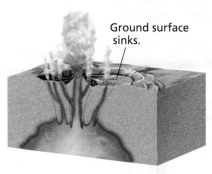

Ground surface sinks.

Volcanic eruptions partially empty the magma chamber.

Caldera

The top of the cone collapses inward to form a caldera.

Calderas

When the magma chamber below a volcano empties, the volcanic cone may collapse and leave a large, basin-shaped depression called a **caldera** (kal DER uh). The process of caldera formation is shown in **Figure 4**.

Eruptions that discharge large amounts of magma can also cause a caldera to form. Krakatau, a volcanic island in Indonesia, is an example of this type of caldera. When the volcanic cone exploded in 1883, a caldera with a diameter of 6 km formed.

Calderas may later fill with water to form lakes. Thousands of years ago, the cone of Mount Mazama in Oregon collapsed during a massive eruption and formed a caldera. The caldera eventually filled with water and is now called Crater Lake.

caldera a large, circular depression that forms when the magma chamber below a volcano partially empties and causes the ground above to sink

Reading Check Describe two ways that calderas form.

SC.912.E.6.4

Quick Lab   Volcanic Cones   25 min

Procedure

❶ Pour 1/2 cup (about 4 oz) of dry plaster of Paris into a measuring cup.

❷ Use a graduated cylinder to measure 60 mL of water, and add the water to the dry plaster in the measuring cup. Use a mixing spoon to blend the mixture until it is smooth.

❸ Hold the measuring cup about 2 cm over a paper plate. Pour the contents slowly and steadily onto the center of the plate. Allow the plaster to dry.

❹ On a clean paper plate, pour dry oatmeal or potato flakes slowly until the mound is approximately 5 cm high.

❺ Without disturbing the mound, use a protractor to measure its slope.

❻ When the plaster cone is hardened, remove it from the plate. Measure the average slope angle of the cone.

Analysis

1. Which cone represents a cinder cone? Which cone represents a shield volcano? Compare the slope angles formed by these cones.

2. How would the slope be affected if the oatmeal were rounder? How would the slope be affected if the oatmeal were thicker?

3. How would you use the same supplies to model a composite volcano?

Figure 5 These scientists are sampling gases emitted from the fumarole field on Vulcano Island in Italy.

www.scilinks.org
Topic: Predicting Volcanic Eruptions
Code: HQX1209

Predicting Volcanic Eruptions

A volcanic eruption can be one of Earth's most destructive natural phenomena. Scientists, such as those in **Figure 5,** look for a variety of events that may signal the beginning of an eruption.

Earthquake Activity

One of the most important warning signals of a volcanic eruption is a change in earthquake activity around the volcano. Growing pressure on the surrounding rock from magma that is moving upward causes small earthquakes. Temperature changes within the rock and fracturing of the rock around a volcano also cause small earthquakes. An increase in the strength and frequency of earthquakes may be a signal that an eruption is about to occur.

Patterns in Activity

Before an eruption, the upward movement of magma beneath the surface may cause the surface of the volcano to bulge outward. Special instruments can measure small changes in the tilt of the ground surface on the volcano's slopes.

Predicting the eruption of a particular volcano also requires some knowledge of its previous eruptions. Scientists compare the volcano's past behavior with current daily measurements of earthquakes, surface bulges, and changes in the amount and composition of the gases that the volcano emits. Unfortunately, only a few of the active volcanoes in the world have been studied by scientists long enough to establish any activity patterns. Also, volcanoes that have been dormant for long periods of time may, with little warning, suddenly become active.

Section 2 Review

LA.910.2.2.3; SC.912.E.6.3; SC.912.E.7.3

Key Ideas

1. **Summarize** the difference between mafic and felsic magma.

2. **Explain** how the composition of magma affects the force of volcanic eruptions.

3. **Compare** three major types of lava flows.

4. **Define** *pyroclastic material,* and list three examples.

5. **Identify** the three main types of volcanic cones.

6. **Describe** how calderas form.

7. **List** three events that may precede a volcanic eruption.

Critical Thinking

8. **Applying Ideas** Would quiet eruptions or explosive eruptions be more likely to increase the steepness of a volcanic cone? Explain your answer.

9. **Drawing Conclusions** Why would a sudden increase in earthquake activity around a volcano indicate a possible eruption?

Concept Mapping

10. Use the following terms to create a concept map: *mafic lava, felsic lava, pahoehoe, aa, shield volcano, pyroclastic material, lapilli, volcanic bomb, volcanic block, volcanic ash,* and *volcanic dust.*

Just How Dangerous Are Volcanoes?

Lava flows can be devastating, but volcanoes have many other powerful ways to cause death and destruction. For example, the 1980 eruption of Mount St. Helens included the initial landslide and explosion followed by heavy falls of volcanic ash and mudflows. Mount St. Helens is one of thirteen active volcanoes in the Cascade Range. Eruptions of Cascade volcanoes tend to be extremely explosive. In addition to other hazards, such eruptions can also produce pyroclastic flows—fast-moving flows of glowing-hot volcanic material mixed with deadly volcanic gases.

A volcanic mudflow partly buried these mailboxes. Many Cascade volcanoes are topped with ice and snow that can melt during an eruption. The water then mixes with volcanic ash to form mudflows resembling fast-moving rivers of cement.

More than one million people live in the Seattle-Tacoma area near Mount Rainier, an active volcano.

A scientist monitors one of the Three Sisters volcanoes in Oregon for signs of an eruption or landslide.

Eruptions of Cascade Volcanoes

Mount Baker
Glacier Peak
WASHINGTON
Mount Rainier
Mount St. Helens
Mount Adams
Mount Hood
Mount Jefferson
Three Sisters
Newberry Volcano
OREGON
Crater Lake
Medicine Lake Volcano
Mount Shasta
Lassen Peak
CALIFORNIA

3,000   Present
Years Before Present

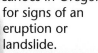

YOUR TURN

UNDERSTANDING CONCEPTS
What dangers are associated with explosive volcanic eruptions?

CRITICAL THINKING
What dangers are associated with volcanoes do not erupt explosively?

357

What You'll Do

> **Create** a working apparatus to test carbon dioxide levels.

> **Analyze** the levels of carbon dioxide emitted from a model volcano.

> **Predict** the possibility of an eruption from a model volcano.

What You'll Need

baking soda, 15 cm³
drinking bottle, 16 oz
box or stand for plastic cup
clay, modeling
coin
cup, clear plastic, 9 oz
graduated cylinder
limewater, 1 L
straw, drinking, flexible
tissue, bathroom (2 sheets)
vinegar, white, 140 mL
water, 100 mL

Safety

Volcano Verdict

You will need to have a partner for this lab. You and your partner will act as geologists who work in a city located near a volcano. City officials are counting on you to predict when the volcano will erupt next. You and your partner have decided to use limewater as a gas-emissions tester. You will use this tester to measure the levels of carbon dioxide emitted from a simulated volcano. The more active the volcano is, the more carbon dioxide it releases.

Procedure

1 Carefully pour limewater into the plastic cup until the cup is three-fourths full. Place the cup on a box or stand. This will be your gas-emissions tester.

2 Now, build a model volcano. Begin by pouring 50 mL of water and 70 mL of vinegar into the drink bottle.

3 Form a plug of clay around the short end of the straw. The clay plug must be large enough to cover the opening of the bottle. Be careful not to get the clay wet.

Step 6

4 Sprinkle 5 cm³ of baking soda along the center of a single section of bathroom tissue. Then, roll the tissue, and twist the ends so that the baking soda cannot fall out.

5 Drop the tissue into the drink bottle, and immediately put the short end of the straw inside the bottle and make a seal with the clay.

6 Put the other end of the straw into the limewater.

7 Record your observations. You have just taken your first measurement of gas levels from the volcano.

8 Imagine that it is several days later and that you need to test the volcano again to collect more data. Before you continue, toss a coin. If it lands heads up, go to step 9. If it lands tails up, go to step 10. Write down the step that you follow.

9 Repeat steps 1–7. But use 2 cm³ of baking soda in the tissue in step 4 instead of 5 cm³. (Note: You must use fresh water, vinegar, and limewater.) Record your observations.

10 Repeat steps 1–7. But use 8 cm³ of baking soda in the tissue in step 4 instead of 5 cm³. (Note: You must use fresh water, vinegar, and limewater.) Record your observations.

Mount Usu, 770 kilometers from Tokyo in Japan, erupted on March 31, 2000.

Analysis

1. **Explaining Events** How do you explain the difference in the appearance of the limewater from one trial to the next?

2. **Recognizing Patterns** What does the data that you collected tell you about the activity in the volcano?

3. **Evaluating Results** Based on your results in step 9 or 10, do you think it would be necessary to evacuate the city?

4. **Applying Conclusions** How would a geologist use a gas-emissions tester to predict volcanic eruptions?

Extension

Evaluating Data Scientists base their predictions of eruptions on a variety of evidence before recommending an evacuation. What other forms of evidence would a scientist need to know to predict an eruption?

The Hawaiian-Emperor Seamount Chain

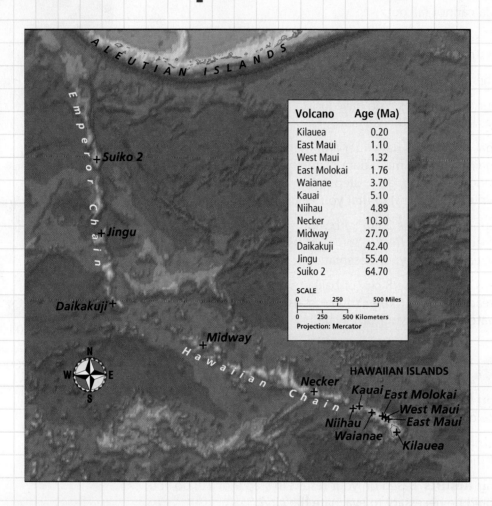

Volcano	Age (Ma)
Kilauea	0.20
East Maui	1.10
West Maui	1.32
East Molokai	1.76
Waianae	3.70
Kauai	5.10
Niihau	4.89
Necker	10.30
Midway	27.70
Daikakuji	42.40
Jingu	55.40
Suiko 2	64.70

SCALE
0   250   500 Miles
0   250   500 Kilometers
Projection: Mercator

Map Skills Activity

This map shows the locations and ages of islands and seamounts in the Hawaiian-Emperor seamount chain, which is located in the Pacific Ocean. Use the map to answer the questions below.

1. **Inferring Relationships** Under which volcano is the hot spot presently located?

2. **Using a Key** Which volcano is the oldest?

3. **Evaluating Data** A seamont is a submarine volcanic mountain. Would you expect older volcanoes to be seamounts or islands? Explain your answer.

4. **Analyzing Data** Which island signifies a change in direction of the movement of the Pacific plate? Explain your answer.

5. **Identifying Trends** In which direction has the Pacific plate been moving since the formation of the islands in the seamount chain changed direction?

6. **Analyzing Relationships** How many years ago did the Pacific plate change its direction?

7. **Analyzing Data** What is the average speed of the Pacific plate over the last 65 million years?

8. **Predicting Consequences** Where would you expect a new volcano to form 1 million years from now?

Summary

Key Ideas

Key Terms

Section 1

Volcanoes and Plate Tectonics

❯ Magma can form when temperature increases in or pressure decreases on mantle rock. Magma also may form when water is added to hot rock.

❯ Volcanism is any activity that includes the movement of magma toward or onto Earth's surface.

❯ Volcanism is common at convergent and divergent boundaries between tectonic plates. Hot spots are areas of volcanic activity that are located over rising mantle plumes, which can exist far from tectonic plate boundaries.

❯ Magma that cools below Earth's surface forms intrusive igneous rock bodies called plutons.

magma, p. 345
volcanism, p. 346
lava, p. 346
volcano, p. 346
hot spot, p. 349

Section 2

Volcanic Eruptions

❯ Hotter, less viscous, mafic lava commonly causes quiet eruptions. Cooler, more viscous, felsic lava commonly causes explosive eruptions, especially if it contains trapped gases.

❯ The five major types of pyroclastic materials are, from smallest to largest, volcanic dust, volcanic ash, lapilli, volcanic bombs, and volcanic blocks.

❯ Volcanic cones are classified into three categories—shield volcanoes, cinder cones, and composite volcanoes—based on composition and form.

❯ A caldera forms where a volcanic cone collapses during a massive eruption and leaves a large, basin-shaped depression.

❯ Events that might signal a volcanic eruption include changes in earthquake activity, changes in the volcano's shape, changes in composition and amount of gases emitted, and changes in the patterns of the volcano's normal activity.

mafic, p. 351
felsic, p. 351
pyroclastic material, p. 352
caldera, p. 355

1. **Everyday Words Used in Science** Find the everyday meanings of the words *mantle* and *plume*. Then, compare the everyday meanings of these words with the scientific meaning of *mantle plume*.

USING KEY TERMS

Use each of the following terms in a separate sentence.

2. *volcanism* SC.912.E.6.2

3. *hot spot* SC.912.E.6.1

4. *pyroclastic material* SC.912.E.6.2

For each pair of terms, explain how the meanings of the terms differ.

5. *magma* and *lava*

6. *mafic* and *felsic*

7. *shield volcano* and *composite volcano* SC.912.E.6.2

8. *crater* and *caldera* SC.912.E.6.2

UNDERSTANDING KEY IDEAS

9. A characteristic of lava that determines the force of a volcanic eruption is SC.912.E.6.2
   a. color.
   b. viscosity.
   c. density.
   d. age.

10. Island arcs form when oceanic lithosphere subducts under SC.912.E.6.2
   a. continental lithosphere.
   b. calderas.
   c. volcanic bombs.
   d. oceanic lithosphere.

11. Areas of volcanism within tectonic plates are called SC.912.E.6.2
   a. hot spots.
   b. cones.
   c. calderas.
   d. fissures.

12. Explosive volcanic eruptions commonly result from SC.912.E.6.2
   a. mafic magma.
   b. felsic magma.
   c. aa lava.
   d. pahoehoe lava.

13. Pyroclastic materials that form rounded or spindle shapes as they fly through the air are called SC.912.E.6.2
   a. ash.
   b. volcanic bombs.
   c. lapilli.
   d. volcanic blocks.

14. A cone formed by only solid fragments built up around a volcanic opening is a SC.912.E.6.2
   a. shield volcano.
   b. cinder cone.
   c. composite volcano.
   d. stratovolcano.

15. The depression that results when a volcanic cone collapses over an emptying magma chamber is a SC.912.E.6.2
   a. crater.
   b. caldera.
   c. vent.
   d. fissure.

16. Scientists have discovered that before an eruption, earthquakes commonly SC.912.E.6.2
   a. stop.
   b. increase in number.
   c. have no relationship with volcanism.
   d. decrease in number.

SHORT ANSWER

17. At what point does magma become lava? SC.912.E.6.2

18. Describe how tectonic movement can form volcanoes. SC.912.E.6.3

19. Name the process that includes the movement of magma onto Earth's surface. SC.912.E.6.2

20. What may happen to magma that does not reach Earth's surface? SC.912.E.6.2

21. How is the composition of magma related to the force of volcanic eruptions? SC.912.E.6.2

22. List and describe the major types of pyroclastic material. SC.912.E.6.2

23. Compare the three main types of volcanic cones. SC.912.E.6.2

24. What signs can scientists study to try to predict volcanic eruptions? SC.912.E.6.2

CRITICAL THINKING

25. **Analyzing Ideas** Why is most lava that forms on Earth's surface unnoticed and unobserved?

26. **Identifying Relationships** The Pacific Ring of Fire is a zone of major volcanic activity because of tectonic plate boundaries. Identify another area of Earth where you might expect to find volcanic activity. SC.912.E.6.3

27. **Analyzing Processes** Why does felsic lava tend to form composite volcanoes and cinder cones rather than shield volcanoes? SC.912.E.6.2

28. **Making Inferences** How might geologists distinguish an impact crater on Earth, such as Meteor Crater in Arizona, from a volcanic crater? SC.912.E.6.2

29. **Making Comparisons** Sinkholes form when the roof of an underground cave is not supported by groundwater. Compare this process to the process by which calderas form. SC.912.E.6.4

CONCEPT MAPPING

30. Use the following terms to create a concept map: *magma, lava, volcano, pluton, mafic lava, felsic lava, pyroclastic material, volcanic ash, volcanic dust, lapilli, volcanic bomb, volcanic block, volcanic cone, shield volcano, cinder cone,* and *composite volcano.* SC.912.E.6.2

MATH SKILLS

31. **Making Calculations** On day 1, a volcano expelled 5 metric tons of sulfur dioxide. On day 2, the same volcano expelled 12 metric tons of sulfur dioxide. What is the percentage increase in sulfur dioxide expelled from day 1 to day 2? SC.912.E.6.2

32. **Interpreting Statistics** A lava flow traveled for 7.3 min before it flowed into the ocean. The speed of the lava was 3 m/s. How far did the lava flow travel? SC.912.E.6.2

WRITING SKILLS

33. **Outlining Topics** Outline the essential steps in the process of caldera formation. SC.912.E.6.2

34. **Communicating Main Ideas** Write an essay describing the formation of a volcano. SC.912.E.6.2

INTERPRETING GRAPHICS

The graphs below show data about earthquake activity; the slope angle, or *tilt*, of the ground; and the amount of gas emitted for a particular volcano over a period of 10 days. Use the graphs to answer the questions that follow.

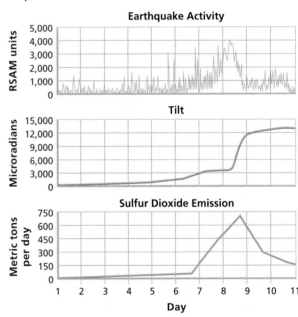

35. On what day did the volcano erupt? Explain your answer. SC.912.E.6.2

36. For how many days before the eruption did gas emission increase? SC.912.E.6.2

37. Why do you think the slope angle of the ground did not return to its original angle after the eruption? SC.912.E.6.2

Understanding Concepts

Directions (1–10): For each question, write on a separate sheet of paper the letter of the correct answer.

1 Magma is liquid rock that forms beneath Earth's surface. Which of the following is NOT a condition under which magma may form?
A. a volcanic eruption
B. increased temperature
C. increased pressure
D. addition of fluids

2 Volcanoes form at various places around Earth, including subduction zones, divergent boundaries, and hot spots. Which of the following is an example of a volcanic formation that is produced at subduction zones?
F. mid-ocean ridges
G. mantle plumes
H. fissures
I. island arcs

3 How does volcanic activity contribute to plate margins where new crust is being formed?
A. Where plates collide at subduction zones, rocks melt and form pockets of magma.
B. Between plate boundaries, hot spots may form a chain of volcanic islands.
C. When plates pull apart at oceanic ridges, magma creates new ocean floor.
D. At some boundaries, new crust is formed when one plate is forced on top of another.

4 An important warning sign of volcanic activity
F. would be a change in local wind patterns.
G. is a bulge in the surface of the volcano.
H. might be a decrease in earthquake activity.
I. is a marked increase in local temperatures.

5 Which aspect of mafic lava is important in the formation of smooth, ropy pahoehoe lava?
A. a fairly high viscosity
B. a fairly low viscosity
C. rapidly deforming crust
D. rapid underwater cooling

6 Which type of volcano is made up of only pyroclastic material that results from violent eruptions?
F. cinder cone
G. composite volcano
H. shield volcano
I. stratovolcano

7 The Pacific Ring of Fire is caused by
A. hot spots throughout the Pacific ocean.
B. subduction of plates along Pacific coasts.
C. mid-ocean ridges in the Pacific.
D. fault lines along Pacific coasts.

8 At which of the following locations does the greatest amount of magma reach the surface, forming a major zone of volcanism?
F. hot spots
G. intrusions
H. mid-ocean ridges
I. subduction zones

9 Which of the following does NOT describe magma that causes explosive eruptions?
A. It is felsic magma.
B. It contains large amounts of trapped and dissolved gases.
C. It is rich in light-colored silicate materials.
D. It has a low viscosity.

10 A scientist is studying a volcanic lava flow in Hawaii. The scientist finds sharp volcanic rock in a large lava field. Which of the following statements best describes the lava that the scientist found?
F. The lava is mafic lava that flowed during a quiet eruption.
G. The lava is the least viscous form of mafic lava.
H. The rocks are lapilli that were produced during an explosive eruption.
I. The lava has a high silica content and flowed during a quiet eruption.

Interpreting Graphics

Directions (11–12): For each question below, record the correct answer on a separate sheet of paper.

Cross-Section of the Juan de Fuca Ridge

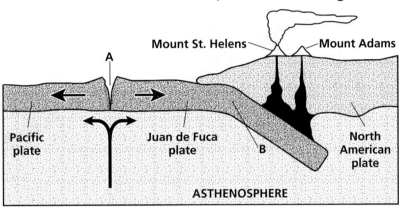

11 The illustration above shows volcanic activity in the Cascade region of the Pacific Northwest. How does activity at point B contribute to volcanic activity at Mount St. Helens and Mount Adams?

A. The Juan de Fuca plate is subducting under the North American plate, producing magma.

B. The Juan de Fuca plate is spreading away from the Pacific plate, producing magma.

C. The volcanic activity is being caused by a hot spot in the North American plate.

D. The North American plate is pushing down on the asthenosphere, producing magma.

Interior of a Volcano

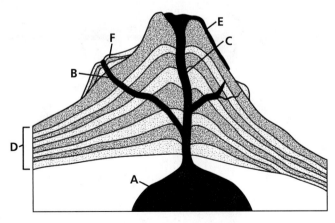

12 What is the term for the underground pool of molten rock, marked by the letter A, that feeds the volcano?

F. fissure

G. intrusion

H. lava pool

I. magma chamber

> **Test Tip**
>
> When using a diagram to answer questions, carefully study each part of the diagram as well as any lines or labels used to indicate parts of the diagram.

Geology Connections

Science, technology, and society are closely linked. This flowchart shows just a few of the connections in the history of geology.

132 C.E. Chinese philosopher Zhang Heng invents a seismoscope.

1880 John Milne invents the predecessor to modern seismometers.

1851 Robert Mallet uses dynamite to create explosions to study seismic waves.

1916 Ludger Mintrop, a German mine engineer, proposes using seismic waves to study underground rock layers.

1906 R.D. Oldham discovers shadow zones, indicating that Earth has a central core.

1936 Inge Lehman uses data from earthquakes to determine that Earth has an inner core that is solid.

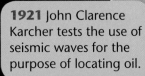

1921 John Clarence Karcher tests the use of seismic waves for the purpose of locating oil.

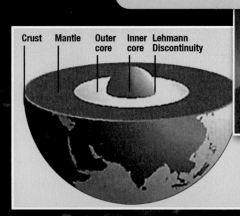

Crust | Mantle | Outer core | Inner core | Lehmann Discontinuity

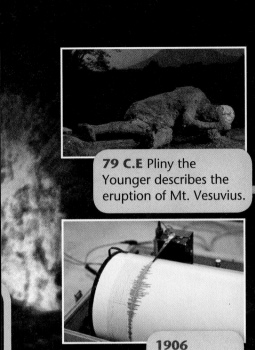

79 C.E Pliny the Younger describes the eruption of Mt. Vesuvius.

1960 A magnitude 9.5 earthquake in Chile causes a tsunami that strikes Hawaii.

1968 The Pacific Tsunami Warning and Mitigation System is established.

TSUNAMI HAZARD ZONE

IN CASE OF EARTHQUAKE, GO TO HIGH GROUND OR INLAND

1906 Seismometers all around the world record an earthquake in California.

1985 Nevada del Ruiz erupts, killing 25,000 people in Colombia.

1912 The Hawaiian Volcano Observatory is formed at Kilauea.

1986 The U.S. forms the Volcano Disaster Assistance Program (V.D.A.P).

1991 The V.D.A.P. successfully predicts the eruption of Mt. Pinatubo.

2004 A tsunami in the Indian Ocean prompts the development of a tsunami warning system in the Indian Ocean.

2006 Thirty nations participate in a test of the Pacific Tsunami Warning System.

YOUR TURN

UNDERSTANDING CONCEPTS
For how many years have people been studying earthquakes?

CRITICAL THINKING
How did John Milne help save thousands of lives in 1991 when Mt. Pinatubo erupted?

Unit 5 Reshaping the Crust

Chapter 14 Weathering and Erosion

Chapter Outline

Why It Matters

This red rock formation in Australia—like Earth's entire surface—is shaped by the processes of weathering and erosion. These processes are essential to the formation of soil, from which the food you eat grows.

Inquiry Lab

🕐 **15 min**

A Disappearing Act

Place two pieces of limestone and two pieces of granite in four separate labeled beakers. Pour a small amount of vinegar into one of the beakers with limestone and one of the beakers with granite. Record your observations. Next, pour water into the remaining two beakers, and observe.

Questions to Get You Started

1. What happens to the materials in vinegar? In water?

2. In general, which type of rock do you predict weathers more rapidly: limestone or granite? Explain.

3. What effect might acid rain have on the rate at which rock weathers? Explain.

4. What is one additional factor that could affect the rate at which rock weathers?

SC.912.E.6.2

371

READING TOOLBOX

These reading tools will help you learn the material in this chapter.

Finding Examples

Examples of Mechanical Weathering Examples can help you picture an idea or concept. Certain words or phrases can serve as signals that an example is about to be introduced. Such signals include

- *for example*   • *such as*   • *for instance*

Your Turn As you read Section 1, make a list of different types of mechanical weathering. See the sample list below to help you get started. Add examples for each type of mechanical weathering. If a word or phrase in the text signals the example, add that word or phrase.

Types of mechanical weathering	Examples	Signal words
exfoliation	overlying rocks erode, granite expands; joints form	for example
ice wedging		
abrasion		

FoldNotes

Tri-Fold A tri-fold can help you track your progress through the process of KWL. The letters KWL stand for "what I **K**now, what I **W**ant to know, and what I **L**earned." These notes help you relate new ideas to those you already know. This can help make new ideas easier to understand.

Your Turn Make a tri-fold FoldNote. In the left column, write what you already know about weathering and erosion. In the middle column, write what you want to know about weathering and erosion. In the right column, write what you learn as you read the chapter.

Know	Want to Know	Learned
Weathering is an important part of soil formation.	What else makes up soil besides weathered rock?	Soil is a combination of weathered rock, water, gases, and organic material.

Graphic Organizers

Spider Maps A spider map divides a topic into ideas and details.

To make a spider map, follow these steps:

❶ For your title, write the main topic. Draw an oval around it.

❷ From the oval, draw legs. Each leg represents a category of the main topic.

❸ From each leg, draw horizontal lines. Write details about each category on these lines.

Your Turn As you read Section 4, complete a spider map like the one started here to organize the ideas you learn about gravity and erosion.

For more information on how to use these and other tools, see **Appendix A.**

Key Ideas	Key Terms		Why It Matters
❯ Identify three agents of mechanical weathering. ❯ Compare mechanical and chemical weathering processes. ❯ Describe four chemical reactions that decompose rock.	weathering mechanical weathering abrasion chemical weathering	oxidation hydrolysis carbonation acid precipitation	Although we say that something that does not change is "like a rock," rocks actually do change over time, through the processes of weathering. These processes also affect buildings, monuments, and other structures made of stone.

Most rocks deep within Earth's crust formed under conditions of high temperature and pressure. When these rocks are uplifted to the surface, they are exposed to much lower temperature and pressure. Uplifted rock is also exposed to the gases and water in Earth's atmosphere.

Because of these environmental factors, surface rocks undergo changes in their appearance and composition. The physical breakdown or chemical decomposition of rock materials exposed at Earth's surface is called **weathering.** There are two main types of weathering: mechanical weathering and chemical weathering. Each type of weathering has different effects on rock.

Mechanical Weathering

The process by which rock is broken down into smaller pieces by physical means is **mechanical weathering.** Mechanical weathering is strictly a physical process and does not change the composition of the rock. Common agents of mechanical weathering are ice, plants and animals, gravity, running water, and wind.

Physical changes within the rock also affect mechanical weathering. For example, when overlying rocks are eroded, granite that formed deep beneath Earth's surface can be exposed, decreasing the pressure on the granite. As a result of the decreasing pressure, the granite expands. Long, curved cracks, called *joints,* develop in the rock. When the joints are parallel to the surface of the rock, the rock breaks into curved sheets that peel away from the underlying rock in a process called *exfoliation.* One example of granite exfoliation is shown in **Figure 1.**

FLORIDA STANDARDS

SC.912.E.6.4 Analyze how specific geologic processes and features are expressed in Florida and elsewhere; **SC.912.E.7.3** Differentiate and describe the various interactions among Earth systems, including: atmosphere, hydrosphere, cryosphere, geosphere, and biosphere.

weathering the natural process by which atmospheric and environmental agents, such as wind, rain, and temperature changes, disintegrate and decompose rocks

mechanical weathering the process by which rocks break down into smaller pieces by physical means

Figure 1 This formation in Kings Canyon National Park is a dome of granite that is shedding large sheets of rock through the process of exfoliation.

Figure 2 Water flows into a crack in a rock's surface. When the water freezes, it expands and causes the crack to widen. Ice wedging is responsible for most of the cracks shown in this photo.

Water

Ice

Water

Ice

www.scilinks.org
Topic: Weathering
Code: HQX1648

Ice Wedging

Another form of mechanical weathering is called *ice wedging*. Ice wedging occurs when water seeps into cracks in rock and then freezes. When the water freezes, its volume increases by about 10% and creates pressure on the surrounding rock. Every time the ice thaws and refreezes, cracks in the rock widen and deepen. This process eventually splits the rock apart, as shown in **Figure 2.** Ice wedging commonly occurs at high elevations and in cold climates. It also occurs in climates where the temperature regularly rises above and then falls below freezing, such as in the northern United States.

Abrasion

The collision of rocks that results in the breaking and wearing away of the rocks is a form of mechanical weathering called **abrasion.** Abrasion is caused by gravity, ice, running water, and wind. Gravity causes loose soil and rocks to move down the slope of a hill or mountain. Rocks break into smaller pieces as they fall and collide. Running water can carry sand or rock particles that scrape against each other and against stationary rocks. Thus, exposed surfaces are weathered by abrasion.

Wind is another agent of abrasion. When wind lifts and carries small particles, it can hurl them against surfaces, such as rock. As the airborne particles strike the rock, they wear away the surface in the same way that a sandblaster would.

abrasion the grinding and wearing away of rock surfaces through the mechanical action of other rock or sand particles

Reading Check **Describe two forms of mechanical weathering.** (See Appendix G for answers to Reading Checks.)

Figure 3 This gray wolf (left) is burrowing into soil to make a den. Prairie dogs also dig into soil to form extensive burrows, where an entire prairie dog community may live.

Plant and Animal Activity

Plants and animals are important <u>agents</u> of mechanical weathering. As plants grow, their roots grow and expand, creating pressure that wedges rock apart. The roots of small plants cause small cracks to form in the rocks. Eventually, the roots of larger plants and trees can fit in the cracks and make the cracks bigger.

The digging activities of burrowing animals, shown in **Figure 3**, affect the rate of weathering. Common burrowing animals include ground squirrels, prairie dogs, ants, earthworms, coyotes, and rabbits. Earthworms and other animals that move soil expose new rock surfaces to both mechanical and chemical weathering. Animal activities and plants can increase the rate of weathering dramatically over a long period of time.

Academic Vocabulary

agent (AY juhnt) a substance or living organism that has an impact on an ecological process

---

SC.912.E.6.2

Quick **Lab** — **Mechanical Weathering**

15 min

Procedure

❶ Examine some **silicate rock chips** by using a **hand lens.** Observe the shape and surface texture.

❷ Fill a **plastic container** that has a **tight-fitting lid** about half full of rock chips. Add **water** to just cover the chips.

❸ Tighten the lid, and shake the container 100 times.

❹ Hold a **strainer** over another container. Pour the water and rock chips into the strainer.

❺ Move your finger around the inside of the empty container. Describe what you feel.

❻ Use the hand lens to observe the rock chips.

❼ Pour the water into a **glass jar,** and examine the water with the hand lens.

❽ Put the rock chips and water back into the container that has the lid. Repeat steps 3 to 7.

❾ Repeat step 8 two more times.

Analysis

1. Did the amount and particle size of the sediment that was left in the container change during your investigation? Explain your answer.

2. How did the appearance of the rock chips change? How did the appearance of the water change?

3. How does the transport of rock particles by water, such as in a river, affect the size and shape of the rock particles?

Chemical Weathering

The process by which rock is broken down because of chemical interactions with the environment is **chemical weathering.** Chemical weathering, or decomposition, occurs when chemical reactions act on the minerals in rock. Chemical reactions commonly occur between rock, water, carbon dioxide, oxygen, and acids. Acids are substances that form *hydronium ions*, H_3O^+, in water. Hydronium ions are electrically charged and can pull apart the chemical bonds of the minerals in rock. Bases can also chemically weather rock. Bases are substances that form *hydroxide ions*, OH^-, in water. Chemical reactions with either acids or bases can change the structure of minerals, which leads to the formation of new minerals. Chemical weathering changes both the chemical composition and physical appearance of rock.

Oxidation

The process by which elements combine with oxygen is called **oxidation.** Oxidation commonly occurs in rock that has iron-bearing minerals, such as hematite and magnetite. In this rock, iron, Fe, combines quickly with oxygen, O_2, that is dissolved in water to form rust, or iron oxide, Fe_2O_3:

$$4Fe + 3O_2 \rightarrow 2Fe_2O_3$$

The red color of much of the soil in the southeastern United States, as shown in **Figure 4,** is mainly due to the presence of iron oxide produced by oxidation. Similarly, the color of many red-colored rocks is caused by oxidized, iron-rich minerals.

Reading Check **Describe two effects of chemical weathering.**

chemical weathering the process by which rocks break down as a result of chemical reactions

oxidation the process by which a metallic element combines with oxygen

Math Skills

Rates of Weathering
Limestone is dissolved by chemical weathering at a rate of 0.2 cm every 100 years. At this rate, after how many years would a layer of limestone 15 m thick completely dissolve?

Figure 4 The red color of the soil surrounding this farmhouse in Georgia is caused by the chemical interaction of iron-bearing minerals in the soil with oxygen in the atmosphere.

Rain, weak acids, and air chemically weather rock.

The bonds between mineral grains weaken as weathering proceeds.

Sediment forms from the weathered rock.

Figure 5 Thousands of years of chemical weathering processes, such as hydrolysis and carbonation, can turn even a hard rock into sediment.

Hydrolysis

Water plays a crucial role in chemical weathering, as shown in **Figure 5.** The change in the composition of minerals when they react chemically with water is called **hydrolysis.** For example, a type of feldspar combines with water and produces a common clay called *kaolin.* In this reaction, hydronium ions displace the potassium and calcium atoms in the feldspar crystals, which changes the feldspar into clay.

Minerals that are affected by hydrolysis often dissolve in water. Water can then carry the dissolved minerals to lower layers of rock in a process called *leaching.* Ore deposits, such as bauxite, the aluminum ore, sometimes form when leaching causes a mineral to concentrate in a thin layer beneath Earth's surface.

hydrolysis a chemical reaction between water and another substance to form two or more new substances

carbonation the conversion of a compound into a carbonate

Carbonation

When carbon dioxide, CO_2, from the air dissolves in water, H_2O, a weak acid called *carbonic acid,* H_2CO_3, forms:

$$H_2O + CO_2 \rightarrow H_2CO_3$$

Carbonic acid has a higher concentration of hydronium ions than pure water does, which speeds up the process of hydrolysis. When certain minerals come in contact with carbonic acid, they combine with the acid to form minerals called carbonates. The conversion of minerals into a carbonate is called **carbonation.**

One example of carbonation occurs when carbonic acid reacts with calcite, a major component of limestone, and converts the calcite into calcium bicarbonate. Calcium bicarbonate dissolves easily in water, so the limestone eventually weathers away.

Organic Acids

Acids are produced naturally by certain living organisms. Lichens and mosses grow on rocks and produce weak acids that can weather the surface of the rock. The acids seep into the rock and produce cracks that eventually cause the rock to break apart.

READING TOOLBOX

Finding Examples
As you read, find examples of each form of chemical weathering. Don't forget to use signal words as clues. Record the examples in a table. See the Reading Toolbox at the beginning of this chapter if you need help getting started.

Figure 6 This stone lion sits outside Leeds Town Hall in England. It was damaged by acid precipitation.

www.scilinks.org
Topic: Acid Precipitation
Code: HQX1690

acid precipitation
precipitation, such as rain, sleet, or snow, that contains a high concentration of acids, often because of the pollution of the atmosphere

Acid Precipitation

Natural rainwater is slightly acidic because it combines with small amounts of carbon dioxide. But when fossil fuels, especially coal, are burned, nitrogen oxides and sulfur dioxides are released into the air. These compounds combine with water in the atmosphere to produce nitric acid, nitrous acid, or sulfuric acid. When these acids fall to Earth, they are called **acid precipitation.**

Acid precipitation weathers some rock faster than ordinary precipitation does. In fact, many historical monuments and sculptures have been damaged by acid precipitation, as shown in **Figure 6.** Between 1940 and 1990, acid precipitation fell regularly in some cities in the United States. In 1990, the Acid Rain Control Program was added to the Clean Air Act of 1970. This program's regulations gave power plants 10 years to decrease sulfur dioxide emissions. The occurrence of acid precipitation has been greatly reduced since power plants have installed scrubbers that remove much of the sulfur dioxide before it can be released.

Section 1 Review

LA.910.2.2.3; SC.912.E.6.4; SC.912.E.7.3

Key Ideas

1. **Identify** three agents of mechanical weathering.

2. **Describe** how ice wedging weathers rock.

3. **Explain** how two activities of plants or animals help weather rocks or soil.

4. **Compare** mechanical and chemical weathering processes.

5. **Identify** and describe three chemical processes that weather rock.

6. **Compare** hydrolysis, carbonation, and oxidation.

7. **Summarize** how acid precipitation forms.

Critical Thinking

8. **Making Connections** Which two agents of weathering would be rare in a desert? Explain your reasoning.

9. **Understanding Relationships** Automobile exhaust contains nitrogen oxides. How might these pollutants affect chemical weathering processes?

Concept Mapping

10. Use the following terms to create a concept map: *weathering, oxidation, mechanical weathering, ice wedging, hydrolysis, abrasion, chemical weathering, carbonation,* and *acid precipitation.*

Key Ideas	Key Terms	Why It Matters
❯ Explain how rock composition affects the rate of weathering. ❯ Discuss how surface area affects the rate at which rock weathers. ❯ Describe the effects of climate and topography on the rate of weathering.	differential weathering	Learning about the different factors that affect weathering can help you understand how your own activities may impact the environment.

The processes of mechanical and chemical weathering generally work very slowly. For example, carbonation dissolves limestone at an average rate of only about one-twentieth of a centimeter (0.05 cm) every 100 years. At this rate, it could take up to 30 million years to dissolve a layer of limestone that is 150 m thick.

The pinnacles in Nambung National Park in Australia are shown in **Figure 1.** Most of the limestone was weathered away by agents of both chemical and mechanical weathering until only the pinnacles remained. The rate at which rock weathers depends on a number of factors, including rock composition, climate, and topography.

Differential Weathering

The composition of rock greatly affects the rate at which rock weathers. The process by which softer, less weather-resistant rock wears away and leaves harder, more resistant rock behind is called **differential weathering.** When rocks that are rich in the mineral quartz are exposed on Earth's surface, they remain basically unchanged, even after all the surrounding rock has weathered away. They remain unchanged because the chemical composition and crystal structure of quartz make quartz resistant to chemical weathering. These characteristics also make quartz a very hard mineral, so it resists mechanical weathering.

Rock Composition

Limestone and other sedimentary rocks that contain calcite weather rapidly because they commonly undergo carbonation. Other sedimentary rocks are affected mainly by mechanical weathering processes. The rates at which these rocks weather depend mostly on the material that holds the sediment grains together. For example, shales and sandstones that are not firmly cemented gradually break up to become clay and sand particles. However, conglomerates and sandstones that are strongly cemented by silicates resist weathering longer than some igneous rocks do.

FLORIDA STANDARDS

LA.910.2.2.3 The student will organize information to show understanding or relationships among facts, ideas, and events (e.g., representing key points within text through charting, mapping, paraphrasing, summarizing, comparing, contrasting, or outlining); **SC.912.E.6.4** Analyze how specific geologic processes and features are expressed in Florida and elsewhere.

differential weathering the process by which softer, less weather-resistant rocks wear away at a faster rate than harder, more weather-resistant rocks do

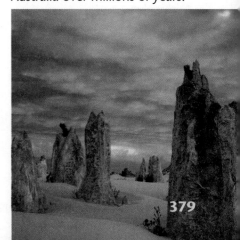

Figure 1 Different rates of weathering formed these limestone pinnacles at Nambung National Park in Australia over millions of years.

379

Figure 2 The Ratio of Total Surface Area to Volume

All cubes have both volume and surface area. The total surface area is equal to the sum of the areas of the six sides.

THINK central
INTERACT ONLINE
(Keyword: HQXWAEF2)

If you split the first cube into eight smaller cubes, you have the same amount of material (volume), but double the surface area. If you split each of the eight small cubes into eight even smaller cubes, the original surface area is doubled again.

Amount of Exposure

The more exposure to weathering agents that a rock receives, the faster the rock will weather. The amount of time that the rock is exposed and the amount of the rock's surface area that is available for weathering are important factors in determining the rate of weathering.

Surface Area

Both chemical and mechanical weathering may split rock into a number of smaller rocks. The part of a rock that is exposed to air, water, and other agents of weathering is called the rock's *surface area*. As a rock breaks into smaller pieces, the surface area that is exposed increases. For example, imagine a block of rock as a cube that has six sides exposed. Splitting the block into eight smaller blocks, as shown in **Figure 2**, doubles the total surface area available for weathering.

Fractures and Joints

Most rocks on Earth's surface contain natural fractures and joints. These fractures and joints are natural zones of weakness within the rock. They increase the surface area of a rock and allow weathering to take place more rapidly. They also form natural channels through which water flows. Water may penetrate the rock through these channels and break the rock by ice wedging. As water moves through these channels, it chemically weathers the rock that is exposed in the fracture or joint. The chemical weathering removes rock material and makes the jointed or fractured area weaker.

Reading Check How do fractures and joints in a rock affect surface area?

Academic Vocabulary

factor (FAK tuhr) a condition or event that brings about or contributes to a result

Quick Lab

10 min

SC.912.E.6.2

Surface Areas

Procedure

❶ Fill two small containers about half full with water.

❷ Add one sugar cube to one container.

❸ Add 1 tsp of granulated sugar to the other container.

❹ Use two different spoons to stir the water and sugar in each container at the same rate.

❺ Use a stopwatch to measure how long the sugar in each container takes to dissolve.

Analysis

1. Did the sugar dissolve at the same rate in both containers?

2. Which do you think would wear away faster—a large rock or a small rock? Explain your answer.

Figure 3 The photo on the left shows Cleopatra's Needle before it was moved to New York City. The photograph on the right shows the 3,000-year-old carvings after only one century in New York City.

Climate

In general, climates that have alternating periods of hot and cold weather allow the fastest rates of weathering. Freezing and thawing can cause the mechanical breakdown of rock by ice wedging. Chemical weathering can then act quickly on the fractured rock. When the temperature rises, the rate at which chemical reactions occur accelerates. In warm, humid climates, chemical weathering is also fairly rapid. The constant moisture is highly destructive to exposed surfaces.

The slowest rates of weathering occur in hot, dry climates. The lack of water limits many weathering processes, such as carbonation and ice wedging. Weathering is also slow in very cold climates.

The effects of climate on weathering rates can be seen on Cleopatra's Needle, which is shown in **Figure 3.** Cleopatra's needle is an obelisk that is made of granite. For 3,000 years, the obelisk remained in Egypt, where the hot, dry climate scarcely changed its surface. Then, in 1880, Cleopatra's Needle was moved to New York City. After only 130 years, the moisture, ice wedging, and pollution, such as acid precipitation, caused more weathering than was caused in the preceding 3,000 years in the Egyptian desert.

Topography and Elevation

Topography, or the elevation and slope of the land surface, also influences the rate of weathering. Because temperatures are generally cold at high elevations, ice wedging is more common at high elevations than at low elevations. On steep slopes, such as mountainsides, weathered rock fragments are pulled downhill by gravity and washed out by heavy rains. As the rock fragments slide down the mountain or are carried away by mountain streams, they smash against each other and break apart. As a result of the removal of these surface rocks, new surfaces of the mountain are continually exposed to weathering.

SCI**LINKS**.

www.scilinks.org
Topic: Rates of Weathering
Code: HQX1269

READING TOOLBOX

Spider Map
Create a spider map and label the center oval "Factors that affect the rate of weathering." Then, fill in the map with at least four factors presented in this section.

Human Activities

Rock can be chemically and mechanically broken down by the action of humans. Mining and construction often expose rock surfaces to agents of weathering. Mining also exposes rock to strong acids and other chemical compounds that are used in mining processes. Construction often removes soil and exposes previously unexposed rock surfaces. Recreational activities, such as hiking and riding all-terrain vehicles, as shown in **Figure 4,** can also speed up weathering by exposing new rock surfaces. Rock that is disturbed or broken by human activities weathers more rapidly than undisturbed rock does.

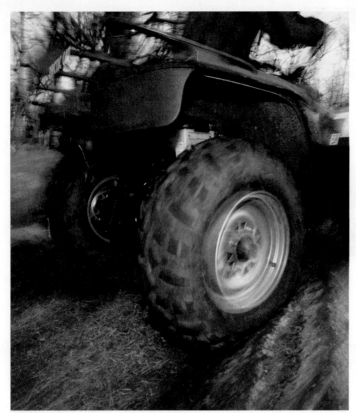

Figure 4 All-terrain vehicles and recreational activities can cause mechanical weathering of exposed rock. These activities may also expose new rock surfaces to chemical weathering.

Plant and Animal Activities

Rock that is disturbed or broken by plants or animals also weathers more rapidly than undisturbed rock does. The roots of plants and trees often break apart rock. Burrowing animals dig holes, exposing new rock surfaces. Some biological wastes of animals can cause chemical weathering. For example, caves that have large populations of bats also have large amounts of bat guano on the cave floors. Bat guano attracts insects, such as millipedes and beetles. The presence of these insects speeds up mechanical weathering, and the presence of the guano increases the rate of certain chemical weathering processes.

Section 2 Review

LA.910.2.2.3; SC.912.E.6.4; SC.912.E.7.3

Key Ideas

1. **Explain** how rock composition affects the rate of weathering.

2. **Discuss** how the surface area of a rock can affect the rate of weathering.

3. **Identify** two ways that climate can affect the rate of weathering.

4. **Describe** two ways that the topography of a region can affect the rate of weathering.

5. **Summarize** three ways that human actions can affect the rate of weathering.

6. **Explain** two ways that animals can affect the rate of weathering.

Critical Thinking

7. **Applying Concepts** Imagine that there is an area of land where mechanical weathering has caused damage. Describe two ways to reduce the rate of mechanical weathering.

8. **Identifying Relationships** How would Cleopatra's Needle probably have been affected if it had been in the cold, dry climate of Siberia for 130 years?

Concept Mapping

9. Use the following terms to create a concept map: *composition, exposure, precipitation, surface area, climate, temperature, topography, weathering, elevation,* and *human activities.*

Key Ideas	Key Terms	Why It Matters
❱ Summarize how soils form. ❱ Explain how the composition of parent rock affects soil composition. ❱ Describe the characteristic layers of mature residual soils. ❱ Predict the type of soil that will form in arctic and tropical climates.	soil soil profile horizon humus	Nearly all the food you eat was grown in soil. Earth scientists study the characteristics of soil to gain a better understanding of how to conserve and use this critical natural resource.

One result of weathering is the formation of *regolith,* the layer of weathered rock fragments that covers much of Earth's surface. *Bedrock* is the solid, unweathered rock that lies beneath the regolith. The lower regions of regolith are partly protected by those above and thus do not weather as rapidly as the upper regions do. The uppermost rock fragments weather to form a layer of very fine particles. This layer of small rock particles provides the basic components of soil. **Soil** is a complex mixture of minerals, water, gases, and the remains of dead organisms.

Soil Characteristics

The characteristics of soil depend largely on the rock from which the soil was weathered, which is called the soil's *parent rock.* Soil that forms and stays directly over its parent rock is called *residual soil.* However, the weathered mineral grains within soil may be carried away from the location of the parent rock by water, wind, or glaciers. Soil that results from the deposition of this material is called *transported soil,* and it may have different characteristics than the bedrock on which it rests.

Soil Composition

Parent rock that is rich in feldspar or other minerals that contain aluminum weathers to form soils that contain large amounts of clay. Parent rock that contains large amounts of quartz, such as granite, weathers to form sandy soils. Soil composition refers to the materials of which it is made. The color of soil is related to the composition of the soil. Black soils are commonly rich in organic material, while red soils may form from iron-rich parent rock. Soil moisture can also affect color, as shown in **Figure 1.**

FLORIDA STANDARDS

SC.912.E.6.2 Connect surface features to surface processes that are responsible for their formation.

soil a loose mixture of rock fragments and organic material that can support the growth of vegetation

Figure 1 These soil scientists are testing soil moisture to determine whether irrigation will be needed. Moister soils are generally darker than drier soils are.

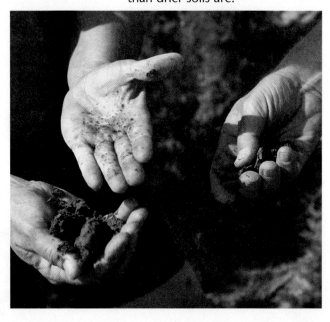

Soil Texture

Rock material in soil can be grouped into three main sizes: clay, silt, and sand. Clay particles have a diameter of less than 0.002 mm. Silt particles have diameters from 0.002 to 0.05 mm. Silt particles are too small to be seen easily, but they make soil feel gritty. Sand particles have diameters from 0.05 to 2 mm. The proportion of clay, silt, and sand in soil determines a soil's texture.

Soil Profile

Transported soils are commonly deposited in unsorted masses by water or wind. However, residual soils commonly develop distinct layers over time. To determine a soil's composition, scientists study a soil profile. A **soil profile** is a cross section of the soil and its bedrock. The different layers of soil are called **horizons.**

Residual soils generally consist of three main horizons. The *A horizon,* or *topsoil,* is a mixture of organic materials and small rock particles. Almost all organisms that live in soil inhabit the A horizon. As organisms die, their remains decay and produce **humus,** a dark, organic material. The A horizon is also the layer from which surface water leaches minerals. The *B horizon,* or *subsoil,* contains the minerals leached from the topsoil, clay, and sometimes humus. In dry climates, the B horizon also may contain minerals that accumulate as water in the soil evaporates. The *C horizon* consists of partially weathered bedrock. The first stages of mechanical and chemical change happen in this bottom layer. **Figure 2** shows the relationships between the three soil horizons.

soil profile a vertical section of soil that shows the layers, or horizons

horizon a horizontal layer of soil that can be distinguished from the layers above and below it

humus dark, organic material formed in soil from the decayed remains of plants and animals

Figure 2 Soil Horizons of Residual Soils

Surface litter fallen leaves and partially decomposed organic matter

Topsoil organic matter, living organisms, and rock particles

Zone of leaching dissolved or suspended materials moving downward

Subsoil larger rock particles with organic matter, and inorganic compounds

Rock particles rock that has undergone weathering

Bedrock solid rock layer

A Horizon

B Horizon

C Horizon

Soil and Climate

Climate is one of the most important factors that influence soil formation. Climate determines the weathering processes that occur in a region. These weathering processes, in turn, help to <u>determine</u> the composition of soil.

Tropical Soils

In humid tropical climates, where much rain falls and where temperatures are high, chemical weathering causes thick soils to develop rapidly. These thick, tropical soils, called *laterites* (LAT uhr IETS), contain iron and aluminum minerals that do not dissolve easily in water. Leached minerals from the A horizon sometimes collect in the B horizon. Heavy rains, which are common in tropical climates, cause a lot of leaching of the topsoil, and thus keep the A horizon thin. But because of the dense vegetation in humid, warm climates, organic material is continuously added to the soil. As a result, a thin layer of humus usually covers the B horizon, as shown in **Figure 3.**

Temperate Soils

In temperate climates, where temperatures range between cool and warm, and where rainfall is not excessive, both mechanical and chemical weathering occur. Temperate soils have the thickest A horizon, as shown in **Figure 3.**

Two main soil types form in temperate climates. In areas that receive more than 65 cm of rain per year, a type of soil called *pedalfer* (pi DAL fuhr) forms. Pedalfer soil contains clay, quartz, and iron compounds. The Gulf Coast states and states east of the Mississippi River have pedalfer soils. In areas that receive less than 65 cm of rain per year, a soil called *pedocal* (PED oh KAL) forms. Pedocal soil contains large amounts of calcium carbonate, which makes it very fertile and less acidic than pedalfer soil. The southwestern states and most states west of the Mississippi River have pedocal soils.

 Reading Check **Compare the formation of tropical soils and temperate soils.**

Desert and Arctic Soils

In desert and arctic climates, rainfall is minimal and chemical weathering occurs slowly. As a result, the soil is thin and consists mostly of regolith—evidence that the soil in these areas forms mainly by mechanical weathering. Also, desert and arctic climates are often too warm or too cold to sustain life, so their soils have little humus.

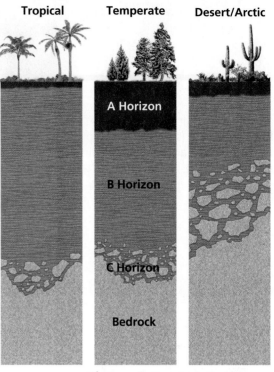

Figure 3 Tropical climates produce thick, infertile soils. Temperate climates produce thick, fertile soils. Desert and arctic climates produce thin soils.

Academic Vocabulary

determine (dee TUHR muhn) to define or decide

Tri-Fold
Create a tri-fold FoldNote to compare soil types in different climates. In the first column, write the type of soil. In the second column, describe the climate. In the third column, describe the soil.

Figure 4 Soil is thick at the top and bottom of a slope. Soil is thin along the slope.

Thin soil

Thick soil

www.scilinks.org
Topic: Soil
Code: HQX1407

Soil and Topography

The shape of the land, or topography, also affects soil formation. Because rainwater runs down a slope, much of the topsoil of the slope washes away. Therefore, as shown in **Figure 4,** the soil at the top and bottom of a slope tends to be thicker than the soil on the slope.

One study of soil in Canada showed that A horizons on flat areas were more than twice as thick as those on 10° slopes. Topsoil that remains on a slope is often too thin to support dense plant growth. The lack of vegetation contributes to the development of a poor-quality soil that lacks humus. The soils on the sides of mountains are commonly thin and rocky, with few nutrients. Lowlands that retain water tend to have thick, wet soils with a high concentration of organic matter, which forms humus. A fairly flat area that has good drainage provides the best surface for the formation of thick, fertile layers of residual soil.

Section 3 Review

LA.910.2.2.3; SC.912.E.6.4; SC.912.E.7.3

Key Ideas

1. **Summarize** how soils form.

2. **Explain** how the composition of the parent rock affects soil composition.

3. **Describe** the three horizons of a residual soil.

4. **Predict** the type of soil that will form in arctic and tropical climates.

Critical Thinking

5. **Applying Ideas** What combination of soil and climate would be ideal for growing deep-rooted crops? Explain your answer.

6. **Analyzing Relationships** Would you expect crop growth to be more successful on a farm that has an uneven topography or on a farm that has level land? Explain your answer.

7. **Analyzing Ideas** Why would tropical soil not be good for sustained farming?

8. **Making Comparisons** Although desert and arctic climates are extremely different, their soils may be somewhat similar. Explain why.

Concept Mapping

9. Use the following terms to create a concept map: *soil, bedrock, regolith, humus, parent rock, residual soil, transported soil, horizon, soil profile, climate,* and *topography.*

SECTION 4 Erosion

Key Ideas	Key Terms	Why It Matters
❯ Define erosion, and list four agents of erosion. ❯ Identify four farming methods that conserve soil. ❯ Discuss two ways that gravity contributes to erosion. ❯ Describe the three major landforms shaped by weathering and erosion.	erosion sheet erosion mass movement solifluction creep landform	Erosion destroys homes, buildings, and lives every year—sometimes through dramatic events such as landslides. By understanding the factors involved in erosion, some of these consequences may be avoided.

When rock weathers, the resulting rock particles do not always stay near the parent rock. Various forces may move weathered fragments of rock away from where the weathering occurred. The process by which the products of weathering are transported is called **erosion.** The most common agents of erosion are gravity, wind, glaciers, and water. Water can move weathered rock in several different ways, including by ocean waves and currents, by streams and runoff, and by the movements of groundwater.

Soil Erosion

As rock weathers, it eventually becomes very fine particles that mix with water, air, and humus to form soil. The erosion of soil occurs worldwide and is normally a slow process. Ordinarily, new soil forms about as fast as existing soil erodes. However, some forms of land use and unusual climatic conditions can upset this natural balance. Once the balance is upset, soil erosion often accelerates.

Soil erosion is considered by some scientists to be the greatest environmental problem that faces the world today. As shown in **Figure 1,** vulnerability to erosion affects fertile topsoil around the world. This erosion prevents some countries from growing the crops needed to prevent widespread famine.

FLORIDA STANDARDS

SC.912.E.7.3 Differentiate and describe the various interactions among Earth systems, including: atmosphere, hydrosphere, cryosphere, geosphere, and biosphere; **SC.912.N.1.3** Recognize that the strength or usefulness of a scientific claim is evaluated through scientific argumentation, which depends one critical and logical thinking, and the active consideration of alternative scientific explanations to explain the data presented.

erosion a process in which the materials of Earth's surface are loosened, dissolved, or worn away and transported from one place to another by a natural agent, such as wind, water, ice, or gravity

Vulnerability
- Low
- Moderate
- High
- Very high

30°N

Equator

30°S

Figure 1 This map shows the vulnerability of soils to erosion by water.

Figure 2 This land in Madagascar can no longer be used for farming because of a form of rapid erosion called *gullying*.

sheet erosion the process by which water flows over a layer of soil and removes the topsoil

Gullying and Sheet Erosion

One farming technique that can accelerate soil erosion is the improper plowing of furrows, or long, narrow rows. Furrows that are plowed up and down slopes allow water to run swiftly over soil. As soil is washed away with each rainfall, the furrows become larger and form small gullies. Eventually, the land can become covered with deep gullies. This type of accelerated soil erosion is called *gullying*. The farmland shown in **Figure 2** has been ruined by gullying.

Another type of soil erosion strips away layers of topsoil. Eventually, erosion can expose the surface of the subsoil. This process is called **sheet erosion.** Sheet erosion may occur where continuous rainfall washes away layers of the topsoil. Wind also can cause sheet erosion during unusually dry periods. The soil, which is made dry and loose by a lack of moisture, is carried away by the wind as clouds of dust and drifting sand. These wind-borne particles may produce large dust storms.

Reading Check **Describe one way that a dust storm may form, and explain how a dust storm can affect the fertility of land.**

Results of Soil Erosion

Constant erosion reduces the fertility of the soil by removing the A horizon, which contains the fertile humus. The B horizon, which does not contain much organic matter, is difficult to farm because it is much less fertile than the A horizon. Without plants, the B horizon has nothing to protect it from further erosion. So, within a few years, all the soil layers could be removed by continuous erosion.

Soil Conservation

Erosion rates are affected not only by natural factors but also by human activities. Certain farming and grazing techniques and construction projects can also increase the rate of erosion. In developing urban areas, vegetation is removed to build houses and roads, such as those shown in **Figure 3.** This land clearing removes protective ground-cover plants and accelerates topsoil erosion. In some areas, such as deserts and mountainous regions, it may take hundreds or thousands of years for the topsoil to be replenished.

But rapid, destructive soil erosion can be prevented by soil conservation methods. People, including city planners and some land developers, have begun to recognize the environmental impact of land development and are beginning to implement soil conservation measures. Some land development projects are leaving trees and vegetation in place whenever possible. Other projects are planting cover plants to hold the topsoil in place. Farmers are also looking for new ways to minimize soil erosion and thus preserve fertile topsoil.

Figure 3 Urban development and agriculture both contribute to the erosion of topsoil.

Why It Matters

Putting Worms to Work

EYE ON THE ENVIRONMENT

Composting breaks down waste to produce nutrient-rich humus-like material. One type of composting, called vermicomposting, uses worms to break down food waste. Vermicomposting can be set up indoors or outdoors, and can be used in agriculture, at home, or at school.

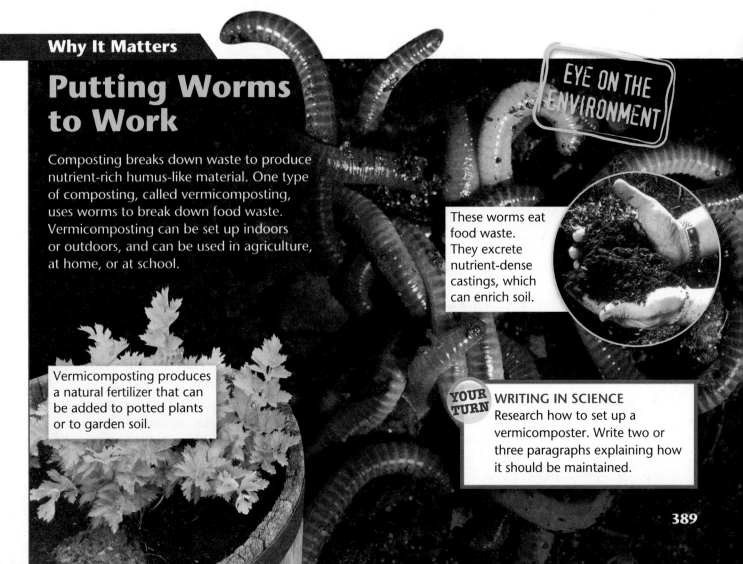

These worms eat food waste. They excrete nutrient-dense castings, which can enrich soil.

Vermicomposting produces a natural fertilizer that can be added to potted plants or to garden soil.

YOUR TURN WRITING IN SCIENCE
Research how to set up a vermicomposter. Write two or three paragraphs explaining how it should be maintained.

Contour Plowing These fields were plowed in contours (or curves) that follow the shape of the land.

Strip-Cropping These fields were planted with alternating strips of different crops.

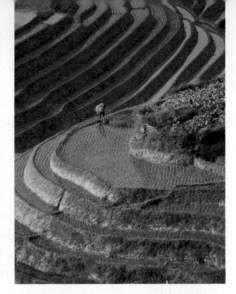

Terracing These terraced fields help slow runoff and prevent rapid soil erosion.

Figure 4 Soil Conservation Methods

Contour Plowing

Farmers in countries around the world use different planting methods to reduce soil erosion. In one method, called *contour plowing,* soil is plowed in curved bands that follow the contour, or shape, of the land. This method of planting, shown in the first part of **Figure 4,** prevents water from flowing directly down slopes, so it prevents gullying.

Strip-Cropping

In *strip-cropping,* crops are planted in alternating bands, also shown in **Figure 4.** A crop planted in rows, such as corn, may be planted in one band, and another crop that fully covers the surface of the land, such as alfalfa, will be planted next to it. The *cover crop* protects the soil by slowing the runoff of rainwater. Strip-cropping is often combined with contour plowing. The combination of these two methods can reduce soil erosion by 75%.

Terracing

The construction of steplike ridges that follow the contours of a sloped field is called *terracing,* as shown in **Figure 4.** Terraces, especially those used for growing rice in Asia, prevent or slow the downslope movement of water and thus prevent rapid erosion.

Crop Rotation

In *crop rotation,* farmers plant one type of crop one year and a different type of crop the next. For example, a farmer might plant a crop that will be harvested one year, and then plant a cover crop the next year. The cover crop does not get harvested. It helps to slow runoff and hold the soil in place. The main purpose of other types of crop rotation is to help maintain soil fertility.

Gravity and Erosion

Gravity causes rock fragments to move down a slope. This movement of fragments down a slope is called **mass movement.** Some mass movements occur rapidly, and others occur very slowly.

Rockfalls and Landslides

The most <u>dramatic</u> and destructive mass movements occur rapidly. The fall of rock from a steep cliff is called a *rockfall*. A rockfall is the fastest kind of mass movement. Rocks in rockfalls often range in size from tiny fragments to giant boulders.

When masses of loose rock combined with soil suddenly fall down a slope, the event is called a *landslide*. Large landslides, in which loosened blocks of bedrock fall, generally occur on very steep slopes. You may have seen a small landslide on cliffs and steep hills overlooking highways, such as the one shown in **Figure 5.** Heavy rainfall, spring thaws, volcanic eruptions, and earthquakes can trigger landslides.

Reading Check What is the difference between a rockfall and a landslide?

Mudflows and Slumps

The rapid movement of a large amount of mud creates a *mudflow*. Mudflows occur in mountainous regions during sudden, heavy rainfall or as a result of volcanic eruptions. Mud churns and tumbles as it moves down slopes and through valleys, and it frequently spreads out in a large fan shape at the base of the slope. The mass movements that sometimes occur in hillside communities, such as the one shown in **Figure 5,** are often referred to as landslides, but they are actually mudflows.

Sometimes, a large block of soil and rock becomes unstable and moves downhill in one piece. The block of soil and rock then slides along the curved slope of the surface. This type of movement is called a *slump*. Slumping occurs along very steep slopes. Saturation by water and loss of friction with underlying rock causes loose soil and rock to slip downhill over the solid rock.

Academic Vocabulary
dramatic (druh MAT ik) vivid or striking

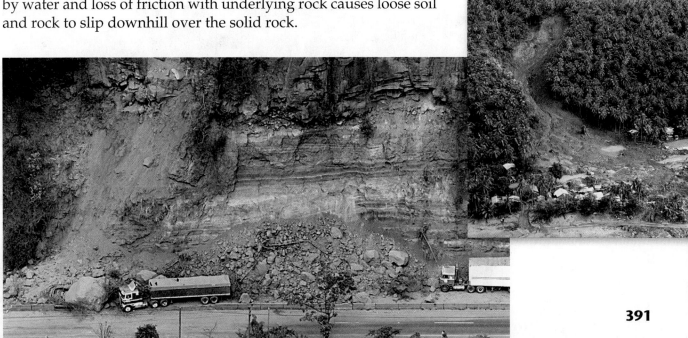

Figure 5 An earthquake in El Salvador caused this dramatic landslide (left). Heavy rains in the Philippines caused this destructive mudflow (right).

Solifluction

Although most slopes appear to be unchanging, some slow mass movement commonly occurs. Catastrophic landslides are the most hazardous mass movement. However, more rock material is moved by the greater number of slow mass movements than by catastrophic landslides.

One form of slow mass movement is called solifluction. **Solifluction** is the process by which water-saturated soil slips over hard or frozen layers. Solifluction occurs in arctic and mountainous climates, where the subsoil is permanently frozen. In spring and summer, only the top layer of soil thaws. The moisture from this layer cannot penetrate the frozen layers beneath. So, the surface layer becomes muddy and slowly flows downslope, or downhill. Solifluction can also occur in warmer regions, where the subsoil consists of hard clay. The clay layer acts like the frozen subsoil in arctic climates by forming a waterproof barrier.

Creep

The extremely slow downhill movement of weathered rock material is known as **creep.** Soil creep moves the most soil of all types of mass movements. But creep may go unnoticed unless buildings, fences, or other surface objects move along with soil.

Many factors contribute to soil creep. Water separates rock particles, which allows them to move freely. Growing plants produce a wedgelike pressure that separates rock particles and loosens the soil. The burrowing of animals and repeated freezing and thawing loosen rock particles and allow gravity to slowly pull the particles downhill.

As rock fragments accumulate at the base of a slope, they form piles called *talus* (TAY luhs), as shown in **Figure 6.** Talus weathers into smaller fragments, which move farther down the slope. The fragments wash into gullies, are carried into successively larger waterways, and eventually flow into rivers.

solifluction the slow, downslope flow of soil saturated with water in areas surrounding glaciers at high elevations

creep the slow downhill movement of weathered rock material

Figure 6 The movement of rock fragments downslope formed these talus cones at the base of the Canadian Rockies.

Figure 7 The mountains in the Patagonian Andes, shown on the left, are still being uplifted and are more rugged than the more eroded Appalachian mountains on the right.

Erosion and Landforms

Through weathering and erosion, Earth's surface is shaped into different physical features, or **landforms.** There are three major landforms that are shaped by weathering and erosion: *mountains*, *plains*, and *plateaus*. Minor landforms that are shaped by weathering and erosion include hills, valleys, and dunes. The shapes of landforms are also influenced by rock composition.

All landforms are subject to two opposing sets of processes. One set of processes bends, breaks, and lifts Earth's crust and thus creates elevated, or uplifted, landforms. The other set of processes includes weathering and erosion, which wear down land surfaces.

landform a physical feature of Earth's surface

Erosion of Mountains

During the early stages in the history of a mountain, the mountain undergoes uplift. Generally, while tectonic forces are uplifting the mountain, it rises faster than it is eroded. Mountains that are being uplifted tend to be rugged and have sharp peaks and deep, narrow valleys. When forces stop uplifting the mountain, weathering and erosion wear down the rugged peaks to rounded peaks and gentle slopes. The formations in **Figure 7** show how the shapes of mountains are influenced by uplift and erosion.

Over millions of years, mountains that are not being uplifted become low, featureless surfaces. These areas are called *peneplains* (PEE nuh PLAYNZ), which means "almost flat." A peneplain commonly has low, rolling hills, as seen in New England.

Reading Check **Describe how a mountain changes after it is no longer uplifted.**

Figure 8 Ancient rivers carved plateaus into mesas, which eventually eroded into the buttes of Monument Valley in Arizona.

Erosion of Plains and Plateaus

A *plain* is a relatively flat landform near sea level. A *plateau* is a broad, flat landform that has a high elevation. A plateau is subject to much more erosion than a plain. Young plateaus, such as the Colorado Plateau in the southwestern United States, commonly have deep stream valleys that separate broad, flat regions. Older plateaus, such as those in the Catskill region in New York State, have been eroded into rugged hills and valleys.

The effect of weathering and erosion on a plateau depends on the climate and the composition and structure of the rock. In dry climates, resistant rock produces plateaus that have flat tops. As a plateau ages, erosion may dissect the plateau into smaller, tablelike areas called *mesas* (MAY suhz). Mesas ultimately erode into small, narrow-topped formations called *buttes* (BYOOTS). In dry areas, such as in the area shown in **Figure 8**, mesas and buttes have steep walls and flat tops. In areas that have wet climates, humidity and precipitation weather landforms into round shapes.

Section 4 Review

LA.910.2.2.3; SC.912.E.6.4; SC.912.E.7.3

Key Ideas

1. **Define** erosion.

2. **List** four agents of erosion.

3. **Summarize** two processes of soil erosion.

4. **Identify** four farming methods that result in soil conservation.

5. **Discuss** two ways gravity contributes to erosion.

6. **Compare** rapid mass movements with slow mass movements.

7. **Describe** the erosion of the three major landforms.

Critical Thinking

8. **Analyzing Relationships** Describe an experiment that could help you determine whether a nearby hill is undergoing creep.

9. **Applying Ideas** Suppose that you wanted to grow grapevines on a hillside in Italy. What farming methods would you use? Explain your answer.

10. **Predicting Consequences** Describe two ways that a small butte would change if it was in a wet climate, rather than a dry climate.

11. **Drawing Conclusions** A hillside community has asked you to help brainstorm ways to prevent future mudflows. Describe three of your ideas.

Concept Mapping

12. Use the following terms to create a concept map: *erosion, gullying, sheet erosion, landslide, mudflow, slump, solifluction, creep, talus, landform, mountain, plain, plateau, mesa,* and *butte.*

Living on the Edge

Weathering and erosion are natural processes that reshape Earth's surface. Mass movements are characteristic of steep hills and shorelines—landforms that humans value, and on which homes are often built. About 25% of the homes and buildings within 150 m of the U.S. coastline and shores of the Great Lakes will be lost due to erosion within the next 60 years, according to the Federal Emergency Management Agency.

Erosion barriers, like these, are intended to slow the movement of sediment. These barriers must be maintained, replaced, and repaired regularly.

Living on the edge can be risky. Each year, landslides in the United States kill over 25 people and cost over $1 billion in damages. In La Conchita, a small coastal town in southern California, a sudden landslide killed ten people and destroyed 18 homes on January 10, 2005.

YOUR TURN

CRITICAL THINKING
What rules or restrictions do you think should govern construction in areas with a high risk of erosion?

ONLINE RESEARCH
Look up *recent landslide news* on the U.S. Geological Survey Web site: www.usgs.gov. Write a description of the most recent landslide reported.

Soil Chemistry

What You'll Do

> **Test** the acidity of soil samples.

> **Identify** the composition of soil samples.

What You'll Need

ammonia solution
stoppers, cork (9)
hydrochloric acid, dilute
medicine dropper
pH paper
subsoil sample (B and C horizons)
test tubes, 9
test-tube rack
topsoil sample (A horizon)
water

Safety

Different soil types contain different kinds and amounts of minerals. To support plant life, soil must have a proper balance of mineral nutrients. For plants to take in the nutrients they need, the soil must also have the proper acidity.

Acidity is measured on a scale called the *pH scale*. The pH scale ranges from 0 (acidic) to 14 (alkaline). A pH of 7 is neutral (neither acidic nor alkaline). In this lab, you will test the acidity of soil samples.

Procedure

❶ pH paper changes color in the presence of an acidic or alkaline substance. Wet a strip of pH paper with tap water. Compare the color of the wet pH paper with the pH color scale. What is the pH of the tap water?

❷ Put some topsoil in a clean test tube until it is one-eighth full. Add water to the test tube until it is three-quarters full. Place a cork stopper on the test tube, and shake the test tube.

❸ Set the soil and water mixture aside in the test-tube rack to settle. When the water is fairly clear, test it with a piece of pH paper. What is the pH of the soil sample? Is the soil acidic or alkaline?

❹ Repeat steps 2 and 3 with the subsoil sample.

❺ Pedalfer soils tend to be acidic. Pedocal soils tend to be alkaline. Based on the pH results in steps 3 and 4, predict whether your soil is pedalfer or pedocal.

Step ❸

6 To test your prediction, you will need to test the soil's composition. Take five rock particles from the subsoil sample. Place each particle in a separate test tube. Use the dropper to add two drops of hydrochloric acid, HCl, to the test tubes. **CAUTION** If you spill any acid on your skin or clothing, rinse immediately with cool water and alert your teacher.

7 HCl has little or no effect on silicates, but HCl reacts with calcium carbonate and causes CO_2 gas to bubble out of solution. How many of the rock particles were silicates? How many were calcium carbonate?

8 Put some of the subsoil in another test tube until it is one-eighth full. Slowly add HCl to the test tube until it is about two-thirds full. Cork the test tube, and gently shake it. **CAUTION** Always shake the test tube by pointing it away from yourself and other students.

Step 6

9 After shaking the test tube, remove the stopper and set the test tube in the rack. Record your observations. After the mixture has settled, draw the test tube and its contents. Label each layer. If iron is present, the solution may look brown. What color is the liquid above the soil sample?

10 Use a medicine dropper to place 10 drops of the liquid in a clean test tube. Carefully add 12 drops of ammonia to the test tube. Test the pH of the solution. If the pH is greater than 8, any iron should settle out as a reddish-brown residue. The remaining solution will be colorless.

11 If the pH is less than 8, add two more drops of ammonia and test the pH again. Continue adding ammonia until the pH reaches 8 or higher. Record your observations, and draw a diagram of the test tube. Label each layer of material in the test tube.

Analysis

1. **Analyzing Results** Is your soil sample most likely pedalfer or pedocal? Explain your answer.

2. **Drawing Conclusions** What type of soil, pedalfer or pedocal, would you treat with acidic substances, such as phosphoric acid, sulfur, and ammonium sulfate, to help plant growth? Explain your answer.

3. **Recognizing Relationships** Explain why acidic substances are usually spread on the surface of the soil.

Extension

Research Use a library or the Internet to learn why the use of phosphate and nitrate detergents has been banned in some areas. Report your findings to the class.

MAPS in Action

Soil Map of North Carolina

SOIL SYSTEMS KEY

Coastal Plain Soil Region
Middle Coastal Plain System
Upper Coastal Plain and Piedmont System
Sandhills System
Lower Coastal Plain—Wicomico and Talbot System
Lower Coastal Plain—Pamlico System
Organic Soil System
Brackish and Freshwater Marsh Systems
Outer Banks System
Large River Valleys and Flood Plain Systems

Piedmont Soil Region
Felsic Crystalline System
Carolina Slate Belt System
Triassic Basin System
Mixed Felsic and Mafic System

Mountain Soil Region
Low and Intermediate Mountain System
Broad Basins, River Terraces, and Flood Plain System
High Mountain System

0   20   40 Miles
0   30   60 Kilometers

Map Skills Activity

This map shows soil systems in the state of North Carolina, including the Outer Banks barrier island system. Use the map to answer the questions below.

1. **Using a Key** How many colors on the map represent soil systems in the Piedmont Soil Region?

2. **Using a Key** Which soil systems are present along the eastern shore of North Carolina?

3. **Analyzing Data** Which city is located on the banks of a large river or in a river valley? Explain your answer.

4. **Inferring Relationships** What landforms would you expect to surround the town of Asheville? Explain your answer.

5. **Analyzing Relationships** Brackish water is water that is somewhat salty but not as salty as sea water. How does this fact explain the location of the Brackish and Freshwater Marsh soil systems?

6. **Identifying Trends** How would you describe the change in elevation of North Carolina, from west to east, based on the locations of soil systems? Explain your answer.

Key Ideas	Key Terms

Section 1

Weathering Processes

❯ Ice, plants and animals, gravity, running water, and wind are all agents of mechanical weathering.

❯ Mechanical weathering physically breaks down rock. Chemical weathering changes the chemical composition of rock.

❯ Oxidation, hydrolysis, carbonation, and acid precipitation are four chemical reactions that decompose rock.

weathering, p. 373
mechanical weathering, p. 373
abrasion, p. 374
chemical weathering, p. 376
oxidation, p. 376
hydrolysis, p. 377
carbonation, p. 377
acid precipitation, p. 378

Section 2

Rates of Weathering

❯ Softer rock weathers more rapidly than harder rock.

❯ Rock weathers faster when more surface area is exposed.

❯ Rock weathers fastest in climates with alternating hot and cold weather and steady moisture. Higher elevations may have more ice wedging. Gravity affects slopes.

differential weathering, p. 379

Section 3

Soil

❯ Weathered rock, water, gases, and organic material form soils.

❯ The composition of parent rock determines the proportion of clay, sand, and silt in the resulting soil.

❯ Mature residual soils contain three layers: the A horizon, B horizon, and C horizon.

❯ Thick soils form in tropical and temperate climates. Thin soils form in arctic and desert climates, where rainfall is minimal.

soil, p. 383
soil profile, p. 384
horizon, p. 384
humus, p. 384

Section 4

Erosion

❯ Erosion transports weathered rock. Gravity, wind, glaciers, and water are four agents of erosion.

❯ Contour plowing, strip-cropping, terracing, and crop rotation are four farming methods that conserve soil.

❯ Gravity contributes to erosion through rapid mass movements, such as rockfalls, and through slow mass movements, such as creep.

❯ Mountains, plains, and plateaus are three major landforms shaped by weathering and erosion.

erosion, p. 387
sheet erosion, p. 388
mass movement, p. 391
solifluction, p. 392
creep, p. 392
landform, p. 393

1. **Finding Examples** Review Section 4. As you review, list four examples of farming practices that increase soil erosion and four examples of farming methods that help to conserve soil.

USING KEY TERMS

Use each of the following terms in a separate sentence.

2. *abrasion* SC.912.E.6.2

3. *humus* SC.912.E.6.2

4. *landform* SC.912.E.6.2

For each pair of terms, explain how the meanings of the terms differ.

5. *weathering* and *erosion* SC.912.E.6.2

6. *mechanical weathering* and *chemical weathering* SC.912.E.6.2

7. *oxidation* and *carbonation* SC.912.E.6.2

8. *soil profile* and *horizon* SC.912.E.6.2

9. *solifluction* and *creep* SC.912.E.6.2

UNDERSTANDING KEY IDEAS

10. A common kind of mechanical weathering is called SC.912.E.6.2
    a. oxidation.
    c. carbonation.
    b. ice wedging.
    d. leaching.

11. Oxides of sulfur and nitrogen that combine with water vapor cause SC.912.E.6.2
    a. hydrolysis.
    b. acid rain.
    c. mechanical weathering.
    d. carbonation.

12. The surface area of rocks exposed to weathering is increased by SC.912.E.6.2
    a. burial.
    c. leaching.
    b. accumulation.
    d. jointing.

13. Chemical weathering is most rapid in SC.912.E.6.2
    a. hot, dry climates.
    b. cold, dry climates.
    c. cold, wet climates.
    d. hot, wet climates.

14. The chemical composition of soil depends to a large extent on SC.912.E.6.2
    a. topography.
    b. the soil's A horizon.
    c. the parent material.
    d. the soil's B horizon.

15. The soil in tropical climates is often SC.912.E.6.2
    a. thick.
    c. dry.
    b. thin.
    d. fertile.

16. All of the following farming methods prevent gullying, *except* SC.912.E.6.2
    a. terracing.
    c. contour plowing.
    b. strip-cropping.
    d. irrigation.

17. The type of mass movement that moves the most soil is SC.912.E.6.2
    a. a landslide.
    c. a rockfall.
    b. a mudflow.
    d. creep.

18. The grinding away of rock surfaces through the mechanical action of rock or sand particles is called SC.912.E.6.2
    a. carbonation.
    c. abrasion.
    b. hydrolysis.
    d. erosion.

19. The process by which softer rock wears away and leaves harder rock behind is SC.912.E.6.2
    a. chemical weathering.
    b. mechanical weathering.
    c. differential weathering.
    d. erosion.

SHORT ANSWER

20. What is the difference between natural rain and acid precipitation? SC.912.E.6.2

21. Explain two reasons why soil conservation is important. SC.912.E.6.2

22. Describe how a mountain changes from a rugged mountain to a peneplain. SC.912.E.6.2

23. Describe three landforms that are shaped by weathering and erosion. SC.912.E.6.2

24. Explain two ways that weathering and erosion are related. SC.912.E.6.2

25. Identify three ways that climate affects the rate of weathering. SC.912.E.6.2

26. Name three landforms that you would expect to find in a desert. SC.912.E.6.2

CRITICAL THINKING

27. Making Comparisons Compare the weathering processes that affect a rock on top of a mountain with those that affect a rock beneath the ground surface. SC.912.E.6.2

28. Understanding Relationships Which do you think would weather faster, a sculpted marble statue or a smooth marble column? Explain your answer. SC.912.E.6.2

29. Making Inferences Mudflows in the southern California hills are usually preceded by a dry summer and widespread fires, which are followed by torrential rainfall. Explain why these phenomena are followed by mudflows. SC.912.E.6.4

30. Evaluating Ideas How can differential weathering help you determine whether a rock is harder or softer than the rock that surrounds it? SC.912.E.6.2

31. Inferring Relationships Suppose that a mountain has been wearing down at the rate of about 2 cm per year for 10 years. After 10 years, scientists find that the mountain is no longer losing elevation. Why do you think the mountain is no longer losing elevation? SC.912.E.6.2

CONCEPT MAPPING

32. Use the following terms to create a concept map: *composition, mechanical weathering, chemical weathering, topography, erosion, conservation, exposure, weathering, surface area,* and *climate.* SC.912.E.6.2

MATH SKILLS

Math Skills

33. Making Calculations A group of scientists calculates that an acre of land has crept 18 cm in 15 years. What is the average rate of creep in millimeters per year? SC.912.E.6.2

34. Making Calculations For a given area of land, the average rate of creep is 14 mm per year. How long will it take the area to move 1 m? SC.912.E.6.2

WRITING SKILLS

35. Writing from Research Research a mudslide or landslide that occurred in the past. Describe the conditions that led to this mass movement and the impact it had. SC.912.E.6.2

36. Communicating Ideas You are in charge of preserving a precious marble statue. Write a paragraph that describes how you would protect the statue from weathering. SC.912.E.6.2

INTERPRETING GRAPHICS

The graph below shows land use in the United States. Use this graph to answer the questions that follow.

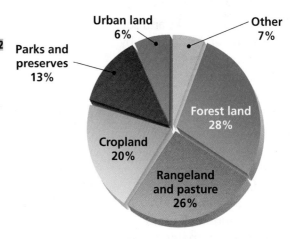

Urban land 6%
Other 7%
Parks and preserves 13%
Forest land 28%
Cropland 20%
Rangeland and pasture 26%

37. How much more land is rangeland and pasture than is urban land? SC.912.E.6.4

38. If cropland increased to 25% and all the other categories remained the same, except for forests, what would the percentage of forests be? SC.912.E.6.4

Understanding Concepts

Directions (1–11): For each question, write on a separate sheet of paper the letter of the correct answer.

1 The processes of physical weathering and erosion shape Earth's landforms by
  A. expanding the elevation of Earth's surface.
  B. decreasing the elevation of Earth's surface.
  C. changing the composition of Earth's surface.
  D. bending rock layers near Earth's surface.

2 Which of the following rocks is most likely to weather quickly?
  F. a buried rock in a mountain
  G. an exposed rock on a plain
  H. a buried rock in a desert
  I. an exposed rock on a slope

3 The red color of rocks and soil containing iron-rich minerals is caused by
  A. chemical weathering.
  B. mechanical weathering.
  C. abrasion.
  D. erosion.

4 In which of the following climates does chemical weathering generally occur most rapidly?
  F. cold, wet climates
  G. cold, dry climates
  H. warm, humid climates
  I. warm, dry climates

5 Which of the following has the greatest impact on soil composition?
  A. the activities of plants and animals
  B. the characteristics of the parent rock
  C. the amount of precipitation
  D. the shape of the land

6 To practice soil conservation, farmers
  F. plant the same type of crop in a field year after year.
  G. plow up and down a slope.
  H. construct steplike ridges that follow the contours of a field.
  I. remove unwanted vegetation.

7 Which of the following statements regarding abrasion, a type of mechanical weathering, is true?
  A. It causes the breakdown of rocks when the rocks collide.
  B. It occurs when water seeps into cracks and freezes.
  C. It results from the growth of plant roots.
  D. It peels a sheet of rock from the layers beneath it.

8 Carbonation, a type of chemical weathering, results in the cycling of materials when
  F. elements combine with oxygen.
  G. organic acids weather rock.
  H. minerals react with water.
  I. carbonic acid reacts with minerals.

9 Gravity causes some types of erosion. Which of the following statements does NOT describe erosion that results from gravity?
  A. Weathered rock moves extremely slowly down a hill.
  B. Topsoil is stripped away from a plain.
  C. Rock falls from a steep cliff.
  D. A large piece of soil and rock move along a slope.

10 Which of the following activities does NOT contribute to erosion?
  F. Farmers rotate crops every other year.
  G. Animal wastes speed up chemical weathering.
  H. Organisms burrow through soil.
  I. A hiker exposes new rock.

11 Which of the following statements about the relationship between surface area and weathering is true?
  A. Surface area is not related to mechanical weathering.
  B. Increased surface area results in increased weathering.
  C. Total surface area decreases as weathering takes place.
  D. Increased surface area results in more ice wedging.

Interpreting Graphics

Directions (12–14): For each question below, record the correct answer on a separate sheet of paper.

Mature Soil Profile

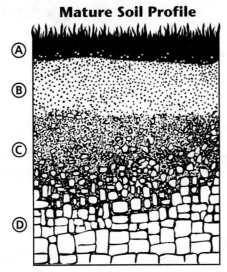

12 Which layer in the soil profile contains the greatest number of soil organisms?

F. layer A **H.** layer C
G. layer B **I.** layer D

13 Which two layers in the soil profile are least likely to contain the dark, organic material humus?

A. layers A and B **C.** layers C and D
B. layers B and C **D.** layers A and D

Blocks of Identical Volume

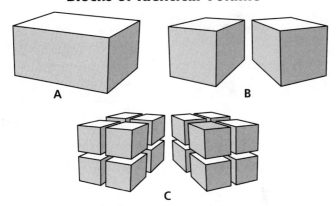

14 The blocks in the figures above have the same volume and are the same mineral. Which figure shows the block or blocks that will weather at the slowest rate?

F. figure A **H.** figure C
G. figure B **I.** The blocks in all three figures will weather at the same rate.

> **Test Tip**
> Whenever possible, highlight or underline numbers or words that are important for correctly answering a question.

River Systems

Chapter Outline

Why It Matters

Water sustains life. Water can also threaten life, in natural disasters called floods. People study river systems to better understand river erosion and deposition—processes that affect humans and shape the land.

Building a Dam

Use clay, sand, soil, and pebbles to build a small model of a landscape with hills and valleys in a large aluminum pan. Gently "rain" water onto your landscape, and observe the flow of the water. Find a place in your landscape that would be suitable for a dam. Use clay to build a dam. Then "rain" water onto your landscape again. Pay attention to how the flow of the water changes and where the water builds up.

Questions to Get You Started

1. Make a labeled diagram to show the paths that the water took as it flowed over your model landscape.

2. When a dam is built, a new lake forms. Describe how and where the lake forms, based on your model.

SC.912.E.6.6

Word Parts

Suffixes The suffixes -ion and -ation turn verbs into nouns. For example, the verb *cooperate* means "to work together." Adding the suffix -ion forms *cooperation,* a noun that means "the process of working together."

Your Turn In Section 1, the key terms *condensation, precipitation,* and *desalination* contain the suffix -ion or -ation. Identify the verb that each term came from, and write its definition. Record your notes in a table like the one started below. The key term *evapotranspiration* also contains the suffix -ation. Split this key term into its component words—*evaporation* and *transpiration*—and add these words to your table.

KEY TERM	RELATED VERB	DEFINITION OF VERB
condensation		
precipitation		
desalination	desalinate	to remove salt from something

Graphic Organizers

Venn Diagram A Venn diagram is useful for showing characteristics that topics share and characteristics that are unique to each topic. As you read, look for topics that have both shared and unique characteristics, and draw a Venn diagram to show how the topics are related.

Your Turn In Section 3, you will read about deltas and alluvial fans. Make a Venn diagram like the one started below, and fill it in with shared and unique characteristics of these two types of sediment deposits.

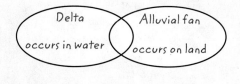

Graphic Organizers

Cause-and-Effect Maps A cause-and-effect map can help you illustrate how, when, or why one event causes another event.

Your Turn As you read Section 3, create a cause-and-effect map like the one started below to help you study the causes and effects of flooding. Remember that you may include as many cause boxes and as many effect boxes as you need.

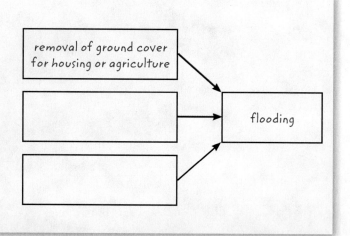

For more information on how to use these and other tools, see **Appendix A.**

The Water Cycle

Key Ideas

❭ Outline the stages of the water cycle.

❭ Describe factors that affect a water budget.

❭ List two approaches to water conservation.

Key Terms

water cycle

evapotranspiration

condensation

precipitation

desalination

Why It Matters

Your survival depends on water, which makes up about two-thirds of your body. When you breathe out, you release water vapor, which becomes part of the water cycle.

The origin of Earth's water supply has puzzled people for centuries. Aristotle and other ancient Greek philosophers believed that rivers such as the Nile and the Danube could be supplied by rain and snow alone. It was not until the middle of the 17th century that scientists could accurately measure the amount of water received on Earth and the amount flowing in rivers. These measurements showed that Earth's surface receives up to 5 times as much water as rivers carry off. So, a more puzzling question than "Where does Earth's water come from?" is "Where does the water go?"

Movement of Water on Earth

Water is essential for humans and all other organisms. Its availability in different forms is critical for the continuation of life on Earth. More than two-thirds of Earth's surface is covered with water. Water flows in streams and rivers. It is held in lakes, oceans, and icecaps at Earth's poles. It even flows through the rock below Earth's surface as groundwater. Water is found not only in these familiar bodies of water but also in the tissues of all living creatures. In the atmosphere, water occurs as an invisible gas. This gas is called *water vapor*. Liquid water also exists in the atmosphere as small particles in clouds and fog, as shown in **Figure 1.**

Earth's water is constantly changing from one form to another. Water vapor falls from the sky as rain. Glaciers melt to form streams. Rivers flow into oceans, where liquid water escapes into the atmosphere as water vapor. This continuous movement of water on Earth's surface from the atmosphere to the land and oceans and back to the atmosphere is called the **water cycle.**

FLORIDA STANDARDS

SC.912.E.7.1 Analyze the movement of matter and energy through the different biogeochemical cycles, including water and carbon; **SC.912.N.3.5** Describe the function of models in science, and identify the wide range of models used in science; **SC.912.N.4.1** Explain how scientific knowledge and reasoning provide an empirically-based perspective to inform society's decision making.

water cycle the continuous movement of water between the atmosphere, the land, and the oceans

Figure 1 The snow, the fog, and the river water in this photo are three of the forms that water takes on Earth. Invisible water vapor is also present in the air.

READING TOOLBOX

Venn Diagram
Make a Venn diagram with two circles. Label one circle "Transpiration" and the other circle "Evaporation." In the area where the circles overlap, write shared characteristics. In each of the other areas, write characteristics that are unique to each process.

evapotranspiration the total loss of water from an area, which equals the sum of the water lost by evaporation from the soil and other surfaces and the water lost by transpiration from organisms

condensation the change of state from a gas to a liquid

precipitation any form of water that falls to Earth's surface from the clouds; includes rain, snow, sleet, and hail

Evapotranspiration

The process by which liquid water changes into water vapor is called *evaporation*. Each year, about 500,000 km³ of water evaporates into the atmosphere. About 86% of this water evaporates from the ocean. The remaining water evaporates from lakes, streams, and the soil. Water vapor also enters the air by *transpiration*, the process by which plants release water vapor into the atmosphere. The total loss of water from an area, which equals the sum of the water lost by evaporation from the soil and other surfaces and the water lost by transpiration from organisms, is called **evapotranspiration.** Evapotranspiration is one part of the water cycle, which is shown in **Figure 2.**

Condensation

Another process of the water cycle is *condensation*. **Condensation** is the change of state from a gas to a liquid. When air rises in the atmosphere, it expands and cools. As the air cools, the water vapor it contains becomes cooler, and some of it condenses, or changes into tiny liquid water droplets, forming clouds.

Precipitation

The third major process of the water cycle is *precipitation*, the process by which water falls from the clouds. **Precipitation** is any form of water that falls to Earth's surface from the clouds and includes rain, snow, sleet, and hail. More than 75% of all precipitation falls on Earth's oceans. The rest falls on land and becomes runoff or groundwater. Eventually, almost all of this water returns to the atmosphere by evapotranspiration, condenses, and falls back to Earth's surface to begin the cycle again.

✓ **Reading Check** **List the forms of precipitation.** (See Appendix G for answers to Reading Checks.)

Figure 2 Evapotranspiration, condensation, and precipitation make up a continuous process called the *water cycle.*

THiNK central
INTERACT ONLINE
Keyword: HQXRVSF2

Water Budget

The continuous cycle of evapotranspiration, condensation, and precipitation establishes Earth's *water budget*. A financial budget is a statement of expected income—money coming in—and expenses—money going out. In Earth's water budget, precipitation is the income. Evapotranspiration and runoff are the expenses. The water budget of Earth as a whole is balanced because the amount of precipitation is equal to the amount of evapotranspiration and runoff. However, the water budget of a particular area, called the *local water budget*, usually is not balanced.

Factors That Affect the Water Budget

Factors that affect the local water budget include temperature, vegetation, wind, and the amount of rainfall. When precipitation exceeds evapotranspiration and runoff in an area, the result is moist soil and possible flooding. When evapotranspiration exceeds precipitation, the soil becomes dry and irrigation may be necessary. Vegetation reduces runoff in an area but increases evapotranspiration. Wind increases the rate of evapotranspiration.

The factors that affect the local water budget vary geographically. For example, the Mojave Desert in California receives much less precipitation than do the tropical rain forests of Queensland, Australia, as **Figure 3** shows.

In most areas of Earth, the local water budget also changes with the seasons. In general, cooler temperatures slow the rate of evapotranspiration. During the warmer months, evapotranspiration increases. As a result, streams generally transport more water in cooler months than they do in warmer months.

Figure 3 Tropical rain forests, such as the one in Queensland, Australia (top photo), receive large amounts of rainfall annually. Deserts, such as the Mojave Desert in California (bottom photo), receive small amounts of rainfall each year.

SC.912.E.7.1

Quick Lab   Modeling the Water Cycle

35 min

Procedure

❶ Place a **short glass** inside a **large plastic mixing bowl**. Add **cold water** to the mixing bowl until about three-fourths of the glass is covered with water. Make sure to keep the inside of the glass dry.

❷ Add drops of **food coloring** (red, blue, or green) to the water in the bowl until the water has a strong color.

❸ Now, add about 1 cup of dry **soil** to the water, and stir gently until the water is muddy as well as colored.

❹ Cover the bowl tightly with a **piece of plastic wrap** secured to the bowl with a **rubber band**,

and place a **coin or stone** in the middle of the plastic wrap above the glass.

❺ Set the bowl in the sun or under a **heat lamp** for 30 minutes to several hours. Then, observe the water that has collected in the glass.

Analysis

1. What are the processes that have taken place to allow water to collect in the glass?

2. Why is the water in the glass not muddy?

3. Is the water in the glass colored? What does this say about pollutants in water systems and the water cycle?

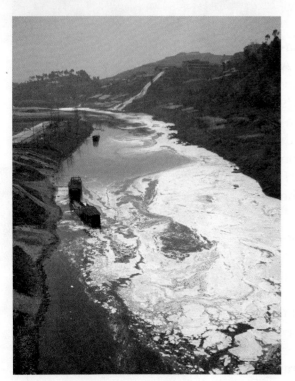

Figure 4 Waste from a paper mill has polluted the Qingai River in China.

Academic Vocabulary

method (METH uhd) a way of doing something

desalination a process of removing salt from ocean water

Water Use

On average, each person in the United States uses about 95,000 L (20,890.5 gal) of water each year. Water is used for bathing, washing clothes and dishes, watering lawns, carrying away wastes, and drinking. Agriculture and industry also use large amounts of water. As the population of the United States increases, so does the demand for water.

About 90% of the water used by cities and industry is returned to rivers or to the oceans as wastewater. Some of this wastewater contains harmful materials, such as toxic chemicals and metals, as shown in **Figure 4.** These toxic materials can pollute rivers and can harm plants and animals in the water.

Conservation of Water

While Earth holds a lot of water, only a small percentage of that water is fresh water that can be used by humans. Scientists have identified two ways to ensure that enough fresh water is available today and in the future. One way is through conservation, or the wise use of water resources. Individuals can conserve water by limiting their water use as much as possible. Governments can help conserve water by enforcing conservation laws and antipollution laws that prohibit the dumping of waste into bodies of water.

A second way to protect the water supply is to find alternative methods of obtaining fresh water. One such method is called **desalination,** which is the process of removing salt from ocean water. However, this method is expensive and is impractical for supplying water to large populations. Currently, the best way of maintaining an adequate supply of fresh water is the wise use and conservation of the fresh water that is now available.

Section 1 Review

LA.910.2.2.3; SC.912.E.7.1; SC.912.N.4.1

Key Ideas

1. **List** two ways in which water reaches the oceans.

2. **Outline** the major stages of the water cycle.

3. **Explain** the difference between condensation and precipitation.

4. **Explain** why most local water budgets are not balanced.

5. **Describe** how vegetation and rainfall affect the local water budget.

6. **List** two ways to ensure the continued supply of fresh water.

Critical Thinking

7. **Applying Concepts** Describe five ways that you can conserve water at home.

8. **Analyzing Processes** Why are the oceans the location of most evaporation and precipitation?

Concept Mapping

9. Use the following terms to create a concept map: *water cycle, evaporation, transpiration, evapotranspiration, condensation, precipitation,* and *water budget.*

Stream Erosion

Key Ideas

❯ Summarize how a river develops.

❯ Describe the parts of a river system.

❯ Explain factors that affect the erosive ability of a river.

❯ Describe how erosive factors affect the development of a river channel.

Key Terms

tributary   gradient

watershed   meander

stream load   braided stream

discharge

Why It Matters

Rivers change course over time. Because they also often form political boundaries, such change can cause problems for people living on both sides of the river.

A river system begins to form when precipitation exceeds evapotranspiration in a given area. Excess water then moves downslope as runoff. As runoff moves across the land surface, it erodes rock and soil and eventually may form a narrow ditch, called a *gully*. Eventually, the processes of precipitation and erosion form a fully developed valley with a permanent stream.

Parts of a River System

A river system is made up of a main stream and **tributaries,** which are all of the feeder streams that flow into the main stream. The land from which water runs off into these streams is called a **watershed.** The ridges or elevated regions that separate watersheds are called *divides*. A river system is shown in **Figure 1.**

The relatively narrow depression that a stream follows as it flows downhill is called its *channel*. The edges of a stream channel that are above water level are called the stream's *banks*. The part of the stream channel that is below the water level is called the stream's *bed*. A stream channel gradually becomes wider and deeper as it erodes its banks and bed.

Channel Erosion

River systems change continuously because of erosion. In the process of *headward erosion*, channels lengthen and branch out at their upper ends, where runoff enters the streams. Erosion of the slopes in a watershed can also extend a river system and can add to the area of the watershed. In the process known as *stream piracy*, a stream from one watershed is "captured" by a stream from another watershed that has a higher rate of erosion. The captured stream then drains into the river system that has done the capturing.

FLORIDA STANDARDS

SC.912.E.7.3 Differentiate and describe the various interactions among Earth systems, including: atmosphere, hydrosphere, cryosphere, geosphere, and biosphere.

tributary a stream that flows into a lake or into a larger stream

watershed the area of land that is drained by a river system

Figure 1 The tributaries that run into this river are fed by runoff from surrounding land. All of the land that drains into a single river makes up the watershed of the river.

Stream Load

A stream transports soil, loose rock fragments, and dissolved minerals as it flows downhill. The materials carried by a stream are called the **stream load.** Stream load takes three forms: suspended load, bed load, and dissolved load. The *suspended load* consists of particles of fine sand and silt. The speed, or rate of downstream travel, of the water keeps these particles suspended, so they do not sink to the stream bed. The *bed load* is made up of larger, coarser materials, such as coarse sand, gravel, and pebbles. This material moves by sliding and jumping along the bed. The *dissolved load* is mineral matter transported in liquid solution.

Stream Discharge

The volume of water moved by a stream in a given time period is the stream's **discharge.** The faster a stream flows, the higher its discharge and the greater the load that the stream can carry. Thus, a swift stream carries more sediment and larger particles than a slow stream does. A stream's speed also affects how the stream cuts down and widens its channel. Swift streams erode their channels more quickly than slow-moving streams do.

Stream Gradient

The speed of a stream depends mainly on gradient. **Gradient** is the change in elevation of a stream over a given horizontal distance. In other words, gradient is the steepness of the stream's slope. Near the *headwaters*, or the beginning of a stream, the gradient generally is steep. This area of the stream has a high rate of flow, which causes rapid channel erosion. As the stream nears its *mouth*, where the stream enters a larger body of water, its gradient often becomes flatter. As a result, the river's speed and erosive power decrease. The stream channel eventually is eroded to a nearly flat gradient by the time the stream channel reaches the sea. Streams with different gradients are shown in **Figure 2.**

---

stream load the materials other than the water that are carried by a stream

discharge the volume of water that flows within a given time

gradient the change in elevation over a given distance

Math Skills

Water Discharge of a River River channels can carry an enormous volume of water. The water that rivers discharge can be calculated by using the following equation:

$$\text{discharge} = \begin{array}{c}\text{speed}\\\text{of the}\\\text{water}\end{array} \times \begin{array}{c}\text{cross-sectional}\\\text{area of the}\\\text{river channel}\end{array}$$

In cubic meters per second (m^3/s), what is the discharge of water carried by a river that moves 1.5 m/s through a cross-sectional area of 520 m^2?

Figure 2 Streams that have steep gradients, such as the stream on the left, have a higher speed than streams that have low gradients, such as the stream on the right, do.

Steep gradient

Low gradient

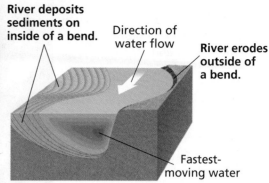

River deposits sediments on inside of a bend.

Direction of water flow

River erodes outside of a bend.

Fastest-moving water

Figure 3 Decreased speed on the inside of a river's curve leads to the deposition of sediment, as this photo of a river in the Banff National Park in Alberta, Canada, shows.

Development of River Channels

As the stream's load, discharge, and gradient decrease, the erosive power of the stream decreases, which influences the development of the stream's channel. Over time, as the channel erodes, it becomes wider and deeper. When the stream becomes longer and wider, it is called a *river*.

Meandering Channels

As a river develops, it may form curves and bends. A river that has a low gradient tends to have more bends than a river that has a steep gradient does. A winding pattern of wide curves, called **meanders,** develops because as the gradient decreases, the speed of the water decreases. When the speed of the water decreases, the river is less able to erode down into its bed. As the water flows through the channel, more energy is directed against the banks, which causes erosion of the banks.

When a river rounds a bend, the speed of the water on the outside of the curve increases. The fast-moving water on the outside of a river bend erodes the outer bank of that bend. However, on the inside of the curve, the speed of the water decreases. This decrease in speed leads to the formation of a *bar* of deposited sediment, such as sand or gravel, as shown in **Figure 3.**

As this process continues, the curve enlarges while further sediment deposition takes place on the opposite bank, where the water is moving more slowly. Meanders can become so curved that they almost form a loop, separated by only a narrow neck of land. When the river cuts across this neck, the meander can become isolated from the river, and an *oxbow lake* forms.

meander one of the bends, twists, or curves in a low-gradient stream or river

www.scilinks.org
Topic: River Systems
Code: HQX1314

✓ **Reading Check** How would you describe the gradient of a river that has meanders?

Figure 4 Braided streams, such as the Chisana River in Alaska, divide into multiple channels.

READING TOOLBOX

Cause-and-Effect Map
Make a cause-and-effect map that is similar to the one you made at the beginning of this chapter. Label the effects "meandering channels" and "braided streams." Then fill in the map with causes of meandering channels and braided streams. Add details about the causes and effects.

Academic Vocabulary

available (uh VAYL uh buhl) able to be used

braided stream a stream or river that is composed of multiple channels that divide and rejoin around sediment bars

Braided Streams

Most rivers are single channels. However, under certain conditions, the presence of sediment bars between a river's banks can divide the flow of the river into multiple channels. A stream or river that is composed of multiple channels that divide and rejoin around sediment bars is called a **braided stream.** Braided streams are a direct result of a high gradient and a large sediment load, particularly when a high percentage of the load is composed of coarse sand and gravel. The bars form on the channel floor when the river is unable to move all of the available load.

Although braided streams, such as those in **Figure 4,** look very different from meandering channels, they can cause just as much erosion. The channel location shifts constantly such that bars between channels erode and new bars form. Sometimes, a single river can change from a braided stream to a meandering stream as the gradient and discharge change.

Section 2 Review

LA.910.2.2.3; SC.912.E.6.2; SC.912.E.7.1

Key Ideas

1. **Summarize** how a river develops.

2. **Describe** the parts of a river system.

3. **Explain** the processes of headward erosion and stream piracy.

4. **List** the three types of stream load.

5. **Explain** how stream discharge and gradient affect the erosive ability of a river.

6. **Describe** the factors that control whether a river is braided or meandering.

7. **Summarize** the process that forms an oxbow lake.

Critical Thinking

8. **Predicting Consequences** If geologic forces were to cause an uplift of the land surface, what would the effect on stream channel erosion be?

9. **Analyzing Processes** Explain how the speed of a stream affects the suspended load.

Concept Mapping

10. Use the following terms to create a concept map: *braided channels, stream load, suspended load, dissolved load, bed load, meanders, stream gradient,* and *headwaters.*

Stream Deposition

Key Ideas	Key Terms	Why It Matters
› Explain the two types of stream deposition. › Describe one advantage and one disadvantage of living in a floodplain. › Identify three methods of flood control. › Describe the life cycle of a lake.	delta alluvial fan floodplain	Building a dam involves risks, but *not* building a dam also has risks. An understanding of floodplains is critical for making good decisions about whether or not to build a dam.

The total load that a stream can carry is greatest when a large volume of water is flowing swiftly. When the speed of the water decreases, the ability of the stream to carry its load decreases. As a result, part of the stream load is deposited as sediment.

FLORIDA STANDARDS

SC.912.E.7.3 Differentiate and describe the various interactions among Earth systems, including: atmosphere, hydrosphere, cryosphere, geosphere, and biosphere; **SC.912.N.4.1** Explain how scientific knowledge and reasoning provide an empirically-based perspective to inform society's decision making.

Deltas and Alluvial Fans

A stream may deposit sediment on land or in water. For example, the load carried by a stream can be deposited when the stream reaches an ocean or a lake. As a stream empties into a large body of water, the speed of the stream decreases sharply. The load is usually deposited at the mouth of the stream in a triangular shape. A triangular-shaped deposit that forms where the mouth of a stream enters a larger body of water is called a **delta.** The exact shape and size of a delta are determined by waves, tides, offshore depths, and the sediment load of the stream.

When a stream descends a steep slope and reaches a flat plain, the speed of the stream suddenly decreases. As a result, the stream deposits some of its load on the level plain at the base of the slope. A fan-shaped deposit called an **alluvial fan** forms on land, and its tip points upstream. In arid and semiarid regions, temporary streams commonly form alluvial fans. Alluvial fans differ from deltas in that alluvial fans form on land instead of being deposited in water. This difference is shown in **Figure 1.**

delta a fan-shaped mass of rock material deposited at the mouth of a stream

alluvial fan a fan-shaped mass of rock material deposited by a stream when the slope of the land decreases sharply

Figure 1 A delta, such as this one in Alaska's Prince William Sound (above), forms when a stream deposits sediment into another body of water. An alluvial fan, such as this one in California's Death Valley (right), forms when a stream deposits sediment on land.

Floodplains

The volume of water in nearly all streams varies depending on the amount of rainfall and snowmelt in the watershed. A dramatic increase in volume can cause a stream to overflow its banks and to wash over the valley floor. The part of the valley floor that may be covered with water during a flood is called a **floodplain.**

Natural Levees

When a stream overflows its banks and spreads out over the floodplain, the stream loses speed and deposits its coarser sediment load along the banks of the channel. The accumulation of these deposits along the banks eventually produces raised banks, called *natural levees*.

Finer Flood Sediments

Not all of the load deposited by a stream in a flood will form levees. Finer sediments are carried farther out into the floodplain by the flood waters and are deposited there. A series of floods produces a thick layer of fine sediment, which becomes a source of rich floodplain soils. Swampy areas are common on floodplains because drainage is usually poor in the area between the levees and the outer walls of the valley. Despite the hazards of periodic flooding, people choose to live on floodplains, as shown in **Figure 2.** Floodplains provide convenient access to the river for shipping, fishing, and transportation. The rich soils, which are good for farming, also draw people to live on floodplains.

Figure 2 Raised on stilts, houses in the Tonle Sap Floodplain in Cambodia stay dry during frequent flooding.

floodplain an area along a river that forms from sediments deposited when the river overflows its banks

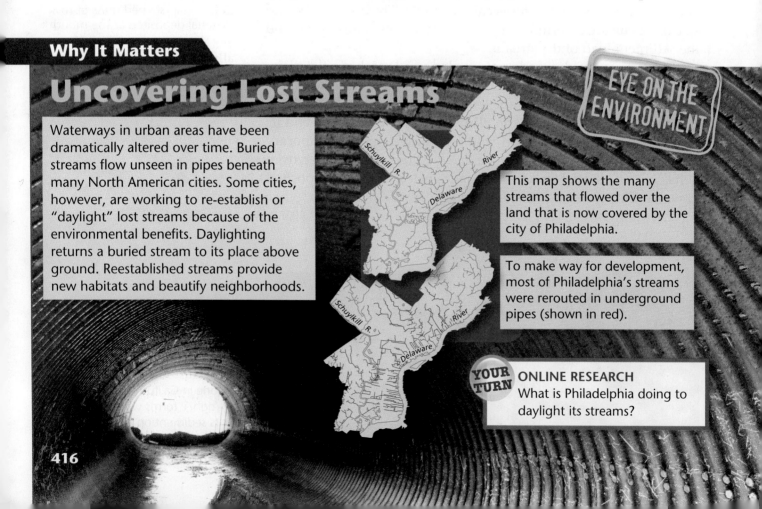

Why It Matters

Uncovering Lost Streams

EYE ON THE ENVIRONMENT

Waterways in urban areas have been dramatically altered over time. Buried streams flow unseen in pipes beneath many North American cities. Some cities, however, are working to re-establish or "daylight" lost streams because of the environmental benefits. Daylighting returns a buried stream to its place above ground. Reestablished streams provide new habitats and beautify neighborhoods.

This map shows the many streams that flowed over the land that is now covered by the city of Philadelphia.

To make way for development, most of Philadelphia's streams were rerouted in underground pipes (shown in red).

YOUR TURN ONLINE RESEARCH
What is Philadelphia doing to daylight its streams?

Quick Lab   Soil Erosion

SC.912.E.6.2

40 min

Procedure

1. Fill a 23 cm × 33 cm pan about half full with moist, fine sand.

2. Place the pan in a sink so that one end of the pan is resting on a brick and is under the water faucet.

3. Position an additional pan or container such that it catches any sand and water that flow out of the first pan.

4. Slowly open the faucet until a gentle trickle of water falls onto the sand in the raised end of the pan. Let the water run for 15 to 20 s.

5. Turn off the water, and draw the pattern of water flow over the sand in your notebook.

6. Press the sand back into place, and carefully smooth the surface by using a ruler. Repeat steps 4 and 5 three more times. Each time, increase the rate of water flow slightly without splashing the sand.

Analysis

1. Describe how the rate of water flow affects erosion.

2. How does the rate of water flow affect gullies?

3. How could erosion on a real hillside be reduced without changing the rate of water flow?

4. How does the shape of a river bend change as water flows?

Human Impacts on Flooding

Human activity can contribute to the size and number of floods in many areas. Vegetation, such as trees and grass, protects the ground surface from erosion by taking in much of the water that would otherwise run off. Where this natural ground cover is removed, water can flow more freely across the surface. As a result, the likelihood of flooding increases. Logging and the clearing of land for agriculture or housing development can increase the volume and speed of runoff, which leads to more frequent flooding. Natural events, such as forest fires, can also increase the likelihood of flooding.

Flood Control

Indirect methods of flood control include forest and soil conservation measures that prevent excess runoff during periods of heavy rainfall. More-direct methods include the building of artificial structures that redirect the flow of water.

The most common method of direct flood control is the building of *dams*. The artificial lakes that form behind dams act as reservoirs for excess runoff. The stored water can be used to generate electricity, supply fresh water, and irrigate farmland. Another direct method of flood control is the building of *artificial levees*. However, artificial levees must be protected against erosion by the river. As **Figure 3** shows, when artificial levees break, flooding and property damage can result. Permanent overflow channels, or *floodways,* can also help prevent flooding. When the volume of water in a river increases, floodways carry away excess water and keep the river from overflowing.

Reading Check Describe two ways that floods can be controlled.

READING TOOLBOX

Suffixes
Add the words *accumulation, transportation,* and *conservation* to the suffix table you started at the beginning of this chapter. Remember to write the verb that each -*ation* word came from, as well as the verb's definition.

Figure 3 This levee near New Orleans broke as a result of Hurricane Katrina, allowing the Mississippi River through.

Precipitation collects in a depression and forms a lake.

A lake loses its water as the water drains away or evaporates.

As water is lost, the lake basin may eventually become dry land.

Figure 4 Compared to rivers, lakes are short lived, and some lakes may eventually dry up.

www.scilinks.org
Topic: Flooding and Society
Code: HQX0585
Topic: Stream Deposition
Code: HQX1457

Academic Vocabulary

exceed (ek SEED) to be more than

The Life Cycle of Lakes

Not all streams flow from the land to the ocean. Sometimes, water from streams collects in a depression in the land and forms a lake. Most lakes are located at high latitudes and in mountainous areas. Most of the water in lakes comes from precipitation and the melting of ice and snow. Springs, rivers, and runoff coming directly from the land are also sources of lake water.

Most lakes are relatively short lived in geologic terms. Many lakes eventually disappear because too much of their water drains away or evaporates, as shown in **Figure 4.** A common cause of excess drainage is an outflowing stream that erodes its bed below the level of a lake basin. Lakes may also lose water if the climate becomes drier and evaporation exceeds precipitation.

Lake basins may also disappear if they fill with sediments. Streams that feed a lake deposit sediments in the lake. Sediments also are carried into the lake by water that runs off the land but does not enter a stream. Most of these sediments are deposited near the shore. These sediments build up over time, which creates new shorelines and gradually fills in the lake. Organic deposits from vegetation also may accumulate in the bottom of a shallow lake. As these deposits grow denser, a bog or swamp may form. The lake basin may eventually become dry land.

Section 3 Review

LA.910.2.2.3; SC.912.E.6.2; SC.912.E.7.1

Key Ideas

1. **Identify** the differences between a delta and an alluvial fan.

2. **Explain** the differences between the deposition of sediment in deltas and alluvial fans with the deposition of sediment on a floodplain.

3. **Describe** the advantages and disadvantages of living in a floodplain.

4. **Summarize** how human activities can affect the size and number of floods.

5. **Identify** three methods of flood control.

6. **Explain** why lakes are usually short lived.

Critical Thinking

7. **Analyzing Ideas** Why are spring floods common in rivers where the headwaters are in an area of cold, snowy winters?

8. **Making Inferences** If you were picking a material to make an artificial levee, what major characteristic would you look for? Explain your answer.

Concept Mapping

9. Use the following terms to create a concept map: *stream deposition, delta, alluvial fan, floodplain, natural levee, dam, artificial levee,* and *lake.*

The Three Gorges Dam

How would you feel if you had to relocate your home because a new dam that is under construction will lead to the flooding of your town? Millions of people in China were affected by the construction of the Three Gorges Dam across the Yangtze River, the largest hydroelectric dam ever built. This enormous project was started with the intention of providing needed electric power and preventing flooding. However, the project also raises many social and environmental issues.

SCIENCE & SOCIETY

Dam construction creates a massive lake upstream that covers old valleys, such as this one. Pollution build-up in the new lake causes problems for nearby ecosystems and residents.

The new lake also covered cities, towns, and historical sites. About 1.3 million people had to relocate their homes.

Area to be flooded

Huang He R.

Jialing R.

Wuxia Gorge
Qutang Gorge   Xiling Gorge
Wanxian   Sandouping   Wuhan   Shanghai
Dam   Yangtze R.   Yellow Sea
Chongqing

CHINA

The dam can provide millions of people with needed power and minimize power shortages in China's growing cities.

YOUR TURN

ONLINE RESEARCH
Use the Internet to research the arguments for and against construction of the Three Gorges Dam.

WRITING IN SCIENCE
Would you have supported or opposed the construction of the dam? Write one page explaining your argument.

Inquiry Lab

⏱ 45 min

Sediments and Water

Running water erodes some types of soil more easily than it erodes others. How rapidly a soil erodes depends on how well the soil holds water. In this lab, you will determine the erosive effect of water on various types of sediment.

What You'll Do

> **Measure** the amount of water that sediment can hold.

> **Identify** the properties that affect how sediment interacts with water.

What You'll Need

graduated cylinder, 100 mL
grease pencil
juice containers, 12 oz (2)
metric ruler
nail, large
pan, 23 cm × 33 cm × 5 cm
  or larger
sand, dry and coarse
silt, dry
stopwatch or clock with
  second hand
water

Safety

Ask a Question

1 Which type of soil would hold more water: sandy soil or silty soil? Which soil would water flow through faster and therefore would erode more rapidly: sandy soil or silty soil?

Form a Hypothesis

2 Write a hypothesis that is a possible answer to the questions above.

Test the Hypothesis

3 Use a graduated cylinder to pour 300 mL of water into each of two juice containers.

4 Place the containers on a flat surface. Using a grease pencil, draw a line around the inside of the containers to mark the height of the water. Label one container "A" and the other "B." Empty and dry the containers.

5 Using silt, fill container A up to the line drawn inside the container. Tap the container gently to even out the surface of the sediment. Repeat this step for container B, but use sand.

Step **5**

420

6 Fill the graduated cylinder with 100 mL of water. Slowly pour the water into container A. Stop every few seconds to allow the soil to absorb the water. Continue pouring until a thin film of water forms on the surface of the sediment. If more than 100 mL of water is needed, refill the graduated cylinder and continue this step.

7 Record the volume of water poured into the container.

8 Using container B, repeat steps 6 and 7. Record your observations.

Step 8

9 Use a metric ruler to measure 1 cm above the surface of the sediment in each container. Using the grease pencil, draw a line to mark this height on the inside of each container. Pour water from the graduated cylinder into containers A and B until the water reaches the 1 cm mark.

10 Poke a nail through the very bottom of the side of container A. Place the container inside the pan. At the same time, start recording the time by using a stopwatch and pull the nail out of the container.

11 Observe the water level, and record the amount of time that the water takes to drop to the sediment surface.

12 Using container B, repeat steps 10 and 11. Record your observations.

Step 12

Analyze the Results

1. **Analyzing Results** In step 8, which type of sediment held more water?

2. **Analyzing Results** Which type of sediment was the water able to flow through faster?

3. **Summarizing Results** What properties of the sediment do you think affected how the water flowed through the sediment? Explain your answer.

Draw Conclusions

4. **Analyzing Results** On the basis of your answers to the questions above, which would water erode more quickly: an area of silt or an area of sand? Explain your answer.

5. **Drawing Conclusions** In which sediment do you think a deep stream channel is most likely to form? In which sediment is a meandering stream likely to form? Explain your answers.

Extension

Applying Conclusions Describe three ways to make slopes covered with soil more resistant to erosion.

MAPS *in Action*

World Watershed Sediment Yield

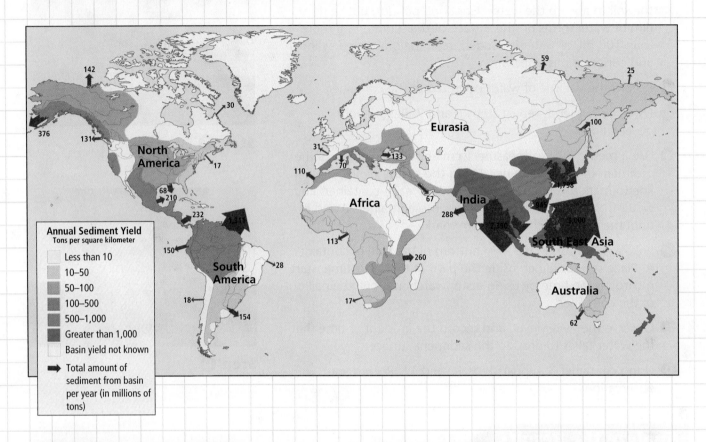

Annual Sediment Yield
Tons per square kilometer

- Less than 10
- 10–50
- 50–100
- 100–500
- 500–1,000
- Greater than 1,000
- Basin yield not known
- ➡ Total amount of sediment from basin per year (in millions of tons)

Map ▸ Skills Activity

This map shows the world's watersheds and identifies the sediment yield of each watershed basin in tons per square kilometer and the total amount of sediment that each basin dumps into the ocean in millions of tons per year. Use the map to answer the questions below.

1. **Using a Key** Which area has the highest total annual sediment yield from one basin?

2. **Using a Key** What is the range of the annual sediment yield in tons per square kilometer for the United States, excluding Alaska?

3. **Analyzing Data** What is the total amount of sediment that basins in South America yield per year?

4. **Analyzing Relationships** Areas that have high relief (where the range of elevations is great) tend to have higher sediment yields than do areas of low relief (where the topography is flatter). Which area would you conclude has higher relief: Africa or South East Asia? Explain your answer.

5. **Making Comparisons** Both the Amazon basin, which is in northern South America, and the India basin have an annual sediment yield range of 100 to 500 tons per square kilometer. However, the total amount of sediment per year from the Amazon basin is 1,311 million tons, while the total amount of sediment per year from the India basin is 288 million tons. Explain why these two basins differ so significantly in their total sediment yield per year.

THINK central
SUPER SUMMARY
Keyword: HQXRVSS

Key Ideas

Key Terms

Section 1

The Water Cycle

❯ The water cycle involves the processes of evapotranspiration, condensation, and precipitation.

❯ A region's water budget is affected by temperature, vegetation, wind, and the amount of rainfall.

❯ Water can be conserved by individuals limiting water use and by governments enforcing conservation laws and antipollution laws.

water cycle, p. 407
evapotranspiration, p. 408
condensation, p. 408
precipitation, p. 408
desalination, p. 410

Section 2

Stream Erosion

❯ A river develops over time, through the processes of precipitation and erosion.

❯ A river system consists of a main stream and tributaries.

❯ The erosive ability of a river is affected by stream load, stream discharge, and stream gradient.

❯ Erosive factors, such as gradient and discharge, can affect the development of a river channel, forming meanders and braided streams.

tributary, p. 411
watershed, p. 411
stream load, p. 412
discharge, p. 412
gradient, p. 412
meander, p. 413
braided stream, p. 414

Section 3

Stream Deposition

❯ Two types of stream deposition are deltas, which form in water, and alluvial fans, which form on land.

❯ Living in a floodplain has advantages, such as access to a river and rich soil, but the risk of flooding is a disadvantage.

❯ Three methods of flood control include forest and soil conservation, dams, and artificial levees.

❯ Over time, a lake may lose its water or fill with sediment and become dry land.

delta, p. 415
alluvial fan, p. 415
floodplain, p. 416

1. **Venn Diagram** Make a Venn diagram with two circles. Label one circle "Meandering channel" and the other circle "Braided stream." In the area where the circles overlap, write shared characteristics. In each of the other areas, write characteristics that are unique to each type of river.

USING KEY TERMS

Use each of the following terms in a separate sentence.

2. *water cycle* SC.912.E.6.2

3. *gradient* SC.912.E.6.2

4. *evapotranspiration* SC.912.E.6.2

5. *floodplain* SC.912.E.6.2

For each pair of terms, explain how the meanings of the terms differ.

6. *condensation* and *precipitation* SC.912.E.6.2

7. *watershed* and *tributary* SC.912.E.6.2

8. *stream load* and *discharge* SC.912.E.6.2

9. *delta* and *alluvial fan* SC.912.E.6.2

UNDERSTANDING KEY IDEAS

10. The change of water vapor into liquid water is called SC.912.E.6.2
    a. runoff.
    b. desalination.
    c. evaporation.
    d. condensation.

11. In a water budget, the income is precipitation and the expense is SC.912.E.6.2
    a. evapotranspiration and runoff.
    b. condensation and saltation.
    c. erosion and conservation.
    d. conservation and sedimentation.

12. The land area from which water runs off into a stream is called a SC.912.E.6.2
    a. tributary.   c. divide.
    b. watershed.   d. gully.

13. Tributaries branch out and lengthen as a river system develops by SC.912.E.6.2
    a. headward erosion.
    b. condensation.
    c. saltation.
    d. runoff.

14. The stream load that includes gravel and large rocks is the SC.912.E.6.2
    a. suspended load.   c. dissolved load.
    b. runoff load.   d. bed load.

15. A fan-shaped formation that develops when a stream deposits its sediment at the base of a steep slope is called a(n) SC.912.E.6.2
    a. delta.
    b. meander.
    c. oxbow lake.
    d. alluvial fan.

16. The part of a valley floor that may be covered during a flood is the SC.912.E.6.2
    a. floodway.
    b. floodplain.
    c. meander.
    d. artificial levee.

17. One way to control floods indirectly is through SC.912.E.6.2
    a. soil conservation.
    b. dams.
    c. floodways.
    d. artificial levees.

SHORT ANSWER

18. How does a local water budget differ from the water budget of the whole Earth? SC.912.E.6.2

19. How is reducing the pollution in streams and groundwater linked to water conservation? SC.912.E.6.2

20. Describe how bank erosion can cause a river to meander. SC.912.E.6.2

21. Why do most rivers that have a large sediment load also have a fast flow of water? SC.912.E.6.2

22. Describe how lakes fill with sediment. SC.912.E.6.2

23. What is the difference between direct and indirect methods of flood control? SC.912.E.6.2

CRITICAL THINKING

24. Evaluating Ideas How would Earth's water cycle be affected if a significant percentage of the sun's rays were blocked by dust or other contaminants in the atmosphere? SC.912.E.6.2

25. Making Comparisons Use an atlas to determine the geographic location of Kolkata, India, and Stockholm, Sweden. How might the local water budgets of these two cities differ? Explain your answer. SC.912.E.6.4

26. Making Inferences The Colorado River is usually grayish brown as it flows through the Grand Canyon. What causes this color? SC.912.E.6.2

27. Making Predictions What do you think would happen to cities in the southwestern United States if rivers in that area could not be dammed? SC.912.E.6.4

CONCEPT MAPPING

28. Use the following terms to create a concept map: *water vapor, condensation, precipitation, channel, stream load, bar, alluvial fan, delta, divides, watersheds, tributaries, floodplains, dams,* and *artificial levees.* SC.912.E.6.2

MATH SKILLS

29. Making Calculations If a river is 3,705 km long from its headwaters to its delta and the average speed of its water is 250 cm/s, use the equation *time = distance ÷ speed* to determine how many days a water molecule takes to make the trip. SC.912.E.6.2

30. Using Equations You wish to examine the annual water budget for the state of Colorado. If p = total precipitation, e = total evapotranspiration, r = total stream runoff, and g = total water soaking into the ground, what equation will allow you to determine whether Colorado experiences a net loss or net gain of water over the course of a year? SC.912.E.6.4

WRITING SKILLS

31. Writing Persuasively Write a persuasive essay of at least 300 words that suggests ways in which your community can conserve water and reduce water pollution. SC.912.E.6.2

32. Communicating Main Ideas Discuss the dangers and advantages of living in a river floodplain. Outline the options for adapting to living in a river floodplain. SC.912.E.6.2

INTERPRETING GRAPHICS

The graph below shows the gradients of several rivers of the United States. Use the graph to answer the questions that follow.

33. Which river has the shallowest average gradient over its entire course? SC.912.E.6.4

34. Which river has the steepest average gradient over its entire course? SC.912.E.6.4

35. Based only on gradient, how would the speed of the Snake River compare with the speed of the Missouri River? SC.912.E.6.4

36. Which end of each line on the graph represents the headwaters of the river system? Explain your answer. SC.912.E.6.4

Understanding Concepts

Directions (1–10): For each question, write on a separate sheet of paper the letter of the correct answer.

1 Condensation is often triggered as water vapor rising in the atmosphere
   A. cools.
   B. warms.
   C. contracts.
   D. breaks apart.

2 The continuous movement of water from the ocean, to the atmosphere, to the land, and back to the ocean is
   F. condensation.
   G. the water cycle.
   H. precipitation.
   I. evapotranspiration.

3 Which of the following statements does NOT describe a practical way to conserve water?
   A. Salt is removed from ocean water.
   B. Water use is limited as much as possible.
   C. Laws are created that protect water resources.
   D. Dumping of wastes into bodies of water is prohibited.

4 Like rivers, lakes have life cycles. Most lakes have short life cycles and eventually disappear. Which of the following conditions may cause a lake to disappear?
   F. when evaporation exceeds precipitation
   G. when precipitation exceeds evaporation
   H. when sediments are removed from the lake
   I. when a local water budget is balanced

5 Which of the following statements about channel erosion is true?
   A. Channel erosion is greatest when the gradient of a stream is steep.
   B. Channel erosion occurs at a greater rate in slow streams.
   C. Channel erosion increases as load decreases.
   D. Channel erosion results in a deeper and narrower stream.

6 How can human activity contribute to increased flooding?
   F. People build dams.
   G. People build artificial levees.
   H. People build housing developments.
   I. People build overflow channels.

7 Water cycles through organisms, the atmosphere, and on Earth's surface. During the water cycle, plants release water into the atmosphere during
   A. condensation.
   B. evaporation.
   C. precipitation.
   D. transpiration.

8 The water budget for a given area is affected by
   F. temperature and precipitation only.
   G. temperature, vegetation, wind, and precipitation.
   H. geology and climate.
   I. the seasons only.

9 A scientist is going to be examining the headwaters of a stream. What can the scientist expect to find at this location?
   A. The stream has a small load.
   B. The stream's discharge is very large.
   C. The stream's gradient is likely steep.
   D. The stream moves very slowly.

10 Which of the following statements best describes how a meander forms?
   F. The gradient increases, and the velocity of the water increases the erosion of the bank, forming a meander.
   G. The river rounds a bend, and its velocity and erosion decrease, which results in a meander.
   H. The river rounds a bend, and the velocity of the water on the outside of the bend increases, which eventually forms a meander.
   I. A river moves more quickly, so it carries more sediment and erodes the banks, which forms a meander.

Interpreting Graphics

Directions (11–12): For each question below, record the correct answer on a separate sheet of paper.

Hydroelectric Power Plant

11 Hydroelectric dams are used to generate electricity for human use. As water rushes past the machinery inside, an electric current is generated. What does water rush past to turn the generator, which produces the current?

A. a transformer
B. the control gate
C. a penstock
D. a turbine

Formation of an Oxbow Lake

12 The illustrations above show the formation of an oxbow lake. What has occurred in figure B?

F. The river cuts across a neck of land, which will isolate the meander from the rest of the river.
G. Erosion in the outer part of the bend is resulting in the meander.
H. The river becomes wider and deeper.
I. The river rounds a bend, and the velocity on the inside of the bend increases, depositing sediment.

Test Tip

If you are permitted to, draw a line through each incorrect answer choice as you eliminate it.

Chapter 16

Groundwater

Chapter Outline

Why It Matters

Groundwater is a major source of fresh water for humans. Where molten rock in Earth's crust heats groundwater and surrounding rock, hot springs form. These macaque monkeys bathe in hot springs in Jigokudani National Park in Japan.

Place two jars on a piece of cardboard. Fill each jar two-thirds full of Epsom salts. Then, fill with warm water to the top of the salt and stir to make a thick solution. Soak a 40 cm piece of twine in the solution until it is thoroughly wet. Then tie a weight onto each end of the twine. Place one end of the twine in each jar. The middle of the twine should hang between the two jars, lower than the water levels, but should not touch the cardboard. Place your set-up somewhere where it will not be disturbed. Observe what happens to the twine over several days.

SC.912.E.6.4

Questions to Get You Started

1. Describe the formation that appears on the twine. How do you think this formed?

2. How is the formation on the twine similar to the natural formation called a stalactite?

429

These reading tools will help you learn the material in this chapter.

Word Origins

Words that Come from Place Names In Section 2, you will learn about *karst topography,* a landscape characterized by caverns, sinkholes, and underground drainage. The term *karst topography* comes from *Karst,* the German name for a region of Slovenia, formerly a part of Yugoslavia, known for its caves.

Your Turn In Section 1, you will learn about *artesian wells.* Use a dictionary or the Internet to learn how these wells got their name. Create a table like the one below and use the information you find to fill it in.

Term	Definition	Etymology (Word Origin)
Artesian wells		

Describing Time

Temporal Language The word *temporal* means "related to time." Temporal language is language that is used to describe time. Paying careful attention to temporal language can help you understand the temporal nature of events and processes.

Your Turn As you read Section 2, make a two-column table. In the first column, write words or phrases in the text that refer to time. In the second column, note the context of the time reference.

Time Reference	Context of Time Reference
slowly	how carbonic acid dissolves limestone
often	when stalactites and stalagmites grow together to form columns

Graphic Organizers

Venn Diagrams A Venn diagram is a graphic representation of the relationships between similar things or ideas. See Appendix A for instructions for making a Venn diagram.

Your Turn As you read Section 2, complete a Venn diagram to represent the relationships between different features formed by chemical weathering.

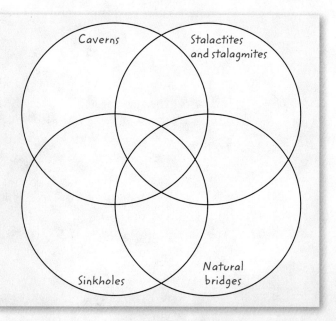

For more information on how to use these and other tools, see **Appendix A.**

Water Beneath the Surface

Key Ideas	Key Terms	Why It Matters
❯ Identify properties of aquifers that affect the flow of groundwater. ❯ Describe the water table and its relationship to the land surface. ❯ Compare wells, springs, and artesian formations. ❯ Describe two land features formed by hot groundwater.	groundwater aquifer porosity permeability water table artesian formation	Almost one-fourth of all fresh water used in the United States comes from groundwater sources. Understanding how water and the ground interact may affect the way you treat the environment.

Surface water that does not run off into streams and rivers may seep down through the soil into the upper layers of Earth's crust. There, the water fills spaces, or *pores,* between rock particles. Water may also fill fractures or cavities in rock that were caused by erosion. Water that fills and moves through these spaces in rock and sediment is called **groundwater.**

Properties of Aquifers

A body of rock or sediment in which large amounts of water can flow and be stored is called an **aquifer.** For water to flow freely through an aquifer, the pores or fractures in the aquifer must be connected. The ease with which water flows through an aquifer is affected by many factors, including porosity and permeability.

Porosity

In a set volume of rock or sediment, the percentage of the rock or sediment that consists of open spaces is **porosity.** One factor that affects porosity is sorting. *Sorting* is the amount of uniformity in the size of the rock or sediment particles, as **Figure 1** shows. Most particles in a well-sorted sediment are about the same size. Poorly sorted sediment contains particles of many sizes. Small particles fill the spaces between large particles, which makes the rock less porous. Particle packing also affects porosity. Loosely packed particles leave many open spaces that can store water, so the rock has high porosity. Rock that has tightly packed particles contains few open spaces and thus has low porosity. Grain shape also affects porosity. In general, the more irregular the grain shape is, the more porous the rock or sediment is.

FLORIDA STANDARDS

MA.912.S.1.2 Determine appropriate and consistent standards of measurement for the data to be collected in a survey or experiment; **SC.912.E.7.3** Differentiate and describe the various interactions among Earth systems, including: atmosphere, hydrosphere, cryosphere, geosphere, and biosphere.

groundwater the water that is beneath Earth's surface

aquifer a body of rock or sediment that stores groundwater and allows the flow of groundwater

porosity the percentage of the total volume of a rock or sediment that consists of open spaces

Figure 1 Differences in Porosity

Well Sorted

Well Sorted

Poorly Sorted

Pores and fractures are empty spaces that make a rock porous. Here, fractures in the rock are filled with water.

Rock is considered permeable if its empty spaces are connected so that water may flow from one space to the next.

Figure 2 Porous rocks do not make good aquifers unless water can move freely through the rocks.

permeability the ability of a rock or sediment to let fluids pass through its open spaces, or pores

Permeability

The ease with which water passes through a porous material is called **permeability.** For a rock to be permeable, the open spaces must be connected, as shown in **Figure 2.** Rock that has high porosity is not permeable if the pores or fractures are not connected. Permeability is also affected by the size and sorting of the particles that make up the rock or sediment. The larger and better sorted the particles are, the more permeable the rock or sediment tends to be. The most permeable rock, such as sandstone, is composed of coarse particles. Other types of rock, such as limestone, may be permeable if they have interconnected cracks. Clay is a sediment composed of flat, very fine-grained particles. Because of this characteristic composition, clay is essentially *impermeable*, which means that water cannot flow through it.

SC.912.E.6.4

Quick **Lab**   Permeability

20 min

Procedure

❶ With a **sharpened pencil**, make seven tiny holes in the bottom of each of **three paper or plastic cups.** Stretch **cheesecloth** tightly over the bottom of each cup. Secure the cloth with a **rubber band.**

❷ Mark a line 2 cm from the top of one cup. Stand the cup on **three thread spools** in a **saucer or pie pan,** and fill the cup to the line with **sand.**

❸ Pour **120 mL of water** into the cup. Use a **stopwatch** to time how long the water takes to drain.

❹ Pour the water from the saucer into a **measuring cup.** Record the amount of water.

❺ Repeat steps 2 to 4 with the two other cups, but fill one cup with **soil** and one with **gravel,** not sand.

❻ Calculate the rates of drainage for each cup by dividing the amount of water that drained by the time the water took to drain.

❼ For each cup, calculate the percentage of water retained by subtracting the amount of water drained from 120 mL. Divide this volume by 120.

Analysis

1. Which cup had the highest drainage rate?

2. A sample with a high drainage rate and a low percentage of water retained is highly permeable. Which sample was the most permeable? Which sample was the least permeable?

Zones of Aquifers

Soil particles attract water molecules and hold water in the soil. When there is more water than the soil can hold, gravity pulls water down through the rock layers until it reaches impermeable rock. As more water soaks into the ground, the water level rises underground and forms two distinct zones of groundwater, as shown in **Figure 3.**

Zone of Saturation

The layer of an aquifer in which the pore space is completely filled with water is the *zone of saturation*. The term *saturated* means "filled to capacity." The zone of saturation is the lower of the two zones of groundwater. The upper surface of the zone of saturation is called the **water table.**

Zone of Aeration

The zone that lies between the water table and Earth's surface is called the *zone of aeration*. The uppermost region of the zone of aeration holds soil moisture—water that forms a film around grains of topsoil. The bottom region, just above the water table, is the capillary fringe. Water is drawn up from the zone of saturation into the capillary fringe by capillary action. *Capillary action* is caused by the attraction of water molecules to other materials, such as soil. For example, when a paper towel soaks up a spill, capillary action draws moisture into the towel. Between the soil moisture region and the capillary fringe is a region that contains both air and water in its pores.

water table the upper surface of underground water; the upper boundary of the zone of saturation

SCI LINKS.
www.scilinks.org
Topic: Groundwater
Code: HQX0699

Reading Check **What are the two zones of groundwater?**
(See Appendix G for answers to Reading Checks.)

Figure 3 Groundwater is divided into zones that are defined by the percentage of water in a given volume of rock.

Capillary fringe

Soil moisture region

Water table

Zone of aeration

Zone of saturation

Movement of Groundwater

Like water on Earth's surface, groundwater flows downward in response to gravity. Water passes quickly through highly permeable rock and slowly through rock that is less permeable. The rate at which groundwater flows horizontally depends on both the permeability of the aquifer and the gradient of the water table. *Gradient* is the steepness of a slope. The speed of groundwater increases as the water table's gradient increases.

Topography and the Water Table

The depth of the water table below the ground surface depends on surface topography, the permeability of the aquifer, the amount of rainfall, and the rate at which humans use the water. Generally, shallow water tables match the contours of the surface, as shown in **Figure 4.** During periods of prolonged rainfall, the water table rises. During periods of drought, the water table falls and flattens because water that leaves the aquifer is not replaced.

Only one water table exists in most areas. In some areas, however, a layer of impermeable rock lies above the main water table. This rock layer prevents water from reaching the main zone of saturation. Water collects on top of this upper layer and creates a second water table, which is called a *perched water table*.

Reading Check What four factors affect the depth of a water table?

Figure 4 The water table generally mirrors surface topography. A perched water table lies above the main water table.

Conserving Groundwater

In many communities, groundwater is the only source of fresh water. Although groundwater is renewable, its long renewal time limits its supply. Groundwater collects and moves slowly, and the water taken from aquifers may not be replenished for hundreds or thousands of years. Communities often regulate the use of groundwater to help conserve this valuable resource. They can monitor the level of the local water table and discourage excess pumping. Some communities recycle used water. This water is purified and may be used to replenish the groundwater supply.

Surface water enters an aquifer through an area called a recharge zone. A *recharge zone* is anywhere that water from the surface can travel through permeable rock to reach an aquifer, as shown in **Figure 4.** Recharge zones are environmentally sensitive areas because pollution in the recharge zone can enter the aquifer. Therefore, recharge zones are often labeled by signs like the one shown in **Figure 5.** Pollution can enter an aquifer from waste dumps and underground storage tanks for toxic chemicals, from fertilizers and pesticides used in agriculture and on lawns, or from leaking sewage systems. If too much groundwater is pumped from an aquifer that is near the ocean, salt water from the ocean can then flow into the aquifer and contaminate the groundwater supply.

Figure 5 Water that enters this drain runs off into the Charles River and surrounding aquifers in Massachusetts.

Recharge zone

Ordinary well

Aquifer

Wells and Springs

Groundwater reaches Earth's surface through wells and springs. A *well* is a hole that is dug to below the level of the water table and through which groundwater is brought to Earth's surface. A *spring* is a natural flow of groundwater to Earth's surface in places where the ground surface dips below the water table. Wells and springs are classified into two groups—ordinary and artesian.

Ordinary Wells and Springs

Ordinary wells work only if they penetrate highly permeable sediment or rock below the water table. If the rock is not permeable enough, groundwater cannot flow into the well quickly enough to replace the water that is withdrawn.

Pumping water from a well lowers the water table around the well and forms a *cone of depression,* as shown in **Figure 6.** If too much water is taken from a well, the cone of depression may drop to the bottom of the well and the well will go dry. The lowered water table may extend several kilometers around the well and may cause surrounding wells to become dry.

Ordinary springs are usually found in rugged terrain where the ground surface drops below the water table. These springs may not flow continuously if the water table in the area has an irregular depth as a result of variable rainfall. Springs that form from perched water tables that intersect the ground surface are very sensitive to the amount of local precipitation. Thus, these springs may go dry during dry seasons or severe droughts.

READING TOOLBOX

Venn Diagrams
Draw a Venn diagram with two circles. Label one circle "Ordinary wells" and the other circle "Artesian wells." In the area where the circles overlap, write shared characteristics. In each of the other areas, write characteristics that are unique to each type of well.

Figure 6 A cone of depression develops in the water table around a pumping well.

Cone of depression

Ordinary well

Flow of water

THINK central
INTERACT ONLINE
Keyword: HQXGWEF6

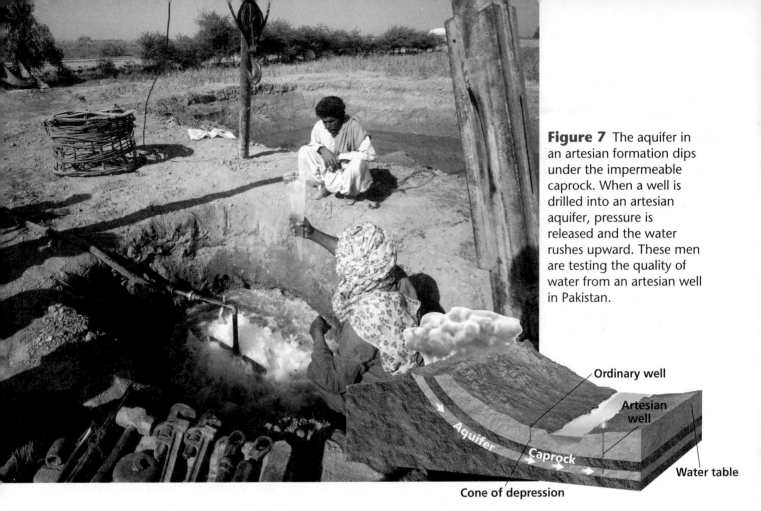

Figure 7 The aquifer in an artesian formation dips under the impermeable caprock. When a well is drilled into an artesian aquifer, pressure is released and the water rushes upward. These men are testing the quality of water from an artesian well in Pakistan.

Ordinary well

Artesian well

Aquifer

Caprock

Water table

Cone of depression

Artesian Wells and Springs

The groundwater that supplies many wells comes from local precipitation. However, the water in some wells may come from as far away as hundreds of kilometers. Water may travel through an aquifer to a distant location. Because the aquifer is so extensive, it may become part of an artesian formation, an arrangement of permeable and impermeable rock.

An **artesian formation** is a sloping layer of permeable rock that is sandwiched between two layers of impermeable rock, as shown in **Figure 7.** The permeable rock is the aquifer, and the top layer of impermeable rock is called the *caprock*. Water enters the aquifer at a recharge zone and flows downhill through the aquifer. As the water flows downward, the weight of the overlying water causes pressure in the aquifer to increase. Because the water is under pressure, when a well is drilled through the caprock, the water quickly flows up through the well and may even spout from the surface. An *artesian well* is a well through which water flows freely without being pumped.

Artesian formations are also the <u>source</u> of water for some springs. When cracks occur naturally in the caprock, water from the aquifer flows through the cracks. This flow forms *artesian springs*.

artesian formation a sloping layer of permeable rock sandwiched between two layers of impermeable rock and exposed at the surface

Academic Vocabulary

source (SOHRS) the thing from which something else comes

✔ **Reading Check** What is the difference between ordinary springs and artesian springs?

Hot Springs

Groundwater is heated when it passes through rock that has been heated by magma. Hot groundwater that is at least 37 °C and that rises to the surface before cooling produces a *hot spring*. When water in a hot spring cools, the water deposits minerals around the spring's edges. The deposits form steplike terraces of calcite called *travertine*. *Mud pots* form when chemically weathered rock mixes with hot water to form a sticky, liquid clay that bubbles at the surface. Mud pots are called *paint pots* when the clay is brightly colored by minerals or organic materials.

Geysers

Hot springs that periodically erupt from surface pools or through small vents are called *geysers*. A geyser consists of a narrow vent that connects one or more underground chambers with the surface. The hot rocks that make up the chamber walls superheat the groundwater. The water in the vent exerts pressure on the water in the chambers, which keeps the water in the chambers from boiling for a time. When the water in the vent finally begins to boil, the boiling water produces steam that pushes the water above it to the surface. Release of the water near the top of the vent relieves the pressure on the superheated water farther down. With the sudden release of pressure, the superheated water changes into steam and explodes toward the surface, as shown in **Figure 8.** The eruption continues until most of the water and steam are emptied from the vent and chambers. After the eruption, groundwater begins to collect again and the process is repeated, often at regular intervals.

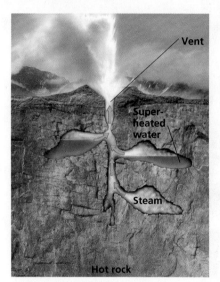

Figure 8 The vent and underground chambers of a geyser enable water to become superheated and to eventually erupt to the surface.

Labels on figure: Vent, Super-heated water, Steam, Hot rock

Section 1 Review

LA.910.2.2.3; SC.912.E.6.2; SC.912.E.7.1

Key Ideas

1. **Identify** the difference between porosity and permeability, and explain how permeability affects the flow of groundwater.

2. **Name and describe** the two zones of groundwater.

3. **Describe** how the contour of a shallow water table compares with the local topography.

4. **Explain** why ordinary springs often flow intermittently.

5. **Define** the term *cone of depression*.

6. **Compare** the rock layers in an artesian formation with those in an ordinary aquifer.

7. **Compare** artesian wells and ordinary wells.

Critical Thinking

8. **Making Inferences** Which type of well would provide a community with a more constant source of water: an ordinary well or an artesian well? Explain your answer.

9. **Identifying Relationships** Why is protecting the environment from pollution important for communities in recharge zones?

10. **Analyzing Ideas** Why don't shallow pools of hot water erupt the way that geysers erupt?

Concept Mapping

11. Use the following terms to create a concept map: *groundwater, water table, zone of saturation,* and *zone of aeration*.

Groundwater and Chemical Weathering

Key Ideas	Key Terms	Why It Matters
❯ Describe how water chemically weathers rock. ❯ Explain how caverns and sinkholes form. ❯ Identify two features of karst topography.	cavern sinkhole karst topography	Water underground causes problems as well as opportunities for adventure and discovery.

As groundwater passes through permeable rock, minerals in the rock dissolve. The warmer the rock is and the longer it is in contact with water, the greater the amount of dissolved minerals in the water. Water that contains relatively high concentrations of dissolved minerals, especially minerals rich in calcium, magnesium, and iron, is called *hard water*. Water that contains relatively low concentrations of dissolved minerals is called *soft water*.

Many people think that using hard water is unappealing. For example, more soap is needed to produce suds in hard water than in soft water. Also, many people prefer not to drink hard water because of its metallic taste. Some household appliances or fixtures may be damaged by the buildup of mineral deposits from hard water. **Figure 1** shows some results of the long-term presence of hard water.

Results of Weathering by Groundwater

One way that minerals become dissolved in groundwater is through chemical weathering. As water moves through soil and other organic materials, the water combines with carbon dioxide to form carbonic acid. This weak acid chemically weathers the rock that the acid passes through by breaking down and dissolving the minerals in the rock.

Figure 1 Soap scum forms when soap reacts with calcium carbonate in hard water (inset). During high-water stages, hard water deposited a residue of calcium carbonate on the canyon walls that border this creek.

FLORIDA STANDARDS

SC.912.E.6.4 Analyze how specific geologic processes and features are expressed in Florida and elsewhere; **SC.912.E.7.3** Differentiate and describe the various interactions among Earth systems, including: atmosphere, hydrosphere, cryosphere, geosphere, and biosphere; **SC.912.N.1.7** Recognize the role of creativity in constructing scientific questions, methods and explanations.

SC.912.E.6.2

Quick Lab
🕐 **25 min**

Chemical Weathering

Procedure

❶ Place limestone, granite, pyrite, and chalk chips into separate small beakers.

❷ Cover the rocks in 1% HCl solution.

❸ After 20 min, observe the rocks.

Analysis

1. How have the rocks changed?

2. How is this process of change like the process of chemical weathering by groundwater?

Figure 2 The formations in Carlsbad Caverns in New Mexico are made of calcite. *Which formations in this photo are stalagmites?*

cavern a natural cavity that forms in rock as a result of the dissolution of minerals; also a large cave that commonly contains many smaller, connecting chambers

Caverns

Rocks that are rich in the mineral calcite, such as limestone, are especially vulnerable to chemical weathering. Although limestone is not porous, vertical and horizontal cracks commonly cut through limestone layers. As groundwater flows through these cracks, carbonic acid slowly dissolves the limestone and enlarges the cracks. Eventually, a cavern may form. A **cavern** is a large cave that may consist of many smaller connecting chambers. Carlsbad Caverns in New Mexico is a good example of a large limestone cavern, as shown in **Figure 2.**

Stalactites and Stalagmites

Although a cavern that lies above the water table does not fill with water, water still passes through the rock surrounding the cavern. When water containing dissolved calcite drips from the ceiling of a limestone cavern, some of the calcite is deposited on the ceiling. As this calcite builds up, it forms a suspended, cone-shaped deposit called a *stalactite* (stuh LAK TIET). When drops of water fall on the cavern floor, calcite builds up to form an upward-pointing cone called a *stalagmite* (stuh LAG MIET). Often, a stalactite and a stalagmite will grow until they meet and form a calcite deposit called a *column*.

Why It Matters

Life in the Dark

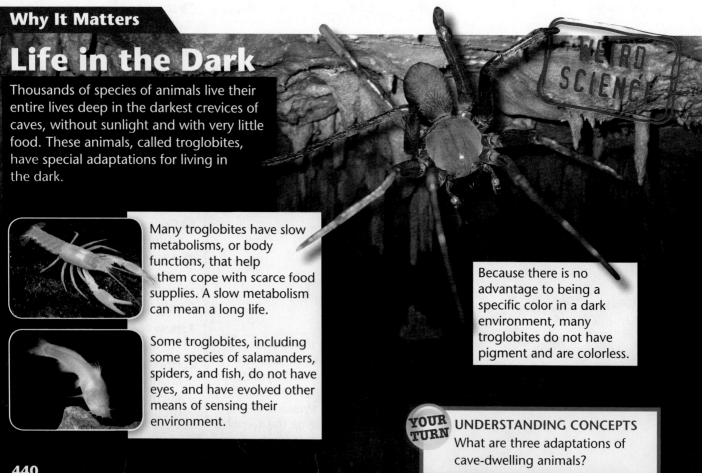

Thousands of species of animals live their entire lives deep in the darkest crevices of caves, without sunlight and with very little food. These animals, called troglobites, have special adaptations for living in the dark.

Many troglobites have slow metabolisms, or body functions, that help them cope with scarce food supplies. A slow metabolism can mean a long life.

Some troglobites, including some species of salamanders, spiders, and fish, do not have eyes, and have evolved other means of sensing their environment.

Because there is no advantage to being a specific color in a dark environment, many troglobites do not have pigment and are colorless.

YOUR TURN
UNDERSTANDING CONCEPTS
What are three adaptations of cave-dwelling animals?

440

Sinkholes

A circular depression that forms at the surface when rock dissolves, when sediment is removed, or when caves or mines collapse is a **sinkhole.** Most sinkholes form by dissolution, in which the limestone or other rock dissolves where weak areas in the rock, such as fractures, previously existed. The dissolved material is carried away from the surface, and a small depression forms. *Subsidence sinkholes* form by a similar process except that as rock dissolves, overlying sediments settle into cracks in the rock and a depression forms.

Collapse sinkholes may form when sediment below the surface is removed and an empty space forms within the sediment layer. Eventually, the overlying sediments collapse into the empty space below. Collapse sinkholes may also form during dry periods, when the water table is low and caverns are not completely filled with water. Because water no longer supports the roof of the cavern, the roof may collapse. Collapse sinkholes may develop abruptly and cause extensive damage. A collapse sinkhole is shown in **Figure 3.**

Natural Bridges

When the roof of a cavern collapses in several places, a relatively straight line of sinkholes forms. The uncollapsed rock between each pair of sinkholes forms an arch of rock called a *natural bridge,* such as the one shown in **Figure 4.** When a natural bridge first forms, it is thick, but erosion causes the bridge to become thinner. Eventually, the natural bridge may collapse.

Reading Check How are sinkholes related to natural bridges?

Figure 3 When land overlying a cavern collapses to form a sinkhole, human-made structures, such as this highway, can be damaged.

sinkhole a circular depression that forms when rock dissolves, when overlying sediment fills an existing cavity, or when the roof of an underground cavern or mine collapses

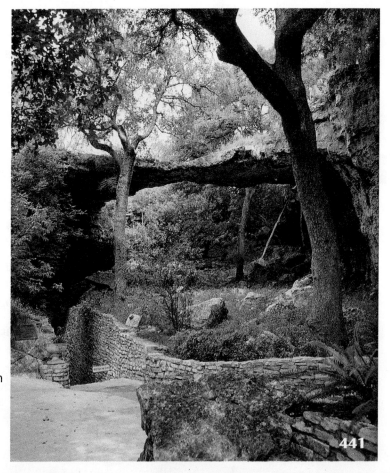

Figure 4 This natural bridge near San Antonio, Texas, formed when the roof of a large cavern room collapsed.

441

Figure 5 The Stone Forest in Yunnan, China, is a dramatic example of karst topography.

karst topography a type of irregular topography that is characterized by caverns, sinkholes, and underground drainage and that forms on limestone or other soluble rock

Academic Vocabulary

feature (FEE chuhr) the shape or form of a thing; characteristic

Karst Topography

Irregular topography caused by the chemical weathering of limestone or other soluble rock by groundwater is called **karst topography.** Common features of karst topography include many closely spaced sinkholes and caverns. In karst regions, streams often disappear into cracks in the rock and then emerge in caves or through other cracks many kilometers away. In the United States, there is extensive karst topography in Kentucky, Tennessee, southern Indiana, northern Florida, and Puerto Rico.

Generally, karst topography forms in regions where the climate is humid and where limestone formations exist at or near the surface. The plentiful precipitation in these regions commonly becomes groundwater. The groundwater flows through the limestone and reacts chemically with the calcite in the limestone. As the groundwater dissolves the limestone, cracks in the rock enlarge to form cave systems. Features of karst topography can form in relatively dry regions, too. In these areas, sinkholes may form very close together and leave dramatic arches and spires, as shown in **Figure 5.** Karst topography in these regions may indicate that the climate is becoming drier.

Section 2 Review

LA.910.2.2.3; SC.912.E.6.2; SC.912.E.7.1

Key Ideas

1. **Describe** how water chemically weathers rock.

2. **Explain** how caverns form.

3. **Explain** the difference between stalactites and stalagmites.

4. **Identify** three common features of karst topography.

5. **Describe** two ways in which a natural bridge might form.

6. **Compare** sinkholes and caverns.

Critical Thinking

7. **Making Inferences** If an area has a dry climate, how can the area have karst topography?

8. **Identifying Relationships** Why might you expect to find springs in regions that have karst topography?

Concept Mapping

9. Use the following terms to create a concept map: *groundwater, stalagmite, stalactite, natural bridge, cavern,* and *sinkhole.*

Is it Possible to Drown in Quicksand?

REAL WORLD

In certain areas where groundwater is near the land surface, quicksand can form. Quicksand is made of fine grains of sand and clay saturated with water. When a person steps on quicksand, the pressure causes water below the sand to move up, turning the sand into a thick jelly-like substance.

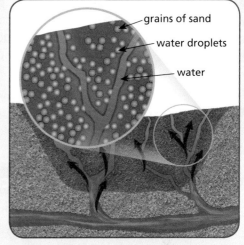

grains of sand
water droplets
water

When force is applied to quicksand, groundwater moves up, resulting in a thick and sandy fluid.

Have you ever seen a movie where a character falls into quicksand and completely disappears? This could not actually happen. A person can sink in quicksand, but only to the waist, because humans are not as dense as quicksand.

It is easy, however, to become trapped in quicksand. If you were stuck in quicksand, you could not simply be pulled out. Instead, you should wiggle your legs to slowly make a space around your body. Water can flow into this space and let you pull yourself free.

WARNING
Soft Sand & Mud

YOUR TURN

UNDERSTANDING CONCEPTS
What happens when someone steps on quicksand?

APPLYING INFORMATION
Describe the porosity and permeability of quicksand.

Porosity

Whether soil is composed of coarse pieces of rock or very fine particles, some pore space remains between the pieces of solid material. Porosity is calculated by dividing the volume of the pore space by the total volume of the soil sample. Thus, if 50 cm³ of soil contains 5.0 cm³ of pore space, the porosity of the soil sample is

$$5.0 \text{ cm}^3/50 \text{ cm}^3 = 0.10 \times 100 = 10\%.$$

The result is generally written as a percentage. In this lab, you will measure and compare the porosity of three samples that represent rock particles.

What You'll Do

> **Measure** the porosity of a given volume of beads for each of three samples: large beads, small beads, and a mix of large and small beads.

> **Describe** how particle size and sorting of a material affect porosity.

What You'll Need

beads, plastic, 4 mm (400)
beads, plastic, 8 mm (200)
beaker, 100 mL
graduated cylinder, 100 mL

Safety

Procedure

1. Fill a beaker to the top with water. Pour the water into a graduated cylinder and record the volume of water.

2. Dry the beaker, and fill it to the top with large (8 mm) plastic beads. Gently tap the beaker to settle and compact the beads. Add more beads to fill the beaker until the beads are level with the top. Record the total volume of the beads, which includes the pore space volume.

3. Fill the graduated cylinder with water to the top mark, and record the volume of water. Carefully pour the water from the cylinder into the beaker filled with the large beads until the water level just reaches the top of the beads.

Step 3

④ To determine the amount of water that you added to the beaker, subtract the volume of water in the graduated cylinder from the volume that you recorded in step 3. This difference is the volume of the pore space between the beads. Record the volume of the pore space.

⑤ Calculate the porosity of the beads. Record the porosity as a decimal and as a percentage.

⑥ Repeat steps 2 to 5 using small (4 mm) beads.

⑦ Drain and dry both sets of beads. Mix together equal volumes of the small and large beads. Using the mixed-size beads, repeat steps 2 to 5.

Step ④

Analysis

1. **Analyzing Methods** Do the 8 mm beads in step 2 represent well-sorted large rock particles, well-sorted small rock particles, or unsorted rock particles?

2. **Analyzing Methods** Do the 4 mm beads in step 6 represent well-sorted large rock particles, well-sorted small rock particles, or unsorted rock particles?

3. **Analyzing Methods** Do the mixed beads in step 7 represent well-sorted or unsorted rock particles?

4. **Making Graphs** Compare your measurements of the porosity of the large beads with your measurements of the porosity of the small beads. Make a graph that shows bead size on the *x*-axis and porosity on the *y*-axis.

5. **Drawing Conclusions** In well-sorted sediment, does porosity depend on particle size? Explain your answer.

6. **Determining Cause and Effect** How did mixing the bead sizes affect the porosity? Explain the effect.

Extension

Designing Experiments How would mixing coarse gravel with fine sand affect the porosity of the gravel? Conduct an experiment to find out if your answer is correct.

Water Level in the Southern Ogallala

EXPLANATION
WATER-LEVEL CHANGE, IN FEET

Declines
- More than 150
- 100 to 150
- 50 to 100
- 25 to 50
- 10 to 25

No substantial change -10 to +10

Rises
- 10 to 25
- 25 to 50
- More than 50

Area of little or no saturated thickness

U — Faults -- U, upthrown side

County line

State line

Map Skills Activity

This map shows water-level change from predevelopment to 2005 in regions of the Ogallala Aquifer, which supplies much of the drinking water in the midwestern United States. Use the map to answer the questions below.

1. **Using a Key** From predevelopment to 2005, how many states had areas in which the water level declined more than 150 feet?

2. **Using a Key** From predevelopment to 2005, how many states had areas in which the water level rose?

3. **Identifying Trends** How has the water level changed overall, from predevelopment to 2005?

4. **Analyzing Relationships** What may have caused the trend that you identified in question 3?

5. **Making Predictions** How do you think the aquifer's overall water level will change over the next 50 years? Explain.

Key Ideas

Key Terms

Section 1

Water Beneath the Surface

❯ The porosity and permeability of an aquifer affect the flow of groundwater.

❯ The water table is the upper surface of the zone of saturation, beneath the land surface and the zone of aeration.

❯ A well is a hole dug to below the water table, while a spring is a natural flow of groundwater to Earth's surface. Water also may flow naturally to Earth's surface through artesian formations.

❯ Hot springs and geysers are two land features formed by hot groundwater.

groundwater, p. 431
aquifer, p. 431
porosity, p. 431
permeability, p. 432
water table, p. 433
artesian formation,
   p. 437

Section 2

Groundwater and Chemical Weathering

❯ Water combines with carbon dioxide to form carbonic acid, which breaks down and dissolves minerals in rock that the water passes through.

❯ Caverns and sinkholes form as limestone or other rock is slowly dissolved by chemical weathering.

❯ Features of karst topography include caverns, sinkholes, and underground drainage.

cavern, p. 440
sinkhole, p. 441
karst topography,
   p. 442

1. **Temporal Language** Create a temporal language table for the page in Section 1 that discusses hot springs and geysers. Find at least five words or phrases that refer to time and record them in the table. Use the table shown in the Reading Toolbox at the beginning of the chapter as a model.

USING KEY TERMS

Use each of the following terms in a separate sentence.

2. *groundwater* SC.912.E.6.2

3. *water table* SC.912.E.6.2

4. *karst topography* SC.912.E.6.2

For each pair of terms, explain how the meanings of the terms differ.

5. *geyser* and *hot spring* SC.912.E.6.2

6. *porosity* and *permeability* SC.912.E.6.2

7. *well* and *spring* SC.912.E.6.2

8. *ordinary well* and *artesian well* SC.912.E.6.2

9. *stalactite* and *stalagmite* SC.912.E.6.2

UNDERSTANDING KEY IDEAS

10. Any body of rock or sediment in which water can flow and be stored is called a(n) SC.912.E.6.2
   a. well.
   b. aquifer.
   c. sinkhole.
   d. artesian formation.

11. The percentage of open space in a given volume of rock is the rock's SC.912.E.6.2
   a. viscosity.
   b. capillary fringe.
   c. permeability.
   d. porosity.

12. The ease with which water can pass through a rock or sediment is called SC.912.E.6.2
   a. permeability.   c. porosity.
   b. carbonation.   d. velocity.

13. The slope of a water table is called the SC.912.E.6.2
   a. gradient.   c. permeability.
   b. porosity.   d. aquifer.

14. A natural flow of groundwater that has reached the surface is a(n) SC.912.E.6.2
   a. spring.   c. aquifer.
   b. well.   d. travertine.

15. Pumping water from a well causes a local lowering of the water table known as a SC.912.E.6.2
   a. cone of depression.
   b. horizontal fissure.
   c. hot spring.
   d. sinkhole.

16. Calcite formations that hang from the ceiling of a cavern are called SC.912.E.6.2
   a. stalagmites.
   b. sinks.
   c. stalactites.
   d. aquifers.

17. Caverns and sinkholes are typical in areas of SC.912.E.6.2
   a. sink topography.
   b. karst topography.
   c. low porosity.
   d. artesian formations.

18. When the roofs of several caverns collapse, the uncollapsed rock between sinkholes can form SC.912.E.6.2
   a. natural bridges.
   b. stalactites.
   c. limestone topography.
   d. artesian formations.

19. A layer of permeable rock that is sandwiched between layers of impermeable rock is called SC.912.E.6.2
   a. a natural bridge.
   b. karst topography.
   c. limestone topography.
   d. an artesian formation.

SHORT ANSWER

20. In regions where the water table is at the surface of the land, what type of terrain would you expect to find? SC.912.E.6.2

21. Explain the process that forms stalactites and stalagmites. Name another process in nature that produces shapes similar to the shapes of stalactites. SC.912.E.6.2

22. How does a mud pot form? SC.912.E.6.2

23. Describe the zones of an aquifer. SC.912.E.6.2

24. What are two ways that groundwater reaches Earth's surface? SC.912.E.6.2

25. How are caverns and sinkholes related? SC.912.E.6.2

26. What causes a geyser to erupt? SC.912.E.6.2

27. Why does it take a long time to replenish a depleted aquifer? SC.912.E.6.2

CRITICAL THINKING

28. **Making Inferences** In what type of location might pumping too much water from an aquifer lead to contamination of the groundwater supply? Explain how the water becomes contaminated. SC.912.E.6.2

29. **Analyzing Relationships** Describe an artesian formation, and explain how the water in an artesian well may have entered the ground many hundreds of kilometers away.

30. **Analyzing Ideas** Explain how a rock can be both porous and impermeable. SC.912.E.6.2

31. **Identifying Relationships** Do you think that an area that has karst topography would have many surface streams or few surface streams? Explain your answer. SC.912.E.6.2

CONCEPT MAPPING

32. Use the following terms to create a concept map: *porosity, sorting, permeability, ordinary well, artesian formation, highly permeable rock,* and *impermeable rock.* SC.912.E.6.2

MATH SKILLS

33. **Evaluating Data** People in Oklahoma use 11 billion gallons of water every day. The renewable water supply in Oklahoma is 68.7 billion gallons per day. What percentage of the renewable water supply do Oklahomans use every day? SC.912.E.6.4

34. **Making Conversions** In an average aquifer, groundwater moves about 50 m per year. At this rate, how long would the groundwater take to flow 1 km? SC.912.E.6.2

WRITING SKILLS

35. **Writing Persuasively** Write a persuasive essay about the importance of conserving groundwater. SC.912.E.6.2

36. **Communicating Main Ideas** Explain how overpumping at one well can affect groundwater availability in surrounding areas. SC.912.E.6.2

INTERPRETING GRAPHICS

The graph below shows the average annual decline in water level for the Ogallala Aquifer over 30 years. Use the graph below to answer the questions that follow.

Average Annual Rate of Decline by Decade for the Ogallala Aquifer, 1969–1999

37. Which region had the highest rate of decline from 1969 to 1999? SC.912.E.6.4

38. Over which decade did the aquifer have the lowest rate of decline? SC.912.E.6.4

39. Which years would you expect to have a higher rate of decline: the years 1999 to 2009 or the years 1989 to 1999? Explain your answer. SC.912.E.6.4

Understanding Concepts

Directions (1–10): For each question, write on a separate sheet of paper the letter of the correct answer.

1 Which of the following statements is FALSE?
  A. Permeability affects flow through an aquifer.
  B. Groundwater can be stored in an aquifer.
  C. Aquifers are always a single rock layer.
  D. Well-sorted sediment holds the most water.

2 The amount of surface water that seeps into the pores between rock particles is influenced by which of the following factors?
  F. rock type, land slope, and climate
  G. rock type, land slope, and capillary fringe
  H. rock type, land slope, and sea level
  I. rock type, land slope, and recharging

3 Shanghai removed 96.03 million cubic meters of groundwater in 2002 but replaced only 13.75 million cubic meters. What was the rate of groundwater depletion in Shanghai that year?
  A. 109.78 million cubic meters of groundwater
  B. 1,320.41 million cubic meters of groundwater
  C. 6.98 million cubic meters of groundwater
  D. 82.28 million cubic meters of groundwater

4 The formation of karst topography is caused by
  F. the physical weathering of limestone.
  G. the chemical weathering of limestone.
  H. closely-spaced sinkholes.
  I. irregular topography.

5 What quality distinguishes an ordinary well from an artesian well?
  A. Water flows freely from an ordinary well.
  B. Water is pressurized in an ordinary well.
  C. Water must be pumped from an ordinary well.
  D. Water comes from rainfall in an ordinary well.

6 Which of the following sediments has the highest porosity?
  F. poorly sorted sediment
  G. tightly packed sediments
  H. coarse-grained sediment
  I. fine-grained sediment

7 Many communities regulate or monitor the use of groundwater to conserve water resources. One way by which communities can conserve ground water is
  A. pumping water from an aquifer and storing it elsewhere.
  B. recycling used water.
  C. allowing water to drain from sewage systems into an aquifer.
  D. enlarging a recharge zone.

8 Which of the following statements best describes the relationship between porosity and permeability?
  F. Porosity and permeability are not related.
  G. Porosity describes how water flows through permeable rock.
  H. Permeability is the ease with which water passes through porous rock.
  I. Porous rock is always permeable.

9 Which of the following statements is NOT a way that sinkholes form?
  A. Rock collapses and dissolves, leaving a sinkhole.
  B. Sediments dissolve, leaving an empty space into which overlying sediments collapse.
  C. Rock dissolves, and overlying sediment settles into cracks.
  D. Rock dissolves and is carried away, leaving a small depression.

10 How does groundwater break down limestone?
  F. by mechanical weathering
  G. by forming a weak acid
  H. by carrying a load
  I. by absorbing minerals

Interpreting Graphics

Directions (11–12): For each question below, record the correct answer on a separate sheet of paper.

The Water Cycle

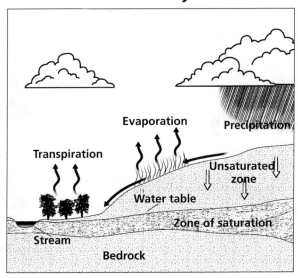

11 Which process occurs where the water table intersects with the surface?
   A. stream formation
   B. runoff
   C. groundwater movement
   D. saturation

Water Use for a Family of Four

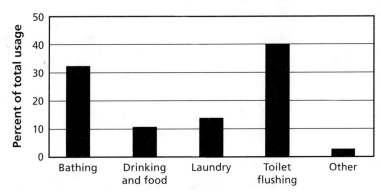

12 A family of four wants to conserve water by halving their water use in one of the five areas described in the graph above. In which area should the family halve their water use to yield the greatest conservation of water?
   F. bathing
   G. drinking and food
   H. laundry
   I. toilet flushing

Test Tip

Remember that if you can eliminate two of four answer choices, your chances of choosing the correct answer will double.

Glaciers

Why It Matters

Glaciers—huge masses of slowly moving ice—reshape Earth's surface by carving valleys, forming lakes, and moving sediment. Glaciers provide information about past and present climates, and they are key indicators of current climate changes.

Inquiry Lab

🕐 **20 min**

Iceberg in a Glass

Find the volume of an **ice cube**. Place your "iceberg" in a **glass** that is two-thirds full of **water**. Determine the volume of the ice that is floating above the water and the volume of the ice that is below the water. Without disturbing the glass, observe what happens as the ice melts. Record your observations.

Fill another **glass** two-thirds full of water. Add **salt**, stirring until no more salt dissolves. Find the volume of a new **ice cube**. Place your new "iceberg" in the glass with the salt water. Determine the volume of the ice above and below the water. Record your observations as the ice melts.

Calculate the percentage of the iceberg that is above the water in each glass.

Questions to Get You Started

1. If a rectangular iceberg with a volume of 60,000 m³ is floating in the ocean, what volume of ice is above the surface of the water? Explain your answer.

2. Describe what happened as the ice melted in each glass. What accounts for any differences between the two glasses?

SC.912.E.6.5

453

READING TOOLBOX

These reading tools will help you learn the material in this chapter.

Word Families

Glacier In this chapter, you will learn many two-word terms, including *alpine glacier* and *glacial drift*, that contain the word *glacier* or *glacial*. Both *glacier* and *glacial* come from the Latin word *glacies,* meaning "ice."

Your Turn As you read this chapter, make a table like the one below. In the first column, write all the terms that include either *glacier* or *glacial*. In the second column, define the other word in each term. Then write your own definition of the whole two-word term.

Term	Definition of second word	Definition of whole two-word term
alpine glacier	*alpine* = of or like mountains	
continental glacier	continent =	
glacial drift	drift =	
glacial period	period =	

Classification

Classifying Glacial Depositions

Classification is a tool for organizing objects and ideas by grouping them into categories. The categories are based on defining characteristics of the objects and ideas. For example, the following table shows how landforms produced by glacial erosion can be classified by their shape and location.

Landform produced by glacial erosion	Shape	Location
cirque	bowl-shaped depression	floor of a valley
arête	sharp, jagged ridge	between cirques

Your Turn As you read Section 2, create a table like the one above to show how glacial depositions can be classified by their composition and by where and how they are deposited.

FoldNotes

Booklet FoldNote A booklet is a useful tool for taking notes as you read a chapter. Each page of the booklet can be used to record details about one of the main topics in the chapter.

Your Turn Create a booklet FoldNote as described in Appendix A. On each page of the booklet, write one of the main topics in Sections 1 and 2: Formation of Glaciers, Types of Glaciers, Movement of Glaciers, Features of Glaciers, Glacial Erosion, Glacial Deposition, and Glacial Lakes. As you read, take notes about each main topic on the appropriate page of your booklet.

Formation of Glaciers

For more information on how to use these and other tools, see **Appendix A.**

SECTION 1 Glaciers: Moving Ice

Key Ideas	Key Terms	Why It Matters
❯ Describe how glaciers form. ❯ Compare two main kinds of glaciers. ❯ Explain two processes by which glaciers move. ❯ Describe three features of glaciers.	glacier alpine glacier continental glacier basal slip internal plastic flow crevasse	Because the size of glaciers depends on climate, glaciers are also an indicator of climate change. Understanding how glaciers form and move can help us make predictions about climate.

A single snowflake is lighter than a feather. However, if you squeeze a handful of snow, you make a firm snowball. In a process similar to making a snowball, natural forces compact snow to make a large mass of moving ice called a **glacier.**

Formation of Glaciers

At high elevations and in polar regions, snow may remain on the ground all year and form an almost motionless mass of permanent snow and ice called a *snowfield*. Snowfields form as ice and snow accumulate above the snowline. The *snowline* is the elevation above which ice and snow remain throughout the year, as shown in **Figure 1.**

Average temperatures at high elevations and in polar regions are always near or below the freezing point of water. So, snow that falls there accumulates year after year. Cycles of partial melting and refreezing change the snow into grainy ice called *firn*.

In deep layers of snow and firn, the pressure of the overlying layers flattens the ice grains and squeezes the air from between the grains. The continued buildup of snow and firn forms a glacier that moves downslope or outward under its own weight.

The size of a glacier depends on the amount of snowfall received and the amount of ice lost. When new snow is added faster than ice and snow melt, the glacier gets bigger. When the ice melts faster than snow is added, the glacier gets smaller. Small differences in average yearly temperatures and snowfall may upset the balance between snowfall and ice loss. Thus, changes in the size of a glacier may indicate climatic change.

FLORIDA STANDARDS

SC.912.E.7.3 Differentiate and describe the various interactions among Earth systems, including: atmosphere, hydrosphere, cryosphere, geosphere, and biosphere.

glacier a large mass of moving ice

SCLINKS

www.scilinks.org
Topic: Glaciers
Code: HQX0675

Figure 1 The snowline on the Grand Teton Mountains at Grand Teton National Park, Wyoming, is more than 3,000 m above sea level.

Figure 2 An alpine glacier (above) descends through Thompson Pass in Alaska. A continental glacier (right) covers much of the land surface in Greenland.

READING TOOLBOX

Classification
As you read this page, create a classification table like the one at the beginning of this chapter. List the two main types of glaciers, describe their characteristics, and give examples.

Types of Glaciers

The two main categories used to classify glaciers are alpine and continental. An **alpine glacier** is a narrow, wedge-shaped mass of ice that forms in a mountainous region and that is confined to a small area by surrounding topography, as shown in **Figure 2**. Alpine glaciers are located in Alaska, the Himalaya Mountains, the Andes, the Alps, and New Zealand.

Continental glaciers are massive sheets of ice that may cover millions of square kilometers, that may be thousands of meters thick, and that are not confined by surrounding topography, as shown in **Figure 2**. Today, continental glaciers, also called *ice sheets*, exist only in Greenland and Antarctica. The Antarctic ice sheet covers an area of more than 13 million km^2 and is more than 4,000 m thick in some places. The Greenland ice sheet covers 1.7 million km^2 of land, and its maximum thickness is more than 3,000 m. If these ice sheets melted, the water they contain would raise the worldwide sea level by more than 50 m.

Reading Check **Where can you find continental glaciers today?** (See Appendix G for answers to Reading Checks.)

Movement of Glaciers

Glaciers are sometimes called "rivers of ice." Gravity causes both glaciers and rivers to flow downward. However, glaciers and rivers move in different ways. Unlike water in a river, glacial ice cannot move rapidly or flow easily around barriers. In a year, some glaciers may travel only a few centimeters, while others may move a kilometer or more. Glaciers move by two basic processes—basal slip and internal plastic flow.

Basal Slip

One way that glaciers move is by slipping over a thin layer of water and sediment that lies between the ice and the ground. The weight of the ice in a glacier exerts pressure that lowers the melting point of ice. As a result, the ice melts where the glacier touches the ground. The water mixes with sediment at the base of the glacier. This mixture acts as a lubricant between the ice and the underlying surface. The process that lubricates a glacier's base and causes the glacier to slide forward is called **basal slip.**

Basal slip also allows a glacier to work its way over small barriers in its path by melting and then refreezing. For example, if the ice pushes against a rock barrier, the pressure causes some of the ice to melt. The water from the melted ice travels around the barrier and freezes again as the pressure is removed.

Internal Plastic Flow

Glaciers also move by a process called **internal plastic flow.** In this process, pressure deforms grains of ice under a glacier. As the grains deform, they slide over each other and cause the glacier to flow slowly. However, the rate of internal plastic flow varies for different parts of a glacier, as shown in **Figure 3.** The slope of the ground and the thickness and temperature of the ice determine the rate at which ice flows at a given point. The edges of a glacier move more slowly than the center because of friction with underlying rock. For this same reason, a glacier moves more quickly near its surface than near its base.

basal slip the process that causes the ice at the base of a glacier to melt and the glacier to slide

internal plastic flow the process by which glaciers flow slowly as grains of ice deform under pressure and slide over each other

 SC.912.E.6.2

Quick Lab

⏱ 15 min

Slipping Ice

Procedure

❶ Squeeze flat a handful of snow or shaved ice until you notice a change in the particles.

❷ Place the squeezed ice on a tray. Place a heavy weight on the squeezed ice.

❸ Lift one end of the tray to a 30° incline, and record your observations.

Analysis

1. What does squeezing do to the particles of snow or ice?

2. How is squeezing the snow or ice similar to the formation of a glacier?

3. What did you observe when you placed the squeezed ice on the tray? What glacial movement process is modeled here?

Fastest rate of ice flow

Figure 3 A line of blue stakes driven into an alpine glacier moves to the position of the red stakes as the glacier flows. This measurement shows that the central part of the glacier moves faster than its edges.

Figure 4 Crevasses (right) are large cracks in a glacier. The composite image below shows what an iceberg might look like if you could see the entire iceberg.

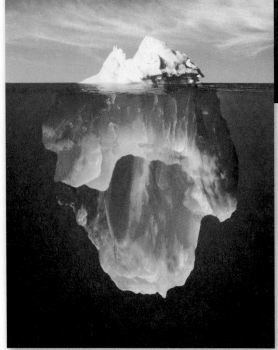

crevasse in a glacier, a large crack or fissure that results from ice movement

Features of Glaciers

While the interior of a glacier moves by internal plastic flow and the entire glacier moves by basal slip, the low pressure on the surface ice causes the surface ice to remain brittle. The glacier flows unevenly beneath the surface, and regions of tension and compression build under the brittle surface. As a result, large cracks, called **crevasses** (kruh VAS uhz), form on the surface, as shown in **Figure 4.** Some crevasses may be as deep as 50 m!

Continental glaciers move outward in all directions from their centers toward the edges of their landmasses. Some parts of the ice sheets may move out over the ocean and form *ice shelves*. When the tides rise and fall, large blocks of ice, called *icebergs*, may break from the ice shelves and drift into the ocean. Because most of an iceberg is below the surface of the water, as shown in Figure 4, icebergs pose a hazard to ships. The area above water of one of the largest icebergs ever observed in the Antarctic was twice the size of Connecticut!

Section 1 Review

LA.910.2.2.3; SC.912.E.6.2; SC.912.E.7.1

Key Ideas

1. **Identify** two regions in which snow accumulates year after year.

2. **Describe** the process by which glaciers form.

3. **Compare** an alpine glacier and a continental glacier.

4. **Explain** how internal plastic flow and basal slip move glaciers.

5. **Describe** two features of glaciers.

6. **Compare** a glacier and a snowfield.

7. **Explain** how a crevasse forms.

Critical Thinking

8. **Making Inferences** If glaciers could move only by internal plastic flow, what might happen to the rate at which glaciers move? Explain your answer.

9. **Identifying Relationships** How can changes in the size of a glacier indicate climate change?

10. **Analyzing Ideas** If icebergs are visible at sea level, why do they pose a hazard to ships?

Concept Mapping

11. Use the following terms to create a concept map: *glacier, firn, snowline, snowfield, alpine glacier, continental glacier, basal slip, internal plastic flow, ice shelf, iceberg,* and *crevasse.*

Glacial Erosion and Deposition

<table>
<tr>
<th>Key Ideas</th>
<th colspan="2">Key Terms</th>
<th>Why It Matters</th>
</tr>
<tr>
<td>
❯ Describe the landscape features that are produced by glacial erosion.

❯ Name and describe five features formed by glacial deposition.

❯ Explain how glacial lakes form.
</td>
<td>
cirque

arête

horn

erratic

glacial drift
</td>
<td>
till

moraine

kettle

esker
</td>
<td>
While glaciers have only affected the surface of the northern part of the United States, they are responsible for many of our nation's natural wonders.
</td>
</tr>
</table>

Many of the landforms in Canada and in the northern United States were created by glaciers. Large lakes, solitary boulders on flat plains, and jagged ridges are just a few examples of landforms created by glaciers. Glaciers created these landforms through the processes of erosion and deposition.

Glacial Erosion

Like rivers, glaciers are agents of erosion. Both a river and a glacier can pick up and carry rock and sediment. However, because of the size and density of glaciers, landforms that result from glacial action are very different from those that rivers form. For example, deep depressions in rock form when a moving glacier loosens and dislodges, or plucks, a rock from the bedrock at the base or side of the glacier. The rock plucked by the glacier is then dragged across the bedrock and causes abrasions. As shown in **Figure 1**, long parallel grooves in the bedrock are left behind and show the direction of the glacier's movement.

FLORIDA STANDARDS

SC.912.E.7.3 Differentiate and describe the various interactions among Earth systems, including: atmosphere, hydrosphere, cryosphere, geosphere, and biosphere; **SC.912.N.3.5** Describe the function of models in science, and identify the wide range of models used in science.

Direction of glacier movement

Grooves

Figure 1 As a glacier moves, it picks up and carries rocks from the bedrock. These grooves at Kelly's Island in Ohio were carved by a glacier 35,000 years ago.

Figure 2 When glaciers erode mountainous regions, characteristic landforms develop. These landforms can be identified after the glaciers retreat. *Identify the jagged ridge that separates bowl-shaped depressions.*

cirque a deep and steep bowl-like depression produced by glacial erosion

arête a sharp, jagged ridge that forms between cirques

horn a sharp, pyramid-like peak that forms because of the erosion of cirques

Academic Vocabulary

projection (proh JEK shuhn) an extension or a structural outgrowth

Landforms Created by Glacial Erosion

Glaciers have shaped many mountain ranges and have created unique landforms by erosive processes. The glacial processes that change the shape of mountains begin in the upper end of the valley where an alpine glacier forms. As a glacier moves through a narrow, V-shaped river valley, rock from the valley walls breaks off and the walls become steeper. The moving glacier also pulls blocks of rock from the floor of the valley. These actions create a bowl-shaped depression called a **cirque** (SUHRK). A sharp, jagged ridge called an **arête** (uh RAYT) forms between cirques. When several arêtes join, they form a sharp, pyramid-like peak called a **horn,** as shown in **Figure 2.**

As the glacier flows down through an existing valley, the glacier picks up large amounts of rock. These rock fragments, which range in size from microscopic particles to large boulders, become embedded in the ice.

Rock particles embedded in the ice may polish solid rock as the ice moves over the rock. Large rocks carried by the ice may gouge deep grooves in the bedrock. Glaciers may also round large rock projections. These rounded projections usually have a smooth, gently sloping side facing the direction from which the glacier came. The other side is steep and jagged because rock is pulled away as the ice passes. The resulting rounded knobs of rock are called *roches moutonnées* (ROHSH ᴍoo tuh NAY), which means "sheep rocks" in French.

✓ **Reading Check** **How does a glacier form a cirque?**

U-Shaped Valleys

A stream forms the V shape of a valley. As a glacier scrapes away a valley's walls and floor, this original V shape becomes a U shape, as shown in **Figure 3**. Because glacial erosion is the only way by which U-shaped valleys form, scientists can use this feature to determine whether a valley has been glaciated in the past.

Small tributary glaciers in adjacent valleys may flow into a main alpine glacier. Because a small tributary glacier has less ice and less cutting power than the main alpine glacier does, the small glacier's U-shaped valley is not cut as deeply into the mountains. When the ice melts, the tributary valley is suspended high above the main valley floor and is called a *hanging valley*. When a stream flows from a hanging valley, a waterfall forms.

Figure 3 Jollie Valley, a U-shaped glaciated valley, is located in the Southern Alps of New Zealand.

Erosion by Continental Glaciers

The landscape eroded by continental glaciers differs from the sharp, rugged features eroded by alpine glaciers. Continental glaciers erode by leveling landforms to produce a smooth, rounded landscape. Continental glaciers smooth and round exposed rock surfaces in a way similar to the way that bulldozers flatten landscapes. Rock surfaces are also scratched and grooved by rocks carried at the base of the ice sheet. These scratches and grooves are parallel to the direction of glacial movement.

SC.912.E.6.2

Quick Lab   Glacial Erosion

⏱ 25 min

Procedure

❶ Put a mixture of sand, gravel, and rock in the bottom of a 15 cm × 10 cm × 5 cm plastic container. Fill the container with water to a depth of about 4 cm. Freeze the container until the water is solid. Remove the ice block from the container.

❷ Use a rolling pin or large dowel to flatten some modeling clay into a rectangle about 20 cm × 10 cm × 1 cm.

❸ Grasp the ice block firmly with a hand towel. Place the block with the gravel-and-rock side down at one end of the clay. Press down on the ice block, and push it along the length of the flat clay surface.

❹ Sketch the pattern made in the clay by the ice block.

❺ Next, press a 2 cm layer of damp sand into the bottom of a shallow, rectangular box. As in step 3, push the ice block along the surface of the sand, but press down lightly.

❻ Repeat steps 3 and 4, but use a soft, wooden board in place of the clay.

Analysis

1. Describe the effects of the ice block on the clay, on the sand, and on the wood.

2. Did any clay, sand, or wood become mixed with material from the ice block? Did the ice deposit material on any surface?

3. What glacial land features are represented by the features of the clay model? the sand model? the wood model?

Section 2   Glacial Erosion and Deposition   **461**

Glacial Deposition

Glaciers are also agents of deposition. Deposition occurs when a glacier melts. A glacier will melt if it reaches low, warm elevations or if the climate becomes warmer. As the glacier melts, it deposits all of the material that it has accumulated, which may range in size from fine sediment to large rocks.

Large rocks that a glacier transports from a distant source are called **erratics.** Because a glacier carries an erratic a long distance, the composition of an erratic usually differs from that of the bedrock over which the erratic lies.

Various other landforms develop as glaciers melt and deposit sediment, as shown in **Figure 4.** The general term for all sediments deposited by a glacier is **glacial drift.** Unsorted glacial drift that is deposited directly from a melting glacier is called **till.** Till is composed of sediments from the base of the glacier and is commonly left behind when glacial ice melts. Another type of glacial drift is *stratified drift.* Stratified drift is material that has been sorted and deposited in layers by streams flowing from the melted ice, or *meltwater.*

erratic a large rock transported from a distant source by a glacier

glacial drift rock material carried and deposited by glaciers

till unsorted rock material that is deposited directly by a melting glacier

Figure 4 Moraines, glacial lakes, drumlins, meltwater streams, and outwash plains are some examples of landforms created by glacial deposition.

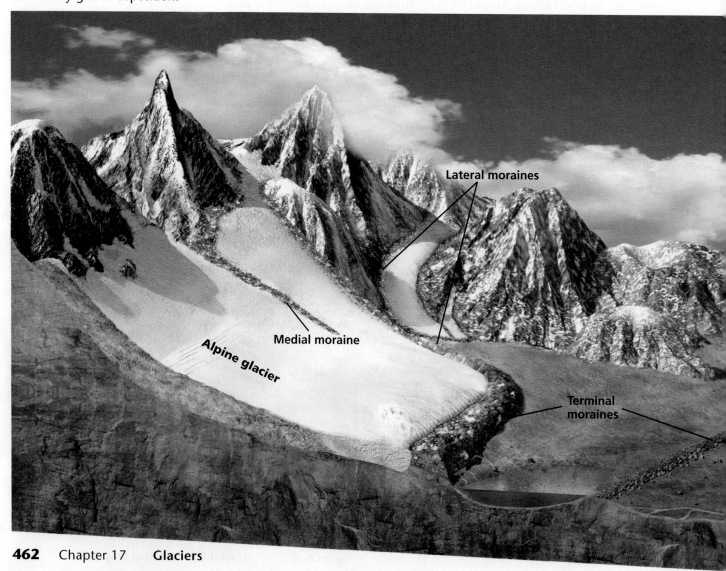

Lateral moraines

Medial moraine

Alpine glacier

Terminal moraines

Till Deposits

Landforms that result when a glacier deposits till are called *moraines*. **Moraines** are ridges of unsorted sediment on the ground or on the glacier itself. There are several types of moraines, as shown in **Figure 4**. A *lateral moraine* is a moraine that is deposited along the sides of an alpine glacier, usually as a long ridge. When two or more alpine glaciers join, their adjacent lateral moraines combine to form a *medial moraine*.

The unsorted material left beneath the glacier when the ice melts is the *ground moraine*. The soil of a ground moraine is commonly very rocky. An ice sheet may mold ground moraine into clusters of drumlins. *Drumlins* are long, low, tear-shaped mounds of till. The long axes of the drumlins are parallel to the direction of glacial movement.

Terminal moraines are small ridges of till that are deposited at the leading edge of a melting glacier. These moraines have many depressions that may contain lakes or ponds. Large terminal moraines, some of which are more than 100 km long, can be seen across the Midwest, especially south of the Great Lakes.

Reading Check Which glacial deposit is a tear-shaped mound of sediment?

moraine a landform that is made from unsorted sediments deposited by a glacier

Erratics

Outwash plain

Drumlins

Kettle

Meltwater streams

Continental glacier

Figure 5 This kettle lake in Saskatchewan, Canada, formed as a result of glacial deposition.

Outwash Plains

When a glacier melts, streams of meltwater flow from the edges, the surface, and beneath the glacier. Glacial meltwater may have beautiful colors, such as milky white, emerald green, or turquoise blue, because it carries very fine sediment. The meltwater carries drift as well as rock particles and deposits them in front of the glacier as a large outwash plain. An *outwash plain* is a deposit of stratified drift that lies in front of a terminal moraine and is crossed by many meltwater streams.

Kettles

Most outwash plains are pitted with depressions called **kettles.** A kettle forms when a chunk of glacial ice is buried in drift. As the ice melts, a cavity forms in the drift. The drift collapses into the cavity and produces a depression. Kettles commonly fill with water to form kettle lakes, such as the one shown in **Figure 5.**

Eskers

When continental glaciers recede, **eskers** (ES kuhrz)—long, winding ridges of gravel and sand—may be left behind. These ridges consist of stratified drift deposited by streams of meltwater that flow through ice tunnels within the glaciers. Eskers may extend for tens of kilometers, like raised, winding roadways.

✓ Reading Check **How do eskers form?**

kettle a bowl-shaped depression in a glacial drift deposit

esker a long, winding ridge of gravel and coarse sand deposited by glacial meltwater streams

www.scilinks.org
Topic: Glaciers and Landforms
Code: HQX0676

Glacial Lakes

Lake basins commonly form where glaciers erode surfaces and leave depressions in the bedrock. Thousands of lake basins in Canada and the northern United States were gouged from solid rock by a continental glacier. Thousands of other glacial lakes form as a result of deposition rather than as a result of erosion. Many lakes form in the uneven surface of ground moraine deposited by glaciers. These lakes exist in many areas of North America and Europe.

Long, narrow *finger lakes*, such as those in western New York, form where terminal and lateral moraines block existing streams. The area south of the Great Lakes, from Minnesota to Ohio, has belts of moraines and lakes. Minnesota, also called the "Land of 10,000 Lakes," was completely glaciated and has evidence of all types of glacial lakes.

Formation of Salt Lakes

Many lakes existed during the last glacial advance. But because of topographic and climatic changes, outlet streams no longer leave these lakes. Water leaves the lakes only by evaporation. When the water evaporates, salt that was dissolved in the water is left behind, which makes the water increasingly salty. Salt lakes, such as the one shown in **Figure 6**, commonly form in dry climates, where evaporation is rapid and precipitation is low.

Figure 6 Many streams and rivers carry dissolved minerals to the Great Salt Lake in Utah. However, because there is no outlet, the lake becomes concentrated with these minerals as continual evaporation removes water.

Why It Matters

Can You Drink a Glacier?

Over 7 billion gallons of bottled water are sold each year in the United States. Companies that bottle water from glacial streams claim that their water is purer than other bottled water because it has been trapped in ice for centuries. Some companies use images of glaciers on their bottles, even if their water does not actually come from glaciers.

REAL WORLD

Water companies often use beautiful images of natural landscapes, but producing, transporting and disposing of plastic bottles causes environmental harm. Over 3 million water bottles are thrown out each day in California alone.

Companies that bottle water from glacial streams want you to think that they sell nature's purest water. Is this true? Atmospheric pollutants—including radioactive waste—can be found in glacial lakes and in ice cores.

YOUR TURN

CRITICAL THINKING
Why do you think many people believe bottled water is healthier than tap water?

465

Early Ice Retreat The ice sheet that covered much of North America formed enormous lakes.

Late Ice Retreat As the ice sheet retreated, the lakes became smaller and the drainage pattern changed.

Today's Great Lakes Uplifting of the land reduced the Great Lakes to their present sizes.

Figure 7 The Great Lakes in the northern United States were formed by a massive continental glacier.

History of the Great Lakes

The Great Lakes of North America formed as a result of erosion and deposition by a continental glacier, as shown in **Figure 7.** Glacial erosion widened and deepened existing river valleys. Moraines to the south blocked off the ends of these valleys. As the ice sheet melted, the meltwater was trapped in the valleys by the moraines, and lakes formed.

In their early stages, the lakes emptied to the south into the Wabash and Illinois Rivers, which flowed into the Mississippi River. Later, the lakes grew larger and also drained into the Atlantic Ocean through the Susquehanna, Mohawk, and Hudson River valleys.

After the glacial period, the crust rose as the weight of the ice was removed. The lake beds uplifted and shrank. The uplift of the land caused the lakes to drain to the northeast through the St. Lawrence River. As a result of this northeasterly flow, Niagara Falls formed between Lake Erie and Lake Ontario.

Section 2 Review

LA.910.2.2.3; SC.912.E.6.2; SC.912.E.7.1

Key Ideas

1. **Describe** the following landscape features: a cirque, an arête, and a horn.

2. **List** five features that form by glacial deposition.

3. **Explain** how terminal and lateral moraines can form glacial lakes.

4. **Compare** the process of glacial deposition with the process of glacial erosion.

5. **Describe** how a kettle forms.

6. **Explain** how an alpine glacier can change the topography of a mountainous area.

7. **Compare** the process of erosion by glaciers with the process of erosion by rivers.

Critical Thinking

8. **Making Comparisons** Compare the processes that form ground moraines with the processes that form eskers.

9. **Analyzing Predictions** On a field trip, you find rock that has long, parallel grooves. Form a hypothesis that explains this feature. What other landforms would you try to find to test this hypothesis?

10. **Making Comparisons** Compare glacial sediment deposited directly by glacial ice with the sediment deposited by glacial meltwater.

Concept Mapping

11. Use the following terms to create a concept map: *cirque, stratified drift, roches moutonnées, moraine, till, glacial drift, kettle, outwash plains,* and *glacier.*

SECTION 3 Ice Ages

Key Ideas	Key Terms	Why It Matters
❯ Describe glacial and interglacial periods within an ice age. ❯ Summarize the theory that best accounts for the ice ages.	**ice age** **Milankovitch theory**	Given global warming, an advance of glaciation seems remote, but it's only a matter of time.

Today, continental glaciers are located mainly in latitudes near the North and South Poles. However, thousands of years ago, ice sheets covered much more of Earth's surface. An **ice age** is a long period of climatic cooling during which the continents are glaciated repeatedly. Several major ice ages have occurred during Earth's geologic history, as shown in **Figure 1**. The earliest known ice age began about 800 million years ago. The most recent ice age began about 4 million years ago. The last advance of this ice age's massive ice sheets reached its peak about 18,000 years ago. Ice ages probably begin with a long, slow decrease in Earth's average temperatures. A drop in average global temperature of only about 5 °C may be enough to start an ice age.

Glacial and Interglacial Periods

Continental glaciers advance and retreat several times during an ice age. The ice sheets advance during colder periods and retreat during warmer periods. A period of cooler climate that is characterized by the advancement of glaciers is called a *glacial period*. A period of warmer climate that is characterized by the retreat of glaciers is called an *interglacial period*. Currently, Earth is in an interglacial period of the most recent ice age.

FLORIDA STANDARDS

SC.912.E.7.3 Differentiate and describe the various interactions among Earth systems, including: atmosphere, hydrosphere, cryosphere, geosphere, and biosphere; **SC.912.N.3.2** Describe the role consensus plays in the historical development of a theory in any one of the disciplines of science.

ice age a long period of climatic cooling during which the continents are glaciated repeatedly

■ Ice age
■ Glacial period
■ Interglacial period

Figure 1 Glacial and Interglacial Periods

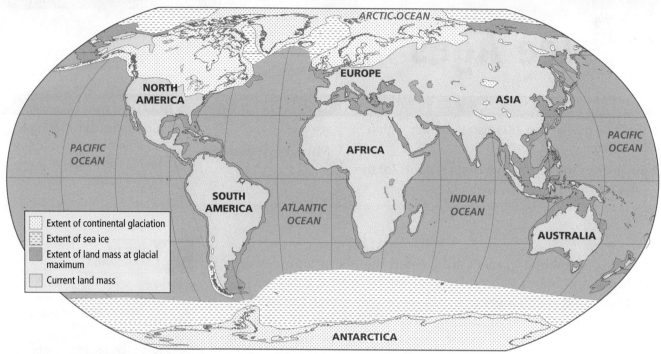

Figure 2 During the last glacial period, about 30% of Earth's surface was covered with ice.

Academic Vocabulary

period (PIR ee uhd) an interval or unit

www.scilinks.org
Topic: Ice Ages
Code: HQX0781

READING TOOLBOX

Booklet FoldNote
Make a Booklet FoldNote to record your notes for Section 3. Use one page for each main topic in the section, and take notes to create an outline.

Glaciation in North America

Glaciers covered about one-third of Earth's surface during the last glacial period. Most glaciation took place in North America and Eurasia. In some parts of North America, the ice was several kilometers thick. So much water was locked in ice during the last glacial period that sea level was as much as 140 m lower than it is today. As a result, the coastlines of the continents extended farther than they do today, as shown in **Figure 2.**

Canada and the mountainous regions of Alaska were buried under ice. In the mountains of the western United States, numerous small alpine glaciers joined to form larger glaciers. These large glaciers flowed outward from the Rocky Mountains and the Cascade and Sierra Nevada Ranges. A great continental ice sheet that was centered on what is now the Hudson Bay region of Canada spread as far south as the Missouri and Ohio Rivers.

Reading Check How did glaciation in the last glacial period affect the sea level?

Glaciation in Eurasia and the Southern Hemisphere

In Europe, a continental ice sheet that was centered on what is now the Baltic Sea spread south over Germany, Belgium, and the Netherlands and west over Great Britain and Ireland. It flowed eastward over Poland and Russia. Long alpine glaciers formed in the Alps and the Himalayas. A continental ice sheet formed in Siberia. In the Southern Hemisphere, the Andes Mountains in South America and much of New Zealand were covered by mountainous ice fields and alpine glaciers. Many land features that formed during the last glacial period are still recognizable.

Causes of Glaciation

The repeated glaciation of Earth's surface is caused by a variety of complex factors. These factors range from very rapid events to very slow processes. For example, the movement of tectonic plates happens very slowly but can cause changes in global circulation patterns of air and ocean water. These changes may lead to ice ages. Scientists have also proposed a number of ideas to explain glacial and interglacial periods. The leading explanation is the Milankovitch theory.

The Milankovitch Theory

A Serbian scientist named Milutin Milankovitch proposed a theory to explain the cause of glacial periods. Milankovitch noticed that climate change occurs in cycles. He thought that these cycles could be linked to cycles in Earth's movement relative to the sun. The **Milankovitch theory** is the theory that cyclical changes in Earth's orbit and in the tilt of Earth's axis occur over thousands of years and cause climatic changes.

Three periodic changes occur in the way that Earth moves around the sun, as **Figure 3** shows. First, the shape of Earth's orbit, or *eccentricity*, changes from nearly circular to elongated and back to nearly circular every 100,000 years. The second change occurs in the tilt of Earth's axis. Every 41,000 years, the tilt of Earth's axis varies between about 22.2° and 24.5°. A third periodic change is caused by the circular motion, or *precession*, of Earth's axis. Precession causes the axis to change its position, which is often described as a wobble. The axis of Earth traces a complete circle every 25,700 years.

Milankovitch calculated how these three factors may affect the distribution of solar energy that reaches Earth's surface. Changes in the distribution of solar energy affects global temperatures, which may cause periods of glacial advance and retreat.

Milankovitch theory the theory that cyclical changes in Earth's orbit and in the tilt of Earth's axis occur over thousands of years and cause climatic changes

Figure 3 According to the Milankovitch theory, the distribution of solar radiation that Earth receives varies because of three kinds of changes in Earth's position relative to the sun.

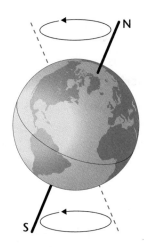

Eccentricity Changes in orbital eccentricity cause an increase in seasonality in one hemisphere and reduce seasonality in the other hemisphere.

Tilt Over a period of 41,000 years, the tilt of Earth's axis varies between 22.2° and 24.5°. The poles receive more solar energy when the tilt angle is greater.

Precession A gradual change, or "wobble," in the orientation of Earth's axis affects the relationship between Earth's tilt and eccentricity.

Figure 4 The microscopic shells of organisms from the order Foraminifera give clues to climate change.

Biological Evidence of Glaciation

Evidence for past glaciation has been discovered in the shells of dead marine animals found on the ocean floor. The formation of the shells of organisms from the order Foraminifera, shown in **Figure 4,** is affected by the temperature of the ocean water. Temperature of the ocean water affects the amount of oxygen that the water dissolves. The amount of oxygen in turn affects how these organisms form their shells. In addition, organisms that lived in ocean waters that were warmer than 8 °C coiled their shells to the right. Organisms that lived in ocean waters that were much cooler coiled their shells to the left.

By studying Foraminifera shells in the layers of sediment on the ocean floor, scientists have discovered evidence of different glacial periods. Scientists have found that the record of changes in marine sediments closely follows the cycle of cooling and warming predicted by the Milankovitch theory.

Other Explanations for Glaciation

Other explanations for the causes of glacial periods have been suggested. Most of these explanations indicate that the glacial periods were caused by changes in the amount of solar energy that reached Earth's surface that were not caused by changes in Earth's position relative to the sun. Some scientists propose that changes in solar energy are caused by varying amounts of energy produced by the sun. Other scientists suggest that glacial periods start when volcanic dust blocks the sun's rays. Volcanic dust in Earth's atmosphere prevents solar radiation from reaching Earth's surface. As a result, Earth's average global temperature drops.

Section 3 Review

LA.910.2.2.3; SC.912.E.6.2; SC.912.E.7.1; SC.912.E.7.7

Key Ideas

1. **Describe** glacial periods and interglacial periods.

2. **Explain** what happens to global sea level during a glacial period.

3. **Identify** the areas of Earth's surface that were covered by ice during the last glacial period.

4. **Summarize** the Milankovitch theory.

5. **Explain** how fossils of marine animals provide evidence of past glaciation.

6. **Describe** two explanations for glacial periods other than the Milankovitch theory.

Critical Thinking

7. **Evaluating Hypotheses** Use the information that you learned about glacial periods within an ice age to explain why volcanic eruptions may not be the cause of ice ages.

8. **Predicting Consequences** If Earth's orbit were always circular, would Earth be more likely to experience ice ages or less likely to experience ice ages? Explain your answer.

Concept Mapping

9. Use the following terms to create a concept map: *ice age, glacial period, interglacial period, Milankovitch theory, eccentricity, tilt, volcanic eruption,* and *precession.*

Watermelon Ice

Believe it or not, glacial ice is home to hundreds of different organisms, including over 60 different species of snow algae in the United States. One type of red snow algae forms the base of the glacial food web. These algae cause pink snow, known as "watermelon ice." When a person walks on the pink snow, the crushed algae release a compound that smells like watermelon!

These red snow algae contain carotene—the pigment found in carrots, oranges, flowers, and flamingoes. Carotene helps another pigment, chlorophyll, in the process of photosynthesis and protects the organism from intense exposure to the sun.

Ice worms come out by the millions at night. They eat snow algae and other microscopic organisms.

Walking on watermelon ice can stain the soles of a person's shoes.

Snow fleas are less than 1 mm long. They eat snow algae and wind-blown pollen. Birds, in turn, eat the snow fleas and ice worms.

YOUR TURN

UNDERSTANDING CONCEPTS
How does the color of red snow algae help them survive the glacial environment?

ONLINE RESEARCH
Use the Internet to find out more about one of the organisms described above. Write a one-page summary to describe your findings.

Making Models Lab

What You'll Do

> **Model** the melting of an ice sheet.

> **Analyze** the effects of melting ice on sea level.

What You'll Need

block, ice,
  5 cm × 5 cm × 5 cm
block, wooden,
  5 cm × 5 cm × 5 cm
pan,
  30 cm × 40 cm × 10 cm
pebbles (1 kg)
ruler, metric
sand (1 kg)
water

Safety

Glaciers and Sea-Level Change

Today, glaciers hold only about 2% of Earth's water. But if the polar ice sheets melted, the coastal areas of many countries would flood. Many major cities, such as New York, New Orleans, Houston, and Los Angeles, would flood if the sea level rose only a few meters. In this lab, you will construct a model to simulate what would happen if the Antarctic ice sheet melted.

Procedure

1. Calculate and record the approximate surface area of the bottom of the pan. Area (*A*) is equal to length (*l*) times width (*w*), or $A = l \times w$, and is expressed in square units.

2. Calculate and record the overall volume of the ice block and the area of one side of the ice block. Volume (*V*) is equal to length (*l*) times width (*w*) times height (*h*), or $V = l \times w \times h$, and is expressed in cubic units.

3. Add the sand and small pebbles to one end of the pan so that they cover about half of the area of the pan and slope toward the middle of the pan. Use the wooden block to elevate the end of the pan containing the sand and pebbles.

4. Slowly add water to the opposite end of the pan. Be sure that the water does not cover the sand and pebbles and touches only the edge of the sand.

Step 3

5 Measure and record the depth of the water at the deepest point.

6 Measure and record the distance from the end of the pan covered with sand to the point where the sand touches the water.

7 Place the block of ice in the pan on top of the sand. Calculate and record the percentage of the total area of the pan that is covered by ice.

8 As the ice begins to melt, pick up the ice block. Note the appearance of the bottom of the ice block and the appearance of the sand under the ice block. Record what is happening to the ice block and what is happening to the sand under the ice block. Place the ice block back on the sand.

Step 4

9 While the ice is melting, calculate the expected rise in the pan's water level by using the following formula:

$$\text{rise in water level} = \frac{\text{volume of water in ice block}}{\text{area of pan covered by water}}$$

10 When the ice is completely melted, measure and record the depth of water at the deepest point.

11 Measure and record the distance from the end of the pan covered with sand to the point where the sand touches the water.

Analysis

1. **Making Comparisons** Compare the depth of the water at the beginning of the lab with the depth at the end of the lab. Explain any differences.

2. **Analyzing Results** How did the distance from the end of the pan covered with sand to the point where the sand touches the water change? Explain your answer.

3. **Compare and Contrast** How does the ice-block model differ from a glacier on Earth?

4. **Drawing Conclusions** How does the ice-block model represent what would happen on Earth if the Antarctic polar ice sheet melted?

Extension

Evaluating Models In this lab, you used a physical model to simulate an occurrence in nature. In what other ways do scientists use models? What kinds of errors can occur when models are used?

Gulkana Glacier

Map Skills Activity

This contour map shows the elevation and boundaries of the Gulkana Glacier located in Alaska. Use the map to answer the questions below.

1. **Using a Key** Estimate the length of the Gulkana Glacier from its northernmost point to its southernmost point.

2. **Analyzing Data** Estimate the latitude and longitude of the glacier's highest point.

3. **Identifying Trends** In which direction do you think Gulkana Glacier is moving at measurement stake D?

4. **Identifying Trends** In which direction do you think Gulkana Glacier is moving at measurement stake A?

5. **Predicting Consequences** Why might you think that the glacier moves in different directions at measurement stake A and measurement stake B?

6. **Analyzing Data** What do you think the scientists are measuring at the measurement stakes?

THINK central
SUPER SUMMARY
Keyword: HQXGLAS

Key Ideas	Key Terms

Section 1

Glaciers: Moving Ice

❯ Glaciers form at high elevations and in polar regions as layers of snow and ice build up.

❯ The two main types of glaciers are alpine glaciers, which form in mountainous areas and are relatively small, and continental glaciers, which are massive ice sheets that cover millions of square kilometers.

❯ Glaciers move by basal slip, sliding over the thin layer of water and sediment that separates the ice from the ground, and internal plastic flow, the process by which grains of ice deform under pressure and slide over each other.

❯ Three features of glaciers are large cracks called crevasses, ice sheets that extend out over the ocean called ice shelves, and large pieces of ice that break off into the ocean called icebergs.

glacier, p. 455
alpine glacier, p. 456
continental glacier, p. 456
basal slip, p. 457
internal plastic flow, p. 457
crevasse, p. 458

Section 2

Glacial Erosion and Deposition

❯ Features produced by glacial erosion include U-shaped valleys, hanging valleys, bowl-shaped depressions called cirques, sharp ridges called arêtes, pointed peaks called horns, and rounded rocks called roches moutonnées.

❯ Features formed by glacial deposition include large transported rocks called erratics, depressions called kettles, ridges called eskers, mounds of till called drumlins, and ridges of sediment called moraines.

❯ Glaciers may form lake basins by eroding the land or by depositing sediments.

cirque, p. 460
arête, p. 460
horn, p. 460
erratic, p. 462
glacial drift, p. 462
till, p. 462
moraine, p. 463
kettle, p. 464
esker, p. 464

Section 3

Ice Ages

❯ During an ice age, cooler glacial periods, characterized by the advancement of glaciers, alternate with warmer interglacial periods, characterized by the retreat of glaciers.

❯ The Milankovitch theory best accounts for the ice ages. It suggests that glacial periods are caused by changes in the distribution of solar energy Earth receives. These changes are caused by regular changes in the eccentricity of Earth's orbit, the tilt of Earth's axis, and precession.

ice age, p. 467
Milankovitch theory, p. 469

1. **Classification** Make a three-column table to classify the two main ways that glaciers move. Label the first column "Type of movement," the second column "Where movement occurs on glacier," and the third column "Description of movement." Fill in your table with details about basal slip and internal plastic flow.

READING TOOLBOX

USING KEY TERMS

Use each of the following terms in a separate sentence.

2. *glacier* **SC.912.E.6.2**

3. *crevasse* **SC.912.E.6.2**

4. *ice age*

For each pair of terms, explain how the meanings of the terms differ.

5. *alpine glacier* and *continental glacier* **SC.912.E.6.2**

6. *till* and *moraine* **SC.912.E.6.2**

7. *basal slip* and *internal plastic flow* **SC.912.E.6.2**

8. *cirque* and *arête* **SC.912.E.6.2**

9. *glacial period* and *interglacial period*

UNDERSTANDING KEY IDEAS

10. Glaciers that form in mountainous areas are called **SC.912.E.6.2**
    a. continental glaciers.
    b. alpine glaciers.
    c. icebergs.
    d. ice shelves.

11. A glacier will move by sliding when the base of the ice and the underlying rock are separated by a thin layer of **SC.912.E.6.2**
    a. water and sediment.
    b. snow.
    c. pebbles.
    d. drift.

12. What part of a glacier moves fastest when the glacier moves by internal plastic flow? **SC.912.E.6.2**
    a. The center of the glacier moves fastest.
    b. The bottom of the glacier moves fastest.
    c. The edges of the glacier move fastest.
    d. The whole ice mass moves at the same speed.

13. Icebergs form when ice breaks off of a(n) **SC.912.E.6.2**
    a. crevasse.   c. alpine glacier.
    b. ice shelf.   d. esker.

14. As a glacier moves through a valley, it carves out a(n) **SC.912.E.6.2**
    a. U shape.   c. V shape.
    b. esker.   d. moraine.

15. A deposit of stratified drift is called a(n) **SC.912.E.6.2**
    a. drumlin.
    b. outwash plain.
    c. ground moraine.
    d. roche moutonnée.

16. One component of the Milankovitch theory is
    a. the circular motion of Earth's axis. **SC.912.E.6.2**
    b. continental drift.
    c. volcanic activity.
    d. landslide activity.

17. Which of the following is not a theory for the cause of ice ages? **SC.912.E.6.2**
    a. volcanic eruptions
    b. variations in Earth's orbit
    c. Foraminifera shell coils
    d. changes in Earth's axial orientation

SHORT ANSWER

18. How does climate change during an ice age? **SC.912.E.7.7**

19. What are the four types of moraines, and how are they different from each other? **SC.912.E.6.2**

20. Identify three types of landforms created by alpine glaciers. **SC.912.E.6.2**

21. In what two ways do glacial lakes form? **SC.912.E.6.2**

22. How do the processes of basal slip and internal plastic flow differ? **SC.912.E.6.2**

CRITICAL THINKING

23. Identifying Relationships Why is it important for scientists to monitor and study the continental ice sheets that cover Greenland and Antarctica? `SC.912.E.7.7`

24. Applying Concepts Antarctic explorers need special training to travel safely over the ice sheet. Besides the cold, what structural aspects of the glaciers may be dangerous? `SC.912.E.6.2`

25. Evaluating Data What phenomenon other than decreased temperature and increased snowfall might signal the beginning of a glacial period? `SC.912.E.7.7`

CONCEPT MAPPING

26. Use the following terms to create a concept map: *snowfield, erosion, deposition, glacier, horn, arête, kettle, moraine, basal slip,* and *internal plastic flow.* `SC.912.E.6.2`

MATH SKILLS   Math Skills

27. Using Equations The area of Earth's surface that is covered with water is 361,000,000 km². The volume of water locked in ice in the Antarctic ice sheet is about 26,384,368 km³. Use the following equation to find the average worldwide rise in sea level, in meters, that would occur if the Antarctic ice sheet melted.

$$\text{rise in water level} = \frac{\text{volume of water in ice sheet}}{\text{area of Earth covered by water}}$$

28. Evaluating Data New York City has an average elevation of 27 m above sea level. Although highly unlikely, what would happen to the city if the Antarctic ice sheet suddenly melted and raised the worldwide sea level by 50 m? `SC.912.E.6.4`

WRITING SKILLS

29. Writing Persuasively Write a research proposal to the National Science Foundation that details a plan of action and reasons for studying the ice sheet in Greenland. `SC.912.E.6.4`

30. Writing from Research Research how ocean currents affect the polar icecaps. Write a short essay that describes global ocean currents and explains how they affect the formation and advancement of polar icecaps. `SC.912.E.7.9`

INTERPRETING GRAPHICS

The graph below shows the relationship between cycles of eccentricity, tilt, and precession. Use the graph to answer the questions that follow.

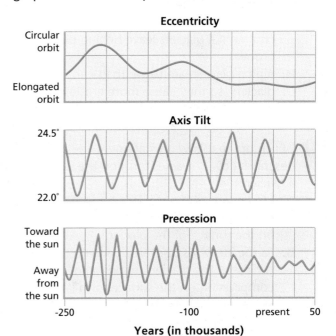

31. What was the angle of Earth's tilt 50,000 years ago? `SC.912.E.7.7`

32. Describe the shape of Earth's orbit 200,000 years ago. `SC.912.E.7.7`

33. How would the seasons 50,000 years from now be different from the seasons 50,000 years ago? `SC.912.E.7.7`

Understanding Concepts

Directions (1–9): For each question, write on a separate sheet of paper the letter of the correct answer.

1 Which statement best compares the movement of glacial ice to the movement of river water?
   A. Glacial ice moves more rapidly than water.
   B. Glacial ice can easily flow around barriers.
   C. Glacial ice moves in response to gravity.
   D. Glacial ice moves in the same way as water.

2 Which of the following statements best describes the difference between alpine and continental glaciers?
   F. Alpine glacier erosion results in rugged features, while continental glacier erosion results in a smooth, rounded landscape.
   G. Alpine glaciers leave grooves in rock that are not parallel to glacial movement while continental glaciers leave behind parallel grooves.
   H. Alpine glaciers are larger than continental glaciers, so they cause more erosion.
   I. Alpine glaciers carry rocks while continental glaciers do not carry rocks.

3 Which of the following statements best describes how crevasses form on the surface of a glacier?
   A. Movement of the glacier's ice from the center toward the edges forms large cracks on the surface of the glacier.
   B. As the ice flows unevenly beneath the surface of the glacier, tension and compression on the surface form large cracks.
   C. Breakage of large blocks of ice from the edges of ice shelves forms large cracks.
   D. Narrow, wedge-shaped masses of ice confined to a small area form large cracks.

4 Which of the following statements about Earth and ice ages is true?
   F. Earth is not in an ice age.
   G. Earth is in a glacial period of an ice age.
   H. Earth is in an interglacial period of an ice age.
   I. Earth is at the beginning of an ice age.

5 Ice ages probably begin due to
   A. increased temperatures.
   B. a drop in average global temperatures.
   C. abundant snowfall.
   D. volcanic eruptions.

6 Glaciers erode rock, but they also leave deposits. Which of the following statements does NOT describe a glacial deposit?
   F. Ridges of unsorted sediment form at the leading edge of a melting glacier.
   G. Stratified drift is left by meltwater.
   H. A pyramid-like peak is left behind after a glacier passes.
   I. Large rocks are moved far from their original source.

7 Scientists have several theories for the causes of ice ages. The Milankovitch theory is based on the idea that ice ages occur in cycles and are caused by
   A. cyclical changes in Earth's orbit and tilt of its axis.
   B. changes in the amount of solar energy Earth receives.
   C. plate tectonics, which change global weather patterns.
   D. sudden drops in temperature.

8 Glacial movement results from two processes. In a glacier undergoing basal slip,
   F. water at the bottom of the glacier mixes with sediments and acts as a lubricant.
   G. pressure deforms grains of ice at the bottom of the glacier, causing the glacier to flow.
   H. the glacier increases in size and flows more quickly as a result.
   I. the glacier moves more slowly at its surface than it does at its base.

9 Glaciers both erode and deposit rock. Cirques and hanging valleys result from
   A. erosion by an alpine glacier.
   B. erosion by a continental glacier.
   C. deposition by an alpine glacier.
   D. deposition by a continental glacier.

Interpreting Graphics

Directions (10–11): For each question below, record the correct answer on a separate sheet of paper.

Basal Slip

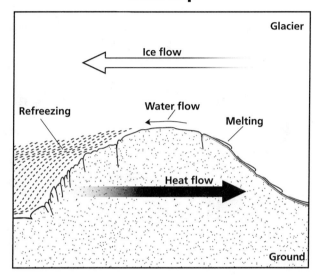

10 Based on the diagram above, what causes the ice to melt?
 F. Pressure decreases the melting point of the ice.
 G. Pressure increases the melting point of the ice.
 H. The ground heats the ice until it melts.
 I. Ice at the base of a glacier does not melt.

World Cities and Their Elevations

New York City	27
Kiev, Ukraine	168
Buenos Aires, Argentina	25
Amsterdam, Netherlands	2

11 Although unlikely, what would happen to the cities listed in the table if the Antarctic ice sheet were to melt and raise the sea level by 50 m?
 A. All of the cities would be covered by water.
 B. Three of the cities would be covered by water.
 C. Two of the cities would be covered by water.
 D. One of the cities would be covered by water.

Test Tip

For a group of questions that refer to a diagram, graph, or table, read all of the questions quickly to determine what information you will need to glean from the graphic.

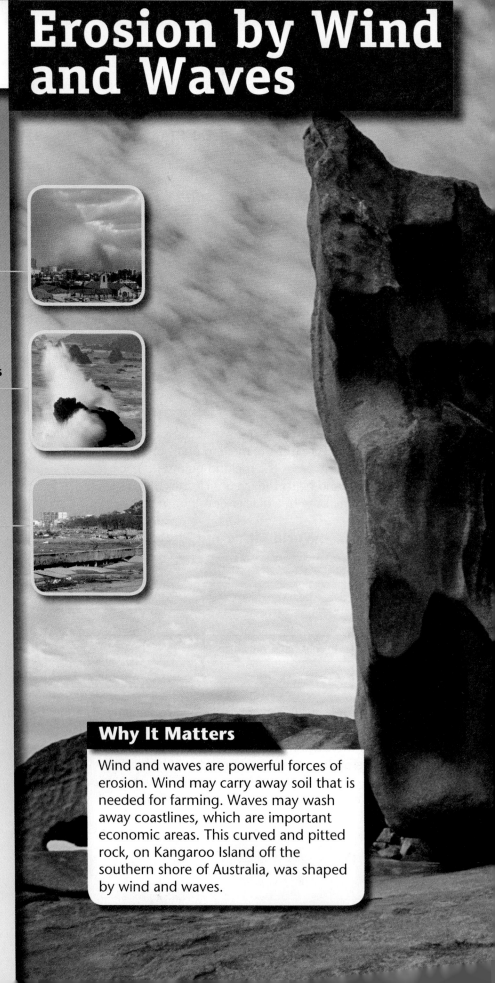

Erosion by Wind and Waves

Why It Matters

Wind and waves are powerful forces of erosion. Wind may carry away soil that is needed for farming. Waves may wash away coastlines, which are important economic areas. This curved and pitted rock, on Kangaroo Island off the southern shore of Australia, was shaped by wind and waves.

Inquiry Lab

 20 min

Shake It Up

Use a magnifying glass or dissecting microscope to observe the samples of shoreline sediment provided by your teacher. Record your observations, noting similarities and differences among the samples. Place all of the samples in the same jar, add water until the jar is three-quarters full, and seal the jar. Shake the jar for 1 min to represent shoreline wave action. Then let the jar rest, and observe the rates of deposition for different-sized particles. Record your observations.

SC.912.E.6.2

Questions to Get You Started

1. Describe the relationship between particle size and rate of deposition in the jar.

2. Based on your observations, how would you expect different-sized particles to settle on a real shoreline?

These reading tools will help you learn the material in this chapter.

Word Parts

Root Words The word *saltation,* a key term in Section 1, may remind you of the salt that you sprinkle on food. Actually, *saltation* is from the Latin word *saltatio,* which means "a dancing" or "dance." This Latin root makes sense, because saltation is the way that wind and water move sand—by bounces and jumps.

Your Turn Choose four key terms or italicized terms in Sections 1 and 2. Using print or online sources, research the root word of each term. Record your findings in a table like the one below.

Term	Root Word	Definition of Root Word	Definition of Term
(desert or stone) pavement	pavimentum (Latin)	beaten floor	a surface of closely packed small rocks

Mnemonics

Longshore Current A mnemonic is a sentence or phrase that can help you remember specific information. For example, a longshore current is a water current that travels near and parallel to the shoreline. You can use the following mnemonic to help you remember the direction and location of a longshore current:

A **long**shore current flows **along** the shoreline.

Your Turn Say this mnemonic a few times to help you learn and remember the direction in which a longshore current flows. Find the other key terms in the chapter, and make up mnemonics that will help you remember their definitions.

FoldNotes

Four-Corner Fold A four-corner fold is useful when you want to compare the characteristics of four topics. You can organize the characteristics of the four topics side by side under the flaps.

Your Turn As you read about dunes in Section 1, make a four-corner fold by following the instructions in **Appendix A.** Label the four outer flaps with the names of the four types of dunes: barchan dunes,

parabolic dunes, transverse dunes, and longitudinal dunes. Take notes about each type of dune underneath the appropriate flap.

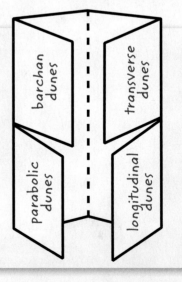

For more information on how to use these and other tools, see **Appendix A.**

Key Ideas	Key Terms		Why It Matters
❯ Describe two ways that wind erodes land. ❯ Compare the two types of wind deposits.	saltation deflation ventifact	dune loess	Blowing wind moves sand, soil, dust, and other particles all over Earth. As a result, wind helps to shape the land, which can be a benefit to those who live there.

Wind contains energy. Some of this energy can move a sailboat or turn a wind turbine, but this energy can also erode the land. As wind passes over the land, the wind can carry sand or dust. Sand is loose fragments of weathered rocks and minerals. Most grains of sand are made of quartz. Other common minerals that make up sand are mica, feldspar, and magnetite.

Dust consists of particles that are smaller than the smallest sand grain. Most dust particles are microscopic fragments of rocks and minerals that come from the soil or volcanic eruptions. Other sources of dust are plants, animals, bacteria, pollution from the burning of fuels, and certain manufacturing processes.

How Wind Moves Sand and Dust

Wind cannot keep sand aloft. Instead, sand grains are rolled by the wind along the ground (surface creep) or are moved by a series of jumps and bounces called **saltation.** Saltation occurs when rolling sand grains collide and some bounce up, as shown in **Figure 1.** Once in the air, a sand grain moves ahead a short distance and then falls. As a sand grain falls, it strikes other sand grains. Saltating sand grains move in the same direction that the wind blows. However, the grains rarely rise more than 1 m above the ground, even in very strong winds.

Because dust particles are very small and light, even gentle air currents can keep dust particles suspended in the air. Dust from volcanic eruptions can remain in the atmosphere for several years. Strong winds may lift large amounts of dust and create dust storms, such as the one shown in **Figure 1.** Some dust storms cover hundreds of square kilometers and darken the sky for several days.

Figure 1 Heavy sand gains move by rolling or by making low, arcing jumps when blown by the wind (left). Dust is light enough to be suspended for days, as shown in this dust storm in Phoenix, Arizona (right).

FLORIDA STANDARDS

LA.910.2.2.3 The student will organize information to show understanding or relationships among facts, ideas, and events (e.g., representing key points within text through charting, mapping, paraphrasing, summarizing, comparing, contrasting, or outlining); **SC.912.E.7.3** Differentiate and describe the various interactions among Earth systems, including: atmosphere, hydrosphere, cryosphere, geosphere, and biosphere; **SC.912.N.3.5** Describe the function of models in science, and identify the wide range of models used in science.

saltation the movement of sand or other sediments by short jumps and bounces that is caused by wind or water

Wind direction

Smaller particles are lifted and carried by the wind.

Larger particles bounce and skip along the ground.

Figure 2 Desert pavement, such as this example in Calico Hills, California, prevents erosion of the material beneath it.

SCi*LINKS*

www.scilinks.org
Topic: Wind Erosion
Code: HQX1669

deflation a form of wind erosion in which fine, dry soil particles are blown away

Effects of Wind Erosion

While wind erosion happens everywhere there is wind, the landscapes that are most dramatically shaped by wind erosion are deserts and coastlines. In these areas, fewer plant roots anchor soil and sand in place to reduce the amount of wind erosion. Also, in the desert, where there is little moisture, soil layers are thin and are likely to be swept away by the wind. Moisture makes soil heavy and causes some soil and rock particles to stick together, which makes them difficult to move.

✓ Reading Check Why does wind erosion happen faster in dry climates than in moist climates? (See Appendix G for answers to Reading Checks.)

Desert Pavement

One common form of wind erosion is deflation. **Deflation** is the process by which wind removes the top layer of fine, very dry soil or rock particles and leaves behind large rock particles. Deflation is one of many processes that may form a surface of closely packed small rocks called *desert pavement*, or *stone pavement*, as shown in **Figure 2.** Desert pavement protects the underlying land from erosion by forming a protective barrier over underlying soil.

Deflation Hollows

Deflation is a serious problem for farmers because it blows away the best soil for growing crops. Deflation may form shallow depressions in areas where the natural plant cover has been removed. As the wind strips off the topsoil, a shallow depression called a *deflation hollow* forms. A deflation hollow may expand to a width of several kilometers and to a depth of 5 to 20 m.

Ventifacts

When pebbles and small stones in deserts and on beaches are exposed to wind abrasion, the surfaces of the rocks become flattened and polished on two or three sides. Rocks that have been pitted or smoothed by wind abrasion are called **ventifacts.** The word *ventifact* comes from the Latin word *ventus*, which means "wind." The direction of the prevailing wind in an area can be determined by the appearance of ventifacts.

Scientists once thought that large rock structures, such as desert basins, natural bridges, rock pinnacles, and rocks perched on pedestals, were formed by wind erosion. However, scientists now think that it is more likely that such large features were produced by erosion due to surface water and weathering. Erosion of large masses of rock by wind-blown sand happens very slowly and happens only close to the ground, where saltation occurs.

ventifact any rock that is pitted, grooved, or polished by wind abrasion

dune a mound of wind-deposited sand that moves as a result of the action of wind

Wind Deposition

The wind drops particles when it slows down and can no longer carry them. These deposited particles are continually covered by additional deposits. Eventually, cementation and pressure from overlying layers bind the fragments together. This process is one way that sedimentary rocks form.

Academic Vocabulary

fragment (FRAG muhnt) a particle or piece that has broken off or been detached from something larger

Dunes

The best-known wind deposits are **dunes,** which are mounds of wind-deposited sand. Dunes form where the soil is dry and unprotected and where the wind is strong, such as in deserts and along the shores of oceans and large lakes. A dune begins to form when a barrier slows the speed of the wind. When wind speed slows, sand accumulates on both sides of the barrier, as shown in **Figure 3.** As more sand is deposited, the dune itself acts as a barrier, grows, and buries the original barrier.

Figure 3 Dune Formation

Barrier

Direction of wind

Wind-driven sand builds up around a barrier, such as a rock, a tuft of grass, or a fence.

Sand buildup

As the dune develops, it becomes a wind barrier and becomes larger.

Dune

Original barrier

The fully formed dune covers the original barrier.

THINK central
INTERACT ONLINE
Keyword: HQXEWWF3

Table 1

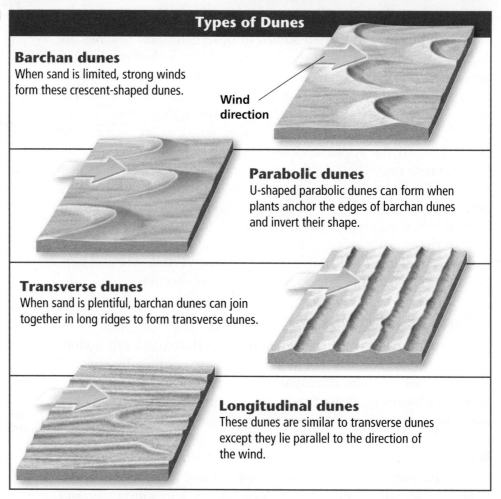

Types of Dunes

Barchan dunes
When sand is limited, strong winds form these crescent-shaped dunes.

Wind direction

Parabolic dunes
U-shaped parabolic dunes can form when plants anchor the edges of barchan dunes and invert their shape.

Transverse dunes
When sand is plentiful, barchan dunes can join together in long ridges to form transverse dunes.

Longitudinal dunes
These dunes are similar to transverse dunes except they lie parallel to the direction of the wind.

Types of Dunes

The force and direction of the wind shapes sand dunes. Commonly, the gentlest slope of a dune is the side that faces the wind. Sand that is blown over the crest of the dune tumbles down the opposite side, which is called the *slipface*. The slipface has a steeper slope than the windward side does. Two long, pointed extensions may form as wind sweeps around the ends of the dune and gives the dune a crescent shape. Crescent-shaped dunes that have an open side facing away from the wind are called *barchan dunes* (BAHR kahn doonz). A *parabolic dune* is a crescent-shaped dune whose open side faces into the wind. The long crescent ends stay behind, held in place by vegetation.

In desert or coastal areas that have a large amount of sand, a series of ridges of sand may form in long, wavelike patterns. These ridges are called *transverse dunes*. Transverse dunes form at right angles to the wind direction. A type of dune that is similar to a transverse dune, called a *longitudinal dune*, also forms in the shape of a ridge. But longitudinal dunes lie parallel to the direction the wind blows. **Table 1** illustrates several types of dunes and explains how the shape of dunes relates to wind direction.

Reading Check How do barchan dunes differ from transverse dunes?

Figure 4 Wind erodes sand from the windward side of the dune and deposits it on the slipface. *Which direction is this sand dune migrating?*

Dune Migration

The movement of dunes is called *dune migration*. If the wind usually blows from the same direction, dunes will move downwind. Dune migration occurs as sand is blown over the crest from the windward side and builds up on the slipface, as shown in **Figure 4.** In mostly level areas, dunes migrate until they reach a barrier. To prevent dunes from drifting over highways and farmland, people often build fences or plant grasses, trees, and shrubs.

SC.912.E.6.2

Quick Lab **Modeling Desert Winds**

20 min

Procedure

❶ Spread a mixture of **dust, sand,** and **gravel** on a table placed outdoors.

❷ Place an **electric fan** at one end of the table.

❸ Put on **safety goggles** and a **filter mask.** Aim the fan across the sediment you have laid out. Start the fan on the lowest speed. Record any observations.

❹ Turn the fan to medium speed and record any observations. Then, turn the fan to its highest speed to imitate a desert windstorm. Record any observations.

Analysis

1. In what direction did the sediment move?

2. What was the relationship between the wind speed and the sediment size that was moved?

3. How does the remaining sediment compare to desert pavement?

4. How did the sand move in this activity? How do your observations relate to dune migration?

5. Using the same materials, how would you model dune migration? How would you model the formation of the different kinds of dunes?

Figure 5 These loess deposits are located in Vicksburg, Mississippi. Much of the surrounding land is fertile farmland.

READING TOOLBOX

Root Words
Use print or online sources to research the root word of *loess*. Add your findings to the table you started at the beginning of the chapter.

loess fine-grained sediments of quartz, feldspar, hornblende, mica, and clay deposited by the wind

Loess

The wind carries dust higher and much farther than it carries sand. Fine dust may be deposited in such thin layers that it is not noticed. However, thick deposits of yellowish, fine-grained sediment, called **loess** (LOH ES), can form by the accumulation of windblown dust. Although loess is soft and easily eroded, it sometimes forms steep bluffs, such as those shown in **Figure 5.**

A large area in northern China is covered in a deep layer of loess. The material in this deposit came from the Gobi Desert, in Mongolia. Deposits of loess are also located in central Europe. In North America, loess is located in the midwestern states, along the eastern border of the Mississippi River valley, and in eastern Oregon and Washington State. These deposits probably formed as dust from dried beds of glacial lakes and from outwash plains blew across the region. Loess deposits are extremely fertile and provide excellent soil for grain-growing regions.

Section 1 Review

LA.910.2.2.3; SC.912.E.6.2; SC.912.E.7.1

Key Ideas

1. **Describe** how wind transports sediment by saltation.

2. **Define** *deflation*, and explain how *deflation hollows* form.

3. **Describe** how ventifacts form.

4. **Describe** how sand dunes form and how dunes migrate.

5. **Explain** how the wind moves loess.

6. **Identify** two reasons why wind erosion has a major effect on deserts.

7. **Compare** the four main shapes of dunes.

Critical Thinking

8. **Analyzing Processes** Explain how wind erosion might contribute to the formation of desert pavement.

9. **Determining Cause and Effect** Why does planting grass, trees, or shrubs help prevent dunes from covering roads?

10. **Analyzing Processes** Explain why the position of dunes would not be helpful for navigation in the desert.

Concept Mapping

11. Use the following terms to create a concept map: *saltation, deflation, dune, deflation hollow, desert pavement, wind, sand particle, top soil layer,* and *migration.*

Key Ideas	Key Terms	Why It Matters
❯ Compare the formation of six features produced by wave erosion. ❯ Explain how beaches form. ❯ Describe the features produced by the movement of sand along a shore.	headland beach longshore current	The endless pounding of the surf produces spectacular shorelines, which, themselves, never stay the same.

As wind moves over the ocean, the wind produces waves and currents that erode the coastline. Wave erosion changes the shape of shorelines, the places where the ocean and the land meet.

Shoreline Erosion

The power of waves striking rock along a shoreline can sometimes shake the ground as much as a small earthquake would. The great force of waves may break off pieces of rock and throw the pieces back against the shore. These sediments grind together in the tumbling water. This abrasive action, which is known as *mechanical weathering*, eventually reduces most of the rock fragments to small pebbles and sand grains.

Much of the erosion along a shoreline takes place during storms, which cause large waves that release tremendous amounts of energy, as shown in **Figure 1**. A severe storm can noticeably change the appearance of a shoreline in a single day.

Chemical weathering also affects the rock along a shoreline. The waves force salt water and air into small cracks in the rock. Chemicals in the air and water react with the rock and enlarge the cracks. Enlarged cracks expose more of the rock to mechanical and chemical weathering.

FLORIDA STANDARDS

LA.910.2.2.3 The student will organize information to show understanding or relationships among facts, ideas, and events (e.g., representing key points within text through charting, mapping, paraphrasing, summarizing, comparing, contrasting, or outlining); **SC.912.E.6.4** Analyze how specific geologic processes and features are expressed in Florida and elsewhere; **SC.912.E.7.3** Differentiate and describe the various interactions among Earth systems, including: atmosphere, hydrosphere, cryosphere, geosphere, and biosphere.

Figure 1 Large waves break apart rock on shorelines and change the shoreline's appearance. *Where is erosion occurring in the photo shown here?*

Sea Cliffs

In places where waves strike directly against rock, the waves slowly erode the base of the rock. The waves cut under the overhanging rock, until the rock eventually collapses to form a steep sea *cliff*. The rate at which sea cliffs erode depends on the amount of wave energy and on the resistance of the rock along the shoreline. Soft rock, such as limestone, erodes very rapidly. Harder rock, such as granite, shows little change over hundreds of years. Resistant rock formations that project out from shore are called **headlands.** Areas that have less resistant rock form *bays*. **Figure 2** shows bays and several other coastal landforms produced by wave erosion.

Sea Caves, Arches, and Stacks

Waves often cut deep into fractured and weak rock along the base of a cliff to form a large hole, or a *sea cave*. When waves cut completely through a headland, a *sea arch* forms. Offshore columns of rock that once were connected to a sea cliff or headland, are called *sea stacks*.

Terraces

As a sea cliff is worn, a nearly level platform, called a *wave-cut terrace*, usually remains beneath the water at the base of the cliff. Eroded material may be deposited offshore to create an extension to the wave-cut terrace called a *wave-built terrace*.

Reading Check List three features that are caused by shoreline erosion.

Figure 2 Wave erosion of sea cliffs causes cliff retreat and forms isolated sea stacks. Sea cliffs develop where waves strike directly against rock that is along a shoreline.

Sea arch

Sea cave

Berm

Beach

Bay

Beaches

Waves create features by eroding the land and depositing sediment. A deposit of sediment along an ocean or lake shore is called a **beach.** Beaches form where more sediment is deposited than is removed. After a beach forms, the rate at which sediment is deposited and the rate at which sediment is removed may vary.

Composition of Beaches

The sizes and kinds of materials that make up beaches vary. In general, the smaller the particle is, the farther it traveled before it was deposited. The composition of beach materials depends on the minerals in the source rock. Some beaches may consist of fragments of shells and coral that are washed ashore. In other locations, sand beaches form from sediment deposited by rivers or glaciers. Other beaches are composed of large pebbles.

The Berm

Each wave that reaches the shore moves sand slightly. The sand piles up to produce a sloping surface. During high tides or large storms, sand is deposited at the back of this slope. So, most beaches have a raised section called the *berm*, as shown in **Figure 2.** The berm is high and steep during the winter because large storms remove sand from the beach on the seaward side of the berm. The sand that is removed may be deposited offshore to form a long underwater ridge called a *sand bar*. In the summer, waves may move the sand back to the shore to widen the beach.

beach an area of the shoreline that is made up of deposited sediment

Headland

Sea stack

Wave-cut terrace

491

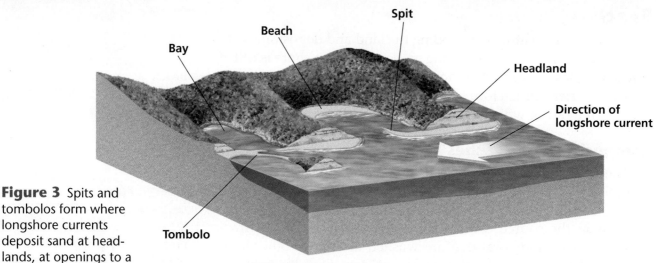

Bay
Beach
Spit
Headland
Direction of longshore current
Tombolo

Figure 3 Spits and tombolos form where longshore currents deposit sand at headlands, at openings to a bay, or on offshore islands.

Academic Vocabulary

individual (IN duh VIJ oo uhl) existing as a single, separate entity; particular

longshore current a water current that travels near and parallel to the shoreline

Longshore-Current Deposits

The direction in which a wave approaches the shore determines how the wave will move sediment. Most waves approach the beach at an angle and retreat in a direction that is more perpendicular to the shore. So, waves move <u>individual</u> sand grains in a zig-zag motion. The general movement of sand along the beach is in the direction in which the waves strike the shore.

Waves moving at an angle to the shoreline often create longshore currents. A **longshore current** is a movement of water parallel to and near the shoreline. Longshore currents transport sand parallel to the shoreline, as shown in **Figure 3.**

Along a relatively straight coastline, sand keeps moving until the shoreline changes direction at bays and headlands. The longshore current slows, and sand is deposited at the far end of the headland. A long, narrow deposit of sand connected at one end to the shore is called a *spit*. Currents and waves may curve the end of a spit into a hook shape. Beach deposits may also connect an offshore island to the mainland. Such connecting ridges of sand are called *tombolos*.

Section 2 Review

LA.910.2.2.3; SC.912.E.6.2; SC.912.E.6.4; SC.912.E.7.1; SC.912.E.7.4; SC.912.E.7.8

Key Ideas

1. **Compare** the formation of six features that are produced by shoreline erosion.

2. **Identify** two factors that determine the composition of beach materials.

3. **Explain** how beaches form.

4. **Compare** sea arches, sea caves, and sea stacks.

5. **Describe** three features produced by the movement of sand along a shore.

Critical Thinking

6. **Making Inferences** How do seasonal changes affect beaches?

7. **Identifying Relationships** How does the speed at which water moves affect the deposition of materials of differing sizes?

Concept Mapping

8. Use the following terms to create a concept map: *shoreline erosion, sea arch, sea cave, sea cliff, wave-cut terrace, wave-built terrace,* and *terrace.*

Coastal Erosion and Deposition

ENVIRONMENTAL CONNECTION

Key Ideas	Key Terms	Why It Matters
❭ Explain how changes in sea level affect coastlines. ❭ Describe the features of a barrier island. ❭ Analyze the effect of human activity on coastal land.	estuary barrier island lagoon	The same wave energy that erodes shorelines can be harnessed to produce electricity.

The boundaries between land and the ocean are among the most rapidly changing parts of Earth's surface. Coastal areas extend from relatively shallow water to several kilometers inland. Coastlines are affected by the long-term rise and fall of sea level and by the long-term uplifting or sinking of the land that borders the water. These and other more rapid processes, such as wave erosion and deposition, constantly change the appearance of coastlines.

Absolute Sea-Level Changes

A change in the amount of ocean water causes sea level to rise or fall, so coastlines are covered or exposed. During the last glacial period, which ended about 15,000 years ago, some of the water that is now in the ocean existed as continental ice sheets. Scientists estimate that the ice sheets held about 70 million cubic kilometers of ice. Now, the ice sheets in Antarctica and Greenland hold only about 25 million cubic kilometers of ice.

During the last glacial period, the water that made up the additional 45 million cubic kilometers of ice is thought to have come from the oceans. As a result, sea level was as much as 140 m lower during the last glacial period than it is today. Since the last glacial period, the ice sheets have been melting, as shown in **Figure 1.** Over the last 5,000 years, sea level has been rising at a rate of about 1 mm per year. If, in the distant future, the polar icecaps were to melt completely, the oceans would rise over 50 m and submerge low-lying coastal regions. The locations of many large cities, such as New York, Los Angeles, Miami, and Houston would be submerged.

FLORIDA STANDARDS

SC.912.E.6.4 Analyze how specific geologic processes and features are expressed in Florida and elsewhere; **SC.912.E.7.3** Differentiate and describe the various interactions among Earth systems, including: atmosphere, hydrosphere, cryosphere, geosphere, and biosphere; **SC.912.N.1.6** Describe how scientific inferences are drawn from scientific observations and provide examples from the content being studied.

Figure 1 This graph shows how sea level has changed during the past 35,000 years.

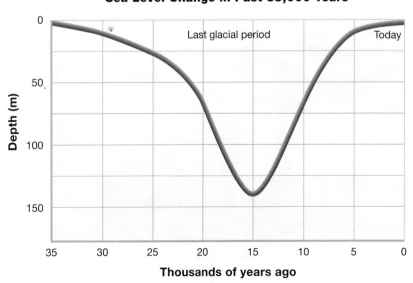

Sea Level Change in Past 35,000 Years

estuary an area where fresh water from rivers mixes with salt water from the ocean; the part of a river where the tides meet the river current

Relative Sea-Level Changes

Absolute sea level changes when the amount of water in the ocean changes. Relative sea level changes when the land or features near the coast change. These changes can be caused by large-scale geologic processes or by localized coastal changes. For example, movements of Earth's crust can cause coastlines to sink or to rise. Coastlines near a tectonic plate boundary may change as tectonic plates move. When coastlines change, the relative sea level of that area also changes.

Submergent Coastlines

When sea level rises or when land sinks, a *submergent coastline* forms. Divides between neighboring valleys become headlands separated by bays and inlets, and submerged peaks may form off-shore islands, as shown in **Figure 2**. Beaches are generally short, narrow, and rocky. When U-shaped glacial valleys become flooded with ocean water as sea level rises, spectacular narrow, deep bays that have steep walls, called *fiords* (FYAWRDZ), form.

The mouth of a river valley that is submerged by ocean water may become a wide, shallow bay that extends far inland. This type of bay, where salt water and fresh water mix, is called an **estuary** (ES tyoo er ee).

Emergent Coastlines

When the land rises or when sea level falls, an *emergent coastline* forms. If an emergent coastline has a steep slope and is exposed rapidly, the coastline will erode to form sea cliffs, narrow inlets, and bays. A series of wave-cut terraces may be exposed as well.

A gentle slope forms when part of the continental shelf is slowly lifted and exposed. The gentle slope forms a smooth coastal plain that has few bays or headlands and that has many long, wide beaches.

Figure 2 The features of a submergent coastline erode over time as sea level rises.

Barrier Islands

As sea level rises over a flat coastal plain, the shoreline moves inland and isolates dunes from the old shoreline to form barrier islands, such as the one shown in **Figure 3**. **Barrier islands** are long, narrow ridges of sand that lie nearly parallel to the shoreline. Barrier islands can be 3 to 30 km offshore and can be more than 100 km long. Between a barrier island and the shoreline is a narrow region of shallow water called a **lagoon**.

Barrier islands also form when sand spits are separated from the land by storms or when waves pile up ridges of sand that were scraped from the shallow, offshore sea bottom. These deposits are then moved toward the shore by waves, currents, and winds. This motion causes most barrier islands to migrate toward the shoreline. Winds blowing toward the land often create a line of dunes that are 3 to 6 m high on the side of the island that faces the shore.

Large waves from storms, especially waves from hurricanes, may severely erode barrier islands. During a storm, sand washes from the ocean side toward the inland side of the island. Some barrier islands are eroding at a rate of about 20 m per year.

Reading Check How do barrier islands form?

Figure 3 Santa Rosa Island is a long, narrow barrier island that is located off the coast of Florida.

barrier island a long ridge of sand or narrow island that lies parallel to the shore

lagoon a small body of water separated from the sea by a low, narrow strip of land

Why It Matters

Wave Power

EYE ON THE ENVIRONMENT

What if we could capture the ocean's energy and use it in our homes? Ocean waves may one day provide trillions of watts of power. Like solar power and wind power, wave power can produce electricity without pollution. This machine, called Pelamis, converts wave energy into electricity.

YOUR TURN
CRITICAL THINKING
On which shorelines is wave power possible? Explain why.

495

Figure 4 This beach area near Biloxi, Mississippi was devastated by Hurricane Katrina.

Academic Vocabulary

economic (ek uh NAHM ik) relating to commerce

SC*LINKS*

www.scilinks.org
Topic: Coastal Changes
Code: HQX0307

Preserving the Coastline

Coastal lands are used for commercial fishing, shipping, industrial and residential development, and recreation. While development of coastal areas is economically important, it can also damage coastal areas in several ways. Pollution is a serious threat to coastal resources. Oil spills are a threat because tankers travel near shorelines and because oil wells are drilled offshore. Garbage, pollution from industry, and sewage from towns on the coast can pollute the coastline. This pollution can damage habitats and kill marine birds and other animals.

Beaches damaged by hurricanes such as Katrina in 2005 will require years of rebuilding, as shown in **Figure 4.** To preserve the coastal zone, private owners and government agencies often work together to set guidelines for coastal protection. Coastal development in some environmentally sensitive areas, such as the North Carolina coast, has been slowed or stopped completely in an attempt to protect these important areas.

Section 3 Review

LA.910.2.2.3; SC.912.E.6.2; SC.912.E.6.4; SC.912.E.7.1; SC.912.E.7.4; SC.912.E.7.9

Key Ideas

1. **Explain** how changes in sea level affect coastlines.

2. **Explain** how the formation of a submergent coastline differs from the formation of an emergent coastline.

3. **Describe** two features of a barrier island.

4. **Explain** why barrier islands are particularly sensitive to erosion.

5. **Describe** two ways in which human activity affects coastlines.

Critical Thinking

6. **Making Predictions** Predict the effect that a season of heavy storms would have on a barrier island.

7. **Identifying Relationships** If Earth were to enter a new glacial period, how might coastlines around the world change?

Concept Mapping

8. Use the following terms to create a concept map: *coastline, emergent coastline, submergent coastline, barrier island,* and *lagoon.*

Where Did All This Sand Come From?

REAL WORLD

It is hard to make a mountain move, but it is just as hard to make a sand dune stop moving. Over decades and centuries, sand dunes have buried many towns and structures. Today, sand dunes threaten to blanket towns and cities in parts of Northern China, Saharan Africa, and the Middle East. The rate of a dune's movement depends on the dune's size and location, as well as wind patterns. Scientists study the movement of dunes to better understand dune migration and to help manage dunes in areas where they threaten human populations.

This house is in a Namibian village built in the early 1900s. Today, the town is covered in sand.

This Danish lighthouse was fully functional in 1900. It was closed in the 1960s, taken over by coastal erosion.

Dunes loom over Nouakchott, Mauritania—the largest city in Saharan Africa. Sooner or later, the dunes will move in on the city.

YOUR TURN

UNDERSTANDING CONCEPTS
List three factors that affect the rate at which a sand dune moves.

ONLINE RESEARCH
Sand dunes move through the process of *granular flow*. Use the Internet to learn more about this process. Write a one-page summary of what you learn.

What You'll Do

› **Model** the effects of wave action and longshore currents on a beach.

› **Identify** ways to decrease the effects of wave action on beach sand.

What You'll Need

block, plaster (2)
block, wooden, large
container, plastic, large
pebbles
ruler, metric
sand, 5 to 10 lb
water

Safety

Beaches

Coastal management is a growing concern because beaches are increasingly used for resources and recreation. The supply of sand for many beaches has been cut off by dams built on rivers and streams that would otherwise carry sand to the shoreline. Waves generated by storms also continuously wear away beaches. In some places, breakwaters have been built offshore to protect beaches from washing away. In this lab, you will examine how wave action may change the shape of beaches and how these changes can be reduced.

Ask a Question

1 How does wave action affect the amount of sand on a beach? How can these effects be reduced?

Form a Hypothesis

2 Form a hypothesis that answers your question. Explain your reasoning.

Test the Hypothesis

3 Make a beach in a large, shallow container by placing a mixture of sand and small pebbles at one end of the container. The beach should occupy about one-fourth of the length of the container.

4 In front of the sand, add water to a depth of 2 to 3 cm. Record what happens.

5 Use the large wooden block to generate several waves by moving the block up and down in the water at the end of the container opposite the beach. Continue this wave action until about half the beach has moved. Describe the beach after this wave action has taken place.

Step ❺

6 Remove the sand, and rebuild the beach.

7 Design three breakwaters that change the flow of water along the beach. Draw your designs on a piece of paper. The two top photos at right are samples of some break-water arrangements.

8 Have your teacher approve your designs before you build them into your model beach.

9 Use the two plaster blocks to model the first breakwater that you designed. Use a wooden block to generate waves as in step 5. Record your observations.

10 Use the wooden block to generate waves that move parallel to the beach. Record your observations.

11 Repeat steps 9 and 10 for each of your other two designs. Record your observations.

Step 7

Analyze the Results

1. **Making Comparisons** How does wave action build up a beach? How does wave action wear away a beach?

2. **Explaining Events** Describe how the sand moved when the waves ran parallel to the beach in step 10.

Step 7

3. **Analyzing Results** How do breakwaters modify the effect that longshore currents have on the shape of a beach?

Draw Conclusions

4. **Making Predictions** Predict what will happen to a beach that is affected by wave action if it had no source of additional sand.

5. **Drawing Conclusions** What effect would a series of jetties have on a beach?

Step 10

Extension

Research and Communications Research what can be done to preserve a recreational beach from erosion that is caused by excessive use by people. Write a letter to a local authority outlining a plan of action to protect that beach.

MAPS in Action

Coastal Erosion Near the Beaufort Sea

**Rapid erosion
(>5 m/per year)**

**Moderate erosion
(1 to 5 m/per year)**

**No detectable erosion
(−1 to 1 m/per year)**

**Deposition
(<−1 m/per year)**

Areas of accretion are shown in purple. Accretion occurs when more material is deposited than is eroded.

Map ▶ Skills Activity

This map shows the coastline of the Beaufort Sea in Canada along with computed amounts of shoreline erosion and accretion. Use the map to answer the questions below.

1. **Using a Key** How many areas of accretion are shown on the map?

2. **Using a Key** What is the level of erosion that is present in most areas shown?

3. **Analyzing Data** Is the estimated overall shoreline change for the entire area shown a positive value (accretion) or a negative value (erosion)?

4. **Making Comparisons** Is there more erosion on the coastal area toward the north or on the area toward the south?

5. **Inferring Relationships** Is the area shown in the map more significantly affected by the effects of waves along the shoreline or by the depositional actions of rivers that enter the ocean? Explain your answer.

6. **Identifying Trends** If present conditions remain the same, what would you expect to happen to the five small islands that are located on the northwest area of the map?

Summary

THINK central
SUPER SUMMARY
Keyword: HQXEWWS

Key Ideas | Key Terms

Section 1

Wind Erosion

> Saltation and deflation are two ways that wind erodes land. Saltation is the movement of particles by a series of jumps or bounces. Deflation is a form of erosion in which dry soil or rock particles are removed by the wind while larger rock particles are left behind.

> The two types of wind deposits are dunes, which are generally made of sand, and loess, which is made of dust particles.

saltation, p. 483
deflation, p. 484
ventifact, p. 485
dune, p. 485
loess, p. 488

Section 2

Wave Erosion

> Wave erosion produces many shoreline features, including steep rock cliffs called *sea cliffs*, holes at the bases of cliffs called *sea caves*, rock bridges called *sea arches*, rock columns called *sea stacks*, flat platforms at the bases of cliffs called *terraces*, and sediment deposits along the shore called *beaches*.

> Beaches form from the deposition of sediments by waves.

> Longshore currents carry sand parallel to the shoreline, forming narrow deposits of sand called *spits*, and ridges of sand that connect islands to the shore called *tombolos*.

headland, p. 490
beach, p. 491
longshore current, p. 492

Section 3

Coastal Erosion and Deposition

> Coastlines migrate as sea level changes.

> Barrier islands are long, narrow offshore ridges of sand.

> Human activities, including development and pollution, threaten coastal resources and habitat.

estuary, p. 494
barrier island, p. 495
lagoon, p. 495

1. **Four-Corner Fold** Make a four-corner fold. Label the outer flaps with the names of different types of landscapes: Coastlines and Beaches, Deserts, Cities and Towns, and Farmland. Under

   the appropriate flap, describe how erosion from wind and water affects each type of landscape.

USING KEY TERMS

Use each of the following terms in a separate sentence.

2. *ventifact* SC.912.E.6.2

3. *longshore current* SC.912.E.6.2

4. *loess* SC.912.E.6.2

For each pair of terms, explain how the meanings of the terms differ.

5. *saltation* and *deflation* SC.912.E.6.2

6. *headland* and *beach* SC.912.E.6.2

7. *barrier island* and *lagoon* SC.912.E.6.2

UNDERSTANDING KEY IDEAS

8. Wind forms desert pavement by removing fine sediment and by leaving large rocks behind in a process called SC.912.E.6.2
   a. saltation.
   b. abrasion.
   c. deflation.
   d. ventifact.

9. Wind moves sand by SC.912.E.6.2
   a. saltation.
   b. emergence.
   c. abrasion.
   d. depression.

10. Dunes move primarily by the process called
    a. abrasion. SC.912.E.6.2
    b. migration.
    c. deflation.
    d. submergence.

11. Thinly layered, yellowish, fine-grained deposits are called SC.912.E.6.2
    a. beaches.
    b. loess.
    c. dunes.
    d. desert pavement.

12. The most important erosion agent on shorelines is SC.912.E.6.4
    a. wave action.   c. wind.
    b. weathering.   d. the tide.

13. Which of the following shoreline features is *not* produced by wave erosion of sea cliffs? SC.912.E.6.2
    a. spits
    b. sea stacks
    c. wave-cut terraces
    d. sea arches

14. Longshore-current deposition of sand at the end of a headland produces a SC.912.E.6.4
    a. sand bar.   c. dune.
    b. spit.   d. sea cliff.

15. Over the last 5,000 years, sea level has changed by SC.912.E.6.2
    a. no significant amount.
    b. falling about 1 mm per year.
    c. rising about 1 cm per year.
    d. rising about 1 mm per year.

16. Barrier islands tend to migrate SC.912.E.6.4
    a. away from the shore.
    b. along the shore.
    c. in the summer.
    d. toward the shore.

SHORT ANSWER

17. What is the difference between an emergent coastline and a submergent coastline? SC.912.E.6.4

18. Explain what may happen if shoreline resources are not protected. SC.912.E.6.4

19. What factors affect the composition of a beach? SC.912.E.6.4

20. Explain the difference between the four main types of dunes. SC.912.E.6.2

21. Explain the difference between absolute sea-level change and relative sea-level change. SC.912.E.6.4

CRITICAL THINKING

22. **Identifying Relationships** The deserts of the southwestern United States contain many tall, sculpted rock formations. Was wind or water erosion the most likely agent responsible for these formations? Explain. SC.912.E.6.4

23. Making Inferences Suppose that one time each month for a year a satellite orbiting Earth takes a photograph of the same sandy, 1 km² area of the Sahara. Would the surface features shown in these 12 photographs remain essentially the same, or would they vary? Explain your answer. `SC.912.E.6.4`

24. Inferring Relationships Wave energy decreases when waves travel through shallow water. Based on this information, what effect do you think development of a wave-built terrace has on erosion of the shoreline? Explain your answer. `SC.912.E.6.4`

CONCEPT MAPPING

25. Use the following terms to create a concept map: *wave erosion, beaches, spit, berm,* and *tombolos.* `SC.912.E.6.4`

MATH SKILLS Math Skills

26. Making Calculations Suppose it was possible for the sea level to continuously rise at the rate of 1 mm per year and that other factors affecting the coastlines do not change. How many kilometers would the sea level rise in 1 million years? `SC.912.E.6.4`

27. Applying Quantities Every year, 25 km³ of sand is deposited on a beach by a nearby river, and 28 km³ of sand is removed by wave action. Is the size of the beach increasing or decreasing? Explain. `SC.912.E.6.4`

WRITING SKILLS

28. Creative Writing Imagine that you are a newspaper reporter who has traveled to another planet. Scientists know that, at one time, both wind and water eroded the surface of the planet. Prepare a news release that describes the landscape you see and explains the processes that produced it. `SC.912.E.6.2`

29. Writing Persuasively You have learned that beautifully colored sunsets and sunrises are the result of dust in the atmosphere. Write a letter or essay to your doubting friend to convince him or her that sunsets and sunrises are caused by dust. Use the evidence that remarkable sunsets were visible around the world for two years after the 1883 eruption of Krakatau, a volcanic island in Indonesia, in your essay. `SC.912.E.6.4`

INTERPRETING GRAPHICS

The graph below shows soil erosion in the United States by wind and water from 1987 to 2003. Use this graph to answer the questions that follow.

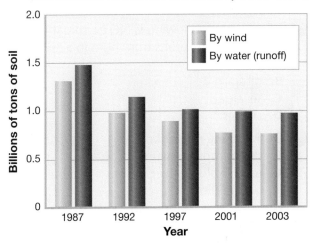

Soil Erosion in the United States, 1987–2003

30. Which year had the most combined soil erosion? `SC.912.E.6.2`

31. Which year had the most soil erosion due to water? `SC.912.E.6.2`

32. Do you predict more or less soil erosion by wind in future years? Explain your answer. `SC.912.E.6.2`

33. Would you expect that the amount of soil erosion in the United States would ever be zero? Explain your answer. `SC.912.E.6.2`

Understanding Concepts

Directions (1–9): For each question, write on a separate sheet of paper the letter of the correct answer.

1 Which of the following factors most affects the rate at which waves erode land features along the shore?
   A. temperature of the waves
   B. direction in which waves approach shores
   C. shape of the rock formation
   D. compostion of the rock formation

2 Why are dust particles more likely to remain in the atmosphere longer and travel farther than sand particles?
   F. Sand grains are carried higher and fall.
   G. Dust particles are smaller and lighter.
   H. Sand grains are made from rocks.
   I. Dust is moved by the process of saltation.

3 Which of the following is NOT a threat to shorelines that results from human activity?
   A. pollution
   B. oil spills
   C. sewage
   D. storms

4 During dune migration,
   F. dunes move upwind.
   G. sand is blown over the crest and builds up on the slipface.
   H. dunes will continue to move, even when they reach a barrier.
   I. sand particles are moved by water.

5 Why is erosion by wind more common in arid climates than in other regions of the world?
   A. Arid climates have much thicker soil layers.
   B. Arid climates have less frequent dust storms.
   C. Arid climates have less plant cover to anchor soil.
   D. Arid climates have more moisture to hold soil.

6 Which of the following statements is true of absolute sea-level changes and relative sea-level changes?
   F. Absolute sea-level changes and relative sea-level changes both result from coastal changes.
   G. Absolute sea-level changes result from changes in the amount of water in the oceans, and relative sea-level changes can be localized.
   H. Absolute sea-level changes affect some shorelines while relative sea-level changes affect all shorelines.
   I. Movements of Earth's crust cause both absolute sea-level changes and relative sea-level changes.

7 Which of the following processes causes erosion along a shoreline?
   A. mechanical weathering
   B. chemical reactions that occur within cracks in the rock
   C. both mechanical and chemical weathering
   D. abrasion

8 Which of the following statements about longshore currents is true?
   F. They deposit sand at the far end of a headland.
   G. They cause most shoreline erosion.
   H. They run perpendicular to shorelines.
   I. They approach the shoreline at an angle.

9 How are sand grains moved by saltation?
   A. The sand grains are carried high into the atmosphere, where they remain suspended.
   B. The sand grains move in the opposite direction of the blowing wind.
   C. The sand grains rise high above the ground, but settle back to Earth.
   D. The sand grains are moved by a series of jumps and bounces.

Interpreting Graphics

Directions (10–11): For each question below, record the correct answer on a separate sheet of paper.

Erosion of a Sea Cliff

10 The coastal landforms shown were most likely formed as a result of the action of

F. glacial movements.

G. seismic activity.

H. sea-level changes.

I. waves and weathering.

Map of Coastal Erosion Patterns

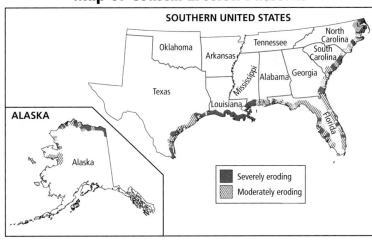

11 Based on the figure above, in which area is shoreline erosion most severe?

A. Louisiana

B. Georgia

C. Texas

D. Alabama

Test Tip

Do not spend a long period of time on any single question. Mark a question that you cannot answer quickly, and come back to it.

Geology Connections

Science, technology, and society are closely linked. This flowchart shows just a few of the connections in the history of geology.

9,500 B.C.E. Systematic farming begins in the Fertile Crescent.

1620 The *Mayflower* carries 102 passengers to Plymouth, Massachusetts.

1790 Farmers make up 90% of the labor force in the United States.

1831 The McCormick reaper makes harvesting grain much more efficient.

1837 John Deere invents a steel walking plow with a curved blade.

1730s Charles "Turnip" Townshend introduces the 4-year crop rotation method.

1935–1938 Overplowing and overgrazing the Great Plains, combined with drought, leads to the creation of the "Dust Bowl."

1916 George Washington Carver publishes *Help for the Hard Times* in which he outlines soil conservation suggestions.

800 B.C.E. Farmers in the Persian empire develop the *qanat* irrigation system.

312 B.C.E. The Romans build the *Aqua Appia*, the first of eleven major aqueducts.

1900 American farmers first use sprinkler irrigation systems.

1954 More farms use tractors than animals, such as horses or mules, for farm production processes.

1911 The Ogallala aquifer in the Midwestern United States is first tapped for irrigation.

2000 Every day, 17 billion gallons of water from the Ogallala aquifer are used for irrigation.

1935 The Natural Resource Conservation Service is established.

2004 Global sales of bottled water exceed $100 billion per year.

2008 The U.S. government offers $20 million in Conservation Innovation Grants.

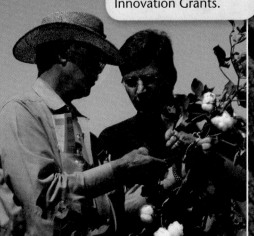

YOUR TURN

UNDERSTANDING CONCEPTS
How is farming related to groundwater use?

CRITICAL THINKING
Why would a government want to give grants for innovative conservation technologies or methods?

Unit 6 Atmospheric Forces

The Atmosphere

Chapter Outline

Why It Matters

The atmosphere makes life as we know it possible on Earth. Gases, such as oxygen and carbon dioxide, which organisms need to live, are contained in the atmosphere. The atmosphere also regulates temperature on Earth and helps to protect living organisms from harmful radiation.

Inquiry Lab

15 min

Colorful Currents

Pour hot water into two beakers, so that the beakers are three-fourths full. To one beaker, add a chunk of dyed ice. To the second beaker, add a chunk of dyed ice that contains a short length of metal chain or several large paper clips strung together. Observe the beakers. Record your observations at 0 min, 1 min, and 5 min.

Questions to Get You Started

1. What is happening in the beakers at 0 min? What is happening at 1 min and at 5 min?

2. What type of energy transfer explains the effect that you see in the first beaker? How can you tell?

3. What type of energy transfer explains the effect that you see in the second beaker? How can you tell?

SC.912.E.7.3

READING TOOLBOX

These reading tools will help you learn the material in this chapter.

Word Parts

Prefixes You can figure out the meanings of many unfamiliar science terms by looking at their word parts. For example, the word *atmosphere* is formed by combining the prefix *atmos-* with the root *sphere*. *Atmos* comes from the Greek word for "vapor" and means "air." *Sphere* is used because the atmosphere is shaped like a sphere around Earth.

Your Turn As you read Section 1, make a table like the one started below. List the layers of the atmosphere, the prefix in the name of each layer, and your guess for the meaning of the prefix. After you have finished, look up the prefixes in a dictionary and correct your table as necessary.

Layer	Prefix	Meaning
troposphere	tropo-	
stratosphere		

Cause and Effect

Signal Words Certain words and phrases signal cause-and-effect relationships. These signal words and phrases are called *cause-and-effect markers*.

Cause markers	Effect markers
cause	therefore
affect	thus
produce	as a result of
as a result of	is an effect of
due to	results from
because	consequently

Your Turn Complete a table of cause-and-effect markers, like the one started below, as you read this chapter.

Cause	Effect	Marker(s)
convection	heating of the lower atmosphere of Earth	the result of; because

Fold Notes

Layered Book FoldNotes are a fun way to help you learn and remember ideas that you encounter as you read. You can use the flaps of the layered book to summarize information you learn into categories.

Your Turn Make a layered book, as described in **Appendix A**. Label the tabs of the layered book

"Troposphere," "Stratosphere," "Mesosphere," and "Thermosphere."

Write notes on the appropriate layers as you read Section 1.

For more information on how to use these and other tools, see **Appendix A**.

SECTION 1 Characteristics of the Atmosphere

Key Ideas	Key Terms	Why It Matters
❯ Describe the composition of Earth's atmosphere. ❯ Explain how two types of barometers work. ❯ Identify the layers of the atmosphere. ❯ Identify two effects of air pollution.	atmosphere ozone atmospheric pressure troposphere stratosphere mesosphere thermosphere	Certain characteristics of the atmosphere have a direct effect on your health and well-being. Whether it's the gases that make up air or the way that it is structured, without the atmosphere, life as we know it would be impossible.

The layer of gases that surrounds Earth is called the **atmosphere.** The atmosphere is made up of a mixture of chemical elements and compounds that is commonly called *air.* The atmosphere protects Earth's surface from the sun's radiation and helps to regulate the temperature of Earth's surface.

Composition of the Atmosphere

As the graph in **Figure 1** shows, the most abundant elements in air are the gases nitrogen, oxygen, and argon. The composition of dry air is nearly the same everywhere on Earth's surface and up to an altitude of about 80 km. The two most abundant compounds in air are the gases carbon dioxide, CO_2, and water vapor, H_2O. In addition to containing gaseous elements and compounds, the atmosphere commonly carries various kinds of tiny solid particles, such as dust and pollen.

Nitrogen in the Atmosphere

Nitrogen makes up about 78% of Earth's atmosphere. Nitrogen in the atmosphere is maintained through a process called the *nitrogen cycle.* During the nitrogen cycle, nitrogen moves from air to the soil and then to plants and animals, and eventually returns to the air.

Nitrogen is removed from the air mainly by the action of nitrogen-fixing bacteria. These microscopic organisms live in the soil and on the roots of certain plants. The bacteria chemically change nitrogen from the air into nitrogen compounds that are vital to the growth of all plants. When animals eat plants, nitrogen compounds enter the animals' bodies. Nitrogen compounds are then returned to the soil through animal wastes or by the decay of dead organisms. Decay releases nitrogen back into the atmosphere. A similar nitrogen cycle takes place between marine organisms and ocean water.

FLORIDA STANDARDS

SC.912.E.7.3 Differentiate and describe the various interactions among Earth systems, including: atmosphere, hydrosphere, cryosphere, geosphere, and biosphere; **SC.912.N.3.5** Describe the function of models in science, and identify the wide range of models used in science; **SC.912.N.4.1** Explain how scientific knowledge and reasoning provide an empirically-based perspective to inform society's decision making.

atmosphere a mixture of gases that surrounds a planet, moon, or other celestial body

Figure 1 This pie graph shows the composition of dry air by volume at sea level.

Section 1 **Characteristics of the Atmosphere 513**

Figure 2 Several processes interact to maintain stable amounts of oxygen, carbon dioxide, and water in the atmosphere.

**READING
TOOLBOX**

Signal Words
Locate the signal words that indicate cause-and-effect relationships on this page. Use a table with three columns to record the causes, the effects, and their markers.

www.scilinks.org
Topic: The Atmosphere
Code: HQX0112

Oxygen in the Atmosphere

Oxygen makes up about 21% of Earth's atmosphere. As shown in **Figure 2,** natural processes maintain the chemical balance of oxygen in the atmosphere. Animals, bacteria, and plants remove oxygen from the air as part of their life processes. Forest fires, the burning of fuels, and the weathering of some rocks also remove oxygen from the air. These processes would quickly use up most atmospheric oxygen if various processes that add oxygen to the air did not take place.

Land and ocean plants produce large quantities of oxygen in a process called *photosynthesis.* During photosynthesis, plants use sunlight, water, and carbon dioxide to produce their food, and they release oxygen as a byproduct. The amount of oxygen produced by plants each year is about equal to the amount consumed by all animal life processes. Thus, the oxygen content of the air remains at about 21% of Earth's atmosphere.

Water Vapor in the Atmosphere

As water evaporates from oceans, lakes, streams, and soil, it enters air as the invisible gas *water vapor.* Plants and animals release water vapor during the life processes of transpiration or respiration, as shown in **Figure 2.** But as water vapor enters the atmosphere, it is removed by the processes of condensation and precipitation. The percentage of water vapor in the atmosphere varies depending on factors such as time of day, location, and season. Because the amount of water vapor in air varies, the composition of the atmosphere is usually given as that of dry air. Dry air has less than 1% water vapor. Moist air may contain as much as 4% water vapor.

Reading Check **Does transpiration increase or decrease the amount of water vapor in the atmosphere?** (See Appendix G for answers to Reading Checks.)

Ozone in the Atmosphere

Although it is present only in small amounts, a form of oxygen called **ozone** is an important component of the atmosphere. The oxygen that we breathe, O_2, has two atoms per molecule, but ozone, O_3, has three atoms. Ozone in the upper atmosphere forms the *ozone layer*, which absorbs harmful ultraviolet radiation from the sun. Without the ozone layer, living organisms would be severely damaged by the sun's ultraviolet rays. Unfortunately, a number of human activities damage the ozone layer. Compounds known as *chlorofluorocarbons*, or CFCs, which were previously used in refrigerators and air conditioners, and exhaust compounds, such as nitrogen oxide, break down ozone and have caused parts of the ozone layer to weaken, as **Figure 3** shows.

Particulates in the Atmosphere

In addition to gases, the atmosphere contains various tiny solid and liquid particles, called *particulates*. Particulates can be volcanic dust, ash from fires, microscopic organisms, or mineral particles lifted from soil by winds. Pollen from plants and particles from meteors that have vaporized are also particulates. When tiny drops of ocean water are tossed into the air as sea spray, the drops evaporate. Left behind in the air are tiny crystals of salt, another type of particulate. Four common sources of particulates are shown in **Figure 4.** Large, heavy particles remain in the atmosphere only briefly, but tiny particles can remain suspended in the atmosphere for months or years.

ozone a gas molecule that is made up of three oxygen atoms

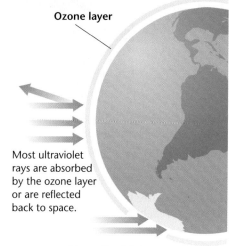

Ozone layer

Most ultraviolet rays are absorbed by the ozone layer or are reflected back to space.

More ultraviolet rays penetrate to Earth's surface through the weakened ozone layer.

Figure 3 Harmful ultraviolet radiation can reach Earth's surface through the weakened ozone layer over Antarctica.

Figure 4 **Sources of Particulates**

Volcanic ash and dust can remain in the atmosphere for months.

The wind carries pollen from plant to plant.

Tornadoes and windstorms carry dirt and dust high into the atmosphere.

As seaspray evaporates, salt particles are left in the atmosphere.

Figure 5 At high altitudes, many climbers carry a supply of oxygen because the density of the atmosphere there is very low. In 2001, Eric Weihenmeyer (above) was the first blind person to reach the summit of Mount Everest.

atmospheric pressure the force per unit area that is exerted on a surface by the weight of the atmosphere

Atmospheric Pressure

Gravity holds the gases of the atmosphere near Earth's surface. As a result, the air molecules are compressed together and exert force on Earth's surface. The pressure exerted on a surface by the atmosphere is called **atmospheric pressure.** Atmospheric pressure is exerted equally in all directions—up, down, and sideways.

Earth's gravity keeps 99% of the total mass of the atmosphere within 32 km of Earth's surface. The remaining 1% extends upward for hundreds of kilometers but gets increasingly thinner at high altitudes, as shown in **Figure 5.** Because there is less weight pressing down from above at higher altitudes, the air molecules are farther apart and exert less pressure on each other at higher altitudes. Thus, atmospheric pressure decreases as altitude increases.

Atmospheric pressure also changes as a result of differences in temperature and in the amount of water vapor in the air. In general, as temperature increases, atmospheric pressure at sea level decreases. The reason is that molecules move farther apart when the air is heated. So, fewer particles exert pressure on a given area, and the pressure decreases. Similarly, air that contains a lot of water vapor is less dense than drier air because water vapor molecules have less mass than nitrogen or oxygen molecules do. The lighter water vapor molecules replace an equal number of heavier oxygen and nitrogen molecules, which makes the volume of the air less dense.

Measuring Atmospheric Pressure

Meteorologists use three units for atmospheric pressure: atmospheres (atm), millimeters or inches of mercury, and millibars (mb). *Standard atmospheric pressure,* or 1 atm, is equal to 760 mm of mercury, or 1,000 mb. The average atmospheric pressure at sea level is 1 atm. Meteorologists measure atmospheric pressure by using an instrument called a *barometer.*

Mercurial Barometers

Meteorologists use two main types of barometers. One type is the *mercurial barometer*, a model of which is shown in **Figure 6.** Atmospheric pressure presses on the liquid mercury in a well at the base of the barometer. The pressure holds the mercury up to a certain height inside a tube. The height of the mercury inside the tube varies with the atmospheric pressure. The greater the atmospheric pressure is, the higher the mercury rises.

Aneroid Barometers

The type of barometer most commonly used today is called an *aneroid barometer*. Inside an aneroid barometer is a sealed metal container from which most of the air has been removed to form a partial vacuum. Changes in atmospheric pressure cause the sides of the container to bend inward or bulge out. These changes move a pointer on a scale. Aneroid barometers can be constructed to keep a continuous record of atmospheric pressure.

An aneroid barometer can also measure altitude above sea level. When used for this purpose, an aneroid barometer is called an *altimeter*. The scale on an altimeter registers altitude instead of pressure. At high altitudes, the atmosphere is less dense and has less pressure exerted on it from above than at low altitudes. So, a lowered pressure reading can be interpreted as an increased altitude reading.

Figure 6 The height of the mercury in this mercurial barometer indicates barometric pressure. *What is the barometric pressure shown?*

Academic Vocabulary

interpret (in TUHR pruht) figure out the meaning of

Reading Check What is inside an aneroid barometer?

SC.912.E.7.3

Quick Lab   Barometric Pressure

25 min (over 5 days)

Procedure

① Use a rubber band to secure plastic wrap tightly over the open end of a coffee can.

② Use tape to secure one end of a 10 cm drinking straw onto the plastic wrap near the center of the can.

③ Use scissors and a metric ruler to cut a piece of cardboard 10 cm wide. The cardboard should also be at least 13 cm taller than the can.

④ Fold the cardboard so that it stands upright and extends at least 3 cm above the top of the straw.

⑤ Place the cardboard near the can so that the free end of the straw just touches the front of the cardboard. Mark an X where the straw touches.

⑥ Draw three horizontal lines on the cardboard: one that is level with the X, one that is 2 cm above the X, and one that is 2 cm below the X.

⑦ Position the cardboard so that the straw touches the X. Tape the base of the cardboard in place.

⑧ Observe the level of the straw at least once per day over a 5-day period. Record any changes that you see.

Analysis

1. What factors affect how your model works? Explain.

2. What does an upward movement of the straw indicate? What does a downward movement indicate?

3. Compare your results with the barometric pressures listed in your local newspaper. What may have caused your results to differ from the newspaper's?

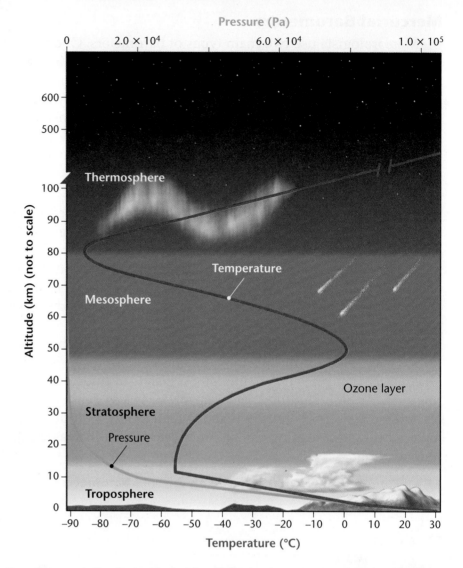

Figure 7 The red line indicates the temperature at various altitudes in the atmosphere. The green line indicates atmospheric pressure at various altitudes.

Layers of the Atmosphere

Earth's atmosphere has a distinctive pattern of temperature changes with increasing altitude, as shown in **Figure 7.** The temperature differences mainly result from how solar energy is absorbed as it moves through the atmosphere. Scientists identify four main layers of the atmosphere based on these differences.

The Troposphere

The atmospheric layer that is closest to Earth's surface and in which nearly all weather occurs is called the **troposphere.** Almost all the water vapor and carbon dioxide in the atmosphere is found in this layer. Temperature within the troposphere decreases as altitude increases because air in this layer is heated from below by thermal energy that radiates from Earth's surface. The temperature within the troposphere decreases at the average rate of 6.5 °C per kilometer as the distance from Earth's surface increases. However, at an average altitude of 12 km, the temperature stops decreasing. This zone is called the *tropopause* and represents the upper boundary of the troposphere. The altitude of this boundary varies with latitude and season.

troposphere the lowest layer of the atmosphere, in which temperature drops at a constant rate as altitude increases; the part of the atmosphere where weather conditions exist

The Stratosphere

The layer of the atmosphere called the **stratosphere** extends from the tropopause to an altitude of nearly 50 km. Almost all the ozone in the atmosphere is concentrated in this layer. In the lower stratosphere, the temperature is almost –60 °C. In the upper stratosphere, the temperature increases as altitude increases because air in the stratosphere is heated by absorption of solar radiation by ozone. The temperature of the air in this layer rises steadily to a temperature of about 0 °C at an altitude of about 50 km above Earth's surface. This zone, called the *stratopause*, marks the upper boundary of the stratosphere.

The Mesosphere

Located above the stratopause and extending to an altitude of about 80 km is the **mesosphere.** In this layer, temperature decreases as altitude increases. The upper boundary of the mesosphere, called the *mesopause*, has an average temperature of nearly –90 °C, which is the coldest temperature in the atmosphere. Above this boundary, temperatures again begin to increase.

The Thermosphere

The atmospheric layer above the mesopause is called the **thermosphere.** In the thermosphere, temperature increases steadily as altitude increases because nitrogen and oxygen atoms absorb solar radiation. Because air particles in the thermosphere are very far apart, they do not strike a thermometer often enough to produce an accurate temperature reading. Therefore, special instruments are needed. These instruments have recorded temperatures of more than 1,000 °C in the thermosphere.

The lower region of the thermosphere, at an altitude of 80 to 400 km, is commonly called the *ionosphere*. In the ionosphere, solar radiation that is absorbed by atmospheric gases causes the atoms of gas molecules to lose electrons and to produce ions and free electrons. Interactions between solar radiation and the ionosphere cause the phenomena known as *auroras*, which are shown in **Figure 8.**

There are not enough data about temperature changes in the thermosphere to determine its upper boundary. However, above the ionosphere is the region where Earth's atmosphere blends into the almost complete vacuum of space. This zone of indefinite altitude, called the *exosphere*, extends for thousands of kilometers above the ionosphere.

Reading Check What is the lower region of the thermosphere called?

stratosphere the layer of the atmosphere that lies between the troposphere and the mesosphere and in which temperature increases as altitude increases; contains the ozone layer

mesosphere the coldest layer of the atmosphere, between the stratosphere and the thermosphere, in which temperature decreases as altitude increases

thermosphere the uppermost layer of the atmosphere, in which temperature increases as altitude increases; includes the ionosphere

Figure 8 Auroras can be seen from space as well as from the ground.

Temperature Inversions

🌿 Any substance that is in the atmosphere and that is harmful to people, animals, plants, or property is called an *air pollutant*. Today, the main source of air pollution is the burning of fossil fuels, such as coal and petroleum. As these fuels burn, they may release harmful chemical substances, such as sulfur dioxide gas, hydrocarbons, nitrogen oxides, carbon monoxide, and lead, into the air.

Certain weather conditions can make air pollution worse. One such condition is a *temperature inversion*, the layering of warm air on top of cool air. Warm air, which is less dense than cool air is, can trap cool, polluted air beneath it. In some areas, topography may make air pollution even worse by keeping the polluted inversion layer from dispersing, as **Figure 9** shows. Under conditions in which air cannot circulate up and away from an area, trapped automobile exhaust can produce *smog*, a general term for air pollution that is a combination of smoke and fog.

Air pollution can be controlled only by preventing the release of pollutants into the atmosphere. International, federal, and local laws have been passed to reduce the amount of air pollutants produced by automobiles and industry. 🌿

Figure 9 During a temperature inversion, polluted cool air becomes trapped beneath a warm-air layer.

Section 1 Review

🌺 LA.910.2.2.3; SC.912.E.7.3

Key Ideas

1. **Describe** the composition of dry air at sea level.

2. **Identify** five main components of the atmosphere.

3. **Explain** the cause of atmospheric pressure.

4. **Explain** how the two types of barometers measure atmospheric pressure.

5. **Identify** the layer of the atmosphere in which weather occurs.

6. **Compare** the four main layers of the atmosphere.

7. **Identify** the two atmospheric layers that contain air as warm as 25 °C.

Critical Thinking

8. **Drawing Conclusions** Why is atmospheric pressure generally lower beneath a mass of warm air than beneath a mass of cold air?

9. **Making Calculations** How much colder is the air at the top of Mount Everest, which is almost 9 km above sea level, than the air at the Indian coastline? (Hint: On average, the temperature in the troposphere decreases by 6.5 °C per kilometer of altitude.)

10. **Applying Ideas** Which industrial city would have fewer air-pollution incidents related to temperature inversions: one on the Great Plains or one near the Rocky Mountains? Explain your answer.

11. **Applying Concepts** In 1982, Larry Walters rose to an altitude of approximately 4,900 m on a lawn chair attached to 45 helium-filled weather balloons. Give two reasons why Walters' trip was dangerous.

Concept Mapping

12. Use the following terms to create a concept map: *oxygen, atmosphere, air, nitrogen, water vapor, ozone,* and *particulates.*

Solar Energy and the Atmosphere

Key Ideas	Key Terms	Why It Matters
❯ Explain how radiant energy reaches Earth. ❯ Describe how visible light and infrared energy warm Earth. ❯ Summarize the processes of radiation, conduction, and convection.	electromagnetic spectrum albedo greenhouse effect conduction convection	By understanding what happens to solar radiation in the atmosphere, scientists can learn more about how the actions of humans affect the atmosphere.

Earth's atmosphere is heated by the transfer of energy from the sun. Some of the heat in the atmosphere comes from the absorption of the sun's rays by gases in the atmosphere. Some heat enters the atmosphere indirectly as ocean and land surfaces absorb solar energy and then give off this energy as heat.

Radiation

All of the energy that Earth receives from the sun travels through space between Earth and the sun as radiation. *Radiation* includes all forms of energy that travel through space as waves. Visible light is the form of radiation that human eyes can detect. However, there are many other forms of radiation that humans cannot see, such as ultraviolet light, X rays, and radio waves.

Radiation travels through space in the form of waves at a very high speed—approximately 300,000 km/s. The distance from any point on a wave to the identical point on the next wave, for example, from crest to crest, is called the *wavelength* of a wave. The various types of radiation differ in the length of their waves. Visible light, for example, consists of waves with various wavelengths that are seen as different colors. The wavelengths of ultraviolet rays, X rays, and gamma rays are shorter than those of visible light. Infrared waves and radio waves have relatively long wavelengths. The waves that make up all forms of radiation are called electromagnetic waves. Almost all the energy that reaches Earth from the sun is in the form of *electromagnetic waves*. The **electromagnetic spectrum,** shown in **Figure 1,** consists of the complete range of wavelengths of electromagnetic waves.

FLORIDA STANDARDS

SC.912.E.7.3 Differentiate and describe the various interactions among Earth systems, including: atmosphere, hydrosphere, cryosphere, geosphere, and biosphere; **SC.912.P.10.4** Describe heat as the energy transferred by convection, conduction, and radiation, and explain the connection of heat to change in temperature or states of matter; **SC.912.P.10.18** Explore the theory of electromagnetism by comparing and contrasting the different parts of the electromagnetic spectrum in terms of wavelength, frequency, and energy, and relate them to phenomena and applications.

electromagnetic spectrum all of the frequencies or wavelengths of electromagnetic radiation

Figure 1 The sun emits radiation whose wavelengths range throughout the electromagnetic spectrum.

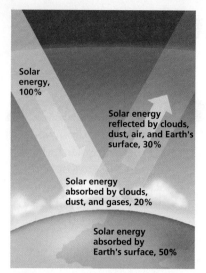

Figure 2 About 70% of the solar energy that reaches Earth is absorbed by Earth's land and ocean surfaces and by the atmosphere. The remainder is reflected back into space.

In the diagram:
- Solar energy, 100%
- Solar energy reflected by clouds, dust, air, and Earth's surface, 30%
- Solar energy absorbed by clouds, dust, and gases, 20%
- Solar energy absorbed by Earth's surface, 50%

The Atmosphere and Solar Radiation

As solar radiation passes through Earth's atmosphere, the atmosphere affects the radiation in several ways. The upper atmosphere absorbs almost all radiation that has a wavelength shorter than the wavelengths of visible light. Molecules of nitrogen and oxygen in the thermosphere and mesosphere absorb the X rays, gamma rays, and ultraviolet rays. In the stratosphere, ultraviolet rays are absorbed and act upon oxygen molecules to form ozone.

Most of the solar rays that reach the lower atmosphere, such as visible and infrared waves, have longer wavelengths. Most incoming infrared radiation is absorbed by carbon dioxide, water vapor, and other complex molecules in the troposphere. As visible light waves pass through the atmosphere, only a small amount of this radiation is absorbed. **Figure 2** shows the percentage of solar energy that is reflected and absorbed by the atmosphere.

Scattering

Clouds, dust, water droplets, and gas molecules in the atmosphere disrupt the paths of radiation from the sun and cause scattering. Scattering occurs when particles and gas molecules in the atmosphere reflect and bend the solar rays. This deflection causes the rays to travel out in all directions without changing their wavelengths. Scattering sends some of the radiation back into space. The remaining radiation continues toward Earth's surface. As a result of scattering, sunlight that reaches Earth's surface comes from all directions. In addition, scattering makes the sky appear blue and makes the sun appear red at sunset.

Why It Matters

Gardens in the Sky

EYE ON THE ENVIRONMENT

Rooftop gardens—such as this one on top of Chicago's City Hall—harness solar radiation, which helps the environment and cuts energy costs. While concrete roofs absorb only 55 to 65% of solar radiation, plants on "green roofs" absorb 75 to 95%. The plants help to decrease indoor temperatures in the summer, which means less air conditioning is needed. In addition, plants filter air pollution and muffle street noise, and provide a habitat for animals such as birds.

The layers of a rooftop garden absorb rainwater, which helps to prevent flooding of the sewage system in the city below.

YOUR TURN

WRITING IN SCIENCE
Design a rooftop garden for a building in your area. Draw plans, and explain your design.

Table 1 Reflection and Absorption Rates of Various Materials

Surface	Percentage of Solar Radiation	
	Reflected	Absorbed
Soil (dark colored)	5–10	90–95
Desert	20–40	60–80
Grass	5–25	75–95
Forest	5–10	90–95
Snow	50–90	10–50
Water (high sun angle)	5–10	90–95
Water (low sun angle)	50–80	20–50

READING TOOLBOX

Prefixes
The prefix ab- in *absorb* means "from" while the prefix re- in *reflect* means "back." Explain how these prefixes give you a clue to the direction of solar radiation when it is absorbed or reflected by different surfaces.

Reflection

When solar energy reaches Earth's surface, the surface either absorbs or reflects the energy. The amount of energy that is absorbed or reflected depends on characteristics such as the color, texture, composition, volume, mass, transparency, state of matter, and specific heat of the material on which the solar radiation falls. The intensity and amount of time that a surface material receives radiation also affects how much energy is reflected or absorbed.

The fraction of solar radiation that is reflected by a particular surface is called the **albedo.** Because 30% of the solar energy that reaches Earth's atmosphere is either reflected or scattered, Earth is said to have an albedo of 0.3. **Table 1** shows the amount of incoming solar radiation that is absorbed and reflected by various surfaces.

albedo the fraction of solar radiation that is reflected off the surface of an object

Absorption and Infrared Energy

The sun constantly emits radiation. Solar radiation that is not reflected is absorbed by rocks, soil, water, and other surface materials. When Earth's surface absorbs solar radiation, the radiation's short-wavelength infrared rays and visible light heat the surface materials. Then, the heated materials convert the energy into infrared rays with longer wavelengths and reemit the energy at those wavelengths. Gas molecules, such as water vapor and carbon dioxide, in the atmosphere absorb the infrared rays. The absorption of thermal energy from the ground heats the lower atmosphere and keeps Earth's surface much warmer than it would be if there were no atmosphere. Sometimes, warm air near Earth's surface bends light rays to produce an effect called a *mirage*, as **Figure 3** shows.

Figure 3 Hot air near the surface of this road bends light rays. *What objects in this photo appear to be reflected?*

2 Energy from the sun is absorbed by Earth's surface and then is radiated into the atmosphere as heat, some of which escapes into space.

3 Greenhouse gases also absorb some of the energy from Earth and radiate it back toward the lower atmosphere and Earth's surface.

1 Solar radiation passes through the atmosphere and warms Earth's surface.

Figure 4 One process that helps to heat Earth's atmosphere is similar to the process that heats a greenhouse.

THINK
central
INTERACT ONLINE
Keyword: HQXATMF4

greenhouse effect the warming of the surface and lower atmosphere of Earth that occurs when carbon dioxide, water vapor, and other gases in the air absorb and reradiate infrared radiation

www.scilinks.org
Topic: Greenhouse Effect
Code: HQX0694

The Greenhouse Effect

One of the ways in which the gases of the atmosphere absorb and reradiate infrared rays, shown in **Figure 4,** can be compared to the process that keeps a greenhouse warm. The glass of a greenhouse allows visible light and infrared rays from the sun to pass through and warm the surfaces inside the greenhouse. But the glass prevents the infrared rays that are emitted by the warmed surfaces within the greenhouse from escaping quickly. Similarly, Earth's atmosphere reduces the escape of energy that radiates from Earth's surface. Because this process is similar to the process that heats a greenhouse, it is called the **greenhouse effect.**

Human Impact on the Greenhouse Effect

Generally, the amount of solar energy that enters Earth's atmosphere is about equal to the amount that escapes into space. However, human activities, in addition to natural causes, are changing this balance and are causing the average temperature of the atmosphere to increase. For example, measurements indicate that the amount of carbon dioxide in the atmosphere has been increasing in recent years. These increases have been attributed to the burning of more fossil fuels and seem likely to continue in the future. Increases in the amount of carbon dioxide may intensify the greenhouse effect and may cause Earth to become warmer.

Variations in Temperature

Radiation from the sun does not heat Earth equally at all places at all times. In addition, a slight delay occurs between the absorption of energy and an increase in temperature. Earth's surface must absorb energy for a time before enough heat has been absorbed and reradiated from the ground to change the temperature of the atmosphere. For a similar reason, the warmest hours of the day are usually mid- to late afternoon even though solar radiation is most intense at noon. The temperature of the atmosphere in any region on Earth's surface depends on several factors, including latitude, surface features, and the time of year and day.

Latitude and Season

Latitude is the primary factor that affects the amount of solar energy that reaches any point on Earth's surface. Because Earth is a sphere, the sun's rays do not strike all areas at the same angle, as shown in **Figure 5.** The rays of the sun strike the ground near the equator at an angle near 90°. At the poles, the sunlight strikes the ground at a much smaller angle. When sunlight hits Earth's surface at an angle smaller than 90°, the energy is spread out over a larger area and is less intense. Thus, the energy that reaches the equator is more intense than the energy that strikes the poles, so average temperatures are higher near the equator than near the poles.

Temperature varies seasonally because of the tilt of Earth's axis. As Earth revolves around the sun once each year, the portion of Earth's surface that receives the most intense sunlight changes. For part of the year, the Northern Hemisphere is tilted toward the sun and receives more direct sunlight. During this time of year, temperatures are at their highest. For the other part of the year, the Southern Hemisphere is tilted toward the sun. During this time, the Northern Hemisphere receives less direct sunlight, and the temperatures there are at their lowest.

Water in the Air and on the Surface

Because water vapor stores energy, the amount of water in the air affects the temperature of a region. The thinner air at high elevations contains less water vapor and carbon dioxide to absorb heat energy. As a result, those areas become warm during the day but cool very quickly at night. Similarly, desert temperatures may vary widely between day and night because little water vapor is present to hold the heat of the day.

Land areas close to large bodies of water generally have more moderate temperatures. In other words, these areas will be cooler during the day and warmer at night than inland regions that have the same general weather conditions. The reason for these moderate temperatures is that water heats up and cools down slower than land does, so the temperature of water changes less than the temperature of land does.

The wind patterns in an area also affect temperature. A region that receives winds off the ocean has more moderate temperatures than a similar region in which the winds blow from the land.

Reading Check **Why are deserts generally colder at night than other areas are?**

Figure 5 Temperatures are higher at the equator because solar energy is concentrated in a small area. Farther north and south, the same amount of solar energy is spread out over a larger area.

Academic Vocabulary

primary (PRIE MER ee) highest in rank or importance

 SC.912.E.7.7

Quick **Lab** ⏱ 5 min

Light and Latitude

Procedure

❶ Hold a flashlight so that the beam shines directly down on a white piece of paper. Use a pencil to trace the outline of the beam of light.

❷ Move the flashlight so that the light shines on the paper at an angle. Trace the outline of the beam of light.

Analysis

1. How does the area of the direct beam differ from the area of the angled beam?

2. How does this lab illustrate how latitude affects incoming solar radiation?

Figure 6 During convection, energy is carried away by heated air as it rises above cooler, denser air.

conduction the transfer of energy as heat through a material

convection the movement of matter due to differences in density that are caused by temperature variations; can result in the transfer of energy as heat

Conduction

The molecules in a substance move faster as they become heated. These fast-moving molecules cause other molecules to move faster. Collisions between the particles result in the transfer of energy, which warms the substance. The transfer of energy as heat from one substance to another by direct contact is called **conduction.** Solid substances, in which the molecules are close together, make relatively good conductors. Because the molecules of air are far apart, air is a poor conductor. Thus, conduction heats only the lowest few centimeters of the atmosphere, where air comes into direct contact with the warmed surface of Earth.

Convection

The heating of the lower atmosphere is primarily the result of the distribution of heat through the troposphere by convection. **Convection** is the process by which air, or other matter, rises or sinks because of differences in temperature. Convection occurs when gases or liquids are heated unevenly. As air is heated by radiation or conduction, it becomes less dense and is pushed up by nearby cooler air. In turn, this cooler air becomes warmer, and the cycle repeats, as shown in **Figure 6.**

The continuous cycle in which cold air sinks and warm air rises warms Earth's atmosphere. Because warm air is less dense than cool air is, warm air exerts less pressure than the same volume of cooler air does. So, the atmospheric pressure is lower beneath a mass of warm air. As dense, cool air moves into a low-pressure region, the less dense, warmer air is pushed upward. These pressure differences, which are the result of the unequal heating that causes convection, create winds.

Section 2 Review

LA.910.2.2.3; SC.912.E.7.3; SC.912.P.10.4; SC.912.P.10.18

Key Ideas

1. **Explain** how radiant energy reaches Earth.

2. **List and describe** the types of electromagnetic waves.

3. **Describe** how gases and particles in the atmosphere interact with light rays.

4. **Describe** how visible light and infrared energy warm Earth.

5. **Explain** how variations in the intensity of sunlight can cause temperature differences on Earth's surface.

6. **Summarize** the processes of conduction and convection.

Critical Thinking

7. **Making Inferences** Why do scientists study all wavelengths of the electromagnetic spectrum?

8. **Applying Concepts** Explain how fans in convection ovens help to cook food more evenly.

9. **Applying Conclusions** You decide not to be outside during the hottest hours of a summer day. When will the hottest hours probably be? How do you know?

Concept Mapping

10. Use the following terms to create a concept map: *electromagnetic waves, infrared waves, greenhouse effect, ultraviolet waves, visible light, scattering,* and *absorption.*

Key Ideas	Key Terms	Why It Matters
❯ Explain the Coriolis effect. ❯ Describe the global patterns of air circulation, and name three global wind belts. ❯ Identify two factors that form local wind patterns.	Coriolis effect trade winds westerlies polar easterlies jet stream	Understanding how wind works was important to early travelers. Such understanding has practical advantages even today.

Air near Earth's surface generally flows from the poles toward the equator. The reason for this flow is that air moves from high-pressure regions to low-pressure regions. High-pressure regions form where cold air sinks toward Earth's surface. Low-pressure regions form where warm air rises away from Earth's surface.

The Coriolis Effect

The circulation of the atmosphere and the oceans is affected by the rotation of Earth on its axis. Because each point on Earth makes one complete rotation every day, points near the equator travel farther and faster in a day than points closer to the poles do. When air moves toward the poles, it travels east faster than the land beneath it does. As a result, the air follows a curved path. The tendency of a moving object to follow a curved path rather than a straight path because of the rotation of Earth is called the **Coriolis effect,** which is shown in **Figure 1.**

The Coriolis effect deflects a moving object along a path that depends on the speed, latitude, and direction of the object. Objects are deflected to the right in the Northern Hemisphere and are deflected to the left in the Southern Hemisphere.

The faster an object travels, the greater the Coriolis effect on the object is. The Coriolis effect also noticeably changes the paths of large masses that travel long distances, such as air and ocean currents. In general, the Coriolis effect is detectable only on objects that move very fast or that travel over long distances.

SC.912.E.7.3 Differentiate and describe the various interactions among Earth systems, including: atmosphere, hydrosphere, cryosphere, geosphere, and biosphere; **SC.912.N.4.1** Explain how scientific knowledge and reasoning provide an empirically-based perspective to inform society's decision making.

Coriolis effect the curving of the path of a moving object from an otherwise straight path due to Earth's rotation

Air moving south from the pole is deflected to the right because the air moves east slower than the ground beneath it does.

North Pole

Air moving north from the equator is deflected to the right because the air is moving east faster than the ground beneath it is.

Equator

Direction of Earth's rotation

Figure 1 Because of Earth's rotation, an object that travels north from the equator will curve to the east. This curving is called the *Coriolis effect*.

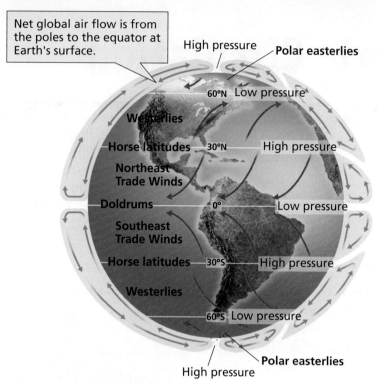

Net global air flow is from the poles to the equator at Earth's surface.

High pressure — Polar easterlies

60°N — Low pressure

Westerlies

Horse latitudes — 30°N — High pressure

Northeast Trade Winds

Doldrums — 0° — Low pressure

Southeast Trade Winds

Horse latitudes — 30°S — High pressure

Westerlies

60°S — Low pressure

High pressure — Polar easterlies

Figure 2 Each hemisphere has three wind belts. Wind belts are the result of pressure differences at the equator, the subtropics, the subpolar regions, and the poles. Winds in the belts curve because of the Coriolis effect. *Do winds in the Northern Hemisphere curve clockwise or counterclockwise?*

trade winds prevailing winds that blow from east to west from 30° latitude to the equator in both hemispheres

westerlies prevailing winds that blow from west to east between 30° and 60° latitude in both hemispheres

polar easterlies prevailing winds that blow from east to west between 60° and 90° latitude in both hemispheres

Global Winds

The air that flows from the poles toward the equator does not flow in a single, straight line. Each hemisphere contains three looping patterns of flow called *convection cells*. Each convection cell correlates to an area of Earth's surface, called a *wind belt*, that is characterized by winds that flow in one main direction. These winds are called *prevailing winds*. All six wind belts are shown in **Figure 2**.

Trade Winds

In both hemispheres, the winds that flow toward the equator between 30° and 0° latitude are called **trade winds.** Like all winds, the trade winds are named according to the direction from which they flow. In the Northern Hemisphere, the trade winds flow from the northeast and are called the *northeast trade winds*. In the Southern Hemisphere, the trade winds are called the *southeast trade winds*. These wind belts are called *trade winds* because many trading ships sailed on these winds from Europe in the 18th and 19th centuries.

Westerlies

Between 30° and 60° latitude, air moving toward the poles is deflected by the Coriolis effect. This flow creates the **westerlies,** which exist in another wind belt in each hemisphere. In the Northern Hemisphere, the westerlies are southwest winds. In the Southern Hemisphere, they are northwest winds. The westerlies blow throughout the contiguous United States.

Reading Check Name two ways in which the trade winds of the Northern Hemisphere differ from the westerlies of the Northern Hemisphere.

Polar Easterlies

Toward the poles, or poleward, of the westerlies—at about 60° latitude—is a zone of low pressure. This zone of low pressure separates the westerlies from a third wind belt in each hemisphere. Over the polar regions themselves, descending cold air creates areas of high pressure. Surface winds created by the polar high pressure are deflected by the Coriolis effect and become the **polar easterlies.** The polar easterlies are strongest where they flow off Antarctica. Where the polar easterlies meet warm air from the westerlies, a stormy region known as a *front* forms.

The Doldrums and Horse Latitudes

As **Figure 2** shows, the trade wind systems of the Northern Hemisphere and Southern Hemisphere meet at the equator in a narrow zone called the *doldrums*. In this warm zone, most air movement is upward and surface winds are weak and variable. As the air approaches 30° latitude, it descends and a high-pressure zone forms. These subtropical high-pressure zones are called the *horse latitudes*. Here, too, surface winds are weak and variable.

Wind and Pressure Shifts

As the sun's rays shift 23.5° northward and southward during the changing seasons of the year, the positions of the pressure belts and wind belts shift in response. Although the area that receives direct sunlight can shift by up to 47°, the average shift for the pressure belts and wind belts is only about 10° of latitude. However, even this small change causes some areas of Earth's surface to be in different wind belts during different times of the year. In southern Florida, for example, westerlies prevail in the winter, but trade winds dominate in the summer.

Jet Streams

Narrow bands of high-speed winds that blow in the upper troposphere and lower stratosphere are **jet streams.** These winds exist in the Northern Hemisphere and Southern Hemisphere.

One type of jet stream is a polar jet stream. Polar jet streams form as a result of density differences between cold polar air and the warmer air of the middle latitudes. These bands of winds, which are about 100 km wide and 2 to 3 km thick, are located at altitudes of 10 to 15 km. Polar jet streams can reach speeds of over 400 km/h and can affect airline routes and the paths of storms.

Another type of jet stream is a subtropical jet stream. In the subtropical regions, very warm equatorial air meets the cooler air of the middle latitudes, and *subtropical jet streams* form. Unlike polar jet streams, subtropical jet streams do not change much in speed or position. A subtropical jet stream is shown in **Figure 3.**

Layered Book
Make a layered book FoldNote, and label the tabs "Trade Winds," "Westerlies," "Polar Easterlies," and "Doldrums and Horse Latitudes." Write notes on the appropriate layers as you read this section.

jet stream a narrow band of strong winds that blow in the upper troposphere

Figure 3 Clouds indicate the path of a jet stream traveling high over Egypt.

Figure 4 Sea breezes keep these kites aloft during the afternoon.

Local Winds

Winds also exist on a scale that is much smaller than a global scale. Movements of air are <u>influenced</u> by local conditions, and local temperature variations commonly cause local winds. Local winds are not part of the global wind belts. Winds that blow at speeds of less than 50 km/h are called *breezes*.

Land and Sea Breezes

Equal areas of land and water may receive the same amount of energy from the sun. However, land surfaces heat up faster than water surfaces do. Therefore, during daylight hours, a sharp temperature difference develops between a body of water and the land along the water's edge. This temperature difference is apparent in the air above the land and water. The warm air above the land rises, creating low pressure. Then, cool air from above the water moves in to replace the warm air. A cool wind moving from water to land, called a *sea breeze*, generally forms in the afternoon, as shown in **Figure 4.** Overnight, the land cools more rapidly than the water does, and the sea breeze is replaced by a *land breeze*. A land breeze flows from the cool land toward the warmer water.

Academic Vocabulary

influence (IN floo uhns) the effect of one thing on another

Mountain and Valley Breezes

During the daylight hours in mountainous regions, a gentle valley breeze blows upslope. This *valley breeze* forms when warm air from the valleys moves upslope. At night, the mountains cool more quickly than the valleys do, and cool air descends from the mountain peaks to create a *mountain breeze*. Areas near mountains may experience a warm afternoon that turns into a cold evening soon after sunset. This evening cooling happens because cold air flows down mountain slopes and settles in valleys.

Section 3 Review

LA.910.2.2.3; SC.912.E.7.3; SC.912.E.7.4

Key Ideas

1. **Describe** the pattern of air circulation between an area of low pressure and an area of high pressure.

2. **Explain** how the Coriolis effect affects wind flow.

3. **Name and describe** Earth's three global wind belts.

4. **Summarize** the importance of jet streams.

5. **Identify** two factors that create local wind patterns.

Critical Thinking

6. **Applying Concepts** Determine whether wind moving south from the equator will curve eastward or westward because of the Coriolis effect.

7. **Inferring Relationships** Which has a lower pressure: the air in your lungs as you inhale or the air outside your body? Explain.

8. **Applying Ideas** While visiting the Oregon coast, you decide to hike toward the ocean, but you are not sure of the direction. The time is 4:00 P.M. How might the breeze help you find your way?

Concept Mapping

9. Use the following terms to create a concept map: *wind, sea breeze, global winds, trade winds, westerlies, local winds, polar easterlies, land breeze, mountain breeze,* and *valley breeze.*

Chasing Rainbows and Sundogs

WEIRD SCIENCE

The interplay of sunlight or moonlight and airborne water droplets, ice crystals, or particulates can create amazing, short-lived effects known collectively as atmospheric optics. Long before computer programs could manipulate images to produce new and surprising versions of reality, atmospheric optics were producing astounding light effects in the sky. Rainbows are the most well-known of these effects. Rainbows are formed when the sun's rays are refracted as they pass through spherical raindrops, causing the white light to split into the colors of the visible spectrum.

Sunset mirages are caused when the rays of the setting sun are refracted through layers of air that are different temperatures.

Crepuscular rays are rays of sunlight that stream through gaps between clouds and alternate with shadowy areas. They are formed when sunlight is partially blocked by clouds, mountains, or anything else that casts a shadow, and then scattered as it hits airborne particulates, water droplets, or ice crystals.

Circumzenithal arcs, which appear as upside-down rainbows, are formed by the refraction of sunlight through horizontally oriented ice crystals. Sunlight enters the top face of an ice crystal and exits through a vertical side face.

Sundogs (also called *parhelia*) are two bright spots that appear on either side of the sun just after sunrise or just before sunset. They are formed when hexagonal, horizontally oriented ice crystals refract sunlight.

YOUR TURN

UNDERSTANDING CONCEPTS
Compare and contrast rainbows and circumzenithal arcs.

ONLINE RESEARCH
Find and describe another example of an atmospheric optic. What causes it to form?

⏱ **45 min**

Energy Absorption and Reflection

When solar energy reaches Earth's surface, the energy is either reflected or absorbed by the material that the surface is made of. Whether the material absorbs or reflects energy, and the amount of energy that is reflected or absorbed, depends on several characteristics of the material. These characteristics include the material's composition, its color and texture, how transparent the material is, the mass and volume of the material, and the specific heat of the material. In this lab, you will study these characteristics to determine which material is best suited for use as roofing material.

What You'll Do

> **Determine** which material would keep the inside of a house the coolest.

> **Explain** which properties of this material determine whether it is a conductor or an insulator.

What You'll Need

cardboard,
  4 cm × 4 cm × 1 cm
  (4 pieces)
paint, black, white, and light
  blue tempera
metal, 4 cm × 4 cm × 1 cm
rubber, beige or tan,
  4 cm × 4 cm × 1 cm
sandpaper,
  4 cm × 4 cm × 1 cm
thermometers, Celsius (4)
watch or clock
wood, beige or tan,
  4 cm × 4 cm × 1 cm

Safety

Ask a Question

1 Which material will keep the interior of a house the coolest?

Form a Hypothesis

2 Identify the material that you think will keep the inside of a house the coolest. List the characteristics of this material that caused you to choose it.

Test the Hypothesis

3 Brainstorm with a partner or with a small group of classmates to design a procedure that will help you determine which materials absorb the most energy and which materials keep the surface below them the coolest. You do not have to test all the materials, if you can explain why you think those materials would not be the coolest. Write down your experimental procedure.

4 Have your teacher approve your experimental design.

Step 3

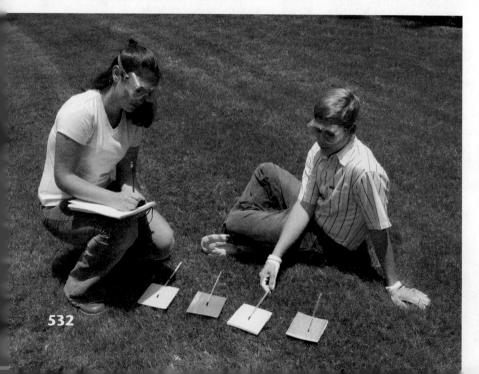

5 Create a table like the one shown on the right. Use this table to record the data you collect as you perform your experiment.

6 Following your design, measure the temperatures that the materials and the surfaces beneath them reach.

Material	Color	Surface temperature (°C)	Temperature below material (°C)
Cardboard	white		
Rubber	beige		
Sandpaper	beige		

DO NOT WRITE IN THIS BOOK

Analyze the Results

1. **Graphing Data** Use the data you collected to create a bar graph. Label the *x*-axis with the materials you tested and the *y*-axis with a range of temperatures.

2. **Analyzing Data** Which material reached the highest temperature on its surface? Which material caused the surface below it to reach the highest temperature?

3. **Analyzing Data** Which material stayed the lowest temperature at its surface? Which material kept the temperature of the surface beneath it the lowest?

4. **Evaluating Results** Did the color of the materials affect whether they absorbed or reflected solar energy? Explain your answer.

Draw Conclusions

5. **Drawing Conclusions** Based on your results, which material would you use for the roof of a house? Did your experimental results support your original hypothesis?

6. **Inferring Relationships** What properties of the material you identified in question 5 do you think make it best for this purpose? Explain your answer.

7. **Making Predictions** Do you think the material you chose would keep the inside of a house warm in colder weather? Explain your answer.

8. **Analyzing Methods** Name two changes in your experimental design that you would make if you were going to repeat the experiment. Explain why you would make each change.

Extension

Applying Ideas Use the materials you tested in the experiment to create a model of Earth's surface that represents how different parts of Earth's surface absorb or reflect solar energy. Which areas of Earth's surface absorb the least energy?

Absorbed Solar Radiation

Absorbed Solar Radiation in January

Absorbed Solar Radiation in July

Longitude

Latitude

Lowest ⟵⟶ Highest

Amount of solar radiation

Map ▶ Skills Activity

These maps show the total amount of solar radiation that is absorbed by Earth in January and July. Use the maps to answer the questions below.

1. **Using a Key** In January, which region has the highest amount of absorbed solar radiation?

2. **Using a Key** In July, which region has the highest amount of absorbed solar radiation?

3. **Comparing Areas** Which area has the greatest difference between the amount of absorbed solar radiation in January and in July: southern Australia or northeastern South America?

4. **Analyzing Data** At what latitudes are January's and July's amounts of absorbed solar radiation similar?

5. **Inferring Relationships** How do these maps explain the differences between the Northern Hemisphere's weather in January and in July?

Key Ideas

Key Terms

Section 1

Characteristics of the Atmosphere

❯ Earth's atmosphere is the mixture of gases, called *air*, that surrounds Earth. Solid and liquid particles, called *particulates*, are mixed with the gases that make up air.

❯ Mercury inside a mercurial barometer rises or sinks as air pressure increases or decreases. In an aneroid barometer, changes in air pressure cause a metal container inside the barometer to bend inward or bulge outward. This moves a pointer on a scale.

❯ The atmosphere is divided into four main layers: the troposphere, the stratosphere, the mesosphere, and the thermosphere.

❯ Air pollution can be harmful to people, animals, plants, and property.

atmosphere, p. 513
ozone, p. 515
atmospheric pressure, p. 516
troposphere, p. 518
stratosphere, p. 519
mesosphere, p. 519
thermosphere, p. 519

Section 2

Solar Energy and the Atmosphere

❯ Most of the energy that reaches Earth from the sun is in the form of electromagnetic radiation.

❯ Visible light and infrared rays from the sun penetrate Earth's atmosphere and heat materials on Earth's surface.

❯ The upper atmosphere is heated by absorption of radiation from the sun. The lower atmosphere is heated by conduction from Earth's surface and by convection of air.

electromagnetic spectrum, p. 521
albedo, p. 523
greenhouse effect, p. 524
conduction, p. 526
convection, p. 526

Section 3

Atmospheric Circulation

❯ The Coriolis effect is the tendency of a moving object to follow a curved path rather than a straight path because of the rotation of Earth.

❯ Each hemisphere contains three convection cells that circulate air. Net global airflow near Earth's surface is from the poles toward the equator. The three global wind belts are the trade winds, the westerlies, and the polar easterlies.

❯ A surface feature, such as a body of water, a mountain, or a valley, can influence local wind patterns.

Coriolis effect, p. 527
trade winds, p. 528
westerlies, p. 528
polar easterlies, p. 528
jet stream, p. 529

Chapter 19 Review

1. **Cause and Effect** Use cause-and-effect signal words to explain the link between Earth's tilt and the seasons.

USING KEY TERMS

Use each of the following terms in a separate sentence.

2. *atmosphere* `SC.912.E.7.3`

3. *electromagnetic spectrum* `SC.912.E.7.3`

4. *Coriolis effect* `SC.912.E.7.3`

For each pair of terms, explain how the meanings of the terms differ.

5. *troposphere* and *stratosphere* `SC.912.E.7.3`

6. *mesosphere* and *thermosphere* `SC.912.E.7.3`

7. *conduction* and *convection* `SC.912.E.7.3`

8. *trade winds* and *westerlies* `SC.912.E.7.3`

9. *polar easterlies* and *westerlies* `SC.912.E.7.3`

UNDERSTANDING KEY IDEAS

10. During one part of the nitrogen cycle, nitrogen is removed from the air mainly by nitrogen-fixing
    a. bacteria. `SC.912.E.7.3`
    b. waves.
    c. minerals.
    d. crystals.

11. The atmosphere contains tiny solid particles called
    a. gases. `SC.912.E.7.3`
    b. particulates.
    c. meteors.
    d. nitrogen.

12. A barometer measures `SC.912.E.7.3`
    a. atmospheric pressure.
    b. wind speed.
    c. ozone concentration.
    d. wavelengths.

13. Almost all the water and carbon dioxide in the atmosphere is in the `SC.912.E.7.3`
    a. exosphere.   c. troposphere.
    b. ionosphere.   d. stratosphere.

14. The process by which the atmosphere reduces Earth's loss of heat to space is called the `SC.912.E.7.3`
    a. greenhouse effect.
    b. Coriolis effect.
    c. doldrums.
    d. convection cell.

15. Energy as heat can be transferred within the atmosphere in three ways: radiation, conduction, and `SC.912.E.7.3`
    a. transpiration.
    b. temperature inversion.
    c. weathering.
    d. convection.

16. A vertical looping pattern of airflow is known as
    a. the Coriolis effect. `SC.912.E.7.3`
    b. a convection cell.
    c. a trade wind.
    d. a westerly.

17. Wind with a speed of less than 50 km/h is called `SC.912.E.7.3`
    a. a jet stream.
    b. the doldrums.
    c. a breeze.
    d. a trade wind.

18. Which of the following layers of the atmosphere is closest to the ground? `SC.912.E.7.3`
    a. troposphere
    b. thermosphere
    c. mesosphere
    d. exosphere

19. Which of the following layers of the atmosphere is closest to space? `SC.912.E.7.3`
    a. troposphere
    b. ionosphere
    c. mesosphere
    d. exosphere

SHORT ANSWER

20. List the three main elemental gases that compose the atmosphere. `SC.912.E.7.3`

21. What is atmospheric pressure, and how is it measured? `SC.912.E.7.3`

22. List and describe the four main layers of the atmosphere. `SC.912.E.7.3`

23. What happens to visible light that enters Earth's atmosphere? SC.912.E.7.3

24. How is heat energy transferred by Earth's atmosphere? SC.912.E.7.3

25. How does latitude affect the temperature of a region? SC.912.E.7.3

26. Explain how the greenhouse effect helps to warm the atmosphere. SC.912.E.7.3

27. What causes the Coriolis effect? SC.912.E.7.3

28. Name and describe the three main wind belts in both hemispheres. SC.912.E.7.3

29. How do surface features influence local wind patterns? SC.912.E.7.3

CRITICAL THINKING

30. Making Inferences If a breeze is blowing from the ocean to the land on the coast of Maine, about what time of day is it? Explain your answer. SC.912.E.7.4

31. Evaluating Ideas What effect might jet streams have on airplane travel? SC.912.E.7.3

32. Inferring Relationships Most aerosol sprays that contain CFCs have been banned in the United States. Which of the four layers of the atmosphere does this ban help to protect? Explain your answer. SC.912.E.7.3

33. Evaluating Information You hear a report about Earth's weather. The reporter says that visible light rays coming from Earth's surface heat the atmosphere in a way similar to the way a greenhouse is heated. Explain why the reporter's statement is incorrect. SC.912.E.7.7

CONCEPT MAPPING

34. Use the following terms to create a concept map: *atmosphere, troposphere, stratosphere, temperature, mesosphere, thermosphere, atmospheric pressure, altitude,* and *exosphere.* SC.912.E.7.3

MATH SKILLS   Math Skills

35. Applying Quantities The albedo of the moon is 0.07. What percentage of the total solar radiation that reaches the moon is reflected? SC.912.E.7.3

36. Making Calculations Maximum local wind speeds for each of the last seven days were 12 km/h, 20 km/h, 11 km/h, 6 km/h, 8 km/h, 19 km/h, and 17 km/h. What was the average maximum wind speed?

WRITING SKILLS

37. Writing from Research Research the debate about global warming. Write one paragraph about evidence that supports global warming and one paragraph about evidence that does not support global warming. SC.912.E.7.7

INTERPRETING GRAPHICS

The graph below shows how the Coriolis effect changes as latitude and wind speed change. Use this graph to answer the questions that follow.

Relationship Between Latitude, Wind Speed, and the Coriolis Effect

38. At what wind speed is the Coriolis effect the greatest? SC.912.E.7.3

39. At what latitude is the Coriolis effect the smallest? SC.912.E.7.3

40. At 90° latitude, is there a direct relationship between the Coriolis effect and wind speed? SC.912.E.7.3

Understanding Concepts

Directions (1–8): For each question, write on a separate sheet of paper the letter of the correct answer.

1 Ozone, a gas molecule made up of three oxygen atoms, is found in the upper atmosphere. Which of the following statements best describes ozone?
  A. It is required for photosynthesis.
  B. It breaks down the protective layer that surrounds Earth.
  C. It absorbs harmful ultraviolet radiation.
  D. It is one of many particulates found in the atmosphere.

2 Which of the following statements best describes the relationship between atmospheric pressure and altitude?
  F. The atmospheric pressure increases as the altitude increases.
  G. The atmospheric pressure increases as the altitude decreases.
  H. The atmospheric pressure varies unpredictably at different altitudes.
  I. The atmospheric pressure is constant at all altitudes.

3 Much of the life on Earth became possible in part because the oxygen levels on Earth increased. Today, the oxygen levels on Earth stay constant. How is this possible?
  A. Plants produce as much oxygen as is used by other organisms.
  B. The oxygen produced by plants is broken down by chlorofluorocarbons.
  C. Oxygen is converted to ozone and is moved to the outer atmosphere.
  D. The oxygen produced by plants is fixed by bacteria.

4 In the Northern Hemisphere, the Coriolis effect causes winds moving toward the North Pole to be deflected in which of the following ways?
  F. Winds are deflected to the right.
  G. Winds are deflected to the left.
  H. Winds are deflected in unpredictable patterns.
  D. Winds are not deflected by the Coriolis effect.

5 Atmospheric nitrogen cannot be used by most organisms. Which of the following statements best describes how this nitrogen is made available to these organisms?
  A. Atmospheric nitrogen is used by plants to make food, which is consumed by other organisms.
  B. Bacteria fix atmospheric nitrogen, adding it to soil so that plants can use it.
  C. Decomposers break down dead organisms and release the nitrogen into the atmosphere so other organisms can use it.
  D. The wastes of animals make nitrogen available.

6 Air pollution is made worse by temperature inversions. Temperature inversions occur when
  F. warm air is mixed with cold air.
  G. cold air is pushed higher in the atmosphere.
  H. warm air is cooled.
  I. warm air lies over cool air.

7 As Earth's atmosphere became warmer over time, more organisms began to live on Earth. Which of the following is NOT a direct factor in the warming of Earth's atmosphere?
  A. reflection of solar energy
  B. the sun's radiation
  C. absorption of the sun's light by Earth's clouds, dust, and gases
  D. the greenhouse effect

8 Venus has more greenhouse gases in its atmosphere than Earth does, and Earth has more greenhouse gases in its atmosphere than Mars does. Based on this information, what can be concluded about the temperatures on each planet?
  F. Venus is warmer than Earth, but Earth is cooler than Mars is.
  G. Venus, Earth, and Mars all have the same temperature.
  H. Mars is the warmest planet of the three.
  I. Earth is cooler than Venus is and warmer than Mars is.

Interpreting Graphics

Directions (9–10): For each question below, record the correct answer on a separate sheet of paper.

Global Wind Belts

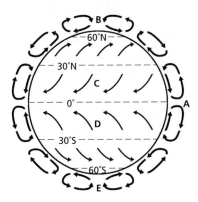

9 Differential heating of Earth's atmosphere results in circulation patterns such as those shown in the figure above. What happens to the air around location A as the air warms and decreases in density?

A. It rises.

B. It sinks.

C. It stagnates.

D. It contracts.

Coastal Land Area on a Summer Day

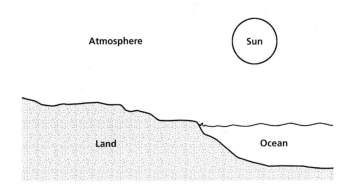

10 The figure above shows a coastal area on a sunny day. The land heats faster than the ocean does. In which direction will the wind blow during the day?

F. from the land to the ocean

G. from the land to the upper atmosphere

H. from the ocean to the land

I. from the ocean and the land

> **Test Tip**
>
> Do not be fooled by answers that may seem correct just because they contain unfamiliar words.

Chapter 20

Water in the Atmosphere

Chapter Outline

Why It Matters

Understanding how water moves through the atmosphere provides a basis for understanding how heat is transferred around the globe and for predicting the weather.

Average Precipitation

Study **local precipitation data.** Each of the four people in your group should choose a season (spring, summer, autumn, or winter) to graph. Use **colored pencils** and a **ruler** to plot the precipitation information for your season on **graph paper.** Then, work together to plot the information for all four seasons on one piece of graph paper. Calculate the average annual precipitation for your area.

Questions to Get You Started

1. What period of time is covered by the local precipitation data?

2. How will you find the average annual precipitation for your area?

3. Compare seasonal precipitation levels for your area. Does one season consistently receive more precipitation than the others? Explain your answer.

SC.912.E.7.8

These reading tools will help you learn the material in this chapter.

Word Parts

Suffixes The suffix *–ion* usually changes verbs into nouns to denote a process. For example, *combination* is a noun formed from the verb *combine*. It means "the result of combining." The suffix *-ly* changes a noun, an adjective, or a verb to an adverb. It means "in the manner of." *Slowly* means "in a slow manner." When you see a word that uses one of these suffixes, the root of the word can help you understand the word's meaning.

Your Turn On a sheet of paper, complete the table below with other words in the chapter that have the suffix *–ion.*

Word	Root	Suffix	Definition
sublimation	sublimate	- ion	the process by which a solid changes directly into a gas
		- ion	

Comparisons

Analyzing Comparisons Comparisons are often signaled by the use of a few key words. The words *like* and *unlike* can tell you whether a comparison is focused on similarities or differences. Comparative words can be formed by using the suffixes *-er* and *-est*. Comparative phrases can be formed by using the words *more* and *less*.

Your Turn As you read this chapter, fill out a table of comparisons like the one below. The entry is for the sentence "Unlike nimbostratus clouds, which produce heavy precipitation, altostratus clouds produce very little precipitation."

First thing	Second thing	Similarities or differences	Signal words or phrases
nimbostratus clouds	altostratus clouds	nimbostratus: heavy precipitation, altostratus: little precipitation	unlike

Fold Notes

Two-Panel Flip Chart FoldNotes help you learn and remember ideas that you encounter as you read. FoldNotes help you organize concepts and see the "big picture."

Your Turn Follow the instructions in **Appendix A** for making a two-panel flip chart. Label the panels as shown here.

Open the appropriate flap to take notes about each topic and draw a sketch.

For more information on how to use these and other tools, see **Appendix A.**

Atmospheric Moisture

Key Ideas

❯ Explain how heat energy affects the changing phases of water.

❯ Explain what absolute and relative humidity are, and describe how they are measured.

❯ Describe what happens when the temperature of air decreases to the dew point or below.

Key Terms

latent heat

sublimation

dew point

absolute humidity

relative humidity

Why It Matters

When the air is humid, you feel warmer than you would if the air were dry, even if the temperature is the same. The humidity affects your body's ability to cool itself by sweating.

Water in the atmosphere exists in three states, or *phases*. One phase is a gas known as *water vapor*. The other two phases of water are the solid phase known as *ice* and the liquid phase known as *water*.

Changing Forms of Water

Water changes from one phase to another when heat energy is absorbed or released, as shown in **Figure 1.** Molecules of ice are held almost stationary in a definite crystalline arrangement. However, when energy is absorbed by the ice, the molecules move more rapidly. They break from their fixed positions and slide past each other in the fluid form of a liquid.

When more energy is absorbed by liquid water, the water changes from a liquid to a gas. Because the additional energy causes the movement of the molecules in liquid water to speed up, the molecules collide more frequently with each other. Such collisions can cause the molecules to move so rapidly that the fastest-moving molecules escape from the liquid to form invisible water vapor in a process called *evaporation*.

Latent Heat

The heat energy that is absorbed or released by a substance during a phase change is called **latent heat.** When liquid water evaporates, the water absorbs energy from the environment. This energy becomes potential energy between the molecules. When water vapor changes back into a liquid through the process of *condensation,* energy is released to the surrounding air and the molecules move closer together. Likewise, latent heat is absorbed when ice thaws, and latent heat is released when water freezes.

FLORIDA STANDARDS

MA.912.S.1.2 Determine appropriate and consistent standards of measurement for the data to be collected in a survey or experiment; **SC.912.E.7.3** Differentiate and describe the various interactions among Earth systems, including: atmosphere, hydrosphere, cryosphere, geosphere, and biosphere; **SC.912.P.10.4** Describe heat as the energy transferred by convection, conduction, and radiation, and explain the connection of heat to change in temperature or states of matter.

latent heat the heat energy that is absorbed or released by a substance during a phase change

Figure 1 Water exists in three states, called *phases*. As it changes from one phase to another, water either absorbs or releases heat energy.

Evaporation

Most water enters the atmosphere through the process of evaporation. Because the largest amounts of solar energy reach Earth near the equator, most evaporation takes place over the oceans of the equatorial region. However, water vapor also enters the atmosphere by evaporation from lakes, ponds, streams, and soil. Plants release water into the atmosphere in a process called transpiration. Volcanoes and burning fuels also release small amounts of water vapor into the atmosphere.

Sublimation

Ice commonly changes into a liquid before changing into a gas. However, in some cases, ice can change directly into water vapor without becoming a liquid. The process by which a solid changes directly into a gas is called **sublimation.** When the air is dry and the temperature is below freezing, ice and snow may sublimate into water vapor. Water vapor can also turn directly into ice without becoming a liquid.

sublimation the process in which a solid changes directly into a gas (the term is sometimes also used for the reverse process)

 Reading Check **Summarize the conditions under which sublimation commonly occurs.** (See Appendix G for answers to Reading Checks.)

Why It Matters

Why Does Humid Air Feel Hotter?

REAL WORLD

You probably have heard people say, "It's not the heat—it's the humidity." When relative humidity is high, the day feels hotter than the temperature you read on the thermometer. Why? Evaporation of sweat is a main mechanism by which the body regulates temperature. Sweat does not evaporate when relative humidity is about 80 percent or higher. When sweat doesn't evaporate, the body does not cool as efficiently.

Smog is worsened by high humidity. Not only do you feel hotter, smog aggravates emphysema, asthma, and other respiratory problems. People can protect themselves by checking the pollution index before going outside.

High temperatures plus high humidity can lead to heatstroke and even death. People can protect themselves by drinking water, restricting outdoor exercise, and checking the Heat Index. The Heat Index (HI) combines temperature with relative humidity to show how hot it really feels.

YOUR TURN ONLINE RESEARCH
What happens in the human body when heatstroke occurs? Why is heatstroke dangerous?

20 °C   20 °C

No vapor pressure

Dry air

Water

Increasing vapor pressure

Water

Water vapor

Moist air

Evaporating water molecules

Figure 2 When water comes into contact with dry air, some of the water molecules evaporate into the dry air. The addition of the water molecules to the air causes the air pressure to increase. This increase in pressure is due to vapor pressure.

Humidity

Water vapor in the atmosphere is known as *humidity*. Humidity is controlled by rates of condensation and evaporation. The rate of evaporation is determined by the temperature of the air. The higher the temperature is, the higher the rate of evaporation is. The rate of condensation is determined by *vapor pressure*. Vapor pressure is the part of the total atmospheric pressure that is caused by water vapor, as shown in **Figure 2.** When vapor pressure is high, the condensation rate is high.

When the rate of evaporation and the rate of condensation are in equilibrium, the air is said to be "saturated." The temperature at which the condensation rate equals the evaporation rate is called the **dew point.** At temperatures below the dew point, net condensation occurs, and liquid water droplets form.

Absolute Humidity

One way to express the amount of moisture in the air is by absolute humidity. **Absolute humidity** is the mass of water vapor contained in a given volume of air. In other words, absolute humidity is a measure of the actual amount of water vapor in the air. Absolute humidity is calculated by using the following equation:

$$absolute\ humidity = \frac{mass\ of\ water\ vapor\ (grams)}{volume\ of\ air\ (cubic\ meters)}$$

However, as air moves, its volume changes as a result of temperature and pressure changes. Therefore, meteorologists prefer to describe humidity by using the mixing ratio of air. The *mixing ratio* is the mass of water vapor in a unit of air relative to the mass of the dry air. For example, the very moist air in tropical regions might have 18 g of water vapor in 1 kg of air, or a mixing ratio of 18 g/kg. On the other hand, the cold, dry air in polar regions commonly has a mixing ratio of less than 1 g/kg. Because this measurement uses only units of mass, it is not affected by changes in temperature or pressure.

dew point at constant pressure and water vapor content, the temperature at which the rate of condensation equals the rate of evaporation

absolute humidity the mass of water vapor per unit volume of air that contains the water vapor, usually expressed as grams of water vapor per cubic meter of air

SCLINKS.

www.scilinks.org
Topic: Atmospheric Moisture
Code: HQX0113

READING TOOLBOX

Two-Panel Flip Chart
Make a two-panel flip chart. Label the first panel "Humidity" and the second panel "Measuring Humidity." Inside each panel, write key ideas about the corresponding topics.

Figure 3 Dew forms on surfaces such as grass and spider webs when the temperature of the air drops lower than the dew point.

relative humidity the ratio of the amount of water vapor in the air to the amount of water vapor needed to reach saturation at a given temperature

Relative Humidity

A more common way to express the amount of water vapor in the atmosphere is by *relative humidity*. **Relative humidity** is a ratio of the actual water vapor content of the air to the amount of water vapor needed to reach saturation. In other words, relative humidity is a measure of how close the air is to reaching the dew point. For example, at 25 °C, air is saturated when it contains 20 g of water vapor per 1 kg of air. If air that is 25 °C contains 5 g of water vapor, the relative humidity is expressed as 5/20, or 25%.

If the temperature does not change, the relative humidity will increase if moisture enters the air. Relative humidity can also increase if the moisture in the air remains constant but the temperature decreases. If the temperature increases as the moisture in the air remains constant, the relative humidity will decrease.

Reaching the Dew Point

When the air is nearly saturated with a relative humidity of almost 100%, only a small temperature drop is needed for the air to reach its dew point. Air may cool to its dew point by conduction when the air comes in contact with a cold surface. During the night, grass, leaves, and other objects near the ground lose heat. Their surface temperatures often drop to the dew point of the surrounding air. Air, which normally remains warmer than surfaces near the ground do, cools to the dew point when it comes into contact with cooler objects, such as grass. When the temperature of air cools below the dew point, condensation, shown in **Figure 3,** called *dew* forms. Dew is most likely to form on cool, clear nights when there is little wind.

If the dew point falls below the freezing temperature of water, water vapor may change directly into solid ice crystals, or *frost*. Because frost forms when water vapor turns directly into ice, frost is not frozen dew. Frozen dew is relatively uncommon. Unlike frost, frozen dew forms as clear beads of ice.

Reading Check **How does dew differ from frost?**

Math Skills

Relative Humidity
Relative humidity can be calculated by using the following equation:

$$\text{relative humidity} = \left[\frac{\text{amount of water vapor in air}}{\text{amount of water vapor needed to reach saturation}} \right] \times 100$$

Air at 20 °C is saturated when it contains 14 g/kg of water vapor. What is the relative humidity of a volume of air that is 20 °C and contains 10 g/kg of water vapor?

Measuring Humidity

Meteorologists are interested in measuring humidity so that they can better predict weather conditions. Relative humidity can be measured by using a variety of instruments, such as an electrical hygrometer, a psychrometer, a dew cell, and a hair hygrometer.

Using an Electrical Hygrometer

Humidity is commonly measured by an electrical hygrometer that uses a *thin polymer film*. The relative humidity of the surrounding air affects the ability of the thin polymer film to absorb or release water vapor. The amount of water vapor that the thin polymer film contains changes the film's ability to conduct electricity. The polymer film's ability to conduct electricity is affected by the relative humidity of the surrounding air. Thus, by measuring the polymer film's ability to conduct electricity, relative humidity can be determined.

Using a Psychrometer

A *psychrometer*, shown in **Figure 4,** is another <u>instrument</u> that is used to measure relative humidity. It consists of two identical thermometers. The bulb of one thermometer is covered with a damp wick, while the bulb of the other thermometer remains dry. When the psychrometer is held by a handle and whirled through the air, the air circulates around both thermometers. As a result, the water in the wick of the wet-bulb thermometer evaporates. Evaporation requires energy, so energy as heat is released by the thermometer. Consequently, the temperature of the wet-bulb thermometer is lower than that of the dry-bulb thermometer. The difference between the dry-bulb temperature and the wet-bulb temperature is used to calculate relative humidity. If there is no difference between the wet-bulb temperature and dry-bulb temperature, no water evaporated from the wet-bulb thermometer. Thus, the air is saturated and the relative humidity is 100%.

Academic Vocabulary

instrument (IN struh muhnt) a mechanical or electronic measuring device

Figure 4 A psychrometer shows differences between wet-bulb and dry-bulb temperatures that can be used to determine relative humidity.

Other Methods for Measuring Humidity

Another instrument that has been used to measure relative humidity is a *dew cell*. A dew cell consists of a ceramic cylinder with electrodes attached to it and treated with lithium chloride, LiCl. When LiCl absorbs water from the air, the dew cell's ability to conduct electricity increases. By detecting the electrical resistance of LiCl as it is heated and cooled, the dew cell can determine the dew point.

A *hair hygrometer* determines relative humidity based on the principle that hair becomes longer as relative humidity increases. As relative humidity decreases, hair becomes shorter.

Figure 5 Scientists use weather balloons, such as this one in Antarctica, to send electrical hygrometers into the high altitudes of the atmosphere.

Measuring Humidity at High Altitudes

To measure humidity at high altitudes, scientists use an electrical hygrometer. The hygrometer may be carried up into the atmosphere in an instrument package known as a *radiosonde*. The radiosonde is attached to a weather balloon, such as the one shown in **Figure 5**. The electrical hygrometer is triggered by passing an electric current through a moisture-attracting chemical substance. The amount of moisture changes the electrical conductivity of the chemical substance. The change can then be expressed as the relative humidity of the surrounding air.

Section 1 Review

LA.910.2.2.3; SC.912.E.7.3; SC.912.P.10.4

Key Ideas

1. **Explain** how most water vapor enters the air.

2. **Identify** the principal source from which most water vapor enters the atmosphere.

3. **Identify** the process by which ice changes directly into a gas.

4. **Define** *humidity*.

5. **Compare** relative humidity with absolute humidity.

6. **Describe** what happens when the temperature of air decreases to the dew point or below the dew point.

7. **Identify** four instruments that are used to measure relative humidity.

Critical Thinking

8. **Predicting Consequences** Explain what would happen to a sample of air whose relative humidity is 100% if the temperature decreased.

9. **Identifying Relationships** Which region of Earth would you expect to have a higher absolute humidity: the equatorial region or the polar regions?

Concept Mapping

10. Use the following terms to create a concept map: *humidity, water vapor, dew point, absolute humidity, dew cell, psychrometer, hygrometer, evaporation, condensation,* and *relative humidity.*

SECTION 2 Clouds and Fog

Key Ideas

❯ Describe the conditions that are necessary for clouds to form.

❯ Explain the four processes of cooling that can lead to the formation of clouds.

❯ Identify the three major types of clouds, noting their characteristic shapes and the altitudes at which they generally form.

❯ Describe four ways in which fog can form.

Key Terms

cloud

condensation nucleus

adiabatic cooling

advective cooling

stratus cloud

cumulus cloud

cirrus cloud

fog

Why It Matters

Often you do not have access to the local weather report. Understanding how clouds form and being able to recognize different cloud types will help you make your own weather predictions and might save you from a drenching.

A cloud is a collection of small water droplets or ice crystals in the air. People commonly think that clouds are high in the sky and fog is close to the ground. However, clouds are not limited to high altitudes. Fog is actually a cloud that forms near or on Earth's surface.

Cloud Formation

For water vapor to condense and form a cloud, a solid surface on which condensation can take place must be available. The lowest layer of the atmosphere, the *troposphere*, contains millions of particles of ice, salt, dust, and other materials that serve as solid surfaces. These particles are so small—less than 0.001 mm in diameter—that they remain suspended in the atmosphere for a long time. The suspended particles that provide the surfaces necessary for water vapor to condense are called **condensation nuclei.** As water molecules collect on the nuclei, water droplets form, as **Figure 1** shows.

In addition, for clouds to form, the air must be "saturated" with water vapor. When the temperature of the air drops, condensation occurs more rapidly than evaporation does. As a result of this net condensation, clouds begin to form. Because the rate of evaporation decreases as temperature decreases, the cooling of air may lead to net condensation.

FLORIDA STANDARDS

LA.910.2.2.3 The student will organize information to show understanding or relationships among facts, ideas, and events (e.g., representing key points within text through charting, mapping, paraphrasing, summarizing, comparing, contrasting, or outlining); **SC.912.E.7.3** Differentiate and describe the various interactions among Earth systems, including: atmosphere, hydrosphere, cryosphere, geosphere, and biosphere.

cloud a collection of small water droplets or ice crystals suspended in the air, which forms when the air is cooled and condensation occurs

condensation nucleus a solid particle in the atmosphere that provides the surface on which water vapor condenses

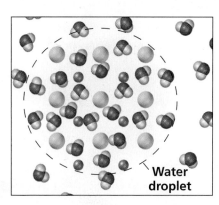

Figure 1 Water molecules are attracted to the sodium and chloride ions in a salt crystal, forming a solution. Additional water molecules are attracted to the solution and the droplet gets bigger.

Salt crystal, Cl⁻, Na⁺, Water molecules, Water droplet

Adiabatic Cooling

As a mass of air rises, the surrounding atmospheric pressure decreases. Because of the lower pressure, the molecules in the rising air move farther apart. Thus, fewer collisions between the molecules happen. The resulting decrease in the amount of energy that is transferred between molecules decreases the temperature of the air. The process by which the temperature of a mass of air decreases as the air rises and expands is called **adiabatic cooling** (AD ee uh BAT ik KOOL ing).

adiabatic cooling the process by which the temperature of an air mass decreases as the air mass rises and expands

Adiabatic Lapse Rate

The rate at which the temperature of a parcel of air changes as the air rises or sinks is called the *adiabatic lapse rate*. The adiabatic lapse rate for clear air is about –1°C for every 100 m that the air rises. Air that is below the dew point—and thus is cloudy—cools more slowly, however. The average adiabatic lapse rate for cloudy air varies between –0.5°C and –0.9°C per 100 m that the air rises. The slower rate of cooling of moist air results from the release of latent heat as the water condenses.

Academic Vocabulary

expand (ek SPAND) to enlarge

Condensation Level

The process through which clouds form by adiabatic cooling is shown in **Figure 2.** Earth's surface absorbs energy from the sun and then reradiates that energy as heat. The air close to Earth's surface absorbs the heat. As the air warms, it rises, expands, and then cools. When the air cools to a temperature that is below the dew point, net condensation causes clouds to form. The altitude at which this net condensation begins is called the *condensation level*. The condensation level is marked by the base of the clouds. Further condensation allows clouds to rise and expand above the condensation level.

Figure 2 Notice in this illustration that temperature and dew point are the same at an altitude of 1,000 m. Above that altitude, condensation begins and clouds, such as the clouds in the image on the right, form.

Reading Check What is the source of energy that warms the air and leads to cloud formation?

1,000 m —
10 °C
Dew point = 10 °C

Rising, expanding, and cooling air

15 °C
500 m —
Dew point = 11 °C

20 °C
0 m —
Dew point = 12 °C

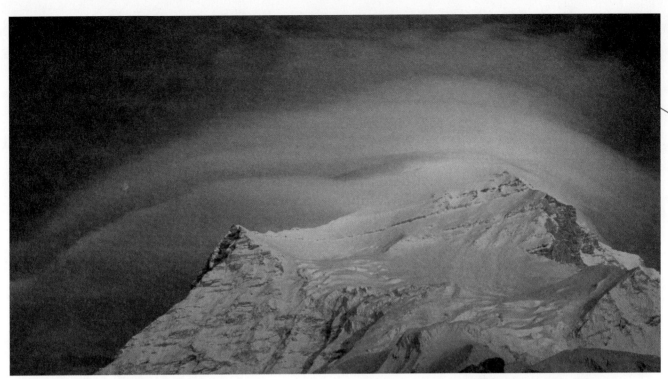

Figure 3 Clouds can form as air is pushed up along a mountain slope and is cooled to below the dew point.

Mixing

Some clouds form when one body of moist air mixes with another body of moist air that has a different temperature. The combination of the two bodies of air causes the temperature of the air to change. This temperature change may cool the combined air to below its dew point, which results in cloud formation.

Lifting

The forced upward movement of air commonly results in the cooling of air and in cloud formation. Air can be forced upward when a moving mass of air meets sloping terrain, such as a mountain range. As the rising air expands and cools, clouds form. As **Figure 3** shows, entire mountaintops can be covered with clouds that formed in this way.

The large cloud formations that are associated with storm systems also form by lifting. These clouds form when a mass of cold, dense air enters an area and pushes a less dense mass of warmer air upward.

Advective Cooling

Another cooling process that is associated with cloud formation is advective cooling. **Advective cooling** is the process by which the temperature of an air mass decreases as the air mass moves over a cold surface, such as a cold ocean or land surface. As air moves over a surface that is colder than the air is, the cold surface absorbs heat from the air and the air cools. If the air cools to below its dew point, clouds form.

www.scilinks.org
Topic: Clouds and Fog
Code: HQX0304

advective cooling the process by which the temperature of an air mass decreases as the air mass moves over a cold surface stratus cloud a gray cloud that has a flat, uniform base and that commonly forms at very low altitudes

Figure 4 A variety of cloud types can be identified by their altitude and shape. *What cloud types form at or above 6,000 m?*

Classification of Clouds

Clouds are classified by their shape and their altitude. The three basic cloud types are stratus clouds, cumulus clouds, and cirrus clouds. There are also three altitude groups: low clouds (0 to 2,000 m), middle clouds (2,000 to 6,000 m), and high clouds (above 6,000 m). This classification system is shown in **Figure 4.**

Stratus Clouds

Clouds that have a flat, uniform base and that begin to form at very low altitudes are called **stratus clouds.** *Stratus* means "sheet-like" or "layered." The base of stratus clouds is low and may almost touch Earth's surface. Stratus clouds form where a layer of warm, moist air lies above a layer of cool air. When the overlying warm air cools below its dew point, wide clouds appear. Stratus clouds cover large areas of sky and often block out the sun. Usually, very little precipitation falls from most types of stratus clouds.

Two variations of stratus clouds are known as *nimbostratus* and *altostratus*. The prefix *nimbo-* and the suffix *-nimbus* mean "rain." Unlike other stratus clouds, the dark nimbostratus clouds can cause heavy precipitation. Altostratus clouds form at the middle altitudes and usually produce very little precipitation.

Figure 5 Cumulus clouds (left) are puffy, vertically growing clouds, while cirrus clouds (right) are wispy.

Cumulus Clouds

Low-altitude, billowy clouds that commonly have a top that resembles cotton balls and a dark bottom are called **cumulus clouds.** *Cumulus* means "piled" or "heaped." Cumulus clouds usually look fluffy, as shown in **Figure 5.** These clouds form when warm, moist air rises and cools. As the cooling air reaches its dew point, the clouds form. The flat base that is characteristic of most cumulus clouds represents the condensation level.

The height of a cumulus cloud depends on the stability of the troposphere, which is the layer of the atmosphere that touches Earth's surface, and on the amount of moisture in the air. On hot, humid days, cumulus clouds reach their greatest heights. High, dark storm clouds known as *cumulonimbus clouds*, or thunderheads, are often accompanied by rain, lightning, and thunder. If the base of cumulus clouds begins at middle altitudes, the clouds are called *altocumulus clouds*. Low clouds that are a combination of stratus and cumulus clouds are called *stratocumulus clouds*.

Cirrus Clouds

Feathery clouds that are composed of ice crystals and that have the highest altitude of any cloud in the sky are **cirrus clouds.** Cirrus clouds are also shown in **Figure 5.** *Cirro-* and *cirrus* mean "curly." Cirrus clouds form at altitudes above 6,000 m. These clouds are made of ice crystals because the temperatures are low at such high altitudes. Because these clouds are thin, light can easily pass through them.

Cirrocumulus clouds are high-altitude, billowy clouds composed entirely of ice crystals. Cirrocumulus clouds commonly appear just before a snowfall or a rainfall. Long, thin clouds called *cirrostratus clouds* form a high, transparent veil across the sky. A halo may appear around the sun or moon when either is viewed through a cirrostratus cloud. This halo effect is caused by the bending of light rays as they pass through the ice crystals.

Reading Check Why are cirrus clouds commonly composed of ice crystals?

cumulus cloud a low-level, billowy cloud that commonly has a top that resembles cotton balls and a dark bottom

cirrus cloud a feathery cloud that is composed of ice crystals and that has the highest altitude of any cloud in the sky

READING TOOLBOX

Analyzing Comparisons
As you read about cumulus clouds and cirrus clouds, look for comparisons between them. Create a table of their similarities and differences.

Fog

Like clouds, **fog** is the result of the condensation of water vapor in the air. The obvious difference between fog and clouds is that fog is very near the surface of Earth. However, fog also differs from clouds because of how fog forms.

Radiation Fog

One type of fog forms from the nightly cooling of Earth. The layer of air in contact with the ground becomes chilled to below the dew point, and the water vapor in that layer condenses into droplets. This type of fog is called *radiation fog* because it results from the loss of heat by radiation. Radiation fog is thickest in valleys and low places because dense, cold air sinks to low elevations. Radiation fog is often quite thick around cities, where smoke and dust particles act as condensation nuclei.

Other Types of Fog

Another type of fog, *advection fog*, forms when warm, moist air moves across a cold surface. Advection fog is common along coasts, where warm, moist air from above the water moves in over a cooler land surface. Advection fog forms over the ocean when warm, moist air is carried over cold ocean currents.

An *upslope fog* forms by the lifting and cooling of air as the air rises along land slopes. *Steam fog* is a shallow layer of fog that forms when cool air moves over an inland warm body of water, such as a river, as shown in **Figure 6**.

Figure 6 Steam fog covers the Yakima River in Washington.

fog water vapor that has condensed very near the surface of Earth because air close to the ground has cooled

---

Section 2 Review

LA.910.2.2.3; SC.912.E.7.3; SC.912.P.10.4

Key Ideas

1. **Describe** the conditions that are necessary for clouds to form.

2. **Explain** the four processes of cooling that can lead to cloud formation.

3. **Identify** the cloud types that form at 8,000 m.

4. **Compare** cirrus, cumulus, and stratus clouds.

5. **Identify** the type of cloud that is known for causing thunderstorms.

6. **Compare** clouds with fog.

7. **Describe** four ways in which fog can form.

Critical Thinking

8. **Applying Ideas** Explain why air expands when it rises.

9. **Making Predictions** How might an increase in pollution affect cloud formation?

10. **Making Comparisons** Which type of cloud has the lowest condensation level? Which type has the highest condensation level?

Concept Mapping

11. Use the following terms to create a concept map: *cloud, cirrus, condensation level, advective cooling, adiabatic cooling, stratus, cumulus,* and *fog.*

SECTION 3 Precipitation

Key Ideas	Key Terms	Why It Matters
❯ Identify the four forms of precipitation. ❯ Compare the two processes that cause precipitation. ❯ Describe two ways that precipitation is measured. ❯ Explain how rain can be produced artificially.	precipitation coalescence supercooling cloud seeding	You may not appreciate the rain when you need to go outside. But rain and other forms of precipitation are an essential part of the water cycle.

Any moisture that falls from the air to Earth's surface is called **precipitation.** The four major types of precipitation are rain, snow, sleet, and hail.

Forms of Precipitation

Rain is liquid precipitation. Normal raindrops are between 0.5 and 5 mm in diameter. They may vary from a fine mist to large drops in a torrential rainstorm. If the raindrops are smaller than 0.5 mm in diameter, the rain is called *drizzle*. Drizzle results in only a small amount of total precipitation.

The most common form of solid precipitation is *snow*, which consists of ice particles. These particles may fall as small pellets, as individual crystals, or as crystals that combine to form snowflakes. Snowflakes tend to be large at temperatures near 0 °C and become smaller at lower temperatures.

When rain falls through a layer of freezing air near the ground, clear ice pellets, called *sleet*, can form. In some cases, the rain does not freeze until it strikes a surface near the ground. There, it forms a thick layer of ice called *glaze ice*, as shown in **Figure 1.** The condition in which glaze ice is produced is commonly referred to as an *ice storm*.

Hail is solid precipitation in the form of lumps of ice. The lumps can be either spherical or irregularly shaped. Hail usually forms in cumulonimbus clouds. Convection currents within the clouds carry raindrops to high levels, where the raindrops freeze before they fall. If the frozen raindrops are carried upward again, they can accumulate additional layers of ice until they are too heavy for the convection currents to carry them. Then they fall to the ground. Large hailstones can damage crops and property.

FLORIDA STANDARDS

SC.912.E.7.3 Differentiate and describe the various interactions among Earth systems, including: atmosphere, hydrosphere, cryosphere, geosphere, and biosphere; **SC.912.N.1.6** Describe how scientific inferences are drawn from scientific observations and provide examples from the content being studied.

precipitation any form of water that falls to Earth's surface from the clouds; includes rain, snow, sleet, and hail

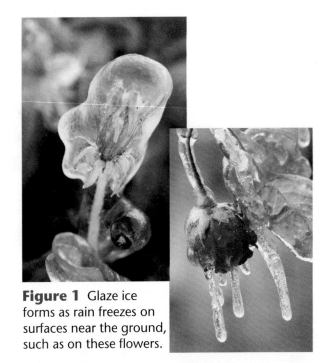

Figure 1 Glaze ice forms as rain freezes on surfaces near the ground, such as on these flowers.

Figure 2 During coalescence, cloud droplets collide and combine with smaller droplets as they fall. The resulting larger droplets fall as rain.

coalescence the formation of a large droplet by the combination of smaller droplets

supercooling a condition in which a substance is cooled below its freezing point, condensation point, or sublimation point without going through a change of state

Causes of Precipitation

Most cloud droplets have a diameter of about 20 μm (micrometers), which is smaller than the period at the end of this sentence. Droplets of this size fall very slowly through the air. A droplet must increase in diameter by about 100 times to fall as precipitation. Two natural processes cause cloud droplets to grow large enough to fall as precipitation: coalescence and supercooling.

Coalescence

The formation of a large droplet by the combination of smaller droplets is called **coalescence** (кон uh LES uhnts) and is shown in **Figure 2.** Large droplets fall much faster through the air than small droplets do. As these larger droplets drift downward, they collide and combine with smaller droplets. Each large droplet continues to coalesce until it contains a million times as much water as it did originally.

Supercooling

Precipitation also forms by the process of supercooling. **Supercooling** is a condition in which a substance is cooled to below its freezing point, condensation point, or sublimation point without changing state. Supercooled water droplets may have a temperature as low as −40 °C. Yet even at this low temperature, the water droplets do not freeze. They cannot freeze because too few *freezing nuclei* on which ice can form are available. Freezing nuclei are solid particles that are suspended in the air and that have structures similar to the crystal structure of ice. Most water from the supercooled water droplets evaporates. The water vapor then condenses on the ice crystals that have formed on the freezing nuclei. The ice crystals rapidly increase in size until they gain enough mass to fall as snow, as shown in **Figure 3.** If the ice crystals melt and turn into rain as they pass through air whose temperature is above freezing, they form the big raindrops that are common in summer thunderstorms.

Figure 3 Most of the rain and snow in the middle and high latitudes of Earth are the result of the formation of ice crystals in supercooled clouds.

Figure 4 Doppler radar helps meteorologists track storms, such as this large thunderstorm system over North Texas. The colors represent the intensity of rainfall. Reds and yellows indicate areas of heaviest rainfall, while blues and greens denote areas of lighter rainfall.

Measuring Precipitation

Meteorologists use a variety of instruments to measure precipitation. For example, a *rain gauge* may be used to measure rainfall.

Amount of Precipitation

In one type of rain gauge, rainwater passes through a funnel into a calibrated container, where the amount of rainfall can then be measured. In another type of rain gauge, rain caught in a funnel fills a bucket. Each time the bucket fills with a given amount of rainwater, the bucket tips and sets off an electrical device that records the amount. As the bucket tips, it activates a switch that releases the water from the bucket.

Snow depth is simply determined with a measuring stick. The water content of the snow is determined by melting a measured volume of snow and by measuring the amount of water that results. On average, 10 cm of snow will melt to produce about 1 cm of water.

Doppler Radar

The intensity of precipitation can be measured using Doppler radar. Doppler radar images, such as the one in **Figure 4,** are commonly used by meteorologists for communicating weather forecasts. Doppler radar works by bouncing radio waves off rain or snow. By timing how long the wave takes to return, meteorologists can detect the location, direction of movement, and intensity of the precipitation. This information is extremely valuable for saving lives because people can be warned of an approaching storm.

Reading Check **What aspects of precipitation can Doppler radar measure?**

READING TOOLBOX

Suffixes
Find two adverbs that end in the suffix *-ly* on this page. Identify which adjective forms the root of each adverb, and give the meaning of the adverb.

www.scilinks.org
Topic: Precipitation
Code: HQX1202

Academic Vocabulary

detect (dee TEKT) to discover the presence of something

Weather Modification

In areas suffering from drought, scientists may attempt to induce precipitation through cloud seeding, as shown in **Figure 5. Cloud seeding** is the process of introducing freezing nuclei or condensation nuclei into a cloud to cause rain to fall.

Methods of Cloud Seeding

One method of cloud seeding uses silver iodide crystals, which resemble ice crystals, as freezing nuclei. The silver iodide is released from burners on the ground or from flares dropped from aircraft. Another method of cloud seeding uses powdered dry ice, which is dropped from aircraft to cool cloud droplets and to cause ice crystals to form. As the ice crystals fall, they may melt to form raindrops.

Improving Cloud Seeding

In some cases, seeded clouds produce more precipitation than unseeded clouds do. In other cases, cloud seeding does not cause a significant increase in precipitation. Sometimes, cloud seeding appears to cause less precipitation. Thus, meteorologists have concluded that cloud seeding may increase precipitation under some conditions but decrease it under others. Research is underway to identify the conditions that cause increased precipitation. Eventually, cloud seeding may become a way to overcome many drought-related problems. In theory, cloud seeding could also help to control a severe storm by releasing precipitation from clouds before the storm can become too large. But scientific experiments have so far failed to prove this.

Figure 5 Special equipment attached to the wings of cloud-seeding planes releases freezing nuclei into clouds. Meteorologists hope that cloud seeding will induce rain to fall on drought-stricken areas.

cloud seeding the process of introducing freezing nuclei or condensation nuclei into a cloud in order to cause rain to fall

Section 3 Review

LA.910.2.2.3; SC.912.E.7.3; SC.912.P.10.4

Key Ideas

1. **Identify** four forms of precipitation.

2. **Compare** coalescence and supercooling.

3. **Identify** the instrument that measures amounts of rainfall.

4. **Describe** how the amount of snowfall can be measured.

5. **Explain** how Doppler radar can be used to measure the intensity of precipitation.

6. **Describe** how precipitation can be induced or increased artificially.

Critical Thinking

7. **Predicting Consequences** If water could not remain liquid during supercooling, how would the potential for precipitation in colder climates be affected?

8. **Making Inferences** Explain how cloud seeding could be dangerous if it is not done properly.

Concept Mapping

9. Use the following terms to create a concept map: *precipitation, rain, snow, glaze ice, hail, coalescence, supercooling, freezing nucleus, sleet,* and *drizzle.*

Ice Storms

Beautiful but dangerous, ice storms are one of weather's most sudden phenomena. Ice storms occur when falling snow, passing through a layer of warmer air, melts into rain. At ground level, the rain then passes through a layer of colder air and freezes when it makes contact with a solid object, coating the object in ice. The rain does not have time to form sleet or snow before it hits Earth's surface because the layer of cold air is very close to the ground.

Ice storms can cover roads with ice in a matter of minutes, causing traffic accidents, as surprised motorists are unable to control their cars. Ice coats power lines and utility poles, which can break when the ice becomes too heavy, causing massive power outages that deprive homes of heat during the coldest part of the year.

People can prepare for ice storms by listening to the radio or watching television for news of winter storm watches, warnings, and advisories. They should have extra food and water at home, plus other supplies such as flashlights, batteries, and a first aid kit.

YOUR TURN

UNDERSTANDING CONCEPTS
Why does freezing rain coat Earth's surface with ice instead of falling as sleet?

WRITING IN SCIENCE
Create a pamphlet that explains what people should do in the event of an ice storm.

559

What You'll Do

> **Measure** humidity in the classroom.

> **Determine** relative humidity.

What You'll Need

cloth, cotton, at least 8 cm × 8 cm
container, plastic
piece of paper
ring stand with ring
rubber band
string
thermometer, Celsius (2)
water

Safety

Relative Humidity

Earth's atmosphere acts as a reservoir for water that evaporates from Earth's surface. However, the amount of water vapor in the atmosphere depends on the relative rates of condensation and evaporation. When the rates of condensation and evaporation are equal, the air is said to be "saturated." When the rate of condensation exceeds the rate of evaporation, water droplets begin to form in the air or on nearby surfaces. The point at which the condensation rate equals the evaporation rate is called the *dew point* and depends on the temperature of the air and on the atmospheric pressure.

Relative humidity is the ratio of the amount of water vapor in the air to the amount of water vapor that is needed for the air to become saturated. This ratio is most commonly expressed as a percentage. When the air is saturated, the air is said to have a relative humidity of 100%. In this lab, you will use wet-bulb and dry-bulb thermometer readings to determine the relative humidity of the air in your classroom.

Procedure

1 Hang two thermometers from a ring stand, as shown in the photo below.

2 Using a rubber band, fasten a piece of cotton cloth around the bulb of one thermometer. Adjust the length of the string so that only the cloth, not the thermometer bulb, is immersed in the water. By using this setup, you can measure both the air temperature and the cooling effect of evaporation.

Step **2**

❸ Predict whether the two thermometers will have the same reading or which thermometer will have the lower reading.

❹ Using a piece of paper, fan both thermometers rapidly until the reading on the wet-bulb thermometer stops changing. Read the temperature on each thermometer.

   a. What is the temperature on the dry-bulb thermometer?

   b. What is the temperature on the wet-bulb thermometer?

   c. What is the difference in the two temperature readings?

❺ Use the table entitled "Relative Humidity" in the Reference Tables section of the Appendix to find the relative humidity based on your temperature readings in step 4. Look at the left-hand column labeled "Dry-Bulb Temperature." Find the temperature that you recorded in step 4a. Then, find the difference in temperature that you recorded in step 4c along the top row of the table. Locate the intersection of the row and column you have identified. The number shown, expressed as a percentage, is the relative humidity. What is the relative humidity of the air in your classroom?

Step ❹

Analysis

1. **Drawing Conclusions** On the basis of the relative humidity you determined, is the air in your classroom close to or far from the dew point? Explain your answer.

2. **Applying Conclusions** If you wet the back of your hand, would the water evaporate and cool your skin?

Extension

Making Inferences Suppose that you exercise in a room in which the relative humidity is 100%.

   a. Would the moisture on your skin from perspiration evaporate easily?

   b. Would you be able to cool off readily? Explain your answer.

Applying Ideas Suppose that you have just stepped out of a swimming pool. The relative humidity is low, about 30%. Would you feel warm or cool? Explain your answer.

MAPS *in Action*

Annual Precipitation in the United States

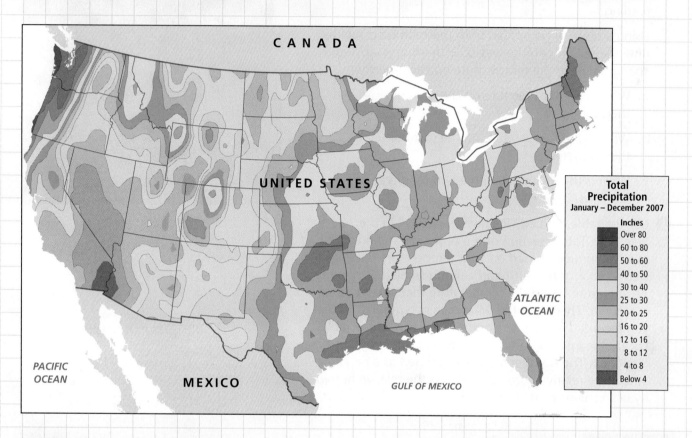

CANADA

UNITED STATES

PACIFIC OCEAN

MEXICO

GULF OF MEXICO

ATLANTIC OCEAN

Total Precipitation
January – December 2007

Inches

Over 80
60 to 80
50 to 60
40 to 50
30 to 40
25 to 30
20 to 25
16 to 20
12 to 16
8 to 12
4 to 8
Below 4

Map Skills Activity

This map shows the total precipitation for the continental United States in 2007. Use the map to answer the questions below.

1. **Using a Key** What is the highest total amount of precipitation for any area in your state?

2. **Making Comparisons** Which area of the United States has the highest total annual precipitation?

3. **Analyzing Methods** Using what you have learned about the formation of precipitation, explain why one area of the United States might have a higher total annual precipitation than another area has.

4. **Making Inferences** List the forms of precipitation that occur in the United States. Identify areas of the United States where you would likely encounter each form.

5. **Evaluating Data** Describe the area of the United States that might be classified as desert.

6. **Making Comparisons** Describe the area of the United States that might have the highest rate of evaporation.

7. **Making Comparisons** Describe the area of the United States that you think might have the highest relative humidity.

THINK
central

SUPER SUMMARY
Keyword: HQXWIAS

Key Ideas

Key Terms

Section 1

Atmospheric Moisture

❯ Latent heat is released or absorbed when water changes from one state to another.

❯ Absolute humidity is the mass of water vapor contained in a given volume of air. Relative humidity is a ratio of the actual amount of water vapor in the air to the amount of water vapor needed to reach saturation. Humidity can be measured using a variety of instruments, including an electrical hygrometer, a psychrometer, a dew cell, and a hair hygrometer.

❯ When air reaches the dew point, the rate of condensation equals the rate of evaporation. Below the dew point, net condensation or deposition causes dew or frost to form.

latent heat, p. 543
sublimation, p. 544
dew point, p. 545
absolute humidity,
   p. 545
relative humidity,
   p. 546

Section 2

Clouds and Fog

❯ Clouds form when water vapor cools and condenses on condensation nuclei.

❯ Water vapor can cool and condense by adiabatic cooling, by the mixing of two bodies of moist air that have different temperatures, by the lifting of air, and by advective cooling.

❯ The three major types of clouds are stratus clouds, cumulus clouds, and cirrus clouds.

❯ Fog forms when air near Earth's surface is chilled below the dew point. Fog can form due to heat loss through radiation, advective cooling, the lifting and cooling of air along land slopes, or when cool air moves over an inland body of warm water.

cloud, p. 549
condensation nucleus,
   p. 549
adiabatic cooling,
   p. 550
advective cooling,
   p. 551
stratus cloud, p. 552
cumulus cloud, p. 553
cirrus cloud, p. 553
fog, p. 554

Section 3

Precipitation

❯ The major forms of precipitation are rain, snow, sleet, and hail.

❯ Coalescence and supercooling are two processes by which cloud droplets become large enough to fall as precipitation.

❯ A rain gauge is used to measure liquid precipitation. Snow is measured by its depth and water content.

❯ Meteorologists utilize cloud seeding to try to induce precipitation.

precipitation, p. 555
coalescence, p. 556
supercooling, p. 556
cloud seeding, p. 558

Chapter 20 Review

1. Comparisons Create a table of the similarities and differences among the different types of precipitation. SC.912.E.7.3

USING KEY TERMS

Use each of the following terms in a separate sentence.

2. *latent heat* SC.912.E.7.3

3. *condensation nucleus* SC.912.E.7.3

4. *precipitation* SC.912.E.7.3

For each pair of terms, explain how the meanings of the terms differ.

5. *coalescence* and *supercooling* SC.912.E.7.3

6. *stratus cloud* and *cumulus cloud* SC.912.E.7.3

7. *adiabatic cooling* and *advective cooling* SC.912.E.7.3

8. *relative humidity* and *absolute humidity* SC.912.E.7.3

9. *cloud* and *fog* SC.912.E.7.3

UNDERSTANDING KEY IDEAS

10. When the temperature of the air decreases, the rate of evaporation SC.912.E.7.3
a. increases.
b. varies.
c. stays the same.
d. decreases.

11. The type of fog that results when moist air moves across a cold surface is SC.912.E.7.3
a. radiation fog.
b. ground fog.
c. advection fog.
d. steam fog.

12. Changes in temperature that result from the cooling of rising air or the warming of sinking air are SC.912.E.7.3
a. adiabatic.
b. relative.
c. advective.
d. latent.

13. Clouds form when the water vapor in air condenses as SC.912.E.7.3
a. the air is heated.
b. the air is cooled.
c. snow falls.
d. the air is superheated.

14. The prefix *nimbo-* and the suffix *-nimbus* mean SC.912.E.7.3
a. high.
b. billowy.
c. rain.
d. layered.

15. The fog that results from the nightly cooling of Earth is called SC.912.E.7.3
a. steam fog.
b. upslope fog.
c. radiation fog.
d. advection fog.

16. Rain that freezes when it strikes a surface produces SC.912.E.7.3
a. sleet.
b. glaze ice.
c. hail.
d. frost.

17. Clouds in which the water droplets remain liquid below 0°C are said to be SC.912.E.7.3
a. saturated.
b. supersaturated.
c. superheated.
d. supercooled.

18. In one method of cloud seeding, silver iodide crystals are used as SC.912.E.7.3
a. freezing nuclei.
b. cloud droplets.
c. dry ice.
d. latent heat.

19. An instrument that uses the electrical conductance of the chemical lithium chloride to measure relative humidity is the SC.912.E.7.3
a. hygrometer.
b. rain gauge.
c. psychrometer.
d. dew cell.

SHORT ANSWER

20. Explain how the transfer of energy affects the changing forms of water. SC.912.E.7.3

21. Explain how a psychrometer measures humidity. SC.912.E.7.3

22. Describe how frost forms. SC.912.E.7.3

23. Describe how precipitation is measured. SC.912.E.7.3

24. Describe how cloud seeding may increase precipitation. SC.912.E.7.3

25. Explain how clouds are classified. SC.912.E.7.3

CRITICAL THINKING

26. Making Inferences Where would air contain more water vapor: over Panama or over Antarctica? Explain your answer. **SC.912.E.7.4**

27. Identifying Relationships One body of air has a relative humidity of 97%. Another has a relative humidity of 44%. At the same temperature, which body of air is closer to its dew point? Explain your answer. **SC.912.E.7.3**

28. Applying Ideas Why would polluted air be more likely to form fog than clean air would?

29. Analyzing Relationships In tropical regions, surface temperatures are very high. However, some precipitation in these regions forms by supercooling. Why might this happen? **SC.912.E.7.3**

30. Predicting Consequences How would a significant decrease in condensation nuclei in the world's atmosphere affect cloud formation and climate? **SC.912.E.7.3**

CONCEPT MAPPING

31. Use the following terms to create a concept map: *hygrometer, condensation nucleus, stratus, cirrus, cloud, cumulus, precipitation, relative humidity, saturated, rain, supercooling, snow, sleet, coalescence, dew cell,* and *psychrometer.* **SC.912.E.7.3**

MATH SKILLS

Math Skills

32. Applying Quantities One day in January, 6 cm of snow falls on your area. If all this snow melts quickly, how deep will the water from the melted snow be? Explain your answer. **SC.912.E.7.3**

33. Making Calculations At 15 °C, air reaches saturation when it contains 10 g of water vapor per 1 kg of air. What is the relative humidity of air at 15 °C if the air contains 7 g of water vapor per 1 kg of air? **SC.912.E.7.3**

WRITING SKILLS

34. Writing from Research Write a report that describes weather conditions necessary to form each type of cloud. Propose regions and describe climates where each cloud type is most likely to be found. **SC.912.E.7.3**

35. Outlining Topics Create an outline of how clouds form and a separate outline of how precipitation forms. Then, explain how the two differ. **SC.912.E.7.3**

INTERPRETING GRAPHICS

The graph below shows variations in temperature and humidity over a 24 h period. Use this graph to answer the questions that follow.

36. Estimate the relative humidity at 6:00 A.M. **SC.912.E.7.3**

37. Estimate the temperature at 6:00 A.M. **SC.912.E.7.3**

38. Explain why relative humidity might be the highest at 6:00 A.M. **SC.912.E.7.3**

39. When is relative humidity the lowest? **SC.912.E.7.3**

40. How does humidity vary relative to temperature? **SC.912.E.7.3**

Understanding Concepts

Directions (1–8): For each question, write on a separate sheet of paper the letter of the correct answer.

1 As water changes state, energy is released or absorbed. During evaporation, the change of state in which liquid water forms a gas, energy is
  A. absorbed from the environment.
  B. released into the surrounding air.
  C. absorbed by the surrounding environment.
  D. released from the surrounding air.

2 Which of the following statements does NOT describe a way to measure humidity?
  F. A psychrometer is used to measure relative humidity.
  G. A thin polymer film is used to measure relative humidity.
  H. A hygrometer measures humidity at high altitudes.
  I. A dew cell is used to measure absolute humidity.

3 Which of the following is necessary for clouds to form?
  A. particles called condensation nuclei
  B. a rate of evaporation that exceeds the rate of condensation
  C. warming of air
  D. sublimation of ice

4 Advective cooling results in the formation of clouds. Which of the following statements best describes this type of cloud formation?
  F. The forced upward movement of air results in the cooling of air and cloud formation.
  G. Moist air mixes with another body of moist air that has a different temperature, forming clouds.
  H. The temperature of an air mass decreases as it moves over a cold surface, forming clouds.
  I. An air mass rises, which results in cooling and expansion and the formation of clouds.

5 Some scientists think that weather can be modified in areas suffering drought. To induce precipitation, scientists might
  A. introduce condensation nuclei.
  B. increase evaporation.
  C. warm clouds.
  D. use Doppler radar.

6 Which of the following processes does NOT result in precipitation?
  F. Smaller droplets combine to form a large droplet.
  G. Water is cooled to below its freezing point, but it does not change state.
  H. Air near the ground becomes chilled below the dew point.
  I. Large water droplets fall, gathering smaller droplets as they fall.

7 Which of the following statements best describes the relationship between absolute humidity and relative humidity?
  A. Relative humidity is not related to absolute humidity.
  B. Absolute humidity is a measure of the relative humidity in a given volume of air.
  C. Relative humidity changes, but absolute humidity is constant.
  D. Relative humidity is a ratio of absolute humidity to the water content of saturated air.

8 Clouds are described by the word roots in their names. For example, cumulus means "piled," cirro and cirrus mean "curly," nimbo and nimbus mean "rain," and stratus means "layered." Which of the following statements describes cumulonimbus clouds?
  F. layered rain clouds
  G. curly layered clouds
  H. piled rain clouds
  I. piled layered clouds

Interpreting Graphics

Directions (9–11): For each question below, record the correct answer on a separate sheet of paper.

MOVEMENT OF AIR OVER A MOUNTAIN

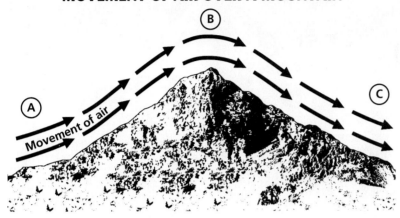

9 As air moves from point A to point B, the air temperature
  A. increases.
  B. decreases.
  C. stays the same.
  D. decreases, then increases.

10 Air moving from point B to point C will become compressed and gain energy as it moves down the mountain, which will cause the air to undergo
  F. adiabatic warming.
  G. adiabatic cooling.
  H. condensation.
  I. sublimation.

PARTS OF A PSYCHROMETER

Wick
Wet bulb   Dry bulb   Handle

11 How does a meteorologist use a psychrometer, such as the one shown in the diagram above, to measure humidity?
  A. It is placed in a pan of water and exposed to the air for one hour.
  B. The handle is used to dip it into a body of water such as a lake.
  C. It is held by the handle and twirled in the air.
  D. It is held until the readings on both thermometers are equal.

> **Test Tip**
>
> If you are not sure of an answer, go to the next question, but remember to skip that number on your answer sheet.

Chapter 21 Weather

Chapter Outline

Why It Matters

Weather—both mild and severe—affects our daily lives. Scientists use weather data and weather patterns to help predict and forecast the weather.

Inquiry Lab

🕐 **20 min**

Build a Wind Vane ◆ ◆ ◆

Use **scissors** to cut a piece of **thin cardboard** or **manila paper** into a triangular arrowhead, 5 cm long, and a rectangular tail, 7 cm long. Make parallel cuts at both ends of a **drinking straw** about 2 cm long, and slide in the arrowhead and the tail. Push a **straight pin** through the balance point of the straw and into the eraser end of a **pencil.** Then push the pointed end of the pencil vertically through the center of an **aluminum pie plate** and into a lump of **modeling clay.** Place the clay in center of a heavy **paper plate** and press down, forming a sandwich of clay between the two plates. (You may also want to steady the pin with a small piece of clay.) Mark the directions N, S, E, and W around the edges of the pie plate with a **marker.** Place your wind vane in front of a **fan** and turn the fan on low speed. Observe what happens.

Questions to Get You Started

1. What does a wind vane measure?

2. How does the design of your wind vane make the arrow point upwind?

3. How is wind direction described? Is it described as the direction from which the wind blows or the direction in which the wind is blowing?

SC.912.E.7.3

These reading tools will help you learn the material in this chapter.

Word Parts

Prefixes, Suffixes, and Root Words The prefix *iso-* is from the Greek word *isos,* meaning "equal." When added to the root word *therm,* which means "heat," you have the word *isotherm,* which means "a line on a weather map that connects points of equal temperature."

Your Turn On a separate sheet of paper, complete a table like the one below with key terms or italicized words from this chapter that contain prefixes, suffixes, or word roots. Use a dictionary or the Internet to find the meanings of the word parts.

Word	Definition	Root	Prefix	Suffix
isobar	a line on a weather map that connects points of equal atmospheric pressure	bar: from the Greek word baros, meaning "weight"	iso: from the Greek word isos, meaning "equal"	

Generalizations

Properties of Severe Weather When you make a generalization, you make a statement that applies to a large group of things or people. If you say, "Most students studied for the test," you are saying that most, but not all, students studied for the test. Words such as *most, usually, typically, commonly,* and *generally,* and phrases such as *in general* and *for the most part,* signal generalizations. Some generalizations do not have a word or phrase signal.

Your Turn As you read Section 2, complete a table like the one below to list the generalizations that you find.

Sentence	Word or phrase that signals generalization	Explanation of why sentence is a generalization
Tornadoes generally cover paths not more than 100 m wide.	generally	The statement applies to most, but not all, tornadoes.

Note Taking

Two-Column Notes Two-column notes can help you learn the key terms, italicized words, and main ideas as you read.

Your Turn Complete two-column notes for Sections 1 and 4.

❶ Write one key term, italicized word, or main idea in each row of the left-hand column.

❷ Add definitions, details, and examples in the right-hand column.

Key term, italicized word, or main idea	Definitions, details, and examples
maritime	• on or near the ocean
maritime air masses	• air masses that form over the ocean • take on the characteristics of the water over which they form (moist, humid) • usually bring precipitation and fog

For more information on how to use these and other tools, see **Appendix A.**

Key Ideas	Key Terms	Why It Matters
❯ Explain how an air mass forms. ❯ List the four main types of air masses. ❯ Describe how air masses affect the weather of North America.	air mass	You may not think about air masses very often, but they influence weather across North America every day.

Differences in air pressure are caused by unequal heating of Earth's surface. The region along the equator receives more solar energy than the regions at the poles do. The heated equatorial air rises and creates a low-pressure center. Conversely, cold air near the poles sinks and creates high-pressure centers. Differences in air pressure at different locations on Earth create wind patterns.

How Air Moves

Air moves from areas of high pressure to areas of low pressure. Therefore, there is a general, worldwide movement of surface air from the poles toward the equator. At high altitudes, the warmed air flows from the equator toward the poles. Temperature and pressure differences on Earth's surface create three wind belts in the Northern Hemisphere and three wind belts in the Southern Hemisphere. These wind belts are influenced by the *Coriolis effect*, which occurs when winds are deflected by Earth's rotation. The processes that affect air movement also influence storms, such as the one shown in **Figure 1**.

Formation of Air Masses

When air pressure differences are small, the air remains relatively stationary. If the air remains stationary or moves slowly over a uniform region, it takes on the characteristic temperature and humidity of that region. A large body of air throughout which temperature and moisture are similar is called an **air mass.** Air masses that form over frozen polar regions are very cold and dry. Air masses that form over tropical oceans are warm and moist.

air mass a large body of air throughout which temperature and moisture content are similar

Figure 1 The motion of Earth's atmosphere can lead to the formation of powerful storms, such as Hurricane Katrina.

Table 1 Air Masses

Source region	Type of air	Symbol
Continental	dry	c
Maritime	moist	m
Tropical	warm	T
Polar	cold	P

Figure 2 A maritime air mass brings fog that rolls in off the coast of California.

Types of Air Masses

Air masses are classified according to their source regions. The source regions determine the temperature and the humidity of the air masses. The source regions for cold air masses are polar areas. The source regions for warm air masses are tropical areas. Air masses that form over oceans are called *maritime*. Air masses that form over land are called *continental*. Maritime air masses are moist, and continental air masses are dry. Air masses and the symbols used to designate them are listed in **Table 1.** The combination of tropical or polar air and continental or maritime air results in air masses that have distinct characteristics.

Continental Air Masses

Continental air masses form over large landmasses, such as northern Canada, northern Asia, and the southwestern United States. Because these air masses form over land, the level of humidity is very low. An air mass may remain over its source region for days or weeks. However, the air mass will eventually move into other regions because of global wind patterns. In general, continental air masses bring dry weather conditions when they move into another region. There are two types of continental air masses: *continental polar* (cP) and *continental tropical* (cT). Continental polar air masses are cold and dry. Continental tropical air masses are warm and dry.

Maritime Air Masses

Maritime air masses form over oceans and other large bodies of water. These air masses take on the characteristics of the water over which they form. The humidity in these air masses tends to be higher than that of continental air masses. When these very moist air masses travel to a new location, they commonly bring precipitation and fog, as shown in **Figure 2.**

The two types of maritime air masses are *maritime polar* (mP) and *maritime tropical* (mT). Maritime polar air masses are moist and cold. Maritime tropical air masses are moist and warm.

North American Air Masses

The four types of air masses that affect the weather of North America come from six locations. These air masses, their source locations, their movements, and the weather they bring are <u>summarized</u> in **Table 2.** The general directions of the air masses' movements are shown in **Figure 3.** An air mass usually brings the weather of its source location, but an air mass may change as it moves away from its source location. For example, cold, dry air may become warmer and more moist as it moves from land to a warm ocean. As the lower layers of the air are warmed, the air rises. This warmed air may then create clouds and precipitation.

Table 2 Air Masses of North America

Air mass	Source location	Movement	Weather
cP	polar regions in Canada	south-southeast	cold and dry
mP	polar Pacific; polar Atlantic	southeast; southwest-south	cold and moist
cT	U.S. southwest	north-northeast	warm and dry
mT	tropical Pacific; tropical Atlantic	northeast; north-northwest	warm and moist

Academic Vocabulary

summarize (SUHM uh RIEZ) explain in a brief way

Tropical Air Masses

Continental tropical air masses form over the deserts of the southwestern United States. These air masses bring dry, hot weather in the summer. They do not form in the winter. Maritime tropical air masses form over the warm water of the tropical Atlantic Ocean, the Caribbean Sea, and the Gulf of Mexico. They bring mild, often cloudy weather to the eastern United States in the winter. In the summer, they bring hot, humid weather and thunderstorms. Maritime tropical air masses also form over warm areas of the Pacific Ocean. But these air masses do not usually reach the Pacific coast. In the winter, maritime tropical air masses bring moderate precipitation to the coast and the southwestern deserts.

SC LINKS.

www.scilinks.org
Topic: Air Masses
Code: HQX0031

Reading Check **Which air mass brings dry, hot weather in the summer?** (See Appendix G for answers to Reading Checks.)

Figure 3 The four types of air masses that influence the weather in North America come from six locations and are named according to their source locations.

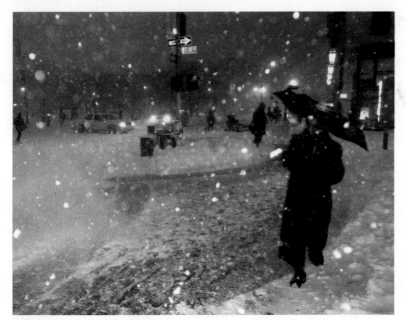

Figure 4 Maritime polar Atlantic air masses can bring heavy snowfall, such as this snowstorm that hit New York City in 2003.

Polar Air Masses

Polar air masses from three regions—northern Canada and the northern Pacific and Atlantic Oceans—influence weather in North America. Continental polar air masses form over ice- and snow-covered land. These air masses move into the northern United States and can occasionally reach as far south as the Gulf Coast of the United States. In summer, these air masses usually bring cool, dry weather. In winter, they bring very cold weather to the northern United States.

Maritime polar air masses form over the North Pacific Ocean and are very moist, but they are not as cold as continental polar Canadian air masses. In winter, maritime polar Pacific air masses bring rain and snow to the Pacific Coast. In summer, they bring cool, often foggy weather. As they move inland and eastward over the Cascades, the Sierra Nevada, and the Rocky Mountains, these cold air masses lose much of their moisture and warm slightly. Thus, they may bring cool and dry weather by the time they reach the central United States.

Maritime polar Atlantic air masses generally move eastward toward Europe, but they sometimes move westward over New England and eastern Canada. In winter, they can bring cold, cloudy weather and snow, as shown in **Figure 4**. In summer, these air masses can produce cool weather, low clouds, and fog.

Section 1 Review

LA.910.2.2.3; SC.912.E.7.3; SC.912.E.7.5

Key Ideas

1. **Define** *air mass.*

2. **Explain** how an air mass forms.

3. **Identify** the location where a cold, dry air mass would form.

4. **List** the four main types of air masses.

5. **Describe** how the four main types of air masses affect the weather of North America.

6. **Describe** the air mass that forms over the warm water of the Atlantic Ocean. What letters designate the source region of this air mass?

Critical Thinking

7. **Making Predictions** How do temperature and humidity change when a maritime tropical air mass is replaced by a continental polar air mass?

8. **Recognizing Relationships** In which direction would you expect a tropical air mass near the coast of Europe to travel? Explain your answer.

Concept Mapping

9. Use the following terms to create a concept map: *maritime polar Pacific, maritime polar, continental polar Canadian, air mass, continental polar,* and *maritime polar Atlantic.*

Key Ideas

❱ Compare the characteristic weather patterns of cold fronts with those of warm fronts.

❱ Describe how a midlatitude cyclone forms.

❱ Describe the development of hurricanes, thunderstorms, and tornadoes.

Key Terms

cold front

warm front

stationary front

occluded front

midlatitude cyclone

thunderstorm

hurricane

tornado

Why It Matters

You've probably heard a weather forecaster use the term *front* and perhaps say that a cold front would pass through your area. Tracking the movement of fronts helps us forecast the weather.

When two unlike air masses meet, density differences usually keep the air masses separate. A cool air mass is dense and does not mix with the less-dense air of a warm air mass. Thus, a boundary, called a *front,* forms between air masses. A typical front is several hundred kilometers long. However, some fronts may be several thousand kilometers long. Changes in middle-latitude weather usually take place along the various types of fronts. Fronts do not exist in the tropics because no air masses that have significant temperature differences exist there.

FLORIDA STANDARDS

SC.912.E.7.5 Predict future weather conditions based on present observations and conceptual models and recognize limitations and uncertainties of such predictions; **SC.912.E.7.6** Relate the formation of severe weather to the various physical factors.

Types of Fronts

For a front to form, one air mass must collide with another air mass. The kind of front that forms is determined by how the air masses move in relationship to each other.

Cold Fronts

When a cold air mass overtakes a warm air mass, a **cold front** forms. The moving cold air lifts the warm air. If the warm air is moist, clouds will form. Large cumulus and cumulonimbus clouds typically form along fast-moving cold fronts, as shown in **Figure 1.** Storms that form along cold fronts are usually short-lived and are sometimes violent. A long line of heavy thunderstorms, called a *squall line,* may occur in the warm, moist air just ahead of a fast-moving cold front. A slow-moving cold front lifts the warm air ahead of it more slowly than a fast-moving cold front does. A slow-moving cold front typically produces weaker storms and lighter precipitation than a fast-moving cold front does.

cold front the front edge of a moving mass of cold air that pushes beneath a warmer air mass like a wedge

Figure 1 As a cold air mass overtakes a warm air mass, a line of thunderstorms called a *squall line* forms.

Cold Front

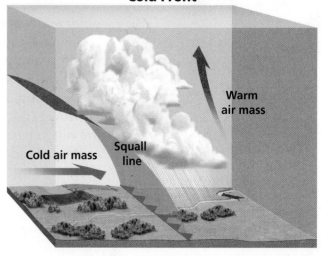

Warm air mass

Cold air mass

Squall line

Warm Front

Occluded Front

Figure 2 As a warm air mass rises over a cold air mass (left), a warm front forms at the boundary of the two air masses. An occluded front (right) forms when a cold air mass lifts a warm air mass off the ground.

warm front the front edge of an advancing warm air mass that replaces colder air with warmer air

stationary front a front of air masses that moves either very slowly or not at all

occluded front a front that forms when a cold air mass overtakes a warm air mass and lifts the warm air mass off the ground and over another air mass

midlatitude cyclone an area of low pressure that is characterized by rotating wind that moves toward the rising air of the central low-pressure region

Two-Column Notes
Use the two-column table that you started at the beginning of the chapter as a model to review the main ideas about fronts in this section.

Warm Fronts

When a warm air mass overtakes a cold air mass, a **warm front** forms. The less dense warm air rises over the cooler air. The slope of a warm front is gradual, as shown in **Figure 2.** Because of this gentle slope, clouds may extend far ahead of the surface location, or *base*, of the front. A warm front generally produces precipitation over a large area and may occasionally cause violent weather.

Stationary and Occluded Fronts

Sometimes, when two air masses meet, the air moves parallel to the front and neither air mass is displaced. A front at which air masses move either very slowly or not at all is called a **stationary front.** The weather produced by a stationary front is similar to the weather produced by a warm front. An **occluded front** usually forms when a fast-moving cold front overtakes a warm front and lifts the warm air off the ground completely, as shown in **Figure 2.**

Polar Fronts and Midlatitude Cyclones

Over each of Earth's polar regions is a dome of cold air that may extend as far as 60° latitude. The boundary where this cold polar air meets the tropical air mass of the middle latitudes, especially over the ocean, is called the *polar front*. Waves commonly develop along the polar front. A *wave* is a bend that forms in a cold front or a stationary front. This wave is similar to the waves that moving air produces when it passes over a body of water. However, the waves that form in a cold front or stationary front are much larger. They are the beginnings of low-pressure storm centers called midlatitude cyclones or *wave cyclones*. **Midlatitude cyclones** are areas of low pressure that are characterized by rotating wind, which moves toward the rising air of the central, low-pressure region. These cyclones strongly influence weather patterns in the middle latitudes.

Stages of a Midlatitude Cyclone

A midlatitude cyclone usually lasts several days. The stages of formation and dissipation of a midlatitude cyclone are shown in **Figure 3.** In North America, midlatitude cyclones generally travel about 45 km/h in an easterly direction as they spin counterclockwise. They follow several storm tracks, or routes, as they move from the Pacific coast to the Atlantic coast. As they pass over the western mountains, they may lose their moisture and energy.

Anticyclones

Unlike the air in a midlatitude cyclone, the air in an *anticyclone* sinks and flows outward from a center of high pressure. Because of the Coriolis effect, the circulation of air around an anticyclone is clockwise in the Northern Hemisphere. Anticyclones bring dry weather, because their sinking air does not promote cloud formation. If an anticyclone stagnates over a region for a few days, it may cause air pollution problems. After being stationary for a few weeks, an anticyclone may cause a drought.

www.scilinks.org
Topic: Fronts and Severe Weather
Code: HQX0624

Reading Check How is the air of an anticyclone different from the air of a midlatitude cyclone?

THINK central
INTERACT ONLINE
Keyword: HQXWTHF3

Figure 3 Stages of a Midlatitude Cyclone

1 Midlatitude cyclones occur along a stationary front. Winds move parallel to the front but in opposite directions on the two sides of the front.

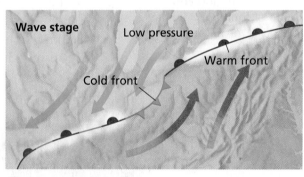

2 A wave forms when a bulge of cold air develops and advances slightly ahead of the rest of the front.

3 As the fast-moving part of the cold front overtakes the warm front, an occluded front forms and the storm reaches its highest intensity.

4 Eventually, the system loses most of its energy and the midlatitude cyclone dissipates.

Severe Weather

Severe weather is weather that may cause property damage or loss of life. Severe weather may include large quantities of rain, lightning, hail, strong winds, or tornadoes. This type of weather causes billions of dollars in damage each year.

Thunderstorms

A heavy storm that is accompanied by rain, thunder, lightning, and strong winds is called a **thunderstorm.** Thunderstorms develop in three distinct stages. In the first stage, or *cumulus stage*, warm, moist air rises, and the water vapor within the air condenses to form a cumulus cloud. In the next stage, called the *mature stage*, condensation continues as the cloud rises and becomes a dark cumulonimbus cloud. Heavy, torrential rain and hailstones may fall from the cloud. While strong updrafts continue to rise, downdrafts form as the air is dragged downward by the falling precipitation. During the final stage, or *dissipating stage*, the strong downdrafts stop air currents from rising. The thunderstorm dissipates as the supply of water vapor decreases.

Lightning

During a thunderstorm, clouds discharge electricity in the form of *lightning*. The released electricity heats the air, and the air expands rapidly and produces the loud noise known as *thunder*. For lightning to occur, the clouds must have areas that carry distinct electrical charges. The upper part of a cloud usually carries a positive charge, while the lower part usually carries a negative charge. Lightning is a huge spark that travels within the cloud, or between the cloud and the ground, to equalize the electrical charges. **Figure 4** shows an example of lightning.

thunderstorm a usually brief, heavy storm that consists of rain, strong winds, lightning, and thunder

Math Skills

Thunderstorm Distance The time between when you see a lightning strike and when you hear thunder indicates how far away the lightning bolt was from you. Sound travels approximately 1 km in 3 s. The lapse time in seconds divided by 3 is roughly the number of kilometers between you and the lightning. If 27 s pass between a flash of lightning and the sound of thunder, how far away was the lightning strike from you?

Figure 4 The average lightning flash lasts only about a quarter of a second, but lightning causes more than $330,000,000 in damage per year in the United States.

Altitude (m)

15,000

10,000

5,000

Sea level

Sinking dry air

Outward-flowing high-level winds

Eye of the hurricane

80 km/h winds   120 km/h winds   Evaporation   Heavy rains

400   300   200   100   0   100   200   300   400

Distance (km)

Figure 5 Although hurricanes are the most destructive storms, the eye at the center of a hurricane is relatively calm.

Hurricanes

Tropical storms differ from midlatitude cyclones in several ways. Tropical storms are concentrated over a smaller area. They lack warm and cold fronts. Also, they are usually much more violent and destructive than midlatitude cyclones. A tropical storm with wind speeds of 120 km/h or more that spiral in toward an intense low-pressure center is called a **hurricane.**

Hurricanes develop over warm, tropical oceans. A hurricane begins when warm, moist air over the ocean rises rapidly. When moisture in the rising warm air condenses, a large amount of energy in the form of latent heat is released. *Latent heat* is heat energy that is absorbed or released during a phase change. This heat increases the strength of the rising air.

A fully developed hurricane consists of a series of thick cumulonimbus cloud bands that spiral upward around the center of the storm, as shown in **Figure 5.** Winds increase toward the center, or eye, of the storm and reach speeds of up to 275 km/h along the eyewall. The eye itself, however, is a region of calm, clear, sinking air.

With a range in diameter of 400 to 800 km, hurricanes are the most destructive storms that occur on Earth. The most dangerous aspect of a hurricane is a rising sea level with large waves, called a *storm surge.* A storm surge can flood vast low-lying coastal areas. This flooding is the reason why most deaths during hurricanes are caused by drowning.

Every hurricane is categorized on the *Saffir-Simpson scale* by using several factors. These factors include central pressure, wind speed, and storm surge. The Saffir-Simpson scale has five categories. Category 1 storms cause the least damage. Category 5 storms can result in catastrophic damage.

Reading Check **Where do hurricanes develop?**

hurricane a severe storm that develops over tropical oceans and whose strong winds of more than 120 km/h spiral in toward the intensely low-pressure storm center

Hurricane Katrina

Hurricane Katrina came marching in to New Orleans, Louisiana, on August 28, 2005. She was accompanied by torrential rain, sustained winds of 282 km/h, and storm surges of up to 8.5 meters. This event taught Americans many lessons about storm preparedness.

Katrina Approaches

Large areas of New Orleans are below sea level. Therefore, city officials were concerned when the hurricane's path turned northward and the storm intensified as it moved toward the coast.

Thousands Homeless

Although a mandatory evacuation order was issued the day before the storm made landfall, many New Orleans residents were unable to leave the city until after the storm. Many of the people who remained sought refuge at the Superdome both before and after the hurricane.

Preventing Future Disasters

In the aftermath of the storm, teams of engineers and scientists reviewed the performance of the city's levees. These teams recommended ways to construct more storm-resistant levees.

Because of Hurricane Katrina, Hurricane Rita—which followed Hurricane Katrina by less than a month—was tracked very carefully, and evacuation orders were issued days in advance.

YOUR TURN

UNDERSTANDING CONCEPTS
Why did Hurricane Katrina particularly endanger New Orleans?

CRITICAL THINKING
What did scientists and government officials learn from Hurricane Katrina?

581

Tornadoes

The smallest, most violent, and shortest-lived severe storm is a tornado. A **tornado** is a destructive, rotating column of air that has very high wind speeds and that is visible as a funnel-shaped cloud, as shown in **Figure 6.**

A tornado forms when a thunderstorm meets high-altitude, horizontal winds. These winds cause the rising air in the thunderstorm to rotate. A storm cloud may develop a narrow, funnel-shaped, rapidly spinning extension that reaches downward and may or may not touch the ground. If the funnel does touch the ground, it generally moves in a wandering, haphazard path. Frequently, the funnel rises and touches down again a short distance away. Tornadoes generally cover paths not more than 100 m wide. Usually, however, everything in that path is destroyed. Tornadoes occur in many locations, but they are most common in *Tornado Alley* in the late spring or early summer. Tornado Alley stretches from Texas up through the midwestern United States.

The destructive power of a tornado is due to mainly the speed of the wind in the funnel. This wind may reach speeds of more than 400 km/h. Most injuries and deaths caused by tornadoes occur when people are trapped in collapsing buildings or are struck by objects blown by the wind.

Figure 6 A powerful tornado in Texas embedded this bucket in a wooden door (inset).

tornado a destructive, rotating column of air that has very high wind speeds and that may be visible as a funnel-shaped cloud

Section 2 Review

LA.910.2.2.3; SC.912.E.7.3; SC.912.E.7.5; SC.912.E.7.6

Key Ideas

1. **Describe** the four main types of fronts.

2. **Compare** the characteristic weather patterns of cold fronts with those of warm fronts.

3. **Identify** the type of front that may form a squall line.

4. **Summarize** how a midlatitude cyclone forms.

5. **Describe** the stages in the development of a thunderstorm.

6. **Describe** the stages in the development of a hurricane.

7. **Explain** why tornadoes are so destructive.

Critical Thinking

8. **Evaluating Methods** What areas of Earth should meteorologists monitor to detect developing hurricanes? Explain your answer.

9. **Making Comparisons** Compare the destructive power of midlatitude cyclones, hurricanes, and tornadoes in terms of size, wind speed, and duration.

Concept Mapping

10. Use the following terms to create a concept map: *tornado, hurricane, warm front, squall line, cold front, severe weather, stationary front, front, midlatitude cyclone,* and *occluded front.*

SECTION 3 Weather Instruments

Key Ideas

❯ Identify four instruments that measure lower-atmospheric weather conditions.

❯ Describe how scientists measure conditions in the upper atmosphere.

❯ Explain how computers help scientists understand weather.

Key Terms

thermometer

barometer

anemometer

wind vane

radiosonde

radar

Why It Matters

When you look at a weather forecast, you see lots of numbers, including temperature, air pressure, and humidity data. These measurements help meteorologists track weather.

Weather observations are based on a variety of measurements, including atmospheric pressure, humidity, temperature, wind speed, and precipitation. These measurements are made with special instruments. Meteorologists then use these measurements to forecast weather patterns.

Measuring Lower-Atmospheric Conditions

During the course of a day, the lower-atmospheric conditions at a given location can change drastically. Meteorologists use the magnitude and speed of these changes to predict future weather events. To obtain accurate data from the lower atmosphere, scientists use instruments such as those shown in **Figure 1.**

Air Temperature

An instrument that measures and indicates temperature is called a **thermometer.** A common type of thermometer uses a liquid—usually mercury or alcohol—sealed in a glass tube to indicate temperature. A rise in temperature causes the liquid to expand and fill more of the tube. A drop in temperature causes the liquid to contract and fill less of the tube. A scale marked on the glass tube indicates the temperature.

Another type of thermometer is an *electrical thermometer.* As the temperature rises, the electric current that flows through the material of the electrical thermometer increases and is translated into temperature readings. A *thermistor,* or thermal resistor, is a type of electrical thermometer that responds very quickly to temperature changes. For this reason, thermistors are extremely useful where temperature change occurs rapidly.

FLORIDA STANDARDS

LA.910.2.2.3 The student will organize information to show understanding or relationships among facts, ideas, and events (e.g., representing key points within text through charting, mapping, paraphrasing, summarizing, comparing, contrasting, or outlining); **MA.912.S.1.2** Determine appropriate and consistent standards of measurement for the data to be collected in a survey or experiment; **SC.912.E.7.5** Predict future weather conditions based on present observations and conceptual models and recognize limitations and uncertainties of such predictions.

thermometer an instrument that measures and indicates temperature

Figure 1 Weather instruments, such as these at Elk Mountain weather research facility in Wyoming, indicate wind speed and direction.

Section 3   **Weather Instruments**   **583**

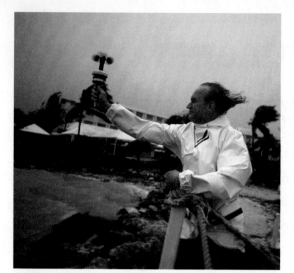

Figure 2 A meteorologist uses an anemometer during Hurricane Luis to measure wind speed.

barometer an instrument that measures atmospheric pressure

anemometer an instrument used to measure wind speed

wind vane an instrument used to determine the direction of the wind

Air Pressure

Changes in air pressure affect air masses at certain locations. The approach of a front is usually indicated by a drop in air pressure. Scientists use instruments called **barometers** to measure atmospheric pressure.

Wind Speed

An instrument called an **anemometer** (AN uh MAHM uht uhr) measures wind speed. A typical anemometer consists of small cups that are attached by spokes to a shaft that rotates freely. The wind pushes against the cups and causes them to rotate, as shown in **Figure 2.** This rotation triggers an electrical signal that registers the wind speed in meters per second or in miles per hour.

Wind Direction

The direction of the wind is determined by using an instrument called a **wind vane.** The wind vane is commonly an arrow-shaped device that turns freely on a pole as the tail catches the wind. Wind direction may be described by using one of 16 compass directions, such as north-northeast. Wind direction also may be described in degrees by moving clockwise, beginning with 0° at the north. Thus, east is 90°, south is 180°, and west is 270°.

Reading Check Which instrument is used to measure air pressure?

SC.912.E.7.3

Quick **Lab** Wind Chill

15 min

Procedure

❶ Place a **23 cm × 33 cm pan** on a level table. Fill the pan to a depth of 1 cm with room-temperature water.

❷ Lay a **thermometer** in the center of the pan, with the bulb submerged. After 5 min, record the water temperature. Do not touch the thermometer.

❸ Place an **electric fan** facing the pan and a few centimeters from the pan. Turn on the fan at a low speed. **CAUTION** Do not get the fan or cord wet.

❹ Record the water temperature every minute until the temperature remains constant.

Analysis

1. How does the moving air affect the temperature of the water?

2. If the moving air is the same temperature as the still air in the room, what causes the water temperature to change?

3. How would you dress on a cool, windy day to stay comfortable? Explain your answer.

How Does Wind Affect Flight?

Airplane pilots must account for wind speed and direction when planning a flight. Wind can speed up or slow down a flight, and airports need to know what time a flight will arrive.

REAL WORLD

Anemometers and windsocks are used to measure wind speed and direction at airports.

N

Heading and airspeed

Wind direction and velocity

Course and groundspeed

S

When wind blows at another angle to an airplane's direction of travel, the pilots must calculate the angle that they need to aim upwind in order to remain on course.

YOUR TURN

UNDERSTANDING CONCEPTS
What are three different ways that wind can affect an airplane trip?

Measuring Upper-Atmospheric Conditions

Conditions of the atmosphere near Earth's surface are only part of the complete weather picture. Scientists use several instruments to measure conditions in the upper atmosphere, to obtain a better understanding of local and global weather patterns.

Radiosonde

An instrument package that is carried high into the atmosphere by a helium-filled weather balloon to measure relative humidity, air pressure, and air temperature is called a **radiosonde.** A radiosonde sends measurements as radio waves to a receiver that records the information. The path of the balloon is tracked to determine the direction and speed of high-altitude winds. When the balloon reaches a very high altitude, the balloon expands and bursts, and the radiosonde parachutes back to Earth.

Radar

Another instrument for determining weather conditions in the atmosphere is radar. **Radar,** which stands for **ra**dio **d**etection **a**nd **r**anging, is a system that uses reflected radio waves to determine the velocity and location of objects. For example, large particles of water in the atmosphere reflect radar pulses. Thus, precipitation and storms, such as thunderstorms, tornadoes, and hurricanes, are visible on a radar screen. The newest Doppler radar can indicate the precise location, movement, and extent of a storm. It can also indicate the intensity of precipitation and wind patterns within a storm.

radiosonde a package of instruments that is carried aloft by a balloon to measure upper atmospheric conditions, including temperature, dew point, and wind velocity

radar a system that uses reflected radio waves to determine the velocity and location of objects

READING TOOLBOX

Two-Column Notes
Create two-column notes to review the main ideas about weather instruments in this section. Put the main ideas in the left column. Add details and examples, in your own words, in the right column.

Figure 3 This satellite image captured Hurricane Wilma in 2005 as it approached Florida.

www.scilinks.org
Topic: Weather Instruments
Code: HQX1646

Weather Satellites

Instruments carried by weather satellites also collect important information about the atmosphere. Satellite images, such as the one shown in **Figure 3,** provide weather information for regions where observations cannot be made from the ground.

The direction and speed of the wind at the level of the clouds can be measured by examining a continuous sequence of cloud images. For night monitoring, satellite images made by using infrared energy reveal temperatures at the tops of clouds, at the surface of the land, and at the surface of the ocean. Satellite instruments can also measure marine conditions. For example, the instruments on satellites can measure the temperature and flow of ocean currents and the height of ocean waves. In addition, satellites can measure land temperatures and soil moisture conditions at remote locations on Earth.

Computers

Meteorologists use supercomputers to understand the weather. Before computers were available, solving the mathematical equations that describe the behavior of the atmosphere was very difficult, and sometimes impossible. In addition to solving many of these equations, computers can store weather data from around the world. These data can provide information that is useful in forecasting weather changes. Computers can also store weather records for quick retrieval. In the future, powerful computers may greatly improve weather forecasts and provide a much better understanding of the atmosphere.

Section 3 Review

LA.910.2.2.3; MA.912.S.1.2

Key Ideas

1. **Identify** four instruments that scientists use to measure lower-atmospheric conditions.

2. **Explain** why scientists are interested in weather conditions in the upper atmosphere.

3. **Describe** the instruments used to measure conditions in the upper atmosphere.

4. **Explain** how meteorologists send weather instruments into the upper atmosphere.

5. **Summarize** how satellites help meteorologists study weather.

6. **Summarize** how computers help scientists study weather.

Critical Thinking

7. **Recognizing Relationships** Wind is named according to the direction from which it blows. Why would a meteorologist need to know the direction that wind is blowing from?

8. **Making Inferences** If weather instruments were moved from a valley to the top of a hill, what changes would you expect in the data? Explain your answer.

Concept Mapping

9. Use the following terms to create a concept map: *thermometer, barometer, anemometer, radar, radio-sonde, satellite, upper atmosphere, lower atmosphere,* and *weather instruments.*

Forecasting the Weather

Key Ideas	Key Terms	Why It Matters
❯ Explain how weather stations communicate weather data. ❯ Explain how a weather map is created. ❯ Explain how computer models help meteorologists forecast weather. ❯ List three types of weather that meteorologists have attempted to control.	station model	Early warnings of severe weather can reduce damage and save lives. Understanding weather information will help you take warnings seriously.

Predicting the weather has challenged people for thousands of years. People in many early civilizations attributed control of weather conditions, such as wind, rain, and thunder, to gods. Some people attempted to forecast the weather by using the positions of the stars and the moon as the basis for their predictions.

Scientific weather forecasting began with the invention of basic weather instruments, such as the thermometer and the barometer. The invention of the telegraph in 1844 enabled meteorologists to share information about weather conditions quickly and led to the creation of national weather services.

Global Weather Monitoring

Weather observers at stations around the world report weather conditions frequently, often several times per hour. They record the barometric pressure and how it has changed, as well as the speed and direction of surface wind. They measure precipitation, temperature, and humidity. They note the type, amount, and height of cloud cover. Weather observers also record visibility and general weather conditions. Similar data are gathered continuously by automated observing systems. Each station in the system sends its data to a collection center. Weather centers around the world exchange the weather information they have collected.

The World Meteorological Organization (WMO) sponsors a program called *World Weather Watch* to promote the rapid exchange of weather information. This organization helps developing countries establish or improve their meteorological services, as shown in **Figure 1.** It also offers advice on the effect of weather on natural resources and on human activities, such as farming and transportation.

FLORIDA STANDARDS

SC.912.E.7.5 Predict future weather conditions based on present observations and conceptual models and recognize limitations and uncertainties of such predictions; **SC.912.N.1.6** Describe how scientific inferences are drawn from scientific observations and provide examples from the content being studied.

Figure 1 One major role of the World Meteorological Organization is to train professionals to use weather instruments, such as this Dobson spectrophotometer installed at Maun, Botswana.

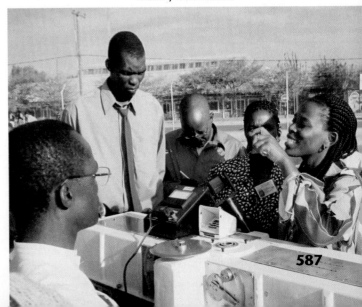

Weather Maps

The data that weather stations collect are transferred onto weather maps. Weather maps allow meteorologists to understand the current weather and to predict future weather events. To communicate weather data on a weather map, meteorologists use symbols and colors. These symbols and colors are understood and used by meteorologists around the world.

Weather Symbols

On some weather maps, clusters of meteorological symbols show weather conditions at the locations of weather stations. Such a cluster of symbols is called a **station model.** Common weather symbols describe cloud cover, wind speed, wind direction, and weather conditions, such as type of precipitation and storm activity. These symbols and a station model are shown in **Figure 2.** Notice that the symbols for cloud cover, wind speed, and wind direction are combined in one symbol in the station model.

Other information included in the station model are the air temperature and the dew point. The *dew point* is the temperature at which the rate of condensation equals the rate of evaporation. The dew point indicates how high the humidity of the air is.

The station model also includes the atmospheric pressure, indicated by a three-digit number in the upper right-hand corner. The digits show pressure to the nearest tenth of a millibar (mb). Therefore you would add a 9 or a 10 to the beginning of the three-digit number to get the number nearest 1,000. For example, a value of 021 would be understood as 1,002.1 mb. A value of 987 would be understood as 998.7 mb. The position of a straight line under this figure—horizontal or angled up or down—shows whether the atmospheric pressure is steady or is rising or falling.

Academic Vocabulary

communicate (kuh MYOO ni KAYT)
make known; tell

station model a pattern of meteorological symbols that represents the weather at a particular observing station and that is recorded on a weather map

Figure 2 Meteorologists use symbols to indicate weather conditions. The station model (lower right) shows an example of conditions around a weather station.

Lt Rain/Drizzle Mod/Hvy Rain Rain/Ice/Snow Lt Snow Mod/Hvy Snow Fog

Plotting Temperature and Pressure

Scientists use lines on weather maps to connect points of equal measurement. Lines that connect points of equal temperature are called *isotherms*. Lines that connect points of equal atmospheric pressure are called *isobars*. The spacing and shape of the isobars help meteorologists interpret their observations about the speed and direction of the wind. Closely spaced isobars indicate a rapid change in pressure and high wind speeds. Widely spaced isobars generally indicate a gradual change in pressure and low wind speeds. Isobars that form circles indicate centers of high or low air pressure. Centers that are marked with an *H* represent high pressure, as you can see in **Figure 3.** Centers that are marked with an *L* represent low pressure.

Plotting Fronts and Precipitation

Most weather maps mark the locations of fronts and areas of precipitation. The weather map in **Figure 3** shows examples of a warm front, a cold front, an occluded front, and a stationary front. Fronts are identified by sharp changes in wind speed and direction, temperature, or humidity.

Areas of precipitation are commonly marked with colors or symbols. Different forms of precipitation are represented by different colors or symbols. For example, the weather map in **Figure 3** indicates light rain by using light green, and snow by using gray and white. Some weather maps use colors to represent different amounts of precipitation so the amounts of precipitation that fall in different areas can be compared.

Figure 3 A typical weather map shows isobars, highs and lows, fronts, and precipitation. *In what parts of the United States are low-pressure areas located?*

www.scilinks.org
Topic: Weather Maps
Code: HQX1647
Topic: Weather Forecasting
Code: HQX1645

✓ Reading Check **How do meteorologists mark precipitation on a weather map?**

Figure 4 With the help of Doppler radar, meteorologists can track severe storms from radar stations, such as this one in Kansas.

SC.912.E.7.3

Quick Lab

10 min

Gathering Weather Data

Procedure

❶ Select an area that is outside your school building, in the shade and away from buildings and pavement.

❷ Use a **thermometer** to measure the air temperature.

❸ Estimate the percentage of cloud cover.

❹ Estimate the wind speed. Use a **magnetic compass** to estimate the wind direction.

Analysis

1. What are the current weather conditions outside your school?

2. Using the data you collected, create a station model that describes the weather at your school.

Weather Forecasts

To forecast the weather, meteorologists use computers to plot the intensity and path of weather systems on maps. Meteorologists then study the most recent weather map and compare it with maps from previous hours. This comparison allows them to follow the progress of large weather systems. By following the progress of weather systems, meteorologists can forecast the weather.

Weather Data

Doppler radar, shown in **Figure 4,** and satellite images supply important information, such as intensity of precipitation. Meteorologists input these data into computers to create weather models. Computer models can show the possible weather conditions for several days. However, meteorologists must carefully interpret these models because computer predictions are based on generalized descriptions.

Some computer models may be better at predicting precipitation for a particular area, while other computer models may be better at predicting temperature and pressure. Comparing models helps meteorologists better predict weather. If weather information on two or more models is similar, a meteorologist will be more confident about a weather prediction. By using all the weather data available, meteorologists can issue an accurate forecast of the weather.

Temperature, wind direction, wind speed, cloudiness, and precipitation can usually be forecast accurately. But it is often difficult to predict precisely the time when precipitation will occur or the exact amount. By using computers, scientists can manipulate data on temperature and pressure to simulate errors in measuring these data. Forecasts are then compared to see if slight data changes cause substantial differences in forecasts. From what they learn, meteorologists can make more accurate forecasts.

Reading Check Why do meteorologists compare models?

Types of Forecasts

Meteorologists make four types of forecasts. *Nowcasts* mainly use radar and enable forecasters to focus on timing precipitation and tracking severe weather. *Daily forecasts* predict weather conditions for a 48-h period. *Extended forecasts* look ahead 3 to 5 days. *Medium-range forecasts* look ahead 3 to 7 days. *Long-range forecasts* look ahead at least 7 days and may cover monthly and seasonal periods.

Accurate weather forecasts can be made for 0 to 5 days. However, accuracy decreases with each day. Extended forecasts are made by computer analysis of slowly changing large-scale movements of air. These changes help meteorologists predict the general weather pattern. For example, the changes indicate if temperature will be warmer or cooler than normal or if conditions will be dry or wet.

Severe Weather Watches and Warnings

One main goal of meteorology is to reduce the amount of destruction caused by severe weather by forecasting severe weather early. When meteorologists forecast severe weather, they issue warnings and watches. A *watch* is issued when the conditions are ideal for severe weather. A *warning* is given when severe weather has been spotted (thunderstorms or tornadoes) or is expected within 24 h (snowstorms or hurricanes). Meteorologists use these alerts to provide people in areas facing severe weather with instructions on how to be safer during the event. **Table 1** lists some safety tips to follow for different types of severe weather.

READING TOOLBOX

Prefixes, Suffixes, and Root Words
The word *forecast* is part of several italicized terms on this page. It contains the prefix *fore-* and the root word *cast*. Use print or online sources to find the meanings of these word parts, and add the meanings to the table you started at the beginning of the chapter.

Table 1 Severe Weather Safety Tips

Type of weather	How to prepare	Safety during the event
Thunderstorm	Have a storm preparedness kit that includes a portable radio, fresh batteries, flashlights, rain gear, blankets, bottled water, canned food, and medicines.	Listen to weather updates. Stay or go indoors. Avoid electrical appliances, running water, metal pipes, and phone lines. If outside, avoid tall objects, stay away from bodies of water, and get into a car, if possible.
Tornado	Have a storm preparedness kit as described above. Plan and practice a safety route.	Listen to weather updates. Stay or go indoors. Go to a basement, storm cellar, or small, inner room, closet, or hallway that has no windows. Stay away from areas that are likely to have flying debris or other dangers. If outside, lie in a low-lying area. Protect your head and neck.
Hurricane	Have a storm preparedness kit as described above. Secure loose objects, doors, and windows. Plan and practice an evacuation route.	Listen to weather updates. Be prepared to follow instructions and planned evacuation routes. Stay indoors and away from areas that are likely to have flying debris or other dangers.
Blizzard	Have a storm preparedness kit as described above. Make sure that you have a way to make heat safely, in the event of power outages.	Listen to weather updates. Stay or go indoors. Dress warmly. Avoid walking or driving in icy conditions.

Controlling the Weather

Some meteorologists are investigating methods of controlling rain, hail, and lightning. Currently, the most researched method for producing rain has been *cloud seeding*. In this process, particles are added to clouds to cause the clouds to precipitate. Cloud seeding can also be used to prevent more-severe precipitation. Scientists in Russia have used cloud seeding, with some success, on potential hail clouds by causing rain, rather than hail, to fall.

Hurricane Control

Hurricanes have also been seeded with freezing nuclei in an effort to reduce their intensity. During Project Stormfury, which took place from 1962 to 1983, four hurricanes were seeded, and the project had mixed results. Scientists have, for the most part, abandoned storm and hurricane control because it is not an attainable goal with existing technology. They do, however, continue to seed clouds to cause precipitation.

Lightning Control

Attempts have also been made to control lightning. Seeding of potential lightning storms with silver-iodide nuclei has seemed to modify the occurrence of lightning. However, no conclusive results have been obtained. Researchers have generated artificial lightning at research facilities to learn more about lightning and how it affects objects it strikes. An example of one of these facilities is shown in **Figure 5**.

Figure 5 An outdoor ultra-high-voltage laboratory generates artificial lightning to test its effects on electrical utility equipment.

Section 4 Review

LA.910.2.2.3; SC.912.E.7.3

Key Ideas

1. **Summarize** how global weather is monitored.

2. **Explain** how a weather map is made.

3. **Explain** which would show stronger winds: widely spaced isobars or closely spaced isobars.

4. **List** six different pieces of information that you can obtain from a station model.

5. **Explain** why meteorologists compare new weather maps with weather maps that are 24 h old.

6. **Describe** how computer models help meteorologists forecast weather.

7. **List** three types of weather that meteorologists have tried to control.

Critical Thinking

8. **Making Inferences** Why might cloud seeding reduce the amount of hail from a storm?

9. **Making Reasoned Judgment** Seeding hurricanes may or may not yield positive results. Each attempt costs a lot of money. If you were in charge of deciding whether to seed a potentially dangerous hurricane, what factors would you consider when deciding what to do? Explain your answer.

Concept Mapping

10. Use the following terms to create a concept map: *isobar, isotherm, weather map, forecast, watch, warning, station model,* and *meteorological symbol*.

When Lightning Strikes!

For thousands of years, most people believed that lightning was caused by the activities of various gods. American inventor Benjamin Franklin was the first person to propose that lightning was actually a giant electrical spark. In the 1750s, Franklin conducted several famous experiments, which involved flying kites in thunderstorms, to test his hypothesis.

1. In the mythology of the Aboriginals of northern Australia, Namarrgon the Lightning Man is a Creation Ancestor. The band from Namarrgon's head to his ankles represents the lightning he creates. **2.** Early sailors noticed a bluish glow, which they called St. Elmo's Fire, coming from the masts on their boats. The glow appeared before or after lightning storms. **3.** Franklin invented the first U.S. lightning rod. Placed on tall buildings, lightning rods channel electricity into the ground, keeping the building and the people inside safe.

YOUR TURN

UNDERSTANDING CONCEPTS
Who was the first person to relate lightning to electricity?

ONLINE RESEARCH
What is St. Elmo's Fire, and what causes it to form?

⏱ **45 min**

Weather Map Interpretation

Weather maps use various map symbols and lines to illustrate the weather conditions in an area at a given time. In this lab, you will study the symbols used on a weather map to gain an understanding of the relationships between temperature, pressure, and winds.

What You'll Do

> **Construct** a pressure and temperature map.

> **Interpret** a weather map.

> **Explain** how weather patterns are related to pressure systems.

What You'll Need

paper
pencil
pencils, red and blue

Procedure

1 Make a copy of the weather map on the following page. You may want to copy a larger version of this map, which can be found in Appendix E. You will use the map symbols on the same page of the Appendix to interpret the weather map. The number on the right of each station on the map represents atmospheric pressure. The number on the left represents temperature.

2 On your copy of the weather map, find stations that have a temperature of 10.0 °C. Use a red pencil to draw a light line through these stations. If two adjacent stations have temperatures above and below 10 °C, there is an estimated point between them that is 10.0 °C. Draw a line through these estimated points to connect the stations that have temperatures of 10.0 °C with an isotherm. Label the isotherm 10 °C.

3 Using the same method as in step 2, draw isotherms for every two degrees of temperature. Examples are isotherms of 12.0 °C, 14.0 °C, and 16.0 °C. Label each isotherm with the temperature it represents.

Step 2

④ Find a station that has a barometric pressure of 1,001.2 mb (millibars), marked 012. Use a blue pencil, and follow the same method that you used in step 2 to create a 1,001.2 mb isobar.

⑤ Using the same method as in step 3, lightly draw isobars for every few millibars of pressure. Examples are isobars of 1,000.6 mb, 1,000.4 mb, and 994 mb. Label each isobar with the pressure it represents.

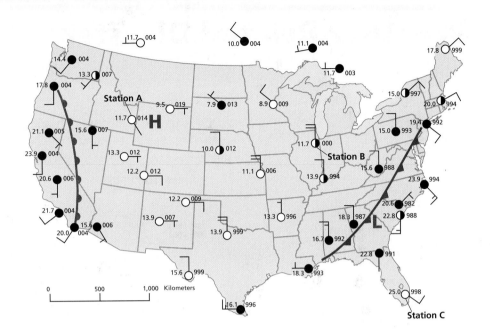

Analysis

1. **Identifying Trends** What is the lowest temperature for which you have drawn an isotherm? What is the highest temperature for which you have drawn an isotherm? Is either isotherm a closed loop? If so, which one?

2. **Making Inferences** Is the air mass that is identified by the closed isotherm a cold air mass or a warm air mass? Explain your answer.

3. **Analyzing Data** Is there a shift in wind direction associated with either front shown on your map? Describe the shift.

4. **Identifying Trends** What is the value of the lowest-pressure isobar that you drew? What is the value of the highest-pressure isobar that you drew? Is either isobar a closed loop? If so, which one?

5. **Drawing Conclusions** At the time that the map represents, were there any areas of low pressure? Were there any areas of high pressure? Identify these areas. What weather conditions would you expect to find in these areas?

Extension

Making Predictions Predict the weather conditions at Station A 24 h after the observations for your map were made. Record your predictions in a table with columns for pressure, wind direction, wind speed, temperature, and sky condition. Also, make and record predictions for Station B and Station C.

Weather-Related Disasters

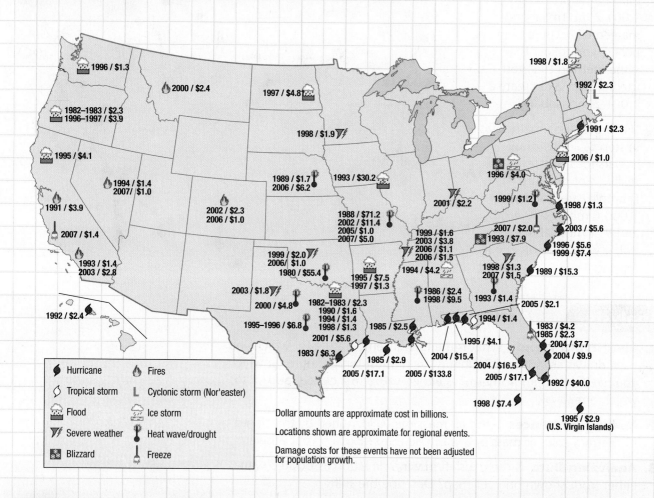

1996 / $1.3

2000 / $2.4

1997 / $4.8

1998 / $1.8

1992 / $2.3

L

1982–1983 / $2.3
1996–1997 / $3.9

1998 / $1.9

1991 / $2.3

1995 / $4.1

1989 / $1.7
2006 / $6.2

1993 / $30.2

1996 / $4.0

2006 / $1.0

1994 / $1.4
2007/ $1.0

2002 / $2.3
2006 / $1.0

2001 / $2.2

1999 / $1.2

1998 / $1.3

1991 / $3.9

1988 / $71.2
2002 / $11.4
2005/ $1.0
2007 / $5.0

1999 / $1.6
2003 / $3.8
2006 / $1.1
2006 / $1.5

2007 / $2.0

1993 / $7.9

2003 / $5.6

2007 / $1.4

1999 / $2.0
2006/ $1.0

1994 / $4.2

1996 / $5.6
1999 / $7.4

1993 / $1.4
2003 / $2.8

1980 / $55.4

1995 / $7.5
1997 / $1.3

1998 / $1.3
2007 / $1.5

1989 / $15.3

2003 / $1.8

2000 / $4.8

1982–1983 / $2.3
1990 / $1.6
1994 / $1.4
1998 / $1.3

1986 / $2.4
1998 / $9.5

1993 / $1.4

1992 / $2.4

1995–1996 / $6.8

2001 / $5.6

1985 / $2.5

1994 / $1.4

2005 / $2.1

1983 / $4.2
1985 / $2.3

1995 / $4.1

2004 / $7.7

1983 / $6.3

1985 / $2.9

2004 / $15.4

2004 / $16.5

2004 / $9.9

2005 / $17.1

2005 / $133.8

2005 / $17.1

1992 / $40.0

1998 / $7.4

1995 / $2.9
(U.S. Virgin Islands)

Key:
- ⬟ Hurricane
- ◇ Tropical storm
- 🌧 Flood
- ⑂ Severe weather
- ❄ Blizzard
- 🔥 Fires
- L Cyclonic storm (Nor'easter)
- Ice storm
- ⬥ Heat wave/drought
- Freeze

Dollar amounts are approximate cost in billions.

Locations shown are approximate for regional events.

Damage costs for these events have not been adjusted for population growth.

Map Skills Activity

This map shows the types and locations of weather disasters that caused at least $1 billion in damage in the United States. Use the map to answer the questions below.

1. **Using a Key** According to the map, how many severe weather events caused more than $10 billion in damage?

2. **Analyzing Data** Which type of weather disaster is more common: floods or fires?

3. **Making Comparisons** How do the types of disasters that happen in the western United States differ from the types of disasters that happen in the eastern United States? Explain why this difference exists.

4. **Inferring Relationships** Why might an ice storm in Alabama cause more damage than an ice storm in Maine?

5. **Identifying Trends** Almost all hurricane damage during this period happened along the coasts of the Atlantic Ocean and the Gulf of Mexico. Explain why.

6. **Analyzing Relationships** In 1996, a blizzard and floods caused $4.0 billion in damage in Ohio, Pennsylvania, and West Virginia. How might these events be related? Explain your answer.

7. **Analyzing Processes** Explain why fires are included in this map of weather-related disasters.

Summary

Key Ideas	Key Terms

Section 1

Air Masses

> An air mass forms when air remains stationary or moves slowly over a uniform region, taking on the characteristic temperature and humidity of that region.

> The four main types of air masses are polar, tropical, continental, and maritime.

> Air masses affect the weather by bringing air that is warm or cold, and dry or moist, to a region. Tropical air masses bring mild weather in the winter, and polar air masses bring cool weather in the summer.

air mass, p. 571

Section 2

Fronts

> Cold fronts usually produce short-lived storms. Warm fronts usually produce precipitation over a large area.

> A midlatitude cyclone forms along a cold or stationary front, in which rotating wind moves toward a low-pressure center.

> Thunderstorms and tornadoes are caused by the interaction of air masses that have different properties. Hurricanes develop when warm, moist air over the ocean rises rapidly.

cold front, p. 575
warm front, p. 576
stationary front, p. 576
occluded front, p. 576
midlatitude cyclone, p. 576
thunderstorm, p. 578
hurricane, p. 579
tornado, p. 582

Section 3

Weather Instruments

> Thermometers, barometers, anemometers, and wind vanes measure lower-atmospheric weather conditions.

> Radiosondes, radar, and satellite equipment measure upper-atmospheric weather conditions.

> Computers are used to solve complicated mathematical equations that describe weather.

thermometer, p. 583
barometer, p. 584
anemometer, p. 584
wind vane, p. 584
radiosonde, p. 585
radar, p. 585

Section 4

Forecasting the Weather

> Each weather station sends data to a collection center.

> Meteorologists prepare weather maps that are based on information from weather stations around the world.

> Computer models predict weather conditions for several days.

> Meteorologists have attempted to control rain, hurricanes, and lightning with only limited success.

station model, p. 588

1. **Prefixes, Suffixes, and Root Words** Look over the table of prefixes, suffixes, and root words that you made while reading this chapter. Identify the word parts that were used most often. Why were these word parts used so often in this chapter?

USING KEY TERMS

Use each of the following terms in a separate sentence.

2. *air mass* SC.912.E.7.3

3. *stationary front* SC.912.E.7.3

4. *station model*

For each pair of terms, explain how the meanings of the terms differ.

5. *midlatitude cyclone* and *hurricane* SC.912.E.7.6

6. *wind vane* and *anemometer*

7. *radiosonde* and *radar*

8. *cold front* and *warm front* SC.912.E.7.3

9. *thermometer* and *barometer*

UNDERSTANDING KEY IDEAS

10. Which of the following is information you would not find in a station model? SC.912.E.7.3
    a. precipitation
    c. front
    b. cloud cover
    d. wind speed

11. Continental polar Canadian air masses generally move SC.912.E.7.3
    a. southeasterly.
    c. northeasterly.
    b. northerly.
    d. westerly.

12. The type of front that forms when two air masses move parallel to the front between them is called SC.912.E.7.3
    a. stationary.
    c. polar.
    b. occluded.
    d. warm.

13. The type of front that forms when warm air is completely lifted off the ground by cold air is called SC.912.E.7.3
    a. cold.
    c. polar.
    b. occluded.
    d. warm.

14. The eye of a hurricane is a region of SC.912.E.7.6
    a. hailstorms.
    c. calm, clear air.
    b. torrential rainfall.
    d. strong winds.

15. The wind of a midlatitude cyclone blows in a circular path around a SC.912.E.7.3
    a. front.
    b. low-pressure center.
    c. high-pressure center.
    d. jet stream.

16. In the mature stage of a thunderstorm, a cumulus cloud grows until it becomes a SC.912.E.7.3
    a. stratocumulus cloud.
    b. altocumulus cloud.
    c. cumulonimbus cloud.
    d. cirrocumulus cloud.

17. An instrument package attached to a weather balloon is
    a. an anemometer.
    c. a thermograph.
    b. a wind vane.
    d. a radiosonde.

18. The lines that connect points of equal atmospheric pressure on a weather map are called
    a. isobars.
    c. highs.
    b. isotherms.
    d. lows.

SHORT ANSWER

19. Describe the weather before and after an occluded front. SC.912.E.7.3

20. What causes lightning? SC.912.E.7.3

21. What is the most likely location for hurricane development? Explain your answer. SC.912.E.7.3

22. How could a meteorologist use a station model to determine whether a cold front is approaching? SC.912.E.7.3

23. Identify the wind direction of wind given as 315°. What direction would a wind vane point in this case? SC.912.E.7.3

24. Identify the type of air mass that is most likely responsible if the air in your area is warm and dry. What letters designate this air mass? SC.912.E.7.3

CRITICAL THINKING

25. Making Predictions Suppose that people on Vancouver Island, off the west coast of Canada, hear reports of a midlatitude cyclone in the Gulf of Alaska. Is it likely that this midlatitude cyclone will reach their area? Explain why. `SC.912.E.7.6`

26. Making Inferences Suppose that a hurricane is passing over a Caribbean island. Suddenly, the rain and wind stop and the air becomes calm and clear. Can a person living on that island safely go outside? Explain your answer. `SC.912.E.7.6`

27. Applying Ideas Is it safe to be in an automobile during a tornado? Explain your answer.

28. Making Inferences An air traffic controller is monitoring nearby airplanes by radar. The controller warns an incoming pilot of a storm that is a few miles away. How did radar help the controller detect the storm?

CONCEPT MAPPING

29. Use the following terms to create a concept map: *air mass, front, warm front, cold front, cyclone, thunderstorm, thermometer, hurricane, barometer,* and *anemometer.* `SC.912.E.7.6`

MATH SKILLS   Math Skills

30. Making Calculations The temperature at a weather station is given as 47°F. Using the equation °C = 5/9 × (°F − 32), find the temperature in degrees Celsius.

31. Making Calculations An average of 124 tornadoes occur each year in Texas. If this is equivalent to 4.7 tornadoes per 10,000 square miles, what is the area of Texas in square miles?

WRITING SKILLS

32. Creative Writing Imagine that you are traveling with friends through the desert in the southwestern United States and a thunderstorm occurs. You tell your friends about the type of front that may have brought the storm. Describe what the stages might look like by types of clouds formed, types of precipitation, and sky color. `SC.912.E.7.6`

33. Communicating Main Ideas Explain how cP and mT air masses travel across the United States, and explain why this information helps meteorologists make forecasts. `SC.912.E.7.4`

INTERPRETING GRAPHICS

The graph below shows the average number of tornadoes that generally occur at different times of day. Use this graph to answer the questions that follow.

34. During which time of day do the least tornadoes occur? `SC.912.E.7.6`

35. Would students be more likely to experience a tornado while they are at school or while they are at home? `SC.912.E.7.6`

36. During which time of day do most tornadoes occur? Why would most tornadoes occur at this time of day? `SC.912.E.7.6`

Understanding Concepts

Directions (1–7): For each question, write on a separate sheet of paper the letter of the correct answer.

1 Making measurements in Earth's upper atmosphere can be difficult. But scientists use several tools to survey weather conditions at high altitudes. Which of the following statements describes one such tool?
  A. A helium-filled balloon carries an instrument package into the atmosphere.
  B. An anemometer measures wind speed.
  C. A barometer measures the atmospheric pressure.
  D. A thermistor measures rapid temperature changes.

2 Storms that have a lot of energy often cause a lot of damage. Of the following storms, which has the greatest amount of energy?
  F. a thunderstorm
  G. a tornado
  H. an anticyclone
  I. a Category 5 hurricane

3 Differences in air pressure result in the formation of air masses and fronts. In turn, these differences in air pressure are caused by
  A. wind.
  B. unequal heating of Earth's surface.
  C. violent storms.
  D. midlatitude cyclones.

4 Continental air masses form over large landmasses. They tend to be dry. The two types of continental land masses are continental polar and continental tropical air masses. How do they differ?
  F. The continental polar air mass is smaller than the continental tropical air mass is.
  G. The continental tropical air mass produces precipitation, but the continental polar air mass does not produce precipitation.
  H. The continental polar air mass is colder than the continental tropical air mass is.
  I. The continental tropical air mass moves into other regions, but the continental polar air mass does not move.

5 Fronts exist because of density differences between air masses. These density differences are typically due to differences in temperature—cold air is denser than warm air. In the tropics, there are few significant temperature differences. What can be concluded about fronts in the tropics?
  A. Because there are no air masses, there are no fronts.
  B. Fronts do not exist because there are no differences in density.
  C. Air masses are less dense, so they do not form fronts.
  D. Fronts do not exist because air masses are warm.

6 The amount of energy in a front can determine how strong a storm it will produce. A slow-moving cold front produces weaker storms than a fast-moving cold front does. What might this indicate about the amount of energy in each front?
  F. Both fronts have the same amount of energy.
  G. A slow-moving cold front does not have enough energy to produce a storm while a fast-moving cold front has enough energy to produce a storm.
  H. A slow-moving cold front has less energy than a fast-moving cold front does.
  I. Both fronts have enough energy to produce very violent storms.

7 Anticyclones bring dry weather, which does NOT promote cloud formation. If an anticyclone stays over an area for a long time, what will likely happen?
  A. The anticyclone produces precipitation over a large area.
  B. The anticyclone produces a squall line.
  C. The anticyclone will lose its moisture and energy.
  D. The anticyclone will cause a drought.

Interpreting Graphics

Directions (8–9): For each question below, record the correct answer on a separate sheet of paper.

Interpreting a Station Model

8 What letter indicates the current barometric reading shown in the model above?
F. letter A
G. letter B
H. letter C
I. letter D

Weather Instruments

9 Which of the weather instruments shown in the figure above uses the cooling effect of evaporation to take measurements?
A. a rain gauge
B. a psychrometer
C. a wind sock
D. an anomometer

> **Test Tip**
>
> Sometimes, only one part of a diagram, graph, or table is needed to answer a question. In such cases, focus on only that information to answer the question.

Chapter 22 Climate

Why It Matters

By learning about climate, we can understand more about the atmospheric conditions of Earth in the past and how human activities may affect atmospheric conditions in the future.

Calculating Average and Yearly Temperatures

Use the Internet or the library to research the average monthly temperatures for the area in which you live. Using graph paper, construct a graph of the average monthly temperatures, with the temperatures on the *y*-axis and the months on the *x*-axis. Next, find the average yearly temperature by calculating the average of the monthly temperatures you used to make the graph. Finally, find the yearly temperature range by determining the difference between the highest average monthly temperature and the lowest average monthly temperature.

SC.912.E.7.8

Questions to Get You Started

1. How does the temperature change throughout the year in your area?

2. Why is it important to know the average yearly temperature and the yearly temperature range of an area?

READING TOOLBOX

These reading tools will help you learn the material in this chapter.

FoldNotes

Key-Term Fold A key-term fold can help you learn the key terms in this chapter.

Your Turn Create a key-term fold as described in **Appendix A.**

1. Write one key term from the Chapter Summary on the front of each tab.

2. As you read the chapter, write the definition of each term under its tab.

3. Use this FoldNote to study the key terms.

Describing Time

Temporal Language *Temporal language* is language that is used to describe time. Paying careful attention to temporal language can help you understand events and processes in the environment.

Your Turn Make a two-column table. As you read this chapter, write words or phrases that refer to time in the first column of your table. In the second column, write whether the word or phrase describes a specific time, duration, frequency, or sequence of events.

Temporal word or phrase	Describes
over millions of years	duration
today	specific time

Graphic Organizers

Cause-and-Effect Maps You can use cause-and-effect maps to show visually how physical processes depend on one another. To make a cause-and-effect map, follow these steps:

1. Draw a box, and write a cause inside the box. You can have as many cause boxes as you want.

2. Draw another box to represent an effect of the cause. You can have as many effect boxes as you want.

3. Connect each cause box to one or more effect boxes with an arrow.

4. If an effect is also the cause of another effect, you may connect the effect box to another effect box.

Your Turn On a separate sheet of paper, complete the cause-and-effect map started below about the causes of climate change. Add at least three more causes.

For more information on how to use these and other tools, see **Appendix A.**

Factors That Affect Climate

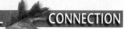
ENVIRONMENTAL CONNECTION

Key Ideas

❯ Identify two major factors used to describe climate.

❯ Explain how latitude determines the amount of solar energy received on Earth.

❯ Describe how the different rates at which land and water are heated affect climate.

❯ Explain the effects of topography on climate.

Key Terms

climate

specific heat

El Niño

monsoon

Why It Matters

Climate change is big in the news these days. Understanding the factors that affect climate can help us evaluate the news and make informed decisions about our role in climate change.

The weather conditions for an area over a long period of time are referred to as **climate.** Climate is different from weather in that weather is the condition of the atmosphere at a particular time. Weather conditions vary from day to day. Climate is a pattern that varies on a much longer basis.

Temperature and Precipitation

Climates are chiefly described by using average temperature and precipitation. To estimate the average daily temperature, add the high and low temperatures of the day and divide by two. The monthly average is the average of all the daily averages for a given month. The yearly average temperature can be found by averaging the 12 monthly averages. However, using only average temperatures to describe climate can be misleading. As you can see in **Figure 1,** areas that have similar average temperatures may have very different temperature ranges. Another way scientists describe climate is by using the *yearly temperature range,* or the difference between the highest and lowest monthly averages.

Precipitation is also described by using monthly and yearly averages, as well as ranges. As with temperature, average yearly precipitation alone is not enough to describe climate. The months that have the largest amount of precipitation are also important. When describing climate, extremes of temperature and precipitation, as well as averages, have to be considered. The factors that have the greatest influence on both temperature and precipitation are latitude, heat absorption and release, and topography.

FLORIDA STANDARDS

SC.912.E.7.3 Differentiate and describe the various interactions among Earth systems, including: atmosphere, hydrosphere, cryosphere, geosphere, and biosphere; **SC.912.E.7.4** Summarize the conditions that contribute to the climate of a geographic area, including the relationships to lakes and oceans; **SC.912.E.7.9** Cite evidence that the ocean has had a significant influence on climate change by absorbing, storing, and moving heat, carbon, and water.

climate the weather conditions in an area over a long period of time

Figure 1 Both St. Louis and San Francisco have the same average yearly temperature. However, St. Louis (right) has a climate of cold winters and hot summers, while San Francisco (left) has a generally mild climate all year.

Average Monthly Temperatures

Temperature (°C) / Month

— San Francisco
— St. Louis

J F M A M J J A S O N D

605

Latitude

One of the most important factors that determines a region's climate is latitude. Different latitudes on Earth's surface receive different amounts of solar energy. Solar energy determines the temperature and wind patterns of an area, which influence the average annual temperature and precipitation.

Solar Energy

www.scilinks.org
Topic: What Affects
Climate?
Code: HQX1652

The higher the latitude of an area is, the smaller the angle at which the sun's rays hit Earth is and the smaller the amount of solar energy received by the area is. At the equator, or 0° latitude, the sun's rays hit Earth at a 90° angle. So, temperatures at the equator are high. Nearer the poles, the sun's rays hit Earth at a smaller angle, and solar energy is spread over a larger area. So, temperatures at the poles are low.

Because Earth's axis is tilted, the angle at which the sun's rays hit an area changes as Earth orbits the sun. During winter in the Northern Hemisphere, the northern half of Earth is tilted away from the sun. Thus, light that reaches the Northern Hemisphere hits Earth's surface at a smaller angle than it does in summer, when the axis is tilted toward the sun. Because of the tilt of Earth's axis during winter in the Northern Hemisphere, areas of Earth at higher northern latitudes directly face the sun for less time than during summer. As a result, the days are shorter and the temperatures are lower during the winter months than during the summer months. **Figure 2** describes these effects.

Figure 2 Average Sea-Level Temperatures During Winter in the Northern Hemisphere

❶ In polar regions, the amount of daylight varies from 24 h of daylight in the summer to 0 h in the winter. Thus, the annual temperature range is very large, but the daily temperature ranges are very small.

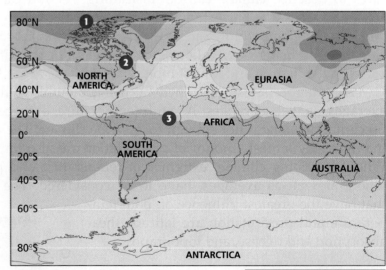

❷ At middle latitudes, the sun's rays strike Earth at an angle of less than 90°. The energy of the rays is spread over a large area. Thus, average yearly temperatures at middle latitudes are lower than those at the equator. The lengths of days and nights vary more than they do at the equator. Therefore, the yearly temperature range is large.

Temperatures (°C)

21 to 32	−23 −12
10 to 21	−34 −23
−1 to 10	−46 to −34
−12 to −1	Below −46

❸ At the equator, the sun's rays strike Earth at nearly a 90° angle for much of the year. In equatorial regions, both days and nights are about 12 h long throughout the year. So, these regions have steady, high temperatures year-round.

Global Wind Patterns

Because Earth receives different amounts of solar energy at different latitudes, belts of cool, dense air form at latitudes near the poles, while belts of warm, less dense air form near the equator. Because cool air is dense, it forms regions of high pressure, while warm air forms regions of low pressure. Differences in air pressure create wind. Because air pressure is affected by latitude, the atmosphere is made up of global wind belts that run parallel to lines of latitude. Winds affect many weather conditions, such as precipitation, temperature, and cloud cover. Thus, regions that have different global wind belts often have different climates.

In the equatorial belt of low pressure, called the *doldrums*, the air rises and cools, and water vapor condenses. Thus, this region generally has large amounts of precipitation. The amount of precipitation generally decreases as latitude increases. In the regions between about 20° and 30° latitude in both hemispheres, or the *subtropical highs*, the air sinks, warms, and decreases in relative humidity. Thus, little precipitation occurs in these regions. Most of the world's deserts are located in these regions. In the middle latitudes, at about 45° to 60° latitude in both hemispheres, warm tropical air meets cold polar air, which leads to belts of greater precipitation. In the high-pressure areas, above 60° latitude, the air masses are cold and dry, and average precipitation is low.

As seasons change, global wind belts shift in a north or south direction, as shown in **Figure 3**. As the wind and pressure belts shift, the belts of precipitation associated with them also shift.

January **July**

Heavy precipitation

Moderate precipitation

Light precipitation

Dry

Figure 3 During winter in the Northern Hemisphere, global wind and precipitation belts shift to the south.

Heat Absorption and Balance

Latitude and cloud cover affect the amount of solar energy that an area receives. However, different areas absorb and release energy differently. Land heats faster than water and thus can reach a higher temperature in the same amount of time. One reason for this difference is that the land surface is opaque and unmoving. Surface ocean water, on the other hand, is transparent and moves continuously. Waves, currents, and other movements continuously replace warm surface water with cooler water from the ocean depths. This action prevents the surface temperature of the water from increasing rapidly. However, the surface temperature of the land can continue to increase as more solar energy is received. In turn, the temperature of the land or ocean influences the amount of heat that the air above the land or ocean absorbs or releases. The temperature of the air then affects the climate of the area.

READING TOOLBOX

Key-Term Fold
Make a FoldNote for terms related to how climate is affected by the temperature differences between land and water. List each term, and explain its effect on climate.

Reading Check **How do wind and ocean currents affect the surface temperature of oceans?** (See Appendix G for answers to Reading Checks.)

Specific Heat and Evaporation

Even if not in motion, water warms more slowly than land does. Water also releases heat energy more slowly than land does. This is because the specific heat of water is higher than that of land. **Specific heat** is the amount of energy needed to change the temperature of 1 g of a substance by 1°C. A given mass of water requires more energy than land of the same mass does to experience an increase in temperature of the same number of degrees.

The average temperatures of land and water at the same latitude also vary because of differences in the loss of heat through evaporation. Evaporation affects water surfaces much more than it affects land surfaces.

Ocean Currents

The temperature of ocean currents that come in contact with the air influences the amount of heat absorbed or released by the air. If winds consistently blow toward shore, ocean currents have a strong effect on air masses over land. For example, the combination of a warm Atlantic current and steady westerly winds gives northwestern Europe a high average temperature for its latitude. In contrast, the warm Gulf Stream has little effect on the eastern coast of the United States. This is because westerly winds usually blow the Gulf Stream and its warm tropical air away from the coast.

Reading Check Why does land heat faster than water does?

---

specific heat the quantity of heat required to raise a unit mass of homogeneous material 1 K or 1°C in a specified way, given constant pressure and volume

Math Skills

Specific Heat Use the following equation to calculate the amount of energy needed to heat 200 kg of water 6 °C, given that the specific heat of water is 4,186 J/kg•K.

energy = specific heat × mass × temperature change

SC.912.E.7.3

Quick Lab   Evaporation

🕐 **30 min**

Procedure

❶ On a **piece of paper**, make a data table similar to the one shown here.

❷ Assemble a **ring stand** on a **table**. Use a **meter-stick** to place the support rings at heights of 20 cm and 40 cm above the base. Position a **portable clamp lamp that has an incandescent bulb** directly over the rings, at a height of 60 cm.

❸ Place **three Petri dishes** or **watch glasses** as follows: one on the base of the stand and one on each of the two rings.

❹ Take **three thermometers**, and lay one across each dish. Turn on the lamp. Use a **stopwatch** to record the temperature every 3 min for 9 min.

❺ Remove the thermometers, and add **30 mL of water** to each of the three dishes.

❻ Keep the lamp on and over the dishes for 24 h.

Dish	Temperature	Amount of water evaporated
1		
2		
3		

DO NOT WRITE IN THIS BOOK

❼ Turn off the lamp. Carefully pour the water from the first dish into a **graduated cylinder**, and record any change in volume. Repeat this process for the other two dishes.

Analysis

1. At what distance from the lamp did the most water evaporate? the least water evaporate?

2. Explain the relationship between temperature and the rate of evaporation.

3. Explain why puddles of water dry out much more quickly in summer than they do in fall or winter.

El Niño–Southern Oscillation

The *El Niño–Southern Oscillation,* or *ENSO,* is a cycle of changing wind and water-current patterns in the Pacific Ocean. Every 3 to 10 years, **El Niño,** which is the warm-water phase of the ENSO, causes surface-water temperatures along the west coast of South America to rise. The event changes the interaction of the ocean and the atmosphere, which can change global weather patterns. During El Niño, an increase in typhoons, cyclones, and floods may occur in the Pacific Ocean region. Droughts may strike other areas around the world, such as Indonesia and Australia. The ENSO has a cool-water phase, called *La Niña,* as well. La Niña also affects weather patterns, such as increasing the number of Atlantic hurricanes.

Seasonal Winds

Temperature differences between the land and the ocean sometimes cause winds to shift seasonally in some regions. During the summer, the land warms more quickly than the ocean. The warm air rises and is replaced by cool air from the ocean. Thus, the wind moves toward the land. During the winter, the land loses heat more quickly than the ocean does, and the cool air flows away from the land. Thus, the wind moves seaward. Such seasonal winds are called **monsoons.**

Monsoon climates, such as that in southern Asia, are caused by heating and cooling of the northern Indian peninsula. In the winter, continental winds bring dry weather and sometimes drought. In the summer, winds carry moisture to the land from the ocean and cause heavy rainfall and flooding, as shown in **Figure 4.** Monsoon conditions also occur in eastern Asia and affect the tropical regions of Australia and East Africa.

El Niño the warm-water phase of the El Niño–Southern Oscillation; a periodic occurrence in the eastern Pacific Ocean in which the surface-water temperature becomes unusually warm

monsoon a seasonal wind that blows toward the land in the summer, bringing heavy rains, and that blows away from the land in the winter, bringing dry weather

Figure 4 Effects of Monsoon Climates

Because monsoon rains cause regular flooding, such as this flood in eastern India, people who live in monsoon regions have adapted to living in flood conditions.

People who live in monsoon climates must adjust to periodic droughts, such as the drought that affected this cropland in southern India.

Topography

The surface features of the land, or *topography*, also influence climate. Topographical features, such as mountains, can control the flow of air through a region.

Elevation

The elevation, or height of landforms above sea level, produces distinct temperature changes. Temperature generally decreases as elevation increases. For example, for every 100 m increase in elevation, the average temperature decreases by 0.7 °C. Even along the equator, the peaks of high mountains can be cold enough to be covered with snow.

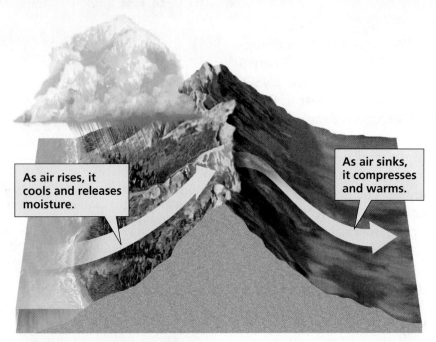

> As air rises, it cools and releases moisture.

> As air sinks, it compresses and warms.

Figure 5 Mountains cause air to rise, cool, and lose moisture as the air passes over them. This process affects the climate on both sides of the mountains.

Rain Shadows

When a moving air mass encounters a mountain range, the air mass rises, cools, and loses most of its moisture through precipitation, as shown in **Figure 5.** As a result, the air that flows down the other side of the range is usually warm and dry. This effect is called a *rain shadow*. One type of warm, dry wind that forms in this way is the *foehn* (FAYN), a dry wind that flows down the slopes of the Alps. Similar dry, warm winds that flow down the eastern slopes of the Rocky Mountains are called *chinooks*.

Section 1 Review

LA.910.2.2.3; SC.912.E.7.3; SC.912.E.7.4; SC.912.E.7.9

Key Ideas

1. **Identify** two factors that are used to describe climate.

2. **Explain** how latitude determines the amount of solar energy received on Earth.

3. **Describe** how latitude determines wind patterns.

4. **Describe** how the different rates at which land and water are heated affect climate.

5. **Explain** the El Niño–Southern Oscillation cycle.

6. **Summarize** the conditions that cause monsoons.

7. **Explain** how elevation affects climate.

8. **Describe** a rain shadow and the resulting local winds.

Critical Thinking

9. **Making Inferences** If land and water had the same specific heat, how might climate be different around the world?

10. **Analyzing Processes** On a mountain, are you likely to find more vegetation on the side facing prevailing winds or on the side facing away from them?

11. **Recognizing Relationships** Why might you find snow-capped mountains in Hawaii even though Hawaii is closer to the equator than Florida is?

Concept Mapping

12. Use the following terms to create a concept map: *climate, temperature range, wind, doldrums, subtropical high, monsoon, El Niño,* and *topography.*

Climate Zones

Key Ideas

> Describe the three types of tropical climates.
> Describe the five types of middle-latitude climates.
> Describe the three types of polar climates.
> Explain why city climates may differ from rural climates.

Key Terms

tropical climate

middle-latitude climate

polar climate

microclimate

Why It Matters

Identifying and studying the different types of climates on Earth helps you better understand the factors that influence the climate where you live.

Earth has three major types of climate zones—tropical, middle-latitude, and polar—each with distinct temperature characteristics. Each zone also has several types of climates because the amount of precipitation within each zone varies.

FLORIDA STANDARDS

SC.912.E.7.4 Summarize the conditions that contribute to the climate of a geographic area, including the relationships to lakes and oceans.

Tropical Climates

Climates characterized by high temperatures and located in the equatorial region are referred to as **tropical climates.** These climates have an average monthly temperature of at least 18 °C, even during the coldest months. Within the tropical zone, there are three types of tropical climates, as shown in **Table 1.**

Tropical rain-forest climates are humid and warm. Central Africa, the Amazon River basin of South America, Central America, and Southeast Asia have areas with tropical rain-forest climates.

Tropical desert climates receive very little precipitation. The largest belt of tropical deserts extends across north Africa and southwestern Asia.

Savanna climates are located in South America, Africa, Southeast Asia, and northern Australia. These climates are described in **Table 1.**

tropical climate a climate characterized by high temperatures and heavy precipitation during at least part of the year

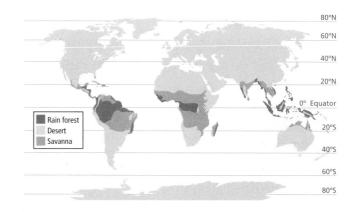

Table 1 Tropical Climates

Climate	Temperature and precipitation	Description
Rain forest	small temperature range; annual rainfall of 200 cm	characterized by dense, lush vegetation; broadleaf plants; and high biodiversity
Desert	large temperature range, with hot days and cold nights; annual rainfall of less than 25 cm	characterized by little to no vegetation and organisms adapted to dry conditions
Savanna	small temperature range; annual rainfall of 50 cm; alternating wet and dry periods	characterized by open grasslands that have clumps of drought-resistant shrubs

Table 2 Middle-Latitude Climates

Climate	Temperature and precipitation	Description
Marine west coast	small annual temperature range; frequent rainfall throughout the year	characterized by deciduous trees and dense forests; mild winters and summers
Steppe	large annual temperature range; annual precipitation of less than 40 cm	characterized by drought-resistant vegetation; cold, dry winters and warm, wet summers
Humid continental	large annual temperature range; annual precipitation of greater than 75 cm	characterized by a wide variety of vegetation and evergreen trees; variable weather
Humid subtropical	large annual temperature range; annual precipitation of 75 to 165 cm	characterized by broadleaf and evergreen trees; high humidity
Mediterranean	small annual temperature range; average annual precipitation of about 40 cm	characterized by broadleaf and evergreen trees; long, dry summers and mild, wet winters

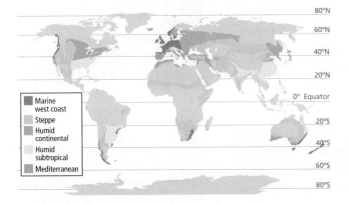

Marine west coast
Steppe
Humid continental
Humid subtropical
Mediterranean

middle-latitude climate a climate that has an average maximum temperature below 18 °C in the coldest month and an average minimum temperature above 10 °C in the warmest month

Middle-Latitude Climates

Climates that have an average maximum temperature below 18 °C in the coldest month and an average minimum temperature above 10 °C in the warmest month are referred to as **middle-latitude climates.** There are five middle-latitude climates, which are described in **Table 2.**

Marine west coast climates receive about 60 to 150 cm of precipitation annually. The average temperature is 20 °C in the summer and 7 °C in the winter. The Pacific Northwest of the United States has a marine west coast climate.

Steppe climates are dry climates that receive less than 40 cm of precipitation per year. The average summer temperature is about 23 °C. The winters are very cold and have an average temperature of −1 °C. The Great Plains of the United States has a steppe climate.

The *humid continental climate* and *humid subtropical climate* both have high annual precipitation. However, the humid continental climate has a much greater temperature range between the summers and winters than the humid subtropical climate. In the United States, the humid subtropical climate is in the southeast and the humid continental climate is in the northeast.

The *mediterranean climate* is a mild climate that has a small temperature range between summer and winter. This climate is named after the sea between Africa and Europe, where this climate is located. However, this climate is also found along the coast of central and southern California.

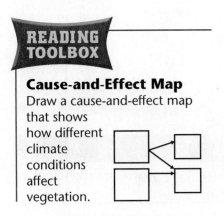

READING TOOLBOX

Cause-and-Effect Map
Draw a cause-and-effect map that shows how different climate conditions affect vegetation.

Reading Check Which subclimates have high annual precipitation?

Figure 1 Subarctic climates, as shown here at Tombstone Valley in Yukon, Canada, support sparse tree growth.

www.scilinks.org
Topic: Polar Climates
Code: HQX1175

Polar Climates

The climates of the polar regions are referred to as the **polar climates.** There are three types of polar climates: the subarctic climate, shown in **Figure 1,** the tundra climate, and the polar icecap climate. The *subarctic climate* has the largest annual temperature range of all climates. The difference between summer and winter temperatures in the subarctic climate has been as much as 63 °C. The *tundra climate* has a smaller annual temperature range than the subarctic climate does. However, the average temperature of the tundra climate is colder than that of the subarctic climate. In the *polar icecap climate,* most of the land surface and much of the ocean are covered in thick sheets of ice year-round. The average temperature never rises above freezing. The polar climates are described in **Table 3.**

polar climate a climate that is characterized by average temperatures that are near or below freezing

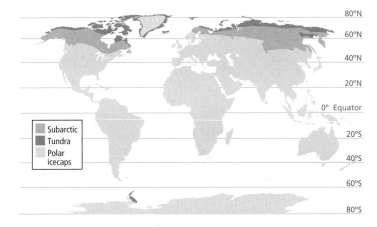

Table 3 Polar Climates

Climate	Temperature and precipitation	Description
Subarctic	largest annual temperature range (63 °C); annual precipitation of 25 to 50 cm	characterized by evergreen trees; brief, cool summers and long, cold winters
Tundra	average temperature below 4 °C; annual precipitation of 25 cm	characterized by treeless plains; nine months of temperatures below freezing
Polar icecap	average temperature below 0 °C; low annual precipitation	characterized by little or no life; temperatures below freezing year-round and high winds

Late afternoon temperatures (°C)

Rural | Commercial | Urban residential | Suburban residential | Rural farmland

Suburban residential | Downtown | Park

Figure 2 The less vegetation and more pavement and buildings an area has, the higher the temperatures in the area tend to be.

microclimate the climate of a small area

Academic Vocabulary

variation (VER ee AY shuhn) a difference in the usual form or function

Local Climates

The climate of a small area is called a **microclimate.** Microclimates are influenced by density of vegetation, by elevation, and by proximity to large bodies of water and structures built by humans. For example, in a city, pavement and buildings absorb solar energy and then reradiate that energy as heat, which raises the temperature of the air above and creates a "heat island," as shown in **Figure 2.** As a result, the average temperature may be a few degrees higher in the city than it is in surrounding rural areas. In contrast, vegetation in rural areas does not reradiate as much energy, so temperatures in those areas are lower.

Effects of Elevation

Elevation also may affect local climates. As elevation increases, temperature decreases and the climate changes. For example, the *highland climate* is characterized by large variations in temperature and precipitation over short distances because of changes in elevation. Highland climates are commonly located in mountainous regions—even in tropical areas.

Effects of Large Bodies of Water

Large bodies of water, such as lakes, influence local climates. The water absorbs and releases heat slower than the land does. Thus, the water moderates the temperature of the nearby land. Large bodies of water can also increase precipitation. Therefore, microclimates near large bodies of water have a smaller range of temperatures and higher annual precipitation than other locations at the same latitude do.

Section 2 Review

LA.910.2.2.3; SC.912.E.7.4

Key Ideas

1. **Identify** the three types of climate zones.

2. **Describe** the three types of tropical climates.

3. **Describe** the five types of middle-latitude climates.

4. **Describe** the three types of polar climates.

5. **Identify** three factors that influence microclimates.

6. **Explain** why city climates may differ from rural climates.

Critical Thinking

7. **Making Inferences** What would happen to the temperature of a rural location if the vegetation were replaced with a parking lot?

8. **Compare and Contrast** Compare latitude lines with the boundaries of major climate zones. Why do they align in some regions but not in others?

Concept Mapping

9. Use the following terms to create a concept map: *tropical climate, subarctic, tundra, steppe, polar icecap, mediterranean, middle-latitude climate, rain forest, savanna, desert,* and *polar climate.*

SECTION 3 Climate Change

Key Ideas	Key Terms	Why It Matters
❯ Compare four methods used to study climate change. ❯ Describe four factors that may cause climate change. ❯ Identify potential impacts of climate change. ❯ Identify ways that humans can minimize their effect on climate change.	**climatologist** **global warming**	There's no doubt that climate changes. Understanding how and why it changes will help guide your response to issues like global warming.

Scientists who study and compare past and present climates are called **climatologists.** Climatologists look at past climates to find patterns in the changes that occur. Identifying those patterns allows the scientists to make predictions about future climates.

Studying Climate Change

When trying to learn about factors that influence climate change, scientists study the evidence left by past climates. This evidence can be left in the remains of plants and animals from earlier time periods. For example, *fossils* of a plant or animal may show adaptations to a particular environment that can reveal clues about the environment's climate. Even polar icecaps contain evidence of past climates. By studying the concentration of gases trapped within *ice cores*, scientists can learn about the gas composition of the atmosphere thousands of years ago. **Table 1** describes some of the methods used to study past climates.

FLORIDA STANDARDS

SC.912.E.7.3 Differentiate and describe the various interactions among Earth systems, including: atmosphere, hydrosphere, cryosphere, geosphere, and biosphere; **SC.912.E.7.4** Summarize the conditions that contribute to the climate of a geographic area, including the relationships to lakes and oceans.

climatologist a scientist who gathers data to study and compare past and present climates and to predict future climate change

Table 1 Methods of Studying Past Climates

Method	What is measured	What is indicated	Length of time measured
Ice cores	concentrations of gases in ice and meltwater	High levels of CO_2 indicate warmer climate; ice ages accompany decreases in CO_2.	hundreds of thousands of years
Sea-floor sediment	concentration of ^{18}O in shells of microorganisms	High ^{18}O levels indicate cool water; lower ^{18}O levels indicate warm water.	hundreds of thousands of years
Fossils	pollen types, leaf shapes, and animal body adaptations	Flower pollens and broad leaves indicate warm climates; evergreen pollens and small, waxy leaves indicate cool climates. Animal fossils show adaptations to climate changes.	millions of years
Tree rings	ring width	Thin rings indicate cool weather and/or less precipitation.	hundreds to thousands of years
Speleothems	concentrations of ^{13}C and ^{18}O in stalagmites	High levels of ^{13}C indicate El Niño events. Low levels of ^{18}O record individual hurricanes.	weeks to hundreds of years

Modeling Climates

Because so many factors influence climate, studying climate change is a complicated process. Currently, scientists use computers to create models to study climate, as shown in **Figure 1.** These models incorporate millions of pieces of data and help sort the complex sets of variables that influence climate. They are called *general circulation models,* or *GCMs.* GCMs simulate changes in one variable when other variables are unchanged. For example, if the sulfur dioxide level is raised in a particular model, the model indicates a decrease in incoming solar radiation because sulfur dioxide reflects sunlight.

Figure 1 Scientists need to use powerful computers to process the amount of data required to study climates.

Climate models simulate many factors of climate, including temperature, precipitation, wind patterns, and sea-level changes. These computer models are complex because they model interactions between oceans, wind, land, clouds, and vegetation. As computers become more powerful, computer-generated climate models will provide greater detail about the global climate system and will help scientists better understand climate change.

Reading Check **Why do scientists use computers to model climate?**

Why It Matters

Ice Tells a Story

EYE ON THE ENVIRONMENT

Have you ever had a frozen treat with several layers that were different colors or textures? You probably inferred that each layer would have a different flavor. Similarly, each layer of ice in the Arctic and Antarctica was formed under different conditions, such as temperature, wind patterns, and amount of precipitation. Scientists study layers of ice in ice cores and make inferences about the conditions under which each layer formed. Ice cores are obtained by drilling thousands of meters down into polar ice. Ice cores can help scientists understand past climate change and develop models to predict future climate change.

Each annual snowfall creates a distinct layer of polar ice, which can provide scientists with annual climate data.

YOUR TURN ONLINE RESEARCH
Research how scientists use ice cores to study past volcanic events.

Potential Causes of Climate Change

By studying computer-generated climate models, scientists have determined several potential causes of climate change. Factors that might cause climate change include the movement of tectonic plates, changes in Earth's orbit, human activity, and atmospheric changes.

Plate Tectonics

The movement of continents over millions of years caused by tectonic plate motion may affect climate change. The changing position of the continents changes wind flow and ocean currents around the globe. These changes affect the temperature and precipitation patterns of the continents and oceans. Thus, the climate of any particular continent is not the same as it was millions of years ago.

Orbital Changes

Periodic changes in the shape of Earth's orbit, changes in Earth's tilt, and the wobble of Earth on its axis can lead to climate change, as shown in **Figure 2.** The combination of these factors is described by the *Milankovitch theory.* Each change of motion has a different effect on climate. Variation in the shape of Earth's orbit, from elliptical to more circular, affects Earth's distance from the sun. Earth's distance from the sun affects the temperature of Earth and therefore affects the climate. Decreasing tilt decreases temperature differences between seasons. The wobble of Earth on its axis changes the direction of Earth's tilt and can reverse the seasons. These changes occur in cycles of 100,000, 41,000, and 26,000 years respectively.

Figure 2 Earth's Orbital Changes

Eccentricity Earth encounters more variation in the energy that it receives from the sun when Earth's orbit is elongated than it does when Earth's orbit is more circular.

Tilt The tilt of Earth's axis varies between 22.2° and 24.5°. The greater the tilt angle is, the more solar energy the poles receive.

Precession A gradual change, or "wobble," in the orientation of Earth's axis affects the relationship between Earth's tilt and eccentricity.

Figure 3 Most deforestation in Brazil is caused by farmers who clear the land for planting crops.

Academic Vocabulary

impact (IM PAKT) the effect of one thing on another

Human Activity

Human activity affects climate through emissions and land use. Pollution from transportation and industry releases carbon dioxide, CO_2, into the atmosphere. Increases in CO_2 concentrations may lead to global warming, an increase in temperatures around Earth. CO_2 is also released into the atmosphere when trees are burned to provide land for agriculture and urban development. Because vegetation uses CO_2 to make food, deforestation, as shown in **Figure 3,** also affects one of the natural ways of removing CO_2 from the atmosphere. As scientists continue to study climate, they will learn more about how human activity affects climate and about how changes in climate may affect us.

Volcanic Activity

Large volcanic eruptions can influence climates around the world. Sulfur and ash from eruptions can decrease temperatures by reflecting sunlight back into space. These changes last from a few weeks to several years and depend on the strength and duration of the eruption.

Potential Impacts of Climate Change

Scientists are concerned about climate changes because of the potential impacts of these changes. Earth's atmosphere, oceans, and land are all connected, and each influences both local and global climates. Changes in the climate of one area can affect climates around the world. Climate change affects not only humans but also plants and animals. Even short-term changes in the climate may lead to long-lasting effects that may make the survival of life on Earth more difficult for both humans and other species. Some of these potential climate changes include global warming, sea-level changes, and changes in precipitation.

Reading Check **What things are influenced by climate change?**

Global Warming

Global temperatures have increased approximately 1 °C over the last 100 years. Researchers are trying to determine if this increase is a natural variation or the result of human activities, such as deforestation and pollution. A gradual increase in average global temperatures is called **global warming.** This process may result from an increase in the concentration of greenhouse gases, such as CO_2, in the atmosphere.

An increase in global temperature can lead to an increase in evaporation. Increased evaporation could cause some areas to become drier than they are now. Some plants and animals would not be able to live in these drier conditions. An increase in evaporation in other areas could cause crops to suffer damage. However, an increase in temperatures due to global warming might improve conditions for crops in colder, northern regions.

An increase in global temperatures could also cause ice at the poles to melt. If a significant amount of ice melts, sea levels around the world could rise. This rise in sea levels would cause flooding around coastlines, where many cities are located.

global warming a gradual increase in the average global temperature

www.scilinks.org
Topic: Global Warming
Code: HQX0681

Sea-Level Changes

Using computer models, some scientists have predicted an increase in global temperature of 2 to 4 °C during this century. An increase of only a few degrees worldwide could melt the polar ice-caps and raise sea level by the addition of water to the oceans and by thermal expansion of the ocean water itself. On a shoreline that has a gentle slope, the shoreline could shift inland many miles, as shown in **Figure 4.** Many coastal inhabitants would be displaced, and freshwater and agricultural land resources would be diminished. Because approximately 50% of the world's population lives near coastlines, this sea-level rise would have devastating effects.

Figure 4 As sea level rises, shore-lines could shift inland many miles. *Which two states would lose the most area if sea level were to rise by 3 m?*

Figure 5 People from the Wangari Maathai Green Belt Movement in Kenya, Africa, prepare seedlings for planting.

What Humans Can Do

Many countries are working together to reduce the potential effects of global warming. Treaties and laws have been passed to reduce pollution. Industrial practices are being monitored and changed. Even community projects to reforest areas, such as the one shown in **Figure 5,** have been developed on a local level.

Individual Efforts

Each individual person can also help to reduce pollution that is caused by the burning of fossil fuels, such as running automobiles and using electricity. These activities increase CO_2 concentrations in the atmosphere. Therefore, humans can have a significant effect on pollution rates by turning lights off when they are not in use, by turning down the heat in the winter, and by reducing air conditioner use in the summer. Recycling is also helpful because less energy is needed to recycle some products than to create them.

Transportation Solutions

Using public transportation and driving fuel-efficient vehicles can also help to release less CO_2 into the atmosphere. All vehicles burn fuel more efficiently when they are properly tuned and the tires are properly inflated. Driving at a consistent speed also allows a vehicle to burn fuel efficiently. Car manufacturers have been developing cars that are more fuel efficient. For example, *hybrid cars* use both gasoline and electricity. These cars release less CO_2 into the atmosphere from burning fuel than other cars do.

Section 3 Review

LA.910.2.2.3; SC.912.E.7.3; SC.912.E.7.4; SC.912.E.7.7

Key Ideas

1. **Compare** four methods that climatologists use to study climate.

2. **Identify** four factors that may cause climate change.

3. **Describe** how orbital changes may affect climate.

4. **Explain** how changes in CO_2 concentrations affect global temperatures.

5. **Explain** one potential negative impact of global warming.

6. **Identify** two ways that countries can work together to reduce their impact on, and the potential effects of, global warming.

7. **Identify** four ways that an individual can reduce their own impact on global warming.

Critical Thinking

8. **Making Predictions** How would the melting of small icebergs affect sea level? Explain your answer.

9. **Evaluating Models** Can short-term climate changes be explained using the cycles described by the Milankovitch theory? Explain your answer.

Concept Mapping

10. Use the following terms to create a concept map: *climatologist, general circulation models, global warming, ice cores, tree rings, fossils,* and *isotopes.*

Polar Bears on Thin Ice

What would you do if a corner store, where you bought milk, juice, and snacks, became farther away each day? What would you do if a trip to this store involved not only a longer distance but also more difficult conditions, which you were not adapted to?

As the ice cover in the Arctic decreases, polar bears are facing these kinds of challenges in their search for food. Many researchers predict that, if climate models are correct, at least two-thirds of the polar bear population will be gone by 2050 and the species will not survive the century.

Some polar bears have drowned trying to travel longer and longer distances between ice floes.

Polar bears depend on ice as a platform from which to hunt seals. With less ice, some bears are starving to death.

2005   **2007**

Sea ice in the Arctic has been decreasing dramatically as temperatures rise.

YOUR TURN

CRITICAL THINKING
Why do you think polar bears are often used to symbolize climate change?

UNDERSTANDING CONCEPTS
Seals give birth and nurse their young on ice. How might this further affect polar bears as the ice cover in the Arctic decreases?

What You'll Do

> **Determine** whether land or water absorbs heat faster.

> **Explain** how the properties of land and water affect climate.

What You'll Need

container (2)
heat lamp
meterstick
soil
thermometer, Celsius (2)
water

Safety

Factors That Affect Climate

Many factors affect climate. One of the most significant factors that influence climate is the distribution of land and water. Because land and water absorb and release thermal energy (or energy as heat) differently, they affect the atmosphere differently. In turn, the differences between land and water affect climate. In this lab, you will explore how the properties of land and water affect climate.

Ask a Question

① How do the properties of land and water affect climate?

Form a Hypothesis

② On a separate piece of paper, write a hypothesis that is a possible answer to the question above.

Test the Hypothesis

③ Fill one container with soil and the other container with water. Place both containers on a flat surface next to each other.

Step ⑤

④ Place the thermometer in the soil, as shown below. The bulb of the thermometer should be covered by no more than 0.5 cm of soil. Record the temperature.

⑤ Place the second thermometer in the container of water, as shown in the photo on the previous page. Make sure that the bulb of the thermometer is covered by no more than 0.5 cm of water.

⑥ Place the heat lamp 25 cm above both containers. Turn on the heat lamp.

⑦ Create a data table like the one at the right. In your table, record the temperature of each sample at 1, 3, 5, and 10 min intervals.

⑧ Disconnect the lamp, and move it aside. Record the temperature of the soil and water after 5 min. **CAUTION** Be sure to let the heat lamp cool before storing it.

Data Table

Time (min)	Temperature of soil (°C)	Temperature of water (°C)
1		
3		
5		
10		
5 (after light off)		

Analyze the Results

1. **Analyzing Data** Which substance absorbed more thermal energy: water or soil?

2. **Analyzing Results** Which substance lost thermal energy faster when the heat source was turned off: water or soil?

Draw Conclusions

3. **Evaluating Conclusions** What conclusion can you draw about how land and water on Earth are heated by the sun?

4. **Analyzing Methods** Does this experiment describe how proximity to a body of water affects the temperature of a region? If so, explain your answer. If not, how could you test that variable?

Extension

Applying Ideas Repeat this experiment, but modify the angle at which the light strikes the surface of the soil and the water. How do your results differ from the results of the original experiment? How does the angle of the light affect temperature change in water and soil?

MAPS in Action

Climates of the World

Tropical Climates
- Rain forest
- Desert
- Savanna

Mid Latitude Climates
- Marine west coast
- Steppe
- Humid continental
- Humid subtropical
- Mediterranean

Polar Climates
- Subarctic
- Tundra
- Polar icecaps
- Highland

Monsoon Air Flow
- Wet monsoon
- Dry monsoon

Major World Ocean Currents
- Cool currents
- Warm currents

Map ▶ Skills Activity

This map shows the climate regions of Earth and the locations of warm and cold ocean currents. Use the map to answer the questions below.

1. **Analyzing Data** Estimate the latitude range for the desert climate of northern Africa.

2. **Making Comparisons** Why does the eastern coast of the United States have a different climate than the western coast does, even though the coasts are at similar latitudes?

3. **Analyzing Ideas** If the ocean current that flows off the western coast of Australia were a warm current, how would it affect the climate of western Australia?

4. **Using a Key** Identify the latitudes where monsoons are located.

5. **Evaluating Data** Explain why the western coast of South America is desert while the inland part of the continent at the same latitude is humid.

THINK central
SUPER SUMMARY
Keyword: HQXCLIS

Key Ideas

Key Terms

Section 1

Factors That Affect Climate

❯ The climate of a region is described by the region's temperature and precipitation.

❯ Latitude determines the angle at which the sun's rays hit Earth. At higher latitudes, the angle is smaller so areas receive less solar energy. At lower latitudes, the angle is larger so areas receive more solar energy.

❯ The temperature of land or water influences the amount of heat that the air above the land or water can absorb or release. The temperature of the air then affects the climate of the area.

❯ Topography affects climate by causing temperature variations due to elevation and by creating rain shadows.

climate, p. 605

specific heat, p. 608

El Niño, p. 609

monsoon, p. 609

Section 2

Climate Zones

❯ The three tropical climates, which are located near the equator, are tropical rain forest, tropical desert, and savanna climates.

❯ The five middle-latitude climates are marine west coast, steppe, humid continental, humid subtropical, and mediterranean climates.

❯ The three polar climates are subarctic, tundra, and polar icecap climates.

❯ Due to the heat island effect, the average temperature in a city is a few degrees higher than it is in surrounding rural areas.

tropical climate, p. 611

middle-latitude climate, p. 612

polar climate, p. 613

microclimate, p. 614

Section 3

Climate Change

❯ By using ice cores, sea-floor sediment, fossils, tree rings, and speleothems, scientists have been able to study past climates.

❯ Natural processes and human activity may be causing changes in Earth's climate, including global warming.

❯ One potential effect of climate change is a rise in sea levels, which could lead to flooding around coastlines.

❯ Humans can minimize their contribution to climate change by reducing pollution from burning fossil fuels, recycling, and using public transportation.

climatologist, p. 615

global warming, p. 619

1. Cause-and-Effect Map Draw a cause-and-effect map that shows how elevation affects climate. SC.912.E.7.4

READING TOOLBOX

USING KEY TERMS

Use each of the following terms in a separate sentence.

2. *specific heat* SC.912.E.7.4

3. *microclimate* SC.912.E.7.4

4. *climatologist*

For each pair of terms, explain how the meanings of the terms differ.

5. *climate* and *microclimate* SC.912.E.7.4

6. *El Niño* and *monsoon* SC.912.E.7.4

7. *tropical climate* and *polar climate* SC.912.E.7.4

UNDERSTANDING KEY IDEAS

8. At the equator, the sun's rays always strike Earth
  a. at a low angle. SC.912.E.7.4
  b. at nearly a 90° angle.
  c. 18 h each day.
  d. no more than 8 h each day.

9. Which of the following is *not* used as evidence of past climates? SC.912.E.7.4
  a. ice cores
  b. general circulation models
  c. tree rings
  d. fossils

10. Water cools SC.912.E.7.4
  a. more slowly than land does.
  b. more quickly than land does.
  c. only during evaporation.
  d. during global warming.

11. Ocean currents influence temperature by
  a. eroding shorelines. SC.912.E.7.4
  b. heating or cooling the air.
  c. washing warm, dry sediments out to sea.
  d. dispersing the rays of the sun.

12. Winds that blow in opposite directions in different seasons because of the differential heating of the land and the oceans are called
  a. chinooks. SC.912.E.7.4
  b. foehn.
  c. monsoons.
  d. El Niño.

13. When a moving air mass encounters a mountain range, the air mass SC.912.E.7.4
  a. stops moving.
  b. slows and sinks.
  c. rises and cools.
  d. reverses its direction.

14. In regions that have a mediterranean climate, almost all of the yearly precipitation falls SC.912.E.7.4
  a. during monsoons.
  b. in the summer.
  c. in the winter.
  d. during hurricanes.

15. The climate that has the largest annual temperature range is the SC.912.E.7.4
  a. subarctic climate.
  b. middle-latitude desert climate.
  c. mediterranean climate.
  d. humid continental climate.

16. The pavement and buildings in cities affect the local climate by SC.912.E.7.4
  a. decreasing the temperature.
  b. increasing the temperature.
  c. increasing the relative humidity.
  d. decreasing the precipitation.

SHORT ANSWER

17. Describe the Milankovitch theory, including how it may explain some climate changes. SC.912.E.7.4

18. What are the possible effects of global warming?

19. Compare marine west coast and humid continental climates. SC.912.E.7.4

20. Making Predictions Describe how the climate in California might be affected if all of the trees in California were cut down. SC.912.E.7.4

21. Making Inferences Explain why the vegetation in areas that have a tundra climate is sparse even though these areas receive enough precipitation to support plant life. SC.912.E.7.4

22. Analyzing Ideas Explain why climates cannot be classified only by latitude. SC.912.E.7.4

23. Predicting Consequences How would global climate be affected if Earth were not tilted on its axis? Explain your reasoning. SC.912.E.7.4

CONCEPT MAPPING

24. Use the following terms to create a concept map: *fossil, ice cores, climate, polar climate, climatologist, steppe, temperature range, tropical climate, middle-latitude climate,* and *savanna.* SC.912.E.7.4

MATH SKILLS   Math Skills

25. Using Equations Temperature generally decreases about 6.5 °C for every kilometer above sea level. If T_N = temperature at a new altitude, a = altitude in kilometers, and T_I = initial temperature at sea level, what equation can be used to find the temperature at a given altitude?

26. Making Calculations From 1970 to 2005, nitrogen-oxide, NO_X, emissions in the United States decreased from about 26.9 million to about 19.0 million tons per year. By what percentage did NO_X emissions decrease over these years?

WRITING SKILLS

27. Researching Topics Research greenhouse gases to determine how they are produced. Then, write a brief essay that outlines how they can be reduced. SC.912.E.7.4

28. Communicating Main Ideas Imagine that you are going to build a vacation house. Research three locations where you would like to build your vacation house, and outline the climate features that would make each location ideal. SC.912.E.7.4

INTERPRETING GRAPHICS

The pie graphs below show world emissions of carbon dioxide, CO_2, in 1995 and predict emissions in 2035. Use these graphs to answer the questions that follow.

Total World Emissions of Carbon Dioxide

*former Soviet Union

29. In 1995, which country or region emitted the most CO_2? Which emitted the least CO_2? SC.912.N.1.1

30. What percentage of the total CO_2 was emitted by developing countries in 1995? SC.912.N.1.1

31. Why do you think researchers predict that CO_2 emissions of developing countries will equal those of developed countries by 2035? SC.912.N.1.1

Understanding Concepts

Directions (1–9): For each question, write on a separate sheet of paper the letter of the correct answer.

1 Which statement best compares how land and water are heated by solar energy?
  A. Water heats up faster and to a higher temperature than land does.
  B. Land heats up faster and to a higher temperature than water does.
  C. Water heats up more slowly but reaches a higher temperature than land does.
  D. Land heats up more slowly and reaches a higher temperature than water does.

2 Which of the following statements best describes the El Niño–Southern Oscillation?
  F. a change in global wind patterns that occurs in the Southern Hemisphere
  G. a warming of surface waters in the eastern Pacific due to the effects of changing wind patterns on ocean currents near the equator
  H. a cooling of surface waters in the eastern Pacific due to the effects of changing wind patterns on ocean currents near the equator
  I. a global wind and precipitation belt between 20°N and 30°N latitude

3 The addition of carbon dioxide to Earth's atmosphere increased average global temperatures. Human activity adds more carbon dioxide to the atmosphere, which may lead to further increases in temperature. What else can increase with these increased temperatures?
  A. evaporation
  B. ice formation
  C. human activity
  D. cloud cover

4 In samples of atmospheric gases taken from ice cores, high levels of carbon dioxide indicate that the sample is from a time period that had
  F. a warm climate.
  G. a cool climate.
  H. high amounts of precipitation.
  I. low amounts of precipitation.

5 Over time, Earth's climate has changed. Which of the following was NOT a factor in that change?
  A. plate tectonics
  B. orbital change
  C. human activity
  D. winds

6 The region of Earth near the equator is called the tropics and has three types of climate. The three types of tropical climate are characterized by high temperatures and amount of precipitation, which in turn determines the vegetation that grows in the area. A tropical climate that has high rainfall results in the growth of
  F. rain forests.
  G. little or no vegetation.
  H. open grasslands that have drought-resistant shrubs.
  I. deciduous trees.

7 Climate is affected by a number of factors, including latitude, elevation, and proximity to mountains. How might mountains affect climate?
  A. They increase temperature as air moves over a mountain.
  B. They cause air to lose moisture as it passes over the mountains.
  C. They absorb heat slower than other areas do, changing the climate.
  D. They moderate area temperatures.

8 Latitude is a determining factor in the type of climate that a region has. This is due primarily to
  F. the amount of solar energy a latitude receives.
  G. global wind patterns.
  H. the proportion of land to water.
  I. ocean currents.

9 Global warming results from increased carbon dioxide in the atmosphere. This carbon dioxide is the product of many human activities. How can people reduce carbon dioxide?
  A. seed clouds
  B. use electricity
  C. drive hybrid cars
  D. eat less

Interpreting Graphics

Directions (10–12): For each question below, record the correct answer on a separate sheet of paper.

Two Cities Separated by Coastal Mountains

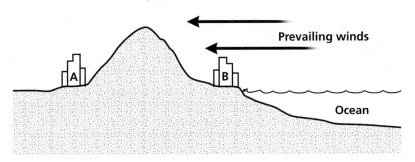

10 Which city is most likely to have the largest yearly temperature range?
  F. City A would likely have the largest yearly temperature range.
  G. City B would likely have the largest yearly temperature range.
  H. Both cities would likely have the same temperature range.
  I. There is not enough information to answer the question.

Climatograms for Two Cities

11 Based on the climatograms above, which of the two cities is in a tropical climate?
  A. Nashville, TN
  B. Manokwari, New Guinea
  C. Both cities are in tropical climates.
  D. Neither city is in a tropical climate.

12 Which month shows the most rainfall for both climates in the climatograms?
  F. March
  G. June
  H. September
  I. December

> **Test Tip**
>
> Read all the information, including the heads, in a table or chart before answering the questions that refer to it.

Meteorology Connections

Science, technology, and society are closely linked. This flowchart shows just a few of the connections in the history of meteorology.

340 B.C.E. Aristotle describes weather patterns in his book titled *Meteorologica*.

1782 The first hot-air balloon is invented by brothers Joseph-Michel and Jacques-Etienne Montgolfier.

1654 Ferdinando II de Medici invents the first sealed, modern-style thermometer.

1887 Heinrich Hertz experiments with creating radio waves in his laboratory.

1930 The first radiosonde is launched, attached to a weather balloon.

1935 Radar is designed for use in air defense in Britain.

2007 The Hartsfield-Jackson International Airport in Atlanta, Georgia, manages 994,346 flights.

1943 Radar is first used for storm tracking.

1946 A radar air-traffic control system is used experimentally.

1926 Robert Goddard invents the first practical liquid-fueled rocket.

1960 The first successful weather satellite, *TIROS*, is launched from Cape Canaveral.

AIRS Retrieved Mid-Tropospheric CO$_2$ Version 5   July 2003

parts per million by volume, ppmv

1957 The Soviet Union launches *Sputnik I*, the first orbital satellite.

2002 The *Aqua* satellite gathers data about Earth's surface and atmosphere.

1969 The first "Internet," ARPANET, becomes functional.

1939 World War II breaks out in Europe.

1946 Scientists develop the first computer, ENIAC.

2007 Local weather information is available for almost any place on Earth.

1988 The National Weather Service initiates a nationwide Doppler radar system.

2005 Accurate prediction of the path of Hurricane Rita allows for evacuations.

YOUR TURN

UNDERSTANDING CONCEPTS
How did Robert Goddard contribute to the study of meteorology?

CRITICAL THINKING
How has the study of weather benefited from the work of scientists outside the field of meteorology?

Unit **7** Oceans

Chapter Outline

Why It Matters

Oceans cover more than 70 percent of Earth's surface. Oceans interact with the atmosphere to influence weather and climate. Exploring and analyzing data about the chemistry of ocean water, the geology of the ocean floor, marine ecosystems, and the physics of water movement is critical to understanding natural processes on Earth.

Inquiry Lab

🕐 **20 min**

Sink or Float?

Fill the bottom half of 3-L soda bottle with water to within about 3 inches from the top and place it on a plastic or metal tray to catch any spills. Using small (3-oz) plastic cups, with some paper clips and metal nuts for ballast, see if you can get a cup to sink with air still trapped inside, simulating a submersible. You may need something pointed to make holes in the cups.

Questions to Get You Started

1. What is buoyancy and why is it so important for maritime travel?

2. Compare techniques for sinking the cup. Does one method consistently work better than others?

3. What challenges do engineers face when designing submersibles?

SC.912.E.7.3

These reading tools will help you learn the material in this chapter.

Science Terms

Everyday Words Used in Science Many words used in science are familiar words from everyday speech. However, the meanings of these everyday words are often different from their meanings in scientific contexts.

Your Turn Before you read this chapter, write down an informal definition of what the word *margin* means to you. As you come across this word in the chapter, write the scientific definition next to your informal definition. For each definition, write a sentence that uses the word *margin* correctly.

Classification

Classifying Sediments Classification is a tool for organizing objects and ideas by grouping them into categories. Groups are classified by defining characteristics. For example, the table below shows how sediments can be classified by their composition.

Your Turn As you read the chapter, complete a table like the one shown here for the three types of sediments described in Section 3.

Type of Sediment	Characteristics
Inorganic	Carried from land to ocean by rivers, wind, and icebergs
Biogenic	
Chemical	

Graphic Organizers

Spider Maps Spider maps show how details are organized into categories, which in turn are related to a main idea. To make a spider map, follow the steps.

❶ Write a main topic title, and draw an oval around it.

❷ From the oval, draw legs. Each leg represents a category of the main topic.

❸ From each leg, draw horizontal lines. Write details about each category on these lines.

Your Turn As you read Section 2, use a spider map to organize the information that you learn about features of the ocean floor.

For more information on how to use these and other tools, see **Appendix A.**

SECTION 1 The Water Planet

Key Ideas	Key Terms	Why It Matters
❯ Name the major divisions of the global ocean. ❯ Describe how oceanographers study the ocean. ❯ Explain how sonar works.	global ocean sea oceanography sonar	New ways to explore the cold, dark ocean depths have revealed to us the bizarre life forms that thrive there.

Nearly three-quarters of Earth's surface lies beneath a body of salt water called the **global ocean.** No other known planet has a similar covering of liquid water. Only Earth can be called the *water planet*.

The global ocean contains more than 97% of all of the water on or near Earth's surface. Although the ocean is the most prominent feature of Earth's surface, the ocean is only about 1/4,000 of Earth's total mass and only 1/800 of Earth's total volume.

Divisions of the Global Ocean

As shown in **Figure 1,** the global ocean is divided into five major oceans. These major oceans are the Atlantic, Pacific, Indian, Arctic, and Southern Oceans. Each ocean has special characteristics. The Pacific Ocean is the largest ocean on Earth's surface. It contains more than one-half of the ocean water on Earth. With an average depth of 4.3 km, the Pacific Ocean is also the deepest ocean. The next largest ocean is the Atlantic Ocean. The Atlantic Ocean has an average depth of 3.9 km. The Indian Ocean is the third-largest ocean and has an average depth of 3.9 km. The Southern Ocean is the fourth-largest ocean and extends from the coast of Antarctica to 60°S latitude. The Arctic Ocean is the smallest ocean, and it surrounds the North Pole.

A **sea** is a body of water that is smaller than an ocean and that may be partially surrounded by land. Examples of major seas include the Mediterranean Sea, the Caribbean Sea, and the South China Sea.

FLORIDA STANDARDS

LA.910.2.2.3 The student will organize information to show understanding or relationships among facts, ideas, and events (e.g., representing key points within text through charting, mapping, paraphrasing, summarizing, comparing, contrasting, or outlining); **MA.912.S.1.2** Determine appropriate and consistent standards of measurement for the data to be collected in a survey or experiment; **SC.912.E.6.5** Describe the geologic development of the present day oceans and identify commonly found features.

global ocean the body of salt water that covers nearly three-fourths of Earth's surface

sea a large, commonly saline body of water that is smaller than an ocean and that may be partially or completely surrounded by land

Figure 1 The global ocean is divided into oceans and seas. *How many oceans are on Earth?*

Exploration of the Ocean

The study of the physical and geological characteristics, chemical composition, and life-forms of the ocean is called **oceanography.** Although some ancient civilizations studied the ocean, modern oceanography did not begin until the 1850s.

oceanography the scientific study of the ocean, including the properties and movements of ocean water, the characteristics of the ocean floor, and the organisms that live in the ocean

www.scilinks.org
Topic: The Oceans
Code: HQX1069

Academic Vocabulary

research (REE SUHRCH) a careful search for and study of information

The Birth of Oceanography

An American naval officer named Matthew F. Maury used records from navy ships to learn about ocean currents, winds, depths, and weather conditions. In 1855, he published these observations as one of the first textbooks about the oceans. Then, from 1872 to 1876, a team of scientists aboard the British Navy ship HMS *Challenger* crossed the Atlantic, Indian, and Pacific Oceans. The scientists measured water temperatures at great depths and collected samples of ocean water, sediments, and thousands of marine organisms. The voyages of the HMS *Challenger* laid the foundation for the modern science of oceanography.

Today, many ships perform oceanographic research. In the 1990s and in the beginning of the 21st century, the research ship *JOIDES Resolution* was the world's largest and most sophisticated scientific drilling ship. Samples drilled by *JOIDES Resolution,* shown in **Figure 2,** provide scientists with valuable information about plate tectonics and the ocean floor. The Japanese ship *CHIKYU,* which is operated by the Integrated Ocean Drilling Program, is one of the most advanced drilling ships now in use.

Reading Check List three characteristics of the ocean that oceanographers study. (See Appendix G for answers to Reading Checks.)

Figure 2 Reentry cones (above) are used so that core samples can later be taken from the same place on the ocean floor. Scientists aboard the research ship *JOIDES Resolution* (right) perform scientific studies of the ocean floor.

Reflected
sound waves

Sound waves
from ship

THINK central

INTERACT ONLINE
Keyword: HQXOBAF3

Figure 3 Active sonar sends out a pulse of sound. The pulse, called a *ping* because of the way it sounds, reflects when it strikes a solid object.

READING TOOLBOX

Classification
Classify each type of tool used to collect data from oceans, including records from ships, samples taken from ships, sonar, and submersibles, as surface tools or deep-ocean tools.

Sonar

Oceanographic research ships are often equipped with sonar. **Sonar** is a system that uses acoustic signals and returned echoes to determine the location of objects or to communicate. Sonar is an acronym for *sound navigation and ranging*. A sonar transmitter sends out a continuous series of sound waves from a ship to the ocean floor, as shown in **Figure 3**. The sound waves travel at about 1,500 m/s through sea water and bounce off the solid ocean floor. The waves reflect back to a receiver. Scientists measure the time that the sound waves take to travel from the transmitter, to the ocean floor, and to the receiver in order to calculate the depth of the ocean floor. Scientists then use this information to make maps and profiles of the ocean floor.

sonar *sound navigation and ranging,* a system that uses acoustic signals and returned echoes to determine the location of objects or to communicate

SC.912.P.10.20

Quick **Lab** Sonar

 30 min

Procedure

❶ Use **heavy string** to tie one end of a **spring** securely to a **doorknob**. Pull the spring taut and parallel to the floor. You will need to keep the tension of the spring constant throughout the lab.

❷ Use **masking tape** to mark the floor directly beneath the hand that is holding the spring taut. Use a **meterstick** to measure and record the distance from that hand to the doorknob.

❸ Note the time on a **stopwatch or clock with a second hand**. Hold the spring taut, and hit the spring horizontally to create a compression wave.

❹ Check the time again to see how long the pulse takes to travel to the doorknob and back to your hand. Record the time.

❺ Repeat steps 2 to 4 three times. Each time, hold the spring 60 cm closer to the doorknob. Keep tension constant by gathering coils as necessary.

❻ Calculate the rate of travel for each trial by multiplying the distance between your hand and the doorknob by 2. Then, divide by the number of seconds the pulse took to travel to the doorknob and back.

Analysis

1. Did the rate the pulse traveled change during the course of the investigation?

2. If a pulse took 3 s to travel to the doorknob and back to your hand, what is the distance from the doorknob to your hand?

3. How is the apparatus you used similar to sonar? How is the apparatus different than sonar? Explain.

Submersibles

Underwater research vessels, called *submersibles,* also enable oceanographers to study the ocean depths. Some submersibles are piloted by people. One such submersible is the *bathysphere,* a spherical diving vessel that remains connected to the research ship for communications and life support. Another type of piloted submersible, called a *bathyscaph,* is a self-propelled, free-moving submarine. One of the most well-known bathyscaphs is the *Alvin.* Another modern submersible, called *Nautile* (NOH teel), is shown in **Figure 4.**

Other modern submersibles are submarine robots. They can take photographs, collect mineral samples from the ocean floor, and perform many other tasks. These robotic submersibles are remotely piloted and allow oceanographers to study the ocean depths for long periods of time.

Underwater Research

Submersibles have helped scientists make exciting discoveries about the deep ocean. During one dive in a submersible, startled oceanographers saw communities of unusual marine life living at depths and temperatures where scientists thought that almost no life could exist. Giant clams, blind white crabs, and giant tube worms were some of the strange life-forms that were discovered. Many of these life-forms have unusual adaptations that allow them to live in hostile environments. The angler fish, shown in **Figure 4,** can produce its own light, which attracts prey.

Figure 4 The submersible *Nautile* (top) carries enough oxygen to keep a three-person crew underwater for more than five hours. Deep-sea submersibles have discovered many strange organisms in the deep ocean, such as this angler fish (bottom).

Section 1 Review

LA.910.2.2.3

Key Ideas

1. **Name** the five major divisions of the global ocean.

2. **Explain** the difference between an ocean and a sea.

3. **Define** *oceanography.*

4. **Describe** two ways that oceanographers study the ocean.

5. **Explain** how sonar works.

6. **Describe** two aspects of the ocean that submersibles are used to study.

7. **List** three types of submersibles.

Critical Thinking

8. **Evaluating Ideas** Most submarines use sonar as a navigation aid. How would sonar enable an underwater vessel to move through the ocean depths?

9. **Analyzing Methods** Why are submarine robots more practical for deep-ocean research than submersibles designed to carry people are?

Concept Mapping

10. Use the following terms to create a concept map: *oceanography, submersible, bathysphere, bathyscaph, robot submersible,* and *sonar.*

Features of the Ocean Floor

Key Ideas	Key Terms	Why It Matters
❯ Describe the main features of the continental margins. ❯ Describe the main features of the deep-ocean basin.	**continental margin** **deep-ocean basin** **trench** **abyssal plain**	Shelves and basins are features not just of your kitchen but of the ocean floor—home to the tallest mountains and flattest plains on Earth.

The ocean floor can be divided into two major areas, as shown in **Figure 1.** The **continental margins** are shallow parts of the ocean floor that are made of continental crust and a thick wedge of sediment. The other major area is the **deep-ocean basin,** which is made of oceanic crust and a thin sediment layer. It forms the deep part of the ocean beyond the continental margin.

Continental Margins

The line that divides the continental crust from the oceanic crust is not abrupt or distinct. Shorelines are not the true boundaries between the oceanic crust and the continental crust. The boundaries are actually some distance offshore and beneath the ocean and the thick sediments of the continental margin.

Continental Shelf

Continents are outlined in most places by a zone of shallow water where the ocean covers the edge of the continent. The part of the continent that is covered by water is called a *continental shelf*. The shelf usually slopes gently from the shoreline and drops about 0.12 m every 100 m. The average depth of the water covering a continental shelf is about 60 m. Though underwater, a continental shelf is part of the continental margin, not the deep-ocean basin.

Changes in sea level affect the continental shelves. During glacial periods, continental ice sheets hold large amounts of water. So, sea level falls and exposes more of the continental shelf to weathering and erosion. But if ice sheets melt adding water to the oceans, sea level rises and covers the continental shelf.

FLORIDA STANDARDS

SC.912.E.6.5 Describe the geologic development of the present day oceans and identify commonly found features; **SC.912.E.7.3** Differentiate and describe the various interactions among Earth systems, including: atmosphere, hydrosphere, cryosphere, geosphere, and biosphere.

continental margin the shallow sea floor that is located between the shoreline and the deep-ocean bottom

deep-ocean basin the part of the ocean floor that is under deep water beyond the continent margin and that is composed of oceanic crust and a thin layer of sediment

Figure 1 The ocean floor includes the continental margins and the deep-ocean basin.

Continental margin

Continental shelf

Continental slope

Continental rise

Submarine canyon

Figure 2 The ocean floor is made of distinct areas and features.

Continental Slope and Continental Rise

At the seaward edge of a continental shelf is a steeper slope called a *continental slope*. The boundary between the continental crust and the oceanic crust is located at the base of the continental slope. Along the continental slope, the ocean depth increases by several thousand meters within an average distance of about 20 kilometers, as shown in **Figure 2.** The continental shelf and continental slope may be cut by deep V-shaped valleys. These deep valleys are called *submarine canyons*. These deep canyons are often found near the mouths of major rivers. Other canyons may form over time as very dense currents called *turbidity currents* carry large amounts of sediment down the continental slopes. Turbidity currents form when earthquakes cause underwater landslides or when large sediment loads run down a slope. These sediments form a wedge at the base of the continental slope called a *continental rise*.

Deep-Ocean Basins

Deep-ocean basins also have distinct features, as shown in **Figure 2.** These features include broad, flat plains; submerged volcanoes; gigantic mountain ranges; and deep trenches. In the deep-ocean basins, the mountains are higher and the plains are flatter than any features found on the continents.

Reading Check What features are located in the deep-ocean basins?

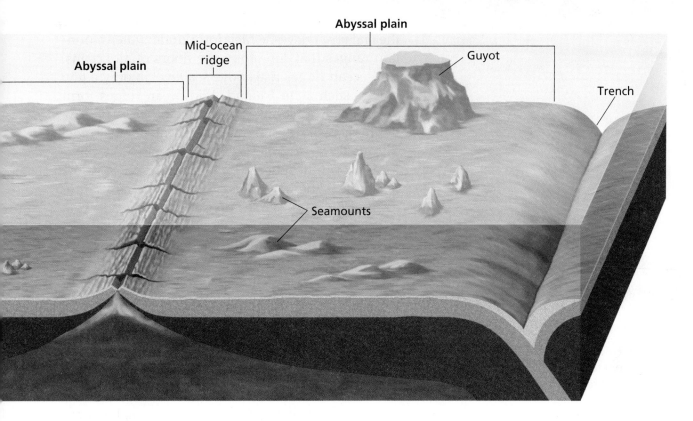

Abssal plain

Mid-ocean ridge

Abyssal plain

Guyot

Trench

Seamounts

Trenches

Long, narrow depressions located in the deep-ocean basins are called **trenches.** At more than 11,000 m deep, the Mariana Trench, in the western Pacific Ocean, is the deepest place in Earth's crust. Trenches form where one tectonic plate subducts below another plate. Earthquakes occur near trenches. Volcanic mountain ranges and volcanic island arcs also form near trenches.

Abyssal Plains

The vast, flat areas of the deep-ocean basins where the ocean is more than 4 km deep are called **abyssal plains** (uh BIS uhl PLAYNZ). Abyssal plains cover about half of the deep-ocean basins and are the flattest regions on Earth. In some places, the ocean depth changes less than 3 m over more than 1,300 km.

Layers of fine sediment cover the abyssal plains. Ocean currents and wind carry some sediments from the continental margins. Other sediment is made when organisms that live in the ocean settle to the ocean floor when they die.

The thickness of sediments on the abyssal plains is determined by three factors. The age of the oceanic crust is one factor. Older crust is generally covered with thicker sediments than younger crust is. The distance from the continental margin to the abyssal plain also determines how much sediment reaches the plain from the continent. Third, the sediment cover on abyssal plains that are bordered by trenches is generally thinner than the sediment cover on abyssal plains that are not bordered by trenches.

trench a long, narrow, and steep depression that forms on the ocean floor as a result of subduction of a tectonic plate, that runs parallel to the trend of a chain of volcanic islands or the coastline of a continent, and that may be as deep as 11 km below sea level; also called an *ocean trench* or a *deep-ocean trench*

abyssal plain a large, flat, almost level area of the deep-ocean basin

Academic Vocabulary

layer (LAY uhr) a separate or distinct portion of matter that has thickness

Figure 3 The white ridges in this photo are coral reefs of an atoll that formed in the shallow waters around a volcanic island. Erosion is changing the island into a guyot.

Mid-Ocean Ridges

The most prominent features of ocean basins are the *mid-ocean ridges,* which form underwater mountain ranges that run along the floors of all oceans. Mid-ocean ridges rise above sea level in only a few places, such as in Iceland. Mid-ocean ridges form where plates pull away from each other. A narrow depression, or rift, runs along the center of the ridge. Through this rift, magma reaches the sea floor and forms new lithosphere. This new lithosphere is less dense than the old lithosphere. As the new lithosphere cools, it becomes denser and begins to sink as it moves away from the rift. Fault-bounded blocks of crust that form parallel to the ridges as the lithosphere cools and contracts are called *abyssal hills.*

As ridges adjust to changes in the direction of plate motions, they break into segments that are bounded by faults. These faults create areas of rough topography called *fracture zones,* which run perpendicularly across the ridge.

Seamounts

Submerged volcanic mountains that are taller than 1 km are called *seamounts.* Seamounts form in areas of increased volcanic activity called *hot spots.* Seamounts that rise above the ocean surface form oceanic islands. As tectonic plate movements carry islands away from a hot spot, the islands sink and are eroded by waves to form flat-topped, submerged seamounts called *guyots* (GEE OHZ) or *tablemounts.* An intermediate stage in this process, called an *atoll,* is shown in **Figure 3.**

Section 2 Review

LA.910.2.2.3; SC.912.E.6.5; SC.912.E.7.3

Key Ideas

1. **Describe** the three main sections of the continental margins.

2. **Describe** where the boundary between the oceanic crust and the continental crust is located.

3. **Explain** how turbidity currents are related to submarine canyons.

4. **List** four main features of the deep-ocean basins, and describe one characteristic of each feature.

5. **Compare** seamounts, guyots, and atolls.

6. **Explain** the difference between the meanings of the terms *continental margin, continental shelf, continental slope,* and *continental rise.*

Critical Thinking

7. **Making Inferences** The Pacific Ocean is surrounded by trenches, but the Atlantic Ocean is not. In addition, the Pacific Ocean is wider than the Atlantic Ocean, and much of the crust under the Pacific Ocean is very young. Which ocean's abyssal plain has thicker sediments? Explain your answer.

8. **Determining Cause and Effect** If sea level were to fall significantly, what would happen to the continental shelves?

Concept Mapping

9. Use the following terms to create a concept map: *continental margin, deep-ocean basin, continental shelf, continental slope, continental rise, trench, abyssal plain,* and *mid-ocean ridge.*

SECTION
3 Ocean-Floor Sediments

Key Ideas	Key Terms	Why It Matters
❯ Describe the formation of ocean-floor sediments. ❯ Explain how ocean-floor sediments are classified by their physical composition.	core sample nodule	Products you use every day contain ocean-floor sediments.

Continental shelves and slopes are covered with sediments. Sediments are carried into the ocean by rivers, are washed away from the shoreline by wave erosion, or settle to the ocean bottom when the organisms that created them die. The composition of ocean sediments varies and depends on which part of the ocean floor the sediments form in. The sediments are fairly well sorted by size. Coarse gravel and sand are usually found close to shore because these heavier sediments do not move easily offshore. Lighter particles are suspended in ocean water and are usually deposited at a great distance from shore.

FLORIDA STANDARDS

SC.912.E.6.5 Describe the geologic development of the present day oceans and identify commonly found features; **SC.912.E.7.3** Differentiate and describe the various interactions among Earth systems, including: atmosphere, hydrosphere, cryosphere, geosphere, and biosphere; **SC.912.N.1.6** Describe how scientific inferences are drawn from scientific observations and provide examples from the content being studied.

Sources of Deep Ocean–Basin Sediments

Sediments found in the deep-ocean basin, which is beyond the continental margin, are generally finer than those found in shallow water. Samples of the sediments in the deep-ocean basins can be gathered by scooping up sediments or by taking core samples. **Core samples** are cylinders of sediment that are collected by drilling into sediment layers on the ocean floor. **Figure 1** shows a core sample being studied aboard the research vessel *JOIDES Resolution*.

The study of sediment samples shows that most of the sediments in the deep-ocean basins are made of materials that settle slowly from the ocean water above. These materials may come from organic or inorganic sources.

core sample a cylindrical piece of sediment, rock, soil, snow, or ice that is collected by drilling

Figure 1 A scientist studies a core sample that was brought up from the drill aboard the research ship *JOIDES Resolution*.

645

Inorganic Sediments

Some ocean-basin sediments are rock particles that were carried from land by rivers. When a river empties into the ocean, the river deposits its sediment load, as shown in **Figure 2**. Most of these sediments are deposited along the shore and on the continental shelf. However, large quantities of these sediments occasionally slide down continental slopes to the ocean floor below. The force of the slide creates powerful turbidity currents that spread the sediments over the continental rise and abyssal plains. Other deep ocean-basin sediments consist of fine particles of rock, including volcanic dust, that have been blown great distances out to sea by the wind. These particles land on the surface of the water, sink, and gradually settle to the bottom of the ocean.

Icebergs also provide sediments that can end up on the ocean basins. As a glacier moves across the land, the glacier picks up rock. The rock becomes embedded in the ice and moves with the glacier. When an iceberg breaks from the glacier, drifts out to sea, and melts, the rock material sinks to the ocean floor.

Even meteorites contribute to deep ocean-basin sediments. Much of a meteorite vaporizes as it enters Earth's atmosphere. The remaining cosmic dust falls to Earth's surface. Because most of Earth's surface is ocean, most meteorite fragments fall into the ocean and become part of the sediments on the ocean floor.

Figure 2 This picture of sediment emptying out of the Mahakam River in Indonesia was taken by astronauts aboard the space shuttle *Columbia*.

Why It Matters

How Do You Turn Mud Into Money?

Oozy mud from underwater may not seem particularly valuable, but ocean sediments are part of a wide variety of familiar products. For example, diatomaceous earth, which comes from the hardened deposits of siliceous oozes, is added to some products for its abrasive qualities. Abrasive qualities are important in such products as toothpaste and metal polishes. Many paints also have diatomaceous earth mixed with them as fine grit.

PURE BRISTLES
63 Italia

YOUR TURN

ONLINE RESEARCH
What are some of the environmental impacts of marine mining?

646

Figure 3 Nodules, such as these mined from the East Pacific Rise, are rich in a variety of minerals.

Biogenic Sediments

In many places on the ocean floor, almost all of the sediments are *biogenic*, meaning that the sediments were originally produced by living organisms. Biogenic sediments are the remains of marine plants, animals, and other organisms. The two most common compounds that make up organic sediments are silica, SiO_2, and calcium carbonate, $CaCO_3$. Silica comes primarily from microscopic organisms called *diatoms* and *radiolarians*. Calcium carbonate comes mostly from the skeletons of tiny organisms called *foraminifera*.

Chemical Deposits

When substances that are dissolved in ocean water crystallize, these materials can form mineral deposits on the ocean floor. Some of these mineral deposits are potato-shaped lumps called **nodules.** Nodules, such as the ones shown in **Figure 3**, are commonly located on the abyssal plains. Nodules are composed mainly of the oxides of manganese, nickel, copper, and iron. Other minerals, such as phosphates, are also carried in the ocean water before they crystallize and form mineral deposits on the ocean floor.

Reading Check How do nodules form?

Math Skills

Ocean-Floor Sediments Ocean-floor sediments are composed of an average of 54% biogenic sediments, 45% Earth rocks and dust, less than 1% precipitation of dissolved materials (nodules and phosphates), and less than 1% of rocks and dust from space. If you collected 10,000 kg of ocean-floor sediment, how many kilograms of each type of ocean-floor sediment would you expect to find?

SC.912.L.14.2

Quick Lab 20 min

Diatoms

Procedure

❶ Observe **diatoms** under a **microscope.**

❷ Sketch what you see. Make sure to note the magnification.

Analysis

1. What characteristics of the diatoms did you observe?

2. Propose one possible function for each of the structures you observed.

nodule a lump of minerals that is made of oxides of manganese, iron, copper, or nickel and that is found in scattered groups on the ocean floor

Figure 4 The remains of diatoms (left) and radiolarians (right), both magnified hundreds of times in these photos, are important components of biogenic sediments on the ocean floor.

READING TOOLBOX

Spider Maps
Create a spider map that has two legs and several lines on each leg. Use the map to compare muds and ooze.

Academic Vocabulary
classify (CLAH sih fie) to arrange or divide into categories according to type

SCiLINKS®
www.scilinks.org
Topic: Ocean-Floor
Sediments
Code: HQX1068

Physical Classification of Sediments

Deep ocean-floor sediments can be classified into two basic types. *Muds* are very fine silt- and clay-sized particles of rock. One common type of mud on the abyssal plains is red clay. Red clay is made of at least 40% clay particles and is mixed with silt, sand, and biogenic material. This clay can vary in color from red to gray, blue, green, or yellow-brown. About 40% of the ocean floor is covered with soft, fine sediment called *ooze*. At least 30% of the ooze is biogenic materials, such as the remains of microscopic sea organisms. The remaining material is fine mud.

Ooze can be classified into two types. *Calcareous ooze* is ooze that is made mostly of calcium carbonate. Calcareous ooze is never found below a depth of 5 km, because at depths between 3 km and 5 km, calcium carbonate dissolves in the deep, cold ocean water. *Siliceous ooze*, which can be found at any depth, is made of mostly silicon dioxide, which comes from the shells of radiolarians and diatoms. Examples of remains of these organisms are shown in **Figure 4.** Most siliceous ooze is found in the cool, nutrient-rich ocean waters around Antarctica because of the abundance of diatoms and radiolarians in that location.

Section 3 Review

LA.910.2.2.3; SC.912.E.6.5; SC.912.E.7.3

Key Ideas

1. **Describe** the formation of two different types of ocean-floor sediments.

2. **Summarize** how icebergs contribute to deep ocean-basin sediments.

3. **Explain** how substances that are dissolved in ocean water travel to the ocean floor.

4. **Explain** how ocean-floor sediments are classified by physical composition.

5. **Describe** how scientists define the word *mud*.

6. **Compare** the compositions of calcareous ooze and siliceous ooze.

Critical Thinking

7. **Making Inferences** What could you infer from a core sample of a layer of sediment that contains volcanic ash and dust?

8. **Applying Ideas** Some businesses have tried to develop methods of extracting nodules from the ocean. Name two factors that businesses should consider when they are determining whether extracting nodules is profitable.

Concept Mapping

9. Use the following terms to create a concept map: *nodule, inorganic sediment, biogenic sediment, diatom, chemical deposit,* and *ocean-floor sediment.*

Underwater Aliens

WEIRD SCIENCE

Thousands of meters underwater, how can any life exist in the extreme pressure, cold, and darkness? These conditions are as inhospitable to humans as another planet might be. Yet, with ever-improving technologies for exploring the ocean depths, scientists have been discovering underwater creatures that are stranger than science fiction. Peculiar traits of deep-sea organisms represent evolutionary adaptations to the extreme pressure, cold, and darkness of their environment. These discoveries raise new scientific questions, such as did shallow water species colonize the deep ocean or vice versa?

This boxfish is one of the new exotic deep-sea creatures recently discovered by scientists exploring Southeast Asia's Celebes Sea.

Nicknamed "big red" because of its unusual deep red color, this bizarre new bell-shaped species of jellyfish is a meter in diameter and was discovered in the deep waters off the California coast.

Known for their mismatched eyes, one of which is larger than the other to scope for prey in the deep's darkness, jewel squid live 500 meters beneath the surface of the North Atlantic.

This carnivorous moonsnail lives in the Antarctic deep sea. The polyps, covering its shell, use the moonsnail as transport to food sources.

Scientists found this cartoon-like squid among other new species while mapping a deep-sea mountain range in the North Atlantic.

 ONLINE RESEARCH
What are some of the more unusual adaptations that allow some marine life to live at extreme ocean depths? Explain why such adaptations are helpful.

CRITICAL THINKING
What harm might human interference from deep-sea mining have on these deep-sea creatures?

This tiny shrimp-like creature is an amphipod. It is nearly transparent and therefore almost invisible in the murky surroundings of the deep ocean.

Ocean-Floor Sediments

What You'll Do

> **Observe and record** the settling rates of four different sediments.

> **Draw conclusions** about how particle size affects settling rate.

> **Identify** factors that affect settling rate of sediments besides particle size.

What You'll Need

balance, metric
column, clear plastic, 80 cm × 4 cm
cup, paper
pencil, grease
ring stand with clamp
ruler, metric
sieve, 4 mm, 2 mm, 0.5 mm
soil, coarse, medium, medium-fine, and fine grain
stopper, rubber
stopwatch
tape, adhesive
teaspoon
towels, paper
water

Safety

Most of the ocean floor is covered with a layer of sediment that varies in thickness from 0.3 km to more than 1 km. Much of this sediment is thought to have originated on land through the process of weathering. Through erosion, the sediment has made its way to the deep-ocean basins. In this lab, you will use sediment samples of four particle sizes to determine the relationship between the size of particles and the settling rate of the particles in water.

Procedure

1. Take one sample of sediment from each of the following size ranges: coarse, medium, medium-fine, and fine.

2. Plug one end of the plastic column with a rubber stopper, and secure the stopper to the column with tape. Place the column in a vertical position using the ring stand and clamp. Carefully fill the column with water to a level about 5 cm from the top, and allow the water to stand until all large air bubbles have escaped.

3. Use the grease pencil to mark the water level on the column. This will be the starting line.

4. Next, draw a line about 5 cm from the bottom of the column. This will be the finish line.

5. Have a member of your lab group put 1 tsp of the coarse sample into the water column. The other group member should record three time measurements as follows:

   a. Using a stopwatch, start timing when the first particles hit the start line on the column, and stop timing when they reach the finish line. Perform this procedure three times. Record the time for each trial in a table similar to the one shown below.

   b. Next, use the stopwatch to determine how long it takes the last particle in the sample to travel from the start line to the finish line. Perform this procedure three times. Record the time for each trial in your table.

Soil samples		Trial 1	Trial 2	Trial 3	Average
Coarse	First time measurment:				
	Second time measurement:				
Medium	First time measurement:				
	Second time measurement:				

6 Determine the average time of the three trials for the first measurement. Do the same for the second measurement. Record the averages.

7 Pour the soil and water from the column into the container provided by your teacher. (Note: Do not pour the soil into the sink.)

8 Refill the plastic column with water up to the original level marked with the grease pencil.

9 Repeat steps 5 through 8 for the remaining sediment sizes. Record the measurements and the averages in your table.

10 With the plastic column filled with water, pour 20 g of unsieved soil into the column, and allow the soil to settle for 5 min. After 5 min, look at the column and record your observations of both the settled sediment and the water. Repeat step 7, and then answer the questions below.

Step 5

Analysis

1. **Organizing Data** Which particles settled fastest? Which particles settled slowest?

2. **Making Comparisons** Compare the settling time of the medium particles with the settling time of the medium-fine particles. Do similar-sized particles fall at the same rate?

3. **Making Inferences** In step 10, why did the water remain slightly cloudy even after most of the particles had settled?

4. **Evaluating Methods** How do the results in step 10 help to explain why the deep-ocean basins are covered with a layer of very fine sediment while areas near the shore are covered with coarse sediment?

5. **Making Predictions** Other than size, what factors do you think would influence the speed at which particles fall in water? Explain your answer.

Extension

Analyzing Predictions Obtain particles of different shapes, such as long, cylindrical grains; flat, disk-shaped grains; round grains; and angular grains. Test the settling times of these grains, and write a brief paragraph that explains how grain shape affects the settling rate of particles in water.

Total Sediment Thickness of Earth's Oceans

Thickness in Meters

Map ▶ Skills Activity

This map shows the total thicknesses of sediments on Earth's ocean floors. Use the map to answer the questions below.

1. **Using a Key** What is the approximate thickness of the sediment located at 45°S and 45°W?

2. **Analyzing Data** Use latitude and longitude to identify two areas that have the thickest sediments.

3. **Comparing Areas** Compare the amount of sediment near the middle of the oceans with the amount of sediment on the continental margins.

4. **Identifying Trends** Rivers deposit massive amounts of sediment when they reach the ocean. Based on this map, at what locations would you expect to find mouths of major rivers?

5. **Inferring Relationships** Which coast of South America—east or west—is most likely bordered by a trench?

6. **Analyzing Relationships** Why does this map contain white spaces even though the key lists no thickness that corresponds with the color white?

THINK central
SUPER SUMMARY
Keyword: HQXOBAS

Key Ideas

Key Terms

The Water Planet

❯ The global ocean can be divided into five major oceans—the Pacific, Atlantic, Indian, Arctic, and Southern Oceans—and many smaller seas.

❯ Oceanography is the study of the oceans and the seas. Oceanographers study the ocean using research ships, sonar, and submersibles.

❯ Sonar is a system that uses acoustic signals and echo returns to determine the location of objects or to communicate.

global ocean, p. 637
sea, p. 637
oceanography, p. 638
sonar, p. 639

Features of the Ocean Floor

❯ Continental margins include the continental shelf, the continental slope, and the continental rise.

❯ Features of deep-ocean basins include trenches, abyssal plains, mid-ocean ridges, and seamounts.

continental margin, p. 641
deep-ocean basin, p. 641
trench, p. 643
abyssal plain, p. 643

Ocean-Floor Sediments

❯ Ocean-floor sediments form from inorganic and biogenic materials as well as from chemical deposits.

❯ Based on physical characteristics, deep ocean-floor sediments are classified as mud or as ooze.

core sample, p. 645
nodule, p. 647

1. **Spider Map** Create a spider map that has two legs and several lines on each leg. Use the map to compare the global ocean and a sea. SC.912.E.6.5

READING TOOLBOX

USING KEY TERMS

Use each of the following terms in a separate sentence.

2. *oceanography*
3. *sonar* SC.912.E.6.5
4. *core sample* SC.912.E.6.5

For each pair of terms, explain how the meanings of the terms differ.

5. *trench* and *abyssal plain* SC.912.E.6.5
6. *submersible* and *nodule* SC.912.E.6.5
7. *continental margin* and *deep-ocean basin* SC.912.E.6.5
8. *oceanography* and *core sample* SC.912.E.6.5
9. *mud* and *ooze* SC.912.E.6.5

UNDERSTANDING KEY IDEAS

10. A self-propelled, free-moving submarine that is equipped for ocean research is a SC.912.E.6.5
    a. turbidity.
    b. bathysphere.
    c. bathyscaph.
    d. guyot.

11. A system that is used for determining the depth of the ocean floor is SC.912.E.6.5
    a. a guyot.
    b. radiolarians.
    c. a bathysphere.
    d. sonar.

12. The parts of the ocean floor that are made up of continental crust are called SC.912.E.6.5
    a. continental margins.
    b. abyssal plains.
    c. mid-ocean ridges.
    d. trenches.

13. The accumulation of sediments at the base of the continental slope is called the SC.912.E.6.5
    a. trench.
    b. turbidity current.
    c. continental margin.
    d. continental rise.

14. The deepest parts of the ocean are called SC.912.E.6.5
    a. trenches.
    b. submarine canyons.
    c. abyssal plains.
    d. continental rises.

15. Large quantities of the inorganic sediment that makes up the continental rise come from SC.912.E.6.5
    a. turbidity currents.
    b. earthquakes.
    c. diatoms.
    d. nodules.

16. Potato-shaped lumps of minerals on the ocean floor are called SC.912.E.6.5
    a. guyots.   c. foraminiferans.
    b. nodules.   d. diatoms.

17. Very fine particles of silt and clay that have settled to the ocean floor are called SC.912.E.6.5
    a. muds.   c. guyots.
    b. seamounts.   d. nodules.

SHORT ANSWER

18. What are the differences between a seamount and a guyot? SC.912.E.6.5
19. Explain how sonar is used to study the oceans.
20. List three ways that scientists can learn about the deep ocean. SC.912.E.6.5
21. How do fine sediments reach the deep-ocean bottom? SC.912.E.6.5
22. What effects do deep-ocean trenches have on the sediment thickness of the abyssal plain?
23. List the three main types of ocean-floor sediments, and describe how they are deposited. SC.912.E.6.5

24. Making Comparisons The exploration of the ocean depths has been compared with the exploration of space. What similarities exist between these two environments and the attempts by people to explore them?

25. Making Predictions What may be the eventual fate of seamounts as they are carried along the spreading oceanic crust? SC.912.E.6.5

26. Analyzing Ideas A type of fish is known to exist only in one river in the central United States. Explain how the fossilized remains of this fish might become part of the sediments on the ocean floor. SC.912.E.6.5

27. Analyzing Relationships Explain how it is possible that scientists have found some red clays on the ocean floor that contain material from outer space. SC.912.E.6.5

CONCEPT MAPPING

28. Use the following terms to create a concept map: *deep-ocean basin, continental shelf, mud, ooze, calcareous ooze, siliceous ooze,* and *sediment.* SC.912.E.6.5

MATH SKILLS   Math Skills

29. Making Calculations The total area of Earth is approximately 511,000,000 km². About 71% of Earth's surface is covered with water. Calculate the area of Earth, in square kilometers, that is covered with water.

WRITING SKILLS

30. Writing from Research Prepare a brief report on the different types of submersibles. Your report should explain the special features of each type of submersible as well as how each type has contributed to oceanographers' knowledge of the oceans.

31. Creative Writing Create an imaginary walking tour of the ocean basins. Your tour should begin at the edge of a continent—perhaps at a beach on the east coast of Florida. Explain exactly what tourists should look for along the continental margin and the ocean floor on their way to the western coast of Africa. SC.912.E.6.5

INTERPRETING GRAPHICS

The graph below compares elevations of land and depths of oceans on Earth's surface. Use the graph to answer the questions that follow.

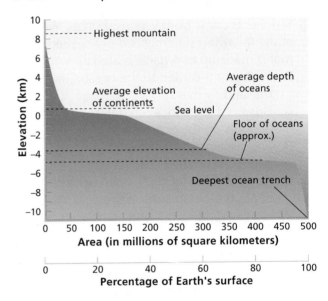

32. What percentage of Earth's surface is covered by land? SC.912.E.6.5

33. Which is greater: the elevation of the highest mountain above sea level or the depth of the deepest ocean trench below sea level? SC.912.E.6.5

34. Relative to sea level, how many times greater is the average depth of the ocean than the average elevation of land? SC.912.E.6.5

35. According to this diagram, how many millions of square kilometers of crust is under ocean water? SC.912.E.6.5

Understanding Concepts

Directions (1–9): For each question, write on a separate sheet of paper the letter of the correct answer.

1 Continental shelves are affected by changes in sea level. Which of the following statements describes such a change?
- **A.** During an ice age, more of the continental shelf is exposed to weathering and erosion.
- **B.** During an ice age, the continental shelf becomes part of the deep-ocean basin.
- **C.** During an ice age, water over the continental shelf is deeper.
- **D.** During an ice age, the slope of the continental shelf drastically increases.

2 Sediments come from various sources. Which of the following statements describes sediment that is made up of organic material?
- **F.** Sediment is carried to the ocean floor from the land by rivers.
- **G.** Dissolved substances crystallize and form deposits on the ocean floor.
- **H.** The remains of marine organisms are deposited on the ocean floor.
- **I.** An iceberg melts in the open ocean, depositing sediments on the ocean floor.

3 To spend a large amount of time identifying and describing organisms that live in the deepest parts of the ocean, scientists might use
- **A.** sonar, which uses acoustic signals.
- **B.** a bathysphere, which is a submersible that remains attached to a ship.
- **C.** a bathyscaph, which is a submersible that is free-moving and self-propelled.
- **D.** a submarine robot, which is remotely piloted and does not carry passengers.

4 The study of deep-ocean sediment samples shows that
- **F.** most of the sediments came from the crust.
- **G.** most of the sediments settled from above.
- **H.** sediments cannot be organic.
- **I.** sediments cannot be inorganic.

5 Ooze is made up of 30% biogenic materials. This ooze is made up of
- **A.** calcareous ooze and siliceous ooze.
- **B.** silt and clay.
- **C.** clay and microscopic organisms.
- **D.** red clay and calcium carbonate.

6 Which of the following is NOT a determining factor in the thickness of sediments on abyssal plains?
- **F.** the location of the abyssal plain near a trench
- **G.** the distance from the continental margin
- **H.** the age of the oceanic crust
- **I.** the depth of the water over the abyssal plain

7 Which of the following is true of boundaries between continental crust and oceanic crust?
- **A.** Shorelines are true boundaries between the oceanic crust and the continental crust.
- **B.** Boundaries between continental crust and oceanic crust are beneath the ocean.
- **C.** Boundaries between continental crust and oceanic crust occur between the continental shelf and the continental slope.
- **D.** Oceanic crust and continental crust form boundaries in the shallowest areas of the continental shelf.

8 In deep ocean basins, volcanic activity does NOT typically occur
- **F.** on the vast, flat abyssal plains.
- **G.** at trenches, which form where a tectonic plate subducts under another plate.
- **H.** at mid-ocean ridges, which form where plates pull apart from each other.
- **I.** at hot spots, including seamounts.

9 Sediments settle throughout the ocean. These sediments are
- **A.** suspended in ocean water.
- **B.** coarser close to shore.
- **C.** inorganic materials.
- **D.** heavier in the deepest parts of the ocean.

Interpreting Graphics

Directions (10–11): For each question below, record the correct answer on a separate sheet of paper.

Studying the Ocean Floor with Sonar

10 Based on the figure above, which of the following best summarizes how sound waves are used?

F. A sound source dragged behind the boat emits waves that penetrate the different layers of the sea floor and bounce back to the receiver.

G. A sound source in front of the boat emits waves that penetrate the different layers of the sea floor and then bounce back to the receiver.

H. A receiver dragged behind the boat emits waves that penetrate the different layers of the sea floor and then bounce back to the receiver.

I. A receiver in front of the boat emits waves that penetrate the different layers of the sea floor and then bounce back to the receiver.

Composition of Ocean-Floor Sediments

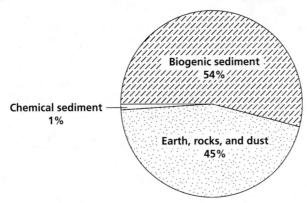

11 Based on the graph above, what percentage of ocean-floor sediments is organic?

A. 1%

B. 45%

C. 46%

D. 54%

> **Test Tip**
>
> Before choosing an answer to a question, try to answer the question without looking at the answer choices on the test.

Chapter 24 Ocean Water

Chapter Outline

Why It Matters

Oceans are home to thousands of species and play a vital role in Earth's ecology. Important resources, including food and fresh water, come from oceans.

Inquiry Lab

Testing Temperature and Gauging Gases

45 min

Open a can of soda at room temperature and a can of chilled soda at the same time. Use a thermometer to measure the temperature of the soda in each can. Pour the soda from each can into a 500 mL beaker, and "swirl" the soda three times. Using a stopwatch, time how long it takes for the "fizziness" in each soda to die down. Return the cold soda to the refrigerator. Repeat the measurements on both sodas at 10 min intervals for the next 40 min. When you have collected all your data, use a pencil to plot your data on graph paper. Your graph should contain two lines: one for the warm soda and one for the cold soda.

SC.912.E.7.3

Questions to Get You Started

1. Compare the ability of the sodas to retain dissolved gases over time. What is the effect of temperature?

2. Do you think temperature affects the exchange of gases between the ocean and the atmosphere in the same way? Explain your answer.

FoldNotes

Key-Term Fold A key-term fold can help you learn the key terms in this chapter.

Your Turn Make a key-term fold, as described in **Appendix A.**

❶ Write each key term from the Chapter Summary on the front of a tab. The first few terms are shown here.

❷ As you read the chapter, write the definition of each term under the appropriate tab.

❸ Use this FoldNote to study the key terms.

Salinity

Pack ice

Thermocline

Comparisons

Analyzing Comparisons Comparisons are often signaled in language by the use of a few key words or structures. The words *similar* and *dissimilar* can tell you whether the comparison is focused on similarities or differences. Often, a comparison describes one thing as *greater than, less than,* or ____ *than* another thing in some way.

Your Turn As you read Sections 1 and 2, fill out a table of comparisons like the one below. The sample entry is for the sentence, "The large amount of dissolved solids in ocean water makes it denser than pure fresh water."

First thing	Second thing	Similarity or difference	Signaling word or phrase
ocean water	fresh water	Ocean water is denser than fresh water.	denser

Note Taking

Comparison Table You can use a comparison table to organize your notes as you compare related topics. A table that compares mineral and energy resources found in the ocean has been started for you. It includes the following:

• topics that you are going to compare
• specific characteristics that you are going to compare

Your Turn Make a table like the one below. As you read Section 3, complete your table. Add columns and rows as needed.

	Petroleum	Nodules	Trace minerals
Resources included	oil, natural gas		
Where found			dissolved in ocean water
Problems involved			

For more information on how to use these and other tools, see **Appendix A.**

Properties of Ocean Water

Key Ideas

❯ Describe the chemical composition of ocean water.

❯ Describe the salinity, temperature, density, and color of ocean water.

Key Terms

salinity   thermocline
pack ice   density

Why It Matters

Ocean water is a complex mixture of chemicals that supports a vast range of living organisms.

Pure liquid water is tasteless, odorless, and colorless. However, the water in the ocean is not pure. Many solids and gases are dissolved in ocean water. In addition to dissolved substances, small particles of matter and tiny organisms are suspended in ocean water. Ocean water is a complex mixture of chemicals that sustains a variety of plant and animal life. Scientists study various properties of ocean water to understand the complex interactions between the oceans, the atmosphere, and the land.

Dissolved Gases

The two main gases in the atmosphere are nitrogen, N_2, and oxygen, O_2. These two gases are also the main gases dissolved in ocean water. While carbon dioxide, CO_2, is not a major component of the atmosphere, a large amount of this gas is dissolved in ocean water. Other atmospheric gases are also present in ocean water in small amounts.

Ocean water dissolves gases from a variety of sources, as shown in **Figure 1.** Gases may enter ocean water from water in streams and rivers. Some of the gases in ocean water come from volcanic eruptions beneath the ocean. Gases are also released directly into ocean water by organisms that live in the ocean. For example, many plants in the ocean make oxygen as a product of photosynthesis. However, most oxygen in the ocean enters at the surface of the ocean from the atmosphere.

FLORIDA STANDARDS

LA.910.2.2.3 The student will organize information to show understanding or relationships among facts, ideas, and events (e.g., representing key points within text through charting, mapping, paraphrasing, summarizing, comparing, contrasting, or outlining); **SC.912.E.7.9** Cite evidence that the ocean has had a significant influence on climate change by absorbing, storing, and moving heat, carbon, and water.

Figure 1 Gases can enter the ocean from streams, volcanoes, organisms, and the atmosphere.

Gases enter the ocean directly from the atmosphere.

Some gases in the ocean come from underwater volcanoes and marine organisms.

Gases enter the ocean from streams and rivers.

Temperature and Dissolved Gases

The temperature of water affects the amount of gas that dissolves in the water. Gases dissolve more readily in cold water than in warm water. You may have noticed this phenomenon when your glass of soda quickly goes "flat" on a warm day. The soda goes flat quickly because the CO_2 that makes the soda bubbly escapes into the air. But if the soda is kept in the refrigerator, the soda will retain its fizz longer. Because cold water dissolves gases more readily, water at the surface of the ocean in cold regions dissolves larger amounts of gases than water in warm tropical regions does.

Gases can return to the atmosphere from the ocean. If the water temperature rises, smaller amounts of gases will remain dissolved, and the excess gases will be released into the atmosphere. For example, warm equatorial ocean water tends to release CO_2 into the atmosphere, but ocean water at cooler, higher latitudes takes up large amounts of CO_2. Therefore, the ocean and the atmosphere are continuously exchanging gases as water temperature changes.

The Ocean as a Carbon Sink

The global ocean contains more than 60 times as much carbon as the atmosphere does. Dissolved CO_2 may be trapped in the ocean for hundreds to thousands of years. Because of this ability to dissolve and contain a large amount of CO_2, the ocean is commonly referred to as a *carbon sink*. Because gaseous CO_2 affects the atmosphere's ability to trap thermal energy from the sun, the ocean is important in the regulation of climate.

Why It Matters

Fresh Water in an Ocean of Salt

Each submarine crewmember needs about 20 liters of water per day. Carrying that much water would take up too much space, so submarines have distillation apparatus.

SCIENCE & SOCIETY

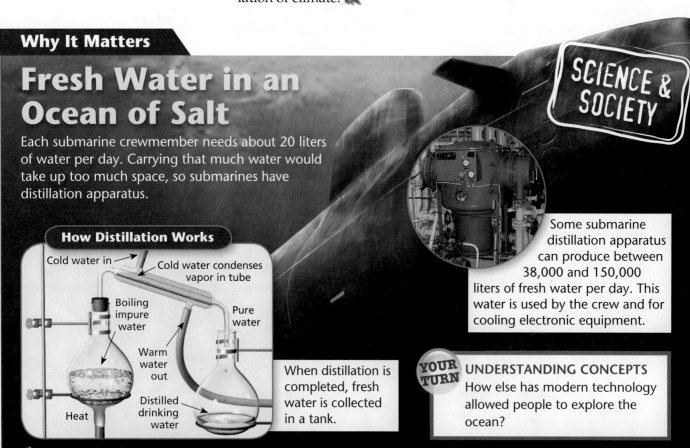

How Distillation Works

Cold water in

Cold water condenses vapor in tube

Boiling impure water

Pure water

Warm water out

Heat

Distilled drinking water

When distillation is completed, fresh water is collected in a tank.

Some submarine distillation apparatus can produce between 38,000 and 150,000 liters of fresh water per day. This water is used by the crew and for cooling electronic equipment.

YOUR TURN
UNDERSTANDING CONCEPTS
How else has modern technology allowed people to explore the ocean?

Figure 2 Dissolved solids make up 3.5% of the mass of ocean water. More than 85% of these dissolved solids are sodium and chlorine.

Magnesium
7.7%

Sulfur
3.7%

Sodium
30.6%

Calcium
1.2%

Potassium
1.1%

Other
0.7%

Chlorine
55.0%

Dissolved Solids

Ocean water is 96.5% pure water, or H_2O. Dissolved solids make up about 3.5% of the mass of ocean water. These dissolved solids, commonly called *sea salts*, give the ocean its salty taste.

Most Abundant Elements

Solids dissolved in ocean water are composed of about 75 chemical elements. The six most abundant elements in ocean water are chlorine, sodium, magnesium, sulfur, calcium, and potassium. The salt halite, which is composed of sodium and chloride ions, makes up more than 85% of the ocean's dissolved solids. The remaining dissolved solids consist of various other salts and minerals, as shown in **Figure 2.** *Trace elements* are elements that exist in very small amounts. Gold, zinc, and phosphorus are some of the trace elements that are found in the ocean.

Sources of Dissolved Solids

Most of the elements that form sea salts come from three main sources: volcanic eruptions, chemical weathering of rock on land, and chemical reactions between sea water and newly formed sea-floor rocks. Each year, rivers carry about 400 billion kilograms of dissolved solids into the ocean. Most of these dissolved solids are salts. As water evaporates from the ocean, salts and other minerals remain in the ocean. Only a small fraction of these salts and minerals are returned to the land in the water that falls as rain and snow during the water cycle.

✔ Reading Check **How do dissolved solids enter the ocean?**
(See Appendix G for answers to Reading Checks.)

 SC.912.E.7.3

Quick Lab
🕐 15 min

Dissolving Solids

Procedure

❶ Heat **200 mL of water** in a **beaker** over a **hot plate** until the water is about 60°C.

❷ Dissolve **table salt** in the water, 1 tsp at a time, until no more salt will dissolve. Record the total amount of salt that dissolves.

❸ Dissolve table salt, 1 tsp at a time, into **200 mL of water** that has been chilled in the refrigerator to about 5°C. Record the total amount of salt that dissolves.

Analysis

1. Which water sample dissolved the most salt?

2. Describe what would happen to the dissolved salt in the hot water if the hot water was chilled to 10°C.

Salinity of Ocean Water

Salinity is a measure of the amount of dissolved salts and other solids in a given liquid. Salinity can be measured by the number of grams of dissolved solids in 1,000 g of ocean water. For example, if 1,000 g of ocean water contained 35 g of solids, the salinity of the sample would be about 35 parts salt per 1,000 parts ocean water. This measurement is written as *salinity* = 35 parts per thousand, or 35‰. Thus, the ocean is about 3.5% salts. However, fresh water is less than 0.1% salt or has a salinity of less than 1‰. Modern instruments measure salinity by recording the conductivity of water, or how easily electricity moves through the water. The higher the salinity of water, the better its conductivity.

Factors That Change Salinity

Precipitation, such as rain and snow, is composed only of fresh water. When ocean surface water evaporates or freezes, only water molecules are removed from the ocean. Dissolved salts and other solids remain behind. Where the rate of evaporation is higher than the rate of precipitation, the salinity of surface water increases. Therefore, in equatorial water, where the rate of precipitation is highest, the salinity is lower than it is in subtropical water, where the rate of evaporation is highest.

Over most of the surface of the ocean, salinity ranges from 33‰ to 36‰. The global ocean has an average salinity of 34.7‰. However, salinity at particular locations can vary greatly, as shown in **Figure 3.** The salinity of the Red Sea, for example, is more than 40‰. The high salinity is due to the hot, dry climate around the Red Sea, which causes high levels of evaporation.

Figure 3 The average surface salinity of the global ocean varies from one location to another. *What effect do river mouths tend to have on the salinity of the surrounding ocean water?*

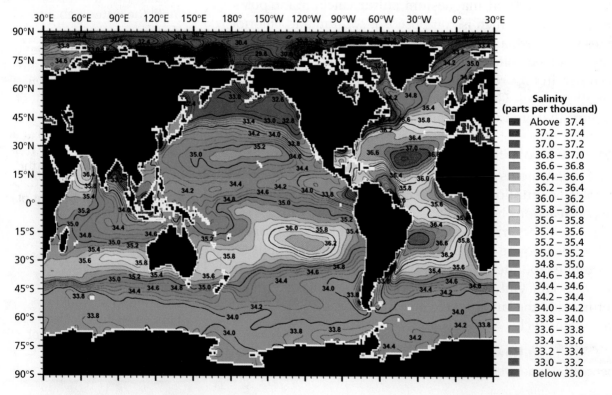

Salinity
(parts per thousand)

	Above 37.4
	37.2 – 37.4
	37.0 – 37.2
	36.8 – 37.0
	36.6 – 36.8
	36.4 – 36.6
	36.2 – 36.4
	36.0 – 36.2
	35.8 – 36.0
	35.6 – 35.8
	35.4 – 35.6
	35.2 – 35.4
	35.0 – 35.2
	34.8 – 35.0
	34.6 – 34.8
	34.4 – 34.6
	34.2 – 34.4
	34.0 – 34.2
	33.8 – 34.0
	33.6 – 33.8
	33.4 – 33.6
	33.2 – 33.4
	33.0 – 33.2
	Below 33.0

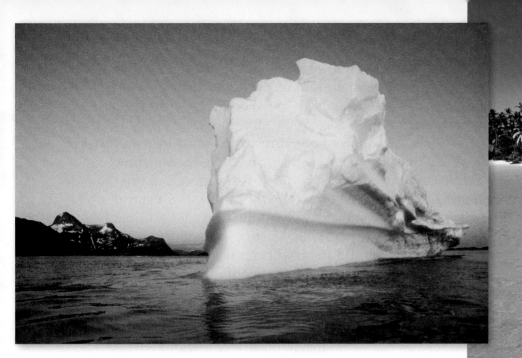

Temperature of Ocean Water

Like ocean salinity, ocean temperature varies depending on depth and location on the surface of the ocean. The range of ocean temperatures is affected by the amount of solar energy an area receives and by the movement of water in the ocean.

Surface Water

The mixing, by waves and currents, of the ocean's surface water distributes heat down-ward to a depth of 100 to 300 m. Thus, the temperature of this zone of surface water is relatively constant and decreases only slightly as depth increases. However, the temperature of surface water does decrease as latitude increases. Therefore, polar surface water is much cooler than the surface water in the tropics, as explained in **Figure 4.**

The total amount of solar energy that reaches the surface of the ocean is much greater at the equator than in areas near the North and South Poles. In tropical water, an ocean surface temperature of about 30 °C is common. The surface temperature in polar oceans, however, often drops as low as –1.9 °C. Because ocean water freezes at about –1.9 °C, vast areas of sea ice exist in polar oceans. A floating layer of sea ice that completely covers an area of the ocean surface is called **pack ice.** Usually, pack ice is no more than 5 m thick because the ice insulates the water below and prevents it from freezing. In the middle latitudes, the ocean surface temperature varies depending on the seasons. In some areas, the ocean surface temperature may vary by as much as 10 °C and 20 °C between summer and winter.

Reading Check **What factors affect the surface temperature of the ocean?**

Figure 4 The surface temperature of tropical ocean water (right) can be as high as 30 °C. However, the surface temperature of polar ocean water (left) is below the freezing point of fresh water.

pack ice a floating layer of sea ice that completely covers an area of the ocean surface

The Thermocline

Because the sun cannot directly heat ocean water below the surface layer, the temperature of the water decreases sharply as depth increases. In most places in the ocean, this sudden decrease in temperature begins close to the surface. The layer in a body of water in which water temperature drops with increased depth faster than it does in other layers is called the **thermocline.**

The thermocline exists because the water near the surface becomes less dense as energy from the sun warms the water. This warm water cannot mix easily with the cold, dense water below. Thus, a thermocline marks the distinct separation between the warm surface water and the cold deep water. Below the thermocline, the temperature of the water continues to decrease, but it decreases very slowly, as shown in **Figure 5.** Changing temperature or shifting currents may alter the depth of the thermocline or cause the thermocline to disappear. Nevertheless, a thermocline is usually present beneath much of the ocean surface.

Deep Water

In the deep zones of the ocean, the temperature of the water is usually about 2 °C. The colder the water is, the denser it is. The density of cold, deep water controls the slow movement of deep ocean currents. This movement occurs when the cold, dense water at the poles sinks and flows beneath warm water toward the equator. Cold, deep ocean water also holds more dissolved gases than warm, shallow ocean water does.

thermocline a layer in a body of water in which water temperature drops with increased depth faster than it does in other layers

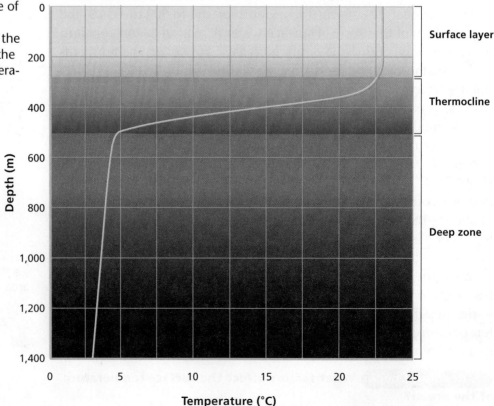

Figure 5 The temperature of ocean water decreases as depth increases. Just below the surface is the thermocline, the area where the water temperature decreases sharply.

Density of Ocean Water

The mass of a substance per unit volume is that substance's **density.** For example, 1 cm³ of pure water has a mass of 1 g. So, the density of pure water is 1 g/cm³. Different liquids have different densities, as shown in **Figure 6.** Two factors affect the density of ocean water: salinity and the temperature of the water. Dissolved solids, which are mainly salts, add mass to the water. The large amount of dissolved solids in ocean water makes it denser than pure fresh water. Ocean water has a density between 1.020 g/cm³ and 1.029 g/cm³.

Ocean water becomes denser as it becomes colder and less dense as it becomes warmer. Water temperature usually affects the density of ocean water more than salinity does. Therefore, the densest ocean water is found in the polar regions, where the ocean surface is coldest. This cold, dense water sinks and moves through the ocean basins near the ocean floor.

✔ Reading Check **Explain why ocean water is denser than fresh water.**

Figure 6 This graduated cylinder contains six liquids that have different densities. From top to bottom, the liquids are corn oil, water, shampoo, dish detergent, antifreeze, and maple syrup. *Which liquid has the lowest density?*

THINK central
INTERACT ONLINE
Keyword: HQXOWAF6

density the ratio of the mass of a substance to the volume of the substance; commonly expressed as grams per cubic centimeter for solids and liquids and as grams per liter for gases

SC.912.E.7.3

Quick Lab   Density Factors

Procedure

❶ Fill a **deep, clear plastic container** half full with **room-temperature water.**

❷ In a **1 L beaker**, mix **1/8 cup of table salt, a few drops of red food coloring,** and 1 L of room-temperature water. Stir the mixture until the salt is dissolved.

❸ Add the red saltwater mixture to the water in the clear plastic container. Record your observations.

❹ In the **1 L beaker**, mix a **few drops of blue food coloring** with water that is 8 °C.

❺ Slowly add the cold, blue water to the clear plastic container in step 3. Record your observations.

Analysis

1. Describe what happened when you added the red salt water to the fresh water. Which is denser: fresh water or salt water?

2. What happened when you added the cold water to the room-temperature water? Which is denser: cold water or room temperature water?

3. What would you expect to happen if the blue water was heated, instead of cooled?

20 min

4. Based on your observations, where would you expect the water in the ocean to be the least dense? the most dense?

5. Describe water layering where a river empties into the ocean.

Color of Ocean Water

Have you ever wondered why the ocean appears blue, as shown in **Figure 7**? The color of ocean water is determined by the way it absorbs or reflects sunlight. White light from the sun contains light from all the visible wavelengths of the electromagnetic spectrum. Much of the sunlight penetrates the surface of the ocean and is absorbed by the water. Water absorbs most of the wavelengths, or colors, of visible light. Only the blue wavelengths tend to be reflected. The reflection of this blue light makes ocean water appear blue.

Figure 7 Ocean water appears blue as far as 100 m below the surface.

Academic Vocabulary

affect (uh FEKT) to change; to have an effect on; to influence

Why Is Ocean Color Important?

Substances or organisms in ocean water, such as phytoplankton, can affect the color of the water. *Phytoplankton* are microscopic plants in the ocean that provide food to many of the ocean's organisms. Phytoplankton absorb red and blue light, but reflect green light. Therefore, the presence and amount of phytoplankton can affect the shade of blue of the ocean.

By studying variations in the color of the ocean, scientists can determine the presence of phytoplankton in the ocean. Because phytoplankton require nutrients, the presence or absence of phytoplankton can indicate the health of the ocean. If the color of an area of the ocean indicates that no phytoplankton are present, a lack of nutrients in the water may be preventing phytoplankton growth.

Section 1 Review

LA.910.2.2.3; SC.912.E.7.9

Key Ideas

1. **Describe** how water temperature affects the ability of the ocean water to dissolve gases.

2. **Summarize** how freezing and evaporation affect salinity.

3. **Describe** the composition of ocean water.

4. **Define** *thermocline*.

5. **Describe** how temperature and salinity affect the density of ocean water.

6. **Explain** how the density of ocean water drives the movement of deep ocean currents.

7. **Explain** why shallow ocean water appears to be blue in color.

Critical Thinking

8. **Making Inferences** Why does the surface temperature of ocean water in middle latitudes vary during the year?

9. **Understanding Relationships** Why would surface water in the North Sea be more likely to contain a high percentage of dissolved gases than surface water in the Caribbean Sea would?

10. **Predicting Consequences** If global temperatures increase, how would this change affect the ability of the ocean to absorb CO_2?

11. **Identifying Relationships** If an area of the ocean has a large decrease in phytoplankton, how would this change affect other ocean organisms? Explain your answer.

Concept Mapping

12. Use the following terms to create a concept map: *ocean water, salinity, temperature, density, dissolved solids,* and *dissolved gas.*

SECTION 2 Life in the Oceans

Key Ideas

❯ Explain how marine organisms alter the chemistry of ocean water.

❯ Explain why plankton can be called *the foundation of life in the ocean.*

❯ Describe the major zones of life in the ocean.

Key Terms

upwelling

plankton

nekton

benthos

benthic zone

pelagic zone

Why It Matters

Variations in sunlight, nutrients, and temperature create different zones in the ocean. These zones are filled with marine organisms especially adapted to the environment.

Most marine organisms depend on two major factors for their survival: sunlight and the essential nutrients available in ocean water. Variations in either of these factors affect the ability of aquatic organisms to survive and flourish.

FLORIDA STANDARDS

SC.912.E.7.3 Differentiate and describe the various interactions among Earth systems, including: atmosphere, hydrosphere, cryosphere, geosphere, and biosphere.

Ocean Chemistry and Marine Life

The chemistry of the ocean is a balance of dissolved gases and solids that are essential to marine life. Marine organisms help to maintain the chemical balance of ocean water. They do this by removing nutrients and gases from the ocean while returning other nutrients and gases to the ocean. For example, marine organisms, such as the giant kelp shown in **Figure 1,** absorb large amounts of carbon, hydrogen, oxygen, and sulfur. They also absorb other elements, such as nitrogen, phosphorus, and silicon. In addition, marine organisms return nutrients and gases to the ocean. For example, photosynthetic marine plants remove carbon dioxide from ocean water to produce oxygen.

Marine organisms, such as the sea horse shown in **Figure 1,** also help to recycle nutrients in the ocean. During a marine organism's lifetime, the organism absorbs and stores nutrients from the ocean. These nutrients are eventually returned to the water when the organism dies. For example, bacteria in the water digest the remains of dead organisms. The bacteria then release the essential nutrients from the dead organisms into the ocean.

Figure 1 Marine organisms, such as giant kelp and sea horses, help to maintain the balance of dissolved gases and solids in ocean water.

Movement of surface water

Surface winds

Upwelling

Figure 2 Upwelling is caused by offshore movement of surface water. *How might stormy weather affect the process of upwelling?*

upwelling the movement of deep, cold, and nutrient-rich water to the surface

plankton the mass of mostly microscopic organisms that float or drift freely in the waters of aquatic (freshwater and marine) environments

nekton all organisms that swim actively in open water, independent of currents

benthos organisms that live at the bottom of oceans or bodies of fresh water

Academic Vocabulary

complex (kahm PLEKS) having many parts or functions

Figure 3 Plankton are so tiny that you need a microscope to see them.

Upwelling

The distribution of life in the ocean depends on the way that life-supporting nutrients cycle in the ocean water. In general, all the elements necessary for life are consumed by organisms near the surface. Elements are then released back into the ocean water when the organisms die, sink to lower depths, and decay. Thus, deep water is a storage area for the nutrients needed for life. These nutrients must, however, return to the surface before most organisms in the ocean can use them.

One way that nutrients return to the surface is through a process called upwelling. **Upwelling** is the movement of deep, cold, and nutrient-rich water to the surface, as shown in **Figure 2.** When the wind blows steadily parallel to a coastline, surface water moves farther offshore. The deep, cold water then rises to replace the surface water that has moved away from the shore.

Marine Food Webs

Because most marine organisms need sunlight as well as nutrients, most marine organisms live in the upper 100 m of water. Free-floating, microscopic organisms, called **plankton**, live within the sunlit zone. Plankton, shown in **Figure 3,** form the base of the complex food webs in the ocean. Plankton are consumed primarily by small marine organisms, which, in turn, become food for larger marine animals. These larger animals fall into two groups. All organisms that swim actively in open water, such as fish, dolphins, and squid, are called **nekton.** The organisms that live on the ocean floor are called **benthos.** Benthos include marine plants and animals, such as oysters, sea stars, and crabs, that live in sunlit, shallow waters.

Ocean Environments

The ocean can be divided into two basic environments, or zones, as shown in **Figure 4.** These zones are the bottom region, or **benthic zone,** and the upper region, or **pelagic zone.** The amount of sunlight, the water temperature, and the water pressure determine the distribution of marine life within these zones.

Benthic Zones

The shallowest benthic zone lies between the low-tide and high-tide lines and is called the *intertidal zone.* Shifting tides and breaking waves make this zone a continually changing environment for the marine organisms that flourish there.

Most of the organisms that live in the benthic zone live in the shallow *sublittoral zone.* This continuously submerged zone is located on the continental shelf and is populated by organisms such as sea stars, brittle stars, and sea lilies.

The *bathyal zone* begins at the continental slope and extends to a depth of 4,000 m. Because little or no sunlight reaches this zone, plant life is scarce. Examples of animals that live in the bathyal zone are octopuses, sea stars, and brachiopods.

The *abyssal zone* has no sunlight because it begins at a depth of 4,000 m and extends to a depth of 6,000 m. Organisms that live in the abyssal darkness include sponges and worms.

The *hadal zone* is confined to the ocean trenches, which are deeper than 6,000 m below the surface of the water. This zone is virtually unexplored, and scientists think that life in the hadal zone is sparse.

Reading Check **Which benthic zone has the most marine life? Why?**

benthic zone the bottom region of oceans and bodies of fresh water

pelagic zone the region of an ocean or body of fresh water above the benthic zone

READING TOOLBOX

Comparison Table
As you read this page, complete a comparison table for the five benthic zones. Label the rows "Depth," "Sunlight," and "Marine life." See the Reading Toolbox at the beginning of this chapter if you need help getting started.

Figure 4 This diagram shows the classification and locations of marine environments.

Figure 5 Fish and marine mammals are examples of organisms that live in the pelagic zone.

www.scilinks.org
Topic: Marine Life
Code: **HQX0912**

Pelagic Zones

The region of the ocean above the benthic zone is the pelagic zone. The area of the pelagic zone above the continental shelf is called the *neritic zone*. The neritic zone has abundant sunlight, moderate temperatures, and relatively low water pressure, which are ideal factors for marine life. Nekton fill the zone's waters and are the source of much of the fish and seafood that humans eat.

The *oceanic zone* extends into the deep waters beyond the continental shelf. It is divided into four zones, based on depth. The epipelagic zone is the uppermost area of the oceanic zone. It is sunlit and populated by marine life, such as the dolphins shown in **Figure 5.** The mesopelagic, bathypelagic, and abyssopelagic zones occur at increasingly greater depths. The amount of marine life in the pelagic zone decreases as depth increases.

Section 2 Review

LA.910.2.2.3; SC.912.E.7.3

Key Ideas

1. **Explain** the effects that marine organisms have on the chemistry of ocean water.

2. **Summarize** the process of upwelling, and describe its importance to marine organisms.

3. **Explain** how plankton form the base of ocean food webs.

4. **Identify** the two major environments, or zones, of the ocean.

5. **Compare** the sublittoral and neritic zones, and name some organisms found in each zone.

Critical Thinking

6. **Analyzing Processes** How can the movement of wind currents alter the chemistry of an area of the ocean?

7. **Making Predictions** How would life in the ocean change if the area of all regions of upwelling decreased?

Concept Mapping

8. Use the following terms to create a concept map: *pelagic zone, neritic zone, benthic zone, ocean environment,* and *oceanic zone.*

SECTION 3 Ocean Resources

Key Ideas	Key Terms	Why It Matters
› Describe three important resources of the ocean. › Explain the threat that water pollution poses to marine organisms.	desalination aquaculture	Resources from the ocean include fresh water, minerals, energy, and food.

The ocean supplies humans with a number of natural resources. It is a major source of food and minerals, and it provides a means of transportation. Furthermore, the growth of Earth's population has created new interest in the ocean as a source of fresh water.

Fresh Water from the Ocean

The increasing demand for fresh water, for things such as drinking water, industry, and irrigation, can be met by converting ocean water to fresh water. One way of increasing the freshwater supply is through desalination, as shown in **Figure 1. Desalination** is the extraction of fresh water from salt water. Although desalination may provide needed fresh water, the process is generally costly.

Methods of Desalination

One method of desalination is distillation. During *distillation,* ocean water is heated to remove the salts. Heat causes the liquid water to evaporate and leaves the dissolved salts behind. When the water vapor condenses, the result is pure fresh water. However, the process of evaporating liquid water often requires a large amount of costly heat energy.

Another method of desalination is *freezing*. When water freezes, the first ice crystals that form do not contain salt. The ice can be removed and melted to obtain fresh water. This process requires about one-sixth of the energy needed for distillation.

Reverse osmosis desalination is a popular method for desalinating ocean water. It includes the use of special membranes that allow water under high pressure to pass through, but block the dissolved salts.

FLORIDA STANDARDS

SC.912.E.7.3 Differentiate and describe the various interactions among Earth systems, including: atmosphere, hydrosphere, cryosphere, geosphere, and biosphere; **SC.912.N.1.6** Describe how scientific inferences are drawn from scientific observations and provide examples from the content being studied; **SC.912.N.4.1** Explain how scientific knowledge and reasoning provide an empirically-based perspective to inform society's decision making.

desalination a process of removing salt from ocean water

Figure 1 After salt water from the Persian Gulf has undergone desalination, much of the resulting fresh water is stored in these towers in Kuwait.

Figure 2 Offshore oil rigs, such as this one in the Gulf of Mexico, produce about one-fourth of the world's oil.

Mineral and Energy Resources

Salt is one mineral resource that can be obtained from the ocean. Other mineral and energy resources can also be obtained from the ocean. While some valuable minerals are easily extracted from the ocean, others are costly or difficult to extract.

Petroleum

The most valuable resource in the ocean is the petroleum found beneath the sea floor. Offshore oil and natural gas deposits exist along continental margins around the world. About one-fourth of the world's oil is now obtained from offshore wells, such as the one shown in **Figure 2.** As a result of new drilling techniques, oil and gas can be extracted far offshore and from great depths.

Math Skills

Ocean's Gold One cubic kilometer of ocean water contains about 6 kg of gold. If you must process 4 million liters of ocean water to get an amount of gold worth 4¢, how many liters of water would have to be processed to get an amount of gold worth $1?

Nodules

Potato-shaped lumps of minerals, called *nodules,* are found on the abyssal floor of the ocean. Nodules are a valuable source of manganese, iron, copper, nickel, cobalt, and phosphates. However, the recovery of nodules is expensive and difficult because they are located in very deep water. Because country borders are observed only close to land, the question of who has the right to mine minerals from the ocean floor can be difficult to answer.

Trace Minerals

The ocean is also the main source of magnesium and bromine. However, the concentration of most other useful chemicals that are dissolved in the ocean is very small. The extraction of minerals found only in trace amounts is too costly to be practical.

Food from the Ocean

Of all the resources that the ocean supplies, the one in greatest demand is food. Seafood, which is an important source of protein, can be harvested through fishing or through aquaculture.

Fishing

Because fish are a significant food source for people around the world, fishing has become an important industry. But when the ocean is overfished, or overharvested, for a long period of time, fish populations can collapse. A collapsed fish population may damage the ecosystem and threaten the fishing industry. To prevent overharvesting, many governments have passed laws to manage fishing.

Aquaculture

Another way to deal with the high demand for seafood is by farming aquatic life. **Aquaculture** is the raising of aquatic plants and animals for human use or consumption. Catfish, salmon, oysters, and shrimp are already grown on large aquatic farms. Similar methods are used to breed fish and seaweed in ocean farms, such as the one shown in **Figure 3.** A major problem for aquaculturalists is that ocean farms are susceptible to pollution and may themselves be a local source of pollution.

Under the best conditions, an ocean farm can produce more food than an agricultural farm of the same size does. For example, in agriculture, only the top layers of soil can be used. In contrast, ocean farms can use a wide range of depths to produce food. Someday, the nutrient-rich bottom water may be pumped to the surface as a way of fertilizing aquatic farms.

Reading Check List the benefits and problems of aquaculture.

READING TOOLBOX

Analyzing Comparisons
As you read about food from the ocean, look for comparisons. Create a comparisons table similar to the one that you started at the beginning of the chapter.

SCiLINKS®

www.scilinks.org
Topic: Ocean Resources
Code: HQX1065

aquaculture the raising of aquatic plants and animals for human use or consumption

Figure 3 Aquaculture establishments, such as this seaweed farm in Madagascar, provide a reliable, economical source of food.

Ocean-Water Pollution

The ocean has been used as a dumping ground for many kinds of wastes, including garbage, sewage, and nuclear waste. Until recently, most wastes were diluted or destroyed as they spread throughout the ocean. But the growth of the world population and the increased use of toxic substances have reduced the ocean's ability to absorb wastes and renew itself.

Productive coastal areas and beaches are in the greatest danger of being polluted because they are closest to sources of pollution, as shown in **Figure 4.** Pollution has destroyed clam and oyster beds, sea birds have become tangled in plastic products, and beaches have been closed because of sewage and oil spills.

Figure 4 Pollution can damage the ocean's ecosystem and make seafood unsafe to eat.

Besides being found in coastal waters, pollutants can be found in most other areas of the ocean. Traces of mercury, the insecticide DDT, and lead from gasoline have been detected in the ocean. In some areas of the world, concentrations of pollutants are so high that the fish have become unsafe for humans to eat. Recognizing the effects of dumping wastes in the ocean, scientists and governments have been working to reduce pollution. For example, the use of DDT has been banned in the United States and the use of leaded gasoline has been greatly reduced.

Section 3 Review

LA.910.2.2.3; SC.912.E.7.3

Key Ideas

1. **Describe** three methods of desalinating ocean water.

2. **Explain** why distillation can be an expensive method of desalination.

3. **List** two important mineral resources in the ocean.

4. **Identify** the most valuable resource that can be obtained from the ocean.

5. **Define** the term *aquaculture,* and explain why aquaculture is important.

6. **Explain** why beaches are especially vulnerable to ocean pollution.

Critical Thinking

7. **Making Inferences** Describe how the mining of nodules may create problems between countries.

8. **Predicting Consequences** How does pollution of the ocean affect the fishing industry?

9. **Analyzing Relationships** How could humans be affected if microscopic marine organisms absorbed small amounts of mercury?

Concept Mapping

10. Use the following terms to create a concept map: *desalination, distillation, freezing, reverse osmosis, petroleum, aquaculture, fishing, salt, ocean resource,* and *pollution.*

Searching for Sunken Treasure

FORENSIC SCIENCE

Shipwrecks full of ancient treasure are not just the stuff of pirate stories. Under some conditions, ocean water can preserve ships and their contents. These artifacts are valuable not just to treasure hunters but to maritime archaeologists, giving them a fascinating insight into days gone by. Sonar, video, and an understanding of how the properties of ocean water affect wood and metals—these tools all help scientists solve the mysteries of how ships sank and what they were used for. In this way, scientists learn more about how people lived in the past.

Many factors affect how a ship decays including water temperature, currents or wave action, the material a ship is made from, and the presence of marine animals.

Sonar Imaging

Side-scan sonar produces images of objects on or under the ocean floor (left). The acoustic reflections from the ocean floor are recorded in a series of "slices" that together form an image (right).

The ocean is not kind to all shipwrecks. Shipworms and bacteria devour wooden wrecks, while dissolved salts attack iron-based metal ships.

YOUR TURN

DRAWING CONCLUSIONS
Explain which combination of water properties you think would be the most destructive to a sunken ship.

ONLINE RESEARCH
Research more about how scientists study shipwrecks. What can be learned from studying shipwrecks?

90 min

Ocean Water Density

What You'll Do

> **Measure** the temperature and density of water.

> **Analyze** the effects of temperature and salinity on the density of water.

What You'll Need

beaker, 250 mL
clay, modeling
freezer (optional)
gloves, heat-resistant
graduated cylinder, 100 mL
hot plate
pencil, grease, red
pencil, grease, yellow
ruler, metric
scissors
straw, plastic
table salt
teaspoon
thermometer
water, distilled

Safety

Step 8

The density of ocean water varies. It is affected by the salinity of the water and the temperature of the water. Furthermore, the salinity of an area of the ocean is affected by the rate of evaporation or freezing and by the addition of fresh water and salts. The temperature of the ocean is determined by the amount of solar radiation that reaches Earth's surface. In this lab, you will observe the effects of temperature and salinity on the density of salt water.

Procedure

1. Make a hydrometer (an instrument used to measure the density of water) by filling 5 cm of one end of a straw with modeling clay.

2. Pour 100 mL of distilled water at room temperature into a glass jar or beaker. Float the straw upright in the jar. If the straw does not float upright, cut off the open end at 1 cm intervals until it floats upright.

3. Use a red grease pencil to mark the water level on the straw. Remove the straw from the water, and draw a continuous line around the straw at the mark.

4. Use a yellow grease pencil to draw lines around the straw at 1 cm intervals above and below the red line. The red line will be used as a reference point.

5. Add 2 tsp of salt to the water, and stir until all the salt has dissolved. Draw a table similar to **Table 1.** Measure the water temperature, and record the measurement in your table.

6. Place the hydrometer in the salt water. In your table, record the density by counting the marks above or below the red line to the water's surface. The higher the hydrometer floats out of the water, the more dense the water.

7. Turn the hot plate on low. Place the beaker of salt water on the hot plate. **CAUTION** Wear heat-resistant gloves.

8. Hold the thermometer in the water. Do not let the thermometer touch the bottom of the beaker.

9 When the temperature of the water reaches 25°C, turn off the hot plate. Immediately place the hydrometer in the water. Record the relative density in your table.

10 Repeat steps 7 to 9, and heat the water until it is 30°C.

11 Turn the hot plate on high. Heat the salt water until it begins to boil. Boil the water for 5 min. Turn off the hot plate.

12 Place the hydrometer in the water. Draw a table similar to **Table 2.** Measure the density of the water, and record the measurement in your table.

13 Boil the water for another 5 min. Measure and record the density of the water.

14 Repeat step 13. Once the water is cool, measure the amount of water that remains in the beaker.

Temperature (°C)	Density (cm above or below the red line)
25	
30	

Table ❶

Minutes of boiling	Density (cm above or below the red line)
5	
10	
15	

Table ❷

Analysis

1. **Analyzing Data** In which trial was the water the most dense? In which trial was it the least dense? Explain your answers.

2. **Identifying Trends** As the temperature of water increases, does the density of the water increase or decrease?

3. **Making Inferences** Based on your observations, infer the density of polar ocean water, and compare it with the density of equally saline water near the equator. Explain your answer.

4. **Analyzing Processes** Why did the amount of water in the beaker change? Explain why boiling the water affected its density.

5. **Forming Hypotheses** How would you expect the density of the water to change if the water was frozen instead of boiled? Explain your answer.

Extension

Evaluating Hypotheses Place a beaker of salt water in a freezer until a crust of ice forms. Break up and remove the ice from the water, and record the density of the remaining water. Is the water more or less dense than it was before it was frozen? Explain.

Sea Surface Temperatures in August

Sea Surface Temperature (°C)

| 0 | 5 | 10 | 15 | 20 | 25 | 30 |

Map ▶ Skills Activity

This map shows global sea surface temperatures in the month of August. Latitude is shown in 15° intervals. Longitude is shown in 30° intervals. The latitude of New York City is 41°N 74°W. Use the map to answer the questions below.

1. **Analyzing Data** Estimate the sea surface temperatures off the east coast of Florida.

2. **Identifying Relationships** Identify areas of the globe that receive the most solar energy.

3. **Inferring Relationships** At which locations would you most likely find pack ice?

4. **Making Comparisons** Where would you expect to find higher surface salinity values: off the coast of North Africa or off the coast of the southern tip of South America?

5. **Analyzing Relationships** As latitude increases, surface temperature decreases. How would you expect the density of surface water to change as latitude increases? Explain your answer.

6. **Making Predictions** Off the coast of New York City, would you expect the density of the ocean water to increase or decrease in December, compared with the density of the water in August? Explain.

Summary

Key Ideas

Key Terms

Section 1

Properties of Ocean Water

❯ Dissolved solids make up 3.5% of the mass of ocean water. Ocean water also contains dissolved gases, such as oxygen, carbon dioxide, and nitrogen.

❯ Salinity is a measure of the amount of dissolved salts in ocean water. The temperature of ocean water is dependent on depth and latitude. The density of ocean water is dependent on temperature and salinity. The color of ocean water is affected by the presence of phytoplankton.

salinity, p. 664
pack ice, p. 665
thermocline, p. 666
density, p. 667

Section 2

Life in the Oceans

❯ Marine organisms help to maintain the chemical balance of ocean water by using nutrients for life processes and by returning the nutrients to the water after death.

❯ Plankton form the base of complex ocean food webs by acting as food for other marine organisms.

❯ There are two major zones of life in the ocean: benthic and pelagic. Each zone supports different types of organisms.

upwelling, p. 670
plankton, p. 670
nekton, p. 670
benthos, p. 670
benthic zone, p. 671
pelagic zone, p. 671

Section 3

Ocean Resources

❯ The ocean is valuable as a source of fresh water, minerals, and food.

❯ Ocean-water pollution threatens both marine organisms and humans by damaging food resources in the ocean.

desalination, p. 673
aquaculture, p. 675

1. **Comparison Table** Make a comparison table to describe the similarities and differences between ocean water and pure fresh water. SC.912.E.7.3

USING KEY TERMS

Use each of the following terms in a separate sentence.

2. *thermocline* SC.912.E.7.2

3. *upwelling* SC.912.E.7.2

4. *desalination* SC.912.E.7.3

For each pair of terms, explain how the meanings of the terms differ.

5. *salinity* and *density* SC.912.E.7.2

6. *plankton* and *nekton* SC.912.L.17.3

7. *benthic zone* and *pelagic zone* SC.912.E.7.3

8. *upwelling* and *aquaculture* SC.912.E.7.2

UNDERSTANDING KEY IDEAS

9. The amount of dissolved salts in ocean water is called the water's SC.912.E.6.5
   a. salinity.
   b. nekton.
   c. plankton.
   d. density.

10. When liquid water is warmed, its density SC.912.E.7.2
    a. increases.
    b. decreases.
    c. remains the same.
    d. doubles.

11. Although most of the wavelengths of visible light are absorbed by ocean water, the one wavelength that is most often reflected is the color SC.912.E.6.5
    a. violet.
    b. green.
    c. yellow.
    d. blue.

12. Drifting marine organisms are known as SC.912.L.17.3
    a. plankton.
    b. benthos.
    c. nekton.
    d. sea stars.

13. Marine animals that can swim to search for food and avoid predators are called SC.912.L.17.3
    a. phytoplankton.
    b. zooplankton.
    c. nekton.
    d. benthos.

14. Which of the following ocean environments experiences the most change? SC.912.E.6.5
    a. intertidal zone
    b. abyssal zone
    c. bathyal zone
    d. neritic zone

15. Which of the following methods is *not* used for producing fresh water by desalination?
    a. distillation
    b. evaporation
    c. reverse osmosis
    d. aquaculture

16. Lumps of minerals on the ocean floor are called SC.912.E.6.5
    a. nekton.
    b. nodules.
    c. benthos.
    d. plankton.

17. Aquaculture is another name for
    a. desalination.
    b. distillation.
    c. ocean farming.
    d. rapid temperature changes.

SHORT ANSWER

18. Describe the process of upwelling, and explain its effects on marine life. SC.912.E.7.2

19. What are the six most abundant elements that are dissolved in ocean water? SC.912.E.6.5

20. How are temperature, salinity, and density related? SC.912.E.7.2

21. Describe how an oil spill would affect a fishing industry. SC.912.E.6.6

22. List three important resources from the ocean, and describe how they are obtained. SC.912.E.6.5

23. What effects does ocean pollution have on humans? SC.912.E.6.6

24. Predicting Consequences If climatic conditions over the ocean caused upwelling and wave action to stop, what would happen to marine life? Explain your answer. SC.912.E.7.2

25. Identifying Relationships How would a significant and global decrease in sunlight affect plankton and other marine organisms?

26. Applying Concepts If you were to start an aquatic farm, in which zone of marine life would you locate your farm? Explain your answer. SC.912.L.17.19

27. Making Inferences When oceanographers first explored the deep-ocean basin along mid-ocean ridges, they discovered a variety of marine life, including sightless crabs. Explain why sightlessness is not a disadvantage to these crabs.

CONCEPT MAPPING

28. Use the following terms to create a concept map: *fishing, marine life, plankton, fish, color, dissolved gas, dissolved solid, desalination, salt, ocean water characteristics,* and *aquaculture.* SC.912.E.6.5

MATH SKILLS

29. Using Equations Using the equation *density = mass ÷ volume,* determine the mass of a 3 cm³ sample of ocean water if the water's density is 1.027 g/cm³.

30. Making Calculations What percentage of dissolved salts would be present in water that has a salinity of 40‰?

31. Making Calculations A 1,000 g sample of ocean water contains 35 g of dissolved solids. Magnesium makes up 7.7% of the 35 g of dissolved solids. How many grams of magnesium are in the 1,000 g sample of ocean water?

WRITING SKILLS

32. Creative Writing Write a descriptive essay about the deep-ocean waters of the oceanic zone. Your essay should include a description of the marine organisms in this zone, as well as a description of what life is like for these marine organisms. SC.912.L.17.2

33. Writing from Research Research the new foods that are being produced through aquaculture and the nations that are investing in this method of farming. Write a short essay that describes these foods, where they are grown, and their nutritional values. SC.912.L.17.19

INTERPRETING GRAPHICS

The graph below shows the depths at which different wavelengths of light penetrate ocean water. Use this graph to answer the questions that follow.

34. Estimate the depth at which yellow light can no longer penetrate ocean water. SC.912.E.6.5

35. Which colors can penetrate ocean water to a depth of 50 m? SC.912.E.6.5

36. Would an object that is painted red appear red at a depth of 50 m? Explain your answer. SC.912.E.6.5

Understanding Concepts

Directions (1–11): For each question, write on a separate sheet of paper the letter of the correct answer.

1 Which of the following statements about the oceans and carbon is true?
  A. The oceans contain very little carbon.
  B. The oceans do not play a role in the cycling of carbon.
  C. The oceans contain more carbon than the atmosphere does.
  D. Because the oceans hold carbon, they do not play a role in climate regulation.

2 Which of the following statements describes ocean salinity?
  F. Salinity is lowest in areas where precipitation is highest.
  G. Salinity is not affected by the freezing of water.
  H. Salinity does not vary, and the ocean has a salinity of 34.7%.
  I. Salinity is high in tropical areas.

3 The temperature of ocean water is dependent on all of the following except
  A. depth.
  B. the amount of solar energy it receives.
  C. water movement.
  D. the number of organisms living in it.

4 As the temperature of ocean water increases from 10°C to 30°C, how does the water's density change?
  F. It increases.
  G. It decreases.
  H. It remains the same.
  I. It is impossible to predict.

5 Which of the following statements describes dissolved gases in the ocean?
  A. N_2 and O_2 do not dissolve in ocean water.
  B. CO_2 can stay dissolved in ocean water for thousands of years.
  C. Ocean water does not release dissolved gases.
  D. Most O_2 enters the ocean from rivers.

6 Which of the following statements is NOT true of the temperature of ocean water?
  F. Temperature varies depending on depth and location.
  G. The amount of solar energy an area receives determines temperature.
  H. Temperature is influenced by salinity.
  I. Ocean water freezes at –1.9°C.

7 The density of ocean water is influenced by what two factors?
  A. dissolved gases and dissolved solids
  B. salinity and temperature
  C. water color and thermocline
  D. dissolved carbon and trace elements

8 How are pollutants harmful to the oceans?
  F. They destroy clam and oyster beds.
  G. They increase water temperatures.
  H. They harm people who swim in the water.
  I. They cannot be controlled.

9 Plankton are the foundation of ocean life because
  A. they are the most numerous organisms in the ocean.
  B. they play a role in dissolving gases and solids in ocean water.
  C. they are the base of complex ocean food webs.
  D. they live in the upper 100 m of water.

10 Plankton live in which zone of the ocean?
  F. abyssal zone, which receives no sunlight
  G. bathyal zone, which receives little light
  H. hadal zone, which is within ocean trenches
  I. neritic zone, which receives a lot of sunlight

11 Upwelling is the movement of deep, cold, and nutrient-rich water to the surface. How might upwelling affect marine organisms?
  A. It would have little effect.
  B. It would promote the growth of organisms.
  C. It would form the base of a food chain.
  D. It would store nutrients.

Interpreting Graphics

Directions (12–13): For each question below, record the correct answer on a separate sheet of paper.

Solids Dissolved in Ocean Water

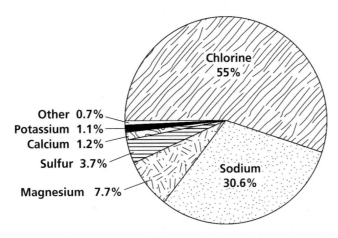

12 Halite is a salt made up of sodium and chloride ions. Based on the graph above, what percentage of the dissolved solids in ocean water are these substances?
   F. 0.7%
   G. 30.6%
   H. 55.0%
   I. 85.6%

Diagram of Upwelling

13 Based on the figure above, which of the following statements describes upwelling?
   A. Nutrient-rich water moves from the ocean bottom to the surface.
   B. Nutrient-rich water moves parallel to the shore.
   C. Nutrient-rich water moves parallel to the direction of the wind.
   D. Nutrient rich water moves from the shore out to the open ocean.

Test Tip

Scan the answer choices for words such as *never* and *always*. Such words are often used in statements that are incorrect because they are too general.

Chapter 25

Movements of the Ocean

Chapter Outline

Why It Matters

Both surface currents and deep currents move heat around Earth. This affects climates worldwide.

Inquiry Lab   Creating Currents

15 min

Fill a **clear cup** half full with **3% salt solution**, which is dyed red using **food coloring**. Fill a **second cup** half full with **10% salt solution**, which is dyed blue. Using a **dropper**, slowly add some of the 10% salt solution to the cup containing the 3% salt solution. Hold the end of the dropper near the edge of the cup, right at the water level. You will need to refill the dropper several times. Observe and record what happens. Repeat the experiment, this time adding some of the 3% salt solution to the cup containing the 10% salt solution.

SC.912.E.7.2

Questions to Get You Started

1. What is density? Explain how adding salt to water changes the density of the water.

2. Explain your observations. How are your observations related to the movement of ocean water?

3. What other factors might affect the density and movement of ocean water? How could you modify this experiment to investigate a different factor?

READING TOOLBOX

These reading tools will help you learn the material in this chapter.

Word Families

Tide You will soon learn many new terms that contain the word *tide* or *tidal*. Both *tide* and *tidal* come from *tid*, the Old English word for "time." The suffix *-al*, meaning "of" or "like," makes *tidal* an adjective. As you read this chapter, you will see some familiar words combined with *tide* or *tidal*, along with their definitions.

Your Turn As you read Section 3, start a table like the one below. Add all the key terms and italicized words that include either *tide* or *tidal*, and write down the definitions of these terms and words, and compare them to each other.

Term	Definition
tidal current	a horizontal movement of water with the tide, toward and away from the coastline

Cause and Effect

Signal Words Certain words and phrases, called markers, can signal cause-and-effect relationships.

Cause markers	Effect markers
cause	therefore
affect	thus
as a result of	as a result
due to	is an effect of
because	consequently

Sentences can also express cause-and-effect relationships, without using markers.

Your Turn As you read Sections 1 and 2, create a table like the one below. When you find a cause-and-effect relationship, add it to your table.

Cause	Effect	Marker
the uneven heating of the atmosphere	winds	caused by

FoldNotes

Pyramid A pyramid can be used to summarize information in three categories, on the three sides of the pyramid.

Your Turn Create a pyramid, as described in Appendix A.

① Along one edge of one side of the FoldNote, write "Global Wind Belts."

② On one edge of another side, write "Continental Barriers."

③ On one edge of the third side, write "The Coriolis Effect."

As you read Section 1, fill in details about the three factors that influence surface currents.

For more information on how to use these and other tools, see **Appendix A**.

Ocean Currents

Key Ideas	Key Terms	Why It Matters
❯ Describe how wind patterns, the rotation of Earth, and continental barriers affect surface currents in the ocean. ❯ Identify the major factor that determines the direction in which a surface current circulates. ❯ Explain how differences in the density of ocean water affect the flow of deep currents.	current surface current Coriolis effect gyre Gulf Stream deep current	Spending time near the coast would let you experience the effects of ocean currents on the local climate. Ocean currents have a large impact on climates around the world.

The water in the ocean moves in giant streams called **currents.** Many ocean currents are complex and difficult to trace. Oceanographers identify ocean currents by studying the physical and chemical characteristics of the ocean water. They also identify currents by mapping the path of debris that is dumped or washed overboard from ships, as shown in **Figure 1.** From these data, scientists have mapped a detailed pattern of ocean currents around the world. Scientists place ocean currents into two major categories: surface currents and deep currents.

FLORIDA STANDARDS

SC.912.E.7.2 Analyze the causes of the various kinds of surface and deep water motion within the oceans and their impacts on the transfer of energy between the poles and the equator; **SC.912.E.7.3** Differentiate and describe the various interactions among Earth systems, including: atmosphere, hydrosphere, cryosphere, geosphere, and biosphere.

Factors That Affect Surface Currents

Currents that move at or near the surface of the ocean and are driven by wind are called **surface currents.** Surface currents are controlled by three factors: air currents, Earth's rotation, and the location of the continents.

All surface currents are affected by wind. Wind is caused by the uneven heating of the atmosphere. Variations in air temperature lead to variations in air density and pressure. Colder, denser air sinks and forms areas of high pressure. Air moves away from high-pressure areas to lower pressure areas. This movement gives rise to wind.

Because *wind* is moving air, wind has kinetic energy. The wind passes this energy to the ocean as the air moves across the ocean surface. As energy is transferred from the air to the ocean, the water at the ocean's surface begins to move.

current a horizontal movement of water in a well-defined pattern, such as a river or stream

surface current a horizontal movement of ocean water that is caused by wind and that occurs at or near the ocean's surface

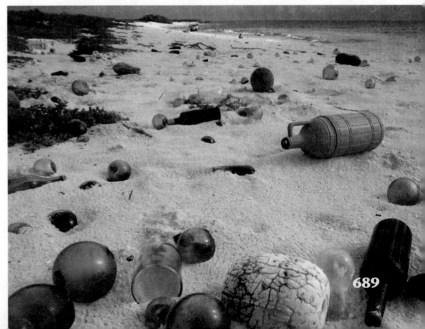

Figure 1 Glass floats, which are used to hold up Japanese fishing nets, have been carried by surface currents from off the coast of Japan to this beach in northwest Hawaii.

689

Global Wind Belts

Global wind belts, such as the trade winds and westerlies shown in **Figure 2,** are a major factor affecting the flow of ocean surface water. The *trade winds* are located just north and south of the equator. In the Northern Hemisphere, the trade winds blow from the northeast. In the Southern Hemisphere, they blow from the southeast. In both hemispheres, trade-wind belts push currents westward across the tropical latitudes of all three major oceans.

The *westerlies* are located in the middle latitudes. In the Northern Hemisphere, westerlies blow from the southwest. In the Southern Hemisphere, they blow from the northwest. Westerlies push ocean currents eastward in the higher latitudes of the Northern and Southern Hemispheres.

Continental Barriers

The continents are another major influence on surface currents. The continents act as barriers to surface currents. When a surface current flows against a continent, the current is deflected and divided.

The Coriolis Effect

As Earth spins on its axis, ocean currents and wind belts curve. The curving of the paths of ocean currents and winds due to Earth's rotation is called the **Coriolis effect.** The wind belts and the Coriolis effect cause huge circles of moving water, called **gyres,** to form.

Figure 3 shows the five main gyres in the ocean. In the Northern Hemisphere, water in the main gyres flows clockwise. In the Southern Hemisphere, water in the main gyres flows counterclockwise.

Coriolis effect the curving of the path of a moving object from an otherwise straight path due to Earth's rotation

gyre a huge circle of moving ocean water found above and below the equator

Figure 2 Global winds and the Coriolis effect together drive the surface currents of the oceans in great circular patterns. The photo at the right shows a small gyre in the Pacific Ocean, off the east coast of Japan.

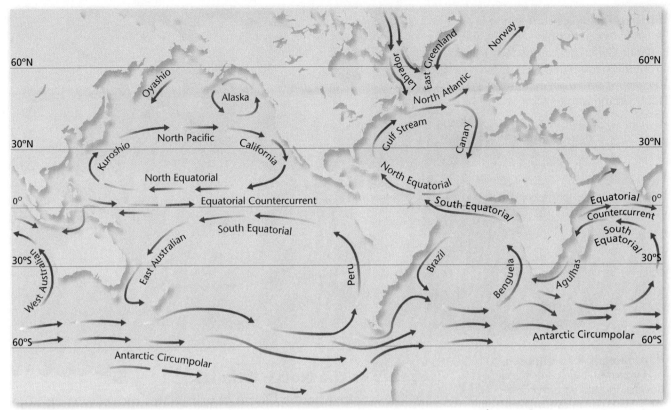

Major Surface Currents

The <u>major</u> surface currents of the world are shown in **Figure 3.** The major currents in the equatorial region and in the Northern and Southern Hemispheres are described below.

Equatorial Currents

Warm equatorial currents are located in the Atlantic, Pacific, and Indian Oceans. Each of these oceans has two warm-water equatorial currents that move in a westward direction. Between these westward-flowing currents lies a weaker, eastward-flowing current called the *Equatorial Countercurrent*.

Currents in the Southern Hemisphere

In the Southern Hemisphere, the currents in the main gyres move counterclockwise. In the most southerly regions of the oceans, constant westward winds produce the world's largest current, the *Antarctic Circumpolar Current*, also known as *West Wind Drift*. No continents interrupt the movement of this current, which completely circles Antartica and crosses all three major oceans.

The Indian Ocean surface currents follow two patterns. Currents in the southern Indian Ocean follow a circular, counterclockwise gyre. Currents in the northern Indian Ocean are governed by *monsoons*, winds whose directions change seasonally.

Reading Check **What is the world's largest ocean current?**
(See Appendix G for answers to Reading Checks.)

Figure 3 This map shows the major surface currents in the oceans of the world. Warm-water currents are shown in red; cold-water currents are shown in blue.

Academic Vocabulary

major (MAY juhr) of great importance; large scale

SCI*LINKS*.
www.scilinks.org
Topic: Ocean Currents
Code: HQX1061

Figure 4 Surface currents in the Atlantic Ocean form the North Atlantic Gyre. The Sargasso Sea results from this pattern of currents. The organisms below are commonly found in the Sargasso Sea.

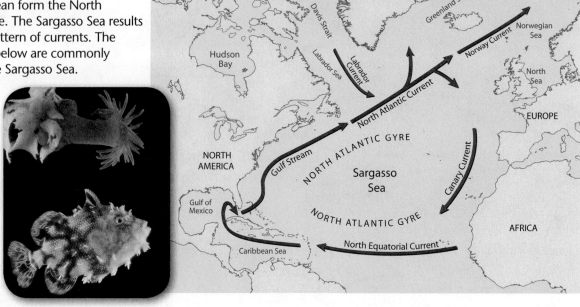

Gulf Stream the swift, deep, and warm Atlantic current that flows along the eastern coast of the United States toward the northeast

Currents in the North Atlantic

In the North Atlantic Ocean, warm water moves through the Caribbean Sea and Gulf of Mexico and then north along the east coast of North America in a swift, warm current called the **Gulf Stream.** Farther north, the cold-water Labrador Current, which flows south, joins the Gulf Stream. South of Greenland, the Gulf Stream widens and slows until it becomes a vast, slow-moving warm current known as the *North Atlantic Current*. Near western Europe, the North Atlantic Current splits. One part becomes the Norway Current, which flows northward along the coast of Norway and keeps that coast ice-free all year. The other part is deflected southward and becomes the cool Canary Current, which eventually warms and rejoins the North Equatorial Current.

As **Figure 4** shows, the Gulf Stream, the North Atlantic Current, the Canary Current, and the North Equatorial Current form the North Atlantic Gyre. At the center of this gyre lies a vast area of calm, warm water called the *Sargasso Sea*. The Sargasso Sea is named after *sargassum*, the brown seaweed that floats on the surface of the water in this area. The pattern of winds and currents around the Sargasso Sea concentrates all kinds of floating debris, such as orange peels and plastic cups, in this area.

Currents in the North Pacific

The pattern of currents in the North Pacific is similar to that in the North Atlantic. The warm Kuroshio Current, the Pacific equivalent of the Gulf Stream, flows northward along the east coast of Asia. This current then flows toward North America as the North Pacific Drift. It eventually flows southward along the California coast as the cool California Current.

Deep Currents

In addition to having wind-driven surface currents, the ocean has **deep currents,** cold, dense currents far below the surface. Deep currents move much more slowly than surface currents do. Deep currents form as cold, dense water of the polar regions sinks and flows beneath warmer ocean water.

The movement of polar waters is a result of differences in density. When water cools, it contracts and the water molecules move closer together. This contraction makes the water denser, and the water sinks. When water warms, it expands and the water molecules move farther apart. The warm water is less dense, so it rises above the cold water. Temperature helps determine density.

Salinity, too, helps determine the density of water. The water in polar regions has high salinity because of the large amount of water frozen in icebergs and sea ice. When water freezes, the salt in the water does not freeze but stays in the unfrozen water. So, unfrozen polar water has a high salt concentration and is denser than water that has a lower salinity. This dense polar water sinks and forms a deep current that flows beneath less dense surface currents, as shown in **Figure 5.**

Antarctic Bottom Water

The temperature of the water near Antarctica is very cold, –2°C. The water's salinity is high. These two factors make the water off the coast of Antarctica the densest and coldest ocean water in the world. This dense, cold water sinks to the ocean bottom and forms a deep current called the *Antarctic Bottom Water*. The Antarctic Bottom Water moves slowly northward along the ocean bottom for thousands of kilometers to a latitude of about 40°N. It takes hundreds of years for the current to make the trip.

Reading Check Why is Antarctic Bottom Water the densest ocean water in the world?

deep current a streamlike movement of ocean water far below the surface

READING TOOLBOX

Pyramid
Create a pyramid to compare three examples of currents in the deep ocean: Antarctic Bottom Water, North Atlantic Deep Water, and Turbidity Currents. Be sure to note the similarities and differences among the currents.

Figure 5 The very dense and highly saline Antarctic Bottom Water travels beneath less dense North Atlantic Deep Water.

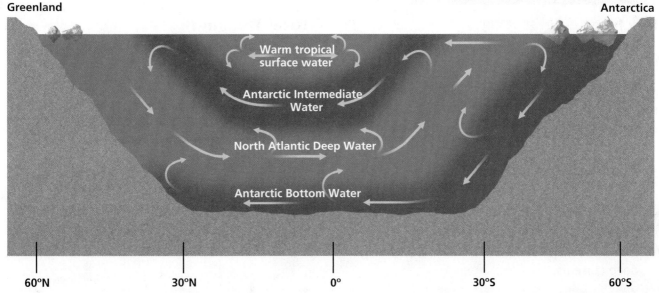

Greenland   Antarctica

- Warm tropical surface water
- Antarctic Intermediate Water
- North Atlantic Deep Water
- Antarctic Bottom Water

60°N   30°N   0°   30°S   60°S

North Atlantic Deep Water

In the North Atlantic, south of Greenland, the water is very cold and has a high salinity. This cold, salty water forms a deep current that moves southward under the northward-flowing Gulf Stream. Near the equator, this deep current divides. One part begins to rise, reverse direction, and flow northward again. The rest of the current continues southward toward Antarctica and flows over the colder, denser Antarctic Bottom Water.

Deep Atlantic currents exist near the Mediterranean Sea, too. Dense water forms in the Mediterranean Sea when evaporation increases and precipitation decreases. These changes increase the salinity, and thus the density, of the water of the Mediterranean Sea. This denser water sinks and flows through the Strait of Gibraltar into the Atlantic Ocean. In turn, surface water from the Atlantic, which is less saline and less dense than deep current water is, flows into the Mediterranean Sea, as shown in **Figure 6.**

Figure 6 The dense, highly saline water of the Mediterranean Sea forms a deep current as it flows through the Strait of Gibraltar and into the less dense Atlantic Ocean.

Turbidity Currents

A turbidity current is a strong current caused by an underwater landslide. Turbidity currents occur when large masses of sediment that have accumulated along a continental shelf or continental slope suddenly break loose and slide downhill. The landslide mixes the nearby water with sediment. The sediment causes the water to become cloudy, or turbid, and denser than the surrounding water. The dense water of the turbidity current moves beneath the less dense, clear water.

Section 1 Review

LA.910.2.2.3; SC.912.E.7.2; SC.912.E.7.3

Key Ideas

1. **Describe** the force that drives most surface currents.

2. **Identify** the winds that affect the surface currents on both sides of the equator.

3. **Identify** the winds that affect the surface currents in the middle latitudes.

4. **Describe** how density affects the flow of deep currents.

5. **List** the factors that affect the density of ocean water.

6. **List** three major surface currents and two major deep currents.

Critical Thinking

7. **Predicting Consequences** Describe how surface currents would be affected if Earth did not rotate.

8. **Identifying Relationships** Explain how the distribution of solar energy around Earth affects ocean surface currents.

Concept Mapping

9. Use the following terms to create a concept map: *ocean currents, surface currents, deep currents, Gulf Stream, North Atlantic Current, Antarctic Bottom Water, gyres,* and *Coriolis effect.*

SECTION 2 Ocean Waves

Key Ideas	Key Terms	Why It Matters
❯ Describe the formation of waves and the factors that affect wave size. ❯ Explain how waves interact with the coastline. ❯ Identify the cause of destructive ocean waves.	wave wave period fetch refraction	Ocean waves, whether small or large, have similar characteristics, which sometimes can cause trouble for people.

A wave is a periodic disturbance in a solid, liquid, or gas as energy is transmitted through the medium. One kind of wave is described as the periodic up-and-down movement of water. Such a wave has two basic parts—a *crest* and a *trough*—as shown in **Figure 1.** The crest is the highest point of a wave. The trough is the lowest point between two crests. The *wave height* is the vertical distance between the crest and the trough of a wave. The *wavelength* is the horizontal distance between two consecutive crests or between two consecutive troughs. The **wave period** is the time required for two consecutive wave crests to pass a given point. The speed at which a wave moves is calculated by dividing the wave's wavelength by its period.

$$wave\ speed = \frac{wavelength}{wave\ period}$$

Wave Energy

The uneven heating of Earth's atmosphere causes pressure differences that make air move. This moving air is called *wind*. Wind then transfers the energy received from the sun to the ocean and forms waves. Small waves, or ripples, form as a result of friction between the moving air and the water. As a ripple receives more energy from the wind, the ripple grows into a larger wave. The longer that the wind blows from a given direction, the more energy that is transferred from the wind to the water and the larger the wave becomes.

The smoothness of the ocean's surface is generally disrupted by many small waves moving in different directions. Because of their large surface area, larger waves receive more energy from the wind than smaller waves do. Thus, larger waves grow larger, and smaller waves die out.

FLORIDA STANDARDS

SC.912.E.7.3 Differentiate and describe the various interactions among Earth systems, including: atmosphere, hydrosphere, cryosphere, geosphere, and biosphere; **SC.912.N.3.5** Describe the function of models in science, and identify the wide range of models used in science; **SC.912.P.10.20** Describe the measurable properties of waves and explain the relationships among them and how these properties change when the wave moves from one medium to another.

wave a periodic disturbance in a solid, liquid, or gas as energy is transmitted through a medium

wave period the time required for identical points on consecutive waves to pass a given point

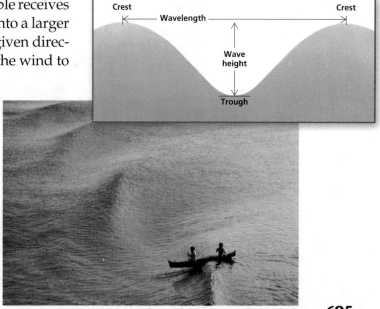

Figure 1 The vertical distance between the crest and the trough of a wave is the wave height.

Figure 2 Like the bottle in this diagram, water molecules do not travel horizontally through the water with the wave.

Water Movement in a Wave

Although the energy of a wave moves from water molecule to water molecule in the direction of the wave, the water itself moves very little. This fact can be demonstrated by observing the movement of a bottle floating on the water as a wave passes. The bottle appears to move up and down, but it moves in a circular path, as shown in **Figure 2.** As the wave passes, the bottle moves only a small distance.

As a wave moves across the surface of the ocean, only the energy of the wave, not the water, moves in the direction of the wave. The water molecules within the wave move in a circular motion. During a single wave period, each water particle moves in one complete circle. At the end of the wave period, a circling water particle ends up almost exactly where it started.

As a wave passes a given point, the circle traced by a water particle initially on the surface of the ocean has a diameter that is equal to the height of the wave. Because waves receive their energy from wind pushing against the surface of the ocean, the energy received decreases as the depth of the water increases. As a result, water at various depths receives varying amounts of energy. Thus, the diameter of a water molecule's circular path decreases as the depth of the water increases, as shown in **Figure 3.** Below a depth of about one-half the wavelength, there is almost no circular motion of water molecules.

Reading Check Why does the diameter of a water molecule's circular path in a wave decrease as depth increases?

Figure 3 Wave energy decreases as depth increases. As a result, the diameter of a water molecule's circular path in a wave also decreases.

Wavelength

Direction of wave movement

Wave height

Negligible water movement below a depth of one-half the wavelength

Wave Size

Three factors determine the size of a wave. These factors are the speed of the wind, the length of time that the wind blows, and fetch. **Fetch** is the distance that the wind can blow across open water. Very large waves are produced by strong, steady winds blowing across a long fetch.

During a storm, steady high winds can cause some waves to gather enough energy to become very large. Strong, gusty winds, on the other hand, produce choppy water that has waves of various heights and lengths, which may come from various directions. Nevertheless, the size of a wave will increase to only a certain height-to-length ratio before the wave collapses.

On calm days, small, smooth waves move steadily across the ocean's surface. One of a group of long, rolling waves that are of similar size is called a *swell*. Swells move in groups in which one wave follows another. Swells that reach the shore may have formed thousands of kilometers out in the ocean.

Whitecaps

 When winds blow the crest of a wave off, *whitecaps* form, as shown in **Figure 4.** Because whitecaps reflect solar radiation, they allow less radiation to reach the ocean. Scientists have been studying how this characteristic may affect climate.

Figure 4 Whitecaps, such as the ones shown here off the coast of North Carolina, may form during storms.

fetch the distance that wind blows across an area of the sea to generate waves

Academic Vocabulary

collapse (kuh LAPS) fall or cave in

 SC.912.P.10.20

Quick **Lab**   **Waves** 🔺

 15 min

Procedure

❶ Fill a **rectangular pan** (40 cm × 30 cm × 10 cm) with **water** to a depth of 7 cm.

❷ Float a **cork** near the center of the pan. On each side of the pan, mark the location of the cork with a small piece of **tape**.

❸ Hold a **spoon** in the water at one end of the pan. Carefully move the spoon up and down in the water to make a slow, regular pattern of waves.

❹ Observe the movement of the cork for 1 min. Sketch how the cork moves in relation to the waves.

❺ Remove the cork from the pan.

❻ Use the spoon to make a strong, steady series of waves.

❼ Remove the spoon from the pan. Observe what happens when the waves reach the edges of the pan. Write down or sketch what you observe.

Analysis

1. Describe the motion of the cork when a wave passes.

2. How does the cork move relative to the tape on the sides of the pan? Explain your answer.

3. When a wave breaks on the shore, the water is carried in the direction of the wave. Based on your observations in step 4, does this statement contradict your model? Explain your answer.

Waves and the Coastline

In shallow water near the coastline, the bottom of a wave touches the ocean floor. A wave touches the ocean floor where the depth of the water is about half the wavelength. Contact with the ocean floor causes the wave to slow and eventually break, as shown in **Figure 5**.

Breakers

The height of a wave changes as the wave approaches the coastline. The water involved in the motion of a wave extends to a depth of one-half the wavelength. As the wave moves into shallow water, the bottom of the wave is slowed. The top of the wave, however, continues to move at its original speed. The top of the wave gets farther and farther ahead of the bottom of the wave. Finally, the top of the wave topples over and forms a *breaker*, a foamy mass of water that washes onto the shore. The height of the wave when the wave topples over is one to two times the height of the original wave.

Breaking waves scrape sediments off the ocean floor and move the sediments along the coastline. The waves also erode rocky coastlines. The size and force of breakers are determined by the original wave height, the wavelength, and the steepness of the ocean floor close to the coastline. If the slope of the ocean floor is steep, the height of the wave increases rapidly and the wave breaks with great force. If the coastline slopes gently, the wave rises slowly. The wave spills forward with a rolling motion that continues as the wave advances up the coastline.

Reading Check As a wave moves into shallow water, what causes the top of the wave to break and topple over?

Figure 5 Breakers begin to form as a wave approaches a coastline. As the wave nears the coastline, wave height increases and wavelength decreases.

Breakers form. Wavelengths shorten. Wavelengths are constant.

Wavelength

1/2 wavelength

Water depth

Water depth is less than 1/2 wavelength.

Water depth is greater than 1/2 wavelength.

Figure 6 Waves strike the shore head-on as a result of refraction. Notice the waves approaching the shore at an angle. These waves bend as they draw closer to the shore.

Direction of wave motion

Refraction

Most waves approach the coastline at an angle. When a wave reaches shallow water, however, the wave bends. This bending is called refraction. **Refraction** is the process by which ocean waves bend toward the coastline as they approach shallow water. As a wave approaches the coastline, the part of the wave that is in shallower water slows, and the part of the wave that is in deeper water maintains its speed. The wave gradually bends toward the beach and strikes the shore head-on, as shown in **Figure 6.**

refraction the process by which ocean waves bend directly toward the coastline as they approach shallow water

Undertows and Rip Currents

Water carried onto a beach by breaking waves is pulled back into deeper water by gravity. This motion forms an irregular current called an *undertow*. An undertow is seldom strong, and only along shorelines that have steep drop-offs do undertows create problems for swimmers.

The generally weak undertow is often confused with the more dangerous *rip current*. Rip currents form when water from large breakers returns to the ocean through channels that cut through underwater sandbars that are parallel to the beach. Rip currents flow perpendicular to the shore through those channels and may be strong enough to carry a swimmer away from the shore quickly. The presence of rip currents can usually be detected by a gap in a line of breakers or by turbid water—water in which sand has been stirred up by the current.

Longshore Currents

Longshore currents form when waves approach the beach at an angle. Longshore currents flow parallel to the shore. Great quantities of sand are carried by longshore currents. If there is a bay or inlet along the coastline where waves refract, sand will be deposited as the energy of the waves decreases. These sand deposits form low ridges of sand called *sandbars*.

Tsunamis

The most destructive waves in the ocean are not powered by the wind. *Tsunamis* are giant seismic ocean waves. Most tsunamis are caused by earthquakes on the ocean floor, but some can be caused by volcanic eruptions and underwater landslides. Tsunamis are commonly called *tidal waves*, which is misleading because tsunamis are not caused by tides.

Tsunamis have long wavelengths. In deep water, the wave height of a tsunami is usually less than 1 m, but the wavelength may be as long as 500 km. A tsunami commonly has a wave period of about 1 h and may travel at speeds of up to 890 km/h (as fast as a jet airplane). Because the wave height of a tsunami is so low in the open ocean, a tsunami cannot be felt by people aboard ships.

Figure 7 The tsunami of 2004 left coastal communities of Sri Lanka in ruins. The tsunami was triggered by an earthquake that had a moment magnitude of 9.0.

www.scilinks.org
Topic: Tsunamis
Code: HQX1561

A Tsunami as a Destructive Force

A tsunami has a tremendous amount of energy. Because its wavelength is so long, the entire depth of the water is involved in the wave motion of a tsunami. All the energy of this mass of water is released against the shore and causes a great deal of destruction, as shown in **Figure 7.** Near the shore, the height of a tsunami greatly increases as the tsunami's speed decreases. As a tsunami approaches the shore, it may reach a height of 30 to 40 m. The arrival of a tsunami may be signaled by the sudden pulling back of the water along the shore. This pulling back occurs when the trough of the tsunami arrives before the crest. If the crest arrives first, a sudden, rapid rise in the water level occurs.

The tsunamis generated by the earthquakes in Chile in 1960 and in the Indian Ocean in 2004 caused widespread destruction. The Chilean tsunami struck the coast of South America and then Hawaii and crossed 17,000 km of ocean to strike Japan.

Section 2 Review

LA.910.2.2.3; SC.912.E.7.3; SC.912.P.10.20

Key Ideas

1. **Explain** how wavelength and wave period can be used to calculate wave speed.

2. **Describe** the formation of waves.

3. **List** three factors that determine the size of a wave.

4. **Explain** why incoming waves refract toward the beach until they strike the shore head-on.

5. **Describe** what factors cause tsunamis.

6. **Explain** why waves slow down in shallow water.

Critical Thinking

7. **Analyzing Processes** Would the breakers on a specific beach always form at the same distance from the shore? Explain your answer.

8. **Predicting Consequences** Explain how whitecaps could affect climate.

Concept Mapping

9. Use the following terms to create a concept map: *wave, wave height, whitecap, trough, crest, fetch, swell,* and *tsunami.*

SECTION 3 Tides

Key Ideas

❯ Describe how the gravitational pull of the moon causes tides.

❯ Compare spring tides and neap tides.

❯ Describe how tidal oscillations affect tidal patterns.

❯ Explain how the coastline affects tidal currents.

Key Terms

tide

tidal range

tidal oscillation

tidal current

Why It Matters

Tides are cyclical and predictable changes in sea level that are important not only to the plants and animals that live along the coast, but to people using the ocean as well.

The periodic rise and fall of the water level in the oceans is called the **tide**. *High tide* is when the water level is highest. *Low tide* is when the water level is lowest. The tide change is most noticeable on the coastline. If you stand on a beach long enough, you can see how the ocean retreats and returns with the tides.

The Causes of Tides

In the late 1600s, Isaac Newton identified the force that causes the rise and fall of tides along coastlines. According to Newton's law of gravitation, the gravitational pull of the moon on Earth and Earth's waters is the major cause of tides. The sun also causes tides, but they are smaller because the sun is so much farther from Earth than the moon is.

As the moon revolves around Earth, the moon exerts a gravitational pull on the entire Earth. However, because the force of the moon's gravity decreases with distance from the moon, the gravitational pull of the moon is stronger on the side of Earth that is nearer the moon. As a result, the ocean on Earth's near side bulges slightly, which causes a high tide within the area of the bulge.

At the same time, another tidal bulge forms on the opposite side of Earth. This tidal bulge forms because the solid Earth, which acts as though all its mass were at Earth's center, is pulled more strongly toward the moon than the ocean water on Earth's far side is. The result is a smaller tidal bulge on Earth's far side. **Figure 1** shows the Earth-moon system and the position of the moon in relation to the tidal bulges.

Low tides form halfway between the two high tides. Low tides form because as ocean water flows toward the areas of high tide, the water level in other areas of the ocean drops.

FLORIDA STANDARDS

SC.912.E.5.6 Develop logical connections through physical principles, including Kepler's and Newton's Laws about the relationships and the effects of Earth, Moon, and Sun on each other; **SC.912.E.7.2** Analyze the causes of the various kinds of surface and deep water motion within the oceans and their impacts on the transfer of energy between the poles and the equator.

tide the periodic rise and fall of the water level in the oceans and other large bodies of water

Figure 1 Because of Earth's rotation, most locations in the ocean have two high tides and two low tides daily.

Math Skills

Tidal Friction As the tidal bulges move around Earth, friction between the water and the ocean floor slows Earth's rotation slightly. Scientists estimate that the average length of a day has increased by 10.8 min in the last 65 million years. How many years does it take for Earth's rotation to slow by 1 s?

tidal range the difference in levels of ocean water at high tide and low tide

READING TOOLBOX

Cause and Effect

As you read this section, add the sentences that describe the multiple causes and effects of tides, tidal variations, and tidal currents to the table that you started at the beginning of the chapter.

Behavior of Tides

Earth rotates on its axis once every 24 h. In that 24 h, the moon moves through about 1/29 of its orbit. Because the moon orbits Earth in the same direction that Earth rotates, all areas of the ocean pass under the moon every 24 h 50 min. As seen from above the North Pole, Earth rotates counterclockwise and the tidal bulges appear to move westward around Earth.

Because there are two tidal bulges, most locations in the ocean have two high tides and two low tides daily. The difference in the levels of the ocean water at high tide and low tide is called the **tidal range.** The tidal range can vary widely from place to place. Because the moon rises about 50 min later each day, the times of high and low tides are also about 50 min later each day.

Spring Tides

The sun's gravitational pull can add to or subtract from the moon's influence on the tides. During the new moon and the full moon, Earth, the sun, and the moon are aligned, as shown in **Figure 2.** The combined gravitational pull of the sun and the moon results in higher high tides and lower low tides. So, the daily tidal range is greatest during the new moon and the full moon. During these two monthly periods, the tides are called *spring tides*.

Neap Tides

During the first-quarter and third-quarter phases of the moon, the moon and the sun are at right angles to each other in relation to Earth, also shown in **Figure 2.** The gravitational forces of the sun and the moon work against each other. As a result, the daily tidal range is small. The tides that occur during this time are called *neap tides*.

Reading Check Describe the location of the sun and the moon in relation to Earth when the tidal range is small.

THINK central
INTERACT ONLINE
Keyword: HQXMOVF2

Figure 2 The alignment of the sun, the moon, and Earth during spring tides differs from their alignment during neap tides. *How often do spring tides occur?*

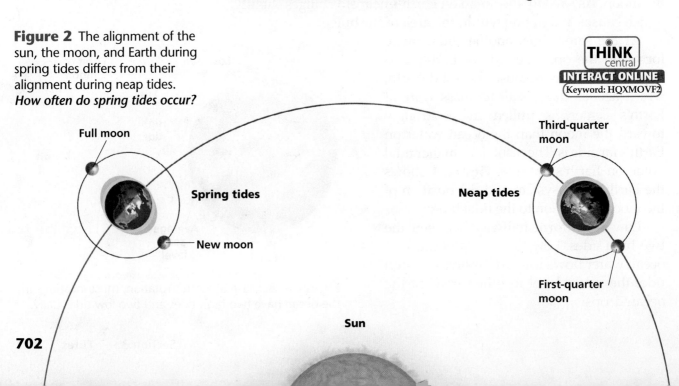

702

Tidal Variations

Although the global ocean is one body of water, continents and irregularities in the ocean floor divide the ocean into several basins. The tidal pattern in an area is greatly influenced by the size, shape, depth, and location of the ocean basin in which the tides occur.

Along the Atlantic coast of the United States, two high tides and two low tides occur each day and have a fairly regular tidal range. Along the shore of the Gulf of Mexico, however, only one high tide and one low tide occur each day. Along the Pacific coast, the tides follow a mixed pattern of tidal ranges. Pacific coast tides commonly have a very high tide followed by a very low tide and then a lower high tide, followed by a higher low tide.

Tidal Oscillations

Tidal patterns are also affected by tidal oscillations. **Tidal oscillations** (TIE duhl AHS uh LAY shunz) are slow, rocking motions of ocean water that occur as the tidal bulges move around the ocean basins. Along straight coastlines and in the open ocean, the effects of tidal oscillations are not very obvious. In some enclosed seas, such as the Baltic and Mediterranean Seas, tidal oscillations reduce the effects of the tidal bulges. As a result, these seas have a very small tidal range. In small basins and narrow bays located off major ocean basins, however, tidal oscillations may amplify the effects of the tidal bulges. An example of the effects of tidal oscillations is shown in **Figure 3.**

Figure 3 A great tidal range of as much as 15 m in the V-shaped Bay of Fundy in Canada is caused by tidal oscillations.

tidal oscillation the slow, rocking motion of ocean water that occurs as the tidal bulges move around the ocean basins

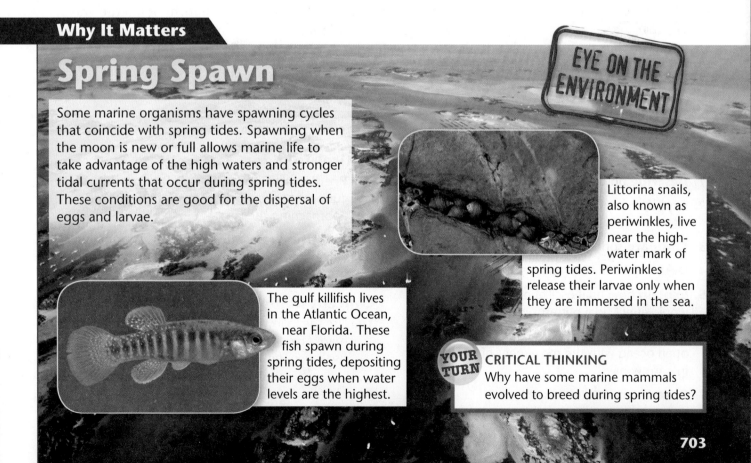

Spring Spawn

EYE ON THE ENVIRONMENT

Some marine organisms have spawning cycles that coincide with spring tides. Spawning when the moon is new or full allows marine life to take advantage of the high waters and stronger tidal currents that occur during spring tides. These conditions are good for the dispersal of eggs and larvae.

Littorina snails, also known as periwinkles, live near the high-water mark of spring tides. Periwinkles release their larvae only when they are immersed in the sea.

The gulf killifish lives in the Atlantic Ocean, near Florida. These fish spawn during spring tides, depositing their eggs when water levels are the highest.

YOUR TURN
CRITICAL THINKING
Why have some marine mammals evolved to breed during spring tides?

703

Figure 4 The photo to the right shows a tidal bore in early spring at Turnagain Arm of Cook Inlet, Alaska.

www.scilinks.org
Topic: Tides
Code: HQX1525

tidal current the movement of water toward and away from the coast as a result of the rise and fall of the tides

Academic Vocabulary

energy (EN uhr jee) the capacity to do work

Tidal Currents

As ocean water rises and falls with the tides, it flows toward and away from the coast. This movement of the water is called a **tidal current.** When the tidal current flows toward the coast, it is called *flood tide*. When the tidal current flows toward the ocean, it is called *ebb tide*. When there are no tidal currents, the time period between flood tide and ebb tide is called *slack water*.

Tidal currents in the open ocean are much smaller than those at the coastline. Tidal currents are strongest between two adjacent coastal regions that have large differences in the height of the tides. In bays and along other narrow coastlines, tides may create rapid currents. Some tidal currents may reach speeds of 20 km/h.

Where a river enters the ocean through a long bay, the tide may enter the river mouth and create a *tidal bore*, a surge of water that rushes upstream, such as the one shown in **Figure 4.** In some areas, the tidal bore rushes upstream in the form of a large wave, up to 5 m high, that eventually loses <u>energy</u>. The tidal bores in the River Severn in England travel almost 20 km/h and reach as far as 33 km inland.

Section 3 Review

LA.910.2.2.3; SC.912.E.7.3; SC.912.P.10.20

Key Ideas

1. **Describe** how the moon causes tides.

2. **Explain** how the sun can influence the moon's effect on tides.

3. **Compare** spring tides and neap tides.

4. **Describe** how ocean basins affect tidal patterns.

5. **Explain** how tidal oscillations in an enclosed sea would affect tidal patterns in that sea.

6. **Compare** the movement of ocean water in the open ocean with the movement of ocean water in narrow bays.

7. **Describe** how a tidal bore forms.

Critical Thinking

8. **Predicting Consequences** Predict where tidal currents may be a concern to ships that are approaching the land.

9. **Identifying Relationships** Describe ways in which tides could be affected if Earth had two moons.

Concept Mapping

10. Use the following terms to create a concept map: *tide, tidal range, spring tide, neap tide, tidal oscillation, tidal current, flood tide,* and *ebb tide.*

Monster Waves: Myth or Fact?

REAL WORLD

Imagine standing on the deck of a ship, watching the approach of a wave taller than a 10-storey building. Such waves do exist. Called rogue waves, they can reach heights of over 30 m and rise out of otherwise steady wave patterns in deep water. Also known as monster waves, freak waves, and extreme waves, they pose a serious threat to even the largest ships.

Rogue wave or tsunami?

Short wave   Large wave   Medium wave

20 m   MEAN SEA LEVEL

Wave direction   **Rogue wave** could reach up to 40 m high

Rogue waves form when two or more waves combine. They can also form when a strong current runs in the opposite direction of waves.

Tsunami

Fault line

Tsunamis are massive movements of water that are not noticeable in deep water and present no threat to ships at sea. They become dangerous when they gain height as they approach shore.

YOUR TURN

UNDERSTANDING CONCEPTS
Why is the deep, open ocean a safe place to be sailing during an earthquake?

CRITICAL THINKING
Why can scientists warn people about tsunamis, but not yet predict with accuracy where and when rogue waves will form?

⏱ **45 min**

Wave Motion

The source of wave motion in water is energy, which is generated primarily from wind. Waves of water appear to move horizontally. However, only the energy of the waves moves horizontally; the water moves horizontally very little. In this lab, you will work with two classmates to simulate wave motion and to observe how energy generates wave motion in water. You will also observe the properties of waves.

What You'll Do

> **Model** the movement of waves.

> **Compare** the characteristics of waves when wave speed changes.

What You'll Need

cloth ties, about 50 cm in length (2)
marker
meterstick
paper, 2 m × 1 m
paper, graph
pen or pencil, colored (3)
rope, thin, 2.5 m in length

Procedure

1 Tie one end of the rope securely to the leg of a chair or table.

2 On the large sheet of paper, use the meterstick to draw a grid like the one shown in the illustration on the next page. The vertical axis should be 2 m long, with marks at intervals of 0.25 m. The horizontal axis should be 1 m long, with marks at intervals of 0.125 m.

3 Place the sheet of paper on the floor, and line up the rope along the 2 m line of the grid.

4 To make waves, move the free end of the rope from side to side. (Note: Be sure to maintain a constant motion with the rope.)

5 While one person moves the rope, another person marks the paper where a crest of a wave hits. The third person marks the paper where a trough of a wave hits.

6 On the graph paper, make a diagram to display your results, with an x axis that has wavelength (in meters) and a y axis that has wave height (in meters).

7 Plot a wave that represents the wave you observed in step 5. Plot the wave height and the wavelength. Indicate the direction of the wave motion.

Step 5

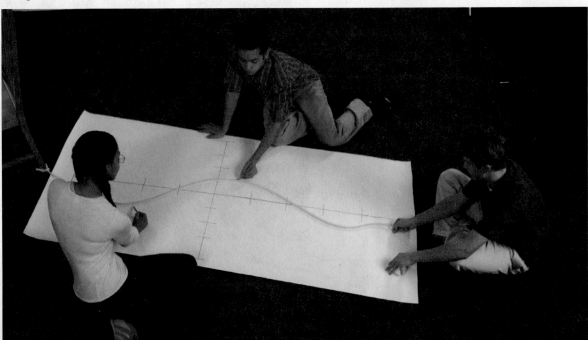

8 Move the rope at a fast speed. Do not change the side-to-side distance that you move the free end of the rope.

9 As soon as a constant motion has been established, repeat step 5. On your diagram, plot a wave that represents the wave you observed when repeating step 5. Use a pen or pencil that is a different color from the color of the first wave plot.

10 Next, generate very small waves. Repeat step 5 and plot the wave, using a third color of pen or pencil.

11 On your diagram, label a crest and a trough on each of the waves you plotted.

12 Use the following formula to calculate the wave speeds of the three waves you plotted, if each wave period is 6 s:

$$wave\ speed = \frac{wavelength}{wave\ period}$$

13 Tie the two pieces of cloth around the middle of the rope, about 15 cm apart.

14 Make waves by moving the end of the rope from side to side. Observe and record the motion of the cloth relative to the motion of the waves.

Analysis

1. **Examining Data** How do the waves you plotted differ from each other? If these waves were real water waves, what might be the cause(s) of the differences?

2. **Recognizing Relationships** How is the motion of the rope similar to wave motion in water?

3. **Analyzing Relationships** How does the motion of the cloth differ from the motion of the wave?

4. **Drawing Conclusions** What does the motion of the cloth tell you about wave motion in water?

Extension

Making Comparisons Use a 4 m rope to repeat the investigation. Construct a diagram similar to your first diagram, but extend the x-axis to provide room to plot a 4 m length. Observe and plot five waves of varying speeds and heights. Compare waves generated on a 2 m rope with those generated on a 4 m rope. Describe your results. Using 6 s as the wave period for each wave you plot, calculate wave speeds.

MAPS *in Action*

Roaming Rubber Duckies

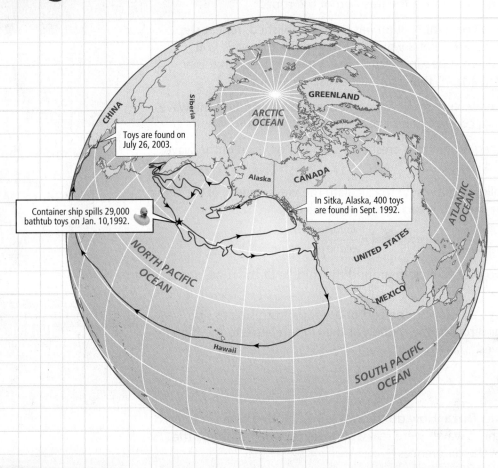

Toys are found on
July 26, 2003.

Container ship spills 29,000
bathtub toys on Jan. 10,1992.

In Sitka, Alaska, 400 toys
are found in Sept. 1992.

CHINA · Siberia · ARCTIC OCEAN · GREENLAND · Alaska · CANADA · UNITED STATES · ATLANTIC OCEAN · NORTH PACIFIC OCEAN · MEXICO · Hawaii · SOUTH PACIFIC OCEAN

Map Skills Activity

This map shows the estimated route taken by
bathtub toys spilled from a cargo ship in the North
Pacific Ocean. Use the map to answer the questions
below.

1. **Analyzing Data** Describe where the toys
   started their journey.

2. **Evaluating Data** How long did it take the toys
   to travel to Sitka, Alaska, by the most direct
   route?

3. **Identifying Relationships** Compare the map
   above with the map of the major surface currents
   in the section entitled "Ocean Currents." Then,
   name the current that carried the toys past
   Hawaii.

4. **Evaluating Sources** Is the current that carried
   the toys along the coast of the western United
   States cold or warm? Explain your answer.

5. **Predicting Consequences** Predict where the
   toys might have been located in December
   2003 if tracking data were plotted on the map.

6. **Identifying Relationships** What is the name
   of the current that carried the toys south along
   the coast of Siberia?

7. **Evaluating Data** How long did it take the toys
   to travel from the location where they were
   spilled to their location on the coast of China on
   July 26, 2003?

Key Ideas	Key Terms

Section 1

Ocean Currents

❯ As wind blows, it moves surface water in the ocean in the same direction. Continents deflect and divide surface currents. The Coriolis effect causes surface currents to curve as they flow.

❯ Surface currents are wind-driven currents.

❯ Deep currents are produced as dense water near the North and South Poles sinks and moves toward the equator beneath less dense water.

current, p. 689
surface current, p. 689
Coriolis effect, p. 690
gyre, p. 690
Gulf Stream, p. 692
deep current, p. 693

Section 2

Ocean Waves

❯ Wind is the primary source of wave energy. Wave size is determined by wind speed, by the length of time that wind blows, and fetch.

❯ As a wave comes into contact with the ocean floor, the wave may undergo refraction or form breakers. Waves near the shoreline can cause currents, such as an undertow and a rip current.

❯ Tsunamis, which are caused by earthquakes on the ocean floor, volcanic eruptions, and underwater landslides, are giant, destructive waves.

wave, p. 695
wave period, p. 695
fetch, p. 697
refraction, p. 699

Section 3

Tides

❯ The gravitational pull of the moon is strongest on the side of Earth that is nearer the moon. As a result, the ocean on this side bulges slightly, which causes a high tide within the area of the bulge. At the same time, a smaller tidal bulge forms on the opposite side of Earth.

❯ Tidal ranges are greatest during spring tides and smallest during neap tides.

❯ In some enclosed seas, tidal oscillations reduce the effects of tidal bulges, resulting in a very small tidal range. In small basins and narrow bays located off major ocean basins, tidal oscillations may amplify the effects of the tidal bulges.

❯ Tidal currents are generally small in the open ocean but may create rapid currents in narrow bays along the coastline.

tide, p. 701
tidal range, p. 702
tidal oscillation, p. 703
tidal current, p. 704

1. **Word Families** Create a table for key terms and italicized words that belong to the word family of the key term *current*. Add the words that are combined with *current* (such as *surface, deep, rip, longshore,* and *tidal*) and their definitions to your table. Combine these words with *current,* and write your own definitions of the new terms. Then compare your definitions with the definitions given in the chapter. SC.912.E.7.3

READING TOOLBOX

USING KEY TERMS

Use each of the following terms in a separate sentence.

2. *current* SC.912.E.7.3
3. *gyre* SC.912.E.7.3
4. *tide* SC.912.E.7.3
5. *wave* SC.912.E.7.3

For each pair of terms, explain how the meanings of the terms differ.

6. *surface current* and *deep current* SC.912.E.7.3
7. *Coriolis effect* and *gyre* SC.912.E.7.3
8. *fetch* and *refraction* SC.912.E.7.3
9. *tidal range* and *tidal oscillation* SC.912.E.7.3

UNDERSTANDING KEY IDEAS

10. The water in the ocean moves in giant streams called SC.912.E.7.2
    a. currents.
    b. westerlies.
    c. waves.
    d. tides.

11. The effect of Earth's rotation on winds and ocean currents is called the SC.912.E.7.2
    a. neap-tide effect.
    b. refraction effect.
    c. Coriolis effect.
    d. tsunami effect.

12. Which of the following currents is the westward warm-water current in the North Atlantic Gyre? SC.912.E.7.2
    a. Canary Current
    b. North Atlantic Current
    c. North Equatorial Current
    d. Gulf Stream

13. Deep currents are the result of SC.912.E.7.2
    a. the Coriolis effect.
    b. changes in the density of ocean water.
    c. the trade winds.
    d. neap tides.

14. The periodic disturbance in water as energy is transmitted through the water is a SC.912.E.7.3
    a. current.   c. fetch.
    b. breaker.   d. wave.

15. The highest point of a wave is the SC.912.E.7.3
    a. trough.   c. crest.
    b. period.   d. length.

16. The distance that a wind blows across an area of the ocean to generate waves is the SC.912.E.7.3
    a. trough.   c. fetch.
    b. sargassum.   d. wave period.

17. The movement of water toward and away from the coast due to tidal forces is called a SC.912.E.7.3
    a. tidal bore.
    b. tidal current.
    c. tidal range.
    d. tidal oscillation.

SHORT ANSWER

18. Describe how a breaker forms. SC.912.E.7.3
19. Define *tide*, and explain why tides form. SC.912.E.7.3
20. What factors control most ocean surface currents? SC.912.E.7.3
21. How does the depth of the ocean affect the shape and speed of a wave? SC.912.E.7.3
22. How do deep currents form? SC.912.E.7.2
23. Explain how wind is the primary source of wave energy. SC.912.E.7.7
24. What is a tidal bore? SC.912.E.7.3

25. Determining Cause and Effect During winter in the northern Indian Ocean, winds called *monsoons* blow in a direction opposite to the direction that they blow during summer. What effect do these winds have on surface currents? `SC.912.E.7.4`

26. Analyzing Processes Suppose that a retaining wall is built along a shoreline. What will happen to waves as they pass over the retaining wall? `SC.912.E.7.3`

27. Making Inferences Imagine that you are fishing from a small boat anchored off the shore in the Gulf of Mexico. You are lulled to sleep by the gently rocking boat but wake up to find your boat on wet sand. What happened? `SC.912.E.7.8`

28. Making Predictions If Earth rotated in the direction opposite to the direction that it now rotates, what effect would this have on the movement of ocean currents? `SC.912.E.7.2`

29. Use the following terms to create a concept map: *currents, surface currents, trade winds, deep currents, Coriolis effect, wave, breaker, rip current, tide, Antarctic Bottom Water,* and *tidal current.* `SC.912.E.7.3`

30. Applying Quantities The Gulf Stream can move 100 million cubic meters of water per second. The Mississippi River moves 15,400 m³ of water per second. How many times more water per second does the Gulf Stream move than the Mississippi River does? `SC.912.E.7.8`

31. Making Calculations If a wave has a wavelength of 216 m and a period of 12 s, what is the speed of the wave?

32. Writing from Research Write a report on the tidal power plant project at La Rance, France. Describe the amount of electricity provided by the project and the impact the project has on the environment of the area.

33. Outlining Topics Create an outline that shows the steps of tide formation. Provide diagrams as needed to illustrate the steps. `SC.912.E.7.3`

The graph below shows the measurements of tides in one location on the Atlantic coast of North America. Use this graph to answer the questions that follow.

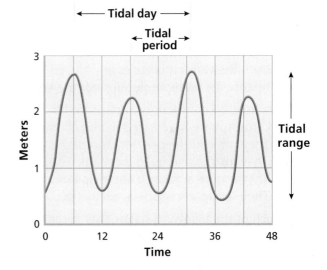

34. How many high tides occur every day in this location? `SC.912.P.10.20`

35. How many hours is the tidal period? `SC.912.P.10.20`

36. How many hours apart are the low tides?

37. What is the average tidal range, in meters?

38. What is the difference in height, in meters, between the first high tide and the second high tide? `SC.912.P.10.20`

Understanding Concepts

Directions (1–10): For each question, write on a separate sheet of paper the letter of the correct answer.

1 Which of the following factors affects the movement of surface currents?
- **A.** Earth's rotation on its axis
- **B.** water salinity
- **C.** human activity
- **D.** sea-floor spreading

2 What is the speed of an ocean wave that has 12 s between crests and a wavelength of 216 m?
- **F.** 6 m/s
- **G.** 3 km
- **H.** 18 m/s
- **I.** 12 m

3 When an ocean wave travels 100 m west, which of the following also travels 100 m west?
- **A.** the energy in the wave
- **B.** the water molecules in the wave
- **C.** both the water molecules and the energy
- **D.** neither the water molecules nor the energy

4 What role do convection currents in the ocean and atmosphere have in regulating climate?
- **F.** They prevent deep-water currents.
- **G.** They restrict energy to local use.
- **H.** They ensure a balance of precipitation.
- **I.** They set up atmospheric circulation.

5 Which of the following statements describes the formation of deep currents?
- **A.** They are driven by wind.
- **B.** They form as warm water moves from the Gulf of Mexico, along the east coast of North America.
- **C.** They occur when cold, dense water sinks in the polar regions and flows beneath warmer water.
- **D.** They form around the Sargasso Sea, isolating this area.

6 The Coriolis effect, or the curving of the path of ocean currents, is due to
- **F.** winds.
- **G.** Earth's rotation.
- **H.** continental barriers.
- **I.** temperature.

7 Which of the following statements best compares currents in the Northern Hemisphere and currents in the Southern Hemisphere?
- **A.** They flow in the same direction, clockwise.
- **B.** Currents in the Northern Hemisphere flow clockwise.
- **C.** Currents in both hemispheres flow in both directions.
- **D.** Currents in both hemispheres change seasonally.

8 Waves frequently vary in size. Which of the following factors does NOT determine the size of a wave?
- **F.** speed of wind
- **G.** length of time wind blows
- **H.** the distance that wind can blow across water
- **I.** the direction of wind

9 Various types of currents have similarities. How is a turbidity current similar to a deep current?
- **A.** Both currents flow beneath less dense water.
- **B.** Both currents are caused by underwater landslides.
- **C.** Both currents result from the cooling of water.
- **D.** Both currents are affected by salinity.

10 Which of the following statements describes the transfer of energy between wind and the ocean?
- **F.** The ocean transfers kinetic energy to the wind, moving the air.
- **G.** Air moves from high-pressure areas to low-pressure areas, giving air kinetic energy that is passed on to ocean water.
- **H.** Water moves from areas of high pressure to low pressure, causing an increase in the kinetic energy of wind.
- **I.** The atmosphere heats the ocean, which increases the kinetic energy of water, and this energy is transferred to wind.

Interpreting Graphics

Directions (11–12): For each question below, record the correct answer on a separate sheet of paper.

Effect of Sun and Moon on Earth's Tides

Diagram A

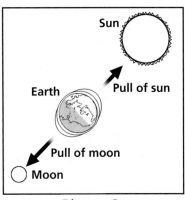

Diagram B

11 Based on the diagrams above, which of the following statements best describes the tides?

   A. The tides in each diagram are the same size.
   B. The tides in diagram B are larger than the tides in diagram A are.
   C. The tides in each diagram are not affected by the pull of the moon.
   D. The tides in diagram B are not affected by the pull of the sun.

Average Yearly Weather Data for San Francisco and Wichita

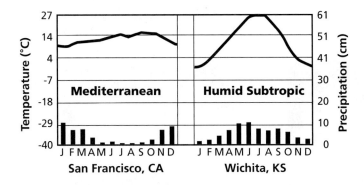

12 Which location shows the most extreme climate variation?

   F. Wichita, Kansas, shows the most extreme climate variation.
   G. San Francisco, California, shows the most extreme climate variation.
   H. Both climates are equally mild.
   I. Both climates are equally variable.

> **Test Tip**
> Allow a few minutes at the end of the test-taking period to check for careless mistakes, such as marking two answers for a single question.

Oceanography Connections

Science, technology, and society are closely linked. This flowchart shows just a few of the connections in the history of oceanography.

1918 The first active sonar system is constructed and used.

1000 C.E. Vikings migrated to North America.

1620 Cornelius Drebbel invents first practical submarine.

1859 The first ocean-going ironclad ships are employed by the French.

1519 Magellan and his crew leave Spain to circumnavigate the world.

1912 The RMS *Titanic* strikes an iceberg and sinks.

TITANIC SINKS FOUR HOURS AFTER HITTING ICEBERG; 866 RESCUED BY CARPATHIA, PROBABLY 1250 PERISH; ISMAY SAFE, MRS. ASTOR MAYBE, NOTED NAMES MISSING

1913 The International Convention for Safety of Life at Sea establishes main shipping routes.

1939 Sonar is used in World War II to find enemy submarines.

1949 American scientists investigate the use of sonar for medical purposes.

1956 Obstetricians begin to use ultrasound technology.

1947 Scientists suggest that dolphins echolocate.

1939–1945 During WWII, whales are mistakenly identified as submarines.

1964 The submersible *Alvin* is first launched.

2000 Sixteen whales beach themselves in the Bahamas after military low- and mid-frequency sonar tests.

1986 Scientists use *Alvin* to explore the wreckage of the RMS *Titanic*.

2003 North Atlantic shipping lanes are shifted to prevent collisions with Right whales off Canada's coast.

YOUR TURN

UNDERSTANDING CONCEPTS
When were modern shipping lanes established?

CRITICAL THINKING
Why might human use of sonar be harmful to animals such as dolphins and whales?

2008 About 90% of all international goods travel some distance by ship.

Florida Close-Up

Florida's natural beauty can teach us a great deal about Earth's physical processes. This photo of the Lake Bedford region shows the cypress-covered wetlands that have infiltrated Florida's low-lying landscape.

FLORIDA STANDARDS

SC.912.E.5.9 Analyze the broad effects of space exploration on the economy and culture of Florida.
SC.912.E.6.2 Connect surface features to surface processes that are responsible for their formation.
SC.912.E.6.4 Analyze how specific geologic processes and features are expressed in Florida and elsewhere.
SC.912.E.7.4 Summarize the conditions that contribute to the climate of a geographic area, including the relationships to lakes and oceans.
SC.912.E.7.8 Explain how various atmospheric, oceanic, and hydrologic conditions in Florida have influenced and can influence human behavior, both individually and collectively.

Florida's Place on Earth

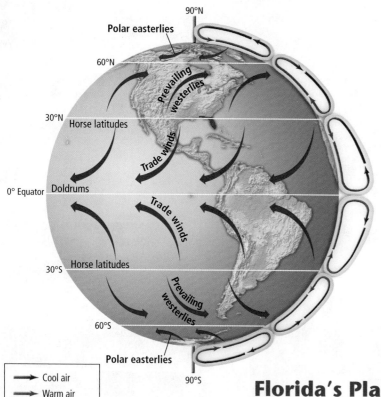

Figure 1 Florida (colored red) is located between 24°30′ and 31° north latitude. Winds in these latitudes blow from east to west.

In this book, you have learned about the physical processes that work in Earth's atmosphere, hydrosphere, and geosphere. On the following pages, you will learn how these physical processes affect Florida.

Florida's Place in the Atmosphere

As you can see in **Figure 1,** Florida is located in the Northern Hemisphere, with the majority of the state below 30°N. This location puts Florida within the trade-wind belt, which means that the winds generally blow from east to west. Florida is cooled by these trade winds and warmed by the surrounding subtropical waters. In winter, northern Florida is influenced by the westerlies wind belt, which brings cool, dry air to that region.

Florida's Place in the Hydrosphere

Florida is a peninsula and has an ocean coastline that is nearly 2,000 km long. Florida is bordered on the west by the Gulf of Mexico and on the south and east by the Atlantic Ocean. **Figure 2** shows how Florida is influenced by the *Florida Current.* This current carries warm, tropical water northward along the east coast of Florida. The Florida Current eventually joins a larger ocean current, called the *Gulf Stream,* which runs along the east coast of North America. As well as the ocean coastline, Florida has many wetlands, lakes, and rivers.

Figure 2 The Florida Current moves north, along the east coast of Florida.

Florida's Place in the Geosphere

Florida is located on the North American plate and is not near any active tectonic plate boundaries. The closest plate boundary is the northern edge of the Caribbean plate, which is an oceanic tectonic plate underlying the Caribbean Sea.

Topographically, Florida is relatively flat. The highest natural point in Florida is Lakewood Park on Britton Hill in Walton County, shown in **Figure 3.** This "high" point is only 105 m above sea level, making it the lowest high point in the United States. The lowest point in Florida is its Atlantic Ocean coastline, at sea level.

As you can see in **Figure 4,** northern and central Florida form the state's highlands, while coastal areas along the Gulf of Mexico and Atlantic Ocean form its lowlands. Within the coastal areas are numerous barrier islands. In addition, Florida has significant wetland areas, such as Big Cypress Swamp and the Everglades. South of Florida's mainland are the Florida Keys, which are home to the third-largest coral reef in the world.

Reading Check In what direction do the winds generally blow over Florida? Why?
(See Appendix G for answers to Reading Checks.)

Figure 3 The 105 m difference in elevation between Florida's highest point, Lakewood Park on Britton Hill (bottom), and its lowest point, sea level on the Atlantic coast (top), reflects how flat Florida is.

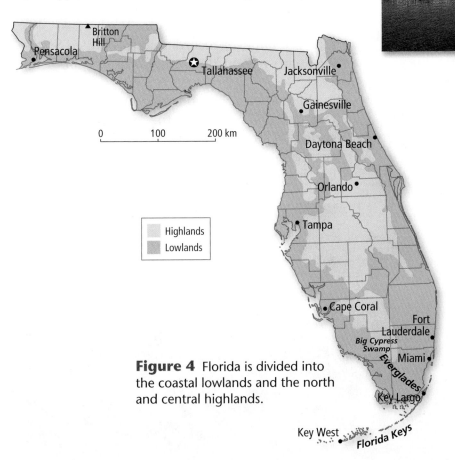

Figure 4 Florida is divided into the coastal lowlands and the north and central highlands.

- Britton Hill
- Pensacola
- Tallahassee
- Jacksonville
- Gainesville
- Daytona Beach
- Orlando
- Tampa
- Cape Coral
- Fort Lauderdale
- Big Cypress Swamp
- Miami
- Everglades
- Key Largo
- Key West
- Florida Keys

0   100   200 km

Highlands
Lowlands

LAKEWOOD PARK
FLORIDA'S HIGHEST POINT
ELEVATION 345 FT.

Maritime tropical air masses originate over the warm waters of the tropics and Gulf of Mexico, where heat and moisture are transferred to the air from the water below. **Figure 1** shows how the maritime tropical Atlantic air mass moves warm moist air northward into Florida, increasing the potential for precipitation and influencing Florida's climate. Northern Florida can also be influenced by the continental polar Canadian air mass, which can bring dry, cold air during the winter.

Rainfall in Florida

Florida is bordered by the Atlantic Ocean and the Gulf of Mexico. In addition, Florida contains numerous inland lakes and swampy areas. Together, these bodies of water account for Florida's high humidity and generally abundant rainfall. Florida's climate, including the amount of rainfall that occurs, is also influenced by the temperatures of the Atlantic Ocean.

As a result, rainfall across Florida is highly variable, according to location and season. There is usually 20 to 25 cm more rainfall on the coast than in the interior of the state. Some parts of Florida, such as the area shown in **Figure 2,** experience frequent torrential downpours. Periods of extremely heavy rainfall are relatively common in Florida. The highest 24 h total rainfall ever recorded in the United States (98.3 cm) fell on the Gulf Coast of Florida in 1950.

In northern Florida, flooding from heavy rain usually occurs in the winter and early spring. In the summer and fall, the entire state is susceptible to flooding from thunderstorms and hurricanes.

Figure 1 The maritime tropical Atlantic air mass directly affects the rainfall and climate of Florida.

Maritime polar Pacific

Continental polar Canadian

Maritime polar Atlantic

Maritime tropical Pacific

Continental tropical

Maritime tropical Atlantic

Figure 2 Florida's wet season is evident in areas such as the Everglades.

Annual Precipitation

The average annual precipitation in Florida is shown in **Figure 3**. Although the average precipitation, usually rainfall, in Florida is 135 cm, there is considerable variation within the state and throughout the year. **Graph 1** compares the average monthly rainfall in Key West and Miami.

The wet season is between May and October, and accounts for about 70% of the annual rainfall. More than half of the annual rainfall usually occurs from June through September. During the wet season, excess water is discharged into the Atlantic Ocean as runoff. Drainage canals have been constructed to facilitate this process and to protect developed areas from flooding. During the dry season, which is between January and May, irrigation is needed to maintain agriculture, golf courses, and urban landscapes.

Precipitation in Florida can vary greatly from year to year. Both serious droughts and serious floods have occurred. Snow is virtually unheard of in southern Florida, but freezing rain occurs on rare occasions in the Panhandle and the northern part of the state, as shown in **Figure 4**.

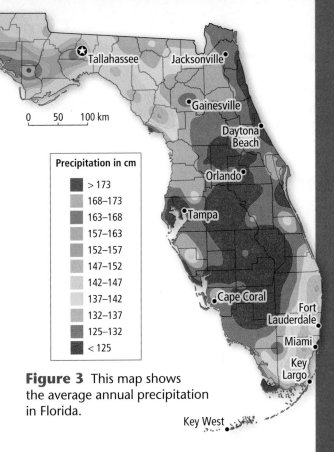

Precipitation in cm
- > 173
- 168–173
- 163–168
- 157–163
- 152–157
- 147–152
- 142–147
- 137–142
- 132–137
- 125–132
- < 125

Figure 3 This map shows the average annual precipitation in Florida.

Graph 1 Although Key West and Miami are not far apart, they experience very different amounts of rainfall.

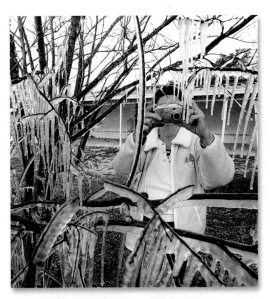

Figure 4 Florida occasionally encounters glaze ice in places like Ormond Beach, near Daytona Beach.

Climate Zones in Florida

As shown in **Figure 5**, there are two primary climate zones in Florida: humid subtropical and humid tropical. Most of the state is in the humid subtropical zone, which is characterized by seasonal temperature variations and sufficient precipitation throughout the year. The southern part of mainland Florida and the Keys are in the humid tropical zone, which is characterized by high temperatures and large amounts of rainfall year-round.

Northern Florida has high humidity year-round, hot summers, cool winters, and occasional freezing. Average annual temperatures range from 18 °C to 21 °C. The central and interior region of Florida is less exposed to cooling breezes, so there are longer periods of high temperature and humidity. The weather is typically warm to hot and humid, allowing central Florida to support a very important citrus industry, shown in **Figure 6.** Arctic air, however, brings periodic hard freezes that can be devastating to citrus crops. South Florida and the Keys are exposed to daytime onshore breezes and have a nearly tropical climate, with high humidity and warm temperatures year-round. Average annual temperatures range from 23 °C to 25 °C. The Keys have frost-free winters.

Florida's climate is an important factor for its tourism industry. Florida's famous beaches, like the one shown in **Figure 7,** and numerous tourist attractions have made it a very popular destination for American and international tourists, particularly during the winter for those who live in colder climates.

Figure 5 Most of Florida is in a humid subtropical climate zone. The southern tip of Florida and the Keys are in a humid tropical climate zone.

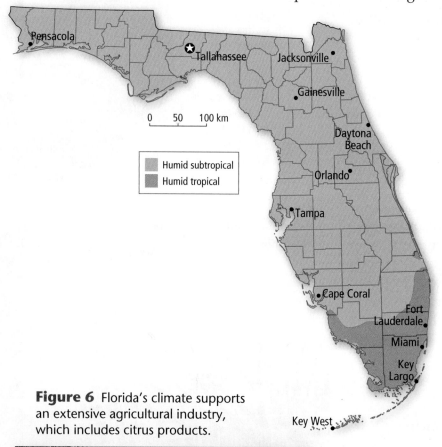

Humid subtropical
Humid tropical

Figure 6 Florida's climate supports an extensive agricultural industry, which includes citrus products.

Figure 7 Many tourists are drawn to Florida's warm climate.

El Niño and La Niña

Florida's weather and climate are affected by El Niño and La Niña. El Niño occurs every 3 to 10 years and usually lasts for about 12 to 15 months. It begins when the top layer of the eastern Pacific Ocean off the coast of Peru warms up, which ultimately causes a change in global weather patterns. In Florida, the effects of El Niño include greater than normal precipitation, as well as less frequent hurricanes in the Gulf of Mexico and Atlantic Ocean. **Figure 8** summarizes some of the effects of the 1982–1983 El Niño in North America. This El Niño event is believed to have been one of the worst ones in history for Florida. The warming of some parts of North America caused weather shifts that resulted in heavier than normal rainfall in the Gulf States. This rainfall caused widespread flooding across the southern United States, including the whole state of Florida!

La Niña is the opposite of El Niño. Stronger Pacific trade winds stir up the water, and deeper, colder water rises to the surface. The colder water cools the Pacific Ocean, causing less moisture to be taken up into the air and, ultimately, a decrease in rainfall. NASA has launched satellites into orbit so Earth scientists can monitor ocean surface temperatures. The data collected, such as the image shown in **Figure 9,** are used to predict El Niño and La Niña events. This image is like a relief map of the oceans. The warming and cooling of the oceans influences sea-surface height, which is indicated by the colors.

Reading Check How is Florida's climate influenced by El Niño?

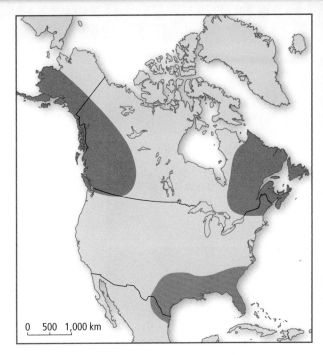

Figure 8 The 1982–1983 El Niño event caused some parts of North America to become warmer (colored red). This ultimately caused heavy rainfall and flooding in other parts (colored blue).

Figure 9 In this satellite map, purple and blue colors indicate cooling of the ocean water. Yellow and red colors indicate warming of the ocean water.

Florida's Geologic History

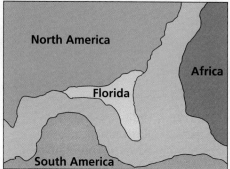

Figure 1 Scientists think that Florida became part of North America only about 200 million years ago.

Florida is located on the North American plate, far from any active tectonic plate boundaries. However, Florida has not always been as tectonically quiet as it is now. Numerous geologic events—including continental drift, mountain-building events on the east coast of the United States, and changing sea levels—have helped to shape Florida. As you learn about the important events in Florida's geologic history, see where they fit on the geologic time scale in Chapter 9.

The Ancient History of Florida

As you read in Chapter 10, scientists think that Earth undergoes supercontinent cycles. In late Precambrian time, the landmass that is now Florida was part of an ancient supercontinent called Rodinia. When Rodinia broke up, about 600 million to 700 million years ago, what we now call Florida is thought to have been part of northwest Africa.

Around 350 million years ago, Earth underwent another supercontinent cycle, resulting in the formation of Pangaea. During the Triassic Period, Pangaea split apart, primarily into the continents Gondwanaland, which included Africa, and Laurasia (ancient North America). A landmass that had been part of Gondwanaland, however, became part of ancient North America, as shown in **Figure 1.** This is the origin of the *basement formation* of present-day Florida.

Florida's *basement rocks* form the geologic foundation located deep under the surface of the state. As you can see in **Figure 2,** the basement rocks include Precambrian-Cambrian and Triassic-Jurrasic igneous rocks, as well as Ordovician-Devonian sedimentary rocks. Fossils of brachiopods and other marine invertebrates that lived in the warm, shallow seas once covering ancient Florida have been used to help date Florida's basement rocks.

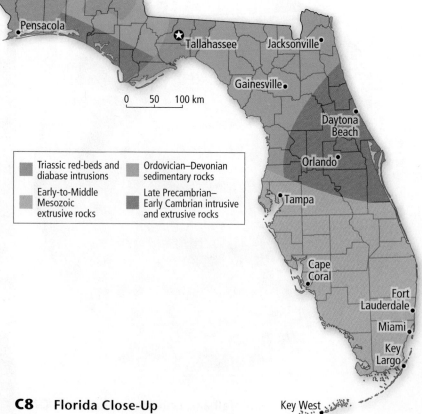

Triassic red-beds and diabase intrusions

Early-to-Middle Mesozoic extrusive rocks

Ordovician–Devonian sedimentary rocks

Late Precambrian–Early Cambrian intrusive and extrusive rocks

Figure 2 This map shows the distribution of Florida's basement rocks.

The Middle History of Florida

When Pangaea started to break apart, the Atlantic Ocean basin began to form. As these events progressed, another basin started to form between the newly formed oceanic crust and the continental crust of what would become North America. This marked the beginning of the formation of Florida's carbonate platform, also called the *Florida Platform.*

Florida's Carbonate Platform

As you can see in **Figure 3,** the Florida Platform is a wide, relatively flat geologic feature that sits between the Gulf of Mexico and the Atlantic Ocean. A large part of it formed during the Cretaceous Period as a result of carbonate deposition on the basement rocks. Most of present-day Florida lies on an exposed part of this platform.

Today, the Florida Platform is 500 km across, from east to west. The eastern edge of the platform is located about 5.5 km off Florida's coast, running from Miami to Palm Beach. The western edge is the Florida escarpment, where the depth of the water plunges to over 3 km in the Gulf of Mexico, more than 160 km west of Tampa.

Carbonate sediment still accumulates on the Florida Platform from the calcium carbonate produced by marine organisms. These carbonate-making organisms, such as the coral in **Figure 4** and certain types of seaweed, help to maintain the platform.

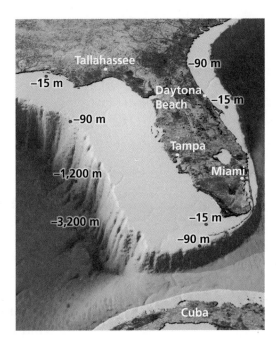

Figure 3 The Florida platform is a vast carbonate formation, most of which is presently underwater.

Figure 4 The base of the Florida escarpment is more than 3 km below sea level. Corals attach themselves to the steep sides of the escarpment to avoid being buried in sediment.

Figure 5 The sea level has fluctuated throughout Florida's geologic history, affecting the types of sediment that have been deposited.

Paleocene **Eocene** **Oligocene** **Miocene** **Pliocene**

Sea-level changes (m)
+200
+100
Present
−100

65 60 55 50 45 40 35 30 25 20 15 10 5 2
Million years ago

Later in the History of Florida

During the Cenozoic Era, regular fluctuations of the sea level occurred over Florida, as shown in **Figure 5.** The sea level varied from up to 200 m above the current level to tens of meters below the current level. Every time the sea level rose, sediment was deposited. As the sea withdrew and the landmass became exposed, erosion removed the deposits. The cycling back and forth between deposition and erosion created the present shape of Florida.

Two main types of sediment have been deposited in Florida throughout the Cenozoic Era, forming carbonate and siliciclastic rocks. Carbonate rocks—mostly dolostone and limestone, shown in **Figure 6**—formed as a result of biological activity. The sediment was primarily made from whole or broken fossils, including foraminifera, bryozoa, molluscs, corals, and other forms of marine life. *Siliciclastic rock* is silica-bearing clastic rock formed from sediment that originated somewhere other than the point of deposition. The most common siliciclastic rocks in Florida are the result of the compaction and cementation of quartz sand, silts, and clays that were the fragments of silica-bearing sedimentary rocks undergoing erosion in areas north of Florida.

Figure 6 Limestone that was deposited as sediment around 30 million years ago is exposed in places like the river banks of Suwanee River State Park.

The Siliciclastic Invasion

The siliciclastic material deposited in Florida is the result of erosion of the Appalachian Mountains, which lie north of Florida. The events related to the so-called *siliciclastic invasion* of Florida are depicted in **Figure 7.**

Before the Oligocene Epoch, very little siliciclastic material was accumulating on the Florida Platform for two main reasons. First, the Gulf Trough, an open seaway from the northern Gulf of Mexico to the Atlantic Ocean, ran across the northern part of the Florida Platform. It diverted the siliciclastic material to the east, away from the Florida Platform. Second, the Appalachian Mountains had been eroding for millions of years, and the amount of siliciclastic material being carried south to the ocean was reduced.

By the late Oligocene Epoch, however, the Gulf Trough had filled in. This occurred when the sea level was low, so rivers draining off the southern Appalachian Mountains created deltas that extended south onto the northern Florida Platform. This was the initial phase of the siliciclastic invasion, which continues today as quartz sand moves south along the beaches of Florida, like that shown in **Figure 8.**

✔ **Reading Check** What is the source of siliciclastic material in Florida?

 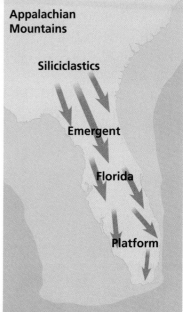

Figure 7 Siliciclastic material from erosion of the Appalachian Mountains began to be deposited in Florida when the Gulf Trough filled in.

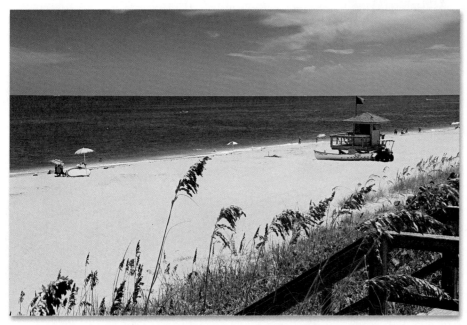

Figure 8 Florida's beautiful beaches are a result of the siliciclastic invasion, which continues today.

Phosphate Deposition

Large-scale marine phosphate deposition started in Florida at the beginning of the Miocene Era. Scientists think that it occurred largely because of an upwelling of cold nutrient-rich water from the deep ocean basins. This upwelling water carried large amounts of phosphorus to the surface of the ocean.

The increased supply of phosphorus contributed to the rapid growth of marine microorganisms, such as the plankton shown in **Figure 9,** for which phosphate is an essential nutrient. As the marine life died, the remaining organic material accumulated on the bottom of the ocean. This organic material mixed with other sediment and became buried. A series of chemical reactions caused it to change into a mineral form of phosphate. The phosphate deposits were then concentrated by ocean currents and waves.

Some of the phosphate-based deposits are now economically important in Florida, as shown in **Figure 10.** Fertilizers are the most important product from the phosphates mined in Florida. You will read more about the contribution of phosphate mining to Florida's economy in a later section, which discusses Florida's natural resources.

Figure 9 Cold water filled with nutrients rose up from deep ocean basins. This upwelling water supported large numbers of microorganisms.

Figure 10 Mining the phosphate that was deposited millions of years ago is important to Florida's economy.

The Ice Age in Florida

Most of Florida's current topography is due to events that occurred during the Pleistocene Epoch. Around 1.8 million years ago, shallow seas covered what is now southern Florida. These seas fluctuated throughout the Pleistocene Epoch, flooding and retreating many times, ranging from 45 m above to 90 m below present sea level. These fluctuations in sea level were due to periods of advancing and retreating glaciers in the Northern Hemisphere, when huge ice sheets either trapped or released massive amounts of sea water.

During the Ice Age, areas north of Florida were covered in thick continental glaciers. Since much of the sea water was trapped as ice, sea level was low and Florida had as much as three times the current land area, as shown in **Figure 11.** When the ice thawed, sea level rose and peninsular Florida probably consisted of only islands. As the sea level fluctuated, shore waves and currents eroded older geologic features or carved out new features. Many of these, such as the Cody Scarp, are now found far inland.

As the last glaciers melted, sea level rose and nutrient-rich water flooded over the southern tip of Florida, covering the area in sediment that included a large quantity of broken shell fragments. The area of the present Everglades was a shallow marine bank, which filled with the carbonate sediment in the shape of ridges. These sediment ridges became covered in mangrove trees, which protected the edges of the shallow bank. Carbonate sediment and shallow reefs made from bryozoa, which are similar to coral, accumulated in the shallow bank. Without high-energy coastal waves, these materials settled and solidified into the limestone that underlies the Everglades today, as shown in **Figure 12.**

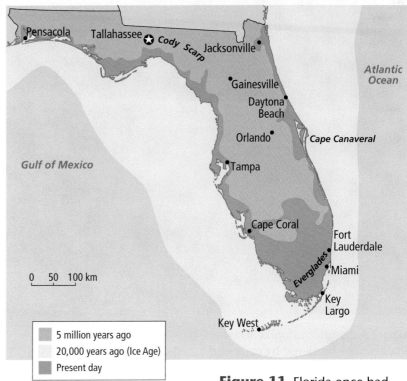

	5 million years ago
	20,000 years ago (Ice Age)
	Present day

0   50   100 km

Figure 11 Florida once had as much as three times its current land area.

Figure 12 Limestone that underlies the Everglades today was formed from the accumulation of sediment, which included shell fragments and bryozoan reefs.

Figure 13 Southern Florida and the Florida Keys are bordered by coral reef formations, visible through the sea water in this photo.

History of the Florida Keys

The Florida Keys, shown in **Figure 13,** are the remains of once-living coral reefs. These islands continue to be surrounded by coral today. During the Pleistocene Epoch, coral colonies grew rapidly and abundantly along the edge of the Florida Platform when sea level was high. The coral colonies became exposed when sea level fell, and the microorganisms died, leaving behind calcium carbonate skeletons that formed reefs. When the sea level rose again, the dead reefs provided an ideal foundation for the growth of new coral. Therefore, when the sea level was high, the coral reefs developed upward. As the sea level decreased, the coral colonies moved to lower depths along the platform.

These successive periods of growth caused Key Largo limestone to accumulate to thicknesses of 23 to 61 m. Key Largo limestone, shown in **Figure 14,** is primarily made of dead coral, shells, and other organic debris. The last significant decrease in sea level exposed some of this limestone, which became the present-day Florida Keys.

During reef growth, sand banks sometimes accumulated behind the reefs, forming lime-sand banks. Miami limestone is granular rock, white to tan in color, that was created from the lime-sand banks covering the southwestern end of the coral reefs. After the last drop in sea level, these banks became exposed and formed the Lower Keys. Miami limestone can be found in layers up to 11 m thick throughout the Lower Keys.

Figure 14 Miami limestone (left) and Key Largo limestone (right) formed in the Florida Keys.

Coral Reefs Continue Today

Corals are colonies of living organisms called polyps, shown in **Figure 15**, that live in a calcium carbonate skeleton. Polyps have a central opening that is surrounded by tentacles, which are used to catch phytoplankton for food.

Coral-reef formation continues in Florida, with corals growing in the shallow water around the Keys and along the southern edge of the Florida Platform. Because the water is shallow, plenty of light can reach the growing corals. The nutrient-rich Gulf Stream flows past, providing an abundance of food for the corals. These conditions have led to Florida's spectacular shallow coral formations, such as the one shown in **Figure 16.** Not only is Florida the only state with abundant shallow coral formations, but its reef tract is the third-largest barrier reef in the world!

Much of southern Florida's coastline would be underwater without these extraordinary formations. The coral reefs reduce the energy of incoming water by causing waves to break along the reef patches, thus protecting the shoreline from the full force of the ocean. This reduces the impact of erosion, which otherwise would remove large quantities of sand and other materials.

Unfortunately, some species of corals are now on the endangered list. Pollution, recreational boating, and shipping, as shown in **Figure 17,** have damaged Florida's coral reefs. Therefore, several state and federal agencies, as well as volunteer groups, now work together in the Coral Reef Conservation Program to help protect Florida's coral reefs.

Reading Check Why does Florida contain high amounts of phosphate deposits?

Figure 15 Coral polyps are surrounded by a limestone skeleton. Coral reefs are formed by many types of polyp colonies.

Figure 16 The reef at John Pennekamp Coral Reef State Park, shown here, is one example of Florida's spectacular coral reefs.

Figure 17 Shipping is one factor that contributes to coral reef damage.

Florida has both nonrenewable and renewable natural resources. Wise management of these resources is necessary if Floridians are to keep their current lifestyle.

Water Resources

A hydrologic divide runs across northern Florida, as shown in **Figure 1.** Neither groundwater nor surface water crosses this divide. While the northern part of the peninsula can access fresh water from neighboring states, the area south of the divide is considered to be a hydrologic island. Therefore, southern Florida's freshwater needs must be met by precipitation. Alternatives include pumping in water from the north and desalinating ocean water. This is a serious concern since about 80% of Florida's population lives in the south. **Table 1** shows the discrepancy between where most of the fresh-water resources are and where most fresh water is consumed.

Surface Water

Florida is covered by over 16,000 km of rivers and streams and 7,800 lakes. As you can see in **Figure 1,** the major rivers are the St. Johns, St. Mary's, and Suwannee Rivers. The major lakes are Lake Okeechobee (the second largest freshwater lake in the nation) and Lake George.

Florida's surface water is also contained within its wetlands, such as the Everglades and Big Cypress Swamp, shown in **Figure 2.**

Table 1

Distribution of Water in Florida		
Location in Florida	Water resources	Water consumed
North of Interstate 4	80%	20%
South of Interstate 4	20%	80%

Figure 1 Florida is covered by more than 30,000 km² of water in the form of rivers, lakes, and streams.

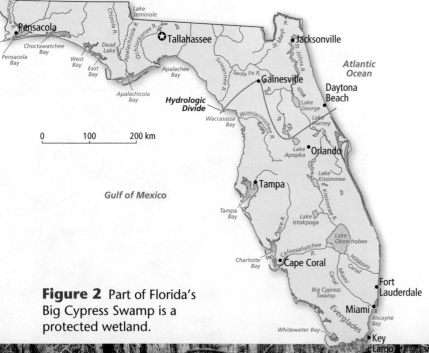

Figure 2 Part of Florida's Big Cypress Swamp is a protected wetland.

Groundwater

There is an abundant supply of groundwater in Florida. In fact, Florida has more available groundwater than any other state. **Figure 3** shows a map of the aquifers in Florida, which contain the groundwater that supplies almost all of the state's drinking water. The major source of groundwater is the Floridan aquifer system. Floridians draw about 9.5 billion liters of water out of the aquifer every day. In southern Florida and the far western panhandle, the Floridan aquifer system is deep underground and produces salty mineralized water. Therefore, in these areas, the sand-and-gravel and Biscayne aquifers are used for water supply.

Surficial aquifers are shallow beds of shells and sand that are only about 30 m below the surface of the ground. They generally produce less water, so they are used primarily for domestic and smaller public-supply wells. The Biscayne aquifer is an intensely used water source, supplying fresh water to Dade, Broward, Palm Beach, and Monroe counties. Because of its proximity to highly populated areas and the surface, it is extremely vulnerable to pollution.

The Floridan aquifer, shown in **Figure 4,** is one of the most productive aquifers in the world and underlies the entire state. Unlike the surficial aquifers, groundwater in the Floridan aquifer is contained under pressure, buried deep within underlying limestone. This gives rise to artesian springs and wells.

Florida's heavy reliance on its aquifer system requires a significant effort from offices such as Florida's Department of Environmental Protection. To protect one of Florida's vital resources, continual monitoring of the effects of human activity on the aquifers is essential.

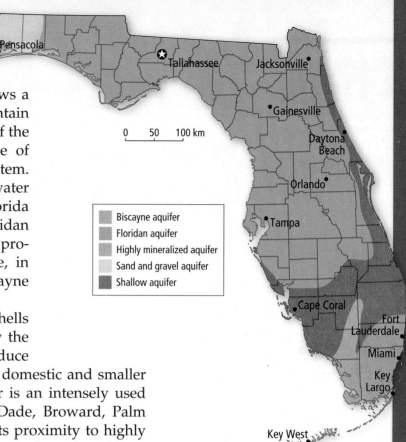

Biscayne aquifer
Floridan aquifer
Highly mineralized aquifer
Sand and gravel aquifer
Shallow aquifer

Figure 3 This map shows the aquifers in Florida, which hold the groundwater resources.

Figure 4 The Floridan aquifer system underlies all of Florida and supplies fresh water to many cities, including Daytona, St. Petersburg, Tallahassee, Gainesville, and Jacksonville.

Figure 5 Wakulla Spring, near Tallahassee, is one of the world's largest and deepest spring systems.

Florida's Springs

Springs form when groundwater is forced up to the surface through openings in the ground. Springs are classified based on the amount of water they discharge. Florida has 33 first magnitude springs (springs that discharge water at a rate of 2.8 m^3 per second or greater), which is more than any other state. The volume of water flowing from a spring depends on many factors, which include the water pressure in the aquifer, the number and size of the caves leading to the opening of the spring, and the size of the opening itself.

North-central Florida has the highest concentration of springs, because the aquifer in this area is closest to the surface. First magnitude springs, such as Silver Spring and Wakulla Spring, shown in **Figure 5**, discharge more than 246 million liters of water a day. Florida's springs support entire river ecosystems, such as the Suwannee and Santa Fe ecosystems. The 320 springs in Florida's spring system make it the largest in the world by volume. Together, these springs discharge over 72 billion liters of fresh water each day. Many of these springs are located in state parks, where they are protected and available for recreational use, such as scuba diving, as shown in **Figure 6.**

Figure 6 Florida's springs attract scuba divers, who can enter a spring through the vent and swim down into the aquifer.

Energy Resources

As you can see in **Figure 7**, Florida relies on natural gas, petroleum, coal, and nuclear energy for electricity generation. Florida has only minor oil and gas reserves, however, and few other energy resources. Since Florida's residential energy consumption is among the highest in the country, looking for sources of renewable energy is particularly important to Floridians. In fact, the state government has set a target for utilities to get 20% of their power from renewable energy sources by 2020.

Legend:
- ■ Nuclear power plant
- ■ Coal-fired power plant
- ▲ Oil-fired power plant
- ■ Natural gas-fired power plant

Figure 7 This map shows Florida's energy resources.

Oil and Natural Gas

Both oil and natural gas are nonrenewable energy resources because they are consumed at a faster rate than they are produced. Geologists think that large deposits of oil and gas are located off Florida's western coast in the Gulf of Mexico, making this area a potential site for exploration.

Oil production on land is relatively small in Florida. The Cretaceous Sunniland Formation in Collier County is the major source of oil, at a depth of 3 to 4 km. The Bear Island and Raccoon Point oil fields are two oil fields that are being worked in the Sunniland Formation.

Nuclear Energy

Since nuclear energy requires uranium, this is also a nonrenewable energy source. Florida has three nuclear power plants: Crystal River, St Lucie, and Turkey Point, shown in **Figure 8**. Together, they supply approximately 20% of the state's electricity. Concerns over fossil-fuel emissions and an increased need for electricity have prompted a heightened interest in using more nuclear power in Florida. After decades of no new developments, there has been a resurgence of proposals for building nuclear power plants in Florida.

Figure 8 The Turkey Point Nuclear Power Plant, on Biscayne Bay, is known for a unique crocodile habitat in its cooling canal system.

Hydroelectric Energy

Florida has little topographical relief, so it produces very little hydroelectric power compared with the other states. In fact, there are only two hydroelectric power plants in the entire state. The Jim Woodruff Lock and Dam, also known as the Lake Seminole project, is built on the Apalachicola River on the Georgia-Florida border. This plant produces enough electricity for 50,000 homes. The other plant, the C.H. Corn Hydroelectric Plant shown in **Figure 9**, is located on Lake Talquin near Tallahassee.

Solar Energy

Since Florida is "the sunshine state," it makes sense to use the power of the sun to generate energy. Florida's strategy has involved expanding the use of solar electric systems (or photovoltaics), which produce electricity from sunlight, as well as solar thermal systems, which produce heat that is used to generate steam. The steam is then used to turn turbines that produce electricity. Florida has also developed several solar energy incentive programs. These programs include the SunSmart Schools Program administered by the Florida Solar Energy Center, which selects schools in Florida to receive photovoltaic systems. In addition, the EnergyWhiz Olympics, shown in **Figure 10**, is an annual event that challenges students to use renewable energy to power cars and other devices.

Figure 9 The C.H. Corn Hydroelectric Plant, on Lake Talquin near Tallahassee, is one of two hydroelectric plants in Florida.

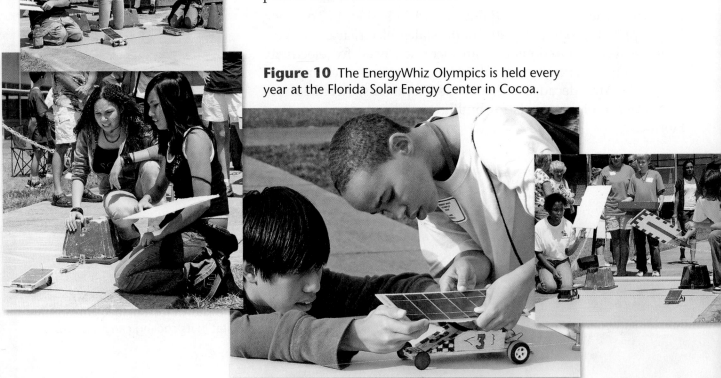

Figure 10 The EnergyWhiz Olympics is held every year at the Florida Solar Energy Center in Cocoa.

Mineral Resources

Florida has significant mineral resources, with almost 200 working mines throughout the state. Florida's primary mineral-resource products are limestone, peat, clay, sand and gravel, phosphate, titanium, zircon, and staurolite. Four of these are shown in **Figure 11.** The annual value of these and other nonfuel mineral-resource products is almost $2 billion, ranking Florida's mineral-resource product value as fifth in the nation. **Table 2** lists some of the important mineral-resource products in Florida.

Phosphate Mining

As you learned earlier, Florida experienced large-scale marine phosphate deposition about 25 million years ago. These deposits are now being mined, as shown in **Figure 12,** and have become the source of Florida's commercial phosphate supply. These deposits provide 75% of the phosphate needed in the United States and 25% of the phosphate needed globally.

Most of the phosphate mined in Florida is chemically treated to make fertilizer. Each year, Florida exports over $1 billion worth of fertilizer. Phosphate has many other uses as well, including its addition to vitamins, soft drinks, and toothpastes. The mining and processing of phosphate creates significant waste, so it is important that this waste is treated and disposed of properly.

Reading Check **Describe the two types of solar energy systems that Florida is using and developing.**

Figure 11 Some of the resources that are mined in Florida include (a) limestone, (b) phosphate, (c) zircon, and (d) staurolite.

Table 2

Florida's Nonfuel Mineral-Resource Products	
cement	magnesium compounds
common clay	phosphate rock
crushed stone	peat
fuller's earth	rutile
gypsum	sand and gravel
kaolin	staurolite
lime	titanium concentrates
limestone	zirconium concentrates

Figure 12 The Hopewell Mine in Hillsborough is one of seven active phosphate mines in Florida.

Natural Hazards in Florida

Florida's warm climate and close proximity to the Atlantic Ocean and Gulf of Mexico make it a prime target for weather-related natural disasters. Although Florida does not experience geologic hazards, such as earthquakes, it does have a significant problem with sinkholes.

Karst Formations

Recall from Chapter 16 that karst terrain develops when underlying rock material is water soluble. The limestone underlying most of Florida dissolves in the naturally acidic groundwater that flows through it, causing cracks, conduits, caves, and caverns. Interestingly, karst formations make north-central Florida one of the world's leading cave-diving destinations. One of these karst formations is shown in **Figure 1.** As the rock continues to dissolve, however, the cavities increase in size and the overlying rock may collapse, causing a sinkhole.

Figure 1 This is the main entrance to the Peacock/Orange Grove Cave System.

Sinkholes

Sinkholes are well known in Florida for the destruction they can cause to roadways and property. In fact, Florida has more sinkholes than any other state. According to the Federal Emergency Management Agency (FEMA), insurance claims for damage as a result of sinkholes have increased significantly over the last two decades. On the other hand, sinkholes give direct entry into groundwater and, therefore, provide access for surface water to enter the aquifer system and replenish Florida's vital groundwater resources.

Lake Jackson, near Tallahassee, is located over sinkholes that drain into the Floridan aquifer. The sinkholes are usually plugged, but occasionally they become unplugged and water in the lake drains into the aquifer. In 1999, this caused over half the water in the lake, as well as fish and alligators, to disappear into the aquifer. Photos of the Lake Jackson sinkhole are shown in **Figure 2.**

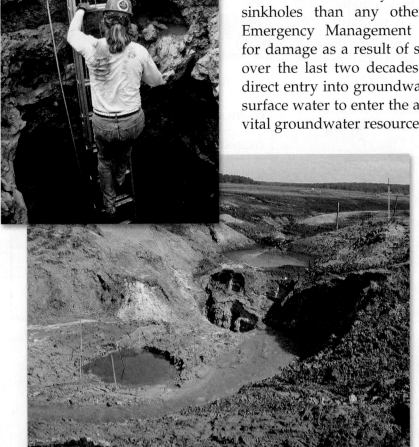

Figure 2 This sinkhole, which is 2.5 m in diameter, caused Lake Jackson to drain in 1999. Geologists climbed into the sinkhole to study how it became unplugged.

Thunderstorms and Lightning

Florida has more thunderstorms and lightning strikes than any other state. Not only is lightning the leading cause of weather-related deaths in Florida, but the state also has the most recorded deaths by lightning in the nation. On average, the interior of central Florida receives the most thunderstorms, on nearly 100 days per year. Although Florida's thunderstorms are generally less than 24 km in diameter, they can grow vertically to great heights, sometimes in excess of 16 km. This explains why a Florida thunderstorm directly overhead can produce a large amount of rain in a short amount of time. Florida's lightning, like the bolt shown in **Figure 3**, is very strongly charged.

Tornadoes and Waterspouts

A tornado forms when a thunderstorm meets horizontal winds, which cause the air in the thunderstorm to rotate. This produces the characteristic column of air that rotates at very high wind speeds. On average, about 45 tornadoes hit Florida each year.

Tornadoes occasionally accompany tropical storms and hurricanes that move over land. Waterspouts, such as the one shown in **Figure 4,** are weak tornadoes that form over warm water. Waterspouts are most common along the Gulf Coast, but they occasionally move inland and become tornadoes.

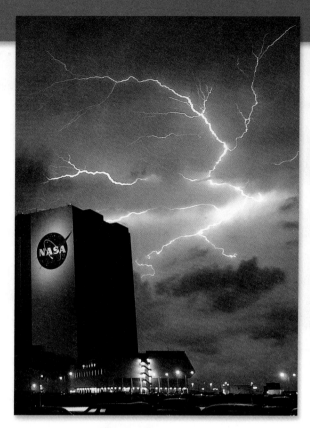

Figure 3 Florida sustains more lightning strikes than any other state.

Figure 4 This waterspout off the Florida Keys shows the characteristic vertical column of water.

Hurricanes

Hurricanes begin as tropical depressions, which are thunderstorms that come together over warm water and begin to spin in an organized way. When a tropical depression strengthens and has winds of 63 to 117 km/h, it is called a tropical storm and assigned a name. Tropical storms that spiral inward toward a center and have sustained winds in excess of 120 km/h are called hurricanes. Hurricanes are the strongest tropical storms on Earth. **Figure 5** shows a distinctive dark spot in the middle, which is the eye. Surrounding the eye is the eye wall, which contains the most intense winds and rainfall.

Figure 5 This photo of Hurricane Fran in 1996 shows the eye of the hurricane.

Florida's hurricane season is between June 1 and November 30, and requires all Floridians to be prepared. Floridians have considerable experience dealing with the intense precipitation and high winds of a hurricane, as shown in **Figure 6**, and know just how destructive a hurricane can be.

Figure 6 Hurricanes bring heavy rainfall and high winds.

Devastating Hurricanes

Unfortunately, Florida has experienced considerable devastation from hurricanes. Recent significant hurricanes include Hurricane Andrew, shown in **Figure 7**, which hit Florida in 1992. There were 25 direct and indirect deaths from Hurricane Andrew, as well as over $25 billion in damage. In 2005, Hurricane Katrina became one of the strongest American coastal storms in the past 100 years. It hit Miami Beach with wind speeds of up to 130 km/h and moved quickly over the Florida peninsula, causing 11 deaths in Florida. Later that year, Hurricane Wilma also caused severe damage to southern Florida.

Figure 7 This radar image shows Hurricane Andrew making landfall in Dade County on August 24, 1992.

Rising Sea Level

Although the exact effects of global warming cannot be predicted, scientists agree that it is occurring and that much of the sea water frozen in the far northern and southern ice sheets and glaciers is beginning to melt. Scientists think that this will cause the sea level to rise, and have predicted the impact on the Florida peninsula. **Figure 8** shows what would happen if the sea level rose by 5 m and 10 m—the predicted scale if significant melting in Greenland or Antarctica occurred. Notice that nearly all of Florida south of Lake Okeechobee, including the Florida Keys, would become submerged!

Coastal Erosion

Natural beach erosion occurs gradually, as drift and currents move water parallel to the shore, and sand is carried along with the water. When sand is being removed by departing currents at the same rate that it is being deposited, no net erosion occurs. Hurricanes and other severe weather can have sudden effects, however, as large storm surges change the distribution of sand along the beaches.

In addition, human-made structures can block or interrupt the natural movement and deposition of sand and other materials along the coastline. Human-made structures can trap sand in one area and inhibit deposition of sand farther along the coast. Although the currents continue to move sand out of that area, there is no sand replacing it and heavy erosion results. **Figure 9** shows an area in Florida with extensive coastal erosion.

Reading Check **Identify three natural hazards that Floridians may face.**

Figure 8 This digitally enhanced NASA satellite image shows the impact that a 5 m rise (dark blue) and a 10 m rise (light blue) in sea level would have on Florida.

Figure 9 Juno Beach in Palm Beach County is an example of a heavily eroded coastline.

Clean Up Your Act

When you wash dishes, the bathroom sink, your clothes, or a car, you wash them with water. But have you ever wondered how water gets clean? Filtration is a common method of removing various pollutants from water. Cities in Florida, such as North Miami and Tampa, use filtration systems to produce high-quality drinking water. Filtration requires very little energy—gravity pulls water down through the layers of filter material. In this lab, you will see how well this energy-efficient method works to clean samples of polluted water. You will test water samples that contain decaying plant matter, powdered clay, vinegar, and laundry detergent.

Materials

beaker, 600 mL (2)
beaker, 1,000 mL (2)
charcoal, activated
clay, powdered
decaying plant matter
gravel
hammer and nail, small
hand lens
laundry detergent
pH test strips
ring stand with ring
sand
scissors
soda bottle, plastic, 2 L
spoon, plastic (2)
vinegar
water, 2,000 mL

Safety

Form a Hypothesis

❶ Form a hypothesis about whether and how filtration will clean each of the four pollutants from the water. Predict whether the pollutant will be completely, partially, or not removed. Then, use the steps below to test your hypothesis.

Test the Hypothesis

❷ Put on your apron, gloves, and goggles. Using scissors, carefully cut the bottom out of the empty soda bottle.

❸ Carefully punch four or five small holes through the plastic cap of the bottle by using a small nail and a hammer. Screw the plastic cap onto the bottle.

❹ Turn the bottle upside down, and set its neck in the ring of a ring stand, as shown on the next page. Put a handful of gravel into the inverted bottle. Add a layer of activated charcoal, followed by thick layers of sand and gravel. Place a 600-mL beaker under the neck of the bottle.

❺ Fill two 1,000-mL beakers with 1,000 mL of clean water. Set one beaker aside to serve as the control. Add three or four spoonfuls of each of the following pollutants to the other beaker: decaying plant matter, powdered clay, household vinegar, and laundry detergent.

6 Copy the table below into a notebook, and record your observations for each beaker in the columns labeled "Before cleaning."

7 Observe the color of the water in each beaker.

8 Use a hand lens to examine the water for visible particles.

9 Smell the water, and note any unusual odor.

10 Stir the water in each beaker rapidly with a plastic spoon, and check for suds. Use a different spoon for each sample.

11 Use a pH test strip to find the pH of the water in each beaker.

12 Gently stir the clean water, and then pour half of it through the filtration device into one of the 600-mL collection beakers.

13 Observe the water in the collection beaker for color, particles, odors, suds, and pH. Be patient. It may take several minutes for the water to travel through the filtration device. Record your observations in the column labeled "After filtration (clean water)" in your table.

14 Repeat steps 12 and 13 using the polluted water. Record your observations in the column labeled "After filtration (polluted water)" in your table.

Results Table				
	Before cleaning (clean water)	Before cleaning (polluted water)	After filtration (clean water)	After filtration (polluted water)
Color				
Particles				
Odor				
Suds				
pH				

DO NOT WRITE IN THIS BOOK.

Analysis and Conclusion

1. How did the color of the polluted water change after filtration? Did the color of the clean water change?

2. Did the filtration method remove all of the visible particles from the polluted water? How do you know?

3. Did any suds form in the "After filtration (polluted water)" step? Explain.

4. How much did the pH of the polluted water change?

5. How did the final pH of the polluted water compare to the pH of the clean water before filtering?

Extension

Applying Your Data
Filtration is only one method that produces high-quality drinking water at water treatment plants. Research other methods that are used to produce high-quality drinking water at water treatment plants in Florida.

Close-Up Review

UNDERSTANDING KEY IDEAS

1. The prevailing winds in Florida blow from SC.912.E.7.8
   a. the north.
   b. the south.
   c. the east.
   d. the west.

2. The highest point in Florida is SC.912.E.6.4
   a. Sugarloaf Mountain.
   b. Britton Hill.
   c. Big Cypress Swamp.
   d. the Everglades.

3. Around 600 million years ago, Florida was part of
   a. Australia. SC.912.E.6.3
   b. west Africa.
   c. the Atlantic Ocean Basin.
   d. the Americas.

4. Rocks that are NOT part of Florida's basement rocks are SC.912.E.6.4
   a. Precambrian-Cambrian igneous rocks.
   b. Ordovician-Devonian sedimentary rocks.
   c. Precambrian carbonate rocks.
   d. Triassic-Jurassic volcanic rocks.

5. El Niño originates in SC.912.E.7.2
   a. the Pacific Ocean, off the coast of California.
   b. the Pacific Ocean, off the coast of Peru.
   c. the Atlantic Ocean, off the coast of Florida.
   d. the Gulf of Mexico.

6. An energy resource that Florida relies on a great deal for electricity is SC.912.E.6.6
   a. hydroelectric power.
   b. geothermal power.
   c. wind power.
   d. nuclear power.

7. Florida's modern coastline has been shaped mainly by SC.912.E.6.4
   a. fluctuations in sea level.
   b. earthquakes.
   c. volcanoes.
   d. sea-floor spreading.

8. Which of the following statements about the Florida Keys is false? SC.912.E.6.4
   a. The Florida Keys were formed about 1.8 million years ago.
   b. The Florida Keys are located near the northern edge of the Florida Platform.
   c. The Florida Keys are the remains of once-living marine microorganisms.
   d. The Florida Keys contain Key Largo limestone.

9. Karst formations occur when SC.912.E.6.4
   a. sinkholes create caverns in the rock below the surface.
   b. the rock below the surface is not very soluble.
   c. the groundwater is very basic.
   d. the rock below the surface is soluble.

10. Which of the following statements about waterspouts is true? SC.912.E.7.6
    a. Waterspouts develop from hurricanes.
    b. Waterspouts strengthen over land.
    c. Waterspouts are weak tornadoes that form over water
    d. Waterspouts are strong tornadoes that form over land.

SHORT ANSWER

11. How does the Florida Current affect Florida's climate? SC.912.E.7.4

12. Describe Florida's geologic location. SC.912.E.6.4

13. How did the Florida Platform form? SC.912.E.6.4

14. Briefly describe two of Florida's aquifers. SC.912.E.6.4

15. Explain how a sinkhole forms. SC.912.E.6.4

16. What are the two main climate zones in Florida? SC.912.E.7.4

17. Describe two factors that influence how much water flows from a spring. SC.912.E.7.3

18. What are key characteristics of a hurricane? SC.912.E.7.6

19. Explain how human-made structures influence coastal erosion.

20. Why is southern Florida referred to as a hydrologic island? SC.912.E.7.3

CRITICAL THINKING

21. Making Comparisons Compare how an El Niño event develops and affects Florida with how a La Niña event develops and affects Florida.

22. Analyzing Relationships Explain the relationship between the erosion of the Appalachian Mountains and the sandy beaches on Florida's coastline. SC.912.E.6.4

23. Analyzing Ideas Explain why hydroelectric power plants are rare in Florida. SC.912.E.6.4

24. Making Inferences What would happen to the Florida coastline if the coral reefs around the Florida Keys were destroyed? Describe two possible effects. SC.912.E.6.4

CONCEPT MAPPING

25. Use the following terms to create a concept map: *erosion, deposition, siliciclastic invasion, Florida Platform, phosphates, coral reefs, microorganisms, sea level, glaciation,* and *limestone.* SC.912.E.6.4

MATH SKILLS

26. Making Calculations At the edges of the Florida Platform, the depth of the water hits 90 m. The Florida Platform is about 500 km across, from east to west, and the edges are 160 km west of Tampa and 5.5 km east of Miami. How wide is the Florida peninsula between Tampa and Miami? SC.912.E.6.4

WRITING SKILLS

27. Writing from Research Imagine that, one day, you notice the ground in your schoolyard beginning to sink. Research sinkholes, and prepare a brief report that describes how you can determine if your schoolyard is in danger of turning into a sinkhole. Also describe the steps you need to take if it is, in fact, turning into a sinkhole. Write a paragraph about how sinkholes can be triggered and how and where to report sinkholes. SC.912.E.6.4

INTERPRETING GRAPHICS

The bar graph below shows sand-dune elevations along the southeast coast of Florida. The *x*-axis indicates the elevations of the sand dunes, and the *y*-axis indicates the percentage of occurrences of sand dunes that are at these elevations. Use this bar graph to answer the questions that follow.

Sand-Dune Elevations

28. What are the maximum and minimum sand-dune elevations on Florida's southeast coast? SC.912.E.6.4

29. What is the mean sand-dune elevation on Florida's southeast coast? SC.912.E.6.4

30. What sand-dune elevation occurs most often on the southeast coast of Florida? SC.912.E.6.4

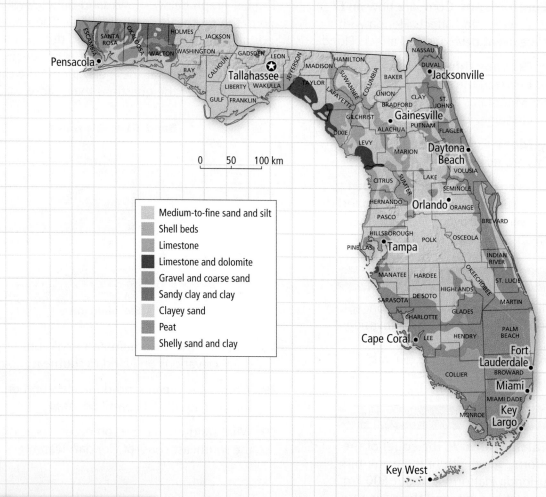

MAPS *in Action*

Environmental Geology Map of Florida

Legend:
- Medium-to-fine sand and silt
- Shell beds
- Limestone
- Limestone and dolomite
- Gravel and coarse sand
- Sandy clay and clay
- Clayey sand
- Peat
- Shelly sand and clay

0   50   100 km

Map ▶ Skills Activity

This map shows environmental geologic data for Florida. The different colors represent different surface and subsurface materials. Use the map to answer the questions below.

1. **Using a Key** What is the dominant material along Florida's east coast?

2. **Using a Key** What is the dominant material in southern Florida?

3. **Analyzing Data** What is the dominant material associated with the northern border of Florida?

4. **Inferring Relationships** Well-developed karst terrain is found where limestone is close to the surface. With this in mind, where do you think the most developed karst terrain is found in Florida?

5. **Identifying Relationships** The southern part of Florida contains some of the most diverse wetlands in the United States. What type of subsurface material is associated with these wetlands? Where else are wetlands likely to be located in Florida? Explain your answer.

6. **Analyzing Data** What material is associated with the Florida Keys? How is this consistent with what you have learned about the geologic history of the Keys?

SCIENCE & SOCIETY

The Kennedy Space Center

Florida is home to the National Aeronautics and Space Administration (NASA) Kennedy Space Center. Merritt Island and Cape Canaveral were chosen to be the location of the Space Center because the area was undeveloped, missiles could be launched without danger to nearby communities, the climate allowed year-round operation, and tracking stations in the Atlantic Ocean could follow the progress of missiles. In turn, space exploration has become a key part of Florida's identity and economy. Center-based activities bring in over $1 billion in out-of-state money each year and provide over 23,000 jobs in Florida.

The Space Center has played a pivotal role in space exploration and scientific research by being a launch site for NASA's space program.

In 2007, almost $3.2 million was spent by tourists who came to see the Space Center's numerous attractions, such as the *Saturn V* moon rocket.

YOUR TURN

UNDERSTANDING CONCEPTS
What are two important contributions that the Kennedy Space Center makes to Florida's economy?

WRITING IN SCIENCE
Research a space-exploration mission that took off from the Kennedy Space Center. Describe what was or is being studied and how the results might benefit Floridians.

Physical Science Connections for Space Science

As you begin your study of space science, here is some important background information on two physical science concepts that are key to space science: gravitation and electromagnetic radiation.

Gravitation and Other Fundamental Forces

Gravitation is a universal force that each mass exerts on any other mass. Gravitation is the force that keeps planets in orbit around the sun and holds planets, stars, and galaxies together. The force of gravitation increases as the mass of an object increases or the distance between objects decreases.

Gravitation is one of four fundamental forces. The other three are (1) the electromagnetic force, (2) the strong nuclear force, and (3) the weak nuclear force. The electromagnetic force exists between any two charged objects, such as protons and electrons in an atom. The strong and weak nuclear forces hold together subatomic particles in atomic nuclei. The table below compares the magnitudes and ranges of the four fundamental forces. Gravitation is by far the weakest force, but it exists between any two objects in the universe no matter how far apart they are.

Force	Relative strength	Range of force
Strong nuclear force	1	Nuclear distances
Electromagnetic force	10^{-2}	Great distances
Weak nuclear force	10^{-13}	Nuclear distances
Gravitational force	10^{-38}	Great distances

Electromagnetic Radiation

Astronomers learn about the universe by studying light and other forms of electromagnetic radiation from distant stars and galaxies. What we refer to as light consists of the wavelengths of radiation that our eyes can detect. In the Space unit, you will learn about many other forms of electromagnetic radiation that have wavelengths shorter or longer than those of visible light.

All objects in the universe emit and absorb electromagnetic radiation. Most objects absorb some incoming radiation and reflect the rest. Physicists call an idealized object that absorbs all incoming radiation a blackbody. For example, stars are close to ideal blackbodies, but everyday objects are not because they reflect as well as emit radiation. The type of radiation emitted by a blackbody depends only on its temperature. At room temperature, most of the radiation is infrared. As the temperature rises above a few hundred degrees Celsius, the blackbody also emits visible light and eventually ultraviolet light.

Why It Matters

In our efforts to study space, we have developed many technologies, from simple telescopes to the International Space Station. Human interest in the regions beyond Earth has impacted life on the surface of the planet, as well as above it, in many ways.

A Model Telescope

Ask a partner to hold up this textbook 1 m away from you. Use a pair of hand lenses to form your model telescope. Hold one lens close to your eye. Hold the second lens in the other hand, and move it back and forth until you can see a clear image of the book cover. Use a meterstick to measure the distance between the two lenses. Have your partner hold the book at different distances, and find the lens arrangement with the clearest image. Then switch roles.

Questions to Get You Started

1. How did you make the textbook image clearer when it was closer to you and farther from you?

2. How could you redesign the telescope so you would not have to hold the lenses?

SC.912.P.10.22

READING TOOLBOX

These reading tools will help you learn the material in this chapter.

Frequency

Always, Sometimes, Never Many statements include a word that tells you about the frequency of the information in the statement. Examples include words such as *always, sometimes, often,* and *never.* Words such as *some, many,* and *most* are examples of words that tell you about frequency in number.

Your Turn As you read this chapter, record examples of statements that contain frequency words. In each statement, underline the word that tells you about the frequency of the information in the statement or about frequency in number in the statement. Here is one example:

> To measure distances in the solar system, astronomers <u>often</u> use astronomical units.

Describing Space

Using Spatial Language Spatial language is used to describe space and the universe. It can be used to describe

- the shape of objects
- the location of objects
- distance
- orientation
- direction of motion

Your Turn As you read this chapter, complete a table like the one below. Add words or phrases that use spatial language to describe something.

Shape	Location	Distance	Orientation	Direction
spherical	in the core	a long way	vertical	outward
cube	at the North Pole	kilometer	tilt	south

FoldNotes

Key-Term Fold The key-term fold can help you learn key terms from this chapter.

Your Turn Create a key-term fold for Section 1, as described in **Appendix A.**

1. Write one key term on the front of each tab.
2. Write a definition or description for each term under its tab.

3. Use this FoldNote to help you review the key terms.

For more information on how to use these and other tools, see **Appendix A.**

Key Ideas	Key Terms	Why It Matters
❯ Describe characteristics of the universe in terms of time, distance, and organization. ❯ Identify the visible and nonvisible parts of the electromagnetic spectrum. ❯ Compare refracting telescopes and reflecting telescopes. ❯ Explain how telescopes for nonvisible electromagnetic radiation differ from light telescopes.	astronomy galaxy astronomical unit electromagnetic spectrum telescope refracting telescope reflecting telescope	Technologies that are developed for space exploration also have spinoffs that allow us to treat illnesses, develop new building materials, predict the weather, and communicate with others around the world.

People studied the sky long before the telescope was invented. For example, farmers observed changes in daylight and the visibility of groups of stars throughout the year to track seasons and to predict floods and droughts. Sailors focused on the stars to navigate through unknown territory. Today, most interest in studying the sky comes from a curiosity to discover what lies within the universe and how the universe changes. This scientific study of the universe is called **astronomy.** Scientists who study the universe are called *astronomers.*

The Value of Astronomy

In the process of observing the universe, astronomers have made exciting discoveries, such as new planets, stars, black holes, and nebulas, such as the one shown in **Figure 1.** By studying these objects, astronomers have been able to learn more about the origin of Earth and the processes involved in the formation of our solar system and other objects in the universe.

Studying the universe is also important for the potential benefits to humans. For example, studies of how stars shine may one day lead to improved or new energy sources on Earth. Astronomers may also learn how to protect us from potential catastrophes, such as collisions between asteroids and Earth. Because of these and other contributions, astronomical research is supported by federal agencies, such as the National Science Foundation and NASA. Private foundations and industry also fund research in astronomy.

FLORIDA STANDARDS

SC.912.E.5.1 Cite evidence used to develop and verify the scientific theory of the Big Bang (also known as the Big Bang Theory) of the origin of the universe; SC.912.E.5.2 Identify patterns in the organization and distribution of matter in the universe and the forces that determine them; SC.912.P.12.7 Recognize that nothing travels faster than the speed of light in vacuum which is the same for all observers no matter how they or the light source are moving.

astronomy the scientific study of the universe

Figure 1 A nebula is a large cloud of gas and dust in space. This nebula is called the Eskimo nebula. It formed as a result of the outer layers of the central star being blown away. Astronomers predict that our sun will reach this state in about 5 billion years.

Figure 2 The Whirlpool galaxy, M51 (above), is 31 million light-years from the Milky Way. Abell 2218 (right) is one of the most massive galaxy clusters known. The cluster's mass has distorted the light from even farther objects into the giant arcs shown here.

Characteristics of the Universe

The study of the origin, properties, processes, and evolution of the universe is called *cosmology*. Astronomers have determined that the universe began about 13.7 billion years ago in one giant explosion, called the *big bang*. Since that time, the universe has continued to expand. In fact, it is expanding faster and faster. The universe is very large, and the objects within it are extremely far apart. Telescopes are used to study distant objects. However, astronomers also commonly use computer and mathematical models to study the universe.

Organization of the Universe

The nearest part of the universe to Earth is our solar system. The solar system includes the sun, Earth, the other planets, and many smaller objects such as dwarf planets, asteroids, and comets. The solar system is part of a **galaxy**, which is a large collection of stars, dust, and gas bound together by gravity. The galaxy in which the solar system resides is called the *Milky Way galaxy*. Beyond the Milky Way galaxy, there are billions of other galaxies, dozens of which are shown in **Figure 2**.

Measuring Distances in the Universe

Because the universe is so large, the units of measurement used on Earth are too small to represent the distance between objects in space. To measure distances in the solar system, astronomers often use astronomical units. An **astronomical unit** (symbol, AU) is the average distance between Earth and the sun, which is 149,597,870.691 km or about 150 million km.

Astronomers also use the speed of light to measure distance. Light travels at 300,000 km/s. In one year, light travels 9.46×10^{12} km. This distance is known as a *light-year*. Aside from the sun, the closest star to Earth is 4.22 light-years away.

galaxy a collection of stars, dust, and gas bound together by gravity

astronomical unit the average distance between Earth and the sun; approximately 150 million kilometers (symbol, AU)

Observing Space

Light enables us to see the world around us and to make observations. When people look at the night sky, they see stars and other objects in space because of the light these objects emit. This visible light is only a small amount of the energy that comes from these objects. By studying other forms of energy, astronomers are able to learn more about the universe. Recall that planets do not emit light. Rather, they reflect the light from stars.

Electromagnetic Spectrum

Visible light is a form of energy that is part of the electromagnetic spectrum. The **electromagnetic spectrum** is all the wavelengths of electromagnetic radiation. Light, radio waves, and X rays are examples of electromagnetic radiation. The radiation is composed of traveling waves of electric and magnetic fields that have fixed wavelengths and therefore fixed frequencies.

electromagnetic spectrum all of the frequencies or wavelengths of electromagnetic radiation

Visible Electromagnetic Radiation

The human eye can see only radiation of wavelengths in the visible light range of the spectrum. When white light passes through a prism, the light is refracted (bent), and a continuous set of colors, as shown in **Figure 3,** results. Every rainbow formed in the sky and any spectrum formed by a prism always has the same colors in the same order. The different colors result because each color of light has a characteristic wavelength that refracts at a different angle when it passes from one medium, such as air, into another, such as a glass prism. For example, the shortest wavelengths of visible light are blue and violet, while the longest wavelengths are orange and red.

Electromagnetic radiation that has wavelengths that are shorter than the wavelengths of violet light or longer than the wavelengths of red light cannot be seen by humans. But these wavelengths can be detected by instruments that are designed to detect electromagnetic radiation that cannot be seen by human eyes. These invisible wavelengths include infrared waves, microwaves, and radio waves (at longer wavelengths than red), as well as ultraviolet rays, X rays, and gamma rays (at shorter wavelengths than blue).

Figure 3 When white light (shown here coming from the upper left) passes from air, through a prism (top right), and then back into air, the light is separated into its different colors.

Reading Check **Which type of electromagnetic radiation can be seen by humans?** (See Appendix G for answers to Reading Checks.)

Invisible Electromagnetic Radiation

If you place a thermometer in any wavelength of the visible spectrum, the temperature reading on the thermometer will rise. In 1800, the scientist William Herschel placed a thermometer just beyond the red end of the visible spectrum. Even though he could not see any light shining on the thermometer, the temperature reading on the thermometer still increased. Herschel had discovered infrared, which means "below the red." Infrared is electromagnetic radiation that has wavelengths that are longer than those of visible light. Other scientists later discovered radio waves, which have even longer wavelengths than infrared.

The ultraviolet wavelengths, which are invisible to humans, are shorter than the wavelengths of violet light. *Ultraviolet* means "beyond the violet." The X-ray wavelengths are shorter than the ultraviolet wavelengths are. The shortest wavelengths are the gamma-ray wavelengths.

Telescopes

Our eyes can see detail, but some things are too small or too far away to see. Our ability to see the detail of distant objects in the sky began with the Italian scientist Galileo. In 1609, he heard of a <u>device</u> that used two lenses to make distant objects appear closer. He built one of the devices and turned it toward the sky. For the first time, he could see that there are craters on the moon and that the Milky Way is made of stars. Later, Isaac Newton invented another kind of telescope. An example of one of these early devices is shown in **Figure 4.**

A **telescope** is an instrument that collects electromagnetic radiation from the sky and concentrates it for better observation. While modern telescopes are able to collect and use invisible electromagnetic radiation, the first telescopes that were developed collected only visible light. Telescopes that collect only visible light are called *optical telescopes*. The two types of optical telescopes are refracting telescopes and reflecting telescopes.

Academic Vocabulary

device (di VIES) a piece of equipment made for a specific use

telescope an instrument that collects electromagnetic radiation from the sky and concentrates it for better observation

Figure 4 An early model of one of the first reflecting telescopes, which was invented by Isaac Newton, can be seen at the Royal Society in London, England.

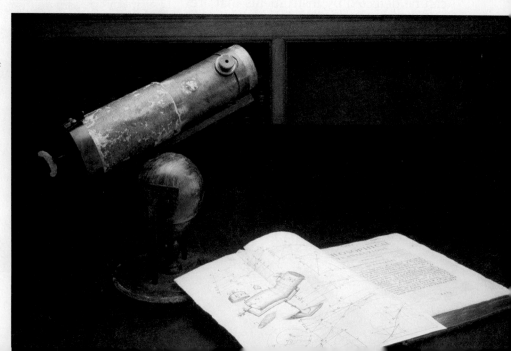

Figure 5 Refracting and Reflecting Telescopes

Refracting telescopes use lenses to gather and focus light from distant objects.

Reflecting telescopes use mirrors to gather and focus light from distant objects.

Refracting Telescopes

Lenses are clear objects shaped to bend light in special ways. The bending of light by lenses is called *refraction*. Telescopes that use a set of lenses to gather and focus light from distant objects are called **refracting telescopes.** Refracting telescopes have an objective lens that bends light that passes through the lens and focuses the light to be magnified by an eyepiece, as shown in **Figure 5.**

One problem with refracting telescopes is that the lens focuses different colors of light at different distances. For example, if an object is in focus in red light, the object will appear out of focus in blue light. Another problem with refracting telescopes is that it is difficult to make very large lenses of the required strength and clarity. The amount of light collected from distant objects is limited by the size of the objective lens.

Reflecting Telescopes

In the mid-1600s, Isaac Newton solved the problem of color separation that resulted from the use of lenses. He invented the **reflecting telescope,** which used a curved mirror to gather and focus light from distant objects, as shown in **Figure 5.** When light enters a reflecting telescope, the light is reflected by a large curved mirror to a second mirror. The second mirror reflects the light to the eyepiece, which is a lens that magnifies and focuses the image.

Unlike objective lenses in refracting telescopes, mirrors in reflecting telescopes can be made very large without affecting the quality of the image. Thus, reflecting telescopes can be much larger and can gather more light than refracting telescopes can. The largest reflecting telescopes that can point anywhere in the sky are a pair called the Keck Telescopes in Hawaii and a slightly larger one in the Canary Islands. Each telescope is 10 m in diameter. Astronomers are tentatively planning to build an ELT (Extremely Large Telescope) that would be about 50 m in diameter and an OWL (Overwhelmingly Large Telescope) that would be 100 m in diameter.

✔ Reading Check What are the problems with refracting telescopes?

refracting telescope a telescope that uses a set of lenses to gather and focus light from distant objects

reflecting telescope a telescope that uses a curved mirror to gather and focus light from distant objects

www.scilinks.org
Topic: Telescopes
Code: HQX1500

Telescopes for Invisible Electromagnetic Radiation

Each type of electromagnetic radiation provides scientists with information about objects in space. Scientists have developed telescopes that detect invisible radiation. For example, a radio telescope, such as the one shown in **Figure 6**, detects radio waves. There are also telescopes that detect gamma rays, X rays, and infrared rays.

One problem with using telescopes to detect invisible electromagnetic radiation is that Earth's atmosphere acts as a shield against many forms of electromagnetic radiation. Atoms and molecules in the atmosphere prevent short wavelengths like gamma rays, X rays, and most ultraviolet rays from reaching Earth's surface. Water vapor blocks infrared rays, so ground-based telescopes that are used to study infrared work best at high elevations, where the air is thin and dry. But the only way to study many forms of radiation is from space.

Space-Based Astronomy

While ground-based telescopes have been critical in helping astronomers learn about the universe, valuable information has also come from spacecraft. Spacecraft that contain telescopes and other instruments have been launched to investigate planets, stars, and other distant objects. In space, Earth's atmosphere cannot interfere with the detection of electromagnetic radiation.

Reading Check Why do scientists launch spacecraft beyond Earth's atmosphere?

Figure 6 Radio telescopes, such as this one (of 27) at the National Radio Astronomy Observatory in New Mexico, provide scientists with information about objects in space.

Why It Matters

The Interstellar Playlist

SCIENCE & SOCIETY

Telescopes gather data from outer space for us to study on Earth. The two Voyager probes carry data in the opposite direction. They carry the Golden Record, which stores 115 images, greetings in 55 languages, sounds from nature, and music from different cultures and eras.

The Voyager probes were launched in 1977 and are still traveling out of the solar system. Their power will last until at least 2025.

The Golden Record has coded instructions to explain its use and origin. The image at right is one of the images stored on the recording.

YOUR TURN CRITICAL THINKING
If you were to make a new Golden Record, what would you put on it? Why?

Space Telescopes

The *Hubble Space Telescope,* shown in **Figure 7,** is an example of a telescope that has been launched into space to collect electromagnetic radiation from objects in space. Another example, the *Chandra X-ray Observatory,* makes remarkably clear images using X rays from objects in space, such as the remnants of exploded stars. The *Swift* spacecraft detects gamma rays and X rays from explosions and collisions of objects such as black holes. The *Spitzer Space Telescope* detects infrared radiation. The *James Webb Space Telescope* is scheduled to be launched in 2013. When deployed in space, this telescope will be used to detect near- and mid-range infrared radiation from objects in space.

Other Spacecraft

Since the early 1960s, spacecraft have been sent out of Earth's orbit to study other planets. Launched in 1977, the space probes *Voyager 1* and *Voyager 2* investigated Jupiter, Saturn, Uranus, and Neptune. These two spacecraft collected images of these planets and their moons. The *Galileo* spacecraft was in orbit around Jupiter and its moons from 1995 to 2003. This space probe gathered information about the composition of Jupiter's atmosphere and storm systems, which are several times larger than Earth's storm systems. The *Cassini* spacecraft began orbiting Saturn in 2004. In December 2004, the *Huygens* probe detached from the *Cassini* orbiter to study the atmosphere and surface of Titan, Saturn's largest moon. The twin Mars rovers *Spirit,* shown in **Figure 8,** and *Opportunity* landed on Mars in January 2004. They confirmed that water had once been present on Mars. In 2008, the *Phoenix* lander found ice on Mars.

Figure 8 The Mars rover *Spirit* and its twin, *Opportunity,* have transmitted thousands of images of the red planet to scientists on Earth. The mission was originally planned to last only three months, but the rovers continued to operate for several years.

Human Space Exploration

Spacecraft that carry only instruments and computers are described as *robotic*. These spacecraft can explore space and travel beyond the solar system. Crewed spacecraft, or those that carry humans, have never gone beyond Earth's moon.

The first humans went into space in the 1960s. Between 1969 and 1972, NASA landed 12 people on the moon. Now, crewed spaceflights only orbit Earth. Flights, such as those aboard the space shuttles, allow people to release or repair satellites, to perform scientific experiments, or to live and work on the International Space Station, as shown in **Figure 9.**

Eventually, NASA would like to send people to explore Mars. However, such a voyage would be expensive, difficult, and dangerous. The loss of two space shuttles and their crews, the *Challenger* in 1986 and the *Columbia* in 2003, have focused public attention on the risks of human space exploration. NASA is planning first to send astronauts back to the moon.

Figure 9 Astronaut Doug Wheelock installs a truss that supports a set of solar panels on the International Space Station.

Spinoffs of the Space Program

Space programs have brought benefits to areas outside the field of astronomy. Satellites in orbit provide information about weather all over Earth. This information helps scientists make accurate weather predictions days in advance. Other satellites broadcast television signals from around the world or allow people to navigate cars and airplanes. Inventing ways to make objects smaller and lighter so that they can go into space has also led to improved electronics. These technological developments have been applied to radios, televisions, and other equipment. Even medical equipment has benefited from space programs. For example, heart pumps have been improved based on NASA's research on the flow of fluids through rockets.

Section 1 Review

SC.912.E.5.2; SC.912.E.5.7; SC.912.E.5.8;
SC.912.P.10.10; SC.912.P.10.18; SC.912.P.12.7

Key Ideas

1. **Describe** characteristics of the universe in terms of time, distance, and organization.

2. **Identify** the parts of the electromagnetic spectrum, both visible and invisible.

3. **Explain** how astronomers use electromagnetic radiation to study space.

4. **Compare** reflecting telescopes and refracting telescopes.

5. **Explain** how a radio telescope differs from an optical telescope.

6. **Identify** two examples of space telescopes and two examples of space probes.

Critical Thinking

7. **Identifying Relationships** Using the development of reflecting telescopes as an example, explain how scientific inquiry leads to advances in technology.

8. **Analyzing Processes** Human space exploration is expensive and dangerous. Explain why NASA should or should not continue doing it.

Concept Mapping

9. Use the following terms to create a concept map: *electromagnetic radiation, reflecting telescope, refracting telescope, telescope, probe, astronomy, universe,* Voyager, and Cassini.

Movements of Earth

Key Ideas	Key Terms	Why It Matters
❯ Describe two lines of evidence for Earth's rotation. ❯ Explain how the change in apparent positions of constellations provides evidence of Earth's rotation and revolution around the sun. ❯ Summarize how Earth's rotation and revolution provide a basis for measuring time. ❯ Explain how the tilt of Earth's axis and Earth's movement cause seasons.	rotation revolution perihelion aphelion equinox solstice	Earth's rotation and revolution are responsible for natural events such as day and night, weather patterns, and the seasons. We also measure and tell time based on Earth's movements.

Understanding the basic motions of Earth helps scientists understand the motions of other bodies in the solar system and the universe. These movements of Earth are also responsible for the seasons and the changes in weather.

The Rotating Earth

The spinning of Earth on its axis is called **rotation.** Each complete rotation takes one day. The most observable effects of Earth's rotation on its axis are day and night. As Earth rotates from west to east, the sun appears to rise in the east in the morning. The sun then appears to cross the sky and set in the west. At any given moment, the part of Earth that faces the sun experiences daylight. At the same time, the part of Earth that faces away from the sun experiences nighttime.

The Foucault Pendulum

In the 19th century, the scientist Jean-Bernard-Leon Foucault provided evidence of Earth's rotation by using a pendulum. He created a long, heavy pendulum that rocks back and forth by attaching a wire to the ceiling and then attaching a weight, called a *bob,* to the wire. Throughout the day, the bob would swing back and forth. The path of the pendulum appeared to change over time. However, it was the floor that was moving while the pendulum's path stayed constant. Because the floor was attached to Earth, one can conclude that Earth rotates. A Foucault pendulum is shown in **Figure 1.**

FLORIDA STANDARDS

SC.912.E.5.7 Relate the history of and explain the justification for future space exploration and continuing technology development; **SC.912.P.10.18** Explore the theory of electromagnetism by comparing and contrasting the different parts of the electromagnetic spectrum in terms of wavelength, frequency, and energy, and relate them to phenomena and applications.

rotation the spin of a body on its axis

Figure 1 The 12 ft arc of this Foucault pendulum in Spokane, Washington, appears to change throughout the day. However, the actual path of the pendulum does not change. Instead, it is the floor that moves as Earth rotates under the pendulum.

A Model Pendulum

Procedure

❶ Use a yo-yo, or tie a small object to one end of a length of string to make a pendulum.

❷ Hold the end of the string in your fingers, and swing the pendulum.

❸ Twist the string in your fingers as you allow the pendulum to continue swinging.

Analysis

1. Does the direction in which the yo-yo swings change?

2. Does the yo-yo twist around with the string?

3. How does this experiment differ from the operation of a Foucault pendulum?

revolution the motion of a body that travels around another body in space; one complete trip along an orbit

perihelion in the orbit of a planet or other body in the solar system, the point that is closest to the sun

aphelion in the orbit of a planet or other body in the solar system, the point that is farthest from the sun

The Coriolis Effect

Evidence of the rotation of Earth can also be seen in the movement of ocean surface currents and wind belts. Ocean currents and wind belts do not move in a straight path. The rotation of Earth causes ocean currents and wind belts to be deflected to the right in the Northern Hemisphere. In the Southern Hemisphere, ocean currents and wind belts deflect to the left. This curving of the path of wind belts and ocean currents is caused by Earth's rotation underneath the atmosphere and the sea and is called the *Coriolis effect*.

The Revolving Earth

As Earth spins on its axis, Earth also revolves around the sun. Even though you cannot feel Earth moving, it is traveling around the sun at an average speed of 29.8 km/s. The motion of a body that travels around another body in space is called **revolution.** Each complete revolution of Earth around the sun takes one year, or about 365 ¼ days.

Earth's Orbit

The path that a body follows as it travels around another body in space is called an *orbit*. Earth's orbit around the sun is not quite a circle. Earth's orbit is an ellipse. An *ellipse* is a closed curve whose shape is determined by two points, or *foci*, within the ellipse. In planetary orbits in our solar system, one focus is located deep within the sun. No object is located at the other focus.

Because its orbit is an ellipse, Earth is not always the same distance from the sun. The point in the orbit of a planet at which the planet is closest to the sun is the **perihelion.** The point in the orbit of a planet at which the planet is farthest from the sun is the **aphelion** (uh FEE lee uhn). As shown in **Figure 2,** Earth's aphelion distance is 152 million km. Its perihelion distance is 147 million km.

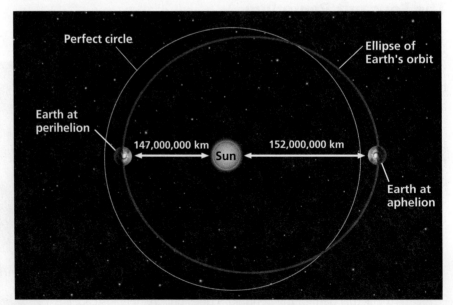

Perfect circle

Ellipse of Earth's orbit

Earth at perihelion

147,000,000 km   Sun   152,000,000 km

Earth at aphelion

Figure 2 As Earth revolves around its elliptical orbit, the planet is farthest from the sun in July and closest to the sun in January. The elliptical orbit in this illustration has been exaggerated for emphasis.

Constellations and Earth's Motion

Evidence of Earth's revolution and rotation around the sun can be seen in the motion of constellations. A *constellation* is a group of stars that are organized in a recognizable pattern. In 1930, the International Astronomical Union divided the sky into 88 constellations. Many of the names given to these constellations came from the ancient Greeks more than 2,000 years ago. Taurus, the bull, and Orion, the hunter, are some examples of names from Greek mythology that have been given to constellations.

Evidence of Earth's Rotation

If you gaze at a constellation in the evening sky, you might notice that it appears to be moving in the shape of an arc, as if it were tracing a circle around a fixed point. The apparent change in its position occurs for the same reason that the sun appears to move across the daytime sky. That is, Earth's rotation makes the constellations appear to move in this way.

Evidence of Earth's Revolution

The position of a constellation in the evening sky changes not only because of Earth's rotation but also because of Earth's revolution around the sun. Examine **Figure 3**, which shows the same region of the sky at the same time of night in February and in March. Notice that all the constellations appear lower in the sky in March than they do in February. This change in the position of the constellations is a result of Earth's revolution. As Earth revolves around the sun, the night side of Earth faces in a different direction of the universe. Thus, as Earth moves, different constellations are visible in the night sky from month to month and from season to season.

Reading Check How does the movement of the constellations provide evidence of Earth's rotation and revolution?

Figure 3 In one month's period, the position of the constellations in the sky seen from Denver, Colorado, at 10 PM change because of the revolution of Earth.

Figure 4 This is a reconstruction of a 3.6 m stone carving that functioned, in part, as a calendar based on solar and lunar cycles.

READING TOOLBOX

Using Spatial Language
How important is spatial language for communicating with people? Choose three sentences in Section 2 that use spatial words or phrases. Try to rewrite each sentence without using the spatial language. Can you do it?

Measuring Time

Earth's motion provides the basis for measuring time. For example, the day and year are based on periods of Earth's motion. The day is determined by Earth's rotation on its axis. Each complete rotation of Earth on its axis is one day, which is then divided into 24 hours.

The year is determined by Earth's revolution around the sun. Each complete revolution of Earth around the sun takes 365 ¼ days, or one year.

A month is based on the moon's motion around Earth. A month was originally determined by the period between successive full moons, which is 29.5 days. The word *month* actually comes from the word *moon*. However, the number of full moons in a year is not a whole number. Therefore, a month is now determined as roughly one-twelfth of a year.

Formation of the Calendar

A *calendar* is a system created for measuring long intervals of time by dividing time into periods of days, weeks, months, and years. Many ancient civilizations created versions of calendars based on astronomical cycles. The ancient Egyptians used a calendar based on a solar year. The Babylonians used a 12-month lunar year. The Aztecs, who lived in what is now Mexico, also created a calendar, which is shown in **Figure 4.**

Because the year is about 365 ¼ days long, the extra ¼ day is usually ignored to make the number of days on a calendar a whole number. To keep the calendars on the same schedule as Earth's movements, we must account for the extra time. So, every four years, one day is added to the month of February. Any year that contains an extra day is called a *leap year*.

More than 2,000 years ago, Julius Caesar, of the Roman Empire, revised the calendar so that an extra day every four years was added. His successor, Augustus Caesar, made the extra day come at the end of the shortest month, February. He also made July and August long months with 31 days each.

The Modern Calendar

Because the year is not exactly 365 days long, over centuries, the calendar gradually became misaligned with the seasons. In the late 1500s, Pope Gregory XIII formed a committee to create a calendar that would keep the calendar aligned with the seasons. We use this calendar today. In this Gregorian calendar, century years, such as 1800 and 1900, are not leap years unless the century years are exactly divisible by 400. Thus, 2000 was a leap year even though it was a century year. However, 2100, 2200, and 2300 will not be leap years.

Time Zones

Using the sun as the basis for measuring time, we define noon as the time when the sun is highest in the sky. Because of Earth's rotation, the sun is highest above different locations on Earth at different times of day. Earth's surface has been divided into 24 standard time zones, as shown in **Figure 5,** to avoid problems created by different local times. In each zone, noon is set as the time when the sun is highest over the center of that zone. Earth's circumference equals 360° measured from Earth's center. If you divide 360° by the 24 hours needed for one rotation, you find that Earth rotates at a rate of 15° per hour. Therefore, each of Earth's 24 standard time zones covers about 15°. The time in each zone is one hour earlier than the time in the zone to the east of each zone.

International Date Line

There are 24 standard time zones and 24 h in a day. But there must be some point on Earth's surface where the date changes. The *International Date Line* was established to prevent confusion. The International Date Line is an imaginary line that runs from north to south through the Pacific Ocean. When it is Friday west of the International Date Line, it is Thursday east of the line. The line is drawn so that it does not cut through islands or continents. Thus, everyone living within one country has the same date. Note where the line is drawn between Alaska and Siberia in **Figure 5.**

Reading Check **What is the purpose of the International Date Line?**

Figure 5 Earth has been divided into 24 standard time zones. A few time zones may differ between 15 and 45 minutes compared to most time zones. *If it is 6 P.M. in Florida, what time would it be in California?*

Academic Vocabulary

significant (sig NIF uh kahnt)
important

Daylight Savings Time

Because of the tilt of Earth's axis, the duration of daylight is shorter in the winter months than in the summer months. During the summer months, days are longer so that the sun rises earlier in the morning when many people are still sleeping. To take advantage of that daylight time, the United States uses *daylight savings time*. Under this system, clocks are set one hour ahead of standard time in March, which provides an additional hour of daylight during the evening. The additional hour also saves energy because the use of electricity decreases. In November, clocks are set back one hour to return to standard time. Countries that are in the equatorial region do not observe daylight savings time because there are not significant changes in the amount of daylight time in the equatorial region. There, daylight is about 12 h every day of the year.

The Seasons

Earth's axis is tilted at 23.5°. As Earth revolves around the sun, Earth's axis always points toward the North Star. Thus, during each revolution, the North Pole sometimes tilts toward the sun and sometimes tilts away from the sun, as shown in **Figure 6.** When the North Pole tilts toward the sun, the Northern Hemisphere has longer periods of daylight than the Southern Hemisphere does. When the North Pole tilts away from the sun, the Southern Hemisphere has longer periods of daylight.

The angle at which the sun's rays strike each part of Earth's surface changes as Earth moves through its orbit. When the North Pole tilts toward the sun, the sun's rays strike the Northern Hemisphere more directly. When the sun's rays strike Earth directly, that region receives a higher concentration of solar energy and is warmer. When the North Pole tilts away from the sun, the sun's rays strike the Northern Hemisphere less directly. When the sunlight is less direct, the concentration of solar energy is less and that region is cooler.

Reading Check What is daylight savings time?

THINK central
INTERACT ONLINE
Keyword: HQXSSPF6

Figure 6 The direction of tilt of Earth's axis remains the same throughout Earth's orbit around the sun. Thus, the Northern Hemisphere receives more direct sunlight during summer months and less direct sunlight during winter months.

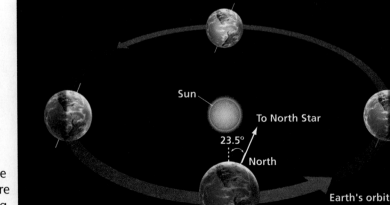

Seasonal Weather

Changes in the angle at which the sun's rays strike Earth's surface cause the seasons. When the North Pole tilts away from the sun, the angle of the sun's rays falling on the Northern Hemisphere is low. As a result, the sun's rays spread solar energy over a large area, which leads to lower temperatures. The tilt of the North Pole away from the sun also causes the Northern Hemisphere to experience fewer daylight hours. Fewer daylight hours also means less energy and lower temperatures. Lower temperatures cause the winter seasons. During winter, the Northern Hemisphere tilts away from the sun, and the Southern Hemisphere tilts toward the sun. The sun's rays strike the Southern Hemisphere at a greater angle than they do in the Northern Hemisphere, and there are more daylight hours in the Southern Hemisphere. Therefore, the Southern Hemisphere experiences summer. So, the seasons are caused by the tilt of Earth's axis and not by Earth's distance from the sun.

Equinoxes

The seasons fall and spring begin on days called equinoxes. An **equinox** is the moment when the sun appears to cross the celestial equator. The *celestial equator* is an imaginary line in the sky directly overhead from the equator on Earth. During an equinox, the sun's rays strike Earth at a 90° angle along the equator. The hours of daylight and darkness are approximately equal everywhere on Earth on that day. The *autumnal equinox* occurs on September 22 or 23 of each year and marks the beginning of fall in the Northern Hemisphere. The *vernal equinox* occurs on March 21 or 22 of each year and marks the beginning of spring in the Northern Hemisphere.

equinox the moment when the sun appears to cross the celestial equator

---

Quick Lab

10 min   **SC.912.E.7.7**

The Angle of the Sun's Rays

Procedure

❶ Turn the lights down low or off in the classroom.

❷ Place a piece of paper on the floor. Using a meterstick, hold a flashlight 1 m above the paper, and shine the light of the flashlight straight down on the piece of paper.

❸ Have a partner outline the perimeter of the circle of light cast by the flashlight on the paper. Label the circle "90° angle." Place a clean piece of paper on the floor.

❹ At a height of 0.5 m from the floor, shine the light of the flashlight on the paper at an angle. Make sure the distance between the flashlight and the paper is 1 m.

❺ Have a partner outline the perimeter of the circle of light cast by the flashlight on the paper. Label the circle "low angle."

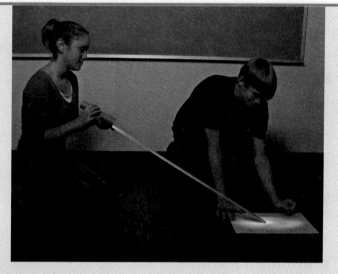

Analysis

1. Compare the two circles drawn in steps 3 and 5. Which circle concentrates the light in a smaller area?

2. Which circle would most likely model the sun's rays striking Earth during the summer season?

Figure 7 In the Northern Hemisphere, the sun appears to follow its highest path across the sky during the summer solstice and its lowest path across the sky during the winter solstice.

solstice the point at which the sun is as far north or as far south of the equator as possible

Summer Solstices

The seasons of summer and winter begin on days called **solstices.** Each year on June 21 or 22, the North Pole's tilt toward the sun is greatest. On this day, the sun's rays strike Earth at a 90° angle along the Tropic of Cancer, which is located at 23.5° north latitude. This day is called the *summer solstice* and marks the beginning of summer in the Northern Hemisphere. *Solstice* means "sun stop" and refers to the fact that in the Northern Hemisphere, the sun follows its highest path across the sky on this day, as shown in **Figure 7,** and then moves lower every day afterward.

The Northern Hemisphere has its most hours of daylight during the summer solstice. The farther north of the equator you are, the longer the period of daylight you have. North of the Arctic Circle, which is located at 66.5° north latitude, there are 24 h of daylight during the summer solstice. At the other extreme, south of the Antarctic Circle, there are 24 h of darkness at that time.

Winter Solstices

By December, the North Pole is tilted to the farthest point away from the sun. On December 21 or 22, the sun's rays strike Earth at a 90° angle along the Tropic of Capricorn, which is located at 23.5° south latitude. This day is called the *winter solstice.* It marks the beginning of winter in the Northern Hemisphere. During the winter solstice, the Northern Hemisphere has the fewest daylight hours. The sun follows its lowest path across the sky. Places that are north of the Arctic Circle then have 24 h of darkness. However, places that are south of the Antarctic Circle have 24 h of daylight at that time.

Section 2 Review

LA.910.2.2.3; SC.912.N.1.7

Key Ideas

1. **Explain** how the apparent change of position of constellations over time provides evidence of Earth's revolution around the sun.

2. **Describe** two lines of evidence that indicate that Earth is rotating.

3. **Summarize** how movements of Earth provide a basis for measuring time.

4. **Explain** why today's calendars have leap years.

5. **Identify** two advantages in using daylight savings time.

6. **Explain** how the tilt of Earth's axis and Earth's movements cause seasons.

7. **Identify** the position of Earth in relation to the sun that causes winter in the Northern Hemisphere.

8. **Describe** the position of Earth in relation to the sun during the Northern Hemisphere's summer solstice.

Critical Thinking

9. **Understanding Relationships** How can it be that Earth is at perihelion during wintertime in the Northern Hemisphere?

10. **Predicting Consequences** Explain how measurements of time might differ if Earth rotated on its axis only once per year.

Concept Mapping

11. Use the following terms to create a concept map: *revolution, perihelion, aphelion, rotation, ellipse, orbit, rotation, Foucault pendulum, Coriolis effect, Earth,* and *constellation.*

What Time Is It?

REAL WORLD

"Synchronizing your watches" is a surprisingly intricate undertaking. Coordinated Universal Time (UTC), also called civil time, is the time we live by. It is based on Earth's rotation rate. Although the time for a full rotation of Earth is usually expressed as 24 h per day, it is actually 23 h 56 min 4s. As well, Earth's rotation rate is not constant—the moon's gravity is slowing it down. Thus, scientists use atomic clocks to establish International Atomic Time (TAI). Atomic clocks are very precise, because they are based on the vibration rate of atoms. To synchronize UTC with TAI, leap seconds may be added to UTC. Since 1972, 23 leap seconds have been added.

International Atomic Time

Data from about 250 atomic clocks, located in about 50 laboratories around the world, are averaged.

International Atomic Time (TAI)

Add leap seconds.

Coordinated Universal Time (UTC)

Civil time as reported on radio, TV, computer networks, and other media

YOUR TURN

UNDERSTANDING CONCEPTS
What is the role of atomic clocks in determining civil time?

CRITICAL THINKING
Why is accurate time necessary? Name two situations in which accurate time is very important.

737

Earth-Sun Motion

During the course of a day, the sun moves across the sky. This motion is due to Earth's rotation. In ancient times, one of the earliest devices used by people to study the sun's motion was the shadow stick. The shadow stick is a type of sundial. Before clocks were invented, sundials were one of the only means of telling time.

In this lab, you will use a shadow stick to identify how changes in a shadow are related to Earth's rotation. You will also determine how a shadow stick can be used to measure time.

What You'll Do

> **Design** an experiment to measure the movement of Earth.

> **Analyze** the effectiveness of your experimental design.

> **Demonstrate** how shadows can be used to measure time.

What You'll Need

board, wooden,
    20 cm × 30 cm
clock or watch
compass, magnetic
dowel, 30 cm long,
    0.64 cm (¼ inch) diameter
paper, lined
pencil
ruler, metric
tape, masking

Ask a Question

1 How can I measure the movement of Earth?

Form a Hypothesis

2 With a partner, build a shadow stick apparatus that is similar to the one in the illustration on the following page. Brainstorm with your partner a way in which you can use the apparatus in an experiment to measure the movement of Earth for 30 min. Write a few sentences that describe your design and your hypothesis about how this experiment will measure Earth's motion.

Step **2**

Test the Hypothesis

3 When you complete your experimental design, have your teacher approve your design before you begin. **CAUTION** Never look directly at the sun.

4 Follow your design to set up and complete your experiment.

5 Take measurements every 5 min, and record this information in a data table.

Analyze the Results

1. **Analyzing Data** In what direction did the sun appear to move in the 30 min period?

2. **Evaluating Methods** If you made your shadow stick half as long, would its shadow move the same distance in 30 min? Explain your answer.

3. **Evaluating Methods** Would you make any changes to your experimental design? Explain your answer.

Draw Conclusions

4. **Drawing Conclusions** In what direction does Earth rotate?

5. **Applying Conclusions** How might a shadow stick be used to tell time?

Extension

Evaluating Methods
Repeat this lab at different hours of the day. Perform the lab early in the morning, early in the afternoon, and early in the evening. Record the results and any differences that you observe. Explain how shadow sticks can be used to tell direction.

MAPS *in Action*

Light Sources

Map ▶ **Skills Activity**

This image of Earth as seen from space at night shows light sources that are almost all created by humans. The image is a composite made from hundreds of nighttime images taken by orbiting satellites. Use the image to answer the questions below.

1. **Comparing Areas** Some climatic conditions on Earth, such as extreme cold, heat, wetness, or a thin atmosphere, make parts of our planet less habitable than other parts. Examples of areas on our planet that do not support large populations include deserts, high mountains, polar regions, and tropical rain forests. Using the image, identify regions of Earth where climatic conditions may not be able to support large human populations.

2. **Inferring Relationships** Using a map of the world and the brightness of the light sources on the image as a key, identify the locations of some of the most densely populated areas on Earth.

3. **Finding Locations** Many large cities are ports on the coastlines of the world's oceans. By using the image, can you look along coastlines and locate light sources that might indicate the sites of large ports? Using a map of the world, name some of these cities.

4. **Inferring Relationships** By looking at the differences in the density of the light sources on the image, can you locate any borders between countries? Identify the countries on both sides of these borders.

Summary

Key Ideas

Section 1

Viewing the Universe

❯ The universe is about 14 billion years old. It is very large, and objects within it are very far apart. The universe is made up of millions of galaxies, each of which is a large collection of stars, dust, and gases. Some stars, such as our own, include planets and other smaller objects.

❯ The visible part of the electromagnetic spectrum is visible light. The nonvisible parts include radio waves, microwaves, infrared waves, ultraviolet rays, X rays, and gamma rays.

❯ Refracting telescopes use lenses to gather and focus light, while reflecting telescopes use curved mirrors to gather and focus light.

❯ Telescopes for nonvisible electromagnetic radiation are designed to gather and focus nonvisible electromagnetic radiation rather than visible light.

Section 2

Movements of Earth

❯ The Foucault pendulum and the Coriolis effect provide evidence of Earth's rotation. As the pendulum swings with a constant motion, the floor beneath it changes position. Wind belts and ocean currents follow a curved, not a straight, path because they are deflected by Earth's rotation.

❯ The apparent movement of constellations in a circular motion provides evidence of Earth's rotation. The apparent movement from night to night and the change in location in the night sky of constellations from season to season provide evidence of Earth's revolution.

❯ Movements of Earth provide a basis for measuring time. One revolution of Earth around the sun is equal to one year. One rotation of Earth on its axis is equal to one day.

❯ The angle of the sun's rays changes throughout the year and leads to seasonal change on Earth.

Key Terms

astronomy, p. 721
galaxy, p. 722
astronomical unit, p. 722
electromagnetic spectrum, p. 723
telescope, p. 724
refracting telescope, p. 725
reflecting telescope, p. 725

rotation, p. 729
revolution, p. 730
perihelion, p. 730
aphelion, p. 730
equinox, p. 735
solstice, p. 736

1. **Two-Column Notes** Use the FoldNote that you made at the beginning of this chapter to study the key terms. See if you know all the definitions. When you have reviewed the terms, use each term in a sentence.

READING TOOLBOX

USING KEY TERMS

Use each of the following terms in a separate sentence.

2. *electromagnetic spectrum* `SC.912.E.5.8`
3. *galaxy* `SC.912.E.5.2`
4. *perihelion* `SC.912.E.5.6`

For each pair of terms, explain how the meanings of the terms differ.

5. *reflecting telescope* and *refracting telescope*
6. *solstice* and *equinox* `SC.912.E.5.6`
7. *rotation* and *revolution* `SC.912.E.5.6`

UNDERSTANDING KEY IDEAS

8. Stars organized into a pattern are `SC.912.E.5.2`
   a. perihelions.
   b. satellites.
   c. constellations.
   d. telescopes.

9. Days are caused by Earth's `SC.912.E.5.6`
   a. perihelion.
   b. aphelion.
   c. revolution.
   d. rotation.

10. The seasons are caused by `SC.912.E.5.6`
    a. Earth's distance from the sun.
    b. the tilt of Earth's axis.
    c. the sun's temperature.
    d. the calendar.

11. Which of the following is a tool that is used by astronomers to study radiation?
    a. a computer model
    b. a ground-based telescope
    c. a Foucault pendulum
    d. a calendar

12. Which of the following is evidence of Earth's revolution? `SC.912.E.5.6`
    a. a Foucault pendulum
    b. the Coriolis effect
    c. night and day
    d. constellation movement

13. Which of the following forms of radiation can be shielded by Earth's atmosphere?
    a. gamma rays
    b. radio waves
    c. visible light
    d. All of the above

14. Which of the following names is not associated with a space telescope?
    a. *Hubble*
    b. *Chandra*
    c. *Cassini*
    d. *Spitzer*

15. Which of the following marks the beginning of spring in the Northern Hemisphere? `SC.912.E.5.6`
    a. vernal equinox
    b. autumnal equinox
    c. summer solstice
    d. winter solstice

16. Which of the following is evidence of Earth's rotation? `SC.912.E.5.6`
    a. a Foucault pendulum
    b. day and night
    c. the Coriolis effect
    d. All of the above

SHORT ANSWER

17. Which two forms of electromagnetic radiation have the shortest wavelengths? `SC.912.P.10.20`

18. What is an advantage of using orbiting telescopes rather than ground-based telescopes?

19. Why does the rotation of Earth require people to establish time zones?

20. What is a leap year, and what purpose does it serve? `SC.912.E.5.6`

21. What line on Earth's surface marks where the date changes?

22. How does the tilt of Earth's axis cause the seasons? `SC.912.E.5.6`

23. **Evaluating Data** If telescopes had not been developed, how would our knowledge of the universe be different?

24. **Analyzing Ideas** In each time zone, it gets dark earlier on the eastern side of the zone than on the western side. Explain why. SC.912.E.5.6

25. **Applying Ideas** How would seasons be different if Earth was not tilted on its axis? SC.912.E.5.6

26. **Making Inferences** What limitation of a refracting telescope could be overcome by placing the telescope in space? Explain your answer.

27. Use the following terms to create a concept map: *Galileo, spacecraft, telescope, constellation, rotation, revolution, Foucault pendulum, Coriolis effect, equinox, solstice,* and *astronomy.* SC.912.E.5.6

28. **Making Calculations** A certain star is 1.135×10^{14} km away from Earth. If light travels at 9.4607×10^{12} km per year, how long will it take for light from the star to reach Earth? SC.912.E.5.11

29. **Applying Quantities** At aphelion, Earth is 152,000,000 km from the sun. At perihelion, the two bodies are 147,000,000 km apart. What is the difference in kilometers between Earth's farthest point from the sun and Earth's closest point to the sun? SC.912.E.5.11

30. **Creative Writing** Imagine that you are the head of a space program that has created the first orbiting telescope. Write a press release that explains to the public why your space agency has spent billions of dollars to build and launch a space telescope. SC.912.E.5.9

31. **Communicating Main Ideas** Explain how a Foucault pendulum and the Coriolis effect provide evidence of Earth's rotation. SC.912.E.5.6

The diagram below shows the different time zones of the world by looking down at the North Pole. Use the diagram to answer the questions that follow.

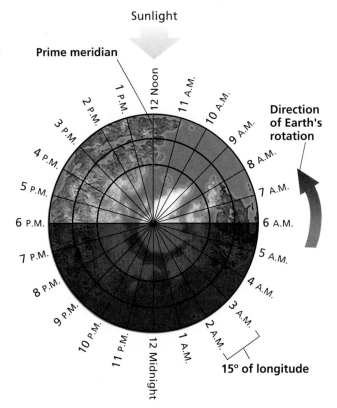

32. If it is 6 P.M. at the prime meridian, what is the time on the opposite side of the world?

33. On the diagram, it is 9 P.M. in Japan and 2 A.M. in Alaska. How many degrees apart are Alaska and Japan?

34. If it is 6 A.M. in Alaska, what time is it in Japan?

35. How many hours are in 120°?

Understanding Concepts

Directions (1–8): For each question, write on a sheet of paper the letter of the correct answer.

1 Which of the following statements best describes the organization of the universe?
  A. It is made up of solar systems, which contain galaxies.
  B. It is made up of a few galaxies and billions of stars.
  C. It is made up of billions of galaxies, which contain billions of stars.
  D. It is made up of solar systems and billions of stars.

2 Scientists use various telescopes to observe the night sky. Which of the following statements best describes the difference between refracting and reflecting telescopes?
  F. Refracting telescopes use lenses, but reflecting telescopes use mirrors.
  G. Refracting telescopes use one lens, but reflecting telescopes use two lenses.
  H. Refracting telescopes have larger lenses than reflecting telescopes do.
  I. Refracting telescopes produce better images than reflecting telescopes do.

3 Telescopes are used both on Earth and in space. What is an advantage of space-based telescopes?
  A. They are less expensive than land-based telescopes are.
  B. Earth's atmosphere does not interfere with space-based telescopes.
  C. They can detect radio waves, which cannot be detected by telescopes on Earth.
  D. They do not require lenses or mirrors as telescopes on Earth do.

4 Which of the following statements about the electromagnetic spectrum is true?
  F. It moves slower than the speed of light.
  G. It consists of waves of varying lengths.
  H. The shortest wavelengths are orange and red.
  I. Scientists can only detect waves of visible light.

5 The most obvious evidence that Earth rotates on an axis is the night and day cycle. What is another way that scientists provided evidence of Earth's rotation?
  A. They used telescopes to observe Earth's motion.
  B. They observed ocean currents.
  C. They observed that Earth is not always the same distance from the sun.
  D. They studied the way constellations move through the sky over several weeks.

6 Foucault used a long, heavy pendulum to observe Earth's rotation. The path of the pendulum appeared to change over time in relation to the floor. How does this provide evidence of Earth's rotation?
  F. The pendulum moved in response to Earth's rotation.
  G. The pendulum moved at dawn and at sunset, providing evidence of rotation.
  H. The floor and the position of the pendulum moved because of Earth's rotation.
  I. The floor moved while the pendulum stayed constant, indicating that Earth rotates.

7 If you wanted to study invisible electromagnetic radiation from space, which type of telescope would you use?
  A. refracting telescope on Earth
  B. reflecting telescope in space
  C. radio telescope on Earth
  D. optical telescope in space

8 People use calendars to measure time. Which of the following statements about the modern calendar is true?
  F. It has not changed over time.
  G. It was aligned with the seasons by Julius Caesar.
  H. It is based on the solar year.
  I. It is based on the lunar year.

Interpreting Graphics

Directions (9–11): For each question below, record the correct answer on a separate sheet of paper.

Seasons and Tilt

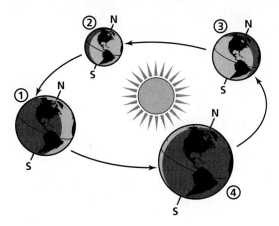

9 In position 1, the Northern Hemisphere tilts toward the sun. Which season is this?

A. winter

B. spring

C. summer

D. fall

10 The Northern Hemisphere experiences a vernal equinox when it is at which of the following positions on the diagram?

F. position 1

G. position 2

H. position 3

I. position 4

Orbit of Earth Around the Sun

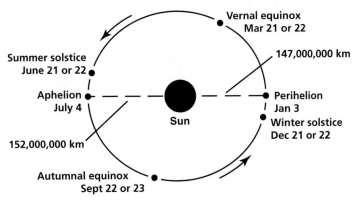

11 Based on the diagram above, which of the following statements describes Earth's orbit?

A. It is circular.

B. It forms an ellipse.

C. At the aphelion and perihelion, Earth is the same distance from the sun.

D. Earth circles the sun in a clockwise direction.

> **Test Tip**
>
> Keep an eye on your time limit. If you begin to run short on time, quickly read the remaining questions to determine which questions might be the easiest for you to answer.

Chapter 27

Planets of the Solar System

Chapter Outline

Why It Matters

Understanding the formation and the characteristics of our solar system and its planets can help scientists plan missions to study planets and solar systems around other stars in the universe.

Inquiry Lab · Planetary Distances

🕐 **20 min**

Turn to Appendix E and find the table entitled "Solar System Data." Use the data from the "semimajor axis" row of planetary distances to devise an appropriate scale to model the distances between planets. Then find an indoor or outdoor space that will accommodate the farthest distance. Mark some **index cards** with the name of each planet, use a **measuring tape** to measure the distances according to your scale, and place each index card at its correct location.

SC.912.E.5.11

Question to Get You Started

How would the distance of a planet from the sun affect the time it takes for the planet to complete one orbit?

READING TOOLBOX

These reading tools will help you learn the material in this chapter.

Word Origins

Names of the Planets The ancient Romans named the five planets that they could see in the night sky after gods from their mythology: Mercury, Venus, Mars, Jupiter, and Saturn. When Uranus and Neptune were discovered, they were also named for Roman gods.

Your Turn Each planet was named for the god in mythology that has something in common with the planet. As you learn about the planets, complete the list of connections between the planets and the Roman gods for which they are named.

Planet	Characteristic of planet	Characteristic of Roman god
Mercury	fastest-moving planet	speedy messenger of the gods
Jupiter	largest planet	ruler of the Roman gods

Mnemonics

Order of the Planets A mnemonic is a sentence or phrase that you can create to help you remember information. For example, the order of the planets from the sun outward is Mercury, Venus, Earth, Mars, Jupiter, Saturn, Uranus, and Neptune. You can use a mnemonic to help you remember this order.

> **M**y **V**ery **E**nergetic **M**other **J**ust **S**erved **U**s **N**achos.

Notice that the first letter of each word is the same as the first letter of the corresponding planet in the order.

Your Turn Practice saying this mnemonic to help you learn and remember the order of the planets. Make up a new mnemonic that you could use to remember the order of the planets.

Graphic Organizers

Chain-of-Events Chart Use a chain-of-events chart when you need to remember the steps of a process.

Your Turn As you read Section 1, create a chain-of-events chart that outlines the formation of the solar system. An example has been started at the right.

❶ Write the first step of the process in the first frame.

❷ Write the next step of the process in the second frame, and use an arrow to show the order of the process.

❸ Continue adding frames and arrows until the process for the formation of the solar system is complete.

The solar nebula formed.

For more information on how to use these and other tools, see **Appendix A**.

Formation of the Solar System

Key Ideas	Key Terms	Why It Matters
❯ Explain the nebular hypothesis of the origin of the solar system. ❯ Describe how the planets formed. ❯ Describe the formation of the land, the atmosphere, and the oceans of Earth.	solar system planet solar nebula planetesimal	Studying the solar system and its various planets can help us understand our own planet and the changes it has been and is going through.

The **solar system** consists of the sun, the planets, the dwarf planets, and all of the other bodies that revolve around the sun. **Planets** are the primary bodies that orbit the sun. Scientists have long debated the origins of the solar system. In the 1600s and 1700s, many scientists thought that the sun formed first and threw off the materials that later formed the planets. But in 1796, the French mathematician Pierre-Simon, marquis de Laplace, advanced a hypothesis that is now known as the *nebular hypothesis*.

The Nebular Hypothesis

Laplace's hypothesis states that the sun and the planets condensed at about the same time out of a rotating cloud of gas and dust called a *nebula*. Modern scientific calculations support Laplace's hypothesis and help explain how the sun and the planets formed from an original nebula of gas and dust.

Matter is spread throughout the universe. Some of this matter gathers into clouds of dust and gas, such as the one shown in **Figure 1.** Almost 5 billion years ago, the amount of gravity near one of these clouds increased as a result of a nearby supernova or other forces. The rotating cloud of dust and gas from which the sun and planets formed is called the **solar nebula.** Energy from collisions and pressure from gravity caused the center of the solar nebula to become hotter and denser. When the temperature at the center became high enough—about 10,000,000 °C—hydrogen fusion began. A star, which is called the sun, formed. The sun is composed of about 99% of all the matter that was contained in the solar nebula.

FLORIDA STANDARDS

SC.912.E.5.5 Explain the formation of planetary systems based on our knowledge of our Solar System and apply this knowledge to newly discovered planetary systems; **SC.912.L.15.8** Describe the scientific explanations of the origin of life on Earth; **SC.912.N.3.4** Recognize that theories do not become laws, nor do laws become theories; theories are well supported explanations and laws are well supported descriptions.

solar system the sun and all of the planets and other bodies that travel around it

planet a celestial body that orbits the sun, is round because of its own gravity, and has cleared the neighborhood around its orbital path

solar nebula a rotating cloud of gas and dust from which the sun and planets formed; *also* any nebula from which stars and exoplanets may form

Figure 1 The Orion nebula is about 1,500 light-years from Earth. Scientists study the nebula to learn about the processes that give birth to stars.

749

Formation of the Planets

While the sun was forming in the center of the solar nebula, planets were forming in the outer regions, as shown in **Figure 2.** Small bodies from which a planet originated in the early stages of formation of the solar system are called **planetesimals.** Some planetesimals joined together through collisions and through the force of gravity to form larger bodies called *protoplanets.* The protoplanets' gravity attracted other planetesimals in the solar nebula. These planetesimals collided with the protoplanets and added their masses to the protoplanets.

Eventually, the protoplanets became very large and formed the planets and moons. *Moons* are the smaller bodies that orbit the planets. Planets and moons are smaller and denser than the protoplanets. Some protoplanets were massive enough to become round but not massive enough to clear away other objects near their orbits. These became the dwarf planets.

Formation of the Inner Planets

The features of a newly formed planet depended on the distance between the protoplanet and the developing sun. The four protoplanets that became Mercury, Venus, Earth, and Mars were close to the sun. They contained large percentages of heavy elements, such as iron and nickel. These planets lost their less dense gases because, at the temperature of the gases, gravity was not strong enough to hold the gases. Other lighter elements may have been blown or boiled away by radiation from the sun. As the denser material sank to the centers of the planets, layers formed. The less dense material was on the outer part of the planet, and the denser material was at the center. Today, the inner planets have solid surfaces that are similar to Earth's surface. The inner planets are smaller, rockier, and denser than the outer planets.

planetesimal a small body from which a planet originated in the early stages of development of the solar system

Academic Vocabulary

formation (fohr MAY shuhn) the act of giving structure or shape to something

www.scilinks.org
Topic: Origins of the Solar
    System
Code: HQX1087

Figure 2 The Nebular Model of the Formation of the Solar System

The young solar nebula begins to collapse because of gravity.

As the solar nebula rotates, it flattens and becomes warmer near its center.

Planetesimals begin to form within the swirling disk.

Formation of the Outer Planets

Four other protoplanets became Jupiter, Saturn, Uranus, and Neptune. As a group, these outer planets are very different from the small, rocky inner planets. These outer planets formed in the colder regions of the solar nebula. They were far from the sun and therefore were cold. Thus, they did not lose their lighter elements, such as helium and hydrogen, or their ices, such as water ice, methane ice, and ammonia ice.

At first, thick layers of ice surrounded small cores of heavy elements. However, because of the intense heat and pressure in the planets' interiors, the ices melted to form layers of liquids and gases. Today, these planets are referred to as *gas giants* because they are composed mostly of gases, have low density, and are huge planets. Jupiter, for example, has a density of only 24% of Earth's density but a diameter that is 11 times Earth's diameter. Uranus and Neptune are different from Jupiter and Saturn, and are sometimes called *ice giants*.

Pluto—The First Dwarf Planet

From its discovery in 1930, Pluto was known as the ninth planet. However, it is quite unlike the other outer planets, which are gas giants or ice giants. In fact, Pluto is smaller than Earth's moon, and it can be best described as an ice ball that is made of frozen gases and rock. Its orbit is very tilted. Because of its characteristics, many astronomers disagreed with Pluto's classification as a planet.

In 2006, astronomers from around the world revised the definition of *planet*. The new definition includes the first eight familiar planets, but it excludes Pluto. Pluto is part of a new category of solar system bodies called *dwarf planets*.

Reading Check **How is Pluto different from the outer planets?** (See Appendix G for answers to Reading Checks.)

SC.912.E.5.5

Quick Lab
5 min

Water Planetesimals

Procedure

❶ Use a **medicine dropper** to place two drops of **water** about 3 cm apart on a **piece of wax paper.**

❷ Lift one edge of the wax paper so that one drop of water moves toward the other drop until the drops collide.

❸ Add a third drop of water to the wax paper. Then, repeat step 2.

Analysis

1. What happened when the water droplets collided?

2. How does this activity model the formation of protoplanets?

As planetesimals grow, their gravitational pull increases. The largest planetesimals begin to collect more of the gas and dust of the nebula.

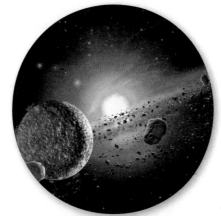

Small planetesimals collide with larger ones, and the planets begin to grow.

The excess dust and gas is gradually removed from the solar nebula, which leaves planets around the sun and thus creates a new solar system.

Formation of Solid Earth

When Earth first formed, it was very hot. Three sources of energy contributed to the high temperature on the new planet. First, much of the energy was produced when the planetesimals that formed the planet collided with each other. Second, the increasing weight of Earth's outer layers compressed the inner layers, which generated more energy. Third, radioactive materials that emit high-energy particles were very abundant when Earth formed. When surrounding rocks absorbed the particles, the energy of the particles' motion led to higher temperatures.

Early Solid Earth

Young Earth was hot enough to melt iron, the most common of the existing heavy elements. As Earth developed, denser materials, such as molten iron, sank to its center, and less dense materials were forced to the outer layers. This process is called *differentiation*. Differentiation caused Earth to form three distinct layers, as shown in **Figure 3.** At the center is a dense *core* that is composed mostly of iron and nickel. Around the core is the very thick layer of iron- and magnesium-rich rock called the *mantle*. The outermost layer of Earth is a thin *crust* of less dense, silica-rich rock. Today, processes that shape Earth, such as plate tectonics, are driven by heat transfer and differences in density.

Present Solid Earth

Eventually, Earth's surface cooled enough for solid rock to form. The solid rock at Earth's surface formed from less dense elements that were pushed toward the surface during differentiation. Earth's surface continued to change as a result of the heat in Earth's interior as well as through impacts and through interactions with the newly forming atmosphere.

READING TOOLBOX

Chain-of-Events Chart
Make a chain-of-events chart. Then, fill in the chart with details about each step of the formation of Earth.

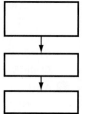

Figure 3 Differentiation of Earth

During its early history, Earth cooled to form three distinct layers.

An atmosphere began to form from the water vapor and carbon dioxide released by volcanic eruptions.

Organisms produced oxygen from photosynthesis to create an oxygenated atmosphere.

Formation of Earth's Atmosphere

Like solid Earth, the atmosphere formed because of differentiation. During the original differentiation of Earth, less dense gas molecules, such as hydrogen and helium, rose to the surface. Thus, the original atmosphere of Earth consisted primarily of hydrogen and helium.

Earth's Early Atmosphere

The high concentrations of hydrogen and helium did not stay with Earth's atmosphere. Earth's gravity would have been too weak to hold these gases unless they were very cold. The sun heated the gases enough so that they escaped Earth's gravity. These gases were probably blown away by the solar wind, which might have been stronger at that time than it is today. Also, Earth's magnetic field, which protects the atmosphere from the solar wind, might not have been fully developed.

Outgassing

As Earth's surface continued to form, volcanic eruptions were much more frequent than they are today. The volcanic eruptions released large amounts of gases, mainly water vapor, carbon dioxide, nitrogen, methane, sulfur dioxide, and ammonia, as shown in **Figure 4.** This process, known as *outgassing*, formed a new atmosphere.

The gases released during outgassing interacted with radiation from the sun. The solar radiation caused the ammonia and some of the water vapor in the atmosphere to break down. Most of the hydrogen that was released during this breakdown escaped into space. Some of the remaining oxygen formed *ozone*, a molecule that contains three oxygen atoms. The ozone collected in a high atmospheric layer around Earth and shielded Earth's surface from the harmful ultraviolet radiation of the sun.

Earth's Present Atmosphere

Organisms that could survive in Earth's early atmosphere developed. Some of these organisms, such as cyanobacteria and early green plants, used carbon dioxide during photosynthesis. Oxygen, a byproduct of photosynthesis, was released. So, the amount of oxygen in the atmosphere slowly increased. About 2 billion years ago, the percentage of oxygen in the atmosphere increased rapidly. Since that time, the chemical composition of the atmosphere has been similar to the present composition of the atmosphere, as shown in **Figure 5.**

Reading Check How did green plants contribute to Earth's present-day atmosphere?

Figure 4 Earth's early atmosphere formed as volcanic eruptions released nitrogen, N_2; water vapor, H_2O; ammonia, NH_3; methane, CH_4; argon, Ar; sulfur dioxide, SO_2; and carbon dioxide, CO_2.

Figure 5 As Earth's surface changed, the gases in the atmosphere changed. Today, the atmosphere is 78% nitrogen, N_2; 21% oxygen, O_2; and 1% other gases.

Formation of Earth's Oceans

Some scientists think that part of Earth's water may have come from space. Early on, icy bodies, such as comets, collided with Earth. Water from these bodies then became part of Earth's atmosphere. As Earth cooled, water vapor condensed to form rain. This liquid water collected on the surface to form the first oceans.

The first ocean was probably made of fresh water. Over millions of years, rainwater fell to Earth and ran over the land, through rivers, and into the ocean. The rainwater dissolved some of the rocks on land and carried those dissolved solids into the oceans. As more dissolved solids were carried to the oceans, the concentration of certain chemicals in the oceans increased. As the water cycled back into the atmosphere through evaporation, some of these chemicals combined to form salts. Over millions of years, water has cycled between the oceans and the atmosphere. Through this process, the oceans have become increasingly salty. Where shallow ocean water has evaporated completely, the salt precipitates and is left behind. This salt may be harvested for human use, as shown in **Figure 6.**

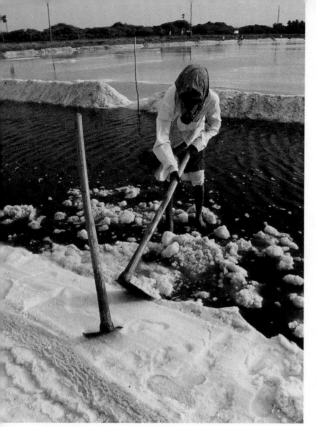

Figure 6 Salt from the ocean can be harvested from salt flats, such as this one in Habantota, Sri Lanka.

The Ocean's Effects on the Atmosphere

The oceans affect global temperatures in a variety of ways. One way the oceans affect temperature is by dissolving carbon dioxide from the atmosphere. Scientists think that early oceans also affected Earth's early climate by dissolving carbon dioxide. Carbon dioxide in the atmosphere keeps energy from escaping into space and thus helps to heat the atmosphere. Over Earth's long history, the concentration of carbon dioxide has increased and decreased for various periods of time. Thus, at different times in its history, Earth likely has experienced climates that are warmer and cooler than the climates we experience today.

Section 1 Review

LA.910.2.2.3; SC.912.E.5.5; SC.912.L.15.8; SC.912.N.3.1; SC.912.N.3.2

Key Ideas

1. **Describe** the nebular hypothesis.

2. **Explain** how planetesimals differ from protoplanets.

3. **Describe** how planets developed.

4. **Explain** why the outer planets are more gaseous than the inner planets.

5. **List** three reasons that Earth was hot when it formed.

6. **Summarize** the process by which the land, atmosphere, and oceans of Earth formed.

Critical Thinking

7. **Identifying Relationships** How does the amount of gas in an outer planet differ from the amount of gas in an inner planet? Explain your answer.

8. **Analyzing Ideas** Explain why Earth is capable of supporting life.

Concept Mapping

9. Use the following terms to make a concept map: *solar system, solar nebula, protoplanet, planetesimal, planet,* and *gas giant.*

<table>
<tr><th>Key Ideas</th><th>Key Terms</th><th>Why It Matters</th></tr>
</table>

Key Ideas	Key Terms	Why It Matters
❯ Compare the models of the universe developed by Ptolemy and Copernicus. ❯ Summarize Kepler's three laws of planetary motion. ❯ Describe how Newton explained Kepler's laws of motion.	eccentricity orbital period inertia	We can send people to the moon and rovers to Mars thanks to models of the solar system.

The first astronomers who studied the sky thought that the stars, planets, and sun revolved around Earth. This idea led to the first model of the solar system. However, the model changed as scientists learned more about how the solar system works.

Early Models

More than 2,000 years ago, the Greek philosopher Aristotle suggested an Earth-centered, or *geocentric,* model of the solar system. In this model, the sun, the stars, and the planets revolved around Earth. However, this model did not explain why planets sometimes appeared to move backward in the sky relative to the stars—a pattern called *retrograde motion.*

By 150 CE, the Greek astronomer Claudius Ptolemy (TAHL uh mee) proposed changes to this model. Ptolemy thought that planets moved in small circles, called *epicycles,* as they revolved in larger circles around Earth. These epicycles seemed to explain why planets sometimes appeared to move backward.

In 1543 CE, a Polish astronomer named Nicolaus Copernicus proposed a sun-centered, or *heliocentric,* model of the solar system. In this model, the planets revolved around the sun in the same direction but at different speeds and distances from the sun. Fast-moving planets passed slow-moving planets. Therefore, planets that were slower than Earth appeared to move backward. **Figure 1** compares Ptolemy's and Copernicus's models. Later, the Italian scientist Galileo Galilei observed four moons traveling around the planet Jupiter. This observation indicated that objects can, and do, revolve around objects other than Earth.

FLORIDA STANDARDS

SC.912.E.5.6 Develop logical connections through physical principles, including Kepler's and Newton's Laws about the relationships and the effects of Earth, Moon, and Sun on each other; **SC.912.E.5.7** Relate the history of and explain the justification for future space exploration and continuing technology development; **SC.912.P.12.4** Describe how the gravitational force between two objects depends on their masses and the distance between them.

Figure 1 Early Solar System Models Ptolemy's solar system model (left) is Earth-centered and has the planets moving in epicycles around Earth. Copernicus's solar model (right) is heliocentric and has the planets moving at different speeds around the sun.

Kepler's Laws

Twenty years before Galileo used a telescope, the Danish astronomer Tycho Brahe made detailed observations of the positions of the planets. After Tycho's death, one of his assistants, Johannes Kepler, worked with Tycho's observations. His studies led Kepler to develop three laws that explained planetary motion.

Law of Ellipses

Kepler's first law, the *law of ellipses*, states that each planet orbits the sun in a path called an ellipse, not in a circle. An *ellipse* is a closed curve whose shape is determined by two points, or *foci*, within the ellipse. In planetary orbits, one focus is located within the sun. No object is located at the other focus. The combined length of two lines, one from each focus to any one point on the ellipse, would always be the same as the length of two other lines, one from each focus, to any other point on the same ellipse.

Elliptical orbits can vary in shape. Some orbits are elongated ellipses. Other orbit shapes are almost perfect circles. The shape of an orbit can be described by a numerical quantity called *eccentricity*. **Eccentricity** is the degree of elongation of an elliptical orbit (symbol, *e*). Eccentricity is determined by dividing the distance between the foci of the ellipse by the length of the major axis. Therefore, the eccentricity of a circular orbit is $e = 0$. The eccentricity of a type of extremely elongated orbit known as a parabolic orbit is $e = 1$.

Reading Check Define and describe an ellipse.

SC.912.E.5.6

Quick Lab   Ellipses

15 min

Procedure

❶ Cover a **cork board** with a **piece of paper**. Put **two push pins** into the cork board, 5 cm apart.

❷ Tie together the ends of a **string** that is 25 cm long. Loop the string around the pins.

❸ Hold the string taut with a **pencil**, and move the pencil to outline an ellipse.

❹ Replace the paper with another **piece of paper**. Place the pins 10 cm apart. Outline another ellipse by using the string.

❺ Use another **piece of paper**. Loop the string around one pin, and outline another ellipse.

Analysis

1. Which ellipse has an eccentricity closest to 0? Which has an eccentricity closest to 1? Describe the shape of your ellipse in terms of eccentricity.

2. Describe the ellipse as you increased the distance between the foci. Describe what would happen to the ellipse if you increased the length of the string without changing the distance between the foci.

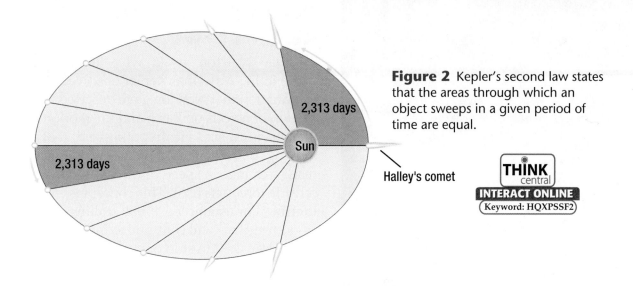

2,313 days

2,313 days

Sun

Halley's comet

Figure 2 Kepler's second law states that the areas through which an object sweeps in a given period of time are equal.

THINK
central
INTERACT ONLINE
Keyword: HQXPSSF2

Law of Equal Areas

Kepler's second law, the *law of equal areas*, describes the speed at which objects travel at different points in their orbits. Kepler discovered that Mars moves fastest in its elliptical orbit when it is closest to the sun. He calculated that a line from the center of the sun to the center of an object sweeps through equal areas in equal periods of time. This principle is illustrated in **Figure 2.**

Imagine a line that connects the center of the sun to the center of an object in orbit around the sun. When the object is near the sun, the imaginary line is short. The object moves relatively rapidly, and the line sweeps through a short, wide, pie-shaped sector. When the object is far from the sun, the line is long. However, the object moves relatively slowly when it is far from the sun, and the imaginary line sweeps through a long, thin, pie-shaped sector in the same period. Kepler's second law states that equal areas are covered in equal amounts of time as an object orbits the sun.

Math Skills

Law of Periods Suppose that scientists discover an asteroid that is 2.0 AU from the sun. If 1 AU = 150 million km, how long would the asteroid's orbital period be in Earth years?

Law of Periods

Kepler's third law, the *law of periods*, describes the relationship between the average distance of a planet from the sun and the orbital period of the planet. The **orbital period** is the time required for a body to complete a single orbit. According to Kepler's third law, the cube of the average distance (a) of a planet from the sun is always proportional to the square of the period (p). The mathematical formula that describes this relationship is $K \times a^3 = p^2$, where K is a constant. When distance is measured in astronomical units (AU) and the period is measured in Earth years, $K = 1$ and $a^3 = p^2$.

Scientists can find out how far away the planets are from the sun by using this law, because they can measure the orbital periods by observing the planets. Jupiter's orbital period is 11.9 Earth years. The square of 11.9 is 142. The cubed number that is equal to 142 is 5.2, so Jupiter is 5.2 AU from the sun.

orbital period the time required for a body to complete a single orbit

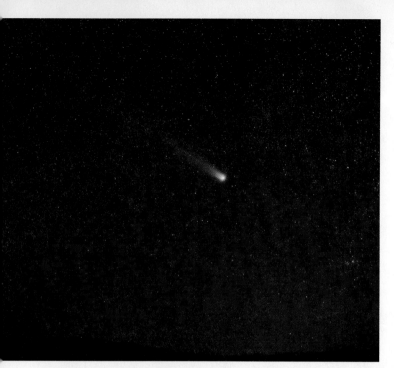

Figure 3 Comet Hyakutake, passing only 0.1 AU from Earth, is kept in orbit by the sun's gravitational pull.

inertia the tendency of an object to resist a change in motion unless an outside force acts on the object

Academic Vocabulary

exist (eg ZIST) to occur or be present

Newton's Explanation of Kepler's Laws

Isaac Newton asked why the planets move in the ways that Kepler observed. The explanation that Newton gave described the motion of objects on Earth and the motion of planets in space. He hypothesized that a moving body will remain in motion and resist a change in speed or direction until an outside force acts on it. This concept is called **inertia.** For example, a ball rolling on a smooth surface will continue to move unless a force causes it to stop or change direction.

Newton's Model of Orbits

Because a planet does not follow a straight path, an outside force must cause the orbit to curve. Newton gave this force the name *gravity,* and he realized that this attractive force exists between any two objects in the universe. The gravitational pull of the sun keeps objects, such as the comet shown in **Figure 3,** in orbit around the sun. While gravity pulls an object toward the sun, inertia keeps the object moving forward in a straight line. The sum of these two motions forms the ellipse of a stable orbit.

The farther from the sun a planet is, the weaker the sun's gravitational pull on the planet is. So, the outer planets are not pulled toward the sun as strongly as the inner ones are. As a result, the orbits of the outer planets are larger and are curved more gently, and the outer planets have longer periods of revolution than the inner planets do.

Section 2 Review

LA.910.2.2.3; SC.912.E.5.6; SC.912.P.12.4

Key Ideas

1. **Compare** Ptolemy's and Copernicus's models of the universe.

2. **Identify** the role that Galileo played in developing the heliocentric theory.

3. **Describe** the shape of planetary orbits.

4. **Explain** the law of equal areas.

5. **Summarize** Kepler's third law of planetary orbits.

6. **Describe** how Newton explained Kepler's laws by combining the effects of two forces.

Critical Thinking

7. **Applying Ideas** A comet's orbit is a highly elongated ellipse. So, why does a comet spend so little time in the inner solar system?

8. **Making Comparisons** How did Kepler's explanation of the orbits of planets differ from Newton's explanation?

Concept Mapping

9. Use the following terms to create a concept map: *retrograde motion, geocentric, heliocentric, ellipse, foci, gravity,* and *inertia.*

Key Ideas	Key Terms	Why It Matters
❯ Identify the basic characteristics of the inner planets. ❯ Compare the characteristics of the inner planets. ❯ Summarize the features that allow Earth to sustain life.	terrestrial planet	Studying other terrestrial planets helps scientists plan for human travel to, and colonization of, Mars.

The planets closest to the sun are called the *inner planets*. These planets are Mercury, Venus, Earth, and Mars. The inner planets are also called **terrestrial planets,** because they are similar to Earth. These planets consist mostly of solid rock and have metallic cores. The number of moons per planet varies from zero to two. The surfaces of inner planets have bowl-shaped depressions, called *impact craters,* that were caused by collisions of the planets with other objects in space.

Mercury

Mercury, the planet closest to the sun, circles the sun every 88 days. The ancient Romans named the planet after the messenger of the gods, who moved quickly. Mercury rotates on its axis once every 59 days.

Images of Mercury reveal a surface that is heavily cratered, as shown in **Figure 1.** The images also show a line of cliffs hundreds of kilometers long. These cliffs may be wrinkles that developed in the crust when the molten core cooled and shrank.

The absence of a significant atmosphere and the planet's slow rotation contribute to the large daily temperature range on Mercury. During the day, the temperature may reach as high as 427 °C. At night, the temperature may plunge to −173 °C.

FLORIDA STANDARDS

LA.910.2.2.3 The student will organize information to show understanding or relationships among facts, ideas, and events (e.g., representing key points within text through charting, mapping, paraphrasing, summarizing, comparing, contrasting, or outlining); **SC.912.E.5.5** Explain the formation of planetary systems based on our knowledge of our Solar System and apply this knowledge to newly discovered planetary systems; **SC.912.E.5.7** Relate the history of and explain the justification for future space exploration and continuing technology development.

terrestrial planet one of the highly dense planets nearest to the sun; Mercury, Venus, Mars, and Earth

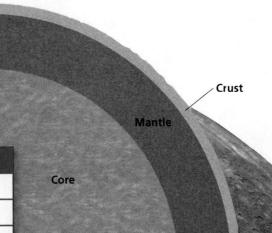

Figure 1 The surface of Mercury, shown in this image captured by the space probe *Messenger,* probably looks much as it did shortly after the solar system formed.

Mercury	
Diameter	4,880 km, or 38% of Earth's diameter
Density	5.4 g/cm³, or 98% of Earth's density
Surface gravity	38% of Earth's surface gravity

Venus

Venus is the second planet from the sun and has an orbital period of 225 days. However, Venus rotates very slowly, only once every 243 days. In some ways, Venus is Earth's twin. The two planets are of almost the same size, mass, and density. However, Venus and Earth differ greatly in other ways.

Venus's Atmosphere

The biggest difference between Earth and Venus is Venus's atmosphere. Venus's atmospheric pressure is about 90 times the pressure on Earth. The high concentration of carbon dioxide in Venus's atmosphere and Venus's relative closeness to the sun have the strongest influences on surface temperatures. Venus's atmosphere is about 96% carbon dioxide.

Solar energy that penetrates the atmosphere heats the planet's surface. The high concentration of carbon dioxide in the atmosphere blocks most of the infrared radiation from escaping. This type of heating is called a *greenhouse effect*. On Earth, the greenhouse effect warms Earth enough to allow organisms to live on the planet. But the greenhouse effect on Venus makes the average surface temperature 464 °C! This phenomenon is commonly referred to as a *runaway greenhouse effect* and makes Venus's surface temperature the highest known in the solar system.

Venus also has sulfur dioxide droplets in its upper atmosphere. These droplets form a cloud layer that reflects sunlight. The cloud layer reflects the sunlight so strongly that, from Earth, Venus appears to be the brightest object in the night sky, aside from Earth's moon and the sun. Because Venus appears near the sun, Venus is usually visible from Earth only in the early morning or evening. Therefore, Venus is commonly called the *evening star* or the *morning star*.

Academic Vocabulary

phenomenon (fuh NAHM uh NUHN) any fact or event that can be sensed or described scientifically (plural, *phenomena*)

Figure 2 Venus's surface is composed of basalt and granite rocks. However, Venus's dense atmosphere is composed primarily of carbon dioxide.

Venus	
Diameter	12,100 km, or 95% of Earth's diameter
Density	5.2 g/cm³, or 95% of Earth's density
Surface gravity	91% of Earth's surface gravity

Figure 3 The scale of this computer-generated image of the Maat Mons volcano on Venus has been stretched vertically to make the topography look more dramatic. The image has also been color enhanced.

Missions to Venus

In the 1970s, the Soviet Union sent six probes to explore the surface of Venus. The probes survived in the atmosphere long enough to transmit surface images of a rocky landscape. The images showed a smooth plain and some rocks. Other instruments carried by the probes indicated that the surface of Venus is composed of basalt and granite. These two types of rock are also common on Earth.

The United States's *Magellan* satellite orbited Venus for four years in the 1990s before the satellite was steered into the planet to collect atmospheric data. *Magellan* also bounced radio waves off Venus to produce radar images of Venus's surface. The European Space Agency's *Venus Express* orbited Venus between April 2006 and May 2009.

Surface Features of Venus

From the radar mapping produced by *Magellan,* scientists discovered landforms such as mountains, volcanoes, lava plains, and sand dunes. Volcanoes and lava plains are the most common features on Venus. At an elevation of 8 km, the volcano Maat Mons, which is shown in **Figure 3,** is Venus's highest volcano.

The surface of Venus is also somewhat cratered. All the craters are about the same age, and they are surprisingly young. This evidence and the abundance of volcanic features on Venus's surface have led some scientists to speculate that Venus undergoes a periodic resurfacing as a result of massive volcanic activity. Energy inside the planet heats the interior over time, which causes the volcanoes to erupt and cover the planet's surface with lava. However, scientists think that another 100 million years may pass before volcanic activity again covers Venus's surface with lava. Venus's surface is very different from Earth's surface, which is constantly changing because of the motion of tectonic plates.

Reading Check How is Venus different from Earth?

Math Skills

Distance from the Sun Earth is about 150 million kilometers from the sun. Venus is 108.2 million kilometers from the sun. How much closer to the sun is Venus than Earth? Express your answer as a percentage.

Earth

The third planet from the sun is Earth. The orbital period of Earth is 365¼ days, and Earth completes one rotation on its axis every day. Earth has one large moon.

Earth has had an extremely active geologic history. Geologic records indicate that over the last 250 million years, Earth's continents separated from a single landmass and drifted to their present positions. Weathering and erosion have changed and continue to change the surface of Earth.

Water on Earth

Earth's unique atmosphere and distance from the sun allow water to exist in a liquid state. Mercury and Venus are so close to the sun that any liquid water on those planets would boil. The outer planets are so far from the sun that water freezes. Earth is the only planet known to have oceans of liquid water, as shown in **Figure 4.** However, scientists think that Jupiter's moon Europa may have an ocean under its icy crust and that Saturn's moon Enceladus may have underground lakes.

Life on Earth

Scientists theorize that as oceans formed on Earth, liquid water dissolved carbon dioxide from the atmosphere. Because of this process, carbon dioxide did not build up in the atmosphere and solar heat was able to escape. Thus, Earth maintained the moderate temperatures needed to support life. Plants and cyanobacteria contributed free oxygen to the atmosphere. Earth is the only known planet that has the proper combination of water, temperature, and oxygen to support life.

Figure 4 Oceans of water and an atmosphere that can support life make Earth a unique planet.

Asthenosphere
Lithosphere
Mesosphere
Outer core
Inner core

Earth	
Diameter	12,756 km
Density	5.515 g/cm³
Surface gravity	9.8 m/s²

Mars	
Diameter	6,800 km, or 53% of Earth's diameter
Density	3.9 g/cm^3, or 71% of Earth's density
Surface gravity	38% of Earth's surface gravity

Figure 5 Mars is called the *Red Planet* because the oxidized rocks on the planet's surface give the planet a red color.

Mars

Mars, shown in **Figure 5,** is the fourth planet from the sun. At an average distance of about 228 million kilometers from the sun, Mars is about 50% farther from the sun than Earth is. Its orbital period is 687 days, and it rotates on its axis every 24 h 37 min. Because its axis tilts at nearly the same angle that Earth's does, Mars's seasons are much like Earth's seasons.

Mars has been geologically active in its past, which is shown in part by the presence of massive volcanoes. A system of deep canyons also covers part of the surface. Valles Marineris is a series of canyons that is as long as the United States is wide—4,000 km. The canyon is thought to be a crack that formed in the crust as the planet cooled. It was later eroded by water.

Martian Volcanoes

Tharsis Montes is one of several volcanic regions on Mars. Volcanoes in this region are 100 times as large as Earth's largest volcano. The largest volcano on Mars is Olympus Mons, which is nearly 24 km tall. It is three times as tall as Mount Everest. At 550 km across, the base of Olympus Mons is about the size of Nebraska. Scientists think that the volcano has grown so large because Mars has no moving tectonic plates. So, Olympus Mons may have had a magma source for millions of years.

Whether Martian volcanoes are still active is a question scientists have yet to answer. A *Viking* landing craft detected two geological events that produced seismic waves. These events, called *marsquakes,* may indicate that volcanoes on Mars are active.

Reading Check **Why are Martian volcanoes larger than Earth's volcanoes?**

READING TOOLBOX

Word Origins
In English, *Olympus Mons* is "Mount Olympus." Look up *Mount Olympus* to see why it is an appropriate name for this particular formation on Mars.

Figure 6 The images above compare the formation of gullies by possible liquid water runoff on Mars (left) with the formation of similar gullies at Mungo National Park in Australia on Earth (right). Mungo National Park is the site of a large lake that dried up more than 10,000 years ago.

Water on Mars

The pressure and temperature of Mars's atmosphere are too low for water to exist as a liquid on Mars's surface. However, several NASA missions—such as the Mars rovers, *Spirit* and *Opportunity*, which landed on Mars in 2004—have found evidence that liquid water did exist on Mars's surface in the past. Mars has many surface features that are characteristic of erosion by water, such as branching paths that look like gullies, as shown in **Figure 6.** Scientists think that other features on Mars might be evidence of vast flood plains produced by a volume of water equal to that of all five of Earth's Great Lakes.

The surface temperature on Mars ranges from 20 °C near the equator during the summer to as low as −130 °C near the poles during the winter. Although most of the water on Mars is trapped in polar icecaps, data from the *Phoenix* lander confirmed in 2008 that water also exists as ice just below the Martian surface. If liquid water were to exist below Mars's surface, the odds of life existing on Mars would dramatically increase. However, no solid evidence of life on Mars has been found.

Section 3 Review

LA.910.2.2.3; SC.912.E.5.5

Key Ideas

1. **Explain** why Mercury has such drastically different temperatures during its day and during its night.

2. **Describe** the main ways in which Venus is similar to and different from Earth.

3. **Identify** the aspects that make Earth hospitable for life.

4. **Explain** why Mars's volcanoes became so tall.

5. **Explain** why Mars does not have liquid water on its surface.

6. **Compare** the characteristics of the inner planets.

Critical Thinking

7. **Making Comparisons** Describe the difference between the greenhouse effect on Venus and the greenhouse effect on Earth.

8. **Understanding Relationships** As rock cools, it contracts. How could this fact explain the presence of Valles Marineris on Mars?

Concept Mapping

9. Use the following terms to create a concept map: *Mercury, Venus, Earth, Mars, terrestrial planet, Olympus Mons, liquid water,* and *Maat Mons.*

Key Ideas

> Identify the basic characteristics that make the outer planets different from terrestrial planets.

> Compare the characteristics of the outer planets.

> Explain why Pluto is now considered a dwarf planet.

Key Terms

gas giant

Kuiper Belt

Why It Matters

Objects beyond the outer planets hold clues to the origin of the solar system. But sending probes to this region is expensive.

The four planets farthest from the sun are called the *outer planets.* They are separated from the inner planets by a ring of debris called the *asteroid belt.* Jupiter, Saturn, Uranus, and Neptune, which are shown in **Figure 1,** are also called **gas giants** because they are large planets that have deep, massive atmospheres made mostly of gas. Uranus and Neptune have more frozen gases and are also known as ice giants. Usually found past the orbit of Neptune is Pluto. Prior to 2006, Pluto was considered to be the most distant outer planet. However, in August of 2006, Pluto was reclassified as a *dwarf planet.*

FLORIDA STANDARDS

SC.912.E.5.5 Explain the formation of planetary systems based on our knowledge of our Solar System and apply this knowledge to newly discovered planetary systems; **SC.912.E.5.6** Develop logical connections through physical principles, including Kepler's and Newton's Laws about the relationships and the effects of Earth, Moon, and Sun on each other.

Gas Giants

Although the gas giants are much larger and more massive than the terrestrial planets, the gas giants are much less dense than the terrestrial planets. Unlike the terrestrial planets, the gas giants did not lose their original gases during their formation. Their large masses give them a huge amount of gravity, which helps them retain the gases.

gas giant a planet that has a deep, massive atmosphere, such as Jupiter, Saturn, Uranus, or Neptune

Each of the gas giants has a thick atmosphere that is made mostly of hydrogen and helium gases. A cloud layer prevents scientists from directly observing more than the topmost part of the atmosphere of the gas giants. But each planet probably has a core made of rock and metals.

Although Saturn's rings may be the most impressive, all four gas giants have ring systems that are made of dust and icy debris that probably came from comets or other bodies.

Figure 1 The four gas giants are much larger than Earth, which is the terrestrial planet shown here at the lower left.

Jupiter

Jupiter, shown in **Figure 2,** is the fifth planet from the sun and is by far the largest planet in the solar system. Its mass is more than 300 times that of Earth and is twice that of all the other planets combined. Jupiter's orbital period is almost 12 years. Jupiter rotates on its axis faster than any other planet rotates—once every 9 h 50 min. Jupiter has at least 63 moons, 4 of which are the size of small planets. It also has several thin rings that are made up of millions of particles.

Jupiter's Atmosphere

Hydrogen and helium make up 92% of Jupiter, so Jupiter's composition is much like the sun's. However, when Jupiter formed about 4.6 billion years ago, it did not have enough mass to allow nuclear fusion to begin. So, Jupiter never became a star.

The alternating light and dark bands on its surface make Jupiter unique in our solar system. Orange, gray, blue, and white bands spread out parallel to the equator. The colors suggest the presence of organic molecules mixed with ammonia, methane, and water vapor. Jupiter's rapid rotation causes these gases to swirl around the planet and form the bands. The average temperature of Jupiter's outer atmospheric layers is −160°C. Jupiter has lightning storms and thunderstorms that are much larger than those on Earth.

Reading Check Why didn't Jupiter become a star?

www.scilinks.org
Topic: Outer Planets
Code: HQX1091

Figure 2 Jupiter is easily identified by its large size and alternating light and dark bands. One of Jupiter's larger moons can be seen in front of the planet.

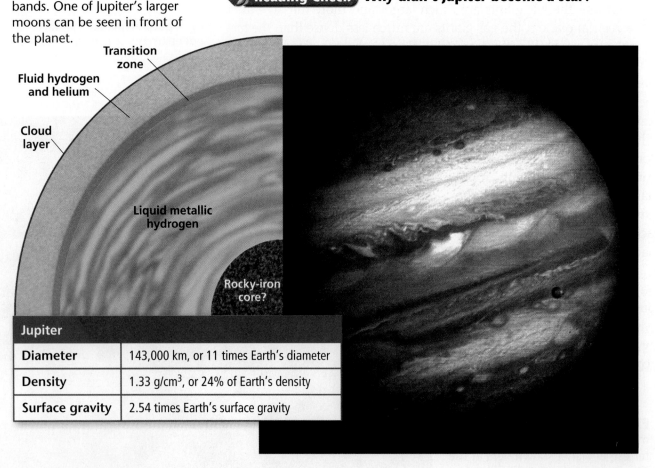

Transition zone

Fluid hydrogen and helium

Cloud layer

Liquid metallic hydrogen

Rocky-iron core?

Jupiter	
Diameter	143,000 km, or 11 times Earth's diameter
Density	1.33 g/cm^3, or 24% of Earth's density
Surface gravity	2.54 times Earth's surface gravity

Weather and Storms on Jupiter

Jupiter's most <u>distinctive</u> feature is its *Great Red Spot*, shown in **Figure 3.** The Great Red Spot is a giant rotating storm, similar to a hurricane on Earth, that has been raging for at least several hundred years. Several other oval spots, or storms, can be seen on Jupiter, although they are usually white. Sometimes, the smaller storms are swallowed up by the larger ones. While storms are common on Jupiter's surface, only a few of the largest storms persist for a long time.

A probe dropped by the *Galileo* spacecraft measured wind speeds of up to 540 km/h on Jupiter. Because winds are caused by temperature differences, scientists have concluded that Jupiter's internal heat affects the planet's weather more than heat from the sun does. From Earth, even using a small telescope, you can see bands of clouds on Jupiter. These bands, which vary depending on latitude, show regions of different wind speeds.

Jupiter's Interior

Jupiter's large mass causes the temperature and pressure in Jupiter's interior to be much greater than they are inside Earth. The intense pressure and temperatures as high as 30,000 °C have changed Jupiter's interior into a sea of liquid, metallic hydrogen. Electric currents in this hot liquid may be the source of Jupiter's enormous magnetic field. Scientists think that Jupiter has a solid, rocky, iron core at its center.

Figure 3 Jupiter's Great Red Spot is an ongoing, massive, hurricane-like storm that is about twice the diameter of Earth.

Academic Vocabulary

distinctive (di STINGK tiv) notable, distinguishing

Why It Matters

What Happens When a Comet Hits a Planet?

Nobody had ever witnessed a collision between a comet and a planet in all of human history. That changed in 1994 when comet Shoemaker-Levy collided with Jupiter.

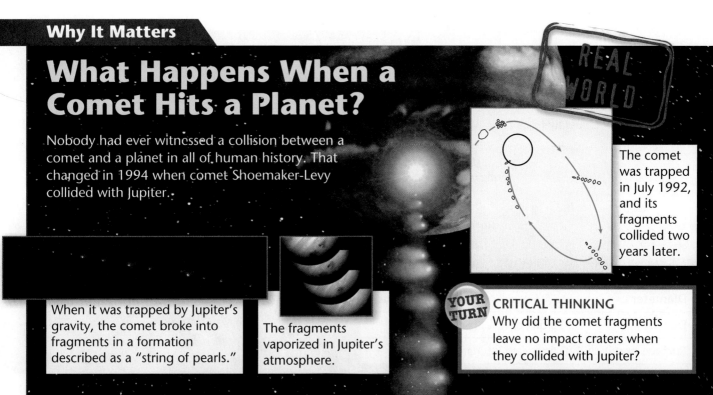

The comet was trapped in July 1992, and its fragments collided two years later.

When it was trapped by Jupiter's gravity, the comet broke into fragments in a formation described as a "string of pearls."

The fragments vaporized in Jupiter's atmosphere.

YOUR TURN

CRITICAL THINKING
Why did the comet fragments leave no impact craters when they collided with Jupiter?

Saturn

Saturn, shown in **Figure 4,** is the sixth planet from the sun and has an orbital period of 29.5 years. Because it is so far from the sun, Saturn is very cold and has an average cloud-top temperature of −176 °C. Saturn has at least 60 moons, and additional small moons continue to be discovered. Its largest moon, Titan, which has a diameter of 5,150 km, is half the size of Earth.

Saturn, like Jupiter, is made almost entirely of hydrogen and helium and has a rocky, iron core at its center. However, Saturn is much less dense than Jupiter. In fact, Saturn is the least dense planet in the solar system.

Saturn's Bands and Rings

Saturn is known for its rings, which are two times the planet's diameter. While the other gas giants also have rings, Saturn has the most complex and extensive system of rings. The rings are made of billions of dust and ice particles. Most of the ring debris probably came from comets or other bodies.

Like Jupiter, Saturn also has bands of colored clouds that run parallel to its equator. These bands are caused by Saturn's rapid rotation. Saturn rotates on its axis about every 10 h 30 min. This rapid rotation, paired with Saturn's low density, causes Saturn to bulge at its equator and to flatten at its poles.

Scientists are learning more about Saturn and its moons from NASA's *Cassini* spacecraft, which reached Saturn on July 1, 2004. Cassini also carried the European Space Agency's *Huygens* probe, which landed on Titan, Saturn's largest moon.

Reading Check How is Saturn similar to Jupiter?

Figure 4 This composite image of Saturn taken from the *Cassini* spacecraft clearly shows the planet's rings.

Liquid hydrogen

Liquid metallic hydrogen

Icy core

Rocky-iron core?

Saturn	
Diameter	120,500 km, or 9.4 times Earth's diameter
Density	0.70 g/cm³, or 13% of Earth's density
Surface gravity	1.07 times Earth's surface gravity

Uranus	
Diameter	51,120 km, or 4 times Earth's diameter
Density	1.3 g/cm^3, or 24% of Earth's density
Surface gravity	91% of Earth's surface gravity

Fluid hydrogen

Icy-liquid mantle

Rocky-iron core?

Figure 5 This exaggerated-color image from the *Hubble Space Telescope* shows Uranus, two of its moons, and some of its rings.

Uranus

Uranus, shown in **Figure 5,** is the seventh planet from the sun and the third-largest planet in the solar system. William Herschel discovered Uranus in 1781. Because Uranus is nearly 3 billion kilometers from the sun, Uranus is a difficult planet to study. But the *Hubble Space Telescope* has taken images that show changes in Uranus's atmosphere. Uranus has at least 27 moons and at least 12 thin rings. Its orbital period is almost 84 years.

Uranus's Rotation

The most distinctive feature of Uranus is its unusual orientation. Most planets, including Earth, rotate with their axes perpendicular to their orbital planes as they revolve around the sun. However, Uranus's axis is almost parallel to the plane of its orbit. The rotation rate of Uranus was not discovered until 1986, when *Voyager 2* passed by Uranus. Astronomers were then able to determine that Uranus rotated once about every 17 h.

Uranus's Atmosphere

Like the other gas giants, Uranus has an atmosphere that contains mainly hydrogen and helium. The blue-green color of Uranus indicates that the atmosphere also contains significant amounts of methane. The average cloud-top temperature of Uranus is –214 °C. However, astronomers believe that the planet's temperature is much higher below the clouds. There may be a mixture of liquid water and methane beneath the atmosphere. Scientists also think that the center of Uranus, which has a temperature of approximately 7,000 °C, is a core of rock and melted elements.

Neptune

Neptune, shown in **Figure 6,** is the eighth planet from the sun and is similar to Uranus in size and mass. Neptune's orbital period is nearly 164 years, and the planet rotates about every 16 h. Neptune has at least 13 moons and six rings.

The Discovery of Neptune

Neptune's existence was predicted before Neptune was actually discovered. After Uranus was discovered, astronomers noted variations from its calculated orbit. They suspected that the gravity of an unknown planet was responsible for the variation. In the mid-1800s, John Couch Adams, an English mathematician, and Urbain Leverrier, a French astronomer, independently calculated the position of the unknown planet. A German astronomer, Johann Galle, discovered a bluish-green disk where Leverrier had predicted the planet would be. Astronomers named the planet Neptune after the Roman god of the sea.

Neptune's Atmosphere

Data from the *Voyager 2* spacecraft indicate that Neptune's atmosphere is made up mostly of hydrogen, helium, and methane. Neptune's upper atmosphere contains some white clouds of frozen methane. These clouds appear as continually changing bands between the equator and the poles of Neptune.

Images taken by *Voyager 2*, the *Hubble Space Telescope,* and earthbound telescopes indicate that Neptune has an active weather system. Neptune has the solar system's strongest winds, which exceed 1,000 km/h. A storm that is the size of Earth and that is known as the *Great Dark Spot* appeared and disappeared on Neptune's surface. Neptune's average cloud-top temperature is about –225 °C.

Figure 6 This Great Dark Spot on Neptune was a giant storm that was similar to the Great Red Spot on Jupiter.

Fluid hydrogen

Icy-liquid mantle

Rocky-iron core?

Neptune	
Diameter	49,530 km, or 3.9 times Earth's diameter
Density	1.6 g/cm^3, or 30% of Earth's density
Surface gravity	1.2 times Earth's surface gravity

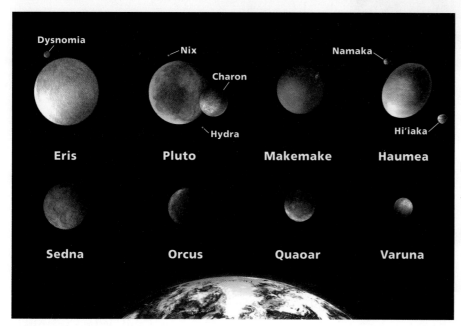

Figure 7 This artist drawing illustrates the largest known trans-Neptunian objects. Note that Pluto, once considered one of the nine planets, is not the largest.

Objects Beyond Neptune

Pluto was discovered in 1930. Until 2006, it was known as the ninth planet. Now, it is defined as a dwarf planet. A *dwarf planet* is any object that orbits the sun, is round because of its own gravity, has not cleared the region around its orbit, and is not a satellite of another planet.

Pluto orbits the sun in an unusual elongated and tilted ellipse. Pluto is usually far beyond Neptune, but it is closer to the sun than Neptune is for about 20 years out of its 248-year orbital period. With a diameter of 2,302 km, Pluto is smaller than Earth's moon. Astronomers think that Pluto is made up of frozen methane, rock, and ice and has an average temperature of –235 °C. Infrared images show that Pluto has extensive methane icecaps and a very thin nitrogen atmosphere. It also has three moons, one of which, named Charon (KER uhn), has a diameter more than half that of Pluto.

Kuiper–Belt Objects

In recent years, scientists have discovered hundreds of objects in our solar system beyond Neptune's orbit. These objects are called *trans-Neptunian objects* (TNOs). Some of these TNOs are similar to Pluto in size and composition, as shown in **Figure 7,** but most are simply small chunks of ice. TNOs exist in a region beyond Neptune's orbit called the **Kuiper Belt** (KIE puhr BELT). Scientists think that these bodies are the remnants of material that formed the early solar system.

Like Pluto, Eris, Makemake (MAH kay MAH kay), and Haumea (HAH oo may uh) are trans-Neptunian dwarf planets or *plutoids*. The other large TNOs have not been classified as such, but may eventually be considered as meeting the definition.

 Reading Check Where is the Kuiper Belt located?

READING TOOLBOX

Word Origins
Eris was a Greek goddess, and Sedna was an Inuit goddess. Quaoar was a god of the Native American Tongva people. Look up these names, and find why they were chosen as names of objects beyond Neptune's orbit.

Kuiper Belt a region of the solar system that starts just beyond the orbit of Neptune and that contains dwarf planets and other small bodies made mostly of ice

Figure 8 This illustration shows an artist's idea of a Jupiter-sized exoplanet in the foreground. This exoplanet orbits a sun-like star called HD209458, which is located 150 light years from Earth.

Exoplanets

Until the 1990s, all the planets that astronomers had discovered were in Earth's solar system. Since then, however, several hundred planetlike objects have been attributed to stars other than Earth's sun. Because these objects circle stars other than Earth's sun, they are called *exoplanets*. The prefix *exo-* means "outside." **Figure 8** shows an artist's rendition of an exoplanet. Most known exoplanets orbit stars that are similar to Earth's sun. Therefore, the existence of exoplanets leads some scientists to wonder if life could exist in another solar system.

Because of their size and distance, exoplanets have only recently been directly observed with telescopes. Most exoplanets can be detected only because their gravity tugs on stars that they orbit. When scientists study some distant stars, they notice that the light coming from the stars shifts in wavelength. This shifting could be explained by the stars' movement slightly toward and then away from Earth. Scientists know that the gravity of an object that cannot be seen can affect a star's movement. In these cases, that object is most likely an exoplanet that orbits the star.

Most of the exoplanets that have been identified are larger than Uranus, but gradually astronomers are discovering exoplanets that are closer to Earth in mass. One may even be the right temperature to support life as we know it. Many exoplanets, though more massive than Jupiter, are closer to their stars than Mercury is to Earth's sun. From studying these many solar systems, scientists hope to learn more about the formation and basic arrangement of solar systems.

Section 4 Review

LA.910.2.2.3; SC.912.E.5.5; SC.912.E.5.6; SC.912.P.12.4

Key Ideas

1. **Explain** what makes Jupiter similar to the sun.

2. **Compare** the characteristics of Jupiter, Saturn, Uranus, and Neptune.

3. **Compare** Jupiter's Great Red Spot with weather on Earth.

4. **Describe** the way in which the tilt of the axis of Uranus's rotation is unusual.

5. **Explain** how Pluto differs from the outer planets of the solar system.

6. **Summarize** the features of objects in the Kuiper Belt.

7. **Describe** what scientists know about exoplanets, planetlike objects outside the solar system.

Critical Thinking

8. **Making Comparisons** How are the compositions of the gas giants similar to the composition of the sun?

9. **Making Inferences** Why is Pluto not considered a planet even though Neptune is sometimes farther from the sun than Pluto is?

10. **Evaluating Conclusions** Should scientists reconsider Pluto to be a planet? Explain your answer.

Concept Mapping

11. Use the following terms to create a concept map: *outer planet, Jupiter, Saturn, Uranus, Neptune, Pluto, gas giant, Kuiper Belt,* and *Great Red Spot.*

New Horizons for Pluto

SCIENCE & SOCIETY

The *New Horizons* spacecraft, on its way to Pluto and the nearby region of icy, rocky solar system bodies called the Kuiper Belt, is the fastest traveler in history. However, despite a speed of 75,000 km/h, the craft will take nine years to reach Pluto in 2015. According to Deputy Associate Administrator for NASA's Science Mission Directorate, Dr. Colleen Hartman, "What we know about Pluto could be written on the back of a postage stamp. After this mission, we'll be able to fill textbooks with new information."

This photo, from 1994, was the first image of Pluto's surface. Taken by the Hubble telescope, it shows 12 distinct surface regions of light and darkness.

The piano-sized craft operates on less power than two 100-watt bulbs. In 2007, it used the gravity of Jupiter to help propel it toward Pluto.

The *New Horizons* spacecraft

During its Jupiter flyby, *New Horizons* photographed this eruption on Io, one of Jupiter's moons. The volcanic plume rises 320 km above the surface.

YOUR TURN

CRITICAL THINKING
New Horizons was launched when Pluto was still called a planet. Should the mission have been cancelled? Why or why not?

ONLINE RESEARCH
Find out where *New Horizons* is right now.

Making Models **Lab**

Crater Analysis

All of the inner planets—Mercury, Venus, Earth, and Mars—have many features in common. They are all made of mostly solid rock and have metallic cores. They have no rings and have from zero to two moons each. And they have bowl-shaped depressions called *impact craters*. Impact craters are caused by collisions between the planets and rocky objects that travel through space. Most of these collisions took place during the formation of the solar system.

Mercury's entire surface is covered with these craters, while very few craters are still evident on the surface of Earth. Many of the moons of the inner and outer planets are also heavily cratered. In this lab, you will experiment with making craters to discover the effect of speed and projectile angle on the way craters form.

What You'll Do

> **Create** a model that demonstrates the formation of impact craters.

> **Analyze** how an object's speed and projectile angle affect the impact crater that the object forms on planets and moons.

What You'll Need

marble, large (1)
marbles, small (5)
marker
meter stick
plaster of Paris
protractor
scissors
shoe box
tape, masking
toothpicks (6)
tweezers

Safety

Procedure

1. Place the top of a toothpick in the center of a piece of masking tape that is 6 cm long. Fold the tape in half around the toothpick to form a "small flag" and "flagpole." On the flag, write the letter A. Repeat this step for the other toothpicks, and label them with the letters B through F.

2. Mix plaster of Paris with water, according to instructions for making plaster of Paris. Spread your mixture in the bottom of the shoe box. Make your plaster layer about 4 cm thick. The surface should be as smooth as possible.

Step 7

774

3. Allow the plaster to dry until it is no longer soupy, but not yet rigid.

4. Drop a large marble onto the plaster from a height of 50 cm above the surface. Quickly remove the marble with tweezers, but do not damage the crater that formed. Place flag A next to the crater to label the crater.

5. Repeat step 4 by using a small marble dropped from a height of 50 cm and another small marble dropped from a height of 25 cm. Use the flags to label craters B (50 cm drop) and C (25 cm drop).

6. Repeat step 4 by using a small marble dropped from a height of 1 m. Label the crater D.

7. Using a protractor as a guide, have your partner tilt the box at a 30° angle to the table. Be sure your partner holds the box steady. Then, drop a small marble vertically from a height of 50 cm. Label the crater E.

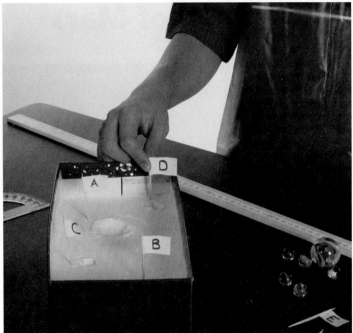

Step 6

8. Repeat step 7 by using an angle of 45°. Label the crater F.

9. Allow the plaster of Paris to harden. Write a description of each crater and the surrounding area.

Analysis

1. **Examining Data** Which crater was formed by the marble that had the highest velocity? What is the effect of velocity on the characteristics of the crater formed?

2. **Explaining Events** Study the shapes of craters B, E, and F. How did the angle of the plaster of Paris affect the shape of the craters that formed?

3. **Making Comparisons** Compare craters A, B, and D. How do they differ from each other? What caused this difference? Is the difference in the masses of the objects a factor? Explain your answer.

Extension

Applying Conclusions Find a map of the surface craters on one of the terrestrial planets. Identify craters that were made by different angles of impact. Label the craters on the diagram, and present your findings to the class.

MOLA Map of Mars

Map Skills Activity

The above map shows the relative elevation of surface features on Mars's surface. The number 0 on the elevation scale marks the average elevation at the equator. This map was created from data collected by the Mars Orbiter Laser Altimeter (MOLA) on the *NASA Mars Global Surveyor*. Use the map to answer the questions below.

1. **Analyzing Data** Estimate the longitude and latitude of Elysium Mons.

2. **Using a Key** Identify three features that have elevations below 0. Identify three features that have elevations above 0.

3. **Comparing Areas** In general, which pole on Mars, the north pole or south pole, has higher elevations?

4. **Using a Key** Which feature, Isidis Planitia or Argyre Planitia, has a higher elevation?

5. **Making Comparisons** Which feature, Hellas Planitia or Olympus Mons, would most likely be a volcano?

6. **Using a Key** Estimate the distance between Olympus Mons and Elysium Mons in degrees of longitude.

7. **Inferring Relationships** Based on what you have learned from the map, what type of features do you think the words *planitia* and *mons* refer to?

THINK central
SUPER SUMMARY
Keyword: HQXPSSS

Key Ideas	Key Terms

Section 1

Formation of the Solar System

❯ The solar system formed from a rotating and contracting region of gas and dust about 5 billion years ago.

❯ The planets formed from collisions of smaller bodies called *planetesimals*.

❯ Earth's land and atmosphere formed by differentiation. Oceans formed as water vapor in the atmosphere condensed and fell.

solar system, p. 749
planet, p. 749
solar nebula, p. 749
planetesimal, p. 750

Section 2

Models of the Solar System

❯ Ptolemy proposed an Earth-centered model of the universe. Copernicus proposed a sun-centered model.

❯ Kepler's first law states that orbits of planets are ellipses with the sun at one focus. The second law states that planets closer to the sun travel faster than those farther away. The third law relates a planet's average distance from the sun to the time it takes to make one orbit.

❯ Newton used the idea of inertia to explain Kepler's laws.

eccentricity, p. 756
orbital period, p. 757
inertia, p. 758

Section 3

The Inner Planets

❯ The four inner (terrestrial) planets consist mainly of solid rock. Their surfaces show cratering, and they have metallic cores.

❯ The terrestrial planets are denser and smaller than the gas giants. Only Earth and Mars have moons. All but Mercury have notable atmospheres.

❯ Liquid water and an oxygen-enriched atmosphere enable Earth to sustain life.

terrestrial planet, p. 759

Section 4

The Outer Planets

❯ The outer planets lack a solid surface and are much less dense and much larger than the terrestrial planets.

❯ The outer planets have rings and many moons, as well as atmospheres rich with hydrogen and helium. Unlike the other outer planets, Uranus's axis of rotation is almost parallel to the plane of its orbit.

❯ Pluto is considered a dwarf planet because astronomers have reclassified objects of the solar system, and Pluto now fits the definition of a dwarf planet.

gas giant, p. 765
Kuiper Belt, p. 771

1. **Chain-of-Events Chart** Make a chain-of-events chart to describe why the outer planets have very different characteristics from those of the inner planets. SC.912.E.5.2

READING TOOLBOX

USING KEY TERMS

Use each of the following terms in a separate sentence.

2. *inertia* SC.912.E.5.6

3. *terrestrial planet*

4. *Kuiper Belt*

For each pair of terms, explain how the meanings of the terms differ.

5. *Kuiper belt* and *orbital period*

6. *planet* and *planetesimal* SC.912.E.5.5

7. *terrestrial planet* and *gas giant*

8. *solar nebula* and *solar system* SC.912.E.5.5

UNDERSTANDING KEY IDEAS

9. Copernicus's model of the solar system is SC.912.E.5.6
   a. geocentric.   c. ethnocentric.
   b. lunocentric.   d. heliocentric.

10. Kepler's first law states that each planet orbits the sun in a path called a(n) SC.912.E.5.6
    a. ellipse.   c. epicycle.
    b. circle.   d. period.

11. The most distinctive feature of Jupiter is its
    a. Great Red Spot.
    b. Great Dark Spot.
    c. ring.
    d. elongated orbit.

12. The planet that has an axis of rotation that is almost parallel to the plane of its orbit is SC.912.E.5.6
    a. Venus.   c. Uranus.
    b. Jupiter.   d. Neptune.

13. The tilt of the axis of Mars is nearly the same as that of SC.912.E.5.6
    a. Mercury.   c. Earth.
    b. Venus.   d. Jupiter.

14. The planet that rotates faster than any other planet in the solar system is SC.912.E.5.6
    a. Earth.   c. Uranus.
    b. Jupiter.   d. Venus.

15. Kepler's law that describes how fast planets travel at different points in their orbits is called the law of SC.912.E.5.6
    a. ellipses.   c. equal areas.
    b. equal speeds.   d. periods.

16. All the outer planets rotate with their axes perpendicular to their orbital planes *except* SC.912.E.5.6
    a. Saturn.   c. Nepture.
    b. Jupiter.   d. Uranus.

17. The first atmosphere of Earth contained a large amount of SC.912.E.5.5
    a. helium.   c. carbon dioxide.
    b. oxygen.   d. methane.

18. The hypothesis that states that the sun and the planets developed out of the same cloud of gas and dust is called the SC.912.E.5.5
    a. Copernicus hypothesis.
    b. solar hypothesis.
    c. nebular hypothesis.
    d. Galileo hypothesis.

19. In the process of photosynthesis, green plants give off
    a. hydrogen.   c. carbon dioxide.
    b. oxygen.   d. helium.

SHORT ANSWER

20. Explain how Earth's early atmosphere differed from Earth's atmosphere today.

21. What is the shape of the planets' orbits?

22. What is Kepler's first law? SC.912.E.5.6

23. How did Newton's ideas about the orbits of the planets differ from Kepler's ideas? SC.912.E.5.6

24. List three features of Earth that allow it to sustain life. SC.912.E.5.5

25. Describe how a planet might form. SC.912.E.5.5

26. How did differentiation help to form solid Earth? SC.912.E.5.5

CRITICAL THINKING

27. Applying Ideas Suppose astronomers discover that exoplanets orbiting stars similar to Earth's sun have similar compositions to the planets in Earth's solar system. What can the astronomers hypothesize about the formation of those solar systems? **SC.912.E.5.5**

28. Identifying Trends If you know the distance from the sun to a planet, what other information can you determine about the orbit of the planet? Explain your answer. **SC.912.E.5.6**

29. Making Inferences How would the layers of Earth be different if the planet had never been hotter than it is today?

CONCEPT MAPPING

30. Use the following terms to create a concept map: *solar system, planet, protoplanet, planetesimal, differentiation, core, mantle, crust, geocentric, heliocentric, Aristotle, Ptolemy, Copernicus, ellipse, Earth, terrestrial planet, outer planet, Jupiter, Saturn, gas giant, Kuiper Belt, solar nebula,* and *inner planet.* **SC.912.E.5.6**

MATH SKILLS   Math Skills

31. Making Calculations Mercury has a period of rotation equal to 58.67 Earth days. Mercury's period of revolution is equal to 88 Earth days. How many times does Mercury rotate during one revolution around the sun?

32. Applying Quantities Uranus's orbital period is 84 years. What is its distance from the sun in astronomical units? **SC.912.E.5.6**

33. Making Calculations Venus's orbital period is 225 days. Calculate your age in Venus years. **SC.912.E.5.6**

WRITING SKILLS

34. Creative Writing Imagine that you are the first astronaut to land on Mars. In a short essay, describe what you hope and expect to find.

35. Communicating Main Ideas Create your own definition for *planet*. Then, write an explanation for why Pluto is or is not a planet.

INTERPRETING GRAPHICS

The graph below shows density in relation to mass for Earth, Uranus, and Neptune. Mass is given in Earth masses. The mass of Earth is equal to 1. Use the graph to answer the questions that follow.

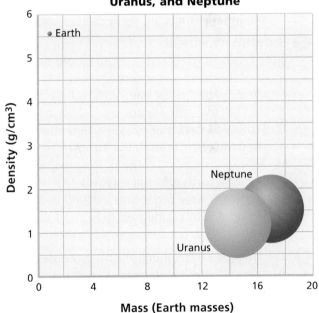

Density Vs. Mass for Earth, Uranus, and Neptune

36. Which planet is denser, Uranus or Neptune? Explain your answer. **SC.912.E.5.6**

37. Which planet has the smallest mass? **SC.912.E.5.6**

38. How can Earth be the densest of the three planets even though Uranus and Neptune have so much more mass than Earth does? **SC.912.E.5.6**

Understanding Concepts

Directions (1–9): For each question, write on a separate sheet of paper the letter of the correct answer.

1 Which of the following statements describes a way in which the formation of the inner planets differs from the formation of the outer planets?
A. The inner planets formed from planetesimals, and the outer planets formed from comets.
B. The inner planets formed more moons than the outer planets did.
C. Because they are closer to the sun, the inner planets formed from heavier elements than the outer planets did.
D. Because they are far from the sun, the outer planets are composed of frozen gases while the inner planets are composed of rock.

2 Scientists hypothesize that Earth's first oceans were made of fresh water. From where did most of this fresh water come?
F. Water vapor in the early atmosphere cooled and fell to Earth as rain.
G. Frozen comets that fell to Earth melted as they traveled through the atmosphere.
H. As soon as icecaps formed, they melted because Earth was still very hot.
I. Early terrestrial organisms exhaled water vapor, which condensed to form fresh water.

3 The original atmosphere of Earth consisted of
A. nitrogen and oxygen gases.
B. helium and hydrogen gases.
C. ozone and ammonia gases.
D. oxygen and carbon dioxide gases.

4 Which of the following processes did NOT happen during the formation of Earth's atmosphere?
F. The amount of carbon dioxide decreased.
G. Volcanic eruptions released large amounts of gases.
H. The amount of oxygen increased.
I. Oxygen formed ozone, which collected in a layer in the upper atmosphere.

5 Scientists estimate that the solar system originated as a solar nebula, and the sun began to produce its own energy through nuclear fusion approximately how many years ago?
A. 50 million years   **C.** 1 billion years
B. 500 million years   **D.** 5 billion years

6 Which of the following statements is true of carbon dioxide in Earth's developing atmosphere?
F. Carbon dioxide entered the atmosphere through the process of outgassing.
G. Earth's earliest atmosphere was made up of carbon dioxide.
H. The earliest organisms used oxygen and released carbon dioxide into the atmosphere.
I. Earth's early atmosphere had more carbon dioxide than it does today.

7 When Earth formed, it was hot enough to melt iron. Which of the following statements does NOT describe a reason why Earth was so hot?
A. collision of planetesimals
B. compression of the inner layers
C. radioactive materials
D. solar energy

8 How to the theories of Ptolemy and Copernicus differ?
F. Ptolemy thought that planets traveled at the same rate of speed, but Copernicus thought that planets had different rates of speed.
G. Ptolemy thought that Earth was the center of the solar system, and Copernicus thought that the sun was the center of the solar system.
H. Ptolemy thought that only Earth had moons, but Copernicus thought that other planets had moons.
I. Ptolemy thought that each planet traveled in a circle, and Copernicus thought that each planet traveled in an ellipse.

9 Why can scientists find only very large planets around other stars?
A. Only large planets can be directly observed.
B. The large planets are far enough from their stars to be observed.
C. Current technology cannot detect the gravitational effects of small planets on stars.
D. Most sun-like stars do not have small planets.

Interpreting Graphics

Directions (10–12): For each question below, record the correct answer on a separate sheet of paper.

Atmospheres of Venus, Earth, and Mars

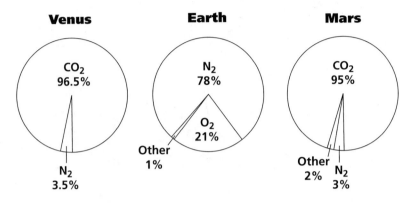

10 What is the percentage of carbon dioxide in the atmosphere of Venus?

F. 3.5% **H.** 95%

G. 21% **I.** 96.5%

Planets of the Solar System

Planet	Orbital period	Rotational period
Mercury	88 days	59 days
Venus	225 days	243 days
Earth	365.25 days	23 hours 56 minutes
Mars	687 days	24 hours 37 minutes
Jupiter	12 years	9 hours 50 minutes
Saturn	29.5 years	10 hours 30 minutes
Uranus	84 years	17 hours
Neptune	164 years	16 hours

11 Which planet's day length is nearly the same as Earth's?

A. Mercury **C.** Saturn

B. Mars **D.** Neptune

12 What is the relationship between distance from the sun and orbital period?

F. Planets that are farther from the sun have a shorter orbital period.

G. Planets that are close to the sun have a shorter orbital period than planets that are far from the sun do.

H. The orbital period of each planet is twice the orbital period of the planet before it in relation to the sun.

I. There is no relationship between distance from the sun and orbital period.

Test Tip

Even if you are sure of the answer to a test question, read all of the answer choices before selecting your response.

Chapter 28

Minor Bodies of the Solar System

Chapter Outline

Why It Matters

Fragments from the formation of the solar system still exist as asteroids, comets, and meteoroids. These objects could demand more than study if they came too close to Earth.

Inquiry Lab

⏱ **20 min**

Suit Up!

Have one partner put on padded work gloves. Wearing the gloves, try to open a CD case, take out the CD, and then close the case. Next, try putting on a pair of socks and shoes and tying up your shoelaces. Your partner will prepare a chart and use a clock to record the time to perform the tasks. Repeat all tasks without the gloves, again recording the times. Trade roles and repeat. See who can perform each task faster.

Questions to Get You Started

1. What can you infer about working in a spacesuit from this exercise?

2. How else can astronauts carry out tasks in space without having to wear spacesuits?

SC.912.E.5.7

These reading tools will help you learn the material in this chapter.

Word Origins

Names of Jupiter's Moons The planet Jupiter was named for the king of the gods in Roman mythology. Jupiter's four largest moons are named after characters associated with Jupiter or Zeus (Jupiter's counterpart in Greek mythology): Io, Europa, Ganymede, and Callisto.

Your Turn The moons of many planets were named for characters in mythology and literature. As you read Section 3, add the planets' moons to a table like the one below. Use a dictionary or other sources to discover the origins of the moons' names.

Planet	Moon	Origin of name
Saturn	Titan	In Roman mythology, the sisters and brothers of Chronos (the Greek counterpart of Saturn) were the Titans. (Other moons of Saturn are named after specific Titans.)

Describing Space

Words and Phrases When you describe the motion of objects through space, you use verbs and phrases that modify the verbs. Paying attention to language that describes motion can help you recognize what kind of motion is described.

Your Turn As you read Section 2, make a three-column table like the one below. Add words or phrases that describe the motion of specific objects.

Objects	Words Describing Motion	Meaning of Motion Words
moon	rotate	spin around a central point (an axis)

Note Taking

Two-Column Notes Two-column notes can help you learn the main ideas from each section. This note-taking strategy will help you review information for quizzes and tests.

Your Turn Complete two-column notes for main ideas in Sections 1 and 4. Follow the example from Section 1 that is shown below.

❶ Write one main idea in each row in the left column.

❷ As you read Sections 1 and 4, add detailed notes and examples in the right column. Be sure to put these details and examples in your own words.

Main Idea	Detail Notes
The lunar surface	• several types of surface features -craters (impact depressions) - rilles (long, deep channels) -ridges (long, narrow rock elevations) -regolith (dust and small rocky fragments) -rocks

For more information on how to use these and other tools, see **Appendix A.**

Key Ideas	Key Terms	Why It Matters
❯ List four kinds of lunar surface features. ❯ Describe the three layers of the moon. ❯ Summarize the three stages by which the moon formed.	satellite moon mare crater	The moon is the only body in the solar system besides Earth that humans have visited in person.

A body that orbits a larger body is called a **satellite.** Six of the planets in our solar system have smaller bodies that orbit around them. These natural satellites are also called **moons.** Our moon is Earth's natural satellite.

In 1957, the Soviet Union launched *Sputnik*, which was the first *artificial satellite* launched into space. In 1958, the United States launched its first artificial satellite, which was named *Explorer 1*. Thousands of artificial satellites are now in orbit around Earth, including weather satellites and space telescopes, such as the *Hubble Space Telescope*.

Exploring the Moon

Between 1969 and 1972, the United States sent six spacecraft to the moon as part of the Apollo space program. Apollo astronauts found that the moon's weak gravity affected the way they moved. They discovered that bouncing was more efficient than walking. Apollo astronauts also explored the moon's surface in a variety of specially-designed vehicles, such as the one shown in **Figure 1.**

The moon has much less mass than Earth does, so the gravity on the moon's surface is about one-sixth of the gravity on Earth. As a result, someone who weighs 690 N (newtons) on Earth would weigh about 115 N on the moon. (The person's mass would remain the same.) The gravity at the moon's surface is not strong enough to hold gases, so the moon has no significant atmosphere. Because it has no atmosphere to absorb and transport thermal energy, the moon's surface temperature varies from 134 °C during the day to −170 °C at night.

FLORIDA STANDARDS

SC.912.E.5.6 Develop logical connections through physical principles, including Kepler's and Newton's Laws about the relationships and the effects of Earth, Moon, and Sun on each other; **SC.912.E.5.7** Relate the history of and explain the justification for future space exploration and continuing technology development.

satellite a natural or artificial body that revolves around a celestial body that is greater in mass

moon a celestial body that revolves around a body that is greater in mass; a natural satellite

Figure 1 *Apollo 17* astronaut Eugene Cernan explores the lunar surface in a Lunar Roving Vehicle.

The Lunar Surface

Because *luna* is the Latin word for "moon," any feature of the moon is referred to as *lunar*. Light and dark patches on the moon can be seen with the unaided eye. The lighter areas are rough highlands that are composed of rocks called *anorthosites*. The darker areas are smooth, reflect less light, and are called *maria* (MAHR ee uh). Each dark area is a **mare** (MAHR ay). *Mare* is Latin for "sea." Galileo named these dark areas *maria* because he thought that they looked like Earth's seas. Today, astronomers know that maria are plains of dark, solidified, basaltic lava. These lava plains formed more than 3 billion years ago when lava slowly filled basins that were created by impacts of massive asteroids.

Craters, Rilles, and Ridges

The surface of the moon, shown in **Figure 2**, is covered with numerous bowl-shaped depressions, called **craters.** Most of the moon's craters formed when debris left over from the formation of the solar system struck the moon about 4 billion years ago. Younger craters are characterized by bright streaks, called *rays*, that extend outward from the impact site. Even these younger craters, however, are almost all billions of years old.

Long, deep channels called *rilles* run through the maria in some places. The moon's rilles are thought to be leftover lava channels from the formation of the maria. Some rilles are as long as 240 km. Another surface feature of the moon is ridges. Ridges are long, narrow elevations of rock that rise out of the surface and criss-cross the maria.

Reading Check **Name two features of the moon.** (See Appendix G for answers to Reading Checks.)

---

mare a large, dark area of basalt on the moon (plural, *maria*)

crater a bowl-shaped depression that forms on the surface of an object when a falling body strikes the object's surface or when an explosion occurs

Academic Vocabulary

depression (dee PRESH uhn) an area lower than the surrounding surface

READING TOOLBOX

Describing Space
As you read Section 1, make a table like the one described at the beginning of the chapter to describe motion words. In the left column, list objects. In the middle column, list verbs (and the phrases the modify them) that describe the motion of the objects. In the right column, state the meaning of the motion words.

Figure 2 More than 1,500 craters on the moon are named for scientists, scholars, and other noteworthy individuals. The lunar surface also has millions of small, overlapping craters. *How does the size of a crater relate to the importance of the individual for which it was named?*

Regolith

More meteorites have reached the surface of the moon than have reached Earth's surface because the moon has no atmosphere for protection. Over billions of years, these meteorites crushed much of the rock on the lunar surface into dust and small fragments. Today, almost all of the lunar surface is covered by a layer of dust and rock, called *regolith*. Regolith is shown in **Figure 3.** The depth of the regolith layer varies from 1 m to 6 m.

Lunar Rocks

Many lunar rocks are very similar to rocks on Earth. Lunar rocks, including the one shown in **Figure 4,** contain many of the same elements as Earth's rocks do, but lunar rocks contain different proportions of those elements. Lunar rocks are igneous, and most rocks near the surface are composed mainly of oxygen and silicon. These surface rocks are similar to the rocks in Earth's crust. Rocks from the lunar highlands are light-colored, coarse-grained anorthosites. Highland rocks are rich in calcium and aluminum. Rocks from the maria are fine-grained basalts and contain large amounts of titanium, magnesium, and iron.

Nevertheless, lunar surface rocks have only small amounts of some elements that are common on Earth. Many of these elements have low melting points and may have boiled off early in the moon's history when the moon was still molten. Also, the minerals in lunar rocks do not contain water.

One type of rock that occurs in both maria and the highlands is *breccia*. Lunar breccia contains fragments of other rocks that have been fused together. These breccias formed when meteorites struck the moon. The force of these impacts broke up rocks, and the heat from the impacts partially melted the fragments.

Figure 4 This rock is 4.3 billion to 4.5 billion years old; it is the oldest rock discovered on the moon. The rock's texture indicates that the rock has a complicated history.

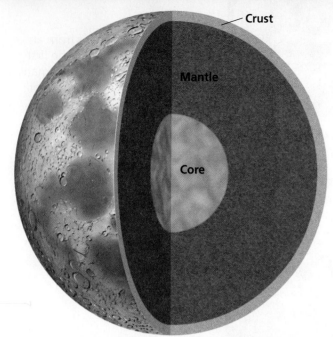

Crust

Mantle

Core

Figure 5 The moon, like Earth, has three compositional layers: the crust, the mantle, and the core.

 SC.912.E.6.1

Quick Lab

⏱ 5 min

Liquid and Solid Cores

Procedure

1 Take one uncooked egg and one hardboiled egg. With your thumb and forefinger, spin both eggs.

2 Record the amount of time each egg spins.

3 Lay one can of solid food and one can of soup on their sides, and spin both cans.

4 Record the amount of time each can spins.

Analysis

1. Which egg stopped spinning first? Which can of food stopped spinning first?

2. Which rotates more steadily: an object that has a solid core or an object that has a liquid core? Explain your answer.

The Interior of the Moon

Rocks of the lunar surface are about as dense as those on Earth's surface. However, the overall density of the moon is only three-fifths the density of Earth. The difference in overall density indicates that the interior of the moon is less dense than the interior of Earth.

Most of the information about the interior of the moon comes from seismographs that were placed on the moon by the Apollo astronauts. Seismographs recorded numerous weak moonquakes, which are similar to earthquakes. More than 10,000 moonquakes have been detected. Most moonquakes occur in the mantle at a depth that is 10 times deeper than the depth at which most earthquakes occur on Earth. From these moonquakes, scientists learned that the moon's interior is layered, as shown in **Figure 5**.

The Moon's Crust

One side of the moon always faces Earth. That side is therefore called the *near side*. The other side always faces away from Earth and is called the *far side*. The pull of Earth's gravity during the moon's formation caused the crust on the far side of the moon to become thicker than the crust on the near side. On the near side, the lunar crust is about 60 km thick. On the far side, the lunar crust is up to 100 km thick. Images of the far side show that the far side's surface is mountainous and has only a few small maria. The crust of the far side appears to consist of materials that are similar to those of the rocks in the highlands on the near side.

Reading Check Name two features of the far side of the moon.

The Moon's Mantle and Core

Beneath the crust is the moon's mantle. The mantle is thought to be made of rock that is rich in silica, magnesium, and iron. Of the moon's 1,738 km radius, the mantle makes up more than half of that distance and reaches 1,000 km below the crust.

Scientists think that the moon has a small iron core that has a radius of less than 700 km. When laser beams were bounced off small mirrors placed on the moon, scientists discovered that the moon's rotation is not uniform. This non-uniform rotation indicates that the core is neither completely solid nor completely liquid. This characteristic may explain why the moon has almost no overall magnetic field. There are, however, small areas on the moon that exhibit local magnetism.

The Formation of the Moon

Rocks taken from the moon by Apollo astronauts provided evidence to help astronomers understand the moon's history. Most scientists generally agree that the moon formed in three stages.

The Giant Impact Hypothesis

Most scientists think that the moon's development began when a large object collided with Earth more than 4 billion years ago. This *giant impact hypothesis* states that a Mars-sized body struck Earth early in the history of the solar system. Before the impact, Earth was molten, or heated to an almost liquid state. The collision ejected chunks of Earth's mantle into orbit around Earth. The debris eventually clumped together to form the moon, as shown in **Figure 6.**

Most of the ejected materials came from Earth's silica-rich mantle rather than from Earth's dense, metallic core. This hypothesis explains why moon rocks share many of the chemical characteristics of Earth's mantle. As the material clumped together, it continued to revolve around Earth because of Earth's gravitational pull.

Differentiation of the Lunar Interior

Early in its history, the lunar surface was covered by an ocean of molten rock. Over time, the densest materials moved toward the center of the moon and formed a small core. The least dense materials formed an outer crust. The other materials settled between the core and the outer layer to form the moon's mantle.

Meteorite Bombardment

The outer surface of the moon eventually cooled to form a thick, solid crust over the molten interior. At the same time, debris left over from the formation of the solar system struck the solid surface and produced craters and regolith.

About 3 billion years ago, the number of small objects in the solar system decreased. Less material struck the lunar surface, and few new craters formed. Craters that have rays formed during the most recent meteor impacts. During this stage of lunar development, virtually all geologic activity stopped. Because the moon cooled more than 3 billion years ago, it looks today almost exactly as it did 3 billion years ago. Therefore, the moon is a valuable source of information about the conditions that existed in the solar system long ago.

Figure 6 The First Stage of Moon Formation

Scientists think that a Mars-sized object collided with Earth and blasted part of Earth's mantle into space.

The resulting debris then began to revolve around Earth.

The material eventually joined to form Earth's moon.

Lava Flows on the Moon

After impacts on the moon's surface formed deep basins, lava flowed out of cracks, or *fissures*, in the lunar crust. This lava flooded the crater basins to form maria. The presence of the maria suggests that fissure eruptions once characterized the moon, even though there is no evidence that large active volcanoes have ever been present on the moon.

Because the moon's crust is thinner on the near side than on the far side, much more lava flowed onto the surface on the near side than onto the surface of the far side of the moon. The near side of the moon has several smooth maria, but the far side has few maria and many more craters, as shown in **Figure 7.**

Scientists do not yet know how magma formed in the lunar interior or how the magma reached the surface. There is no evidence of plate tectonics or convection currents in the moon's mantle, so the magma must have formed in some other way. A large amount of energy would have been needed to produce the magma in the upper layers of the moon. Some scientists think this energy may have come from a long period of intense meteorite bombardment. Other scientists think that radioactive decay of materials may have also heated the moon's interior enough to cause magma to form. Scientists agree that the lava flows ended about 3.1 billion years ago, when the interior cooled completely.

Figure 7 The near side of the moon (top) has fewer visible craters than the far side (bottom) does in part because lava flows on the near side covered many of the impact sites with maria.

Section 1 Review

LA.910.2.2.3; SC.912.E.5.5; SC.912.E.5.6

Key Ideas

1. **Describe** what maria on the surface of the moon look like and how they came to be known as maria.

2. **Compare** the thickness of the moon's crust on the near side with the thickness of the crust on the far side.

3. **Summarize** how and when the maria formed.

4. **Describe** how the surface of the moon would be different today if meteorites had continued to hit it at the same rate as they did 3 billion years ago.

5. **Describe** breccias and how they formed on the moon.

6. **Summarize** how scientists think the moon formed.

Critical Thinking

7. **Analyzing Ideas** Explain how Earth's gravity affected the moon's near side and far side differently.

8. **Making Comparisons** Compare the features of the lunar surface created by lava flows and the features created by impacts.

Concept Mapping

9. Use the following terms to create a concept map: *moon, meteorite, crater, rille, maria, highlands,* and *basalt.*

Movements of the Moon

Key Ideas

❯ Describe the shape of the moon's orbit around Earth.

❯ Explain why eclipses occur.

❯ Describe the appearance of four phases of the moon.

❯ Explain how the movements of the moon affect tides on Earth.

Key Terms

apogee   solar eclipse
perigee   lunar eclipse
eclipse   phase

Why It Matters

Understanding the movements of the moon enables us to predict solar and lunar eclipses as well as low and high tides.

If you looked down on the moon from above its north pole, you would see the moon rotate once on its axis every 27.3 days. However, if you stood on the moon's surface and measured the lunar day by the amount of time between sunrises, you would find that a lunar day is 29.5 Earth days long. This discrepancy is due to the fact that, while the moon is revolving around Earth, Earth and the moon are also revolving around the sun.

The Earth-Moon System

To observers on Earth, the moon appears to orbit Earth. However, if you could observe Earth and the moon from space, you would see that Earth and the moon revolve around each other. Together, they form a single system that orbits the sun.

The mass of the moon is only 1/80 that of Earth. So, the balance point of the Earth-moon system is not halfway between the centers of the two bodies. The balance point is located within Earth's interior because Earth's mass is greater than the moon's mass. This balance point is called the *barycenter*. The barycenter follows a smooth orbit around the sun, as shown in **Figure 1.**

The Moon's Elliptical Orbit

The orbit of the moon around Earth forms an ellipse that is about 5% more elongated than a circle is. Therefore, the distance between Earth and its moon varies over a month's time. When the moon is farthest from Earth, the moon is at **apogee.** When the moon is closest to Earth, the moon is at **perigee.** The average distance of the moon from Earth is 384,000 km.

FLORIDA STANDARDS

SC.912.E.5.6 Develop logical connections through physical principles, including Kepler's and Newton's Laws about the relationships and the effects of Earth, Moon, and Sun on each other; **SC.912.N.3.5** Describe the function of models in science, and identify the wide range of models used in science.

apogee in the orbit of a satellite, the point that is farthest from Earth

perigee in the orbit of a satellite, the point that is closest to Earth

Figure 1 The Earth-moon system.

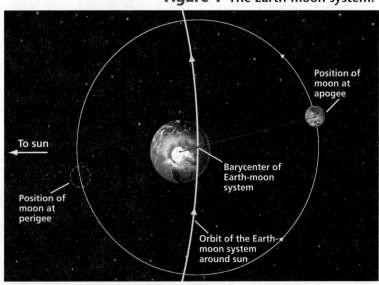

Moonrise and Moonset

The moon appears to rise and set at Earth's horizon because of Earth's rotation on its axis. If you were to watch the moon rise or set on <u>successive</u> nights, however, you would notice that it rises or sets approximately 50 minutes later each night. This happens because of both Earth's rotation and the moon's revolution. While Earth completes one rotation each day, the moon also moves in its orbit around Earth. It takes an extra 1/29 of Earth's rotation, or 50 minutes, for the horizon to catch up to the moon.

Lunar Rotation

In addition to orbiting Earth and revolving around the sun, the moon also spins on its axis. The moon rotated rapidly when it formed, but the pull of Earth's gravity has slowed the moon's rate of rotation. The moon now spins very slowly and completes a rotation only once during each orbit around Earth. The moon revolves only once around Earth in about 27.3 days relative to the stars. Because the rotation and the revolution of the moon take the same amount of time, observers on Earth always see the same side of the moon. Therefore, images of the far side of the moon must be taken by spacecraft orbiting the moon.

As the moon orbits Earth, the part of the moon's surface that is illuminated by sunlight changes. The sun's light always illuminates half of the moon and, as shown in **Figure 2,** half the Earth. The near side of the moon is sometimes fully illuminated by the sun. At other times, depending on where the moon is in its orbit, the near side is partly or completely darkened.

Reading Check Why are we unable to photograph the far side of the moon from Earth?

READING TOOLBOX

Two-Column Notes
Create two-column notes to review the main ideas for Section 2. Put the main ideas in the left column, and add details and examples in your own words in the right column. Use as a model the two-column notes table that you started at the beginning of the chapter.

Figure 2 The lunar landing module, which was also called *The Eagle*, flew to meet the command module at the end of the *Apollo 11* mission. Seen from this viewpoint, Earth is illuminated from above.

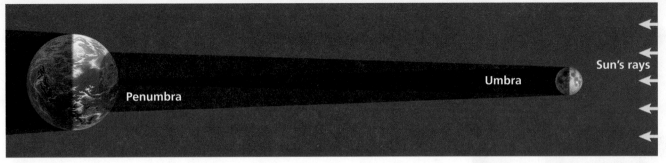

Figure 3 During a solar eclipse, the shadow of the moon falls on Earth. The distance between Earth and the moon in this diagram is not to scale.

Eclipses

Bodies orbiting the sun, including Earth and its moon, cast long shadows into space. An **eclipse** occurs when one celestial body passes through the shadow of another. Shadows cast by Earth and the moon have two parts. In the inner, cone-shaped part of the shadow, the *umbra*, sunlight is completely blocked. In the outer part of the shadow, the *penumbra*, sunlight is only partially blocked, as shown in **Figure 3.**

Solar Eclipses

When the moon is directly between the sun and part of Earth, the shadow of the moon falls on Earth and causes a **solar eclipse.** During a *total solar eclipse*, the sun's light is completely blocked by the moon. The umbra falls on the area of Earth that lies directly in line with the moon and the sun. Outside the umbra, but within the penumbra, people see a *partial solar eclipse*. The penumbra falls on the area that immediately surrounds the umbra.

The umbra of the moon is too small to make a large shadow on Earth's surface. The part of the umbra that hits Earth during an eclipse, as shown in **Figure 4,** is never more than a few hundred kilometers across. So, a total eclipse of the sun covers only a small part of Earth and is seen only by people in particular parts of Earth along a narrow path. A total solar eclipse also never lasts more than about seven minutes at any one location. A total eclipse will not be visible in the United States until 2017, even though there is a total eclipse somewhere on Earth about every 18 months.

eclipse an event in which the shadow of one celestial body falls on another

solar eclipse the passing of the moon between Earth and the sun; during a solar eclipse, the shadow of the moon falls on Earth

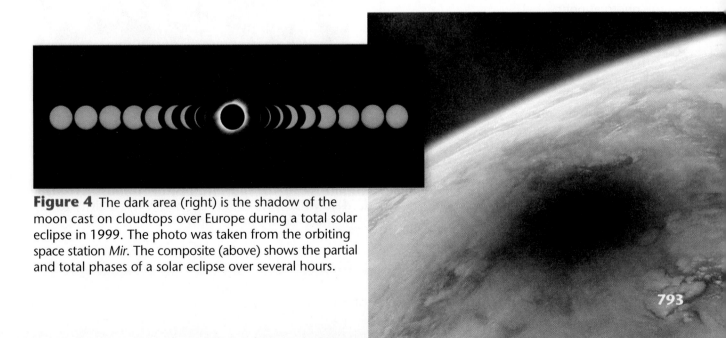

Figure 4 The dark area (right) is the shadow of the moon cast on cloudtops over Europe during a total solar eclipse in 1999. The photo was taken from the orbiting space station *Mir*. The composite (above) shows the partial and total phases of a solar eclipse over several hours.

Effects of Solar Eclipses

During a total solar eclipse, people on the ground are in the moon's umbra. In the areas on Earth's surface under the umbra, the sky becomes as dark as it does at twilight. During this period of darkness, the sunlight that is not eclipsed by the moon shows the normally invisible outer layers of the sun's atmosphere. The last bits of normal sunlight before darkness often glisten like the diamond on a ring and cause what is known as the *diamond-ring effect*. The diamond-ring effect is shown in **Figure 5.** Therefore, many people think that total solar eclipses are very beautiful.

If the moon is at or near apogee when it comes directly between Earth and the sun, the moon's umbra does not reach Earth. If the umbra fails to reach Earth, a ring-shaped eclipse occurs. This type of eclipse is called an *annular eclipse*, because *annulus* is the Latin word for "ring." During an annular eclipse, the sun is never completely blocked out. Instead, a thin ring of sunlight is visible around the outer edge of the moon. The brightness of this thin ring of ordinary sunlight prevents observers from seeing the outer layers of the sun's atmosphere that are visible during a total solar eclipse. An annular eclipse will be visible from the American Southwest on May 20, 2012.

Reading Check **What is one difference between a total solar eclipse and an annular eclipse?**

Figure 5 The diamond-ring effect produced by a solar eclipse can be stunning for observers on the part of Earth that falls under the moon's shadow.

SC.912.E.5.6

Quick Lab   Eclipses   15 min

Procedure

❶ Make two balls from **modeling clay**, one about 4 cm in diameter and one about 1 cm in diameter.

❷ Using a **metric ruler**, position the balls about 15 cm apart on a **sheet of paper**, as shown in the photo at right.

❸ Turn off any nearby lights. Place a **penlight** approximately 15 cm in front of and almost level with the larger ball. Shine the light on the larger ball. Sketch your model, and note the effect of the beam of light.

❹ Repeat step 3, but reverse the positions of the two balls. You may need to raise the smaller ball slightly to center its shadow on the larger ball. Sketch your model, and again note the effect of the light beam.

Analysis

1. Which planetary bodies do the larger clay ball, the smaller clay ball, and the penlight represent?

2. As viewed from Earth, what event did your model in step 3 represent? As viewed from the moon, what would your model represent?

3. As viewed from Earth, what event did your model in step 4 represent? As viewed from the moon, what would your model represent?

4. In what ways could you modify this activity to more closely model how eclipses occur?

Sun's rays

Umbra

Penumbra

Lunar Eclipses

A **lunar eclipse** occurs when Earth is positioned between the moon and the sun and when Earth's shadow crosses the lighted half of the moon. For a total lunar eclipse to occur, the entire moon must pass into Earth's umbra, as shown in **Figure 6.** When only part of the moon passes into Earth's umbra, a *partial lunar eclipse* occurs. The remainder of the moon passes through Earth's penumbra. When the entire moon passes through Earth's penumbra, a *penumbral eclipse* occurs. During a penumbral eclipse, the moon darkens so little that the eclipse is barely noticeable.

A lunar eclipse lasts for several hours. Even during a total lunar eclipse, sunlight is bent around Earth through our atmosphere. Mainly red light reaches the moon, so the totally eclipsed moon appears to have a reddish color, as shown in the middle portion of the composite image in **Figure 7.**

Frequency of Solar and Lunar Eclipses

As many as seven eclipses may occur during a calendar year. Four may be lunar, and three may be solar or vice versa. However, total eclipses of the sun and the moon occur infrequently. Solar and lunar eclipses do not occur during every lunar orbit. This is because the orbit of the moon is not in the same plane as the orbit of Earth around the sun. The moon crosses the plane of Earth's orbit only twice in each revolution around Earth. A solar eclipse will occur only if this crossing occurs when the moon is between Earth and the sun. If this crossing occurs when Earth is between the moon and the sun, a lunar eclipse will occur.

Lunar eclipses are visible everywhere from the dark side of Earth. A total solar eclipse, however, can be seen only by observers in the small path of the moon's shadow as it moves across Earth's lighted surface. A partial solar eclipse can be seen for thousands of kilometers on either side of the path of the umbra.

Figure 6 During a lunar eclipse, the shadow of Earth falls on the moon. The distance between Earth and the moon in this diagram is not to scale.

lunar eclipse the passing of the moon through Earth's shadow at full moon

Figure 7 This composite image shows a total lunar eclipse as seen from Earth over several hours.

Phases of the Moon

On some nights, the moon shines brightly enough for you to read a book by its light. But moonlight is not produced by the moon. The moon merely reflects light from the sun. Because the moon is spherical, half of it is always lit by sunlight. As the moon revolves around Earth, however, different amounts of the near side of the moon, which faces Earth, are lighted. Therefore, the apparent shape of the visible part of the moon varies. These varying shapes, lighted by reflected sunlight, are called **phases** of the moon and are shown in **Figure 8.**

When the moon is directly between the sun and Earth, the sun's rays strike only the far side of the moon. As a result, the entire near side of the moon is dark. When the near side is dark, the moon is said to be in the *new-moon* phase. During this phase, no lighted area of the moon is visible from Earth.

phase the change in the illuminated area of one celestial body as seen from another celestial body; phases of the moon are caused by the changing positions of Earth, the sun, and the moon

Figure 8 Phases of the Moon

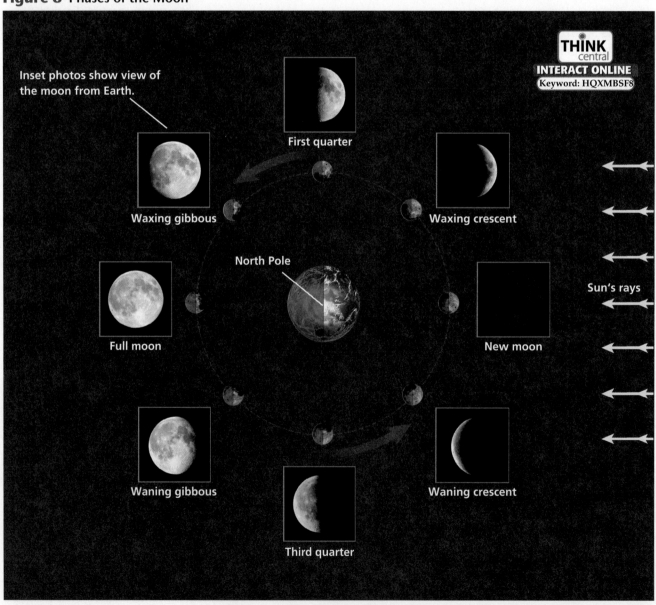

Inset photos show view of the moon from Earth.

THINK central
INTERACT ONLINE
Keyword: HQXMBSF8

First quarter

Waxing gibbous

Waxing crescent

North Pole

Full moon

New moon

Sun's rays

Waning gibbous

Third quarter

Waning crescent

Waxing Phases of the Moon

As the moon continues to move in its orbit around Earth, part of the near side becomes illuminated. When the size of the lighted part of the moon is increasing, the moon is said to be *waxing*. When a sliver of the moon's near side is illuminated, the moon enters its *waxing-crescent* phase.

When the moon has moved through one-quarter of its orbit after the new moon phase, the moon appears to be a semicircle. Half of the near side of the moon is lighted. When a waxing moon becomes a semicircle, the moon enters its *first-quarter* phase. When the lighted part of the moon's near side is larger than a semicircle and still increasing in size, the moon is in its *waxing-gibbous* phase. The moon continues to wax until it appears as a full circle. At *full moon*, Earth is between the sun and the moon. Consequently, the entire near side of the moon is illuminated by the light of the sun.

www.scilinks.org
Topic: Lunar Cycle
Code: HQX0887

Waning Phases of the Moon

After the full moon phase, when the lighted part of the near side of the moon appears to decrease in size, the moon is *waning*. When it is waning but the lighted part is still larger than a semicircle, the moon is in the *waning-gibbous* phase. When the lighted part of the near side becomes a semicircle, the moon enters the *third-quarter* phase. When only a sliver of the near side is visible, the moon enters the *waning-crescent* phase. After the waning-crescent phase, the moon again moves between Earth and the sun. The moon once more becomes a new moon, and the cycle of phases begins again.

Before and after a new moon, only a small part of the moon shines brightly. However, the rest of the moon is not completely dark. It shines dimly from sunlight that reflects first off Earth's clouds and oceans and then reflects off the moon. Sunlight that is reflected off Earth is called *earthshine*. The darker part of the moon shown in **Figure 9** is lit by earthshine.

Time from New Moon to New Moon

Although the moon revolves around Earth in 27.3 days, a longer period of time is needed for the moon to go through a complete cycle of phases. The period from one new moon to the next one is 29.5 days. This difference of 2.2 days results from the orbiting of the Earth-moon system around the sun. In the 27.3 days in which the moon orbits Earth, the two bodies move slightly farther along their orbit around the sun. Therefore, the moon must go a little farther to be directly between Earth and the sun. About 2.2 days are needed for the moon to travel this extra distance. The position directly between Earth and the sun is the position of the moon in each new moon phase.

Figure 9 The darker portion of this crescent moon is not completely dark because some sunlight is reflected from Earth, to the moon, and back to Earth.

Reading Check **Describe two phases of the waning moon.**

Figure 10 The moon's pull on Earth is greatest at point A, on Earth's near side, and weakest at point C, on Earth's far side. Point B represents Earth's center of mass. Earth's rotation causes two low tides and two high tides each day on most shorelines.

Tides on Earth

Bulges in Earth's oceans, called tidal bulges, form because the moon's gravitational pull on Earth decreases with distance. Thus, the ocean on Earth's near side is pulled toward the moon with the greatest force. The solid Earth, which acts as though all of its mass were its center, experiences less force. The ocean on the far side is subject to less force than the solid Earth is. As shown in **Figure 10,** these differences cause tidal bulges. Because Earth rotates, tides occur regularly at any given point on the surface each day. The sun also causes tides, but they are smaller because the sun is much farther from Earth than the moon is. Twice each month, when the sun, moon, and Earth are almost in line, the gravitational pulls combine to produce especially high tides.

Section 2 Review

LA.910.2.2.3; SC.912.E.5.6

Key Ideas

1. **Explain** why the moon rises and sets about 50 minutes later each successive night.

2. **Describe** what causes a total solar eclipse.

3. **Explain** why a lunar eclipse does not occur every time the moon revolves around Earth.

4. **Summarize** how a solar eclipse differs from a lunar eclipse.

5. **Describe** the relative locations of the sun, Earth, and the moon during a new moon phase.

6. **Describe** how the appearance of the moon changes when it is waxing.

7. **Explain** why the moon repeats phases every 29.5 days but completes an orbit in 27.3 days.

8. **Explain** how the moon causes tidal bulges on Earth.

Critical Thinking

9. **Analyzing Ideas** Explain why observers on Earth always see the same side of the moon.

10. **Making Comparisons** Explain why more people see each total lunar eclipse than each total solar eclipse.

11. **Analyzing Relationships** The sun's gravity also affects tides on Earth. Why does the moon have a larger effect on tides than the sun does?

Concept Mapping

12. Use the following terms to create a concept map: *Earth, moon, sun, eclipse, solar eclipse, lunar eclipse, umbra,* and *penumbra.*

Satellites of Other Planets

Key Ideas	Key Terms	Why It Matters
❭ Compare the characteristics of the two moons of Mars. ❭ Describe how volcanoes were discovered on Io. ❭ Name one distinguishing characteristic of each of the Galilean moons. ❭ Compare the characteristics of the rings of Saturn with the rings of the other outer planets.	Galilean moon	Studying the moons of other planets helps scientists better understand our own moon as well as the forces that have helped to shape the solar system.

Until the 1600s, astronomers thought that Earth was the only planet that had a moon. In 1610, Galileo discovered four moons orbiting Jupiter. He also observed what later were identified as the rings of Saturn. Since the time of Galileo, astronomers have discovered that all of the planets in our solar system except Mercury and Venus have moons. In addition, the gas giants Saturn, Jupiter, Uranus, and Neptune all have rings.

Moons of Mars

Mars has two tiny moons, named Phobos and Deimos. They revolve around Mars relatively quickly. Phobos and Deimos are irregularly shaped chunks of rock and are thought to be captured asteroids. Phobos is 27 km across at its longest, and Deimos is about 15 km across at its longest.

The surfaces of Phobos and Deimos are dark, like maria on Earth's moon. Both moons have many craters. The large number of craters shows that the moons have been hit by many asteroids and comets, and suggests that the moons are fairly old.

Moons of Jupiter

Galileo observed four large moons revolving around Jupiter. Since that discovery was made, scientists have observed dozens of smaller moons around Jupiter. Smaller moons continue to be discovered today. Most of Jupiter's moons have diameters of less than 200 km, but of the largest four, known as the **Galilean moons,** three are bigger than Earth's moon. Until spacecraft flew near the moons, scientists knew little about them. Now, scientists have identified many unique characteristics of the Galilean moons. One of the four Galilean moons is shown in **Figure 1.**

FLORIDA STANDARDS

LA.910.2.2.3 The student will organize information to show understanding or relationships among facts, ideas, and events (e.g., representing key points within text through charting, mapping, paraphrasing, summarizing, comparing, contrasting, or outlining); **SC.912.E.5.7** Relate the history of and explain the justification for future space exploration and continuing technology development.

Galilean moon any one of the four largest satellites of Jupiter—Io, Europa, Ganymede, and Callisto—that were discovered by Galileo in 1610

Figure 1 The stormy surface of Jupiter is visible in the background. In the foreground is Io, which orbits Jupiter once every 42 hours.

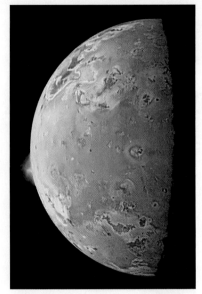

Figure 2 In this image taken by the *Galileo* spacecraft you can see a volcanic eruption on the left side of Io against the background of space.

Academic Vocabulary

extraterrestrial (eks truh tuh RES tree uhl) not of Earth

Io

Io is the innermost of Jupiter's four Galilean moons. An engineer examining images from the *Voyager* spacecraft discovered volcanoes on Io. Io is the first extraterrestrial body on which active volcanoes have been seen. Since the discovery of Io's volcanoes, scientists realize that volcanism is more widespread in the solar system than they had thought. Volcanoes on Io eject thousands of metric tons of material each second. The lava that erupts on Io is much hotter than the lava that erupts on Earth. The temperature of the lava on Io is higher because the lava has more magnesium and iron than lava on Earth does. Plumes of volcanic material on Io reach heights of hundreds of kilometers, as shown in **Figure 2**. Because parts of Io's surface are yellow-red, scientists think that the volcanic material is mostly sulfur and sulfur dioxide.

Io moves inward and outward in its orbit around Jupiter because of the gravitational pull of the other moons of Jupiter. This movement produces differences in gravitational pull on opposite sides of the moon called *tidal forces*. These forces are similar to tides on Earth caused by the pull of the moon. As Io is pulled back and forth, its surface also moves in and out. Calculations show that tidal forces make Io's surface move in and out by 100 m. Heat from the friction caused by this surface flexing results in the melting of the interior of Io and leads to volcanism. Data from the *Galileo* spacecraft show that Io has a giant iron core and may possess a magnetic field. Much of what we know about Jupiter's moons came from information gathered by the *Galileo* spacecraft, which orbited Jupiter from 1995 to 2003.

Why It Matters

Early Telescope Images

To the unaided eye, the only moon visible from Earth is our own. Imagine the surprise about 400 years ago when the Italian scientist and inventor, Galileo Galilei, turned his newly improved telescope to Jupiter and discovered four more moons.

The telescope was invented in the late 1500s. In 1610, with this improved model, Galileo discovered Jupiter's largest moons.

The four objects changed position each night but stayed close to Jupiter. He concluded that they must be moons.

YOUR TURN ONLINE RESEARCH How many moons orbit Jupiter now? Why would the number keep changing?

Europa

Europa is the second closest Galilean moon to Jupiter. Europa is about the size of Earth's moon and it is slightly less dense than Earth's moon. Astronomers think that Europa has a rock core that is covered with a crust of ice that is about 100 km thick. Images of Europa, such as the one shown in **Figure 3**, show cracks in this enormous ice sheet.

Scientists have concluded from observations made from spacecraft that an ocean of liquid water may exist under this blanket of ice. If liquid water exists, simple forms of life could also exist there. Astronomers have no evidence of life on Europa, but many think Europa would be a good place to investigate the possibility of extraterrestrial life.

Figure 3 This false-color image of Europa shows immense cracks across its ice sheets.

Ganymede

Ganymede is the third Galilean moon from Jupiter. Ganymede is also the largest moon in the solar system, even larger than the planet Mercury. However, Ganymede has a relatively small mass because it is probably composed mostly of ice mixed with rock.

Images of Ganymede, such as **Figure 4,** show dark, crater-filled areas. Other light areas show marks that are thought to be long ridges and valleys. The *Galileo* spacecraft provided evidence to support the existence of a magnetic field around Ganymede. Ganymede is the only moon in the solar system that is known to have its own magnetic field. This magnetic field is completely surrounded by Jupiter's much more powerful magnetic field.

Figure 4 Much of Ganymede's surface is covered with ridges and valleys.

Callisto

Of the four Galilean moons, Callisto is the farthest from Jupiter. Callisto is similar to Ganymede in size, density, and composition. However, Callisto has a much rougher surface than Ganymede does. In fact, Callisto is one of the most densely cratered moons in our solar system.

Like craters on Earth's moon and other bodies in our solar system, craters on Callisto are the result of collisions that occurred early in the history of the solar system. **Figure 5** shows a giant impact basin that is 600 km across and a set of concentric rings that extend about 1,500 km outward in all directions from the crater.

Reading Check **Name one feature of each of the Galilean moons.**

Figure 5 "Ripples" of ice and rock radiate out from this impact crater, called *Valhalla*, on Callisto.

Telesto
Calypso

Helene

Prometheus Janus

Pan   Atlas

Pandora Epimetheus

Mimas Enceladus Tethys

Dione

Rhea

Hyperion

Titan

Iapetus

Phoebe

Saturn

Figure 6 This composite image shows Saturn and many of Saturn's largest moons. The distances of the moons from Saturn and from each other are not to scale.

Moons of Saturn

Saturn has dozens of moons. Most of them are small, icy bodies that have many craters. However, five of Saturn's moons are fairly large. These five moons and many of Saturn's other moons are shown in **Figure 6.**

Titan

Saturn's largest moon, called Titan, has a diameter of more than 5,000 km. Only Jupiter's moon Ganymede is larger. Unlike any of the other moons in our solar system, Titan has a thick atmosphere that is composed mainly of nitrogen. Titan's atmosphere is so thick that hydrocarbon smog conceals most of the surface.

In 2005, the *Huygens* (HIE guhnz) probe, part of the Cassini mission, gathered data about Titan's atmosphere. The information it gathered is giving scientists clues about how Titan and its atmosphere formed. When the probe got below much of the atmosphere's haze, it sent back clear images of the surface, which showed signs of flowing liquid, probably methane. *Cassini* also sent back many images of Titan, an example of which is shown in **Figure 7.**

Saturn's Other Moons

Saturn's icy moons resemble Jupiter's icy Galilean moons. Enceladus has erupting geysers and so may have underground water near its surface. For that reason, it may be a better place to look for life than Europa. Saturn's other smaller moons have irregular shapes. Scientists think that many of the smallest moons, such as Janus, were captured by Saturn's gravity.

Figure 7 This image of Titan was taken by the Cassini mission in 2008. The image shows Titan in polarized infrared wavelengths by which clouds can be seen in its atmosphere.

Moons of Uranus and Neptune

Uranus's four largest moons, Oberon, Titania, Umbriel, and Ariel, were known by the mid-1800s. A fifth, Miranda, was discovered in 1948 and is shown in **Figure 8.** Other much smaller moons have been discovered recently by using spacecraft and orbiting observatories such as the *Hubble Space Telescope.* Astronomers know that Uranus has at least two dozen small moons.

Neptune has at least 13 moons. Triton, a large icy moon, is unusual because it revolves around Neptune in a backward, or *retrograde,* orbit. Some astronomers think that Triton has an unusual orbit because the moon was captured by the gravity of Neptune after forming elsewhere in the solar system and then coming too close to the planet. Triton's diameter is 2,705 km, and the moon has a thin atmosphere.

Figure 8 Uranus's moon called Miranda shows intriguing evidence of past geologic activity.

Pluto's Moons

Although Pluto is no longer officially considered a planet, it does have at least three moons. Pluto's largest moon, Charon (KER uhn), is almost half the size of Pluto. In fact, because Pluto and Charon are so similar in mass, they both orbit a common balance point, or *barycenter,* that is located between them. Charon orbits Pluto in 6.4 days, the same length of time as a day on Pluto. Because of these equal lengths, Charon stays in the same place in Pluto's sky. In the same way that one side of Earth's moon always faces Earth, one side of Pluto always faces Charon.

Pluto's other two moons, Hydra and Nix, are much smaller. These moons were discovered in 2005 by astronomers using the *Hubble Space Telescope.* These moons also orbit the barycenter between Pluto and Charon.

Reading Check **Identify two ways Charon is different from other moons.**

SCI
LINKS.

www.scilinks.org
Topic: Moons of Other
    Planets
Code: HQX0993

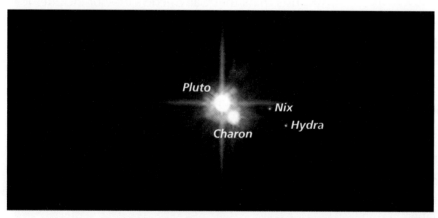

Figure 9 Pluto was discovered in 1930, Charon was discovered in 1978, and two smaller moons, Nix and Hydra, were discovered in 2005. (The spikes of light in the image are effects of the telescope.)

Rings of the Gas Giants

Saturn's spectacular set of rings, shown in **Figure 10,** was discovered more than 300 years ago. Each of the rings circling Saturn is divided into hundreds of small ringlets. The ringlets are composed of billions of pieces of rock and ice. These pieces range in size from particles the size of dust to chunks the size of a house. Each piece follows its own orbit around Saturn. The ring system of Saturn is very thin.

Originally, astronomers thought that the rings formed from material that was unable to clump together to form moons while Saturn was forming. However, evidence indicates that the rings are much younger than originally thought. Now, most scientists think that the rings are the remains of a large cometlike body that entered Saturn's system and was ripped apart by tidal forces. Particles from the rings continue to spiral into Saturn, but the rings are replenished by particles given off by Saturn's moons.

The other gas giants have rings as well. These rings are relatively narrow. Jupiter's were not discovered until the *Voyager 1* spacecraft flew by Jupiter in 1979. Jupiter has a single, thin ring made of microscopic particles that may have been given off by Io or one of Jupiter's other moons. The particles may also be debris from collisions of comets or meteorites with Jupiter's moons. Uranus also has a dozen thin rings. Neptune's relatively small number of rings are clumpy rather than thin and uniform.

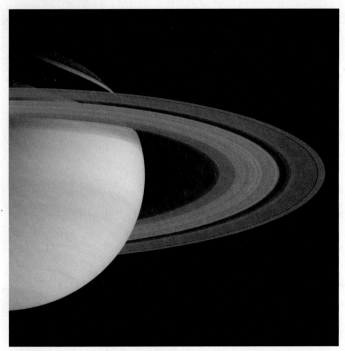

Figure 10 Saturn has the most extensive system of rings in the solar system. The angle at which its rings are visible changes as Saturn orbits the sun.

Section 3 Review

LA.910.2.2.3; SC.912.E.5.5

Key Ideas

1. **Compare** the characteristics of Phobos and Deimos.

2. **List** the four moons of Jupiter that were discovered by Galileo, and identify one distinguishing characteristic of each.

3. **Describe** how volcanoes were discovered on Io.

4. **Explain** why Io remains volcanically active.

5. **Describe** how the smaller moons of Uranus were discovered.

6. **Explain** why Triton has an unusual orbit.

7. **Compare** the characteristics of Saturn's rings with the rings of the other outer planets.

Critical Thinking

8. **Analyzing Relationships** Explain why scientists think that Ganymede's interior includes ice.

9. **Inferring Relationships** Compare and contrast the way in which moons and ring systems form.

10. **Making Comparisons** Explain why Triton retains an atmosphere while Phobos does not.

Concept Mapping

11. Use the following terms to create a concept map: *moon, ring, Mars, Uranus, Jupiter, Saturn, Phobos, Deimos, Pluto, Galilean moon, natural satellite, Charon, Titania,* and *Titan.*

Asteroids, Comets, and Meteoroids

Key Ideas	Key Terms	Why It Matters
❯ Describe the physical characteristics of asteroids and comets. ❯ Describe where the Kuiper Belt is located. ❯ Compare meteoroids, meteorites, and meteors. ❯ Explain the relationship between the Oort cloud and comets.	asteroid comet **Kuiper Belt** **Oort cloud** meteoroid meteor	Some asteroids are close enough to Earth that they could cause significant damage if one were to strike Earth. For this reason, some scientists keep track of known asteroids and their orbits.

In addition to the sun, the planets, and the planets' moons, our solar system includes millions of smaller bodies. Some of these small bodies are tiny bits of dust or ice that orbit the sun. Other bodies are as big as small moons. Astronomers theorize that these smaller bodies are leftover debris from the formation of the solar system.

Asteroids

The largest of the minor bodies in the solar system are called asteroids. **Asteroids** are fragments of rock that orbit the sun. Astronomers have discovered more than 300,000 asteroids. Millions of asteroids may exist in the solar system. The orbits of asteroids, like those of the planets, are ellipses. The largest known asteroid, Ceres, has a diameter of about 1,000 km. Because it is large enough that gravity has caused it to become round, Ceres is also considered to be a dwarf planet. Two other asteroids are shown in **Figure 1.**

Most asteroids are located in a region between the orbits of Mars and Jupiter known as the *asteroid belt*. This main belt extends from about 299 million to about 598 million kilometers from the sun. However, not all asteroids are located in the main asteroid belt. The closest asteroids to the sun are inside the orbit of Mars, about 224 million kilometers from the sun. The *Trojan asteroids* are concentrated in groups just ahead of and just behind Jupiter as it orbits the sun. In fact, the Trojan asteroids almost share Jupiter's orbit. These asteroids are named for the Trojan and Greek warriors of the famous Trojan War of Greek mythology. Asteroids also exist beyond Jupiter's orbit.

FLORIDA STANDARDS

SC.912.N.1.6 Describe how scientific inferences are drawn from scientific observations and provide examples from the content being studied;
SC.912.E.5.5 Explain the formation of planetary systems based on our knowledge of our Solar System and apply this knowledge to newly discovered planetary systems.

asteroid a small, rocky object that orbits the sun; most asteroids are located in a band between the orbits of Mars and Jupiter

Figure 1 This image of the asteroids Ida (left) and Dactyl (right) were taken by the spacecraft *Galileo* as it passed through the asteroid belt on its way to Jupiter. Ida is 56 km long, and Dactyl is 1.5 km across.

Academic Vocabulary

composition (KAHM puh ZISH uhn)
the substances that make up an object

www.scilinks.org
Topic: Comets, Asteroids,
and Meteoroids
Code: HQX0317

READING TOOLBOX

Word Origins

The asteroid Pallas is named after the Greek goddess of wisdom, war, and the arts, Pallas Athena. As you read Section 4, find the origins of the names of asteroids and comets. Add them to the table that you started at the beginning of the chapter.

Composition of Asteroids

The <u>composition</u> of asteroids is similar to that of the inner planets. Asteroids are classified according to their composition into three main categories. The most common of the three types of asteroids is made mostly of carbon materials, which give this type of asteroid a dark color. The second type of asteroid is made of mostly silicate minerals. These asteroids look like Earth rocks. The third, and rarest, type of asteroid is composed of mostly iron and nickel. These asteroids have a shiny, metallic appearance, especially on fresh surfaces.

Many astronomers think that asteroids in the asteroid belt are made of material that was not able to form a planet because of the strong gravitational force of Jupiter. Scientists estimate that the total mass of all asteroids is less than the mass of Earth's moon.

Near-Earth Asteroids

More than a thousand asteroids have orbits that sometimes bring them very close to Earth. These asteroids have wide, elliptical orbits that bring them near Earth's orbit. Thus they are called *near-Earth asteroids*. Near-Earth asteroids make up only a small percentage of the total number of asteroids in the solar system.

Interest in near-Earth asteroids has increased in recent years with the realization that these asteroids could inflict great damage on Earth if they were to strike the planet. Meteor Crater, in Arizona, which is shown in **Figure 2**, formed when a small asteroid that had a diameter of less than 50 m struck Earth about 49,000 years ago. Several recently established asteroid detection programs have begun to track all asteroids whose orbits may approach Earth. By identifying and monitoring these asteroids, scientists hope to predict and possibly avoid future collisions.

Reading Check **What are the three types of asteroids by composition?**

Figure 2 Barringer Meteorite Crater, also known simply as Meteor Crater, in Arizona, has a diameter of more than 1 km. Dozens of such craters have resulted from past impacts on Earth, but most craters have eroded or have been covered by sediment.

Comets

Every few years, an object that looks like a star that has a tail is visible in the evening sky. This object is a comet. **Comets** are small bodies of ice, rock, and cosmic dust that follow highly elliptical orbits around the sun. The most famous is Halley's Comet, which passes by Earth every 76 years. It last passed Earth in 1986 and will return in 2061. Every 5 to 10 years, another very bright comet will be visible from Earth. Comet Hale-Bopp, shown in **Figure 3,** was particularly spectacular as it passed Earth in 1997, as was comet McNaught in 2007.

Composition of Comets

A comet has several parts. The core, or nucleus, of a comet is made of rock, metals, and ice. Cores of comets are commonly between 1 km and 100 km in diameter. A spherical cloud of gas and dust, called the *coma,* surrounds the nucleus. The coma can extend as far as 1 million kilometers from the nucleus. A comet's bright appearance largely results from sunlight reflected by the comet's coma. The nucleus and the coma form the head of the comet. In 2004, the spacecraft *Stardust* flew by a comet named Wild 2. It returned samples from the comet's coma to Earth in 2006. In 2005, the spacecraft, *Deep Impact,* slammed a probe into the nucleus of comet Temple 1. The probe released a plume of dust, giving scientists a look at what a comet's nucleus is made of. The *Rosetta* spacecraft will go into orbit around a comet in 2014 and will drop a lander onto its surface.

The most spectacular parts of a comet are its tails. Tails form when sunlight causes the comet's ice to change to gas. The gas, or ion, tail of a comet streams from the comet's head. The solar wind—electrically charged particles expanding away from the sun—pushes the gas away from the comet's head. Thus, regardless of the direction the comet travels, its ion tail points away from the sun. The comet's second tail is made of dust and curves backward along the comet's orbit. Some comets have tails that are more than 80 million kilometers long.

comet a small body of rock, ice, and cosmic dust that follows an elliptical orbit around the sun and that gives off gas and dust in the form of a tail as it passes close to the sun

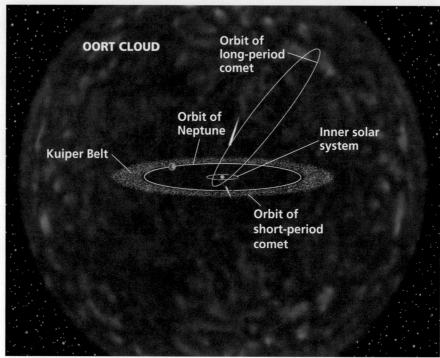

Figure 4 Most comets come from the Oort cloud, a region in the outer solar system that is far beyond the orbit of Neptune.

The Kuiper Belt

Recent advances in technology have allowed scientists to observe thousands of small objects beyond the orbit of Neptune. Most of these objects, including some comets, are from a ring of icy bodies called the **Kuiper Belt** (KIE puhr BELT), which is located just beyond Neptune's orbit. The Kuiper Belt is also illustrated in **Figure 4.** The dwarf planets Pluto and Eris are located in the Kuiper Belt. Several other objects that are candidates for dwarf-planet status also reside in the Kuiper Belt.

The Oort Cloud

Astronomers think that most comets originate in the Oort cloud, which is illustrated in **Figure 4.** The **Oort cloud** is a spherical cloud of dust and ice that lies far beyond Neptune's orbit and that contains the nuclei of billions of comets. The total mass of the Oort cloud is estimated to be between 10 and 40 Earth masses.

The Oort cloud surrounds the solar system and may reach as far as halfway to the nearest star. Scientists think that the matter in the Oort cloud was left over from the formation of the solar system. Studying this distant matter helps scientists understand the early history of the solar system.

Bodies within the Oort cloud circle the sun so slowly that they take a few million years to complete one orbit. But the gravity of a star that passes near the solar system may cause a comet to fall into a more elliptical orbit around the sun. The orbits of comets that pass by Jupiter may also be changed by Jupiter's gravitational force. If a comet takes more than 200 years to complete one orbit of the sun, the comet is called a *long-period comet*.

Short-Period Comets

Comets called *short-period comets* take less than 200 years to complete one orbit around the sun. In recent years, astronomers have discovered that most short-period comets come from the Kuiper Belt. Some of the comets that originate in the Kuiper Belt have been forced outward into the Oort cloud by Jupiter's gravity. Many comets in the Kuiper Belt are the result of collisions between larger Kuiper-Belt objects there. Halley's comet, which has a period of 76 years, is a short-period comet.

Meteoroids

In addition to relatively large asteroids and comets, very small bits of rock or metal move throughout the solar system. These small, rocky bodies are called **meteoroids.** Most meteoroids have a diameter of less than 1 mm. Scientists think that most meteoroids are pieces of matter that become detached from passing comets. Large meteoroids—more than 1 cm in diameter—are probably the result of collisions between asteroids.

Meteors

Meteoroids that travel through space on an orbit that takes them directly into Earth's path may enter Earth's atmosphere. When a meteoroid enters Earth's atmosphere, friction between the object and the air molecules heats the meteoroid's surface. As a result of this friction and heat, most meteoroids burn up in the atmosphere. As a meteoroid burns up in Earth's atmosphere, the meteoroid produces a bright streak of light called a **meteor.** Meteors are commonly called *shooting stars*. Meteoroids sometimes also vaporize very quickly in a brilliant flash of light called a *fireball*. Observers on Earth may hear a loud noise as a fireball disintegrates.

When a large number of small meteoroids enter Earth's atmosphere in a short period of time, a *meteor shower* occurs. During the most spectacular of these showers, several meteors are visible every minute. A composite photo of a meteor shower is shown in **Figure 5.** Meteor showers occur at the same time each year. This happens because Earth intersects the orbits of comets that have left behind a trail of dust. As these particles burn up in Earth's atmosphere, they appear as meteors streaking across the sky.

Reading Check What is the difference between a meteor and a meteoroid?

Math Skills

Matter From Space
Astronomers estimate that about 1 million kg of matter from meteoroids falls to Earth each day. Based on this estimate, how many kilograms of matter from meteoroids would fall on Earth in three weeks?

meteoroid a relatively small, rocky body that travels through space

meteor a bright streak of light that results when a meteoroid burns up in Earth's atmosphere

Figure 5 The straight lines in this composite photo are meteors burning up as they move through Earth's atmosphere.

Meteorites

Figure 6 Types of Meteorites

Stony

Iron

Stony-iron

Figure 6 Types of Meteorites

Millions of meteoroids enter Earth's atmosphere each day. A few of these meteoroids do not burn up entirely in the atmosphere because they are relatively large. These meteoroids fall to Earth's surface. A meteoroid or any part of a meteoroid that is left when a meteoroid hits Earth is called a *meteorite*. Most meteorites are small and have a mass of less than 1 kg. However, large meteorites occasionally strike Earth's surface with the force of a large bomb. These impacts leave large impact craters.

Meteorites can be classified into three basic types: stony, iron, and stony-iron. These three types of meteorites are shown in **Figure 6**. *Stony meteorites* are similar in composition to rocks on Earth. Some stony meteorites contain carbon-bearing compounds that are similar to the carbon compounds in living organisms. Although most meteorites are stony, *iron meteorites* are easier to find. Iron meteorites are easier to find because they have a distinctive metallic appearance. This distinctive appearance makes iron meteorites easy to distinguish from common Earth rocks. The third type of meteorites, called *stony-iron meteorites,* contain iron and stone. Stony-iron meteorites are rare.

Astronomers think that almost all meteorites come from collisions between asteroids. The oldest meteoroids may be 100 million years older than Earth and its moon. Therefore, meteorites may provide information about how the early solar system formed.

Some rare meteorites originated on the moon or Mars. Computer simulations have shown that meteorites that hit the moon or Mars can eject rocks that then fall to Earth. Many of these rare meteorites have been found in Antarctica. Finding meteorites in Antarctica is relatively easy because they stand out against the background of snow and ice.

Section 4 Review

LA.910.2.2.3; SC.912.E.5.5

Key Ideas

1. **Identify** where the asteroid belt is located in the solar system.

2. **Describe** the physical characteristics of asteroids.

3. **List** the four main parts of a comet, and identify their physical characteristics.

4. **Compare** the ion and dust tails of a comet.

5. **Explain** the relationship between the Oort cloud and comets.

6. **Describe** the location of the Kuiper Belt.

7. **Distinguish** between a meteor, a meteoroid, and a meteorite.

Critical Thinking

8. **Analyzing Relationships** Explain why a comet's ion tail always points away from the sun.

9. **Making Comparisons** Explain how iron meteorites can be distinguished from common rocks of Earth's crust.

10. **Making Comparisons** You find a meteorite on the ground. What kind of meteorite did you most likely find? Describe two steps of its journey from space.

Concept Mapping

11. Use the following terms to create a concept map: *comet, asteroid, Kuiper Belt, Oort cloud, long-period comet, short-period comet,* and *meteoroid.*

Dodging Space Debris

SCIENCE & SOCIETY

The glove that astronaut Edward White lost during the first U.S. spacewalk in 1965 was certainly the fastest-moving glove in history. It circled Earth repeatedly at a speed of 28,000 km/h before burning up in the atmosphere about a month later. The same fate awaits an average of 100 to 200 basketball-sized (or larger) objects each year, as well as innumerable objects 1 cm in size or smaller. NASA calls these objects orbital debris, but their more colorful name is space junk.

Lottie Williams, in Turley, Oklahoma, was grazed in the shoulder by a lightweight fragment. This is the only known case of a person being struck by space debris.

This graphic shows the estimated 100,000-plus pieces of space debris larger than 1 cm. Pieces less than 1 cm number many millions. Most do not survive reentry, so there is little danger to people or property.

This windshield damage was caused by a 0.2 mm fragment of space debris traveling 3 to 6 km/s—equivalent to the damage from a rifle bullet.

In 1997, this 32 kg pressure sphere and two other items from a Delta II rocket booster landed in Texas. A fourth booster item struck Lottie Williams.

YOUR TURN

UNDERSTANDING CONCEPTS
Even though most pieces of space debris are tiny, why are they an important concern?

CRITICAL THINKING
How can tiny pieces of debris cause such significant damage?

Galilean Moons of Jupiter

What You'll Do

› **Calculate** the value of a constant, K.

› **Explain** how Kepler's law of periods explains orbits of moons of Jupiter.

What You'll Need

calculator
metric ruler

Kepler's third law of motion—the law of periods—explains the relationship between a planet's distance from the sun and the planet's period (the time required to make one revolution around the sun). According to the law of periods, the cube of the average distance of the planet from the sun is proportional to the square of the planet's period. Kepler's third law can be expressed mathematically as $K \times a^3 = p^2$, in which a is the average distance from the sun, p is the period, and K is a constant. Kepler's third law also may be applied to moons orbiting a planet, in which a is the average distance of a moon to the planet and p is the moon's period. In this activity, you will verify that the orbital motions of Jupiter's moons obey Kepler's third law.

Procedure

① Two telescope eyepiece views at the left show how Jupiter and its four largest, or Galilean, moons appear through a telescope on Earth at midnight on the 9th and 19th day of a month. Compare these illustrations with the chart below, which shows the path of each moon as it orbits Jupiter during the same month.
  a. List the days when each of Jupiter's moons crosses in front of the planet.
  b. List the days when each of the moons is behind Jupiter.

② Use the data in the table on the next page to test Kepler's third law. Calculate p^2 and a^3 for each of the planets. Record your results in a table of your own. Then, calculate K for each planet by using Kepler's third law, $K = p^2/a^3$. Record your results in a similar table.

③ Draw Jupiter and its moons as they would appear from Earth at midnight on the 2nd and 26th of the month.

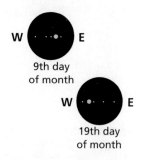

9th day of month

19th day of month

Step 1 The central horizontal band on the chart below represents Jupiter. When a moon's path crosses in front of this band, the moon is in front of the planet. When a moon's path crosses behind this band, the moon is behind Jupiter.

4 Draw Jupiter's moons on the first day of the month that all four moons are on the same side of the planet. Identify the date.

5 Give a date when only two moons will be visible. Name the two visible moons.

6 Follow each moon's motion on the chart. Find the length of time, in Earth days, required for each moon to orbit Jupiter. To do this, measure the time between two points when the moon is in exactly the same position on the same side of Jupiter. Record your answers in a table with columns for moons, p (in Earth days), a (in mm), p^2, a^3, and K.

Kepler's Third Law

Planet	p (in Earth years)	a (in billions of km)	a^3	p^2	K
Mercury	0.24	0.058			
Venus	0.62	0.108			
Earth	1	0.150			
Mars	1.88	0.228			
Jupiter	11.86	0.778			
Saturn	29.46	1.427			
Uranus	83.8	2.871			
Neptune	163.7	4.497			

DO NOT WRITE IN THIS BOOK

7 Measure the scale distance between the maximum outward swing of each moon and the center of Jupiter in millimeters. Record your answers in your table.

8 Square each period measurement, and record the answer in your table. Cube each distance measurement, and record the answer.

9 Use your results to test Kepler's third law. Because $K = p^2/a^3$, divide p^2 by a^3 for each moon to find K. Record your results in your table.

Analysis

1. **Analyzing Events** Will you see all four of Jupiter's largest moons each time you look at Jupiter through a telescope or binoculars? Explain your answer.

2. **Making Inferences** If you look at Jupiter's moons through a telescope, they look like dots. If you had no charts, how could you identify each moon?

3. **Drawing Conclusions** After you solve for K for each moon, study your results. Is K a constant for the moons of Jupiter? Explain your answer.

Extension

Making Calculations Recalculate the values of K for the planets by using astronomical units instead of kilometers. How does this affect the amount of variation in the value of the constant?

Lunar Landing Sites

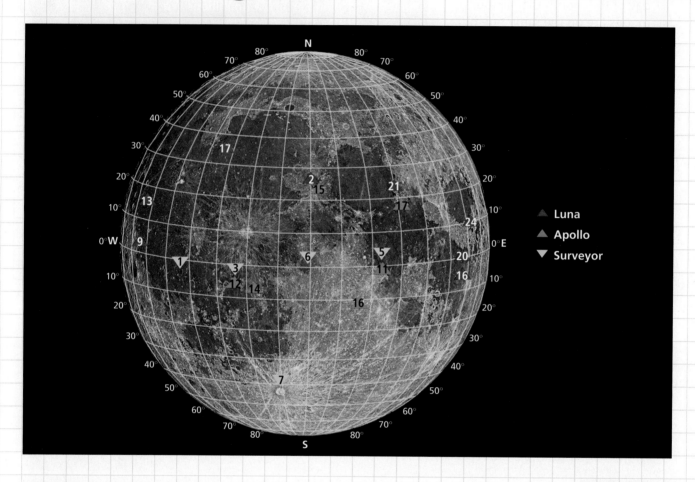

Map Skills Activity

This map shows the surface of the near side of the moon and the landing sites of both lunar missions that had crews and lunar missions that did not have crews. Most Surveyor missions took place before the Apollo missions. The Luna missions were launched by the former Soviet Union. Use the map to answer the questions below.

1. **Using a Key** How many Luna missions landed on the moon?

2. **Using a Key** How many Surveyor missions landed on the moon's southern hemisphere?

3. **Analyzing Data** How many Apollo missions landed close to Surveyor mission landing sites?

4. **Making Comparisons** At which areas of latitude are no landing sites located?

5. **Making Comparisons** In what 10° range of latitude are most landing sites located?

6. **Inferring Relationships** Based on the locations of most landing sites, what surface features do you think interested scientists?

7. **Identifying Trends** The missions to the moon used radio communications. Radio communications require a clear path between the transmitter and receiver. Taking these facts into consideration, how many landing sites would you expect to find on the far side of the moon? Explain your answer.

Key Ideas	Key Terms

Section 1

Earth's Moon

❯ Lunar surface features include maria, craters, rilles, ridges, regolith, and rocks.

❯ The moon's crust averages about 80 km deep. Extending about 1,000 km below the crust is the rocky mantle, which may be surrounded by a partly solid and partly liquid iron core that is less than 700 km in radius.

❯ The moon is thought to be a chunk of Earth's early mantle ejected as a result of a giant impact with a Mars-sized body. As the early molten moon cooled, it developed its three layers. Craters and regolith formed from meteorite impacts.

satellite, p. 785
moon, p. 785
mare, p. 786
crater, p. 786

Section 2

Movements of the Moon

❯ The shape of the moon's orbit around Earth is an ellipse.

❯ Eclipses occur when one planetary body passes through the shadow of another.

❯ The full moon phase shows a fully illuminated moon. Third quarter shows a half-moon (left side lit). New moon is not visible. First quarter shows a half-moon (right side lit).

❯ Tides result largely from the moon's gravitational pull on Earth.

apogee, p. 791
perigee, p. 791
eclipse, p. 793
solar eclipse, p. 793
lunar eclipse, p. 795
phase, p. 796

Section 3

Satellites of Other Planets

❯ Phobos and Deimos are irregularly shaped with many craters. They revolve around Mars quickly.

❯ The Voyager spacecraft discovered volcanoes on Io.

❯ The four Galilean moons of Jupiter are Io (known for its volcanoes), Europa (with an icy coating and possibly liquid water), Ganymede (the largest moon in the solar system), and Callisto (a very densely cratered moon).

❯ Saturn has many more rings than other planets do.

Galilean moon, p. 799

Section 4

Asteroids, Comets, and Meteoroids

❯ Asteroids are large, rocky bodies. Comets are smaller and are made of rock, ice, and dust.

❯ The Kuiper Belt is located beyond the orbit of Neptune.

❯ Meteoroids are small rocky bodies. The streak of light made when they burn up in the atmosphere is called a meteor. Any part that reaches the ground is called a meteorite.

❯ Most comets are thought to originate in the Oort cloud.

asteroid, p. 805
comet, p. 807
Kuiper Belt, p. 808
Oort cloud, p. 808
meteoroid, p. 809
meteor, p. 809

1. **Describing Space** Name two words that describe the motion of all minor bodies of the solar system, and explain how the meanings of these words differ.

USING KEY TERMS

Use each of the following terms in a separate sentence.

2. *crater* SC.912.E.5.2

3. *mare*

4. *Galilean moon*

For each pair of terms, explain how the meanings of the terms differ.

5. *perigee* and *apogee* SC.912.E.5.6

6. *Oort cloud* and *Kuiper Belt*

7. *solar eclipse* and *lunar eclipse* SC.912.E.5.6

8. *comet* and *asteroid*

9. *meteoroid* and *meteorite*

UNDERSTANDING KEY IDEAS

10. Dark areas on the moon that are smooth and that reflect little light are called
    a. rilles.
    b. rays.
    c. maria.
    d. breccia.

11. What happened in the most recent stage in the development of the moon?
    a. The densest material sank to the core.
    b. The crust began to break.
    c. Earth's gravity captured the moon.
    d. The number of meteorites hitting the moon decreased.

12. During each orbit around Earth, the moon spins on its axis SC.912.E.5.6
    a. 1 time.
    b. about 29 times.
    c. about 27 times.
    d. 365 times.

13. In a lunar eclipse, the moon SC.912.E.5.6
    a. casts a shadow on Earth.
    b. is in Earth's shadow.
    c. is between Earth and the sun.
    d. blocks part of the sun from view.

14. When the size of the lighted part of the moon's near side is decreasing, the moon is
    a. full. SC.912.E.5.6
    b. waxing.
    c. annular.
    d. waning.

15. Compared with the other moons of Jupiter, the four Galilean moons are
    a. larger.
    b. farther from Jupiter.
    c. lighter.
    d. younger.

16. The main asteroid belt exists in a region between the orbits of
    a. Mercury and Venus.
    b. Earth and Mars.
    c. Venus and Earth.
    d. Mars and Jupiter.

17. Meteorites can provide information about
    a. the composition of the solar system before the planets formed.
    b. the size of Earth.
    c. the destiny of the solar system.
    d. the size of the universe.

SHORT ANSWER

18. Describe how maria formed on the moon.

19. Are craters on the moon caused by volcanism or by impacts with other bodies? Explain your answer.

20. Do total eclipses of the sun occur only at full moons? Explain your answer. SC.912.E.5.6

21. Are any moons in the solar system bigger than planets? Explain. SC.912.E.5.6

22. Which planets have rings?

23. Which two places in the solar system do comets come from?

24. What is the difference between natural and artificial satellites?

CRITICAL THINKING

25. Analyzing Relationships If Earth had two moons that traveled on the same orbit and were the same distance from Earth, but formed a 90° angle with Earth, how would Earth's tides be different? `SC.912.E.5.6`

26. Making Inferences How would the craters on the moon be different today if the moon had developed a dense atmosphere that moved as wind and that contained water?

27. Determining Cause and Effect If meteorites had stopped hitting the moon before the outer surface of the moon cooled, how would the moon's surface be different than it is today?

28. Evaluating Information Suppose that the moon spun twice on its axis during each orbit around Earth. How would the study of the moon from Earth be easier than it is currently?

29. Applying Ideas The surfaces of some `SC.912.E.5.6` asteroids reflect only small amounts of light. Other asteroids reflect up to 40% of the light that falls on them. Of what kind of materials would each type of asteroid probably be composed?

CONCEPT MAPPING

30. Use the following terms to create a concept map: *moon, Earth, apogee, perigee, new moon, full moon, waxing, waning, solar eclipse, lunar eclipse, umbra, penumbra,* and *phase.* `SC.912.E.5.6`

MATH SKILLS

31. Making Calculations There are 60 s in 1 min, 60 min in 1 h, 24 h in 1 day, and 365 1/4 days in a year. How many seconds are in a year? `SC.912.E.5.6`

32. Making Calculations The radius of Earth's moon is 1,738 km. The diameter of Neptune's moon Triton is 2,705 km. What percentage of Earth's moon's size is Triton?

WRITING SKILLS

33. Creative Writing Imagine that you want to live on the moon. Describe how you would get your water and how you would acquire food and other supplies. `SC.912.E.5.7`

34. Communicating Ideas Summarize how the moon's gravity and the rotation of Earth cause tides. `SC.912.E.5.6`

INTERPRETING GRAPHICS

The graph below shows the number of near-Earth asteroids discovered each year. Use the graph below to answer the questions that follow.

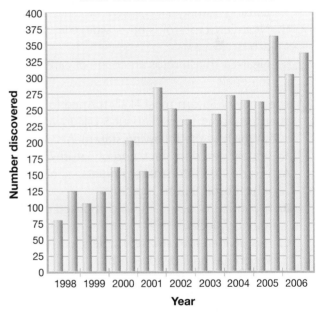

35. Was the rate of discovery of near-Earth asteroids in 2006 higher or lower than the rate in 2005?

36. How many near-Earth asteroids were discovered in the half-year in which the most discoveries were made?

37. Which calendar year had the highest total number of near-Earth asteroid discoveries?

38. What is the total number of near-Earth asteroids discovered in the last three years shown on the graph?

Understanding Concepts

Directions (1–9): For each question, write on a separate sheet of paper the letter of the correct answer.

1 Because of differences in surface gravity, how much does a person who weighs 360 newtons (360 N) on Earth weigh on the moon if the moon has one-sixth the gravity of Earth?
  A. 36 N
  B. 60 N
  C. 180 N
  D. 90 N

2 Why are scientists concerned about near-Earth asteroids?
  F. Near-Earth asteroids make up only a small percentage of asteroids.
  G. Near-Earth asteroids might strike Earth, causing damage.
  H. Near-Earth asteroids have wide, elliptical orbits.
  I. Near-Earth asteroids are made of carbon materials.

3 The rings of Saturn most likely formed long after the planet formed about 5 billion years ago. Which of the following statements accurately describes each ring of Saturn?
  A. It is divided into smaller ringlets, all of which orbit Saturn together.
  B. It consists of a single ring composed of rock and ice pieces.
  C. It is divided into smaller ringlets, each of which has an individual orbit.
  D. It is part of a set of rings that are unlike those found anywhere else.

4 Which of the following statements describes why temperature variation on the moon is so large?
  F. The moon has no atmosphere to provide insulation.
  G. The atmosphere of the moon is made up of cold gases.
  H. Gases are dense and close to the surface.
  I. Dark, smooth rocks absorb the sun's heat.

5 The asteroid belt did NOT become a planet during the formation of the solar system because
  A. the material is continually colliding with itself.
  B. comets break up in the belt.
  C. of Jupiter's gravity.
  D. the asteroids are not massive enough.

6 Why does the moon look today almost exactly as it did 3 billion years ago?
  F. The number of small objects in the solar system decreased.
  G. Geologic activity on the moon increased.
  H. The outer surface of the moon solidified.
  I. The densest materials had moved away from the moon's surface to the core.

7 The oldest lunar rocks discovered are about 4.5 billion years old. How do these rocks compare to Earth rocks?
  A. Lunar rocks contain different proportions of the elements that make up Earth rocks.
  B. Lunar rocks contain water, but Earth rocks do not contain water.
  C. Lunar rocks are igneous, but Earth rocks are sedimentary.
  D. Lunar rocks are older than Earth rocks.

8 How do meteorites from the moon or Mars reach Earth?
  F. Earth's gravity pulls meteoroids from the moon and Mars.
  G. Meteorites hit the moon or Mars and eject rocks onto Earth.
  H. The moon and Mars lose meteoroids into space.
  I. Comets carry rocks from the moon and Mars to Earth.

9 Why have more meteorites made it to the surface of the moon than to Earth's surface?
  A. The moon shields Earth from meteorites.
  B. Earth is mostly covered by water.
  C. The meteorites that hit the moon are larger, so they do not break up.
  D. The moon has no atmosphere for protection.

Interpreting Graphics

Directions (10–12): For each question below, record the correct answer on a separate sheet of paper.

Phases of the Moon in the Northern Hemisphere

1	2	3	4	5	6	7	8
New Moon	Waxing Crescent	First Quarter	Waxing Gibbous	Full Moon	Waning Gibbous	Last Quarter	Waning Crescent

10 How would the appearance of the moon in the Southern Hemisphere be different from its appearance in the Northern Hemisphere?

F. The phases of the moon would appear exactly the same.

G. The Southern Hemisphere would see a full moon when the Northern Hemisphere sees a new moon.

H. The moon would wax from left to right instead of from right to left.

I. The Southern Hemisphere would see a waxing moon when the Northern Hemisphere sees a waning moon.

11 What part of the moon is facing Earth during the new moon in stage 1?

A. the near side

B. the far side

C. the north pole

D. the south pole

Structure of the Moon

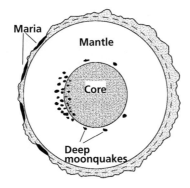

Maria
Mantle
Core
Deep moonquakes

12 Where is the crust of the moon the thickest?

F. at the poles

G. at the equator

H. on the near side

I. on the far side

Test Tip

Test questions are not necessarily arranged in order of difficulty. If you are unable to answer a question, mark it and move on to other questions.

Chapter 29 The Sun

Chapter Outline

Why It Matters

The sun provides Earth with more than just heat. All living things on Earth depend, either directly or indirectly, on the sun as a source of energy to permit and sustain life processes.

Inquiry Lab   Making a Spectrum

15 min

Fill a **shallow dish** or basin about halfway with **water**. Lean a **flat mirror** against one side of the dish so that the mirror is on an angle. Make sure that part of the mirror is submerged in the water. Darken the classroom, and shine a **flashlight** at the mirror. Observe the reflected image. What do you see?

SC.912.E.5.8

Questions to Get You Started

1. Why do you see colors even though you started with white light?

2. What would you see if you placed a red filter over the flashlight?

Word Parts

Suffixes The suffix *-ive* changes nouns and verbs to adjectives and adds the meaning "relating or tending to." For example, *supportive* is an adjective formed from the noun *support*. It means "tending to give support." The suffix *-tion* changes verbs to nouns, or nouns to other nouns, and adds the meaning "the act or state of." For example, *connection* is a noun formed from the verb *connect*. It means "the state of joining."

Your Turn Make a table like the one below. In Section 1, there are two key terms with the suffix *-ive* and an italicized word with the suffix *-tion*. Add them to your table, along with other *-ive* or *-tion* words.

Word	Suffix	Related noun or verb	Definition of word
reaction	-tion	react	a response to something

Generalizations

Signal Words Generalizations are statements applied to a large group of things. Generalizations may be signaled by words such as *commonly, usually, normally,* or *generally*. Sometimes they are signaled by words such as *most, mostly,* and *much,* and by phrases such as *in general* and *for the most part*. Many generalizations, however, are not signaled by a word or phrase.

Your Turn As you read Section 2, look for sentences that are generalizations. Make a table like the one below to list the generalizations that you find.

Sentence	Word or phrase that signals generalization	Why sentence is a generalization
Many other solar activities are affected by the sunspot cycle.	many	The statement applies to many, but not all, solar activities.

Graphic Organizers

Chain-of-Events Chart A chain-of-events chart shows the order in which steps occur.

Your Turn As you read Section 1, complete the chain-of-events chart that outlines each step in the process of nuclear fusion.

❶ The first step in the process is written in the first box.

❷ The second step in the process is written in the second box, and an arrow shows the order of the first and second steps.

❸ Continue adding boxes and arrows until the process of nuclear fusion is complete.

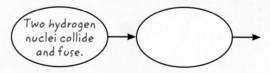

For more information on how to use these and other tools, see **Appendix A.**

Key Ideas	Key Terms	Why It Matters
❯ Explain how the sun converts matter into energy in its core. ❯ Compare the radiative and convective zones of the sun. ❯ Describe the three layers of the sun's atmosphere.	nuclear fusion radiative zone convective zone photosphere chromosphere corona	Scientists hope that their research will one day result in the technology to create safe, controlled nuclear fusion reactions on Earth, which could then be used as a source of plentiful, reliable energy.

Throughout much of human history, people thought that the sun's energy came from fire. People knew that burning a piece of coal or wood produced energy as heat and light. They assumed that the sun, too, burned some type of fuel to produce its energy. But less than 100 years ago, scientists discovered that the source of the sun's energy is quite different from fire.

The Sun's Energy

The sun appears to the unaided eye as a dazzling, brilliant ball that has no distinct features. Because the sun's brightness can damage your eyes if you look directly at the sun, astronomers look at the sun only through special filters. Astronomers often use other specialized scientific instruments to study the sun.

Composition of the Sun

Scientists break up the sun's light into a spectrum by using a device called a *spectrograph*. Dark lines form in the spectra of stars when gases in the stars' outer layers absorb specific wavelengths of the light that passes through the layers. Because each element produces a unique pattern of spectral lines, astronomers can match the spectral lines of starlight to those of Earth's elements, as shown in **Figure 1**, and identify the elements in the star's atmosphere.

About 75% of the sun's mass is hydrogen, and hydrogen and helium together make up about 99% of the sun's mass. The sun's spectrum reveals, however, that the sun contains traces of almost all other chemical elements.

FLORIDA STANDARDS

SC.912.E.5.4 Explain the physical properties of the Sun and its dynamic nature and connect them to conditions and events on Earth; **SC.912.N.3.4** Recognize that theories do not become laws, nor do laws become theories; theories are well supported explanations and laws are well supported descriptions; **SC.912.N.3.5** Describe the function of models in science, and identify the wide range of models used in science.

Figure 1 When light passes through hydrogen gas and then through a slit in a prism, dark lines appear in the spectrum. Hydrogen and lines from other elements in the solar spectrum are shown in the bottom spectrograph.

Hydrogen

Solar spectrum

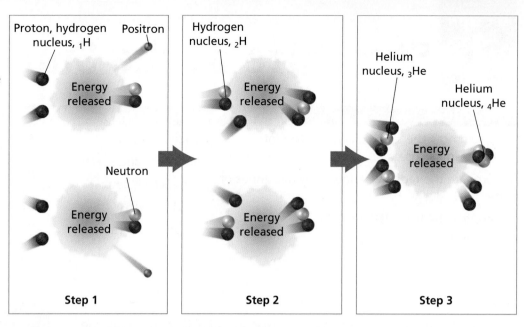

Figure 2 In the core of the sun, the nuclei of hydrogen atoms fuse to form helium. The fusion process converts some of the mass into energy.

INTERACT ONLINE
Keyword: HQXSUNF2

Step 1 | **Step 2** | **Step 3**

Labels in figure:
Proton, hydrogen nucleus, $_1H$
Positron
Energy released
Neutron
Energy released
Hydrogen nucleus, $_2H$
Energy released
Energy released
Helium nucleus, $_3He$
Helium nucleus, $_4He$
Energy released

Generalizations
As you read Section 1, look for sentences that contain generalizations, and list them in a table. Remember that some generalizations are not signaled by a word or phrase.

Academic Vocabulary

convert (cohn VUHRT) change from one form to another

Nuclear Fusion

A powerful atomic process known as nuclear fusion occurs inside the sun. **Nuclear fusion** is the process of combining nuclei of small atoms to form more-massive nuclei. Fusion releases huge amounts of energy. Nuclei of hydrogen atoms are the primary fuel for the sun's fusion. A hydrogen atom, the simplest of all atoms, commonly consists of only one electron and one proton. Inside the sun, however, electrons are stripped from the protons by the sun's intense heat.

Nuclear fusion produces most of the sun's energy and consists of three steps, as shown in **Figure 2.** In the first step, two hydrogen nuclei, or *protons*, collide and fuse. In this step, the positive charge of one of the protons is neutralized as a particle called a *positron* is emitted. As a result, the proton becomes a neutron and the original two protons become a proton-neutron pair. In the second step, another proton combines with this proton-neutron pair to produce a nucleus made up of two protons and one neutron, a rare type of helium. In the third step, two nuclei made up of two protons and one neutron collide and fuse. As this fusion happens, two protons are released. The remaining two protons and two neutrons are fused together as a helium nucleus of the common type. During each step of the reaction, energy is released.

The Final Product

One of the final products of the fusion of hydrogen in the sun is always a helium nucleus. The helium nucleus has about 0.7% less mass than the hydrogen nuclei that combined to form it do. The lost mass is converted into energy during the series of fusion reactions that forms helium. The energy released during the three steps of nuclear fusion causes the sun to shine and gives the sun its high temperature.

Mass Changing into Energy

The sun's energy comes from fusion, and the mass that is lost during fusion becomes energy. In 1905, the physicist Albert Einstein, then an unknown patent-office worker, proposed that a small amount of matter yields a large amount of energy. At the time, the existence of nuclear fusion was unknown. In fact, scientists had not yet discovered the nucleus of the atom. Einstein's proposal was part of his special theory of relativity. This theory included the equation $E = mc^2$. In this equation, E represents energy produced; m represents the mass, or the amount of matter, that is changed; and c represents the speed of light, which is about 300,000 km/s. Einstein's equation can be used to calculate the amount of energy produced from a given amount of matter.

By using Einstein's equation, astronomers were able to explain the huge quantities of energy produced by the sun. The sun changes about 4 million tons of mass into energy every second. Yet this amount of mass is small compared with the total mass of the sun.

During fusion, a type of subatomic particle called a *neutrino* is given off. Neutrinos escape the sun and reach Earth in about eight minutes. Studies of these particles confirm that the sun is fueled by the fusion of hydrogen into helium. One apparatus that collects these particles is shown in **Figure 3.** Elements other than hydrogen can fuse, too. In stars that are hotter than the sun, energy is produced by fusion reactions of the nuclei of carbon, nitrogen, and oxygen.

Figure 3 In Japan, this giant tank of pure water, which was only partly filled when the photo was taken, captures subatomic particles that fly out of the sun during nuclear fusion.

SC*L*INKS.

www.scilinks.org
Topic: The Sun
Code: HQX1477

Reading Check How did the equation $E = mc^2$ help scientists understand the energy of the sun? (See Appendix G for answers to Reading Checks.)

SC.912.P.10.11

Quick Lab Modeling Fusion

10 min

Procedure

1 Mark six coins by using a marker or wax pencil. Put a *P* for "proton" on the head side of each coin and an *N* for "neutron" on the tail side of the coins.

2 Place two coins P-side up. These two protons each represent hydrogen's simplest isotope, H. Model the fusion of these two H nuclei by placing them such that their edges touch. When they touch, flip one of them to be N-side up. This flip represents a proton becoming a neutron during fusion. The resulting nucleus, which consists of one proton and one neutron, represents the isotope hydrogen-2, ^{2}H.

3 To model the next step of nuclear fusion, place a third coin, P-side up, against the ^{2}H nucleus from step 2. This forms the isotope helium-3, or ^{3}He.

4 Repeat steps 2 and 3 to form a second ^{3}He nucleus.

5 Next, model the fusion of two ^{3}He nuclei. Move the two ^{3}He nuclei formed in step 3 so that their edges touch. When the two ^{3}He nuclei touch, move two of the protons in the two ^{3}He nuclei away from the other four particles. These four particles form a new nucleus: helium-4, or ^{4}He.

Analysis

1. Large amounts of energy are released when nuclei combine. How many energy-producing reactions did you model?

2. Create a diagram that shows the formation of ^{4}He.

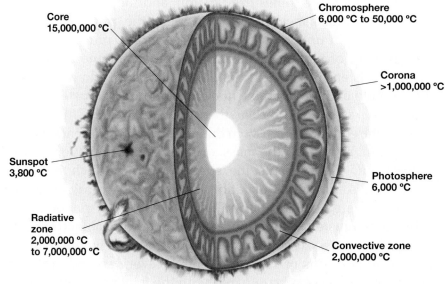

Figure 4 Energy released by fusion reactions in the core slowly works its way through the layers of the sun by the processes of radiation and convection.

Core
15,000,000 °C

Chromosphere
6,000 °C to 50,000 °C

Corona
>1,000,000 °C

Sunspot
3,800 °C

Photosphere
6,000 °C

Radiative zone
2,000,000 °C
to 7,000,000 °C

Convective zone
2,000,000 °C

SC.912.E.5.11

The Sun's Interior

Scientists can't see inside the sun. But computer models have revealed what the invisible layers may be like. In recent years, careful studies of motions on the sun's surface have supplied more detail about what is happening inside the sun. The parts of the sun are shown in **Figure 4.**

The Core

At the center of the sun is the core. The core makes up 25% of the sun's total diameter of 1,390,000 km. The temperature of the sun's core is about 15,000,000 °C. No liquid or solid can exist at such a high temperature. The core, like the rest of the sun, is made up entirely of ionized gas. The mass of the sun is 300,000 times the mass of Earth. Because of the sun's large mass, the pressure from the sun's material is so great that the center of the sun is more than 10 times as dense as iron.

The enormous pressure and high temperature of the sun's core cause the atoms to separate into nuclei and electrons. On Earth, atoms generally consist of a nucleus surrounded by one or more electrons. Within the core of the sun, however, the energy and pressure strip electrons away from the atomic nuclei. The nuclei have positive charges, so they tend to push away from each other. But the high temperature and pressure force the nuclei close enough to fuse. The most common nuclear reaction that occurs inside the sun is the fusion of hydrogen into helium.

The Radiative Zone

Before reaching the sun's atmosphere, the energy produced in the core moves through two zones of the sun's interior. The zone surrounding the core is called the **radiative zone.** The temperature in this zone ranges from about 2,000,000 °C to 7,000,000 °C. In the radiative zone, energy moves outward in the form of electromagnetic waves, or radiation.

The Convective Zone

Surrounding the radiative zone, comprising the outer 30 percent of the sun, is the **convective zone,** where temperatures are about 2,000,000 °C. Energy produced in the core moves through this zone by convection. *Convection* is the transfer of energy by moving matter. On Earth, boiling water carries energy upward by convection. In the sun's convective zone, hot gases carry energy to the sun's surface. As the hot gases move outward and expand, they lose energy. The cooling gases become denser than the other gases and sink to the bottom of the convective zone. There, the cooled gases are heated by the energy from the radiative zone and rise again. Thus, energy is transferred to the sun's surface as the gases rise and sink.

The Sun's Atmosphere

Surrounding the convective zone is the sun's atmosphere. Although the sun is made of gases, the term *atmosphere* refers to the uppermost region of solar gases. This region has three layers—the photosphere, the chromosphere, and the corona.

The Photosphere

The innermost layer of the solar atmosphere is the **photosphere.** *Photosphere* means "sphere of light." The photosphere is made of gases that have risen from the convective zone. The temperature in the photosphere is about 6,000 °C. Much of the energy given off from the photosphere is in the form of visible light. The layers above the photosphere are transparent, so the visible light is the light that is seen from Earth. A photo of the sun's photosphere is shown in **Figure 5.** The dark spots are cool areas of about 3,800 °C and are called *sunspots.*

Reading Check What layers make up the sun's atmosphere?

radiative zone the zone of the sun's interior that is between the core and the convective zone and in which energy moves by radiation

convective zone the region of the sun's interior that is between the radiative zone and the photosphere and in which energy is carried upward by convection

photosphere the visible surface of the sun

Figure 5 The photosphere is referred to as the sun's surface because this layer is the visible surface of the sun. Sunspots are cooler regions in the photosphere.

Figure 6 The corona of the sun becomes visible during a total solar eclipse. The black disk is the silhouette of the moon, which is blocking the photosphere.

chromosphere the thin layer of the sun that is just above the photosphere and that glows a reddish color during eclipses

corona the outermost layer of the sun's atmosphere

The Chromosphere

Above the photosphere lies the **chromosphere,** or color sphere. This is a thin layer of gases that glows with reddish light that is typical of the color given off by hydrogen. The chromosphere's temperature ranges from 6,000 °C to 50,000 °C. The gases of the chromosphere move away from the photosphere. In an upward movement, gas regularly forms narrow jets of hot gas that shoot outward to form the chromosphere and then fade away within a few minutes. Some of these jets reach heights of 16,000 km.

Spacecraft study the sun from above Earth's atmosphere. These spacecraft can detect small details on the sun. They can also measure wavelengths of light that are blocked by Earth's atmosphere. Movies made from these spacecraft images show how features on the sun rise, change, and sometimes twist.

The Sun's Outer Parts

Just above the chromosphere is a thin zone called the transition region where the temperature rises dramatically. The outermost layer of the sun's atmosphere is the **corona** (kuh ROH nuh), or crown. The corona is a huge region of gas with a temperature above 1,000,000 °C. The corona is not very dense, but its magnetic field can stop most subatomic particles from escaping into space. However, electrons and electrically charged particles called *ions* do stream out into space as the corona expands. These particles make up the *solar wind*, which flows outward from the sun to the rest of the solar system.

The chromosphere and the corona are normally not seen from Earth because the sky during the day is too bright. Occasionally, however, the moon moves between Earth and the sun and blocks out the light of the photosphere. The sky darkens, and the corona becomes visible, as shown in **Figure 6.**

Section 1 Review

LA.910.2.2.3; SC.912.E.5.4

Key Ideas

1. **Describe** how scientists use spectra to determine the composition of stars.

2. **Identify** the two elements that make up most of the sun.

3. **Identify** the end products of the nuclear fusion process that occurs in the sun.

4. **Explain** how the sun converts matter into energy in its core.

5. **Compare** the radiative and convective zones of the sun.

6. **Describe** the three layers of the sun's atmosphere.

7. **Explain** why the sun's corona can be seen during an eclipse but not at other times.

Critical Thinking

8. **Making Inferences** Describe whether the amount of hydrogen in the sun will increase or decrease over the next few million years. Explain your reasoning.

9. **Analyzing Ideas** Why does fusion occur in the sun's core but not in other layers?

10. **Predicting Consequences** What might happen to the solar wind if the sun lost its corona?

Concept Mapping

11. Use the following terms to create a concept map: *sun, hydrogen, helium, nuclear fusion, core, radiative zone,* and *convective zone.*

Solar Activity

Key Ideas	Key Terms	Why It Matters
❯ Explain how sunspots are related to powerful magnetic fields on the sun. ❯ Compare prominences, solar flares, and coronal mass ejections. ❯ Describe how the solar wind can cause auroras on Earth.	sunspot prominence solar flare coronal mass ejection aurora	Solar flares and coronal mass ejections can cause geomagnetic storms on Earth that disrupt communications technologies such as radio, television, and cellular telephones.

The gases that make up the sun's interior and atmosphere are in constant motion. The energy produced in the sun's core and the force of gravity combine to cause the continuous rising and sinking of gases. The gases also move because the sun rotates on its axis. Because the sun is a ball of hot gases rather than a solid sphere, not all locations on the sun rotate at the same speed. Places close to the equator on the surface of the sun take 25.3 Earth days to rotate once. Points near the poles take 33 days to rotate once. On average, the sun rotates once every 27 days.

Sunspots

The movement of gases within the sun's convective zone and the movements caused by the sun's rotation produce magnetic fields. These magnetic fields cause convection to slow in parts of the convective zone. Slower convection causes a decrease in the amount of gas that is transferring energy from the core of the sun to these regions of the photosphere. In some places, the magnetic field is thousands of times stronger than it is in other places. Because less energy is being transferred, these regions of the photosphere are up to 3,000 °C cooler than surrounding regions.

Although they still shine brightly, these cooler areas of the sun appear darker than the areas that surround them do. These cool, dark areas of gas within the photosphere are called **sunspots.** The rest of the photosphere has a grainy appearance called *granulation.* The area around the sunspots shown in **Figure 1** has visible granulation. A large sunspot can have a diameter of more than 100,000 km, which is more than seven times the diameter of Earth.

FLORIDA STANDARDS

SC.912.P.10.16 Explain the relationship between moving charges and magnetic fields, as well as changing magnetic fields and electric fields, and their application to modern technologies.

sunspot a dark area of the photosphere of the sun that is cooler than the surrounding areas and that has a strong magnetic field

Figure 1 The diameter of this large sunspot is bigger than Earth's diameter. This image also shows the granulation on the sun's surface.

Relative size of Earth

Sunspot

Granules

Sunspots Recorded

Figure 2 The sunspot cycle lasts an average of 11 years. *When will the next high point in the cycle occur?*

READING TOOLBOX

Suffixes
In Section 2, one key term and two italicized words contain the suffix *-tion*. Find and add these words to your table.

The Sunspot Cycle

Astronomers have carefully observed sunspots for hundreds of years. Observations of sunspots showed astronomers that the sun rotates. Later, astronomers observed that the numbers and positions of sunspots vary in a cycle that lasts about 11 years.

A sunspot cycle begins when the number of sunspots is very low but begins to increase. Sunspots initially appear in groups about midway between the sun's equator and poles. The number of sunspots increases over the next few years until it reaches a peak of 100 or more sunspots. Then, sunspots at higher latitudes slowly disappear, and new ones appear closer to the sun's equator. **Figure 2** shows that after the peak, the number of sunspots begins to decrease until it reaches a minimum. Another 11-year cycle begins when the number of sunspots begins to increase again.

Solar Eruptions

Many other solar activities are affected by the sunspot cycle. The *solar-activity cycle* is caused by the changing solar magnetic field. This cycle is characterized by increases and decreases in various types of solar activity, including solar eruptions. Solar eruptions are events in which the sun lifts substantial material above the photosphere and emits atomic or subatomic particles. These events include prominences, solar flares, and coronal mass ejections.

Why It Matters

SOHO, So Helpful

On November 4, 2003, the most violent solar flare ever recorded ejected billions of tons of hot gases and particles from the sun's surface at 2,700 km/s. Had Earth been in its direct path, we would have had only 17 hours warning. Without the Solar and Heliospheric Observatory (SOHO), we might not have seen it coming. SOHO images the sun in visible, X-ray, and (as shown here) UV frequencies. Initially planned for two years, the mission has been extended at least three times.

In addition to its sun-related duties, SOHO has discovered more than 1,000 new comets.

YOUR TURN **ONLINE RESEARCH**
When was the last major solar flare that affected Earth?

Prominences

The magnetic fields that cause sunspots also create other disturbances in the sun's atmosphere. Great clouds of glowing gases, called **prominences,** form huge arches that reach high above the sun's surface. Each solar prominence follows curved magnetic field lines from a region of one magnetic polarity to a region of the opposite magnetic polarity. Some prominences may last for several weeks, while others may erupt and disappear in hours. The gas in prominences is very hot and is commonly associated with the chromosphere.

Solar Flares

The most violent of all solar disturbances is a **solar flare,** a sudden outward eruption of electrically charged particles, such as electrons and protons. The trigger for these eruptions is unknown. However, scientists know that solar flares release the energy stored in the strong magnetic fields of sunspots. This release of energy can lead to the formation of coronal loops, such as the ones shown in **Figure 3.**

Solar flares may travel upward thousands of kilometers within minutes, but few eruptions last more than an hour. During a peak in the sunspot cycle, 5 to 10 solar flares may occur each day. The temperature of the gas in solar flares may reach 20,000,000 °C. Some of the particles from a solar flare escape into space. These particles increase the strength of the solar wind.

Coronal Mass Ejections

Particles also escape into space as **coronal mass ejections,** or parts of the corona that are thrown off the sun. As the gusts of particles strike Earth's *magnetosphere,* or the space around Earth that contains a magnetic field, the particles can generate a sudden disturbance in Earth's magnetic field. These disturbances are called *geomagnetic storms.* Although several small geomagnetic storms may occur each month, the average number of severe storms is less than one per year.

Geomagnetic storms have been known to interfere with radio communications on Earth. The high-energy particles that circulate in Earth's outer atmosphere during geomagnetic storms can also damage satellites. They can also lead to blackouts when power lines become overloaded. Not all solar activity is so dramatic, but the activity of the sun affects Earth every day.

Reading Check How do coronal mass ejections affect communications on Earth?

Figure 3 A coronal loop, shown here curving from left to right, can arch more than 500,000 km above the sun's surface.

prominence a loop of relatively cool, incandescent gas that extends above the photosphere and above the sun's edge as seen from Earth

solar flare an explosive release of energy that comes from the sun and that is associated with magnetic disturbances on the sun's surface

coronal mass ejection coronal gas that is thrown into space from the sun

Math Skills

Magnetic Fields
Solar magnetic field densities at the sun's poles are 0.001 teslas (T); those near sunspots are up to 0.3 T. How many times the field densities at the poles are field densities near sunspots?

Figure 4 Auroras, such as these over Finland, can fill the entire sky. The different colors in an aurora result from high-energy particles from the sun colliding with atoms of different elements in Earth's atmosphere.

Academic Vocabulary

interaction (IN tuhr AK shuhn) the action or influence between things

aurora colored light produced by charged particles from the solar wind and from the magnetosphere that react with and excite the oxygen and nitrogen of Earth's upper atmosphere; usually seen in the sky near Earth's magnetic poles

www.scilinks.org
Topic: Solar Activity
Code: HQX1413

Auroras

On Earth, a spectacular effect of the interaction between the solar wind and Earth's magnetosphere is the appearance in the sky of bands of light called **auroras** (aw RAWR uhz). **Figure 4** shows an example of an aurora. Auroras are usually seen close to Earth's magnetic poles because electrically charged particles are guided toward Earth's magnetic poles by Earth's magnetosphere. The electrically charged particles strike the atoms and gas molecules in the upper atmosphere and produce colorful sheets of light. Depending on which pole they are near, auroras are called *northern lights*—or *aurora borealis* (aw RAWR uh BAWR ee AL is)—or *southern lights*—or *aurora australis*.

Auroras normally occur between 100 and 1,000 km above Earth's surface. They are most frequent just after a peak in the sunspot cycle, especially after solar flares occur. Across the northern contiguous United States, auroras are visible about five times per year. In Alaska, however, people can see auroras almost every clear, dark night. Astronauts in orbit can also look down on Earth and see auroras. But Earth is not the only planet that has auroras. Spacecraft have imaged auroras on Jupiter and Saturn.

Section 2 Review

LA.910.2.2.3; SC.912.E.5.4

Key Ideas

1. **Explain** why sunspots are cooler than surrounding areas on the sun's surface.

2. **Identify** the number of sunspots that are on the sun during the peak of the sunspot cycle.

3. **Summarize** how the latitude of sunspots varies during the sunspot cycle.

4. **Explain** how prominences are different from solar flares.

5. **Summarize** the cause of auroras on Earth.

Critical Thinking

6. **Identifying Relationships** How can a sunspot be bright but look dark?

7. **Analyzing Ideas** Why doesn't the whole sun rotate at the same rate?

Concept Mapping

8. Use the following terms to create a concept map: *sunspot, prominence, solar flare, solar-activity cycle,* and *coronal mass ejection.*

REAL WORLD

Seasonal Sunlight

Visible light makes up a small fraction of the sun's total energy and is the only part of its energy that your eyes can detect. But this tiny "sliver" of the electromagnetic spectrum helps to feed the world, guide animals on their yearly migrations, and even let you know when it's time to wake up. Earth's green plants and other producers use about 2% of the solar energy that reaches Earth for photosynthesis, generating between 150 and 200 billion tons of organic matter each year. This is the matter that we use for food, fuel, and countless other applications.

Sunlight motivates us to go outside and helps keep our bodies fit. Our skin uses sunlight to make vitamin D, which we need for strong bones and a healthy immune system.

In winter, when there is less natural light available, some people experience seasonal affective disorder (SAD) and use methods known as light therapy to help them cope.

Some migratory animals, such as butterflies and birds, use the sun to help them determine direction when they travel. Fish use patterns of reflected sunlight for the same purpose.

YOUR TURN

UNDERSTANDING CONCEPTS
What are three ways that people depend on sunlight?

CRITICAL THINKING
In what other ways do organisms rely on sunlight?

90 min

Energy of the Sun

The sun is, on average, 150 million kilometers away from Earth. Scientists use complex astronomical instruments to measure the size and energy output of the sun. However, it is possible to estimate the sun's energy output by using simple instruments and the knowledge of the relationship between the sun's size and its distance from Earth. In this lab, you will collect energy from sunlight and estimate the amount of energy produced by the sun.

Objectives

> **Estimate** the sun's energy output.

> **Evaluate** the differences between known values and experimental values.

Materials

aluminum foil, 8 cm × 64 cm
clay, modeling
desk lamp with 100 W bulb
jar, glass, with lid
paint or magic marker, black,
  flat finish
pencil
ruler, metric
tape, masking
thermometer, Celsius

Safety

Procedure

1 Construct a solar collector in the following way.

  a. Carefully punch a hole in the jar lid, or use a lid that is already prepared by your teacher.

  b. Cut an 8 cm × 64 cm piece of aluminum foil. Place the piece of foil with the shorter (8 cm) edge in front of you. Fold the strip over three times. Then rotate the foil 90°, and fold it over two times. The resulting foil strip is now 2 cm × 8 cm. Wrap the strip snugly around at least half the bulb of the thermometer. Bend the edges out so that they form "wings," as shown in the photo. **CAUTION** Thermometers are fragile. Do not squeeze the bulb of the thermometer too tight or let the thermometer strike any solid object. Bend the remaining foil outward to collect as much sunlight as possible.

  c. Paint the wings black using a marker or flat black paint.

  d. Slip the top of the thermometer through the hole in the jar's lid. On the top and bottom of the lid, mold the clay around the thermometer to hold the thermometer steady. Place the lid on the jar. Adjust the thermometer so that the aluminum-foil wings are centered in the jar. Then, secure the thermometer and clay to the lid with masking tape.

2 Place the solar collector in sunlight. Tilt the jar so that the sun shines directly on the metal wings. Carefully hold the jar in place. You may want to prop the jar up carefully with books.

3 Watch the temperature reading on the thermometer until it reaches a maximum value or until 5 min have elapsed. Record this value. Allow the collector to cool for 2 min.

④ Place the lamp or heat lamp at the end of a table. Remove any reflector or shade from the lamp.

⑤ Place the collector about 30 cm from the lamp, and turn the collector toward the lamp.

⑥ Turn on the lamp, and wait 1 min. Then, gradually move the collector toward the lamp in 2 cm increments. Watch the temperature carefully. At each position, let the collector sit until the temperature reading stabilizes. Stop moving the collector when the temperature reaches the maximum temperature that was achieved in sunlight.

⑦ Once the temperature has stabilized at the same level reached in sunlight, record the distance between the center of the lamp and the thermometer bulb.

Analysis

1. **Analyzing Results** Because the collector reached the same temperature in both trials, the collector absorbed as much energy from the sun at a distance of 150 million km as it did from the light bulb at the distance that you measured. Using 1.5×10^{13} cm as the distance to the sun, calculate the power of the sun in watts by using the equation that follows. The power of the lamp is equal to the wattage of the light bulb.

$$\frac{power_{sun}}{(distance_{sun})^2} = \frac{power_{lamp}}{(distance_{lamp})^2}$$

2. **Evaluating Models** The sun's power is generally given as 3.7×10^{26} W. Calculate your experimental percentage error by first subtracting your experimental value from the accepted value. Divide this difference by the accepted value, and multiply by 100. Describe two possible sources for your calculated error.

Extension

Evaluating Models How would using a fluorescent bulb instead of an incandescent bulb in the experiment affect the results of the experiment? Explain your answer.

XRT Composite Image of the Sun

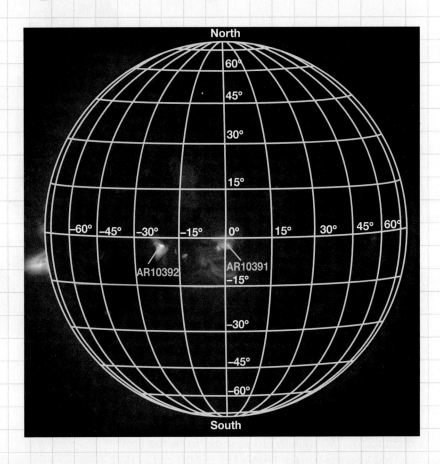

Map Skills Activity

This map is an X-ray telescope (XRT) image of the sun that includes latitude and longitude lines. Yellow represents the strongest X-ray radiation. Red represents moderate X-ray radiation. Black represents the weakest X-ray radiation. Active regions (AR) are numbered. Use the map to answer these questions.

1. **Analyzing Data** What is the latitude and longitude of the active region numbered 10392?

2. **Analyzing Data** How would you describe the intensity of the X-ray radiation in the region at 15° north latitude and –15° west longitude?

3. **Inferring Relationships** Why do the lines of solar longitude appear to be close to each other near the left side and the right side of the map?

4. **Interpreting Data** Dark regions of the corona that are visible in X-ray images are called *coronal holes*. They are the source of the solar wind. What is the range of longitudes covered by the coronal hole in the southwestern quadrant of the map?

5. **Analyzing Relationships** Sunspots emit large amounts of X-ray radiation. Where on this map would you expect to find sunspots?

Key Ideas | Key Terms

Section 1

Structure of the Sun

❯ The sun's core converts matter into energy through the process of nuclear fusion. In nuclear fusion, four hydrogen nuclei are combined to form one helium nucleus, releasing much energy.

❯ Energy produced by nuclear fusion moves from the sun's core through the hotter radiative zone (in the form of electromagnetic waves) and then the cooler convective zone (in the form of gaseous convection currents) before it enters the sun's atmosphere.

❯ The sun's atmosphere is composed of three layers: the photosphere (the inner layer, but the layer that is visible to us on Earth), the hotter chromosphere, and the much hotter and much larger corona (the outer layer).

nuclear fusion, p. 824
radiative zone, p. 827
convective zone, p. 827
photosphere, p. 827
chromosphere, p. 828
corona, p. 828

Section 2

Solar Activity

❯ Sunspots are regions of the photosphere that have stronger magnetic fields than the regions that surround them. They are cooler than the surrounding regions because less energy is being transferred to them from the core.

❯ Prominences are loops of relatively cool gas that extend above the photosphere. They are usually associated with the chromosphere. Solar flares are explosive releases of the energy stored in the magnetic fields of sunspots. Coronal mass ejections cause disturbances in Earth's magnetosphere called geomagnetic storms.

❯ Auroras are colorful sheets of light that occur in Earth's polar regions when charged particles from the interaction between the solar wind and Earth's magnetosphere collide with atoms and molecules in the atmosphere.

sunspot, p. 829
prominence, p. 831
solar flare, p. 831
coronal mass ejection, p. 831
aurora, p. 832

1. **Chain-of-Events Chart** Create a chain-of-events chart to show how the solar wind interacts with Earth's magnetosphere to form auroras. SC.912.E.5.4

USING KEY TERMS

Use each of the following terms in a separate sentence.

2. *photosphere* SC.912.E.5.4

3. *solar flare* SC.912.E.5.4

4. *solar wind* SC.912.E.5.4

5. *sunspot cycle* SC.912.E.5.4

For each pair of terms, explain how the meanings of the terms differ.

6. *chromosphere* and *corona* SC.912.E.5.4

7. *photosphere* and *core* SC.912.E.5.4

8. *solar flare* and *prominence* SC.912.E.5.4

9. *aurora* and *solar wind* SC.912.E.5.4

UNDERSTANDING KEY IDEAS

10. According to Einstein's theory of relativity, in the formula $E = mc^2$, the c stands for SC.912.E.5.4
    a. corona.
    b. core.
    c. the speed of light.
    d. the length of time.

11. A nuclear reaction in which atomic nuclei combine is called SC.912.E.5.4
    a. fission.
    b. fusion.
    c. magnetism.
    d. granulation.

12. The part of the sun in which energy moves from atom to atom in the form of electromagnetic waves is called the SC.912.E.5.4
    a. radiative zone.
    b. convective zone.
    c. solar wind.
    d. chromosphere.

13. The number of hydrogen atoms that fuse to form a helium atom is SC.912.E.5.4
    a. two.
    c. six.
    b. four.
    d. eight.

14. The part of the sun that is normally visible from Earth is the SC.912.E.5.4
    a. core.
    c. corona.
    b. photosphere.
    d. solar nebula.

15. Sunspots are regions of SC.912.E.5.4
    a. intense magnetism.
    b. the core.
    c. high temperature.
    d. lighter color.

16. The sunspot cycle repeats about every SC.912.E.5.4
    a. month.
    c. 11 years.
    b. 5 years.
    d. 19 years.

17. Sudden outward eruptions of electrically charged particles from the sun are called
    a. prominences.
    c. sunspots. SC.912.E.5.4
    b. coronas.
    d. solar flares.

18. Gusts of solar wind can cause SC.912.E.5.4
    a. rotation.
    b. magnetic storms.
    c. nuclear fission.
    d. nuclear fusion.

19. *Northern lights* and *southern lights* are other names for SC.912.E.5.4
    a. prominences.
    b. auroras.
    c. granulations.
    d. total solar irradiance.

SHORT ANSWER

20. What is the outermost layer of the sun? SC.912.E.5.4

21. How is the solar activity cycle related to the sunspot cycle? SC.912.E.5.4

22. What is unusual about the magnetic field in a sunspot? SC.912.E.5.4

23. From what process does the sun gets its energy? What steps does this process follow? SC.912.E.5.4

24. Compare two types of solar activity. SC.912.E.5.4

25. Describe the corona, and identify when it is visible from Earth. SC.912.E.5.4

26. How does the transfer of energy in the radiative zone differ from the transfer of energy in the convective zone? SC.912.E.5.4

CRITICAL THINKING

27. Making Comparisons How is the transfer of energy in a pan of hot water similar to the transfer of energy in the sun's convective zone? SC.912.E.5.4

28. Making Comparisons Explain how the radiative zone in the sun is similar to the region between the sun and Earth. SC.912.E.5.4

29. Making Predictions Predict what would happen to the number of sunspots if parts of the sun's magnetic field suddenly increased in strength. SC.912.E.5.4

30. Drawing Conclusions If Earth's magnetosphere shifted so that solar wind was not deflected toward the poles but was deflected toward the equator, what would happen to the area where auroras are most often visible? SC.912.E.5.4

31. Analyzing Relationships Magnetic fields create electric currents that can damage electric power grids and interrupt the flow of electricity. How does this information help explain why strong magnetic storms can knock out power in cities? SC.912.E.5.4

32. Predicting Consequences How do scientists predict magnetic storms? List two ways that scientists on Earth could help people prepare for a very large magnetic storm. SC.912.E.5.4

CONCEPT MAPPING

33. Use the following terms to create a concept map: *sun, nuclear fusion, core, radiative zone, convective zone, photosphere,* and *corona.* SC.912.E.5.4

MATH SKILLS

34. Making Calculations On average, Earth is 1.5×10^8 km from the sun. A coronal mass ejection, or CME, can have a speed of 7×10^6 km/h. At this speed, how long would a CME take to reach Earth? SC.912.E.5.4

35. Applying Information A peak of the sunspot cycle occurred in the years 2000–2001. In what years will the next two peaks occur? SC.912.E.5.4

WRITING SKILLS

36. Creative Writing Write a short story that describes an imaginary trip to the center of the sun. Describe each layer and zone through which you would pass. SC.912.E.5.4

37. Writing from Research Research the northern lights. Write a short travel brochure that describes when and where to go to see the most spectacular and frequent displays of the auroras. SC.912.E.5.4

INTERPRETING GRAPHICS

The graph below shows how the latitudes of sunspots vary over time. Use the graph to answer the questions that follow.

Average Daily Sunspot Area

38. How many complete sunspot cycles are illustrated by the graph? SC.912.E.5.4

39. How does the range of latitudes of sunspots change over time? How is this change related to the sunspot cycle? SC.912.E.5.4

40. According to the graph, how many sunspots were located at the sun's north pole? SC.912.E.5.4

Understanding Concepts

Directions (1–8): For each question, write on a separate sheet of paper the letter of the correct answer.

1 What is the source of the sun's energy?
  A. nuclear fission reactions that break down massive nuclei to form lighter atoms
  B. nuclear fusion reactions that combine smaller nuclei to form more massive ones
  C. reactions that strip away electrons to form lighter atoms
  D. reactions that strip away electrons to form more massive atoms

2 The elements that make up the sun can be identified by using a spectrograph to
  F. count the number of dark lines in the spectrum of the sun.
  G. compare the spectrum of the sun to the spectra of various elements.
  H. subtract the number of dark lines in the spectrum hydrogen from the spectrum of the sun.
  I. identify which wavelengths of light are absorbed in the spectrum of the sun.

3 Which of the following statements does NOT describe a step of fusion?
  A. Two hydrogen nuclei collide and fuse.
  B. A proton joins a proton–neutron pair.
  C. Neutrinos escape the sun.
  D. Two nuclei made up of two protons and one neutron collide and fuse.

4 On average, the sun rotates every 27 days. Which of the following statements describes the rotation of the sun?
  F. Not all locations on the sun rotate at the same rate.
  G. Points near the poles rotate faster than points near the equator do.
  H. Only the sun's atmosphere rotates.
  I. The sun's rotation does not form a magnetic field.

5 What does the equation $E = mc^2$ describe?
  A. the amount of energy lost during fusion
  B. the speed of neutrinos
  C. the rate of fusion
  D. the amount of energy produced from a given amount of matter

6 Solar ejections are events that result in the emission of atomic particles. Which of the following statements does NOT describe a solar ejection?
  F. Clouds of glowing gases form huge arches that reach above the sun's surface.
  G. Electrically charged particles suddenly erupt outwards.
  H. Less energy is transferred in regions of the photosphere.
  I. Parts of the corona are thrown off the sun.

7 Which of the following statements best describes the relationship between the temperature of a region of the sun and the amount of fusion that takes place in that region?
  A. Fusion occurs in equal amounts in all regions of the sun, regardless of temperature.
  B. Fusion takes place in sunspots, which have the coolest temperatures on the sun.
  C. Fusion takes place in the region of the sun that has the highest temperature.
  D. Fusion takes place in regions of the sun that have moderate temperatures.

8 In addition to the sun, fusion occurs in all other active stars. Which of the following statements about fusion in stars is true?
  F. Only hydrogen undergoes fusion.
  G. Hydrogen undergoes fusion and forms many different types of elements.
  H. The only product of fusion is helium.
  I. Various types of elements can undergo fusion.

Interpreting Graphics

Directions (9–10): For each question below, record the correct answer on a separate sheet of paper.

Structure of the Sun

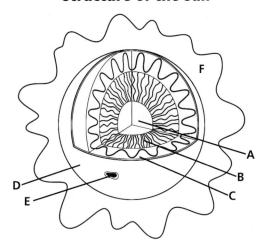

9 Fusion reactions provide power for the stars, such as the sun. In which part of the sun do these fusion reactions take place?

A. layer A
B. layer B
C. layer C
D. layer D

Earth's Magnetosphere

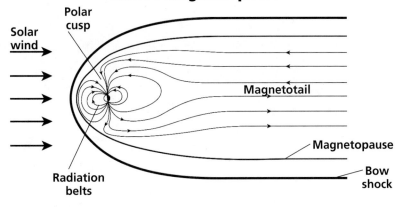

10 The figure above shows what happens when Earth's magnetic field interacts with solar wind. Based on the figure, which of the following statements is *most* likely true?

F. The magnetic field extends into space and protects Earth from solar wind.
G. Solar wind can reach Earth through the magnetotail.
H. The radiation belts completely surround Earth.
I. Solar wind cannot reach Earth's surface.

> **Test Tip**
>
> Choose the best possible answer for each question, even if you think there is another possible answer that is not given.

Chapter 30

Stars, Galaxies, and the Universe

Why It Matters

Our solar system is one small part of the universe. By studying stars and galaxies, we can learn more about the formation and evolution of the universe.

These reading tools will help you learn the material in this chapter.

Science Terms

Everyday Words Used in Science Many terms that are used in science are familiar words, taken from everyday speech. Scientists sometimes choose familiar words to describe things that are new, unfamiliar, or difficult to understand.

Your Turn In Section 2, you will learn about the objects listed in the table below. Based on your understanding of the familiar words that make up these terms, explain what you would expect them to mean in a table of your own. After reading Section 2, write the scientific definitions in your table.

Term	What I think it means	Scientific definition
white dwarf		
red giant		
supergiant		
black hole		

Fact, Hypothesis, or Theory?

Scientific Theories A scientific law describes or summarizes a pattern in nature. Scientific theories are sometimes confused with scientific laws, but they are not the same. The following statements apply to scientific theories:

- They explain observations or patterns in nature.
- They can be used to predict other observations or patterns.
- They may be revised or abandoned if reliable evidence contradicts them.

Your Turn In Section 4, the big bang theory is discussed in detail. On a sheet of paper, write "Big Bang Theory" and a definition of this theory. Then write a paragraph explaining why it is a theory.

Note Taking

Pattern Puzzles Pattern puzzles can help you remember information in the correct order. They can also help you review the steps of a process, such as a lab procedure or math solution. Below are the instructions for making a pattern puzzle.

1. Write down the steps of a process on a sheet of paper. Write one step per line.
2. Cut the sheet of paper into strips, with only one step per strip. Shuffle the strips.
3. Put the strips in their proper order. Then check the order in your textbook.

Your Turn As you read Section 2, write down the steps in the life cycle of a main-sequence star in order. If a step is long, divide it into two or three shorter steps. Then cut the steps into strips, shuffle them, and put them in order again. The first two steps are shown below.

> • An outside force compresses a nebula.

> • Some of the particles of the nebula are pulled toward each other by gravity.

For more information on how to use these and other tools, see **Appendix A**.

<table>
<tr><th>Key Ideas</th><th>Key Terms</th><th>Why It Matters</th></tr>
</table>

Key Ideas

> Describe how astronomers determine the composition and temperature of stars.
> Explain why stars appear to move in the sky.
> Describe one way astronomers measure the distances to stars.
> Explain the difference between absolute magnitude and apparent magnitude.

Key Terms

star
Doppler effect
light-year
parallax
apparent magnitude
absolute magnitude

Why It Matters

By analyzing sunlight, scientists discovered the element helium in the sun, a star, even before they found it on Earth. Today, we use helium in high-tech applications as well as in party balloons.

A star is a ball of gases that gives off a tremendous amount of electromagnetic energy. This energy comes from nuclear fusion within the star. *Nuclear fusion* is the combination of light atomic nuclei to form heavier atomic nuclei.

As seen from Earth, most stars in the night sky appear to be tiny specks of white light. However, if you look closely at the stars, you will notice that they vary in color. For example, the star Antares shines with a slightly reddish color, the star Rigel shines blue-white, and the star Arcturus shines with an orange tint. Our own star, the sun, is a yellow star.

Analyzing Starlight

Astronomers learn about stars primarily by analyzing the light that the stars emit. Astronomers direct starlight through *spectrographs*, which are devices that separate light into different colors, or wavelengths. Starlight passing through a spectrograph produces a display of colors and lines called a *spectrum*. There are three types of spectra: *emission*, or bright-line; *absorption*, or dark-line; and *continuous*.

All stars have *dark-line spectra*—bands of color crossed by dark lines where the color is diminished, as shown in **Figure 1.** A star's dark-line spectrum reveals the star's composition and temperature.

Stars are made up of different elements in the form of gases. While the inner layers of a star's photosphere are very hot, the outer layers are somewhat cooler. Elements in the outer layers absorb some of the light radiating from lower in the photosphere. Because different elements absorb different wavelengths of light, scientists can study the elements that make up a star, and find out from them how hot the star is by studying its spectrum.

FLORIDA STANDARDS

SC.912.E.5.3 Describe and predict how the initial mass of a star determines its evolution; **SC.912.E.5.8** Connect the concepts of radiation and the electromagnetic spectrum to the use of historical and newly-developed observational tools; **SC.912.E.5.11** Distinguish the various methods of measuring astronomical distances and apply each in appropriate situations.

star a large celestial body that is composed of gas and that emits light

Figure 1 The solar spectrum is shown here with each colored section on a new band.

Classification of Stars		
Color	Surface temperature (°C)	Examples
Blue	above 30,000	10 Lacertae
Blue-white	10,000–30,000	Rigel, Spica
White	7,500–10,000	Vega, Sirius
Yellow-white	6,000–7,500	Canopus, Procyon
Yellow	5,000–6,000	sun, Capella
Orange	3,500–5,000	Arcturus, Aldebaran
Red	less than 3,500	Betelgeuse, Antares

Figure 2 Stars in the sky show tinges of different colors, which reveal the temperatures of the stars' surfaces. Blue stars shine with the hottest temperatures, and red stars shine with the coolest.

READING TOOLBOX

Pattern Puzzle
Make a pattern puzzle that outlines the steps used by scientists to determine the elements that make up a star. Follow the instructions for making a pattern puzzle, given at the beginning of the chapter. See Appendix A for further instructions.

The Compositions of Stars

Every chemical element has a characteristic spectrum in a given range of temperatures. The colors and lines in the spectrum of a star indicate the elements that make up the star. Through spectrum analysis, scientists have learned that stars are made up of the same elements that compose Earth. But while the most common element on Earth is oxygen, the most common element in stars is hydrogen. Helium is the second most common element in stars. Elements such as carbon, oxygen, and nitrogen, usually in small quantities, make up most of the remaining one percent or so of the mass of stars.

The Temperatures of Stars

The surface temperature of a star is indicated by its color, as shown in **Figure 2.** Most star temperatures range from 2,800 °C to 24,000 °C, although some are hotter. Generally, blue stars have an average surface temperature of 35,000 °C. Red stars are the coolest, with average surface temperatures of 3,000 °C. Yellow stars, such as the sun, have surface temperatures of about 5,500 °C.

The Sizes and Masses of Stars

Stars also vary in size and mass. The smallest stars are slightly bigger than Jupiter, about one-seventh the size of our sun. Most stars are smaller and less massive than the sun. The sun, a medium-sized star, has a diameter of about 1,390,000 km. Some giant stars have diameters that are 1,000 times the sun's diameter. Most of the stars you can see in the night sky are medium-sized stars that are similar in size to our sun.

Many stars also have about the same mass as the sun, though some stars may be significantly more or less massive. Stars that are very dense may have more mass than the sun and still be much smaller than the sun. Less-dense stars may have a larger diameter than the sun has but still have less mass than the sun.

Stellar Motion

Two kinds of motion are associated with stars—actual motion through space and apparent motion across the night sky. Because stars are so far from Earth, their actual motion can be measured only with high-powered telescopes and specialized spacecraft. Apparent motion on any given night, on the other hand, is much more noticeable.

Apparent Motion of Stars

The *apparent motion* of stars, or motion as it appears from Earth, is caused by the movement of Earth. By aiming a camera at the sky and leaving the shutter open for a few hours, you can photograph the apparent motion of the stars. The curves of light in **Figure 3** record the apparent motion of stars in the northern sky. The circular trails make it seem as though the stars are moving counterclockwise around a central star called Polaris, or the North Star. The circular pattern is caused by the rotation of Earth on its axis. Polaris, which is not a very bright star, is almost directly above the North Pole, and thus the star does not appear to move much.

Earth's revolution around the sun causes the stars to appear to move in a second way. Stars located on the side of the sun opposite Earth are obscured by the sun. As Earth orbits the sun, however, different stars become visible during different seasons. The visible stars appear slightly to the west at a given time every night. Each night, most stars appear a small distance farther across the sky than they were at the same time the night before. After many months, some stars may finally disappear below the western horizon.

Reading Check **Why does Polaris appear to remain stationary in the night sky?** (See Appendix G for answers to Reading Checks.)

Figure 3 Stars appear as curved trails in this long-exposure photograph. These trails result from the rotation of Earth on its axis.

Circumpolar Stars

Some stars are always visible in the night sky. These stars never pass below the horizon in either their nightly or annual movements. In the Northern Hemisphere, the movement of these stars makes them appear to circle Polaris, the North Star. These circling stars are called *circumpolar stars*. The stars of the Little Dipper are circumpolar for most observers in the Northern Hemisphere. For a person at the North Pole, all visible stars are circumpolar. The farther the observer moves from the North Pole toward the equator, the fewer circumpolar stars the observer will be able to see.

Actual Motion of Stars

Most stars have several types of *actual motion*. First, they move across the sky, which can be seen only for the closest stars. Second, they may revolve around another star. Third, they either move away from or toward our solar system.

From a star's spectrum, astronomers can learn more about how that star is moving in space toward or away from Earth. The spectrum of such a star appears to shift, as shown in **Figure 4.** The apparent shift in the wavelength of light emitted by a light source moving toward or away from an observer is called the **Doppler effect.** The colors in the spectrum of a star moving toward Earth are shifted slightly toward blue. This shift, called *blue shift*, occurs because the light waves from a star appear to have shorter wavelengths as the star moves toward Earth.

A star moving away from Earth has a spectrum that is shifted slightly toward red. This shift, called *red shift*, occurs because the wavelengths of light appear to be longer. Distant galaxies all have red-shifted spectra, which indicates that all these galaxies are moving away from Earth.

Reading Check **What causes starlight to shift toward the red end of the spectrum?**

Doppler effect an observed change in the frequency of a wave when the source or observer is moving

Academic Vocabulary

occur (uh KUHR) happen

THINK central
INTERACT ONLINE
Keyword: HQXSTGF4

Figure 4 The light from stars is shifted based on the star's movement in relationship to Earth. For example, light from stars that are moving away from Earth is shifted slightly toward the red end of the spectrum.

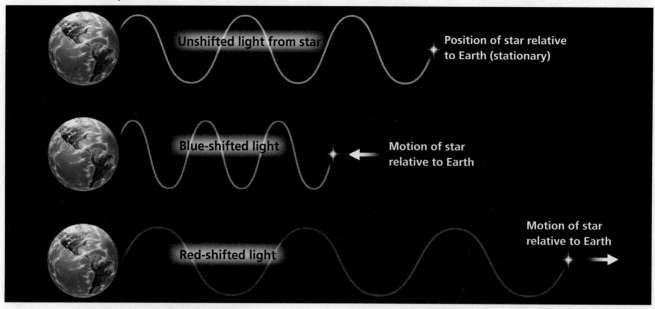

Unshifted light from star — Position of star relative to Earth (stationary)

Blue-shifted light — Motion of star relative to Earth

Red-shifted light — Motion of star relative to Earth

Distances to Stars

Because space is so vast, distances between the stars and Earth are measured in light-years. A **light-year** is the distance that light travels in one year. Because the speed of light is 300,000 km/s, light travels about 9.46 trillion km in one year. The light you see when you look at a star left that star sometime in the past. Light from the sun, for example, takes about 8 minutes to reach Earth. The sun is therefore 8 light-minutes from Earth. When we witness an event on the sun, such as a solar flare, the event actually took place about 8 minutes before we saw it.

Apart from the sun, the star nearest Earth is Proxima Centauri. This star is 4.2 light-years from Earth, nearly 300,000 times the distance from Earth to the sun. Polaris is about 430 light-years from Earth. When you look at Polaris, you see the star the way it was 430 years ago.

For relatively close stars, scientists can determine a star's distance by measuring **parallax,** the apparent shift in a star's position when viewed from different locations. As Earth orbits the sun, observers can study the stars from different perspectives, as shown in **Figure 5.** As Earth moves halfway around its orbit, a nearby star will appear to shift slightly relative to stars that are farther from Earth. The closer the star is to Earth, the larger the shift will be. Using this method from a spacecraft, astronomers measured the distance to about a million stars within 1,000 light-years of Earth.

Figure 5 Observers on Earth see nearby stars against those in the distant background. The movement of Earth causes nearby stars to appear to move.

light-year the distance that light travels in one year

parallax an apparent shift in the position of an object when viewed from different locations

---

SC.912.E.5.11

Quick Lab — Parallax

15 min

Procedure

❶ Use a metric ruler and scissors to cut five 1 m lengths of thread. Use masking tape to tape one end of each piece of thread to the edge of a paper plate. Each plate should have the same diameter. One plate should be red, and four should be blue.

❷ Stand on a ladder, and tape the free end of each piece of thread to the ceiling at various heights. Place the threads 30 cm apart in a staggered pattern. Hang the plates in a location that allows the widest field of view and movement.

❸ Stand directly in front of and facing the red plate at a distance of several meters.

❹ Close one eye, and sketch the position of the red plate in relation to the blue plates.

❺ Take several steps back and to the right. Repeat step 4.

❻ Take several more steps and make another sketch.

❼ Repeat step 6.

Analysis

1. Compare your drawings. Did the red plate change position as you viewed it from different locations? Explain your answer.

2. What results would you expect if you continued to repeat step 6? Explain your answer.

3. If you noted the positions of several stars by using a powerful telescope, what would you expect to observe about their positions if you saw the same stars six months later? Explain.

Figure 6 The sun, which has an apparent magnitude of –26.8, is the brightest object in our sky. All other objects appear dimmer in the sky, so their apparent magnitudes are higher on the scale.

Stellar Brightness

More than 3 billion stars can be seen through telescopes on Earth. Of these, only about 6,000 are visible without a telescope. Billions more stars can be observed from Earth-orbiting telescopes, such as the *Hubble Space Telescope*. The visibility of a star depends on its brightness and its distance from Earth. Astronomers use two scales to describe the brightness of a star.

The brightness of a star as it appears to us on Earth is called the star's **apparent magnitude.** The apparent magnitude of a star depends on both how much light the star emits and how far the star is from Earth. The lower the number of the star on the scale shown in **Figure 6,** the brighter the star appears to observers on Earth. The true brightness, or **absolute magnitude,** of a star is how bright the star would appear if all the stars were at a standard, uniform distance from Earth. The brighter a star actually is, the lower the number of its absolute magnitude.

apparent magnitude the brightness of a star as seen from the Earth

absolute magnitude the brightness that a star would have at a distance of 32.6 light-years from Earth

Section 1 Review

SC.912.E.5.3; SC.912.E.5.8; SC.912.E.5.11; SC.912.P.10.11; SC.912.P.12.7

Key Ideas

1. **Describe** what astronomers analyze to determine the composition and surface temperature of a star.

2. **Compare** the mass of the sun with the masses of most other stars in the universe.

3. **Explain** why, as you observe the night sky over time, stars appear to move westward across the sky.

4. **Describe** the units used to measure the distance to stars in terms of whether their starlight takes minutes or years to reach Earth.

5. **Describe** the method astronomers use to measure the distance to stars that are less than 1,000 light-years from Earth.

6. **Explain** the difference between apparent magnitude and absolute magnitude.

Critical Thinking

7. **Identifying Relationships** How does the movement of Earth affect the apparent movement of stars in the sky?

8. **Analyzing Ideas** Why is it better for astronomers to measure parallax by observing every six months instead of observing every year?

9. **Understanding Relationships** If two stars have the same absolute magnitude, but one of the stars is farther from Earth than the other one, which star would appear brighter in the night sky?

Concept Mapping

10. Use the following terms to create a concept map: *star, apparent magnitude, red shift, Doppler effect, light-year, absolute magnitude,* and *blue shift.*

Stellar Evolution

Key Ideas

❯ Describe how a protostar becomes a star.

❯ Explain how a main-sequence star generates energy.

❯ Describe the evolution of a star after its main-sequence stage.

Key Terms

main sequence

nebula

giant

white dwarf

nova

neutron star

pulsar

black hole

Why It Matters

Theories of stellar evolution help us to predict the age of our sun, as well as when it will stop shining. In fact, there's nothing to worry about.

FLORIDA STANDARDS

SC.912.E.5.3 Describe and predict how the initial mass of a star determines its evolution; **SC.912.P.10.19** Explain that all objects emit and absorb electromagnetic radiation and distinguish between objects that are blackbody radiators and those that are not; **SC.912.P.12.4** Describe how the gravitational force between two objects depends on their masses and the distance between them.

main sequence the location on the H-R diagram where most stars lie; it has a diagonal pattern from the lower right to the upper left

Because a typical star exists for billions of years, astronomers will never be able to observe one star throughout its entire lifetime. Instead, they have developed theories about the evolution of stars by studying stars in different stages of development.

Classifying Stars

Plotting the surface temperatures of stars against their *luminosity*, or the total amount of energy they give off each second, reveals a consistent pattern. The graph that illustrates this pattern is the *Hertzsprung-Russell diagram*, or *H-R diagram*, a simplified version of which is shown in **Figure 1.** The graph is named for Ejnar Hertzsprung and Henry Norris Russell, the astronomers who discovered the pattern nearly 100 years ago.

Astronomers plot the highest temperatures on the left and the highest luminosities at the top. The temperature and luminosity for most stars fall within a band that runs diagonally through the middle of the H-R diagram. This band, which extends from cool, dim, red stars at the lower right to hot, bright, blue stars at the upper left, is known as the **main sequence.** Stars within this band are called *main-sequence stars* or *dwarfs.* The sun is a main-sequence star.

Figure 1 The Hertzsprung-Russell Diagram

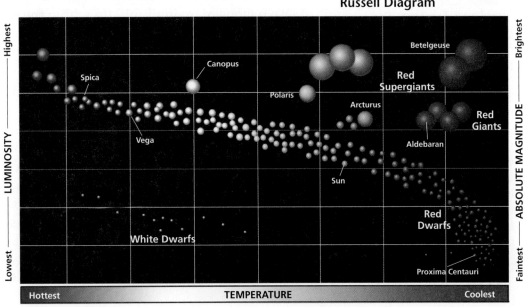

Figure 2 The Eagle Nebula is a region in which star formation is currently taking place. This false-color image of a small part of the Eagle Nebula was captured by the *Hubble Space Telescope*.

READING TOOLBOX

Scientific Theories vs. Scientific Laws
On a sheet of paper, write the name and definition of the law given on this page. Explain why it is a law, not a theory.

nebula a large cloud of gas and dust in interstellar space; a region in space where stars are born

Math Skills

Nuclear Fusion The sun converts nearly 545 million metric tons of hydrogen to helium every second. In the process, approximately 3.6 million metric tons of that hydrogen mass are changed into energy and radiated into space. What percentage of the converted hydrogen is changed into radiated energy? If the sun loses 3.6 million metric tons of mass per second, how many metric tons of mass will it lose in one year?

Star Formation

A star begins in a **nebula** (NEB yu luh), a cloud of gas and dust, such as the one shown in **Figure 2.** A nebula commonly consists of about 70% hydrogen, 28% helium, and 2% heavier elements. When an outside force, such as the explosion of a nearby star, compresses the cloud, some of the particles move close to each other and are pulled together by gravity. Alternatively, the collapse may start randomly, without an identifiable force.

According to Newton's *law of universal gravitation,* all objects in the universe attract each other with a force that increases as the mass of any object increases or as the distance between the objects decreases. Thus, as gravity pulls particles closer together, the attraction on each other increases. This pulls more nearby particles toward an area of increasing mass. As more particles come together, dense regions of matter build up within the nebula.

Protostars

As gravity makes these dense regions more compact, any spin the region has is greatly amplified. The shrinking, spinning region begins to flatten into a disk that has a central concentration of matter called a *protostar*. Gravitational energy is converted into heat energy as more matter is pulled into the protostar. This heat energy causes the temperature of the protostar to increase.

The protostar continues to contract and increase in temperature for several million years. Eventually, the gas becomes so hot that its electrons are stripped from their parent atoms. The nuclei and free electrons move independently, and the gas is then considered a separate state of matter called *plasma*. Plasma is a hot, ionized gas that has an equal number of free-moving positive ions and electrons.

The Birth of a Star

Temperature continues to increase in a protostar to about 10,000,000 °C. At this temperature, nuclear fusion begins. *Nuclear fusion* is a process that occurs when extremely high temperature and pressure cause less-massive atomic nuclei to combine to form more-massive nuclei and, in the process, release enormous amounts of energy. The onset of fusion marks the birth of a star. Once nuclear fusion begins in a star, the process can continue for billions of years.

A Delicate Balancing Act

As gravity increases the pressure on the matter within the star, the rate of fusion increases. In turn, the energy radiated from fusion reactions heats the gas inside the star. The outward pressures of the radiation and the hot gas resist the inward pull of gravity. The stabilizing effect of these forces is shown in **Figure 3.** This equilibrium makes the star stable in size. A main-sequence star maintains a stable size as long as the star has an ample supply of hydrogen to fuse into helium.

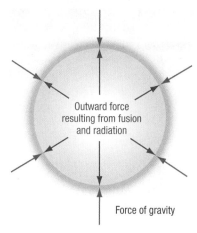

Outward force resulting from fusion and radiation

Force of gravity

Figure 3 Stellar equilibrium is achieved when the inward force of gravity is balanced by the outward pressure from fusion and radiation inside the star.

✔ Reading Check How does the pressure from fusion and hot gas interact with the force of gravity to maintain a star's stability?

The Main-Sequence Stage

The second and longest stage in the life of a star is the main-sequence stage. During this stage, energy continues to be generated in the core of the star as hydrogen fuses into helium. Fusion releases enormous amounts of energy. For example, when only 1 g of hydrogen is converted into helium, the energy released could keep a 100 W light bulb burning for more than 200 years.

A star that has a mass about the same as the sun's mass stays on the main sequence for about 10 billion years. More-massive stars, on the other hand, fuse hydrogen so rapidly that they may stay on the main sequence for only 10 million years. Because the universe is about 14 billion years old, massive stars that formed long ago have long since left the main sequence. Less massive stars, which are at the bottom right of the main sequence on the H-R diagram, are thought to be able to exist for hundreds of billions of years.

The stages in the life of a star cover an enormous period of time. Scientists estimate that over a period of almost 5 billion years, the sun, shown in **Figure 4,** has converted only 5% of its original hydrogen nuclei into helium nuclei. After another 5 billion years, though, with 10% of the sun's original hydrogen converted, the rate of fusion in the core will decrease significantly, causing the sun's temperature and luminosity to change. Then the sun will move off the main sequence.

Figure 4 Our sun is a yellow dwarf star. It is located in the diagonal band of main-sequence stars on the H-R diagram.

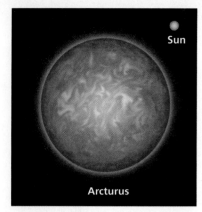

Figure 5 Arcturus is an orange giant that is about 23 times larger than the sun. Despite being about 1,000°C cooler than the sun, Arcturus gives off more than 100 times as much light as the sun does because it has so much surface area.

giant a very large and bright star whose hot core has used most of its hydrogen

Leaving the Main Sequence

A star enters its third stage when about 20% of the hydrogen atoms within its core have fused into helium atoms. The core of the star begins to contract under the force of its own gravity. This contraction increases the temperature in the core. As the helium core becomes hotter, it transfers energy into a thin shell of hydrogen surrounding the core. This energy causes hydrogen fusion to continue in the shell of gas. The on-going fusion of hydrogen radiates large amounts of energy outward, which causes the outer shell of the star to expand greatly.

Giant Stars

A star's shell of gases grows cooler as it expands. As the gases in the outer shell become cooler, their glow becomes reddish. These large, red stars are known as **giants** because they are larger than main-sequence stars of the same surface temperature.

Because of their large surface areas, giant stars are bright. Giants, such as the star Arcturus shown in **Figure 5,** are 10 or more times larger than the sun. Stars that contain about as much mass as the sun will become giants. As they become larger, more luminous, and cooler, they move off the main sequence. Giant stars are above the main sequence on the H-R diagram.

Supergiants

Main-sequence stars that are more massive than the sun will become larger than giants in their third stage. These highly luminous stars are called *supergiants*. These stars appear along the top of the H-R diagram. Supergiants are often at least 100 times larger than the sun. Betelgeuse, the large, orange-red star shown in **Figure 6,** is one example of a supergiant. Located in the constellation Orion, Betelgeuse is 1,000 times larger than the sun.

Though such supergiant stars make up only a small fraction of all the stars in the sky, their high luminosity makes the stars easy to find in a visual scan of the night sky. However, despite the high luminosity of supergiants, their surfaces are relatively cool.

Reading Check Where are giants and supergiants found on the H-R diagram?

Figure 6 If the sun were replaced by the red supergiant Betelgeuse, the surface of this star would be farther out than Jupiter's orbit. *How does the temperature of Betelgeuse compare with that of the sun?*

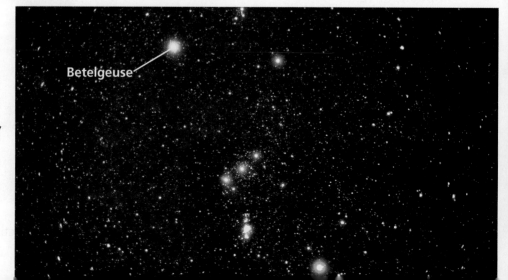

The Final Stages of a Sunlike Star

In the evolution of a medium-sized star, fusion in the core will stop after the helium atoms have fused into carbon and oxygen. With energy no longer available from fusion, the star enters its final stages.

Planetary Nebulas

As the star's outer gases drift away, the remaining core heats these expanding gases. The gases appear as a *planetary nebula*, a cloud of gas that forms around a sunlike star that is dying. Some of these clouds may form a simple sphere or ring around the star. However, many planetary nebulas form more-complex shapes. For example, the Ant nebula has a double-lobed shape, as shown in **Figure 7**.

White Dwarfs

As a planetary nebula disperses, gravity causes the remaining matter in the star to collapse inward. The matter collapses until it cannot be pressed further together. A hot, extremely dense core of matter—a **white dwarf**—is left. White dwarfs shine for billions of years before they cool completely.

White dwarfs are in the lower left of the H-R diagram. They are hot but dim. These stars are very small, about the size of Earth. As white dwarfs cool, they become fainter. This is the final stage in the life cycle of many stars.

Figure 7 The Ant nebula is a planetary nebula that is located more than 3,000 light-years from Earth in the southern constellation Norma.

white dwarf a small, hot, dim star that is the leftover center of an old sunlike star

Novas and Supernovas

Some white dwarf stars are part of binary star systems. If a white dwarf revolves around a red giant, the gravity of the very dense white dwarf may capture loosely held gases from the red giant. As these gases accumulate on the surface of the white dwarf, pressure begins to build up. This pressure may cause large explosions, which release energy and stellar material into space. Such an explosion is called a **nova.**

A nova may cause a star to become many thousands of times brighter than it normally is. However, within days, the nova begins to fade to its normal brightness. Because these explosions rarely disrupt the stability of the binary system, the process may start again and a white dwarf may become a nova several times.

A white dwarf star in a binary system may also become a *supernova*, a star that has such a tremendous explosion that it blows itself apart. Unlike an ordinary nova, a white dwarf can sometimes accumulate so much mass on its surface that gravity overwhelms the outward pressure. The star collapses and becomes so dense that the outer layers rebound and explode outward. Supernovas are thousands of times more violent than novas. The explosions of supernovas completely destroy the white dwarf star and may destroy much of the red giant.

The Final Stages of Massive Stars

Stars that have masses of more than 8 times the mass of the sun may produce supernovas without needing a secondary star to fuel them. In 1054, Chinese astronomers saw a supernova so bright that it was seen during the day for more than three weeks. At its peak, the supernova radiated an amount of energy that was equal to the output of about 400 million suns.

nova a star that suddenly becomes brighter

Life Cycle of Stars

Nebula

Protostar

Star like the sun

Protostar

Massive star

Supernovas in Massive Stars

While only a small percentage of white dwarfs become supernovas, massive stars become supernovas as part of their life cycle, which is shown in **Figure 8.** After the supergiant stage, these stars contract with a gravitational force that is much greater than that of small-mass stars. The collapse produces such high pressures and temperatures that nuclear fusion begins again. This time, carbon atoms in the core of the star fuse into heavier elements such as oxygen, magnesium, or silicon.

Fusion continues until the core is almost entirely made of iron. Because iron has a very stable nuclear <u>structure</u>, fusion of iron into heavier elements takes energy from the star rather than giving off energy. Having used up its supply of fuel, the core begins to collapse under its own gravity. Energy released as the core collapses is transferred to the outer layers of the star, which explode outward with tremendous force. Within a few minutes, the energy released by the supernova may surpass the amount of energy radiated by a sunlike star over its entire lifetime.

✓ Reading Check What causes a supergiant star to explode as a supernova?

Neutron Stars

Stars that contain about 8 or more times the mass of the sun do not become white dwarfs. After a star explodes as a supernova, the core may contract into a very small but incredibly dense ball of neutrons, called a **neutron star.** A single teaspoon of matter from a neutron star would have a mass of 2×10^{30} kilograms (a 2 followed by 30 zeroes). A neutron star that has more mass than the sun may have a diameter of only about 20 km but may emit the same amount of energy as 100,000 suns. Neutron stars rotate very rapidly.

Academic Vocabulary

structure (STRUHK chuhr) the arrangement of the parts of a whole; a whole that is built or put together from parts

neutron star a star that has collapsed under gravity to the point that the electrons and protons have smashed together to form neutrons

Figure 8 A star the mass of the sun becomes a white dwarf near the end of its life cycle. A more massive star may become a neutron star.

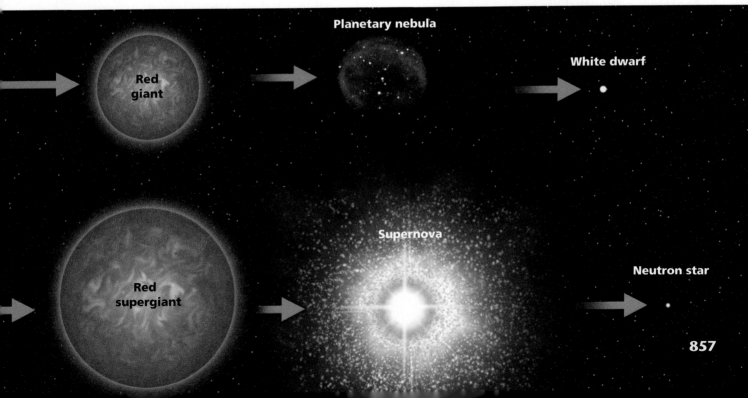

Red giant — Planetary nebula — White dwarf

Red supergiant — Supernova — Neutron star

Pulsars

Some neutron stars emit a beam of radio waves that sweeps across space like a lighthouse light beam sweeps across water. Because we detect pulses of radio waves every time the beam sweeps by Earth, these stars are called **pulsars.** For each pulse we detect, we know that the star has rotated within that period. Newly formed pulsars, such as the one shown in **Figure 9,** are commonly surrounded by the remnants of a supernova. But most known pulsars are so old that these remnants have long since dispersed and have left behind only the spinning star.

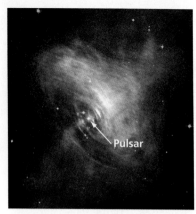

Figure 9 This pulsar, located in the heart of the Crab nebula, is still surrounded by the remains of a supernova explosion that took place less than 1,000 years ago.

pulsar a rapidly spinning neutron star that emits pulses of radio and optical energy

black hole an object so massive and dense that even light cannot escape its gravity

Black Holes

Some massive stars produce leftovers too massive to become stable neutron stars. If the remaining core of a star contains more than 3 times the mass of the sun, the star may contract further under its greater gravity. The force of the contraction crushes the dense core of the star and leaves a **black hole.** The gravity of a black hole is so great that nothing, not even light, can escape it.

Because black holes do not give off light, locating them is difficult. But a black hole can be observed by its effect on a companion star. Matter from the companion star is pulled into the black hole. Just before the matter is absorbed, it swirls around the black hole. The gas becomes so hot that X rays are released. Astronomers locate black holes by detecting these X rays. Scientists then try to find the mass of the object that is affecting the companion star. Astronomers conclude that a black hole exists only if the companion star's motion shows that a massive, invisible object is present nearby.

Section 2 Review

SC.912.E.5.3; SC.912.E.5.6; SC.912.P.10.10;
SC.912.P.10.11; SC.912.P.10.19; SC.912.P.12.4

Key Ideas

1. **Explain** the steps that the gas in a nebula goes through as it becomes a star.

2. **Describe** the process that generates energy in the core of a main-sequence star.

3. **Explain** how a main-sequence star like the sun is able to maintain a stable size.

4. **Describe** how nuclear fusion in a main-sequence star is different from nuclear fusion in a giant star.

5. **Describe** how a star similar to the sun changes after it leaves the main-sequence stage of its life cycle.

6. **Describe** what causes a nova explosion.

7. **Explain** why only very massive stars can form black holes.

8. **Describe** two types of supernovas.

Critical Thinking

9. **Identifying Relationships** How do astronomers conclude that a supergiant star is larger than a main-sequence star of the same temperature?

10. **Analyzing Ideas** Why would an older main-sequence star be composed of a higher percentage of helium than a young main-sequence star?

11. **Compare and Contrast** Why does temperature increase more rapidly in a more massive protostar than in a less massive protostar?

12. **Analyzing Ideas** How can astronomers detect a black hole if it is invisible to an optical telescope?

Concept Mapping

13. Use the following terms to create a concept map: *main-sequence star, nebula, supergiant, white dwarf, planetary nebula, black hole, supernova, protostar, giant, pulsar,* and *neutron star.*

Key Ideas

❯ Describe the characteristics that identify a constellation.

❯ Describe the three main types of galaxies.

❯ Explain how a quasar differs from a typical galaxy.

Key Terms

constellation

galaxy

quasar

Why It Matters

People have used the stars for thousands of years to help them navigate and to know when to plant crops.

FLORIDA STANDARDS

SC.912.E.5.2 Identify patterns in the organization and distribution of matter in the universe and the forces that determine them.

When you look into the sky on a clear night, you see what appear to be individual stars. These visible stars are only some of the trillions of stars that make up the universe. Most of the ones we see are within 100 light-years of Earth. However, in the constellation Andromeda, there is a hazy region that is actually a huge collection of stars, gas, and dust. This region is more than two million light-years from Earth. It is the farthest one can see with the unaided eye.

Constellations

By using a star chart and observing carefully, you can identify many star groups that form star patterns or regions. Although the stars that make up a pattern appear to be close together, they are not all the same distance from Earth. In fact, they may be very distant from one another, as shown in **Figure 1.**

If you look at the same region of the sky for several nights, the positions of the stars in relation to one another do not appear to change. Because of the tremendous distance from which the stars are viewed, they appear fixed in their patterns. For more than 3,000 years, people have observed and recorded these patterns. These patterns of stars and the region of space around them are called **constellations.**

constellation one of 88 regions into which the sky has been divided in order to describe the locations of celestial objects; a group of stars organized in a recognizable pattern

Dividing Up the Sky

In 1930, astronomers around the world agreed upon a standard set of 88 constellations. The stars of these constellations and the regions around them divide the sky into sectors. Just as you can use a road map to locate a particular town, you can use a map of the constellations to locate a particular star. Star charts can be found in Appendix F.

Figure 1 The Constellation Orion

Distance (ly)

Academic Vocabulary

association (uh SOH see AY shuhn) a connection or combination

galaxy a collection of stars, dust, and gas bound together by gravity

Multiple-Star Systems

Stars are not always solitary objects isolated in space. When two or more stars are closely associated, they form multiple-star systems. *Binary stars* are pairs of stars that revolve around each other and are held together by gravity. In systems where the two stars have similar masses, the center of mass, or *barycenter*, will be somewhere between the stars. If one star is more massive than the other, the barycenter will be closer to the more massive star.

Multiple-star systems sometimes have more than two stars. In such a star system, two stars may revolve rapidly around a common barycenter, while a third star revolves more slowly at a greater distance from the pair. Astronomers estimate that more than half of all sunlike stars are part of multiple-star systems.

Reading Check What percentage of stars similar to the sun are in multiple-star systems?

Star Clusters

Sometimes, nebulas collapse to form groups of hundreds or thousands of stars, called clusters. *Globular clusters* have a spherical shape and can contain up to one million stars. An *open cluster*, such as the one shown in **Figure 2**, is loosely shaped and rarely contains more than a few hundred stars.

Galaxies

A large-scale group of stars, gas, and dust that is bound together by gravity is called a **galaxy**. Galaxies are the major building blocks of the universe. A typical galaxy, such as the Milky Way galaxy in which we live, has a diameter of about 100,000 light-years and may contain more than 200 billion stars. Astronomers estimate that the universe contains hundreds of billions of galaxies.

Distances to Galaxies

Some stars allow astronomers to find distances to the galaxies that contain the stars. For example, giant stars called *Cepheid* (SEF ee id) *variables* brighten and fade in a regular pattern. Most Cepheids have regular cycles that range from 1 to 100 days. The longer a Cepheid's cycle is, the brighter the star's visual absolute magnitude is. By comparing the Cepheid's absolute magnitude and the Cepheid's apparent magnitude, astronomers calculate the distance to the Cepheid variable. This distance, in turn, tells them the distance to the galaxy in which the Cepheid is located.

Figure 2 The open cluster M50 is made up of hundreds of stars. It is located about 3,000 light-years from Earth.

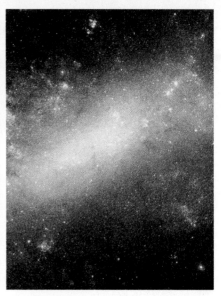

Figure 3 The three main types of galaxies are spiral (left), elliptical (center), and irregular (right).

Types of Galaxies

In studying galaxies, astronomers found that galaxies could be classified by shape into the three main types shown in **Figure 3.** The most common type of large galaxy, called a *spiral galaxy*, has a nucleus of bright stars and flattened arms that spiral around the nucleus. The spiral arms consist of billions of young stars, gas, and dust. Some have a straight bar of stars that runs through the center. These galaxies are called *barred spiral galaxies*.

Galaxies of the second type vary in shape from nearly spherical to very elongated, like a stretched-out football. These galaxies are called *elliptical galaxies*. They are extremely bright in the center and do not have spiral arms. Elliptical galaxies have few young stars and contain little dust and gas.

The third type of galaxy, called an *irregular galaxy*, has no particular shape. These galaxies usually have low total masses and are fairly rich in dust and gas. Irregular galaxies make up only a small percentage of the total number of observed galaxies.

The Milky Way

If you look into the night sky, you may see what appears to be a cloudlike band that stretches across the sky. Because of its milky appearance, this part of the sky is called the Milky Way. We see this band of stars when looking through the dense plane of our own galaxy.

The *Milky Way galaxy* is a spiral galaxy in which the sun is one of hundreds of billions of stars. Each star orbits around the center of the Milky Way galaxy. It takes the sun about 225 million years to complete one orbit around the galaxy.

Two irregular galaxies, the Large Magellanic Cloud and Small Magellanic Cloud, are our closest neighbors. Even so, these galaxies are each more than 170,000 light-years away from Earth. Within 5 million light-years of the Milky Way are about 30 other galaxies. These galaxies and the Milky Way galaxy are collectively called the *Local Group*.

SC*LINKS.*

www.scilinks.org
Topic: Galaxies
Code: HQX0632

Figure 4 The jets of gas projected from a quasar can extend for more than 100,000 light-years. Quasars are too distant to be clearly photographed. The image shown is an artist's rendition of a quasar. The smaller inset is an actual image taken by the *Chandra X-Ray Observatory.*

Quasars

Discovered in 1963, quasars used to be the most puzzling objects in the sky. Viewed through an optical telescope, a quasar appears as a point of light, almost in the same way that a small, faint star would appear. The word **quasar** is a shortened term for *quasi-stellar radio source.* The prefix *quasi-* means "similar to," and the word *stellar* means "star." Quasars are not related to stars, but quasars are related to galaxies. Some quasars project a jet of gas, as shown in **Figure 4.**

Astronomers have discovered that quasars are located in the centers of galaxies that are distant from Earth. Galaxies that have quasars in them differ from other galaxies in that the quasars in their centers are very bright. The large amount of energy emitted from such a small volume could be explained by the presence of a giant black hole. The mass of such black holes is estimated to be billions of times the mass of our sun. Quasars are among the most distant objects that have been observed from Earth.

quasar quasi-stellar radio source; a very luminous object that produces energy at a high rate

Section 3 Review

LA.910.2.2.3; SC.912.E.5.2

Key Ideas

1. **Identify** the characteristics of a constellation.

2. **List** the three basic types of galaxies.

3. **Describe** the Milky Way galaxy in terms of galaxy types.

4. **Describe** the difference between a typical galaxy and a quasar.

Critical Thinking

5. **Identifying Relationships** Explain how stars can form a constellation when seen from Earth but can still be very far from each other.

6. **Making Calculations** The sun orbits the center of the Milky Way galaxy every 225 million years. How many revolutions has the sun made since the formation of Earth 4.6 billion years ago?

7. **Analyzing Ideas** Why are the constellations that are seen in the winter sky different from those seen in the summer sky?

Concept Mapping

8. Use the following terms to create a concept map: *galaxy, elliptical galaxy, Milky Way galaxy, irregular galaxy, barred spiral galaxy,* and *spiral galaxy.*

The Big Bang Theory

Key Ideas	Key Terms	Why It Matters
❯ Explain how Hubble's discoveries led to an understanding that the universe is expanding. ❯ Summarize the big bang theory. ❯ List evidence for the big bang theory.	cosmology big bang theory cosmic background radiation	Studying the origin, structure, and future of the universe helps us better understand our origins and our place in the universe.

The study of the origin, structure, and future of the universe is called **cosmology.** Cosmologists, or people who study cosmology, are concerned with processes that affect the universe as a whole. Like the parts found within it, the universe is always changing. While some astronomers study how planets, stars, or galaxies form and evolve, a cosmologist studies how the entire universe formed and tries to predict how it will change in the future.

Like all scientific theories, theories about the origin and evolution of the universe must constantly be tested against new observations and experiments. Many current theories of the universe began with observations made less than 100 years ago.

Hubble's Observations

Just as the light from a single star can be used to make a stellar spectrum, scientists can also use the light given off by an entire galaxy to create the spectrum for that galaxy. In the early 1900s, finding the spectrum of a galaxy could take the whole night, or even several nights. Although collecting new spectra was very time consuming, the astronomer Edwin Hubble used these galactic spectra to uncover new information about our universe.

Measuring Red Shifts

Near the end of the 1920s, Hubble found that the spectra of galaxies, except for the few closest to Earth, were shifted toward the red end of the spectrum. By examining the amount of red shift, he determined the speed at which the galaxies were moving away from Earth. Hubble found that the most distant galaxies showed the greatest red shift and thus were moving away from Earth the fastest.

Many distant galaxies are shown in **Figure 1.** Modern telescopes that have electronic cameras can take images of hundreds of spectra per hour. These spectra all confirm Hubble's original findings.

cosmology the study of the origin, properties, processes, and evolution of the universe

Figure 1 This image from the *Hubble Space Telescope* shows hundreds of galaxies. These galaxies all have large red shifts, so they are moving away from Earth very fast.

Figure 2 Like raisins in expanding cake batter, the farther galaxies are from each other, the faster they move away from each other.

THINK
central
INTERACT ONLINE
(Keyword: HQXSTGF2)

big bang theory the theory that all matter and energy in the universe was compressed into an extremely small volume that 13 to 15 billion years ago exploded and began expanding in all directions

The Expanding Universe

Imagine a raisin cake rising in a kitchen oven. If you were able to sit on one raisin, you would see all the other raisins moving away from you. Raisins that are farther away in the dough when it begins rising move away faster because there is more cake between you and them and because the whole cake is expanding. The situation is similar with galaxies and the universe, as shown in **Figure 2.** By using Hubble's observations, astronomers were able to determine that the universe was expanding.

A Theory Emerges

Although cosmologists have proposed several different theories to explain the expansion of the universe, the current and most widely accepted is the big bang theory. The **big bang theory** states that billions of years ago, all the matter and energy in the universe was compressed into an extremely small volume. If you trace the expanding universe back in time, all matter would have been close together at one point in time. About 14 billion years ago, a sudden event called the *big bang* sent all of the matter and energy outward in all directions.

As the universe expanded, some of the matter gathered into clumps that evolved into galaxies. Today, the universe is still expanding, and the galaxies continue to move apart from one another. This expansion of space explains the red shift that we detect in the spectra of galaxies. **Figure 3** shows a timeline of events following the big bang.

By the mid-20th century, almost all astronomers accepted the big bang theory. An important discovery in the 1960s finally convinced most of the remaining scientists that a sudden event, the big bang, had taken place.

Reading Check What does the big bang theory tell us about the early universe?

Figure 3 A Big Bang Timeline

Quick Lab   The Expanding Universe

SC.912.E.5.1

15 min

Procedure

❶ Use a **marker** to make 3 dots in a row on an uninflated **balloon.** Label them "A," "B," and "C." Dot B should be closer to A than dot C is to B.

❷ Blow the balloon up just until it is taut. Pinch the balloon to keep it inflated, but do not tie the neck.

❸ Use **string** and a **ruler** to measure the distances between A and B, B and C, and A and C.

❹ With the balloon still inflated, blow into the balloon until its diameter is twice as large.

❺ Measure the distances between A and B, B and C, and A and C. For each set of dots, subtract the original distances measured in step 3 from the new distances. Then, divide by 2, because the balloon is about twice as large. This

calculation will give you the rate of change for each pair of dots.

❻ Repeat steps 4 and 5.

Analysis

1. Did the distance between A and B, between B and C, or between A and C show the greatest rate of change?

2. Suppose dot A represents Earth and that dots B and C represent galaxies. How does the rate at which galaxies are moving away from us relate to how far they are from Earth?

Cosmic Background Radiation

In 1965, researchers using radio telescopes detected **cosmic background radiation,** or low levels of energy evenly distributed throughout the universe. Astronomers concluded that this background radiation formed shortly after the big bang.

The universe soon after the big bang would have been very hot and would have cooled to a great extent by now. The energy of the background radiation has a temperature of only about 3 °C above *absolute zero,* the coldest temperature possible. Because absolute zero is about –273 °C, the cosmic background radiation's temperature is about 270 °C below zero.

Like any theory, the big bang theory must continue to be tested against each new discovery about the universe. But the big bang theory has been well tested, and any changes are likely to be modifications of the general concept.

cosmic background radiation radiation uniformly detected from every direction in space; considered a remnant of the big bang

Figure 4 This display is shown on half a globe that represents the sky as seen from Earth orbit. The temperature difference between the red spots and the blue spots is only 2/10,000 °C.

Ripples in Space

Maps of cosmic background radiation over the whole sky look very smooth. But on satellite maps that show where temperatures differ from the average background temperature, "ripples" become apparent, as shown in **Figure 4.** These ripples are irregularities in the cosmic background radiation, which were caused by small fluctuations in the distribution of matter in the early universe. The ripples are thought to indicate the first stages in the formation of the universe's first galaxies.

865

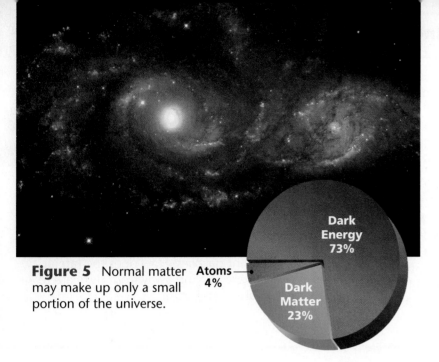

Figure 5 Normal matter may make up only a small portion of the universe.

Dark Energy 73%

Atoms 4%

Dark Matter 23%

A Universe of Surprises

Recent data based on the ripples in the cosmic background radiation and studies of the distance to super-novas found in ancient galaxies have forced astronomers to rethink some of the theories about what makes up the universe. Astronomers now think that the universe is made up of more mass and energy than they can currently detect.

Dark Matter

Surprisingly, analyzing the ripples in the cosmic background radiation suggests that the kinds of matter that humans, the planets, the stars, and the matter between the stars are made of makes up only 4% of the universe, as shown in **Figure 5**. Another 23% of the universe is made up of a type of matter that does not give off light but that has gravity that we can detect. Because this type of matter does not give off light, it is called *dark matter*.

Dark Energy

Another surprise is that most of the universe is composed of something that we know almost nothing about. The unknown material is called *dark energy*, and scientists think that it acts as a force that opposes gravity. Recent evidence suggests that distant galaxies are farther from Earth than current theory would indicate. So, many scientists conclude that some form of undetectable dark energy is pushing galaxies apart. Because of dark energy, the universe is not only expanding, but the rate of expansion also seems to be accelerating.

SCiLINKS

www.scilinks.org
Topic: Big Bang
Code: HQX0146

READING TOOLBOX

Everyday Words Used in Science
How would you define *dark matter* and *dark energy*? Compare your definitions with those on this page.

Section 4 Review

🏴 LA.910.2.2.3; SC.912.E.5.1; SC.912.E.5.2; SC.912.E.5.3; SC.912.E.5.7

Key Ideas

1. **Describe** how red shifts were used by cosmologists to determine that the universe is expanding.

2. **Summarize** the big bang theory.

3. **List** evidence that supports the big bang theory.

4. **Compare** the amount of visible matter in the universe with the total amount of matter and energy.

Critical Thinking

5. **Inferring Relationships** How did the distribution of matter in the early universe affect how we are able to detect cosmic background radiation today?

6. **Evaluating Theories** Use the big bang theory to explain why scientists do not expect to find galaxies that have large blue shifts.

7. **Identifying Relationships** Why do observations made of distant galaxies indicate that dark energy exists?

Concept Mapping

8. Use the following terms to create a concept map: *cosmic background radiation, dark energy, red shift, dark matter, big bang theory,* and *galaxies.*

A Cool Telescope

Every year, over 100 researchers brave the coldest, windiest place on Earth to use a special telescope that looks deep inside Earth. Why? This special telescope, called IceCube, is searching for hints of the origins of the universe. Pure, deep Antarctic ice provides the perfect observatory for detecting subatomic particles called neutrinos that reach Earth from far across space.

The average depth of an IceCube hole is nearly 2.5 km below the surface. These holes are drilled using hot water, producing approximately 750,000 L of melted ice in the process. It took about 57 hours to drill IceCube's first hole.

 YOUR TURN

UNDERSTANDING CONCEPTS
What is the telescope IceCube designed to do?

CRITICAL THINKING
How might life at a research station on Antarctica be similar to, and different from, life on the International Space Station?

Star Magnitudes

What You'll Do

› **Construct** a model photometer and two model stars.

› **Demonstrate** how distance affects the brightness of stars.

› **Explain** how color is related to the temperature of stars.

What You'll Need

aluminum foil, 12 cm × 12 cm
batteries, AA (3)
desk lamp with incandescent bulb
flashlight bulbs, 3-volt (2)
paraffin, 12 cm × 6 cm bricks (2)
rubber band, large
ruler, metric
tape, electrical
wire, plastic-coated with stripped ends, 15 cm
wire, plastic-coated with stripped ends, 20 cm

Safety

Among other things, astronomers study the brightness, or magnitude, of stars. Except for the sun, stars are very faint and visible only at night. Thus, their brightness must be measured with a device called a *photometer* or, more recently, a CCD (charge-coupled device). An astronomical photometer consists of a surface that is sensitive to light and a device that measures the amount of light that reaches the surface. Photometers can also be used to compare the colors of different light sources. In this lab, you will determine the effect of distance on brightness and the relationship between temperature and color.

Procedure

1. Construct two flashlights:

   a. Arrange the bulbs and batteries as shown in the figure below. Using electrical tape, attach the wires to the batteries and bulbs. The bulbs should be on. If they are not on, study the illustration again and make adjustments.

   b. Tape the flashlight arrangements together so that they can be moved. Be sure to leave the wires loose at the negative ends of the batteries so that you can turn your flashlights on and off.

2. Construct a model photometer by folding the aluminum foil in half with the shiny side facing out, and placing it between two paraffin bricks. Hold the pieces together using a rubber band.

3. Place the two flashlights about 2 m apart on a table. Place the photometer between them with the largest sides of the bricks facing each flashlight bulb, as shown in the figure below.

4. Turn on both flashlights, and turn off all room lights.

5. Move the photometer until both sides are equally bright. Measure the distance, in centimeters, from each flashlight bulb to the center of the photometer. Record these measurements.

Step ❶

Rubber band

Paraffin bricks

Aluminum foil

6 Square the distances you recorded in step 5. Record these values.

7 Incandescent light bulbs have filaments that emit light at a temperature that is much cooler than the sun's surface. Place the photometer between the desk lamp and a window on a bright day. Sunlight coming through a window will be the same color as the sunlight outdoors. Turn off any fluorescent ceiling lighting, and turn on the desk lamp.

8 Compare the color differences between the paraffin sides of your photometer.

9 Darken the room once again, and compare the colors of the bulb powered by one battery with the colors of the bulb powered by two batteries.

Step 8

Analysis

1. **Analyzing Data** The ratio of the square of the distances you calculated in step 6 is equal to the ratio of the brightnesses of the bulbs. What is the ratio of the square of the distance of the two-battery flashlight to that of the one-battery flashlight? What does this information tell you about the relationship between the brightness of the two flashlights?

2. **Drawing Conclusions** Based on the results of the investigation, would you expect a white star to be hotter or cooler than a yellow star?

3. **Applying Conclusions** Using your knowledge of the spectrum, would you expect a white star to be hotter or cooler than an orange star? Predict whether a blue star is hotter or cooler than a white star. Also, predict whether a red star is hotter or cooler than an orange star.

Extension

Explaining Observations Find an incandescent bulb controlled by a dimmer. Watch the color of the light as it fades. Does it become more yellow or more white? Explain why.

MAPS in Action

The Milky Way

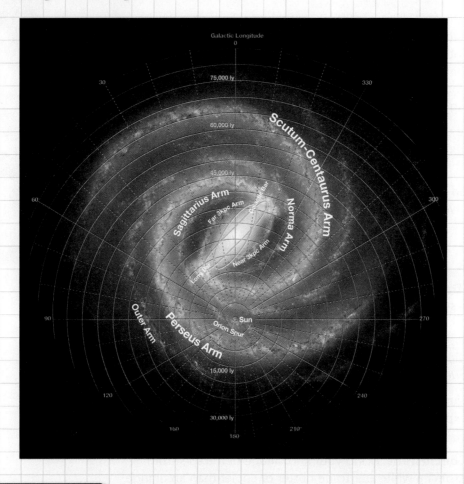

Map ▶ Skills Activity

The map above shows what astronomers think the Milky Way galaxy looks like. Because of Earth's position within the galaxy, scientists must hypothesize what our galaxy looks like from a perspective outside of the galaxy. They must also form a hypothesis about the shape and location of those spiral arms that are obscured by either the galactic core or other spiral arms that are closer to Earth. Use the map to answer the questions below.

1. **Using a Key** What is the approximate distance from one edge of the Milky Way to the other edge?

2. **Analyzing Data** What is the approximate width of the galactic core through its long axis?

3. **Inferring Relationships** How are the Sagittarius Arm and the Orion Spur related to each other?

4. **Identifying Locations** In which feature of the galaxy is the solar system located?

5. **Identifying Trends** What happens to the arms of the Milky Way as they radiate outward from the center of the galaxy?

6. **Evaluating Data** As shown on this map, the Milky Way is a barred spiral galaxy with two major arms each attached to opposite ends of the galactic core. Considering the shape of these arms, in which direction is the galaxy rotating when viewed from this perspective?

Key Ideas

Key Terms

Characteristics of Stars

> To determine its composition and surface temperature, astronomers study a star's spectrum.

> Stars appear to move in the sky because of the Earth's rotational movement.

> Astronomers measure the distance to stars using the distance light travels in one year (the light-year) and the apparent shift in a star's position when viewed from different locations (parallax).

> Apparent magnitude is a star's brightness as it appears to us on Earth. Absolute magnitude is its true brightness if all stars were at a standard, uniform distance from Earth.

star, p. 845
Doppler effect, p. 848
light-year, p. 849
parallax, p. 849
apparent magnitude, p. 850
absolute magnitude, p. 850

Stellar Evolution

> A protostar becomes a star when its hydrogen begins to fuse to form helium.

> Main-sequence stars generate energy through hydrogen fusion.

> Sunlike stars may become planetary nebulas and then white dwarfs. Massive stars may become supernovas and then neutron stars, pulsars, or black holes.

main sequence, p. 851
nebula, p. 852
giant, p. 854
white dwarf, p. 855
nova, p. 856
neutron star, p. 857
pulsar, p. 858
black hole, p. 858

Star Groups

> A constellation contains a recognizable star pattern and can be used to locate celestial objects.

> The three types of galaxies are spiral, elliptical, and irregular.

> Quasars are very bright, distant galaxies that are thought to have enormous black holes in their centers.

constellation, p. 859
galaxy, p. 860
quasar, p. 862

The Big Bang Theory

> Hubble found that the spectra of galaxies are red-shifted, indicating they are moving away from Earth and from each other.

> The big bang theory states that, about 14 billion years ago, all matter and energy in the universe was compressed into an extremely small volume that began to expand in all directions.

> Evidence for the big bang theory includes red shifts, cosmic background radiation, and ripples in space.

cosmology, p. 863
big bang theory, p. 864
cosmic background radiation, p. 865

1. **Scientific Theories vs. Scientific Laws**
As you review Newton's law of universal gravitation and the big bang theory, think about why one is a law and the other is a theory. Write a paragraph to explain your thoughts about this. SC.912.E.5.1

USING KEY TERMS

Use each of the following terms in a separate sentence.

2. *light-year* SC.912.E.5.11
3. *cosmology* SC.912.E.5.1
4. *big bang theory* SC.912.E.5.1

For each pair of terms, explain how the meanings of the terms differ.

5. *constellation* and *cluster* SC.912.E.5.2
6. *spiral galaxy* and *elliptical galaxy* SC.912.E.5.2
7. *galaxy* and *quasar* SC.912.E.5.2
8. *cosmic background radiation* and *red shift* SC.912.E.5.1

UNDERSTANDING KEY IDEAS

9. The most common element in most stars is SC.912.E.5.1
   a. oxygen.
   c. helium.
   b. hydrogen.
   d. sodium.

10. Cosmic background radiation SC.912.E.5.1
    a. is very hot.
    b. is blue-green.
    c. comes from supernovas.
    d. comes almost equally from all directions.

11. Stars appear to move in circular paths through the sky because
    a. Earth rotates on its axis.
    b. Earth orbits the sun.
    c. the stars orbit Polaris.
    d. the Milky Way is a spiral galaxy.

12. A nebula begins the process of becoming a protostar when the nebula SC.912.E.5.5
    a. develops a red shift.
    b. changes color from red to blue.
    c. begins to shrink and increases its spin.
    d. explodes as a nova.

13. The brightest star in the night sky is
    a. Polaris.
    b. Mars.
    c. Arcturus.
    d. Sirius.

14. A main-sequence star generates energy by fusing
    a. nitrogen into iron.
    b. helium into carbon.
    c. hydrogen into helium.
    d. nitrogen into carbon.

15. Which of the following choices lists the colors of stars from hottest to coolest?
    a. red, yellow, orange, white, blue
    b. orange, red, white, blue, yellow
    c. yellow, orange, red, blue, white
    d. blue, white, yellow, orange, red

16. The heaviest element formed in the core of a star is SC.912.E.5.3
    a. iron.
    b. carbon.
    c. helium.
    d. nitrogen.

17. The change in position of a nearby star as seen from different points on Earth's orbit compared with the position of a faraway star is called SC.912.E.5.11
    a. parallax.
    b. blue shift.
    c. red shift.
    d. a Cepheid variable.

SHORT ANSWER

18. Describe what scientists think will happen to the sun in the next 5 billion years. SC.912.E.5.3

19. How can a black hole be detected if it is invisible? SC.912.E.5.8

20. How does a galaxy that contains a quasar differ from an ordinary galaxy?

21. What evidence indicates that the universe is expanding? SC.912.E.5.1

22. How does the presence of cosmic background radiation support the big bang theory? SC.912.E.5.1

CRITICAL THINKING

23. **Inferring Relationships** If the spectrum of a star indicates that the star shines with red light, what is the approximate surface temperature of the star? SC.912.E.5.8

24. **Analyzing Ideas** Why are different constellations visible during different seasons?

25. **Analyzing Ideas** Explain why Polaris is considered to be a very significant star even though it is not the brightest star in Earth's sky.

26. **Making Comparisons** Why does energy build up more rapidly in a massive protostar than in a less massive one? SC.912.E.5.3

27. **Analyzing Ideas** Explain why an old main-sequence star is made of a higher percentage of helium than a young main-sequence star is.

28. **Analyzing Ideas** If all galaxies began to show blue shifts, what would this change indicate about the fate of the universe? SC.912.E.5.8

CONCEPT MAPPING

29. Use the following terms to create a concept map: *galaxy, star, black hole, white dwarf, neutron star, giant, spiral galaxy, supergiant, elliptical galaxy, planetary nebula, main sequence, irregular galaxy,* and *protostar.*

MATH SKILLS

30. **Making Calculations** The Milky Way galaxy has about 200 billion stars. If only 10% of an estimated 125 billion galaxies thought to exist in the universe were as large as the Milky Way, how many total stars would be in those galaxies?

31. **Making Calculations** Given that the nearest star is about 4 light-years from Earth and a light-year is about 10,000,000,000,000 km, how many years would it take to travel to the nearest star if your spaceship goes 100 times faster than a car traveling 100 km/h? SC.912.E.5.11

WRITING SKILLS

32. **Creative Writing** Imagine that you are navigating through the galaxy and seeing many kinds of objects. Write a brief tour article for a magazine that describes your trip.

33. **Writing from Research** Use the Internet and library resources to research the function of constellations in ancient cultures. Write a short essay describing three different ways that ancient cultures used constellations.

INTERPRETING GRAPHICS

The graph below shows the relationship between a star's age and mass. Use the graph to answer the questions that follow.

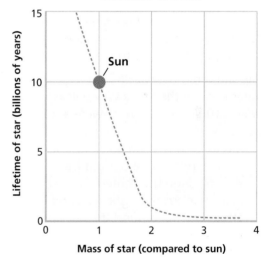

Relationship Between Age and Mass of a Star

34. Which star would live longer, a star that has half the mass of the sun or a star that has 2 times the mass of the sun? SC.912.E.5.3

35. Approximately how long would a main-sequence star that has a mass about 1.5 times that of our sun live? SC.912.E.5.3

36. If the mass of the sun was reduced by one-half, approximately how much longer would the sun live than it would with its current mass? SC.912.E.5.3

Understanding Concepts

Directions (1–10): For each question, write on a separate sheet of paper the letter of the correct answer.

1 What accounts for different stars being seen in the sky during different seasons of the year?
- **A.** stellar motion around Polaris
- **B.** Earth's rotation on its axis
- **C.** Earth's revolution around the sun
- **D.** position north or south of the equator

2 How do stellar spectra provide evidence that stars are actually moving?
- **F.** Dark line spectra reveal a star's composition.
- **G.** Long exposure photos show curved trails.
- **H.** Light separates into different wavelengths.
- **I.** Doppler shifts occur in the star's spectrum.

3 What happens to main sequence stars when energy from fusion is no longer available?
- **A.** They expand and become supergiants.
- **B.** They collapse and become white dwarfs.
- **C.** They switch to fission reactions.
- **D.** They contract and turn into neutron stars.

4 The sun orbits every 225 million years in the outer edge of the Milky Way galaxy. The Milky Way is 100,000 light years wide and a spiral galaxy, which is a type of galaxy that
- **F.** has a nucleus of bright stars, flattened and curled arms, and a straight bar of stars that runs through the center.
- **G.** has a nucleus of bright stars and flattened arms that curl around the nucleus.
- **H.** has a shape like a stretched-out football.
- **I.** has no particular shape.

5 Evidence for the big-bang theory is provided by
- **A.** cosmic background radiation.
- **B.** apparent parallax shifts.
- **C.** differences in stellar luminosity.
- **D.** star patterns called constellations.

6 Which of the following statements does NOT describe the typical galaxy?
- **F.** It has a diameter of 100,000 light years.
- **G.** It contains billions of stars.
- **H.** It is one of billions of galaxies.
- **I.** It is loosely shaped and carries few stars.

7 The H-R diagram is one tool used by astronomers. Which of the following statements describes the H-R diagram?
- **A.** It describes the life cycles of stars.
- **B.** It is used to plot absolute magnitude against luminosity.
- **C.** It identifies which elements are found in a star.
- **D.** It relates temperature and the amount of fusion within a star.

8 Why do scientists use light years to describe the distance between Earth and other stars?
- **F.** Other stars are too close for the distance to be measured in other units.
- **G.** Space is extremely vast.
- **H.** Stars move through space at the speed of light.
- **I.** Scientists measure the amount of light a star emits to find out how far it is from Earth.

9 When a star is moving toward or away from Earth, the star's spectrum is shifted. Which of the following statements describes the spectrum of a star moving toward Earth?
- **A.** The spectrum is shifted toward red wavelengths of light.
- **B.** The spectrum has more dark bars in it.
- **C.** The spectrum has a greater variety of colors in it.
- **D.** The spectrum is shifted toward blue wavelengths of light.

10 A star that has the mass of the sun will cease fusion at its core when it is 10 billion years old. What happens to the star?
- **F.** It leaves the main sequence.
- **G.** It has the same temperature but different luminosity.
- **H.** It becomes more stable.
- **I.** It forms a new star.

Interpreting Graphics

Directions (11–13): For each question below, record the correct answer on a separate sheet of paper.

Changing Shape of the Big Dipper over Time

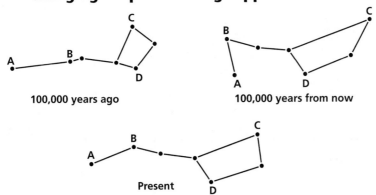

100,000 years ago

100,000 years from now

Present

11 Based on the figures of the Big Dipper above, which of the following statements is most likely true?
  A. New stars have replaced some of the stars in the constellation.
  B. The stars that make up the constellation are moving relative to each other.
  C. People use different stars to describe the Big Dipper constellation.
  D. Only the stars at position A and position C are moving.

Stellar Characteristics

Name	Color	Magnitude	Distance
Arcturus	orange	0.0	36.8 ly
Betelgeuse	red	0.5	400 ly
Canopus	yellow-white	−0.6	310 ly
Capella	yellow	0.1	42.2 ly
Mintaka	blue-violet	2.2	915 ly
Rigel	blue-white	0.2	800 ly
Sirius	white	−1.4	8.6 ly
Vega	white	0.0	25.3 ly

12 Which star has the brighest apparent magnitude as seen from Earth?
  F. Rigel
  G. Betelgeuse
  H. Mintaka
  I. Sirius

13 Which of these stars is the coolest?
  A. Arcturus
  B. Betelgeuse
  C. Mintaka
  D. Vega

Test Tip

If you are unsure of an answer, eliminate the answers that you know are wrong before choosing your answer.

Reference

Reading Toolbox Overview

Science textbooks can be hard to read because you have to learn new words and new ideas. The Reading Toolbox page at the beginning of each chapter in this book contains tools that can help you get the most out of your reading. Each of the sections on these pages is designed to help you analyze words, language, or ideas.

Analyzing Words

Analyzing Words tools will help you learn and understand specific words or phrases in a chapter.

- **FoldNotes** The key-term fold will help you learn the key terms in the chapter. Instructions for making a key-term fold are on page 884.

- **Science Terms** This tool will help you understand how the common meanings of words can differ from the scientific meanings. A table of everyday words used in science can be found on page 894.

- **Word Parts** If you understand the meanings of the prefixes, suffixes, or word roots, you can understand many science terms. A table of word parts used in science terms is on page 896.

- **Word Origins** Learning the origin of words and phrases used in science can help you remember the word.

- **Word Families** Because similar words can be grouped together into word families, understanding one word can help you understand all of the words in the family.

Analyzing Language

Analyzing Language tools will help you discover connections between ideas and specific kinds of language.

- **Analogies, Comparisons, and Cause and Effect** These tools help you understand the relationship between various words and phrases.

- **Generalizations, Making Predictions, Frequency, and Finding Examples** These tools help you identify language that can key you into when generalizations or predictions are being made, how often something occurs, and when an example is being used.

- **Fact, Hypothesis, or Theory?; Describing Time and Space; Reading Equations; and Word Problems** These tools can help you understand language that is used to describe science concepts and mathematical language.

- **Classification** This tool will help you understand how language is used to organize items.

- **Mnemonics** A mnemonic is a useful study tool to help you remember related words.

Analyzing Ideas

Analyzing Ideas tools will help you organize ideas and create materials that you can use to study.

- **Note Taking** These tools are various methods for taking notes while you read. For details about note-taking methods, see pages 879–883.

- **FoldNotes** There are various types of FoldNotes that you can make to help you learn information. Instructions for making FoldNotes can be found on pages 884–887.

- **Graphic Organizers** These tools are a visual way of showing relationships between ideas. Information on how to create various types of graphic organizers can be found on pages 888–893.

Note Taking

It is important to organize the information that you learn while you are reading a chapter so that you can use those notes to study for your tests. There are many ways to take notes. Each of these note-taking methods is a way to create a clear summary of the key points that you will need to remember for exams.

Comparison Table

A comparison table is useful when you want to compare the characteristics of two or more topics in science. Organizing information in a table helps you compare several topics at one time. In a table, all topics are described in terms of the same list of characteristics, which helps you make a thorough comparison.

1 **Create Table** Draw as many columns and rows as you need to compare the topics of interest, as shown below.

2 **Identify Topics** In the top row, write the topics that you want to compare.

3 **Identify Characteristics** In the left-column, write the general characteristics that you want to compare. As you read the chapter, fill in the characteristics for each topic in the appropriate boxes.

	Solid	Liquid	Gas	Plasma
Definite volume	yes	yes	no	no
Definite shape	yes	no	no	no
Possible changes of state	melting, sublimation	freezing, evaporation	condensation	

Practice

1. Make a comparison table to compare apples, oranges, and broccoli. Compare the following characteristics: color, shape, fruit or vegetable, and vitamins contained.

APPENDIX A

Outlining

Outlining is one of the most widely used methods for taking notes. A well-prepared outline can be an effective tool for understanding, comprehending, and achieving success on tests. Most outlines follow the same structure. This textbook is organized in such a way that you can easily outline the important ideas in a chapter or section.

1 **List Main Ideas** List main ideas or topics first. Each topic can be a section title and is listed after a Roman numeral.

2 **Add Major Points** Add major points that give you important information about the topic. Each major point will appear in red type in the section. You should add the points to your outline following capitalized letters.

3 **Add Subpoints** Add subpoints that describe parts of the major points. The first subpoint should be the green heading that appears after the red main topic. Subpoints should be added after numerals in your outline.

4 **Include Supporting Details** Finally, add supporting details for each subpoint. Pick important details from the text that follow the green headings. Add the details to your outline following lower-case letters.

II. Igneous Rock
   A. The Formation of Magma
      1. Partial Melting
         a. minerals melt at different temperatures
         b. magma composition changes
      2. Fractional Crystallization
         a. minerals freeze at different temperatures
         b. crystallization removes minerals from magma

Practice

1. Outline one of the sections in the chapter that you are currently covering in class.

Pattern Puzzles

You can use pattern puzzles to help you remember information in the correct order. Pattern puzzles are not just a tool for memorization. They can also help you better understand a variety of scientific processes, from the steps used to solve a mathematical conversion to the procedure used to write a lab report. Pattern puzzles are useful tools to practice and to review before tests. They also work very well in problem solving.

1 Write Steps In your own words, write down the steps of a process on a sheet of paper. Write one step per line, and do not number the steps. You should divide longer steps into two or three shorter steps.

2 Separate Steps Cut the sheet of paper into strips with only one step per strip of paper. Shuffle the strips of paper so that they are out of sequence.

3 Reorganize Steps Place the strips in their proper sequence. Confirm the order of the process by checking your text or your class notes.

How to determine the density of a mineral

- Place the mineral on a balance beam.

- Read and record the mass indicated by the balance, in grams.

- Place the mineral in a graduated cylinder with a given volume of water.

- Subtract the difference in volume, and record the difference, in cubic centimeters.

- Divide the mass by the volume to find the density.

- Place the mineral in a graduated cylinder with a given volume of water.

- Place the mineral on a balance beam.

- Divide the mass by the volume to find the density.

- Read and record the mass indicated by the balance, in grams.

- Subtract the difference in volume, and record the difference, in cubic centimeters.

Practice

1. Create a pattern puzzle that describes the steps that you take during one of your favorite activities (for example, baking cookies, writing a short story, playing a song on the guitar, or scoring a soccer goal). See if a friend can put the pieces of your puzzle in the correct order.

Summarizing

Summarizing is a simple method of taking notes in which you restate what you read in your own words. A summary is simply a brief restatement of a longer passage. Summarizing is a useful way to take notes because it helps you focus on the most important ideas. You can use your notes when you are reviewing for a test so that you can study all of the main points without having to reread the entire chapter.

❶ Identify Main Ideas Identify the main idea in a paragraph by reading completely through the paragraph. Sometimes, the first or last sentence of a paragraph states the main idea directly. Key-idea sentences may also be used as the main idea.

❷ Create Summary Statement Write a short statement that expresses the main idea. It is best to use complete sentences. You can use abbreviations as long as you will remember later what they mean. You may be able to summarize more than one paragraph in a single statement. In other cases, you may need more than one sentence to summarize a paragraph. Skip a couple of lines, and then repeat these first two steps for each paragraph in the section or chapter that you are reading.

❸ Include Additional Notes Add important notes or facts in the lines in between your summary statements. Read the text in Section 4 of Chapter 6 that follows the heading "Nonfoliated Rocks." The heading, "Nonfoliated Rocks," is too simple to be a summary statement because it does not tell you what nonfoliated rocks are nor any of their characteristics. On the other hand, you don't need to include any of the information about the Parthenon in your summary. A good summary for this text is given below.

Nonfoliated rocks do not have bands or aligned minerals.

The rock they come from contains mainly grains of only one mineral, which are usually round or square.

Quartzite and marble are common nonfoliated rocks.

Practice

1. Summarize the first paragraph of this page.

Two-Column Notes

Two-column notes can be used to learn and review definitions of vocabulary terms or details of specific concepts. One strategy for using two-column notes is to organize main ideas and their details. The two-column method of review is great for preparing for quizzes or tests. Cover the information in the right-hand column with a sheet of paper, and after reciting what you know, uncover the notes to check your answers.

❶ **Make Table** Divide a blank sheet of paper into two columns. Label the left-hand column "Main idea" and the right-hand column "Detail notes."

❷ **Identify Main Ideas** Identify the main ideas. Key ideas are listed at the beginning of each section. However, you should decide which ideas to include in your notes. Key words can include boldface terms as well as any other terms that you may have trouble remembering. Questions may include those that the author has asked or any questions that your teacher may have asked during class.

❸ **Add Main Ideas** In the right-hand column, write the main ideas as questions, key words, or a combination of both. The table below shows some of the main ideas from sections 1 and 2 of Chapter 1, "Introduction to Earth Science."

❹ **Create Detail Notes** Do not copy ideas from the book or waste time writing in complete sentences. Summarize your ideas using by phrases that are easy to understand and remember. Decide how many details you need for each main idea, and include that number to help you focus on the necessary information.

❺ **Include Detail Notes** Write the detail notes in the right-hand column. Be sure to list as many details as you designated in the main-idea column.

Main idea	Detail notes
Branches of Earth science (3 important details)	• natural science—observation and experimentation • four branches—geology, oceanography, meteorology, astronomy • branches of science overlap (environmental science)
Scientific methods (4 important details)	• ask a question • form a hypothesis • test the hypothesis • draw conclusions

Practice

1. Make your own two-column notes using the periodic table. Include in the details the symbol and the atomic number of each of the following elements.

   a. neon   c. copper   e. lead
   b. oxygen   d. calcium   f. sodium

FoldNotes

FoldNotes are a useful study tool that you can use to organize concepts. One FoldNote focuses on a few main concepts. By using a FoldNote, you can learn how concepts fit together. FoldNotes are designed to make studying concepts easier so that you can remember the ideas for tests.

Key-Term Fold

A key-term fold is useful for studying definitions of key terms in a chapter. Each tab can contain a key term on one side and its definition on the other. Use the key-term fold to quiz yourself on the definitions of the key terms in a chapter.

❶ Fold a **sheet of lined notebook paper** in half from left to right.

❷ Using **scissors,** cut along every third line from the right edge of the paper to the center fold to make tabs.

Booklet

A booklet is a useful tool for taking notes as you read a chapter. Each page of the booklet can contain a main topic from the chapter. Write details of each main topic on the appropriate page to create an outline of the chapter.

❶ Fold a **sheet of paper** in half from left to right. Then, unfold the paper.

❷ Fold the sheet of paper in half again from the top to the bottom. Then, unfold the paper.

❸ Refold the sheet of paper in half from left to right.

❹ Fold the top and bottom edges to the center crease.

❺ Completely unfold the paper.

❻ Refold the paper from top to bottom.

❼ Using **scissors,** cut a slit along the center crease of the sheet from the folded edge to the creases made in step 4. Do not cut the entire sheet in half. Unfold the paper.

❽ Fold the sheet of paper in half from left to right. While holding the bottom and top edges of the paper, push the bottom and top edges together so that the center collapses at the center slit. Fold the four flaps to form a four-page book.

Double-Door Fold

A double-door fold is useful when you want to compare the characteristics of two topics. The double-door fold can organize characteristics of the two topics side by side under the flaps. Similarities and differences between the two topics can then be easily identified.

❶ Fold a **sheet of paper** in half from the top to the bottom. Then, unfold the paper.

❷ Fold the top and bottom edges of the paper to the center crease.

Four-Corner Fold

A four-corner fold is useful when you want to compare the characteristics of four topics. The four-corner fold can organize the characteristics of the four topics side by side under the flaps. Similarities and differences between the four topics can then be easily identified.

❶ Fold a **sheet of paper** in half from top to bottom. Then, unfold the paper.

❷ Fold the top and bottom of the paper to the crease in the center of the paper.

❸ Fold the paper in half from side to side. Then, unfold the paper.

❹ Using **scissors,** cut the top flap creases made in step 3 to form four flaps.

Layered Book

A layered book is a useful tool for taking notes as you read a chapter. The four flaps of the layered book can summarize information into four categories. Write details of each category on the appropriate flap to create a summary of the chapter.

1 Lay one **sheet of paper** on top of **another sheet.** Slide the top sheet up so that 2 cm of the bottom sheet is showing.

2 Holding the two sheets together, fold down the top of the two sheets so that you see four 2 cm tabs along the bottom.

3 Using a **stapler,** staple the top of the FoldNote.

Pyramid

A pyramid provides a unique way for taking notes. The three sides of the pyramid can summarize information into three categories. Use the pyramid as a tool for studying information in a chapter.

1 Place a **sheet of paper** in front of you. Fold the lower left-hand corner of the paper diagonally to the opposite edge of the paper.

2 Cut off the tab of paper created by the fold (at the top).

3 Open the paper so that it is a square. Fold the lower right-hand corner of the paper diagonally to the opposite corner to form a triangle.

4 Open the paper. The creases of the two folds will have created an X.

5 Using **scissors,** cut along one of the creases. Start from any corner, and stop at the center point to create two flaps. Use **tape** or **glue** to attach one of the flaps on top of the other flap.

Table Fold

A table fold is a useful tool for comparing the characteristics of two or three topics. In a table fold, all topics are described in terms of the same characteristics so that you can easily make a thorough comparison.

1 Fold a **piece of paper** in half from the top to the bottom. Then, fold the paper in half again.

2 Fold the paper in thirds from side to side.

3 Unfold the paper completely. Carefully trace the fold lines by using a pen or pencil.

Tri-Fold

A tri-fold is a useful tool that helps you track your progress. By organizing the chapter topic into what you know, what you want to know, and what you learn, you can see how much you have learned after reading a chapter.

1 Fold a piece a paper in thirds from the top to the bottom.

2 Unfold the paper so that you can see the three sections. Then, turn the paper sideways so that the three sections form vertical columns.

3 Trace the fold lines by using a **pen** or **pencil.** Label the columns "Know," "Want," and "Learn."

Three-Panel Flip Chart

A three-panel flip chart is useful when you want to compare the characteristics of three topics. The three-panel flip chart can organize the characteristics of the three topics side by side under the flaps. Similarities and differences between the three topics can then be easily identified.

1 Fold a **piece of paper** in half from the top to the bottom.

2 Fold the paper in thirds from side to side. Then, unfold the paper so that you can see the three sections.

3 From the top of the paper, cut along each of the vertical fold lines to the fold in the middle of the paper. You will now have three flaps.

Two-Panel Flip Chart

A two-panel flip chart is useful when you want to compare the characteristics of two topics. The two-panel flip chart can organize the characteristics of the two topics side by side under the flaps. Similarities and differences between the two topics can then be easily identified.

1 Fold a **piece of paper** in half from the top to the bottom.

2 Fold the paper in half from side to side. Then, unfold the paper so that you can see the two sections.

3 From the top of the paper, cut along the vertical fold line to the fold in the middle of the paper. You will now have two flaps.

Graphic Organizers

Graphic Organizers are a way to draw or map concepts. Graphic Organizers can show simply how concepts are connected, when steps occur in a process, or how events are related. When you outline a concept using Graphic Organizers, you will understand the concept better and have a study tool that you can use later.

Concept Map

Concept maps are useful when you are trying to identify how several ideas are connected to a main concept. Concept maps may be based on vocabulary terms or on main topics from the text. As you read about science, look for terms that can be organized in a concept map.

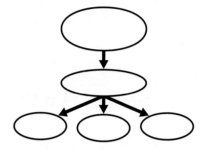

How to Make a Concept Map

1 **Main Ideas** Identify main ideas from the text. Write the ideas as short phrases or single words.

2 **Main Concepts** Select a main concept. Place this concept at the top or center of a piece of paper.

3 **More Ideas** Place other ideas under or around the main concept based on their relationship to the main concept. Draw a circle around each idea.

4 **Connections** Draw lines between the concepts. Add linking words to connect the ideas.

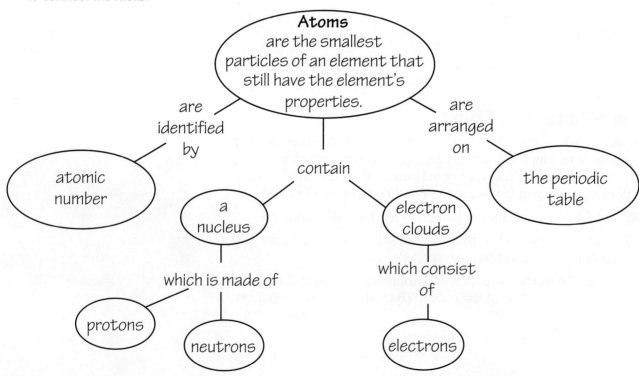

Flow Chart

Science is full of processes. A flow chart shows the steps that a process takes to get from one point to another point. Timelines and cycles are examples of the kinds of information that can be organized well in a flow chart. As you read, look for information that is described in steps or in a sequence, and draw a process chart that shows the progression of the steps or sequence.

How to Make a Flow Chart

1 **Box First Step** Draw a box. In the box, write the first step of a process or cycle.

2 **Add Next Step** Under the box, draw another box, and draw an arrow to connect the two boxes. In the second box, write the next step of the process.

3 **Add More Steps** Continue adding boxes until each step of the process or cycle is written in a box. For cycles only, draw an arrow to connect the last box and the first box.

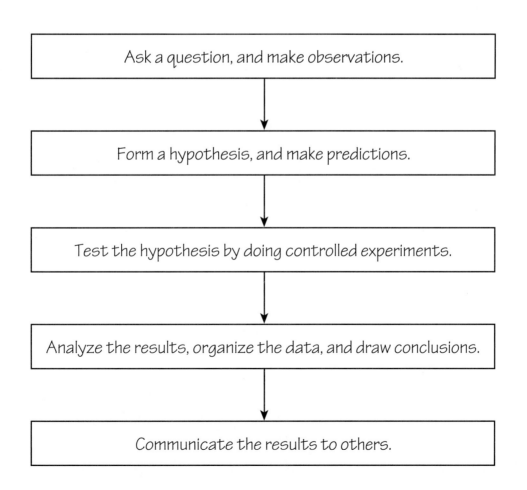

Ask a question, and make observations.

Form a hypothesis, and make predictions.

Test the hypothesis by doing controlled experiments.

Analyze the results, organize the data, and draw conclusions.

Communicate the results to others.

Chain-of-Events Chart

When to Use a Chain-of-Events Chart
A chain-of-events chart is similar to a flow chart. A chain-of-events chart shows the order in which steps occur. As you read, look for information that occurs in a sequence, and draw a chain-of-events chart that shows the order of the sequence.

How to Make a Chain-of-Events Chart

❶ Box First Event Draw a box. In the box, write the first event of a chain of events.

❷ Add Next Event Draw another box to the right of the first box. Draw an arrow to connect the two boxes. In the second box, write the next event in the timeline.

❸ Add More Events Continue adding boxes until each step of the chain of events is written in a box.

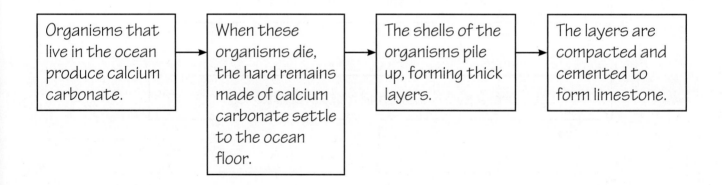

| Organisms that live in the ocean produce calcium carbonate. | → | When these organisms die, the hard remains made of calcium carbonate settle to the ocean floor. | → | The shells of the organisms pile up, forming thick layers. | → | The layers are compacted and cemented to form limestone. |

Cause-and-Effect Map

A cause-and-effect map is a useful tool for illustrating a specific type of scientific process. Use a cause-and-effect map when you want to describe how, when, or why one event causes another event. As you read, look for events that are either causes or results of other events, and draw a cause-and-effect map that shows the relationships between the events.

How to Make a Cause-and-Effect Map

1 **Cause Box** Draw a box, and write a cause in the box. You can have as many cause boxes as you want. The diagram shown here is one example of a cause-and-effect map.

2 **Effect Boxes** Draw another box to the right of the cause box to represent an effect. You can have as many effect boxes as you want. Draw arrows from each cause box to the appropriate effect boxes.

3 **Descriptions** In the cause boxes, explain the process that makes up the cause. In the effect boxes, write a description of the effect or details about the effect.

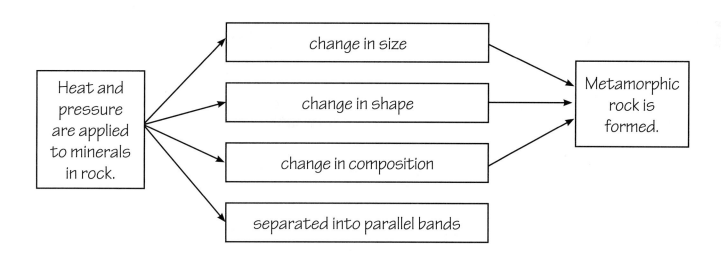

Spider Map

A spider map is an effective tool for classifying the details of a specific topic in science. A spider map divides a topic into ideas and details. As you read about a topic, look for the main ideas or characteristics of the topic. Within each idea, look for details. Use a spider map to organize the ideas and details of each topic.

How to Make a Spider Map

1 Main Topic Write the main topic in the center of your paper. Draw a circle around the topic.

2 Main Ideas From the circle, draw legs to represent the main ideas or characteristics of the topic. Draw as many legs as you want. Write an idea or characteristic along each leg.

3 Details From each leg, draw horizontal lines. As you read the chapter, write details about each idea on the idea's horizontal lines. To add more details, make the legs longer and add more horizontal lines.

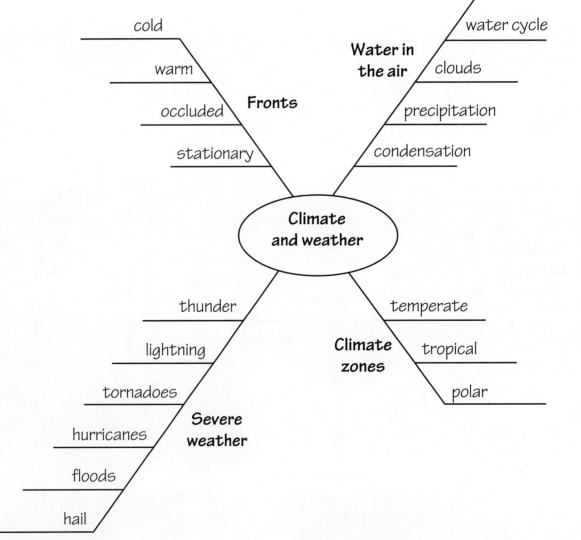

Venn Diagram

A Venn diagram is a useful tool for comparing two or three topics in science. A Venn diagram shows which characteristics that the topics share and which characteristics are unique to each topic. Venn diagrams are ideal when you want to illustrate relationships in a pair or small group of topics. As you read, look for topics that have both shared and unique characteristics, and draw a Venn diagram that shows how the topics are related.

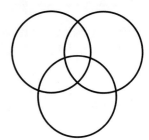

How to Make a Venn Diagram

1 Circles Draw overlapping circles. Draw one circle for each topic, and make sure that each circle partially overlaps the other circles.

2 Main Topics In each circle, write a topic that you want to compare with the topics in the other circles.

3 Shared Characteristics In the areas of the diagram where circles overlap, write the characteristics that the topics in the overlapping circles share.

4 Unique Characteristics In the areas of the diagram where circles do not overlap, write the characteristics that are unique to the topic of the particular circle.

Physical properties

- can be observed or measured without changing the identity of a substance

- color, odor, mass, volume, weight, density, strength, flexibility, magnetism, and electrical conductivity

- help describe and define matter

- can be characteristic properties

Chemical properties

- describe matter based on its ability to change into new matter that has different properties

- cannot always be observed

- reactivity, including flammability

Everyday Words Used in Science

Scientific words may have common meanings that you already know.
Understanding the difference between everyday meanings and
scientific meanings will help you develop a scientific vocabulary.
The table here provides common and scientific meanings for words
that you will see in this textbook.

Word	Common meaning	Scientific meaning
abrasion	a spot, such as on the skin, that has been scraped or worn away	the grinding and wearing away of rock surfaces through the mechanical action of other rock or sand particles
atmosphere	general mood of the social environment	a mixture of gases that surrounds a planet, moon, or other celestial body
carbonation	full of carbon dioxide, as in soda water	the conversion of a compound into a carbonate
concentration	the act of focusing one's attention on something	the amount of a particular substance in a given quantity of a mixture, solution, or ore
condensation	the droplets of liquid on the outside of a glass or window	the change of state from a gas to a liquid
conservation	protection of something	the preservation and wise use of natural resources
creep	a crawling motion; an annoying or disgusting person	the slow downhill movement of weathered rock material
crust	the outer edge of a slice of bread	the thin and solid outermost layer of Earth above the mantle
eccentricity	a change in manner or conduct from what is ordinary or customary	the degree of elongation of an elliptical orbit (symbol, e)
element	a fundamental constituent part	a substance that cannot be separated or broken down into simpler substances by chemical means
energy	the ability to be active	the capacity to do work
fault	a weakness or shortcoming in one's character; responsibility for wrong actions	a break in a body of rock along which one block slides relative to another; a form of brittle strain
fetch	to chase and retrieve; go after and return with	the distance that wind blows across an area of the sea to generate waves
fluid	smooth; graceful (for example, fluid movement)	a nonsolid state of matter in which the atoms or molecules are free to move past each other, as in a gas or liquid
force	violence used to compel a person or thing	an action exerted on a body in order to change the body's state of rest or motion; force has magnitude and direction
friction	conflict between people who have opposing views	a force that opposes motion between two surfaces that are in contact
gas	short for gasoline; a liquid fuel used by vehicles, such as cars and buses	a form of matter that does not have a definite volume or shape

Word	Common meaning	Scientific meaning
gravity	seriousness (for example, the gravity of the situation)	a force of attraction between objects that is due to their masses and that decreases as the distance between the objects increases
inertia	resistance to change	the tendency of an object to resist a change in motion unless an outside force acts on the object
kettle	a metal pot used for cooking or boiling water	a bowl-shaped depression in a glacial drift deposit
legend	a person who has done great deeds; an old story of such deeds	a list of map symbols and their meanings
mass	a quantity of material that has an unspecified shape	a measure of the amount of matter in an object
matter	a subject of concern or topic of discussion	anything that has mass and takes up space
mineral	a substance required by animals or plants for proper development	a natural, usually inorganic solid that has a characteristic chemical composition, an orderly internal structure, and a characteristic set of physical properties
model	a miniature representation of a larger object	a pattern, plan, representation, or description designed to show the structure or workings of an object, system, or concept
motion	movement	an object's change in position relative to a reference point
organic	an organism or object produced without the use of synthetic drugs, fertilizers, or hormones	a covalently bonded compound that contains carbon, excluding carbonates and oxides
period	a punctuation mark used to indicate the end of a sentence	a unit of geologic time that is longer than an epoch but shorter than an era
phase	a distinguishable stage in a cycle	the change in the illuminated area of one celestial body as seen from another celestial body
pressure	the burden of mental stress	the amount of force exerted per unit area of a surface
product	something available for sale (for example, a computer product)	a substance that forms in a chemical reaction
relief	a lessening of pain or discomfort; aid given in time of trouble	the difference between the highest and lowest elevations in a given area; the variations in elevation of a land surface
revolution	the overthrow of one government and the substitution with another (for example, the American Revolution)	the motion of a body that travels around another body in space; one complete trip along an orbit
solution	the answer to a problem	a homogeneous mixture throughout which two or more substances are uniformly dispersed
star	a person who is highly celebrated in a particular field	a large celestial body that is composed of gas and that emits light
table	a piece of furniture that has a flat, horizontal surface	an orderly arrangement of data
theory	an assumption based on limited knowledge	a system of ideas that explains many related observations and is supported by a large body of evidence acquired through scientific investigation
volume	a measure of how loud a sound is	a measure of the size of a body or region in three-dimensional space

Analyzing Science Terms

You can unlock the meaning of an unfamiliar science term by analyzing its word parts. Many parts of scientific words carry a meaning that derives from Latin or Greek. The parts of words listed below provide clues to the meanings of many science terms.

Word part or root	Meaning	Application
a-	not, without	abiotic
astr-, aster-	star	astronomy
bar-, baro-	weight, pressure	barometer
batho-, bathy-	depth	batholith, bathysphere
circum-	around	circum-Pacific, circumpolar
-cline	lean, slope	anticline, syncline
-duct-	to lead, draw	conduction
eco-	environment	ecology, ecosystem
epi-	on	epicenter
ex-, exo-	out, outside of	exosphere, exfoliation, extrusion
geo-	earth	geode, geology, geomagnetic
-graph	write, writing	seismograph
hydro-	water	hydrosphere
hypo-	under	hypothesis
iso-	equal	isoscope, isostasy, isotope
-lith, -lithic	stone	Neolithic, regolith
-log-	study	ecology, geology, meteorology
magn-	great, large	magnitude
mar-	sea	marine
meta-	among, change	metamorphic, metamorphism
-meter	to measure	thermometer, spectrometer
micro-	small	microquake
-morph, -morphic	form, shape	metamorphic
nebula-	mist, cloud	nebula
neo-	new	Neolithic
paleo-	old	paleontology, Paleozoic
ped-, pedo-	ground, soil	pediment
per-	through	permeable
peri-	around	perigee, perihelion
seism-, seismo-	shake, earthquake	seismic, seismograph
sol-	sun	solar, solstice
spectro-	look at, examine	spectroscope, spectrum
-sphere	ball, globe	geosphere, lithosphere
strati-, strato-	spread, layer	stratification, stratovolcano
terra-	earth, land	terracing, terrane
thermo-	heat	thermosphere, thermometer
top-, topo-	place	topographic
trop-, tropo-	turn, respond to	tropopause, troposphere

Math Skills

Fractions

Fractions represent numbers that are less than 1. In other words, fractions are a way of using numbers to represent a part of a whole. For example, if you have a pizza with 8 slices and you eat 2 of the slices, you have 6 out of the 8 slices, or $\frac{6}{8}$, of the pizza left. The top number in the fraction is called the *numerator*. The bottom number is called the *denominator*.

There are special rules for adding, subtracting, multiplying, and dividing fractions. **Figure 1** summarizes these rules.

Figure 1 Basic Operations for Fractions

Rule and example	
Multiplication	$\left(\frac{a}{b}\right)\left(\frac{c}{d}\right) = \left(\frac{ac}{bd}\right) \qquad \left(\frac{2}{3}\right)\left(\frac{4}{5}\right) = \frac{8}{15}$
Division	$\frac{a}{b} \div \frac{c}{d} = \frac{\left(\frac{a}{b}\right)}{\left(\frac{c}{d}\right)} = \frac{ad}{bc}$ $\frac{2}{3} \div \frac{4}{5} = \frac{\left(\frac{2}{3}\right)}{\left(\frac{4}{5}\right)} = \frac{(2)(5)}{(3)(4)} = \frac{10}{12}$
Addition and subtraction	$\frac{a}{b} \pm \frac{c}{d} = \frac{ad \pm bc}{bd}$ $\frac{2}{3} - \frac{4}{5} = \frac{(2)(5) - (3)(4)}{(3)(5)} = -\frac{2}{15}$

Practice

1. Perform the following calculations:

    a. $\frac{7}{8} + \frac{1}{3} =$

    b. $\frac{7}{8} \times \frac{1}{3} =$

    c. $\frac{7}{8} \div \frac{1}{3} =$

    d. $\frac{7}{8} - \frac{1}{3} =$

Percentages

Percentages are the same as other fractions except that in a percentage the whole (or the number in the denominator) is considered to be 100. Any percentage, $x\%$, can be read as x out of 100. For example, if you completed 50% of an assignment, you completed $\frac{50}{100}$, or $\frac{1}{2}$, of the assignment.

Percentages can be calculated by dividing the part by the whole. Your calculator displays a decimal value when it solves a division problem that has an answer that is less than 1. The decimal value can be written as a fraction. For example, 0.45 can be written as the fraction $\frac{45}{100}$.

An easy way to calculate a percentage is to divide the part by the whole and then multiply by 100. This multiplication moves the decimal point two positions to the right and gives you the number that would be over 100 in a fraction. So, $0.45 = 45\%$.

Try this example:

> You scored 73 out of 92 problems on your last exam. What was your percentage score?

First, divide the part by the whole to get a decimal value. The fraction $\frac{73}{92} = 0.7935$, which is equal to $\frac{79.35}{100}$.

Then, multiply by 100 to find the percentage: $0.7935 \times 100 = 79.35\%$.

Practice

1. The mass of the oxygen atom in a water molecule is 16.00 u. A water molecule has a total molar mass of 18.01 u. What percentage of the mass of water is made up of oxygen?

2. A candy bar contains 14 g of fat. The total fat contains 3.0 g of saturated fat and 11 g of unsaturated fat. What percentage of the fat is saturated? What percentage is unsaturated?

Exponents

An exponent is a number that is a superscript to the right of another number. The best way to explain how an exponent works is with an example. In the value 5^4, 4 is the exponent on 5. The number with its exponent means that 5 is multiplied by itself 4 times.

$$5^4 = 5 \times 5 \times 5 \times 5 = 625$$

Exponent are powers.

You will frequently hear exponents referred to as *powers*. Using this terminology, one could read the above equation as *five to the fourth power equals 625.* Keep in mind that any number raised to the zero power is equal to 1. Also, any number raised to the first power is equal to itself:

$$5^1 = 5$$

Figure 2 summarizes the rules for dealing with exponents.

Figure 2 Rules for Dealing with Exponents

	Rule	Example
Zero power	$x^0 = 1$	$7^0 = 1$
First power	$x^1 = x$	$6^1 = 6$
Multiplication	$(x^n)(x^m) = x^{(n+m)}$	$(x^2)(x^4) = x^{(2+4)} = x^6$
Division	$\dfrac{x^n}{x^m} = x^{(n-m)}$	$\dfrac{x^8}{x^2} = x^{(8-2)} = x^6$
Exponents that are fractions	$x^{1/n} = \sqrt[n]{x}$	$4^{1/3} = \sqrt[3]{4} = 1.5874$
Exponents raised to a power	$(x^n)^m = x^{nm}$	$(5^2)^3 = 5^6 = 15{,}625$

Roots are the opposite of exponents.

The symbol for a square root is $\sqrt{}$. The value underneath this symbol is equal to a number times itself. It is also possible to have roots other than the square root. For example, $\sqrt[3]{x}$ is a cube root, which means that if you multiply some number, n, by itself 3 times, you will get the number x, or $x = n \times n \times n$.

We can turn our example of $5^4 = 625$ around to solve for the fourth root of 625.

$$\sqrt[4]{625} = 5$$

Taking the nth root of a number is the same as raising that number to the power of $1/n$. Therefore, $\sqrt[4]{625} = 625^{1/4}$.

Use a calculator to solve exponents and roots.

You can solve problems involving exponents and roots easily by using a scientific calculator. Many calculators have dedicated keys for squares and square roots. But what do you do if you want to find other powers, such as cubes and cube roots? Most scientific calculators have a key with a caret symbol, (^), that is used to enter exponents. If you type in "5^4" and hit the equals sign or the enter key, the calculator will display the answer 625.

Many scientific calculators have a key with the symbol $\sqrt[x]{}$ that you can use to enter roots. When using this key, enter the root first. To solve the problem of the fourth root of 625, you would type "4 $\sqrt[x]{}$ 625," and the calculator would return the answer 5. If your calculator does not have the root key, you may be able to enter the root as a fraction if your calculator has a key that allows you to enter fractions. In this case you would use the exponent key and the fraction key to enter "625^ $\frac{1}{4}$." If your calculator does not have a fraction key, you can enter the decimal equivalent of the fractional exponent to find the root. Instead of entering $\frac{1}{4}$ as the exponent, enter "625^0.25," because 0.25 is equal to $\frac{1}{4}$.

Practice

1. Perform the following calculations:

   a. $9^1 =$

   b. $(3^3)^5 =$

   c. $\dfrac{2^8}{2^2} =$

   d. $(14^2)(14^3) =$

   e. $11^0 =$

   f. $6^{1/6} =$

Order of Operations

Use the following phrase to remember the correct order for long mathematical problems: *Please Excuse My Dear Aunt Sally*. This phrase stands for "Parentheses, Exponents, Multiplication, Division, Addition, Subtraction." **Figure 3** summarizes these rules.

Figure 3 Order of Operations

Step	Operation
1	**Parentheses** Simplify groups inside parentheses. Start with the innermost group, and work out.
2	**Exponents** Simplify all exponents.
3	**Multiplication and Division** Perform multiplication and division in order from left to right.
4	**Addition and Subtraction** Perform addition and subtraction in order from left to right.

Try the following example:

$$4^3 + 2 \times [8 - (3 - 1)] = ?$$

1 Simplify the operations inside parentheses. Begin with the innermost parentheses:

$$(3 - 1) = 2$$
$$4^3 + 2 \times [8 - 2] = ?$$

Move on to the next-outer brackets:

$$[8 - 2] = 6$$
$$4^3 + 2 \times 6 = ?$$

2 Simplify all exponents:

$$4^3 = 64$$
$$64 + 2 \times 6 = ?$$

3 Perform multiplication:

$$2 \times 6 = 12$$
$$64 + 12 = ?$$

4 Solve the addition problem:

$$64 + 12 = 76$$

Practice

1. $2^3 \div 2 + 4 \times (9 - 2^2) =$

2. $\dfrac{2 \times (6 - 3) + 8}{4 \times 2 - 6} =$

Geometry

Shapes are a useful way to model many objects and substances studied in science. For example, many of the properties of a wheel can be understood by using a perfect circle as a model.

Therefore, knowing how to calculate the area or the volume of certain shapes is a useful skill in science. Equations for the area and volume of several geometric shapes are provided in **Figure 4.**

Figure 4 Geometric Areas and Volumes

Geometric shape		Useful equations
Rectangle		$area = lw$
Circle		$area = \pi r^2$ $circumference = 2\pi r$
Triangle		$area = \dfrac{1}{2}bh$
Sphere		$surface\ area = 4\pi r^2$ $volume = \dfrac{4}{3}\pi r^3$
Cylinder		$volume = \pi r^2 h$
Rectangular box		$surface\ area = 2(lh + lw + hw)$ $volume = lwh$

Practice

1. A cylinder has a diameter of 14 cm and a height of 8 cm. What is the cylinder's volume?

2. Calculate the surface area of a 4 cm cube.

3. Will a sphere with a volume of 76 cm^3 fit in a rectangular box that is 7 cm × 4 cm × 10 cm?

Algebraic Rearrangements

Often in science, you will need to determine the value of a variable from an equation written as an algebraic expression.

Algebraic expressions contain constants and variables. *Constants* are numbers that you know and that do not change, such as 2, 3.14, and 100. *Variables* are represented by letters, such as x, y, a, and b. Variables in equations are unspecified quantities and are also called the *unknowns*.

An algebraic expression contains one or more of the four basic mathematical operations: addition, subtraction, multiplication, and division. Constants, variables, or terms made up of both constants and variables can be involved in the basic operations.

Solve for the variable.

To find the value of some variable, you need to simplify the expression by rearranging the equation. Ideally, after you have finished rearranging the equation, you will end up with a simple equation that tells you the value of the variable.

To get from a complicated equation to a simpler one, you need to isolate the variable on one side of the equation. You can do so by performing the same operations on both sides of the equation until the variable is alone. Because both sides of the equation are equal, if you do the same operation on both sides of the equation, the results will still be equal.

Look at the following simple problem:

$$8x = 32$$

In this equation, you need to solve for the variable x. You can add, subtract, multiply, or divide anything to or from one side of an equation as long as you do the same thing to the other side of the equation. In this case, we need to get rid of the 8 so that the x is by itself. If we divide both sides by 8, we have this equation:

$$\frac{8x}{8} = \frac{32}{8}$$

The 8s on the left side of the equation cancel each other out, and the fraction $\frac{32}{8}$ can be reduced to give the whole number 4.

$$x = 4$$

Next, consider the following equation:

$$x + 2 = 8$$

Remember that you can add or subtract the same quantity from each side. To isolate x, you need subtract 2 from each side:

$$x + 2 - 2 = 8 - 2$$
$$x + 0 = 6$$
$$x = 6$$

Now, consider one more equation:

$$-3(x - 2) + 4 = 29$$

One way to solve this more complicated expression is to follow the order of operations in reverse order to isolate x. First, subtract the 4.

$$-3(x - 2) + 4 - 4 = 29 - 4$$
$$-3(x - 2) = 25$$

Now, divide by −3.

$$\frac{-3(x - 2)}{-3} = \frac{25}{-3}$$
$$x - 2 = -8.3$$

Now, only the expression that was inside the parentheses remains on the left side of the equation. You can find the value of x by adding 2 to both sides of the equation.

$$x - 2 + 2 = -8.3 + 2$$
$$x = -6.3$$

Practice

1. Rearrange each of the following equations to give the value of the variable indicated with a letter:

   a. $8x - 32 = 128$

   b. $6 - 5(4a + 3) = 26$

   c. $-2(3m + 5) = 14$

   d. $\left[8\frac{(8 + 2z)}{32} \right] + 2 = 5$

   e. $\frac{(6b + 3)}{3} - 9 = 2$

Scientific Notation

Often, scientists deal with very large or very small quantities. For example, in one second, about 3,000,000,000,000,000,000 electrons' worth of charge pass through a standard light bulb; and the ink required to make the dot over an *i* in this textbook has a mass of about 0.000000001 kg.

Obviously, it is very time-consuming to read and write such large and small numbers. It is also easy to lose track of the zeros and make an error when doing calculations with numbers that have many zeros. Powers of the number 10 are used to keep track of the zeros in large and small numbers. Numbers that are expressed as some power of 10 multiplied by another number with only one digit to the left of the decimal point are said to be written in *scientific notation.*

Use exponents to write large numbers.

Study the positive powers of 10 shown in **Figure 5.** The number of zeros corresponds to the exponent to the right of the 10. The number for 10^4 is 10,000; it has 4 zeros.

But how can you use the powers of 10 to simplify large numbers such as the number of electron-sized charges passing through a light bulb? The number 3,000,000,000,000,000,000 can be written as $3 \times 1,000,000,000,000,000,000$. To write the large number as an exponent, count the zeros—there are 18 zeros. Therefore, the exponent is 10^{18}. So, 3,000,000,000,000,000,000 can be expressed as 3×10^{18} in scientific notation.

Use exponents to write small numbers.

Now, you know how to simplify really large numbers, but how do you simplify really small numbers, such as 0.000000001? To simplify numbers that are less than 1, use negative exponents.

Next, study the negative powers of 10. To determine the exponent that you need to use, count the number of decimal places that you must move the decimal point to the right so that only one digit is to the left of the decimal point. To simplify the mass of the ink in the dot on an *i*, 0.000000001 kg, you must move the decimal point 9 decimal places to the right for the numeral 1 to be on the left side of the decimal point. In scientific notation, the mass of the ink is 1×10^{-9} kg.

Figure 5 Powers of 10

Power of 100	Decimal equivalent
10^4	10,000
10^3	1,000
10^2	100
10^1	10
10^0	1
10^{-1}	0.01
10^{-2}	0.001
10^{-3}	0.0001

Use scientific notation to write any number.

Values that have more than one nonzero number can also be written using scientific notation. For example, 5,943,000,000 is 5.943×10^9 when expressed in scientific notation. The number 0.0000832 is 8.32×10^{-5} when expressed in scientific notation.

When you use scientific notation in calculations, follow the rules for using exponents in calculations. When you multiply two numbers expressed in scientific notation, add the exponents, as shown below.

$$(4 \times 10^5) \times (2 \times 10^3) = [(4 \times 2) \times 10^{(5+3)})] = 8 \times 10^8$$

When you divide two numbers expressed in scientific notation, subtract the exponents.

Practice

1. Rewrite the following values using scientific notation:
   a. 12,300,000 m/s
   b. 0.0000000000045 kg
   c. 0.0000653 m
   d. 55,432,000,000,000 s
   e. 273.15 K
   f. 0.00062714 kg

SI

One of the most important parts of scientific research is being able to communicate your findings to other scientists. Today, scientists need to be able to communicate with other scientists all around the world. They need a common language in which to report data. If you do an experiment in which all of your measurements are in pounds and you want to compare your results to those of a French scientist whose measurements are in grams, you will need to convert all of your measurements. For this reason, the *Système International d'Unités*, or SI, was created in 1960.

You are probably accustomed to measuring distance in inches, feet, and miles. Most of the world, however, measures distance in centimeters (cm), meters (m), and kilometers (km). The meter is the official SI unit for measuring distance. **Figure 6** lists the SI units for some common measurements.

Prefixes are used to indicate quantities.

Notice that centi*meter* and kilo*meter* each contain the word *meter*. When dealing with SI units, you frequently use the base unit, in this case the meter, and add a prefix to indicate that the quantity that you are measuring is a multiple of that unit. Most SI prefixes indicate multiples of 10. For example, the centimeter is 1/100 of a meter. Any SI unit with the prefix *centi-* will be 1/100 of the base unit. A centigram is 1/100 of a gram.

Figure 6 Some SI Units

Quantity	Unit name	Symbol
Length	meter	m
Mass	kilogram	kg
Time	second	s
Temperature	kelvin	K
Amount of substance	mole	mol
Electric current	ampere	A
Pressure	pascal	Pa
Volume	cubic meters	m^3

Figure 7 Some SI Prefixes

Prefix	Symbol	Exponential factor
giga-	G	10^9
mega-	M	10^6
kilo-	k	10^3
hecto-	h	10^2
deka-	da	10^1
deci-	d	10^{-1}
centi-	c	10^{-2}
milli-	m	10^{-3}
micro-	μ	10^{-6}
nano-	n	10^{-9}
pico-	p	10^{-12}
femto-	f	10^{-15}

How many meters are in a *kilo*meter? The prefix *kilo-* indicates that the unit is 1,000 times the base unit. A kilometer is equal to 1,000 meters. Multiples of 10 make dealing with SI values much easier than values such as feet or gallons. To convert from feet to miles, you must remember a large conversion factor, 1.893939×10^{-4} miles per foot. To convert from kilometers to meters, you need to look only at the prefix to know that you will multiply by 1,000.

Figure 7 lists possible prefixes and their meanings. When working with a prefix, simply take the unit symbol and add the prefix symbol to the front of the unit symbol. For example, the symbol for *kilometer* is written "km."

Practice

1. Convert each value to the requested units:
   a. 0.035 m to decimeters
   b. 5.24 m^3 to cubic centimeters
   c. 13,450 g to kilograms

Significant Figures

Significant figures indicate the precision of a value. You can use the rules in the following list to determine the number of significant figures in a reported value. After you have reviewed the rules, use **Figure 8** to check your understanding of the rules. Cover up the second column of the table, and try to determine how many significant figures each number has.

You can use a few rules to determining the number of significant figures in a measurement.

① All nonzero digits are significant.

> **Example** 1,246 (four significant figures, shown in red)

② Any zeros between significant digits are also significant.

> **Example** 1,206 (four significant figures)

③ If the value does not contain a decimal point, any zeros to the right of a nonzero digit are not significant.

> **Example** 1,200 (two significant figures)

④ Any zeros to the right of a significant digit and to the left of a decimal point are significant.

> **Example** 1,200. (four significant figures)

⑤ If a value has no significant digits to the left of a decimal point, any zeros to the right of the decimal point and to the left of a nonzero digit are not significant.

> **Example** 0.0012 (two significant figures)

⑥ If a measurement is reported that ends with zeros to the right of a decimal point, those zeros are significant.

> **Example** 0.1200 (four significant figures)

If you are adding or subtracting two measurements, your answer can have only as many decimal positions as the value with the least number of decimal places. The final answer in the following problem has five significant figures. It has been rounded to two decimal places because 0.04 g has only two significant figures.

$$\begin{array}{r} 134.050 \text{ g} \\ -0.04 \text{ g} \\ \hline 134.01 \text{ g} \end{array}$$

Figure 8 Significant Figures

Measurement	Number of significant figures	Rule
12,345	5	1
2,400 cm	2	3
305 kg	3	2
2,350. cm	4	4
234.005 K	6	2
12.340	5	6
0.001	1	5
0.002450	4	5 and 6

When you multiply or divide measurements, your final answer can have only as many significant figures as the value with the least number of significant figures. Examine the following multiplication problem.

$$\begin{array}{r} 12.0 \text{ cm}^2 \\ \times 0.04 \text{ cm} \\ \hline 0.5 \text{ cm}^3 \end{array}$$

The final answer has been rounded to one significant figure because 0.04 cm has only one. When performing both types of operations (addition/subtraction and multiplication/division), round the result after you complete each type of operation, and round the final result.

Practice

1. Determine the number of significant figures in each of the following measurements:
   a. 65.04 mL   c. 0.007504 kg
   b. 564.00 m   d. 1,210 K

2. Perform each of the following calculations, and report your answer with the correct number of significant figures and units:
   a. 0.004 dm + 0.12508 dm
   b. 340 m ÷ 0.1257 s
   c. 40.1 kg × 0.2453 m²
   d. 1.03 g – 0.0456 g

Graphing Skills

Line Graphs

Usually, in laboratory experiments, you will control one variable and see how changes in that variable affect another variable. Line graphs can show these relationships clearly. Suppose that you want to determine the rate of a plant's growth by measuring the growth of a plant over time. In this experiment, you would control the time intervals at which the plant height is measured. Thus, time is the *independent variable*. The change in the height of the plant that you measure depends on the time interval that you choose. So, plant height is the *dependent variable*. The table in **Figure 1** shows some sample data from an experiment that measured the rate of plant growth.

When you make a line graph, always plot the independent variable on the *x*-axis. For the plant-height experiment, the axis will be labeled "Time (days)." Remember to include the units in your axis label. Pick a range for your graph that is just large enough to enter all of your data points. From the data in **Figure 1,** you can see that plant height was measured over 35 days. Therefore, the *x*-axis should have a range of 0 days to 35 days.

Plot the dependent variable on the *y*-axis. In this case, the *y*-axis is labeled "Plant height (cm)" and has a range from 0 cm to 5 cm.

When you draw the axes for your graph, you want to use as much of the available space as possible. You should label the grid marks for each axis at intervals that evenly divide up the data range. In the graph in **Figure 2,** the *y*-axis has grid marks at intervals of 1, and the *x*-axis has grid marks at intervals of 5. Notice that the interval of the grid marks on the *x*-axis is not the same interval at which the data were measured.

Think of your graph as a grid with lines running horizontally from the *y*-axis and vertically from the *x*-axis. To plot a point, find the *x*-value for that point on the *x*-axis. Follow the vertical line from the *x*-axis until it intersects the horizontal line from the *y*-axis at the corresponding *y*-value. At the intersection of these two lines, place your point. After you have plotted all of your data points, connect each point with a straight line. **Figure 2** shows a line graph of the data in **Figure 1.**

Figure 1 Data for Plant Growth Versus Time

Time (days)	Plant height (cm)
0	1.43
7	2.16
14	2.67
21	3.25
28	4.04
35	4.67

Figure 2 Line Graph for Plant Growth Versus Time

Practice

1. Create a line graph of the data below.

Time (days)	Plant height (cm)
0	1.46
7	2.67
14	3.89
21	4.82

2. Compare the graph you made with **Figure 9.** What can you conclude about the two groups of plants?

Scatter Plots

Some groups of data are best represented in a graph called a *scatter plot*. Scatter plots are often used to find trends, or general patterns, in data. A scatter plot is similar to a line graph. The data points are plotted on the graph that has an *x*-axis and a *y*-axis, but each point is not connected with a line. Instead, a straight best-fit line is drawn through the data points to show the overall trend. A best-fit line is a single, smooth line that represents all of the data points without necessarily going through all of them. To find a best-fit line, pick a line that is equidistant from as many data points as possible. Examine the graph in **Figure 3.**

If we connected all of the data points with lines, the lines would create a zigzag pattern. It would be hard to see the general pattern in the data. But if we find a best-fit line, we can see a trend more clearly. The trend in a scatter plot depends on the data. The best-fit line in **Figure 4** shows that magazine subscriptions increased.

If you pick two points on the best-fit line, you can estimate the line's slope. The slope will tell you the average rate of increase in magazine subscriptions. By using the dotted lines in **Figure 4,** you can estimate the data point for 1940 as 18 magazine subscriptions per 1,000 households and for 1960 as 42 magazine subscriptions per 1,000 households. The slope is (42 subscriptions – 18 subscriptions) divided by (1960 – 1940). The slope tells you that there is an increase of 24 subscriptions per 1,000 households every 20 years.

Figure 3

Figure 4

Practice

1. Create a scatter plot, and draw a best-fit line for the data below.

Year	Magazine subscriptions per 1,000 households
1918	17
1931	15
1942	42
1954	36
1967	64
1980	73
1992	60
2008	70

2. What does the best-fit line represent?

3. If these data are from a different city than the data in **Figure 4,** what conclusions could you draw about the two cities?

Bar Graphs

Bar graphs should be used for noncontinuous data. They make it easy to compare data quickly when you have one value for multiple items. You can see from **Figure 5** that Jupiter has the largest radius and Mercury has the smallest radius. You could easily arrange the planets in order of size.

Figure 5

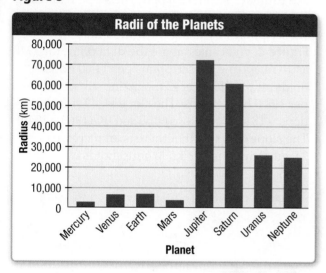

Choosing the scale of a bar graph will make identifying trends in the data easier. Examine **Figure 6** below.

Figure 6

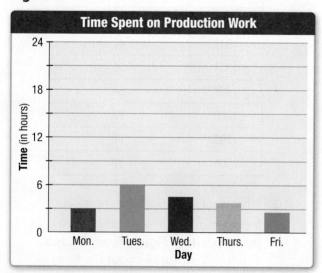

The data are represented accurately in **Figure 6,** but you cannot draw conclusions quickly. Remember that when you create a graph, you want the graph to be as clear as possible. The same data are graphed in **Figure 7,** but the range and scale of the y-axis are smaller than they are in **Figure 6.** The trend in the data is much easier to see in **Figure 7.**

Figure 7

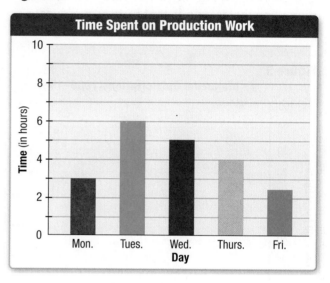

Practice

1. Which day of the week is most productive, according to **Figure 14**?

2. Which day of the week is least productive, according to **Figure 14**?

3. Using the following data, create an easily readable bar graph.

Fiscal period	Money spent (in millions)
First quarter	89
Second quarter	56
Third quarter	72
Fourth quarter	41

Pie Graphs

Pie graphs are an easy way to visualize how parts make up a whole. Often, pie graphs are made from percentage data, such as the data in **Figure 8.**

To create a pie graph, begin by drawing a circle. Because percentages represent parts of 100, imagine dividing the circle into 100 equal parts. Then, you need to figure out how much of the pie each part takes up. It is easiest to start with the largest piece. To graph the data in **Figure 8,** you would start with the data for oxygen. Half of the circle equals 50 parts, so you know that 46% will be slightly less than half of the pie. Shade a piece that is less than half, and label it "Oxygen." Continue making pie pieces for each element until the entire pie graph has been filled. Each element should be a different color to make the graph easy to read as the pie graph in **Figure 9** shows.

You can also use a protractor to construct a pie graph. This method is especially helpful when your data cannot be converted into simple percentages. First, convert the percentages to degrees by dividing each number by 100 and multiplying that result by 360. Next, draw a circle, and make a vertical mark across the top of the circle. Use a protractor to measure the largest angle from your table. Mark this angle along the circumference. For example, 32.9% would be 118° because 32.9/100 = 0.329 and 0.329 × 360 = 118.

To create the next pie piece, measure a second angle from the second mark to make a third mark along the circumference. Continue measuring the angles for each segment until all of your slices are measured. Draw lines from the marks to the center of the circle, and label each slice.

Figure 9 Composition of Earth's Crust

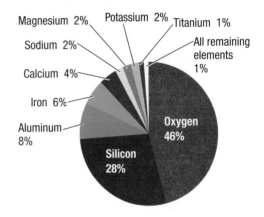

Figure 8 Composition of Earth's Crust

Element	Percentage of Earth's crust
Oxygen	46%
Silicon	28%
Aluminium	8%
Iron	6%
Calcium	4%
Sodium	2%
Magnesium	2%
Potassium	2%
Titanium	1%
All remaining elements	1%

Practice

1. Use the data below to make a pie graph.

Kind of land use	Percentage of total land
Grassland and rangeland	29
Wilderness and parks	13
Urban	7
Wetlands and deserts	4
Forest	30
Cropland	17

2. If humans use half of forests and grasslands, as well as all croplands and urban areas, how much of the total land do humans use?

Ternary Diagrams

Ternary graphs, or ternary diagrams, show three variables on the same plot. Earth scientists use ternary diagrams to show composition of rocks and minerals and the physical states of rock material. The most common use of ternary diagrams is to represent the relative percentage of three components, such as three minerals or three elements.

The composition of any point on a ternary diagram can be described by first determining the percentage of each of the three components, as shown in **Figure 10.** In a ternary diagram, any point represents the relative percentage of three components: A, B, and C. The three components must always add up to 100%. In other words, the total composition of the mineral or rock represented by a given point on a ternary diagram is a combination of A, B, and C, so that

$$x\% \text{ A} + y\% \text{ B} + z\% \text{ C} = 100\%$$

Readings of composition are stated as % A, % B, and % C. For example, the point in the diagram below has a composition of 40% A, 50% B, and 10% C. In most ternary diagrams, areas of the triangle are given names so that scientists can identify a rock or mineral by its name, rather than by its composition.

Figure 10 How to Read a Ternary Diagram

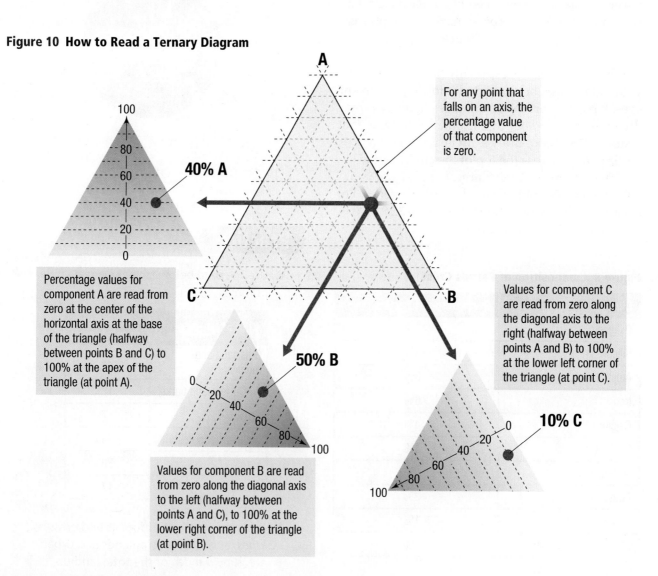

For any point that falls on an axis, the percentage value of that component is zero.

Percentage values for component A are read from zero at the center of the horizontal axis at the base of the triangle (halfway between points B and C) to 100% at the apex of the triangle (at point A).

Values for component B are read from zero along the diagonal axis to the left (halfway between points A and C), to 100% at the lower right corner of the triangle (at point B).

Values for component C are read from zero along the diagonal axis to the right (halfway between points A and B) to 100% at the lower left corner of the triangle (at point C).

Chemistry Skills Refresher

Atoms and Elements

Every object in the universe is made up of particles of matter. Matter is anything that has mass and takes up space. An element is a substance that cannot be separated into simpler substances by chemical means. Elements cannot be separated in this way because each element consists of only one kind of atom. An atom is the smallest unit of an element that maintains the properties of that element.

Atomic Structure Atoms are made up of small particles called *subatomic particles*. The three major types of subatomic particles are **electrons, protons,** and **neutrons** as shown in **Figure 1.** Electrons have a negative electrical charge, protons have a positive charge, and neutrons have no electrical charge. The protons and neutrons are packed close to one another and form the **nucleus.** The protons give the nucleus a positive charge. The electrons of an atom are located in a region around the nucleus known as an **electron cloud.** The negatively charged electrons are attracted to the positively charged nucleus.

Figure 1 Atomic Structure

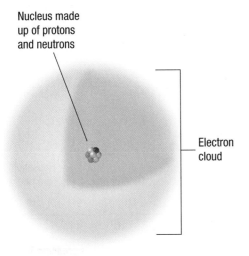

Nucleus made up of protons and neutrons

Electron cloud

Atomic Number To help in the identification of elements, scientists have assigned an **atomic number** to each kind of atom. The atomic number is equal to the number of protons in the atom. Atoms that have the same number of protons are all of the same element. An uncharged, or electrically neutral, atom has an equal number of protons and electrons. Therefore, the atomic number is also equal to the number of electrons in an uncharged atom. The number of neutrons, however, can vary for a given element. Atoms that have different numbers of neutrons but are of the same element are called **isotopes.**

Periodic Table of the Elements In a periodic table, the elements are arranged in order of increasing atomic number. Each element in the table is found in a separate box. In each horizontal row of the table, each element has one more electron and one more proton than the element to its left. Each row of the table is called a **period.** Changes in chemical properties across a period correspond to changes in the elements' electron arrangements. Each vertical column of the table, known as a **group,** contains elements that have similar properties. The elements in a group have similar chemical properties because they have the same number of electrons in their outer energy level. For example, the elements helium, neon, argon, krypton, xenon, and radon all have similar properties and are known as the noble gases.

Molecules and Compounds

When the atoms of two or more elements are joined chemically, the resulting substance is called a **compound.** A compound is a new substance that has properties different from those of the elements that compose it. For example, water, H_2O, is a compound formed when atoms of hydrogen, H, and oxygen, O, combine. The smallest complete unit of a compound that has all of the properties of that compound is called a **molecule.**

Chemical Formulas

A chemical formula indicates the elements that make up a compound. The chemical formula also indicates the relative number of atoms of each element present. For example, the chemical formula for water is H_2O, which indicates that each water molecule consists of two atoms of hydrogen and one atom of oxygen.

Chemical Equations

A chemical reaction occurs when a chemical change takes place. (During a chemical change, new substances that have new properties form.) A chemical equation is a useful way of describing a chemical reaction by means of chemical formulas. The equation indicates the substances that react and the products. For example, when carbon and oxygen combine, they can form carbon dioxide. The equation for this reaction is as follows:

$$C + O_2 \rightarrow CO_2$$

Acids, Bases, and pH

An ion is an atom or group of atoms that has an electrical charge because it has lost or gained one or more electrons. When an acid, such as hydrochloric acid, HCl, is mixed with water, the acid separates into ions. An acid is a compound that produces hydrogen ions, H^+, in water. The hydrogen ions then combine with a water molecule to form a hydronium ion, H_3O^+. A solution that contains hydronium ions is an acidic solution. A base, on the other hand, is a substance that produces hydroxide ions, OH^-, in water.

To determine whether a solution is acidic or basic, scientists measure pH. **pH** is a measure of how many hydronium ions are in solution. The pH scale ranges from 0 to 14. The middle point, pH = 7, is neutral, neither acidic nor basic. Acids have a pH of less than 7; bases have a pH of more than 7. The lower the number is, the stronger the acid is. The higher the number is, the stronger the base is. **Figure 2** shows the pH of some common substances.

Figure 2 pH Measurements of Some Common Substances

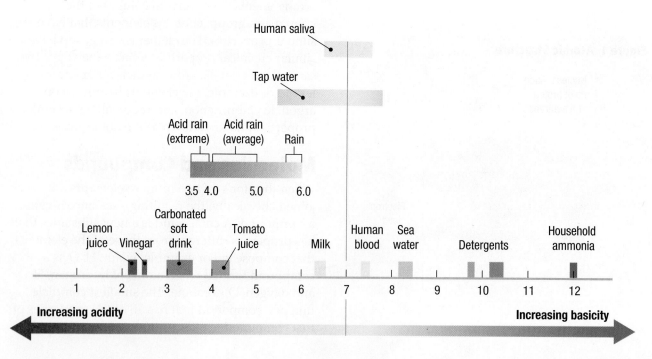

Physics Skills Refresher

Mass

All matter has mass. Mass is the amount of matter that makes up an object. For example, Earth is made of a very large amount of matter and therefore has a large mass. An object's mass can be changed only by changing the amount of matter in the object.

Weight

Weight is different from mass. Weight is a measure of the gravitational force that is exerted on an object. Objects that have large mass are heavier than objects that have a small mass, even if the objects are the same size.

Density

The mass per unit of volume of a substance is density. Thus, a material's density is the amount of matter it has in a given space. To find density, both mass and volume must be measured. Density is calculated by using the following equation:

$$density = \frac{mass}{volume}$$

Density is expressed in units of mass over units of volume. Most commonly, density is expressed as grams per cubic centimeter (g/cm^3) or as kilograms per cubic meter (kg/m^3).

The density of a particular substance is always the same at a given temperature and pressure. The density of one substance is usually different from the density of other substances. Therefore, density is a useful property for identifying substances.

Concentration

A measure of the amount of one substance that is dissolved in another substance is concentration. The substance that is dissolved is the solute. The substance that dissolves another substance is the solvent. Concentration is calculated by using the following equation:

$$concentration = \frac{mass\ of\ solute}{volume\ of\ solvent}$$

Concentration is expressed as mass of solute divided by volume of solvent. Most commonly, concentration is expressed as grams per milliliter (g/mL) or as kilograms per liter (kg/L).

Forces

In science, a force is simply a push or a pull. All forces have both magnitude and direction. Force is expressed using a unit called a newton (N). All forces are exerted by one object on another object.

More than one force can be exerted on an object at the same time. The net force is the force that results from combining all the forces exerted on an object. When forces are in the same direction, net force is calculated by using the following equation:

$$net\ force = force\ A + force\ B$$

When forces are in the opposite direction, net force is calculated by using the following equation:

$$net\ force = force\ A - force\ B$$

Pressure

The force exerted over a given area is pressure. Pressure can be calculated by using the following equation:

$$pressure = \frac{force}{area}$$

The SI unit for pressure is the pascal (Pa). Other common units of pressure include bars and atmospheres.

Speed

The rate at which an object moves is its speed. Speed depends on the distance traveled and the time taken to travel that distance. Speed is calculated by using the following equation:

$$speed = \frac{distance}{time}$$

The SI unit for speed is meters per second (m/s). Other units commonly used to express speed are kilometers per hour, feet per second, and miles per hour.

Velocity

The speed of an object in a particular direction is velocity. Speed and velocity are not the same, even though they are calculated using the same equation. Velocity must include a direction, so velocity is described as speed in a certain direction. For example, the speed of a plane that is traveling south at 600 km/h is 600 km/h. The velocity of a plane that is traveling south at 600 km/h is 600 km/h south.

Velocity can also be thought of as the rate of change of an object's position. An object's velocity remains constant only if its speed and direction don't change. Therefore, constant velocity occurs only along a straight line.

Acceleration

The rate at which velocity changes is called acceleration. Acceleration can be calculated by using the following equation:

$$acceleration = \frac{final\ velocity - starting\ velocity}{time\ it\ takes\ to\ change\ velocity}$$

Velocity is expressed in meters per second (m/s), and time is expressed in seconds (s). Therefore, acceleration is expressed in meters per second per second (m/s/s), or meters per second squared (m/s^2).

Inertia

The tendency of an object to resist any change in motion is called *inertia.* Because of inertia, an object at rest will remain at rest until something causes it to move. A moving object continues to move at the same speed and in the same direction unless something acts on it to change its speed or direction.

Momentum

The property of a moving object that is equal to the product of the object's mass and velocity is momentum. Momentum is calculated by using the following equation:

$$momentum = mass \times velocity, \text{ or } p = mv$$

The SI unit for momentum is kilograms multiplied by meters per second (kg•m/s). When a moving object hits another object, some or all of the momentum of the first object is transferred to the other object. If only some of the momentum is transferred, the rest of the momentum stays with the first object.

Thermodynamics

The study of the behavior of the flow of energy in natural systems is thermodynamics. The laws of thermodynamics describe some of the basic truths of how energy behaves in the universe. Many Earth processes involve the flow of energy through the Earth system.

The First Law of Thermodynamics This law is often called the Law of Conservation of Energy. Simply stated, this law states that energy can be changed from one form to another but that it cannot be created or destroyed. Energy constantly changes from one form to another, but the total amount of energy available in the universe is constant.

The Second Law of Thermodynamics This law states that in all energy exchanges, if no energy enters or leaves the system, the potential energy of the new state will always be less than that of the initial state. In other words, no form of energy converts entirely to another form of energy without losing some energy as heat. So, the entropy of an isolated system always increases as time increases. Entropy is a measure of disorder, or randomness, of energy and matter.

The Third Law of Thermodynamics This law states that if all of the thermal motion of molecules, or kinetic energy, were removed from a system, a temperature called absolute zero would be reached. Absolute zero is in a temperature of 0 Kelvin or –273.15 degrees Celsius.

$$absolute\ zero = 0\ K = -273.15\ °C$$

Technology Skills

Using Search Engines

The World Wide Web is filled with information on almost any topic imaginable. Search engines make it possible to sort through this vast amount of information to find what you need.

A search engine is software that you use to search for Web pages by using keywords. Some search engines let you search huge databases that cover large portions of the Web. Other search engines may search a limited but more focused range of pages, such as the pages on a single Web site or journal articles in a specific subject area.

Although the scope of search engines may differ, most search engines work in a similar way. For example, consider Scirus, a search engine that searches for scientific information. You can access Scirus by entering the Web address *www.scirus.com* into the address bar of your Web browser, as **Figure 1** shows.

Figure 1 Address Bar of Web Browser

Once you are on the Scirus home page, you will see a search box. To find information on a specific topic, type into the search box keywords that you think are most likely to target the web pages about that topic. Then, click on the Search button to start the search. For example, if you are researching black holes, you would type the keywords "black hole." The search engine will return a list of pages containing those keywords. You can then click on the links to visit the pages that seem most promising for your research goals.

Use the help pages to improve your searches.

Although all search engines work in a similar way, they are all slightly different. To make your searches more effective on a particular site, look at the site's help page or advanced search page for helpful tips and advanced search options.

If you search a broad topic, you may get too many Web sites in your search results. The help page or advanced search page can also help you determine the best way to narrow your search so that you will find a more manageable number of Web sites. For example, these pages may allow you to select other keywords to include or exclude from your search, tell you where to look for the keywords on Web pages, and tell you what types of Web sites to include in the search. Suppose that you wanted to find only Web pages that contain information about neutrinos and black holes. You could use the advanced search page to help narrow your results, as **Figure 2** shows.

Figure 2 Advanced Search Page

Check the reliability of Web sites.

When you visit a site to find factual information, remember to check the source of the information. Anyone can post information on the Internet, but the information does not have to be correct. Usually, government and educational institutions are reliable sources of information; personal Web sites may not contain accurate information.

Practice

1. Use an Internet search engine to find information about gamma rays. List three Web sites, and discuss how reliable each one might be.

How Search Engines Work

Most search engines rely on Boolean logic. Boolean logic uses three words—*AND, OR,* and *NOT*—to define the relationships between topics. These three words, known as *Boolean operators*, can be used to make very effective searches.

Use the AND operator to find multiple terms.

When you use the AND operator between two search terms, both of the terms must be present in the results. For example, to find Web pages that contain both the words *work* and *power,* you would enter both search terms, as **Figure 3** shows. The shaded area of the Venn diagram in **Figure 3** represents the results of this search.

Figure 3 Search Results Using AND

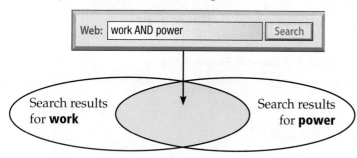

Note that the AND operator is in all capital letters. Some search engines require that you use all capital letters to distinguish the operators from the search terms.

Use the OR operator to find either term.

When you use the OR operator between two search terms, the results should show pages that contain either one or both of the terms. If you use the OR operator, your search result will have more Web pages, as the shaded area in **Figure 4** shows.

Figure 4 Search Results Using OR

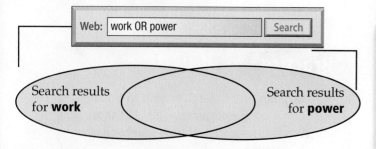

Use the NOT operator to exclude a term.

When you use the NOT operator before a word, your search results should not contain that term. This operator will help you narrow your search by excluding a certain set of Web pages that commonly have the word of the topic that you are looking for. **Figure 5** shows a Venn diagram of the search results for the search "work NOT power."

Figure 5 Search Results Using NOT

Using more than one Boolean operator will make your searches more specific. For example, to find Web sites that contain information about work and power, but not electricity, you would search "work AND power NOT electricity."

Some search engines do not support the direct use of Boolean operators. You may have to go to the advanced search page to do Boolean searches. Many advanced search pages allow you to fill in search fields that are similar to the Boolean operators, as **Figure 6** shows.

Figure 6 Search Fields and Boolean Operators

Advanced search field	Boolean operator
All of the words	AND
Any of the words	OR
None of the words	NOT

Practice

1. Write a Boolean search query to find Web pages that must contain the word *rock* and either the word *sedimentary* or the word *metamorphic.*

2. Draw a Venn diagram to represent the search query that you wrote in item 1.

Technology in the Library

Libraries are one of the best places to find highly reliable reference materials, such as encyclopedias, dictionaries, and nonfiction books. Printed materials are often subject to editing and peer review, unlike much of the information on the Internet. Libraries also have books, magazines, newspapers, and journals that may not be available on the Internet or are expensive to access.

If you do not have a specific source in mind, the best place to start your library research is the library's catalog. Most libraries now have systems for searching their catalogs by computer. So, searching the catalog is similar to using a search engine on the Web. When you are doing a library search, you should specify whether the keywords are for a subject, a title, or an author.

Once you have the results of a catalog search, you will need to know where to find the books that come up in your search results. Most libraries use one of two classification systems—the Library of Congress system or the Dewey decimal system. Whichever system your library uses, you should write down the call numbers for the books that you want to find from your catalog search. Then, use a map or directory of the library to find the books.

Both classification systems organize nonfiction books by subject, as **Figure 7** and **Figure 8** show. Most large libraries use the Library of Congress system, whereas many smaller libraries use the Dewey decimal system.

Figure 8 Library of Congress Classification System

Letter on book binding	Subject
A	General works
B	Philosophy, psychology, and religion
C–F	History
G–H	Geography and social sciences (e.g., anthropology)
J	Political science
K	Law
L	Education
M	Music
N	Fine arts
P	Literature
Q	Science
R	Medicine
S	Agriculture
T	Technology
U–V	Military and naval science
Z	Bibliography and library science

Figure 7 Dewey Decimal System

Number on book binding	Subject
000–099	General works
100–199	Philosophy and psychology
200–299	Religion
300–399	Social studies
400–499	Language
500–599	Pure sciences
600–699	Technology
700–799	Arts
800–899	Literature
900–999	History

Practice

1. What system does your school library use to classify books?

2. List three magazines or journals in your school or local library that could contain current information on scientific research.

3. Name the title and call number for a book on science.

Scientific Methods

Scientists gain new knowledge and understanding of the natural world by using scientific methods. These methods are sometimes presented in a series of ordered steps. However, there is no single scientific method. The steps may be done in a different order, or certain steps may be repeated in some scientific investigations.

Making Observations Observing objects and events in the natural world is an important step in any scientific method. Observation is usually the starting point of any scientific study. You also make observations when doing experiments. It is important to keep detailed records of observations so that you can accurately remember them.

Asking Questions Careful observations eventually lead to questions. A good question should be specific and should serve as the focus for the entire investigation.

Forming a Hypothesis A hypothesis is a possible explanation or answer to your question. You do not know whether a hypothesis is the right answer until it is tested. You should be able to test your hypothesis to determine whether it is true or false. You should make predictions about what you think will happen if your hypothesis is true and what will happen if your hypothesis is false. These predictions can help you design an experiment to test the hypothesis.

Testing a Hypothesis Once you have a question, a hypothesis, and a set of predictions, you are ready to do an experiment to test the hypothesis. You should design your experiment to be as simple as possible, and you should consider which variables you want to control. Your design should also include plans about what instruments and materials you will use and how you will analyze the data that you collect.

Drawing Conclusions After you finish an experiment, you will determine whether your hypothesis is correct by examining your results. You may evaluate your hypothesis by seeing if your original predictions were correct. If your results do not support your hypothesis, they may lead you to ask more questions. You may need to form a new hypothesis, make new predictions, and perform a new or modified version of your experiment.

Communicating Results If you carry out an investigation that provides new information, you should publish your results. Others who read about your investigation may try to understand how you drew your conclusions. They may try your experiment to see if they get the same results or use your results to form new hypotheses and do new experiments.

Making observations

Asking questions

Forming a hypothesis

Testing a hypothesis

Drawing conclusions

Communicating results

Conducting Experiments

Many scientific experiments try to determine a cause-and-effect relationship—"When *A* happens, *B* happens." The *A* and the *B* in this relationship are variables, or changing quantities. The variable that you change intentionally in an experiment is called the *independent variable* and, in this case, is *A*. The *dependent variable*, *B*, changes in response to the changes in the independent variable.

Suppose that your experiment is seeking to answer the following question: "What happens to the rate of crystal formation when the temperature of the solution changes?" In this case, temperature would be the independent variable, and the rate of crystal formation would be the dependent variable. You would change the temperature and then measure the resulting change in rate. When you graph your results, independent variables are represented on the *x*-axis, and dependent variables are represented on the *y*-axis.

Make observations in the lab.

You should write down any observations that you make during an experiment, along with any data that you collect. Record the characteristics of the materials that you use, the conditions during your experiment, any changes that occur, and anything that you think might be relevant to the experiment. These observations will help you when you are reporting your results. They can also help you figure out why your experimental results may not be what you expected. Usually, a pen is used to record your observations in a lab notebook because people reading the notes later can be sure that you did not change your notes after the experiment.

Avoid measurement pitfalls.

One common error in taking measurements results from parallax. *Parallax* is an apparent shift in position caused by a change in viewing angle. To avoid parallax errors, always line up your eyes with the part of the measurement scale that you are reading.

Another common measurement error is recording the wrong units of measurement. Always check the instrument to make sure that you know which units it uses, and record those units.

Taking Measurements

It is important to note the limits of the tools that you use to collect data. The exactness of a measurement is called *precision*, and it is determined by the instrument that you use. Precision is reflected in the number of significant figures. When you record measurements, you should use the correct number of significant figures. Usually, instruments with a digital readout give you the correct number of significant figures. So, you can record the measurement exactly as you see it on the instrument. When you need to read the measurement from a scale on an instrument, you should record as many digits as are marked on the scale and estimate one more digit beyond that.

Measure volume with a graduated cylinder.

You should use a graduated cylinder when you need precise measurements of volume.

① Place the graduated cylinder on a flat, level surface.

② Make sure that you are at eye level with the surface of the liquid.

③ Read the mark closest to the liquid level. Because most liquids climb slightly up the glass walls of a graduated cylinder, they produce a curved surface called a *meniscus*, shown in **Figure 1.** You should always take volume readings from the bottom of the meniscus.

Tip Holding a piece of white paper behind the graduated cylinder can make the meniscus easier to see.

Figure 1 Meniscus in a Graduated Cylinder

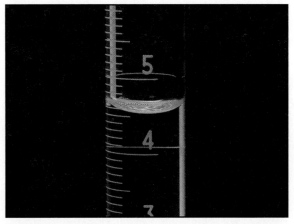

Measure mass with a balance.

A triple-beam balance, shown in **Figure 2,** can measure mass to a precision of 0.01 g.

1 Make sure that the balance is properly "zeroed." First, make sure that the balance is on a level surface. Then, slide all of the slider weights to zero. Turn the zero adjustment knob until the pointer is in line with the zero at the center of the arrow.

2 Place the object to be measured on the pan. **CAUTION** Never place chemicals or hot objects directly on the balance pan.

3 To determine the total mass of the object, add the readings from all three beams.

4 Move the largest slider weight to the right along the beam until the balance tips. Then, move the slider back one notch so that the beam tips back the other way. Repeat this step for the next-largest slider weight. Then, move the smallest slider weight to the right until the pointer points to the zero on the right end.

5 If you are measuring solid chemicals, start by putting a piece of weighing paper on the pan. Record the mass of the weighing paper. Then, place the chemical on the weighing paper. Measure the total mass of the chemical and paper. Then, subtract the mass of the paper to determine the mass of the chemical alone. You may use a similar method for measuring the mass of a liquid in a container.

Tip If you want to use a specified amount of a substance, move the sliders to the right by the amount of mass that you want to obtain. The balance will tip. Slowly add the substance until the balance points to zero.

Measure temperature with a thermometer.

Digital thermometers and bulb thermometers are often used in the lab. Bulb thermometers consist of a column of liquid—either mercury or colored alcohol—in a glass tube, as shown in **Figure 3.** As the liquid heats up, it expands, so the column of liquid rises up the tube.

1 To measure temperature with a digital thermometer, immerse the probe in the liquid or touch it to an object. Wait for the digital readout to stabilize, and then record the temperature. Make sure that the thermometer is set to the desired scale (Celsius or Fahrenheit).

2 To measure temperature with a bulb thermometer, put the thermometer in the liquid to be measured. Wait for the level of liquid inside the thermometer to stabilize.

3 With your eyes level with the top of the liquid inside the thermometer, take the reading on the scale next to the column of liquid. Pay attention to the scale on the thermometer. The smallest unit marked on a bulb thermometer is usually 1 °C. These markings are close together, so you can only estimate half a unit between marks, or 0.05 °C.

CAUTION A glass thermometer can break if it hits a solid object or overheats. In addition to producing broken glass, the liquid inside will spill. If a mercury thermometer should ever break, immediately notify your teacher or another adult. Let your teacher clean up the spill. Do not touch the mercury. Because mercury is a hazardous substance, mercury thermometers are rarely used in class laboratories.

Figure 2 Triple-Beam Balance

Figure 3 Alcohol Thermometer

Communicating Scientific Results

Whether you are writing a laboratory report for your teacher or submitting a paper to a scientific journal, you should use a similar structure to report the results of an experiment. Your lab report should contain enough information so that others can use it to reproduce your experiment and compare their results to yours. Laboratory reports should contain the same basic parts.

Start with a title.

Choose a title that clearly conveys the nature of the experiment. The title could describe the subject, the hypothesis, or the result. If you are doing an experiment from a lab manual, this title could be the same as the title of the experiment given in the manual.

Include background information.

The background section should briefly explain why your experiment is important. State the question that your experiment is trying to answer. You could also include a description of the initial observations that led you to the question. Sometimes, the background section includes the basic principles that you will use when you analyze your experiment.

State your hypothesis.

This section should state your hypothesis and your predictions of what will happen if the hypothesis is true and what will happen if the hypothesis is false. Your hypothesis is what you think will happen in the experiment. Often, a hypothesis is written as an "If . . . then" statement. The independent variable, or variable that you will change, should follow the "If" in the statement. The effect on the dependent variable should follow the "then" in the statement. Suppose that you want to find out if adding salt to water changes the boiling temperature of water. You would change the amount of salt that you add to water and measure the temperature at which the water boils. So, the amount of salt would be your independent variable, and the boiling temperature would be your dependent variable. Your hypothesis statement could be "If salt is added to water, the temperature at which water boils will increase."

List your materials before you start your experiment.

To make sure that you have everything that you need for your experiment, list all of the equipment and other supplies that you use in the experiment. For experiments taken from a lab manual, these materials are usually listed in the manual.

Describe the procedure that you used.

Detailed steps that describe exactly how you did your experiment are included in the procedure. Include details about how you set up the equipment, how you took your measurements, and what analysis or calculations you did with your data after collecting it. Your description should be detailed enough that someone else could reproduce the experiment exactly as you did it. If you are doing an experiment from a lab manual, you should write the steps in your own words and note anything that you did that was different from the procedure in the manual.

Record your observations, data, and analysis.

You should list all of the data you collected and show the results of any analysis or calculations that you performed with the data. It is often useful to present data or other results using tables or graphs. Also, include any observations that you made that might be relevant to your conclusions. Some experiments in lab manuals list specific questions that you should answer in your analysis.

End the report with your conclusions.

In your conclusions, you should discuss whether or not your experiment supports your original hypothesis. Remember that your experiment may not support your hypothesis. You can still explain why you think that the experiment did not turn out the way that you expected. You can also present a new or modified hypothesis and briefly describe additional experiments that could be done if you were to continue or expand your investigation. Some experiments in lab manuals list specific questions that you should answer in your conclusions.

Mapping Expeditions

Journey to Red River

New Mexico

Materials
compass, magnetic, with
  degree markings (optional)
ruler, metric

How do you get from one place to another when you don't know the route? Whether you are planning a trip on foot or by car or boat, a map can be very handy. The ability to read a map can help you reach your destination quickly and safely and can help you avoid becoming disoriented and lost.

The topographic map on the facing page shows the area around Red River, New Mexico. Imagine that you are traveling to Red River to do some camping, hiking, and sightseeing. Study the map for a few moments, and note the locations of roads, creeks, hills, and other features. Then, answer the questions below.

1 Red River lies in northeastern New Mexico near the Colorado border. The magnetic declination in Red River is about 13°E. Draw a diagram that shows how you would adjust a magnetic compass to determine true north in Red River. Why is distinguishing true north from geomagnetic north important?

2 You set up a tent at Mallette Campground. If you walk in a straight line from your campsite to the cemetery at the base of Graveyard Canyon, how far will you walk? Show your work.

3 You decide to hike from St. Edwin Chapel to location A. What is your elevation at location A? How much higher than your starting point is your destination? (Elevations on the map are given in feet.)

4 Notice that the road in the lower-right corner of the map winds back and forth to make a series of hairpin turns. Why did the road designers build the road this way?

5 Most United States Geological Survey maps, including this one, were created in the early 1960s. Like most towns, Red River has changed in the last few decades. Which features of the map might not reflect how Red River looks today? Which features are probably still accurate?

**Red River Area
Taos County, New Mexico**

Scale 1:24,000

Roads

Buildings

Campground

Cemetery

Chapel

A Case of the Tennessee Shakes

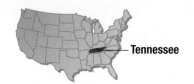

Tennessee

Materials
road map of Tennessee

Did you know that almost 10,000 earthquakes occur every day? In fact, an earthquake likely is occurring right now somewhere in the world. Fortunately, less than 2% of the earthquakes that seismographs record are strong enough to do serious damage.

You might think that scientists are most interested in strong earthquakes. But weak earthquakes can tell a seismologist (a scientist who studies earthquakes) as much as strong ones can.

Earthquake Frequency (based on observations since 1900)

Descriptor	Magnitude	Average occurring annually
Great	8.0 and higher	1
Major	7.0 to 7.9	18
Strong	6.0 to 6.9	120
Moderate	5.0 to 5.9	800
Light	4.0 to 4.9	about 6,200
Minor	3.0 to 3.9	about 49,000
Very minor	2.0 to 2.9 1.0 to 1.9	about 365,000 about 29,200,000

Part 1

❶ Examine the map below. Which tectonic plates are involved in most earthquakes that occur in North America?

❷ At tectonic plate boundaries, most earthquake epicenters are densely distributed, or closely packed. Why do most earthquakes occur along tectonic plate boundaries?

Eurasian plate

North American plate

Eurasian plate

African plate

Pacific plate

Nazca plate

South American plate

Australian plate

Antarctic plate

— Plate boundary
• Recorded earthquake

Each dot on this map represents the epicenter of an earthquake. Most of these earthquakes, which occurred over a 20-year period, were too weak to be felt by people.

❸ Some earthquakes, however, occur in the interior of the United States, which is far from any plate boundary. Propose a hypothesis that explains these earthquakes.

Part 2

The map above shows the epicenters of earthquakes in eastern Tennessee. However, Tennessee is far from any plate boundary. Some scientists think that the earthquakes in this region are the result of an ancient fault that has been reactivated. Other scientists think that a new fault zone is forming in eastern Tennessee. If they are correct, eastern Tennessee may experience a major earthquake in this zone.

❶ Use the map to describe the location of the eastern Tennessee seismic zone (ETSZ) in terms of longitude and latitude.

❷ Name at least two major cities that are located in the ETSZ. How could a major earthquake affect these cities?

❸ Two nuclear power plants are located in the ETSZ. Imagine that a company has plans to build a plant near McMinnville, Tennessee. The United States Geological Survey has hired you to advise this company about the risk of a major earthquake. Briefly describe what you would say in a letter to the company. Explain your reasoning as clearly as possible.

By using trench excavations, seismologist Karl Mueller can study sediments across the New Madrid fault in Tennessee to estimate the dates and magnitudes of past earthquakes.

Buried Treasure

ENVIRONMENTAL CONNECTION

United States

By many standards, the United States is one of the wealthiest countries in the world. Although this wealth is largely due to the ingenuity and hard work of the people who live in the country, it is also due to good fortune. The crust that lies beneath the United States holds a huge supply of natural resources. These resources include ores that contain precious metals, such as copper, silver, and gold, as well as fossil fuels, such as petroleum, coal, and natural gas. The availability and distribution of these resources have been important in shaping U.S. history.

This worker in California cuts through steel, an iron alloy, at 2,000 °F!

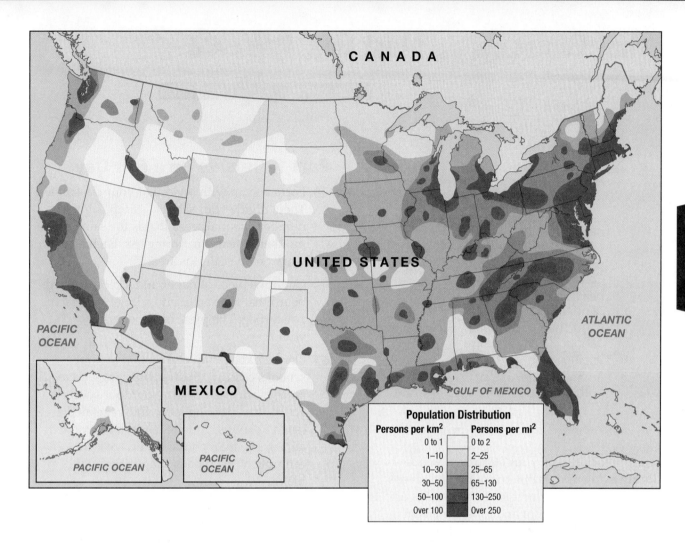

C A N A D A

UNITED STATES

PACIFIC OCEAN

ATLANTIC OCEAN

MEXICO

GULF OF MEXICO

PACIFIC OCEAN

PACIFIC OCEAN

Population Distribution

Persons per km²	Persons per mi²
0 to 1	0 to 2
1–10	2–25
10–30	25–65
30–50	65–130
50–100	130–250
Over 100	Over 250

1 Find your state on the map of natural resources on the previous page. What resources are produced in your state?

2 Look at the locations of the various resources. Which resources are commonly located near each other? Why do certain resources commonly occur together?

3 When tectonic plates collide, pockets of hot magma may come into contact with cooler, solid rock. Using what you know about plate tectonics and the ways in which minerals form, describe why California has more iron-ore deposits than Nebraska does.

4 Describe the conditions that existed in the United States millions of years ago and that resulted in the formation of the modern petroleum and natural-gas deposits.

5 Compare the map on this page with the map on the previous page. What areas have both high concentrations of people and a large reserve of natural resources? What areas have many people but few resources? How could resources be transported to areas in which they are needed?

6 Using these two maps, would you say that most cities have grown up in places in or near which there are natural resources? Why or why not? What other factors could have influenced the location of cities?

7 Imagine that you work for a company that builds electrical equipment made primarily of copper. Why might southern Arizona be a good place to locate a new plant? What might be a disadvantage of locating your plant there?

What Comes Down Must Go... WHERE?

Materials

cardboard, about
    23 cm × 33 cm
paper, about
    23 cm × 33 cm
pencils, red, blue, and
    purple
permanent marker,
    fine-tipped
plastic bag, reclosable,
    about 23 cm × 33 cm
scissors
umbrella, raincoat, or
    other rain gear

Imagine looking out your classroom window during a downpour. Billions of tiny raindrops splatter off of everything in sight. Streams of water fall from the roof and form dozens of puddles and streams on the ground. These miniature lakes and rivers swirl together, and tiny torrents carry away leaves, bits of trash, and other debris. A day or two later, the ground outside looks completely dry. Where did all of the water go?

In this activity, you will create a map of your school. After observing the type of ground cover and the slope of the terrain at various locations, you will predict whether rainwater will collect or run off at those locations. You will also look for possible sources of pollution and places where erosion might occur. Later, you will go outside in the rain and find out whether your predictions are correct.

Part 1: Outside on a Fair Day

❶ Form a team with several of your classmates. Then, divide your school's campus into the number of equal areas that is the same as the number of teams in your class. Each team will work on one campus area.

❷ Cut out a piece of paper and a piece of cardboard that fit exactly into a large reclosable plastic bag. The piece of paper will be your map.

❸ On the paper, map one section of your school's campus. Include buildings, paved areas (such as sidewalks, outdoor sports courts, and parking lots), and vegetated areas (such as lawns, athletic fields, and wooded areas). The map on the next page is an example of the type of map that you will make.

❹ **a.** Use a red pencil to mark the areas on your map. Draw arrows to indicate a downhill slope. Use a narrow arrow to indicate a steep slope and a wider arrow to indicate a gradual slope. Use circles to indicate flat areas.

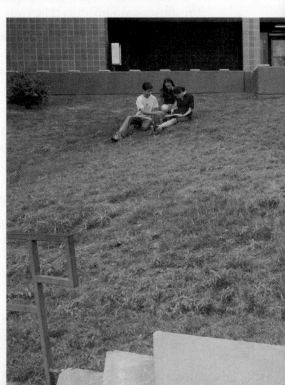

b. Use a blue pencil to draw arrows and circles that indicate where you think surface water may collect or flow during a steady rain. These areas may include low-lying areas, the roofs of buildings, gutters, and drainage ditches.

c. Use a purple pencil to mark the locations that you think might contribute pollution to the runoff. (These areas may include parking lots that contain oil stains or places where trash is usually found on the ground, such as near a dumpster.)

5 Seal your map and the piece of cardboard in the reclosable bag. When you are outside in the rain, use a permanent marker to write your observations on the outside of the bag.

Part 2: Outside During a Steady Rain

6 Dress appropriately, and go outside. Using the marker, write on your plastic-covered map the places where water collects and runs. In places where water moves along the ground, use arrows to show the water's direction. Use the letter *P* to mark the locations of pollutants that you observe in the water. Use the letter *E* to mark the locations where erosion seems to be occurring. (Look for soil or natural debris that is being washed along by moving water.)

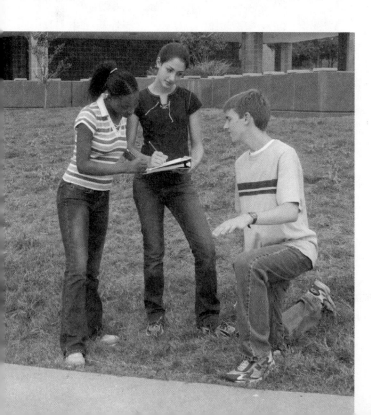

Part 3: Back in the Classroom

7 Discuss your predictions for some of the locations. Were your predictions correct? How do you explain differences between your predictions and your observations?

8 Was the pollution that you observed suspended load, bed load, or dissolved load? Explain how there may have been pollution that you could not observe.

9 Explain how erosion on your school's campus could affect the erosion and deposition that occurs downstream from the campus.

10 Assemble the maps from your class into a single map of your school's campus. In your opinion, does most of the rainfall at your school become groundwater or runoff? Where does runoff go when it leaves your school's campus? Your school is probably part of a larger, local watershed. Find out what stream or other body of water the surface runoff in your area empties into.

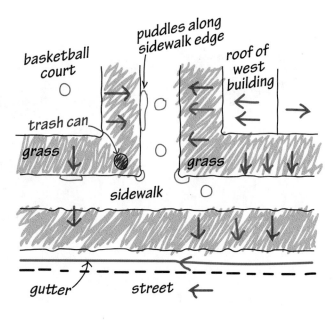

Where the **hippos** Roam

Africa

Materials
pencils, assorted colors
ruler, metric

Millions of years ago, ancestors of modern crocodiles lurked in the shallow waters of lakes and other bodies of water. Like their current descendents, they hunted fish and other animals. If you could travel back in time to visit one of those lakes, you might see the ancestors of today's hippopotamuses there, too. Antelopes might browse along the edges of the lake, and rodents of various sizes might scurry back and forth.

When paleontologists examine the fossil of a prehistoric organism, they may discover clues about the organism's life. They may also answer questions about the organism's environment: Was the area hot or cold? Was it humid or dry? Then, by putting all of these clues together, the paleontologists may be able to learn a little more about how organisms and environments change over time.

Unfortunately, studying a fossil site is no easy task! Discoveries of complete organisms are rare. More often, a paleontologist may find a few teeth scattered over a very large area. In such cases, keeping track of where the fossils were found is very important. In this activity, you will use the data from a fossil site to create a map of fossil locations at that site. Then, you will draw some conclusions about the past environment, or *paleoenvironment*, at that location.

The animals that lived near lakes millions of years ago probably had lives similar to the lives of animals that live near lakes today.

Location of Fossil Teeth				
Layer	Hippos	Rodents	Crocodiles	Bovids*
A	B11, C6, D3, I15, J10, L7, M6		C14, F7, G13, I3, L13, O2	
B	F2, J3, K1, K2	B10, B11, F13	H2, I7, K2, N5, N7	G14
C		B3, C10, D1, H8, M9, N4		A5, A6, E2, E4, E14, H7, H8, H12, K4, M1, N15

*Bovids are antelopes and other such animals.

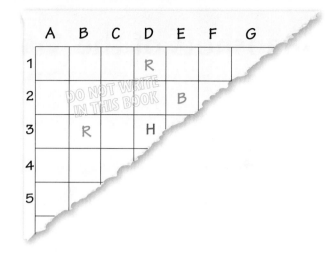

The table above shows the locations of fossils that were found spread out over 22,500 m². A team of paleontologists decided that this site, which measured 150 m × 150 m, was too large to work on all at once. So, the paleontologists decided to create a grid of 10 m squares. Starting in the northwest corner of the site, they labeled the squares from west to east with the letters *A–O*. Then, they numbered the squares 1–15 from north to south. Thus, each fossil could be labeled with a letter and a number that would identify where the fossil was found. For example, A1 would signify the 10 m × 10 m square in the northwest corner of the site, and O15 would signify the square in the southeast corner.

① Create a map of the fossil site by drawing a grid similar to the one described above. The scale should be 1 cm = 10 m. Use letters to label across the top edge of the grid, and use numbers to label down the left edge of the grid. For each fossil, place a letter (*H* for a hippo fossil, *R* for a rodent fossil, *C* for a crocodile fossil, and *B* for a bovid fossil) in the square that corresponds to where the fossil was found. Use pencil color to represent the different layers of sediment, and make a key that shows which layer each color represents.

② From the distribution of fossils in the layer of sediment just below the surface layer, what part of this site might have been under water? Explain your answer, and devise a way to show that area on your map.

③ Describe how the environment at this site changed over time.

④ One team member wished to search this site for fossils of dry-climate plants. Which layer or layers would most likely yield fossils of such plants? Explain your answer.

⑤ One paleontologist suggested that tectonic uplift had raised the area's elevation over time and thus caused the climate to change. A second paleontologist thought that the area had probably lost elevation over time. With which scientist do you agree? Explain your answer.

Fossils, such as these crocodile teeth, help scientists learn what an area was like millions of years ago.

Snapshots of the Weather

United States

Materials
paper, tracing
pencil

From looking at a weather map, you might get the impression that the clouds, fronts, and other features shown are standing still. However, weather patterns change constantly, and a weather map can show only what is happening at one particular instant. For this reason, meteorologists rely on a sequence of maps to make predictions about local weather.

In this activity, you will analyze a sequence of weather maps. The maps were taken from a daily newspaper and show weather patterns that occurred in the United States during a 4-day period. You will note what information the maps show and do not show, and you will make a few predictions based on your observations.

1 Look carefully at the maps on the next page. What weather information do they show? Now, look at the weather symbols in the Reference Tables section of Appendix E. What information is not included on these maps? Why might a newspaper exclude certain types of information on daily weather maps?

2 Why would a newspaper that serves only a specific geographic region publish the weather for the entire continental United States?

3 Describe how the weather patterns in your location changed during the 4-day period shown.

4 During what season do you think this 4-day period occurred? Explain your answer.

5 Trace the outline of one weather map on a separate piece of paper, but do not include any information on the map. Predict the locations of the fronts on the day following this 4-day period. Note the locations of the fronts on your new map.

6 Predict the temperature and precipitation patterns that occur in your location on the day following this 4-day period.

This tornado twisted through Manchester, South Dakota, on June 24, 2003. On the same day, South Dakota had its largest recorded outbreak of twisters ever!

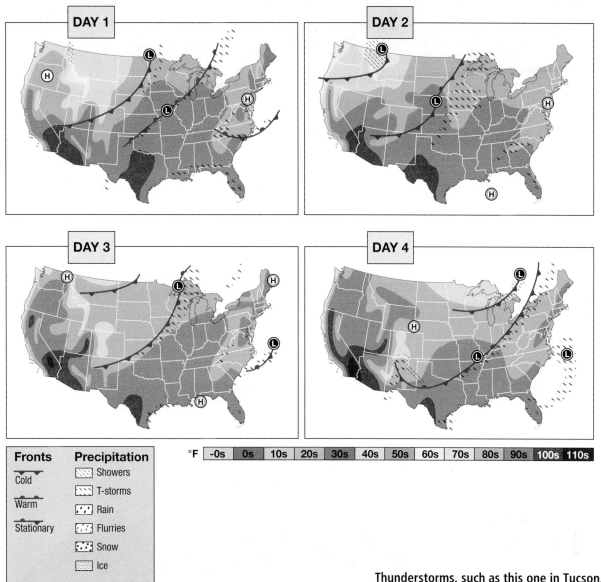

Fronts
Cold
Warm
Stationary

Precipitation
Showers
T-storms
Rain
Flurries
Snow
Ice

°F -0s 0s 10s 20s 30s 40s 50s 60s 70s 80s 90s 100s 110s

Thunderstorms, such as this one in Tucson, Arizona, bring much-needed moisture to dry regions.

Stars in Your Eyes

A constellation is an arbitrary grouping of stars. The map to the right shows constellations that can be seen from the Northern Hemisphere of Earth. A Southern Hemisphere sky map, which is not provided, would show stars that can be seen from the Southern Hemisphere of Earth. Refer to the map to the right as you answer the questions below.

1 For many years, the best way to navigate at night was to use the stars as a guide. Many people used Polaris—the North Star—to orient themselves. This approach would not have worked for people all over the world, however. Why not?

2 What is the name of the constellation that contains Polaris?

3 What is the temperature of the star in the Bootes constellation, with magnitude 0?

4 The constellation Virgo can be observed from the Northern Hemisphere during the summer but not during the winter. Explain why.

5 Compare the constellation Draco on the map below with the constellation on the map to the right. What type of animal was this constellation named after?

6 Pick a group of stars that have not been connected into a constellation. Sketch the star group on a separate piece of paper. Connect the stars into a new constellation, and name your constellation.

People, such as Sumerians, Greeks, Chinese, and Egyptians, have been grouping stars into constellations like these for thousands of years.

Magnitude Scale		Spectral Type		
		Temperature (K)		
0		50,000–25,000		O-B
1		11,000		A
2		7,500		F
3		6,000		G
4		5,000		K
5		3,500		M

⊙ Variable star
⁖ Open cluster
✳ Globular cluster
⬭ Galaxy
— Constellation boundary

There are 88 constellations recognized by modern astronomers. The Northern Hemisphere sky map shows those that can be seen from the Northern Hemisphere of Earth.

Long-Term Projects

Introducing Long-Term Projects

Scientific investigations that lead to important discoveries are almost never short term. Usually, these investigations last months, years, and even decades before results are considered complete and dependable. Investigations in Earth science are no exception. The long-term projects included in this section will give you practical experience in investigating Earth science the way that Earth scientists do—over extended periods of time. You will observe changes over time, keep detailed records of your observations, and draw conclusions from your data. By following these steps, you will learn firsthand what it is like to be an Earth scientist.

Safety First!

Many of the long-term projects require you to make field trips to an observation site or to conduct your activities outdoors. Advance planning is essential. You should plan carefully for these investigations and should be certain that you are aware of the safety guidelines that must be followed. The following are general guidelines for fieldwork and lab work.

Conducting Fieldwork

Find out about on-site hazards before setting out. Determine whether there are poisonous plants or dangerous animals where you are going, and know how to identify them. Also, find out about other hazards, such as steep or slippery terrain.

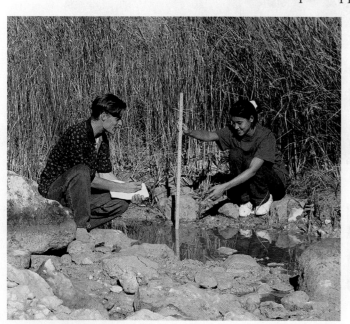

Wear protective clothing. Dress in a manner that will keep you warm, comfortable, and dry. Wear sunglasses, sunscreen, a hat, gloves, rain gear, or other gear to suit local weather conditions. Wear waterproof shoes if you will be near water or mud.

Do not approach or touch wild animals unless you have permission from your teacher. Avoid animals that may sting, bite, scratch, or otherwise cause injury.

Do not touch wild plants or pick wildflowers without permission from your teacher. Many wild plants can cause irritation or can be toxic, and many are protected by law. Never taste a wild plant.

Do not wander away from the group. Do not go beyond where you can be seen or heard. Travel with a partner at all times.

Report any hazards or accidents to your teacher immediately. Even if an incident seems unimportant, tell your teacher about it.

Consider the safety of the ecosystem that you will be visiting as well as your own safety. Do not remove anything from a field site without your teacher's permission. Stay on trails when possible to avoid trampling delicate vegetation. Never leave garbage behind at a field site. Strive to leave natural areas just as you find them.

Conducting Lab Work

Be aware of safety hazards. Any field or lab exercises in which there are known safety hazards will include safety cautions and icons to identify specific hazards. By being aware of safety concerns, you may avoid accidents. Know where safety equipment and emergency exits are located so that you are prepared in the event of an emergency.

Do not engage in inappropriate behavior. Most laboratory accidents are caused by carelessness, lack of attention, or inappropriate behavior. Always be aware of your surroundings, and pay attention to safety cautions.

Be neat. Keep your work area free of unnecessary clutter. Tie back loose hair and loose articles of clothing. Do not wear dangling jewelry or open-toed shoes in the lab. Never eat or drink in the laboratory.

Clean your lab station when your lab time is over. Before leaving the lab, clean up your work area. Put away all equipment and supplies, and dispose of chemicals and other materials as directed by your teacher. Turn off water, gas, and burners, and unplug electrical equipment. Wash your hands with soap and water after working on any lab.

For additional information about safety in the lab and in the field, refer to the Lab and Field Safety section in the front of this book. Don't take any chances with safety!

What safety concerns are being ignored in this photograph?

Long-Term Project 1

Duration
8 or 9 months

Objectives

> **Observe and record** the positions of sunrise and sunset once per month.

> **Graph and analyze** collected data that describe the positions of sunrise and sunset.

> **Predict** the positions of sunrise and sunset for 3 or 4 months.

Materials
compass, magnetic
glue
paper
paper, graph
pen
pencil
poster board
scissors
twist tie (or pipe cleaner)

Safety

Positions of Sunrise and Sunset

You are probably aware that the sun rises in the east and sets in the west each day. What may not be obvious to you is that the positions of sunrise and sunset along the horizon differ from day to day in a specific pattern. As the positions of sunrise and sunset change, the amount of sunlight that an area receives also changes. In this investigation, you will observe the changes in the sun's position along the horizon at sunrise and at sunset. You will be making two observations on or near the 21st of each month for approximately 8 or 9 months (depending on the schedule of your school year).

Procedure

① Construct the bearing chart before taking any measurements. Copy the bearing chart from the next page onto a piece of paper.

② Glue your copy of the chart to a piece of poster board. When the glue is dry, trim away the excess poster board.

③ Wrap the center of a twist tie once around the center of a pencil. Poke the ends of the twist tie through the center of the bearing chart to make a pointer for your chart.

The sun appears to rise and set at different positions relative to landmarks, such as these skyscrapers in Los Angeles, California.

④ On a cloudless morning just before sunrise, place the bearing chart on a level spot where no buildings or trees block your view of sunrise and sunset. **CAUTION** Although sunlight is less intense at sunrise and sunset, you should never stare at the sun for extended periods of time.

⑤ Use the magnetic compass to determine the direction of north. Set the bearing chart so that 0° is pointing north and 180° is pointing south. (Note: Have the chart face the same direction for every observation, even months from now.) Try to align an edge of the chart with some permanent object near your observation point.

Step ① Copy the chart below on a separate piece of paper, and use it to construct your bearing chart.

Long-Term Project 1, *continued*

Step ❼

Date	Position of sunrise (in degrees)	Position of sunset (in degrees)

DO NOT WRITE IN THIS BOOK

6 When the bearing chart is in place and properly aligned, measure the position of sunrise. (Note: Sunrise occurs at the instant the top of the sun appears on the horizon.) Without looking at the sun, measure its position by pointing the chart's pencil toward the sun. The shadow of the eraser end of the pencil will mark the sun's position.

7 In your lab notebook, draw a table like the one shown above. Record the position of sunrise (in degrees) in your table. That evening, measure and record the position of sunset (in degrees). (Note: Sunset occurs when the top edge of the sun drops below the horizon.)

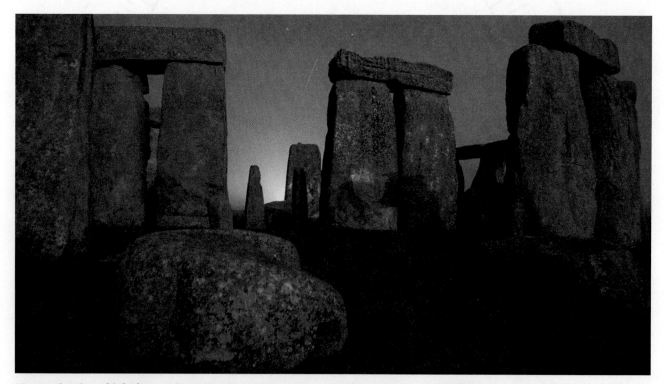

Many scientists think that ancient people used structures, such as Stonehenge in England, to predict astronomical occurrences and to determine the timing of solstices and equinoxes.

Step ❾

Position of Sun at Sunrise

Position of the sun at sunrise (degrees)

0°
30°
60°
90°
120°
150°
180°

9/21 10/21 11/21 12/21 1/21 2/21 3/21 4/21 5/21 6/21 7/21 8/21

Observation dates

DO NOT WRITE IN THIS BOOK

❽ Repeat steps 6 and 7 on the same date each month. (Note: On the equinoxes, the sun will rise due east and set due west. On the solstices, the sunrise and sunset will be shifted from these directions. The amount of the maximum shift will depend on the observer's latitude.)

❾ On a sheet of graph paper, prepare a graph similar to the one shown above. Label the graph's *y*-axis, which represents the position (in degrees) of the sun at sunrise, from 0° to 180°. The position of 90° will be in the center of the *y*-axis scale. The *x*-axis represents observation dates. Next, make a graph on which to plot the position of the sun at sunset. Label the *y*-axis of this graph from 180° to 360°.

❿ On each graph, connect the points by drawing a smooth line. Estimate the positions of points between the plotted points.

Analysis

1. **Analyzing Data** On which date does the sun appear to follow the highest path across the sky? What happens to the length of daylight during this season?

2. **Analyzing Data** On which date does the sun appear to follow the lowest path across the sky? What happens to the length of daylight during this season?

3. **Analyzing Results** On which dates are the positions of the sun at sunrise and again at sunset about 180° apart? Those dates mark the beginning of which seasons?

4. **Describing Events** What general statement can you make about the pattern of sunrise and sunset according to the graphs?

5. **Forming a Hypothesis** Expand your graph to include the predicted position of the sun in June and July. Describe the pattern that you predicted.

Extension

Evaluating Hypotheses
Use the process described in the investigation to chart the positions of sunrise and sunset for the months of June and July. How do your observations compare with your prediction?

Making Comparisons
Use the same process to chart the positions of the moon at moonrise and moonset. Refer to an almanac when you choose the times at which you will make measurements. Do the positions of sunrise and sunset correlate to those of moonrise and moonset? What can you conclude from your observations?

Long-Term Project 2 ENVIRONMENTAL CONNECTION

Duration
2 weeks

Objectives
> **Count and record** the number of particulates in the air over a 2-week period.

> **Analyze** how wind direction and particulate source are related.

Materials
compass, magnetic
microscope
microscope slides (8 or more)
paper, graph
pencil, grease
petroleum jelly
slide box
tape, masking or packaging, or rubber bands

Safety

Air-Pollution Watch

When certain types of pollutants are present in high concentrations, they threaten the general health and well-being of humans. Some substances that can be air pollutants include dust and smoke particles, pollen, mold spores, and waste gases. If these tiny particles remain suspended in the air for long periods of time, they are called *particulates*.

Wind direction affects the number of particulates in the air. If there is a source of particulates in an area, there will be a large number of particulates in the air when the wind blows from the direction of that source. There will be fewer particulates in the air when the wind blows from the direction opposite the source.

In this investigation, you will collect and view a few types of particulates. You will collect particulates from an outdoor site every day for 2 weeks. Then, you will examine those particulates.

Procedure

1 Select a collection site in an open area, such as a large field or pasture, where the wind can blow past the site from every direction.

2 Locate a four-sided post, such as a 4 in. × 4 in. fence post, that is firmly driven into the ground. Try to choose a post whose top is at least 1 m above ground level. If there are no fences in your area, look for another four-sided structure that you could use.

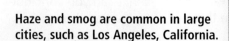

Haze and smog are common in large cities, such as Los Angeles, California.

Step **3**

Day	Date	Wind direction	Slide direction	Number of particulates					Total
				1	2	3	4	5	
1			N						
			S						
			E						
			W						

DO NOT WRITE IN THIS BOOK

3 Use a compass to establish north, south, east, and west directions from the post's location. Determine the direction from which the wind is blowing by watching objects, such as a flag, move in the wind. Record the wind direction and the date in a table like the one shown above.

4 Look for any phenomena that may affect air quality, such as smoke-stacks or heavy traffic. Record these observations and the day's weather conditions.

5 Use a grease pencil to mark on the back of each microscope slide the direction that the slide will face when placed on the post. Place each slide on the appropriate side of the post.

6 Use tape or rubber bands to attach the slides to the post, as shown on the lower-right side of this page. Use your finger to spread a thin, even film of petroleum jelly on one side of each slide.

7 Return to the site the following day. Remove the slides. Place each slide carefully in the slide box. (Note: Do not touch the greased surface.)

Step **6**

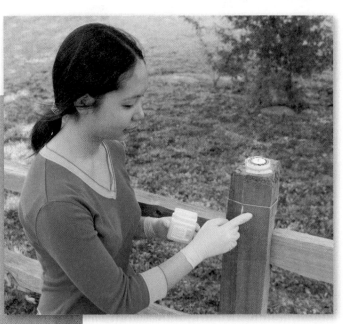

Long-Term Projects **941**

Long-Term Project 2, *continued*

8 Place new slides on the post, and record the wind direction and weather conditions.

9 Examine each slide under the microscope at 100×. Focus on one section that you have chosen at random. Count the number of particulates that you observe in the section. Record this number in column 1 of your table.

10 Move the slide, and examine another section that you have chosen at random. Count the number of particulates in this section. Record this number in column 2 of your table.

11 Repeat step 10 three more times so that you have a total of five observations per slide. Record the total number of particulates counted in the five sections.

12 Repeat steps 7 through 11 each weekday for 2 weeks.

13 When you have finished examining the slides and recording your results, total the number of particulates counted for each of the wind directions.

14 Using the data in your table, construct a bar graph. On the *y*-axis, plot the total number of particulates obtained in the past 5 days. On the *x*-axis, plot the day and wind direction. A sample graph is shown on the next page.

Step **9**

Step **14**

Number of particulates

DO NOT WRITE IN THIS BOOK

Day 1   Day 2   Day 3   Day 4   Day 5

Day and wind direction

Analysis

1. **Analyzing Results** For your location, did any one wind direction or group of wind directions result in more particulates than any other direction or directions did?

2. **Interpreting Information** What are possible sources of these particulates?

3. **Applying Conclusions** What would your results likely be if you set up this investigation near a populated urban area?

4. **Evaluating Methods** Did weather conditions have any effect on your results? Explain your answer.

5. **Graphing Data** Construct a second graph that uses data from all 10 days on which you collected samples. How does this graph differ from your previous graph?

6. **Identifying Patterns** Did you see a different pattern in the data when you plotted data from more than 5 days? Explain your answer.

Extension

Research Use the library or the Internet to research common particulates. Use your research to identify common particulates on several of the slides from this investigation. Which particulates are most common in your area? Explain why these particulates are most common.

Long-Term Project 3

Duration

1 month

Objectives

› **Measure and record** weather variables twice every day.

› **Predict** weather conditions based on data that you collected.

Materials

aneroid barometer or barograph
compass, magnetic
paper, graph
thermometer, Celsius

Safety

Correlating Weather Variables

Identifying weather patterns that exist in an area is the first step in making weather predictions. Weather records are used to identify relationships between variables. Although weather cannot be predicted with complete accuracy, the probability that certain weather conditions will happen at a given time and place can be established.

In this investigation, you will gather and organize weather information in a data table and will present the information as a graph. Then, you will analyze the relationships between the data collected and will make predictions about the weather.

Procedure

1 Use graph paper to make two charts like the one shown at lower left. One chart will hold data from the first 15 days of the project. The other will hold data from the second 15 days of the project. At the top of each column, write the date on which the observation was made.

2 Twice daily for a month, at about the same times every day (about 10 hours apart), measure and record the following weather variables: temperature (°C), barometric pressure (mb), wind direction, cloud cover, and weather conditions. The chart on the following page explains how to measure and record these variables.

3 Use the month's data to make two graphs. Do so by connecting the points for temperature with one smooth line and the points for pressure with a second smooth line.

Step 1

How to Measure Weather Variables

Weather variable	How to measure and record the variable
Temperature	Place a thermometer where it is in the shade and is not exposed to precipitation. Wait at least 3 min, and then read the temperature. Plot a point for that temperature on your chart.
Barometric pressure	Using a barometer, record the barometric pressure to the nearest tenth of a millibar. If your barometer is calibrated in "inches of mercury," change inches to millibars by using the Barometric Conversion Scale at right. Plot a point for the barometric pressure.
Wind direction	Determine the wind direction by using a weather vane or by observing objects moved by the wind. Wind direction is named according to the direction from which the wind blows. Use a compass to help determine direction. Using the symbols shown in the Table of Weather Symbols in the Reference Tables section of Appendix E of this book, record wind direction on the circles at the bottom of your chart.
Cloud cover	Estimate the amount of sky that is covered by clouds. Using the symbols shown in the Table of Weather Symbols in the Reference Tables section of Appendix E of this book, shade the circles at the bottom of your chart.
Weather conditions	Observe the present weather conditions. Using the Table of Weather Symbols in the Reference Tables section of Appendix E of this book, draw in your chart the symbol that most accurately indicates the weather conditions.

Step **2**

One Atmosphere 1013.2

APPENDIX D

Analysis

1. **Evaluating Data** According to your graph, on how many days was the temperature falling? On how many days was the barometric pressure falling?

2. **Identifying Patterns** Of the days that had falling temperature, how many had rising barometric pressure?

3. **Inferring Relationships** In general, what is the relationship between temperature and pressure?

4. **Analyzing Results** What sky cover and wind direction are generally associated with falling barometric pressure?

5. **Interpreting Results** What weather conditions are generally associated with high barometric pressure? with low barometric pressure?

6. **Drawing Conclusions** How do the relationships between certain weather variables help you predict the weather?

7. **Evaluating Methods** Which weather variables are most useful in predicting precipitation?

Extension

Research Find out what the normal temperature, pressure, and precipitation are for your area during the time period in which you recorded your data. Do your observations match the normal conditions for that time period? How can you explain differences between your observations and the normal conditions?

Long-Term Project 4

Duration
1 week

Objectives

› **Observe and record** locations of weather fronts.

› **Predict** weather conditions based on data you collected.

› **Compare** the movement of weather fronts in different seasons.

Materials

pencils, colored daily weather maps for consecutive days (5)

Weather Forecasting

The National Weather Service collects data from hundreds of weather stations located around the world. Daily newspapers summarize this weather data in the form of national weather maps. The data include temperature, precipitation, cloud cover, and barometric pressure. The patterns produced by the data allow meteorologists to identify weather fronts and to provide information about weather conditions around the globe.

In this investigation, you will use a series of daily weather maps to track the movements of weather systems in the winter months. Then, you will use these data to predict weather conditions.

Procedure

1. Find a local or national newspaper that prints a daily weather map from the National Weather Service. You may also use the Internet to find daily weather maps.

2. Cut out or print out the map, and write on it the date that it represents.

3. Make a data table similar to the sample table shown at the bottom of this page.

4. Fill in your table with the information from the weather map.

5. Make at least one copy of the blank weather map on the third page of this exercise.

Step 3

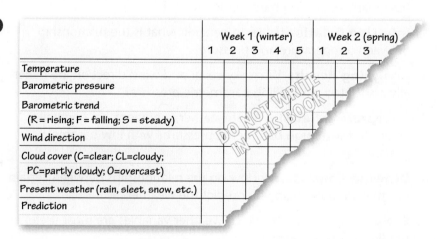

	Week 1 (winter)					Week 2 (spring)		
	1	2	3	4	5	1	2	3
Temperature								
Barometric pressure								
Barometric trend (R = rising; F = falling; S = steady)								
Wind direction								
Cloud cover (C=clear; CL=cloudy; PC=partly cloudy; O=overcast)								
Present weather (rain, sleet, snow, etc.)								
Prediction								

A meteorologist from the National Weather Service tracks the path of a hurricane in the Gulf of Mexico.

6 On your copy of the map, put an *L* at any locations where low-pressure centers are shown on the daily weather map that you collected in step 1. Circle the *Ls* with a colored pencil, and label each circle with the date.

7 Put an *H* on your map at the locations of any high-pressure centers. Circle the *Hs* with a second colored pencil, and label each circle with the date.

8 Repeat steps 1–7, but use four consecutive daily weather maps that follow the first day's map, and reuse your data table and weather map. For each symbol, use the same colors that you used for the first day's map.

9 Draw arrows to connect the daily positions of each high-pressure center and of each low-pressure center.

10 Use the formula below to calculate the average velocity (in kilometers per day) of each high-pressure center and each low-pressure center. The average velocity equals the total distance traveled divided by the number of days traveled, or

$$average\ velocity = \frac{total\ distance\ traveled}{number\ of\ days}$$

Long-Term Project 4, *continued*

Step **5**

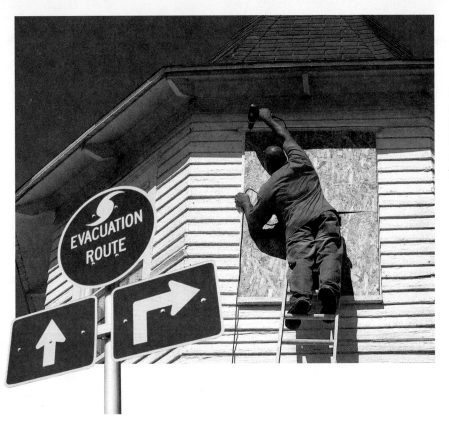

Many hurricane-prone areas have established evacuation routes to help people reach safety before a hurricane hits. This man is boarding up windows in his house to prepare for an imminent hurricane.

Analysis

1. **Analyzing Data** Generally, in which direction do the pressure centers over the United States move?

2. **Analyzing Results** From your calculations, what is the average rate of movement (in kilometers per day) of low- and high-pressure centers in winter?

3. **Making Predictions** Predict where the low- and high-pressure centers will be located on the day following the date of the last map in your series.

4. **Forming a Hypothesis** Refer to your series of daily weather maps to predict the weather for your hometown on the sixth day of the series. Write a forecast with your predictions of weather conditions.

5. **Evaluating Predictions** Was your prediction about the locations of the low- and high-pressure centers from question 3 accurate? Explain why or why not.

6. **Evaluating Hypotheses** Compare your weather prediction with the daily weather map for the appropriate day. Check the accuracy of your prediction. What factors could have caused errors in your prediction?

7. **Explaining Events** Describe the general weather conditions associated with regions of low and high atmospheric pressure.

Extension

Designing Experiments
In the spring, repeat the entire investigation. What is the average rate of movement (in kilometers per day) of low- and high-pressure centers in the spring? Compare the rate of movement of pressure systems during spring and winter.

Long-Term Project 5

Duration
6 months (October 1 to April 1)

Objectives
> **Record** temperature and precipitation data for eight regions.
> **Graph and analyze** climate features for eight regions.
> **Classify** regions by using two climate classification systems.

Materials
almanac
atlas
paper, graph
rain gauge (optional)
thermometer (optional)
weather reports, daily

Safety

Comparing Climate Features

A graph of the monthly temperatures and amounts of precipitation for a region is called a *climatograph.* Climatographs can be used to compare the climates of different areas or to classify an area's climate.

In this investigation, you will use climate data to compare your local climate with the climates of other regions of the United States. You will keep a daily temperature and precipitation log. You will record data every day from the first day of October until the first day of April. You will then compare your graphed data with information about the world's climates. You will use this comparison to develop a conclusion about the type of climate that your location has.

Procedure

1. Listen to or watch a daily weather report for your area, or find this information in a daily newspaper or on the Internet. You may also keep your own records by using a thermometer and a rain gauge.

2. Beginning on the first day of October, keep a daily record of the high and low temperatures and of the amount of precipitation that occurs. During winter, snow should be melted before determining the amount of precipitation (in centimeters).

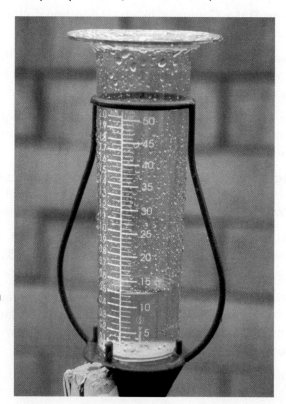

Rain gauges collect precipitation for scientists to measure.

3 Calculate the average temperature for each day by dividing the sum of the day's high and low temperatures by 2. Record this information.

4 At the end of each month, record the average monthly temperature given by the weather report, or calculate the average monthly temperature by dividing the sum of the daily averages by the number of days in the month. Also, record the total monthly precipitation given by the weather report.

5 Use the Internet or an almanac to look up climate data for your town or city and for seven other cities in the United States. Select one city from each of the following regions: New England, the Gulf Coast, the Midwest, the Southwest, the Pacific Northwest, the interior of Alaska, and the Hawaiian Islands.

6 Look up the average monthly temperatures and precipitation for your town or city and for each city that you chose. Record these data in a table.

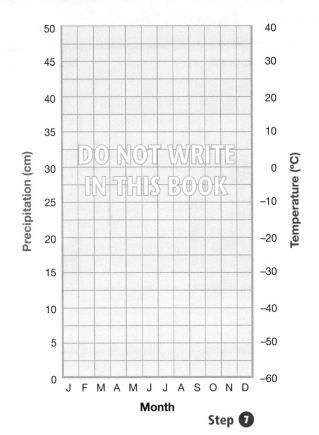

Step **7**

7 On your graph paper, make eight copies of the blank climatograph shown on the upper-right side of this page.

8 Label each blank climatograph with the name of one of the seven cities. Label the eighth climatograph with the name of your town or city.

9 If you recorded temperature and precipitation in English (American) units, such as degrees Fahrenheit or inches, convert your measurements to SI units, such as degrees Celsius or centimeters. Use the SI Conversions table in Appendix E of this book to convert English units to SI units.

10 For each of the eight locations, plot the average temperature for January by placing a dot in the center of the square that is located in the column representing January and in the row representing that average temperature.

11 Using the same method, plot the average precipitation for January.

12 Repeat steps 10 and 11 for each month's data for each location. Then, connect the temperature points in order of consecutive months to form a line, and shade the columns from 0 up to the recorded precipitation amount for each month.

Long-Term Project 5, *continued*

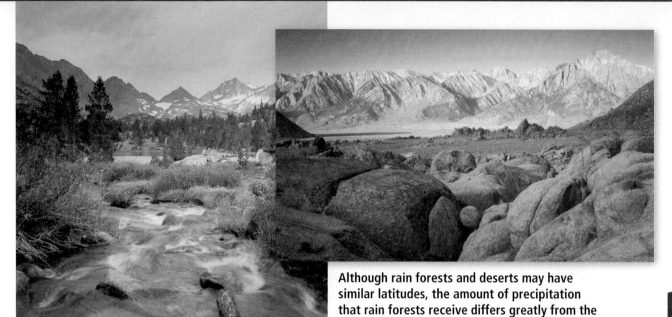

Although rain forests and deserts may have similar latitudes, the amount of precipitation that rain forests receive differs greatly from the amount that deserts receive.

Analysis

1. **Making Comparisons** Compare each of the climatographs of your seven chosen U.S. cities with the sample climatographs on the previous page. Identify the climate type or types for each location that you selected. What features of each climatograph helped you classify each region?

2. **Analyzing Results** Use the climatograph for your area to classify your regional climate. What features of your climatograph helped you identify the climate type?

3. **Examining Data** Compare the average temperatures and precipitation amounts for your location that you collected to the values that you obtained from the Internet or an almanac. Do you think that this year's climate data are typical for your region? Explain your answer.

4. **Classifying Information** How would each of the climatographs, including the one for your region, fit into the climate classification system outlined in the chapter entitled "Climate"?

5. **Evaluating Methods** In this investigation, you compared climates by looking at average precipitation and temperature. What other factors might affect the climate of an area? Give examples of each factor.

Extension

Making Comparisons
Bermuda is a small island in the Atlantic Ocean. Bermuda is at about the same latitude as St. Louis, Missouri, which lies in the middle of a continent. In which of the two locations does the temperature vary least from month to month? Explain the cause of the temperature pattern in the location that has the more moderate pattern.

Long-Term Project 6

Duration
8 months

Objectives
› **Observe** the position of Mars in the night sky for 8 months.

› **Graph** the apparent movement of Mars through the night sky.

› **Identify** changes in the relative positions of Earth and Mars.

Materials
celestial sphere
 model (optional)
compass, magnetic
constellation charts
flashlight
metric ruler

Planetary Motions

While observing the evening sky over a period of time, you might have noticed that some objects look like stars but do not maintain fixed positions relative to the celestial sphere. These objects are the planets. As viewed from Earth at various times during the year, the patterns in the planets' motions differ from the patterns that you might expect.

In this investigation, you will observe the planet Mars in the night sky on the 1st and 15th of each month over a period of 8 months. Then, you will use your observations to draw conclusions and make predictions about planetary motion.

Procedure

❶ Obtain data on the positions of Mars in the night sky throughout the last year from an astronomical yearbook or from the Internet. Astronomical yearbooks can be found at most libraries.

❷ Check the Internet, an almanac, or the weather section of a newspaper to find the time of night that Mars will be visible in your area.

❸ Copy the star chart on the third and fourth pages of this lab onto a separate piece of paper.

❹ Practice measuring angular distance by using the method shown at the bottom of this page. Always use the same hand when measuring angular distance. To have confidence in the accuracy of your measurements, you may need to practice measuring angular distance for a few days or weeks before beginning this lab.

Step ❹

Estimating Angular Distance in Degrees
Hold your hand at arm's length.

1°   5°   10°   15°

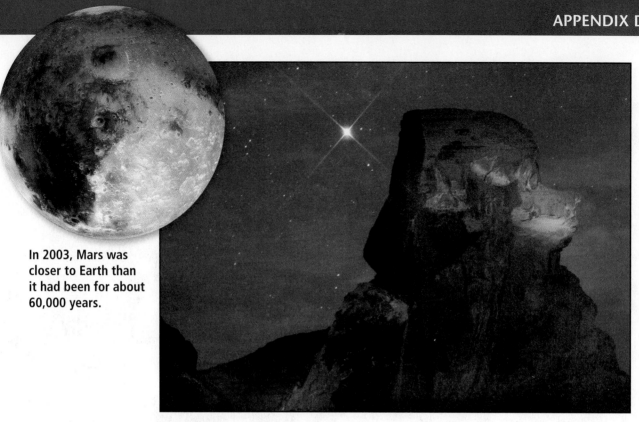

In 2003, Mars was closer to Earth than it had been for about 60,000 years.

5 On the 1st and 15th of each month, go at night to an area that gives you a clear view of the eastern, southern, and western skies. (Note: If the skies are not clear on the 1st and 15th, make observations as close to these dates as possible.)

6 At the same time each night, locate Mars in the night sky. Mars will have a dull red appearance.

7 Use your magnetic compass to position yourself facing south, and observe the position of Mars relative to the background stars.

8 Choose a constellation. Use the method illustrated at the bottom of the previous page to estimate Mars's angular distance (in degrees) from the constellation.

9 On your star chart, locate the constellation from which you measured Mars's angular distance. Draw Mars in the appropriate position relative to the constellation, and label the planet's position with the date.

10 Compare the apparent brightness of Mars with that of the background stars. Record your observation on a separate sheet of paper.

11 Repeat steps 6–10 on the 1st and 15th of each month for the next 8 months.

12 After each observation, draw an arrow from Mars's previous position to the position that you just observed. The progression of arrows will show Mars's apparent path.

Long-Term Project 6, *continued*

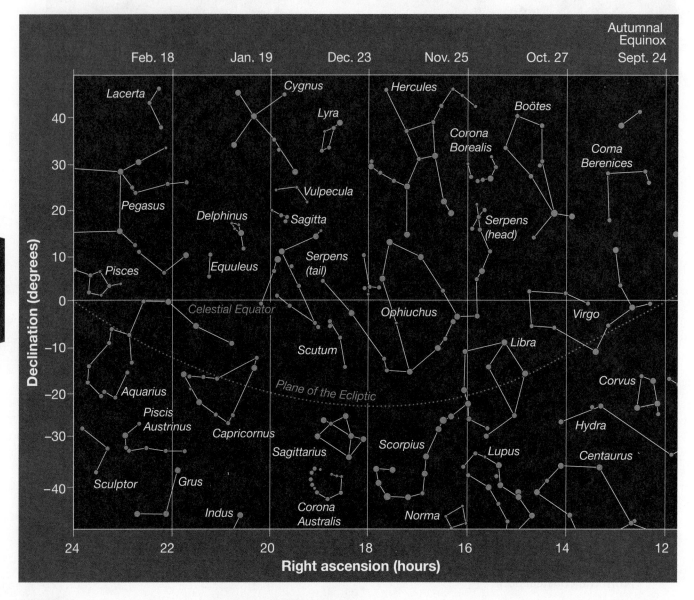

Step ❸

Analysis

1. **Examining Data** In which months does Mars appear highest in the night sky? lowest in the night sky?

2. **Evaluating Results** In which direction does Mars appear to move across the sky? At any point during the year, does Mars appear to deviate from this apparent path?

3. **Making Predictions** In one year from today, will Mars be in the same position that it is in today? Explain.

4. **Drawing Conclusions** From your observations of the apparent brightness of Mars at different times of the year, what can you infer about the distance between Mars and Earth? Explain your answer.

Extension

Evaluating Predictions In the Analysis section of this investigation, you predicted the position of Mars in one year. Use the Internet or library to research where astronomers predict Mars will be in one year. Was your prediction accurate? Explain why or why not.

Evaluating Hypotheses Repeat this investigation, but measure the positions of another planet, such as Venus, over the course of 8 months. Write a brief essay that explains how the paths of Mars and Venus differ.

REFERENCE TABLES

SI Conversions

The metric system is used for making measurements in science. The official name of this system is the Système Internationale d'Unités, or International System of Measurements (SI).

SI Units	From SI to English	From English to SI
Length		
kilometer (km) = 1,000 m	1 km = 0.62 mile	1 mile = 1.609 km
meter (m) = 100 cm	1 m = 3.28 feet	1 foot = 0.305 m
centimeter (cm) = 0.01 m	1 cm = 0.394 inch	1 inch = 2.54 cm
millimeter (mm) = 0.001 m	1 mm = 0.039 inch	
micrometer (μm) = 0.000 001 m		
nanometer (nm) = 0.000 000 001 m		
Area		
square kilometer (km^2) = 100 hectares	1 km^2 = 0.386 square mile	1 square mile = 2.590 km^2
hectare (ha) = 10,000 m^2	1 ha = 2.471 acres	1 acre = 0.405 ha
square meter (m^2) = 10,000 cm^2	1 m^2 = 10.765 square feet	1 square foot = 0.093 m^2
square centimeter (cm^2) = 100 mm^2	1 cm^2 = 0.155 square inch	1 square inch = 6.452 cm^2
Volume		
liter (L) = 1,000 mL = 1 dm^3	1 L = 1.06 fluid quarts	1 fluid quart = 0.946 L
milliliter (mL) = 0.001 L = 1 cm^3	1 mL = 0.034 fluid ounce	1 fluid ounce = 29.577 mL
microliter (μL) = 0.000 001 L		
Mass		* Equivalent weight at Earth's surface
kilogram (kg) = 1,000 g	1 kg = 2.205 pounds*	1 pound* = 0.454 kg
gram (g) = 1,000 mg	1 g = 0.035 ounce*	1 ounce* = 28.35 g
milligram (mg) = 0.001 g		
microgram (μg) = 0.000 001 g		
Energy		
British Thermal Units (BTU)	1 BTU = 1,055.056 joules	1 joule = 0.00095 BTU

Temperature

°F 0 20 40 60 80 100 120 140 160 180 200 220

°C -20 -10 0 10 20 30 40 50 60 70 80 90 100

Freezing point of water   **Normal human body temperature**
Room temperature

Conversion of Fahrenheit to Celsius:
$$°C = \frac{5}{9}(°F - 32)$$

Conversion of Celsius to Fahrenheit:
$$°F = \frac{9}{5}(°C) + 32$$

Mineral Uses

Metallic Minerals

Mineral and chemical formula	Location of economically important deposits	Important uses
Chalcopyrite, $CuFeS_2$	Chile, U.S., and Indonesia	electrical and electronic products, wiring, telecommunications equipment, industrial machinery and equipment
Chromite, $FeCr_2O_4$	South Africa, Kazahkstan, and India	production of stainless steel, alloys, and metal plating
Galena, PbS	Australia, China, and U.S.	batteries, ammunition, glass and ceramics, and X-ray shielding
Gold, Au	South Africa, U.S., and Australia	computers, communications equipment, spacecraft, jet engines, dentistry, jewelry, and coins
Ilmenite, $FeTiO_3$	Australia, South Africa, and Canada	jet engines; missile components; and white pigment in paints, toothpaste, and candy
Magnetite, Fe_3O_4	China, Brazil, and Australia	steelmaking
Uraninite, UO_2	Canada and Australia	fuel in nuclear reactors and manufacture of radioisotopes

Nonmetallic Minerals

Mineral and chemical formula	Location of economically important deposits	Important uses
Barite, $BaSO_4$	China, India, and U.S.	weighting agent in oil well drilling fluids, automobile paint primer, and X-ray diagnostic work
Borax, $Na_2B_4O_7 \cdot 10H_2O$	Turkey, U.S., and Russia	glass, soaps and detergents, agriculture, fire retardants, and plastics and polymer additives
Calcite, $CaCO_3$	China, U.S., and Russia	cement, lime production, crushed stone, glassmaking, chemicals, and optics
Diamond, C	Australia, Democratic Republic of the Congo, and Russia	jewelry, cutting tools, drill bits, and manufacture of computer chips
Fluorite, CaF_2	China, Mexico, and South Africa	hydrofluoric acid, steelmaking, water fluoridation, solvents, manufacture of glass, and enamels
Gypsum, $CaSO_4 \cdot 2H_2O$	U.S., Iran, and Canada	wallboard, building plasters, and manufacture of cement
Halite, NaCl	U.S., China, and Germany	chemical production, human and animal nutrition, highway deicer, and water softener
Sulfur, S	Canada, U.S., and Russia	sulfuric acid, fertilizers, gunpowder, and tires
Kaolinite, $Al_2Si_2O_5(OH)_4$	U.S., Uzbehkistan, and Czech Republic	glossy paper and whitener and abrasive in toothpaste
Orthoclase, $KAlSi_3O_8$	Italy, Turkey, and U.S.	glass, ceramics, and soaps
Quartz, SiO_2	U.S., Germany, and France	glass, computer chips, ceramics, abrasives, and water filtration
Talc, $Mg_3Si_4O_{10}(OH)_2$	China, U.S., and Republic of Korea	ceramics, plastics, paint, paper, rubber, and cosmetics

Guide to Common Minerals

This table is used in the chapter lab for the chapter entitled "Minerals of Earth's Crust."

	Luster		Hardness	Cleavage	Fracture	Color/opacity	
Nonmetallic; light color	glassy to pearly	Scratches glass	6	two cleavage planes at nearly right angles		various colors but often white or pink; opaque	
	glassy		6	two cleavage planes at 86° and 94°		colorless, white, pink, or various colors; translucent to opaque	
	glassy and waxy		7	no cleavage	conchoidal fracture	various colors; transparent to opaque	
	glassy		6.5–7	no cleavage	conchiodal to irregular fracture	olive green; transparent to translucent	
	glassy	Does not scratch glass	2.5–3	three cleavage planes at right angles		colorless to gray; transparent to opaque	
	glassy		3	three cleavage planes at 75° and 105°		colorless or white and may be tinted; transparent to opaque	
	glassy, pearly, or silky		1–2.5	one perfect cleavage plane	conchoidal and fibrous fracture	white, pink, or gray to colorless; transparent to opaque	
	pearly to waxy		1	one cleavage plane		white to green; opaque	
	glassy or pearly		2–2.5	one cleavage plane		colorless to light gray or brown; translucent to opaque	
	glassy		4	eight cleavage planes (octahedral)		green, yellow, purple, and other colors; transparent to translucent	
	glassy		4.5–5	no cleavage	conchiodal to irregular fracture	green, blue, violet, brown, or colorless; translucent to opaque	
	silky		3.5–4	no cleavage	irregular, splintery fracture	green; translucent to opaque	
Nonmetallic; dark color	glassy and silky	Scratches glass	5–6	two cleavage planes at 56° and 124°		dark green, brown, or black; translucent to opaque	
	resinous and glassy		6.5–7.5	no cleavage	irregular fracture	dark red or green; transparent to opaque	
	pearly and glassy	Does not scratch glass	2.5–3	one cleavage plane		black to dark brown; translucent to opaque	
	metallic to earthy		1–2	one cleavage plane		black to gray; opaque	
Metallic	metallic or earthy	Does not scratch glass	5.5–6.5	no cleavage	irregular fracture	reddish brown to black; opaque	
	metallic		2.5	three cleavage planes at right angles		lead gray; opaque	
	metallic	Scratches glass	5–6	two cleavage planes at 56° and 124°		iron black; opaque	
	metallic		6–6.5	no cleavage	conchoidal to irregular fracture	brass yellow; opaque	

Streak	Specific gravity	Other properties	Mineral name and chemical formula
white	2.6	prismatic, columnar, or tabular crystals	orthoclase, $KAlSi_3O_8$
blue-gray to white	2.6 to 2.7	striations	plagioclase, $(Na, Cl)(Al, Si)_4O_8$
white	2.65	six-sided crystals	quartz, SiO_2
white to pale green	3.2 to 3.3	stubby, prismatic crystals	olivine, $(Mg, Fe)_2SiO_4$
white	2.2	cubic crystals and salty taste	halite, $NaCl$
white	2.7	may produce double image when you look through it	calcite, $CaCO_3$
white	2.2 to 2.4	thin layers and flexible	gypsum, $CaSO_4 \cdot 2H_2O$
white	2.7 to 2.8	soapy feel and thin scales	talc, $Mg_3Si_4O_{10}(OH)_2$
white	2.7 to 3	thin sheets	muscovite, $KAl_2Si_3O_{10}(OH)_2$
white	3.2	fluorescent under UV light; cubic and six-sided crystals	fluorite, CaF_2
white or pale red-brown	3.1	six-sided crystals	apatite, $Ca_5(OH, F, Cl)(PO_4)_3$
emerald green	4	fibrous, radiating aggregates or circular, banded structure	malachite, $CuCO_3 \cdot Cu(OH)_2$
pale green or white	3.2	six-sided crystals	hornblende, $(Ca, Na)_{2-3}(Mg, Fe, Al)_5$ $Si_6(Si, Al)_2O_{22}(OH)_2$
white	4.2	12- or 24-sided crystals	garnet, $Fe_3Al_2(SiO_4)_3$
white to gray	2.7 to 3.2	thin, flexible sheets	biotite, $K(Mg, Fe)_3AlSi_3O_{10}(OH)_2$
black to dark green	2.3	greasy feel, soft, and flaky	graphite, C
red to red-brown	5.25	granular masses	hematite, Fe_2O_3
lead gray to black	7.4 to 7.6	very heavy	galena, PbS
black to dark green	5.2	8- or 12-sided crystals; may be magnetic	magnetite, Fe_3O_4
greenish black	5	cubic crystals	pyrite, FeS_2

Guide to Common Rocks

This table is used in the chapter lab for the chapter entitled "Rocks."

Rock class	Grain size	Description	Rock class	Rock name
Made of crystals	Coarse grained	mostly light in color; shades of pink, gray, and white are common	igneous	granite
		dark in color; commonly black and white; heavy heft	igneous	gabbro
		foliated; layers of different minerals give a banded appearance	metamorphic	gneiss
		foliated; contains abundant amount of quartz, and may contain garnet; flaky minerals	metamorphic	schist
		nonfoliated; reacts with acid	metamorphic	marble
	Fine grained	usually light in color; many holes and spongy appearance; may float in water	igneous	pumice
		light to dark in color; glassy luster; conchoidal fracture	igneous	obsidian
		dark in color; may ring like a bell when struck with a hammer	igneous	basalt
		fine grained; foliated; cleaves into thin, flat plates	metamorphic	slate
Made of rock particles	Coarse grained	coarse-grained particles, more than 2 mm; rounded pebbles; some sorting; clay and sand are visible	sedimentary	conglomerate
		well-preserved fossils are common; can be scratched with a knife; many colors but usually white-gray; reacts with acid	sedimentary	limestone
		cube-shaped crystals; commonly colorless; does not react with acid	sedimentary	halite
	Medium grained	1/16 to 2 mm grains; mostly quartz fragments; surface feels sandy	sedimentary	sandstone
	Fine grained	soft and porous; commonly white or buff color	sedimentary	chalk
		microscopic grains; clay composition; smooth surface; hardened mud appearance	sedimentary	shale

Radiogenic Isotopes and Half-Life

Unstable isotopes, called *radiogenic isotopes* or *radioactive isotopes,* decay to form different isotopes called *daughter isotopes.* Each radiogenic isotope breaks down at a predictable rate, called its *half-life,* into a daughter isotope. Because of this predictable decay pattern, radiogenic isotopes are used to determine numeric dates for rocks. The table below describes several common radiometric dating methods.

Radiometric dating method	How it works	Parent isotope	Daughter isotope	Half-life	Effective dating range
Argon-argon dating ($^{39}Ar/^{40}Ar$)	Comparison made between ^{39}Ar and ^{40}Ar in a sample specially irradiated to form ^{39}Ar; ^{39}Ar is equivalent to ^{40}K in potassium-argon dating.	potassium-40, ^{40}K irradiated to form argon-39, ^{39}Ar	argon-40, ^{40}Ar	1.25 billion years	10,000 to 4.6 billion years
Fission track dating	Tracks of damage created by charged particles from radioactive decay that pass through a mineral's crystal lattice are counted under an electron microscope.	uranium, U	ultimately, lead, Pb, but also several other daughter isotopes	not applicable	500 years to 1 billion years
Potassium-argon dating ($^{40}K/^{40}Ar$)	Comparison is made between the amount of ^{40}K and amount of ^{40}Ar; over time, ^{40}K decreases and ^{40}Ar increases.	potassium-40, ^{40}K	argon-40, ^{40}Ar	1.25 billion years	50,000 to 4.6 billion years
Radiocarbon dating ($^{14}C/^{12}C$)	Comparison is made between the amount of ^{14}C in organic matter and the amount of ^{12}C; ^{12}C remains constant over time, and ^{14}C breaks down.	carbon-14, ^{14}C	nitrogen-14, ^{14}N	5,730 years	<70,000 years
Rubidium-strontium dating ($^{87}Rb/^{87}Sr$)	Comparison made between the ratio of $^{87}Sr/^{86}Sr$ and the ratio of $^{87}Rb/^{86}Sr$ to find the amount of ^{87}Sr formed by radioactive decay.	rubidium-87, ^{87}Rb	strontium-87, ^{87}Sr	48.1 billion years	10 million to 4.6 billion years
Thorium-lead dating ($^{232}Th/^{208}Pb$)	Comparison made between amount of ^{232}Th and the ratio of $^{208}Pb/^{204}Pb$; ^{232}Th breaks into ^{208}Pb, and ^{204}Pb remains constant.	thorium-232, ^{232}Th	lead-208, ^{208}Pb	14.0 billion years	>200 million years
Uranium-lead dating ($^{235}U/^{207}Pb$)	Comparison made between amount of ^{235}U and the ratio of $^{207}Pb/^{204}Pb$; ^{235}U breaks into ^{207}Pb, and ^{204}Pb remains constant.	uranium-235, ^{235}U	lead-207, ^{207}Pb	704 million years	10 million to 4.6 billion years
Uranium-lead dating ($^{238}U/^{206}Pb$)	Comparison made between amount of ^{238}U and the ratio of $^{206}Pb/^{204}Pb$; ^{238}U breaks into ^{206}Pb, and ^{204}Pb remains constant.	uranium-238, ^{238}U	lead-206, ^{206}Pb	4.5 billion years	10 million to 4.6 billion years

APPENDIX E

Topographic and Geologic Map Symbols

Topographic Map Symbols

Elevation markers

Contour lines	
Index contour lines	100
Depression contour lines	
Water elevation	9600
Spot elevation	x 9136

Boundaries

National	
State	
County, parish, municipal	
Township, precinct, town	
Incorporated city, village, or town	
National or state reservation	
Small park, cemetery, airport, etc.	
Land grant	

Buildings and Structures

Buildings	
School	
Church	
Cemetery	cem
Barn and warehouse	
Wells (non-water)	oil gas
Open-pit mine, quarry, or prospect	
Tunnel	
Benchmark	BM 8025
National Park	
Campsite	
Bridge	

Roads and Railroads

Divided highway	
Road	
Trail	
Railroad	

Geologic Map Symbols

Sedimentary Rocks

Breccia	
Conglomerate	
Dolomite	
Limestone	
Mudstone	
Sandstone	
Siltstone	
Shale	

Igneous and Metamorphic Rocks

Extrusive	
Intrusive	
Metamorphic	

Features

River	
Water well	water
Spring	
Lake	
Glacier	

Contour Map

This map is used in the chapter lab for the chapter entitled "Models of the Earth."

Humidity and Air Pressure

The Relative Humidity table below is used in the chapter lab for the chapter entitled "Water in the Atmosphere." The Barometric Conversion Scale is used in the Long-Term Project entitled "Correlating Weather Variables" in the Appendix.

Relative Humidity (%)

Dry-bulb temperature (°C)	Difference in temperature (°C)									
	1.0	**2.0**	**3.0**	**4.0**	**5.0**	**6.0**	**7.0**	**8.0**	**9.0**	**10.0**
10	88	77	66	55	44	34	24	15	6	—
11	89	78	67	56	46	36	27	18	9	—
12	89	78	68	58	48	39	29	21	12	—
13	89	79	69	59	50	41	32	23	15	7
14	90	79	70	60	51	42	34	26	18	10
15	90	80	71	61	53	44	36	27	20	13
16	90	81	71	63	54	46	38	30	23	15
17	90	81	72	64	55	47	40	32	25	18
18	91	82	73	65	57	49	41	34	27	20
19	91	82	74	65	58	50	43	36	29	22
20	91	83	74	66	59	51	44	37	31	24
21	91	83	75	67	60	53	46	39	32	26
22	92	83	76	68	61	54	47	40	34	28
23	92	84	76	69	62	55	48	42	36	30
24	92	84	77	69	62	56	49	43	37	31
25	92	84	77	70	63	57	50	44	39	33
26	92	85	78	71	64	58	51	46	40	34
27	92	85	78	71	65	58	52	47	41	36
28	93	85	78	72	65	59	53	48	42	37
29	93	86	79	72	66	60	54	49	43	38
30	93	86	79	73	67	61	55	50	44	39
31	93	86	80	73	67	61	56	51	45	40
32	93	86	80	74	68	62	57	51	46	41
33	93	87	80	74	68	63	57	52	47	42
34	93	87	81	75	69	63	58	53	48	43
35	94	87	81	75	69	64	59	54	49	44
36	94	87	81	75	70	64	59	54	50	45
37	94	87	82	76	70	65	60	55	51	46
38	94	88	82	76	71	66	60	56	51	47
39	94	88	82	77	71	66	61	57	52	48
40	94	88	82	77	72	67	62	57	53	48

Barometric Conversion Scale

One Atmosphere 1013.2

Weather Map of the United States

This map is used in the chapter lab for the chapter entitled "Weather."

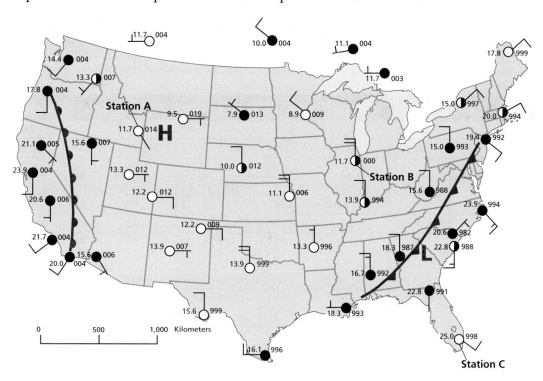

Weather Map Symbols

This chart is used in the Long-Term Project entitled "Weather Forecasting."

Cloud cover (fraction of sky covered)	◯ Clear	◐ $\frac{1}{8}$	◕ Scattered	◕ $\frac{3}{8}$	◑ $\frac{4}{8}$
	◕ $\frac{5}{8}$	● Broken	◕ $\frac{7}{8}$	● Overcast	⊗ Obscured ⊗ No data
Wind speed (knots)	◎ Calm	│ 1 to 2	⌐ 3 to 7	⌐ 8 to 12	⌐ 13 to 17
	⌐ 18 to 22	⌐ 23 to 27	▛ 48 to 52	▛ 73 to 77	▜ 103 to 107
Wind direction	◯ North	◯ Northeast	◯— East	◯ Southeast	
	◯ South	◯ Southwest	—◯ West	◯ Northwest	
Weather conditions	𝄖 Drizzle	☰ Fog	△ Hail	∞ Haze	● Rain	▽ Shower
	Freezing rain	Smoke	✳ Snow	Thunderstorm	Hurricane	Tropical storm

Solar System Data

Notes

The **semimajor axis** is the average distance between an object and its primary (the body the object revolves around).

Surface gravity indicated for the gas giants is calculated for the altitude at which the atmospheric pressure equals 1 bar.

Rotation period and **orbital period** are sidereal measurements (relative to the stars, not the sun).

* This value indicates distance from the sun in AU.

† This value represents the rate of rotation at the sun's equator. The sun displays differential rotation; in other words, it rotates faster at its equator than at its poles.

R This value indicates retrograde rotation or retrograde revolution.

	Sun	Mercury	Venus	Earth	Mars	Jupiter	Saturn	Uranus	Neptune
Mass (10^{24} kg)	1,989,100	0.33	4.87	5.97	0.642	1,899	568	86.8	102
Diameter (km)	1,390,000	4,880	12,100	12,756	6,800	143,000	120,535	51,120	49,530
Density (kg/m^3)	1,408	5,427	5,243	5,515	3,933	1,326	687	1,270	1,638
Surface gravity (m/s^2)	274	3.7	8.9	9.8	3.7	23.1	9	8.7	11
Escape velocity (km/s)	617.7	4.3	10.4	11.2	5	59.5	35.5	21.3	23.5
Rotation period (h)	609.12	1,407.6	5,832.5 R	23.9	24.6	9.9	10.7	17.2 R	16.1
Length of day (hours)	609.6†	4,222.6	2,802	24	24.7	9.9	10.7	17.2	16.1
Semimajor axis (10^6 km)	N/A	57.9	108.2	149.6	227.9	778.6	1,433.5	2,872.5	4,495.1
Perihelion (10^6 km)	N/A	46	107.5	147.1	206.6	740.5	1,352.6	2,741.3	4,444.5
Aphelion (10^6 km)	N/A	69.8	108.9	152.1	249.2	816.6	1,514.5	3,003.6	4,545.7
Orbital period (days)	N/A	88	224.7	365.2	687	4,331	10,747	30,589	59,800
Orbital velocity (km/s)	N/A	47.9	35	29.8	24.1	13.1	9.7	6.8	5.4
Orbital inclination (degrees)	N/A	7	3.4	0	1.9	1.3	2.5	0.8	1.8
Orbital eccentricity	N/A	0.205	0.007	0.017	0.094	0.049	0.057	0.046	0.011
Axial tilt (degrees)	7.25	0.01	2.6	23.5	25.2	3.1	26.7	82.2	28.3
Mean surface temperature (°C)	6,073	167	464	15	−65	−110	−140	−195	−200
Global magnetic field?	yes	yes	no	yes	no	yes	yes	yes	yes

	Earth's moon	Major moons of Jupiter				Major moons of Saturn			
		Io	Europa	Ganymede	Callisto	Dione	Rhea	Titan	Iapetus
Mass (10^{20} kg)	0.073	893.2	480.0	1,481.9	1,075.9	0.375	11.0	1,345.5	15.9
Diameter (km)	3,475	3,643.2	3,121.6	5,262.4	4,820.6	1,120	1,528	5,150	1,436
Density (kg/m^3)	3,340	3,530	3,010	1,940	1,830	1,500	1,240	1,881	1,020
Rotation period (days)	655.7	1.77	3.55	7.15	16.69	2.74	4.52	15.95	79.33
Semimajor axis (10^3 km)	0.384*	421.6	670.9	1,070.4	1,882.7	377.40	527.04	1,221.83	3,561.3
Orbital period (days)	27.32	1.77	3.55	7.15	16.69	2.74	4.52	15.95	79.33

	Major moons of Uranus			Major moons of Neptune		Pluto's moon	Selected asteroids		Selected comets	
	Umbriel	Titania	Oberon	Triton	Nereid	Charon	Vesta	Ceres	Chiron	Hale-Bopp
Mass (10^{20} kg)	11.7	35.2	30.1	214	0.2	19	3	8.7	—	—
Diameter (km)	1,169	1,578	1,523	2,707	340	1,186	530	960 × 932	—	—
Density (kg/m^3)	1,400	1,710	1,630	2,050	1,000	2,000	—	—	—	—
Rotation period	4.14 days	8.71 days	13.46 days	5.87 days R	unknown	6.39 days	5.342 h	9.075 h	—	—
Semimajor axis (10^3 km)	266.30	435.91	583.52	354.76	5,513.4	19,600	2.362 *	2.767 *	13.7 *	250 *
Orbital period	4.14 days	8.71 days	13.46 days	5.87 days R	360.14 days	6.39 days	3.63 y	4.60 y	50.7 y	4,000 y

REFERENCE MAPS
Topographic Provinces of North America

Geologic Map of North America

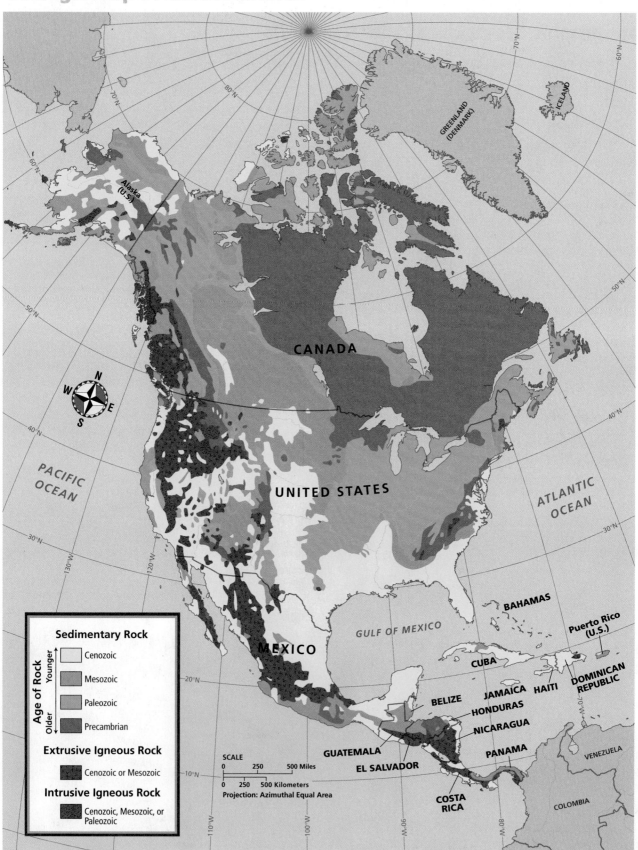

Sedimentary Rock

Age of Rock
Younger — Older

Cenozoic
Mesozoic
Paleozoic
Precambrian

Extrusive Igneous Rock

Cenozoic or Mesozoic

Intrusive Igneous Rock

Cenozoic, Mesozoic, or Paleozoic

SCALE

0   250   500 Miles

0   250   500 Kilometers

Projection: Azimuthal Equal Area

Mineral and Energy Resources of North America

Resources

- Cu Copper
- Au Gold
- Salt
- Ag Silver
- S Sulfur
- U Uranium
- ✳ Major nuclear power plant
- Hydroelectric power

Fossil Fuel Deposits of North America

SCALE

0 — 250 — 500 Miles

0 — 250 — 500 Kilometers

Projection: Azimuthal Equal Area

Fossil Fuels

- Oil (Petroleum)
- Natural gas
- Coal

Topographic Maps of the Moon

Near Side

90°W — 0° — 90°E
50°N — 50°N

OCEANUS PROCELLARUM

Mare Iridum
Mare Imbrium
Apollo 15
Crater Copernicus
Mare Serenitatis
Apollo 17
Mare Crisium
Mare Marginis
Mare Insularum
Mare Tranquillitatis
Apollo 11
Mare Smythii
Apollo 12
Apollo 14
Apollo 16
Mare Fecunditatis
Mare Nubium
Mare Nectaris
Mare Humorum
Crater Tycho

0° — 0°
90°W — 0° — 90°E
50°S — 50°S

Far Side

90°E — 180° — 90°W
50°N — 50°N

Mare Moscoviense
Crater Mendeleev
Crater Hertzsprung
Crater Korolev
Mare Orientale
Mare Ingenii
Crater Apollo
Mare Australe

0° — 0°
90°E — 180° — 90°W
50°S — 50°S

• Apollo landing sites

-9,900 -8,000 -6,000 -4,000 -2,000 0 2,000 4,000 6,000 8,200 METERS

Color-coded topography key

Star Charts for the Northern Hemisphere

Spring

Summer

Constellations	
1	Ursa Minor
2	Draco
3	Cepheus
4	Cassiopeia
5	Auriga
6	Ursa Major
7	Boötes
8	Hercules
9	Cygnus
10	Perseus
11	Gemini
12	Cancer
13	Leo
14	Serpens
15	Sagitta
16	Pegasus
17	Pisces

Autumn

Winter

Constellations	
18	Aries
19	Taurus
20	Orion
21	Virgo
22	Libra
23	Ophiuchus
24	Aquila
25	Lepus
26	Canis Major
27	Hydra
28	Corvus
29	Scorpius
30	Sagittarius
31	Capricornus
32	Aquarius
33	Cetus
34	Columba

Maps of the Solar System

The diagram at top shows the relative sizes of the eight planets. The order of the planets from the sun is the following: Mercury, Venus, Earth, Mars, Jupiter, Saturn, Uranus, and Neptune. The diagrams at bottom show the orbits of the planets around the sun.

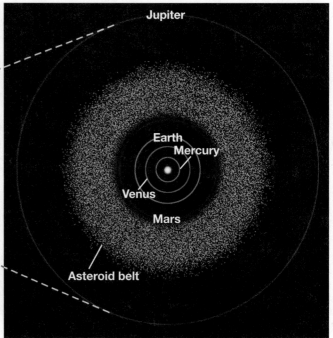

Answers to Reading Checks

Chapter 1

Page 7: Meteorologists use information gathered by satellites, radar, and other technologies on factors such as wind speed, temperature, and rainfall to create weather maps.

Page 10: Observations may lead to interesting scientific questions and may help scientists formulate reasonable and testable hypotheses.

Page 13: Answers may vary but should include three of the following types of models: physical models, graphic models, conceptual models, computer models, and mathematical models.

Page 14: Scientists present the results of their work at professional meetings and in scientific journals.

Chapter 2

Page 30: Indirect observations are the only means available for exploring Earth's interior at depths too great to be reached by drilling.

Page 34: Dust and rock come to Earth from space, while hydrogen atoms in the atmosphere enter space from Earth.

Page 36: An energy budget is the total distribution of energy to, from, and between Earth's various spheres.

Page 38: soil and plants

Page 42: The amount of matter and energy in an ecosystem can supply a population of a given size, and no larger. This maximum population is the carrying capacity of the ecosystem.

Chapter 3

Page 58: because the equator is the only parallel that divides Earth into halves

Page 62: Because both the parallels and the meridians are equally spaced straight lines on a cylindrical projection, the parallels and meridians form a grid.

Page 65: by using a graphic scale, or a printed line divided into proportional parts that represent units of measure; a fractional scale, in which a ratio shows how distance on Earth relates to distance on a map; or a verbal scale, which expresses scale in sentence form

Page 69: Water moves from areas of higher elevation to areas of lower elevation. Because the V shape points toward higher elevation, it points upstream.

Page 71: Scientists create soil maps to classify, map, and describe soils.

Chapter 4

Page 89: The atomic number is the number of protons in an atom's nucleus. The mass number is the sum of the number of protons and the number of neutrons in an atom. The unified atomic mass unit is used to express the mass of subatomic particles or atoms.

Page 95: Atoms form chemical bonds by transferring electrons or by sharing electrons.

Page 97: The oxygen atom has a larger and more positively charged nucleus than the hydrogen atoms do. As a result, the oxygen nucleus pulls the electrons from the hydrogen atoms closer to it than the hydrogen nuclei pull the shared electrons from the oxygen. This unequal attraction forms a polar-covalent bond.

Chapter 5

Page 113: Nonsilicate minerals never contain compounds of silicon bonded to oxygen.

Page 114: The building block of the silicate crystalline structure is a four-sided structure known as the silicon-oxygen tetrahedron, which is one silicon atom surrounded by four oxygen atoms.

Page 119: The strength and geometric arrangement of the bonds between the atoms that make up a mineral's internal structure determine the hardness of a mineral.

Page 121: Chatoyancy is the silky appearance of some minerals in reflected light. Asterism is the appearance of a six-sided star when a mineral reflects light.

Chapter 6

Page 137: As magma cools and solidifies, minerals crystallize out of the magma in a specific order that depends on their melting points.

Page 141: Fine-grained igneous rock forms mainly from magma that cools rapidly; coarse-grained igneous rock forms mainly from magma that cools more slowly.

Page 143: A batholith is an intrusive structure that covers an area of at least 100 km^2. A stock covers an area of less than 100 km^2.

Page 147: Three groups of clastic sedimentary rock are conglomerates and breccias, sandstones, and shales.

Page 149: Graded bedding is a type of stratification in which different sizes and types of sediments settle to different levels.

Page 152: The high pressures and temperatures that result from the movements of tectonic plates may cause chemical changes in the minerals.

Chapter 7

Page 168: Water creates ore deposits by eroding rock and releasing minerals, and by carrying the mineral fragments and depositing them in streambeds.

Page 173: Cap rock is a layer of impermeable rock at the top of an oil- or natural gas-bearing formation through which fluids cannot flow.

Page 174: As neutrons strike neighboring nuclei, the nuclei split and release additional neutrons that strike other nuclei and cause the chain to continue.

Page 179: Answers may vary but should include three of the following: geothermal, solar, hydroelectric, and biomass.

Page 182: The use of fossil fuels affects the environment when coal is mined from the surface, which destroys the land. When fossil fuels are burned, they affect the environment by creating air pollution.

Chapter 8

Page 202: Hutton reasoned that the extremely slow-working forces that changed the land on his farm had also slowly changed the rocks that make up Earth's crust. He concluded that large changes must happen over a period of millions of years.

Page 204: Because ripple marks form at the top of a rock layer, scientists can use the orientation of the ripple marks to determine which direction was "up" when the rock layers formed.

Page 208: Varves are like tree rings in that varves are laid down each year. Thus, counting varves can reveal the age of sedimentary deposits.

Page 211: An isotope that has an extremely long half-life will not show significant or measurable changes in a young rock. In a very old rock, an isotope that has a short half-life may have decayed to the point at which too little of the isotope is left to give an accurate age measurement. So, the estimated age of the rock must be correlated to the dating method used.

Page 215: A trace fossil is fossilized evidence of past animal movement, such as tracks, footprints, borings, or burrows, that can provide information about prehistoric life.

Chapter 9

Page 229: You would find fossils of extinct animals in older layers of a geologic column.

Page 234: Earth is approximately 4.6 billion years old.

Page 236: Answers may vary but should include three of the following: trilobites, brachiopods, jellyfish, worms, snails, and sponges.

Page 240: Answers may vary but could include *Archaeopteryx*, pterosaurs, *Apatosaurus*, and *Stegosaurus*.

Page 243: During ice ages, water from the ocean was frozen as ice on the continents, so the amount of liquid water in the seas decreased and sea level fell.

Chapter 10

Page 261: Many scientists rejected Wegener's hypothesis because the mechanism that Wegener suggested was physically impossible.

Page 263: New sea floor forms as magma rises to fill the rift that forms when two plates pull apart at a divergent boundary.

Page 265: The symmetrical magnetic patterns in sea-floor rocks show that rock formed at one place (at a ridge) and then broke apart and moved away from the center in opposite directions.

Page 268: Scientists use the locations of earthquakes, volcanoes, trenches, and mid-ocean ridges to outline tectonic plates.

Page 270: Collisions at convergent boundaries can happen between two oceanic plates, between two continental plates, or between one oceanic plate and one continental plate.

Page 273: When denser lithosphere sinks into the asthenosphere, the asthenosphere must move out of the way. As the asthenosphere moves, it drags or pushes on other parts of the lithosphere, which causes movement.

Page 276: As a plate subducts beneath another plate, islands and other land features on the subducting plate are scraped off the subducting plate and become part of the overriding plate.

Page 279: The continents Africa, South America, Antarctica, and Australia formed from Gondwanaland. The subcontinent of India was also part of Gondwanaland.

Chapter 11

Page 295: Tension and shear stress can both pull rock apart.

Page 297: limbs and hinges

Page 299: A thrust fault is a type of reverse fault in which the fault plane is at a low angle relative to the surface.

Page 303: The Himalayas are growing taller because the two plates are still colliding and causing further compression of the rock, which further uplifts the mountains.

Page 305: Answers may include three of the following: folded mountains, fault-block mountains, dome mountains, and volcanic mountains.

Chapter 12

Page 321: Rayleigh waves cause the ground to move in an elliptical, rolling motion. Love waves cause rock to move side-to-side and perpendicular to the direction the waves are traveling.

Page 322: The speed of seismic waves changes as they pass through different layers of Earth.

Page 327: Moment magnitude is more accurate for larger earthquakes than the Richter scale is. Moment magnitude is directly related to rock properties and so is more closely related to the cause of the earthquake than the Richter scale is.

Page 331: Scientists think that stress on a fault builds up to a critical point and is then released as an earthquake. Seismic gaps are areas in which no earthquakes have happened in a long period of time and thus are likely to be under a high amount of stress.

Chapter 13

Page 347: The denser plate of oceanic lithosphere subducts beneath the less dense plate of continental lithosphere.

Page 349: As the lithosphere moves over the mantle plume, older volcanoes move away from the mantle plume. A new hot spot forms in the lithosphere above the mantle plume as a new volcano begins to form. In addition, a long plume can produce several volcanoes at once.

Page 352: The faster the rate of flow is and the higher the gas content is, the more broken up and rough the resulting cooled lava will be.

Page 355: A caldera may form when a magma chamber empties or when large amounts of magma are discharged, causing the ground to collapse.

Chapter 14

Page 374: Two types of mechanical weathering are ice wedging and abrasion. Ice wedging is caused by water that seeps into cracks in rock and freezes. When water freezes, it expands and creates pressure on the rock, which widens and deepens cracks. Abrasion is the grinding away of rock surfaces by other rocks or sand particles. Abrasive agents may be carried by gravity, water, and wind.

Page 376: Two effects of chemical weathering are changes in the chemical composition and changes in the physical appearance of a rock.

Page 380: Fractures and joints in a rock increase surface area and allow weathering to occur more rapidly.

Page 385: Large amounts of rainfall and high temperatures cause thick soils to form in both tropical and temperate climates. Tropical soils have thin A horizons because of the continuous leaching of topsoil. Temperate soils have three thick layers, because leaching of the A horizon in temperate climates is much less than leaching of the A horizon in tropical climates.

Page 388: Dust storms may form during droughts when the soil is made dry and loose by lack of moisture and wind-caused sheet erosion carries it away in clouds of dust. If all of the topsoil is removed, the remaining subsoil will not contain enough nutrients to raise crops.

Page 391: Landslides are masses of loose rock combined with soil that suddenly fall down a slope. A rockfall consists of rock falling from a steep cliff.

Page 393: When a mountain is no longer being uplifted, weathering and erosion wear down its jagged peaks to low, featureless surfaces called *peneplains*.

Chapter 15

Page 408: Precipitation is any form of water that falls to Earth from the clouds, including rain, snow, sleet, and hail.

Page 413: A river that has meanders probably has a low gradient.

Page 417: Floods can be controlled indirectly through forest and soil conservation measures that reduce or prevent runoff, or directly by building artificial structures, such as dams, levees, and floodways, to redirect water flow.

Chapter 16

Page 433: The two zones of groundwater are the zone of saturation and the zone of aeration.

Page 434: The depth of a water table depends on topography, aquifer permeability, the amount of rainfall, and the rate at which humans use the groundwater.

Page 437: Ordinary springs occur where the ground surface drops below the water table. An artesian spring occurs where groundwater flows to the surface through natural cracks in the overlying caprock.

Page 441: A natural bridge may form when two sinkholes form close to each other. The bridge is the uncollapsed rock between the sinkholes.

Chapter 17

Page 456: Continental glaciers exist only in Greenland and Antarctica.

Page 460: A moving glacier forms a cirque by pulling blocks of rock from the floor and walls of a valley and leaving a bowl-shaped depression.

Page 463: A drumlin is a long, low, tear-shaped mound of till.

Page 464: Eskers form when meltwater from receding continental glaciers flows through ice tunnels and deposits long, winding ridges of gravel and sand.

Page 468: The sea level was up to 140 m lower than it is now.

Chapter 18

Page 484: Moisture makes soil heavier, so the soil sticks and is more difficult to move. Therefore, erosion happens faster in dry climates.

Page 486: Barchan dunes are crescent shaped; transverse dunes form linear ridges.

Page 490: Answers should include three of the following: sea cliffs, sea caves, sea arches, sea stacks, wave-cut terraces, and wave-built terraces.

Page 495: As sea levels rise over a flat coastal plain, the shoreline moves inland and isolates dunes from the old shoreline. These dunes become barrier islands.

Chapter 19

Page 514: Transpiration increases the amount of water vapor in the atmosphere.

Page 517: An aneroid barometer contains a sealed metal container that has a partial vacuum.

Page 519: The lower region of the thermosphere is called the *ionosphere.*

Page 525: Deserts are colder at night than other areas are because the air in deserts contains little water vapor that can absorb heat during the day and release heat slowly at night.

Page 528: They flow in opposite directions from each other, and they occur at different latitudes.

Chapter 20

Page 544: When the air is very dry and the temperature is below freezing, ice and snow change directly into water vapor by sublimation.

Page 546: Dew is liquid moisture that condenses from air on cool objects when the air is nearly saturated and the temperature drops. Frost is water vapor that condenses as ice crystals onto a cool surface directly from the air when the dew point is below freezing.

Page 550: The source of energy that warms the air and leads to cloud formation is solar energy that is reradiated as heat by Earth's surface. As the process continues, latent heat released by the condensation may allow the clouds to expand beyond the condensation level.

Page 553: because cirrus clouds form at very high altitudes where air temperature is low

Page 557: Doppler radar measures the location, direction of movement, and intensity of precipitation.

Chapter 21

Page 573: a continental tropical air mass

Page 577: The air of an anticyclone sinks and flows outward from a center of high pressure. The air of a midlatitude cyclone rotates toward the rising air of a central low-pressure region.

Page 579: over warm tropical seas

Page 584: A barometer is used to measure atmospheric pressure.

Page 589: Areas of precipitation are marked by using colors or symbols.

Page 590: Meteorologists compare models because different models are better at predicting different weather variables. If information from two or more models matches, scientists can be more confident of their predictions.

Chapter 22

Page 607: Waves, currents, and other water motions continually replace warm surface waters with cooler water from the ocean depths, which keeps the surface temperature of the water from increasing rapidly.

Page 608: The temperature of land increases faster than that of water because the specific heat of land is lower than that of water, and thus the land requires less energy to heat up than the water does.

Page 612: marine west coast, humid continental, and humid subtropical

Page 616: Scientists use computer models to incorporate as much data as possible to sort out the complex variables that influence climate and to make predictions about climate.

Page 618: Climate change influences humans, plants, and animals. It also affects nearby climates, sea level, and precipitation rates.

Chapter 23

Page 638: Oceanographers study the physical characteristics, chemical composition, and life-forms of the ocean.

Page 642: Trenches; broad, flat plains; mountain ranges; and submerged volcanoes are part of the deep-ocean basins.

Page 647: When chemical reactions take place in the ocean, dissolved substances can crystallize to form nodules that settle to the ocean floor.

Chapter 24

Page 663: Dissolved solids enter the oceans from the chemical weathering of rock on land, from volcanic eruptions, and from chemical reactions between sea water and newly formed sea-floor rocks.

Page 665: Ocean surface temperatures are affected by the amount of solar energy an area receives and by the movement of water in the ocean.

Page 667: Ocean water contains dissolved solids (mostly salts) that add mass to a given volume of water. The large amount of dissolved solids in ocean water makes ocean water denser than fresh water.

Page 671: Most marine life is found in the sublittoral zone. Life in this zone is continuously submerged, but waters are still shallow enough to allow sunlight to penetrate.

Page 675: Aquaculture provides a reliable, economical source of food. However, aquatic farms are susceptible to pollution, and they may become local sources of pollution.

Chapter 25

Page 691: Because no continents interrupt the flow of the Antarctic Circumpolar Current, also called the *West Wind Drift*, it completely encircles Antarctica and crosses three major oceans and is therefore the world's largest ocean current. All other surface currents are deflected and divided when they meet a continental barrier.

Page 693: Antarctic Bottom Water is very cold. It also has a high salinity. The extreme cold and high salinity combine to make the water extremely dense.

Page 696: Because waves receive energy from wind that pushes against the surface of the water, the amount of energy decreases as the depth of water increases. As a result, the diameter of the water molecules' circular path also decreases.

Page 698: Contact with the ocean floor slows down the bottom of the wave but not the top of the wave. Because of the difference in speed between the top and bottom of the wave, the top gets farther ahead of the bottom until the wave becomes unstable and falls over.

Page 702: When the tidal range is small, the sun and the moon are at right angles to each other relative to Earth's orbit.

Florida Close-Up

C3: Florida is located below 30°N latitude, within the trade-winds belt. Therefore, winds generally blow from east to west.

C7: The effects of El Niño include greater than normal precipitation and fewer hurricanes in the Gulf of Mexico and Atlantic Ocean.

C11: The siliciclastic rock that invades Florida is eroding sediment from the Appalachian Mountains, which are north of Florida.

C15: The phosphate deposits in Florida are the result of upwelling of cold nutrient-rich water, which supplied phosphorus to marine microorganisms that flourished. As dead organisms and other organic matter died and became buried, chemical reactions caused conversion to the phosphate mineral form.

C21: Florida is using and developing solar electric systems (or photovoltaics), which produce electricity from sunlight, and solar thermal systems, which produce heat that is used to generate steam.

C25: Answers should include three of the following: sinkholes, tornadoes, waterspouts, hurricanes, thunderstorms, and rising sea levels/coastal erosion.

Chapter 26

Page 723: The only kind of electromagnetic radiation the human eye can detect is visible light.

Page 725: Images produced by refracting telescopes are subject to distortion because of the ways different colors of visible light are focused at different distances from the lens and because of size limitations on the objective lens.

Page 726: Scientists launch spacecraft into orbit to detect radiation screened out by Earth's atmosphere and to avoid light pollution and other atmospheric distortions.

Page 731: Constellations provide two kinds of evidence of Earth's motion. As Earth rotates, the stars appear to change position during the night. As Earth revolves around the sun, Earth's night sky faces a different part of the universe. As a result, different constellations appear in the night sky as the seasons change.

Page 733: Because time zones are based on Earth's rotation, as you travel west you eventually come to a location where, on one side of the time zone border, the calendar moves ahead one day. The purpose of the International Date Line is to locate the border so that the transition would affect the least number of people. So that it will affect the least number of people, the International Date Line is in the middle of the Pacific Ocean, instead of on a continent.

Page 734: Daylight savings time is an adjustment that is made to standard time by setting clocks ahead one hour to take advantage of longer hours of daylight in the summer months and to save energy.

Chapter 27

Page 751: Unlike the outer planets, Pluto is very small and is composed of rock and frozen gas, instead of thick layers of gases.

Page 753: Green plants release free oxygen as part of photosynthesis, which caused the concentration of oxygen gas in the atmosphere to gradually increase.

Page 756: An ellipse is a closed curve whose shape is defined by two points inside the curve. An ellipse looks like an oval.

Page 761: Answers may vary but should address differences in distance from the sun, density, atmospheric pressure and density, and tectonics.

Page 763: Martian volcanoes are larger than volcanoes on Earth because Mars has no moving tectonic plates. Magma sources remain in the same spot for millions of years and produce volcanic material that builds the volcanic cone higher and higher.

Page 766: When Jupiter formed, it did not have enough mass for nuclear fusion to begin.

Page 768: Saturn and Jupiter are made almost entirely of hydrogen and helium and have rocky-iron cores, ring systems, many satellites, rapid rotational periods, and bands of colored clouds.

Page 771: The Kuiper Belt is located beyond the orbit of Neptune.

Chapter 28

Page 786: Answers should include two of the following features: maria, highlands, craters, ridges, and rilles.

Page 788: The crust of the far side of the moon is thicker than the crust of the near side is. The crust of the far side also consists mainly of mountainous terrain and has only a few small maria.

Page 792: The far side of the moon is never visible from Earth, because the moon's rotation on its axis and the moon's revolution around Earth take the same amount of time.

Page 794: During a total eclipse, the entire disk of the sun is blocked, and the outer layers of the sun become visible. During an annular eclipse, the disk of the sun is never completely blocked out, so the sun is too bright for observers on Earth to see the outer layers of the sun's atmosphere.

Page 797: When the lighted part of the moon is larger than a semicircle but the visible part of the moon is shrinking, the phase is called *waning gibbous.* When only a sliver of the near side is visible, the phase is called a *waning crescent.*

Page 801: Io's surface is covered with many active volcanoes. Europa's surface is covered by an enormous ice sheet. Ganymede is the largest moon in the solar system and has a strong magnetic field. Callisto's surface is heavily cratered.

Page 803: Charon is almost half the size of the body it orbits. Charon's orbital period is the same length as Pluto's day, so only one side of Pluto always faces its largest moon.

Page 806: The most common type is made mostly of carbon materials. The second type is made mostly of silicate minerals. Other asteroids are made mostly of metals such as iron and nickel.

Page 809: A meteoroid is a rocky body that travels through space. When a meteoroid enters Earth's atmosphere and begins to burn up, the meteoroid produces a meteor.

Chapter 29

Page 825: Einstein's equation helped scientists understand the source of the sun's energy. The equation explained how the sun could produce huge amounts of energy without burning up.

Page 827: The sun's atmosphere consists of the photosphere, the chromosphere, and the corona.

Page 831: Coronal mass ejections generate sudden disturbances in Earth's magnetic field. The high-energy particles that circulate during these storms can damage satellites, cause power blackouts, and interfere with radio communications.

Chapter 30

Page 847: Polaris is almost exactly above the pole of Earth's rotational axis, so Polaris moves only slightly around the pole during one rotation of Earth.

Page 848: Starlight is shifted toward the red end of the spectrum when the star is moving away from the observer.

Page 853: The forces balance each other and keep the star in equilibrium. As gravity increases the pressure on the matter within a star, the rate of fusion increases. This increase in fusion causes a rise in gas pressure. As a result, the energy from the increased fusion and gas pressure generates outward pressure that balances the force of gravity.

Page 854: Giants and supergiants appear in the upper right part of the H-R diagram.

Page 857: As supergiants collapse because of gravitational forces, fusion begins and continues until the supply of fuel is used up. The core begins to collapse under its own gravity and causes energy to transfer to the outer layers of the star. The transfer of energy to the outer layers causes the explosion.

Page 860: More than 50% of all stars similar to the sun are in multiple-star systems.

Page 864: All matter and energy in the early universe was compressed into a small volume at an extremely high temperature until the temperature cooled and all of the matter and energy was forced outward in all directions.

Glossary · Glosario

A

abrasion (uh BRAY zhuhn) the grinding and wearing away of rock surfaces through the mechanical action of other rock or sand particles (374)

abrasion proceso por el cual las superficies de las rocas se muelen o desgastan por medio de la acción mecánica de otras rocas y partículas de arena (374)

absolute age (AB suh LOOT AYJ) the numeric age of an object or event, often stated in years before the present, as established by an absolute-dating process, such as radiometric dating (207)

edad absoluta la edad numérica de un objeto o suceso, que suele expresarse en cantidad de años antes del presente, determinada por un proceso de datación absoluta, tal como la datación radiométrica (207)

absolute humidity (AB suh LOOT hyoo MID uh tee) the mass of water vapor per unit volume of air that contains the water vapor; usually expressed as grams of water vapor per cubic meter of air (545)

humedad absoluta la masa de vapor de agua por unidad de volumen de aire que contiene al vapor de agua; normalmente se expresa por metro cúbico de aire (545)

absolute magnitude (AB suh LOOT MAG nuh TOOD) the brightness that a star would have at a distance of 32.6 light-years from Earth (850)

magnitud absoluta el brillo que una estrella tendría a una distancia de 32.6 años luz de la Tierra (850)

abyssal plain (uh BIS uhl PLAYN) a large, flat, almost level area of the deep-ocean basin (643)

llanura abisal un área amplia, llana y casi plana de la cuenca oceánica profunda (643)

acid precipitation (AS id pree SIP uh TAY shuhn) precipitation, such as rain, sleet, or snow, that contains a high concentration of acids, often because of the pollution of the atmosphere (378)

precipitación ácida precipitación tal como lluvia, aguanieve o nieve, que contiene una alta concentración de ácidos debido a la contaminación de la atmósfera" (378)

adiabatic cooling (AD ee uh BAT ik KOOL ing) the process by which the temperature of an air mass decreases as the air mass rises and expands (550)

enfriamiento adiabático el proceso por medio del cual la temperatura de una masa de aire disminuye a medida que ésta se eleva y se expande (550)

advective cooling (ad VEK tiv KOOL ing) the process by which the temperature of an air mass decreases as the air mass moves over a cold surface (551)

enfriamiento advectivo el proceso por medio del cual la temperatura de una masa de aire disminuye a medida que ésta se mueve sobre una superficie fría (551)

air mass (ER MAS) a large body of air throughout which temperature and moisture content are similar (571)

masa de aire un gran volumen de aire, cuya temperatura y cuyo contenido de humedad son similares en toda su extension (571)

albedo (al BEE doh) the fraction of solar radiation that is reflected off the surface of an object (523)

albedo porcentaje de la radiación solar que la superficie de un objeto refleja (523)

alluvial fan (uh LOO vee uhl FAN) a fan-shaped mass of rock material deposited by a stream when the slope of the land decreases sharply; for example, alluvial fans form when streams flow from mountains to flat land (415)

abanico alluvial masa de materiales rocosos en forma de abanico, depositados por un arroyo cuando la pendiente del terreno disminuye bruscamente; por ejemplo, los abanicos aluviales se forman cuando los arroyos fluyen de una montaña a un terreno llano (415)

alpine glacier (AL PIEN GLAY shuhr) a narrow, wedge-shaped mass of ice that forms in a mountainous region and that is confined to a small area by surrounding topography; examples include valley glaciers, cirque glaciers, and piedmont glaciers (456)

glaciar alpino una masa de hielo angosta, parecida a una cuña, que se forma en una región montañosa y que está confinada a un área pequeña por la topografía que la rodea; los glaciares de valle, los circos glaciares y los glaciares de pie de monte son algunos ejemplos de esto (456)

anemometer (AN uh MAHM uht uhr) an instrument used to measure wind speed (584)

anemómetro un instrumento que se usa para medir la rapidez del viento (584)

aphelion (uh FEE lee uhn) in the orbit of a planet or other body in the solar system, the point that is farthest from the sun (730)

afelio en la órbita de un planeta u otros cuerpos en el sistema solar, el punto que está más lejos del Sol (730)

apogee (AP uh JEE) in the orbit of a satellite, the point that is farthest from Earth (791)

apogeo en la órbita de un satélite, el punto en el que el satélite está más alejado de la Tierra (791)

apparent magnitude (uh PER uhnt MAG nuh TOOD) the brightness of a star as seen from Earth (850)

magnitud aparente el brillo de una estrella como se percibe desde la Tierra (850)

aquaculture (AHK wuh KUHL chuhr) the raising of aquatic plants and animals for human use or consumption (675)

acuacultura el cultivo de plantas y animales acuáticos para uso o consumo humano (675)

aquifer (AHK wuh fuhr) a body of rock or sediment that stores groundwater and allows the flow of groundwater (431)

acuífero un cuerpo rocoso o sedimento que almacena agua subterránea y permite que fluya (431)

arête (uh RAYT) a sharp, jagged ridge that forms between cirques (460)

cresta una cumbre puntiaguda e irregular que se forma entre circos glaciares (460)

artesian formation (ahr TEE zhuhn fawr MAY shuhn) a sloping layer of permeable rock sandwiched between two layers of impermeable rock and exposed at the surface (437)

formación artesiana capa inclinada de rocas permeables que está en medio de dos capas de rocas impermeables y expuesta en la superficie (437)

asteroid (AS tuhr OYD) a small, rocky object that orbits the sun; most asteroids are located in a band between the orbits of Mars and Jupiter (805)

asteroide un objeto pequeño y rocoso que se encuentra en órbita alrededor del Sol; la mayoría de los asteroides se ubican en una banda entre las órbitas de Marte y Júpiter (805)

asthenosphere (as THEN uh SFIR) the solid, plastic layer of the mantle beneath the lithosphere; made of mantle rock that flows very slowly, which allows tectonic plates to move on top of it (31, 267)

astenosfera la capa sólida y plástica del manto, que se encuentra debajo de la litosfera; está formada por roca del manto que fluye muy lentamente, lo cual permite que las placas tectónicas se muevan en su superficie (31, 267)

astronomical unit (AS truh NAHM i kuhl YOON it) the average distance between Earth and the sun; approximately 150 million kilometers (symbol, AU) (722)

unidad astronómica la distancia promedio entre la Tierra y el Sol; aproximadamente 150 millones de kilómetros (símbolo: UA) (722)

astronomy (uh STRAHN uh mee) the scientific study of the universe (7, 721)

astronomía el estudio científico del universo (7, 721)

atmosphere (AT muhs FIR) a mixture of gases that surrounds a planet, moon, or other celestial body (35, 513)

atmósfera una mezcla de gases que rodea un planeta, una luna, u otras cuerpos celestes (35, 513)

atmospheric pressure (AT muhs FIR ik PRESH uhr) the force per unit area that is exerted on a surface by the weight of the atmosphere (516)

presión atmosférica la fuerza por unidad de área que el peso de la atmósfera ejerce sobre una superficie (516)

atom (AT uhm) the smallest unit of an element that maintains the chemical properties of that element (88)

átomo la unidad más pequeña de un elemento que conserva las propiedades químicas de ese elemento (88)

aurora (aw RAWR uh) colored light produced by charged particles from the solar wind and from the magnetosphere that react with and excite the oxygen and nitrogen of Earth's upper atmosphere; usually seen in the sky near Earth's magnetic poles (832)

aurora luz de colores producida por partículas con carga del viento solar y de la magnetosfera, que reaccionan con los átomos de oxígeno y nitrógeno de la parte superior de la atmósfera de la Tierra y los excitan; normalmente se ve en el cielo cerca de los polos magnéticos de la Tierra (832)

B

barometer (buh RAHM uht uhr) an instrument that measures atmospheric pressure (584)

barómetro un instrumento que mide la presión atmosférica (584)

barrier island (BAR ee uhr IE luhnd) a long ridge of sand or narrow island that lies parallel to the shore (495)

isla barrera un largo arrecife de arena o una isla angosta ubicada paralela a la costa (495)

basal slip (BAY suhl SLIP) the process that causes the ice at the base of a glacier to melt and the glacier to slide (457)

deslizamiento basal el proceso que hace que el hielo de la base de un glaciar se derrita y que éste se deslice (457)

beach (BEECH) an area of the shoreline that is made up of deposited sediment (491)

playa un área de la costa que está formada por sedimento depositado (491)

benthic zone (BEN thik zohn) the bottom region of oceans and bodies of fresh water (671)

zona bentónica la región del fondo de los océanos y de las masas de agua dulce (671)

benthos (BEN THAHS) organisms that live at the bottom of oceans or bodies of fresh water (670)

benthos organismos que viven en el fondo de los océanos o de las masas de agua dulce (670)

big bang theory (BIG BANG THEE uh ree) the theory that all matter and energy in the universe was compressed into an extremely small volume that 13 billion to 15 billion years ago exploded and began expanding in all directions (864)

teoría del Big Bang la teoría que establece que toda la materia y la energía del universo estaban comprimidas en un volumen extremadamente pequeño que explotó hace aproximadamente 13 a 15 mil millones de años y empezó a expandirse en todas direcciones (864)

biomass (BIE oh MAS) plant material, manure, or any other organic matter that is used as an energy source (179)

biomasa materia vegetal, estiércol o cualquier otra materia orgánica que se usa como fuente de energía (179)

biosphere (BIE oh SFIR) the part of Earth where life exists; includes all of the living organisms on Earth (35)

biosfera la parte de la Tierra donde existe la vida; comprende todos los seres vivos de la Tierra (35)

black hole (BLAK HOHL) an object so massive and dense that even light cannot escape its gravity (858)

hoyo negro un objeto tan masivo y denso que ni siquiera la luz puede salir de su campo gravitacional (858)

body wave (BAHD ee WAYV) in geology, a seismic wave that travels through the body of a medium (320)

onda interna en geología, una onda sísmica que se desplaza a través del cuerpo de un medio (320)

Bowen's reaction series (BOH inz ree AK shuhn SIR eez) the simplified pattern that illustrates the order in which minerals crystallize from cooling magma according to their chemical composition and melting point (137)

serie de reacción de Bowen el patrón simplificado que ilustra el orden en que los minerales se cristalizan a partir del magma que se enfría, de acuerdo con su composición química y punto de fusion (137)

braided stream (BRAYD uhd STREEM) a stream or river that is composed of multiple channels that divide and rejoin around sediment bars (414)

corriente anastomosada una corriente o río compuesto por varios canales que se dividen y se vuelven a encontrar alrededor de barreras de sedimento (414)

caldera (kal DER uh) a large, circular depression that forms when the magma chamber below a volcano partially empties and causes the ground above to sink (355)

caldera una depresión grande y circular que se forma cuando se vacía parcialmente la cámara de magma que hay debajo de un volcán, lo cual hace que el suelo se hunda (355)

carbonation (KAHR buh NAY shuhn) the conversion of a compound into a carbonate (377)

carbonación la transformación de un compuesto a un carbonato (377)

carrying capacity (KAR ee ing kuh PAS i tee) the largest population that an environment can support at any given time (42)

capacidad de carga la población más grande que un ambiente puede sostener en cualquier momento dado (42)

cavern (KAV uhrn) a natural cavity that forms in rock as a result of the dissolution of minerals; also a large cave that commonly contains many smaller, connecting chambers (440)

caverna una cavidad natural que se forma en la roca como resultado de la disolución de minerales; también, una gran cueva que generalmente contiene muchas cámaras más pequeñas comunicadas entre sí (440)

cementation (SEE men TAY shuhn) the process in which minerals precipitate into pore spaces between sediment grains and bind sediments together to form rock (145)

cementación el proceso en el cual los minerales se precipitan entre los poros de granos de sedimento y unen los sedimentos para formar rocas (145)

Cenozoic Era (SEN uh ZOH ik ER uh) the current geologic era, which began 65.5 million years ago; also called the *Age of Mammals* (242)

era Cenozoica la era geológica actual, que comenzó hace 65.5 millones de años; también llamada *Edad de los Mamíferos* (242)

chemical sedimentary rock (KEM i kuhl SED uh MEN tuhr ee RAHK) sedimentary rock that forms when minerals precipitate from a solution or settle from a suspension (146)

roca sedimentaria química roca sedimentaria que se forma cuando los minerales precipitan a partir de una solución o se depositan a partir de una suspensión (146)

chemical weathering (KEM i kuhl WETH uhr ing) the process by which rocks break down as a result of chemical reactions (376)

desgaste químico el proceso por medio del cual las rocas se fragmentan como resultado de reacciones químicas (376)

chromosphere (KROH muh SFIR) the thin layer of the sun that is just above the photosphere and that glows a reddish color during eclipses (828)

cromosfera la delgada capa del Sol que se encuentra justo encima de la fotosfera y que resplandece con un color rojizo durante los eclipses (828)

cirque (SUHRK) a deep and steep bowl-like depression produced by glacier erosion (460)

circo una depresión profunda y empinada, con forma de tazón, producida por erosión glaciar (460)

cirrus cloud (SIR uhs KLOWD) a feathery cloud that is composed of ice crystals and that has the highest altitude of any cloud in the sky (553)

nube cirro una nube liviana formada por cristales de hielo, la cual tiene la mayor altitud de todas las nubes en el cielo (553)

clastic sedimentary rock (KLAS tik SED uh MEN tuhr ee RAHK) sedimentary rock that forms when fragments of preexisting rocks are compacted or cemented together (147)

roca sedimentaria clástica roca sedimentaria que se forma cuando los fragmentos de rocas preexistentes se unen por compactación o cementación (147)

cleavage (KLEEV ij) in geology, the tendency of a mineral to split along specific planes of weakness to form smooth, flat surfaces (118)

exfoliación en geología, la tendencia de un mineral a agrietarse a lo largo de planos débiles específicos y formar superficies lisas y planas (118)

climate (KLIE muht) the weather conditions in an area over a long period of time (605)

clima las condiciones del tiempo en un área durante un largo período de tiempo (605)

climatologist (KLIE muh TAHL uh jist) a scientist who gathers data to study and compare past and present climates and to predict future climate change (615)

climatólogo un científico que recopila datos para estudiar y comparar los climas del pasado y del presente y para predecir cambios climáticos en el futuro (615)

cloud (KLOWD) a collection of small water droplets or ice crystals suspended in the air, which forms when the air is cooled and condensation occurs (549)

nube un conjunto de pequeñas gotitas de agua o cristales de hielo suspendidos en el aire, que se forma cuando el aire se enfría y ocurre condensación (549)

cloud seeding (KLOWD SEED ing) the process of introducing freezing nuclei or condensation nuclei into a cloud in order to cause rain to fall (558)

sembrado de nubes el proceso de introducir núcleos congelados o núcleos de condensación en una nube para producir lluvia (558)

coalescence (KOH uh LE suhns) the formation of a larger droplet by the combination of smaller droplets (556)

coalescencia la formación de una gota más grande al combinarse gotas más pequeñas (556)

cold front (KOHLD FRUHNT) the front edge of a moving mass of cold air that pushes beneath a warmer air mass like a wedge (575)

frente frío el borde del frente de una masa de aire frío en movimiento que empuja por debajo de una masa de aire más caliente como una cuña (575)

comet (KAHM it) a small body of ice, rock, and cosmic dust that follows an elliptical orbit around the sun and that gives off gas and dust in the form of a tail as it passes close to the sun (807)

cometa un cuerpo pequeño formado por hielo, roca y polvo cósmico que sigue una órbita elíptica alrededor del Sol y que libera gas y polvo, los cuales forman una cola al pasar cerca del Sol (807)

compaction (kuhm PAK shuhn) the process in which the volume and porosity of a sediment is decreased by the weight of overlying sediments as a result of burial beneath other sediments (145)

compactación el proceso en el que el volumen y la porosidad de un sedimento disminuyen por efecto del peso al quedar el sedimento enterrado debajo de otros sedimentos superpuestos (145)

compound (KAHM POWND) a substance made up of atoms of two or more different elements joined by chemical bonds (93)

compuesto una sustancia formada por átomos de dos o más elementos diferentes unidos por enlaces químicos (93)

condensation (KAHN duhn SAY shuhn) the change of state from a gas to a liquid (408)

condensación el cambio de estado de gas a líquido (408)

condensation nucleus (KAHN duhn SAY shuhn NOO klee uhs) a solid particle in the atmosphere that provides the surface on which water vapor condenses (549)

núcleo de condensación una partícula sólida en la atmósfera que proporciona la superficie en la que el vapor de agua se condensa (549)

conduction (kuhn DUHK shuhn) the transfer of energy as heat through a material (526)

conducción la transferencia de energía en forma de calor a través de un material (526)

conservation (KAHN suhr VAY shuhn) the preservation and wise use of natural resources (183)

conservación la preservación y el uso inteligente de los recursos naturales (183)

constellation (KAHN stuh LAY shuhn) one of 88 regions into which the sky has been divided in order to describe the locations of celestial objects; a group of stars organized in a recognizable pattern (859)

constelación una de las 88 regiones en las que se ha dividido el cielo con el fin de describir la ubicación de los objetos celestes; un grupo de estrellas organizadas en un patrón reconocible (859)

contact metamorphism (KAHN TAKT MET uh MAWR FIZ uhm) a change in the texture, structure, or chemical composition of a rock due to contact with magma (152)

metamorfismo de contacto un cambio en la textura, estructura o composición química de una roca debido al contacto con el magma (152)

continental drift (KAHN tuh NENT'l DRIFT) the hypothesis that a single large landmass broke up into smaller landmasses to form the continents, which then drifted to their present locations; the movement of continents (259)

deriva continental la hipótesis de que una sola masa de tierra se dividió en masas de tierra más pequeñas para formar los continentes, los cuales se fueron a la deriva hasta terminar en sus ubicaciones actuales; el movimiento de los continents (259)

continental glacier (KAHN tuh NENT'l GLAY shuhr) a massive sheet of ice that may cover millions of square kilometers, that may be thousands of meters thick, and that is not confined by surrounding topography (456)

glaciar continental una enorme capa de hielo que puede cubrir millones de kilómetros cuadrados, tener un espesor de miles de metros y que no está confinada por la topografía que la rodea (456)

continental margin (KAHN tuh NENT'l MAHR jin) the shallow sea floor that is located between the shoreline and the deep-ocean bottom (641)

margen continental el suelo marino poco profundo que se ubica entre la costa y el fondo profundo del océano (641)

contour line (KAHN TOOR LIEN) a line that connects points of equal elevation on a map (68)

curva de nivel una línea en un mapa que une puntos que tienen la misma elevación (68)

convection (kuhn VEK shuhn) the movement of matter due to differences in density that are caused by temperature variations; can result in the transfer of energy as heat (526)

convección el movimiento de la materia debido a diferencias en la densidad que se producen por variaciones en la temperatura; puede resultar en la transferencia de energía en forma de calor (526)

convective zone (kuhn VEK tiv ZOHN) the region of the sun's interior that is between the radiative zone and the photosphere and in which energy is carried upward by convection (827)

zona convective la región del interior del Sol que se encuentra entre la zona radiactiva y la fotosfera y en la cual la energía se desplaza hacia arriba por convección (827)

convergent boundary (kuhn VUHR juhnt BOWN duh ree) the boundary between tectonic plates that are colliding (270)

límite convergente el límite entre placas tectónicas que chocan (270)

core (KAWR) the central part of Earth below the mantle; also the center of the sun (30)

núcleo la parte central de la Tierra, debajo del manto; también, el centro del Sol (30)

core sample (KAWR SAM puhl) a cylindrical piece of sediment, rock, soil, snow, or ice that is collected by drilling (645)

muestra de sondeo un fragmento de sedimento, roca, suelo, nieve o hielo que se obtiene taladrando (645)

Coriolis effect (KAWR ee OH lis e FEKT) the curving of the path of a moving object from an otherwise straight path due to Earth's rotation (527, 690)

efecto de Coriolis la desviación de la trayectoria recta que experimentan los objetos en movimiento debido a la rotación de la Tierra (527, 690)

corona (kuh ROH nuh) the outermost layer of the sun's atmosphere (828)

corona la capa externa de la atmósfera del Sol (828)

coronal mass ejection (KAWR uh nuhl MAS ee JEK shuhn) coronal gas that is thrown into space from the sun (831)

eyección de masa coronal gas coronal que el Sol expulsa al espacio (831)

cosmic background radiation (KAHZ mik BAK GROWND RAY dee AY shuhn) radiation uniformly detected from every direction in space; considered a remnant of the big bang (865)

radiación cósmica de fondo radiación que se detecta de manera uniforme desde todas las direcciones en el espacio; se considera un resto del Big Bang (865)

cosmology (kahz MAHL uh jee) the study of the origin, properties, processes, and evolution of the universe (863)

cosmología el estudio del origen, propiedades, procesos y evolución del universo (863)

covalent bond (koh VAY luhnt BAHND) a bond formed when atoms share one or more pairs of electrons (97)

enlace covalente un enlace formado cuando los átomos comparten uno o más pares de electrones (97)

crater (KRAY tuhr) a bowl-shaped depression that forms on the surface of an object when a falling body strikes the object's surface or when an explosion occurs; a similar depression around the central vent of a volcano or geyser (786)

crater una depresión con forma de tazón, que se forma sobre la superficie de un objeto cuando un cuerpo en caída impacta sobre ésta o cuando se produce una explosión; una depresión similar alrededor de la chimenea de un volcán o géiser (786)

creep (KREEP) the slow downhill movement of weathered rock material (392)

arrastre el movimiento lento y descendente de materiales rocosos desgastados (392)

crevasse (kruh VAS) in a glacier, a large crack or fissure that results from ice movement (458)

grieta en un glaciar, una fractura o fisura grande debida al movimiento del hielo (458)

crust (KRUHST) the thin and solid outermost layer of Earth above the mantle (30)

corteza la capa externa, delgada y sólida de la Tierra, que se encuentra sobre el manto (30)

crystal (KRIS tuhl) a solid whose atoms, ions, or molecules are arranged in a regular, repeating pattern (114)

cristal un sólido cuyos átomos, iones o moléculas están ordenados en un patrón regular y repetitivo (114)

cumulus cloud (KYOO myoo luhs KLOWD) a low-level, billowy cloud that commonly has a top that resembles cotton balls and a dark bottom (553)

nube cúmulo una nube esponjada ubicada en un nivel bajo, cuya parte superior normalmente parece una bola de algodón y es obscura en la parte inferior (553)

current (KUHR uhnt) in geology, a horizontal movement of water in a well-defined pattern, such as a river or stream; the movement of air in a certain direction (689)

corriente en geología, un movimiento horizontal de agua en un patrón bien definido, como por ejemplo, un río o arroyo; el movimiento del aire en una cierta dirección (689)

D

deep current (DEEP KUHR uhnt) a streamlike movement of ocean water far below the surface (693)

corriente profunda un movimiento del agua del océano que es similar a una corriente y ocurre debajo de la superficie (693)

deep-ocean basin (DEEP OH shuhn BAYS uhn) the part of the ocean floor that is under deep water beyond the continental margin and that is composed of oceanic crust and a thin layer of sediment (641)

cuenca oceánica profunda la parte del fondo del océano que está bajo aguas profundas más allá del margen continental y que se compone de corteza oceánica y una delgada capa de sedimento (641)

deflation (dee FLAY shuhn) a form of wind erosion in which fine, dry soil particles are blown away (484)

deflación una forma de erosión del viento en la que se mueven partículas de suelo finas y secas (484)

deformation (DE fawr MAY shuhn) the bending, tilting, and breaking of Earth's crust; the change in the shape of rock in response to stress (293)

deformación el proceso de doblar, inclinar y romper la corteza de la Tierra; el cambio en la forma de una roca en respuesta a la tensión (293)

delta (DEL tuh) a fan-shaped mass of rock material deposited at the mouth of a stream; for example, deltas form where streams flow into the ocean at the edge of a continent (415)

delta un depósito de materiales rocosos en forma de abanico ubicado en la desembocadura de un río; por ejemplo, los deltas se forman en el lugar donde las corrientes fluyen al océano en el borde de un continente (415)

density (DEN suh tee) the ratio of the mass of a substance to the volume of the substance; commonly expressed as grams per cubic centimeter for solids and liquids and as grams per liter for gases (120, 667)

densidad la relación entre la masa de una sustancia y su volumen; comúnmente se expresa en gramos por centímetro cúbico para los sólidos y líquidos, y como gramos por litro para los gases (120, 667)

dependent variable (dee PEN duhnt VER ee uh buhl) in an experiment, the factor that changes as a result of manipulation of one or more other factors (the independent variables) (11)

variable dependiente en un experimento, el factor que cambia como resultado de la manipulación de uno o más factores (las variables independientes) (11)

desalination (DEE sal uh NAY shuhn) a process of removing salt from ocean water (410, 673)

desalación (o desalinización) un proceso de remoción de sal del agua del océano (410, 673)

dew point (DOO POYNT) at constant pressure and water vapor content, the temperature at which the rate of condensation equals the rate of evaporation (545)

punto de rocío a presión y contenido de vapor de agua constantes, la temperatura a la que la tasa de condensación es igual a la tasa de evaporación (545)

differential weathering (DIF uhr EN shuhl WETH uhr ing) the process by which softer, less weather resistant-rocks wear away at a faster rate than harder, more weather-resistant rocks do (379)

desgaste diferencial el proceso por medio cual las rocas más blandas y menos resistentes al clima se desgastan a una tasa más rápida que las rocas más duras y resistentes al clima (379)

discharge (dis CHAHRJ) the volume of water that flows within a given time (412)

descarga el volumen de agua que fluye en un tiempo determinado (412)

divergent boundary (die VUHR juhnt BOWN duh ree) the boundary between two tectonic plates that are moving away from each other (269)

límite divergente el límite entre dos placas tectónicas que se están separando una de la otra (269)

dome mountain (DOHM MOWN tuhn) a circular or elliptical, almost symmetrical elevation or structure in which the stratified rock slopes downward gently from the central point of folding (305)

domo una elevación o estructura circular o elíptica, casi simétrica, en la cual la roca estratificada se encuentra en una ligera pendiente hacia abajo a partir del punto central de plegamiento (305)

Doppler effect (DAHP luhr e FEKT) an observed change in the frequency of a wave when the source or observer is moving (848)

efecto Doppler un cambio que se observa en la frecuencia de una onda cuando la fuente o el observador está en movimiento (848)

dune (DOON) a mound of wind-deposited sand that moves as a result of the action of wind (485)

duna un montículo de arena depositada por el viento que se mueve como resultado de la acción de éste (485)

Earth science (UHRTH SIE uhns) the scientific study of Earth and the universe around it (5)

ciencias de la Tierra el estudio científico de la Tierra y del universo que la rodea (5)

earthquake (UHRTH KWAYK) a movement or trembling of the ground that is caused by a sudden release of energy when rocks along a fault move (319)

terremoto un movimiento o temblor del suelo causado por una liberación súbita de energía que se produce cuando las rocas ubicadas a lo largo de una falla se mueven (319)

eccentricity (EK sen TRIS uh tee) the degree of elongation of an elliptical orbit (symbol, *e*) (756)

excentricidad el grado de alargamiento de una órbita elíptica (símbolo: *e*) (756)

eclipse (i KLIPS) an event in which the shadow of one celestial body falls on another (793)

eclipse un suceso en el que la sombra de un cuerpo celeste cubre otro cuerpo celeste (793)

ecosystem (EE koh SIS tuhm) a community of organisms and their abiotic environment (41)

ecosistema una comunidad de organismos y su ambiente abiótico (41)

El Niño (el NEEN yoh) the warm-water phase of the El Niño–Southern Oscillation; a periodic occurrence in the eastern Pacific Ocean in which the surface-water temperature becomes unusually warm (609)

El Niño la fase caliente de la Oscilación Sureña "El Niño"; un fenómeno periódico que ocurre en el océano Pacífico oriental en el que la temperatura del agua superficial se vuelve más caliente que de costumbre (609)

elastic rebound (ee LAS tik REE bownd) the sudden return of elastically deformed rock to its undeformed shape (319)

rebote elástico ocurre cuando una roca deformada elásticamente vuelve súbitamente a su forma no deformada (319)

electromagnetic spectrum (ee LEK troh mag NET ik SPEK truhm) all of the frequencies or wavelengths of electromagnetic radiation (521, 723)

espectro electromagnético todas las frecuencias o longitudes de onda de la radiación electromagnética (521, 723)

electron (ee LEK TRAHN) a subatomic particle that has a negative charge (88)

electron una partícula subatómica que tiene carga negative (88)

element (EL uh muhnt) a substance that cannot be separated or broken down into simpler substances by chemical means; all atoms of an element have the same atomic number (87)

elemento una sustancia que no se puede separar o descomponer en sustancias más simples por medio de métodos químicos; todos los átomos de un elemento tienen el mismo número atómico (87)

elevation (EL uh VAY shuhn) the height of an object above sea level (67)

elevación la altura de un objeto sobre el nivel del mar (67)

epicenter (EP i SENT uhr) the point on Earth's surface directly above an earthquake's starting point, or focus (320)

epicentro el punto de la superficie de la Tierra que queda justo arriba del punto de inicio, o foco, de un terremoto (320)

epoch (EP uhk) a subdivision of geologic time that is longer than an age but shorter than a period (232)

época una subdivisión del tiempo geológico que es más larga que una edad pero más corta que un período (232)

equinox (EE kwi NAHKS) the moment when the sun appears to cross the celestial equator (735)

equinoccio el momento en que el Sol parece cruzar el ecuador celeste (735)

era (IR uh) a unit of geologic time that includes two or more periods (232)

era una unidad de tiempo geológico que incluye dos o más períodos (232)

erosion (ee ROH zhuhn) a process in which the materials of Earth's surface are loosened, dissolved, or worn away and transported from one place to another by a natural agent, such as wind, water, ice, or gravity (387)

erosion un proceso por medio del cual los materiales de la superficie de la Tierra se aflojan, disuelven o desgastan y son transportados de un lugar a otro por un agente natural, como el viento, el agua, el hielo o la gravedad (387)

erratic (er RAT ik) a large rock transported from a distant source by a glacier (462)

errática una piedra grande transportada de una fuente lejana por un glacial (462)

esker (ES kuhr) a long, winding ridge of gravel and coarse sand deposited by glacial meltwater streams (464)

esker una cumbre larga y con curvas, compuesta por grava y arena gruesa depositada por corrientes de aguas glaciares (464)

estuary (ES tyoo er ee) an area where fresh water from rivers mixes with salt water from the ocean; the part of a river where the tides meet the river current (494)

estuario un área donde el agua dulce de los ríos se mezcla con el agua salada del océano; la parte de un río donde las mareas se encuentran con la corriente del río (494)

evapotranspiration (ee VAP oh TRAN spuh RAY shuhn) the total loss of water from an area, which equals the sum of the water lost by evaporation from the soil and other surfaces and the water lost by transpiration from organisms (408)

evapotranspiración la pérdida total de agua de un área, igual a la suma del agua perdida por evaporación del suelo y otras superficies, y el agua perdida debido a la transpiración de los organismos (408)

evolution (EV uh LOO shuhn) the process of change by which new species develop from preexisting species over time (233)

evolución el proceso de cambio por el cual se desarrollan nuevas especies a partir de especies preexistentes a lo largo del tiempo (233)

extrusive igneous rock (eks TROO siv IG nee uhs RAHK) rock that forms from the cooling and solidification of lava at Earth's surface (141)

roca ígnea extrusive roca que se forma a partir del enfriamiento y la solidificación de la lava en la superficie de la Tierra (141)

fault (FAWLT) a break in a body of rock along which one block slides relative to another; a form of brittle strain (299)

falla una grieta en un cuerpo rocoso a lo largo de la cual un bloque se desliza respecto a otro; una forma de tensión quebradiza (299)

fault zone (FAWLT ZOHN) a region of numerous, closely spaced faults (324)

zona de fallas una región donde hay muchas fallas, las cuales están cerca unas de otras (324)

fault-block mountain (FAWLT BLAHK MOWN tuhn) a mountain that forms where faulting breaks Earth's crust into large blocks, which causes some blocks to drop down relative to other blocks (305)

montaña de bloque de falla una montaña que se forma cuando una falla rompe la corteza de la Tierra en grandes bloques, lo cual hace que algunos bloques se hundan respecto a otros bloques (305)

felsic (FEL sik) describes magma or igneous rock that is rich in feldspars and silica and that is generally light in color (142, 351)

félsico término que describe un tipo de magma o roca ígnea que es rica en feldespatos y sílice y generalmente tiene un color claro (142, 351)

fetch (FECH) the distance that wind blows across an area of the sea to generate waves (697)

alcance la distancia que el viento sopla en un área del mar para generar olas (697)

floodplain (FLUD playn) an area along a river that forms from sediments deposited when the river overflows its banks (416)

llanura de inundación un área a lo largo de un río formada por sedimentos que se depositan cuando el río se desborda (416)

focus (FOH kuhs) the location within Earth along a fault at which the first motion of an earthquake occurs (320)

foco el lugar dentro de la Tierra a lo largo de una falla donde ocurre el primer movimiento de un terremoto (320)

fog (FAWG) water vapor that has condensed very near the surface of Earth because air close to the ground has cooled (554)

niebla vapor de agua que se ha condensado muy cerca de la superficie de la Tierra debido al enfriamiento del aire próximo al suelo (554)

fold (FOHLD) a form of ductile strain in which rock layers bend, usually as a result of compression (297)

pliegue una forma de tensión dúctil en la cual las capas de roca se curvan, normalmente como resultado de la compression (297)

folded mountain (FOHLD uhd MOWNT uhn) a mountain that forms when rock layers are squeezed together and uplifted (304)

montaña de plegamiento una montaña que se forma cuando las capas de roca se comprimen y se eleven (304)

foliation (FOH lee AY shuhn) the metamorphic rock texture in which mineral grains are arranged in planes or bands (153)

foliación la textura de una roca metamórfica en la que los granos de mineral están ordenados en planos o bandas (153)

food web (FOOD WEB) a diagram that shows the feeding relationships between organisms in an ecosystem (43)

red alimenticia un diagrama que muestra las relaciones de alimentación entre los organismos de un ecosistema (43)

fossil (FAHS uhl) the trace or remains of an organism that lived long ago, most commonly preserved in sedimentary rock (213)

fósil los indicios o los restos de un organismo que vivió hace mucho tiempo, comúnmente preservados en las rocas sedimentarias (213)

fossil fuel (FAHS uhl FYOO uhl) a nonrenewable energy resource formed from the remains of organisms that lived long ago; examples include oil, coal, and natural gas (171)

combustible fósil un recurso energético no renovable formado a partir de los restos de organismos que vivieron hace mucho tiempo; algunos ejemplos incluyen el petróleo, el carbón y el gas natural (171)

fracture (FRAK chuhr) in geology, a break in a rock, which results from stress, with or without displacement, including cracks, joints, and faults; also the manner in which a mineral breaks along either curved or irregular surfaces (118)

fractura en geología, un rompimiento en una roca, que resulta de la tensión, con o sin desplazamiento, incluyendo grietas, fisuras y fallas; también, la forma en la que se rompe un mineral a lo largo de superficies curvas o irregulars (118)

galaxy (GAL uhk see) a collection of stars, dust, and gas bound together by gravity (722, 860)

galaxia un conjunto de estrellas, polvo y gas unidos por la gravedad (722, 860)

Galilean moon (GAL uh LEE uhn MOON) any one of the four largest satellites of Jupiter—Io, Europa, Ganymede, and Callisto—that were discovered by Galileo in 1610 (799)

satélite galileano cualquiera de los cuatro satélites más grandes de Júpiter (Io, Europa, Ganímedes y Calisto) que fueron descubiertos por Galileo en 1610 (799)

gas giant (GAS JIE uhnt) a planet that has a deep, massive atmosphere, such as Jupiter, Saturn, Uranus, or Neptune (765)

gigante gaseoso un planeta con una atmósfera masiva y profunda, como por ejemplo, Júpiter, Saturno, Urano o Neptuno (765)

gemstone (JEM stohn) a mineral, rock, or organic material that can be used as jewelry or an ornament when it is cut and polished (169)

piedra preciosa un mineral, roca o material orgánico que se puede usar como joya u ornamento cuando se corta y se pule (169)

geologic column (JEE uh LAHJ ik KAHL uhm) an ordered arrangement of rock layers that is based on the relative ages of the rocks and in which the oldest rocks are at the bottom (229)

columna geológica un arreglo ordenado de capas de rocas que se basa en la edad relativa de las rocas y en el cual las rocas más antiguas están al fondo (229)

geology (jee AHL uh jee) the scientific study of the origin, history, and structure of Earth and the processes that shape Earth (6)

geología el estudio científico del origen, la historia y la estructura del planeta Tierra y los procesos que le dan forma (6)

geosphere (JEE oh sfir) the mostly solid, rocky part of Earth; extends from the center of the core to the surface of the crust (35)

geosfera la capa de la Tierra que es principalmente sólida y rocosa; se extiende desde el centro del núcleo hasta la superficie de la corteza terrestre (35)

geothermal energy (JEE oh THUHR muhl EN uhr jee) the energy produced by heat within Earth (177)

energía geotérmica la energía producida por el calor del interior de la Tierra (177)

giant (JIE uhnt) a very large and bright star whose hot core has used most of its hydrogen (854)

gigante una estrella muy grande y brillante que tiene un núcleo caliente que ha usado la mayor parte de su hidrógeno (854)

glacial drift (GLAY shuhl DRIFT) the rock material carried and deposited by glaciers (462)

deriva glacial el material rocoso que es transportado y depositado por los glaciares (462)

glacier (GLAY shuhr) a large mass of moving ice (455)

glaciar una masa grande de hielo en movimiento (455)

global ocean (GLOH buhl OH shuhn) the body of salt water that covers nearly three-fourths of Earth's surface (637)

océano global la masa de agua salada que cubre cerca de tres cuartas partes de la superficie de la Tierra (637)

global warming (GLOH buhl WAWRM ing) a gradual increase in average global temperature (619)

calentamiento global un aumento gradual de la temperatura global promedio (619)

gradient (GRAY dee uhnt) the change in elevation over a given distance (412)

gradiente el cambio en la elevación a lo largo de una distancia determinada (412)

greenhouse effect (GREEN hows e FEKT) the warming of the surface and lower atmosphere of Earth that occurs when carbon dioxide, water vapor, and other gases in the air absorb and reradiate infrared radiation (524)

efecto invernadero el calentamiento de la superficie terrestre y de la parte más baja de la atmósfera, el cual se produce cuando el dióxido de carbono, el vapor de agua y otros gases del aire absorben radiación infrarroja y la vuelven a irradiar (524)

groundwater (GROWND wawt uhr) the water that is beneath Earth's surface (431)

agua subterránea el agua que está debajo de la superficie de la Tierra (431)

Gulf Stream (GULF STREEM) the swift, deep, and warm Atlantic current that flows along the eastern coast of the United States toward the northeast (692)

corriente del Golfo la corriente rápida, profunda y cálida del océano Atlántico que fluye por la costa este de los Estados Unidos hacia el noreste (692)

gyre (JIER) a huge circle of moving ocean water found above and below the equator (690)

giro un círculo enorme de agua oceánica en movimiento que se encuentra debajo del ecuador (690)

half-life (HAF LIEF) the time required for half of a sample of a radioactive isotope to break down by radioactive decay to form a daughter isotope (210)

vida media el tiempo que se requiere para que la mitad de una muestra de un isótopo radiactivo se descomponga por desintegración radiactiva y forme un isótopo hijo (210)

headland (HED LAND) a high and steep formation of rock that extends out from shore into the water (490)

promontorio una formación rocosa alta y empinada que se extiende de la costa hacia el agua (490)

horizon (huh RIE zuhn) a horizontal layer of soil that can be distinguished from the layers above and below it; also a boundary between two rock layers that have different physical properties (384)

horizonte una capa horizontal de suelo que puede distinguirse de las capas que están por encima y por debajo de ella; también, un límite entre dos capas de roca que tienen propiedades físicas distintas (384)

horn (HAWRN) a sharp, pyramid-like peak that forms because of the erosion of cirques (460)

cuerno un pico puntiagudo en forma de pirámide que se forma debido a la erosión de los circos (460)

hot spot (HAHT spaht) a volcanically active area of Earth's surface, commonly far from a tectonic plate boundary (349)

mancha caliente un área volcánicamente activa de la superficie de la Tierra que comúnmente se encuentra lejos de un límite entre placas tectónicas (349)

humus (HYOO muhs) dark, organic material formed in soil from the decayed remains of plants and animals (384)

humus material orgánico obscuro que se forma en la tierra a partir de restos de plantas y animales en descomposición (384)

hurricane (HUHR i kayn) a severe storm that develops over tropical oceans and whose strong winds of more than 120 km/h spiral in toward the intensely low-pressure storm center (579)

huracán tormenta severa que se desarrolla sobre océanos tropicales, con vientos fuertes que soplan a más de 120 km/h y que se mueven en espiral hacia el centro de presión extremadamente baja de la tormenta (579)

hydroelectric energy (HIE DROH ee LEK trik EN uhr jee) electrical energy produced by the flow of water (179)

energía hidroeléctrica energía eléctrica producida por el flujo del agua (179)

hydrolysis (hie DRAHL i sis) a chemical reaction between water and another substance to form two or more new substances; a reaction between water and a salt to create an acid or a base (377)

hidrólisis una reacción química entre el agua y otras sustancias para formar dos o más sustancias nuevas; una reacción entre el agua y una sal para crear un ácido o una base (377)

hydrosphere (HIE droh sfir) the portion of Earth that is water (35)

hidrosfera la porción de la Tierra que es agua (35)

hypothesis (hie PAHTH uh sis) a testable idea or explanation that leads to scientific investigation (10)

hipótesis una idea o explicación que conlleva a la investigación científica y que se puede probar (10)

I

ice age (IES AYJ) a long period of climatic cooling during which the continents are glaciated repeatedly (467)

edad de hielo un largo período de enfriamiento del clima, durante el cual los continentes se ven repetidamente sometidos a la glaciación (467)

igneous rock (IG nee uhs RAHK) rock that forms when magma cools and solidifies (139)

roca ígnea una roca que se forma cuando el magma se enfría y se solidifica (139)

independent variable (IN di PEN duhnt VER ee uh buhl) in an experiment, the factor that is deliberately manipulated (11)

variable independiente el factor que se manipula deliberadamente en un experimento (11)

index fossil (IN DEKS FAHS uhl) a fossil that is used to establish the age of a rock layer because the fossil is distinct, abundant, and widespread and the species that formed that fossil existed for only a short span of geologic time (216)

fósil guía un fósil que se usa para establecer la edad de una capa de roca debido a que puede diferenciarse bien de otros, es abundante y está extendido; la especie que formó ese fósil existió sólo por un corto período de tiempo geológico (216)

inertia (in UHR shuh) the tendency of an object to resist a change in motion unless an outside force acts on the object (758)

inercia la tendencia de un objeto a resistir un cambio en el movimiento a menos que actúe una fuerza externa sobre el objeto (758)

intensity (in TEN suh tee) in Earth science, the amount of damage caused by an earthquake (328)

intensidad en las ciencias de la Tierra, la cantidad de daño causado por un terremoto (328)

internal plastic flow (in TUHR nuhl PLAS tik FLOH) the process by which glaciers flow slowly as grains of ice deform under pressure and slide over each other (457)

flujo plástico interno el proceso por medio del cual los glaciares fluyen lentamente a medida que los granos de hielo se deforman por efecto de la presión y se deslizan unos sobre otros (457)

intrusive igneous rock (in TROO siv IG nee uhs RAWK) rock formed from the cooling and solidification of magma beneath Earth's surface (141)

roca ígnea intrusiva una roca formada a partir del enfriamiento y solidificación del magma debajo de la superficie terrestre (141)

ion (IE AHN) an atom, radical, or molecule that has gained or lost one or more electrons and has a negative or positive charge (96)

ion un átomo, radical o molécula que ha ganado o perdido uno o más electrones y que tiene una carga negativa o positiva (96)

ionic bond (ie AHN ik BAHND) the attractive force between oppositely charged ions, which form when electrons are transferred from one atom to another (96)

enlace iónico la fuerza de atracción entre iones con cargas opuestas, que se forman cuando se transfieren electrones de un átomo a otro (96)

isogram (IE soh GRAM) a line on a map that represents a constant or equal value of a given quantity (66)

isograma una línea en un mapa que representa un valor constante o igual de una cantidad dada (66)

isostasy (ie SAHS tuh see) a condition of gravitational and buoyant equilibrium between Earth's lithosphere and asthenosphere (293)

isostasia una condición de equilibrio gravitacional y flotante entre la litosfera y la astenosfera de la Tierra (293)

isotope (IE suh TOHP) one of two or more atoms that have the same number of protons (atomic number) but different numbers of neutrons (atomic mass) (89)

isótopo uno de dos o más átomos que tienen el mismo número de protones (número atómico) pero diferente número de neutrones (masa atómica) (89)

J

jet stream (JET STREEM) a narrow band of strong winds that blow in the upper troposphere (529)

corriente en chorro un cinturón delgado de vientos fuertes que soplan en la parte superior de la troposfera (529)

K

karst topography (KAHRST tuh PAHG ruh fee) a type of irregular topography that is characterized by caverns, sinkholes, and underground drainage and that forms on limestone or other soluble rock (442)

topografía de karst una tipo de topografía irregular que se caracteriza por cavernas, depresiones y drenaje subterráneo y que se forma en piedra caliza o algún otro tipo de roca soluble (442)

kettle (KET'l) a bowl-shaped depression in a glacial drift deposit (464)

marmita una depresión con forma de tazón en un depósito de deriva glaciar (464)

Kuiper Belt (KIE puhr BELT) a region of the solar system that starts just beyond the orbit of Neptune and that contains dwarf planets and other small bodies made mostly of ice (771, 808)

cinturón de Kuiper una región del Sistema Solar que comienza justo después de la órbita de Neptuno y que contiene planetas enanos y otros cuerpos pequeños formados principalmente de hielo (771, 808)

L

lagoon (luh GOON) a small body of water separated from the sea by a low, narrow strip of land (169)

laguna una masa pequeña de agua separada del mar por una tira de tierra baja y angosta (169)

landform (LAND FAWRM) a physical feature of Earth's surface (393)

accidente geográfico una característica física de la superficie terrestre (393)

latent heat (LAYT'nt HEET) the heat energy that is absorbed or released by a substance during a phase change (543)

calor latente la energía calorífica que es absorbida o liberada por una sustancia durante un cambio de fase (543)

latitude (LAT uh TOOD) the angular distance north or south from the equator; expressed in degrees (57)

latitud la distancia angular hacia el norte o hacia el sur del ecuador; se expresa en grados (57)

lava (LAH vuh) magma that flows onto Earth's surface; the rock that forms when lava cools and solidifies (346)

lava magma que fluye a la superficie terrestre; la roca que se forma cuando la lava se enfría y se solidifica (346)

law of crosscutting relationships (LAW UHV KRAWS KUHT ing ri LAY shuhn SHIPS) the principle that a fault or body of rock is younger than any other body of rock that it cuts through (206)

ley de las relaciones entrecortadas el principio que establece que una falla o cuerpo rocoso siempre es más joven que cualquier otro cuerpo rocoso que atraviese (206)

law of superposition (LAW UHV soo puhr puh ZISH uhn) the principle that a sedimentary rock layer is older than the layers above it and younger than the layers below it if the layers are not disturbed (203)

ley de la sobreposición el principio de que una capa de roca sedimentaria es más vieja que las capas que se encuentran arriba de ella y más joven que las capas que se encuentran debajo de ella si las capas no han sido alteradas (203)

legend (LEJ uhnd) a list of map symbols and their meanings (65)

leyenda una lista de símbolos de un mapas y sus significados (65)

light-year (LIET YIR) the distance that light travels in one year; about 9.46 trillion kilometers (849)

año luz la distancia que viaja la luz en un año; aproximadamente 9.46 trillones de kilómetros (849)

lithosphere (LITH oh sFIR) the solid, outer layer of Earth that consists of the crust and the rigid upper part of the mantle (31, 267)

litosfera la capa externa y sólida de la Tierra que está formada por la corteza y la parte superior y rígida del manto (31, 267)

lode (LOHD) a mineral deposit within a rock formation (168)

veta un depósito mineral que se encuentra dentro de una formación rocosa (168)

loess (LOH es) fine-grained sediments of quartz, feldspar, hornblende, mica, and clay deposited by the wind (488)

loess sedimentos de grano fino de cuarzo, feldespato, horneblenda, mica y arcilla depositados por el viento (488)

longitude (LAHN juh TOOD) the angular distance east or west from the prime meridian; expressed in degrees (58)

longitud la distancia angular hacia el este o hacia el oeste del primer meridiano; se expresa en grados (58)

longshore current (LAWNG SHAWR KUHR uhnt) a water current that travels near and parallel to the shoreline (492)

corriente de ribera una corriente de agua que se desplaza cerca de la costa y paralela a ella (492)

lunar eclipse (LOO nuhr i KLIPS) the passing of the moon through Earth's shadow at full moon (795)

eclipse lunar el paso de la Luna frente a la sombra de la Tierra cuando hay luna llena (795)

luster (LUHS tuhr) the way in which a mineral reflects light (118)

brillo la forma en que un mineral refleja la luz (118)

M

mafic (MAF ik) describes magma or igneous rock that is rich in magnesium and iron and that is generally dark in color (142, 351)

máfico término que describe un tipo de magma o roca ígnea que es rica en magnesio y hierro y generalmente tiene un color oscuro (142, 351)

magma (MAG muh) liquid rock produced under Earth's surface; igneous rocks are made of magma (345)

magma roca líquida producida debajo de la superficie terrestre; las rocas ígneas están hechas de magma (345)

magnitude (MAG nuh TOOD) a measure of the strength of an earthquake (327)

magnitud una medida de la intensidad de un terremoto (327)

main sequence (MAYN SEE kwuhns) the location on the H-R diagram where most stars lie; it has a diagonal pattern from the lower right (low temperature and luminosity) to the upper left (high temperature and luminosity) (851)

secuencia principal la ubicación en el diagrama H-R donde se encuentran la mayoría de las estrellas; tiene un patrón diagonal de la parte inferior derecha (baja temperatura y luminosidad) a la parte superior izquierda (alta temperatura y luminosidad) (851)

mantle (MAN tuhl) in Earth science, the layer of rock between Earth's crust and core (30)

manto en las ciencias de la Tierra, la capa de roca que se encuentra entre la corteza terrestre y el núcleo (30)

map projection (MAP proh JEK shuhn) a flat map that represents a spherical surface (62)

proyección cartográfica un mapa plano que representa una superficie esférica (62)

mare (MAH ray) a large, dark area of basalt on the moon (plural, *maria*) (786)

mar lunar una gran área oscura de basalto en la Luna (786)

mass extinction (MAS ek STINGK shuhn) an episode during which large numbers of species become extinct (239)

extinción masiva un episodio durante el cual grandes cantidades de especies se extinguen (239)

mass movement (MAS MOOV muhnt) the movement of a large mass of sediment or a section of land down a slope (391)

movimiento masivo el movimiento hacia abajo por una pendiente de una gran masa de sedimento o una sección de terreno (391)

matter (MAT uhr) anything that has mass and takes up space (87)

materia cualquier cosa que tiene masa y ocupa un lugar en el espacio (87)

meander (mee AN duhr) one of the bends, twists, or curves in a low-gradient stream or river (413)

meandro una de las vueltas, giros o curvas de un arroyo o río de bajo gradiente (413)

mechanical weathering (muh KAN i kuhl WETH uhr ing) the process by which rocks break down into smaller pieces by physical means (373)

desgaste mecánico el proceso por medio del cual las rocas se rompen en pedazos más pequeños mediante medios físicos (373)

meridian (muh RID ee uhn) any semicircle that runs north and south around Earth from the geographic North Pole to the geographic South Pole; a line of longitude (58)

meridiano cualquier semicírculo que va de norte a sur alrededor de la Tierra, del Polo Norte geográfico al Polo Sur geográfico; una línea de longitud (58)

mesosphere (MES oh SFIR) literally, the "middle sphere"; the strong, lower part of the mantle between the asthenosphere and the outer core (31); *also* the coldest layer of the atmosphere, between the stratosphere and the thermosphere, in which temperature decreases as altitude increases (519)

mesosfera literalmente, la "esfera media"; la parte fuerte e inferior del manto que se encuentra entre la astenosfera y el núcleo externo (31); *también*, la capa más fría de la atmósfera que se encuentra entre la estratosfera y la termosfera, en la cual la temperatura disminuye al aumentar la altitud (519)

Mesozoic Era (MES oh ZOH ik ER uh) the geologic era that lasted from 251 million to 65.5 million years ago; also called the Age of Reptiles (239)

era Mesozoica la era geológica que comenzó hace 251 millones de años y terminó hace 65.5 millones de años; también llamada Edad de los Reptiles (239)

metamorphism (MET uh MAWR FIZ uhm) the process in which one type of rock changes into metamorphic rock because of chemical processes or changes in temperature and pressure (151)

metamorfismo el proceso en el que un tipo de roca cambia a roca metamórfica debido a procesos químicos o cambios en la temperatura y la presión (151)

meteor (MEET ee uhr) a bright streak of light that results when a meteoroid burns up in Earth's atmosphere (809)

meteoro un rayo de luz brillante que se produce cuando un meteoroide se quema en la atmósfera de la Tierra (809)

meteoroid (MEET ee uhr OYD) a relatively small, rocky body that travels through space (809)

meteoroide un cuerpo rocoso relativamente pequeño que viaja en el espacio (809)

meteorology (MEET ee uhr AHL uh jee) the scientific study of Earth's atmosphere, especially in relation to weather and climate (7)

meteorología el estudio científico de la atmósfera de la Tierra, sobre todo en lo que se relaciona al tiempo y al clima (7)

microclimate (MIE kroh KLIE mit) the climate of a small area (614)

microclima el clima de un área pequeña (614)

middle-latitude climate (MID'l LAT uh TOOD KLIE muht) a climate that has an average maximum temperature below 18 °C in the coldest month and an average minimum temperature above 10 °C in the warmest month (612)

clima de latitud media un clima que tiene una temperatura promedio máxima de 18 °C en el mes más frío y una temperatura promedio mínima de 10 °C en el mes más caliente (612)

mid-latitude cyclone (MID LAT uh TOOD SIE KLOHN) an area of low pressure that is characterized by rotating wind that moves toward the rising air of the central low-pressure region; the motion is counterclockwise in the Northern Hemisphere (576)

ciclón de latitud media un área de baja presión caracterizada por la presencia de viento en rotación que se desplaza hacia el aire ascendente de la región central de baja presión; en el hemisferio norte, el movimiento se produce en sentido contrario al de las manecillas del reloj (576)

mid-ocean ridge (MID OH shuhn RIJ) a long, undersea mountain chain that has a steep, narrow valley at its center, that forms as magma rises from the asthenosphere, and that creates new oceanic lithosphere (sea floor) as tectonic plates move apart (262)

dorsal oceánica una larga cadena submarina de montañas que tiene un valle empinado y angosto en el centro, se forma a medida que el magma se eleva a partir de la astenosfera y produce una nueva litosfera oceánica (suelo marino) a medida que las placas tectónicas se separan (262)

Milankovitch theory (MUH lan KOH vich THEE uh ree) the theory that cyclical changes in Earth's orbit and in the tilt of Earth's axis occur over thousands of years and cause climatic changes (469)

teoría de Milankovitch la teoría que establece que los cambios cíclicos en la órbita de la Tierra y en la inclinación de su eje se producen a lo largo de miles de años y provocan cambios climáticos (469)

mineral (MIN uhr uhl) a natural, usually inorganic solid that has a characteristic chemical composition, an orderly internal structure, and a characteristic set of physical properties (111)

mineral un sólido natural, normalmente inorgánico, que tiene una composición química característica, una estructura interna ordenada y propiedades físicas y químicas características (111)

mineralogist (MIN uhr AL uh jist) a person who examines, analyzes, and classifies minerals (117)

minerólogo una persona que examina, analiza y clasifica los minerales (117)

mixture (MIKS chuhr) a combination of two or more substances that are not chemically combined (98)

mezcla una combinación de dos o más sustancias que no están combinadas químicamente (98)

Mohs hardness scale (MOHZ HAHRD nis SKAYL) the standard scale against which the hardness of minerals is rated (119)

escala de dureza de Mohs la escala estándar que se usa para clasificar la dureza de un mineral (119)

molecule (MAHL i KYOOL) a group of atoms that are held together by chemical forces (93)

molécula un conjunto de átomos que se mantienen unidos por acción de las fuerzas químicas (93)

monsoon (mahn SOON) a seasonal wind that blows toward the land in the summer, bringing heavy rains, and that blows away from the land in the winter, bringing dry weather (609)

monzón viento estacional que sopla hacia la tierra en el verano, ocasionando fuertes lluvias, y que se aleja de la tierra en el invierno, ocasionando tiempo seco (609)

moon (MOON) a celestial body that revolves around a body that is greater in mass; a natural satellite (785)

luna un cuerpo celeste que gira alrededor de un cuerpo que tiene mayor masa; un satélite natural (785)

moraine (moh RAYN) a landform that is made from unsorted sediments deposited by a glacier (463)

morrena un accidente geográfico que se forma a partir de varios tipos de sedimentos depositados por un glaciar (463)

mountain range (MOWN tuhn RAYNJ) a series of mountains that are closely related in orientation, age, and mode of formation (301)

cinturón de montañas una serie de montañas que están íntimamente relacionadas en orientación, edad y modo de formación (301)

N

nebula (NEB yu luh) a large cloud of gas and dust in interstellar space; a region in space where stars are born (852)

nebulosa una nube grande de gas y polvo en el espacio interestelar; una región en el espacio donde las estrellas nacen (852)

nekton (NEK tuhn) all organisms that swim actively in open water, independent of currents (670)

necton todos los organismos que nadan activamente en las aguas abiertas, de manera independiente de las corrientes (670)

neutron (NOO TRAHN) a subatomic particle that has no charge and that is located in the nucleus of an atom (88)

neutrón una partícula subatómica que no tiene carga y que está ubicada en el núcleo de un átomo (88)

neutron star (NOO TRAHN STAHR) a star that has collapsed under gravity to the point that the electrons and protons have smashed together to form neutrons (857)

estrella de neutrones una estrella que se ha colapsado debido a la gravedad hasta el punto en que los electrones y protones han chocado unos contra otros para formar neutrones (857)

nodule (NAHJ ool) a lump of minerals whose composition differs from the composition of the surrounding sediment or rock; also a lump of minerals that is made of oxides of manganese, iron, copper, or nickel and that is found in scattered groups on the ocean floor (647)

nódulo un bulto de minerales que tienen una composición diferente a la de los sedimentos o rocas de los alrededores; también, un bulto de minerales compuesto por óxidos de manganeso, hierro, cobre o níquel y que se encuentra en grupos esparcidos en el fondo del océano (647)

nonfoliated (NAHN FOHL ee ayt id) the metamorphic rock texture in which mineral grains are not arranged in planes or bands (154)

no foliada la textura de una roca metamórfica en la que los granos de mineral no están ordenados en planos ni bandas (154)

nonrenewable resource (NAHN ri NOO uh buhl REE SAWRS) a resource that forms at a rate that is much slower than the rate at which the resource is consumed (171)

recurso no renovable un recurso que se forma a una tasa que es mucho más lenta que la tasa a la que se consume (171)

nonsilicate mineral (NAHN SIL i kit MIN uhr uhl) a mineral that does not contain compounds of silicon and oxygen (113)

mineral no-silicato un mineral que no contiene compuestos de sílice y oxígeno (113)

nova (NOH vuh) a star that suddenly becomes brighter (856)

nova una estrella que súbitamente se vuelve más brillante (856)

nuclear fission (NOO klee uhr FISH uhn) the process by which the nucleus of a heavy atom splits into two or more fragments; the process releases neutrons and energy (174)

fisión nuclear el proceso por medio del cual el núcleo de un átomo pesado se divide en dos o más fragmentos; el proceso libera neutrones y energía (174)

nuclear fusion (NOO klee uhr FYOO zhuhn) the process by which nuclei of small atoms combine to form a new, more massive nucleus; the process releases energy (176, 824)

fusión nuclear el proceso por medio del cual los núcleos de átomos pequeños se combinan y forman un núcleo nuevo con mayor masa; el proceso libera energía (176, 824)

O

observation (AHB zuhr VAY shuhn) the process of obtaining information by using the senses; the information obtained by using the senses (10)

observación el proceso de obtener información por medio de los sentidos; la información que se obtiene al usar los sentidos (10)

occluded front (uh KLOOD id FRUHNT) a front that forms when a cold air mass overtakes a warm air mass and lifts the warm air mass off the ground and over another air mass (576)

frente ocluido un frente que se forma cuando una masa de aire frío supera a una masa de aire caliente y la levanta del suelo por encima de otra masa de aire (576)

oceanography (OH shuh NAHG ruh fee) the scientific study of the ocean, including the properties and movements of ocean water, the characteristics of the ocean floor, and the organisms that live in the ocean (6, 638)

oceanografía el estudio científico del océano, incluyendo las propiedades y los movimientos del agua, las características del fondo y los organismos que viven en él (6, 638)

Oort cloud (AWRT KLOWD) a spherical region that surrounds the solar system, that extends from the Kuiper Belt to almost halfway to the nearest star, and that contains billions of comets (808)

nube de Oort una región esférica que rodea al Sistema Solar, que se extiende desde el cinturón de Kuiper hasta la mitad del camino hacia la estrella más cercana y contiene miles de millones de cometas (808)

orbital period (AWR buh tuhl PIR ee uhd) the time required for a body to complete a single orbit (757)

período de órbita el tiempo que se requiere para que un cuerpo complete una órbita (757)

ore (AWR) a natural material whose concentration of economically valuable minerals is high enough for the material to be mined profitably (167)

mena un material natural cuya concentración de minerales con valor económico es suficientemente alta como para que el material pueda ser explotado de manera rentable (167)

organic sedimentary rock (awr GAN ik SED uh MEN tuhr ee RAHK) sedimentary rock that forms from the remains of plants or animals (146)

roca sedimentaria orgánica roca sedimentaria que se forma a partir de los restos de plantas o animales (146)

oxidation (AHKS i DAY shuhn) the process by which a metallic element combines with oxygen (376)

oxidación el proceso por medio del cual un elemento metálico se combina con oxígeno (376)

ozone (OH zohn) a gas molecule that is made up of three oxygen atoms (515)

ozono una molécula de gas que está formada por tres átomos de oxígeno (515)

P

P wave (PEE WAYV) a primary wave, or compression wave; a seismic wave that causes particles of rock to move in a back-and-forth direction parallel to the direction in which the wave is traveling; P waves are the fastest seismic waves and can travel through solids, liquids, and gases (321)

onda P una onda primaria u onda de compresión; una onda sísmica que hace que las partículas de roca se muevan en una dirección de atrás hacia delante en forma paralela a la dirección en que viaja la onda; las ondas P son las ondas sísmicas más rápidas y pueden viajar a través de sólidos, líquidos y gases (321)

pack ice (PAK IES) a floating layer of sea ice that completely covers an area of the ocean surface (665)

manto de hielo marino una capa flotante de hielo marino que cubre completamente un área de la superficie del océano (665)

paleomagnetism (PAY lee oh MAG nuh TIZ uhm) the study of the alignment of magnetic minerals in rock, specifically as it relates to the reversal of Earth's magnetic poles; *also* the magnetic properties that rock acquires during formation (263)

paleomagnetismo el estudio de la alineación de los minerales magnéticos en la roca, específicamente en lo que se relaciona con la inversión de los polos magnéticos de la Tierra; también, las propiedades magnéticas que la roca adquiere durante su formación (263)

paleontology (PAY lee uhn TAHL uh jee) the scientific study of fossils (213)

paleontología el estudio científico de los fósiles (213)

Paleozoic Era (PAY lee OH ZOH ik ER uh) the geologic era that followed Precambrian time and that lasted from 542 million to 251 million years ago (236)

era Paleozoica la era geológica que vino después del período Precámbrico; comenzó hace 542 millones de años y terminó hace 251 millones de años (236)

Pangaea (pan JEE uh) the supercontinent that formed 300 million years ago and that began to break up 200 million years ago (278)

Pangea el supercontinente que se formó hace 300 millones de años y que comenzó a separarse hace 200 millones de años (278)

Panthalassa (PAN thuh LAH suh) the single, large ocean that covered Earth's surface during the time the supercontinent Pangaea existed

Panthalassa el único gran océano que cubría la superficie de la Tierra cuando existía el supercontinente Pangea

parallax (PAR uh LAKS) an apparent shift in the position of an object when viewed from different locations (849)

paralaje un cambio aparente en la posición de un objeto cuando se ve desde lugares distintos (849)

parallel (PAR uh LEL) any circle that runs east and west around Earth and that is parallel to the equator; a line of latitude (57)

paralelo cualquier círculo que va hacia el Este o hacia el Oeste alrededor de la Tierra y que es paralelo al ecuador; una línea de latitud (57)

peer review (PIR ri VYOO) the process in which experts in a given field examine the results and conclusions of a scientist's study before that study is accepted for publication (14)

evaluación de pares el proceso en el cual los expertos en un campo dado examinan los resultados y las conclusiones de un estudio científico antes de aceptar su publicación (14)

pelagic zone (pi LAJ ik ZOHN) the region of an ocean or body of fresh water above the benthic zone (671)

zona pelágica la región de un océano o una masa de agua dulce sobre la zona bentónica (671)

perigee (PER i JEE) in the orbit of a satellite, the point that is closest to Earth (791)

perigeo en la órbita de un satélite, el punto que está más cerca de la Tierra (791)

perihelion (PER i HEE lee uhn) in the orbit of a planet or other body in the solar system, the point that is closest to the sun (730)

perihelio en la órbita de un planeta u otros cuerpos en el sistema solar, el punto que está más cerca del Sol (730)

period (PIR ee uhd) a unit of geologic time that is longer than an epoch but shorter than an era (232)

período una unidad de tiempo geológico que es más larga que una época pero más corta que una era (232)

permeability (PUHR mee uh BIL uh tee) the ability of a rock or sediment to let fluids pass through its open spaces, or pores (432)

permeabilidad la capacidad de una roca o sedimento de permitir que los fluidos pasen a través de sus espacios abiertos o poros (432)

phase (FAYZ) in astronomy, the change in the illuminated area of one celestial body as seen from another celestial body; phases of the moon are caused by the changing positions of Earth, the sun, and the moon (796)

fase en astronomía, el cambio en el área iluminada de un cuerpo celeste según se ve desde otro cuerpo celeste; las fases de la Luna se producen como resultado de los cambios en la posición de la Tierra, el Sol y la Luna (796)

photosphere (FOHT oh SFIR) the visible surface of the sun (827)

fotosfera la superficie visible del Sol (827)

placer deposit (PLAS uhr dee PAHZ it) a deposit that contains a valuable mineral that has been concentrated by mechanical action (168)

yacimiento de aluvión un yacimiento que contiene un mineral valioso que se ha concentrado debido a la acción mecánica (168)

planet (PLAN it) a celestial body that orbits the sun, is round because of its own gravity, and has cleared the neighborhood around its orbital path (749)

planeta un cuerpo celeste que orbita alrededor del Sol, es redondo debido a su propia fuerza de gravedad y ha despejado los alrededores de su trayectoria orbital (749)

planetesimal (PLAN i TES i muhl) a small body from which a planet originated in the early stages of development of the solar system (750)

planetesimal un cuerpo pequeño a partir del cual se originó un planeta en las primeras etapas de desarrollo del Sistema Solar (750)

plankton (PLANGK tuhn) the mass of mostly microscopic organisms that float or drift freely in the waters of aquatic (freshwater and marine) environments (670)

plancton la masa de organismos casi microscópicos que flotan o se encuentran a la deriva en aguas (dulces y marinas) de ambientes acuáticos (670)

GLOSSARY/GLOSARIO

plate tectonics (PLAYT tek TAHN iks) the theory that explains how large pieces of the lithosphere, called *plates*, move and change shape (267)

tectónica de placas la teoría que explica cómo las grandes partes de litosfera, denominadas placas, se mueven y cambian de forma (267)

polar climate (POH luhr KLIE muht) a climate that is characterized by average temperatures that are near or below freezing; typical of polar regions (613)

clima polar un clima caracterizado por temperaturas cercanas o inferiores al punto de congelación; típico de las regiones polares (613)

polar easterlies (POH luhr EES tuhr leez) prevailing winds that blow from east to west between 60° and 90° latitude in both hemispheres (528)

vientos polares del este vientos preponderantes que soplan de este a oeste entre los 60° y los 90° de latitud en ambos hemisferios (528)

porosity (poh RAHS uh tee) the percentage of the total volume of a rock or sediment that consists of open spaces (431)

porosidad el porcentaje del volumen total de una roca o sedimento que está formado por espacios abiertos (431)

Precambrian time (pree KAM bree uhn TIEM) the interval of time in the geologic time scale from Earth's formation to the beginning of the Paleozoic era, from 4.6 billion to 542 million years ago (234)

período Precámbrico el intervalo en la escala de tiempo geológico que abarca desde la formación de la Tierra hasta el comienzo de la era Paleozoica; comenzó hace 4,600 millones de años y terminó hace 542 millones de años (234)

precipitation (pree SIP uh TAY shuhn) any form of water that falls to Earth's surface from the clouds; includes rain, snow, sleet, and hail (408, 555)

precipitación cualquier forma de agua que cae de las nubes a la superficie de la Tierra; incluye a la lluvia, nieve, aguanieve y granizo (408, 555)

prominence (PRAHM uh nuhns) a loop of relatively cool, incandescent gas that extends above the photosphere and above the sun's edge as seen from Earth (831)

protuberancia una espiral de gas incandescente y relativamente frío que, vista desde la Tierra, se extiende por encima de la fotosfera y la superficie del Sol (831)

proton (PROH tahn) a subatomic particle that has a positive charge and that is located in the nucleus of an atom; the number of protons in the nucleus is the atomic number, which determines the identity of an element (88)

protón una partícula subatómica que tiene una carga positiva y que está ubicada en el núcleo de un átomo; el número de protones que hay en el núcleo es el número atómico, y éste determina la identidad del elemento (88)

pulsar (PUHL sahr) a rapidly spinning neutron star that emits pulses of radio and optical energy (858)

pulsar una estrella de neutrones que gira rápidamente y emite pulsaciones de energía radioeléctrica y óptica (858)

pyroclastic material (PIE roh KLAS tik muh TIR ee uhl) fragments of rock that form during a volcanic eruption (352)

material piroclástico fragmentos de roca que se forman durante una erupción volcánica (352)

Q

quasar (KWAY zahr) quasi-stellar radio source; a very luminous object that produces energy at a high rate; quasars are thought to be the most distant objects in the universe (862)

cuasar fuente de radio cuasi-estelar; un objeto muy luminoso que produce energía a una gran velocidad; se piensa que los cuasares son los objetos más distantes del universo (862)

R

radar (RAY dahr) radio detection and ranging, a system that uses reflected radio waves to determine the velocity and location of objects (585)

radar detección y exploración a gran distancia por medio de ondas de radio; un sistema que usa ondas de radio reflejadas para determinar la velocidad y ubicación de los objetos (585)

radiative zone (RAY dee ay tiv ZOHN) the zone of the sun's interior that is between the core and the convection zone and in which energy moves by radiation (827)

zona radiactiva la zona del interior del Sol que se encuentra entre el núcleo y la zona de convección y en la cual la energía se mueve por radiación (827)

radiometric dating (RAY dee oh MET rik DAYT ing) a method of determining the absolute age of an object by comparing the relative percentages of a radioactive (parent) isotope and a stable (daughter) isotope (209)

datación radiométrica un método para determinar la edad absoluta de un objeto comparando los porcentajes relativos de un isótopo radiactivo (precursor) y un isótopo estable (hijo) (209)

radiosonde (RAY dee oh SAHND) a package of instruments that is carried aloft by a balloon to measure upper atmospheric conditions, including temperature, dew point, and wind velocity (585)

radiosonda un conjunto de instrumentos que se colocan en un globo para medir condiciones de la atmósfera superior, como la temperatura, el punto de rocío y la velocidad del viento (585)

recycling (ree SIE kling) the process of recovering valuable or useful materials from waste or scrap; the process of reusing some items (183)

reciclar el proceso de recuperar materiales valiosos o útiles de los desechos o de la basura; el proceso de reutilizar algunas cosas (183)

reflecting telescope (ri FLEKT ing TEL uh SKOHP) a telescope that uses a curved mirror to gather and focus light from distant objects (725)

telescopio reflector un telescopio que utiliza un espejo curvo para captar y enfocar la luz de objetos lejanos (725)

refracting telescope (ri FRAKT ing TEL uh SKOHP) a telescope that uses a set of lenses to gather and focus light from distant objects (725)

telescopio refractante un telescopio que utiliza un conjunto de lentes para captar y enfocar la luz de objetos lejanos (725)

refraction (ri FRAK shuhn) the process by which ocean waves bend directly toward the coastline as they approach shallow water (699)

refracción el proceso por medio del cual las olas oceánicas se curvan directamente hacia la costa a medida que se acercan a agua poco profunda (699)

regional metamorphism (REE juhn uhl MET uh MAWR FIZ uhm) a change in the texture, structure, or chemical composition of a rock due to changes in temperature and pressure over a large area, generally as a result of tectonic forces (152)

metamorfismo regional un cambio en la textura, estructura o composición química de una roca debido a cambios en la temperatura y presión en un área extensa, generalmente como resultado de la acción de fuerzas tectónicas (152)

relative age (REL uh tiv AYJ) the age of an object in relation to the ages of other objects (202)

edad relativa la edad de un objeto en relación con la edad de otros objetos (202)

relative humidity (REL uh tiv hyoo MID uh tee) the ratio of the amount of water vapor in the air to the amount of water vapor needed to reach saturation at a given temperature (546)

humedad relativa la proporción de la cantidad de vapor de agua que hay en el aire respecto a la cantidad de vapor de agua que se necesita para alcanzar la saturación a una temperatura dada (546)

relief (ri LEEF) the difference between the highest and lowest elevations in a given area; the variations in elevation of a land surface (68)

relieve la diferencia entre las elevaciones más altas y las más bajas en un área dada; las variaciones en elevación de una superficie de terreno (68)

remote sensing (ri MOHT SENS ing) the process of gathering and analyzing information about an object without physically being in touch with the object (61)

teledetección el proceso de recopilar y analizar información acerca de un objeto sin estar en contacto físico con el objeto (61)

renewable resource (ri NOO uh buhl REE SAWRS) a natural resource that can be replaced at the same rate at which the resource is consumed (177)

recurso renovable un recurso natural que puede reemplazarse a la misma tasa a la que se consume (177)

revolution (REV uh LOO shuhn) the motion of a body that travels around another body in space; one complete trip along an orbit (730)

revolución el movimiento de un cuerpo que viaja alrededor de otro cuerpo en el espacio; un viaje completo a lo largo de una órbita (730)

rifting (RIFT ing) the process by which Earth's crust breaks apart; can occur within continental crust or oceanic crust (275)

fracturación el proceso por medio del cual la corteza de la Tierra se fractura; puede producirse dentro de la corteza continental u oceánica (275)

rock cycle (RAHK SIE kuhl) the series of processes in which rock forms, changes from one type to another, is destroyed, and forms again by geologic processes (136)

ciclo de las rocas la serie de procesos por medio de los cuales una roca se forma, cambia de un tipo a otro, se destruye y se forma nuevamente por procesos geológicos (136)

rotation (roh TAY shuhn) the spin of a body on its axis (729)

rotación el giro de un cuerpo alrededor de su eje (729)

S

S wave (ES WAYV) a secondary wave, or shear wave; a seismic wave that causes particles of rock to move in a side-to-side direction perpendicular to the direction in which the wave is traveling; S waves are the second-fastest seismic waves and can travel only through solids (321)

onda S una onda secundaria u onda rotacional; una onda sísmica que hace que las partículas de roca se muevan en una dirección de lado a lado, en forma perpendicular a la dirección en la que viaja la onda; las ondas S son las segundas ondas sísmicas en cuanto a velocidad y únicamente pueden viajar a través de sólidos (321)

salinity (suh LIN uh tee) a measure of the amount of dissolved salts in a given amount of liquid (664)

salinidad una medida de la cantidad de sales disueltas en una cantidad determinada de líquido (664)

saltation (sal TAY shuhn) the movement of sand or other sediments by short jumps and bounces that is caused by wind or water (483)

saltación el movimiento de la arena u otros sedimentos por medio de saltos pequeños y rebotes debido al viento o al agua (483)

satellite (SAT'l IET) a natural or artificial body that revolves around a celestial body that is greater in mass (785)

satélite un cuerpo natural o artificial que gira alrededor de un cuerpo celeste que tiene mayor masa (785)

scale (SKAYL) the relationship between the distance shown on a map and the actual distance (65)

escala la relación entre la distancia que se muestra en un mapa y la distancia real (65)

sea (SEE) a large, commonly saline body of water that is smaller than an ocean and that may be partially or completely surrounded by land; also a subdivision of an ocean (637)

mar una gran masa de agua, generalmente salada, que es más pequeña que un océano y que puede estar parcial o totalmente rodeada de tierra; también, una subdivisión de un océano (637)

sea-floor spreading (SEE FLAWR SPRED ing) the process by which new oceanic lithosphere (sea floor) forms when magma rises to Earth's surface at mid-ocean ridges and solidifies, as older, existing sea floor moves away from the ridge (263)

expansión del suelo marino el proceso por medio del cual se forma nueva litósfera oceánica (suelo marino) cuando el magma sube a la superficie de la Tierra en las dorsales oceánicas y se solidifica, a medida que el antiguo suelo marino existente se aleja de la dorsal oceánica (263)

seismic gap (SIEZ mik GAP) an area along a fault where relatively few earthquakes have occurred recently but where strong earthquakes are known to have occurred in the past (331)

brecha sísmica un área a lo largo de una falla donde han ocurrido relativamente pocos terremotos recientemente, pero donde se sabe que han ocurrido terremotos fuertes en el pasado (331)

seismogram (SIEZ muh GRAM) a tracing of earthquake motion that is recorded by a seismograph (325)

sismograma una traza del movimiento de un terremoto registrada por un sismógrafo (325)

seismograph (SIEZ muh GRAF) an instrument that records vibrations in the ground (325)

sismógrafo un instrumento que registra las vibraciones en el suelo (325)

shadow zone (SHAD oh ZOHN) an area on Earth's surface where no direct seismic waves from a particular earthquake can be detected (322)

zona de sombra un área de la superficie de la Tierra donde no se detectan ondas sísmicas directas de un determinado terremoto (322)

sheet erosion (SHEET ee ROH zhuhn) the process by which water flows over a layer of soil and removes the topsoil (388)

erosión laminar el proceso por medio del cual el agua fluye sobre el suelo y remueve la capa superior de éste (388)

silicate mineral (SIL i kit MIN uhr uhl) a mineral that contains a combination of silicon and oxygen and that may also contain one or more metals (112)

mineral silicato un mineral que contiene una combinación de silicio y oxígeno y que también puede contener uno o más metales (112)

silicon-oxygen tetrahedron (SIL i KAHN AHKS i juhn TE truh HEE druhn) the basic unit of the structure of silicate minerals; a silicon ion chemically bonded to and surrounded by four oxygen ions (114)

tetraedro de sílice-oxígeno la unidad fundamental de la estructura de los minerales silicatos: un ion de silicio unido químicamente a cuatro iones de oxígeno, los cuales lo rodean (114)

sinkhole (SINGK HOHL) a circular depression that forms when rock dissolves, when overlying sediment fills an existing cavity, or when the roof of an underground cavern or mine collapses (441)

depresión una depresión circular que se forma cuando la roca se funde, cuando el sedimento suprayacente llena una cavidad existente, o al colapsarse el techo de una caverna o mina subterránea (441)

soil (SOYL) a loose mixture of rock fragments and organic material that can support the growth of vegetation (383)

suelo una mezcla suelta de fragmentos de roca y material orgánico en la que puede crecer vegetación (383)

soil profile (SOYL PROH FIEL) a vertical section of soil that shows the layers, or horizons (384)

perfil del suelo una sección vertical de suelo que muestra las capas u horizontes (384)

solar eclipse (SOH luhr i KLIPS) the passing of the moon between Earth and the sun; during a solar eclipse, the shadow of the moon falls on Earth (793)

eclipse solar el paso de la Luna entre la Tierra y el Sol; durante un eclipse solar, la sombra de la Luna cae sobre la Tierra (793)

solar energy (SOH luhr EN uhr jee) the energy received by Earth from the sun in the form of radiation (178)

energía solar la energía que la Tierra recibe del Sol en forma de radiación (178)

solar flare (SOH luhr FLER) an explosive release of energy that comes from the sun and that is associated with magnetic disturbances on the sun's surface (831)

erupción solar una liberación explosiva de energía que proviene del Sol y que se asocia con disturbios magnéticos en la superficie solar (831)

solar nebula (SOH luhr NEB yuh luh) a rotating cloud of gas and dust from which the sun and planets formed; *also* any nebula from which stars and exoplanets may form (749)

nebulosa solar una nube de gas y polvo en rotación a partir de la cual se formaron el Sol y los planetas; también, cualquier nebulosa a partir de la cual se pueden formar estrellas y exoplanetas (749)

solar system (SOH luhr SIS tuhm) the sun and all of the planets and other bodies that travel around it (749)

Sistema Solar el Sol y todos los planetas y otros cuerpos que se desplazan alrededor de él (749)

solifluction (SAHL uh FLUHK shuhn) the slow, downslope flow of soil saturated with water in areas surrounding glaciers at high elevations (392)

soliflucción el flujo lento y descendente de suelo saturado con agua en áreas que rodean glaciares a altas elevaciones (392)

solstice (SAHL stis) the point at which the sun is as far north or as far south of the equator as possible (736)

solsticio el punto en el que el Sol está tan lejos del ecuador como es posible, ya sea hacia el norte o hacia el sur

solution (suh LOO shuhn) a homogeneous mixture throughout which two or more substances are uniformly dispersed (98)

solución una mezcla homogénea en la cual dos o más sustancias se dispersan de manera uniforme (98)

sonar (SOH NAHR) **s**ound **n**avigation **a**nd **r**anging, a system that uses acoustic signals and returned echoes to determine the location of objects or to communicate (639)

sonar navegación y exploración por medio del sonido; un sistema que usa señales acústicas y ondas de eco que regresan para determinar la ubicación de los objetos o para comunicarse (639)

specific heat (spuh SIF ik HEET) the quantity of heat required to raise a unit mass of homogeneous material 1 K or 1 °C in a specified way, given constant pressure and volume (608)

calor específico la cantidad de calor que se requiere para aumentar una unidad de masa de un material homogéneo 1 K ó 1° C de una manera especificada, dados un volumen y una presión constantes (608)

star (STAHR) a large celestial body that is composed of gas and that emits light; the sun is a typical star (845)

estrella un cuerpo celeste grande que está compuesto de gas y emite luz; el Sol es una estrella típica (845)

station model (STAY shuhn MAHD'l) a pattern of meteorological symbols that represents the weather at a particular observing station and that is recorded on a weather map (588)

estación modelo el modelo de símbolos meteorológicos que representan el tiempo en una estación de observación determinada y que se registra en un mapa meteorológico (588)

stationary front (STAY shuh NER ee FRUHNT) a front of air masses that moves either very slowly or not at all (576)

frente estacionario un frente de masas de aire que se mueve muy lentamente o que no se mueve (576)

strain (STRAYN) any change in a rock's shape or volume caused by stress; deformation (296)

tensión cualquier cambio en la forma o volumen de una roca causado por el estrés; deformación (296)

stratosphere (STRAT uh SFIR) the layer of the atmosphere that lies between the troposphere and the mesosphere and in which temperature increases as altitude increases; contains the ozone layer (519)

estratosfera la capa de la atmósfera que se encuentra entre la troposfera y la mesosfera y en la cual la temperatura aumenta al aumentar la altitud; contiene la capa de ozono (519)

stratus cloud (STRAT uhs KLOWD) a gray cloud that has a flat, uniform base and that commonly forms at very low altitudes (552)

nube estrato una nube gris que tiene una base plana y uniforme y que comúnmente se forma a altitudes muy bajas (552)

streak (STREEK) the color of a mineral in powdered form (118)

veta el color de un mineral en forma de polvo (118)

stream load (STREEM LOHD) the materials other than the water that are carried by a stream (412)

carga de un arroyo los materiales que lleva un arroyo, además del agua (412)

stress (STRES) in geology, the amount of force per unit area that acts on a rock (295)

estrés en geología, la cantidad de fuerza por unidad de área que se ejerce sobre una roca (295)

sublimation (SUHB luh MAY shuhn) the process in which a solid changes directly into a gas (the term is sometimes also used for the reverse process) (544)

sublimación el proceso por medio del cual un sólido se transforma directamente en un gas (en ocasiones, este término también se usa para describir el proceso inverso) (544)

sunspot (SUHN spaht) a dark area of the photosphere of the sun that is cooler than the surrounding areas and that has a strong magnetic field (829)

mancha solar un área oscura en la fotosfera del Sol que es más fría que las áreas que la rodean y que tiene un campo magnético fuerte (829)

supercontinent cycle (soo puhr KAHN tuh nuhnt SIE kuhl) the process by which supercontinents form and break apart over millions of years (278)

ciclo de los supercontinentes el proceso por medio del cual los supercontinentes se forman y se separan a lo largo de millones de años (278)

supercooling (SOO puhr KOOL ing) a condition in which a substance is cooled below its freezing point, condensation point, or sublimation point without going through a change of state (556)

superfrío una condición en la que una sustancia se enfría por debajo de su punto de congelación, punto de condensación o punto de sublimación sin pasar por un cambio de estado (556)

surface current (SUHR fis KUHR uhnt) a horizontal movement of ocean water that is caused by wind and that occurs at or near the ocean's surface (689)

corriente superficial un movimiento horizontal del agua del océano que es producido por el viento y que ocurre en la superficie del océano o cerca de ella (689)

surface wave (SUHR fis WAYV) in geology, a seismic wave that travels along the surface of a medium and that has a stronger effect near the surface of the medium than it has in the interior (320)

onda superficial en geología, una onda sísmica que se desplaza a lo largo de la superficie de un medio, cuyo efecto es más fuerte cerca de la superficie del medio que en el interior de éste (320)

system (SIS tuhm) a set of particles or interacting components considered to be a distinct physical entity for the purpose of study (33)

sistema un conjunto de partículas o componentes que interactúan unos con otros, el cual se considera una entidad física independiente para fines de estudio (33)

T

telescope (TEL uh skohp) an instrument that collects electromagnetic radiation from the sky and concentrates it for better observation (724)

telescopio un instrumento que capta la radiación electromagnética del cielo y la concentra para mejorar la observación (724)

terrane (tuh RAYN) a piece of lithosphere that has a unique geologic history and that may be part of a larger piece of lithosphere, such as a continent (276)

macizo autóctono un fragmento de litosfera que tiene una historia geológica única y que puede formar parte de un fragmento de litosfera mayor, como por ejemplo, un continente (276)

terrestrial planet (tuh RES tree uhl PLAN it) one of the highly dense planets nearest to the sun; Mercury, Venus, Mars, and Earth (759)

planeta terrestre uno de los planetas muy densos que se encuentran más cerca del Sol; Mercurio, Venus, Marte y la Tierra (759)

theory (THEE uh ree) a system of ideas that explains many related observations and is supported by a large body of evidence acquired through scientific investigation (15)

teoría un sistema de ideas que explica muchas observaciones relacionadas y que está respaldado por una gran cantidad de pruebas obtenidas mediante la investigación científica (15)

thermocline (THUHR moh klien) a layer in a body of water in which water temperature drops with increased depth faster than it does in other layers (666)

termoclina una capa en una masa de agua en la que, al aumentar la profundidad, la temperatura del agua disminuye más rápido de lo que lo hace en otras capas (666)

thermometer (thuhr MAHM uht uhr) an instrument that measures and indicates temperature (583)

termómetro un instrumento que mide e indica la temperatura (583)

thermosphere (THUHR moh sfir) the uppermost layer of the atmosphere, in which temperature increases as altitude increases; includes the ionosphere (519)

termosfera la capa más alta de la atmósfera, en la cual la temperatura aumenta a medida que la altitud aumenta; incluye la ionosfera (519)

thunderstorm (THUHN duhr stawrm) a usually brief, heavy storm that consists of rain, strong winds, lightning, and thunder (578)

tormenta eléctrica una tormenta fuerte y normalmente breve que consiste en lluvia, vientos fuertes, relámpagos y truenos (578)

tidal current (TIED'l KUHR uhnt) the movement of water toward and away from the coast as a result of the rise and fall of the tides (704)

corriente de marea el movimiento del agua hacia la costa y de la costa hacia el mar, como resultado del ascenso y descenso de las mareas (704)

tidal oscillation (TIED'l АНs uh LAY shuhn) the slow, rocking motion of ocean water that occurs as the tidal bulges move around the ocean basins (703)

oscilación de las mareas el movimiento lento y mecedor del agua del océano que se produce cuando los abultamientos de marea se mueven alrededor de las cuencas oceánicas (703)

tidal range (TIED'l RAYNJ) the difference in levels of ocean water at high tide and low tide (702)

rango de marea la diferencia en los niveles del agua del océano entre la marea alta y la marea baja (702)

tide (TIED) the periodic rise and fall of the water level in the oceans and other large bodies of water (701)

marea el ascenso y descenso periódico del nivel del agua en los océanos y otras masas grandes de agua (701)

till (TIL) unsorted rock material that is deposited directly by a melting glacier (462)

arcilla glaciárica material rocoso desordenado que deposita directamente un glaciar que se está derritiendo (462)

topography (tuh PAHG ruh fee) the size and shape of the land surface features of a region, including its relief (67)

topografía el tamaño y la forma de las características de una superficie de terreno, incluyendo su relieve (67)

tornado (tawr NAY doh) a destructive, rotating column of air that has very high wind speeds and that may be visible as a funnel-shaped cloud (582)

tornado una columna destructiva de aire en rotación cuyos vientos se mueven a velocidades muy altas y que puede verse como una nube con forma de embudo (582)

trace fossil (TRAYS FAHS uhl) a fossilized mark that formed in sedimentary rock by the movement of an animal on or within soft sediment (215)

fósil traza una marca fosilizada que se formó en una roca sedimentaria por el movimiento de un animal sobre sedimento blando o dentro de éste (215)

trade winds (TRAYD WINDZ) prevailing winds that blow from east to west from 30° latitude to the equator in both hemispheres (528)

vientos alisios vientos prevalecientes que soplan de este a oeste desde los 30° de latitud hacia el ecuador en ambos hemisferios (528)

transform boundary (TRANS FAWRM BOWN duh ree) the boundary between tectonic plates that are sliding past each other horizontally (271)

límite de transformación el límite entre placas tectónicas que se están deslizando horizontalmente una sobre otra (271)

trench (TRENCH) a long, narrow, and steep depression that forms on the ocean floor as a result of subduction of a tectonic plate, that runs parallel to the trend of a chain of volcanic islands or the coastline of a continent, and that may be as deep as 11 km below sea level; also called an *ocean trench* or a *deep-ocean trench* (643)

fosa submarina una depresión larga, angosta y empinada que se forma en el fondo del océano debido a la subducción de una placa tectónica; corre paralela al curso de una cadena de islas montañosas o a la costa de un continente; y puede tener una profundidad de hasta 11 km bajo el nivel del mar; también denominada *fosa oceánica* o *fosa oceánica profunda* (643)

tributary (TRIB yoo TER ee) a stream that flows into a lake or into a larger stream (411)

afluente un arroyo que fluye a un lago o a otro arroyo más grande (411)

tropical climate (TRAHP i kuhl KLIE muht) a climate characterized by high temperatures and heavy precipitation during at least part of the year; typical of equatorial regions (611)

clima tropical un clima caracterizado por temperaturas altas y precipitación fuerte durante al menos una parte del año; típico de las regiones ecuatoriales (611)

troposphere (TROH poh SFIR) the lowest layer of the atmosphere, in which temperature drops at a constant rate as altitude increases; the part of the atmosphere where weather conditions exist (518)

troposfera la capa inferior de la atmósfera, en la que la temperatura disminuye a una tasa constante a medida que la altitud aumenta; la parte de la atmósfera donde se dan las condiciones del tiempo (518)

tsunami (tsoo NAH mee) a giant ocean wave that forms after a volcanic eruption, submarine earthquake, or landslide (329)

tsunami una ola gigante del océano que se forma después de una erupción volcánica, terremoto submarino o desprendimiento de tierras (329)

unconformity (UHN kuhn FAWRM uh tee) a break in the geologic record created when rock layers are eroded or when sediment is not deposited for a long period of time (205)

disconformidad una ruptura en el registro geológico, creada cuando las capas de roca se erosionan o cuando el sedimento no se deposita durante un largo período de tiempo (205)

uniformitarianism (YOON uh FAWRM uh TER ee uhn IZ uhm) a principle that geologic processes that occurred in the past can be explained by current geologic processes (201)

uniformitarianismo un principio que establece que es posible explicar los procesos geológicos que ocurrieron en el pasado en función de los procesos geológicos actuales (201)

upwelling (UHP WEL ing) the movement of deep, cold, and nutrient-rich water to the surface (670)

surgencia el movimiento de las aguas profundas, frías y ricas en nutrientes hacia la superficie (670)

varve (VAHRV) a pair of sedimentary layers (one coarse, one fine) that is deposited in an annual cycle, commonly in glacial lakes, and that can be used to determine absolute age (208)

varva un par de capas sedimentarias (una gruesa y otra fina) que se deposita en un ciclo anual. Esto ocurre comúnmente en lagos glaciares , y que puede usarse para determinar la edad absoluta (208)

ventifact (VEN tuh FAKT) any rock that is pitted, grooved, or polished by wind abrasion (485)

ventifacto cualquier roca que es marcada, estriada o pulida por la abrasión del viento (485)

volcanism (VAHL kuh NIZ uhm) any activity that includes the movement of magma toward or onto Earth's surface (346)

volcanismo cualquier actividad que incluye el movimiento de magma hacia la superficie de la Tierra o sobre ella (346)

volcano (vahl KAY noh) a vent or fissure in Earth's surface through which magma and gases are expelled (346)

volcán una chimenea o fisura en la superficie de la Tierra a través de la cual se expulsan magma y gases (346)

warm front (WAWRM FRUHNT) the front edge of an advancing warm air mass that replaces colder air with warmer air (576)

frente cálido el borde del frente de una masa de aire caliente en movimiento que reemplaza al aire más frío (576)

water cycle (WAWT uhr SIE kuhl) the continuous movement of water between the atmosphere, the land, and the oceans (407)

ciclo del agua el movimiento continuo del agua entre la atmósfera, la tierra y los océanos (407)

water table (WAWT uhr TAY buhl) the upper surface of underground water; the upper boundary of the zone of saturation (433)

capa freática el nivel más alto del agua subterránea; el límite superior de la zona de saturación (433)

watershed (WAWT uhr SHED) the area of land that is drained by a river system (411)

cuenca hidrográfica el área del terreno que es drenada por un sistema de ríos (411)

wave (WAYV) a periodic disturbance in a solid, liquid, or gas as energy is transmitted through a medium (695)

onda una perturbación periódica en un sólido, líquido o gas que se transmite a través de un medio en forma de energía (695)

wave period (WAYV PIR ee uhd) the time required for identical points on consecutive waves to pass a given point (695)

período de onda el tiempo que se requiere para que puntos idénticos de ondas consecutivas pasen por un punto dado (695)

weathering (WETH uhr ing) the natural process by which atmospheric and environmental agents, such as wind, rain, and temperature changes, disintegrate and decompose rocks (373)

meteorización el proceso natural por medio del cual los agentes atmosféricos o ambientales, como el viento, la lluvia y los cambios de temperatura, desintegran y descomponen las rocas (373)

westerlies (WES tuhr leez) prevailing winds that blow from west to east between 30° and 60° latitude in both hemispheres (528)

vientos del oeste vientos preponderantes que soplan de oeste a este entre 30° y 60° de latitud en ambos hemisferios (528)

white dwarf (WIET DWAWRF) a small, hot, dim star that is the leftover center of an old sunlike star (855)

enana blanca una estrella pequeña, caliente y tenue que es el centro sobrante de una estrella vieja parecida al Sol (855)

wind vane (WIND VAYN) an instrument used to determine the direction of the wind (584)

veleta un instrumento que se usa para determinar la dirección del viento (584)

Index

INDEX

INDEX

Z

Photo Credits

Royalty Free/CORBIS; 515 (tl), Roger Ressmeyer/CORBIS ; 515 (tr), Wolfgang Kaehler/CORBIS; 515 (bl), Carol Hughes; Gallo Images/CORBIS; 516 (tl), Didrik Johnck/CORBIS; 516 (tr), Chris Noble/Stone/Getty Images; 517, HMH/Andy Christiansen; 519, NASA/CORBIS; 520, Martin Thomas/Reuters NewMedia Inc./CORBIS; 521 (infrared), NOAO/SPL/Photo Researchers, Inc.; 521 (ultraviolet), SOHO/ESA/NASA; 521 (visible), NASA/JIAS/SPL/Photo Researchers, Inc.; 521 (x-ray), NASA/JIAS/SPL/Photo Researchers, Inc.; 521 (radio), NRAO/AUI/NSF; 522 (b), Tim Boyle/Getty Images; 523, Jeremy Woodhouse/Photodisc/Getty; 529, NASA/Photo Researchers, Inc.; 530, Charles Benes/Index Stock Imagery, Inc.; 531 (bkgd), Design Pics Inc./Alamy; 531 (l), Morgan David de Lossy/CORBIS; 531 (tr), Pekka Parviainen/Photo Researchers, Inc.; 531 (c), Marko Mikkila; 531 (cr), Mark Duffy/Alamy; 532 (b), HMH/Andy Christiansen; 534, NASA; 535 (b), NASA/Photo Researchers, Inc.; 535 (c), Jeremy Woodhouse/Photodisc/Getty; 535 (t), Wolfgang Kaehler/CORBIS; 540-541 (all), Charles Doswell III/Getty Images; 540 (c), Michael S. Yamashita/CORBIS; 540 (b), Gary W. Carter/CORBIS; 540 (t), Paul Zahl/National Geographic Image Collection; 541, HMH/Victoria Smith Photo; 544 (bkgd), Craig Aurness/CORBIS; 544 (br), David Vintiner/CORBIS; 544 (bl), Jon Hicks/CORBIS; 546 (t), Paul Zahl/National Geographic Image Collection; 547 (b), Breck Kent/Animals Animals/Earth Scenes; 548 (tl), Graham Neden/Ecoscene/CORBIS; 550 (br), Michael S. Yamashita/CORBIS; 551 (t), Beth Wald/Aurora; 553 (tr), Gary Braasch/CORBIS; 553 (tl), Royalty Free/CORBIS; 554 (tl), Charles O'Rear/CORBIS; 555 (bc), Gary W. Carter/CORBIS; 555 (bl), Darrell Gulin/CORBIS; 556 (b), Ted Kinsman/Photo Researchers, Inc.; 557 (t), Gene Rhoden/Weatherpix; 558 (tl), Jim Brandenburg/Minden Pictures; 560 (br), HMH/Victoria Smith; 561 (tr), HMH/Victoria Smith; 563 (bl), Gary W. Carter/CORBIS; 563 (cl), Michael S. Yamashita/CORBIS; 563 (t), Paul Zahl/National Geographic Image Collection; 568-569 (all), Getty Images/Taxi; 568 (t), Benjamin Lowy/CORBIS; 568 (c), A & J Verkaik/CORBIS; 568 (b), NASA; 569, HMH/Victoria Smith Photo; 571, NOAA; 572, Rick Doyle/CORBIS; 574, Benjamin Lowy/Corbis; 578, A & J Verkaik/CORBIS; 580 (c), CIMSS/NOAA; 580 (b), Smiley N. Pool/ Dallas Morning News/CORBIS; 581 (b), ROBERT GALBRAITH/Reuters/CORBIS; 581 (cr), Brian Collins/USGS; 581 (tr), David J. Phillip/AP Images; 582 (tl), Howard B. Bluestein/Photo Researchers, Inc.; 582 (inset), Jim Reed/CORBIS; 583, Jonathan Blair/CORBIS; 584 (b), HMH/Victoria Smith; 584 (t), Philippe Giraud/CORBIS SYGMA ; 585 (bkgd), RF123; 585 (t), Direccao dos Servicos Meteorologicos e Geofisicos; 586 (t), NASA; 587, Courtesy World Meteorological Organization; 589 (t), Courtesy, The Weather Channel; 590, Jim Reed/CORBIS; 592, H. David Seawell/CORBIS; 593 (bkgd), Dale O'Dell/Veer/Getty; 593 (bl), Michael S. Yamashita/CORBIS; 593 (br), John Tinning/Frank Lane Picture Agency/CORBIS; 593 (bc), ON PAGE CREDIT; 594 (b), HMH; 597 (4), Jim Reed/CORBIS; 597 (1), A & J Verkaik/CORBIS; 597 (1), Benjamin Lowy/CORBIS; 597 (3), NASA; 599 (bkgd), Kim Morris/ZUMA; 599 (tr), Gene Rhoden/weatherpix; 599 (cl), Gary Gardiner/ZUMA; 599 (b), Southern Stock/Brand X/CORBIS; 599 (cr), Tulsa World/WPN; 602-603 (all), Theo Allofs/CORBIS; 602 (t), Wolfgang Kaehler/CORBIS; 602 (c), Bryan and Cherry Alexander Photography; 602 (b), Wendy Stone/CORBIS; 603, HMH/Victoria Smith Photo; 605 (br), Andrea Pistolesi/Getty Images; 605 (b), Wolfgang Kaehler/CORBIS; 609 (bl), Reuters NewMedia, Inc./CORBIS; 609 (br), Indranil Mukherjee/AFP/Getty Images; 613 (tl), Bryan and Cherry Alexander Photography; 616 (tl), Bojan Brecelj/CORBIS; 616 (inset), Simon Fraser/Photo Researchers, Inc.; 616 (bkgd), Arctic-Images/CORBIS; 618 (tr), Yann Arthus-Bertrand/CORBIS; 620 (bl), Wendy Stone/CORBIS; 620 (tl), Wendy Stone/CORBIS; 621 (bkgd), Norbert Rosing/Getty Images; 621 (t), Johnny Johnson/Getty Images; 621 (r), Ralph Lee Hopkins/Getty Images; 621 (bl), NASA; 621 (br), NASA; 622 (b), Victoria Smith/Harcourt; 625 (cl), Bryan and Cherry Alexander Photography; 625 (tl), Wolfgang Kaehler/CORBIS; 630 (tr), Kunsthistorisches Museum, Vienna, Austria/ Bridgeman Art Library; 630 (1654), Alamy; 630 (1783), The Gallery Collection/CORBIS; 630 (1930), Hulton-Deutsch Collection/CORBIS; 630 (1887), Bettmann/CORBIS (1935), Bettmann/CORBIS; 630 (1943), Jim Reed/CORBIS; 630 (1946), Gabe Palmer/CORBIS; 630 (2007), Robin Nelson/ZUMA; 630-631 (all), Anthony Redpath/CORBIS; 631 (1939), The Dmitri Baltermants Collection/CORBIS; 631 (1926), Bettmann/CORBIS; 631 (1957), Bettmann/CORBIS; 631 (1946),

Bettmann/CORBIS; 631 (1960), AP IMAGES/NASA; 631 (2002), NASA; 631 (2005), NASA; 631 (1988), National Oceanic and Atmospheric Administration/Department of Commerce; 631 (1969), Reuters/CORBIS; 631 (2005), National Oceanic and Atmospheric Administration/Department of Commerce;

UNIT SEVEN: 633 (cr), Tom Stewart/CORBIS; 633 (l), G. R. Roberts/Natural Sciences Image Library (NSIL) of New Zealand; 633 (br), Craig Tuttle/CORBIS; 634-635 (all), Jeffrey L. Rotman/CORBIS; 634 (t), Ocean Drilling Program - Texas A&M University; 634 (c), B. Tanaka/Getty Images/Taxi; 634 (b), Tom McHugh/Photo Researchers, Inc.; 635, HMH/Victoria Smith Photo; 638 (l, br), Ocean Drilling Program - Texas A&M University; 639 (ship), National Oceanic and Atmospheric Administration/Department of Commerce; 640 (inset), David Shale/naturepl.com; 640 (t), Alexis Rosenfeld/SPL/Photo Researchers, Inc.; 644, B. Tanaka/Getty Images/Taxi; 645, Ocean Drilling Program - Texas A&M University; 646 (b), Courtesy Stephen Morris, Experimental Nonlinear Physics Group, University of Toronto; 646 (bkgd), Nautilus Mining; 646 (bc), Rob Cousins/Alamy; 646 (bl), Brian North/Alamy; 647 (nodules), Tom McHugh/Photo Researchers, Inc.; 647 (bkgd), Darryl Torckler/Getty Images/Stone; 647 (nodules), Tom McHugh/Photo Researchers, Inc.; 648 (r), Andrew Syred/SPL/Photo Researchers, Inc.; 648 (l), Jim Zuckerman/CORBIS; 649 (bkgd), Science Source/Photo Researchers, Inc.; 649 (red jelly), AP IMAGES/Ocean Geographic Magazine through WHOI/ISSP,Michael Aw,HO; 649 (t), AP IMAGES/Ocean Geographic Magazine through WHOI/ISSP,Michael Aw,HO; 649 (larval squid), AP IMAGES/Dr. Ross Hopcroft, University of Alaska through WHOI/ISSP/HO; 649 (moonsnail), Katrin Linse/British Antarctic Survey; 649, David Shale; 649 (bl, cr), David Shale; 651, HMH/Victoria Smith; 652, NGDC/NOAA; 653 (c), B. Tanaka/Getty Images/Taxi; 653 (t), Ocean Drilling Program - Texas A&M University; 658-659 (all), David Hall/seaphotos.com; 658 (t), Sean Davey/AllSport/Getty Images; 658 (c), David Hall/seaphotos.com; 658 (b), Chris Hellier/CORBIS; 659, Sam Dudgeon/Harcourt; 662 (bkgd), BAE Systems; 662 (br), Nordtec; 663 (tl), Sean Davey/AllSport/Getty Images; 665 (tr), Craig Tuttle/CORBIS; 665 (tl), Tom Stewart/CORBIS; 667 (br), HMH/Victoria Smith; 667 (tc), HMH/Sam Dudgeon; 668 (tl), Lawson Wood/CORBIS; 669 (bl), David Hall/seaphotos.com; 670 (bl), IQ3d/Bruce Coleman, Inc.; 672 (tr), Craig Tuttle/CORBIS; 673 (bl), Steve Raymer/National Geographic Image Collection; 674 (tr), Bohemian Nomad Picturemakers/CORBIS; 675 (b), Chris Hellier/CORBIS; 676 (t), Simon Fraser/SPL/Photo Researchers, Inc.; 677 (bkgd), Stephen Frink/CORBIS; 677 (b), John Daniels/Alamy; 677 (tr), David Noble/Alamy; 677 (tr, inset), Victor R. Boswell Jr./National geographic/Getty Images; 677 (cr), Klein Sonar Side Scan; 677 (t), Richard T. Nowitz/CORBIS; 678 (bl), HMH/Victoria Smith; 680, Courtesy of N.R. Nalli, NOAA/NESDIS, Washington, D.C.; 681 (tl), Sean Davey/AllSport/Getty Images; 681 (b), Chris Hellier/CORBIS; 681 (cl), David Hall/seaphotos.com; 686-687 (all), Chris Walsh/IFA Bilderteam/Jupiterimages; 686 (c), Darrell Wong; 686 (t), Jonathan Blair/CORBIS; 686 (b), Paul A. Souders/CORBIS; 687, Sam Dudgeon/Harcourt; 689 (bl), Jonathan Blair/CORBIS; 690 (br), Provided by the SeaWiFS Project, NASA/Goddard Space Flight Center, and ORBIMAGE; 692 (inset), Peter David/Natural Visions; 694 (cl), M-SAT LTD/Photo Researchers, Inc.; 695 (bl), Jack Ficlds/CORBIS; 697 (br), HMH/Victoria Smith; 697 (tr), Darrell Wong; 699 (tr), G. R. Roberts/Natural Sciences Image Library (NSIL) of New Zealand; 700 (inset), Connie Rica/CORBIS; 700 (tl), John Stanmeyer/VII/AP/Wide World Photos; 703 (cl), Paul A. Souders/CORBIS; 703 (tl), Buddy Mays/CORBIS; 703 (bkgd), V. Mouchel/MAXPPP /ZUMA; 703 (br), Sally Morgan / Ecocsene; 703 (bl), Department of Biological and Environmental Sciences,Samford University; 704 (tl), Bruce M. Herman/Photo Researchers, Inc.; 705 (bkgd), Karsten Petersen; 706 (b), HMH/Victoria Smith; 709 (cl), Darrell Wong; 709 (tl), Jonathan Blair/CORBIS; 709 (bl), Paul A. Souders/CORBIS; 714-715 (all), Stephen Frink/zefa/Corbis; 714 (1000 C.E.), Wolfgang Kaehler/Alamy; 714 (1859), London Art Archive/Alamy; 714 (1620), ©London Photos-Homer Sykes/Alamy; 714 (1519), North Wind Picture Archives/ Alamy; 714 (t), Naval Historical Foundation; 714 (1913), Dr.Jean-Paul Rodrigue, Department of Economics and Geography, Hofstra University; 714 (1912), The Granger Collection, New York; 715 (1939), The Granger Collection, New York; 715 (1944), James L. Amos/Corbis; 715 (1949), R. Ludwig Turner and the Ludwig Family; 715

(2008), Kos Picture Source/Alamy; 715 (2003), Carl D. Walsh/Aurora Photos; 715 (1964), Emory Kristof and Alvin Chandler/National Geographic Image Collection; 715 (1986), Emory Kristof/National Geographic Image Collection; 715 (1967), Vincenzo Lombardo/Getty Images; 715 (1939-1945), Denis Scott/Corbis; 715 (2000), Tim Aylen/AP Images;

UNIT EIGHT: 717 (cr), NASA; 717 (l), NASA/Gemini Observatory, GMOS Team; 717 (br), Fred Espenak; 718-719 (all), Stocktrek Images/Getty Images; 718 (b), Visuals Unlimited/CORBIS; 718 (t), Jean-Charles Cuillandre/Canada-france-Hawaii Telescope/SPL/Photo Researchers, Inc.; 719, HMH/Victoria Smith Photo; 721 (bl), NASA; 722 (tl), Jean-Charles Cuillandre/Canada-france-Hawaii Telescope/SPL/Photo Researchers, Inc.; 722 (tr), NASA; 723 (tr), Alfred Pasieka/SPL/Photo Researchers, Inc.; 724 (br), Michael Freeman/CORBIS; 726 (tl), Glen Alison/PhotoDisc Green/gettyimages; 726 (bkgd), NASA; 726 (bl), NASA; 726 (dna), ©Jon Lomberg; 727 (br), NASA-JPL; 727 (tl, bl), NASA; 728 (t), NASA; 729, Visuals Unlimited/CORBIS; 732 (tl), Gianni Dagli Orti/CORBIS; 735 (br), HMH/Andy Christiansen; 737 (bkgd), Atlantide Phototravel/CORBIS; 737 (cl), The National Institute of Standards and Technology; 737 (tr), HMH/Victoria Smith Photo; 738 (br), HMH/Peter Van Steen; 740 (t), C. Mayhew & R. Simmon/NASA/GSFO; 741 (tl), Jean-Charles Cuillandre/Canada-france-Hawaii Telescope/SPL/Photo Researchers, Inc.; 743, Visuals Unlimited/CORBIS; 746-747 (all), Denis Scott/CORBIS; 746 (t), Royal Observatory, Edinburgh/SPL/Photo Researchers, Inc.; 746 (c), NASA/SPL/Photo Researchers, Inc.; 746 (b), CORBIS; 746 (b), Ctein /Getty Images; 747, HMH/Victoria Smith Photo; 749 (bl), Royal Observatory, Edinburgh/SPL/Photo Researchers, Inc.; 754 (tl), Lindsay Hebberd/CORBIS; 756 (br), HMH/Victoria Smith; 758 (t), Ctein/Getty Images; 759 (b), JPL/NASA; 760 (br), NASA/SPL/Photo Researchers, Inc.; 761 (tl), NASA/SPL/Photo Researchers, Inc.; 762 (br), ESA/PLI/CORBIS; 763 (t), NASA; 764 (tr), Gordon Garradd/Photo Researchers, Inc.; 764 (tl), NASA; 765 (bl), Kevin Kelley/Getty Images; 766 (br), NASA; 767 (tr), CORBIS; 767 (bkgd), Science Source/Photo Researchers, Inc.; 767 (bl), NASA; 767 (bc), NASA; 768 (br), NASA/JPL/Space Science Institute; 769 (tl), Lawrence Sromovsky, University of Wisconsin-Madison,Keck Observatory; 770 (br), JPL/NASA; 771, Wikipedia based on a NASA image; 772 (tl), Lynette R. Cook; 773 (bkgd), www.launchphotography.com; 773 (t), NASA; 773 (tl), NASA; 773 (bl), NASA; 774 (b), HMH/Victoria Smith; 775 (tr), HMH/Victoria Smith; 776 (tc), NASA/SPL/Photo Researchers, Inc.; 777 (b), CORBIS; 777 (bl), NASA/SPL/Photo Researchers, Inc.; 777 (t), Royal Observatory, Edinburgh/SPL/Photo Researchers, Inc.; 777 (cl), Ctein /Getty Images; 782 (t), NASA; 782 (c), CNES/GAMMA; 782 (c), Galileo Project/JPL/NASA; 782 (b), Wally Pacholka/AstroPics.com; 783, HMH/Victoria Smith Photo; 785, NASA; 786 (b), Courtesy U.S. Geological Survey; 787 (b), NASA; 787 (t), NASA; 790 (b,t), USGS; 792, NASA; 793 (br), CNES/GAMMA; 793 (bl), Jay Pasachoff & Roger Ressmeyer/Science Faction; 794 (t), Royalty Free/CORBIS; 794 (b), HMH/Victoria Smith; 795 (b), Dr. Fred Espenak/Photo Researchers, Inc.; 796, NASA; 796 (moons), John Bova/Photo Researchers, Inc.; 797, John Sanford/Photo Researchers, Inc.; 799, NASA/JPL/University of Arizona; 800 (b), Galileo Project/JPL/NASA; 800 (bc), AstronomyOnline.org; 800 (br), Scala /Art Resource, NY; 800 (bl), Galleria Palatina,Palazzo Pitti,Florence,Italy/Bridgeman Art Library; 800 (bkgd), Special Collection Library, University of Michigan; 801 (t), Galileo Project/JPL/NASA; 801 (b,c), NASA; 802 (t,b), NASA; 803 (b), Dr. R. Albrecht, ESA/ESO Space Telescope European Coordinating Facility; NASA ; 803 (b), NASA; 803, NASA, ESA, H. Weaver (JHU/APL), A. Stern (SwRl), and the HST Pluto Companion Search Team; 804 (t), NASA; 805, NASA; 806, Getty Images/PhotoDisc; 809, Juan Carlos Casado; 810 (b), Ken Nichols/Institute of Meteorites; 810 (c), Breck P. Kent/Animals Animals/Earth Scenes; 810 (t), E.R. Degginger/Bruce Coleman, Inc.; 811 (bkgd), NASA; 811 (r), NASA; 811 (tl), Tulsa World; 811 (cl), NASA; 811 (b), Enver Essop; 814, NASA; 815 (4), Wally Pacholka/AstroPics.com; 815 (3), Galileo Project/JPL/NASA; 815 (2), CNES/GAMMA; 815 (1), NASA; 820-821 (all), SOHO/ESA/NASA; 820 (t), Fred Espenak; 820 (b), Pekka Parviainen/Photo Researchers, Inc.; 821, HMH/Victoria Smith Photo; 825 (b), HMH/Andy Christiansen; 825 (t), Kamioka Observatory, ICRR (Institute for Cosmic Ray Research), The University of Tokyo; 827 (inset), NOAO/AURA/NSF; 827 (b),

1035

Staff Credits

The people who contributed to this edition of **Holt McDougal Earth Science** are listed below. They represent design, editorial, marketing, multimedia, and production.

Wesley M. Bain, Kelly Ballew, Kimberly Barr, Angela Beckmann, Sara Butler, Soojinn Choi, Clarissa Cochran, Lorraine Cooper, Lana Cox, Eddie Dawson, Juliet Dervin, Michelle Dike, Lydia Doty, Sam Dudgeon, Holly Everett, Jenevieve Eyre, Leigh Ann García, Diana Goetting, Kristin Hay, Tim Hovde, John Koonz, Denise Mahoney, Stuart McKenzie, Ivonne Mercado, Richard Metzger, Erin Miller, Jessica Mraz, Ali Nagib, Mercedes Newman, David Parisotto, Sara Rider, Jeff Robinson, Karen Ross, Tara Ross, Beth Sample, Kay Selke, Susan Skinner, Chris Smith, Victoria Smith, Kim Soriano, Sherry Sprague, Jeannie Taylor, Bob Tucek, Kira J. Watkins, and Nadyne Wood.